HISTORICAL COLLECTIONS
of the
STATE *of* NEW YORK

CONTAINING

A GENERAL COLLECTION OF THE MOST INTERESTING FACTS,
TRADITIONS, BIOGRAPHICAL SKETCHES, ANECDOTES ETC.,

RELATING TO ITS

HISTORY AND ANTIQUITIES,

WITH GEOGRAPHICAL DESCRIPTIONS OF
EVERY TOWNSHIP IN THE STATE

John W. Barber
Author of Connecticut, and Massachusetts Historical Collections

&

Henry Howe
Author of "The Memoirs of Eminent American Mechanics," Etc.

[Arms of the State of New York.]

[More elevated.]

HERITAGE BOOKS
2009

HERITAGE BOOKS
AN IMPRINT OF HERITAGE BOOKS, INC.

Books, CDs, and more—Worldwide

For our listing of thousands of titles see our website
at
www.HeritageBooks.com

A Facsimile Reprint
Published 2009 by
HERITAGE BOOKS, INC.
Publishing Division
100 Railroad Ave. #104
Westminster, Maryland 21157

Entered according to Act of Congress, in the year 1841
By John W. Barber and Henry Howe,
In the Clerk's Office of the District Court of Connecticut.

— Publisher's Notice —
In reprints such as this, it is often not possible to remove blemishes from the original. We feel the contents of this book warrant its reissue despite these blemishes and hope you will agree and read it with pleasure.

International Standard Book Numbers
Paperbound: 978-0-7884-1338-4
Clothbound: 978-0-7884-8147-5

PREFACE.

The design of this volume is to give an account of the most important and interesting events relating to the history of the state of New York, from its settlement to the present time, with geographical descriptions, illustrated by numerous engravings. In collecting the materials and preparing them for publication, the compilers of this work have unitedly spent more than two years of close and laborious application. We have visited every part of the state, and besides travelling thousands of miles in the public conveyances, we have journeyed many hundreds on foot.

Although feeling conscious that we have used all the efforts, and taken every precaution which could be reasonably expected, in order to have this work accurate in every respect, yet we do not claim an entire exemption from those imperfections ever attendant on works of this kind. A degree of diffidence is felt, when it is considered who are to be the readers. Travellers in giving accounts of foreign countries, may make statements at random, which may pass for truth, when there is no one at hand able to correct their errors. This volume will come before many persons, who, on some subjects introduced, have better means of information, and possess more knowledge than the compilers. A certain writer defines history to be merely "an approximation towards truth." Although this humiliating statement will not be allowed to its full extent, yet when the imperfection of every thing human is considered, it must be confessed to have some foundation in truth.

In the prosecution of this work, we have availed ourselves of the labors of those who have preceded us. The historian, of necessity, derives his information from others. It will be observed, that quotations have been made from a great variety of publications; in most instances of which, credit has been given. As a general rule, we have preferred to have each account appear as it was originally given to the public, in the author's own words, from which the reader can draw his own inferences. Truth ought always to be preferred before elegance of language. In the geographical department much information has been derived from Spafford's and Gordon's Gazetteers, and the state maps, published at Ithaca by Messrs. Stone & Clark. Spafford may be considered as the pioneer in furnishing geographical descriptions of the state: his first gazetteer was published in 1813, the second in 1824. The gazetteer by Mr. Gordon, consisting of 800 closely printed octavo pages, containing a map of the state, and one of each county, was published in 1836, and is by far the most complete and valuable work of the kind relating to New York, which has as yet been issued. To this able work, we would refer our readers for a full statistical and geographical account of the various places in the state. It not only contains a great amount of statistical information, but also the political history of the state, abstracts of its laws, and other valuable information. It is a volume which ought to be placed in every public library in the state.

The numerous engravings interspersed throughout this volume, were, with few exceptions, copied from drawings taken on the spot by the compilers of the work. In these engravings, our principal object was to give faithful representations, rather than picturesque views, or beautiful specimens of art. Before deciding that any of these representations are incorrect, we wish our readers to consider that the appearance of any place will be materially altered, as viewed from different points. In order to form an entirely correct judgment, it will be necessary to stand on the spot from whence the drawing was taken.

COUNTIES, TOWNSHIPS, VILLAGES.

Acra, 183
Acron, 153
Acquabogue, 540
Adams, 200
Adams Basin, 265
Adamsport, 531
Adamsville, 572
Addison, 528
Alabama, 175
Albion, 431
Alden, 143
Albany, 44
ALBANY COUNTY, 44
Alfred, 56
Albion, 431, 429
Alexandria, 158, 201
All n, 56
Alexander, 175
Almond, 56
ALLEGANY COUNTY, 56
Allegany City, 82
Allen's Hill, 409
Alloway, 579
Amagansett, 536
Amber, 392
Amboy, 383, 431
Amenia, 133
Amherst, 143
Amity, 56, 428
Amsterdam, 272
Ancram, 114
Andes, 126
Andover, 57, 375
Angelica, 57
Annsville, 360
Antwerp, 201
Appling, 201
Apulia, 384
Arcade, 603
Arcadia, 578
Argyle, 567
Arietta, 191
Arkport, 531
Arkwright, 87
Ashford, 82
Ashville, 90
Astoria, 461
Athens, 181
Athol, 562
Attica, 602
Attlebury, 142
Auburn, 74
Augusta, 360
Aurelius, 79
Auriesville, 278
Aurora, 143
Austerlitz, 114
Au Sable, 106
Avoca, 528
Avon, 242

Babylon, 539
Bainbridge, 99
Barker's Mills, 466
Baker's Bridge, 56
Bakersville, 113
Baldwinsville, 384
Ballston, 491
Ballston Spa, 492
Bangor, 163
Barcelona, 93
Barbersville, 132
Baremarket, 142

Barker, 66
Barre, 429
Barrington, 605
Barrytown, 140
Barton, 549
Batavia, 175
Batestown, 468
Bath, 464, 528
Bathhouse, 237
Battenville, 572
Bayleytown, 525
Bearysville, 525
Beaverdam, 543
Bedford, 584
Beekman, 106, 133
Belfast, 57
Bell Port, 535
Belleisle, 383
Belleville, 202, 428
Belmont, 163
Bennet's Flats, 531
Bennet Settlement, 179
Bennington, 602
Benton, 605
Bergen, 178
Berkshire, 549
Berlin, 464
Berne, 50
Bethany, 179
Bethel, 547
Bethlehem, 50
Betts' Corners, 384
Big Flats, 94
Binghamton, 66
Birdsall, 59
Black Brook, 106
Black Rock, 143
Bleeker, 167
Blenheim, 516
Bloomingsburg, 547
Blooming Grove, 411
Bloomville, 130
Blossomsville, 263
Bluff Point, 605
Bolivar, 59
Bolton, 562
Bombay, 163
Boonville, 360
Borodino, 403
Boston, 143
Bouckville, 260
Bovina, 126
Boylston, 431
Bradford, 530
Branchport, 605
Branch, 541
Brandon, 164
Brasher, 483
Brant, 152
Breakabeen, 518
Bridgehampton, 543
Bridgeport, 260
Bridgewater, 360
Brighton, 263, 447
Bristol, 404, 561
Broadalbin, 167
Brockport, 271
Brookfield, 255
Brookhaven, 533
Brooklyn, 219
BROOME COUNTY, 66
Broome, 516
Bronx, 587

Brownville, 201, 408
Brunswick, 464
Brutus, 80
Buffalo, 147
Bullville, 417
Burdette, 552
Burlingham, 547
Burlington, 440
Burns, 59
Bushnell's Basin, 266
Bushwick, 233
Burton, 82
Buskirk's Bridge, 567
Busti, 87
Butler, 578
Butternuts, 440
Byersville, 251
Byron, 179
Byrnville, 518

Cackemyer's Mills, 135
Cadiz, 85
Cadysville, 59
Cairo, 183
Cahoes, 54
Caldwell, 562
Caledonia, 244
Cambridge, 567
Camillus, 383
Campbell, 530
Cambria, 348
Camden, 361
Cameron, 530
Canaan, 114
Canaderaga, 447
Canajoharie, 274
Canandaigua, 404
Candice, 404
Canaseraga, 260
Canastota, 260
Candor, 549
Caneadea, 59
Canisteo, 530
Canning, 365
Cannonsville, 132
Canoga, 525
Canterbury, 411
Canton, 403, 483
Cape Vincent, 212
Cardiff, 384
Carlton, 430
Caroline, 552
Careysville, 179
Carlisle, 516
Carmel, 448
Carrol, 88
Carr's Corners, 152
Carter, 242
Caton, 530
Carthage, 135
Casadaga, 92
Casety Hollow, 360
Castile, 602
Castleton, 474
CATTARAUGUS COUNTY, 82
Catherines, 94
Catlin, 95
Cato, 80
Catskill, 183
Caughnawaga, 280
CAYUGA COUNTY, 74
Cayuga, 79
Cayuta, 95

Cazenovia, 255
Cedarville, 196
Centre Port, 540
Centreville, 59, 80, 92, 114, 532
Chamberlain, 85
Champion, 201
Champlain, 106
Chapinsville, 408
Charlotte, 88
Charlotteville, 524
Charleston, 278
Charlton, 491
Chaumont, 212
Chateaugua, 164
Chatham, 114
CHATAUQUE COUNTY, 87
Chatauque, 88
Chazy, 106
Checktowaga, 152
Chelsea, 475
Chemung, 95
CHEMUNG COUNTY, 94
Chenango, 66
CHENANGO COUNTY, 99
Chenango Forks, 66
Cherry Valley, 440
Cherry Creek, 88
Chester, 417, 565
Chesterfield, 155
Chili, 263
China, 603
Chittenango, 260
Chittenden Falls, 122
Churchtown, 114
Churchville, 266, 484
Cincinnatus, 123
Cicero, 383
Clarendon, 430
Clarence, 152
Clarke's Settlement, 73
Clarkson, 263
Clarkstown, 476
Clarkesville, 59, 255, 79
Clavernck, 114
Clay, 383
Clayton, 201
Clear Creek, 89
Cleaveland, 431
Clermont, 115
Clifton Park, 491
CLINTON COUNTY, 105
Clinton, 133
Clintonville, 106, 133, 453
Clockville, 260
Clyde, 578
Clymer, 89
Cobleskill, 516
Cochecton, 547
Coeyman's, 50
Concord, 153
Colchester, 126
Colden, 152
Coles' Mills, 449
Colesville, 72
Cold Spring, 83, 449, 463
Collierville, 444
Collins, 152
Collinsville, 242
Colosse, 432
Columbia, 192
COLUMBIA COUNTY, 113
Columbiaville, 122, 485

COUNTIES, TOWNSHIPS, VILLAGES.

Columbus, 100
Conesville, 518
Conesus, 244
Coney Island, 237
Conhocton, 530
Conklin, 72
Connewango, 84
Conquest, 80
Constable, 165
Constableville, 242
Constantia, 431
Coonsville, 408
Copake, 116
Cooperstown, 445
Copenhagen, 239
Corbeau, 106
Corfu, 180
Corinth, 492
Cornwall, 411
Cornwallsville, 188
Corum, 534
Cortlandt, 585
CORTLANDT COUNTY, 123
Cortlandtville, 123
Coventry, 100
Covert, 525
Covington, 603
Cowlesville, 602
Coxsackie, 188
Craigsville, 411
Crawford, 417
Croton, 585
Crown Point, 156
Cuba, 59
Cuddebackville, 417
Currytown, 283
Cutchogue, 545

Danby, 552
Danube, 192
Dansville, 249, 530
Darien, 179
Dashville, 559
Davenport, 126
Day, 492
Dayanville, 242
Dayton, 84
Deansville, 365
Decatur, 444
Deerfield, 361
Deer Park, 417
Defriestville, 464
De Kalb, 484
Delavan, 87
DELAWARE COUNTY, 125
Delanti, 92
Delhi, 126
Delphi, 392
Denmark, 239
Depauville, 201, 484
Depeyster, 484
Deposit, 132
De Ruyter, 256
Dewit, 383
Dexter, 201
Dexterville, 89
Diana, 239
Dickenson, 165
Dix. 95
Dobb's Ferry, 587
Dover, 133
Dora, 72
Dresden, 567, 605
Dryden, 552
Duane, 165
Duanesburg, 507
Dublin, 525
Dundee, 608
Dunkirk, 91
Durham, 188
Durhamville. 375
DUTCHESS COUNTY, 132

Eagle, 60

Eagle Harbor, 430
East Bloomfield, 408
East Chester, 587
East Hampton, 535
Easton, 568
Eaton, 256
Eddysville, 557
Edenville, 428
Eden, 153
Edinburg, 492
Edmeston, 444
Edwards, 484
Elba, 179
Elbridge, 383
Ellenburg, 106
Ellenville, 560
Ellery, 89
Ellicott, 89
Ellicottville, 85
Ellington, 89
Ellisburg, 202
Elmira, 95
Elizabethtown, 156
Elmore's Corners, 556
Enfield, 552
Ephrata, 167
ERIE COUNTY, 142
Erieville, 260
Erwin, 530
Erin, 99
Esopus, 556
Esperane, 523
Essex, 156
ESSEX COUNTY, 154
Etna, 552
Evans, 153
Evans' Mills, 211
Exeter, 444

Fabius, 384
Factoryville, 474, 549
Fairfield, 193
Fairhaven, 430
Fairport Basin, 266
Fall Creek, 552
Fallsburg, 547
Farmersville, 84, 525
Farmington, 408
Far Rockaway, 456
Fayetteville, 387
Federal Store, 137
Fenner, 258
Felt's Mill, 212
Finchville, 423
Fishkill, 134
Flanders, 543
Flatbush, 235
Flatlands, 235
Fleming, 80
Florence, 361
Florida, 278, 428
Floyd, 361
Flushing, 453
Fluvanna, 89
Fonda's Bush, 167
Forrestburg, 547
Forestville, 90
Fort Ann, 568
Fort Edward, 569
Fort Miller, 569
Fort Covington, 165
Fort Hunter, 278
Fort Plain, 279
Fosterdale, 79
Fowlersville, 251
Fowler, 484
Frankfort, 194
Franklin, 127, 165
FRANKLIN COUNTY, 162
Franklinville, 85, 135, 384
Frankville, 105
Fredonia, 90
Freedom, 85
Freedom Plains, 137

Freehold, 188
Freetown, 124
French Creek, 89, 201
French Mills, 165
Friendship, 60
Fulloms Basin, 266
Fulton, 439, 518
Fultonville, 278

Gaines, 430
Gainesville, 603
Galen, 578
Gallatin, 116
Galway, 492
Gardner's Island, 536
Garretsville, 444
Gasport, 359
Gates, 263
Gayhead, 135, 188
Geddes, 394
Genesee, 60
GENESEE COUNTY, 174
Geneseo, 245
Genoa, 80
Geneva, 409
Georgetown, 259
German Flats, 194
German, 100
Germantown, 116
Gerry, 89
Ghent. 116
Gilboa, 516
Gilbertsville, 440
Gilman, 191
Glen, 278
Glenn Falls, 566
Glencadia, 122
Glencoe, 119
Glenham, 135
Glenville, 507
Gorham, 408
Goshen, 417
Gouverneur, 484
Grafton, 464
Granby, 431
Granger, 60
Granville, 570
Gravesend, 236
Great Bend, 201
Great Valley, 85
Greece, 263
Greenbush, 464
GREENE COUNTY, 181
Green Haven, 133
Greene, 100
Greenport, 545
Greenfield, 492
Green River, 114
Green's Corners, 270
Greensburg, 587
Greenville, 188
Greenwich, 571
Greenwood, 531
Greig, 239
Greggsville, 251
Griffin's Mills, 143
Groton, 552
Grove, 60
Groveland, 246
Grosvenor's Corners, 516
Guilderland, 51
Guilford, 101

Hadley, 492
Hague, 565
Half Moon, 492
Hallet's Cove, 461
Hall's Mills, 52
Halseyville, 553
Hamburg, 153
Hamilton, 259
HAMILTON COUNTY, 189
Hammertown, 137
Hammond's Port, 533

Hammond, 484
Hamden, 128
Hampton, 376, 572
Hamptonburg, 418
Hague, 565
Hancock, 128
Hanford's Landing, 264
Hannibal, 431
Hanover, 89
Harlaem, 338
Harmony, 90
Harpersfield, 128
Harpersville, 72
Harrisburg, 239
Hartfield, 88
Harrison, 590
Hartford, 125, 572
Hartland, 348
Hartsville, 142
Hartwick, 444
Hartville, 337
Hastings, 431, 587
Havana, 94
Hebron, 572
Haverstraw, 476
Head-of-the-river, 541
Hebron, 572
Hector, 552
Helena, 483
Hempstead, 455
Hempstead Harbor, 462
Henderson, 202
Henrietta, 264
HERKIMER COUNTY, 191
Herkimer, 194
Hermitage, 604
Hermon, 484
Hicksville, 463
High Falls, 558
Hillsdale, 116
Hinsdale, 85
Hitchcock's Corners, 133
Hobart, 132
Hoffman, 158
Hogansburg, 163
Holland, 153
Holley, 430
Homer, 124
Hoosick, 466
Hope, 191
Hopkinton, 484
Hopewell, 135, 408, 417
Horicon, 565
Hornby, 531
Hornelsville, 531
Hounsfield, 202
Houseville, 242
Howard, 531
Hoytes, 525
Hudson. 116
Hughsonville, 135
Hull's Mills, 142
Hume, 60
Humphrey, 85
Hunter, 188
Huntington, 539
Hurley, 556
Huron, 579
Hyde Park, 137

Independence, 60
Ira, 80
Irelandville, 532
Irondequoit, 265
Islip, 540
Italy, 605
Ithaca, 552

Jackson, 444, 572
Jacksonburg, 444
Jacksonville, 248, 553
Jamaica, 458
Jamestown, 89
Janesville, 383

COUNTIES, TOWNSHIPS, VILLAGES. 7

Jasper, 531
Jay, 157
Java, 603
Jefferson, 95, 518, 532
JEFFERSON COUNTY, 201
Jerusalem, 456, 605
Jerusalem Corners, 153
Johnsburg, 566
Johnstown, 119, 167
Johnsonville, 135, 469
Jordan, 383
Junius, 525

Keene, 157
Keesville, 155
Kempsville, 352
Kendall, 430
Kennadayville, 528
Kennedy's Mills, 90
Kent, 449
Kinderhook, 118
Kinderhook Landing, 122
Kingsboro', 168
Kingsbridge, 601
Kingsbury, 572
KINGS COUNTY, 219
Kingston, 556
Kinney's Corners, 431
Kirkland, 361
Kirkville, 387
Knowlesville, 430
Knox, 51
Knoxville, 532
Kortright, 130
Kysorville, 251

Lafayette, 384
Lafayette Corners, 137
La Grange, 137, 603
Lairdsville, 376
Lake Pleasant, 191
Lakeville, 248, 462
Lancaster, 153
Lansing, 553
Little Britain, 418
Lansingburg, 468
Laona, 91
Lawyersville, 516
Lasselsville, 167
Lathrop's Corners, 82
Latintown, 559
Laurens, 444
Lawrence, 484
Lebanon, 260
Lee, 365
Leesville, 524
Ledyard, 80
Le Fargeville, 212
Leicester, 246
Lenox, 260
Leon, 85
Leonardsville, 255
Le Ray, 211
Le Roy, 179, 444
Levanna, 80
Lewis, 157
Lewisboro', 590
LEWIS COUNTY, 238
Lewiston, 348
Lexington, 189
Leyden, 239
Liberty, 530, 547
Lima, 248
Lincklaen, 101
Lindley, 531
Lindon, 430
Lisbon, 484
Lisle, 72
Litchfield, 196
Little Falls, 196
Little Valley, 85
Little Utica, 384
Liverpool, 394
Livingston, 119

LIVINGSTON COUNTY, 242
Livingstonville, 516
Livonia, 248
Locke, 80
Lockport, 212, 351
Lockville, 578
Lodi, 525
LONG ISLAND, 251
Long Lake, 191
Lorraine, 211
Louisville, 484
Lowville, 239
Lloydsville, 447
Ludlowville, 553
Lumberland, 547
Luzerne, 566
Lyme, 211
Lyndon, 85
Lyons, 579
Lysander, 384

Machias, 86
Macedon, 579
Macksville. 403
McLeansville, 552
McDonough, 101
McGrawsville, 124
Madison, 260
MADISON COUNTY, 255
Madrid, 484
Malden, 559
Malone, 165
Malta, 492
Mamakating, 547
Mamaroneck, 591
Manhattanville, 338
Mann's Valley, 516
Mansville, 202
Marbleborough, 558
Marcellus, 387
Manchester, 408
Manheim, 198
Manlius, 384
Mansfield, 86
Marathon, 125
Marbletown, 558
Marion, 580
Marcy, 365
Marshall. 365
Martinsburg, 240
Maryland, 444
Mason's Corners, 105
Masonville, 130
Massena, 485
Mattatuck, 545
Mattawan, 134
Matthews Mills, 387
Matildaville, 485
Mayfield, 174
Mayville, 88
Mechanicsville, 142, 499
Mecklenburg, 552
Medina, 430
Mendon, 265
Mentz, 80
Meredith, 130
Mexico, 432
Middleburg, 603
Middleburg, 518
Middlefield, 444
Middleport, 199, 359
Middle Settlement, 265
Middlesex, 607
Middleville, 194
Middletown, 130, 428, 492, 478
Milan, 80, 137
Mill Brook, 158
Millers Place, 534
Milford, 444
Milltown, 449, 452
Milton, 492, 558
Millville, 430, 464
Milo, 607

Mina, 90
Minaville, 278
Minden, 279
Minerva, 157
Minisink, 419
Mixville, 60
Mohawk, 194, 280
Moira, 166
Monroe, 421
MONROE COUNTY, 263
Montezuma, 80
Montgomery, 423
MONTGOMERY Co., 272
Monticello, 447, 548
Mooers, 106
Mooersville, 130
Moravia, 81
Moreau, 493
Morehouse, 191
Morgansville, 180
Moriah, 158
Moriches, 535
Morrisiana, 597
Morrisville, 257
Morristown, 485
Moscow, 246
Motts' Corners, 552
Mount Hope, 423
Mount Morris, 248
Mount Pleasant, 593
Mount Upton, 101
Mud Creek, 528
Murray, 430

Nanticoke, 72
Naphanock, 560
Naples, 408
Napoli, 86
Narrowsburg, 547
Nassau, 468
Natural Bridge, 219
Navarino, 389
Near Rockaway, 456
Nelson, 260
Neskayuna, 54, 508
Netterville, 509
Nettlehill, 93
Neversink, 547
New Albion, 86
Newark, 549, 578
New Baltimore, 189
New Berlin, 101
New Brighton, 474
Newburg, 424
New Castle, 596
New City, 476
Newcomb, 158
Newfield, 553
New Fane, 352
New Hackensack, 135
New Hartford, 365
New Haven, 432
New Hudson, 60
New Lebanon, 120
New Lisbon, 444
New London, 375
New Ohio, 72
New Paltz, 559
Newport, 199
New Rochelle, 596
Newry, 188
New Scotland, 51
Newstead, 153
Newtown, 460
New Utretcht, 237
New Windsor, 425
New York, 284
NEW YORK COUNTY, 284
Niagara, 352
NIAGARA COUNTY, 347
Nicholas Point, 582
Nicholas, 549
Nicholsville, 174
Nicholville, 484

Niles, 81
Nineveh, 72
Nisbets Corners, 365
Nobleville, 444
Norfolk, 485
North Armenia, 137
Northampton, 174
North Castle, 596
Northfield, 475
North Hempstead, 462
North East, 137
North Port, 540
North Salem, 596
Northville, 174
Northumberland, 493
Norway, 199
Norwich, 102, 463
Nunda, 60
Nyack, 478

Oakfield, 179
Oakhill, 188
Oak Orchard, 430
Oaksville, 445
Ohio, 199
Ogden, 265
Ogdensburg, 485
Old Attlebury, 142
Olean, 86
Olive, 559
Omar, 92
Oneida Castleton, 375
ONEIDA COUNTY, 360
Oneonta, 444
Onondaga, 389
ONONDAGA COUNTY, 383
Ontario, 580
ONTARIO COUNTY, 403
Oppenheim, 174
Oquago. 70
Oran, 392
ORANGE COUNTY, 411
Orange, 532
Orangetown, 478
Orangeville, 603
Oriskany, 377
Oriskany Falls, 360
Orleans, 212
ORLEANS COUNTY, 429
Orville, 383
Orwell, 432
Osborn's Bridge, 174
Osborneville, 189
Ossian, 60
Oswegatchie, 485
Oswego, 432
OSWEGO COUNTY, 431
Owego, 549
Otego, 445
Otisco, 392
Otisville, 423
Otto, 86
Otsego, 445
OTSEGO COUNTY, 439
Otselic, 102
Ovid, 525
Owasco, 81
Owensville, 597
Oxbow, 201
Oxford, 102, 411
Oyster Bay, 462
Oyster Ponds, 545

Painted Post, 532
Palatine, 282
Palermo, 438
Palmers' Corners, 105
Pamelia, 212
Palmyra, 580
Paradox, 158
Panama, 90
Paris, 366
Parish. 438
Parishville, 489

COUNTIES, TOWNSHIPS, VILLAGES.

Parma, 265
Patchogue, 535
Paterson, 449
Patroon's Mills, 464
Pavilion, 180
Pawling, 137
Peekskill, 585
Peckville, 135
Pekin, 348
Pelham, 596
Pembroke, 180
Pendleton, 357
Penfield, 266
Penn Yan, 607
Perrinton, 266
Perry, 552, 603
Perrysburg, 86
Perrysville, 106, 258
Persia, 86
Peru, 106
Peruville, 552
Peterboro', 260
Petersburg, 469
Perth, 174
Pharsalia, 104
Phelps, 409
Philadelphia, 212
Philipsburg, 56, 428
Philipsport, 547
Philipstown, 449
Phœnix, 439, 444
Pierpont, 489
Piermont, 478
Pike, 61
Pinckney, 242
Pine Hill, 179
Pine Bridge, 601
Pine Plains, 137
Piseco, 191
Pitcairn, 489
Pitcher, 104
Pitts Flats, 409
Pittsfield, 447
Pittsford, 266
Pittstown, 469
Plainfield, 447
Plainville, 384
Plattakill, 516
Plattekill, 559
Plattsburg, 108
Pleasant Plains, 133
Pleasant Valley, 137, 167
Pleasantville, 593
Plymouth, 104
Poesten Kill, 469
Poland, 90, 199
Pomfret, 90
Pompey, 392
Poolville, 259
Portage, 61, 365
Porter, 357
Portland, 92
Port Byron, 80
Port Benjamin, 560
Port Chester, 597
Port Douglas, 155
Port Genesee, 263
Port Gibson, 408
Port Henry, 158
Port Hickson, 560
Port Jackson, 278
Port Jarvis, 417
Port Jefferson, 534
Port Kent, 155
Port Randall, 155
Port Richmond, 475
Portville, 86
Potsdam, 489
Potter, 607
Potters Hollow, 52
Poughkeepsie, 137
Poughquake, 133
Poundridge, 597
Prattsburg, 532

Prattsville, 189
Pratts Hollow, 257
Preble, 125
Preston, 105
Princetown, 509
Providence, 493
Pulaski, 438
Pulteney, 532
Pulteneyville, 583
PUTNAM COUNTY, 448
Putnam Valley, 452
Putnam, 575
Pulvers Corners, 137
Punchkill, 516

Quaker Hill, 137
Queensbury, 566
QUEENS COUNTY, 452
Queenston Heights, 349
Quincy, 92
Quogue, 543

Ramapo, 482
Ramerton, 464
Randolph, 87
Ransomville, 551
Rawsonville, 167
Raynertown, 456
Reading, 532
Redfield, 438
Redford, 113
Redhook, 140
Red Mills, 449
Remsen, 366
Rensselaer, 469
RENSSELAER COUNTY, 463
Rensselaerburg, 484
Rensselaer's Mills, 469
Rensselaerville, 51
Reynales Basin, 359
Reynoldsville, 552
Rhinebeck, 141
Riceville, 86
Ridgeway, 430
Richfield, 447
Richford, 551
Richland, 438
Richmond, 409
RICHMOND COUNTY, 473
Richmondville, 516
Richville, 180, 484
Riga, 266
Ripley, 92
Riverhead, 540
Roanoke, 180
Rochester, 266, 559
Rock City, 137, 492
Rock Glen, 135
Rockland, 547
ROCKLAND COUNTY, 475
Rodman, 212
Rome, 366
Romulus, 525
Rondoubt, 557
Root, 283
Rossie, 490
Rose, 582
Rosendale, 556
Rossville, 475
Rouses Point, 106
Rotterdam, 509
Roxbury, 130
Royalton, 359
Rush, 270
Rushville, 408, 549, 607
Rushford, 65
Russel, 490
Russia, 199
Rutland, 212
Rutledge, 84
Rye, 597

Sacketts Harbor, 202
Sagg Harbor, 543

St. Johnsville, 283
St. Regis, 163
Salem, 92, 575
Salina, 393
Salisbury, 199, 411
Salt Point, 137
Sampsondale, 476
Sanford, 73
Sandusky, 85
Sandlake, 469
Sandy Creek, 430, 438
Sandy Hill, 572
Sangerfield, 370
Saranac, 113
Saratoga, 493
Sardinia, 153
SARATOGA COUNTY, 491
Saratoga Springs, 498
Saugerties, 559
Saquoit, 366
Savannah, 582
Sawpitts, 597
Scarsdale, 597
Scotchtown, 428
Schaghticoke, 469
Schenectady, 509
Schoharie, 520
SCHOHARIE COUNTY, 515
Schodac, 469
Schroon, 158
Schroeppel, 439
Schultz Corners, 133
Schuyler, 199
Schuylerville, 493
Scienceville, 189
Scio, 65, 430
Scipio, 81
Scotia, 507
Scott, 125
Scottsville, 271
Scriba, 439
Searsburg, 417, 552
Sempronius, 81
Seneca, 409
SENECA COUNTY, 525
Seneca Falls, 525
Sennet, 81
Separate, 142
Seward, 524
Setauket, 534
Shandaken, 559
Sharon, 524
Shawangunk, 559
Shelby, 430
Shelter Island, 541
Sheldon, 603
Shenandoah, 135
Sherburne, 105
Sheridan, 92
Sherman, 92
Sherman's Mills, 469
Shookville, 137
Shortsville, 408
Shumla, 92
Sibley's Corners, 270
Sidney, 130
Siloam, 260
Silver Creek, 90
Sinclairville, 88
Sing Sing, 593
Skanandoa, 375
Skeneateles, 401
Sloansville, 523
Slaterville, 552
Sleepy Hollow, 595
Smithborough, 551
Smith's Corners, 82
Smithfield, 260
Smithtown, 516, 541
Smithville, 105, 201, 202
Smoky Hollow, 114
Smyrna, 105
Sodus, 582
Solesville, 260

Solon, 125
Somers, 597
Somerville, 490
Somerset, 359
South Bristol, 411
South East, 452
Southfield, 475
Southampton, 543
Southold, 545
Southport, 99
South Salem, 590
Spafford, 403
Sparta, 249, 593
Speigleton, 468
Speedville, 552
Spencer's Basin, 265
Spencer, 551
Spencertown, 114
Spencer's Corners, 137
Speunk, 543
Spracker's Basin, 283
Springfield, 447
Springmill, 60
Springport, 81
Springtown, 559
Springwater, 251
Springville, 122
Stamford, 132
Stafford, 180
Stanford, 142
Stanton Hill, 189
Stapleton, 475
Stark, 199
Starkey, 608
Stephentown, 469
Sterling, 81
Steuben, 371
STEUBEN COUNTY, 527
Stewart's Corners, 142
Stillwater, 499
St. Johnsville, 283
St. Helena, 602
ST. LAWRENCE CO., 482
Stockbridge, 260
Stockholm, 490
Stockport, 122
Stockton, 92
Stone Arabia, 282
Stone Mill, 212
Stonybrook, 534
Stormville, 135
Stowe's Square, 239
Stratford, 174
Strykersville, 518, 603
Stuart's Corners, 82
Stuyvesant, 122
SUFFOLK COUNTY, 533
Sugar Loaf, 428
Sullivan, 260
SULLIVAN COUNTY, 546
Summer Hill, 81
Summer Valley, 57
Summit, 524
Sweden, 271
Syracuse, 395

Taberg, 360
Taghkanic, 123
Talcott's Corners, 82
Talcottville, 239
Tannersville, 189
Tappan, 478
Tarrytown, 588
Theresa, 201
Thompson, 547
Thompsonville, 548
Throopsville, 80
Ticonderoga, 158
Tioga, 551
TIOGA COUNTY, 548
Tomhenick, 469
Tompkins, 132
TOMPKINS COUNTY, 551
Tompkinsville, 474

COUNTIES, TOWNSHIPS, VILLAGES. 9

Tonawanda, 153, 359
Trenton, 372
Triangle, 73
Troupsburg, 532
Troy, 469
Trumansburg, 553
Truxton, 125
Tully, 403
Tunesassah, 82
Tupper's Corners, 82
Turin, 242
Tylersville, 212
Tyre, 526
Tyrone, 532

Ullines, 469
ULSTER COUNTY, 555
Ulsterville, 559
Ulysses, 553
Unadilla, 447
Unadilla Forks, 447
Union, 73
Union Corners, 251
Union Falls, 166
Union Square, 432
Union Mills, 167
Union Springs, 81
Union Vale, 142
Union Village, 571
Unionville, 420, 593
Upper Landing, 135
Urbana, 532
Utica, 373

Valatie, 118
Varysburg, 603
Van Buren, 403
Vanhornsville, 199
Varick, 526
Venice, 82
Verbank, 142

Vermont, 89
Verna, 552
Vernon, 375
Verona, 375
Versailles, 86
Vesper, 403
Vestal, 74
Veteran, 99
Victor, 411
Victory, 82
Vienna, 375, 409
Villenova, 92
Virgil, 125
Volney, 439
Vorheesville, 278

Waddington, 485
Wadham's Mills, 162
Wainscott, 536
Waits Corners, 576
Walden, 423
Wales, 154
Wallkill, 428
Walton, 132
Walworth, 583
Wampsville, 260
Warren, 199, 476
WARREN COUNTY, 561
Warrensburgh, 567
Warsaw, 604, 605
Warwick, 428
Washington, 142
WASHINGTON Co., 567
Washingtonville, 411, 439
Washington Hollow, 137
Waterburg, 553
Waterborough, 90
Waterford, 505
Waterloo, 526
Watertown, 212
Waterville, 371

Waterville Corners, 153
Water Valley, 153
Watervliet, 54
Watson, 242
Wawarsing, 560
Wayne, 533
WAYNE COUNTY, 578
Webster, 271
Wellsburg, 99
Weedsport, 80
Wells, 191
West Almond, 65
West Bloomfield, 411
West Farms, 597
Westfield, 93
West Galway, 167
West Milford, 92
West Point, 411
Westchester, 597
WESTCHESTER Co., 584
Westerlo, 55
Western, 376
Westfield, 475
Westford, 448
Westhampton, 543
Westmoreland, 376
Westport, 162
West Troy, 54
West Turin, 242
Westville, 166, 448
Wethersfield, 604
Wheatfield, 359
Wheatland, 271
Wheeler, 533
White's Corners, 153
White Creek, 576
Whitehall, 577
Whitehaven, 153
White Plains, 598,
Whitesborough, 377
Whitestown, 377

Whitestone, 453
Whitesville, 60, 212
Whitlockville, 584
Willet, 125
Williamsburg, 234
Williamson, 583
Williamstown, 212, 439
Williamsville, 143
Willsborough, 162
Wilmington, 162
Wilmurt, 199
Wilna, 219
Wilson, 359
Wilton, 506
Winansville, 188
Windham, 189
Windsor, 70
Winfield, 199
Winton, 199
Wirt, 66
Wolcott, 583
Woodburn, 547
Woodhull, 533
Woodstock, 256, 561
Woodville, 202
Worcester, 448
Wurtzboro', 547
Wynantskill, 464
Wyoming, 603
WYOMING COUNTY, 601

Yates, 430
YATES COUNTY, 604
Yatesville, 605, 608
Yaughcrippiebush, 558
Yonkers, 601
York, 251
Yorkshire, 87
Yorktown, 601
Yorkville, 338, 377
Youngstown, 357

POPULATION OF THE COUNTIES IN THE STATE OF NEW YORK IN 1840.

Albany,	68,546	Herkimer,	37,378	Richmond,	10,985
Allegany,	40,920	Jefferson,	61,064	Rockland,	11,874
Broome,	22,348	Kings,	47,613	Saratoga,	40,450
Cattaraugus,	28,803	Lewis,	17,849	Schenectady,	17,233
Cayuga,	50,362	Livingston,	35,710	Schoharie,	32,351
Chautauque,	47,641	Madison,	40,007	Seneca,	24,868
Chemung,	20,731	Monroe,	64,912	St. Lawrence,	56,693
Chenango,	40,779	Montgomery,	35,801	Steuben,	45,992
Clinton,	28,178	New York,	312,932	Suffolk,	32,469
Columbia,	44,237	Niagara,	31,114	Sullivan,	15,630
Cortland,	24,605	Oneida,	85,327	Tioga,	20,350
Delaware,	35,363	Onondaga,	67,914	Tompkins,	38,113
Dutchess,	52,488	Ontario,	43,501	Ulster,	45,724
Erie,	62,153	Orange,	50,733	Warren,	13,470
Essex,	23,611	Orleans,	25,015	Washington,	41,095
Franklin,	16,450	Oswego,	43,820	Wayne,	42,160
Fulton,	18,038	Otsego,	49,412	Westchester,	48,687
Genesee,	59,640	Putnam,	12,825	Yates,	20,442
Greene,	30,446	Queens,	30,324		
Hamilton,	1,907	Rensselaer,	60,303	Total,	2,429,476

INDEX.

Adirondack Mountains.......................... 157
Amsterdam, Nieuw, in 1659................... 287
Andre, taking of................................ 479
Andre, execution of............................ 588
Anecdotes, ludicrous........................... 446
Anecdotes, singular............................ 187
Allen, William H. epitaph..................... 118
Ararat, city of.................................. 153
Arnold the traitor, anecdote of................ 283
Antone, Abram, trial of....................... 257
Astor House.................................... 334

Barber, Lieutenant-colonel, death of........... 137
Baker, Miss Rachel, the sleeping preacher..... 387
Backus, Azel, D. D. epitaph................... 364
Barber, Robert, murder of..................... 261
Ballad, on the destruction of Schenectady..... 513
Battery and Castle Garden..................... 331
Bennington, battle of........................... 466
Beach, Timothy, adventures of................. 130
Bear, conflict with............................. 554
Bishop, Sarah, hermitess....................... 590
Big Kettle, notice of........................... 84
Bowne Mansion House......................... 453
Boyd, Lieutenant, horrible death of........... 247
Black Kettle, notice of......................... 390
Black Rock, attack on.......................... 144
Brock, Sir James, death of..................... 349
Brant, Joseph, notice of........................ 275
Brant, conference with......................... 447
Brown, Colonel, notice of...................... 283
Bread, scarcity of............................... 550
British officers, description of................. 308
Bristol, wreck of................................ 457
Burgess, Daniel, escape of...................... 61
Burgoyne, surrender of......................... 497
Buffalo, burning of.............................. 151
Butler House, Mohawk......................... 282
Butlers, fac-simile of........................... 273
Butler, Walter, death of........................ 172

Captive boys of Rensselaerville................. 52
Cahoes Falls..................................... 54
Canajoharie, invasion of........................ 275
Caroline, burning of............................ 357
Cameron, Dugald, epitaph..................... 530
Carthage Bridge................................. 269
Catskill Mountain House....................... 185
Cayuga Bridge................................... 79
Census, New York city, State, and the United States............................ 235
Chateaugay, skirmish at........................ 164
Chatauque gas springs.......................... 91
Child, first born in Long Island................ 220
Chimney Point Gulf............................ 241
Church, ancient, at Caughnawaga.............. 281
Church, ancient, Albany........................ 46
Churches, number of, in New York............ 329
Cholera in New York........................... 314
Chippewa, battle of............................. 354
Cherry Valley, destruction of................... 442
Chemung, battle of.............................. 96
City Hall, New York............................ 316
Clinton, George, notice of...................... 419
Clinton, De Witt, notice of..................... 426
Clinton Liberal Institute....................... 362
Cornplanter, notice of........................... 83

Cork Island, Oxford............................ 104
Colden, Governor, effigy of.................... 297
Colbraith, Colonel, anecdote of................ 366
Cozier, E. S., epitaph.......................... 375
Colden, Cadwallader, notice of................. 454
Cochran, Dr. John, epitaph.................... 375
Cobelskill, attack on............................ 516
Corn, early method of pounding............... 531
Crosby, Enoch, notice of....................... 135
Croton Aqueduct................................ 336
Customhouse.................................... 323

Dana, General James, notice of................ 517
Deserter, execution of.......................... 464
De Fonclaire, J. B. V., epitaph................ 173
Dean, Esq., James, notice of................... 376
Diploma for the Indians........................ 173
Dodd, Rev. Bethuel, epitaph................... 382
Downie, Commodore, epitaph.................. 113
Dover stone church............................. 134
Doxtader, J., the tory, defeat of................ 524
Dream, remarkable.............................. 171
Dutch, ancient, church......................... 46
Dutch church, Fishkill.......................... 136
Dutch church, ancient.......................... 595
Dwight's, Dr., description of Westchester County in the revolution............. 592

Edwards, George C. epitaph.................... 530
Edwards, D. D., Jonathan, epitaph............ 514
Erie Canal celebration.......................... 334
Emmet, Thomas Addis, epitaph................ 347
Esopus, Indian attack on....................... 557

Fire, great, in New York, 1776................. 303
Fire, great, in New York, 1835................. 321
Fort Erie, assault on............................ 145
Fort Erie, sortie of.............................. 146
Fort Plain, block-house......................... 279
Fort Ann, battle near........................... 568
Fort Edward, plan of........................... 569
Fox, George, notice of.......................... 454
Frazer, General, death of....................... 504
French colony, account of...................... 392
French emigrants in Greene County........... 100
Fulton, Robert, notice of....................... 340

Gardner, Lyon, notice of....................... 536
Garretson, Freeborn, notice of................. 141
Genesee Falls.................................... 269
Glenns Falls..................................... 566
Glenville, incursion into........................ 507
Gray, Colonel, death of......................... 210
Granger, Gideon, epitaph...................... 407
Greig, Captain, remarkable preservation of... 369
Gothic or Temperance Hall.................... 329

Harpers, William and John, adventures of.... 128
Hamilton, Miss Sally, murder of............... 181
Hanford's Landing.............................. 264
Hale, Captain Nathan, notice of................ 308
Halls of Justice.................................. 318
Harlem Tunnel.................................. 338
Hamilton, Alexander, notice of................. 344
Hamilton, Alexander, epitaph.................. 347
Hamilton College................................ 361
Hathaway, Hon. Joshua, epitaph.............. 370

INDEX.

Han Yerry, anecdote of	379
Herkimer, General, notice of	192
Herkimer, burning of	195
Hendrick, King, notice of	280
Hendy, Colonel, anecdote of	98
Hornby Lodge	64
Hosack, Rev. S., D. D. epitaph	173
Holland Land Company's Office	176
Hughes, John, Welsh epitaph on	375
Hurlgate	461
Indian forts at Philipsburg	56
Indian antiquities, Oxford	103
Indians, interview with, in 1691	235
Irving, Washington, residence of	588
Jay, John, LL. D. notice of	584
Jefferson barracks	211
Jemison, Mary, the "white woman"	602
Johnson Hall	168
Johnson, Sir William, notice of	168
Johnson, Sir John, incursion of	170
Johnson, Sir Guy, residence of	272
Johnsons, the fac-similes of	273
Kalm, Professor, visit to Albany	47
Kidd's Heights, Albany	45
Kidd, William, the pirate	536
Kirtland, Rev. Mr. notice of	362
King, Rufus, notice of	460
Kingston destroyed	557
Knickerbocker, extract from	290
Kosciusko, notice of	415
Kunze, J. C., D. D. notice of	347
Lake George, battle of	563
Lawrence, Captain J., epitaph	346
Lee, Ann, notice of	55
Leverich, Rev. Mr. notice of	461
Letter, anonymous, Newburg	425
Livingston, Robert R. notice of	115
Livingston, Philip, notice of	339
Livingston, William, notice of	340
Livingston, Brockholst	342
Livingston's Manor	119
Liberty-pole, first, in Mohawk Valley	194
Little Falls, Indian descent at	198
Lindesay, Mr. notice of	440
Louis Philippe, King, visit to Elmira	98
Long Island, battle of	228
Long Island, history of	251
Long Island, Indians of	253
Lundy's Lane, battle of	355
Mann, J. D. Milton, epitaph	118
McCrea, Miss Jane, murder of	569
McKenzie, A. epitaph	173
Mersereau, Judge, notice of	73
Merrick, Martha, epitaph of	124
Merchants' Exchange, New York	325
Mexico, wreck of	457
Meigs, Colonel, expedition of	544
Minisink, invasion of	420
Montour, Catharine, notice of	94
Mooers, General, epitaph on	112
Morgan, William, abduction of	177
Monumental inscription, Sackett's Harbor	211
Moody, Lady, notice of	236
Mohawk Castles, taking of	277
Monument at Hempstead	456
Monumental pile, Indian	278
Monument at Goshen	418
Montgomery, General, notice of	343
Montgomery, epitaph	346
Montgomery, Fort, capture of	422
Montgomery, Fort, shocking appearance at	423
Montauk Point, view of	537
Morris, Gouverneur, notice of	597
Mormonism, origin of	580
Musquetoes, Indian tradition respecting	81
Murder near the Sterling Iron Works	428
Murphy, T. adventures of	518
Navy Yard, Brooklyn	221
Negro plot	295
New York, evacuation of	310
New York in 1800	315
New York University	326
New York Deaf and Dumb Asylum	327
Newspapers, ancient, extracts from	296
Niagara Falls, view of	353
Niagara Fort, account of	358
Norton, Seth M. epitaph	364
Novel marriage	514
Oak, ancient, at Lyons	579
Oak openings	180
Officers, Dutch names of	287
Ogdensburg, attack on	486
Oneida Institute, view of	378
Onondagas, account of	389
Onondaga, French colony at, in 1656	398
Oriskany, battle of	390
Oswego, attack on	436
Oswego Fort, surrender of	435
Palatinates, settlement of	521
Painted Post, the history of	530
Parson's, Gen. correspondence with Gov. Tryon	591
Penitentiary, Blackwell's island	320
Perkins, Capt. S. epitaph	370
Peekskill, incursion into	586
Phœnix, burning of	107
Phelps and Gorham's surveys	406
Phelps, Hon. Oliver, epitaph	408
Phillips' patent	595
Pine, large	130
Pike, Gen. Z. M. death of	205
Pike, Gen. Z. M. monumental inscription	211
Pixley, Colonel D. epitaph	551
Plattsburg, battle of	110
Portage Falls, view of	62
Pompey, ancient remains at	392
Prison at Auburn	77
Prison ships, revolutionary	222
Prescott, battle of	487
Proudfit, Rev. J. epitaph	576
Publications, periodical, in New York	333
Putnam's battle with Indians	573
Pulteneyville, invasion of	583
Queenstown Heights, battle of	349
Red Jacket, notice of	149
Red Jacket, conference with	406
Rensselaer tenants, riot of	114
Rensselaer, manor of	472
Rensselaer, Hon. Stephen, notice of	50
Revolutionary incidents in New York	304
Rivington press destroyed	300
Robbery at Fishkill	136
Rochester, O'Reilly's sketches of	267
Rockwell, J. O. notice of	386
Robinson House, the	450
Roger's Rock	565
Royalists executed at Kingston	558
Salt procured by Indians	74
Sammons, Sampson, adventures of	171
Sackett's Harbor, attack on	207
Sandy Creek, battle at	202
Sanger, Jedidiah, notice of	365
Salina salt works	396
Sailor's Snug Harbor	474
Sabbath Day Point	565
Sandy Hill, Indian barbarities at	573
Schlosser Landing, view of	356
Schenando, notice of	363
Schuyler, Honyost, stratagem of	369
Schuyler, General Philip, notice of	498
Schuyler Mansion House	494
Schenectady, destruction of	511
Schoharie, middle fort, attack on	518
Schoharie stone church	522
Seneca oil spring	59
Seneca Mission House	149
Senecas invaded by the French	243
Senecas, sacrifice of	268

INDEX.

Shakers, notice of.................................. 55
Shakers at New Lebanon..................... 120
Silliman, Major-general, capture of............ 463
Sing Sing Prison................................. 593
Skeene, Major, royalist........................... 577
Smith, Richard, notice of........................ 541
Smith, Joseph, the Mormon.................... 580
Sleepy Hollow..................................... 595
Spanish Hill, Chemung........................... 95
Spy, Indian, death of.............................. 508
Standard, first, taken in last war................ 163
Stadt Huys in 1642................................ 236
Stuyvesant, Governor, notice of................ 339
Sterling, Lord, notice of.......................... 343
Stanwix, Fort, siege of........................... 368
Steuben, Baron, notice of........................ 371
Stillwater, battle at................................ 499
Steamboat, Fulton, first American.............. 342

Tammany Hall, New York...................... 330
Tallmadge, Colonel, expedition of.............. 534
Ticonderoga, Fort................................. 158
Ticonderoga, capture of, by Allen............... 159
Ticonderoga, St. Clair's evacuation of.......... 161
Tornado in Allegany County..................... 57
Tripe's Hill, first settlers at...................... 281
Trenton Falls....................................... 373
Truxton, Commodore, notice of................ 460
Troy Female Seminary........................... 471
Tryon, correspondence with..................... 591
Tunnel at Portage.................................. 63

Union College..................................... 510
Union Race Course................................ 459

Van Buren, President, birthplace............... 119
Van Buren, Abraham A. epitaph................ 119
Van Kleek House.................................. 138
Van Renselaer, S. notice of...................... 50
Van Tassel Mansion.............................. 588
Van Wart, Isaac, epitaph......................... 588

Warrant, ancient.................................. 140
Wadsworth, James and William, notice of..... 245
Washington, Fort, capture of.................... 600
Washington inaugurated......................... 324
Washington's head-quarters, Newburg......... 424
Walnut tree, large................................. 90
Walker, Rev. Elnathan........................... 124
Wawarsing, burning of........................... 560
Wedding, curious.................................. 384
West Point Academy............................. 412
West Point, ancient view of..................... 416
Wheat, &c. price of, 1804........................ 174
White, Hugh, notice of........................... 378
White, Hugh, epitaph............................. 382
White Plains, battle of........................... 598
Williams, Rev. Mr. capture of................... 163
Willet, Colonel Marinus, notice of.............. 460
Williamson, Captain, first settler at Bath...... 529
Wilkinson, Jemima, "the Universal Friend"... 605
William Henry, Fort, capture of................ 564
Woolsey, Major, cowardice of................... 520

Yeo, Sir James, amusing alarm of, near Rochester, 270
Yellow Fever in New York...................... 311
York Island, military movements on........... 301
York, U. C. attack on............................ 203
Young, Major G. D. notice of................... 163

OMISSIONS AND CORRECTIONS.

Page 50, the *Albany Medical College* is a flourishing Institution. Its officers are a President, Registrar, Librarian, and eight Professors. Number of students in 1841, one hundred and twenty-three.

Page 95, the village of *Horseheads* is about five miles north of Elmira, so called, it is said, from the sculls of horses found near it, slaughtered for food by Sullivan's army.

Page 120, Pop. of New Lebanon, 2,534.

Page 282, for *Tryon*, read Campbell.

Page 308, for DAVID, read NATHAN HALE.

Page 472, there are at this time (1841) 17 churches in Troy, viz: 3 Episcopal, 4 Presbyterian, 1 Scotch Presbyterian, 2 Baptist, 2 Methodist, 1 Friends, 1 Universalist, 1 Catholic, and 2 African.

NEW YORK.

OUTLINE HISTORY.

THERE is reason to believe that the first Europeans who landed on the soil of New York, were the crew of a French vessel under the command of John de Verrazzano, a Florentine, in the service of Francis I., of France. "Verrazzano had been for some time intrusted with the command of four ships, in cruising against the Spaniards. These vessels being separated in a storm, the commander resolved with one of them, the *Dauphin*, to undertake a voyage for the purpose of discovering new countries." About the middle of March, 1524, he arrived on the American coast near Wilmington, N. C. From this point he proceeded as far south as Georgia. He then turned and proceeded northward, until he came to about the latitude of 41° north, where he entered a harbor, which, from his description, is believed to be that of New York.*

It appears from Verrazzano's account, that he stayed in the harbor about fifteen days. It seems he had much intercourse with the natives of the country. "They came on board his ship frequently, and without reserve; traded with him freely for such articles as he needed, and generally attended his men, in greater or smaller numbers, whenever they went on shore." He sailed from the harbor on the 5th of May, and proceeded as far north as the coast of Labrador; from thence he sailed for France, where he arrived in July. In a letter to the king, he gave an account of his voyage, giving the name of *New France* to the country he visited. As his voyage neither produced nor promised any addition to the revenues of France, his discoveries were not pursued, and even the memory of it was almost forgotten. It is supposed that Verrazzano, in a subsequent voyage, was cut to pieces and devoured by the savages.

In 1607, a London company fitted out a ship under the command of Henry Hudson, for the purpose of discovering a northwestern passage to the East Indies. This voyage, and another the next year

---

* An account of this voyage, given in a letter to the French king, is found in Richard Hakluyt's Voyages, Navigations, &c., published in 1600, in London, in three vols. folio. It is republished in vol. i. of the Coll. of the New York Hist. Soc.

for the same purpose, both proving unsuccessful, the company suspended their patronage. Hudson then went to Holland, and entered into the service of the celebrated Dutch East India Company. This company fitted out a small ship, named *Half Moon*, under the command of Hudson, with a crew it is said of twenty men, Dutch and English. Hudson left Amsterdam on the 4th, the Texel on the 6th of April, and arrived on the American coast on the 18th of July, 1609, near Portland, in the state of Maine.

Pursuing his course southward, Hudson came to Cape Cod, where he landed, about the 3d of August. After this, he sailed southward and westward for one-and-twenty days, " making remarks on the soundings and currents," until he came to the entrance of Chesapeak Bay, about the 24th of August. From this point, he returned northward along the coast, and on the 28th discovered Delaware Bay During the six following days, Hudson pursued his northerly course, until, on the 3d of September, 1609, he anchored within Sandy Hook.

" The next day, the 4th of September, he sent a boat on shore for the purpose of fishing. The tradition is that his men first landed on Coney Island, which lies near to Long Island, and now makes a part of Kings county. On the same day the natives came on board his ship, as she lay at anchor, conducting themselves with great apparent friendliness, and discovering a strong disposition to barter the produce of their country for knives, beads, clothes, and other articles of a similar kind. The next day, the 5th of September, Hudson again sent his boat on shore, for the purpose, as appears from the journal, of exploring and sounding the waters lying to the south, within Sandy Hook, and forming what is now called the Horse Shoe. Here the boat's crew landed and penetrated some distance into the woods, in what is now Monmouth county, in New Jersey. They were very well received by the natives, who presented them very kindly with what the journal calls 'green tobacco,' and also with 'dried currants;' [these were probably whortleberries,] which are represented as having been found in great plenty, and of a very excellent quality.

"On the 6th of September, Hudson sent a boat manned with five hands to explore what appeared to be the mouth of a river, at the distance of about four leagues from the ship. This was no doubt the strait between Long and Staten islands, generally called the Narrows. Here, the writer of the journal observes, 'a good depth of water was found;' and within, a large opening, and a narrow river to the west; in which it is evident he refers to what is now called the Kills, or the channel between Bergen Neck and Staten Island. In exploring the bay and the adjacent waters, the boat's crew spent the whole day. On their way in returning to the ship towards night, they were attacked by the natives, in two canoes; the one carrying fourteen men, and the other twelve. A skirmish ensued, in which one of Hudson's men, named John Colman, was killed by an arrow, which struck him in the throat, and two more were wounded. The next day the remains of Colman were interred on a point of land not far from the ship, which from that circumstance received the name of Colman's Point; and which, probably, was the same that is now called Sandy Hook.

"On the 8th, 9th and 10th days of September, Hudson still rode cautiously at anchor, without the Narrows, and seems to have been chiefly employed in trading with the natives, and in guarding against any insidious attacks which might have been meditated by them, and which he evidently feared. On the 11th, he sailed through the Narrows, and found, as the writer of the journal expresses it, 'a very good harbor for all winds.' On the 12th, he first entered the river which bears his name, and sailed up about two leagues. On these two days the ship was visited by great numbers of the natives, who brought Indian corn, beans, tobacco, and oysters, in abundance, and exchanged them for such trifles as the ship's company were disposed to barter. They had pipes of 'yellow copper,' in which they smoked. They had also various ornaments of copper; and earthen pots, in which they dressed their meat. But, although they were 'civil,' as the writer of the journal tells us, and 'made show of love,' Hudson did not think proper to trust them; and by no means would suffer any of them to remain on board during the night.

"From the 12th to the 22d of September, Hudson was employed in ascending the river. The journal represents it in general about a mile wide, and of a good depth, abounding with fish, among which were 'great store of salmons.' As he advanced, he found the land on both sides growing higher, until it became 'very mountainous.' This high land, it is observed, 'had many points; the channel was narrow, and there were many eddy winds.' In his passage up the river, the natives frequently came on board of his ship, and sometimes in considerable numbers, but always in an amicable manner.

"Hudson appears to have sailed up the river a little above where the city of Hudson now stands; and beyond that point, he himself never ascended. Not considering it as safe to proceed farther with his ship, he sent a boat with five hands, (the mate, who had the command of the expedition, being one,) to explore and sound the river higher up. The boat proceeded eight or nine leagues beyond where the ship lay at anchor; but finding the soundings extremely irregular, and the depth, in some places, not more than seven feet, it was judged unadvisable to attempt any farther progress. It is evident, from the whole account, that the boat went as far as where the city of Albany now stands.

"It is worthy of notice, that the farther they went up the river, the more friendly and hospitable the natives appeared. After they had passed the highlands, the writer of the journal observes: 'There we found a very loving people, and very old men; and were well used.' On the 18th of September, when the ship was lying about twenty-five or thirty miles below the present situation of Albany, 'the mate,' it is farther observed, 'went on shore with an old savage, a governor of the country, who took him to his house and made him good cheer.' At this place the savages flocked on board the ship in considerable numbers, bringing with them corn, tobacco, pumpkins, and grapes, and some of them beaver and otter skins, which they exchanged for hatchets, knives, beads, and other trifles. On the 20th of September, Hudson and his crew, for the purpose of making an experiment on the temper of the Indians, attempted to make a number of their principal men drunk. But though they 'were all merry,' as the journalist expresses it, only one of them appears to have been completely intoxicated. This phenomenon excited great surprise and alarm among his companions. They knew not what to make of it, and it was not until the next day, when he had completely recovered, that they became composed. This, so far as we know, is the first instance of intoxication by *ardent spirits*, among the Indians on this part of the American continent. It is very remarkable that among the Six Nations there is a tradition, still very distinctly preserved, of a scene of intoxication which occurred with a company of the natives when the ship first arrived....... On the 22d of the month, confidence on the part of the natives being restored, a number of their chiefs came on board the ship as she lay at anchor. This interview the writer of the journal describes in the following manner: 'At three o'clock in the afternoon they came on board, and brought tobacco and beans, and gave them to our master, and made an oration, and showed him all the country round about. Then they sent one of their company on land, who presently returned and brought a great platter of venison, dressed by themselves; and they caused him to eat with them. Then they made him reverence and departed.'

"On the 23d of September, Hudson began to descend the river. On his way down, his men went frequently on shore, and had several very friendly interviews with the natives, who expressed a desire that they might reside among them; and made them an offer of lands for that purpose. But when the ship came below the highlands, the savages appeared to be of a different character, and were extremely troublesome; especially those who inhabited the western side of the river. They attempted to rob the ship, and repeatedly shot at the crew with bows and arrows from several points of land. Hudson's men discharged several muskets at them, and killed ten or twelve of them. In these conflicts, which were frequently renewed during the first and second days of October, none of the ship's crew appears to have been injured. The land on the eastern side of the river, near its mouth, was called by the natives '*Manna-hatta.*'

"On the 4th day of October, (just one month from the day on which he landed within Sandy Hook,) Hudson came out of the river which bears his name; and without anchoring in the bay, immediately stood out to sea. By twelve o'clock at noon that day he was entirely clear of land. He steered directly for Europe; and on the 9th of November following he 'arrived,' as the writer of the journal expresses it, 'in the range of Dartmouth, Devonshire.' Here the journal ends.

"Whether Hudson immediately landed in England, cannot now be clearly ascertained; but it appears that he left that country in April, **1610**, and reached the American coast early in the summer. He soon discovered the great northern bay which bears his name. There, after an unwise delay, he was compelled to pass a distressing and dangerous winter. In the spring, in addition to all his other misfortunes, he found a spirit of dissatisfaction and mutiny growing among his crew, and at length manifesting itself in open violence. This proceeded so far, that on the 22d of June, 1611, a majority of the crew arose, took command of the ship, put Hudson, his son, and seven others, most of whom were sick or lame, into a boat, turned them adrift in the ocean, and abandoned them to their fate. They never were heard of more.

"Hudson did not give his own name to the river which he discovered. The Iroquois Indians called it *Cahohatatea*. The Mahicans, *Mahakaneghtuc*, and sometimes *Shatemuck*. Hudson styled it emphatically the 'Great River,' or the 'Great River of the Mountains;' no doubt from the extraordinary circumstance of such a body of water flowing through the mountains without a cataract. The name of its discoverer, however, was early attached to it. I find it familiarly called Hudson's river, in some of the public documents of the Dutch colonial government; but more frequently the North river, to distinguish it from the Delaware, which was discovered by the same navigator, and which being within the territory claimed by the Dutch, was called by them the South river.

"The Dutch immediately began to avail themselves of the advantage which the discovery of Hudson presented to their view. In 1610, it appears that at least one ship was sent hither by the East India Company, for the purpose of trading in furs, which it is well known continued for a number of years to be the principal object of commercial attraction to this part of the new world. In 1614, a fort and trading-house were erected on the spot where Albany now stands, and called Fort Orange; and about the same time another fort and trading-house were established on the southwest point of Manhattan Island, and called New Amsterdam. The whole colony received the name of New Netherlands."—*Hist. Discourse by Samuel Miller, D. D., vol. i. Coll. New York Hist. Soc.*

In 1621, "the Privileged West India Company" was formed in Holland; this company in 1623 began its operations along the Hudson, with a direct view to colonization. A number of settlers during this year were sent out, under the command of *Cornelis Jacobse Mey*, who were most heartily welcomed by the few previous inhabitants. Before these arrived they had been two years without supplies, and had been obliged to cut up the sails of some of their boats for necessary clothing. In compliment to Capt. Mey, they named the bay of New York *Port Mey*. During the same year the forts *New Amsterdam* and *Orange* were erected, upon the sites of the present cities of New York and Albany.

In 1625, the West India Company freighted two ships, in one of which Peter Minuit arrived in New Netherland, with a company of Waloons, who settled on Long Island opposite New Amsterdam. Minuit is considered by some as the first Governor or Director of

New Netherland. Subordinate to him, the gradation of authority and rank seems to have been: 1. *Opper-Koopman;* 2. *Onder-Koopman;* 3. *Koopman;* 4. *Assistant.* The office of *Opper-Koopman,* chief-merchant or commissary, was vested in Isaac de Raiser. In four or five years the trade with the natives was greatly extended, attracting dealers even from the lakes, and from the banks of the St. Lawrence near Quebec.

In 1629, the company adopted a charter of " Liberties and exemptions for patroons, masters, and private individuals, who should plant colonies in New Netherland, or import thither any neat cattle." The terms of encouragement to those who should send out settlers, were great. Such as should undertake to plant a colony of fifty souls, upwards of fifteen years old, were to be acknowledged *Patroons,* a name denoting something baronial and lordly in rank and means. They were allowed to select lands for miles in extent, which should descend to their posterity for ever. Under this charter, several directors of the company determined to avail themselves of these privileges, among whom were Samuel Goodyn, Samuel Bloemart, Killian Van Rensselaer, the Heer Pauw, and Jan de Laet. These persons sent out Wouter Van Twiller, as agent, to inspect the condition of the country, and to purchase the lands of the natives for the purpose of settlement.

Owing to some disturbances in the colony, Minuit was recalled in 1633, and Wouter Van Twiller was appointed in his place. The arrival of Van Twiller, as governor, gave a fresh impulse to the settlements. During his administration, the controversy occasioned by the encroachments of the English was begun. In 1638, William Kieft succeeded Van Twiller as governor of New Netherland. In 1642, he broke up the English settlement on Long Island, and fitted up two sloops to drive them out of the Schuylkill, of which they had possessed themselves. In 1643, the New England colonies entered into a league both against the Dutch and Indians. In 1646, a severe battle was fought on part of Strickland's Plain, called Horse Neck, between the Dutch and Indians. There appears not to have been any particulars of the action preserved ; but it is said the battle was contested with mutual obstinacy, and great numbers were killed on both sides. The Dutch ultimately remained masters of the field.

In 1647, Peter Stuyvesant arrived at Fort Amsterdam, as governor. He was a brave old officer, and had been commissioned governor-general of Curacoa and the Dutch West Indies. He laid claim to all the lands and streams from Cape Henlopen to Cape Cod ; he went to Hartford, and demanded a surrender to the Dutch of all the lands on Connecticut river. These claims were opposed, and left to the decision of arbitrators. Long Island was divided : the eastern part was to be held by the English, the western by the Dutch ; to the main, the boundaries were amicably adjusted.

In 1664, Charles II. of England, disregarding the Dutch claim on New Netherland, made a grant to his brother, the Duke of York and Albany, which included all the mainland of New England, beginning at St. Croix, extending to the rivers Connecticut and Hudson, "together with the said river called Hudson's river, and all the lands from the west side of Connecticut river, to the east side of Delaware Bay." In order to enforce this claim of England for the New Netherland, an expedition, consisting of three ships, 130 guns, and six hundred men, was sent against it, under the command of Col. Richard Nichols. On his arrival at Manhattan, Nichols demanded the surrender of the fort. Gov. Stuyvesant was exceeding loth to surrender without an attempt at defence, but the favorable terms offered to the inhabitants disposed them to an immediate capitulation. After some fruitless negotiation, during which Gov. Stuyvesant pleaded the justice of the title of the States-General, and the existing peace between them and the English nation, the province was surrendered, August 27th, 1664, upon the most liberal terms to the vanquished.

Having taken possession of the country, Nichols assumed the government, with the title of "Deputy-governor under his royal highness the Duke of York, of all his territories in America." New Amsterdam was now called, in honor of the Duke, New York, and Fort Orange, Albany. Gov. Nichols proceeded to erect a Court of Assizes, consisting of the governor, council, and justices of the peace This court compiled a body of laws, collected from the ancient customs and usages, with additional improvements, such as the times required, regarding English law as the supreme rule. These ordinances were sent to England, and confirmed by the Duke of York the following year.

It is supposed that, at the time Nichols took possession of the province, the Dutch inhabitants were about 6000 in number. New Amsterdam, the metropolis, it is said, contained about 3000 persons, about half of whom returned to Holland. Their habitations, however, were soon occupied by emigrants, partly from Great Britain, but mostly from New England. Upon Hudson river there were many Dutch settlers; and upon the shores of the Delaware, there were numerous plantations of Dutch and Swedes.

Col. Nichols, after having governed the province about three years, resigned his office, and Col. Francis Lovelace was appointed by the duke to succeed him. Lovelace assumed the government in 1667, and continued his administration till the colony was re-surrendered to the Dutch. War having been declared against Holland, a small squadron was sent over by the Dutch, which arrived at Staten Island July 30th, 1673. Lovelace being absent from New York, Captain Manning, who had the charge of the town, rejected the aid of the English inhabitants, who offered to defend the place, sent a messenger to the enemy, and struck his flag before their vessels appeared in sight. As the fleet advanced, the garrison showed their willingness to fight; but Manning forbade a gun to be fired, under pain of death, and surrendered the place unconditionally to the invaders. He was afterwards tried by a court-martial, and pleaded guilty to all the charges preferred. His sentence was as extraordinary as his conduct; it was, that, "though he deserved death, yet, because he had since the surrender been in England, and seen the king and duke, it was adjudged that his sword should be broke over his head, in public, before the City Hall; and himself rendered incapable of wearing a sword, and of serving his majesty for the future, in any public trust in the government."

Anthony Clove was constituted the Dutch governor, but he remained in the office but a short period. A treaty of peace, in 1674, was concluded between the Dutch and English, by which New Netherland was restored to the English. The Duke of York, to remove all controversy respecting his property in America, took out a new patent from the king, and commissioned Major Edmund Andros "Governor of New York, and all his territories in these parts." Andros, as the agent of a despotic master, was unpopular to the people under his government, and involved himself in disputes with the neighboring government of Connecticut.

The province of New York, about the year 1678, contained twenty-four towns, villages, and parishes. Fifteen vessels, on an average, traded yearly with England, importing English manufactures to the value of £50,000 sterling. Its annual exports, besides pease, beef, pork, tobacco, and peltry, consisted of about sixty thousand bushels of wheat. The city of New York contained 3,430 inhabitants, and owned only three ships, eight sloops, and seven boats. "A trader worth £500 was considered a substantial merchant; and the planter, worth half that sum in movables, was accounted rich. All the estates in the colony were valued at £150,000. Ministers were scarce, and religions many. The duke maintained a chaplain at New York, which was the only certain endowment of the church of England. There were about twenty houses for public worship, of which about half were vacant. The law made it obligatory upon every district to build churches, and provide for their ministers, whose compensation varied from £40 to £70 a-year, besides a house and garden. But the Presbyterians and Independents, the greater and more substantial portion of the inhabitants, only, showed much willingness to comply with the requisition. There were no beggars in the province, and the poor were well cared for. The militia amounted to 2000, including 140 horsemen; and some regular troops were maintained for the forts at Albany and New York."

Col. Thomas Dongan arrived at New York, in August, 1683, as the successor of Andros in the government. He immediately, on the request of the magistrates of New York, gave orders that an assembly should be elected by the freeholders. This assembly, consisting of a council of ten, and eighteen representatives, convened at Hempstead on the 17th of October. They passed an act of general naturalization; an act declaring the liberties of the people, or a Bill of Rights; one for defraying the expense of government; and a few others, regulating the internal affairs of the province. In 1686, James II. having come to the throne, on the renewal of Gov. Dongan's commission, refused to confirm the privileges granted when he was Duke of York. The assembly was prohibited, and orders were given to Dongan to "*suffer no printing-press in his government.*" Much disaffection arose at this time, among the colonists, on account of the appointment of professed Catholics to the principal crown offices. At this period there were in the province 4000 foot, 300 horse, and one company of dragoons. The shipping, belonging to the city of New York, had increased to nine or ten three-masted vessels, of about 80 or 90 tons; 200 or 300 ketches or barks, of 40 tons; and about twenty sloops, of twenty-five tons.

In 1687, the French court aimed a blow, which threatened the British interests in North America. M. Denonville, with 1500 French and 500 Indians, took the field against the Senecas, one of the confederated tribes of the "*Five Nations,*" who were the friends of the English. An action took place near the principal Seneca village, in which 100 Frenchmen, ten French Indians, and about eighty of the Senecas were killed. Denonville, the next day, marched forward to burn the village, but found it in ashes. The Senecas had burnt it, and fled. After destroying the corn in this and several other villages, the French returned to Canada. For this attack, and other outrages committed by the French, the confederated Five Nations thirsted for revenge. "On the 26th of July, 1688, twelve hundred of their men landed on the south side of the island of Montreal, while the French were in perfect security, burnt their houses, sacked their plantations, and put to the sword all the men, women, and children, without the skirts of the town. A thousand French were slain in this invasion, and twenty-six carried into captivity, and burnt alive. Many more were taken prisoners in another attack, in October, and the lower part of the island wholly destroyed; only three of the confederates were lost, in all this scene of misery and desolation." Nothing but the ignorance of the Indians, in the art of attacking fortified places, saved Canada from being utterly cut off.

In 1688, it was determined to add New York and the Jerseys to the jurisdiction of New England, and Sir Edmund Andros was appointed captain-general and vice-admiral over the whole. Governor Dongan was removed from his office of governor, and Francis Nicholson, who had been lieutenant-governor under him, was appointed in his stead. The constitution, established on this occasion, was a legislative and executive governor, and a council, who were appointed by the king, without the consent of the people. The news of the accession of William and Mary, in 1689, to the throne of England, was joyfully received in New York. Andros, the tyrant of New England, was seized at Boston. Jacob Leisler, with forty-nine men, seized the fort at New York, and held it for the protestant king and queen of England.

Leisler's assumption of the command at New York excited a spirit of envy and hatred among many of the people, at the head of whom were Col. Bayard and the Mayor, who, unable to make any effectual resistance, retired to Albany. A letter arriving from the English ministry, addressed " To Francis Nicholson, Esq., or, in his absence, to such as, for the time being, take care for preserving the peace and administering the laws in his majesty's province of New York, &c.," to do every thing pertaining to the office of lieutenant-governor, till farther orders—Nicholson having absconded, Leisler considered the letter as addressed to himself, and accordingly assumed the office of governor. The people of Albany, though friendly to William and Mary, refused subjection to Leisler. They were however compelled to submit to his authority by an armed force under Milborn, his son-in-law. The colonists continued in a state of contention nearly two years. During this period, the French and Indians from Canada, in 1690, surprised Schenectady, and massacred sixty men, women, and children.

In 1691, Col. Henry Sloughter arrived at New York, as governor of the province; which was, at this time, by an act of the assembly, divided into ten counties. The arbitrary acts of James were repealed, and the former privileges of the colonists were restored. Leisler and Milborn, having made a foolish attempt to retain their authority, were imprisoned on a charge of high treason. They were tried by a special commission, and sentenced to suffer death. Gov. Sloughter hesitated to command their execution, and wrote to the English ministers for directions how to dispose of them. Their enemies, fearing the result of this application, made a petition for, and earnestly pressed their execution. "The governor resisted, until, having been invited by the petitioners to a sumptuous entertainment, he was, when his reason was drowned in wine, seduced to sign the death-warrant. Before he recovered his senses, the prisoners were executed." Sloughter died suddenly, in July, 1691, and ended a short, weak, and turbulent administration.

Upon the death of Sloughter, the government, pursuant to the late act for declaring the rights of the people, committed the chief command to Richard Ingoldsby. His authority was terminated by the arrival of Col. Benjamin Fletcher, who arrived with the commission of governor, in August, 1692. Fletcher is represented as a man of violent temper, shallow capacity, and avaricious disposition. He made considerable disturbance, by his efforts to establish the Episcopal form of church government in the province. By virtue of a commission which he held, Fletcher attempted to take the command of the militia of Connecticut; and went to Hartford, in that colony, while the legislature were in session, to compel obedience. While attempting to have his commission read to the train-bands at that place, Capt. Wadsworth, their senior officer, ordered the drums to beat, and told Fletcher, who commanded "silence," that if he was interrupted he would "make the sun shine through him." Fletcher upon this desisted, and returned to New York.

Early in 1693, Count Frontenac, with a force of 6 or 700 French and Indians, made an incursion into the Mohawk country, and surprised an Indian village on the river, slew many of the inhabitants, and took 300 prisoners. Col. Schuyler hastened to the assistance of his allies, and with about 300 Indians, mostly boys, followed the retreating enemy, and several skirmishes ensued. When the French reached the north branch of Hudson's river, a cake of ice opportunely served them to cross it; and Schuyler, who had retaken about fifty Indians, desisted from the pursuit. The French, in this expedition, lost about eighty men, and such were their sufferings, that they were compelled to eat their own shoes; the Iroquois, while in pursuit, fed upon the dead bodies of their enemies. In 1696, Frontenac made another descent, with a large force, and spread devastation among the possessions of the Five Nations. After this expedition, the Indians in the English interest continued to harass the inhabitants near Montreal, and similar parties in the French interest to harass those near Albany, until the peace of Ryswick, in 1697.

In 1698, Richard, Earl of Bellamont, arrived as the successor of Fletcher, and his commission included the governments of Massachusetts and New York: and for the latter, he brought with him his kinsman, John Nanfan, as lieutenant-governor. Piracy, at this time, prevailed in the American seas to a great extent, and the inhabitants of several colonies were accused of giving the pirates aid. The most noted of these marauders was a Captain Kidd, the remembrance of whom is kept alive by the belief that he buried immense sums of money along the coast. To suppress piracy was one of the avowed purposes of the king, in selecting a man of the high rank, resolution, and integrity of the Earl of Bellamont. The earl died in 1701, and Nanfan, the lieutenant-governor, assumed the command. Lord Cornbury was appointed governor the following year.

Cornbury began his administration by espousing one of the factions in the colony which had its rise from Leisler, who was executed for treason. By a series of outrageous acts, he endeavored to establish the Episcopal party. He prohibited the Dutch ministers and teachers from exercising their functions without his special license, and imprisoned some of them for disobeying his orders. This tyrant was the grandson of the Earl of Clarendon, and first cousin of the queen. "Having dissipated his substance in riot and debauchery, and being compelled to fly from his creditors, he obtained from his patron the government of New York, which was confirmed by the queen, who added the government of New Jersey. His character is portrayed as a compound of bigotry and intolerance, rapacity and prodigality, voluptuousness and cruelty, united with the loftiest arrogance and the meanest chicane." His dissolute habits and ignoble manners completed the disgust with which he was universally regarded; and when he was seen rambling abroad in the *dress of a woman*, the people beheld with indignation and shame the representative of their sovereign and the ruler of the colony. In 1709, the queen was compelled to revoke his commission by the complaints of the people of New York and New Jersey. When deprived of his office, his creditors put him in prison in the province he had governed, where he remained till the death of his father elevated him to the peerage, which entitled him to liberation.

John, Lord Lovelace, Baron of Hurley, the successor of Cornbury, arrived in the province, December, 1708. The hopes entertained, from his exalted character, of a happy administration, were frustrated by his death on the succeeding 5th of May. The government now devolved upon Richard Ingoldsby, lieutenant-governor. His administration of eleven months is chiefly distinguished by an unsuccessful attempt on Canada. In this attempt, the province of New York discovered much zeal. Besides raising several companies, she procured six hundred warriors of the Five Nations, paid their wages, and maintained a thousand of their wives and children at Albany while they were in the campaign, at the expense of about twenty thousand pounds. In 1710, Colonel Schuyler went to England, to press upon the ministry the importance of subduing Canada. The more effectually to accomplish this object, he took with him five Indian chiefs, who gave Queen Anne assurances of their fidelity, and solicited her assistance against their common enemies, the French.*

Brigadier-general Robert Hunter, a native of Scotland, arrived as governor of the province, in June, 1710. He brought with him three thousand *Palatines,* who, in the previous year, had fled to England from the rage of persecution in Germany. Many of these persons settled in the city of New York, others in Livingston Manor in Columbia county, while others went into Pennsylvania. In 1711, the assembly of New York, in order to assist the enterprise under the command of Colonel Nicholson for the reduction of Canada, passed an act for raising troops, restricted the price of provisions, and issued 10,000*l.* in bills of credit, to be redeemed by taxation in five years. Nicholson mustered at Albany two thousand colonists, one thousand

---

* "The arrival of the five sachems in England, made a great bruit through the whole kingdom. The mob followed wherever they went, and small cuts of them were sold among the people. The court was at that time in mourning for the death of the Prince of Denmark; these American kings were, therefore, dressed in black underclothes, after the English manner; but instead of a blanket, they had each a scarlet-in-grain cloth mantle edged with gold, thrown over all their other garments. This dress was directed by the dressers of the play-house, and given by the queen, who was advised to make a show of them. A more than ordinary solemnity attended the audience they had of her majesty. Sir Charles Cotterel conducted them in two coaches to St. James's; and the Lord Chamberlain introduced them into the royal presence. Their speech on the 19th of April, 1710, is preserved by Oldmixon, and is in these words:

"GREAT QUEEN—We have undertaken a long voyage, which none of our predecessors could be prevailed upon to undertake, to see our great queen, and relate to her those things which we thought absolutely for the good of her, and us her allies, on the other side of the water.

"We doubt not but our great queen has been acquainted with our long and tedious war, in conjunction with her children against her enemies, the French, and that we have been as a strong wall, for their security, even to the loss of our best men. We were mightily rejoiced when we heard our great queen had resolved to send an army to reduce Canada; and immediately, in token of friendship, we hung up the kettle, and took up the hatchet, and with one consent, assisted Colonel Nicholson, in making preparations on this side the lake: but at length, we were told our great queen, by some important affairs, was prevented in her design at present, which made us sorrowful, lest the French, who had hitherto dreaded us, should now think us unable to make war against them. The reduction of Canada is of great weight to our free hunting; so that if our great queen should not be mindful of us, we must, with our families, forsake our country, and seek other habitations, or stand neuter, either of which will be much against our inclinations.

"In token of the sincerity of these nations, we do, in their names, present our great queen with these belts of wampum, and in hopes of our great queen's favor, leave it to her most gracious consideration."

Palatines, and one thousand Indians, who commenced their march towards Canada on the 28th of August. A fleet, under the command of Admiral Walker, sailed from Boston with a land force of six thousand four hundred men, with the intention of joining Colonel Nicholson before Quebec. The admiral arrived in the St. Lawrence early in August, but owing to fogs and tempestuous weather, eight or nine transports, with about a thousand men, were lost by shipwreck. This put an end to the expedition, and the admiral sailed for England. Nicholson, who had proceeded as far as Lake George, was compelled to retreat. The peace of Utrecht, signed March, 1713, put an end to hostilities, and continued till 1739.

Governor Hunter, after a wise and popular administration, left the province in 1719, and the command devolved on Colonel Peter Schuyler. In September, 1720, William Burnet, son of the celebrated Bishop Burnet, arrived as the successor of Governor Hunter. His administration of seven years was prosperous. Soon after his arrival, for the purpose of securing the trade and friendship of the Six Nations, he erected a trading-house at Oswego, in the country of the Senecas. The great merit of Governor Burnet's administration consisted in his effectual efforts to diminish the trade and influence of the French with the northern Indians. He failed, however, in his endeavors to prevent the establishment of a French fort at Niagara, by which they secured to themselves the possession of the west end of Lake Ontario, as they had previously that of the east by the erection of Fort Frontinac many years before. The persecutions in France at this period, which ensued the revocation of the edict of Nantz, drove many of the protestant subjects of Louis XIV. into foreign countries. Many fled to this province. The most wealthy settled in the city: others planted New Rochelle on the East river, and a few seated themselves at New Paltz in Ulster county.

In 1728, Colonel John Montgomery received from Governor Burnet the seal of the province, and assumed the government. His short administration, terminated by his death in 1731, was one of tranquillity, and not distinguished by any important event. During his term, in 1731, the boundary between New York and Connecticut was finally settled; and a tract of land upon the Connecticut side, of 60,000 acres, called the *Oblong*, was ceded to the former in consideration of another near the Sound, surrendered to the latter.

Governor Montgomery was succeeded by Rip Van Dam, the oldest member of the council, and an eminent merchant of the city, who held the government until August, 1732, when William Cosby arrived, with a commission to govern this, and the province of New Jersey. The French, during this year, erected Fort Frederic at Crown Point, which gave to them the command of Lake Champlain. The finances at this period were much embarrassed; while the frequent calls for supplies imposed a heavy burden upon the colony.

In 1734, the establishment of a court of equity was agitated in the assembly. The governors had previously exercised the office of chancellor, which had at times excited the jealousy, and produced much controversy among the colonists. The court party insisted that the governor was, *ex officio,* chancellor of the colony, while the popular party warmly opposed this position. After the close of the session, there appeared in the paper called "Zenger's New York Weekly Journal," severe animadversions on the government. Several printed ballads likewise appeared, which ridiculed some of the members of the legislature. The governor and council considering the subject worthy of notice, voted that the obnoxious numbers of Zenger's paper, and two printed ballads, were derogatory to the dignity of his majesty's government, and tended to raise sedition and tumult. They likewise voted that said papers and ballads should be burnt by the common hangman. Zenger was imprisoned for eight months, and much ferment was produced in the colony.

Governor Cosby died in March, 1736. One of his last acts was the suspension of Rip Van Dam from his seat as councillor of the province. After Cosby's death, the council immediately convened, and George Clarke, the senior councillor, next after Rip Van Dam, was declared president, and assumed the government. A powerful party, however, was formed in favor of Mr. Van Dam, as his suspension from the council was by many declared illegal. The sharp controversy on this point was ended in October, when Mr. Clarke received his commission as lieutenant-governor.

During the administration of Governor Clarke, the colony was embroiled in controversies principally relating to the prerogatives of the governor on one hand, and the rights of the people on the other. In their second session, 1737, the house departed from their accustomed mode of proceeding, and instead of voting to take the governor's speech into consideration, voted that his honor the lieutenant-governor be addressed. This address is a remarkable production for the times in which it was formed. On the subject of the revenue, the house adopted the following bold and energetic language:

"The true causes of the deficiency in the revenue, we believe are too well known to your honor, to make it necessary for us to say much on that head. Had the conspicuous loyalty of the inhabitants of this province met with a suitable treatment in return, it is not unlikely that we should now be weak enough to act like others before us, in being lavish beyond our abilities, and raising sums unnecessary to be given, and continued the donation like them for a longer time than what was convenient for the safety of the inhabitants; but experience has shown the imprudence of such a conduct; and the miserable condition to which the province is reduced, renders the raising of large sums very difficult if not impracticable. We therefore beg leave to be plain with your honor, and hope you will not take it amiss when we tell you, that you are not to expect that we will raise sums unfit to be raised, or put what we shall raise into the power of a governor to misapply, if we can prevent it; nor shall we make up any other deficiencies than what we conceive are fit and just to be paid, or continue what support or revenue we shall raise for any longer time than one year; nor do we think it convenient to do even that, until such laws are passed as we conceive necessary for the safety of the inhabitants of this colony, who have reposed a trust in us for that only purpose, and which we are sure you will think it reasonable we should act agreeable to, and by the grace of God, we shall endeavor not to deceive them."

In 1738, Captain Norris, of the ship Tartar, then lying in the city of New York, made application to the mayor for liberty to impress thirty seamen to man his vessel. The governor and council ordered the mayor to cause the impressment to be made. The mayor refused to obey the order, and the governor and council prudently declined taking measures to enforce obedience. At the close of Clarke's administration, the finances of the colony were in a depressed condition. "The duties on negro slaves, wine, rum, brandy, cocoa, and dry goods, from September, 1741, to September, 1742, amounted to £2,197 7s. 1¾d. only; while the expenses of government, for about the same period, amounted to upwards of £4,600."

In 1743, George Clinton, the son of the Earl of Lincoln, was appointed to supersede Mr. Clarke as governor of the colony. His arrival was highly gratifying to the colonists, and a spirit of harmony prevailed. In 1744, war was declared between France and England, and great preparations were made on both sides, to carry it on with vigor. A similar spirit prevailed in their respective colonies in America. Large appropriations were made by the assembly of New York to carry on the war. In 1745, the English colonies united in an expedition against Louisburg, on Cape Breton Island. This important fortress was surrendered in June. Eight thousand pounds was voted by the assembly for the promotion of this enterprise.

The country north of Albany was kept in a continued state of alarm by Indian warriors, who ranged in small parties, marking their course by conflagration and indiscriminate slaughter. The fort at Hoosic was captured by M. De Vaudreuil, in August, 1746; and the settlements at Saratoga were surprised, and many of the inhabitants killed or carried into captivity. These events caused much distress, and occasioned much alarm even in Ulster and Orange counties. The plan of the war, in 1746, was, that a squadron under the command of Admiral Warren, with a body of land forces, should proceed up the St. Lawrence; while the troops from New York, and other colonies at the south, should be collected at Albany, and proceed against Crown Point and Montreal. The assembly of New York entered with great zeal upon this design: they levied a tax of £40,000, to redeem bills issued for the occasion. In July, a congress of the Six Nations was held with the governor, at Albany, who was attended by Dr. Colden, Mr. Livingston, and Mr. Rutherford, members of the council. The indisposition of the governor prevented him from opening the council in person, and that duty fell upon Dr. Colden. The Indians formally renewed their pledge to unite zealously in the war against the French. The efforts of the colonies were, however, rendered nearly useless by the failure of the promised assistance from England.

In April, 1748, the preliminaries of peace were signed at Aix-la-Chapelle, and hostilities soon after ceased. After the close of the war, the colony enjoyed a period of general tranquillity. The inhabitants vigorously pursued the arts of peace, and by industry, economy, and enterprise, repaired, in a great measure, the losses sustained in the preceding war. In 1750, the entries at New York were two hundred and thirty-two, and the clearances two hundred and eighty-six. Above six thousand tons of provisions, chiefly flour, were exported, besides large quantities of grain.

Governor Clinton having resigned, Sir Danvers Osborne arrived as his successor, in October, 1753. " Clinton is represented to have been mercenary; to have used every plausible device, for enhancing the profits of his government; to have sold offices and even the reversions of such as were ministerial; and to have amassed a fortune, during his administration of ten years, of more than £80,000 sterling. He became, afterward, governor of Greenwich Hospital." The administration of Sir Danvers Osborne endured but a few days only. Five days after his arrival, he was found suspended by the neck in the garden of Mr. Murray, with whom he resided. This unfortunate gentleman is supposed to have committed suicide on account of grief for the loss of his wife, and by the embarrassments which he apprehended would attend the exercise of his office as governor.

James de Lancey, who had been appointed lieutenant-governor by one of the last acts of Governor Clinton, on the death of Osborne assumed the administration of government. At this period, the English and French extended their settlements in the colonies, and each were anxious to secure the most eligible situations for trading-houses and forts. Mutual complaints of aggression were soon followed by open acts of hostility.

In 1754, a convention of delegates from New Hampshire, Massachusetts, Connecticut, Rhode Island, Pennsylvania, and Maryland, with the lieutenant-governor and council of New York, was held at Albany, for the purpose of uniting upon some scheme for the common defence. The plan for a political union, drawn up by Dr. Franklin, a delegate from Pennsylvania, was adopted on the 4th of July. This plan had the singular fortune to be rejected by the provincial assemblies, because it gave too much power to the crown; and, at the same time, to be rejected by the crown, because it gave too much power to the people.

In September, 1755, Sir Charles Hardy, a distinguished naval officer, arrived in New York with commission of governor. Being ignorant of civil affairs, he put himself into the hands of Mr. De Lancey, and was guided altogether by his counsels. Early in the spring of this year, the colonies made preparations for vigorous exertions against the enemy. An expedition was planned against the French in Nova Scotia, another against the French on the Ohio, a third against Crown Point, and a fourth against Niagara. The first expedition resulted in the reduction of Nova Scotia. That against the French on the Ohio failed by the defeat of General Braddock, who was drawn into an ambuscade of French and Indians near Fort du Quesne. The expedition against Crown Point, commanded by Gen. Wm. Johnson, though unsuccessful in its main object, served, in a measure, to dispel the gloom occasioned by the defeat of Braddock. Governor Shirley, of Massachusetts, took the command of the expedition against Niagara. He advanced to Oswego, where, being poorly supplied with provisions, the expedition was abandoned, and the troops returned to Albany. During the winter and spring following, marauding parties of western Indians committed many atrocities in the counties of Orange and Ulster.

In the plan of operations for the campaign of 1756, Niagara and Crown Point, then in possession of the French, were the principal points of attack. Owing to the improvidence of Gen. Abercrombie, then in command, in the absence of Lord Loudon, nothing of importance was effected by the English forces. In August, Marquis de Montcalm, commander of the French troops in Canada, captured the two forts at Oswego, which he demolished, took 1,600 men prisoners, with 120 cannon, 14 mortars, two sloops-of-war, 200 boats and batteaux, with a large quantity of stores and provisions. The campaign of 1757 was equally unsuccessful on the part of the English. Fort William Henry, on Lake George, with a garrison of 3,000 men under Col. Munro, was compelled, after a brave defence, to surrender to Montcalm. This event gave the French the command of the lake and the western frontier.

In 1758, the celebrated William Pitt, Lord Chatham, now placed at the head of the British ministry, gave a new tone to their measures, and a fresh impulse to the colonies. The tide of success was soon turned in favor of the English, which continued, with few exceptions, till Canada was subjected to their arms. The plan for this year comprehended three expeditions, viz, *Louisburg, Ticonderoga,* and *Fort du Quesne.* Louisburg surrendered to Gen. Amherst in July. Gen. Abercrombie, with an army of 16,000 men, passed Lake George and made an attack on Ticonderoga. After a contest of four hours, he was compelled to retire with the loss of nearly two thousand in killed and wounded. Abercrombie, after his defeat, sent Col. Bradstreet, with 3,000 men, against Fort Frontenac, on the northeastern side of the outlet of Lake Ontario. Bradstreet sailed down the lake, landed within a mile of the fort, and in two days compelled it to surrender.* The garrison at Fort du Quesne, unsustained by their savage allies, on the 24th of November abandoned and burnt this fortress on the approach of the British army under Gen. Forbes.

Great Britain, having resolved to annihilate the French power in

---

* The expedition under Col. Bradstreet consisted of the following troops:—Regulars, 135; Royal artillery, 30; New York provincials, 1,112; Massachusetts do., 675; New Jersey do., 412; Rhode Island do., 318; batteau-men, 300; and about 60 rangers; in all 3,035. The regulars were commanded by Capt. Ogilvie, and the artillery by Lieut. Brown, The New York troops consisted of two detachments. The first commanded by Lieutenant-colonel Charles Clinton, of Ulster, amounting in the whole to 440, under Capts. Ogden, of Westchester, Peter Dubois, of New York, Samuel Bladgely, of Dutchess, and Daniel Wright, of Queens. The second was commanded by Lieutenant-colonel Isaac Corse, of Queens, and Major Nathaniel Woodhull, of Suffolk, amounting to 668, under Captains Elias Hand, of Suffolk, Richard Hewlett, of Queens, Thomas Arrowsmith, of Richmond, William Humphrey, of Dutchess, Ebenezer Seeley, of Ulster, and Peter Yates and Goosen Van Schaick, of Albany. The troops left Fort Stanwix, August 14th, 1758, and the fort capitulated on the 27th. The commander of the fort was exchanged for Col. Peter Schuyler. Col. Corse, who had distinguished himself in the three preceding campaigns, with a part of his troops, volunteered to erect a battery, in the night of the 26th, in the midst of the enemy's fire, which in the morning commanded their fort, and led to an immediate surrender. The colonel received a slight wound, but not so severe as to unfit him for duty. The detachment returned to Fort Stanwix the 10th of September."—*Gordon's Gaz. of New York.*

America, made adequate preparations for the campaign of 1759. The colonies now displayed that zeal with which men pursue their interests when animated with well-founded hopes of success. The legislature of New York authorized a levy of 2,680 men, and issued the sum of £100,000 in bills of credit, bearing interest, and redeemable in 1768, by the proceeds of an annual tax. The impositions, in the space of five months of the year 1759, amounted to $625,000. At the instance of Gen. Amherst, a loan of £150,000 was made to the crown, which was paid in specie.

The contemplated points of attack, in 1759, were *Ticonderoga, Crown Point, Niagara,* and *Quebec.* Gen. Amherst took Ticonderoga, and proceeded to Crown Point, which surrendered without opposition. In July, Gen. Prideaux invested Niagara, but was slain by the bursting of a cohort in the trenches. The fort was, however, captured by Sir William Johnson, who succeeded him in command. On the 13th of September, a severe battle was fought between the British forces under Gen. Wolfe, and the French under Montcalm. Both these commanders were killed, the French were defeated, and Quebec surrendered to the British arms. In the ensuing spring of 1760, the French made a fruitless attempt to recover Quebec. On the 8th of September, Montreal, Detroit, Michilimackinac, and all other places within the government of Canada, were surrendered to his Britannic majesty.

The conquest of Canada, by preventing the incursions of the French and Indians into the territory of New York, removed a great obstacle to the prosperity of the colony. Gov. De Lancey died suddenly, July 30th, 1760. Cadwallader Colden assumed the government, as president of the council, and received the appointment of lieutenant-governor in August, 1761. Mr. Colden was superseded by General Robert Monckton on the 26th of October. This gentleman being placed at the head of an expedition against Martinique, on the 15th of November, left the government of the province to Mr. Colden, under an agreement for an equal division of the salary and perquisites.

In 1763, the celebrated controversy with New Hampshire, respecting boundaries, commenced. The territory in question comprised the country between Connecticut river and Lake Champlain, since known as Vermont. The original character of the colonies, owing to imperfect surveys of the country, were many of them extremely indefinite, vague, and often contradictory. A grant was made in 1664 and 1674, by Charles II. to his brother, the Duke of York, containing, among other parts of America, " all the lands, from the west side of Connecticut river, to the east side of Delaware bay." This territory was, however, by many supposed to fall within the limits of New Hampshire, although claimed by New York, by virtue of the grant made to the Duke of York.

The government of New Hampshire, in 1760, made large grants of land to settlers *west* of Connecticut, and the settlements progressed with astonishing rapidity. In 1763, one hundred and thirty-eight townships had been granted by New Hampshire, extending as far west as the shore of Lake Champlain, and to what was esteemed twenty miles east of Hudson river. To check these proceedings, Gov. Colden issued a proclamation, claiming jurisdiction as far east as Connecticut river. He also commanded the sheriff of Albany county to make return of all persons, who, under the New Hampshire grants, had taken possession of lands west of the river. In opposition to this, the governor of New Hampshire issued a proclamation, declaring the grant of the Duke of York to be obsolete, and that New Hampshire extended as far west as Massachusetts and Connecticut.

Application having been made to the crown, a decision was obtained in 1764, by which the western bank of Connecticut river was declared to be the boundary line between the provinces of New Hampshire and New York. The government of New York proceeded to organize the new territory, and to exercise jurisdiction. The new district was divided into four counties. The southwestern part was annexed to the county of Albany, and the northwestern part formed into a county, by the name of Charlotte; east of the Green Mountains were formed the counties of Gloucester and Cumberland. Courts were held in these counties, the grants of land under New Hampshire were declared illegal, and the settlers required to take out new charters from New York. Some of the towns complied, and purchased their lands the second time, but the greater part refused. Actions of ejectment were commenced in Albany against several of the ancient settlers, which were decided in favor of the New York titles. When the executive officers came to eject the inhabitants, they generally met with opposition, and were not allowed to proceed in the execution of their offices. The militia were called out to support the sheriff; but as they agreed in sentiment with the settlers, they disbanded themselves on the appearance of armed opposition. As the efforts of the government were continued, mobs were raised, the opposition of the settlers became more bold and daring, and was frequently characterized by acts of outrage and violence.

In 1765, much excitement was produced by the *stamp act*, passed by the British parliament, for the purpose of raising a revenue from the colonies. This act ordained that all instruments of writing, such as deeds, bonds, notes, &c., among the colonies, should be null and void, unless executed on *stamped paper*, for which a duty should be paid to the crown. In October, a congress of twenty-eight delegates, from Massachusetts, Connecticut, Rhode Island, New York, New Jersey, Pennsylvania, Delaware, Maryland, and South Carolina, was held at New York, to consult on the common interest. They made a declaration of the rights and grievances of the colonies, and petitioned for redress. In Connecticut and New York originated an association of persons styling themselves the "*Sons of Liberty*," which extended into other colonies, who bound themselves, among other things, to march to any part of the continent, at their own expense, to support the British constitution in America: by which was understood, the prevention of any attempt to carry the stamp act into operation.

In New York, Peter de Lancey, James M'Evers, and other stamp officers, obeyed the public voice, and renounced their commissions. Gov. Colden, having taken the oath to execute the stamp act, became the object of popular indignation. His effigy was carried about the city and hung; his carriage and other property were burned; and his person was probably preserved from violence, only by his advanced age. When the stamps arrived, they were lodged in the fort, which the governor, contrary to the advice of his council, put into a state for defence. He was obliged to surrender their custody to the city corporation, on the assurance of being responsible for their value, and to declare that he would take no measures to enforce the act, but leave the subject to his successor, who was hourly expected. Sir Henry Moore, Bart., who was commissioned governor in July, 1765, met the council on the 13th of November following, and proposed at once to attempt the execution of the stamp act. The unanimous advice of his council, and the demonstration of public feeling, induced him to a more prudent course.

Gov. Moore's administration was terminated by his death, in September, 1769. During his term of service efforts were made, unsuccessfully, to settle the boundaries between this province and Massachusetts, who claimed territory to the Pacific Ocean. Emigrants from Massachusetts intruded into the counties along the Hudson, and settled even in the manor of Rensselaerwyck. They were frequently removed by force, and blood was shed more than once in the attempt. Commissioners from both colonies met at New Haven, October, 1767, who agreed that the western line of Massachusetts should be fixed at twenty miles east from Hudson river, but differed as to the manner in which that line should be determined.

At the termination of Gov. Moore's administration, the supreme court consisted of four judges: Daniel Horsemanden, chief justice; David Jones, second; William Smith, third; and Robert R. Livingston, the fourth justice. The first received £300, and the others £200 per annum. The salary of the governor had been increased, from time to time, to £2,000 per annum, with a perquisite of £400, granted as an appropriation for fire-wood and candles for Fort George. The attorney had £150, and the colonial agent, Mr. Charles, at London, £500 per annum. The colony of New York contained, at this period, upwards of one hundred and sixty thousand inhabitants.

By the death of Sir Henry Moore, the government again devolved on Mr. Colden. This his third administration, continued till November, 1770, when he was superseded by John, Lord Dunmore. With the service of this nobleman commenced the practice of paying the governor by the crown. This practice was afterward denounced by most of the colonies as a serious grievance, as it made the governor independent of the assembly. Dunmore governed the colony until his removal to Virginia, when his place was supplied on the 8th of July, 1771, by William Tryon, the last of the royal governors.

In 1772, Governor Tryon made an unsuccessful attempt to conciliate the minds of the settlers of the New Hampshire grants. In 1774, the assembly passed an act by which it was declared felony, punishable by death, for any of these settlers to oppose the government by force. The governor at the same time made proclamation offering a reward of fifty pounds for the apprehension of Ethan Allen, Seth Warner, and six others of the most obnoxious of the settlers. The inhabitants of the New Hampshire grants became still more violent in their opposition. The proscribed persons, in an address to the people of the county of Albany, made this public declaration:— "We will kill and destroy any person or persons whomsoever, who shall presume to be accessary, aiding, or assisting in taking any of us."

In the spring of 1775, an event took place in the New Hampshire grants which exasperated both parties. At the time appointed for the session of the court at Westminster, in the disputed territory, some of the inhabitants in this and the adjacent towns took possession of the courthouse, to prevent the officers under the authority of New York from entering. The judges, on being refused admittance, retired to their quarters. About eleven o'clock at night, the sheriff and other officers, attended by an armed force, repaired to the courthouse, when, being again refused admittance, some of the party fired into the house, killed one man, and wounded several. The people were highly inflamed by these rash proceedings. Some of the officers were seized, and carried to the jail at Northampton, Massachusetts. Matters now appeared about to be brought to a sanguinary crisis. But at this period, an event took place, which arrested the attention of all, and gave a new channel to the torrent of popular fury. The breaking out of the revolutionary war at Lexington, caused a suspension of local and provincial contests; and the public mind was exclusively directed to the great contest now opening between Britain and America.

In May, 1775, the second continental congress was to be assembled at Philadelphia. The subject of sending delegates to this body was agitated in the assembly of New York; and on the refusal of that body to appoint them, a provincial convention was called by the people for this purpose. The convention assembled at New York on the 22d of April, and proceeded to make the appointments. This convention was composed of deputies from New York, Albany, Dutchess, Ulster, Orange, Westchester, Kings, and Suffolk counties. They appointed Philip Livingston, George Clinton, James Duane, John Alsop, Simon Boerum, William Floyd, John Jay, Henry Wisner, Philip Schuyler Lewis Morris, Francis Lewis, and Robert R. Livingston, Jr., delegates to the continental congress, who, or any five of them, were intrusted with full power to concert with the other colonies, and adopt those measures best adapted to sustain their rights.

The news of the battle of Lexington, (19th of April, 1775,) caused a violent agitation in the city of New York, which prevailed for some days, until a new committee of superintendence, consisting of one hundred of the most respectable citizens, was formed at the instance of the "committee of observation." It was resolved that a provincial congress ought to be speedily assembled, to assume the government of the colony, to prepare for defence, &c. It submitted at the same time the form of an association, to be signed by the inhabitants, declaratory of their rights and liberties, and of their determination to sustain them. This association was signed by the whigs with great cordiality, and by the tories under the fear of, or by actual constraint. The inhabitants generally began to arise under the direction of committees. Six hundred stands of arms were seized in the city arsenal and distributed among the people: another parcel was taken from the soldiery by Colonel Willet, when on the way to the harbor to be exported to Boston.

It was deemed of importance, in order to put the country in a posture of defence, to secure the fortresses at Ticonderoga and Crown Point. On the 10th of May, Colonel Ethan Allen took possession of Ticonderoga by surprise: on the same day, Crown Point was surrendered to Colonel Warner; a third party surprised Skeensborough, (now Whitehall.) The capture of an armed sloop at St. Johns soon after, gave to the Americans the entire command of Lake Champlain. Governor Tryon, who had been absent on a visit to Europe, returned to New York on the 24th of June. He was much esteemed by many of the citizens, and received a complimentary address from the city authorities. His exertions to promote the royal cause, soon rendered him extremely unpopular. In October, he became alarmed for his personal safety, and retired on board of the Halifax packet.

On the 22d of May, 1775, a provincial congress, consisting of about seventy members, convened at New York. The proceedings of the convention were determined by counties; New York having four, Albany three, and each of the others two votes. Two regiments were authorized to be levied; bounties were offered for the manufacture of gunpowder and muskets in the province; fortifications were projected at Kingsbridge, and the Highlands; and Philip Schuyler and Richard Montgomery were recommended, the first as major-general, the second as brigadier, to be appointed by the continental congress.

Upon the adjournment of the congress, in September, for a month, they delegated their powers to a "*Committee of Safety;*" and this expedient was resorted to upon every subsequent adjournment. Ordinarily, this committee was composed of three members from the city, and one from each of the other counties. When on the re-assembling of the congress, and at other times, a quorum was not present, the members resolved themselves into a "committee of safety," and thus the public business was never interrupted. The committee was empowered to execute the resolves of the provincial and general congresses, to superintend the military affairs of the province, to appropriate money for the public service, and to convene the congress when and where they deemed necessary.

While General Washington was engaged in organizing the main body of the American army in Massachusetts, an important expedition was planned against Canada, the command of which was assigned to Generals Schuyler and Montgomery. General Schuyler having retired on account of ill health, Montgomery, with a force of one thousand men, proceeded to Montreal, and from thence led his gallant little army to Quebec. During his progress, Colonel Arnold, with a boldness and perseverance rarely surpassed, passed up the Kennebec river and pursued his course through a trackless wilderness of three hundred miles, and joined Montgomery at Quebec. On the last day of the year, (1775,) General Montgomery, with a force of less than eight hundred, attempted to take Quebec by storm. This brave commander fell in the assault, and the Americans were repulsed with the loss of about half their number. Arnold, now in the command, encamped about three miles from Quebec, where he maintained his position till spring. He was afterward compelled to make a disastrous retreat, and by the 1st of July the whole army was driven from Canada.

Congress being informed that a large number of the inhabitants of Tryon county were disaffected to the American cause, and, under the direction of Sir John Johnson, were making military preparation, resolved to disarm them. General Schuyler, to whom this business was committed, in January, 1776, called out seven hundred of the Albany militia, and commenced his march. But such was the enthusiasm of the people that, on his arrival at Caghnewaga, his force amounted to near three thousand, including nine hundred of the Tryon county militia. The approach of this formidable body awed the royalists into submission. The whole number disarmed was supposed to amount to about six hundred. About the same time, a considerable number were entrenching themselves on Long Island, in order to support the royal cause. A detachment of the Jersey militia was sent over, by whom they were disarmed, and their leaders secured.

The fourth provincial congress convened at White Plains on the 9th of July. This body took the title of "*The Representatives of the State of New York*," and exercised all the powers of sovereignty, until the establishment of the government under the constitution. On the first day of their meeting, they received from the continental congress *The Declaration of Independence*. They immediately passed an unanimous resolution, fully approving of the measure, and expressing their determination at all hazards to support it. The convention, on the 16th of July, on the motion of Mr. Jay, declared that all persons abiding in the state, and who were entitled to the protection of the laws, who should aid or abet its enemies, should on conviction suffer death.

In 1776, it was expected that the enemy would make New York their principal point of attack. Gen. Washington arrived in the city on the 14th of April, and great exertions were made for putting the place in a posture of defence. On the 22d of August, Lord Howe landed a force, estimated at 24,000 men, on Long Island, at Gravesend bay. The Americans, amounting to 15,000, under the command of

Gen. Sullivan, were encamped on a peninsula near the village of Brooklyn. On the 27th, an obstinate battle was fought, and the Americans were compelled to retire to their entrenchments with great loss. On the night of the 30th, a safe retreat was effected from the island. On the 15th of September, the British took possession of New York, the American troops having retired to Harlaem and King's Bridge. A few days after the British took possession, a fire broke out, in which about one thousand houses were destroyed, being about one fourth part of the city.

A large proportion of the distinguished and wealthy inhabitants of the city of New York, and many in the adjacent country, were loyalists, and, of course, enemies to American independence. On the arrival of the British army, the disaffected in this part of the state and the neighboring parts of New Jersey, embodied themselves under officers selected by themselves. Oliver de Lancey was appointed a general, with authority to raise a brigade of tories, and a like commission was given to Courtland Skinner, of New Jersey. These troops committed many murders and robberies on both sides of the Hudson river, but more especially in Westchester county. The provincial congress now adopted energetic measures. The "Council of Safety" were empowered to send for persons and papers, and to employ military force. By its dread power numerous arrests, imprisonments, and banishments, were made throughout the state. Many tories and their families were sent into New York, others expelled the state, others required to give security to reside within prescribed limits; and occasionally the jails, and even the churches, were crowded with its prisoners, and many were sent for safe-keeping to the jails of Connecticut. The personal property of those who had joined the enemy was confiscated.

The American army being in point of numbers greatly inferior to that of the British, General Washington drew off the main body of his army from York Island, and encamped at White Plains. Lord Howe advanced upon him with 15,000 men. An engagement ensued on the 28th of October, but no decisive advantage was obtained; the Americans retired to a strong position on the heights of North Castle, which the enemy declined to attack. General Washington, leaving about 7,500 men under General Lee to defend North Castle, crossed the Hudson and continued his retreat to the southward. The American army continuing to retire from New York, Sir William Howe embraced the opportunity of reducing Fort Washington and Fort Lee, on the Hudson. While these operations were going on in the southern part of the state, the northern division of the army, under General Gates, was engaged at the north in putting Ticonderoga in a state of defence, and made preparations to secure the command of Lake Champlain. General Arnold, who commanded the American fleet, being pursued, was obliged to blow up his vessels, and, after firing the fortress at Crown Point, retreated to Ticonderoga. The British general, Carlton, after reconnoitering the latter place, deemed it prudent on the approach of winter to return to Canada.

The state convention, driven from New York, convened from time to time at Harlaem, King's Bridge, Philip's Manor, Fishkill, White Plains, Poughkeepsie, and Kingston. On the 1st of August, 1776, a committee was appointed to report a constitution. The draft of this instrument, which was prepared by Mr. Jay, was reported on the 12th of March, and finally adopted on the 20th of April, 1777. It was amended by convention in October, 1801, and superseded by the present constitution in November, 1821. The constitution of 1777 was republican in its character. The supreme executive power was vested in a governor and lieutenant-governor, who was to preside over the senate, and perform the duties of the governor in case of vacancy. The legislative power was vested in the senate and house of assembly, who were to hold at least one session every year. The governor and members of the senate and house of assembly, were to be elected by the *freeholders* of the state of New York.

The returns of the first elections under the new constitution were made to the Council of Safety, July 9th, 1777. General George Clinton was chosen governor, and was sworn into office on the 30th of the same month, at Kingston, being then in the active command of the New York militia. He did not quit the field until after the defeat of Burgoyne, but discharged such civil duties as devolved on him, by correspondence with the Council of Safety. At the adoption of the constitution, the state was divided into fourteen counties: New York, Richmond, Kings, Queens, Suffolk, Westchester, Dutchess, Orange, Ulster, Albany, Tryon, Charlotte, Cumberland, and Gloster; the two last form part of the present state of Vermont. The first six (except part of Westchester and part of Orange) remained in possession of the enemy until the peace, the highlands forming the great barrier to his farther advance from the south.

The principal object of the British in the campaign of 1777, was to open a communication between the city of New York and Canada, and to separate the New England from the other states. The plan consisted of two parts: General Burgoyne, with the main body of the army from Canada, was to advance by the way of Lake Champlain, and effect a junction, at Albany, with the royal army from New York. A detachment of British soldiers and a large body of Indians, under Colonel St. Leger, with a regiment of New York loyalists, under Sir John Johnson, were to ascend the St. Lawrence to Lake Ontario, and penetrate towards Albany by way of the Mohawk river. General Burgoyne, with an army of more than 7,000 men, exclusive of a corps of artillery and a large body of Indians, invested Ticonderoga on the 30th of June. This fortress was abandonded by General St. Clair, on the approach of the enemy. The rear-guard of the American army, consisting of 1,000 men, under Colonel Warner, was overtaken and defeated at Hubbardston. General Schuyler, who commanded at Fort Edward, was obliged to retire to Saratoga before the superior force of the enemy. While the British were encamped at Fort Edward, a detachment, under Colonel Baum, was sent to take possession of the American stores at Bennington, in the

New Hampshire grants. General Stark collected the militia in that vicinity, and an obstinate engagement took place, in which the British were totally defeated. On the 3d of August, St. Leger, with about 1,800 men, invested Fort Schuyler, under the command of General Gansevoort. He had a severe conflict with General Herkimer, who was advancing to the relief of the garrison, and was obliged to abandon the siege and return to Montreal. General Burgoyne, having advanced as far as Saratoga, found himself surrounded by a brave army, from which he endeavored in vain to effect a retreat. In this extremity, on the 17th of October, he was compelled to surrender his whole army, consisting of more than 5,700 men, to General Gates.

During the operations at Saratoga, Sir Henry Clinton, with three thousand men, proceeded up the Hudson, with the view of effecting a diversion in favor of Burgoyne. On the 6th of October, he made an attack on forts Montgomery and Clinton. These works were carried at the point of the bayonet, but most of the garrisons escaped. Forts Independence and Constitution were evacuated, and General Putnam, who had the command on the Hudson, retreated to Fishkill. General Tryon on the following day burned Continental Village, where considerable stores were deposited; General Vaughan with a strong detachment, proceeding up the river, devastated the settlements along its banks, burned the village of Kingston, and then embarked for New York.

In the campaigns of 1778 and 1779, nothing decisive was effected; the British engaged in no enterprise of much importance, and appear to have aimed at little more than to plunder and devastate the unprotected parts of the country. Many acts of cruelty were committed, and a great amount of public and private property destroyed. The main body of the American army was concentrated near West Point, for the protection of that important fortress. General Clinton, having seized the works at Verplanck's Neck and Stoney Point, General Washington formed a design for their recovery. The reduction of the fortress at Stoney Point by Gen. Wayne, by assault, on the 16th of July, 1779, was one of the most bold and daring enterprises which occurred during the war.

The Indians of the Six Nations (with the exception of the Oneidas and a few others) had been induced by the presents and promises of Sir John Johnson, and with the desire of plunder, to invade the frontiers, and wherever they went they carried slaughter and devastation. To put a stop to these incursions, congress, in August, 1779, sent General Sullivan with an army against them. Sullivan, with a force of 3,000 men, marched from Easton, Pennsylvania, to Tioga Point, where he was joined by General Clinton, who marched from the Mohawk with a force of about one thousand men. The Indians collected their forces, and took a strong position near Newtown, Tioga county, determining to resist the advance of Sullivan. They stood a cannonade for more than two hours, during which time they repelled several assaults; they were, however, compelled to give way and abandon their works. Generals Sullivan and Clinton penetrated without obstruction into the heart of the Seneca country, and spread desolation on every side. Eighteen towns and villages, besides hamlets and detached habitations, were burnt. All their fields of corn, their orchards and gardens, were entirely destroyed. By this summary proceeding the ardor of the Indian warriors was damped, and their inroads became much less frequent and destructive.

At the period of this expedition, different parts of the state suffered severely from the depredations of detached parties of Indians. In July, Colonel Brandt, with a party of Indians and royalists, burned the Minisink settlement and took several prisoners. In August, the Indians with their tory associates destroyed the settlements at Canajoharie, and burnt a number of houses at Schoharie and Norman's creek. In October, these irruptions were renewed, a great extent of country about the Mohawk was laid waste, and many of the settlers were killed or made prisoners.

During the year 1780 and 1781, the operations of the war were chiefly conducted in the southern states, the British occupying the city of New York and its vicinity. In 1780, a plot, fraught with imminent danger to the American cause, was happily discovered. General Arnold having solicited and obtained the command of West Point, entered into a negotiation with Sir Henry Clinton, to deliver that important fortress into the hands of the enemy. To facilitate the correspondence, John Andre, the adjutant-general of the British army, proceeded up the Hudson in the Vulture sloop-of-war, as near West Point as practicable, without exciting suspicion. On the night of September 21st, Andre went on shore in a boat, and met Arnold on the beach. Failing to get on board the Vulture again, Andre attempted to return to New York by land, in disguise. Receiving a passport from Arnold, he passed the guards and outposts without suspicion. When about thirty miles from New York, he was met by three militia-men, *Paulding*, *Williams*, and *Van Wert*, who, refusing the bribes which Andre offered, carried him to their commanding officer. He was tried as a spy by a board of officers, condemned, and executed.

The capture of Cornwallis at Yorktown, Virginia, convinced the British government of the impracticability of conquering the United States. The provisional articles of peace between the two countries were signed at Paris, November 30th, 1782. On the 19th of April, 1783, a formal proclamation of the cessation of hostilities was made throughout the army, and the definitive treaty, acknowledging the independence of the United States, was signed on the 30th of September. The British troops evacuated New York on the 25th of November, and the Americans took possession the same day.

The termination of the revolutionary war, and the adoption of the federal constitution in 1788, gave a new aspect to the affairs of the country. During the war a considerable portion of New York was in possession of the enemy, and many of its most fertile tracts open to their ravages: many of the new settlements were broken up. On the return of peace these were resumed, and many others commenced, which progressed with astonishing rapidity. Commerce, also, experienced a rapid revival on the return of peace. In 1791, the exports to foreign ports amounted to above two million five hundred thousand dollars. In 1793, six hundred and eighty-three foreign vessels, and one thousand three hundred and eighty-one coasting vessels, entered the port of New York.

The controversy relative to the New Hampshire grants still continued. Frequent application had been made by both parties to the general congress for the interference of that body, but no decisive result was obtained. In 1789, the legislature passed an act in order to settle this controversy, and acknowledging the territory as an independent state. Commissioners were mutually appointed, and in 1790, after a controversy of twenty-six years, the subject was brought to an amicable adjustment. In 1791, the new state was admitted into the Union, with the name of Vermont.

In 1786, the state of New York, to quiet or put at rest certain antiquated claims of Massachusetts to a portion of her territory, granted that state large tracts of vacant lands. These lands consisted of two parts: one part comprehended all that part of the state lying west of a line beginning at the north at the mouth of Great Sodus bay, on Lake Ontario, and running thence southerly to the north line of Pennsylvania, except one mile on the east side of Niagara river, and the islands in that stream. This tract consisted of six millions one hundred and forty-four thousand acres, and was called the *Genesee Country*. The other tract comprehended ten or twelve townships, of six square miles each, embraced in the counties of Broome and Tioga. These cessions embraced about 10,000 square miles, nearly one fourth of the state, New York ceding every thing, save sovereignty, to Massachusetts without an equivalent. The government of Massachusetts sold the first tract to Oliver Phelps and Nathaniel Gorham, for one million of dollars, and the other to John Brown and others, for three thousand three hundred dollars and some cents.

The "*Military Lands*," as they were called, were set apart by the legislature, in 1782, for the officers and soldiers of the state of New York, who should serve in the army of the United States till the end of the war, according to law. The military tracts contained about one million eight hundred thousand acres, comprehending, generally speaking, the counties of Onondaga, Cortlandt, Cayuga, Tompkins, and Seneca, and parts of the counties of Oswego and Wayne. Previous to the cession made to Massachusetts, and the grant made to the soldiers, the Indian title was not extinguished. Messrs. Phelps and Gorham, and the government of New York, had to extinguish these before settlements could be made. The first permanent settlement made in the western territory was by Hugh White, in 1784, in company with four or five families from Connecticut, who seated themselves at Whitestown, near Utica.

A party of emigrants, in 1790 or 1791, made a road through the woods from the settlements of Whitestown to Canandaigua. Emigration now increased from year to year. The winter was the season usually chosen for emigrating from New England to the western country. Then, as the country was shaded by forest trees, there was commonly snow enough for sleighing. In 1796, the British evacuated forts Oswegatchie and Oswego, and immediately afterward settlements were begun at these places. In 1797 and 1798, settlements were commenced at Lowville, Watertown, and Brownville, in the counties of Lewis and Jefferson. Settlements were now rapidly extended on every side. The settlements along the great road from Utica to Genesee river, were mostly connected by the year 1800, and from that year the western country began to attain consequence in the councils of the state.

In 1795, Governor Clinton, having for eighteen years discharged the office of governor, declined a re-election on account of sustaining the republican principle of rotation in office. He was succeeded by John Jay, who continued in the office till 1801, when Mr. Clinton again accepted a re-election. In 1796, the legislature granted the Oneida Indians an annuity of $5,552, in lieu of all former stipulations for lands purchased in 1795; $2,300 to the Cayugas; and $2,000 to the Onondagas. A general organization act was passed in 1801, dividing the state into thirty counties. Mr. Clinton, having been elected vice-president of the United States, Morgan Lewis succeeded him as governor, in 1804. Mr. Lewis was succeeded by Daniel D. Tompkins, in 1807. Albany, the same year, was made the capital of the state.

In 1810, an act was passed by the legislature "for exploring the route of an inland navigation from Hudson's river to Lake Ontario and Lake Erie." Commissioners were appointed for this purpose, who made a report the following year.* The subject now began to excite general interest, and a bill being introduced by Mr. Clinton, an act was passed, "to provide for the improvement of the internal navigation of the state." Commissioners were again appointed to solicit

---

* The first legislative movement with reference to a communication like the present canal between the Hudson and Lake Erie, was brought about by the exertions of Mr. Joshua Forman, then a member of assembly from Onondaga county, who proposed to the House, February 4th, 1808, that "a joint committee be appointed, to take into consideration the propriety of exploring and causing an accurate survey to be made of the most eligible and direct route for a canal, to open a communication *between the tide waters of the Hudson and Lake Erie*, to the end that congress may be enabled to appropriate such sums as may be necessary to the accomplishment of that great object." "The proposition," says Gordon, in his very able Gazetteer, "was received by the House ' with such expressions of surprise and ridicule, as are due to a very wild and foolish project.' It was fortunately, however, firmly sustained by the proposer and his friends, and finally sanctioned upon the principle, ' that it could do no harm and might do some good.' But the joint committee, prepossessed in favor of the Oswego route, directed the surveyor-general to cause a survey of the rivers, streams, and waters in the *usual route* between Hudson river and Lake Erie, *and such other route as he might deem proper:* shifting to the surveyor-general the responsibility of countenancing a project deemed absurd. Six hundred dollars, only, could be procured for the exploration. .... When in January, 1809, Mr. Forman waited upon President Jefferson, and informed him that in view of his proposal to expend the surplus revenues of the nation in making roads and canals, the state of New York had explored the route of a canal from the Hudson to Lake Erie, and had found it practicable; and when he had described all the advantages anticipated, the president replied, ' that it was a very fine project, and *might be executed a century hence.*' "

aid from the congress of the United States. De Witt Clinton and Governeur Morris were appointed to lay the subject before the general government. They proceeded to Washington, and presented a memorial to congress; but were unsuccessful in their application to that body for assistance. In March, 1812, the commissioners again made a report to the legislature, and insisted that *now* sound policy demanded that the canal should be made by the state on her own account. The subject was, however, soon after suspended by the breaking out of the war with Great Britain.

War having been declared in 1812, the attention of the Americans was early directed to the invasion of Canada, and troops to the number of eight or ten thousand were collected along the line for this purpose. They were distributed into three divisions; the *northwestern* army, under General Harrison; the army of the *centre*, under General Stephen Van Rensselaer, at Lewiston; and the army of the *north*, in the vicinity of Plattsburg, under General Dearborn, the commander-in-chief. Great exertions were also made in preparing a naval force upon the lakes, the command of which was intrusted to Commodore Chauncey. About the 1st of October, Commodore Chauncey, with a body of seamen, arrived at Sacketts Harbor; several schooners which had been employed as traders on the lake were purchased, and fitted out as vessels of war. Lieutenant Elliot was despatched to Black Rock, to make arrangements there for building a naval force superior to that of the enemy on Lake Erie.

On the 13th of October, a detachment of one thousand men under Colonel Van Rensselaer crossed the Niagara river at Lewiston, and attacked the British on the heights of Queenston. They succeeded in dislodging the enemy, but not being reinforced from the American side, as was expected, were afterward repulsed, and compelled to surrender. During the ensuing winter, the operations of the war on the New York frontier were mostly suspended. Some skirmishing took place along the St. Lawrence; but the opposing enemies being divided by a barrier of ice, not sufficiently strong to admit of the transportation of artillery, no enterprise of importance was attempted. In April, 1813, General Dearborn made dispositions for a descent upon York, the capital of Upper Canada. The enterprise was committed to a detachment of one thousand seven hundred men, under the command of General Pike, assisted by the fleet under the command of Commodore Chauncey. General Pike was killed in the attack, but the place, with large quantities of military stores, fell into the hands of the Americans. Commodore Chauncey having returned with the fleet to Fort Niagara, it was immediately resolved to make a descent upon Fort George, situated upon the opposite shore. An attack was made on the 27th of May, and after a short contest the place fell into the hands of the Americans.

During these operations of the Americans, several enterprises were undertaken by the enemy. About the last of May, a detachment of about one thousand British soldiers, under Sir George Prevost, made an attack on Sacketts Harbor, but were repulsed with considerable loss. On the 10th of September, Commodore Perry captured the British fleet on Lake Erie. The operations on Lake Ontario were less decisive. During the latter part of summer and autumn, frequent skirmishes took place, but no important advantage was obtained by either party. After the victory on Lake Erie, great preparations were made for the conquest of Montreal. This object was to be effected by two divisions under Generals Wilkinson and Hampton, who were to effect a junction on the St. Lawrence. The division under Wilkinson moved down the river early in November; on the 11th, a severe but indecisive engagement with the enemy took place at Williamsburg. General Hampton made a short incursion into Canada, but no junction was effected. The enterprise against Montreal was abandoned, and the troops retired to winter quarters at French Mills, near St. Regis. Fort George was evacuated and blown up by the Americans. In December, the British crossed over above Fort Niagara, and took that place by storm. After the capture of the fort, they proceeded up the river and burnt Lewiston, Youngstown, Manchester, and the Indian village of Tuscarora. On the 30th, a detachment of the British crossed over near Black Rock. They were feebly opposed by the militia, who soon gave way, and were totally routed. Having set fire to Black Rock, the enemy advanced to Buffalo, which they laid in ashes, thus completing the desolation of the Niagara frontier.

Early in July, 1814, Fort Erie was taken by the Americans, and during the same month sanguinary battles were fought at Chippewa and Bridgewater. On the 11th of September, Sir George Prevost, with an army of fourteen thousand men, made a descent upon Plattsburg, and after a severe engagement was compelled to retire with great loss. The British fleet, under Commodore Downie, was captured by Commodore Macdonough, on the same day. The war was terminated by the treaty of Ghent, signed by the commissioners of both countries, December 24th, 1814, and ratified by the president and senate on the 17th of the following February.

On the termination of the war, the consideration of the great plan for the internal navigation of the state was resumed. During the session of 1817, a memorial was presented, signed by upwards of one hundred thousand citizens, calling upon the legislature to pass laws for the commencement and execution of the proposed canals. An act was accordingly passed, and large appropriations made for this purpose. The Erie and Champlain canals were immediately commenced and vigorously prosecuted. The Erie canal, from Albany to Buffalo, was completed in 1825, at an expense of about eight millions of dollars, and is one of the most magnificent works of the kind ever constructed. The Champlain canal, seventy-one miles in length, was completed in 1823, at an expense of $875,000.

In 1817, Governor Tompkins was chosen vice-president of the United States, and De Witt Clinton was elected to succeed him as governor of New York. In 1822, Mr. Clinton declining a re-election, he was succeeded by Joseph C. Yates. During this year, (1822,) the constitution of the state having been revised by a convention at Albany the preceding year, was accepted by the people in January. In 1824, De Witt Clinton was again re-elected to the office of governor. He died suddenly, February 11th, 1828, and the duties of his office devolved on Nathaniel Pitcher, the lieutenant-governor. Martin Van Buren was next elected governor. He entered on the duties of the office on the 1st of January, 1829, which, after holding for three months, he resigned. He was succeeded by Enos T. Throop, who exercised the office of governor from 1829 to 1833, when he was succeeded by William L. Marcy. Governor Marcy was succeeded in the office of governor by William H. Seward, in 1837.

ALBANY COUNTY.

ALBANY COUNTY was originally organized in 1683; but its limits have since been greatly altered. In the year 1768, there were but ten counties in the state, viz: New York, Westchester, Dutchess, Orange, Ulster, Albany, Richmond, Kings, Queens, and Suffolk. This county then embraced the whole of the territory of New York lying north of Ulster and west of the Hudson river, as well as all northward of Dutchess on the east side of the Hudson. Its greatest length now is 28, and greatest breadth 21 miles. The surface and soil are very much diversified. Along the Hudson are alluvial flats, nowhere exceeding a mile in width, susceptible in some places of high cultivation. From these flats, the surface rises abruptly 140 feet, and thence gradually westward to the mountains. On the Mohawk, the land is broken, rugged, and naturally sterile; on the west are the Helderberg Hills, precipitous and craggy, with a soil of calcareous loam. Centrally the county consists of undulating grounds and plains, with small marshes and tracts of cold, wet sands and clay, but which of late years have been greatly fertilized by gypsum, converting the piney and sandy desert into fragrant clover and fruitful wheat fields. Still, large tracts in this county are unimproved and perhaps unimprovable; but the greater portion is productive of wheat, of which a large surplus is annually sent to the New York market. The country is well watered by streams which, flowing from the highlands, empty into the Hudson, affording valuable hydraulic power. This county is divided into ten towns. Population in 1840 was 68,536.

ALBANY, the capital of New York, and the oldest city in the United States, lies in 42° 39′ 3″ N. Lat., and 3° 12′ E. Lon., from Washington. It received its present name in the year 1664, in honor of James, duke of York and Albany, who afterward mounted the throne of England as James II. Its original Indian name was *Scagh-negh-ta-da*, signifying, "*the end of the pine woods*," and this

J. W. Barber del.

Sherman & Smith, sc. N.Y.

SOUTH VIEW OF ALBANY, FROM GREENBUSH FERRY.

The city and State Halls each surmounted with a dome, are seen towering above the other buildings on the hill, on which Albany is mostly built. The entrance of the Erie Canal is seen on the north; the South or Greenbush Ferry Landing, on the left.

name for the same reason was applied by the aborigines to the site of the city of Schenectady, where it is yet retained with a slight variation in the orthography. The Dutch named Albany "Beaverwyck," [i. e. Beaver-town,] and afterward, " Willemstadt." It was never known as Fort Orange, or Urania, as has been asserted; but the fort only was called Fort Orange.* Albany was probably never visited by a *white man* till Sept., 1610, when Hendricke Chrystance, who was sent up the river by Henry Hudson to explore the country, first landed here; and as far as can be learned from tradition and some documentary evidence, he landed somewhere in the present North Market street. In that or the succeeding year, a party of the Dutch built a blockhouse on the north point of Boyd's Island, a short distance below the Albany ferry.

This house was erected for a two-fold purpose; first, to open a trade with the Indians for furs; the next, to secure themselves against any sudden attack from the savages. But it was soon demolished, for the next spring's freshet and ice swept the whole of it away. This party then chose a hill, subsequently called " *Kiddenhooghten*,"† within two miles of Albany, for the erection of another trading-house. The Indians called this hill "Ta-wass-a-gun-shee," or the " Look-out Hill." Not long afterward, this spot was abandoned, and a more convenient post selected. The place last chosen was in the vicinity of the house now called " Fort Orange Hotel," in South Market street. The Dutch there erected a Fort, " mounting eight *stone pieces*,"‡ and called it " Fort Orange."

Until after the year 1625, the Dutch did not contemplate making any permanent settlements in this state. They merely visited the country in the autumn and winter, with a view to the fur trade with the Indians, returning in the spring to Holland, or "Vaderlandt." But in that year, the Dutch West India Company first entertained the idea of colonizing their newly discovered territories in America, and accordingly offered large appropriations of land to such families as should " settle" in their colony of New Netherlands. This soon brought many over, and from that period till 1635, several of our most respectable Dutch families arrived; among them were the ancestors of the Van Schelluyne, Quackenboss, Lansing, Bleeker, Van Ness, Pruyn, Van Woert, Wendell, Van Eps, and Van Rensselaer families.

It does not appear that any stone or brick building was erected here (the fort excepted) until the year 1647, when, according to

---

* For most of the statements given respecting the early history of Albany, the authors are indebted to the " Historical Reminiscences," published in the American Journal, 1835.

† *Kiddenhooghten*, or *Kidds-heights or hill*, received its name about the year 1701; and, according to tradition, in memory of the pirate *Kidd*, so celebrated "in song and story," who it is supposed concealed much of his ill-gotten treasure in the vicinity. It is, however, doubted whether Kidd ascended the Hudson as far as Albany.

‡ According to Mr. Vander Kempt, the translator of our Dutch records, they were called " Stien-gestucken," or stone pieces, because they were loaded with *stone* instead of *iron ball*. They were formed of long and strong iron bars, longitudinally laid, and bound with iron hoops, and were of immense caliber.

a "letter from Commissary De la Montagnie" to the Dutch governor at New Amsterdam, (New York,) a *stone building* was erected near the fort, and he complains of the " enormous libations" upon the occasion of celebrating its completion: " No less" (he says) " than 8 ankers (128 gallons) of brandy were consumed."

About 100 years since, Albany was protected against sudden irruptions from the Indians by the erection of palisades,* part of the remains of which were visible within the last forty years. Barrack (now Chapel) street, was the principal place for business. The government of the city was extremely rigid, and often cruel; it bore the character more of a *military* despotism than that of a civil police; heavy penalties were imposed for the least infraction of the laws regulating the trade with the Indians, and many families consequently ruined. This severity drove some of the "traders" to the Schenectady flats, where they intercepted a considerable portion of the fur on its way to Albany, and which occasioned for many years the most bitter animosities between the inhabitants of both places. The circulating medium then in use consisted principally of *sewant*, or wampum.

Ministers of the reformed religion were regularly sent out from Holland to the colony. In 1657, the Rev. Gideon Schaats sailed from Amsterdam for this colony, and about the same time the Dutch West India Company wrote a letter, stating that they would send a *bell* and a *pulpit*, " for the inhabitants of Fort Orange, and of the village of Beaverwick, for their newly constructed *little church*." In

Ancient Dutch Church, Albany.

1715, this church became too small for the congregation, and the proprietors adopted a singular mode of enlarging it. Beyond and on every side of the ancient building, they sunk a new stone wall;

---

* These palisades consisted of large pieces of timber in close contact with each other, driven endwise into the ground, and GATES or openings were made at suitable intervals, which were closed at night.

on this foundation they raised a larger structure. Having thus completely enclosed the first church, they took it down and removed the whole, with only the loss of public worship for three sabbaths. The new edifice, which had been constructed in this manner, was one story high, of Gothic appearance, having its windows richly ornamented with coats of arms. This church, of which the preceding engraving is a representation, stood about ninety-two years in the open area formed by the angle of State, Market, and Court streets. It was taken down in 1806, and the stone of which it was constructed was used in the erection of the South Dutch Church, between Hudson and Beaver streets. Fort Orange, on the river bank, appears to have been but a slight fortification. In 1639, a complaint was made by the commandant of the fort to Gov. Stuyvesant, stating "that the fort was in a miserable state of decay, *and that the hogs had destroyed a part of it.*" A later work built of stone was erected on the river hill, at the west end of State-street. The English Church was just below it, at the west end of a market.

As has been stated, the government of Beaverwick, or Albany, while under the Dutch rule was rigid and arbitrary. It was in the hands of three or more "commissaries," appointed by the governor and council, who usually held their offices for one year. Without the permission of the commissaries, no one was allowed to build houses, buy or sell, or to establish manufactories, stores, shops, taverns, or beer-houses. In 1647, Jan La Battie applied for permission "to build a brewery," which was granted "on his paying yearly *six beavers*, a duty of perhaps of about eighty dollars. The duties were generally *farmed out*, or sold at auction; and during this year and several years afterward, the duties on beer in Beaverwick exceeded eight hundred dollars. The fines imposed for the violation of ordinances were generally distributed in the sentence in this way: "one third to the church, one third to the public, and one third to the attorney-general."

"Professor Kalm, who visited Albany in 1749, has left us some facts. All the people then understood Dutch. All the houses stood gable end to the street; the ends were of brick, and the side walls of planks or logs. The gutters on the roofs went out almost to the middle of the street, greatly annoying travellers in their discharge. At the stoopes (porches) the people spent much of their time, especially on the shady side; and in the evenings they were filled with both sexes. The streets were dirty by reason of the cattle possessing their free use during the summer nights. They had no knowledge of stoves, and their chimnies were so wide that one could drive through them with a cart and horses. Many people still made wampum to sell to Indians and traders. Dutch manners everywhere prevailed; but their dress in general was after the English form. They were regarded as close in traffic; were very frugal in their house economy and diet. Their women were over-nice in cleanliness, scouring floors and kitchen utensils several times a week; rising very early and going to sleep very late. Their servants were chiefly negroes. Their breakfast was *tea* without milk, using sugar by putting a small bit into the mouth. Their dinner was buttermilk and bread; and if to that they added sugar, it was deemed delicious."—*Watson's Sketches of Olden Times in New York.*

Albany was incorporated as a city, under Governor Dongan's administration, in 1686. The charter limits were one mile on the river, and extended northwest to the north line of the manor of Rensselaer, and retaining that width thirteen and a half miles; the fee simple of which was vested in the corporation. Its bounds were enlarged by the addition of part of the small town of Colonie, in 1815, which now forms the fifth ward. The government of the city is now lodged in a mayor, recorder, ten aldermen, and ten assistant aldermen, who are annually elected on the first Tuesday of May. The plat on which the city is built is uneven. A low alluvial flat extends along the river from fifteen to one hundred rods wide; west of which rises abruptly a hill of clay and sand, in the first half mile one hundred and fifty-three feet, and in the next about sixty-seven feet high; from this summit the country extends in nearly an even plain to Schenectady.

The position of Albany, necessarily makes it a great thoroughfare. The completion of the canals has given it a great commercial importance, making it the entrepot for a great proportion of the products destined for the New York market. To accommodate this trade, a basin has been constructed by the citizens on the river, in which all the northern and western canal boats are received. It consists of part of the river included between the shore and a pier eighty feet wide, and four thousand three hundred feet long. The pier contains about eight acres, on which stores have been built, and where immense quantities of lumber and other articles of trade are deposited. The basin has an area of thirty-two acres.

State and City Halls, Albany.

The above is a west view of the State and City Halls, the fronts of which face the Academy Park, a small section of which appears on the left. The building on the right is the City Hall, constructed of white marble, hewed out by the state prisoners, at Sing Sing, and distinguished above all other edifices in this country by its *gilded dome,* like the Invalides at Paris. It was completed in December, 1832. In the rotunda of this building there is a statue of Hamilton, a copy of that by Greenough, in the Merchants' Exchange, destroyed by the great fire in New York, in 1835. There are also two designs in bass-relief, executed by W. Coffee, at the cost of the citizens, commemorative of De Witt Clinton and Sir Walter Scott. A bust of each is introduced in the designs; that of Clinton is surrounded by figures, representing Commerce, Agriculture, Science, a canal lock, &c. The bust of Scott is accompanied with a female figure, presenting a volume inscribed " Marmion ;" the words " Minstrel" and " Waverly" appear on a scroll below ; the Genius of History, Fame, and the emblems of death and immortality, are also introduced. The New State Hall, partially seen on the left, was commenced in 1835. It covers an area of one hundred and thirty-eight by eighty-eight feet, and is sixty-five feet in height. The materials of the building are brick and stone ; the exterior faced with marble, from Mount Pleasant; the ceilings are arched with brick, and the whole fire-proof. This edifice contains the offices of the secretary of state, comptroller, treasurer, attorney-general, surveyor-general, &c.

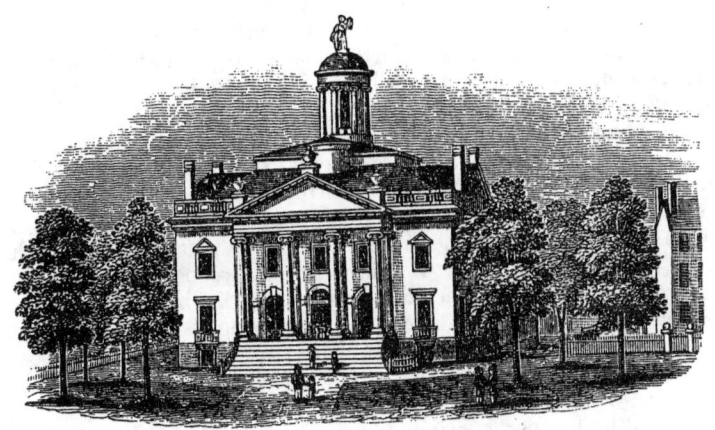

East View of the Capitol at Albany.

The above is an eastern view of the capitol, situated at the head of State-street, one hundred and thirty feet above the level of the river. It is substantially built of stone, at an expense of $120,000, of which the city corporation paid $34,000. The hall of the representatives and the senate chamber, each contain full length portraits of Washington, and of several governors of the state. The *Academy* is on the north side of the public square ; is a fine building, constructed of Nyac stone, three stories high and ninety feet front; cost, at the city charge, $90,000, exclusive of the site and some important donations. The *Albany Institute* has commodious apartments in the Academy. Its library contains about two thousand volumes, and its museum more than ten thousand specimens in geology, mineralogy, botany, coins, engravings, casts, &c. It publishes its transactions from time to time, and has a high reputation abroad. The *Albany Female Academy*, is a beautiful building, erected by a company incorporated February, 1821 ; this institution has a high reputation. The Exchange, Stanwix Hall, the Museum, and several of the churches, are fine buildings. The *Atheneum*, was established in 1827; the *Albany Library*, established in 1792, and now connected with the Atheneum, has about nine thousand volumes.

There are six banks, viz:—Bank of Albany, incorporated in 1792; capital, $240,000. New York State Bank, incorporated 1803; capital, $369,600. Mechanics and Farmers' Bank, incorporated 1811; capital, $442,000. Commercial Bank, incorporated 1825; capital, $300,000. Canal Bank, incorporated 1829; capital, $300,000. Albany City Bank, incorporated 1834; capital, $500,000. The Albany Savings Bank was incorporated in 1820.

There are 25 churches: 4 Presbyterian; 1 Associate do.; 3 Dutch Reformed; 4 Methodist Episcopal; 1 Protestant Methodist; 1 Colored do.; 3 Baptist; 1 Colored do.; 2 Catholic; 3 Episcopalian; 1 Friends; 1 Universalist. Population, 33,663. Albany is distant from New York 148 miles; from Washington city, 376; Philadelphia, 237; Boston, 171; Hartford, 92; Montreal, 247; Quebec, 394; Detroit, 664; Buffalo via Utica by land, 296; via Cherry Valley, 282; by the canal, 363.

Upon the northern bounds of the city is the mansion house of the late Stephen Van Rensselaer, Esq., the patroon of the manor of Rensselaerwick. It is almost entirely surrounded by a thick forest of trees, giving it an unusually retired aspect. " The name of this gentleman can scarcely be mentioned without a passing tribute to his merit. Blessed with great wealth, which so frequently leads to selfish egotism and exclusiveness, he has through life been distinguished as an active and efficient public man ; bestowing his personal services and his fortune, to the encouragement of every species of improvement in literature, science, and art. His name, as a benefactor, is associated with most of the charitable and scientific institutions of the state ; and he has perhaps done more than any other citizen to foster agriculture and internal improvements."—*Gordon's Gaz*.

BERNE, centrally distant west from Albany 20 miles, was taken from Rensselaerville in 1795. Population, 3,740. This town was settled during the revolutionary war, by a number of Scotch families. Berne, East Berne, and Readsville, are the names of postoffices. Centreville, is a small village. The lands in this town are leased by Mr. Van Rensselaer.

BETHLEHEM, the first town south from Albany, was taken from Watervliet, in 1793. Pop. 3,225. The flats on Hudson river are inhabited by the descendants of the early Dutch settlers. There are here extensive limestone caves, one of which has been explored for about a quarter of a mile. Coeyman's creek and the Normans kill, afford valuable hydraulic power. Cedar Hill postoffice, on the Hudson, is 8 miles south from Albany. Mills Island, a fertile tract in the Hudson, lies partly in the town.

COEYMANS, taken from Watervliet in 1791. Pop. 3,107. It was early settled by the Dutch, and received its name from one of the first settlers, himself a proprietor. Coeyman's village, at the junction of Coeyman's creek with the Hudson, 14 miles south of Albany, including the *Square*, contains 150 dwellings. Coeyman's Hollow, is a post village, in the central part of the town on Hawnakrans kill.

GUILDERLAND, taken from Watervliet in 1803. Pop. 2,790. Guilderland, West Guilderland, Guilderland Centre, and Dunsville, are postoffices. The town is centrally distant from Albany 10 miles.

KNOX, taken from Berne in 1822. Pop. 2,143. The lands are leased by Mr. Van Rensselaer. Knoxville, or Union Street, 21 miles west from Albany, has about 30 dwellings.

NEW SCOTLAND, taken from Bethlehem in 1832. Pop. 2,914. New Scotland, 8 miles southwest of Albany, has about 40 dwellings. New Salem, Clarksville, Union Church, are postoffices. Callagan's Corners, is a small settlement in the southeast part of the town.

RENSSELAERVILLE, taken from Watervliet in 1790. Pop. 3,712. Rensselaerville, a village of about 125 dwellings, is situated on Ten Mile creek, at the junction of the Albany, Delaware, and Greenville turnpikes, 24 miles southwest from Albany. The following view

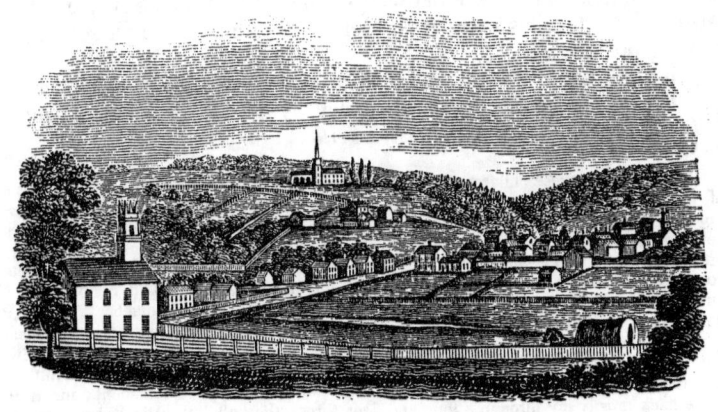

Northeastern View of Rensselaerville.

was taken near the Episcopal church seen on the left. The church on the hill is the Presbyterian, and that on the right the Methodist. The Baptist church is not seen from this point. On the Ten Mile creek there is an artificial reservoir or dam, flooding 80 or 100 acres, which affords great hydraulic power. This stream approaches the village through the ravine, seen between the hills in the engraving, and in the course of half a mile falls 150 or 200 feet. In 1788, the first mill in this town was erected by Messrs. Samuel Jenkins and Joel Culver on this creek, near the site of the village. This town was first settled during the revolution by Mr. Henry Vandyke, an elderly gentleman, who located himself in the southwest part. Samuel Jenkins, Melatiah and Nathaniel Hatch, Joseph Woodford, Thomas Brown, Joel Culver, Jonathan Crocker, Ashbel Culver and others, settled here about 1788. They were mostly young men, from Connecticut, Massachusetts, and Dutchess county. They built their log cabins, cooked their provisions, remained during warm weather, and in winter returned east. These first settlers were very poor. For the first year or two, not a horse was owned within a mile of the village, and they were obliged to carry their maple sugar 20 or 30 miles on their backs, exchange it for corn, and return in the same manner. The first log cabin in the village was located on the spot where Mr. Charles L. Mumford's store now stands, and was erected by Mr. Samuel Jenkins. In the hollow near the village, the tories, during the revolutionary war, had a secret place of rendezvous. Here they built a hut of bass-wood logs, oblong in its form, with the logs meeting at the top, and capable of holding 50 or 100 men. An unsuccessful attempt was made to surprise them. The military road, built during the old French war, between Athens and Schoharie, passed a little west of the village site. Preston Hollow, 30 miles southwest of Albany, on the Athens and Cherry Valley turnpike, has about 40 dwellings. Potter's Hollow, 2 miles south of the above, and Hall's Mills, about 5 miles south from Rensselaerville, are small settlements, having postoffices.

The following account of the captivity of two lads, John and Robert Brice, is drawn from a pamphlet by Mr. Josiah Priest, entitled "*The Captive Boys of Rensselaerville.*"

The parents of these children emigrated from Scotland in 1774, and settled in that part of the Rensselaerwick patent formerly comprised in the limits of this town, but now in those of Berne. The war of the revolution had raged with various success for about four years, when the few scattered families of this vicinity began to be in constant fear from the incursions of the tories and Indians, who had now commenced their depredations and acts of cold-blooded cruelty upon the inhabitants in the neighborhood of Old Schoharie. The family of Mr. Brice, having got out of bread, sent one morning on horseback, Robert, the youngest of the two boys, who was then about eleven years of age, with a bag of meal to get ground at a place called the Beaver Dam, eight or nine miles distant from their dwelling. He arrived safely at the mill, in company with three other lads, who went thither on a similar errand. By the time their meal was ready, the day was far spent; and as their route back mostly lay through a long and deep forest, they all but little Robert concluded to remain with the miller overnight. John Brice, the elder of the two boys, was at this time at work with a farmer by the name of Johannes Deitz, who resided about three miles from the mill, and thither Robert was determined to go and spend the night, and return the remainder of the way home on the next morning. The bag of meal being placed on the horse, the little fellow pursued his lonely way through the wilderness. It was near the commencement of twilight, the last beams of the descending sun were flashing their golden glare among the peaks of the mountains, when, on approaching the house where he intended to have passed the night, an Indian horribly painted rose up suddenly from the roadside, and seizing the bridle of the horse, without saying a word, or seeming to notice the rider, lead the horse directly towards the house. On passing the barn door, the boy was inspired with additional terror on beholding old Mr. Deitz lying on the ground weltering in his blood. Between the house and barn, he saw in a similar situation the wives of old Mr. Deitz and son, with four small children of the latter, and a servant girl, in all eight persons, their newly shed blood scarcely yet cooled in the evening air. He now perceived the house to be full of Indians, hideously painted, busily and silently employed in carrying out its contents—provisions, clothing, &c. In casting his eye around, he beheld at a little distance from the house his brother John and Captain Deitz, the son of the old man, tied to a tree, prisoners. The work of robbery and butchery being accomplished, the Indians packed their plunder on the backs of several horses which they had stolen, and hurried from the place. They had gone but a little way from the scene of butchery, when hearing a crackling noise behind them, the lads looked back, and saw the house, barn, and outhouses all in flames. The first night of their captivity they slept within a mile of their parents, in the arms of the savages. Early the next morning they resumed their flight; their progress was slow through the woods, occasioned by the bulkiness of their baggage, while they directed their way towards the head waters of the Cattskill creek, sleeping that night somewhere in the neighborhood of what is now called Potter's Hollow, a few miles southwest of Oakhill, in Greene county. From this place they again set off in the morning towards the Schoharie river, and at the close of the day, while ascending to the height of land aiming to reach the river above Middleburgh, the Indians suddenly became very much alarmed. News, it appeared, had reached the garrison at Schoharie of the outrage, and they had sent out a party to intercept the Indians in their retreat; but the savages had discovered them in season not to be surprised. Abandoning their horses, plunder and all, the three prisoners and eight scalps excepted, the Indians fled into the woods on the side of the ridge, and the darkness of night soon hid them from the fury of their pursuers. If they had not been disturbed in their course, their intention was to have availed themselves of the warrior's path on the Schoharie river, leading to the place called *Brake-a-bin*, from thence to Harpersfield, and so on to the Susquehannah, the Chemung, Genesee, and Niagara. As soon as it was day, having slept that night without fire, they set forward again, much cast down in their minds; pursuing the range of the mountain till somewhere near Gilboa, they crossed the creek, and passed on through the woods to Harpersfield; from thence to the Charlotte river, coming to the Susquehannah at McDaniel's Mills, since so called, and thence onward down that river to the Oquago.

Having now lost all their provisions, they felt the sufferings of hunger, and had no way to relieve themselves, lest their tell-tale guns should report them to their pursuers. Three days and nights they were compelled to subsist on nothing except what the bushes might afford—wintergreens, birch bark, and now and then a few wild berries. Captain Deitz was a peculiar sufferer, as suspended from a stick were the aged scalps of his father and mother, his wife and the four bloody memorials of his babes, adorned with the half-grown hair of their infant heads. These were constantly in his view, and often slapped in his face by the savage warrior. Captain Deitz finally died at Montreal with a broken heart. On the third day, when not far from the mouth of the Unadilla river, they considered themselves out of danger, consequently travelled more at leisure, stopping frequently to hunt. At such times, as when they went out to hunt a day, intending to return by night, the Indians always bound Captain Deitz and Robert's brother to a tree, laying them flat on their backs, with their legs a little elevated to a limb; in this uneasy posture they were compelled to suffer till their return. The owner of Robert had received a wound in the leg, when the party were pursued by the detachment from the garrison at Schoharie, and after a few days travelling, he became so lame as to be unable to travel as fast as his companions. The poor boy was now separated from his brother and Captain Deitz, and was left behind with his master and two other Indians. The first intimation to the boy that they had arrived in the Genesee or Indian country, were the yells which they uttered, and the responses they received from a great distance, which were continued until within sight of each other. Here commenced a persecution which the little fellow had not anticipated; for the Indian children about his size and age immediately fell upon him with their whips and fists, amusing themselves to see him jump about and cry. He fled for protection to his master, but obtained none from that quarter. His next resort was to fly to a hut, although full of Indians, all laughing at his misfortunes; he sprang in among them, trembling, pale, and bleeding, when his pursuers desisted. Whenever they approached an Indian settlement, the same ominous yells were renewed, when the same sort of persecution again befell him; but as necessity at first had taught him to fly to a hut, so he now had learned to press forward with all his power to the door of the first wigwam which offered to his view, never being repulsed on his entry. Four times on passing from one settlement to another, he experienced the same sort of treatment; which custom at one time had nearly cost him his life. An Indian lad much larger than himself, who ought, even according to their notions of dignity and manners, to have known better, knocked him down with a club, but he sprang up, and soon found the accustomed asylum, drenched in blood. At length, the three Indians came to a place called the Nine Mile Landing, on Lake Ontario, where was the home of his master. Here they shaved his head and adorned it with feathers, and painted him after their manner, intending to bring him up as an Indian, taking him with them on their fishing and hunting parties, initiating him as fast as possible into their mode of living. A few weeks after, his master took him to Fort Erie, opposite to where Buffalo now stands, and sold him for fifteen dollars to the captain of a vessel on Lake Erie, who was a Scotchman. From this time he saw his Indian acquaintance no more, going immediately with his new master to Detroit. Supposing that if he continued with the captain, and followed a sea-faring life, all opportunity would be forever lost of returning to his parents, he contrived a plea to be left at Detroit, to which his master consented. At this place he remained until the close of the revolutionary war, when, according to the articles of peace, the prisoners of both countries were to be sent to their homes. His brother, at the time of their separation, was sent to Fort Niagara, and he, in company with Robert and many others, were released and sent to their respective homes.—Robert Brice is now, or was recently, still living in Bethlehem in this county; a respected citizen of the farmer class.

WATERVLIET was organized in 1788. Pop., including West Troy, 10,146. It includes the islands in the Hudson on the east; centrally distant north from Albany 6 miles, extending 10 miles along the Mohawk river, and its lowest branch or sprout, and 6½ along the Hudson. Havers, Van Schaicks or Cahoes, and Green or Tibbets islands, are formed by sprouts of the Mohawk. They were occupied by the American army under General Gates, in 1777. The lands of the town are principally comprised in the manor of Rensselaerwick. Cahoes, Neskayuna, and West Troy, are villages. The small but flourishing manufacturing village of Cahoes is situated near the falls, on the bank of the Mohawk, within a short distance of the junction of the Erie and Champlain canals. The water-power developed here is very great, and the advantages of this position for manufactures, are among the best in the state.

"The Cahoes Falls, in full view of the village, and seen with special advantage from the bridge, have a total descent of 78 feet, and a perpendicular pitch of about 40. Above the cataract, the bank on the left has nearly 100 feet perpendicular elevation, and below, 170 feet. On the right above the pitch, the bank is low; but below it, the shore is between 80 and 90 feet high; below the falls the river runs in a deep, rocky and broken bed for a short distance, expanded into the placid pool formed by the state dam, and glides over that dam in one lovely sheet of about ⅓ of a mile in length, whose gentle fall of 7 feet makes a pleasant contrast with the great cataract above. In floods, the whole bed at the latter is covered with water, which descends in one unbroken torrent about 900 feet wide. At such seasons, the high rocky barriers which confine the stream, the roar of the cataract, the dashing of the troubled waters as they descend the rapids, and the striking assimilation of the torrent with the wilderness above, give to the scene unusual sublimity."

West Troy, incorporated in 1836, comprising Gibbonsville, Watervliet, and Port Schuyler, is situated upon the Hudson, opposite Troy, and may be considered as a part of that city. [*See view of Troy.*] A communication is constantly kept up with it by ferries, and a fine macadamized road 6 miles in length along the river connects it with Albany. A valuable water-power is derived from the Junction canal, and used at the arsenal and other works. The village has, by the census of 1840, a population of 4,607; and enjoying all the advantages of navigation possessed by Troy, grows rapidly. The United States arsenal, located here, comprises several extensive buildings of stone and brick, in which there are a large quantity of arms, with workshops for their repair. Among the cannon are some pieces taken at Saratoga and at Yorktown; others, presented to the United States by Louis XIV., with some cast in New York and Philadelphia during the revolution. Another suburb of Troy, called North Troy, has been laid out upon Tibbets island, upon which is the railroad depot.

At Neskayuna, there is a small society of Shakers, which was established here in September, 1776, by Ann Lee. They own 2,000 acres of good land, well cultivated and divided into four farms, on each of which is a *family*, the whole amounting to about 80 persons of both sexes and all ages. From a very small beginning, the society has grown into several communities, the largest of which is established at New Lebanon, Columbia county.

Ann Lee, or "*Mother Ann*," (as she is usually called,) was born at Manchester, England. About the year 1758, she joined herself to the society of Shakers, so called from the singular tremblings and shakings with which these people were affected at their religious meetings. According to the account given by her biographer, she passed through great trial and distress of mind for the space of nine years, during which period she had many visions and revelations. She set up herself as a religious teacher, and soon collected a number of followers, who believed her to be the "elect lady," spoken of in the 2d of John. After having been imprisoned in England and confined in a madhouse, she set sail for America, in the spring of 1774, with a number of her followers; particularly, Abraham Stanley, her husband, William Lee, her brother, James Whitaker and John Hocknell; and arrived at New York the following August. It appears that Mother Ann remained in New York nearly two years, and then went to Albany, and thence, in the following September, to Neskayuna. In 1781, she began a progress through various parts of the country, particularly of New England, which lasted, we are told, about two years and four months. She died in 1784. The following lines are from a book entitled "Christ's Second Appearing;" they are extracted from a poem called "A Memorial to Mother Ann," and will serve to show in what light she is viewed by her followers.

> At Manchester, in England, this burning truth began,
> When Christ made his appearance in blessed Mother Ann;
> A few at first received it and did their lust forsake,
> And soon their testimony brought on a mighty shake.
>
> For Mother's safe protection, good angels flew before,
> Towards the land of promise, Columbia's happy shore;
> Hail, thou victorious Gospel, and that auspicious day,
> When Mother safely landed in North America.
>
> About four years she labor'd with the attentive throng,
> While all their sins they open'd and righted ev'ry wrong;
> At length she closed her labors and vanish'd out of sight,
> And left her faithful children increasing in the light.
>
> How much they are mistaken who think that Mother's dead,
> When through her ministrations so many souls are fed!
> In union with the Father, she is the second Eve,
> Dispensing full salvation to all who do believe.

WESTERLO, taken from Coeymans and Rensselaer in 1815. Pop. 3,096. Centrally distant from Albany, southwest, 21 miles. The western part pertains to the manor of Rensselaerwick; the eastern part is in Coeyman's Patent. The Dutch and Germans commenced settlements in 1759, around the lowlands. In 1794, they were much increased by the arrival of many emigrants from New England. Disbrows and South Westerlo are postoffices.

ALLEGANY COUNTY.

ALLEGANY COUNTY was taken from Genesee in 1806. It is 44 miles long, 28 wide, being part of the tract ceded to Massachusetts. The two western tiers of towns are within the Holland Land Company's purchase. The Genesee river flows through the county by a deep channel, depressed from five hundred to eight hundred feet below the higher hills. By an act passed in 1828, this river was declared a public highway from Rochester to the Pennsylvania line. The soil is of a good quality, there being extensive tracts of alluvion, and the uplands embrace a variety. The northern part is best for grain, but as a whole it is better for grazing. Wheat and corn thrive well in the valley and on the river flats. Of the former, twenty-five bushels an acre are an average crop, and of the latter forty. On the upland, corn, rye, potatoes, oats, and buckwheat, are productive crops. The growth of forest trees being heavy, lumbering is carried on extensively. The Rochester and Olean canal, chartered in 1836, and now constructing, enters the county at Portage and terminates at Olean, in the adjoining county of Cattaraugus. The line of the Erie railroad also passes through it. The county contains 30 towns. Pop. 40,917.

ALFRED, taken from Angelica in 1808, distant from Albany 246, and from Angelica, east, 10 miles. Pop. 1,637. The town is a good one for farming. Alfred and Vandemark are postoffices. Baker's Bridge and Alfred Centre are villages. In 1821, Almond and Independence were taken from the town.

ALLEN, taken from Angelica in 1823, since reduced; distant from Albany 244, from Angelica, north, 6 miles. There is a postoffice at Allen, and one at Allen Centre. Pop. 870.

ALMOND, taken from Alfred; since reduced in area. Pop. 1,434. The Bath and Angelica turnpike passes through it. Almond, the largest village, 16 miles east from Angelica, has about thirty-five dwellings. Centre Almond and North Almond are postoffices.

AMITY, taken from Angelica and Scio in 1830; distant from Albany 258, from Angelica, south, 6 miles. Pop. 1,356. The Genesee crosses it northwestwardly, upon which are flats from half a mile to a mile wide. Phillipsburg, a very flourishing post village, lies on the river and line of the Erie railroad in the northeast angle of the town, and has one Presbyterian and one Methodist church. There is a fall here of twelve or fourteen feet, yielding an excellent water-power. Phillipsville, Hobbieville, and Genesee Valley, are postoffices.

In the vicinity of Phillipsburg are the remains of three Indian forts, on the largest of which there formerly stood eight aged trees. On the bark of one of them was carved a figure of a *turtle*, underneath which there was also cut a canoe, with *seven* Indians in it, headed down stream. This was done, according to the account given by the natives to the first settlers, by a party of *seven* Indians of the *Turtle* tribe, to inform their companions that they had gone down the river.

ANDOVER, taken from Independence in 1824; distant from Albany 252, from Angelica, southeasterly, 15 miles. Pop. 864.

ANGELICA, formed from Leicester in 1805; from Albany 256, and from New York 327 miles. The Genesee crosses the southwestern angle of the town. Pop. 1,261.

View of the Public Buildings at Angelica.

Angelica Village, 2 miles east of the Genesee river, 40 miles west from Bath, 52 S. from Batavia, incorporated 2d of May, 1835, is the county seat. The above view, taken near the residence of Mr. John T. Wright, shows all the public buildings excepting the Baptist church. The gothic structure, on the left, is the Episcopal church; the building with a spire, the Presbyterian; the one with a cupola, the courthouse; and that on the extreme right, the Methodist church. There are in the village about one hundred and thirty dwellings and two printing-offices, each issuing a weekly paper. About three miles southwest of the village, is the seat of Philip Church, Esq., called Belvidere, where there is a fine house with a farm under high cultivation. The county was first settled by this gentleman, in 1804, and the town is named after his mother, Mrs. Angelica Church, the eldest daughter of General Philip Schuyler.

BELFAST, taken from Caneadea, by the name of Orrinsburg, in 1824; name changed in 1825; distant from Albany 264, and from Angelica, west, 6 miles. Pop. 1,684. Summer's Valley, Rockville, and Belfast, are post-offices.

The following account of a tornado, which passed over this region a few years since, is taken from Silliman's Journal for July, 1839 :—

" Having visited and examined the scene of the tornado, so well described by Mr. Willis Gaylord, of Otisco, Onondaga County, N. Y., in the Genesee Farmer, Nov. 10, 1838, we also can bear witness to the tremendous devastation which that whirlwind produced.

" We were on the ground in September, about two months after the event. Before the tornado, a region of 4 or 500 acres had been covered by a dense forest of pine trees, many of them very tall and large; roads had been cut through this forest, and a few solitary houses were planted in it, here and there. Now we looked in vain over the whole tract for a single perfect tree. Those which had not been uprooted or broken in two near the ground, were shivered and twisted off at different elevations, leaving only a portion of a shattered trunk, so that not a single tree top, and hardly a single branch, were found standing in the air: there were instead only mutilated stems, presenting a striking scene of desolation wherever our eyes ranged over the now almost empty aerial space. On the ground the appearances were still more remarkable. The trees were interwoven in every possible way, so as to form a truly military abattis of the most impassable kind; nor immediately after the gale could any progress be, in fact, made through the gigantic thickets of entangled trunks and branches, without the labor of bands of pioneers, who cut off the innumerable logs that choked every avenue. We had before seen many avenues made through forests by winds, prostrating the trees and laying them down in the direction of its course: but never had we seen such a perfect desolation by a gyratory movement, before which the thick and lofty forest and the strongest framed buildings vanished, in an instant, and their ruins were whirled irresistibly around like flying leaves or gossamer.

"Still, it was truly wonderful that people were buried in the ruins of their houses, and travellers with their horses and cattle were exposed to this driving storm of trees which literally filled the air, and still not a single life was lost, although some persons were wounded.

"We were assured that this wind had marked a track of devastation for twenty miles or more, but this was the scene of its greatest ravages. Two or three miles from this place, we saw a wing of a house which had been moved quite around, so as to form a right angle with its former position, and still the building was not broken."—*Editors.*

"The first appearance of severe wind, (says Mr. Gaylord,) was, as we learned, in the town of Rushford, some fifteen miles from the place where we observed its effects. The day was hot and sultry, and the course of the gale was from the N. of W. to S. of East. At its commencement in Rushford, it was only a violent thunder gust, such as are frequently experienced, but it soon acquired such force as to sweep in places every thing before it. In its passage the same violence was not at all times exerted; some places seemed wholly passed over, while in the same direction and at only a small distance whole forests were crushed. In the language of one who had suffered much from the gale, 'it seemed to move by bounds, sometimes striking and sometimes receding from the earth,' which indeed was most likely the case.

"It passed the Genesee river in the town of Belfast, a few miles below Angelica, and its fury was here exerted on a space of country perhaps a mile or a mile and a half in width. The country here is settled and cleared along the river, but the road passes at a little distance from the river, and at this point wound round one of the finest pine woods to be found on the stream. Of course when it came over the higher lands from the N. W., the tornado crossed the river and the plain before encountering the groves of pine. In the space occupied by the central part of the tornado, say three fourths of a mile in width, nothing was enabled to resist its fury. Strong framed houses and barns were crushed in an instant, and their fragments and contents as quickly scattered to every point of the compass; while those out of the direct line were only unroofed or more or less damaged. Large oaks and elms were literally twisted off, or crushed like reeds.

"The road from the north approached the pine woods on what was the northern verge of the tornado, and the first appearance of the country in front was that of woodlands, in which all the trees had been broken off at the height of 20 or 30 feet, leaving nothing but countless mutilated trunks. On entering the narrow passway, however, which with immense labor had been opened through the fallen trunks, it was perceived that much of the largest part of the trees had been torn up by the roots, and lay piled across each other in the greatest apparent confusion imaginable. Fortunately for our view of the whole ground, a few days before our arrival, fire had been put in the 'windfall,' and aided by the extreme dry weather, the whole was burned over so clean, that nothing but the blackened trunks of the trees were remaining, thus disclosing their condition and position most perfectly. This position was such as to demonstrate beyond the possibility of a doubt, the fact, that the tornado had a rotary motion against the sun, and in perfect accordance with the course which we in a former volume of the Farmer have ascribed to such electric aerial currents, a theory first developed by Mr. Redfield of New York.

"The first tree met with, prostrated by the tornado, was a large pine, which lay with its top exactly to the N. of West, or precisely against the general course of the storm. Hundreds of others lay near in the same direction on the outer part of the whirl, but immediately after entering the fallen timber, the heads of the trees began to incline to the centre of the space torn down, and south of this, the inclination was directly the reverse until the

ALLEGANY COUNTY.   59

outside of the whirl was reached, when they all lay with their tops to the east. This almost regular position of the fallen timber, was most distinct in the bottom courses, or that which was first blown down, those that resisted the longest, being, as was to be expected, pitched in the most diverse directions. That there was also an upward spiral motion, causing a determination of the rushing air to the centre of the whirl, would appear probable from the fact that articles from the buildings destroyed were carried high in the air, and then apparently thrown out of the whirl, into the common current; and also from the fact, that a large majority of the trees both from the south and to the north of the centre of the gale, lay with their heads inclined to that point, while the centre was marked by the greatest confusion imaginable. A diagram formed of a continued succession of circles moving from the right to the left, would illustrate the position of the trees first uprooted, as these lay as when first crushed by the approach of the whirlwind.

"Many curious facts illustrative of the force of the wind were related by the inhabitants in and near the place. A farmer attempted to drive his team of horses to the barn, but the tempest was too soon upon him. When the rush was over, and it was seemingly but a moment, he found the barn torn to pieces, himself about thirty rods in one direction from it, and his horses as many rods the other, and what was most remarkable, with scarcely a fragment of harness upon them. A wagon was blown away, and a month afterward one of the wheels had not been found. A house standing near the Genesee river, and a little out of the line of the gale, was completely covered with mud that must have been taken from the bed of the river. And appearances render it very evident that near the centre of the whirl the water was entirely taken from the channel."

BIRDSALL, taken from Allen and Almond in 1829; distant from Albany, southwest, 245 miles. Pop. 328. Birdsall post-office is 12 miles northeast from Angelica.

BOLIVAR was taken from Friendship, in 1825; from Albany 275, and from Angelica, southwest, 19 miles. Pop. 408. Bolivar Village has about twenty-five dwellings.

BURNS, taken from Ossian in 1826; distant centrally from Angelica, northeast, 16, and from Albany 239 miles. De Witt's Valley and Whitney's Valley are post-offices. Pop. 847.

CANEADEA, taken from Angelica in 1808; distant from Albany 267, from Angelica, northwest, 11 miles. Pop. 1,647. Caneadea Village is centrally situated. The Caneadea Indian reservation commences here, and extends northward on the river about ten miles, through Hume into Portage and Granger.

CENTREVILLE, taken from Pike in 1819; from Angelica, northwest, 18 miles. Pop. 1,504. Centreville Village, centrally situated in the town, has about thirty-five dwellings.

CLARKSVILLE, taken from Cuba in 1835; from Angelica, southwest, 18 miles. Clarksville is a post-office. Pop. 326.

CUBA, taken from Friendship in 1822; distant from Albany 275, and from Angelica, southwest, 18 miles. Pop. 1,761. Cuba Village, centrally situated, near which the lines of the Erie railroad and the Rochester and Olean canal intersect, is a very flourishing place, and has about eighty dwellings, one Presbyterian, and one Baptist church. Cadysville is 2 miles north of the village.

The famed Seneca Oil Spring is in this town, within eighty rods of the county line. The spring rises in a marsh, distant three and a half miles from the village. It is a muddy, circular, stagnant pool, about eighteen feet in diameter, with no visible outlet. The water is coated with a thin layer of mineral oil, giving it a yellowish-brown color, similar to dirty molasses. The oil is collected by skimming it from the fountain, and is used for rheumatism in man, and sprains and sores for man or beast. The spring was highly valued by the Indians, and a square mile around it has been reserved for the Senecas. The oil sold in the eastern states is obtained from Oil Creek, in Venango county, Pennsylvania, where it is more pure and abundant. The spring gives name to a post-office.

EAGLE, taken from Pike in 1823; centrally distant from Albany 264, from Angelica, northwest, 24 miles. Pop. 1,222.

FRIENDSHIP, taken from Caneadea in 1815. Pop. 1,230. Friendship Village, on the line of the Erie railroad, 10 miles southwest from Angelica, contains about sixty dwellings.

GENESEE, taken from Cuba in 1830; from Angelica, southwest, 25 miles. Pop. 569. Little Genesee and West Genesee are names of post-offices. Little Genesee is a small village.

GRANGER, taken from Grove; centrally distant from Angelica, north, 12 miles. Grove, Short Tract, and Hickory Swale, are post-offices. Pop. 1,064.

GROVE, taken from Nunda in 1827; from Angelica, north, 14 miles. East Grove is a post-office. Pop. 625.

NEW HUDSON, formerly named Haight, and taken from Rushford in 1825; from Albany 268, and from Angelica, west, 13 miles. Black Creek is a post-office. The summit level of the Rochester and Olean canal is in this town. Pop. 1,488.

HUME, taken from Pike in 1822; from Albany, southwest, 260 miles; drained by the Genesee on the southeast. Pop. 2,305. Hume and Cold Creek are post-offices. At Mixville, a post village, 15 miles northwest from Angelica, there are about twenty dwellings, and an excellent hydraulic power, comprising four perpendicular falls, making in the whole seventy-five feet descent.

INDEPENDENCE, taken from Alfred in 1821; from Albany 262, and from Angelica, southeast, 20 miles. Pop. 1,398. Independence Centre, Independence, Whitesville, and Spring Mill, are post villages.

NUNDA, taken from Angelica in 1808; from Albany 253, and from Angelica, northeast, 18 miles. Pop. 2,614. The name is a corruption of an Indian word signifying "potatoe ground," applied when this town comprehended the rich flats of the Genesee. Nunda and East Hill are post-offices. The village of Nunda Valley, upon the Cashaqua creek, is a place of much and increasing business; the Rochester and Olean canal is to pass through it.

The following is a southern view of the open square in the business portion of the place, taken at Whitcomb and Co.'s store. The village was first settled about the year 1826, by Deacon Rawson, Asa Heath, Samuel Swain, David Basset, James M. Heath, and others. The latter-named person built the first tavern, in 1826, of logs. The Baptist and Presbyterian churches were erected in 1832. The village contains about one hundred dwellings.

OSSIAN, taken from Angelica in 1808; from Albany 233, and from Angelica, northeast, 20 miles. Pop. 945. Ossian village is centrally situated.

Central Part of Nunda Valley Village.

Pike, taken from Nunda, March, 1818; from Albany 255, and from Angelica, northwest, 18 miles. Pop. 2,181. Pike, centrally situated, has one Presbyterian, one Methodist, and one Baptist church, and about ninety dwellings. East Pike and East Koy are post-offices.

Portage, taken from Nunda in 1827; centrally distant from Albany 247, and from Angelica, north, 18 miles. Pop. 4,715. Portageville, on the Genesee river at the head of the rapids, is a flourishing village, containing about sixty or seventy dwellings. The line of the Olean and Rochester canal passes through it. Hunt's Hollow and Oakland are post-offices.

This town is located in an exceedingly interesting region, both from the wild grandeur of its river scenery, and the exhibition of human enterprise and skill in the construction of a tunnel for the canal, through the solid rock, which here bounds the valley of the Genesee. " There are three distinct falls on the river, respectively sixty, ninety, and one hundred and ten feet high, within the space of two miles, each differing in character, and each having peculiar beauties. Although the cascades are highly admirable, they are almost disregarded in the wonder and fear caused by the stupendous, perpendicular walls of the river, rising to four hundred feet in height, and extending along the stream for three miles, with almost as much regularity as if constructed by art. To this great depth the river has worn its bed in the solid rock, in turns as short and graceful, as if winding through the softest meadow." The middle falls, which are the highest, have been the scene of several narrow escapes, of which, perhaps the following is the most remarkable. Early in the spring of 1827, a boy about fourteen, named Joel Burgess, took a boat into the river above the falls, for the purpose of obtaining a duck which he had shot. In his eagerness to secure the prize, he lost sense of his peril and floated down the stream. On going over the dam, which is situated about twelve rods above the cataract, he was thrown out of the boat, but still held on with both hands. Thus clinging to the frail bark, he was fast hurrying to an awful death, when his feet struck a small projecting rock in the bed of the river. With admirable presence of mind, he let go of the boat and stood fast. His situation was even now full of danger. On each side the water was deep, and the current running with an irresistible force. Chilled and exhausted by the coldness of the element, he was about losing hold of the slippery rock, when those ashore succeeded in throwing him a rope, which he tied around his waist and was dragged exhausted to land. Under these falls, on the northern side, is the "Devil's Oven," a cave fifteen feet in height, and sixty feet deep.

Pass of the Genesee at Portage Falls.

The above is a representation of the gorge, at that point where the river, coming from the south, takes a sudden and abrupt bend to the east. It is situated below the middle and upper falls; both of which are in full sight from near this point. The spectator is supposed to be standing in the valley, and looking eastwardly in the direction of the lower falls, which are about a mile and a half distant. Immediately in front rise massy, perpendicular rocks, to the height of four hundred feet, their summits crowned with gigantic pines and hemlocks, the aged sentinels of an hundred years. In the perspective, the river meanders along its rocky bed, until finally lost to the view behind projecting precipices. Far in the distant horizon is seen the hills of the Cashaqua, and to the right " Hornby Lodge," standing on the verge of the precipice, resembling an ancient chateau; its rude, gothic architecture in keeping with the wildness of the situation. The sketch for the above engraving was taken at the close of the year. Winter had thrown her snowy mantle upon the face of nature. The huge evergreens and naked limbs of the other forest trees were enveloped in their drapery of white; immense icicles hung from the rocks; while the blue of the distant hills, contrasting with the icy splendor and sublimity of the foreground, combined to render it a scene of indescribable grandeur. Some years since, a party of surveyors cut down an immense pine, standing on the verge of the precipice. It turned one somerset in its descent, and struck its butt perpendicularly upon the rocky bottom of the gorge. Every limb fell to the earth with the shock. It stood for a moment, a tall, limbless trunk, quivered, and fell with a crash.

The tunnel, eleven hundred and eighty feet in length, to which allusion has been made, commences at a point on the southern side of the gorge, about six hundred feet east of the lodge, and has a southwestern termination near the middle falls. The following description of this work, and the "lodge," is from an interesting series of letters, entitled "Midsummer Rambles," published in the New York Commercial Advertiser in the summer and autumn of 1840. "The trunk of the tunnel is to be twenty-seven feet wide and twenty feet high. Fortunately, the character of the rock (sandstone) is favorable to the progress of the work. The contractor for this section is ELISHA JOHNSON, Esq., formerly mayor of Rochester, and one of its most enterprising citizens. Mr. Johnson commenced this vast excavation last year, first running a shaft or 'heading' five and a half feet nearest the roof, and of the entire width required, through the whole length of the tunnel. One of the lateral drifts, for the introduction of air and light from the river brink to the main tunnel, had also been previously completed," the opening to which is seen in the engraving on the rock in front of the " Lodge."

"The entire excavation of this tunnel, including the gallery, shaft, and lateral drifts, will amount to more than twenty-five thousand cubic yards, for which the price paid is four dollars per yard. This, however, will not, by a great amount, cover the entire cost of the tunnel; for since the excavation has been commenced, such is the character of the rock—thrown together apparently by nature in loose masses and blocks—that it now appears that the entire roof and sides of the tunnel will require arching with solid mason work. Indeed, temporary arches of wood have been found necessary during the progress of almost every successive yard of the work. It is by far the greatest undertaking of the kind that has been attempted in our country.

"Perceiving, at the outset, that his contract would require a long time for its completion, Mr. Johnson, whose daily presence was

Hornby Lodge at Portage Falls.

necessary, wisely determined to surround himself by his family. He accordingly prepared 'a lodge' for them in the 'wilderness.' The site selected is wild and picturesque in a high degree. It stands upon a small plain or table, upon the highest verge of the precipitous bank of the river so often adverted to, a few yards only from the edge, which juts out, and almost impends over the abyss, threatening to descend and overwhelm all that may be below. The site of the building is near the southwestern entrance of the tunnel.* Facing that direction, a full view is presented of the chasm of the river, and the upper and middle falls; the roar of which is incessant, and the ascending clouds of vapor of which form objects of ever-varying and incessant interest and beauty. '*Hornby Lodge*' is the name of Mr. Johnson's castle, and the grounds around it—purposely kept as wild as nature herself has made them—are called '*Tunnel Park.*'

"The house, or lodge, is of itself a great curiosity. In shape it is an octagon, sixty feet in diameter, and two stories high—with wings—according to the ground-plan annexed. It is supported by the trunk of a huge oak tree, standing in the centre, from which the beams and rafters radiate to the outward circumference. It stands directly over the main tunnel, the roof of which is 100 feet beneath the base of the lodge. The work is prosecuted by relief parties night and day; and while the miners were at work directly beneath the lodge, the explosions of the powder used in blasting were both heard and felt by the family, essentially disturbing their slumber at night. The ornaments of the lodge, over the doors and windows, and much of the furniture, are truly Gothic, being formed from the crookedest limbs of trees that could be found. On the whole, it is a most picturesque establishment, standing alone in its rustic beauty, and looking out fearfully

---

* Having formerly been some years engaged on public works, we were naturally interested in the construction at this place. Much credit is due to Mr. Edward A. Stillman, a young man of 22, who is the resident *instrumental* engineer. His lines have been run with uncommon success as compared with similar works in Europe.—*H. H.*

upon the confined deep. I was a partaker of Mr. Johnson's hospitality for one night. It was a beautiful moonlight night; and both by day and night I enjoyed the scene to the full."

To the foregoing description, we would add that the building presents a similar appearance from every direction. There is between each pair of wings a door which opens into an octagonal saloon, occupying the whole of the basement, excepting the wings. This saloon is in true "log cabin" style. The trunk of the huge oak, previously alluded to, with its shaggy bark covering, rises from the floor in the centre of the room as a pillar to support the ceiling. The furniture, chairs, sofas, &c., in this apartment are formed of the rough limbs of the forest. The wings are divided into rooms of convenient size answering the respective purposes of parlor, library, office, conservatory, kitchen, &c. &c. The structure approaches to the Swiss Gothic style, and its peculiar and novel feature is, that while the lower story is an octagon, the upper is a quadrilateral, *diamonding* with the base.

We will close our account of this region by a description of the lower falls, taken from the "Rambles." "The water at the lower falls rushes around an immense rock in its descent, close under the southeastern bank. Fortunately for visiters, as yet the scene has been thus far permitted by man to remain in a state of nature. It is therefore as wild and romantic as can be desired. A dark screen of evergreen, hanging over the cataract so near and thick as to render it unsafe to push through it, partially hides the descending torrent of foam, which dots after its final plunge the river to a considerable distance with cream-like ornaments. Partly detached from the main wall which confines the river to its narrow bed, a huge rock partially conceals the fall, tapering upward like a sugar-loaf, and crested with evergreens. On the opposite, or western side, the top of the rock around which the waters hurry in their maddened wrath, is level as the house-floor, and large enough for a company of

> Those gallant sons who shoulder guns
> And twice a year go out a-training,

to perform their martial exercises upon. Midway from the top, the sugar-loaf is united to the main buttress. The depth of this fall is 96 feet."

RUSHFORD, taken from Caneadea in 1827, is centrally situated from Albany 270, and from Angelica, northwest, 20 miles. Pop. 1,502. Rushford village contains 1 Methodist church, and about 70 dwellings.

SCIO, taken from Angelica in 1823, and centrally distant, south, 16 miles. Scio and Wellsville are post-offices. Pop. 1,150. In its territorial limits, this town is far the largest in the county. Its surface is high and much broken by streams, and heavily timbered with pines, hemlock, &c. Most of the township is in its primitive wilderness state.

WEST ALMOND comprises township No. 4 in the first range of Morris' Reserve, and was taken from Almond, Angelica and Alfred in 1835; from Angelica, east, 7 miles. Pop. 810.

WIRT, taken from Friendship and Bolivar; from Angelica, southwest, 14 miles. Pop. 1,208. South Branch and Richburg are post-offices.

BROOME COUNTY.

BROOME COUNTY, named after Lieut. Gov. Broome, was taken from Tioga in 1806. Length, on the Pennsylvania line, 37 miles; breadth, on the Tioga boundary 28, on the Delaware 13, and midway 17 miles. Centrally distant from New York, northwest, 252, and from Albany, southwest, 145 miles. The surface of the country is broken and mountainous. Among its principal elevations are the Cookquago, the Oquago, and the Randolph mountains. The valleys bordering on its numerous streams are extensive and fertile, producing large quantities of wheat. The soil is generally better adapted to grazing than the culture of grain. Fruit succeeds well. The inhabitants are principally farmers, and its agriculture is respectable. The Chenango canal enters the county on the north, follows down the valley of the Chenango river, and enters the Susquehannah river at Binghamton. The line of the Erie railroad passes through the county. The county is divided into 11 towns. Population, 22,348.

BARKER was taken from Lisle in 1831; drained by the Tioughnioga river crossing it diagonally from northwest to southeast. Population, 1,258. Chenango Forks, post village, 12 miles north from Binghamton, has about 30 dwellings. There is a small collection of houses at Hyde settlement.

CHENANGO was organized in February, 1791; since reduced in limits. It is centrally intersected by Chenango river, which enters the Susquehannah at Chenango Point. Along the valleys of both these streams are rich alluvial flats from one to two miles wide. The land is broken and hilly, containing large quantities of pine and other timber for market. Population, 5,475. The village of BINGHAMTON in this town, formerly called *Chenango Point,* the shire village of the county, was incorporated in 1813, 1824, and 1834. It derived its present name from William Bingham, a munificent benefactor of the village in its infant state. This gentleman was possessed of a large estate, and was the proprietor of a large patent of land lying on both sides of the Susquehannah, including the site of the village. Mr. Bingham was a native of England, and came to this country when a young man, and went into the mercantile business in Philadelphia. He was a member of congress for some years while it held its sessions at Philadelphia. His two daughters married, the one Alexander, the other Henry Baring, two noted bankers in London. Mr. Bingham died in London in 1804.

Western View of Binghamton.

The above shows the appearance of the village as it is entered from the west side of Chenango river, by the *red bridge*, (so called,) which is 600 feet long. The village is principally on the east side of the Chenango, and contains about 400 houses, 30 stores, and 2,000 inhabitants. There are six churches, viz: 1 Episcopal, 1 Methodist, 1 Presbyterian, 1 Congregational, 1 Baptist, and 1 Catholic. There are two female seminaries, a large school for boys, two printing-offices, the courthouse and prison; two banks—the Broome County Bank incorporated 1831, with a capital of $100,000, and the Binghamton Bank, which commenced its operations in 1839, with a capital of $100,000, and the privilege of extending it to one million. The village of Binghamton is 150 miles from Albany, 90 from Utica, 40 from Norwich, 22 from Owego, and 7 from the Pennsylvania line. The great medium of transportation to the place is by the *Chenango canal*. This canal, which terminates at Binghamton and Utica, is 95 miles long, 46 feet wide, and 4½ deep. The number of locks in the whole route is 105. The canal was commenced in 1834 and completed in 1837, and cost nearly two millions of dollars.

The tract of country in which Binghamton is situated, became first known to the whites by the expedition of Gen. Sullivan against the Indians in 1779. Upon the site of Binghamton, a brigade of American troops under the command of Gen. James Clinton, the father of De Witt Clinton, encamped for one or two nights on their way to join the main body under Sullivan, then penetrating westward. The first white man who made a permanent settlement in what is claimed for the village vicinity, was Capt. Joseph Leonard, who was originally from Plymouth, Massachusetts. He first emigrated to Wyoming, Pennsylvania. He owned a farm in that place, and was under arms there at the time of the massacre, though not on the field of action. He moved from Wyoming in 1787, with a young wife and two little children. His wife and children were put on board a canoe, with what goods he brought up, and the canoe rowed by a hired man; while he himself went up on land with two horses, keeping the shore, and regulating his progress by that of his family on the river. A Capt. Baldwin, who settled on the Chemung river, moved up at the same time in company with him.*

Capt. Leonard received his first information of this region from Amos Draper, then an Indian trader in these parts. On his first arrival, he found a Mr. Lyon, who lived in a temporary log house near where Col. Page's ashery now stands. In two or three weeks afterward, Col. Wm. Rose and his brother, from Connecticut, came on to Binghamton, and fixed their location a little above Capt. Leonard's. During this year, (1787,) Joshua Whitney, Gen. Wm. Whitney, and Henry Green, from Hillsdale, Columbia county, came to this place, and settled on the west side of the Chenango, about two miles above its junction with the Susquehannah, on what was afterward called Whitney's flats. At the time the above families settled here, their nearest white neighbors were at Tioga, a distance of forty miles.

Previous to the settlement of these first emigrants, a number of persons from Massachusetts came on an exploring tour to this region; on their return they obtained a grant from the legislature of Massachusetts of a large tract, which they afterward purchased of the Indians. This tract contained 230,000 square acres, for which the company paid to the state £1,500. It appears that when the agents of the company came on, they found that patents had already been granted to Bingham, Wilson, and Cox, by the state of New York, which interfered with their grants. This claim of Massachusetts to this part of the state, originating in some ancient colonial claims, was finally satisfied by the grant of the right of pre-emption to certain lands in western New York. The facts respecting the treaty with the Indians, &c., is from the *Annals of Binghamton.*

"They made their propositions to the Indians for the purchase of it, appointed a time and place for the negotiation of the bargain, and returned home. These individuals, at first, designed to form a company to consist only of eleven persons; but conceiving the purchase too heavy for so small a number, and having so many applications for co-partnership, the number of the company was finally fixed at sixty. This company appointed as commissioners to treat with the Indians, Elijah Brown, Gen. Oringh Stoddard, Gen. Moses Ashley, Capt. Raymond, and Col. David Pixley. These gentlemen met the Indians in treaty, in the first instance on the Chenango river, the east side, two or three miles above the present village of Binghamton, in the forepart of winter. But at this treaty the negotiation was not fully completed, and they adjourned to meet at the Forks of the Chenango. At this second treaty, there were between three and four hundred Indians.

---

* The authors are indebted for the history of Binghamton, to a work published at that place in 1840, entitled "Annals of Binghamton, and of the country connected with it, from the earliest settlement, by J. B. Wilkinson."

"At this and the former treaty, it is said, the Indians, who were furnished with provisions and liquor at the expense of the company, would get drunk, almost to a man, by night, but be sober through the day. While the subjects of the treaty were under discussion from day to day, they would sit in circles upon the ground, and listen with the utmost decorum. Their chiefs, when they spoke, would speak in substance, if not in form, in accordance with parliamentary rule. Captain, and afterward Esquire Dean, was their interpreter, and did their business.

"The nominal sum paid for this tract is not now known, but the payment was made, one half in money, and the other moiety in goods, consisting of rifles, hatchets, ammunition, blankets, and woollen cloths. The last, it is said, the savages, in perfect character with their taste, immediately tore into strings for ornament.

"An estimation was made of the entire cost of these ten townships, to wit: the purchase price, the expense of the treaties, and the survey made of it, and found to amount to about one shilling per acre. The number of acres contained in the tract, as has just been stated, was 230,000 square acres. This, equally divided among the sixty proprietors, would give to each 3,833 acres, with a fraction over. The price for which the land was sold, in the earliest sale of it, was uniformly at twenty-five cents per acre; but it, after a little, rose to one dollar per acre, and even to more.

"The land upon the shores of the two rivers, and for some distance back, was, even at the time of the purchase, partially cleared, so far as the Indians have their lands cleared. The under-brush was cleared, having been kept down by burning; and grass growing on the flats. The Indians uniformly keep down the shrubby part of their hunting grounds, that they may, with the more facility, discover and pursue their game. Col. Rose says, that he could see deer upon the mountains immediately back of him for half a mile, so free were they of under-brush. He observes, also, that the woods exhibited a sombre appearance, from their annual burnings. The large island opposite Judge Stoddard's, was, when the first settlers came, covered with grass and the anacum weed, a tall kind of weed, the roots of which they were in the habit of digging and drying, and then grinding or pounding for bread stuff; or rather its apology, perhaps, when their corn failed them.

"The Indians, in their treaty with the New England commissioners, reserved to themselves the right of hunting upon the lands they had sold, for the term of seven years; and also made a reserve of one half mile square, as their own possession. This reserve was situated near the mouth of Castle creek, and went by the name of the Castle Farm. Upon this reserve the Indians of the neighborhood who did not remove to New Stockbridge, or Oneida, resided. Their number on the farm is said to have been about twenty families. They by no means confined themselves to this little spot. They cultivated the ground of the farm, more or less, but depended chiefly, in accordance with their long custom and native propensity, upon hunting and fishing."

In the summer of 1789, a very considerable accession was made by persons who settled in the Susquehannah and Chenango valleys. Daniel Hudson, afterward a major and judge, settled between Capt. Leonard and Col. Rose; Jonathan Fitch settled upon the creek that took his name: he was a merchant from Wyoming, and had been sheriff of the county; it is believed he was the first representative to the state legislature from the new county of Tioga. The first religious society formed within the bounds of the settlement was a Baptist church, consisting of 10 or 12 members, formed by Elder Howe, a very early settler in the place. He was succeeded by Elder Fisk. This society became extinct about the year 1800. A Dutch Reformed church was founded about 1798, by the Rev. Mr. Manly, who was succeeded in his ministrations by the Rev. Mr. Palmer: this church was afterward merged into the Presbyterian. The present *Presbyterian church* was organized in 1817. Mr. Niles, their minister, was ordained the next year. He died in 1828, and was succeeded by Mr. Lockwood, who continued his pastoral relation till 1833. He was succeeded, in 1836, by the Rev. John A. Nash: in 1838, Mr. Nash was succeeded by Rev. David D. Gregory. The *Episcopal church* was incorporated in 1816. Rev. Mr. Keeler was the first officiating clergyman. He was succeeded by Rev. F. H. Cumming. In 1821, Mr. Cumming was succeeded by Rev. Mr. Gear. The clergymen succeeding have been in the following order: Rev. Nathaniel Huse, in 1824; Rev. Mr. Cumming, in 1829; Rev. Hiram Adams, in 1831; Rev. Mr. Shimeall, in 1835; and Rev. Edward Andrews, in 1836. The *Methodist* society was formed in 1817. In 1822, the Methodist chapel was purchased of the Episcopalians, and moved from the site of the present Episcopal church to where it now stands. The present *Baptist* church was instituted in 1829. Elder Frederick was its first pastor. The succeeding pastors have been in the order following: Revs. Jason Corwin, Henry Robertson, Davis Dimmick, William Storrs, and Rev. James M. Coley. The *Congregational* church was organized in 1836, and the Rev. John Starkweather was called to be their pastor; he was succeeded by Rev. Samuel W. Bush. A Catholic church was finished in 1837. In Jan. 1838, a Universalist society was organized.

WINDSOR, the ancient Oquago, was taken from Chenango in 1807; has a mountainous surface, and is centrally intersected by the Susquehannah. Great quantities of locust timber, valuable for shipbuilding, have been taken from this town. The principal settlement is on the west side of the Susquehannah, and has about 60 dwellings, and 350 inhabitants; 16 miles from Binghamton, and 128 from Albany. Pop. 2,368.

The valley of Oquago was settled by the whites about the year 1788. The most of the earlier inhabitants were from Waterbury and Watertown, in Connecticut. The Rev. Mr. Buck was the first minister who preached in the place. He was called by the first settlers Major Buck, as he had held that office during the revolutionary war. Mr. Williston, a missionary from Connecticut, appears to have been the next. Soon after the formation of the Presbyterian church, Rev. Seth Sage became the settled pastor, and remained such till his death. The Episcopal church was organized in 1803, by Bishop chase, then a missionary in Western New York. The Presbyterian meeting-house was erected in 1800, the Methodist in 1833.

Oquago was the residence of a tribe of Indians. It appears to have been a half-way resting-place for the "Six Nations" as they passed south of Wyoming, and also for the tribes of the Wyoming valley as they passed north. Jonathan Edwards, the celebrated divine, while a minister at Stockbridge, Mass., took a deep interest in the welfare of the Indians in this place. He procured a missionary for them, Rev. Mr. Hawley, and three other persons, Mr. Woodbridge, Mr. and Mrs. Ashley. The three latter returned. Mrs. Ashley, it appears, was employed during her stay as an interpreter. Mr. Hawley remained their missionary until the commencement of the French war, when it was considered unsafe for him to remain longer. About one year previous to this time, Mr. Edwards sent one of his sons, a lad of about nine years of age, to Oquago, under the care of Mr. Hawley, to learn the Indian language, in order to become an Indian missionary. When the war commenced, a faithful Indian, who had special care of the lad, took him and conveyed him to his father, part of the way on his back. This lad was afterward President of Union College.

The following, relating to the privations and difficulties encountered by the first settlers of Oquago valley, is from *Wilkinson's Annals of Binghamton.*

"In about the year 1794, there was what was called the *pumpkin* freshet, in the month of August; the Susquehannah rising much above its usual height, and sweeping down in its tide the productions of the fields—corn, pumpkins, potatoes, &c. A great scarcity was the natural consequence. During this scarcity, Maj. Stow shouldered a bushel of wheat, in which the *whole neighborhood* had a common share, and started for Wattles' ferry to mill, a distance of more than forty miles, carrying his grist the whole distance on foot. He got his wheat ground, and returned in the same trudging manner. During his journey, he purchased one quarter of a pound of tea—at that time a rare article with the settlers—to help out the repast which he anticipated at his return. Upon his arrival home, the neighbors, who held an interest in the grist of wheat—and most probably others also—collected at the major's house, to hold a sort of thanksgiving; which was to be celebrated by preparing and partaking of as sumptuous a feast as their stores would admit. Out of the flour they made *short-cake;* but having no hog's lard, they would have come short of this luxury, had not the major bethought himself of some *bear's grease* which he had in the house, and which answered as a substitute. Their tea was quite a new article to them, for which they were not prepared. They had no teakettle, no teapot, no teacups. Instead of the first, a small kettle was furnished to boil the water in; they put the tea into the same to steep it; and instead of cups and saucers, they used a wooden bowl, which they passed around from one to the other. Still they made a merry cheer of it; *felt* the glow of sociability, and told each his best anecdote. These early inhabitants, when they became old, would tell the story to their children and more recent inhabitants, with moistened eyes; but said, it was then a heart-felt thanksgiving and a merry time."

COLESVILLE, taken from Windsor in 1821; drained centrally by the Susquehannah river; from Albany 123 miles. Pop. 2,517. Harpersville, 17 miles N. E. from Binghamton, has about 30 dwellings. Colesville, New Ohio, Nineveh, Dora, and Susquehannah, are post-offices. Bellona springs in this town, so named from some sulphur springs, has been frequented for health and pleasure.

CONKLIN, taken from Chenango in 1824; having the Susquehannah river running N. W. through it in a deep valley with fertile flats. Pop. 1,471. Conklin and Corbotville are post-offices: the former of which is about 4 miles E. of Binghamton.

LISLE, taken from Union in 1801; from Binghamton, N. E., 18 miles. Lisle, Lisle Centre, and Union Village, are post-offices. This town was settled in 1792 by emigrants from the eastern states. Pop. 1,558.

" A congregational church was organized in what is called Lisle, in the year 1797, by the Rev. Seth Williston, who had, a short time previously, been sent there by the Connecticut Missionary Society, upon the personal application of Mr. Edwards. The church consisted, in its first formation, of sixteen members, eleven of whom were by profession. In 1801, William Osborn was *elected* to the office of a deacon; but it was not till 1810 that he was *consecrated* by the imposition of hands from the presbytery; and his colleague, Andrew Squires, was consecrated at the same time.

" Mr. Williston employed about half of his time in pastoral duties in this congregation; the rest of his time he missionated in Union, Owego, and in Oquago. He was installed pastor of the church in Lisle, in October, 1803; and from this period he appears to have employed all his time within the pastoral limits of this one congregation, until he was dismissed from it in 1810. The church of Lisle was the earliest organized, it is believed, of any west of the Catskill and south of Utica. At the time of Mr. Williston's installation, the council organized what then was called ' The Susquehannah Association,' taking in some of the northern counties of Pennsylvania.

" In the year 1796, Mr. E. Edwards built the first saw-mill on the Onondaga or its waters; and was nearly, if not quite, the first that came down the Chenango with a *raft*. He subsequently carried on lumbering to a great extent; and the pine timber of that section being of a superior quality, compensated for his being so far back from the broader stream of the Susquehannah. The first grist-mill was built much later, by Dr. Wheeler. Previous to this, the inhabitants came down to Castle creek for their grinding; and when that mill failed for want of water, they were obliged to go to Tioga Point."

NANTICOKE, taken from Lisle in 1831; from Albany 144 miles.

There are sulphur springs in the N. W. part of the town; 14 miles N. W. from Binghamton. Pop. 418.

SANDFORD, taken from Windsor in 1821; from Albany 121, from Binghamton, E., 24 miles. The town is thinly settled, being stony and mountainous. Pop. 1,172.

TRIANGLE, so named from its shape, taken from Lisle in 1831; from Albany 132, from Binghamton, N., 17 miles. Pop. 1,692. Triangle post-office is at Clarke's settlement, near the E. line, where there are about 30 dwellings. At Union Village is the post-office named Upper Lisle.

UNION was organized in 1791; lies on the north side of the Susquehannah; its surface is undulating, with a fertile soil of gravelly loam. The village of Union is on the Susquehannah, 9 miles W. from Binghamton, containing about 50 houses and 300 inhabitants. Maine post-office is in the northern part of the town. Pop. 2,600.

The town appears to have been first settled about the year 1789. One of the most prominent settlers was Gen. Oringh Stoddard, one of the commissioners appointed by the Boston Company to treat with the Indians. Amos Patterson, afterward judge of Broome county, and Joshua Mersereau, one of the earliest judges of old Tioga county, were early settlers in Union. Judge Mersereau and his brother John, were originally from New Jersey. Previous to the revolutionary war, these two brothers removed to Staten Island, where they kept a large tavern. It is stated that they were the first persons who commenced a line of stages from New York to Philadelphia, uniting their line with the boats that plied between their own dock and New York.

When Staten Island fell into the hands of the British, Judge Mersereau and his brother, being zealous in the American cause, left the island and entered into the American service. These two brothers were the principal agents in preventing the British from crossing the Delaware in their pursuit of Washington. Judge Mersereau, who was a commissary through the war, was much about the person of Washington. When he had crossed the Delaware, he was asked if he was sure that he had removed every thing that could be employed to transport the enemy over. Washington replied he thought he had. Judge Mersereau begged the privilege of re-crossing with his brother and making search. They went back and searched the opposite shore, and found, below the surface of the water, two Durham boats, which had been *timely sunk* by a royalist who lived near. They raised them up and took them to the Pennsylvania side.

"Several of the Indians, whose particular location was at the Castle farm, had temporary huts or wigwams in Union, near the river, and on both sides. These they occupied more or less for several years after the country was settled. Where, and in what manner, they obtained their salt was always a mystery to the whites. They would strike a course over the mountain about opposite Judge Mersereau's, on the south side of the river, and after an absence of about twelve hours, would return with a pail or kettle of salt; and that, too, immediately upon their return, would be warm. Old Mr. Richards used to say, that the Indians would cross the river below Willow Point, rise the mountain, and bring back salt. Sometimes it would be warm. He inferred that there must be a salt spring near, but it never could be found. John D. Mersereau relates, that when a lad, his father and himself have endeavored to follow the Indians when they were known to have set out for salt; but they soon would appear to be apprehensive that they were watched, and would either remain where they were, or turn from their course. Never more than *two* would set out upon the expedition. They used the utmost precaution to prevent the whites from ever discovering the secret spot. They had other places to which they resorted for salt, one or more in the neighborhood of Oquago. Why these sources of salt have never been found by the whites, is a mystery.

VESTAL was taken from Union in 1823, being divided from that town by the Susquehannah. It is a lumbering town, being but a small part of it cultivated. Major David Barney was one of the first settlers. He came down the river from Cooperstown with a large family of children in a canoe. Vestal is 8 miles S. W. from Binghamton. Pop. 1,250. There are two post-offices, Vestal, S. Vestal.

CAYUGA COUNTY.

CAYUGA COUNTY was formed from Onondaga in 1799; but other counties have since been taken from it. Greatest length N. and S. 55, greatest breadth E. and W. 23 miles. From Albany, W., 156 miles, from New York, 301. Upon the S. the surface rises into ridges, along the Cayuga lake, the Owasco lake and inlet, and the Skaneateles lake. The disposition of the waters shows an irregular surface. The Poplar ridge, E. of the Cayuga lake, rises in some places to 600 feet above, but has a gentle slope towards the lake, displaying finely cultivated farms. The eastern declivity of this and other hills are more abrupt. On the N. of Auburn, the country is comparatively level, yet has a rolling appearance from the many large gravel hills scattered over the plain, assuming in many places the semblance of stupendous mounds formed by art. This gravel has much limestone, and produces excellent wheat. Few portions of the state possess more fertile lands, or can boast of higher cultivation. In all the fruits of the climate, this county is prolific. About two thirds of the land is under improvement. The southern portion is most thickly settled. The Cayuga lake, which forms a large part of the western boundary, is a beautiful sheet of water, 36 miles long, and from 1 to 4 broad. The county is divided into 22 towns. Pop. 50,364.

AUBURN was taken from Aurelius in 1823. The town, 3 miles by

2, comprehending 6 lots of the old military tract, is included within the chartered limits of the village. The compact part of the village lies 2½ miles from Lake Owasco, on the outlet of that name. It is 156 miles from Albany, 314 from New York, 7 from Weedsport on the Erie canal, and 339 from Washington. Pop. 5,626. There are 2 Presbyterian churches, 1 Episcopal, 1 Baptist, 1 Universalist, and 1 Catholic; a state prison, courthouse, theological seminary, an academy, 2 banks, 4 printing-offices, and a number of splendid hotels. Auburn is one of the most thriving and beautiful villages in the state. Its principal streets are adorned with lofty buildings of brick and limestone.

Eastern part of Genesee-street, Auburn.

Auburn was first settled in 1793, by Col. John L. Hardenbergh, and was for many years called "*Hardenbergh's Corners.*" It became a post village in 1800, and in 1805 the county town; and received its present name from Dr. Crosset. At this time, the village consisted of but a few log dwellings, a store or two, a grist-mill, &c., all situated near the bank of the creek, not far from the spot occupied by the establishment of Messrs. Leonard & Warden.

In 1807, the building of the courthouse was commenced, and the county courts removed to this place from Aurora. In 1811, the village is supposed to have contained about 300 inhabitants; the courthouse was the only public building; even this was in an unfinished state. The construction of an academy, a three-story brick building, and a neat little Episcopal church were commenced, and a Presbyterian society formed during this year.

In 1815, Auburn was incorporated a village, at which time it contained 1,000 inhabitants. From this period, its improvement became more rapid and uniform; walks were now put down on the principal streets, which before were muddy and uneven. In 1816, the state prison was founded in this place; the first Presbyterian church in North-street was commenced, and the Bank of Auburn, capital $200,000, was chartered. In April, 1817, the village contained 1,506 inhabitants, 148 dwellings, 20 stores, and 40 mechanic shops.

A railroad connects Auburn with Syracuse. This road is 26 miles long, and was constructed at an expense of $460,000. A railroad is now constructing between this place and Rochester, which passes some distance S. of the Erie canal, through the flourishing villages of Canandaigua and Geneva, a distance by this route of $77\frac{1}{2}$ miles.

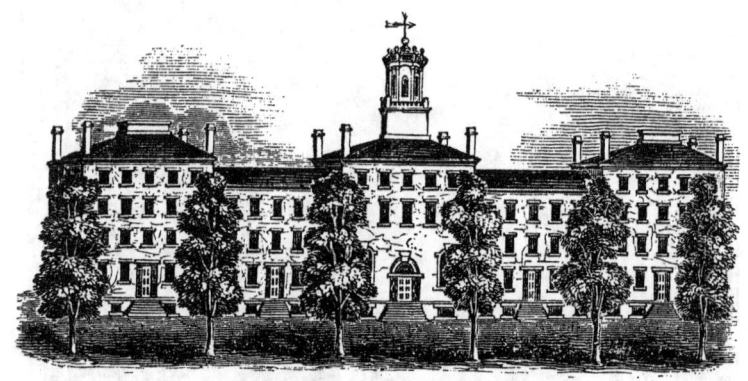

Auburn Theological Seminary.

The *Auburn Theological Seminary* was established by the synod of Geneva in 1819, and by the act of incorporation, in 1820, was placed under commissioners, chosen by the synods of Genesee, Geneva, and Oneida. There are four professors in the institution. Over 300 clergymen have been educated since its establishment. In 1839, the number of students was 71. The principal building is of stone, presenting a front of 200 feet. The library exhibits a valuable collection of choice theological works, and contains upwards of 5,000 vols. No charge is made for the use of the library, rooms, or furniture. The *Methodist Episcopal* society was organized in 1821; their house, on Chapel-street, was erected soon after, and has been since sold to the Catholics; their present stone chapel, on North-street, was erected in 1833. The *Baptist* society was organized in 1825, and built a church on South-street, (since sold to the Universalists,) in 1829; their church on Genesee-street was erected in 1834. The *Second Presbyterian* society was organized in 1829, and the foundation of their house laid. In 1833, the Universalist society was organized; and in 1834, the Catholics fitted up their church on Chapel-street.

The following is a representation of the state prison as viewed from the N.; the cupola of the courthouse is seen in the distance. The

State Prison at Auburn.

erection of this prison commenced in 1816. "It occupies a plot of ground forming a square 500 feet each way, enclosed with a boundary wall 2,000 feet in extent, 30 feet high, and 4 feet thick at the base. A small river or creek runs along the S. side of the boundary, and sufficient power from the stream is obtained, by means of a water-wheel and shaft through the wall, to work the machinery within the prison. The prison buildings stand back about 80 feet from the road, and form three sides of a square; the front part being about 280 feet long; each of the return wings is 240 feet long and 45 in depth." The cost of erecting the prison was more than $500,000. The usual number of prisoners of late years has been between 6 and 700. The earnings of the prison during the year ending Sept. 1839, was $60,161.46; the expenditures during the same period, $51,671.21. Religious instruction is regularly given by the chaplain. Sunday schools are instituted in the prisons, in which the students in the theological seminary and other pious persons assist; the younger portion of the convicts, if illiterate, are taught to read, write, and cast accounts.

"The building contained originally 550 cells. More, we believe, have lately been added. They are principally distributed into four tiers or stories, and constructed on each side of the block or wing. The cells are each 7 feet long, 7 feet high, and 3½ wide. They are sufficiently lighted, well warmed, and ventilated. The area between the cells and the parallel walls, 10 feet wide, is open from the ground to the roof; and of this interval, 3 feet adjoining the cells are occupied by the galleries. This space in front of the cells forms a complete sounding-gallery, so that the watchman in the open area on the ground can hear even a whisper, from a distant cell in the upper story.

"Such are the provisions and precautions for the separate confinement of the prisoners *at night.* In the daytime, they are compelled to labor together, in an orderly and penitential manner. Soon after daylight, on a signal given by the prison bell, the turnkey unlocks the

Prisoners at the State Prison at Auburn.

doors of the cells, when the convicts, each with his night tub, water can, and mush kid, march out; and having disposed of these articles according to the order of the prison, proceed to the workshops, where they commence the labor of the day. At a fixed hour another bell is rung, when they form again in line, and march in silence, with closed files, to the mess-room, where they breakfast at narrow tables. so arranged that they are unable to exchange even looks or signs. After an interval of 20 to 30 minutes, they return in the same manner to the workshops. At 12 o'clock, they dine under the same care to prevent intercourse. On the approach of night, they wash their faces and hands, and at the ringing of the bell, form a line according to the number of their cells, march out of the shops to their tubs, and at the word of command take them up, step forward and empty into the drain the water which had been placed in them in the morning to purify them. They then proceed, with closed files, the tubs hanging on their arms, to the wash-room, adjoining the kitchen, where their mush and molasses in a kid, and water in a can for drinking, have been placed together, in rows, by the cooks; and, without breaking their step, they stoop and take up the can and kid, march to their respective galleries, enter their cells as they arrive at them, and pull the doors partly shut. Each gallery is occupied by one company, which is marched and locked up by one turnkey, with two keys, differing from each other, and from all the rest. The convicts then eat supper in their respective cells. At an early hour they are required, by the ringing of a bell, to take off their clothes and go to bed, upon their canvass hammocks; when well, they are not permitted to lie down before the bell rings. nor to get up again, but from necessity, until the ringing of the morning bell. During the night, turnkeys are constantly moving round the galleries, wearing woollen socks on their feet, and walking so noiselessly that the convicts are not able to discover their presence or absence; and thus the whole wing, containing several hundred convicts, is preserved in perfect stillness and order. It is obvious that no communication can take place between the convicts at night, without the connivance or negligence of the turnkeys, which is guarded against by the visits of the keeper and his deputies at different hours."—*Gordon's Gaz.*

The following inscriptions are copied from monuments in the graveyard N. of the village.

"Professori Hist. Eccles Politiaeque nostro Reverendo Matthaeo La Rue Perrine D. D. quindecim annos a principio in Seminario Auburnensi theologico qui eruditus dilectus modestus impietate erga deum a'que homines cunctos imagine Dei creatos sincerus vixit nato maii V MDCCLXXVII moriturus exitum prospexit tranquillus patiens benignus spe in Christo solo radiatus christum esse verum deum et redemptorem suum gloriosissimum gaudens confessus et precatus triumphavit suis benedixit gloriae ascendit Feb. XII MDCCCXXXVI Hunc lapidem amici nonnulli orbati posuere."

[To the memory of Rev. Matthew La Rue Perrine, D. D., Professor of Ecclesiastical History and Polity, for fifteen years, in the Theological Seminary at Auburn. He was learned, amiable, and modest, and lived in sincere piety towards God and good will towards all men created in the image of God. He was born May 5, 1777. In the near prospect of death he was tranquil and patient, illumined by hope in Christ alone, whom he joyfully confessed to be the true God and his most glorious Redeemer. Having prayed, he triumphed over death, blessed his friends, and ascended to glory, Feb. 12, 1836.—Some of his bereaved friends have erected this monument to his memory.]

"1 Cor. 15; 57. 'But thanks be to God which giveth us the victory through our Lord Jesus Christ,' Rev. *William Lewis, Jr.*, son of Wm. and Mary Lewis of 'his vicinity. After his course of preparatory studies in Williams College and Auburn Theo. Seminary, and successfully devoting himself to the cause of Education, Temperance and Piety in Canada, New York, Indiana, and Ohio, he went home to God, 4 April, 1838, aged 36 years. From the bible class, his interest in religion began. His faith and character were formed on the Bible; and he went down the dark valley saying 'all is light.'"

Aurelius, organized in 1789; bounds since altered; from Albany 159 miles. Pop. 2,644. Cayuga, 8 miles W. from Auburn, has about 30 dwellings. Aurelius and Fosterdale are small villages. Clarksville, 1 mile W. from Auburn, has about 50 dwellings.

Cayuga Bridge.

The above view of Cayuga Bridge, which crosses the Cayuga lake on the great western turnpike, was taken on the western bank, and shows on the opposite side of the lake a portion of the little village of Cayuga. The large building on the right is the well-known tavern of Mr. Titus, having superior accommodations. This bridge, so famous in political estimates, was commenced in May, 1799, and finished in September, 1800. It was built by the Manhattan Company of New York, and cost $150,000. Its length is one mile. "This bridge is the longest in America, perhaps in the world, and yet five years ago," says a traveller in 1800, " the Indians possessed the shores of the lake, imbosomed in almost impenetrable woods." The first bridge was built on mud sills—the second on piles—the third and last was erected in 1833, and cost about $15,000.

BRUTUS, taken from Aurelius in 1802. Pop. 2,045. Weedsport, incorporated in 1831, on the canal 7 miles N. of Auburn, 26 from Syracuse, 87 W. of Utica, and 197 by canal from Albany, is a flourishing village, with about 120 dwellings. Centreville is a small village on the canal.

CATO, taken from Aurelius in 1802; bounds since altered; from Albany 155, from Auburn, N. E., 13 miles. Cato Corners and Cato are small villages. Pop. 2,380.

CONQUEST, taken from Cato in 1821; from Albany 162 miles. Pop. 1,911. The post-office is 19 miles N. N. W. of Auburn.

FLEMING, taken from Aurelius in 1823; from Albany 160 miles. Pop. 1,330. Fleming, 5 miles S. of Auburn, has about 20 dwellings.

GENOA, organized by the General Sessions of Ontario county, in 1789, by the name of Milton; name and bounds since altered; from Albany 185, from Auburn centrally distant, S., 20 miles. Pop. 2,591. Genoa, formerly called the "Indian Fields," has about 40 dwellings. Northville has about 20 dwellings. Kings Ferry, Five Corners, and East Genoa are post-offices.

IRA, taken from Cato in 1821; from Albany 189 miles. Pop. 2,282. Ira, 24 miles N. of Auburn, has about 25 dwellings.

LEDYARD, taken from Scipio in 1823. Aurora, post village 18 miles S. W. from Auburn, is beautifully situated upon the lake in a fertile country, and has several churches, the Cayuga Academy, and about 125 dwellings. Levana, also upon the lake, 14 miles from Auburn, is a small village. Pop. 2,500.

LOCKE, taken from Milton, original name of Genoa, in 1802; from Albany 166, from Auburn centrally distant, S. E., 21 miles. Milan, at which is the post-office of the town, has about 50 dwellings. Pop. 1,800.

MENTZ, originally named Jefferson, and taken from Aurelius in 1808; from Albany 161 miles. Pop. 4,215. Port Byron, on the canal, 3 miles W. from Weedsport, and 8 from Auburn, has about 150 dwellings. Throopsville is a small manufacturing village on the Owasco outlet, 3 miles N. W. from Auburn. Montezuma Village is situated at the junction of the Seneca, Cayuga, and Erie canals. It contains an Episcopal and a Baptist church, a collector's office, and about 75 dwellings: distant, 10 miles from Auburn, 21 from Geneva, 64 from Rochester, 7 from Cayuga, 35 from Syracuse, and 205 from Albany. In 1839, the state was successful in sinking a shaft about 300 feet, from which issues a large quantity of the best salt water in the state. The salt made from it is remarkably free from impurities, and the facilities for its manufacture are great, the ground being good and fire-wood plenty. No lime is used in the manufacture of salt from these springs. The Montezuma marshes commence about a mile westward of the village: they are gradually drying away, and it is believed that the healthfulness of this town is now equal to any in the vicinity.

"This marshy tract," says a well known writer, "is the *paradise of musquetoes*," which tiny and troublesome insect are here notorious for their numbers, size, and "penetrating proboscis." The following is said to be the tradition of the Onondagas respecting the origin of this " musical insect:"

"There were, in times of old—many hundred moons ago—two huge feathered monsters permitted by the Manitou to descend from the sky and light upon the banks of the Seneca river, near the present route of the canal, at Montezuma. Their form was exactly that of a musquetoe, and they were so large that they darkened the sun like a cloud, as they flew between the earth and it. Standing the one upon one side of the river, and the other opposite on the other bank, they guarded the river, and stretching their long necks into the canoes of the Indians as they attempted to paddle along the stream, gobbled them up as the stork king in the fable did the frogs. The destruction of life was great, for the embargo was so strictly enforced that not an Indian could pass without being devoured in the attempt. It was long before the monsters could be exterminated, and then only by the combined efforts of all the warriors of the Cayuga and Onondaga nations of Indians. The battle was terrible, but the warriors finally triumphed, and the mammoth musquetoes were slain. But, sad to relate, as their carcases decomposed in the sun, every particle became vivified, and flew off daily in myriads of clouds of musquetoes! And they have filled the country ever since."

MORAVIA, taken from Sempronius in 1833; from Albany 157, from Auburn centrally distant, S. E., 20 miles. Settlements were commenced here in 1794. A branch of the Owasco inlet here falls perpendicularly 70 feet. Pop. 2,010. Moravia is a small village.

NILES, taken from Sempronius in 1833; from Albany 160, from Auburn centrally distant, S. E., 15 miles. Kellogsville and West Niles are post-offices. Pop. 2,234.

OWASCO, taken from Aurelius in 1802; from Albany 164 miles. Owasco, a small village, is 8 miles S. E. from Auburn. Pop. 1,331.

SCIPIO, organized as part of Ontario county in 1789; bounds since altered; from Albany 180, centrally distant S. from Auburn, 10 miles. Scipio, N. Scipio, Sherwood's Corners, and Scipioville are post-offices. Pop. 2,255.

SEMPRONIUS, organized in 1799; from Albany 153, from Auburn centrally distant, S. E., 16 miles. Skaneateles lake touches it on the N. Pop. 1,304.

SENNET, taken from Brutus in 1807; from Albany 160 miles. Sennet, 5 miles N. of Auburn, has about 30 dwellings. Pop. 2,060.

SPRINGPORT, taken from Scipio and Aurelius in 1823; from Albany 166 miles. Pop. 1,891. Union Springs, so called from two springs whose united waters form a useful mill-stream, laid out in 1813, on the Cayuga lake, 10 miles S. W. from Auburn, has about 50 dwellings.

STERLING, the northernmost town, formed from Cato in 1812; from Albany 172, from Auburn, N., centrally distant 28 miles. Sterling, Martville, and Little Sodus are post-offices. Pop. 2,536.

SUMMER HILL, originally named Plato, and taken from Locke in

1821; from Albany 147, from Auburn, S. E., centrally distant 25 miles. Summer Hill, in the south part, has about 20 dwellings. Pop. 1,446.

VENICE, taken from Scipio in 1823; W. from Albany 162 miles. Smith's Corners, 14 miles S. W. of Auburn, Talcott's 15, Tupper's 17, and Stuart's Corners, are small villages. Pop. 2,105.

VICTORY, taken from Cato in 1821; from Albany 167, from Auburn N., 20 miles. Lathrop's Corners has about 25 or 30 dwellings. Pop. 2,371.

CATTARAUGUS COUNTY.

CATTARAUGUS COUNTY, taken from Genesee in 1803; centrally distant from New York via Catskill, 384; from Albany, 292; from Buffalo, S. E., 50 miles. Length, E. and W., 39, and greatest breadth N. and S. 36 miles. It derives its name from the Indian word *Gah-ta-ra-ke-ras*, signifying stinking shore or beach, originally applied to Lake Erie, and thence extended over the adjacent country. This county is highly elevated, being from 500 to 1200 feet above Lake Erie. Its surface is broken by some hills of no mean pretensions to the character of mountains, but in general it is but moderately uneven, and in some parts quite level. In the S., along the Allegany river, there are broad belts of white pine, behind which there are marshes; excepting these, the lands are generally firm, and timbered with a variety of trees of lofty growth. No region of this state, and probably none of any other in the Union, was originally covered with an equal amount of valuable timber. Some of the trees have measured 230 feet in height, and five of them have been known to furnish an hundred "lumber-man's" logs. Shingles and boards for the supply of the whole western world, have been manufactured in the shingle shanties and saw-mills upon the Allegany and its tributaries. The lands in the N. part are warmer and better adapted to grain and grass crops than in the south, except at the S. W. corner. This county formed part of the Holland Land Company's purchase, who originally owned it all excepting the Indian reservations. About one eighth of the county is under improvement. The county is divided into 26 towns. Pop. 28,803.

ASHFORD, taken from Ellicottville in 1824; from Albany 282, from Buffalo 40, from Ellicottville, N., 10 miles. Pop. 1,462. Not more than a tenth part of the town is yet under improvement. The valley of the Cattaraugus creek, on the northern line of the town, is from 1 to 2 miles broad, and fertile. Ashford is a small village.

BURTON was taken from Great Valley in 1831; centrally distant from Ellicottville, S. E., 16 miles. Pop. 511. "Allegany city," is a plot laid out some years since upon the Allegany river, near the eastern boundary. Not more than one thirtieth part of this town is under improvement.

COLD SPRING was taken from Napoli, of which it formed the southern part. Pop. 673. This township is intersected by the Allegany river. At the mouth of Cold Spring creek, which enters this stream, is an "Indian village called *Tunes-assah;* the reservation, one mile in width along the river, extends some miles above and several below this point into Pennsylvania; this remnant lately had at its head the celebrated chief *Cornplanter,* who died early in the year 1836, aged about 100 years. Some of the tribe are wealthy; have large stocks of cattle, and some saw-mills. Much is due for the improvement of their condition to the judicious efforts of the society of 'Friends,' of Philadelphia, who have long maintained instructers among them, teaching the primitive arts of civilization, and who have a settlement in the southern part of the town." Some of the last of the Indian prophets incorporated a part of the tenets of Christianity into their pagan system. A few years since, a portion of the Indians in this town were in the practice of collecting around a log about 30 feet long, worked into a resemblance of the human form, to which they performed a kind of worship. The son of Cornplanter subsequently persuaded them to throw it into the river.

Cornplanter, the chief above-mentioned, it appears, was the son of a white man, who lived in the vicinity of Fort Plank; his mother was a young woman of the Seneca tribe. The Seneca Indians, during the revolutionary war, were led on against the Americans in the Mohawk valley, by Cornplanter, who, in one of his incursions, took his father prisoner. He however treated him well, and released him from confinement. In a letter written by Cornplanter to the governor of Pennsylvania in 1822, complaining of the attempt to impose taxes upon him and the Senecas residing on the Allegany, he began as follows:

"When I was a child, I played with the butterfly, the grasshopper, and the frogs. As I grew up, I began to pay some attention, and play with the Indian boys in the neighborhood, and they took notice of my skin being a different color from theirs, and spoke about it. I inquired of my mother the cause, and she told me that my father was a resident of Albany. I ate still my victuals out of a bark dish: I grew up to be a young man, and married me a wife, but I had no kettle or gun. I then knew where my father lived, and went to see him, and found he was a white man and spoke the English language. He gave me victuals while I was at his house, but when I started to return home he gave me no provision to eat on the way. He gave me nei'her kettle nor gun, neither did he tell me that the United States were about to rebel against the government of England," &c. &c.

"Cornplanter lived to a great age, having deceased within the last eight or ten years. He was an able man, distinguished in subsequent negotiations. He was eloquent, and a great advocate for temperance. He made a very effective and characteristic speech upon that subject in 1822. 'The Great Spirit first made the world, and next the flying animals, and found all things good and prosperous. He is immortal and everlasting. After finishing the flying animals, he came down upon the earth and there stood. Then he made different kinds of trees, and woods of all sorts, and people of every kind. He made the spring and other seasons, and the weather suitable for planting. These he did make. But *stills,* to make whiskey to give to Indians, he did not make.' * * * * 'The Great Spirit told us that there were three things for people to attend to. First, we ought to take care of our wives and children. Secondly, the white people ought to attend to their farms and cattle. Thirdly, the Great Spirit has given the bears and deers to the Indians.' * * * 'The Great Spirit has ordered me to quit drinking. He wishes me to inform the people that they should quit drinking intoxicating drink.' In the course of the same speech, he gave evidence that he was not overmuch pleased with the admixture of his own blood. * * * 'The different kinds the Great Spirit made separate, and not to mix with and disturb each other. But the white people have broken this command, by mixing their color with the Indians. The Indians have done better by not doing so.' "—*Stone's Life of Brant.*

Ganothjowaneh, a distinguished chief of the Seneca tribe, was, it is said, a superior orator to Red Jacket. He was called by the whites, *Big Kettle,* that being the signification of his Indian name. It is stated that he never tasted ardent spirits, and opposed the practice among the Indians, and suffered some persecutions on this account. During the early period of his life, he was opposed to the introduction of Christianity, but latterly was rather in favor of it. Mr. Wright, the missionary, now living among the Senecas, near Buffalo, attempted to persuade him to embrace the Christian religion. When told that he was a sinner in the sight of God, Big Kettle appeared to be somewhat surprised; throwing himself in an oratorical attitude, he recounted a long list of his good deeds, and endeavored to make it appear that he was not a sinner. He once came to Mr. Wright, and asked him the question, " Does God overrule all things ?" " Certainly," replied Mr. Wright. " I tell my people so, in council," replied Big Kettle; " but when I am alone, and think how much iniquity is practised by the white people in getting away our lands, &c., and how they go on without being punished, I have my doubts." He said that the preaching of the missionaries was good, and that the Indians would listen to, and follow it, but he said it would be useless: the bad habits of his people were so strong, the attempt to break them up would be as idle as to " stop the wind from blowing down Lake Erie."

CONNEWANGO, formed from Little Valley in 1823; from Albany, 312, from Ellicottville, S. W., 20 miles. The soil is excellent. Pop. 1,316. Rutledge is a small post village.

DAYTON, taken from Perrysburg in 1835; from Albany 302, from Ellicottville, N. W., 25 miles. Pop. 922. The surface of the town is undulating, and generally heavily timbered.

ELLICOTTVILLE, taken from Ischua in 1820; was named after Joseph Ellicott, late principal agent of the Holland Land Company. Pop. 1,088.

Ellicottville, the county seat, is from Albany 292, from New York, by the way of Cattskill, 384, from Mayville, E., 50, from Angelica, W., 35, and from Buffalo, S. W., 50 miles. Grove Hurlburt and Orrin Pitcher were the first settlers, and came here in 1815. The following view of the county buildings was taken near Gregory's tavern. The Episcopal church is seen on the left. The courthouse is the larger building, fronting the spectator. The jail, a stone structure, is seen on the right. There are here, besides the above, 2 land and 2 weekly newspaper offices, a fine hotel, a Presbyterian church, and about 90 dwellings. The scenery of the valley and surrounding hills is beautiful, and has been compared to the Italian.

FARMERSVILLE, taken from Olean in 1812; area since much reduced; from Albany 280, and from Ellicottville, N. E., 19 miles.

Pop. 1,294. Farmersville is a small post village. About one fourth part of the town is under cultivation.

Southern View of the Public Buildings, Ellicottville.

FRANKLINVILLE, taken from Olean, by the name of Ischua, in 1812. Pop. 1,276. Franklinville Village in the N. E. angle of the town, 13 miles N. E. from Ellicottville, has about 60 dwellings. Cadiz, a mile below on the Ischua creek, has about 40 dwellings.

FREEDOM, formed from Ischua, or Franklinville, in 1820. Pop. 1,831. Freedom Village, 26 N. E. from Ellicottville, Chelsea 21, and Sandusky 24 miles, are small settlements. There is here an oil spring, similar in many respects to the famous Seneca oil spring at Cuba, Allegany county.

GREAT VALLEY, taken from Olean in 1818; from Albany 299, centrally distant S. from Ellicottville 11 miles. Chamberlain is a village. Kilbuck and Great Valley are post-offices. The Indian reservation, about a mile wide, extends along the river to the east line of the town. Pop. 843.

HINSDALE, taken from Olean in 1820. Pop. 1,937. Hinsdale, 26 S. E., and West Hinsdale, 16 miles from Ellicottville, are post villages.

HUMPHREY, taken from Burton; from Ellicottville, S. E., centrally distant 10 miles. Chapelsburg is a post-office. Pop. 459.

LEON, taken from Connewango in 1832; from Albany 307, from Ellicottville, W., 18 miles. Leon Centre is a small village. Leon and Leon Mills are post-offices. Pop. 1,325.

LITTLE VALLEY, taken from Perry in 1818; Little Valley village is a small settlement, 7 miles S. W. from Ellicottville. Bucktooth is a post-office. Not one fortieth part of the town is settled. The Indian reservation extends along the Allegany river through this town. Pop. 671.

LYNDON, taken from Franklinville in 1829; from Albany 277, and from Ellicottville, E., 20 miles. Hopkins is a post-office. Pop. 628.

MACHIAS, taken from Yorkshire in 1827; from Albany 288, from Ellicottville, N. E., 10 miles. Machias, a post-office, and Machias Corners, are small settlements. Pop. 1,085.

MANSFIELD, taken from Little Valley in 1830, originally named Cecilius; from Albany 296, and from Ellicottville, W., 5 miles. Pop. 960.

NAPOLI, originally named Cold Spring, and taken from Little Valley. Seeleysburg, 13 miles S. W. from Ellicottville, is a post-office. Napoli is a small village. Pop. 1,142.

NEW ALBION, taken from Little Valley in 1830; from Albany 302, from Ellicottville, W., 10 miles. New Albion is a post-office. Pop. 1,033.

OLEAN, organized in 1808; bounds since much reduced. Pop. 638. Olean Village, at the junction of the Olean creek with the Alleghany river, is the oldest place in the county. It was founded by Major Hoops, and named by him, in honor of Gen. Hamilion, "Hamilton on the Allegany." Major Hoops was originally from Philadelphia, and served as an aid under Washington during the revolutionary war. This is a flourishing village, and is destined to become a place of importance. The New York and Erie railroad is to pass through it; and the Genesee Valley canal, now constructing from Rochester south, is to terminate here. The width of the Allegany river is 20 rods, with a channel free from obstructions. The amount of lumber annually sent to market by it, is about 200 millions of feet, board measure, of superior quality.

OTTO, taken from Perrysburg in 1823; from Albany, W., 300 miles. Waverly, 11 miles N. W. from Ellicottville, is a small village. Otto and East Otto are names of post-offices. Pop. 2,125.

PERRYSBURG, originally named Perry, was taken from Olean and Ischua in 1814. It is in the northwestern angle of the county; from Albany 304, and from Ellicottville 30 miles. Perrysburg and Versailles are small villages, and North Perrysburg a post-office. Pop. 1,672.

PERSIA, taken from Perrysburg in 1835; from Albany, W., 300 miles. Pop. 870. Lodi, 25 miles N. W. from Ellicottville, upon both sides of the Cattaraugus creek, is partly in Erie county. It was first settled on the Erie county side of the creek, in 1811, by Mr. Turner Aldrich, one of the society of Friends; and on the Cattaraugus side, about the year 1813, by Benjamin Waterman, Thomas Farnsworth, Daniel and Ahaz Allen, and others. Both of the churches, the Presbyterian and Methodist, were built in 1832. At its first settlement, there was not a white inhabitant south of here in the western half of the county, and no road to Pennsylvania in the county, excepting an Indian trail. The village contains about 100 houses, an academy, and a weekly newspaper office. The creek in this town affords a valuable water-power.

PORTVILLE, the S. E. town of the county, recently taken from Olean; from Albany 296 miles. Pop. 462. Riceville is a small settlement; Mill Grove a post-office.

RANDOLPH, taken from Connewango in 1826; from Ellicottville, S. W., centrally distant about 35 miles. East and West Randolph are small settlements. Pop. 1,283.

YORKSHIRE, taken from Ischua in 1820; from Albany, W., 281, from Ellicottville, N. E., 15 miles. Yorkshire, Yorkshire Forks, and Delavan are small post villages. Pop. 1,292.

CHATAUQUE COUNTY.

CHATAUQUE COUNTY, the southwestern county of the state, was formed from Genesee in 1808. The name is a corruption of the Indian word Ots-ha-ta-ka, which signifies a foggy place, and was applied to the country around the head of the Chatauque lake, even now famous for its fogs. Its greatest length N. and S. is 40, and greatest breadth E. and W. 36 miles; centrally distant from Albany, W., 330, and from New York, by way of Cattskill, N. W., 428 miles. The soil generally is strong clay loam, very productive of large crops of wheat, barley, and corn; the last is however destroyed sometimes by the early frosts to which the country is subject. The plain upon the lake is highly fertile, and produces the finest fruits adapted to the climate.

This county, though bordering on Lake Erie, is situated on the elevated ground known as the "Chatauque Ridge," which divides the waters of the northern lakes from those of the Allegany river. This ridge is generally from 5 to 10 miles from the shore of Lake Erie, and elevated from 790 to 1400 feet above it. The general surface of the county, though hilly, is not mountainous, and the highest hills are arable to their summits and frequently adorned with valuable farms. The soil along the shore of Lake Erie from 1 to 4 miles wide is a border of rich alluvion, and along the margin of the rivers. The upland is generally a moist loam. Grain is raised in considerable quantities, and the county is generally well adapted to grazing. Fruit, such as apples, pears, and plums, succeeds well.

Chatauque Lake is a fine sheet of water 16 miles long, and from 1 to 4 wide. Its elevation is 1,305 feet above the ocean, and it is navigated by steamboats. This county formed part of the Holland Land Company's purchase; and wild lands were offered by them at $1 50 to $4, per acre; but a company from Batavia bought their interest in the wild land of the county. More than three quarters of the county are yet unimproved. The county is divided into 20 towns. Pop. 47,641.

ARKWRIGHT, taken from Pomfret and Villenova in 1829; distant from Albany 310, centrally situated from Mayville, N. E., 16 miles. Pop. 1,418.

BUSTI, formed from Ellicott and Harmony in 1823; from Albany

334, from Mayville, S. E., 17 miles. Its surface is hilly, and the soil good. Pop. 1,749.

CARROLL, taken from Ellicott in 1825; from Albany 336, from Mayville, S. E., 29 miles. Carroll and Frewsburgh are small settlements. Scarcely one third of the town is yet improved. Pop. 1,632.

CHARLOTTE, taken from Gerry in 1829; from Albany 325, and from Mayville, N. E., 13 miles. Charlotte Centre is a post-office, and Sinclairville a small post village. Pop. 1,428.

CHATAUQUE, organized as part of Genesee county in 1804; since much reduced in area. It is upon the "dividing ridge," but chiefly on its eastern declivity, and produces excellent crops of corn, wheat, and grass. Pop. 2,980.

Western entrance into Mayville.

Mayville the county seat, incorporated in 1830; distant, 336 miles W. of Albany; from New York, via Cattskill, 434; from Buffalo, S. W., 66; from Erie, Penn., 35; from Warren, Penn., 40; from Portland Harbor, E., 7 miles. This is one of the most beautiful sites for a village in the state, and is situated upon the high grounds at the head of the lake. The above view was taken near the residence of Mr. M. P. Bemas, on the road to Westfield, at a point commanding a view of the principal street and the lake in the distance. The top of the courthouse, a substantial edifice, costing $9,000, is seen on the left. Further down is the spire of the Episcopal church, nearly opposite to it the Baptist, and on the right of the engraving the Academy. The Methodist and Presbyterian churches are not seen from this point. The Episcopal, the first church built here, was erected about 1824. Mayville has about 80 dwellings. In the northern part are two springs on the "dividing ridge" within ten minutes walk of each other. One of which flows into those streams which empty into the Gulf of Mexico, and the other into those which flow into the Atlantic by the St. Lawrence. Hartfield, 2 miles E. of Mayville, is a small village. There is a post-office at De Wittville, and one called Magnolia.

CHERRY CREEK, taken from Ellington in 1829; from Albany 320,

CHATAUQUE COUNTY. 89

and from Mayville, E., 18 miles. There is a post-office at Cherry Creek village. Pop. 1,141.

CLYMER, formed from Chatauque in 1821; from Albany 353, and from Mayville, S. W., 15 miles. Clymer is a small village, and Clymer Centre a post-office. Pop. 800.

ELLERY, on Chatauque lake, taken from Chatauque in 1821; from Albany 342, and from Mayville, S. E., 13 miles. Pop. 2,252. Ellery Centre is a small post village.

ELLICOTT, taken from Pomfret in 1812; limits since reduced; from Albany 330, and from Mayville, S. E., 22 miles. Pop. 2,568.

Southern view of Jamestown.

Jamestown, the principal village in the county, is on the Chatauque outlet, 4 miles below the lake, and contains about 200 dwellings. The above view was taken near the sawmill on the Chatauque outlet, seen in front, and shows the principal portion of the place. The spire in the centre of the view, is that of the Congregational church. The steeple on the left is the Presbyterian, and that on the right the Academy. There are also a Methodist and a Baptist church, and 2 weekly newspaper offices in the place. A steamboat plies on the lake between here and Mayville. James Pendergrast, Esq., from Pittstown, Rensselaer co., established himself here in 1811 or '12, and laid the foundation of the village. The first tavern was built shortly after by Jacob Fenton. But few dwellings were erected till 1816, when the place rapidly increased by emigrants principally from the eastern part of the state. Fluvanna and Dexterville are villages.

ELLINGTON, taken from Gerry in 1824; from Albany 320, from Mayville, E., 20 miles. Pop. 1,709. Ellington and Clear Creek are small villages.

FRENCH CREEK, taken from Clymer in 1829; from Albany 355, from Mayville, S. W., 17 miles. Pop. 621. The greater part of the town is yet in its wilderness state.

GERRY, divided from Pomfret in 1812; from Albany 326, from Mayville, S. E., 13 miles. Vermont is a small village. Pop. 1,246. About three fourths of the town is yet unimproved.

HANOVER, taken from Pomfret in 1812. Pop. 3,998.

Silver creek, 33 miles from Buffalo, lies on a harbor on Lake Erie, and has about 100 dwellings. Forestville, on Walnut creek, 6 miles from the Lake, has about 100 dwellings, and a weekly newspaper office. Nashville, Smith's Mills, Irving, and Le Grange, are small settlements.

<small>"Walnut creek in this town has its name from a black walnut tree, which formerly stood a mile above its mouth, and was 36 feet in circumference at its base, gradually and gracefully tapering 80 feet to the first limb. Its entire height was 150 feet, and was estimated to contain 150 cords of wood, or 50,000 feet of inch boards. The bark was a foot thick. The tree was entirely sound when blown down in 1822, and was supposed to have been 500 years old. The butt, 9 feet in length, was transported to Buffalo, having been excavated, and was there occupied as a grocery. It was subsequently carried by the canal to the Atlantic cities, and, splendidly adorned, was exhibited for money to thousands of admirers."—*Gordon's Gaz.*</small>

HARMONY, taken from Chatauque in 1816; from Albany 338, from Mayville, S., 13 miles. Ashville and Panama are small villages. Pop. 3,333. About one fourth of the town is under improvement.

MINA, taken from Clymer in 1824; from Albany 353, from Mayville, S. W., 13 miles. Pop. 870. There is a small settlement at Mina, and one at Finley's mills. Most of the town is yet in its wilderness state.

POLAND, taken from Ellicott in 1832; from Albany 316, from Mayville, S. E., 20 miles. Kennedy's Mills and Waterborough are small hamlets. Pop. 1,082.

POMFRET, taken from Chatauque in 1808, is on the "divided ridge." Pop. 4,556. Fredonia village was incorporated in 1829; is on the Canadawa creek, 315 miles from Albany, 22 N. E. from Mayville, 45 S. W. from Buffalo, and 3 from Lake Erie at Dunkirk. It is the oldest village in the county, and was formerly called Canadawa, from the creek. It contains about 120 dwellings. The annexed view was

Southern view of Fredonia.

taken near the residence of Samuel Johnson, Esq. The large building with a square tower is the Johnson House; the steeple next to it is that of the Baptist church; the third is the Academy, incorporated in 1836; the fourth the Presbyterian, and the fifth, on the extreme right, the Episcopal church. The Methodist and Universalist churches are not seen in the drawing. Laona, 2 miles above Fredonia, has a valuable water-power and about 45 dwellings.

The following account of the Gas springs in this vicinity, is from the Report of Dr. Lewis C. Beck, published in the New York Geological Reports for 1832.

"*Chatauque Gas Springs.*—By far the most interesting exhibitions of the evolution of carburetted hydrogen, which occur in this state, are to be observed in the county of Chatauque. The village of Fredonia, indeed, has attracted much attention in consequence of the gas springs found in its immediate vicinity, although they are by no means confined to this particular locality. The gas springs seem to have their origin in the strata of slate which form the bed of the stream, and which are everywhere met with in this vicinity, a short distance from the surface of the earth. This slate has a bluish color, and some of the layers are exceedingly fragile, requiring only a few years exposure to be completely converted into a clayey soil. The lower strata, however, resist atmospheric agencies, and are sometimes used as a building material. When recently broken, this slate always emits a strong bituminous odor, and it frequently contains thin seams of a substance resembling bituminous coal. Most commonly, however, this bituminous matter occurs in patches, having more the appearance of detached vegetable impressions than a regular stratum. Through fissures in this rock in the creek near the village, are everywhere to be seen bubbles of gas rising through the water. The evolution, however, is most abundant at the bridge, and about three quarters of a mile below. The gas, when collected in a proper vessel and fired, burns with a white flame tinged with yellow above, and blue near the orifice of the burner. Its illuminating power is not inferior to that of ordinary coal gas. When mixed with atmospheric air and ignited, it explodes violently. It contains no admixture of sulphuretted hydrogen.

"The illuminating power of this gas, and its abundant supply, suggested the idea of its employment in lighting the village. A copious discharge of the gas was observed issuing from a fissure in the rock, which forms the bed of the creek, which it was thought could be diverted to a boring on the bank. A shaft was accordingly sunk through the slate about 22 feet in depth, which occasionally passed through layers of the bituminous substance, already described, and the result was that the gas left the creek and issued through the shaft. By means of a tube, the gas was now conducted to a gasometer, and from thence to different parts of the village. The gasometer had a capacity of about 220 cubic feet, and was usually filled in about 15 hours, affording a sufficient supply of gas for 70 or 80 lights. Bubbles of the same gas are here and there seen rising through the water in this creek for nearly three quarters of a mile below the village. But the largest quantity is evolved at the latter point. It was not possible for me, with any apparatus which I could command, to determine the amount of gas given out at this place in a given time; but bubbles rise with great rapidity from an area of more than 20 feet square, and I should probably be warranted in asserting that it is 5 or 6 times greater than that obtained at the village.

"At Van Buren harbor, on Lake Erie, 4 miles from Fredonia, bubbles of inflammable gas may be seen rising through the water, when the lake is calm, a rod or two from the shore. In the town of Sheridan, six and a half miles from Fredonia, the same gas is also abundantly evolved in various places; and a short distance below Portland harbor, near the shore of the lake, there is supposed to be a sufficient supply to light a city. It is employed in the lighthouse at the harbor, 75 feet above the level of the lake."

Dunkirk, formerly owned by the Dunkirk Land Company, is pleasantly situated on Lake Erie, and is destined to be a place of great importance from its being the terminating point of the line of the New York and Erie railroad. The distance from Buffalo is 44 miles, and to Piermont, on the Hudson, (about 22 miles N. of New York,) by the line of the railroad, 446 miles. This whole distance from Dunkirk to New York, on the completion of the road, will be accomplished in from 20 to 24 hours. The U. S. government, viewing the growing importance of the place, has expended large sums in the improvement of its harbor. This port is occasionally open many days, and even weeks, earlier in the spring and later in the fall, than

Northeastern view of Dunkirk Harbor.

that of Buffalo. The above view was taken about a mile from the village, seen on the left. The large cupola is that of the hotel, a capacious brick structure; the steeple next to it is that of the Presbyterian church, and the smaller one the Academy. The opposite shore of the harbor is seen beautifully curving around in the distance, and is lined to near the water's edge with a fine growth of forest trees. Van Buren is the name of a place laid out as a city 2 miles above Dunkirk, where there is a good harbor. Shumla and West Milford are small villages. Cassadaga is a post-office.

PORTLAND, taken from Chatauque in 1813; distant from Albany 354, and from Mayville, N., 6 miles. Salem and Centreville are small settlements. Pop. 2,136. About half the town is under improvement.

RIPLEY, taken from Portland in 1817, on the "dividing ridge," has a hilly surface. Distant from Albany 348, and from Mayville, W., 12 miles. Pop. 2,197. Quincy, formerly called Ripley, contains the post-office and about 50 dwellings.

SHERIDAN, taken from Pomfret and Hanover in 1827; 340 miles from Albany, and 20 N. E. of Mayville. East Sheridan and Orrington are post-offices. Pop. 1,883.

SHERMAN, taken from Mina in 1822; from Albany 348, from Mayville, S. W., 12 miles. Sherman is a small village. Pop. 1,100. More than two thirds of the town is yet a forest.

STOCKTON, formed from Chatauque in 1821; distant from Albany 323, from Mayville, N. E., 8 miles. Delanti and Casadaga are small villages. Pop. 2,078.

VILLENOVA, taken from Hanover in 1823; distant from Albany 318, from Mayville, N. E., 22 miles. Omar is a small village. Pop. 1,655. About one fourth part of the town is under cultivation.

WESTFIELD, formed from Portland and Ripley in 1829. Pop. 3,199. Near the shore of Lake Erie, about three quarters of a mile below Portland harbor, is a carburetted hydrogen spring, the gas of which is sufficiently abundant to light a city, and is used for the lighthouse at the harbor, seventy-five feet above the lake level. McIntyre's sulphur spring, on the banks of the Chatauque creek, 3 miles from the lake, was formerly much frequented.

Westfield village, from Albany 342, from Mayville, N. W., 6, and from Buffalo, S. W.. 60 miles; was incorporated in 1833. It is a pleasant, bustling little village, situated on the border of a handsome

View in central part of Westfield Village.

plain, and containing about 100 dwellings. The above view was taken at Edson & Son's store, and shows on the left the Episcopal, and on the right the Presbyterian churches. The other public buildings are the Methodist church, Academy, and Westfield Hotel, a substantial brick edifice, with a cupola. About two and a half miles from the village, near the road to Mayville, is a remarkable gulf, known as the "Hogs Back," which is much resorted to in the summer. The first settler with a family in the county, was a Mr. John McMahan, from Northumberland county, Penn. He came here about the year 1803, and bought of the Holland Land Company a tract six miles square, on the Chatauque creek, in this town. Portland, or Barcelona. one mile from Westfield, on the lake, was early occupied by the French, who had a military post at this place. The lighthouse, 40 feet in height, standing on a bluff, is a conspicuous object, and visible at a great distance on the lake. The village contains about 40 dwellings. Rogersville, Volusia, and Nettle Hill are post-offices.

CHEMUNG COUNTY.

CHEMUNG* COUNTY was formed from the western part of Tioga in 1836. Greatest length, N. and S., 28; greatest breadth, E. and W., 20 miles. The surface of the county is hilly. The soil consists generally of sandy and gravelly loam, interspersed with patches of marl and clay. The uplands are commonly better adapted to grass than grain; but the valleys give fine crops of wheat and corn; oats, beans, barley, peas, and hops thrive almost everywhere. The pine plains, principally in the towns of Elmira and Big Flats, formerly considered almost worthless, are now deemed highly valuable; producing by treatment with plaster, and due succession of crops, abundant returns in wheat, Indian corn, and clover. The Chemung canal, connecting Elmira with Cayuga lake, is about 20 miles in length. The New York and Erie railroad passes through the towns of Chemung, Southport, Elmira, and Big Flats. Chemung county is divided into ten towns. Pop. 20,731.

BIG FLATS, taken from Elmira in 1822; from Albany 207, from Elmira centrally distant, NW., 10 miles. The navigable feeder of the Chemung canal passes centrally through the town in an easterly direction. There are extensive flats on the Chemung river. Pop. 1,375.

CATHERINES was taken from Newtown in 1798; from Albany 184 miles. Havanna, founded in 1829 by Mr. David Ayres, and incorporated in 1836, 18 miles N. from Elmira, is a very thriving village, containing about 700 inhabitants. It is situated upon a small stream rushing over a high hill from the west, with three cascades, making together a fall of over 100 feet.

This town appears to have derived its name from its having been the residence of *Catherine Montour*, the wife of an Indian sachem or king. She has sometimes been called Queen Esther. This remarkable woman, it is said, was a native of Canada, a half-breed, her father being one of the French governors, probably Count Frontenac. During the wars between the Six Nations and the French and Hurons, Catherine was taken prisoner, when she was about ten years old, and carried into the Seneca country, and adopted as one of their children. At a suitable age she was married to a distinguished chief of her tribe, by whom she had several children. Her husband was killed in battle about 1730. She is represented as having been a handsome woman when young, genteel, and of good address. She frequently accompanied the chiefs of the Six Nations to Philadelphia, and other places where treaties were holden. On account of her character and manners, she was much caressed by the American ladies of the first respectability, and invited and entertained at their houses. Her residence was at the head of Seneca lake. She has

---

* Chemung is said to be *big horn*, or *great horn*, in the ancient Indian dialect. And that a very large horn was found in the Chemung or Tioga river, has been well ascertained.

CHEMUNG COUNTY.   95

been accused of perpetrating some savage atrocities at the massacre at Wyoming, but the account does not appear to be well authenticated. At the period of the revolutionary war, Catherine's town consisted of thirty houses, cornfields, orchards, &c.; these were all destroyed by Gen. Sullivan, Sept. 3, 1779, in his expedition into the Indian country.

CATLIN, taken from Catherine in 1823; from Albany 190, from Elmira, NW., 12 miles. A great portion of the town is yet unsettled. Catlin, West Catlin, and Martins Hill, are post-offices. Pop. 1,119.

CAYUTA, taken from Spencer in 1824; from Albany, SW., 188, from Elmira, NE., 20 miles. It is rather thinly settled. Cayuta, West Cayuta, and Van Eltensville, are post-offices. Pop. 835. The surface of the township is hilly and broken; the hills are covered with pines and hemlocks.

CEHMUNG, organized in 1791; from Albany, SW., 198, from Elmira, E., 12 miles. Surface is hilly, and broken with fertile flats along the Chemung river. Pop. 2,377. The Chemung upper and lower *Narrows* are formed by high, rocky cliffs, projecting into the river, along which the road is conducted with great labor.

"In the south part of the town is a mound, called *Spanish Hill*, elevated 110 feet above the plain, and near the river bank, described as a work of art; but this suggestion is rendered incredible from the fact, that the area of its summit comprises four acres. Upon this summit, however, are vestiges of fortifications, displaying much skill in the art of defence; having regular entrenchments, which perfectly commanded the bend in the river.—*Gordon's Gazeteer.*

DIX, taken from Catlin in 1835, is the NW. town of the county; from Elmira 20 miles. Pop. 1,990. Townsend, Moreland, and West Catlin are post-offices. Jefferson, post village, partly in Steuben county, at the head of Seneca lake, 3 miles N. of Havanna, was founded in 1828 by Dr. Watkins, and has about 50 dwellings.

ELMIRA was taken from Chemung by the name of Newtown, in 1792. Much of the land in this township is rich and productive, particularly the flats on Chemung river. Pop. 4,791. Elmira village is situated at the confluence of Newtown creek with the Chemung river. It was formerly the half-shire village of Tioga county, and is now the seat of justice for Chemung co. It was incorporated in 1815 by the name of Newtown, which name was changed to Elmira in 1828: its ancient Indian name was Conewawah, a word signifying "*a head on a pole.*" Elmira is admirably situated for the purposes of trade, in the midst of a fertile valley, eight to ten miles in extent from N. to S., and from twelve to fifteen miles E. and W. The place is connected with Pennsylvania and Maryland, in trade, by the Chemung and Susquehannah rivers, and with almost every portion of the state by means of the Chemung canal, which leads through Seneca lake, and thence by the Seneca to the Erie canal.

The village contains about 230 dwellings, 4 churches—1 Presbyterian, 1 Baptist, 1 Methodist, and 1 Episcopal—2 newspaper establishments, 1 bank, and a number of select schools. The village is on the line of the Erie railroad.

CHEMUNG COUNTY.

Distant view of the Village of Elmira.

The above view was taken near the Sullivan mill,* about a mile eastward of the village, near the junction of Newtown creek with the Chemung river. The first spire on the right is that of the Presbyterian church, the next to the left the courthouse; the others are those of the Episcopal and Baptist churches. The bridge seen extending across the Chemung is 600 feet in length.

The section of country in which Elmira is situated became known to the whites during the revolutionary war. When Gen. Sullivan was penetrating into the Indian country, in 1779, the Indians under Brant, and the tories under Colonels Butler and Johnson, made a stand to oppose his progress at the SE. point of this town. They entrenched themselves by a breast-work of about a half a mile in length, so covered by a bend in the river as to expose only their front and one of their flanks to attack. On Sullivan's approach, Aug. 29th, an action commenced which is sometimes called the "Battle of the Chemung;" the force of the Indians and tories has been estimated from 800 to 1,500, while that of the Americans was between 4,000 and 5,000. The following account of the battle is extracted from the 2d vol. of "*Stone's Life of Brant.*"

"The enemy's position was discovered by Major Parr, commanding the advance guard, at about 11 o'clock in the morning of the 29th of August. General Hand immediately formed the light infantry in a wood, at the distance of about 400 yards from the breastwork, and waited until the main body of the army arrived on the ground. A skirmishing was, however, kept up by both sides—the Indians sallying out of their works by small parties, firing, and suddenly retreating—making the woods at the same time to resound with their war-whoops, piercing the air from point to point as though the tangled forest were alive with their grim-visaged warriors. Correctly judging that the hill upon his right was occupied by the savages, Gen. Sullivan ordered Poor's brigade to wheel off, and endeavor to gain their left flank, and, if possible, to surround them, while the artillery and main body

---

* So called from its being only a few rods above Sullivan's landing place, where he encamped both on the advance of, and return from his expedition against the Indians. The site of the fortress which Sullivan built, can be distinctly seen from the south windows of this mill.

of the Americans attacked them in front. The order was promptly executed; but as Poor climbed the ascent, the battle became animated, and the possession of the hill was bravely contested. In front the enemy stood a hot cannonade for more than two hours. Both tories and Indians were entitled to the credit of fighting manfully. Every rock, and tree, and bush, shielded its man, from behind which the winged messengers of death were thickly sent, but with so little effect as to excite astonishment. The Indians yielded ground only inch by inch; and in their retreat darted from tree to tree with the agility of the panther, often contesting each new position to the point of the bayonet—a thing very unusual even with militiamen, and still more rare among the undisciplined warriors of the woods. Thayendanegea was the animating spirit of the savages. Always in the thickest of the fight, he used every effort to stimulate his warriors, in the hope of leading them to victory. Until the artillery began to play, the whoops and yells of the savages, mingled with the rattling of musketry, had well-nigh obtained the mastery of sound. But their whoops were measurably drowned by the thunder of the cannon. This cannonade 'was elegant,' to adopt the phraseology of Sullivan himself, in writing to a friend, and gave the Indians a great panic. Still, the battle was contested in front for a length of time with undiminished spirit. But the severity of fighting was on the flank just described. As Poor gallantly approached the point which completely uncovered the enemy's rear, Brant, who had been the first to penetrate the design of the American commander, attempted once more to rally his forces, and with the assistance of a battalion of the rangers, make a stand. But it was in vain, although he exerted himself to the utmost for that purpose—flying from point to point, seeming to be everywhere present, and using every means in his power to reanimate the flagging spirits, and reinvigorate the arms of his followers. Having ascended the steep, and gained his object without faltering, the enemy's flank was turned by Poor, and the fortunes of the day decided. Perceiving such to be the fact, and that there was danger of being surrounded, the retreat-halloo was raised, and the enemy, savages and white men, precipitately abandoned their works, crossed the river, and fled with the utmost precipitation— the Indians leaving their packs and a number of their tomahawks and scalping-knives behind them. The battle was long, and on the side of the enemy bloody. Eleven of their dead were found upon the field—an unusual circumstance with the Indians, who invariably exert themselves to the utmost to prevent the bodies of their slain from falling into the hands of their foes. But being pushed at the point of the bayonet, they had not time to bear them away. They were pursued two miles, their trail affording indubitable proof that a portion of their dead and wounded had been carried off. Two canoes were found covered with blood, and the bodies of 14 Indian warriors were discovered partially buried among the leaves. Eight scalps were taken by the Americans during the chase. Considering the duration of the battle, and the obstinacy with which it was maintained, the loss of the Americans was small almost to a miracle. Only 5 or 6 men were killed, and between 40 and 50 wounded. Among the American officers wounded, were Maj. Titcomb, Capt. Clayes, and Lieut. Collis—the latter mortally. All the houses of the contiguous Indian town were burnt, and the cornfields destroyed."

The first settler of Newtown, now Elmira, was Col. John Hendy, a native of Pennsylvania and a veteran of the revolution. In the summer of 1788, he came into this town and erected a log hut on the point where Sullivan had encamped, about half a mile from the present centre of the village of Elmira. He brought his family to this place in the fall of the same year. It was during this year that this section of the country was surveyed by Gen. James Clinton, Gen. John Hathorn, and John Cantine, Esq., as commissioners on the part of the state. The land at this time was estimated and sold by the state at *eighteen pence* per acre to the first settlers. The second log house was built by John Miller near the bank of the river on the farm now occupied by Capt. Partridge. The same year, and the year following, (1789,) several families came in and settled on the south side of the river, in Southport. In the same year, Thomas Hendy and a Mr. Marks built log houses at the east end of the site of the village. When Col. Hendy built his log cabin on the pine plain of Conewawah, the only highway or road existing in the country for hundreds of miles round, was what was called the Indian pathway, extending from Wilkesbarre, Penn., to Canada. This pathway crossed the lot of Col. Hendy, and was for a long period the only avenue by which emigrants from the south reached Niagara and the northwestern part of the state.

The following anecdote relative to Col. Hendy, is taken from a publication, in a pamphlet form, entitled "Views of Elmira," by Solomon Southwick, Esq. It is from this publication that the historic notices of this place are mostly taken.

"They [the Indians] knew nothing of ceremony, and never waited for an invitation to visit the cabins of the white settlers; but would stalk in and sit themselves down as freely as they had been used to do in their own huts; nor were they less scrupulous in their attacks upon whatever food or beverage presented itself. If any of the whites disliked this freedom, they found it their best policy to bear patiently with the oft-repeated demands upon their hospitality which flowed from it; but in spite of their philosophy were sometimes involved in serious strife with their lawless visiters. One evening of a summer's day, Col. Hendy, having returned from the labors of the field, found two Indians at his house, one of whom was John Harris, celebrated for his quarrelsome and malignant temper, as well as vigorous and athletic frame. He had insulted Mrs. Hendy, and evinced such bad intentions, that his companion, aided by Col. Hendy's son, had found it necessary to bind him down in a chair, which operation they had just performed when Col. Hendy came in. Whilst the friendly Indian laid down and went quietly to sleep, the Colonel seated himself to watch the motions of the unruly savage. The fellow was so mortified by the compulsion and restraint imposed upon him, that he became apparently humble, and the Colonel, on his promise to behave well, unbound him, and ordered him to lay down on the floor and go to sleep, whilst he threw himself on the bed, but did not think it safe to undress or sleep; and the event proved the necessity and prudence of his precaution. For the savage, ruminating on the disgraceful circumstance of his having been bound, till his revengeful temper was roused to a high degree, rose up suddenly crying out "*Me be many*," a well known exclamation of the Indians when prepared to commence a fight single-handed with one of their own, or that of the white race. This was a critical moment for Hendy, who quickly perceived there was no time to be lost; he therefore rose up, exclaiming "*You be many—You none at all—I be many!*" and as the Indian sprang forward to grapple with him, brandishing a long knife, the veteran gave him a blow on the side of his head which laid him prostrate on the hearth; and then seizing him by the hair, beat his head upon the hearth, till the savage yielded up his knife, well convinced by the Colonel's demonstrations, that if he was *many*, his host was *many more*, or at least *too many* for him—and the next morning he was as quiet and peaceable as a lamb."

"In 1790, we believe it was, Elmira was visited by some ten or twelve hundred Indians; one of the oldest settlers assures us there were not less than eleven hundred. Their object was the negotiation of a treaty with the United States. On our part the venerable TIMOTHY PICKERING was the principal negotiator. GUY MAXWELL acted as his secretary, and transcribed the treaty. On the part of the Indians there were chiefs of all the Six Nations, among whom were Red Jacket, Big Tree, Trench Peter, Farmer's Brother, &c. Jasper Parish, of Canandaigua, was their interpreter. It was on this occasion that Red Jacket made one of his most eloquent and powerful speeches. One of the chiefs, and several of the subordinates, died during the negotiation; and their bones, it is said, have been recently found in digging the cellars for the elegant row of buildings, called *Benjamin's Block*, on Front-street. The treaty was held immediately east of the present courthouse in Lake-street, under an ancient oak-tree, which thenceforth, if not before, was known by the name of the council tree."

In 1792, Nathaniel Seely built the first frame house in the village of Newtown, now Elmira. The original patentee of the towns of Southport and Newtown was Moses De Witt; he sold out to a Mr. White. In 1794, Guy Maxwell and Samuel Hepburn purchased the village plot of Elmira from Mr. White. In 1797, Elmira received a visit from Louis Phillipe, the present king of France, the Duke de Nemours, and the Duke de Berri. These distinguished personages had been spending some time at Canandaigua, under the hospitable roof of Thomas Morris, Esq., son of Robert Morris, to whom the United States are so much indebted for his services as a financier in the revolution. Mr. Morris gave the royal exiles a letter of introduction to Henry Tower, Esq., who then resided here. They travelled *on foot* through the Indian pathway from Canandaigua to Elmira, a distance of more than 70 miles. Mr. Tower, on their arrival, fitted up a boat—an American ark or batteau—in which he took them down to Harrisburg, through the Chemung and Susquehannah rivers.

ERIN, taken from Chemung in 1822; from Albany 186, from Elmira, NE., 12 miles. Erin is a post-office, centrally located. Pop. 1,441. The surface of the town is hilly and broken and the soil rather of an indifferent quality.

SOUTHPORT, taken from Elmira in 1822; from Albany 203 miles. It has broad and rich flats upon the Chemung river, which forms in part the northern boundary. Wellsburg on the Chemung river, 6 miles SE. from Elmira, is a small post village. Southport and Seeleys Creek are post-offices. Pop. 2,100.

VETERAN, taken from Catherines in 1823; from Albany 190, from Elmira, N., centrally distant 12 miles. Pop. 2,279. Millport, Pine Valley, and Veteran are post-offices.

CHENANGO COUNTY.

CHENANGO COUNTY was formed from Herkimer and Tioga counties in 1798; the northern part of which was erected into Madison county in 1806. Its form is irregular; the greatest length N. and S., 35 miles; greatest width, 28. The general surface of the county is broken and hilly, though not mountainous. Its valleys are extensive, rich, and fertile, producing large crops of grain; while the uplands are well adapted to grazing. Its agriculture is respectable, and its inhabitants are generally farmers. Live-stock is one of their principal exports. The Susquehannah river crosses the SE. corner of the county. The Chenango river, one of its principal branches, flows southerly through the centre of the county. The Unadilla river forms most of the eastern bounds of the county. The numerous streams in this county furnish abundance of fine mill sites. The Chenango canal passes through the county in the valley of the Chenango river. This county was principally settled by emigrants from the eastern states. It originally included the twenty townships of the " Governor's purchase," a part of which are now in Madison county. The county is divided into 19 towns. Pop. 40,779.

BAINBRIDGE, organized as part of Tioga county, by the name of Jericho, in 1791; name since altered and limits much reduced. Pop.

3,324. The town forms part of a tract given by the state to sufferers in former grants to the present state of Vermont.

Bainbridge, incorporated in 1829; a large and thriving village, pleasantly situated upon the W. branch of the Susquehannah, upon the Ulster and Delaware turnpike; 110 miles from Albany, and 14 S. from Norwich; has about 90 dwellings. E. Bainbridge, N. Bainbridge, and S. Bainbridge are names of post-offices.

COLUMBUS, taken from Brookfield in 1805; from Albany 83, from Norwich, NE., 16 miles. Columbus is a small village, and Columbus Corners a post-office. Pop. 1,561.

COVENTRY, taken from Greene in 1806; from Albany 117, from Norwich 16 miles. Coventry and Coventryville are post villages, on the Cattskill turnpike. Pop. 1,681.

GERMAN, taken from De Ruyter in 1806; from Albany 115, from Norwich, W., 15 miles. Pop. 975.

GREENE was formed from Union and Jericho in 1798; limits since reduced. The Chenango river passes in a SW. direction through the town, upon which are rich alluvial flats. Pop. 3,452. Greene, the principal village, is on the river, 20 miles SW. from Norwich, and 19 N. from Binghamton. It contains 3 churches, 11 stores, and about 90 dwellings. It was laid out in village form in 1806, and was at first called Hornby. East Green and Genegansette are post-offices.

The first person who settled in the vicinity of the village of Greene, is supposed to have been Conrad Sharp, a Dutchman, who located himself about two miles above the village in 1794; a number of other Dutchmen came in and formed quite a settlement in his vicinity. The names of some of the other principal settlers were, Stephen Ketchum, David Bradley, Derick Race, Joseph Tillotson, Mr. Gray, a Baptist elder, and Elisha Smith, who was the agent, for a number of years, in behalf of the Hornby Patent; he surveyed the town of Greene and laid out the village.

The first white inhabitants who located themselves on the site of the village, were eight or ten French families, who fled from their country during the revolutionary period. The first one who came appears to have been Simon Barnet, who is said to have been a creole from the West Indies. He came to this place from Philadelphia, probably sent as a pioneer for the French company. One of the emigrants, M. Dutremont, was a man of considerable talents, learning, and wealth. This gentleman contracted for the lands settled by the company. The purchase was made of William W. Morris and Malachi Treat, the patentees. Capt. Juliand, one of the French emigrants, came into the place in 1797, a little after the first company. About the year 1795, the celebrated French statesman, Talleyrand, visited this place, when on a sylvan jaunt on horseback from Philadelphia to Albany in company with a French gentleman. When here, he became acquainted with the son of M. Dutremont, with whom he was so much pleased, that he obtained the consent of his parents to take him to France, where he became his private secretary. By the death of M. Dutremont, the financial affairs of the little colony became deranged. He was drowned while fording a river on horseback, on his way to Philadelphia. As he had not paid for the land occupied by the emigrants, it reverted back to the patentees. The emigrants became discouraged, and after a few years left the place, moved down below Towanda, and joined a French settlement at a place called Frenchtown, now Asylum. Capt. Juliand, however, remained in Greene, and to him and Judge Elisha Smith the foundation of the village is to be ascribed.

" There were no Indians in this particular section, when first settled by the whites. But we have to record a most remarkable mound, the relic of Indian superstition and industry. There are now to be seen only some imperfect traces of it. It was situated about two miles south of the village, and about thirty rods from the river bank, on what is now the farm of Mr. Lott. The mound, before it was dug down or ploughed over, was about six or seven feet above the surface of the ground, and forty feet in diameter; being nearly circular. There was also, till within a few years, a large pine stump in the centre of it, the remains of a large pine-tree which was standing when the whites came in. It was *then*, however, a *dead* tree. When it was cut down, there were counted 180 concentric circles or yearly growths. Estimating the age of the mound by the concentric circles of the stump, it must have been over 200 years old when this section of the country was settled. An examination of this mound was made in 1829, by digging, and there were found human bones to a great number; and lower from the surface, there were found bones that had been evidently burnt; suggesting the idea, that the mode of disposing of the dead, when these bones were deposited, was *burning the dead body*. No conjecture could be formed as to the number of bodies buried here. They were found lying without order, very much *jumbled*, and so far decayed as to crumble, or fall apart, when brought to the air and handled. The supposition would not be an unlikely one, that these bones were the remains of bodies which had fallen in battle, and were afterward hurriedly thrown together and buried. * * * * In the mound near Greene, there were found, lying quite in one pile, 200 arrow heads, cut after their usual form, and all either of yellow or black *flint*. It will be recollected that there are no stones of this kind found in this part of the state of New York. In another part of the mound there were found, lying together, about sixty, made after the same form. A silver band or ring was also found, of about two inches in diameter, extremely thin, but wide, with the remains—in appearance—of a reed pipe, lying within it. The supposition is, that it was some sort of musical instrument. There was also found a number of stone chisels, of different shapes, evidently fitted to perform different species of work. A large piece of mica also, cut into the form of a heart; the border much decayed, and the different laminæ separated."—*Annals of Binghamton.*

GUILFORD, taken from Oxford in 1813, by the name of Eastern; name since changed; from Norwich, centrally distant S., 10 miles. Pop. 2,828. Guilford is a small post village, Rockdale a post-office, and Mount Upton a small settlement.

LINCKLAEN, taken from German in 1823; since reduced in area; from Albany 128, from Norwich, NW., 20 miles. Lincklaen and West Lincklaen are post-offices. Pop. 1,249.

McDONOUGH, named in honor of Commodore McDonough, taken from Preston in 1816; from Albany 128, from Norwich, W., 14 miles. Pop. 1,369. Near the south line of the town is a sulphur spring much frequented. McDonough is a small village.

NEW BERLIN, taken from Norwich in 1807. Pop. 3,086. New Berlin, an incorporated village, 13 miles NE. from Norwich, and 90 W. from Albany, on the Unadilla river, has 1 Presbyterian, 1 Episcopal, 1 Baptist, and 1 Methodist church. There are here 154 dwellings, 10 mercantile stores, a weekly newspaper office, and several large manufacturing establishments. South New Berlin, 9 miles east from Norwich, has about 40 dwellings. New Berlin Centre is a small village.

NORWICH, formed from Jericho and Union, as part of Tioga county, in 1793; area since much reduced. Pop. 4,146. Norwich village, the county seat, is delightfully situated upon the Chenango river. Its site is much admired by travellers. It is surrounded by lands in a

Courthouse and other buildings in Norwich.

high state of cultivation, and well supplied with pure and wholesome water. There is a mineral spring near the village resorted to for cutaneous diseases. The above view shows the courthouse in the centre of the engraving; the building with a spire on the left, is the Presbyterian church. The courthouse has been but recently erected. It is built of freestone, and is one of the most splendid structures of the kind in the state. Besides the above, there are in the village 1 Episcopal, 1 Baptist, and 1 Methodist church, 2 weekly newspaper offices, the Chenango Bank, several manufactories, and about 200 dwellings.

OTSELIC, taken from German in 1817; distant from Albany 110, from Norwich, NW., 20 miles. Otselic is a small village, and South Otselic a post-office. Pop. 1,621.

OXFORD.* "The present town of Oxford was originally a part of the township of Fayette, a tract which was laid out soon after the war of the revolution, and sold at auction in New York, in lots of a mile square. This township, and a tract called the Gore, bought by Gen. Hovey and Judge Melancton Smith, containing about 7,000 acres, were incorporated into a town in 1793, and in 1794 the first town meeting was held at the house of Gen. Hovey; this building stood on the site of the Fort Hill house, (burnt in 1839.) Previous to 1791,

---

* Communicated to the authors by Henry M. Hyde, Esq.

there were no settlers on the western part of Fayette except two, Mr. Elijah Blackman, and a man named Phelps. They lived on lot 92, in the bounds of the present village.

"From the time the settlement was commenced, by the exertions of Gen. Hovey, whose enterprise and hardihood surmounted every obstacle, the population rapidly increased. The pioneers who composed the settlement, were distinguished for qualifications rarely possessed by men in their laborious occupations. Their intelligence was proverbial. In fact, many of them were persons of considerable scientific attainments. They obtained an act of incorporation for an academy as early as 1794, and sustained the institution in the most creditable manner, under all difficulty. Gen. Hovey, whose name seems to be connected with nearly all the occurrences in the early days of the town, was a man of uncommon business abilities, and was a favorite of the distinguished men who were at that time at the head of affairs in this state. He was a member of assembly in 1798, and was also a judge of the county. He afterward removed to the Ohio, and at the time of Burr's expedition down the Mississippi, he was the general agent of a company, composed of some of the first men of the Union, for the purpose of canalling the Ohio at the falls opposite Louisville. The project failed, and Gen. Hovey was a severe sufferer in consequence. He died about 1815.

"Nearly all the settlers were natives of New England, and a majority were from the state of Connecticut. There are at present living many of the hardy pioneers who commenced the settlement. Of these, Mr. Francis Balcom, Mr. Jonathan Baldwin, Judge Anson Cary, Col. Samuel Balcom, James Padgett, and some few others, are now residing in this town. Judge Uri Tracy, who was some years since a member of congress from this district, and who died three or four years since, was likewise an early resident, and principal of the academy."

"The Indian antiquities in and about the village of Oxford are worthy of notice. Of these, the Old Fort has always attracted the most attention. This fort stood upon the hill in about the middle of the village, and the ditch is yet to be distinguished, in front of the house of Ira Wilcox, Esq. When discovered, it was a regular semicircle from the river, and enclosed about three quarters of an acre, and the ditch, when the ground was cleared, was in many places four feet deep. The interior of the fort was covered with the largest kind of maple and beach trees, and on the top of the bank hove up, stood a dead pine stump, which, when cut, left a stump on which was counted two hundred grains or circles. This tree evidently sprang up after the ditch was dug. There were upon the north and south sides of the fort, two places where the ground had evidently never been disturbed. These are supposed to have been gates. The ditch was four or five feet wide, and on the river side, the bank having been almost perpendicular. The fort must have been a strong position. Nothing short of cannon from the neighboring hills could annoy the fort. In the course of subsequent excavations in and about it, human bones, cooking utensils, and other relics, have been found. Of course, nothing is known about the object of this fortification, or by whom built. The Oneidas have a tradition running many generations back, but they can tell us nothing definite. The Oneidas leave us this tradition: that about a century or more since, a gigantic chief occupied it, who destroyed all their hunters who came into this quarter. They called this chief *Thick Neck*. The Oneidas made several attempts to decoy him from his stronghold, but without success. They at length managed to go between him and the fort, when he ran down the river about six miles and secreted himself in the marsh around the pond called Warn's Pond. Here he was discovered and killed by the Oneidas, who buried him and scratched the leaves over his grave that no vestige of him should remain. The remnant of his tribe were adopted by the Oneidas, and an Indian who was hung at Morrisville many years since named Abram Antone, was a descendant from *Thick Neck*.

"There is an incident connected with a small island a few rods above the bridge over the Chenango. Some years ago, two worthies residing in the town, having quarrelled about some trifling matter, resolved to exchange shots, in vindication of their honor. The place selected for the transaction was this island. On the day appointed, the belligerents made their appearance on the spot. The seconds, however, were agreed that neither should suffer harm, and loaded the pistols with cork instead of ball. Each second inspired his principal with courage, by imparting to him the information that his antagonist's pistol was loaded with cork, at the same time assuring him that his own contained the lead. The consequence was, the duellists manifested great bravery—no one was hurt, and the actors were highly complimented for their chivalry, and unhesitatingly pronounced men of *honor*. The island has since been called *Cork Island*."

Central part of the Village of Oxford.

The above view was taken on the banks of the Chenango canal, and shows the principal public buildings in the village. The church on the left is the Presbyterian, the smaller building with a cupola in the centre is the Academy, and the two spires seen on the right are those of the Episcopal and Baptist churches, which latter structures stand near the site of the old fort. There is also a Methodist church in the village, 2 weekly newspaper offices, and about 170 dwellings. There are several bridges over the Chenango river, and the Appian way, from Newburg, terminates here. The village is 8 miles south of Norwich. There is a post-office at South Oxford. Population of the town, 3,177.

PHARSALIA, first settled in 1798, and taken from Norwich in 1806, by the name of Stonington; name afterward changed; distant from Albany 114, from Norwich, NE., 11 miles. Pop. 1,213. Pharsalia is a small post village, and East Pharsalia a post-office.

PITCHER, formed from German and Lincklaen in 1827; from Albany 127, from Norwich, W., 17 miles. Pitcher is a small post village. Pop. 1,561.

PLYMOUTH, taken from Norwich in 1806; from Albany 107, from

Norwich, NW., 7 miles. Frankville, formerly known by the name of the French settlement, has 30 or 40 dwellings. Pop. 1,625.

PRESTON, taken from Norwich in 1806; from Albany 115, from Norwich, centrally distant W., 7 miles. Pop. 1,117. The Chenango river and canal pass through the SE. section of the town. Mason and Palmer's Corners are small villages.

SHERBURNE, taken from Genoa in 1806; from Albany 96, from Norwich, N., 11 miles. Pop. 2,791. The flats on the Chenango river, which flows through this town, are remarkably fertile. The portion of the town called "the Quarter," was early settled by 20 families from Connecticut, who bought one quarter of the township. They formed themselves into a religious society of the Presbyterian denomination before emigrating. They arrived on a Thursday, and by the succeeding Sabbath had erected a log meeting-house, in which they assembled for public worship; and not a single Sunday has since passed without divine service being performed. Sherburne, post village, has about 100 dwellings.

SMITHVILLE, taken from Greene in 1806; from Albany 131, from Norwich, SW., 20 miles. Pop. 1,762. Smithville is a village of about 40 or 50 dwellings.

SMYRNA was taken from Sherburne in 1808. Pop. 2,240. The first settler was Joseph Porter, who emigrated here in 1792. The first post-office was established in 1808. The village of Smyrna was incorporated in 1834; it is 101 miles from Albany and 11 NW. of Norwich, and contains about 60 dwellings.

CLINTON COUNTY.

CLINTON COUNTY lies on the western shore of Lake Champlain, at the northeastern extremity of the state, about 170 miles N. from Albany. Soon after the conquest of Canada, in 1759, the shores of Lake Champlain were visited by speculators in quest of pine and oak timber, but no permanent settlements were made until about the close of the revolution. Its greatest length N. and S. is $40\frac{1}{2}$ miles, greatest breadth 37 miles. The northern boundary being latitude 45°, indicates the rigors of a cold northern country. The natural advantages enjoyed by this county have been undervalued. Along the whole eastern border, adjoining the shore of Lake Champlain, a wide tract of land extends, moderately uneven or quite level, with a pretty strong inclination or depression eastward, averaging 8 miles in width of no inferior quality. It amply repays the labor of the husbandman. The western part is mountainous, but these mountains are covered with timber, and the county with rapid streams and mill sites, and abounds with the richest and best of iron ores, already extensively manufactured. The soil is of various qualities. On the broad belt of comparatively level land above noticed, it is principally a clayey with some tracts of a sandy loam. The streams supply a profusion of good natural sites for all sorts of hydraulic work. With these advantages, this county looks forward with confidence to increased sources of business and profit. About one fifth part is settled. Pop. 28,180. The county is divided into 10 towns.

AU SABLE, taken from Peru in 1839; distant 155 miles N. from Albany, centrally distant from Plattsburg 15 miles. Pop. 3,229. The village of Clintonville on the Au Sable river, partly in Clinton and partly in Essex counties, was incorporated in 1825. It contains 2 churches, 1 Presbyterian and 1 Methodist, 8 mercantile stores, upwards of 80 dwellings, and 730 inhabitants. It is 6 miles W. of Keesville, 17 from Elizabeth, and 18 from Plattsburg. The extensive works of the "Peru Iron Company" are located in this village. They have a forge of 18 fires, an extensive rolling-mill, a nail and a cable factory, furnace, &c. All these works were commenced when the place was comparatively new, by I. Aiken, Esq., but little was done till the organization of the company by the legislature about the year 1825.

BEEKMAN, taken from Plattsburg in 1820; distant from Albany 167, NW. from Plattsburg, 18 miles. The township is 6 miles in width, and stretches across the country 37 miles; the eastern part of the town is level or undulating, the western mountainous. Pop. 2,763.

BLACK BROOK, taken from Peru in 1839; from Albany 163, from Plattsburg, SW., 25 miles. Black Brook and Union Falls are small villages. Pop. 1,054.

CHAMPLAIN, organized in 1788; from Albany, N., 185 miles. Champlain village, on the left bank of the Chazy, 5 miles from Lake Champlain, has about 40 dwellings. Rouses Point, 23 miles N. from Plattsburg, Corbeau, and Perrysville, are small villages. Pop. 2,950.

CHAZY, taken from Champlain in 1804. Pop. 3,592. Chazy, 15 miles N. of Plattsburg on the state road from Albany to Canada, and West Chazy, are small villages. Chazy Landing, on Lake Champlain, is 3 miles from Chazy village.

ELLENBURG, taken from Mooers in 1830; from Plattsburg, NW., 25 miles. Pop. 1,164.

MOOERS, named in honor of Gen. B. Mooers, was taken from Champlain in 1804; from Plattsburg, NNW., 18 miles. Pop. 1,701. Mooers is a small post village on the Chazy river.

PERU, taken from Plattsburg and Willsburg in 1792; bounds since altered. Pop. 3,183. Peru, post village, 10 miles S. of Plattsburg and 4 from Lake Champlain, has 1 Presbyterian, 1 Methodist, and 1 Catholic church, 70 dwellings, and 360 inhabitants. Unionville and Port Jackson are post-offices. The first settler in Peru village was John Cochran, who came here in 1794. Rev. Hernan Garlick was one of the first ministers who preached in this section. It is said that he used to cross the lake, in a boat, and walk 30 miles to preach to a congregation.

CLINTON COUNTY.

The following is an account of the conflagration of the steamer Phœnix, which took place near here, on Lake Champlain, September 5, 1819.

The steamboat left Burlington for Plattsburg about midnight, and had proceeded by one o'clock in the morning as far as Providence island, when the alarm was given. The boat at this time was temporarily commanded by a son of the captain, Richard M. Sherman, a young man of twenty-two. "Amid the confusion, danger, and difficulties attendant on this terrible disaster, he displayed an energy and presence of mind, not only worthy of the highest praise, but which we might seek for in vain, even among those of riper years. To qualities like these, rightly directed as they were, was it owing that *not a person was lost on that fearful night.* In that burning vessel, at the dead of night, and three miles from the nearest land, was the safety of *every one* cared for, and ultimately secured, by the promptness, energy, and decision of this young commander."

Shortly after the fire was discovered, it raged with irresistible violence. "The passengers, roused by the alarm from their slumbers, and waking to a terrible sense of impending destruction, rushed in crowds upon the deck, and attempted to seize the small-boats. Here, however, they were met by young Sherman, who, having abandoned all hope of saving his boat, now thought only of saving his passengers, and stood by the gangway with a pistol in each hand, determined to prevent any person from jumping into the boats before they were properly lowered into the water, and prepared to receive their living freight. With the utmost coolness and presence of mind he superintended the necessary preparations, and, in a few minutes, the boats were lowered away, and the passengers received safely on board. They then shoved off, and pulled through the darkness for the distant shore. As soon as this was reached, and the passengers landed, the boats returned to the steamboat and took off the crew, and, as the captain supposed, every living soul except himself. But, shortly after the boats had left the second time, he discovered, under a settee, the chambermaid of the Phœnix, who, in her fright and confusion, had lost all consciousness. Lashing her to the plank which he had prepared for his own escape, this gallant captain launched her towards the shore; and was thus left alone with his vessel, now one burning pile. Having satisfied himself that no living thing remained on board his boat, and with the proud consciousness that he had saved every life intrusted to his care, he sprung from the burning wreck as it was about to sink beneath the waters, and, by the means of a settee, reached the shore in safety.—This is no exaggerated story. It is the simple narrative of one of the most heroic acts on record. We have only to add, that the captain who so faithfully and fearlessly discharged his duty on this trying occasion, is still (1840) in command of a noble boat on Lake Champlain, and is known to every traveller as Captain Sherman, of the steamboat Burlington."

The following description of this terrific scene was written by one of the passengers:—
"I awoke at the time of the alarm, but whether aroused by the cry of fire, the noise of feet trampling on deck, or by that restlessness common to persons who sleep in a strange place, with a mind filled with sorrow and anxiety, I am unable to tell. I thought I heard a faint cry of fire, and, after a short interval, it seemed to be renewed. But it came so weakly upon my ear, and seemed to be flung by so careless a voice, that I concluded it was an unmeaning sound uttered by some of the sailors in their sports on deck. Soon, however, a hasty footstep was heard passing through the cabin, but without a word being uttered. As I approached the top of the cabin stairs, an uncommon brilliancy at once dispelled all doubts. Instantly the flames and sparks began to meet my eyes, and the thought struck me that no other way of escape was left but to plunge half naked through the blaze into the water. One or two more steps assured me that this dreadful alternative was not yet arrived: I hastily stepped aft,—a lurid light illuminated every object beyond with the splendor of a noon-day sun; I fancied it was the torch of death, to point me and my fellow-travellers to the tomb. I saw no person on deck; but, on casting my eyes towards the boat which was still hanging on the larboard quarter, I perceived that she was filled, and that her stern-sheets were occupied with ladies. I flew to the gangway, and assisted in lowering the boat into the water. I then descended the steps, with an intention of entering the boat; but perceiving that she was loaded deep, and that there was a strong breeze and a high sea, I desisted. The painter was soon cut, and the boat dropped astern. I ascended the steps with the design of submitting myself to the water upon a plank; for I had great confidence in my skill in swimming, and I acted under an impression that the shore was only a few rods, certainly not half a mile distant. Judge of what would have been my astonishment, and probably also my fate, had I done as I contemplated; when the fact was, that the steamboat at this period was in the broadest part of Lake Champlain, and at least

three miles from any land. I had left the deck about two hours before, and this change had occurred in the mean time. I looked round upon the deck to find a suitable board, or something of sufficient buoyancy, that I could trust to amid such waves as I saw were running. There was nothing large enough to deserve such confidence; I looked aft over the taffrail, every thing there looked gloomy and forbidding; I cast my eyes forward, the wind was directly ahead, and the flames were forced, in the most terrific manner, towards the stern, threatening every thing in its range with instant destruction. I then thought if I could pass the middle of the boat, which seemed also to be the centre of the fire, I might find security in standing to windward on the bowsprit. I made the attempt. It was vain. The flames were an insurmountable barrier. I was obliged to return towards the stern. There was then no one in sight. I stepped over upon the starboard side of the quarterdeck. I thought all was gone with me. At that moment I saw a lady come up to the cabin door; she leaned against the side of it, and looked with a steadfast gaze and distracted air towards the flames; she turned and disappeared in the cabin. It was Mrs. Wilson, the poor unfortunate lady who, afterward, with the captain's assistance, as he informed me, committed herself, with many piercing shrieks and agonizing exclamations, to the treacherous support of a small bench, on the troublous bosom of the lake. I then looked over the starboard quarter to know whether the other boat was indeed gone. I had the happiness to see her; she seemed to be full, or nearly so; one or two passengers were standing on the lower steps of the accommodation ladder, apparently with the design of entering the boat when she came within reach. I was determined to enter her at all risks, and instantly leaped over the quarter and descended into her. I found her knocking under the counter, and in danger of foundering. The steam-vessel still continued to advance through the water: the waves dashed the boat with considerable violence against her, and most of those who had sought safety in the boat, being unacquainted with water scenes, were much alarmed, and by their ill-directed efforts were adding to the risk. Under these circumstances it became necessary to cut the fast, which was done, and the boat, and those that were in it, were instantly secure. All these incidents occurred in a shorter time than I have consumed in writing them. From the moment of my hearing the first alarm to that of leaving the steamboat, was not, I am satisfied, near ten minutes; I believe it was not five."

View of Plattsburg.

PLATTSBURG, organized in 1785. Pop. 6,397. Plattsburg, an incorporated village and county seat, is distant from New York 319, from Albany 164, from Whitehall 112, and from Ogdensburg, E., 120 miles. The accompanying view was taken on the eastern bank of the Saranac, about 30 rods above the bridge. The first steeple on the left is that of the Presbyterian church, the second the Methodist, the third the courthouse, the fourth the Episcopal, and the fifth the Catholic.

Besides the above-mentioned public buildings, there is an academy, the Clinton county bank, and about 300 buildings.

A settlement was commenced in this village " previous to the revolution, by a Count Vredenburg, a German nobleman, who, marrying a lady of the household of the queen of England, obtained a warrant for 30,000 acres of land, which he located on Cumberland bay, whither he removed, although he did not perfect his title by patent. He built a large house on the spot now occupied by the United States Hotel in Plattsburg, where he resided, as tradition reports, in extraordinary luxury, having his floors covered with carpets, and his windows shaded with damask curtains. When the revolutionary struggle commenced, he sent his family to Montreal, but remained some time after their departure, and then suddenly and mysteriously disappeared: his house, and a saw-mill he had built 3 miles above, on the Saranac, ' at Vredenburg's Falls,' being at the same time burned. He was generally supposed to have been robbed and murdered by some one covetous of the money and plate which he displayed.

" In July, of 1783, after the preliminaries of peace had been settled, Lieut. (since Maj. Gen.) Benjamin Mooers, adjutant of Hazen's regiment of Canadian and Nova Scotia refugees stationed at Newburg, on the Hudson, with 2 other officers and 8 men, left Fishkill Landing in a boat, and by way of the Hudson, the portage from Fort Edward to Lake George, and by that lake and Champlain, reached Point au Roche, 9 miles N. of Plattsburg, where he and his companions, on the 10th August, commenced the first permanent settlement of the county.

" A company, consisting of Judge Zephaniah Platt and others, formed soon after the war for the purchase of military warrants, located their warrants on Lake Champlain. In August, 1784, the judge. Capt. Nathaniel Platt, and Capt. Reeve, personally surveyed the Plattsburg patent on Cumberland bay, and laid off, among others, 10 lots of 100 acres each, to be given to the first 10 settlers who came on with families. Another tract of 100 acres was allotted as a donation to the first male child born on the patent. Messrs. Jacob Ferris, John Burke, Derrick Webb, Jabez Pettit, and Cyrenus Newcomb, were the first settlers on the '*gift lots*,' and Platt Newcomb, Esq., was the fortunate first born male, but not the first child born on the patent; Mrs. Henry Ostrander having previously given birth to a daughter, who intermarried with a Mr. Wilson, of Chateaugua, of Franklin county. From this period the settlement of the county steadily progressed.

" The first court was holden at Plattsburg on the 28th day of Oct., 1788, of which the following persons were officers: Charles Platt, *judge;* Peter Saily, Wm. McAuley, and Pliney Moore, *assistant justices;* Theodorus Platt, *justice;* Benjamin Mooers, *sheriff;* John Fautfreyde, *coroner;* Robert Paul, John Stevenson, Lott Elmore, Lewis Lezotte, and Jonathan Lynde, *constables. Grand jury,* Clement Goslin, Allen Smith, Abner Pomeroy, Jonas Allen, Joseph Shelden, Peter Payn, Moses Soper, Edward Everett, Elnathan Rogers, John Hoffnagle, Cyrenus Newcomb, Melchor Hoffnagle, Stephen Cuyler, Jacob Ferris, John Ransom, and John Cochran."—*Gordon's Gaz.*

Plattsburg is rendered memorable as the place of the victory of Com. McDonough and Gen. Macomb, over the British naval and land forces, in Sept. 1814. The following account of the military movements on the land are copied from the statements given by Maj. A. C. Flagg and Gen. St. J. B. L. Skinner, who both were actors in the scenes described.

"'On the 31st Aug., (says Maj. Flagg,) the advance of the British army under Gen. Brisbane entered Champlain, and encamped on the north side of the great Chazy river, and on the same day Maj. Gen. Mooers ordered out the militia of the counties of Clinton and Essex,' *en masse.* ' The regiment from Clinton co., under Lieut. Col. Miller, immediately assembled, and on the 2d Sept. took a position on the west road near the village of Chazy; and on the 3d, Gen. Wright, with such of his brigade as had arrived, occupied a position on the same road, about 8 miles in advance of this place. On the 4th, the enemy having brought up his main body to Champlain, took up his line of march for Plattsburg. The rifle corps, under Lieut. Col. Appling on the lake road, fell back as far as Dead creek, blocking up the road in such a manner as to impede the advance of the enemy as much as possible. The enemy advanced on the 5th, within a few miles of Col. Appling's position, and finding it too strong to attack, halted, and caused a road to be made west into the Beekmantown road, in which the light brigade under Gen. Powers advanced; and on the morning of the 6th, about 7 o'clock, attacked the militia, which had at this time increased to nearly 700, under Gen. Mooers; and a small detachment of regulars under Maj. Wool, about 7 miles from this place. After the first fire, a considerable part of the militia broke and fled in every direction. Many, however, manfully stood their ground, and with the small corps of Maj. Wool, bravely contested the ground against five times their number, falling back gradually, and occupying the fences on each side of the road, till they arrived within a mile of the town, when they were reinforced by two pieces of artillery under Capt. Leonard; and our troops occupying a strong position behind a stone wall, for some time stopped the progress of the enemy.'

" At this point, one of the finest specimens of discipline ever exhibited, was shown by the British troops on the occasion of the opening Capt. Leonard's battery upon them. The company to which I was attached, formed a part of the left flank of our little army, and was on the rise of ground west of the road leading from Mr. Halsey's corner to Isaac C. Platt's, and about midway between the artillery and the head of the British column; and the whole scene was open to our view. Here, (at Halsey's corner,) was a battery of two field-pieces, so perfectly masked by a party of the infantry, that the enemy probably was not aware of it, until it opened upon him. There a dense column of men, with a front equal to the width of the road, and extending nearly half a mile in length, pressing on with a buoyancy and determination of spirit, betokening an expectation that they would be permitted to walk into our works without much opposition. How sad the disappointment to the victorious veterans of so many bloody fields of Europe! So perfect was the motion of the troops in marching, that they seemed a great mass of living matter moved by some invisible machinery. Yet I can now almost fancy we could hear them cracking their jokes, and each claiming for himself the honor of being the first to make a lodgment in the Yankee forts; when suddenly, with the noise of thunder, the sound of a cannon came booming through the air. It sent forth a round shot which took effect near the centre of the front platoon, about breast high, and ploughed its way through, sweeping all before it, the whole length of the column; opening a space apparently several feet wide, which, however, was immediately closed, as if by magic; and on the column pressed as if nothing had happened. A second shot was fired with the like effect, and similar consequences; but when the third discharge came, with a shower of grape shot, there was a momentary confusion. Immediately, however, the charge was sounded by some dozen British bugles; which through the clear and bland atmosphere of a bright September morning, was the most thrilling and spirit-stirring sound that could greet a soldier's ears. In an instant of time, the men forming the advance of the column had thrown their knapsacks on either side the road, and bringing their pieces to the charge, advanced in double quick time upon our miniature battery.

"' Our troops being at length compelled to retire, contested every inch of ground, until they reached the south bank of the Saranac, where the enemy attempted to pursue them, but was repulsed with loss. The loss of the British in this skirmish, was Col. Wellington, and a Lieut. of the 3d Buffs, and two Lieuts. of the 58th, killed; and one Capt. and one Lieut. of the 58th light company wounded, together with about 100 privates killed and wounded, while that on our part did not exceed 25. The corps of riflemen under Col. Appling, and detachment under Capt. Sproul, fell back from their position at Dead creek in time to join the militia and regulars just before they entered the village, and fought with their accustomed bravery. The British got possession of that part of the village north of the Saranac about 11 o'clock, but the incessant and well-directed fire of our artillery and musketry from the forts and opposite banks, compelled them to retire before night beyond the reach of our guns.' The bridge in the village was defended during this day by Capt. Martin I. Aikin's company* of volunteers, who were stationed in the saw-mill on the south bank of the river for that purpose. The enemy arrived towards night with his heavy artillery and baggage on the lake road, and crossed the beach, where he met with a warm reception from our row-galleys; and it is believed, suffered a heavy loss in killed and wounded. On our side, Lieut. Duncan of the navy lost an arm by a rocket, and 3 or 4 men were killed by the enemy's artillery. The enemy encamped on the ridge west of the town, his right near the river, and occupying an extent of nearly 3 miles, his left resting on the lake about a mile north of the village. From the 6th until the morning of the 11th, an almost continual skirmishing was kept up between the enemy's pickets and our militia and volunteers stationed on the river, and in the mean time both armies were busily engaged—ours in strengthening the works of the forts, and that of the enemy in erecting batteries, collecting ladders, bringing up his heavy ordnance, and making other preparations for attacking the forts. On the morning of the 7th, a body of the enemy under Capt. Noadie, attempted to cross at the upper bridge about 7 miles west of the village, but were met by Capt. Vaughn's company of about 25 men, and compelled to retire with the loss of two killed, and several wounded. On the morning of the 11th, the enemy's fleet came round the Head with a tight breeze from the north, and attacked ours which lay at anchor in Cumberland bay, two miles from shore east of the fort.

" 'The enemy commenced a simultaneous bombardment of our works from 7 batteries, from which several hundred shells and rockets were discharged, which did us very little injury; and our artillery had nearly succeeded in silencing them all before the contest on the lake was decided.

" 'The enemy attempted at the same time to throw his main body in the rear of the fort, by crossing the river 3 miles west of the town, near the site of Pike's cantonment. He succeeded in crossing, after a brave resistance by the Essex militia and a few of the Vermont volunteers, in all about 350, stationed at that place, who retired back a mile and a half from the river, continually pouring in upon them an incessant fire from behind every tree, until Lieut. Sumpter brought up a piece of artillery to their support, when the enemy commenced a precipitate retreat.

" 'The Vermont volunteers, who had hastened to the scene of action on the first alarm, fell upon the enemy's left flank, and succeeded in making many prisoners, including 3 officers.

" 'Had the British remained on the south side of the river 30 minutes longer, he must have lost nearly the whole detachment that crossed. Our loss in this affair was five killed and eight or ten wounded, some mortally.

" 'Immediately on ascertaining the loss of the fleet, Sir George Prevost ordered preparations to be made for the retreat of the army, and set off himself, with a small escort, for Canada, a little after noon. The main body of the enemy, with the artillery and baggage, were taken off in the afternoon, and the rear guard, consisting of the light brigade, started at daybreak and made a precipitate retreat; leaving their wounded and a large quantity of provisions, fixed ammunition, shot, shells, and other public stores, in the different places of deposit about their camp. They were pursued some distance by our troops, and many prisoners taken; but owing to the very heavy and incessant rain, we were compelled to return. The enemy lost upon land more than 1,000 men, in killed, wounded, prisoners, and deserters, while our aggregate loss did not exceed 150.' "

The following account of the naval action is from *"Perkins' History of the late War."*

" The American fleet, under Commodore McDonough, lay at anchor in the bay, on the right flank of the American lines, and two miles distant. Great exertions had been made

---

* "This company was composed of young men and boys of the village, most of whom were not subject to military duty, who volunteered after the militia had gone out on the Chazy road, offered their services to Gen. Macomb, who accepted their offer, armed the company with rifles, and ordered them to repair to the head-quarters of Gen. Mooers, and report for duty." Three only, it is said, of the members of this corps were over 18 years of age.

by both parties to produce a superior naval force on this lake; the Americans at Otter creek, and the British at the Isle aux Noix. On comparing their relative strength on the 11th of September, the American fleet consisted of the Saratoga, flag-ship, mounting 26 guns; Eagle, 20 guns; Ticonderoga, 17 guns; Preble, 7 guns; 6 galleys, of 2 guns each, 12 guns; four, of one, 4 guns; making in the whole, 86 guns; and 820 men. The British fleet consisted of the frigate Confiance, flag-ship, mounting 39 guns; Linnet, 16 guns; Cherub, 11 guns; Finch, 11 guns; five galleys, of 2 guns each, 10 guns; eight, of one, 8 guns; making in the whole 95 guns, and 1,020 men.

"The British land forces employed themselves from the 7th to the 11th, in bringing up their heavy artillery, and strengthening their works on the north bank of the Saranac. Their fortified encampment was on a ridge a little to the west of the town, their right near the river, and their left resting on the lake, 1 mile in the rear of the village. Having determined on a simultaneous attack by land and water, they lay in this position on the morning of the 11th, waiting the approach of their fleet. At 8 o'clock, the wished-for ships appeared under easy sail, moving round Cumberland head; and were hailed with joyous acclamations. At 9, they anchored within 300 yards of the American squadron in line of battle; the Confiance opposed to the Saratoga, the Linnet to the Eagle; 13 British galleys to the Ticonderoga, Preble, and a division of the American galleys. The Cherub assisting the Confiance and Linnet, and the Finch aiding the galleys. In this position, the weather being perfectly clear and calm, and the bay smooth, the whole force on both sides became at once engaged.* At an hour and a half after the commencement of the action, the starboard guns of the Saratoga were nearly all dismantled. The commandant ordered a stern anchor to be dropped, and the bower cable cut, by means of which the ship rounded to, and presented a fresh broadside to her enemy. The Confiance attempted the same operation and failed. This was attended with such powerful effects, that she was obliged to surrender in a few minutes. The whole broadside of the Saratoga was then brought to bear on the Linnet, and in 15 minutes she followed the example of her flag-ship. One of the British sloops struck to the Eagle; 3 galleys were sunk, and the rest made off; no ship in the fleet being in a condition to follow them, they escaped down the lake. There was no mast standing in either squadron, at the close of the action, to which a sail could be attached. The Saratoga received 55 round shot in her hull, and the Confiance 105. The action lasted without any cessation, on a smooth sea, at close quarters, 2 hours and 20 minutes. In the American squadron 52 were killed, and 58 wounded. In the British, 84 were killed, and 110 wounded. Among the slain was the British commandant, Com. Downie. This engagement was in full view of both armies, and of numerous spectators collected on the heights, bordering on the bay, to witness the scene. It was viewed by the inhabitants with trembling anxiety, as success on the part of the British would have opened to them an easy passage into the heart of the country, and exposed a numerous population on the borders of the lake to British ravages. When the flag of the Confiance was struck, the shores resounded with the acclamations of the American troops and citizens. The British, when they saw their fleet completely conquered, were dispirited and confounded."

"A short distance from the village, are the ruins of the cantonment and breastworks occupied by Gen. Macomb and his troops. A mile north, is shown the house held by Gen. Prevost, as his head-quarters, during the siege; between which and the village the marks of cannon-shot on the trees and other objects are still visible. Further onward about 5 miles, on a hill overlooking the village of Beekmantown, is the spot where a sanguinary engagement took place between the American and British troops, which resulted in the death of the British Col. Wellington and several men of both armies."—*Gordon's Gaz.*

The following inscriptions were copied from monuments in the graveyard in Plattsburg.

"In memory of GEN. BENJAMIN MOOERS, who died Feb. 20, 1838. He served as lieutenant and adjutant during the revolutionary war. He commanded the militia at the battle

---

* "I will mention one circumstance for the purpose of showing the frame of mind in which the brave McDonough entered the battle, and in whom he put his trust for success. After the enemy's fleet hove in sight, the men of his ship were assembled on the quarter-deck, when he kneeled down, and in humble, and fervent prayer, commended himself, his men, and the cause in which they were engaged, to the God of Battles, and arose from that posture, with a calmness and serenity depicted on his brow, which showed he had received comfort and assurance from above. One other little incident, and I will proceed with my subject. During the hottest part of the battle, the hen-coop was shot away, when a cock escaped and flew up into the rigging, flapped his wings, and crowed most manfully! The sailors considered this as a sure omen of success, and, cheering from one end of the ship to the other, went to their work of dealing death to the enemy with redoubled exertion. The cock remained in the rigging during the whole of the engagement, ever and anon cheering the men on to a greater exertion by his clear shrill voice."—*Gen. Skinner's account of the Battle of Plattsburg.*

of Plattsburg, Sept. 11th, 1814. He was the first settler in this county who remained here through life. He was the first sheriff of the county, and for 30 years county treasurer. He repeatedly represented this section of country in the assembly and senate of the state, and discharged the important duties which devolved upon him as a citizen, a soldier, and a Christian, with fidelity to his country, and integrity to his God."

Grave of Commodore Downie at Plattsburg.

"Sacred to the memory of GEORGE DOWNIE, ESQ., a post-captain in the British navy, who gloriously fell on board his B. M. S. Confiance, while leading the vessels under his command to the attack of the American Flotilla, at anchor in Cumberland Bay, off Plattsburg, on the 11th of Sept., 1814."

"To mark the spot where the remains of a gallant officer and sincere friend were honorably interred, this stone has been erected by his affectionate sister-in-law, Mary Downie."

SARANAC, taken from Plattsburg in 1834; from Albany, N., 145 miles. Pop. 1,464. Redford, 21 miles southwesterly from Plattsburg, has about 60 dwellings. Here are the extensive works of the Redford Crown Glass Company. Bakersville is a small village about 5 miles NE. from Redford.

COLUMBIA COUNTY.

COLUMBIA COUNTY, taken from Albany in 1786: its greatest length on the E. line 36, medium breadth 18 miles. Centrally distant N. from New York 125, from Albany, SE., 34 miles. The surface of the county is considerably diversified, though no part can be called mountainous. Ranges of small hillocks are interspersed with extensive plains or valleys, and much of rich alluvion. There are some excellent lands, and much of the larger portion may be, by judicious culture, rendered highly productive. Nature, in the abundant beds of lime, has furnished the means, as if by a special providence, of tempering the cold and ungrateful constituents of the clay; and in many places the lime in the form of marl does not require burning to become a stimulant. Scarce any portion of the state is better adapted to the raising of sheep, and the profits from this source, already great, are yearly increasing. This county is famed for the quantity and quality of its Indian corn Lead and iron ore are found in this county. It is divided into 19 towns. Pop. 44,237.

ANCRAM, originally named Gallatin, and taken from Livingston in 1803; from Albany, S., 51, centrally distant S. E. from Hudson 21 miles. Pop. 1,769. The Ancram Iron Works operate quite extensively in castings and bar iron from the celebrated ore of Salisbury, in Connecticut. Ancram is a small village near the W. line of the town.

AUSTERLITZ, taken from Hillsdale, Canaan, and Chatham, in 1818; surface hilly and mountainous. Pop. 2,090. Spencertown, 15 miles NE. of Hudson, and Green River, are small villages.

CANAAN, organized in 1788; bounds since altered. Canaan Corners 24, Canaan 18 miles NE. from Hudson, and Red Rock are small settlements. The surface of the town is mountainous, with some fertile valleys. Pop. 1,957.

CHATHAM, taken from Canaan and Kinderhook in 1795. Pop. 3,650. Chatham Four Corners, on the Albany and Hartford and the Hudson and New Lebanon roads, is a small settlement, 20 miles SE. of Albany and 14 NE. from Hudson. Chatham, North Chatham, New Concord, and ... ... are post-offices.

CLAVERACK, organized in 1788. Pop. 3,053. This name is derived from Klauver-rack literally Clover-reach; so called in its early settlement from the immense fields of clover which abounded here. Claverack post village, 4 miles E. of Hudson, was the seat of justice for the county, from 1787 to 1806, when it was removed to Hudson. It is a beautiful village, and contains about 60 dwellings. Churchtown, Smoky Hollow, and Centreville are small villages. This country was settled at a very early period by the Dutch. The following extracts from ancient newspapers, show that difficulties between the landlords and tenants are not confined to our time.

To the printer of the New York Gazette, dated May 20th, 1766.

Sir,—*For many months* past we have heard a great deal of the uneasiness and riotous behavior of the tenants upon several of the large manors of this government. And as these disorders have risen to a very great and dangerous height, and the causes of them variously spoken of, and not well understood, (some imputing the fault to the landlords, and others the tenants,) it is surprising that more care has not been taken to set the whole affair in a clearer light; which, besides that it might tend to an amicable settlement of the difference, would dispose the public to join in discountenancing the blameable party, and obtain redress for the injured. On the one hand, it seems strange that the landlords should draw upon themselves so much trouble and vexation, so much ill-will and opposition from their tenants, unless the matters they insist on are just and reasonable, and of very great importance. On the other hand, it seems equally strange that the tenants should take such desperate steps, and hazard the ruin of their families, the loss of property, and even life itself, unless their grievances are of the most insupportable kind, and such as it is worse than death to bear. If these matters were explained by an impartial narrative, it would, I believe, do service to the parties and oblige the public, &c.   A. B.

Extracts from letters from Claverack, near Albany, dated June 27th, 1766.

" For some months a mob has frequently assembled and ranged the eastern part of the manor of Rensselaer. Last week they appeared at Mr. Livingston's with some proposals to him; but he being from home, they returned to Mr. Rensselaer's son's, about two miles from Claverack, where, not finding him at home, they used some insulting words, and left a message for Mr. Rensselaer, that if he did not meet them next day at their rendezvous, they would come to him. On the 26th, the sheriff of Albany, with 150 men under his command, went to disperse the rioters, who were assembled it is supposed to the number of 60 in a house on the manor. On the sheriff's advancing to the house they fired upon him, and shot off his hat and wig, but he escaped unhurt—many shots were exchanged on both sides. Of the militia, Mr. Cornelius Tenbrook, of Claverack, was killed, and seven wounded. Of the rioters, three were killed (two of whom were the ringleaders) and many wounded, among whom was Capt. Noble (one of the chief instigators) in the back. The rioters retreated to Capt. Noble's house, where they formed a breastwork, and did not quit the house till the sheriff's party left the place. He afterward went to Poughkeepsie to get assistance from the regulars to disperse the whole; but the regulars were gone to Pendergraft's house, on Philip's Patent, in Dutchess county.

"We hear from Fredericksburg, in Dutchess county, that on Saturday last, as a party of regulars stationed there, under the command of Major Brown, were crossing a bridge, they were met by about 30 of the rioters, who were going to join Pendergraft, their chief's party—a skirmish ensued, whereon two of the regulars were wounded, and it is supposed a much greater number of the rioters, who generally dismounted and fled to the cornfields and bushes, leaving some of their horses and guns, which were taken, and one prisoner. Several more were taken that night. The next evening they sent a flag of truce with 50 followers, who were all lodged in the meeting-house, and the next day several more parties came in. Pendergraft's wife was gone to persuade her husband to accept of the governor's mercy, as were many more wives of the rioters. We hear of no lives lost. It was reported that 300 of the rioters lodged at Quaker Hill, intending to attack the regulars on the 13th ult." [How many uneasy moments must such of these *sensible* regulars feel, who are persuaded that they are employed to support IN EQUITY?]

From the New York Gazette, dated November 10th, 1768.

"On Saturday last, the great cause between the Crown and Mr. John Van Rensselaer was ended. It was tried by a struck jury, and came on before the Hon. Justice Jones, on Tuesday the 25th of October, and continued (with evening adjournments by the consent of parties) until the 5th inst. The suit was for intrusion upon the crown lands, to try the limits of that part of the old Rensselaerwick manor and estate called Claverack. It was promoted by certain reduced officers upon a supposition that there was a great unpatented vacancy between the manor of Rensselaerwick and Livingston, and the patents of Kinderhook and Westenhook, and carried on at the expense of the crown. There never was a trial in this colony so solemn, important, and lengthy. The counsel spent about eleven hours in summing up the evidence: Mr. Attorney General, Mr. Mayor, Mr. Duane, and Mr. Kissam, were of the counsel for the crown; and Mr. Smith, jr., Mr. Scott, and Mr Thomas Smith conducted the defence. The judge was clear in his charge upon the construction of the old patent in the Rensselaer family, and the jury in two hours agreed on their verdict for the defendant. . . . . This estate was attached upon the same principles, by certain petitioners a few years ago; but their petitions were dismissed by the governor and council, in the administration of Gen. Monckton, on the 20th October, 1762."

CLERMONT, organized in 1788; from Albany, S., 43 miles. Pop. 1,231. Clermont, 12 miles S. of Hudson, is a small post village. It was the ancient seat of the Livingston family, and the residence of Chancellor Livingston, the well-known patron of Fulton, who named his first American steamboat the "Clermont." The following biographical sketch is extracted from the Encyclopædia Americana.

"Robert R. Livingston, an eminent American politician, was born in the city of New York, November 27th, 1746. He was educated at King's College, and graduated in 1765. He studied and practised law in that city with great success. Near the commencement of the American revolution he lost the office of recorder, on account of his attachment to liberty, and was elected to the first general congress of the colonies; was one of the committee appointed to prepare the Declaration of Independence; in 1780, was appointed secretary of foreign affairs; and throughout the war of the revolution, signalized himself by his zeal and efficiency in the revolutionary cause. At the adoption of the constitution of New York, he was appointed chancellor, which office he held until he went, in 1801, to France, as minister plenipotentiary, appointed by President Jefferson. He was received by Napoleon Bonaparte, then first consul, with marked respect and cordiality, and during a residence of several years in the French capital, the chancellor appeared to be the favorite foreign envoy. He conducted, with the aid of Mr. Monroe, the negotiation which ended in the cession of Louisiana to the United States, took leave of the first consul, (1804,) and made an extensive tour on the continent of Europe. On his return from Paris, Napoleon, then emperor, presented to him a splendid snuff-box, with a miniature likeness of himself, (Napoleon,) painted by the celebrated Isabey. It was in Paris that he formed a friendship and close personal intimacy with Robert Fulton, whom he materially assisted with counsel and money, to mature his plan of steam navigation. In 1805, Mr. Livingston returned to the United States, and thenceforward employed himself in promoting the arts and agriculture. He introduced into the state of New York the use of gypsum, and the Merino race of sheep. He was president of the New York Academy of fine arts, of which he was a chief founder. He died March 26th, 1813, with the reputation of an able statesman, a learned lawyer, and a most useful citizen."

COPAKE, taken from Taghkanic in 1824; from Albany, S., 57 miles; from Hudson, SE., 16 miles. The town is part of the Livingston manor. Pop. 1,505. The eastern part of this township is mountainous; on the western border is Copake lake, which covers about 600 acres, and embosoms an island of about 20 acres, which has been the residence of members of the Livingston family.

GALLATIN, taken from Ancram in 1830; from Hudson, SE., 15 miles. Pop. 1,645.

GERMANTOWN, organized in 1788; from Albany, S., 39, and from Hudson, S., 12 miles: commonly known by the name of the German or East Camp. Pop. 968. There are three landings on the Hudson. In June, 1710, seventy of the palatines sent out by Queen Anne settled on this spot, then part of Livingston manor. In 1725, pursuant to an arrangement between George I. and the proprietor. this tract was granted by letters patent to the persons belonging to East Camp, as the settlement was called, in trust to appropriate 40 acres for the use of a church and school, and to divide the rest equally among the inhabitants. The settlement first commenced by three small lodges, or dorfs, the German word for village, named respectively after the superintendent of each, as Weiser's Dorf, Kneiskerns Dorf, &c.

GHENT, taken from Claverack, Kinderhook, and Chatham in 1818. Population 2,557. Ghent is a small village, 10 miles NE. of Hudson.

GREENPORT, recently formed from Hudson. Pop. 1158.

HILLSDALE was organized in 1788; centrally distant 14 miles E. of Hudson. Pop. 3,470. Green river and Hillsdale are post-offices. Unhappy disputes relative to titles to land in this town, long agitated the inhabitants, and several lives were lost in the controversy before it was finally settled by arbitration.

HUDSON, the capital of Columbia county, is situated on the E. bank of Hudson river, 116 miles from New York, 29 from Albany, and 28 from West Stockbridge, Mass. Lat. 42° 14′ N., long. 14′ E. from New York. The city is finely situated on an elevation of about 50 feet above the Hudson, the western part of which is a bold cliff or promontory projecting into the river, more than 60 feet high. The principal part of the city is built on a street one mile long, extending in a straight line from the foot of Prospect Hill, to the promenade on the extremity of the cliff. Nearly all the streets intersect each other at right angles, except near the river, where they conform

SOUTH EASTERN VIEW OF HUDSON CITY, N. Y., FROM ACADEMY, OR PROSPECT HILL.

The principal street in Hudson, one mile in length, is seen in the central part of the engraving. The village of Athens appears on the opposite bank of the Hudson; the Cattskill mountains are seen in the extreme distance, on the left.

COLUMBIA COUNTY. 117

to the shape of the ground. The promenade at the western extremity, and fronting the principal street, commands a beautiful view of the river, the village of Athens opposite, the country beyond, and the towering Catskill mountains. The bay south of the city is locked in by a lofty eminence, anciently termed *Rorabuck*, now called *Mount Merino*, in consequence of there being a sheep farm established here some years since. The city contains 5 churches—1 Presbyterian, 1 Episcopal, 1 Baptist, 1 Methodist, and 1 Universalist. There is an academy, a number of classical schools, the Hudson Lunatic Asylum, a private hospital for the reception and cure of lunatics, 1 bank, and 3 printing-offices. An elegant courthouse has been recently erected. Water is brought in subterranean pipes from the foot of Becraft's mountain for the use of the city. Pop. 5,671.

Hudson was founded in 1783, by enterprising men of property from Rhode Island and Nantucket, of the names of Jenkins, Paddock, Barnard, Coffin, Thurston, Greene, Minturn, Lawrence, and others, in all thirty persons. About twenty of this company, in the early part of 1783, sailed up the Hudson to find some navigable situation on which to commence a new settlement. They selected and purchased the site on which the city now stands, which at that time was occupied as a farm, with a single store-house on the bank of the river. In the fall of this year, two families arrived and commenced a settlement. In the spring of 1784, the other proprietors arrived, bringing with them several vessels; they were soon followed by other emigrants from the eastward. Between the spring of 1784 and that of 1786, there were 150 dwelling-houses erected, besides wharves, warehouses, shops, barns, &c., and several works connected with manufactures; and the population had increased to 1,500 persons. In 1795, Mr. Ashbel Stoddard removed from Connecticut, established a printing-office, and issued a weekly paper, the "Hudson Gazette."

Hudson was incorporated a city in 1785. At this period about *twenty-five* vessels were owned in the place, which were mostly employed in the West India trade; a few were engaged in the whale and seal fishery, which was carried on with considerable success, and Hudson rapidly increased in wealth and population. During the revolutionary struggle in France, and the long protracted war in Europe, such was the demand for neutral vessels, and such the high prices of freight, that the vessels owned here were engaged in the carrying trade. This trade was not long enjoyed, for British orders in council and French decrees swept many of them from their owners. Other losses followed by shipwreck, and the embargo, non-intercourse, and the war which succeeded, almost finished the prosperity of Hudson. The city was a port of entry till 1815. The immense losses at sea produced much embarrassment and many failures, and kept the place in a state of depression for a considerable period. From this depression it is gradually and steadily advancing. The Hudson and Berkshire railroad proceeds from this city, across the route of the New York and Albany railroad, 31 miles to the west line of Massachusetts at West Stockbridge, whence it is continued for two miles, till it unites with the great western railroad of that state.

The following inscriptions are copied from monuments in the graveyard in this place:

"To the memory of WILLIAM HOWARD ALLEN, lieutenant in the U. S. Navy, who was killed in the act of boarding a piratical schooner on the coast of Cuba, near Matanzas, on the 9th of November, 1822, Æ 32.—William Howard Allen. His remains, first buried at Matanzas, were removed to this city by the U. S. government, and interred under the direction of the Common Council of this city, beneath this marble erected to his honor by the citizens of his native place, 1833. William Howard Allen was born in the city of Hudson, July 8, 1790; appointed a midshipman in 1801, and a lieutenant in 1811; took a conspicuous part in the engagement between the Argus and Pelican in 1813, and was killed while in the command of the U. S. schooner Alligator.

"Pride of his country's banded chivalry,
His fame their hope, his name their battle cry,
He lived as mothers wish their sons to live,
He died, as fathers wish their sons to die."

Allen's Monument.

"In memory of JOHN MILTON MANN, M. D., who was drowned crossing the Hudson from this city to Athens, August 24, A. D. 1809, aged 43 years. This monument is erected as a token of their love by his bereaved wife and children. Doctor Mann was born in Attlebury, Massachussetts; he was educated at Brown's University in Providence, Rhode Island; and came to reside in Hudson, A. D. 1800. This city is indebted to him for the introduction of vaccine innoculation, though here as elsewhere, the philanthropic enterprise was obliged to contend against prejudice and misrepresentation. The Common Council of Hudson, of which body he was a member, voted that they would attend his funeral and wear crape on the left arm thirty days on account of their respect for his character, and their regret for his loss. Here are laid the remains of one whom society respected and his kindred loved. He was a wise scholar, a skilful physician, a kind husband and father, and a sincere Christian. Deeply is he bewailed. Few men of his time possessed a mind more happily turned to the acquisition of science, or exhibited more perspicuously patience and vigor, than Doctor Mann. Alas! just as his faculties had become mature, and society had learned their value—just when in the prime of bodily and mental manhood, with his honors thickening upon him, death struck him down. But let not infidel grief regard his mind as having been cultivated or his knowledge accumulated in vain; for so he was enabled to enter the future life with enlarged capacities of enjoyment, with more worthy views of his own nature and destiny, with a clearer apprehension of his heavenly FATHER's will, and with added incitement to constant obedience. We will not mourn, then, as they who have no hope."

KINDERHOOK was organized in 1788; the surface of the town is diversified, soil gravelly clay of sandy loam, and generally well cultivated. Pop. 3,512. This place was settled at an early period by some Dutch and Swedish families. Its name is of curious origin, and signifies *children's corner*, or point; so called from the number of children belonging to a Swedish family that anciently lived on a point of land about half a mile above the present upper landing. Several of their descendants are now living of the fourth and fifth generation. Valatie is a large manufacturing village in this town, 14 miles N. of Hudson, at the junction of the Valatie and Kinderhook creeks. It contains 1 Presbyterian, 1 Methodist, and 1 Lutheran church, 8 mercantile stores, 300 dwellings, and 1,700 inhabitants. Kinderhook village on the old post-road to Albany, 12 N. of Hudson, 5 E. from the river, and 20 miles S. from Albany, is finely situated on a beautiful level plain. Many of the dwellings have spacious yards and gardens decorated with shrubbery; and groves of trees interspersed here and there give this place a pleasing aspect. There are several churcnes, an academy in high repute, and about 90 dwellings.

Birthplace of President Van Buren, Kinderhook.

The above is a representation of the house in which Martin Van Buren, recently president of the United States, was born. It is situated about 60 rods E. of the central part of the village, near the banks of the creek. It was at that time occupied by his father, Abraham Van Buren, as a tavern, and the town meetings of former days were held within its walls. Originally it had a gable roof with two attic windows, in Dutch style; and the small building seen on the right stood in the rear and was used as a kitchen. On a beam in the cellar, cut rudely with a penknife, are the initials, M. V. B; a memento of the president's youthful days.

The following epitaph of president Van Buren's brother was copied from a tablet in the new graveyard, about three fourths of a mile N. of the village.

"In memory of ABRAHAM A. VAN BUREN, who died at Hudson, Oct. 30th, 1836, in the 49th year of his age. He had been for many years, and was at the time of his death, surrogate of the county of Columbia; and by his talents and integrity, secured universal respect and esteem. Peace be to his ashes."

LIVINGSTON was organized in 1788. Glenco, 9 miles SE. from Hudson, and Johnstown, are small villages. Pop. 2,534.

"Livingston manor or lordship, originally contained that tract which now composes the towns of Livingston, Taghkanic, Copake, Ancram, Gallatin, Clermont, and Germantown It was granted by the English government, while America was a colony, to Robert Livingston, who had been some years settled in this country and who was a member of the British king's council. This consisted of several distinct grants made in the years 1684, 1685, and 1686. In 1710, agreeable to an arrangement with Queen Anne, the proprietor conveyed a tract containing 6,000 acres adjoining the Hudson from the SE. part of the manor, to a number of Palatines, who had served in her armies, and were now driven from Germany by the French army. This tract constituted the township of Germantown. In 1714 a new grant, or grant and confirmation, was made of the manor to the original proprietor, and erected into a lordship, with the usual privileges and royalties at that day annexed to baronies. He was authorized to constitute a Court Baron, and appoint the officers thereof; and the manor tenants were entitled to elect a member to the legislative assembly for the manor, and without losing their votes in the county elections, which privilege they exercised until the revolution."

NEW LEBANON was taken from Canaan in 1818. Lebanon Springs village is 25 miles from Albany, 32 NE. from Hudson. There are here about 35 dwellings, and several taverns for the accommodation of visiters at the spring. The spring is ten feet in diameter and four deep, and discharges water sufficient to turn several mills near its source. The water is tasteless, inodorous, and soft, and is deemed beneficial in internal obstructions, salt-rheum, and cutaneous affections generally. The place is much resorted to for health and amusement. The surrounding country is salubrious and picturesque. New Lebanon is a small settlement, one mile and a half SE. of the spring.

Shaker Buildings in New Lebanon.

New Lebanon, Shaker village, called by its inhabitants the village of the "*Millennial Church,*" is two and a half miles S. of the spring, on the western side of the Taghkanic mountain, and contains about six hundred inhabitants. The annexed view shows one of their dwellings (containing a *family* of 150 persons,) and their meeting-house, which was erected in 1823. This place of worship is somewhat singular in its construction. It is eighty feet long by sixty-five wide, all in one room, without beams or pillars, having a domical roof covered with tin; and a porch thirty-four by twenty-seven feet, roofed and covered the same way. The building is of wood, but the foundation and flights of steps are of marble.

"This edifice," says a visiter, " stands in a beautiful grass plat, in the centre of the village. There are no seats in the house, except for spectators of their worship. Their stone walls and other fences are constructed with the utmost regularity and precision, and their gate-posts are of massive marble columns, of many tons weight. They manufacture a great variety of articles for sale, which are remarkable for their neatness and durability; and, in short, their farms, their gardens, their manufactories, and houses, all exhibit the pleasing effects of industry and rural economy. Indeed, they are one independent community;—their property is all held in common, and 'nowhere,' says Professor Silliman, 'in any community, can the moralist, the philosopher, or the statesman, see such a demonstration of the power of industry and economy.' They cheerfully pay their proportion of the public taxes, and share all the burdens of government except the bearing of arms, which they deem to be unlawful. They never ask charity for any purpose, but always have hands and hearts to give. We were conducted through the whole establishment in every department. Their internal domestic arrangement is excellent. Their standing motto seems to be, to save time and labor, and all their various machines and utensils are constructed to this end. We visited their extensive dairy, their washing-house, mills and manufactories, all of which evinced the most consummate skill and nicety. We also visited their school, consisting of about one hundred hearty, rosy-cheeked, and contented children, from eight to fifteen years of age. They underwent a very creditable examination in the various branches of astronomy, grammar, reading, spelling, arithmetic, &c., and gave us the most satisfactory proof that they are not trained up in ignorance. . . . . As far as our observation extended, they are as willing to let others think for themselves, as they are to cherish their own peculiarities; and, surely, if they are tolerant we should not be intolerant. They are indeed a most singular people, but they have many, very many, excellent qualities. They are plain in their deportment and manners, close though honest in their dealings, but kind, benevolent, and hospitable; and they remember and treasure up every kindness shown to them. In short, they are inoffensive, quiet, and valuable citizens; and notwithstanding the idle, and even abominable stories that have been put forth against them, after close observation for many years past, it is our deliberate conviction that among themselves they strictly live up to their professions, and that their conduct and morals are irreproachable."*

The society own about 2,000 acres of land in this town, and about half as much more in Hancock, Mass., the adjoining town. Within a few years after "Mother Ann," as she is usually called, made an establishment at Neskayuna, (see *Watervliet, p. 55,*) another was begun at New Lebanon, which is now the principal Shaker establishment in the state. Their religious tenets must, of course, necessarily affect the order of their societies, by producing an entire separation of the men from the women.

The leading characteristic in the worship of this people, is their dancing. This they describe as the involuntary result of the exhilirating and overpowering delight received through the outpouring of divine grace upon their hearts. The evolutions and changes in the dance, by constant practice, become as precisely correct as the manœuvres of a regiment of experienced soldiers; it becomes in fact a

---

* New York Commercial Advertiser.

mechanical movement. No one ever makes a mistake, or throws the rank in disorder from inattention or inexperience; but every thing is conducted in the most exact order, as if every step and movement of the body was directed by a gauge and rule. Dances are sometimes held in private houses, when variations are frequently introduced. On some occasions it is said their movements are so rapid, that the eye can scarce follow or keep pace with their swift motions.

"The principal doctrines of the Shakers are a belief in the *second appearance of Christ* in the person of the holy mother. They admit of but two persons in the Godhead, God the Father, and God the Mother, which they say is according to the order of nature, being male and female. To relieve the depraved race of man, they believe that it became necessary for God to take upon him the real character of human nature as it is, male and female, and that his first appearance was in the person of man, and the second in the person of woman, whereby the work of redemption was finished and completed. The confusion and wickedness that prevailed in the Catholic Church, during the long period which preceded and followed the reformation, they ascribe to the work of redemption not being completed in Christ's first appearance, it being the necessary period that must intervene between the making and fulfilment of the promise of Christ, that he would establish his law of righteousness on earth. They believe in perfect holiness, and insist that salvation from *sin* here is necessary to salvation from misery hereafter. They regard the Bible as a testimony of Christ's first appearance, but deny that it contains the word of God, or of life, as they consider a belief in the second appearance of Christ, or in the spiritual character and mission of the holy mother, as indispensable to salvation."

STOCKPORT, so named from Stockport, England, the native place of Mr. Wilde, the proprietor of the mills at Columbiaville, was taken from Hudson, Ghent, and Stuyvesant, in 1833. The Claverack and Kinderhook creeks unite near the centre of the town. In breaking through the high bank of the river, these streams, within three miles, have several falls which amount to about one hundred and sixty feet, and this water-power has given rise to the several flourishing manufacturing villages named below. Columbiaville, six miles N. of Hudson, has very extensive cotton factories, and about forty-five dwellings. The Hudson river Seminary is located here. The *print works* for printing calicoes, were established fourteen years since, by J...... Marshall & Co., and employ about two hundred and fifty hands. There are in this vicinity about seventy dwellings. Chittenden's Falls are seven, and Springville two and a half miles from Hudson. At Glencadia, on the Kinderhook creek, three and a half miles from Hudson river, there are two falls amounting to about seventy feet, on which are situated extensive cotton factories. Pop. 1814.

STUYVESANT was taken from Kinderhook in 1823. Stuyvesant or Kinderhook Landing, on the Hudson, is one hundred and twenty-five miles N. of New York, five W. from Kinderhook, twenty S. of Albany, and contains about fifty dwellings. Pop. 1,946.

TAGHKANIC, taken from Livingston, in 1823, by the name of Granger; name and bounds since altered. It is one of the towns of Livingston manor, and lies SE. of Hudson fifteen miles. Pop. 1,724.

CORTLAND COUNTY.

CORTLAND COUNTY, taken from Onondaga in 1808, and named in honor of Gen. Pierre Van Cortlandt, who was a large landholder here: centrally distant NW. from New York 200, and from Albany, W., 145 miles. This county forms part of the high central section of the state. It has the dividing ridge between the northern and southern waters across its northern and western borders. It is consequently elevated. Its surface is composed of easy hills and broad valleys, giving it a gently waving and diversified aspect. The soil is generally a gravelly loam, rich and productive. This county comprises four whole and two half townships of the tract granted by the state to the soldiers of the revolution, and is settled chiefly by emigrants from the eastern states. Pop. 24,605. It is divided into 11 towns.

CINCINNATUS, taken from Solon in 1804; W. from Albany 131, from Cortland, SE., 15 miles. Pop. 1,301. Cincinnatus, the post village, contains about 30 dwellings.

CORTLANDVILLE, taken from Homer in 1829; 142 miles from Albany. Pop. 3,799. The following view shows the principal public

Public buildings in Cortlandville.

buildings in the village. The first building on the right is the Methodist church, the second the Academy, the third the Presbyterian, the fourth the Baptist, and the last the Universalist church. The courthouse is seen on the opposite side of the street. The village is pleasantly situated and laid out in regular squares. There are here two weekly newspaper offices and about 120 dwellings, some of them splendid, with neat door-yards adorned with trees, shrubbery, &c. &c. McGrawsville, a small village, is 4 miles E. from Cortlandville. South Cortland and Port Watson are post-offices.

The following epitaph was copied from a monument in the graveyard at Cortlandville.

"In memory of Martha Merrick, wife of David Merrick, who died April 8, 1831, in the 62d year of her age. She had passed the last 32 years of her life in this town and Homer, having been among the first settlers in this county. She departed this life in the full faith of a blessed Saviour. She lived respected and died regretted."

FREETOWN, taken from Cincinnatus in 1818; from Albany 140, and from Cortland, SE., 10 miles. Freetown Corners is a small village, and Freetown is a post-office. Pop. 949.

HOMER, organized in 1794. The township is level; the soil a sandy and clay loam. Pop. 3,572. Homer village, the largest in the county, is beautifully situated upon a plain, upon the W. bank of the Tioughnioga river; from Albany 138 miles, 40 N. from Oswego, 30 S. from Syracuse, 2½ N. from Cortland village. The following view shows on the right the Episcopal church, the building next is

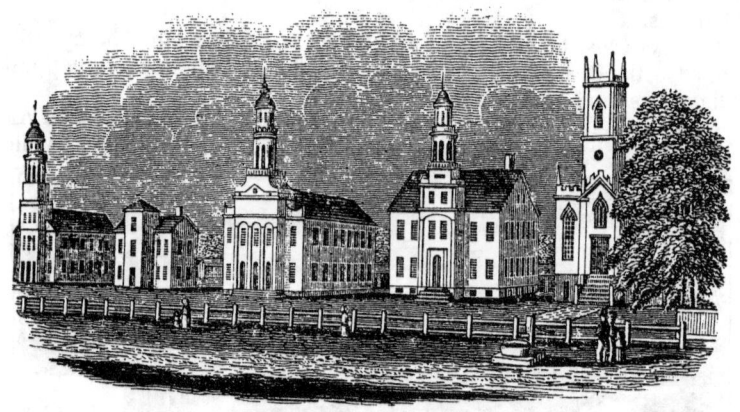

Public buildings in Homer.

the Academy, the third the Presbyterian, the fourth the Methodist, and the fifth the Baptist church. The Cortland Academy is a highly flourishing institution, having a collection of philosophical apparatus and a cabinet of minerals. The public buildings are upon a square of 6 acres. The village was incorporated in 1825, and has about 200 buildings.

The following is the copy of an inscription on a monument in the graveyard in this village.

"REV. ELNATHAN WALKER, was born at Taunton, Mass., Feb. 7th, 1780; graduated at Brown's College, Rhode Island, Sept. 7th, 1803. Joined the church in Dighton, Mass.,

Jan. 31, 1805, was ordained and installed Pastor of this church, Oct. 25th, 1809. Died June 4th, 1820. This monument is erected by an affectionate people as the last testimony of respect to their beloved pastor. Rev. Mr. Walker settled over this church when it consisted of 99 members. Admitted during his ministry 481. Left when he died 440. Having ended his labors and called upon God, saying Lord Jesus receive my spirit, he fell asleep.

MARATHON, originally named Harrison; taken from Cincinnatus in 1818; from Albany 145, and from Cortland, SE., 15 miles. Pop. 1,063. Marathon is a small village about 4 miles from the county line, on the south.

PREBLE, taken from Tully in 1808; from Albany 138, from Cortland, N., 10 miles. Preble, a small post village, is seven miles N. of Cortland. Pop. 1,247.

SCOTT, taken from Preble in 1815; from Albany 146 miles. The surface of the township is broken by ridges of hills running N. and S., with valleys of good land. Pop. 1,332. Scott Centre, post village 10 miles NW. of Cortland, has about 20 dwellings.

SOLON, organized in 1798; from Albany 140, from Cortland, E., 10 miles. Solon and East Solon are post-offices. Pop. 2,311. This township has a soil of good quality, and the inhabitants have been much engaged in rearing cattle.

TRUXTON, taken from Solon and Fabius in 1808; limits since changed; from Albany 128, NE. from Cortland 12 miles. Pop. 3,658. Truxton village, pleasantly situated on the right bank of the river, has about 40 dwellings. Cuyler is a post-office.

VIRGIL, organized in 1804; from Albany 148, from Cortland, S., 6 miles. Virgil and Hartford are small post villages. Pop. 4,501.

WILLET, taken from Cincinnatus in 1818; from Albany 137, from Cortland, SE., 17 miles. Pop. 870. This is a hilly township and but thinly settled.

DELAWARE COUNTY.

DELAWARE COUNTY, formed from Ulster and Otsego counties in 1797, is centrally distant from New York via Cattskill 166, SW. from Albany 77 miles. Greatest length NE. and SW. 60; greatest breadth SE. and NW. 37 miles.

The county has a broken and diversified surface—from the rugged, lofty, and barren mountain side and summit, to the subsiding hill and the high and low plain, with the rich valley, and the low and fertile alluvion. Its climate is subject to sudden and great changes of temperature, yet not unfriendly to health and longevity. It is principally watered by the northeastern sources of the Delaware, a large navigable river of Pennsylvania, on which stands the city of Philadelphia. The east branch of the Susquehannah, another large stream of Pennsylvania, forms a part of the northeastern boundary, as does the Delaware a part of its southwestern. The Cookquago branch of the Delaware, or the true Delaware, as it ought to be called, runs nearly centrally through the county from NE. to SW.; the Popacton branch runs nearly parallel with this, a short distance to the south of it. These streams with their branches, and many smaller streams, spread plentifully over the whole county, and supply a vast profusion of fine sites for mills. The quality of the soil is as various as the surface. On the upland there is a large proportion of chocolate-colored loam, and the valleys and alluvial flats have a rich mould. The whole may be pronounced a good country for farming, well watered by small springs and rivulets. The heavy trade of this county follows the course of its lumber, which goes in rafts by the Delaware and Susquehannah rivers to Philadelphia and Baltimore; while considerable traffic is carried on with the towns on the Hudson, to which there are turnpikes in various directions. The value of the wild lands in the county is from two to three dollars an acre, and the improved lands in the valleys average about 30 dollars, while those on the hills are worth about 5 dollars the acre. West of the Mohawk branch of the Delaware, the county was divided into several patents; but east of it was included in the Hardenburgh patent. In 1768, William, John, Alexander, and Joseph Harper, with eighteen others, obtained a patent here for 22,000 acres of land, and soon after the Harpers removed from Cherry Valley, and made a settlement which was called Harpersfield, but which was broken up by the Indians and tories during the revolutionary war. About one quarter of the county is under improvement. Pop. 32,933. The county has 18 towns.

ANDES, taken from Middletown in 1819; from Albany 90, centrally distant SE. from Delhi 15 miles. Shavertown and Andes are post-offices. This town and Bovina were principally settled by the Scotch. Pop. 2,176.

BOVINA, taken from Middletown, Delhi, and Stamford, in 1820; distant from Albany 89, from Delhi centrally situated E. 10 miles. Bovina and Fish Lake are post-offices. Pop. 1,403.

COLCHESTER, taken from Middletown, part of Ulster county, in 1792; bounds since reduced; from Albany 91, from Delhi S. 21 miles. Colchester and Popacton are post-offices. Pop. 1,567. The surface is hilly, somewhat mountainous. The settlements are principally on a branch of the Susquehannah, which passes through the town.

DAVENPORT, formed in 1817; from Albany 65, from Delhi centrally situated N. 11 miles. Davenport, West Davenport, and Davenport Centre, are post-offices. Pop. 2,054.

DELHI, taken from Middletown, Kortwright, and Walton, in 1798; area since much reduced; from Albany 77, west from Cattskill 68, from Kingston 67 miles. Pop. 2,555.

The following view of Delhi village, the county seat, was taken on the eastern bank of the Delaware. This village was incorporated in 1821. The building with a steeple seen on the extreme right is a factory—the spire near the centre of the view is that of the Epis-

Eastern view of Delhi Village.

copal church, the one to the left the Presbyterian, and the cupolas are respectively those of the Courthouse, Jail, and Academy. The academy here, under the charge of the Rev. Daniel Shepherd, is incorporated and flourishing. The village contains about 100 dwellings.

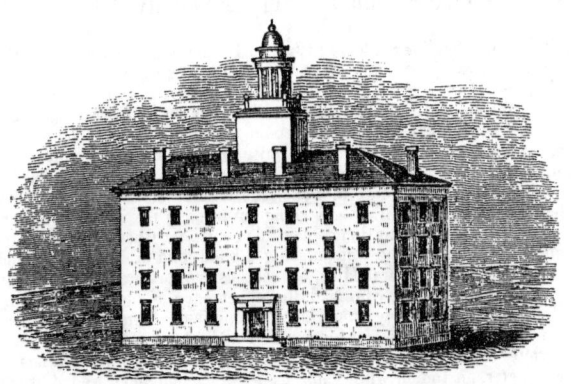

Delaware Literary Institute, Franklin.

FRANKLIN, taken from Harpersfield whilst part of Otsego county, in 1792; area since much altered. It was settled in 1785. Pop. 3,025. Franklin village is pleasantly situated 16 miles W. from Delhi, 80 from Kingston, and 60 S. of Utica, and contains 1 Presbyterian, 1 Baptist, and 1 Methodist church, and about 500 inhabitants. " The Delaware Literary Institute was incorporated in 1835. The building is of stone, 86 feet long, 42 wide, and 4 stories high. It contains, besides rooms to accommodate 80 male students, a chapel, two recitation rooms, and one for apparatus. Cost, including the site, $7,500. It has a chemical, a philosophical apparatus, and a library. It is directed by a board of 24 trustees. It has a male and female department, and five teachers are employed in instruction. Rev. Silas Fitch is principal, and Merit Platt lecturer and instructer in natural science. It has 110 students. The moral influence and pecuniary advantages it affords are considered highly favorable." East Franklin and North Franklin are post-offices.

HAMDEN, taken from Walton and Delhi in 1825; from Albany 85, from Delhi, SW., 8 miles. Hamden is a small post village on the Delaware. Pop. 1,469.

HANCOCK, a large and somewhat mountainous township, was taken from Colchester in 1806; from Albany 129, and from Delhi centrally distant SW. 27 miles. Hancock, East Branch, Bloomfield, Paulina, and Partridge Island are the post-offices. Pop. 1,027. The inhabitants, who are principally engaged in lumbering, are chiefly settled upon the Popacton branch of the Delaware.

HARPERSFIELD, organized in 1788 as part of Montgomery county; bounds since much reduced; from Albany 62 miles. It has a mountainous surface. Pop. 1,696. Harpersfield, 18 miles NE. of Delhi, and West Harpersfield, are small post villages. North Harpersfield is a post-office.

The following is extracted from Mr. Campbell's interesting and valuable work entitled " Annals of Tryon County:"

" In 1768, William, John, Alexander, and Joseph Harper, with eighteen other individuals, obtained a patent for twenty-two thousand acres of land lying in the now county of Delaware. The Harpers removed from Cherry Valley soon after, and made a settlement there which was called Harpersfield. This settlement had begun to flourish at the commencement of the war. Col. John Harper had the command of one of the forts in Schoharie.

The following account of a successful enterprise of Col. Harper, was furnished by the Rev. Mr. Fenn, who received the information from him. He informed me that in the year 1777, he had the command of the fort in Schoharie, and of all the frontier stations in this region. He left the fort in Schoharie, and came out through the woods to Harpersfield in the time of making sugar, and from thence laid his course for Cherry Valley to investigate the state of things there; and as he was pursuing a blind kind of Indian trail, and was ascending what are now called Decatur Hills, he cast his eye forward and saw a company of men coming directly towards him, who had the appearance of Indians. He knew that if he attempted to flee from them they would shoot him down; he resolved to advance right up to them, and make the best shift for himself he could. As soon as he came near enough to discern the white of their eyes, he knew the head man and several others; the head man's name was Peter, an Indian with whom Col. Harper had often traded at Oquago before the revolution began. The colonel had his great-coat on, so that his regimentals were concealed, and he was not recognised; the first word of address of Col. Harper's was, 'How do you do, brothers?' The reply was, 'Well—how do you do, brother? Which way are you bound, brother?' 'On a secret expedition: and which way are you bound, brothers?' 'Down the Susquehannah, to cut off the Johnston settlement.' (Parson Johnston and a number of Scotch families had settled down the Susquehannah, at what is now called Sidney's Plains, and these were the people whom they were about to destroy.) Says the colonel, 'Where do you lodge to-night?' 'At the mouth of Schenevas creek,' was the reply. Then shaking hands with them, he bid them good speed, and proceeded on his journey.

" He had gone but a little way from them before he took a circuit through the woods, a distance of eight or ten miles, on to the head of Charlotte river, where were a number of men making sugar; ordered them to take their arms, two days' provisions, a canteen of rum, and a rope, and meet him down the Charlotte, at a small clearing called Evans's place, at a certain hour that afternoon; then rode with all speed through the woods to Harpersfield; collected all the men who were there making sugar, and being armed and victualled, each man with his rope laid his course for Charlotte; when he arrived at Evans's place he found the Charlotte men there, in good spirits; and when he mustered his men, there were fifteen, including himself, exactly the same number as there were of the enemy; then the colonel made his men acquainted with his enterprise.

"They marched down the river a little distance, and then bent their course across the hill to the mouth of Schenevas creek; when they arrived at the brow of the hill where they could overlook the valley where the Schenevas flows, they cast their eyes down upon the flat, and discovered the fire around which the enemy lay encamped. 'There they are,' said Col. Harper. They descended with great stillness, forded the creek, which was breast-high to a man; after advancing a few hundred yards, they took some refreshment, and then prepared for the contest—daylight was just beginning to appear in the east. When they came to the enemy, they lay in a circle with their feet towards the fire, in a deep sleep; their arms and all their implements of death, were all stacked up according to the Indian custom when they lay themselves down for the night: these the colonel secured by carrying them off a distance, and laying them down; then each man taking his rope in his hand, placed himself by his fellow; the colonel rapped his man softly, and said, 'Come, it is time for men of business to be on their way;' and then each one sprang upon his man, and after a most severe struggle they secured the whole of the enemy.

"After they were all safely bound, and the morning had so far advanced that they could discover objects distinctly, says the Indian Peter, 'Ha! Col. Harper! now I know thee—why did I not know thee yesterday?' 'Some policy in war, Peter.' 'Ah, me find em so now.' The colonel marched the men to Albany, delivered them up to the commanding officer, and by this bold and well-executed feat of valor he saved the whole Scotch settlement from a wanton destruction.

"Early in the spring of 1780, a party of tories and Indians, under the command of Brant, destroyed Harpersfield. The inhabitants had generally left the place; but a few of the men were at the time engaged in making maple sugar. Nineteen were taken prisoners, and several killed. A consultation was held in the Indian language in presence of the prisoners relative to a contemplated attack upon the upper fort, in Schoharie; the Indians, satisfied with the booty and prisoners already obtained, were unwilling to risk any thing in an uncertain expedition; some of the tories represented the plan as promising success, and advised the Indians to kill the prisoners, that they might not be encumbered with them. Brant came up to Capt. Alexander Harper, one of the prisoners, and drawing his sword, asked him if there were any troops in the fort; saying his life should be taken if he did not inform him correctly. Harper knew enough of the Indian language to have learned the subject of the foregoing conversation, and immediately answered that it was well garrisoned, believing that they would all be killed should he answer differently. Another prisoner, not knowing the determination of the Indians, and fearing their vengeance should the falsehood be detected, stated truly that there were few if any troops in the fort. Harper insisted that his statement was true; he was believed, and they returned to Niagara. The last night of their journey they encamped a short distance from the fort. In the morning the prisoners were to run the gauntlet. Harper, knowing the hostility of the Indians towards him, and fearing they might take his life, requested Brant to interfere and protect him, which he promised to do. The Indians arranged themselves in two parallel lines, facing inward, with clubs and whips in their hands.

"Harper was selected first; he was a tall, athletic man, and on the first signal sprang from the mark with extraordinary swiftness. An Indian near the end of the line fearing he might escape with little injury, stept before him; Harper struck him a blow with his fist, and then springing over him, ran towards the fort; the Indians, enraged, broke their ranks and followed him. The garrison, who had been apprised of the movements of the Indians, were upon the walls when they saw Harper approaching; they threw open the gate, and he rushed in, when they immediately closed it. It was with difficulty they could keep the Indians back. The other prisoners took different courses and got into the fort without passing through this, if not fiery, yet bloody ordeal."*

---

* "William Harper was an active member of the provincial congress, and after the war was several times a member of the state legislature. When Otsego county was formed, he was appointed one of the assistant judges, William Cooper, Esq., being first judge. He lived to a great age, and died a few years since at Milford, in Otsego county, retaining to the last that strong desire for information which had characterized his public life. Col. John Harper died in Harpersfield, and Alexander and Joseph, soon after the war, obtained a grant of some land in the western part of the state of Ohio, whither they removed. The quiet of the country, and the approach of civilization, was not congenial to them. They preferred the life of a borderer, and sought it amid the boundless forests which then covered that beautiful state."

KORTRIGHT, organized as part of Otsego county in 1793; from Albany 68 miles. Bloomville, 7 miles NE., and Kortright 14 miles from Delhi, are small villages. South Kortright and North Kortright are names of post-offices. Pop. 2,442.

MASONVILLE, taken from Sidney in 1811; from Albany 105, and from Delhi NW. centrally distant 24 miles. Pop. 1,420. This town contains great quantities of pine, and lumbering is the principal occupation of its inhabitants.

MEREDITH, taken from Franklin and Kortright in 1800; from Albany 77, and from Delhi centrally situated N. 8 miles. Meredith and West Meredith are small settlements. Pop. 1,640. Dr. Dwight, in his journey to the Niagara Falls in 1804, passed through this town. He says: " Meredith is in the fullest sense a new settlement. In the year 1800 it contained only 213 inhabitants, and in the year 1810, 726. Peculiar efforts have been made by Mr. Law to introduce into this township sober, industrious, virtuous settlers. In this manner he has probably secured its prosperity, both moral and physical, for a century. Since the date of my journal, the inhabitants have built an academy, in which they assemble for public worship. .... From the house of Mr. Law, a handsome mansion in the centre of the town, the prospect stretches to the south, over a valley ultimately bounded by mountains at the distance of thirty miles; and to the north, over another valley which extends ten miles. The hill which limits the northern prospect is covered with a magnificent growth of white pines; one of which having fallen down was measured by Mr. Law, and was found to be *two hundred and forty-seven feet* in length. .... It is not improbable that the next generation may never see a white pine of the full size, and may regard an exact account of this noble vegetable production as a mere fable."—*Dwight's Travels, vol.* 4.

MIDDLETOWN, taken from Rochester and Woodstock as part of Ulster county, in 1789; area since much reduced; settled by emigrants from New England, and by Scotch, Dutch, Irish, and German emigrants; from Albany 79, from Delhi centrally situated SE. 20 miles. Middletown, Ashville, Colesville, and Halcottsville, are post-offices. Pop. 2,608.

ROXBURY, taken from Stamford in 1799; area since altered; permanently settled by New England emigrants in 1790; from Albany 63 miles. Roxbury, formerly called Beaver Dam village, and Mooresville, 28 miles E. of Delhi, are small villages. Pop. 3,004.

SIDNEY, taken from Franklin in 1801; from Albany 100, and from Delhi, NW., 24 miles. Sidney Plains, Sidney, and New Road, are post-offices. Near here is a locality called " the Beaverdam," where there are the timbers remaining of a dam constructed by the beavers which flooded 30 or 40 acres of land. Pop. 1,720.

One of the first settlers of this town was Timothy Beach, originally from Fairfield county, Connecticut. At the close of the revolutionary war, Mr. Beach, with his son, a lad of about 12 years, proceeded up the Hudson river to Cattskill, and from thence struck across the wilderness to Wattle's Ferry, a distance of about one hundred miles.

Being considered dangerous to penetrate that distance without a guide, they procured the services of an Indian conductor. Mr. Beach selected his farm near Wattle's ferry, on the Susquehannah, then in a wilderness state, since known as the *Ketchum farm*. He then returned through the same woods, carrying his boy on his horse behind him, till he arrived in Connecticut. On November 11th, 1784. Mr. Beach with his family went up to Albany, and from thence continued their journey till they arrived at Otsego lake, the head waters of the Susquehannah. Here they left their teams, as the road proceeded no further, put their effects on board of a batteau, and glided gently down the lake, a distance of nine miles to its outlet, where they encamped in the open air, on the spot where the village of Cooperstown is now built. On the third day after leaving this place, Mr. Beach arrived at his farm, on which was a small clearing, having a log house in a ruinous state, in the centre. It appears that the place had belonged to a Scotchman who was killed by the Indians in the revolutionary war.

"The shortness of time," says Mr. Priest, (in a pamphlet giving an account of the adventures of this family,) "between their arrival here and the setting in of winter, prevented the building a larger and a better log house. During this winter they became experimentally acquainted with cold, hunger, and a variety of sorrows, known only to the pioneers of an entire new country. Money was of but little use, as food was not to be bought where there was none for sale, as scarcely any as yet had been produced. There were but five families in the whole community, who having come in the spring of the same season, had not therefore had time to raise but little, consequently food of any kind was scarcely to be found among them. To procure it from a distance was also extremely difficult, there being no settlement where it could be had, nearer than old Schoharie, a distance of about seventy miles, to which place at that time the road was not much better than none at all.

"This dreadful winter at length passed away, and with it, in a measure, their sufferings; as by this time they had learned of the Indians how to catch fish, which abounded in the river, coves, and creeks of the country. Without this relief they must have finally perished. But now a new scene of things, such as they had never before witnessed, says Mrs. Priest, were about to captivate their attention. March had begun to yield its rains; the snow to feel its dissolving power; every rill and creek of the mountains to swell and roar, plunging forward over crag and cliff to the vales below. The devious Susquehannah began to put on majesty, drinking largely of its annual libation from earth and sky, swelling the headlong waters, which as they rose lifted and tore away the ice from the shores and promontories. Loud sounds were heard to moan along the thick-ribbed ice, the covering of the waters bursting in ten thousand places with the noise of tempests. But now commenced a more amazing display of the power of the waters. Already its banks were overflown, and the distant forests of the flats along the river, inundated with the sweeping flood to the very base of the hills. The broken ice began to move, large islands of it to rush upon each other, still breaking more and more, urging its way forward with resistless fury. Now the roar increases, large fields of ice plunge into the woods on either shore; the trees bending, groan and snap asunder beneath the overwhelming load, still passing on till thrown in huge heaps along the shores and in the adjacent woods. Still the main channel pursues its way, every moment adds to the enormous weight it bears. As far as the eye can view from the tops of commanding eminences, above, below, all its commotion, plunging onward with a loud and steady roar till stayed on some long level in the river. Here it makes a stand, or but slowly moves; as a vast army on the verge of battle, which halts to adjust its prowess, then to move again. So the river in its grandeur resumed its course a moment, while from shore to shore the ice stood piled in pyramids, chafing up and down as if in anger. But now the level narrows to a defile between the mountains, when all at once the mass for many miles above, with whirling eddies, stood at bay. So halts the embattled host, whose scouts descry the foe; the council, cool in war, debate the safest mode to bring their legions fiercely to the fight. Now suddenly the waters rise and boil and foam through all its heaps and ranks of massive ice; as generals do, inspiring courage in the soldier's breast. The upper floods having gathered head, urge on with augmented power its course;

expectation stands aghast; the lowing herds with stupid gaze wonder at the noise, deer from their coverts scamper to the hills, dogs howl from fear at the dismal sounds, horses snort, bounding with staring eyeballs both right and left; when all at once the frozen dam gives way and rushes on with sound of thunder. Fury and desolation mark its progress, trees torn from their roots plunge here and there, old timber with fences swept from the fields and woods, mingle in the ruin; onward roars the unconquered deluge, till from Otsego lake to where the frightful Caughnawaga dashes to foam the descending river with the subdued and shivered ice: which ends the scene.

STAMFORD, taken from Woodstock, and organized as part of Ulster co. in 1792; from Albany 58, from Delhi, centrally distant NE., 16 miles. Pop. 1,681. Hobart, upon the Delaware river, is a village containing about 80 dwellings. Stamford is a small village near the head of the river.

TOMPKINS, originally named Pinefield, and taken from Walton in 1808; it has a mountainous surface. Pop. 2,032. Deposit village, upon the Delaware, and partly in Broome co., 116 miles from Albany, 40 SW. from Delhi, and on the Erie railroad, has about 70 dwellings. Cannonsville and Barbersville are small settlements.

WALTON, taken from Franklin in 1797; from Albany 94, from Delhi, centrally situated SW., 17 miles. Walton village, on the Delaware, has about 70 dwellings, within the area of a mile. Pop. 1,844.

DUTCHESS COUNTY.

DUTCHESS COUNTY was organized in 1683. It is on the E. side of the Hudson river, 75 miles S. of Albany, and 74 N. of New York. Greatest length N. and S. 38, greatest breadth E. and W. 26 miles. This county is one of the most opulent in the state, though its area has been reduced by the erection of the small county of Putnam from its southern end. Along the eastern border towns there are ranges of hills called the Fishkill or Matteawan mountains. Along the western borders of these, the surface is tossed into ridges and valleys, knolls and dales, fancifully diversified, producing a great variety of position, of soil and aspect, and a multitude of brooks and springs. In the southern part are some of the highest peaks of the Highlands. That called the Old Beacon, two miles from Matteawan village, and three from Fishkill Landing, raises its crest 1,471 feet, and the New Beacon or Grand Sachem, half a mile southward, towers 1,685 above tide. Their names are derived from the Beacons placed on their summits during the revolution. From the top of the latter, the view on the S. embraces the country upon the Hudson, for 25 miles to Tappan bay; on the SE. includes Long Island and the sound; and upon the NE. and W. comprehends, in the diameter of a circle 50 miles in extent, scenery of every diversity, blending the beauties of cultivation with the stern and unchangeable features of nature. The principal streams are the Hudson river on its western boundary, Ten

Mile, Fishkill, and Wappinger's creeks. As a whole, the county is highly fertile, producing abundantly wheat, rye, corn, oats, and grass, and an immense amount of produce is annually exported to New York. This county is divided into 18 towns. Pop. 50,926.

AMENIA, from Albany 75, and from New York 95 miles. Pop. 2,179. Until 1761, Amenia was part of the Crom Elbow precinct, when it was erected into a separate one, and in 1788, into a township with its present name. Ameniaville, 24 miles E. of Poughkeepsie, is a small village. The Amenia Seminary, in Ameniaville, has been in operation about 5 years, and is in a flourishing condition. The village of Hitchcock's Corners, 29 miles from Poughkeepsie, lies partly in this town, and partly in Sharon, in the state of Connecticut. It is pleasantly situated in a beautiful and populous valley, rich in the resources of agricultural wealth. The township comprises the width of the *oblong* tract, and the E. tier of lots, in the Great Nine Partners,—a large tract from the Hudson to the W. line of Connecticut, granted to *nine* proprietors or partners. It is stated in Spafford's Gazetteer, that "in 1711, Richard Sackett and family lived on this tract, and continued the only white family until 1724, when Ulric or Oliver Winegar removed thither from the German Camp in Livingston manor, with a few other families. But the improvements were very small until 1741, when several families emigrated here from Connecticut."

BEEKMAN, organized in 1788; from New York, NE., 87, from Albany, S., 90 miles. Pop. 1,400. The Clove vale in this town, which was early settled by the Dutch, is extremely fertile. "On the Sprout creek, which rises in this town, a great quantity of human bones have accidentally been discovered, lying promiscuously, as if a vast pile of human bodies had here been made, and left to rot. No tradition has been preserved of this event, but it is supposed the spot was once the scene of a bloody Indian battle, and that the slain were hastily thrown together, probably friends and foes, and left to the raven, the fox, and the worm." Beekmanville, on the Fishkill, 16 miles E., Greenhaven, 18, and Poughquake, 18 E. of Poughkeepsie, are small settlements. At the Beekman furnace 1,000 tons of pig iron are annually manufactured.

CLINTON, organized in 1788; NE. from New York 90, from Albany, SE., 70, and from Poughkeepsie, NE., 16 miles. Clintonville, Pleasant Plains, Clinton Hollow, and Schultz Corners, are small settlements. Pop. 1,830.

DOVER, taken from Pawling in 1807; from New York, N., 80, and from Albany, S., 90 miles. This town was early settled by the Dutch. Pop. 1,999. Dover, South Dover, 24 E. from Poughkeepsie, and Chestnut Ridge, 2 miles S. from Dover village, are small settlements.

Near Dover village is a remarkable cavern, which, from the resemblance of the entrance to the pointed Gothic arch, is called the Stone Church. The following description is from the pen of a late visitor:—

"The Stone Church consists of a fissure in the rock on a declivity

Dover Stone Church.

of the mountain, and near its base, through which passes a rippling streamlet, which, in its passage down until it reaches the ground-work or floor of the church, forms numerous and extensive cascades, some of thirty feet in height, and from ten to fifteen in breadth. This current has been looked upon as the great architect of the work. The opening, though so narrow at the top as to appear almost closed, gradually widens to its base, so that it forms a vast arch of very considerable regularity, of perhaps twenty feet span and upwards. Its greatest depth is probably two hundred feet; and the inner or principal apartment, (it being divided into two spacious halls,) is about seventy feet in length, and is well lighted and aired from above. The ante-chamber, as it may be termed, or hall of entrance, is separated from the church by a huge mass of rock, which has detached itself from the side or roof, and is aptly styled the pulpit. The view is well fitted to inspire feelings of devotion. The heart, touched by the religious gloom and solemnity of the place, acknowledges the power of the Creator, and rises in admiration of his works."

FISHKILL was organized in 1788. Pop. 10,436. This town was settled by the Dutch, previous to any other in the county. Its early inhabitants called it Vis-kill, that is, fish creek; kill being the Dutch for creek,—hence its present name. Matteawan is a beautiful manufacturing village upon the Fishkill creek, about a mile from the landing, at the foot of the Matteawan mountain. It was founded in 1814, by Messrs. Schenck and Leonard, about which time the Matteawan company was formed. There are here several large cotton mills, and factories of various descriptions. There are about 2,000 persons connected with and employed in the works. S. Grosvenor & Company, are the agents of the company in New York. There are many neat dwellings, and two beautiful churches, one Presbyterian and one Episcopalian, at whose sabbath schools 250 children attend. No intoxicating liquors are permitted to be sold, and almost the whole population have pledged themselves to abstain from their use. "The deep valley, with its cascades and rapids; the village, with its neat white dwellings, magnificent factories, and ornamental churches, overhung by the stupendous mountain, render this one of the most beautiful scenes in the state, where enlightened, cheerful, and perse-

DUTCHESS COUNTY.   135

Factory Buildings in Matteawan, Fishkill.

vering industry is reaping its due reward. It attracts much attention, and is greatly resorted to in the summer season."

Glenham, Franklinville, and Rocky Glen, are small manufacturing villages. Fishkill Landing, Hopewell, New Hackensack, Carthage, Upper Landing, Johnsonville, Hughsonville, Stormville, Shenandoah, Cackemeyer's Mills, Gayhead, and Peckville, are small villages or hamlets. Fishkill village, on the creek, 5 miles from the Hudson river, and 16 from Poughkeepsie, is situated upon a beautiful plain, in a fertile country, and has about eighty dwellings, an academy, one Episcopal, and one Dutch church. A portion of the American army were located here in the revolutionary war. Their barracks were about half a mile south of the village. The head-quarters of the officers was the dwelling now occupied by Isaac Van Wyck. Esq., generally known by the name of the "Wharton House."* The barracks commenced about 30 rods north of this dwelling, from the residence of the widow, Mrs. Cornelius Van Wyck, and extended southwardly near the line of the road, to the foot of the mountain. The soldiers' graveyard was situated near the base of the mountain, where a road turns off from the turnpike to the east. While the army was here, the tory and other prisoners were confined in the old Dutch stone church, represented in the following engraving. In this church, it is said that Enoch Crosby was confined, and escaped in an apparently miraculous manner.

The following is an inscription on a monument in the graveyard, adjoining the church:

---

* This dwelling and its vicinity is the scene of "The Spy," by J. Fennimore Cooper. Some years since a work was published, entitled "Enoch Crosby, or the Spy Unmasked," which attempted to identify the hero of Cooper's novel with a person then living. This production is generally believed to have but slight foundation in truth. It is not, however, questioned, but that there was such a person as Enoch Crosby, and that some of the adventures attributed to him actually happened. He died at South East, in Putnam co., about 10 or 12 years since.

"Glory to God alone! Sacred to the memory of the Reverend Nicholas Van Vrancken, minister of Jehovah Jesus, and Pastor of the Dutch Reformed Congregations of Fishkill, Hopewell, and New Hackensack. This excellent man lived tenderly beloved, and died deeply lamented, by the people of his charge. He was born the 24th of May, 1762, and departed in peace and rested in hope, the 20th of May, 1804, aged 41 years, 11 months and 19 days. The Lord gave, and the Lord taketh away; blessed be the name of the Lord."

Old Dutch Stone Church, Fishkill.

The following extracts are from newspapers published at the time to which they refer :—

"*July 12th*, 1765.—We hear from the Fishkills, that for a week or two past, a tiger or panther has been seen in the woods in that neighborhood, not far from Mr. Depeyster's house. It had killed several dogs, torn a cow so that she died the same day, and carried off the calf; it likewise carried off a colt of about a week old. Eight men with their guns went in search of it, and started it at a distance; it fled with great swiftness, and has been since seen at the Fishkills."

"*August 28th*, 1776.—A few days since about 100 women, inhabitants of Dutchess county, went to the house of Colonel Brinkerhoff, at Fishkill, and insisted upon having tea at the lawful price of six shillings per pound, and obliged that gentleman to accommodate them with one chest from his store for that purpose. Shortly after he sold his cargo to some Yorkers, who, for fear of another female attack, forwarded the nefarious stuff to the North river precipitately, where it is now afloat, but the women have placed their guard on each side."

"Forty Dollars Reward will be paid by the subscriber, besides all reasonable expences, for detecting and bringing to justice, one or more of a gang of villains, eight or ten in number, who, on the night of the 17th of August last, armed with guns, bayonets, and swords, surrounded the house of Mrs. Phebe Thomas, on Quaker Hill, in Dutchess county, which some of their number forcibly entered, and after many threatening expressions, robbed the subscriber of the following articles, viz. 180 silver dollars, 28 guineas, 9 half Johanneses, 1 green silk purse, opening with a spring with a large silver hook, and containing between £4 and £5 in small silver, with one guinea; two pairs of silver shoe buckles; 1 silver table-spoon, marked with the letters R. M., with a T at top between them; 1 small silver snuff-box, marked A. S.; 1 large paper snuff-box; one silver thimble; two penknives, (one with a mother-of-pearl handle,) in cases; one carved ivory tooth-pick case; one lawn handkerchief; one red and white linen do.; three cotton stockings, and one pair of white yarn knit garters. One pair of buckles has been found upon a fellow, who went by the name of Williams, who formerly used to profess himself a painter in New York; was lately taken up on a charge of some other felonies, and imprisoned at Kingston, in Ulster county,

from whence, on the approach of the British incendiaries, he was removed (with the other prisoners,) into the state of Connecticut, where he is now confined.
"Quaker Hill, Nov. 5, 1777. MARY FERRARI."

"*Fishkill, February 7th*, 1783.—It is with pain and regret, that we mention the death of Lieutenant-Colonel Barber, who was unfortunately killed at camp the 11th ult. The circumstances which led to this unhappy catastrophe, we are told, are as follows: Two soldiers were cutting down a tree; at the instant he came riding by it was falling, which he did not observe, till they desired him to take care; but the surprise was so sudden, and embarrassed his ideas so much, that he reined his horse to the unfortunate spot where the tree fell, which tore his body in a shocking manner, and put an immediate period to his existence."

HYDE-PARK, so called from the country seat of the late Dr. S. Bard; taken from Clinton in 1821; from New York, N., 81, and from Albany, S., 68 miles. Pop. 2,364. Hyde Park village and landing are about 7 miles N. from Poughkeepsie. The village has several churches, about 80 dwellings, a distinguished female seminary and a classical school for boys. The magnificent seat of the late Dr. Hosack is here. Staatsburg is a post-office, 2 miles N. of Hyde Park.

LA GRANGE, originally named Freedom, and taken from Beekman and Fishkill in 1821; from Albany, S., 77, and from Poughkeepsie, SE., 8 miles. Freedom Plains, Spouts Creek, and Arthursburg, are names of post-offices. Pop. 1,851.

MILAN, taken from North East in 1818; from Albany 63 miles. Milan, Shookville, 25 N., and Lafayette Corners and Rock City, each 24 miles from Poughkeepsie, are small villages. Pop. 1,726.

NORTH EAST, organized in 1788. The surface of this township is covered with portions of the Taghkanic and Matteawan mountains. The western mountains are cultivated to their summits, and have excellent lands for sheep pasturage. Spencer's Corners, 31 NE., North Amenia, 28 NE., and Federal Store, 25 miles NE. from Poughkeepsie, are small villages. The form of this town is nearly that of a boot, 10 miles long E. and W., 5 wide at the top or W. end, 3 across the ancle, and with a foot 7 miles in length. Pop. 1,381.

PAWLING, organized in 1788; from Poughkeepsie, SE., 22 miles. Pop. 1,571. Pawlingville and Quaker Hill are small post villages; the latter was first settled by Friends in 1740.

PINE PLAINS, taken from North East in 1823; from Albany 72 miles. Pine Plains, 28 miles NE. from Poughkeepsie, has about 40 dwellings. Hammertown and Pulver's Corners are small settlements. The western part of this township is mountainous. In the northeastern part there was formerly an extensive plain covered with pines,—hence the name of the town. Pop. 1,324.

PLEASANT VALLEY, taken from Clinton in 1821; from New York 84, and from Albany 82 miles. Pleasant Valley is a manufacturing village, 7 miles NE. from Poughkeepsie, beautifully situated upon the right bank of Wappinger's creek, and has 1 Presbyterian, 1 Methodist, 1 Friends, and 1 Episcopal church, and about 100 dwellings. Salt Point, 12 miles NE. from Poughkeepsie, and Washington Hollow, are small villages. Pop. 2,219.

POUGHKEEPSIE was organized in 1788: its name is said to have been derived from the Indian word *Apokeepsing*, signifying *safe har-*

bor. The face of the country along the Hudson river is somewhat broken, but the general surface is but moderately uneven. Pop. 10,006. The village of Poughkeepsie, one of the most thriving and substantial places in the state, was first founded by a number of Dutch familes somewhere about the year 1700. Being situated about half-way between New York and Albany, it occasionally became, in early periods of its history, the place of legislative deliberations. The convention which met to deliberate on the Federal Constitution, and voted for its adoption, met in this place in 1788. The annexed engraving, taken from one published in the Family Magazine, Dec. 1838, is a representation of the first house erected in this place. It

Van Kleek House.

was built in the year 1702, by Myndert Van Kleek, one of the earliest settlers of Dutchess county. The house and grounds attached are still in possession of his descendants. It belonged to Matthew Vassar, Esq., in 1835, the year in which this house was demolished.— The distant building seen on the left, is that of the old brewery, this ancient edifice exhibited its port-holes, a feature so common in the buildings of the early settlers, they being necessary for defence against the original possessors of the soil. In 1787, this building, then a public house of some note, was used as a stadt-house; the eleventh session of the legislature of this state was held therein. George Clinton was then governor of the state, and Pierre Van Cortlandt, afterward mayor of New York, lieutenant-governor.

Poughkeepsie is by the river, 70 miles from Albany, and 75 from New York, 18 from Kingston, 14 from Newburg, and 42 from Hudson. Population of the village in 1840, was 7,710. The central part of the village is nearly a mile from the landing place on the Hudson, standing on an elevated plain about 200 feet from the river. Several roads conveniently graded, and the principal one paved, lead from the shore to the plain above, which on the north is overlooked by a beautiful slate hill, from which is a commanding prospect of the adjacent country. The Fall creek or kill meanders through the plain on which the village is built, and finally passes into the Hudson by a succession of cataracts and cascades, which together fall more than 160 feet, affording water-power for a number of mills and factories. There are 11 churches, viz: 2 Presbyterian, 2 Episcopal, 2 Methodist, 2 Friends, 1 Baptist, 1 Catholic, and 1 African; there is also a Universalist society. There are 3 banks, having an aggregate capital of $850,000, 3 newspaper offices, and a variety of manufacturing establishments. Within the limits of the village are twelve male and female schools, all of which are of a superior order.

Poughkeepsie Collegiate School.

The above is a representation of the Poughkeepsie Collegiate School, erected on the summit of an elevated hill about a mile from the Hudson, and half a mile northward from the business part of the village. This structure is modelled after the Parthenon at Athens, and is 35 by 115 feet in size, exclusive of the colonnade; inclusive, 77 by 137 feet. It cost, exclusive of the ground, about forty thousand dollars. This institution was opened for the reception of pupils in Nov., 1836, under the superintendence of Mr. Charles Bartlett, assisted by eight competent teachers. During the first term, there were 50 pupils; the second, 84; the third, 94; and the fourth term, 108. "Its situation is truly a noble one; standing on an eminence commanding an extensive view of almost every variety of feature necessary to the perfection of a beautiful landscape. From the colonnade, which entirely surrounds it, the eye of the spectator can compass a circuit of nearly fifty miles: on the south, at a distance of twenty miles, the Highlands terminate the view, within which an apparent plain stretches to their base, covered with highly cultivated farms, neat mansions, and thriving villages. Similar scenery meets the eye on the east, but more undulating. On the west and north, the Hudson rolls on in its pride and beauty, dotted with the sails of inland commerce and numerous steamboats, all laden with products of industry and busy men. In the dim distance, the azure summits of the Cattskill, reared to the clouds, stretch away to the north, a distance of forty miles, where the far-famed 'Mountain House' is distinctly seen, like a pearl, in its mountain crest, at an elevation of nearly three thousand feet above the river. At our feet, like a beautiful panorama, lies the village of Poughkeepsie, with its churches, its literary institutions, and various improvements in view, indicating the existence of a liberal spirit of well-directed, enterprise." The *Dutch-*

ess County Academy was erected in 1836, in the southeast part of the village, at an expense of about $14,000. The average number of its pupils is about one hundred. " The objects of this institution are to prepare young men for college, for teachers of common schools, for the counting-house, or any of the active pursuits of life."

The following is copied from the ancient records in Poughkeepsie, and will serve to show one form of a legal instrument in olden times.

DUTCHESS COUNTY } ss. Thomas Sanders Esqr. Justice of the peace for said County Assigned.

[L. S.]   To all Constables and other officers as well within the said County as Elsewhere within the Collony of New York to whom the Execution hereof doth or may Concern Greeting

WHEREAS I have Received Information and Charge against one James Jones Lately Come from Lebanon In ye County of Windham In ye Collony of Conecticut and Liveing in Dutchess County at the house of one Ellexander Griggs Calls him self a Weaver a Lusty Well Sott Likely man full faced Brown Complextioned and wares a Black Wigg Irishman; by birth by the brogue on his Speach Who is Charged before me to be a Dangerous person and is suspected to have Stolen a Silver Spoon or the bigest part of a Silver Spoon; as by a Warrant Produced; and the Complaint of William Derddy of Lebanon in County afores^d Some time in the month of this Present November.

Notwithstanding Seavvrall Endeavours for apprehensions of him he hath not as yett been apprehended but hath withdrawn himself and fled—Lately from Lebanon in ye County of Windham In ye Colloney of Conecticut and is Come to our County of Dutchess These are therefore in his majesties name to Command you and Every of You to make diligent Search within your Severall Precincts and Districts for said James Jones and to make hue and Cry after him from Town to Town and from County to County and that as well by horsemen as footmen according to Law and if you shall find the said James Jones that then you do Carry him before some one of his majesties Justice of the Peace Within the County or place Whare he shall be taken to be Dealth withall according to Law Hereof fails not at your perrills⁓   Given Under my Hand In Dutchess County this Seventeenth Day of November In the fourth year of our Reaign And In the Year of our Lord God Everlasting An^o 1730

To Franc Cooll High Constapel
In Dutchess County pursue After   The mark of 💲 Thomas Sanders
the Person In this Hue and Cry   Justice of the Peace.

RED HOOK, taken from Rhinebeck in 1812; from Albany 55, and from New York 96 miles. Pop. 2,833. Red Hook is a small village, 25 miles N. from Poughkeepsie. Upper Red Hook, Barrytown, and Tivoli, are post-offices.

WESTERN VIEW OF POUGHKEEPSIE, N. Y.

The above shows the appearance of Poughkeepsie, as seen from the elevated bank on the west side of the Hudson, a short distance below New Paltz landing. The Hotel at the Steamboat landing, is seen on the extreme right.

RHINEBECK, organized in 1788, is centrally distant from Poughkeepsie 17, from Albany 57, and from N. York 91 miles. Pop. 2,749. The surface of the township in the eastern part is rolling, in the western it is level. The Rhinebeck flats, near the centre, are noted for easy culture and fertility: the *Wirtemburg tract*, in the SE. part of the town, has a light soil, which has been rendered productive by the use of plaster. This town was settled at an early period, by some German families, and derives its name from the river *Rhine* in Germany, and *Beekman*, an original proprietor. Much of the land was formerly holden in large tracts, and leased out to tenants in small farms. The village of *Rhinebeck Flats* was incorporated in 1834, and is 3 miles E. from the Hudson. It contains a Dutch Reformed and a Methodist church, an Academy, with upwards of 100 houses in the vicinity. *Rhinebeck Landing*, on the river, is 90 miles from New York and 55 from Albany.

Methodist Church and Academy, at Rhinebeck.

The above is an eastern view of the Methodist church and the Academy in the central part of the village. The Methodist church, a plain but substantial stone structure, is seen on the left, and the Academy on the right. The church was erected in 1822; the Rev. Freeborn Garrettson, a resident of this town, contributed largely to its erection. Mr. Garrettson was one of the pioneers of the Methodist denomination in this part of the state, and on account of his labors to promote the cause of Christianity, and of his exemplary life, his memory is deservedly cherished with respect and affection. Mr. G. was born in Maryland in 1752. His parents were members of the Church of England, and educated their children in the same faith. About the beginning of the American revolution, some of the first Methodist preachers who came over to America labored in the vicinity of his father's residence. He joined the Methodist society, and soon after became a travelling preacher. He was remarkably conscientious in the performance of whatever he considered his duty. Being convinced that slaveholding was wrong, he gave his slaves their freedom, telling them, that they did not belong to him, and he did not desire their services, without making them a compensation. Having conscientious scruples which deterred him from taking the prescribed state oath, during the revolutionary period, he suffered some persecutions on this account. In one instance, he was seized by a mob, who took him to a magistrate, by whom he was ordered to prison. While part of the mob were taking him thither, they were dispersed by a remarkable flash of lightning, and he was left unmolested. In 1788, Mr. Garrettson was appointed presiding elder for the district north of New York, then including all the circuits from New Rochelle to Lake Champlain. In 1793, he was married to Miss Livingston, daughter of Judge Livingston, of Clermont, in the manor of Livingston. In 1799, a mansion-house was erected on the bank of the Hudson, in Rhinebeck, where his family were settled during the remainder of his life. The following is a copy of the inscription on his monument, in the graveyard attached to the church represented in the engraving.

"Sacred to the memory of the REV. FREEBORN GARRETTSON, an itinerant minister of the Methodist Episcopal church. He commenced his itinerant ministry in the year 1775. In this work he continued until his death, laboring with great diligence and success in various parts of the United States and of Nova Scotia. He died in peace, in the city of New York, September 27th, 1827, in the 76th year of his age, and 52d of his ministry.—' Mark the perfect man, and behold the upright, for the end of that man is peace,' Psalm xxxvi. 37.—' I have fought the good fight, I have finished my course, I have kept the faith :— Henceforth there is laid up for me a crown of righteousness, which the Lord, the righteous judge shall give me at that day, and not to me only, but all them also that love his appearing,' 11 Tim. iv. 7, 8."

STANFORD, taken from Washington in 1788; from New York 110, and from Albany 78 miles. Pop. 2,278. Stanford, with Clinton and Washington, comprised Charlotte precinct before the revolution. This precinct has been settled about 100 years. Bangall, 20 miles NE. from Poughkeepsie, Attlebury, Old Attlebury, Separate, Hull's Mills, Stewart's Corners, and Bare Market, are small settlements.

UNION VALE, taken from Beekman and La Grange in 1827; from New York 75, from Albany 90, and from Poughkeepsie, E., 15 miles. Pop. 1,499. Verbank and Clove are post-offices.

WASHINGTON, organized in 1788; from Poughkeepsie, E., 16 miles. Pop. 2,833. The principal portion of the early settlers were Friends or Quakers, from Long Island and the eastern states. Mechanicsville, 15 miles E. of Poughkeepsie, and Hartsville, are small villages. At the former place is the Nine Partners Orthodox Friends school which was established in 1797, and is now flourishing.

ERIE COUNTY.

ERIE COUNTY was taken from Niagara county in 1821. Greatest length N. and S. 44, and greatest breadth E. and W. 30 miles. Centrally distant from New York 357, from Albany, W., 298 miles. Lake Erie and the Niagara river form its western boundary, the

Tonawanta creek its northern, and the Cattaraugus its southern. The many streams which empty into Lake Erie furnish fine mill sites. The Erie canal enters the Tonawanta creek on the northern border; from which a towing path has been constructed along the bank of the creek, which is used as a canal 12 miles to the Tonawanda village, a short distance above its junction with Niagara river, near Grand Island. A railroad connects Buffalo with the village at Niagara Falls, and one with the Black Rock ferry. The surface in the northern part of the county is level or gently undulating; the southern is more diversified, but no part is hilly. Generally the soil is good; consisting in the northern half, of warm, sandy, and gravelly loam, occasionally mixed with clay, and adapted to wheat; in the southern, clay prevails, and is productive of grass. Both portions yield excellent and various fruits. About one third of the land is under improvement. The whole county was within the Holland Land Company's purchase, excepting a strip a mile wide on the Niagara river. The county has 21 towns. Pop. 62,251.

ALDEN, taken from Clarence in 1823; from Albany 272 miles. Pop. 1,984. Alden, 20 miles E. of Buffalo, is a small village.

AMHERST, taken from Buffalo in 1818; from Albany 283 miles. Pop. 2,440. Williamsville, 10 miles NE. from Buffalo, is a thriving village containing about 50 dwellings.

AURORA was erected in 1818, when the former town of Willink was divided into 3 towns, Aurora, Wales, and Holland, abolishing the name of Willink, which had been given in honor of one of the principal proprietors of the Holland Land Company. It has an undulating surface, soil clay and gravelly loam. Pop. 2,909. Aurora village is 15 miles SE. from Buffalo; it contains about 700 inhabitants, 1 Presbyterian and 1 Methodist church, and 150 dwellings. The Baptists are the most numerous denomination in the village, and occupy the Presbyterian church one half of the time. The hydraulic privileges within one fourth of a mile from the village are very great, and can be used to almost any extent. Griffin's Mills is a small settlement 3 miles SW. from Aurora. The Aurora Seminary was incorporated in 1833.

BOSTON, taken from Eden in 1817; from Albany 289, from Buffalo, SE., 18 miles. The land is elevated, the soil a moist or wet loam, and adapted for grass. Boston, Boston Centre, and North Boston, are small settlements. Pop. 1,746.

BLACK ROCK, recently organized, comprises what was formerly the southern part of the town of Buffalo. The village of Black Rock is in two divisions, the upper and lower. The post-office, which is in the south part, is 3 miles from Buffalo, opposite the village of Waterloo on the Canada side.

The following is a distant northern view of part of the village of Black Rock; the Canada side, on which is the village of Waterloo, is seen on the right and Lake Erie in the extreme distance. A ferry boat plies between Waterloo and the south part of Black Rock village. Niagara river at this point is three fourths of a mile wide, 20 feet

ERIE COUNTY.

Distant view of Black Rock and vicinity.

deep, and runs with a current of 6 miles an hour. The harbor of Black Rock is 4,565 yards long from N. to S., and from 88 to 220 yards broad, containing an area of 136 acres. It begins in the lake opposite Buffalo, at Bird island, and is continued, by a mole of double wooden cribs filled in with stone 18 feet wide and 2,915 yards long, to Squaw island, and is raised from 1 to 4 feet above the surface of the river, rising gradually towards the north. A dam at the end of Squaw island, connecting it with the main land, raises the water about 4½ feet to the level of the lake. The average depth of the water in this harbor is 15 feet. By means of the dam, great water-power is obtained, and mills of various kinds are established at the lower village. The village of Black Rock contains about 350 dwellings, and 2,000 inhabitants.

Black Rock, in common with other places on the Niagara frontier, was ravaged and burnt by the enemy in December, 1813. On the 11th of July previous, the British made an attack on the place. The following particulars of this event are compiled from the Buffalo Gazette.

" The British troops which crossed over at Black Rock on the 10th inst. were commanded by Cols. Bishop and Warren. They crossed the Niagara below Squaw island, and marched far above the navy yard before any alarm was given. The detached militia being surprised, retreated up the beach, and left the enemy in quiet possession of the village, who proceeded to burn the sailors' barracks and block-houses at the great battery. They then proceeded to the batteries, dismounted and spiked three 12 pounders, and took away 3 field-pieces and one 12 pounder; they took from a storehouse a quantity of whiskey, salt, flour, pork, &c., which, with four citizens, they took across the river. At the first moment of the alarm, Gen. Porter left Black Rock for Buffalo, at which place he assembled a body of volunteers and a few regulars, which, with 100 militia and 25 Indians, formed a junction about a mile from the enemy. After being formed, with the militia and Indians on the flanks and the volunteers and the regulars in the centre, they attacked, and the enemy, after a contest of 20 minutes, retreated in the utmost confusion to the beach, embarked in several of our boats, and pulled for the opposite shore; all the boats got off without injury, except the last, which suffered severely from our fire, and from appearance nearly all the men in her were killed or wounded. The British lost 8 killed on the field, besides those killed and wounded in the boats. We took 15 prisoners, who were sent to Batavia. Capt. Saunders, of the British 49th, was wounded while stepping into his boat; he was conveyed to Gen. Porter's house. He states that Col. Bishop was badly wounded and carried into the boat, and says also, that several killed and wounded were carried into the boats. On our side, Sergeant Hartman, Jonathan Thompson, and Joseph Wright were killed, and 5 wounded, 2 of whom were Indians. The Indians behaved well and committed no act of cruelty. They fought because they were friendly to the United States, and because their own possessions, which are very valuable, were in danger of invasion. They are opposed to crossing the river to fight, but are ready to meet the enemy at the threshold in defence of the country which protects them. Maj. King was at Black Rock overnight, and was present and assisted in the action. Two hundred regulars have arrived from Erie at Black Rock, where they are to be stationed."

Fort Erie, about a mile S. from the ferry at Waterloo on the Canada side, was a post of much importance during the last war. After the battle at Niagara, the Americans fell back to Fort Erie, of which they had previously taken possession. This fortress is situated on the margin of the lake, at its outlet into the Niagara river; being nearly a horizontal plain 15 feet above the level of the water, it possesses no natural advantages. On the 13th of Aug., 1814, the British troops, having invested the fort, opened a brisk cannonade, which was returned from the American batteries. At sunset on the 14th, one of their shells lodged in a small magazine, which blew up without any injurious effects. The following account of the assault which took place a few hours afterward, is taken from "*Perkins' History of the Late War.*"

"Gen. Gaines, expecting an assault in the course of the night, kept his men constantly at their posts. The night was dark, and the early part of it rainy; at 2 o'clock in the morning, the British columns, enveloped in darkness, were distinctly heard approaching the American lines. The infantry under Maj. Wood, and Captain Towson's artillery, opened a brisk fire upon them. The sheet of fire from this corps, enabled Gen. Gaines to discover this column of the British, 1,500 strong, approaching the American left. The infantry were protected by a line of loose brush representing an abattis bordering on the river. The British, in attempting to pass round this, plunged into the water breast high. The commanding general was about to order a detachment of riflemen to support Maj. Wood, but was assured by him that he could maintain his position without a reinforcement. The British columns were twice repulsed, and soon afterward fled in confusion. On the right, the lines were lighted by a brilliant discharge of musketry and cannon, which announced the approach of the centre and left columns of the enemy. The latter met the veteran 9th regiment, and Burton's and Harding's companies of volunteers, aided by a 6 pounder, and were repulsed. The centre column, under Col. Drummond, approached at the same time the most assailable points of the fort, and with scaling ladders ascended the parapet, but were driven back with great carnage. The assault was twice repeated, and as often checked; this column, concealed by the darkness of the night and the clouds of smoke which rolled from the cannon and musketry, then passed round the ditch, repeated their charge, reascended their ladders, and with their pikes, bayonets, and spears, fell upon the artillerists. Most of the officers, and many of the men, received deadly wounds. Lieut. McDonough being severely wounded, and in the power of the enemy, surrendered and demanded quarter; Col. Drummond, refusing it, drew a pistol and shot him dead. In a moment afterward, as he was repeating the order to give no quarters, Col. Drummond was shot through the heart. The bastion was now in the possession of the British. The battle raged with increased fury on the right; reinforcements were ordered and promptly furnished from Maj. Wood's corps on the left. Capt. Fanning kept up a spirited and destructive fire from his artillery on the enemy as they were approaching the fort. Majs. Hindman and Trimble, failing to drive the British from the bastion, with the remaining artillerists and infantry, and Capt. Birdsall's detachment of riflemen, rushed in through the gateway, to the assistance of the right wing, and made a resolute charge. A detachment, under Maj. Hall, was introduced over the interior of the bastion, for the purpose of charging the British, who still held possession, but the narrowness of the passage, admitting only 2 or 3 abreast, prevented its accomplishment, and they were obliged to retire. At this moment, every operation was arrested by the explosion of the principal magazine, containing a large quantity of cartridges and powder, in the end of a stone building adjoining the contested bastion. Whether this was the effect of accident or design, was not known. The explosion was tremendous, and its effects decisive. The British in possession of the bastion were destroyed in a moment. As soon as the tumult occasioned by that event had subsided, Capt. Biddle posted a field-piece, so as to enfilade the exterior plain, and the salient glacis. Fanning's battery at the same time opened on the British who were now returning. In a few minutes they were all driven from the works, leaving 222 killed, 174 wounded on the field, and 186 prisoners. To these losses are to be added, those killed on the left flank by Maj. Wood's infantry and Towson's artillery, and floated down the Niagara, estimated in the official reports at 200. The American loss during the bombardment of the 13th and 14th, was 9 killed, and 36 wounded, and in the assault of the night of the 14th, 17 killed, 56 wounded, and 11 missing."

The British troops still continuing their investment of Fort Erie, on the 17th of September a part of the American garrison made a *sortie*, and took the British works about 500 yards in front of their line. The British had two batteries on their left, which annoyed the fort, and were about opening a third. Their camp was about 2 miles distant, sheltered by a wood; their works were garrisoned with one third of their infantry, from 1,200 to 1,500 men, and a detachment of artillery.

"Early on the morning of the 17th, General Porter, with a large detachment, was ordered to penetrate through the woods by a circuitous route, and get between the British main body and their batteries; while General Miller was directed to take a position in the ravine, between the American lines and the batteries, and attack them in front. The advance of Gen. Porter's command consisted of two hundred riflemen, under Colonel Gibson. The right column, of 400 infantry, commanded by Col. Wood; the left, under Gen. Davis, of 500 militia, designed to act as a reserve, and to hold in check any reinforcements from the British main body. Gen. Porter's corps carried the blockhouse in the rear of the third battery by storm, the magazine was blown up, and the garrison made prisoners. The leaders of the 3 divisions under Gen. Porter, all fell nearly at the same time; Col. Gibson, at the head of the riflemen, at the second battery, and Gen. Davis and Col. Wood in an assault upon the first. While these transactions were taking place in the rear of the enemy's works, General Miller in front penetrated between the first and second batteries, and aided by the operations of Gen. Porter in the rear, succeeded in carrying them. Within 30 minutes from the commencement of the action, 2 batteries, 2 blockhouses, and the whole line of entrenchments were in possession of the Americans; and immediately afterward, the other battery was abandoned by the British. Gen. Ripley was now ordered up with the reserve, and at the close of the action, was dangerously wounded in the neck. Strong reinforcements from the British main body arrived while the Americans were engaged in destroying the works, and took part in the action. The object of the sortie being fully accomplished, the American troops were ordered to return to the fort. During the action, Gen. Porter, in passing from the right to the left column of his detachment, accompanied with only 2 or 3 officers, suddenly found himself within a few yards of a body of 60 British soldiers, who had just emerged from a ravine, and were hesitating which way to go. The general immediately advanced, and ordered them to surrender; approaching the first man on the left, he took his musket, and pushed him towards the American lines: in this way he proceeded nearly through the whole company, most of the men voluntarily throwing down their arms, and retiring towards the fort: when on a sudden, a soldier, whose musket the general was about to seize, presented the bayonet to his breast, and demanded *his* surrender. Gen. Porter seized the musket, and was about wrenching it from him, when he was seized by a British officer, and 3 or 4 men who stood in the ranks, and thrown on the ground. He succeeded in gaining his feet, when he found himself surrounded by 15 or 20 men, with their guns presented at him, demanding his surrender. By this time, several American officers with a number of men were advancing to the scene of action. Gen. Porter, now assuming an air of composure and decision, told them they were now surrounded and prisoners, and if they fired a gun they should all be put to the sword. By this time a company of Cayuga riflemen had arrived, and after a momentary scene of confusion and carnage, the whole British party were killed, or made prisoners."

The American loss was 79 killed, 432 wounded and missing. The British loss, as estimated by the American commander, was 500 in killed and wounded: 385 prisoners were taken, and their advance works were destroyed. On the night of the 21st, Gen. Drummond, after an investment of 56 days, broke up his camp, and retired to his intrenchments behind Chippewa river.

Immediately after the unfortunate termination of the battle of Queenstown, Gen. Van Rensselaer resigned the command to Gen. Smyth, and retired from the service. Upon taking the command, Gen. Smyth issued two proclamations to the citizens of New York, one of which was an appeal to their patriotism, and calling upon them to join him in an expedition to conquer Canada and secure peace to the American frontier. This call was answered, and a highly respectable force assembled for the expedition. The result of this enterprise is thus given in Perkins' History of the Late War.

"On the 27th of November, 1812, the military force collected at Black Rock, under Gen. Smyth, prepared for the invasion of Canada, amounted to 4,500 effective men, consisting of New York volunteers under Gen. Porter, and regulars and volunteers from Pennsylvania and Baltimore: 85 boats were prepared for crossing the river, capable of transporting at once the necessary artillery and 3,500 men. On the night of the 27th, two parties were sent over, one under Colonel Boerlster, and the other under Capt. King, assisted by a company of marines, under Lieut. Angus, to destroy the British batteries. They effectually accomplished this object, routed the enemy, spiked their guns, and drove them from the shore. Capt. King, in attempting to return, was captured, with two boats belonging to his party. Colonel Winder, with a party of 250 men, in attempting to land at a difficult point on the river, was prevented by the rapidity of the current, and obliged to return to the American side. The general embarkation commenced in the morning of the 28th, but was not completed until afternoon. They then moved up the stream from the navy yard to Black Rock, and were ordered by Gen. Smyth to disembark and dine. After dinner, the expedition was postponed to a future day. This attempt gave the enemy full notice of the plans of the American general. The two following days were employed in preparations for a second attempt. At 3 o'clock in the morning of the 1st of December, the embarkation commenced a second time; the regulars on the right, Gen. Tanehills's brigade in the centre, and the New York volunteers on the left. Gen. Porter, accompanied by Majs. Chapin and Macomb, Capt. Mills of the cavalry, and Adj. Chace, with two pilots, took his station in the front boat, hoisted his flag, and advanced to the head of the line to lead the expedition.

"The troops, in fine spirits and in eager expectation, awaited their orders from Gen. Smyth, when, after considerable delay, they were given, not to proceed to the Canada shore, but to disembark and go into winter quarters. Nothing could exceed the chagrin and disappointment of the troops upon this occasion; disorder and insubordination ensued; Gen. Smyth's life was threatened, and in imminent danger; the militia disbanded and sent home; and Gen. Smyth, finding the Canadas were not to be taken by proclamation, and being disinclined to make use of more powerful means, retired from the service."

BUFFALO CITY is situated at the outlet of Lake Erie, at the head of Niagara river, at the mouth of the Buffalo creek, and at the western extremity of the Erie canal; Lat. 42° 53' N., long. 2° west from Washington. Distant from Albany by the great western road 298 miles; by the Erie canal, 364; from New York, by Albany and Utica, 445; by Morristown. N. J., Owego, and Ithaca, 357; from Rochester, 73; from Niagara Falls, 22; from Erie, Penn., 90; from Cleveland, Ohio, 103; from Detroit, Mich., 290; from Toronto, U. C., 72; from Montreal, L. C., 427; and from Washington City, 376 miles. Buffalo is the port of entry for the Niagara district, including Silver Creek, Dunkirk, and Portland, and all above the falls. It is an *entrepot* for the great and growing trade between New York and a large portion of Upper Canada and the great west.

Buffalo was originally laid out in 1801, by the Holland Land Company, on a bluff or terrace rising 50 feet above the water, and partly on the low and marshy ground extending from the terrace to the creek and lake. This marsh has been drained, and a large portion of the business part of the city lies upon it. The Erie canal from Tonewanda village is continued along the margin of Niagara river and the shore of the lake to the city. A mole or pier of wood and stone, 1,500 feet long, extends from the south side of the mouth of the creek, forming a partial breakwater to protect the shipping from the gales which are felt here. For the better accommodation of trade, a ship canal, 80 feet wide and 13 deep, was completed in 1833, across the harbor near the mouth of the creek, a distance of 700 yards. A lighthouse built of limestone stands on the end of the pier, 46 feet in height.

From the time of the foundation of this place to 1812, it increased slowly. In that year it became a military post, and in December, 1813, every building in it was burnt save two, by the British and Indians. Many of the inhabitants were taken prisoners to Montreal. The place was soon rebuilt, and by 1817, it contained 100 houses, some of which were large and elegant. It was incorporated as a village in 1822, and, in 1823, had the courthouse and jail, and upwards of 300 buildings. It had then felt in advance the influence of the Erie canal, and much improvement was made in anticipation of the completion of that great work. In 1829, it had 400 houses and more than 2,000 inhabitants. It was incorporated as a city in 1832, and contains at this time about 2,000 houses, and 18,041 inhabitants. There are 13 churches, viz: 1 Presbyterian, 1 Episcopal, 1 Free Congregational, 1 German Lutheran, 1 Unitarian, 1 Methodist Episcopal, 1 Methodist Reformed, 1 Baptist, 1 Universalist, 2 Catholic, 1 German Evangelical, and 1 Bethel, a literary and scientific academy, incorporated in 1827, 3 banks, 5 weekly and 2 daily newspapers, and many hotels and taverns required for the great concourse of strangers here. The buildings, public and private, are generally good, many of them four stories high, among which are fine specimens of architecture. An enterprising citizen, Mr. Rathbun, during the year 1835, erected 99 buildings, at an aggregate cost of about $500,000; of these, 52 were stores of the first class, 32 dwellings, a theatre, &c."

The following is a western view of the Seneca Mission church, on the Indian reservation, four miles from the main street in Buffalo. The church is somewhat on the congregational plan. This building was erected in 1829, almost wholly at the expense of the Indians. The Rev. Asher Wright is their minister, and resides a short distance from the church. In order to render himself more useful to them, he has acquired their language, as they are but partially acquainted with the English. They seem to be much attached to him. The Indian burying ground is about 25 rods north of the church. This spot is the site of an Indian fort, on which some vestiges of the wall are still remaining. The Senecas have a tradition that there was a great battle fought here against a hostile tribe; that the bodies of the slain were collected, and burnt-sacrifices were offered, &c. This is strongly corroborated by the fact of human bones, those of animals, and corn in a burnt state, having been dug up on this spot. Four or five graves

NORTH WEST VIEW OF BUFFALO, N. Y.

The above view was taken on a gentle elevation, a short distance westwardly of the city. A small portion of Lake Erie is seen on the extreme right.

ERIE COUNTY.

Seneca Mission House, Buffalo Reservation.

only have monuments. The following inscriptions were copied from two of them. Red Jacket's monument was erected by some persons connected with the theatre in Buffalo:

"SAGOYEWATHA, Keeper Awake, *Red Jacket;* chief of the Wolf Tribe of the Senecas, the friend and protector of his people. Died Jan. 20, 1832, aged 78 years. Erected by —."

"In memory of 'The White Woman,' Mary Jemison, daughter of Thomas Jemison and Jane Irwin, born on the ocean between Ireland and Philadelphia in 1742, or '43, taken captive at Marsh Creek, Penn., in 1755, carried down the Ohio, adopted into an Indian family in 1759, removed to Genesee river, was naturalized in 1817, removed to this place in 1831, and having survived two husbands and five children, leaving three still alive, she died Sept. 19th, 1833, aged about 91 years, having a few weeks before expressed a hope of pardon through Jesus Christ. The council of the Lord shall stand."

There are about nine hundred Indians on the Buffalo creek reservation; of this number about six hundred and seventy-five are Senecas, the rest Onondagas, Oneidas, Tuscaroras, a few Mohawks, and four or five Stockbridge Indians. They have eight peace and two war chiefs, who have a seat in the council of the confederated Six Nations. There are about ninety chiefs in the Seneca nation, persons authorized to sign treaties, &c. These chiefs preside over about 2,400 Indians, who live on the Buffalo creek, Tonewanda, Allegany, and Cattaraugus reservations. Many attempts have been made, by treaty and otherwise, to get possession of the Indian lands in the vicinity of Buffalo. It is believed that the full extent of the bribery, fraud, and villany which has been practised upon the Indians, in order to make them sign treaties for their lands, will never be fully known. At present, only about one fourteenth part of the Indians are willing to remove. Whether the recent attempts of the land speculators to get the Indian territory into their possession will prove successful, remains to be seen.

The following is an eastern view of the house of William Jones, and the cabin of Red Jacket, both situated about 80 rods from the Mission church. The house of Jones, which is seen on the right, is a fair specimen of the better sort of Indian houses. It is said that Jones was offered ten thousand dollars by the land speculators, if he

House of Red Jacket, on the Buffalo Reservation.

would sign his name to the treaty, conveying away the Indian lands. Although as anxious and diligent as most white men in the pursuit of wealth, yet considering it would be injurious to his Indian brethren, he refused the bribe. The cabin seen on the left, is constructed of hewed logs, and was the residence of the celebrated chief Red Jacket, during the latter period of his life. It stands back a few rods from the road, and is quite humble in its appearance.

The following biographical sketch of Red Jacket is taken principally from the 14th vol. of the New York Mirror, and partly from persons on the reservation, who were acquainted with the subject of it.

Red Jacket was born in 1756. His birthplace is supposed to have been at a place formerly called "Old Caste," about 3 miles west of Geneva, in the present limits of the town of Seneca. His Indian name was *Sa-go-you-wat-ha*, a word signifying one who keeps awake by magical influence. During the revolution, the Senecas fought under the British standard. Although quite young, his activity and intelligence attracted the attention of the British officers. By them he was presented with a richly embroidered scarlet jacket. This he wore on all occasions, and from this circumstance arose the name by which he is known among the whites. During the revolution he took little or no part as a warrior, but his personal activity and transcendent talents won the esteem of his tribe. A gentleman who knew him intimately for more than 30 years in peace and in war, speaks of him in the following terms. "Red Jacket was a perfect Indian in every respect, in costume, in his contempt of the dress of the white men, in his hatred and opposition to the missionaries, and in his attachment to, and veneration for the ancient customs and traditions of his tribe. He had a contempt for the English language, and disdained to use any other than his own. He was the finest specimen of the Indian character that I ever knew, and sustained it with more dignity than any other chief. He was second to none in authority in his tribe. As an orator he was unequalled by any Indian I ever saw. His language was beautiful and figurative, as the Indian language always is, and delivered with the greatest ease and fluency. His gesticulation was easy, graceful, and natural. His voice was distinct and clear, and he always spoke with great animation. His memory was very strong. I have acted as interpreter to most of his speeches, to which no translation could do adequate justice."

The following interesting anecdotes are illustrative of his peculiar points of character, as well as of his ready eloquence. At a council held with the Senecas, a dispute arose between Gov. Tompkins and Red Jacket, connected with a treaty of some years standing. The governor stated one thing, and the Indian chief insisted that the reverse was true. But, it was rejoined, "you have forgotten—we have it written down on paper." "The paper then tells a lie," was the confident answer; "I have it written here," continued the chief, placing his hand with great dignity upon his brow. "You Yankees are born with a feather between your fingers; but your paper does not speak the truth. The Indian keeps his knowledge here—this is the book the Great Spirit gave us—it does not lie!" A reference was immediately made to the treaty in question, when, to the astonishment of all present, and to the triumph of the tawny statesman, the document confirmed every word that he had uttered.

It happened during the revolution that a treaty was held with the Indians at which Lafayette was present, the object of which was to unite the various tribes in amity with America. The majority of the chiefs were friendly, but there was much opposition made to it, especially by a young warrior, who declared that when an alliance was entered into with America, he should consider that the sun of his country had set forever. In his travels through the Indian country, when last in America, it happened at a large assemblage of chiefs, that Lafayette referred to the treaty in question, and turning to Red Jacket, said, "Pray tell me, if you can, what has become of that daring youth who so decidedly opposed all propositions for peace and amity?" "I myself am the man," replied Red Jacket; "the decided enemy of the Americans, so long as the hope of successfully opposing them remained, but now their true and faithful ally until death."

During the late war, Red Jacket with his tribe enlisted on the American side. He fought through the whole war, and displayed the most undaunted intrepidity; while in no instance did he exhibit the ferocity of the savage, or disgrace himself by any act of inhumanity.

Red Jacket was the foe of the white man. His nation was his god; her honor, preservation, and liberty, his religion. He hated the missionary of the cross, because he feared some secret design upon the lands, the peace, or the independence of the Senecas. He never understood Christianity. Its sublime disinterestedness exceeded his conceptions. He was a keen observer of human nature; and saw that among white and red men, sordid interest was equally the spring of action. He therefore naturally enough suspected every stranger who came to his tribe, of some design on their little and dearly prized domains. His tribe was divided into two factions, one of which, from being in favor of the missionaries, was called the Christian, and the other, from their opposition, the pagan party. His wife, who would attend the religious meetings of the Christian party, received much persecution from him on this account. During his last sickness there seemed to be quite a change in regard to his feelings respecting Christianity. He repeatedly remarked to his wife, that he was sorry that he had persecuted her,—that she was right and he wrong, and as his dying advice, told her, "*Persevere in your religion, it is the right way!*"

A few days before his decease, he sent for Mr. Harris, the missionary; but he was attending an ecclesiastical council, and did not receive the message until after the death of the chief. In his last wandering moments it is said that he directed that a vial of cold water should be placed in his coffin, so that he might have something with which to fight the evil spirit. A considerable number of people from Buffalo attended his funeral, some of whom wished him buried in the ancient or pagan style. He was, however, interred in the Christian manner, in accordance with the wishes of his relatives. He left two wives, but none of his children survived him. Two of his sons are supposed to have died Christians. Rev. Jabez B. Hyde, a teacher to the Senecas before the war of 1812, states that one of the sons of Red Jacket was the first convert to Christianity from this tribe.

For some months previous to his death, time had made such ravages on his constitution as to render him fully sensible of his approaching dissolution. To that event he often adverted, and always in the language of philosophic calmness. He visited successively all his most intimate friends at their cabins, and conversed with them upon the condition of the nation in the most affecting and impressive manner. He told them that he was passing away, and his counsels would soon be heard no more. He ran over the history of his people from the most remote period to which his knowledge extended, and pointed out, as few could, the wrongs, the privations, and the loss of character, which almost of themselves constituted that history. "I am about to leave you," said he, "and when I am gone, and my warning shall no longer be heard or regarded, the craft and the avarice of the white man will prevail. Many winters have I breasted the storm, but I am an aged tree, and can stand no longer. My leaves are fallen, my branches are withered, and I am shaken by every breeze. Soon my aged trunk will be prostrate, and the foot of the exulting foe of the Indian may be placed upon it in safety; for I leave none who will be enabled to avenge such an indignity. Think not I mourn for myself. I go to join the spirits of my fathers, where age cannot come; but my heart fails when I think of my people, who are soon to be scattered and forgotten."

At the time of the burning of Buffalo in the last war, most of the regular American troops were removed from the Niagara frontier. Gov. Tompkins, on being informed of this, ordered out the militia for its defence. On the 25th December, 1813, Gen. Hall had assembled at Black Rock and Buffalo 2,000 men. On the night of the 29th, the enemy were discovered approaching the American shore in great force. The militia were ordered to oppose their landing, but the main body fled on the approach of the enemy. Col. Blakesley's regiment, with other detached corps, amounting in the whole to about 600 men, formed in a line, and poured a destructive fire on the enemy as they approached the shore. They were, however, overpowered by numbers, and forced to retire. Gen. Hall retired with the remains of the dispersed militia to Eleven Mile creek, where he was able to collect only about 300 men to cover the flying inhabitants. The frontier presented one scene of universal desolation. "The miserable inhabitants who escaped the Indian tomahawk, fled into the interior, without shelter or means of support, in the depth of winter, and subsisted on the charity of their friends." The following, relative to these events, is extracted from an official letter to Gov. Tompkins:

"On my arrival at Batavia, I found that the inhabitants of that place, and the country west, as far as Buffalo on the main road, had, on receiving information of the landing of the enemy, fled and left their homes, but were generally returning. I proceeded to Buffalo, and found that flourishing village totally destroyed. The only buildings remaining in it are a jail, which is built of stone, a small frame house, and an armorer's shop. All the houses east of Buffalo on the Batavia road, for two miles, excepting log-houses, are also destroyed, and almost every building between Buffalo and Niagara along the river, had, I was informed, shared the same fate. The enemy had with him at Black Rock and Buffalo, a number of Indians, (the general opinion in that country is about two hundred,) who pursued their accustomed mode of horrid warfare, by tomahawking, scalping, and otherwise mutilating the persons who fell into their hands. Among the victims of their savage barbarity, was a Mrs. Lovejoy, of Buffalo, who was tomahawked and afterward burnt in her own house. The conduct of these savages has struck the minds of the people on the Niagara frontier with such horror, as to make it absolutely necessary that a more efficient force than the ordinary militia of the country should be employed for its protection, to prevent its becoming entirely depopulated. There was, when I left Batavia, between five and six hundred militia at Williamsville and in its vicinity, under the command of Gen. Hopkins, and about the same number on the ridge road near the arsenal, under the command of Col. Hopkins. It was the intention of Gen. Hall, who was at Batavia, to make up the number at each of these stations to 1,000 men. There was also at Batavia about 100 regulars, under the command of Major Riddle, who had received orders to march to Williamsville."

BRANT, recently formed from Collins, is situated in the southwestern corner of the county, bounded partly on the S. by Cattaraugus creek; centrally distant from Buffalo 26 miles. Pop. 1,068.

CHEEKTOWAGA, recently erected from the southern portion of Amherst; from Buffalo, W., 7 miles. The line of the Buffalo and Batavia railroad passes centrally through the town. Pop. 1,137.

CLARENCE, organized in 1808; bounds since altered; from Albany 265 miles. Clarence, 18 miles NE. from Buffalo, has about 50 dwellings. Pop. 2,271.

COLDEN, taken from Holland in 1827; from Albany 287, from Buffalo. SE., 21 miles. Pop. 1,085.

COLLINS, taken from Concord in 1821; from Buffalo, S., 30 miles. Lodi village is partly in this town and partly in Cattaraugus co. (See Persia, Cattaraugus co.) A large portion of this town was settled by Friends. Pop. 4,227. Collins Centre and Carr's Corners are small villages.

ERIE COUNTY.   153

CONCORD, taken from Willink in 1812; from Albany 282 miles. Springville village, incorporated in 1834, 28 miles SE. from Buffalo, has 1 Baptist, 1 Methodist, and 1 Presbyterian church, a flourishing Academy, 110 dwellings, 7 mercantile stores, a large flouring mill, erected at the expense of $20,000, two woollen factories, &c., and about 700 inhabitants. Concord Centre and Waterville Corners are small villages. Pop. 3,004.

EDEN, organized in 1812; centrally distant from Buffalo, S., 16 miles. Eden and Eden Valley are small villages. Many German and Swiss emigrants have settled in this town. Pop. 2,172.

EVANS, taken from Eden in 1821; from Albany 293, from Buffalo, SW., 19 miles. Jerusalem Corners and Evans are small villages. Pop. 1,822.

HAMBURG, taken from Willink in 1812; from Buffalo centrally distant, SE., 10 miles. Hamburg, E. Hamburg, Water Valley, Whites Corners, and Hamburg on the lake, are small settlements. Pop. 3,734.

HOLLAND, taken from Aurora in 1818; bounds since altered; from Buffalo, SE., 24 miles. Holland is a small village. Pop. 1,242.

LANCASTER, taken from Clarence in 1833; from Albany 280 miles. Lancaster, 10 miles E. of Buffalo, is a small village. Town Line, on the Lancaster and Alden line, is a post-office. Pop. 2,083.

NEWSTEAD, originally organized by the name of Erie, as part of Genesee county, and taken from Batavia in 1804; from Albany 260 miles. Akron, 24 miles NE. from Buffalo, and Fisher's Falls, are small villages. Newstead is a post-office. Pop. 2,653.

SARDINIA, taken from Concord in 1821; from Albany 273 miles. Sardinia on the Cattaraugus creek, 34 miles SE. from Buffalo, has about 50 dwellings. Pop. 1,741.

TONEWANDA was recently taken from Buffalo. It comprises Grand Island, in the St. Lawrence, and a small tract of the adjoining mainland. Pop. 1,250. Tonewanda village lies at the mouth and on both sides of Tonewanda creek, the portion lying on the north side of the creek being in Wheatfield, Niagara co. It is 16 miles SW. from Lockport, 11 N. from Buffalo, on the lines of the Buffalo and Niagara railroad and the Erie canal, which latter here runs in the Tonewanda creek. Grand Island, called by the Indians Owanungah, in the Niagara river, commences about 5 miles below the termination of Lake Erie, runs down 8 miles, and ends within 3 of Niagara Falls. Its breadth varies from 3 to 6 miles. Originally this with the small islands of Strawberry, Snake, Squaw, and Bird, belonged to the Senecas, and were purchased of them by the state for $1,000, and an annuity of $500. "The state, in 1833, sold Grand Island to the East Boston Co., who have erected upon it, on the site of the proposed Jewish city of Ararat, opposite to the mouth of the Tonewanda creek, the village of White Haven, (named after Mr. Stephen White, who resides upon Tonewanda island nearly opposite,) where they have a steam grist-mill and saw-mill 150 feet square, with room for 15 gangs of saws, said to be the largest in the world, several dwellings, a building used for a school and church, a commodious

20

wharf, several hundred feet long, and a spacious dock of piles for storing and securing floating timber. The principal object of the company is to prepare timber for vessels on the lakes and the ocean, fitting the frames to the models given; in which they avail themselves, not only of their special resources on the island, but of all which the vast region around the upper lakes affords." The opertions of this company are at present suspended.

"In 1816 and '17, a number of persons from the United States and Canada went on this island. They marked out the boundaries of their different possessions; elected magistrates and other officers from among themselves; and gave out that they were amenable to neither government, but an independent community. After the question of boundary was settled, the state of New York passed a law to drive them off; but that was not effected till the severe measure was resorted to of destroying their houses, which was done by the sheriff and posse of Erie county. 'Grand Island was selected by Major Noah, (now of the city of New York,) on which to build a city, and establish a colony of Jews, with the view of making it the Ararat, or resting-place of that dispersed people. There it was anticipated that their government would be organized, and thence the laws would emanate which again were to bring together the children of Israel, and re-establish them as a nation upon the earth. The European Rabbi did not sanction the scheme, and it vanished as a day-dream of the learned and worthy projector."—*Steele's Book of Niagara Falls.*

The monument erected by Major Noah is now standing. It is about 14 feet in height. The lower part is built of brick,—the upper or pyramidal portion is of wood, and the whole painted white. The following is inscribed upon the tablet, which faces the east.

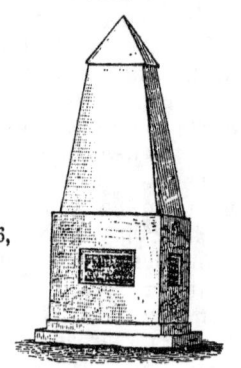

שמע ישראל יי אלהינו *

יי אחד

ARARAT,

A CITY OF REFUGE FOR THE JEWS,

Founded by MORDECAI M. NOAH, *in the Month* TIZRI, 5586,

September, 1825, and in the 50th year of American

Independence.

WALES, taken from Willink in 1818; from Buffalo, SE., 20 miles. Wales, S. Wales, and Wales Centre, are villages. Pop. 2,441.

ESSEX COUNTY.

ESSEX COUNTY, formed from Clinton in 1799, was originally settled from New England. Its greatest length N. and S. 43, greatest breadth E. and W. 41 miles; centrally distant from New York 271,

---

* *Trans.*—" Hear, O Israel, the Lord our God is one Lord."—Deut. vi. 4.

and from Albany 126 miles. Pop. 23,620. The county is divided into 15 towns. "The surface of this county is decidedly mountainous, in which respect it bears a striking contrast to the St. Lawrence. In addition to this, it may be remarked, that the hills, as well as the mountains, are steep and abrupt, and almost uniformly present, on one side, a precipice nearly perpendicular. In this county there are no long and gradual slopes, or gentle risings towards the mountain summit, but they are always bold and difficult of ascent. A surface of country thus characterized, combined also with great height, both of the general surface and especially of numerous peaks, alters to a very great extent its agricultural character. By this combination, the mean temperature of the county is reduced so low, that the cultivation of some of the most useful vegetables is prevented, or they are crops so uncertain, on account of late springs and early autumnal frosts, that little inducement is held out for trying them even as matters of experiment. There are, however, some bright and favored places where most of the essential vegetable productions are raised, and even grow luxuriantly, as along the shores of Lake Champlain and the valleys of the upper Hudson." But the agricultural poverty of this county is amply compensated by her immense mineral resources. "Many years must elapse before a correct estimate can be formed in regard to their real extent and value. To say that there are here numerous beds of magnetic iron ore, would scarcely convey a true idea of the enormous deposits of that mineral which are found in various parts of the county. The ore is everywhere of sufficient purity for the manufacturer, and if only a small portion of it can be wrought, Essex must become one of the most thriving counties in the state."—*State Geol. Rep.*

CHESTERFIELD, taken from Willsborough in 1802. Pop. 2,697. Port Kent, a small village 25 miles from Elizabethtown, upon the lake, is the stopping place for the steamboats. Port Douglass, also upon the lake, is the shipping place for the Clintonville iron works. Port Randall is a village in the SE. part. Keeseville is a flourishing manufacturing village on the Au Sable river, which forms here the boundary line between the counties of Clinton and Essex. It is 21 miles from Elizabethtown, and 16 from Plattsburg. There are 1 Presbyterian, 1 Baptist, and 1 Catholic church, an Academy, 10 mercantile stores, 225 dwellings, the Essex County Bank, and 1,800 inhabitants. This place is now the centre of business for the great iron and lumber district of the Au Sable valley. A railroad $4\frac{3}{4}$ miles in length connects it with Port Kent. Keeseville was originally named "Anderson's Falls," from a Mr. John W. Anderson, who settled here about the year 1813. At this time he was almost the only inhabitant in the place. In 1819, a post-office was established, and the present name was given to the village in honor of Mr. Richard Keese, a partner of Anderson's. The first clergyman was the Rev. Elijah Crane. a pious and devoted minister of the Methodist persuasion, who located himself here in 1825, and was very efficient in reforming the morals of the place. Near here is the High Bridge of Keeseville, on the Au Sable river, which is one of the greatest natural curiosities in the state.

CROWN POINT, organized in 1780; from Albany 100 miles; centrally distant SE. from Elizabeth 20 miles. Pop. 2,212. Crown Point, whence the name of the town and ancient fort are derived, is situated at the NE. extremity, and is formed by an extensive deep bay on the west, skirted by a steep mountain, and on the north and east by the body of the lake. Fort Frederick, at this place, was built by the French in 1731. This fortress was a star work, being in the form of a pentagon, with bastions at the angles, and surrounded by a ditch walled in with stone. This post secured the command of Lake Champlain, and guarded the passage into Canada. It was through this lake, by the route of Crown Point, that the parties of French and Indians made their bloody incursions upon the frontiers of New England and New York. This fort was subsequently blown up; and its site is now marked by a heap of ruins. This place being abandoned by the French, in 1759, to Gen. Amherst, fort Crown Point was afterward erected, about a quarter of a mile from the shore, and has at a distance something the appearance of Ticonderoga. The walls were of wood and earth, 16 feet high, 22 thick, enclosing an area of 1,500 yards square, surrounded by a deep broad ditch cut into granite. There were here a double row of stone barracks, and on the north, a gate with a drawbridge and covered way leading to the lake. These works and those adjoining, which were extensive, are now mostly heaps of rubbish. Crown Point fell into the hands of the Americans at the time of the capture of Ticonderoga, in May, 1775, but was evacuated the next year. The disastrous expedition against Canada was terminated near this place, by the destruction of the lake fleet under the command of Gen. Arnold, Oct. 13th, 1776. Arnold, on his retreat from Canada, on board his fleet, was pursued by the enemy so closely, that he was obliged to run his vessel on shore and blow up five gondolas. The British soon established themselves, with their army and fleet, at Crown Point, and strengthened the fortifications; but ere long they abandoned the station and retired to Canada.

ELIZABETHTOWN, settled in 1785, and organized in 1798; from Albany 126, from Lake Champlain, W., 8 miles. Pop. 1,061. Elizabeth, the county seat, is a small village of 30 or 40 dwellings. About a mile SW. of the village is a detached mountain called the *Giant of the valley*, the summit of which is elevated 1,200 feet above the plain, and commands a very extensive prospect to the eastward. It embraces a view of the whole valley of Lake Champlain, comprising Plattsburg, Burlington, Vergennes, Middlebury, and many other villages.

ESSEX, taken from Willsborough in 1805; from Albany 133 miles. Pop. 1,681. Essex village, handsomely situated upon Lake Champlain, has about 40 or 50 dwellings. About 12 miles NE. of Elizabeth is the noted Split Rock. This curiosity is part of a rocky promontory projecting into the lake about 150 feet, and elevated 40 above the water. The part broken off contains half an acre covered with trees, and is separated about 20 feet from the main rock. The opposing sides fit the prominences of the one, corresponding with the cavities of the other. Through this fissure a line has been let down to the depth of 500 feet without reaching the bottom. There is a third post-office called Wessex.

JAY, settled in 1790, by emigrants from New England. "The Forks," Upper Village, and Jayville, are manufacturing villages; the latter is 20 miles NW. of Elizabeth, the county seat. There is a large quantity of iron annually manufactured in this town. Pop. 2,260.

KEENE, taken from Elizabeth and Jay in 1808; from Albany 138, from Elizabeth, W., 12 miles. The settlements at the "Flats" were commenced in 1797, and those at the "Great Plains," in 1804. Pop. 730.

Adirondack Mountains.

The Adirondack mountains, which are partially in this town, were comparatively but little known until explored by the state geologists. They named them from the Adirondack Indians, who formerly dwelt in this region. The group, as a whole, is more lofty than the White Hills of New Hampshire, though the main summit, Mount Washington, exceeds the highest by 767 feet. Mount Marcy (named in honor of ex-governor Marcy) is the most lofty, being 5,337 feet, or 57 feet *over a mile in height*. Large banks of snow have been observed on this peak as late as the middle of July; and there is reason to believe that ice is formed there every night in summer.

LEWIS, settled about 1800, and taken from Willsborough in 1805. This township has its surface much broken by high mountains. Iron ore is abundant. Lewis, 5 miles N. from Elizabeth, is the post village. Pop. 1,500.

MINERVA, taken from Schroon in 1804. Minerva Four Corners, in the SE., 92 miles NE. from Albany, 40 SW. from Elizabethtown, is the post village. Pop. 455.

MORIAH, on Lake Champlain, taken from Crown Point and Elizabethtown in 1808; from Albany 114, from Elizabethtown centrally distant S. 10 miles. Iron ore of excellent quality abounds here. Pop. 2,595. This place was first settled about 1785, by William Mackenzie, Esq. Moriah, West Moriah, Port Henry, and Millbrook, are post villages. Pondsville is a post-office.

NEWCOMB, taken from Minerva and Moriah in 1828; N. from Albany 120, centrally distant SW. from Elizabethtown 30 miles. Pop. 74. The Adirondack mountains are partially in this town, Mount Marcy, the highest, being on the dividing line between this and Keene. Newcomb is a small settlement, centrally situated.

SCHROON, taken from Crown Point in 1804. Schroon, 30 miles S. from Elizabeth, Paradox, and Hoffman, are small post villages. Pop. 1,660.

Ruins of Fort Ticonderoga.

TICONDEROGA,* taken from Crown Point in 1804; from Albany 196, S. from Elizabeth 30 miles. Alexandria and Ticonderoga are thriving villages; the former at the upper fall, near Lake George, and the latter on the lower falls, near Lake Champlain, about one mile apart. Pop. 2,168.

The above is a representation of the ruins of Fort Ticonderoga, the fortress so celebrated in colonial and revolutionary history. These ruins are situated on a peninsula of about 500 acres, elevated upwards of 100 feet above Lake Champlain, at the mouth of Lake George's outlet. This fortress was originally erected by the French in 1756, and was called by them Carillon, and was a place of much strength by nature and art, surrounded on three sides by water, and having half the fourth covered by a swamp, and the only approachable point defended by a breastwork. It was, however, commanded by Mount Defiance on the south side of the creek or outlet, which,

---

" * Ticonderoga is a corruption from the Indian word Che-onderoga, signifying *noisy*, probably in allusion to the falls on the outlet of Lake George.

towers 750 feet above the lake. It was on the summit of this mountain that Gen. Burgoyne's troops showed themselves on the morning of July 4th, 1777, with a battery of heavy cannon, which they had drawn up along the ridge during the night. The distance from the summit to the fort, in a straight line, is about a mile. The position was so commanding that they could count all the men in the fort, and fully justified Gen. St. Clair in ordering an immediate retreat of the garrison. Mount Independence, connected in history with Ticonderoga, lies in Vermont, one mile from the fort on the east side of the lake. There are here also remains of military works.

The following account of the defeat of Gen. Abercrombie before Ticonderoga, July 8, 1758, is from the 3d volume of Macauley's History of New York:

"The expedition against Ticonderoga and Crown Point was conducted by Abercrombie in person. In the beginning of July he embarked his forces, amounting to nearly seven thousand regulars and ten thousand provincials, on Lake George, on board of nine hundred batteaux, and one hundred and thirty-five whale boats, with provisions, artillery, and ammunition. Several pieces of cannon were mounted on rafts, to cover the proposed landing at the outlet of the lake. Early the next morning he reached the landing place, which was in a cove on the west side of the lake near its issue, leading to the advanced guard of the enemy, composed of one bat alion, in a logged camp. He immediately debarked his forces, and after having formed them into three columns, marched to the enemy's advanced post, which was abandoned with precipitation. He continued his march with the army towards Ticonderoga, with the intention of investing it; but the route lying through a thick wood that did not admit of any regular progression, and the guides proving extremely ignorant, the troops were bewildered, and the columns broken by falling in one on another. Lord Howe being advanced at the head of the right centre column, encountered a French detachment, that had likewise lost its way in the retreat from the advanced post, and a warm skirmish ensuing, the enemy were routed with considerable loss; and one hundred and forty-eight were taken prisoners. This advantage was purchased at a dear rate. Lord Howe, and one other officer, besides privates, were killed. The former is spoken of in very high terms for his bravery.* Abercrombie perceiving the troops were greatly fatigued and disordered, deemed it advisable to fall back to the landing place. Then he detached Lieutenant-colonel Bradstreet, with a detachment, to take possession of a saw-mill in the vicinity of Ticonderoga, which the enemy had abandoned. This post being secured, Abercrombie advanced again towards Ticonderoga, where, he understood from the prisoners, the enemy had assembled eight battalions, with a body of Canadians and Indians, amounting in all to six thousand men. The actual number, however, was considerably less, not exceeding four thousand men, as was afterward ascertained. These, they said, being encamped before the fort, were employed in making a formidable intrenchment, where they intended to wait for a reinforcement of three thousand men, who had been detached, under the command of M. de Levi, to make a diversion on the side of the Mohawk; but upon intelligence of Abercrombie's approach, were now recalled for the defence of Ticonderoga. This information induced Abercrombie to strike, if possible, some decisive blow before the junction could be effected. He therefore early next morning sent his engineer to reconnoitre the enemy's intrenchments; and he, upon his return, reported that the works being still unfinished, might be attempted with good prospect of success. A disposition was made accordingly for the attack, and after proper guards had been left at the saw-mill and the landing place, the whole army was put in motion. The troops advanced with great alacrity towards the intrenchments, which, however, they found altogether impracticable. The breastwork was raised eight feet high, and the ground before it covered with an abattis,

---

* "This young officer was the idol of the army. From his first arrival in America, he had accommodated himself and his regiment to the peculiar nature of the service. He cut his hair short, and induced the regiment to follow the example. He fashioned their clothing for the activity of service, and divested himself and them of every article of superfluous baggage. When near Ticonderoga, major, afterward Gen. Putnam, with about 100 men, advanced in front of the army as a kind of scouting party. Putnam endeavored to prevent Lord Howe from accompanying him, saying, 'My Lord, if I am killed, the loss of my life will be of little consequence, but the preservation of yours is of infinite importance to this army.' The only answer was, 'Putnam, your life is as dear to you, as mine is to me: I am determined to go.' They soon met the left flank of the enemy's advance, by whose first fire his lordship fell."—*Humphrey's Life of Putnam.*

or felled trees, with their boughs pointing outward, and projecting in such a manner as to render the intrenchment almost inaccessible. Notwithstanding these discouraging difficulties, the troops marched up to the assault with an undaunted resolution, and sustained a terrible fire. They endeavored to force their way through these embarrassments, and some of them even mounted the parapet; but the enemy were so well covered, and defended their works with so much gallantry, notwithstanding their greatly inferior numbers, that no impression could be made ; the carnage became fearfully great, and the assailants began to fall into great confusion, after several attacks, which lasted several hours. Abercrombie by this time saw plainly that no hope of success remained ; and in order to prevent a total defeat, sounded a retreat, leaving about *two thousand* men on the field. Every corps of the army behaved, on this unfortunate day, with remarkable intrepidity; the greatest loss sustained among the corps, was that of the regiment of Lord John Murray."

The seizure of the fortress of Ticonderoga, by Col. Ethan Allen, on the 10th of May, 1775, is thus related by Ramsay, in his history of the American Revolution :

" It early occurred to many, that if the sword decided the controversy between Great Britain and her colonies, the possession of Ticonderoga would be essential to the security of the latter. Situated on a promontory, formed at the junction of the waters of Lake George and Lake Champlain, it was the key of all communication between New York and Canada. Messrs. Deane, Wooster, Parsons, Stevens, and others of Connecticut, planned a scheme for obtaining possession of this valuable post. Having procured a loan of 1,800 dollars of public money, and provided a sufficient quantity of powder and ball, they set off for Bennington, to obtain the co-operation of Colonel Allen of that place. Two hundred and seventy men, mostly of that brave and hardy people who are called green mountain boys, were speedily collected at Castleton, which was fixed on as the place of rendezvous. At this place Colonel Arnold, who, though attended only with a servant, was prosecuting the same object, unexpectedly joined them. He had been early chosen a captain of a volunteer company by the inhabitants of New Haven, among whom he resided. As soon as he received news of the Lexington battle, he marched off with his company for the vicinity of Boston, and arrived there, though 150 miles distant, in a few days. Immediately after his arrival he waited on the Massachusetts committee of safety, and informed them, that there were at Ticonderoga many pieces of cannon and a great quantity of valuable stores, and that the fort was in a ruinous condition, and garrisoned only by about 40 men. They appointed him a colonel, and commissioned him to raise 400 men, and to take Ticonderoga. The leaders of the party which had previously rendezvoused at Castleton, admitted Colonel Arnold to join them, and it was agreed that Colonel Allen should be the commander in chief of the expedition, and that Colonel Arnold should be his assistant. They proceeded without delay, and arrived in the night at Lake Champlain, opposite to Ticonderoga. Allen and Arnold crossed over with 83 men, and landed near the garrison. They contended who should go in first, but it was at last agreed that they should both go in together. They advanced abreast, and entered the fort at the dawning of day. A sentry snapped his piece at one of them, and then retreated through the covered way to the parade. The Americans followed, and immediately drew up. The commander, surprised in his bed, was called upon to surrender the fort. He asked, By what authority ? Colonel Allen replied, '*I demand it in the name of the great Jehovah, and of the continental congress.*' No resistance was made, and the fort, with its valuable stores and forty-eight prisoners, fell into the hands of the Americans. The boats had been sent back for the remainder of the men, but the business was done before they got over. Colonel Seth Warner was sent off with a party to take possession of Crown Point, where a sergeant and 12 men performed garrison duty. This was speedily effected. The next object, calling for the attention of the Americans, was to obtain the command of Lake Champlain, but to accomplish this, it was necessary for them to get possession of a sloop of war, lying at St. Johns, at the northern extremity of the lake. With the view of capturing this sloop it was agreed to man and arm a schooner lying at South Bay, and that Arnold should command her, and that Allen should command some batteaux on the same expedition. A favorable wind carried the schooner ahead of the batteaux, and Colonel Arnold got immediate possession of the sloop by surprise. The wind again favoring him, he returned with his prize to Ticonderoga, and rejoined Colonel Allen. The latter soon went home, and the former with a number of men agreed to remain there in garrison. In this rapid manner the possession of Ticonderoga and the command of Lake Champlain were obtained, without any loss, by a few determined men."

The following account of the evacuation of Ticonderoga by General St. Clair, on July 6, 1777, and some of the events which followed, is from the 3d volume of Macauley's History of New York:

"From Crown Point, the British army advanced on both sides of the lake; the naval force keeping its station in the centre; the frigate and gun-boats cast anchor just out of cannon-shot from the American works. On the near approach of the right wing, which advanced on the west side of the lake, on the second of July, the Americans abandoned and set fire to their works, block-houses and saw-mills, towards Lake George; and without attempting any serious opposition, suffered General Phillips to take possession of Mount Hope. This post commanded the American lines in a great degree, and cut off their communication with Lake George. The enemy charged the Americans, on this occasion, with supineness and want of vigor; but this charge seems not well-founded; they had not men enough to make any effectual opposition to the powerful force which threatened to enclose them.

"In the mean time, the British army proceeded with such expedition in the construction of their works, the bringing up of their artillery, stores, and provisions, and the establishment of posts and communications, that by the fifth, matters were so far advanced as to require but one or two days more to completely invest the posts on both sides of the lake. Mount Defiance had also been examined, and the advantages which it presented were so important, that it had been determined to take possession, and erect a battery there. This work, though attended with extreme difficulty and labor, had been carried on by General Phillips with much expedition and success. A road had been made over very rough ground, to the top of the mount; and the enemy were at work in constructing a level for a battery, and transporting their cannon. As soon as this battery should be ready to play, the American works would have been completely invested on all sides.

"The situation of General St. Clair was now very critical. He called a council of war, to deliberate on measures to be taken. He informed them that their whole effective number was not sufficient to man one half of the works; that as the whole must be constantly on duty, it would be impossible for them to endure the fatigue for any considerable length of time; that General Schuyler, who was then at Fort Edward, had not sufficient forces to relieve them; and that, as the enemy's batteries were nearly ready to open upon them, and the place would be completely invested in twenty-four hours, nothing could save the troops but an immediate evacuation of the posts.

"It was proposed that the baggage of the army, with such artillery stores and provisions as the necessity of the occasion would admit, should be embarked with a strong detachment on board of two hundred batteaux, and despatched under convoy of five armed galleys, up the lake to Skeensborough, (Whitehall,) and that the main body of the army should proceed by land, taking its route on the road to Castleton, which was about thirty miles southeast of Ticonderoga, and join the boats and galleys at Skeensborough. It was thought necessary to keep the matter a secret till the time should come, when it was to be executed. Hence, the necessary preparations could not be made, and it was not possible to prevent irregularity and disorder, in the different embarkations and movements of the troops.

"About two o'clock in the morning of July the sixth, General St. Clair left Ticonderoga, and about three, the troops at Mount Independence were put in motion. The house which had been occupied by General de Fermoy was, contrary to orders, set on fire. This afforded complete information to the enemy of what was going forward, and enabled them to see every movement of the Americans—at the same time, it impressed the latter with such an idea of discovery and danger, as precipitated them into great disorder. About four o'clock, Colonel Francis brought off the rear-guard, and conducted their retreat in a regular manner; and soon after, some of the regiments, through the exertions of their officers, recovered from their confusion. When the troops arrived at Hubbardton they were halted for nearly two hours, and the rear-guard was increased by many who did not at first belong to it, but were picked up on the road, having been unable to keep up with their regiments. The rear-guard was here put under the command of Colonel Seth Warner, with orders to follow the army, as soon as the whole came up, and to halt about a mile and a half short of the main body. The army then proceeded to Castleton, about six miles further—Colonel Warner, with the rear-guard and stragglers, remaining at Hubbardton.

"The retreat of the Americans from Ticonderoga and Mount Independence, was no sooner perceived by the British, than General Frazer began an eager pursuit with his brigade. Major-general Reidesel was ordered to join in the pursuit with the greater part of his Germans. General Frazer continued the pursuit through the day, and having received intelligence that the rear of the American army was at no great distance, ordered his men to lie that night upon their arms. On July seventh, at five in the morning, he came up with Colonel Warner, who had about one thousand men. The British advanced boldly to the attack, and the two bodies formed within sixty yards of each other. The conflict was fierce and bloody. Colonel Francis fell at the head of his regiment, fighting with great gallantry. Warner was so well supported by his officers and men, that the assailants broke and gave way. They soon, however, recovered from their disorder, formed again, and charged the Americans with the bayonet, when they, in their turn, were put into disorder; these, however, rallied and returned to the charge, and the issue of the battle became dubious. At that moment, General Reidesel appeared with the advance party of his Germans. These being led into action, soon decided the fortune of the day, and the Americans had to retreat. The loss in this action was very considerable on the American side. Colonel Hale, who had not brought his regiment, which consisted of militia, into action, although ordered so to do, in attempting to escape by flight, fell in with an inconsiderable party of the enemy, and surrendered himself, and a number of his men, prisoners. In killed, wounded, and prisoners, the Americans lost in this action three hundred and twenty-four men, and the British one hundred and eighty-three in killed and wounded."

WESTPORT, taken from Elizabethtown in 1815. Iron ore abounds. Pop. 1,932. Westport, a thriving village at the head of NW. bay of Lake Champlain, 8 miles east of Elizabethtown, contains about sixty dwellings. Wadhams Mills, on the Boquet, is a small village.

WILLSBOROUGH, originally organized as part of Clinton county in 1788; since modified. Pop. 1,667. Willsborough, 2 miles from the mouth of the Boquet river, N. from Albany 138, and from Elizabeth E. 13 miles, is a manufacturing village, and has about 50 dwellings.

WILMINGTON, taken from Jay in 1821; name and boundaries since altered; from Albany 148, from Elizabeth NW. 20 miles. The White Face Mountain here commands a view of more than 100 miles in extent, including Montreal, Ogdensburg, and Lake Ontario. Pop. 928.

FRANKLIN COUNTY.

FRANKLIN COUNTY, taken from Clinton in 1808, is centrally distant from New York 287, from Albany NW. 142 miles. Greatest length 60, greatest breadth 30 miles. The high northern latitude sufficiently indicates the rigors of the climate. The forests are very dense, consisting of trees of immense size. In the southwestern part are some lofty ridges of mountains, but of all the rest a large portion is rather level than hilly. The settlements are almost wholly in the northern part, extending about 15 miles S. from the N. line, and even here are sparse; much the larger portion of the county being as yet covered with the primitive forests. The soil is a sandy loam, occasionally mixed with clay, stony, and the fields commonly among thrifty farmers are fenced with stones gathered from the surface. Some wheat is raised, but it is an uncertain crop, whilst grass, oats, barley, corn, &c., generally are very productive. No portion of the state is perhaps better adapted to the sugar-beet. Grazing and lumbering are the chief pursuit of the inhabitants, who find their market upon the

St. Lawrence river. Pop. 16,450. The county is divided into 13 towns.

BANGOR, taken from Dickenson in 1812; distant NW. from Albany 221 miles. Pop. 1,218. Bangor, 5 miles W. of Malone, and W. Bangor, are post villages. The population is principally distributed along two roads about 3 miles asunder, known as the North and South streets.

BELMONT, taken from Chateaugua, in 1833; NW. from Albany 185. Pop. 470. Belmont is a small village, 12 miles SE. of Malone.

BOMBAY, taken from Fort Covington in 1833; NW. from Malone 20 miles. Pop. 1,446. The Indian village of St. Regis lies on the left bank of the St. Regis river, upon the northern boundary. The reservation of this tribe lies partly in this town and partly in Fort Covington, extending 3 by 11 miles. Hogansburg and Bombay Four Corners are villages. The present or late chief of the St. Regis Indians, is or was a descendant of the daughter of the Rev. John Williams the minister of Deerfield, Mass., who was with most of his family and neighbors taken prisoners to Canada in 1704. Mr. Williams was carried to Lake Champlain, and from thence to Montreal and Quebec. In 1706, a flag-ship was despatched to the latter place, and Mr. Williams and 57 other captives were redeemed and sent to Boston: all his children returned with the exception of his daughter Eunice, who, at the age of 10 years, was left behind. She adopted the manners of the Indians, to one of whom she was married, and became converted to the Catholic faith. Some time after the war, she, with her husband, visited her relations at Deerfield, dressed in the Indian costume: and though every persuasive was in vain tried to induce her to abandon him and remain among her connections, she still persisted in wearing her blanket and counting her beads, and returned to Canada, where she ended her days. Her descendants still continue to visit their relatives in New England, by whom they are hospitably received. One of them, by the name of Eleazer Williams, has been educated by his friends in New England and employed as a missionary to the Indians at Green Bay. Mr. Williams some years since, when on a visit to Canada, found the Bible of his great-grandfather, the Rev. John Williams, with his name in it. He states, that when Deerfield was destroyed, the Indians took a small church bell, which is now hanging in the Indian church at St. Regis. It was conveyed on a sledge as far as Lake Champlain and buried, and was afterward taken up and conveyed to Canada.

The first standard captured from the enemy in the late war was taken at this place by Maj. Guilford Dudley Young, on the 22d of Oct., 1812. The following account of this event is extracted from newspapers published at the time.

"Major Young, of the Troy militia, commandant of a detachment stationed at French Mills, on the St. Regis river, having received information that a party of the enemy had arrived at the village of St. Regis, and that more were shortly expected, formed a resolution to take them before they were reinforced. For this purpose, he marched a detachment, at 11 o'clock on the night of the 21st of October, crossed the river at Gray's Mills about 3, and at 5 in the morning arrived within half a mile of the village unexpected by the enemy. Here the major made such a judicious disposition of his men, that the enemy were entirely surrounded, and after a few discharges, surrendered themselves prisoners with the loss of 5 killed. The result of this affair was the capture of 40 prisoners with their arms, equipments, &c., one stand of colors and two batteaux, without a man of our party being hurt. They got safe back to camp at 11 o'clock in the morning. The prisoners were sent off to Plattsburg. Maj. Young has thus had the honor of taking the first standard from the enemy in the present war."

From the Albany Gazette of January, 1813.

" On Thursday, the 5th inst., at 1 o'clock, a detachment of the volunteer militia of Troy entered this city, with the British colors taken at St. Regis. The detachment, with 2 superb eagles in the centre, and the British colors in the rear, paraded to the music of Yankee Doodle and York Fusileers, through Market and State streets, to the capitol, the officers and colors in the centre. The remainder of the vestibule, and the grand staircase leading to the hall of justice, and the galleries of the senate and assembly chambers, were crowded with spectators. His excellency the governor, from illness, being absent, his aids, Cols. Lamb and Lush, advanced from the council chamber to receive the standard." Upon which Maj. Young, in a truly military and gallant style, and with an appropriate address, presented it to the people of New York; to which Col. Lush, on the part of the state, replied in a highly complimentary speech, and the standard* was deposited in the council room, amid the loud huzzas of the citizens and military salutes. Subsequently to this achievement, Maj. Young† was appointed a colonel in the U. S. army.

BRANDON, taken from Bangor in 1828; centrally distant SW. from Malone 30 miles. The settlements are in the north part of the town. Pop. 560.

CHATEAUGUA, taken from Plattsburg and Champlain as part of Clinton county. Chateaugua Four Corners, 13 miles E. from Malone on the turnpike to Plattsburg, is a small village. West Chateaugua is a post-office. Pop. 2,820. There is in this town a cascade on the Chateaugua river of 90 feet perpendicular, over granite rock. Chateaugua was settled in April, 1804, by Benjamin Roberts, from Manchester, Vermont; William Bailey, Esq., and Mr. Nathan Beman, came about the same time. Mr. Beman acted as a guide in conducting Col. Ethan Allen into Ticonderoga. At the first settlement of this place, there were no other settlers in the limits of the county, excepting a few Canadians at French mills, now Fort Covington.

A skirmish took place in this vicinity during the late war, between the British and a portion of the American army under General Hampton, which was designed for the co-operation upon Montreal. The following account of this affair is taken from "*Perkins' History of the Late War.*"

---

* The standard is at present remaining in the capitol at Albany.

† This officer was a native of Lebanon, Conn. " After the war he entered the patriot service under Gen. Mina, and lost his life in the struggle for Mexican independence in 1817. The patriots, 269 in number, had possession of a small fort which was invested by a royalist force of 3,500 men. The supplies of provision and water being cut off, the sufferings of the garrison and women and children in the fort became intolerable; many of the soldiers deserted, so that not more than 150 effective men remained. Col. Young, however, knowing the perfidy of the enemy, determined to defend the fort to the last. After having bravely defeated the enemy in a number of endeavors to carry the fort by storm, Col. Young was killed by a cannon shot, from the battery raised against the fort. 'On the enemy's last retreat, the colonel, anxious to observe all their movements, fearlessly exposed his person, by stepping on a large stone on the ramparts; and while conversing with Dr. Hennessey on the successes of the day, and on the dastardly conduct of the enemy, the last shot that was fired from their battery carried off his head. Col. Young was an officer, whom, next to Mina, the American part of the division had been accustomed to respect and admire. In every action he had been conspicuous for his daring courage and skill. Mina reposed unbounded confidence in him. In the hour of danger he was collected, gave his orders with precision, and, sword in hand, was always in the hottest of the combat. Honor and firmness marked all his actions. He was generous in the extreme, and endured privations with a cheerfulness superior to that of any other officer of the division. He has been in the U. S. service as Lieut. Col. of the 29th regiment of infantry. His body was interred by the few Americans who could be spared from duty with every possible mark of honor and respect; and the general gloom which pervaded the division on this occasion was the sincerest tribute that could be offered by them to the memory of their brave chief.' "—*Barber's Historical Collections and Antiquities of Connecticut.*

"On the morning of the 21st of October, 1813, the army commenced a movement down the Chateaugay. An extensive wood of 10 or 12 miles in front, blocked up with felled timber, and covered by the Indians and British light troops, impeded the progress of the army. Gen. Izard was detached with the light troops and one regiment of the line to turn these impediments in flank, and seize on the open country below, while the army, preceded by a working party, advanced in a more circuitous, but practicable route. The measure succeeded, and the main body reached the advanced position on the Chateaugay, on the evening of the 22d. The 23d and 24th were employed in getting up the artillery and stores. There was now in front of the army 7 miles of open country, at the end of which commenced a wood of some miles in extent, which had been formed into an entire abattis, filled with a succession of wooden breastworks, the rearmost of which was supplied with ordnance. The Indians and light troops were placed in front, and a heavy force in the rear. On the evening of the 25th, Col. Purdy, with the light troops, was detached to gain the rear of this position, while Gen. Izard made a simultaneous attack in front. Col. Purdy was misled by his guides, the attempt failed, and the advanced corps retired, with a loss of 50 killed, wounded, and missing, to a position 3 miles in the rear. On the 28th, Gen. Hampton, under an impression that Sir George Prevost might be in the way of his further advance, fell back to his former position at the Chateaugay Four Corners," and immediately conducted his army back to Plattsburg for winter quarters.

CONSTABLE, taken from Harrison as part of Clinton county in 1807; bounds since altered. Pop. 1,121. Constable is a small village 7 miles N. of Malone. East Constable is a post-office.

DICKENSON, taken from Harrison (original name of Malone) in 1808; from Malone centrally distant SW. 30 miles. Pop. 1,005. This town is about 50 miles long, N. and S., and 6 broad. The settlements are in the northern part.

DUANE, taken from Malone in 1828; centrally distant S. of Malone 20 miles. The post village lies in the N. part of the town, where there is a considerable quantity of iron and steel manufactured from ore in the vicinity. Pop. 324.

FORT COVINGTON, named after Gen. Covington, who was slain at the battle of Williamsburg in Canada, November 11, 1813; taken from Constable in 1817; from Malone N. 7 miles. In the Fork, 5 miles S. of the St. Lawrence, is the post village of Fort Covington, formerly called "French Mills," which contains about 150 dwellings. Fort Covington of the late war was in this township. A large lumber business is here conducted by the way of the St. Lawrence. Pop. 2,098.

FRANKLIN, recently formed from Belmont; centrally distant 28 miles SE. from Malone. The post-office is at Merritsville. Pop. 192.

MALONE, taken from Harrison, and organized as part of Clinton county in 1805; from Albany 212 miles, from Plattsburg W. 51, and from Ogdensburg E. 70 miles. Pop. 3,229. Malone village, the county seat, is situated upon both sides of the Salmon river. This stream is here crossed by a stone bridge, having an arch of 97 feet span and a roadway of 70 feet above the original bed of the stream. This town was first settled by Nathan Wood, an emigrant from Vermont, who located himself about a mile north of the village. The following view was taken near Hosford's tavern, and shows the principal part of the village. The public building on the extreme left is the academy, the one adjacent, the Baptist church; the steeple of a large cotton factory is seen near the centre of the engraving, at the foot of the hill, and the courthouse on the right; the Presbyterian

View of Malone.

church, a large and substantial stone structure, is not brought into this view, being at the eastern end of the village.

During the late war, (Feb., 1814,) a detachment of British made an incursion into this place, and proceeded as far as Chateaugua Four Corners. They were commanded by Col. Scott, of the 103d British regiment, and numbered about 2,300 men, including many Indians. Hearing of the approach of the American troops, they retreated in great confusion, though not without destroying the bridges in their rear. The whole party suffered severely in their retreat by a tremendous storm of snow and hail which prevailed at the close of the day, and lost upwards of 200 men by desertion.

MOIRA, taken from Dickenson in 1827; from Albany 225, centrally distant W. of Malone 14 miles. Pop. 964. Moira is a small village.

WESTVILLE, taken from Constable in 1829; from Albany 233, from Malone centrally distant NW. 9 miles. Westville is a small village. Pop. 1,033.

FULTON COUNTY.

FULTON COUNTY was taken from the northern part of Montgomery county in 1838; NW. from Albany 40 miles; length E. and W. 32 miles, breadth N. and S. 17. The surface of the northern part of this county is hilly, with some ranges of a mountainous character. The Kayaderosseras range of mountains enters the county on the NE., but sinks to the general level in the town of Northampton. The county is well watered and contains several small lakes. It is divided into 9 towns. Pop. 18,038.

FULTON COUNTY. 167

BLEEKER, taken from Johnstown in 1831; from Albany 53 miles, from Johstown N. 13. There are three inconsiderable settlements in the town. The soil is quite poor and covered with small evergreens. Pop. 346.

BROADALBIN, taken from Caughnawaga in 1793; from Albany 47 miles, from Johnstown NE. 10. A settlement was made in this town in 1776, by Daniel McIntyre, and a few other emigrants from Scotland; but it was broken up during the revolutionary war. Fonda's Bush or Rawsonville, 10 miles from Johnstown, incorporated in 1815, has about 800 inhabitants. West Galway and Union Mills are small post villages. Pop. 2,728.

EPHRATA, taken from Palatine in 1827; from Albany 58 miles, from Johnstown centrally distant W. 10. This town was settled in 1724, by Germans. Pop. 2,009. Pleasant Valley, Ephrata, and Lasselsville, are small villages.

Southern view of Johnstown.

JOHNSTOWN, originally named Caughnawaga, was founded about the year 1770, by Sir William Johnson, who resided here during the latter period of his life, essentially in the rank, and with much of the splendor of a nobleman. Sir William and his family, by various means, became possessed of vast tracts of valuable land in this section of the country, and had many tenants and retainers under them. Their great possessions, however, were confiscated during the revolutionary war, on account of their adherence to the British cause. The village of Johnstown is about 4 miles N. of Fonda, the seat of justice for Montgomery county, and 44 from Albany. The accompanying engraving shows the appearance of the village as viewed from the first elevation south, on the road to Caughnawaga or Fonda village. The courthouse is the first building seen on the left with a spire; Mayfield mountains appear in the extreme distance. The village contains a bank, an academy, 4 churches—1 Presbyterian, 1 Episcopal, 1 Dutch Reformed, and 1 Methodist—and about 250 dwellings. It is situated on a handsome plain, skirted on the N. and W. by Cayadutta creek, and on the S. by a hill of moderate elevation. It was regularly laid out by Henry Oothoudt, Jeremiah Van Rensselaer, and Christopher P. Yates, state commissioners, in 1784, and was incorporated in 1807. The village of Kingsboro is 4 miles NE. from Johnstown; it has a Presbyterian church, an academy, and about 40 or 50 dwellings. This village has acquired some celebrity, as being the place where great quantities of dressed deer-skin gloves and mittens have been manufactured. The town of Johnstown was originally organized by the name of Caughnawaga in 1798; its territorial limits have since been much reduced. Pop. 5,408.

Johnson Hall, in Johnstown.

The above is a southeastern view of the mansion-house built by Sir William Johnson, called *"Johnson Hall."* This house, now occupied by Mr. Wells, is situated about three fourths of a mile NW. of the courthouse, on ground gently elevated above the village. The hall itself is built of wood, but the buildings or wings on each side are of stone, pierced with loop-holes for musketry. When Sir William occupied these buildings, he had them surrounded by a stone breastwork. While in possession of the Johnson family, this was a place of resort for the sachems of the Six Nations, and all the Mohawks repaired thither to receive their presents from the British government.

William Johnson was born in Ireland about the year 1714; he was a nephew of Sir Peter Warren, the naval commander who distinguished himself at the siege of Louisburg in 1745. Sir Peter having married a sister of Chief-justice De Lancey of New York, purchased a large tract of land on the Mohawk, and about the year 1734, sent for his nephew to come to America and superintend this estate. Young Johnson first established himself at the mouth of the Schoharie, afterward erected a house in the town of Amsterdam, and subsequently the hall at Johnstown. To fulfil the duties of his commission, he learned the language of the Indians, studied their manners and cultivated their acquaintance. His situation between Albany and Oswego presented a fine opportunity for trade, and he carried on a large traffic with them, supplying them with goods, and receiving in return beaver and other skins. By a course of sagacious measures he obtained an influence over the Indians greater than was ever possessed by any other white man.

In 1757, Johnson was intrusted with the command of the provincial troops of New York, whom he led to Lake George, where was achieved the first victory gained on the British side, in the war commencing at that period. For this victory, towards which he did but little more than barely hold the place of commander-in-chief, he received from the house of commons £5,000 sterling; and from the king, the title of baronet, and the office of superintendent of Indian affairs. In 1759, being at the head of the provincial troops employed under Gen. Prideaux to besiege Fort Niagara, he became, when that officer was killed, the commander-in-chief: by his activity and skill he defeated the enemy and obtained possession of the fort and garrison. In 1760, when Gen. Amherst embarked at Oswego on his expedition to Canada, Sir William brought to him at that place 1,000 Indians of the Iroquois or Six Nations, which was the largest number that had ever been seen in arms at one time in the cause of England. "Sir William Johnson possessed considerable talents as an orator, and his influence over the Indians was not a little owing to the impression made upon them by means of his elocution. . . . . He had wives and concubines, sons and daughters, of different colors." By Lady Johnson he had 3 children—1 son and 2 daughters. His son, Sir John Johnson, took side with the British, in the revolutionary war, and became the scourge of the Mohawk valley. One of the daughters married Col. Claus, and the other Sir Guy Johnson. Sir William died suddenly, at Johnson Hall, July 11th, 1774, aged 60 years; and was succeeded by his son in his title, and also to his post as major-general of the militia.

The following anecdote respecting Sir William, seems to evince, that in his dealings with the Indians, who have a good reputation for cunning, he was not outwitted. Hendrick, the chief of the Mohawks, was at the house of Sir William when he received several rich suits of laced clothes. Soon after, the chief came to him and said, "I dream." "Well! what did you dream?" "I dream you give me one suit of clothes." This hint could not be mistaken or well avoided, and accordingly Hendrick received a suit. Some time afterward Sir William meeting Hendrick, said to him, "I dreamed last night. Did you! What did you dream?" "I dreamed you gave me a tract of land," describing it. Hendrick at first paused at the enormity of the demand, but at length said, "You may have the land; *but we no dream again, you dream too hard for me.*" The tract of land thus obtained, is stated to have been 12 miles square, in the present county of Herkimer; the title to it was confirmed by the king, and was called the "Royal Grant."

The power which Sir William Johnson acquired over the Indians descended to his son and to his nephew, Col. Guy Johnson, who succeeded him in the agency of Indian affairs. As the family had derived most of their wealth and consideration from the crown, they were, as might be supposed, devoted loyalists. In 1775, Gen. Schuyler prevailed upon the Indians to agree to be neutral in the coming conflict. It appeared, however, that the influence of the Johnson family prevailed with the Indians, and induced them to join the British cause. It also appeared that Sir John was fortifying his house and arming the Scotch Highlanders, his tenants and adherents. Congress having heard of these movements, sent Gen. Schuyler to disarm these persons, and take other measures to secure the tranquillity of Tryon county. Schuyler set out on this mission with 700 militia, but before he reached Caughnawaga his force had increased to three thousand. At Schenectady a deputation of Mohawks under the influence of the Johnsons met him, and with much artfulness endeavored to dissuade him from advancing. On the 16th of January, 1776, Gen. Schuyler despatched a letter to Sir John, requesting him to meet him on the morrow; they accordingly met, and after some subsequent delay, he and the Scotch gentlemen agreed to make a delivery of the arms of the inhabitants. Sir John likewise agreed that he would not go westward of German Flats and Kinsland district, and that six Scotch inhabitants might be taken as hostages. On the 19th, Schuyler marched into Johnstown and drew up his men in a line; the Highlanders were drawn up facing them, and grounded their arms. The military stores were surrendered: and this service being performed, Schuyler and the militia returned. It was found afterward that the Highlanders had not delivered up their broadswords or ammunition.

Gen. Herkimer was left by Gen. Schuyler to complete the disarming of the hostile inhabitants. Sir John, notwithstanding his word of honor, continued his hostile intrigues with the Indians, and otherwise forfeited his promises. It was found necessary to secure him, and in May, 1776, Col. Dayton was sent on this duty. The tories in Albany gave notice to Sir John of his approach, and the knight and his followers fled to the woods, and escaped to Canada, arriving at Montreal after nineteen days of suffering and starvation. He left his residence in much haste: an iron chest with the family Bible and papers were buried in the garden. On arriving in Canada, the baronet was commissioned a British colonel, and raised the regiment of tories called the *Royal Greens.* By his adherence to the British, his immense estate was forfeited, and this appears to have inspired him with implacable revenge. On Sunday, the 21st of May, 1780, at dead of night, Sir John Johnson, with a force of about 500 men, part of whom were Indians, made an incursion into Johnstown. He had penetrated the country by way of Lake Champlain to Crown Point, and thence through the woods to the Sacondaga river. The following account of this incursion is from a newspaper published June 15th, 1780.

"By the latest intelligence from Schenectady, we are informed that Sir John Johnson, (who styles himself Lieut. colonel commanding the King's Royal Yorkers, in the parcels given to some of the prisoners,) on Lord's day evening, the 21st ult., made his first appearance at Johnson Hall, undiscovered by any but his friends, who no doubt were in the secret. On Monday, about daybreak, they began to burn all the houses except those of the tories, beginning at Aaron Putnam's, below Tripe's Hill, and continued burning to Anthony's Nose, or Acker's house, except a few which by the vigilance of the people were put out after the enemy had set them on fire. There have been burnt 33 houses and out-houses and a mill; many cattle were killed in the field, and 60 or 70 sheep burnt in a barn. Eleven persons were killed. Col. Fisher [Visscher] and his two brothers fought with great bravery, when the two brothers were killed and scalped; the colonel went up stairs and there defended himself, but being overpowered, was knocked down and scalped, on which they plundered the house, set it on fire, and then went off. The colonel recovering a little, though he was left by the enemy for dead, he pulled one of his dead brothers out of the house then in flames; the other was consumed in the house. It is said that the doctors have hopes that Col. Fisher will recover. His mother had a narrow escape for her life, being knocked on her head by an Indian; but she is like to do well. Capt. Hansen was killed by an Indian, who had formerly been used by him with kindness, and professed much gratitude. Old Mr. Fonda was cut in several parts of his head with a tomahawk. Had it not been for the alertness of Mr. Van Vrank, probably more would have been butchered by their savage hands; he alarmed the people along the way to Caughnawaga, who by crossing the river saved their lives. Having done all the mischief to the distressed inhabitants they possibly could, they returned to Johnson Hall in the afternoon; when Johnson dug up his plate, and about sundown marched for the Scotch Bush, about four miles, that evening. He has 15 or 20 of his negroes who had been sold; several of his tenants and others have gone with him. He has permitted some of his prisoners to return on parole. His whole force when he landed at Crown Point, is said to be about 500 men, 200 of them British, part of his own regiment, and Indians. Capt. Putnam and four men followed them in their retreat four days, on their way to Lake Champlain. He saw him 24 miles from Johnson Hall. Some think they will take their route to Oswagatchie; but this seems improbable, as they have not provisions sufficient with them. His excellency the governor has collected a body of militia to intercept their way to Lake Champlain; a number have also marched from the New Hampshire grants for the same purpose: Col. Van Schaick, with 800 men, is in pursuit of him by the way of Johnstown. We hear that the enemy had their feet much swelled by their long march; and being greatly fatigued, it is hoped our people may come up with and give a good account of the Lieut. colonel and his murdering banditti."

In this incursion, Mr. Sampson Sammons and his three sons, all stanch whigs, residing in Johnstown, were captured by the enemy and their dwelling laid in ashes. The elder Mr. Sammons and his youngest son, a youth of eighteen, were released by Sir John, but Jacob and Frederick, the other sons, were taken to Canada and confined in the fortress of Chamblee. From this place they made their escape, and after a series of dreadful suffering, in their flight through the wilderness, arrived in safety among their friends. A long and interesting account of their adventures is given in Col. Stone's Life of Brant.

"A singular but well-attested occurrence," says Col. Stone, "closes this interesting personal narrative. The family of the elder Sammons had long given up Frederick as lost. On the morning after his arrival at Schenectady, he despatched a letter to his father, by the hand of an officer on his way to Philadelphia, who left it at the house of a Mr. Levi De Witt, five miles distant from the residence of the old gentleman. The same night on which the letter was thus left, Jacob dreamed that his brother Frederick was living, and that there was a letter from him at De Witt's announcing the joyful tidings. The dream was repeated twice, and the contents of the letter were so strongly impressed upon his mind, that he repeated what he believed was the very language, on the ensuing morning—insisting that such a letter was at the place mentioned. The family, his father in particular, laughed at him for his credulity. Strong, however, in the belief that there was such a communication, he repaired to the place designated, and asked for the letter. Mr. De Witt looked for it, but replied there was none. Jacob requested a more thorough search, and behold the letter was found behind a barrel, where it had fallen. Jacob then requested Mr. De Witt to open the letter, and examine while he recited its contents. He did so, and the creamer repeated it word for word."

In the summer of 1781, another expedition was sent against Johnstown. This was conducted with so much secrecy, that on the 24th of Oct., the enemy, about one thousand in number under Majors Ross and Butler, were upon the settlement at Warrensbush before their approach was suspected. Col. Willet, who was at Fort Rensselaer about twenty miles distant, on hearing the news, immediately marched for Fort Hunter, which he reached early on the following morning with all the forces he could muster, being but 416 men in all. When he arrived here, he learned that Ross and Butler had the preceding day crossed the river some distance below Tripe's Hill, and arrived at Johnstown about the middle of the day, killing and taking the people prisoners, destroying buildings and cattle on their way. Having effected the passage of the river, Col. Willet pushed on in pursuit of the enemy. Having ascertained their position, he detached Major Rowley, of Massachusetts, with part of his force, by a circuitous march, to fall upon the rear of the enemy while he attacked them in front, a short distance above the Hall. The battle became spirited and general, but the militia under Col. Willet gave way, and ran in the utmost confusion to the stone church in the village. Here the colonel succeeded in bringing them to a halt. But the defeat would have been complete, had not Major Rowley, at this period of the action, emerged from the woods and fell upon the enemy's rear in the very moment of their exultation at their easy victory. The fight was now maintained on both sides with obstinacy till near sunset, when Willet was enabled to collect a respectable force, with which he returned to the field, and again mingled in the fight. The battle was kept up till dark, when the enemy, pressed on all sides, fled in disorder to the woods—nor stopped short of a mountain six miles distant. The loss of the Americans in this conflict was about forty. The enemy lost about the same number killed, and about fifty prisoners.

"Major Ross retreated up the north side of the Mohawk, marching all night, after the battle. In the morning he was pursued by Col. Willet, but was not overtaken. The region of country over which Ross retreated, after he had passed the settlements, lies twenty or thirty miles north of Fort Schuyler, and at that time was uncultivated and desolate. His army suffered much from hunger.—It was on this retreat that Walter Butler was killed: he was pursued by a small party of Oneida Indians; when he arrived at West Canada creek, about 15 miles above Herkimer, he swam his horse across the stream, and then turning round, defied his pursuers, who were on the opposite side. An Oneida immediately discharged his rifle and wounded him; he fell. Throwing down his rifle and his blanket, the Indian plunged into the creek and swam across; as soon as he had gained the opposite bank, he raised his tomahawk, and with a yell, sprang like a tiger upon his fallen foe. Butler supplicated, though in vain, for mercy; the Oneida with his uplifted axe, shouted in his broken English,—' *Sherry Valley! remember Sherry Valley!*' and then buried it in his brains: he tore the scalp from the head of his victim still quivering in the agonies of death, and ere the remainder of the Oneidas had joined him, the spirit of Walter Butler had gone to give up its account. The place where he crossed is called *Butler's Ford* to this day."— *Campbell's Annals of Tryon County.*

The following is a copy of a kind of diploma, in possession of the New York Historical Society, which it would seem the Johnson family were in the habit of giving to those Indians in whom they confided. In the vignette, a British officer is seen presenting a medal, or something resembling it, to an Indian dressed in the aboriginal style,—the council fire, the pipe of peace, the chain of friendship, &c., are all represented.

"By the Honorable Sir William Johnson, Bart., His Majesty's sole Agent and Superintendant of Indian Affairs for the Northern Department of North America, Colonel of the Six United Nations, their Allies and Dependants, &c. &c.

"To   Whereas, I have received repeated proofs of your attachment to his Britannic Majesty's Interests and Zeal for his service upon sundry occasions, more particularly   I do therefore give you this public Testimonial thereof, as a proof of his Majesty's Esteem and Approbation, Declaring you, the said   to be a   of your   and recommending it to all his Majesty's Subjects and faithful Indian Allies to Treat and Consider you upon all occasions agreeable to your character, Station and services Given under my hand and seal at Arms at Johnson Hall the   day of   17
By Command of Sir W: Johnson.

The following inscriptions are copied from monuments in the graveyard in the village of Johnstown:

"Sacred to the memory of the Rev. *Simon Hosack*, D.D., minister of the Presbyterian church, Johnstown, who died May 19, 1833, in the 79th year of his age. He was born in Rosshire, in the north of Scotland, in March, A.D., 1755. He received a finished education in the University of Aberdeen, and completed his theological course in the seminary connected with that institution. As a man, he was judicious and prudent—as a Christian, his conversation was in Heaven, and whatsoever things were true, honest, just, pure, lovely, and of good report, these were his—as a minister of the gospel, he was evangelical in his sentiments, circumspect in his walk, and watchful of the spiritual welfare of his people, of which he had the oversight for the extended period of 42 years. His death, which, though deeply and sensibly felt to be a great loss by all who well knew and rightly appreciated his sterling worth, was to him great gain."

"This stone was erected by *Anne McKenzie*, in grateful remembrance of her affectionate husband, Dugald McKenzie, who departed this life on the 7th of Sept., 1809, aged 27 years and 7 months.
No private interest did his soul invade,
No foe he injured, no kind friend betrayed;
He followed virtue as his surest guide,
Lived like a Christian, like a Christian died."

"In memory of *John Baptiste Vaumane De Fonclaire*, formerly a captain in the Martinique regiment, in the service of his most Christian Majesty, Louis the XVI., and for thirty years past a citizen of the United States, who departed this life 5th January, 1811, in the 71st year of his age."

MAYFIELD, taken from Caughnawaga in 1793; from Albany 40, and from Johnstown, NE., 8 miles. Cranberry Creek, Mayfield, and Ricefield, are post-offices. Pop. 2,615.

NORTHAMPTON, taken from Broadalbin in 1801. At the confluence of the Scandaga river and the Mayfield creek, lies the small village of "Fish House," where Sir William Johnson had his sporting lodge, or summer retreat. Northampton, or Fish House village, 17 miles NE. from Johnstown, is a small village. There is here a splendid bridge across the river, costing about $60,000. Northville and Osborn's Bridge are small settlements. Pop. 1,526.

OPPENHEIM, taken from Palatine in 1808; from Albany 63, from Johnstown, W., 18 miles. This town was settled in 1724, by Germans. Its present inhabitants are characterized by the hardy industry and frugality of that nation. Oppenheim and Bracket's Bridge are post-offices. Pop. 2,169.

PERTH, recently taken from Amsterdam, of Montgomery county; it is 10 miles E. of Johnstown, and is the smallest town in the county. Pop. 737.

STRATFORD, taken from Palatine in 1805; from Albany 63 miles. Nicholsville is a small settlement, 23 miles NW. from Johnstown, on the west line of the county. Pop. 500.

GENESEE COUNTY.

GENESEE COUNTY was taken from Ontario in 1802, and has since been much reduced by the formation of several counties from it; centrally distant from New York 321, from Albany 258 miles. This county pertains to the great plain of the west, and forms with Wyoming the highest portion of it. Upon the west, the streams run to Lake Erie, and on the east to the Genesee river: as in limestone countries generally, the streams are subject to much fluctuation. The soil is generally highly fertile, and produces as fine crops of wheat as any part of the state. By the recent erection of Wyoming county from the southern portion, this county is reduced to twelve towns, and a population of about 30,000.

The following is a list of articles and rates of wages, taken from a history of Genesee county, published in 1804, by Robert Munroe:

"Wheat from 62 cents to $1 per bushel; corn, from 30 to 50 cents a bushel; hay, from $6 to $12 a ton; butter and cheese, from 10 to 16 cents a pound; a yoke of oxen, from $50 to $80; milch cows, $16 to $25; a pair of good working horses, $100 to $125; sheep, $2 to $4; pork, freshed killed in winter, $4 to $6 a 100 lb.—salted in Spring, $8 to $10; whiskey, 60 to 75 cents a gallon; salt, $1 a bushel, weighing 56 lbs., field ashes, 4 to 9 cents a bushel: 600 bushels may be manufactured into a ton of pot or pearl ashes, which has been sold at market at $1.25 to $1.50; and some persons by saving their ashes, or by manufacturing them, have nearly cleared the cost of improving land.

The wages of a laborer, $10 to $15 a month and board; a suit of clothes, made from $4 to $5; a pair of shoes, $1.75 to $2.50. Store goods are sold at very moderate prices, the expense of carriage from New York to Albany being about $2 a hundred weight."

ALABAMA, taken from Pembroke and Shelby in 1826; from Albany 257 miles. The greater part of the town was in the Tonawanta Indian reservation, part of which was sold in 1827-8. The Indians have yet here, and in Niagara and Erie counties, a tract of 12,000 acres. Their village, containing about 300 inhabitants, is situated in this town. Alabama post-office is 12 miles NW. from Batavia. Pop. 1,798.

ALEXANDER, taken from Sheldon in 1812; from Albany 247 miles; drained NE. by the Tonawanta creek. Alexander, on the Tonawanta railroad, incorporated in 1834, has about seventy dwellings. Brookville is a small settlement, 6 miles south of Batavia. The Alexander classical school, in this town, was incorporated in 1834. Pop. 2,241.

BATAVIA was organized in 1802; it has a level surface and is drained by the Tonawanta creek. Batavia, the shire village, incorporated in 1823, is laid out upon a plat about 2 miles square. The village is principally built on a single street upwards of a mile long, on the eastern side of Tonawanta creek, distant from Albany 244 miles, Buffalo 40, Rochester 34, Canandaigua 49, Genesee 29, Lockport 32 miles. Population of the town, 4,219. A railroad connects Batavia with Rochester.

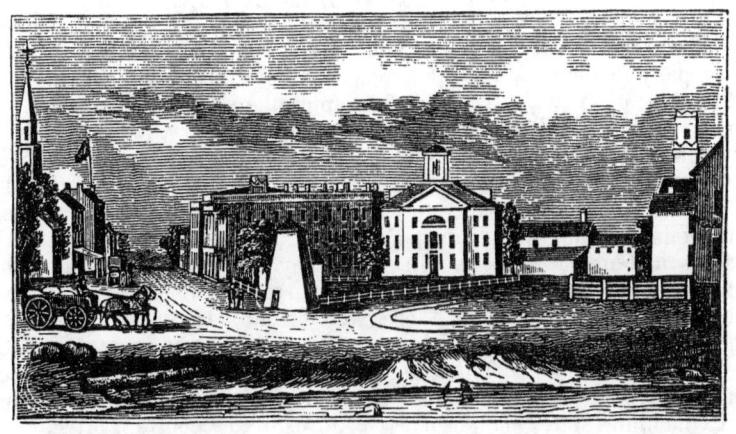

Western view of the central part of Batavia.

The above is a western view of the central part of Batavia, as seen from the bridge over the Tonawanta creek, about 40 rods NW. from the courthouse seen in the central part of the engraving. The village consists of about 300 dwellings, many of which are finely constructed of brick. The spire of the Presbyterian church is seen on the left, the tower of the Episcopal on the right. The state arsenal is about a mile NW. of the courthouse. There are in the village,

1 bank, and 2 printing offices, and the office of the Holland Land Company. Dr. Dwight, who on his visit to Niagara Falls passed through Batavia in Oct., 1804, states that at that time it contained "from 20 to 30 houses; a considerable number of them built of logs; the rest small, and chiefly of one story. The courthouse, a well-looking structure, has three stories, the second of which is the county jail." He also says, "in the season when we were on the ground, so many persons were ill of the diseases common to this region, that those who remained well, were scarcely able to nurse the sick."

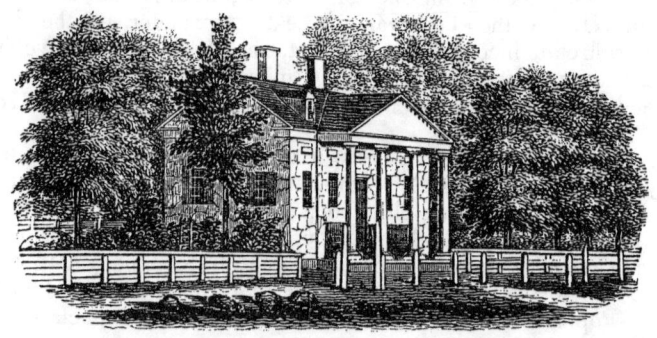

Office of the Holland Land Company.

The above is an eastern view of the office of the Holland Land Company in Batavia, about 80 rods northward from the courthouse. The state of New York, in 1786, granted the state of Massachusetts more than six million acres of her western territory, [*see page* 40,] which that state sold to Oliver Phelps and Nathaniel Gorham, for one million of dollars. These gentlemen soon after extinguished the Indian title to a part of this territory; they surveyed it into tracts, denominated ranges and townships, and sold large parcels to speculators and actual settlers. In 1790, they sold nearly the whole of the residue of the survey, 1,204,000 acres, to Robert Morris, of Philadelphia, for eight pence the acre, who resold it to Sir William Pultney. Phelps and Gorham being unable to fulfil their contract in full with Massachusetts, compromised and surrendered that part of the land to which the Indian title was unextinguished; in consideration of which, the state relinquished two thirds of the contract price. In 1796, Robert Morris purchased from the state this portion also—extinguished the Indian title—sold off several large tracts upon the east side, and along the Genesee, and mortgaged the residue to Wilhem Willink, of Amsterdam, and 11 associates, called the "*Holland Land Company.*" This company, by the foreclosure of the mortgage, acquired full title to the land, surveyed it, and opened their first land-office in Batavia in 1801. "Having sold a large proportion of the country, they, in 1805, conveyed the residue of the wild lands to several companies, who have undertaken to retail them."

"The Holland purchase was bounded on the east by a transit meridian line due north from latitude 42°, embracing the two western ranges of the county of Allegany, and with an offset, west, of two and a quarter miles, extending north to Lake Ontario, on the west line of Murraytown, Orleans county—two fifths of Allegany county, the greater portion of Genesee and Orleans counties, and all of Niagara, Erie, Chatauque and Cattaraugus," with the exception of some small Indian reservations.

Batavia has acquired celebrity from its being the place from which *William Morgan* was abducted in 1826, for attempting to reveal the secrets of *free masonry*. Morgan, it appears, was born in 1774, in Culpepper county, Va. His occupation was originally that of a bricklayer and stone mason. He removed from Virginia in 1821, and went to York, U. C.; from thence he removed to Rochester. From various misfortunes, he became quite reduced in his circumstances, and in the summer of 1826 he resided in the village of Batavia. While here, he became connected with D. C. Miller, a printer, for the purpose of publishing a work disclosing masonic obligations, secret signs, &c. Morgan, it appears, was a royal arch mason; and when the fact became known that he was preparing a work to reveal the secrets of masonry, many of the masonic fraternity became much excited, and appeared determined to put an end to his disclosures. For this purpose, his character was assailed in the public prints. In July, 1826, Morgan was arrested on a civil suit at Batavia, and gave bail; he was afterward arrested and hurried to jail, without time being given him to procure bail, and search was made at his lodgings for his papers on some pretended process, the sheriff in the mean time absenting himself. An attempt was afterward made to burn down Miller's printing office, where "Morgan's Book" was printing.

On Sunday, Sept. 10th, application was made to J. Chipman, Esq., a magistrate of Canandaigua, for a warrant to apprehend Morgan for stealing a shirt and cravat, which it appeared afterward he had only borrowed. The warrant being issued, the constable at Canandaigua, attended by five other persons from that place, immediately set out for Batavia, where they arrived in the evening. Early the next morning, (Monday,) Morgan was arrested and taken to the public house where the party had slept; an extra stage-coach was procured, and the party left Batavia for Canandaigua, with Morgan in their custody. Miller attempted to procure the release of Morgan just as the carriage was starting, but he was pushed aside, and the driver was urged to drive fast till he should get out of the county. Having arrived in Canandaigua, Morgan in the evening was taken before the magistrate who had issued the warrant, and was by him examined and discharged. One of the party then immediately applied to the same magistrate for a warrant against Morgan for a debt of about $2, which he said had been assigned to him by a tavern keeper. Judgment was entered against Morgan for $2.69, debt and costs, and an execution immediately issued. Morgan took off his coat, and offered it to the constable to levy upon for the debt. The constable declined receiving it, and Morgan was committed to the Canandaigua jail the same evening, where he remained till the evening of the next day.

On the 12th of Sept., about 9 o'clock in the evening, the wife of the jailer, at the request of the plaintiff in the execution, consented to let Morgan out of the prison. As he was leaving the jail steps, he was violently seized by two persons; he struggled, and cried "murder," a number of times. Two other persons now came up, one of whom stopped Morgan's outcry by thrusting a handkerchief, or something similar, into his mouth. At a signal given by one of the party, a two-horse carriage now drove up; two of the party thrust Morgan into the carriage, and then got in themselves. This carriage arrived in Rochester about day-dawn the next morning. Another carriage was procured, and relays of horses were obtained. When the party arrived at New Fane, about 3 miles from Lockport, they sent to the sheriff of Niagara county, to assist them in getting Morgan into Canada. The sheriff accordingly left Lockport, attended the party, and assisted them in procuring horses, &c. They arrived at Lewiston about midnight; here another carriage was procured, and the party was driven to the burying ground near Fort Niagara. Here they left the carriage and proceeded with Morgan in their custody to the ferry, and crossed over to the Canada side. After conferring with a number of persons in Niagara village, Morgan was brought back, as arrangements had not been completed for his reception. This event it appears had been anticipated. Morgan was taken to the magazine of Fort Niagara, and locked in before day-dawn, on the morning of the 14th of September.

On the day that Morgan was put into the magazine, a royal arch chapter was installed at Lewiston, which event called together a considerable assemblage of masons from the vicinity. " In the evening, 20 or 30 persons came to the fort from Lewiston. About midnight, 7 persons, stated to be royal arch masons, held a consultation on the plain near the graveyard, as to the manner in which Morgan should be disposed of. The prevailing opinion among them appeared to be, that Morgan had forfeited his life for a breach of his masonic obligations, and that they ought to see the penalty executed by drowning him in the river; some of the company discovering a reluctance to go to such lengths, the project was abandoned at that time. On the night of the 15th, a similar consultation was held between four persons, but nothing was decided on. " As to the disposition of Morgan, after the evening of the 14th of September, nothing has yet been known judicially, but circumstances are strong, to induce the belief that he was put to death on the night of the 19th of Sept., 1826, by being cast into the depths of Niagara river."*

BERGEN, taken from Murray in 1818; bounds since altered. Ber-

---

* Report of Mr. Whittlesey and others, at the United States anti-masonic convention, held at Philadelphia, Sept. 11th, 1830.

gen is a small village, 16 miles NE. from Batavia. North Bergen and Stone Church are post-offices. Pop. 1,835.

BETHANY, taken from Batavia in 1812; from Albany 241 miles. Bethany, 8 miles SE., Linden 10 miles S. from Batavia, Bennet's Settlement, and East Bethany, are small villages. Pop. 2,288. The Genesee Manual Labor Seminary, in this town, was incorporated in 1832—capital $20,000, with a farm annexed.

BYRON, taken from Bergen in 1820; from Albany 247, from Batavia, NE., 10 miles. Byron and South Byron are small villages,—the latter of which is on the line of the Batavia and Rochester railroad. Pop. 1,908. In the SW. part of the town, sulphuric acid is produced in great quantities in a diluted and concentrated state, in a hillock 230 feet long and 100 broad, elevated 5 feet above the plain.

DARIEN, taken from Pembroke in 1832; from Albany 255 miles. Darien, 13 miles SW. from Batavia, and Darien Centre, are small villages. Pop. 2,406.

ELBA, taken from Batavia in 1820; from Albany 250 miles. Pine Hill, 6 miles N. from Batavia, Oakfield, and Careysville, are small villages. Pop. 3,161.

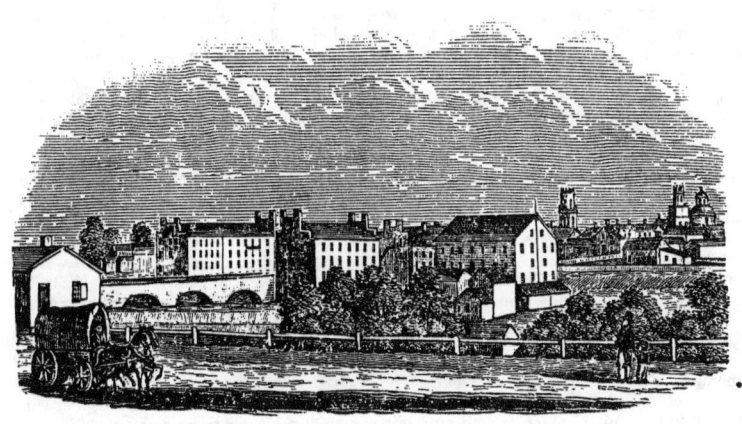

Eastern view of Le Roy Village.

LE ROY, named after Mr. Jacob Le Roy, a French gentleman from Paris, who was a large proprietor, was taken from Caledonia in 1812, and organized by the name of Bellona; from Albany 234 miles. Le Roy village was founded in 1810, by Mr. Le Roy, and incorporated in 1834. It contains 1 Episcopal, 1 Baptist, 1 Methodist, and 1 Presbyterian church, and about 260 dwellings, surrounded by ample lots and of very neat appearance. The annexed view was taken on the eastern bank of Allen's creek, near the Baptist church. The fall in the creek here, and in the vicinity, is considerable. At the village it is 18 feet; within a mile is another fall of 27, and within 2 miles a third of 80 feet. South Le Roy is a small settlement, 12 miles from Batavia. Pop. 4,335.

PAVILION, organized in 1841. This township comprises the northern part of the original town of Covington, now in Wyoming county. Pavilion is a small village, 11 miles SE. from Batavia.

PEMBROKE, taken from Batavia in 1812; bounds since altered; from Albany 257 miles. Richville, 14 miles W. from Batavia, and Corfu, are small villages. East Pembroke is a post-office. Pop.

Dr. Dwight, who travelled through this town in Oct., 1804, notices the circumstance of his passing, when in this part of the state, through oak plains or *openings*. These grounds are described as having a varied surface, and in a great degree destitute of forests, but covered with grass, weeds, and shrubs of various kinds: he supposes these openings to have been caused by the Indians burning them over, to produce pasture for deer. The following is extracted from the 4th vol. of his Travels.

"When one of these plains is seen at a little distance, a traveller emerging from the forest naturally concludes, that it is the commencement of a settled country, and as he advances towards it, is instinctively led to cast his eye forward to find the village of which it is the outskirt. From this impression his mind will be unable to free itself: for the thought, though given up, will recur again and again, in spite of his absolute conviction that he is in the heart of an immense wilderness. At the same time a sense of stillness and solitude, a feeling of absolute retirement from the world, deeper and more affecting than any which he has even suspected before, will be forced upon him while he is roving over one of these sequestered regions. No passage out of them is presented to his eye. Yet though the tract around him is seemingly bounded everywhere, the boundary is everywhere obscure; being formed by trees thinly dispersed, and retired beyond each other, at such distances, as that while in many places they actually limit the view, they appear rather to border dim, indistinct openings into other tracts of country. Thus he always feels the limit to be uncertain; and until he is actually leaving one of these plains, will continually expect to find a part of the expansion still spreading beyond the reach of his eye. At every little distance, especially on the higher grounds, the view is widely, though indefinitely extended along the surface; and a little above where he looks through the stems of the trees, is bounded only by the horizon. On every side a multitude of chasms conduct his eye beyond the labyrinth by which he is surrounded; and present an imaginary passage back into the world, from which he is withdrawn; bewildering him with expectation, continually awakened to be continually disappointed. Thus in a kind of wild, romantic rapture, he wanders over these plains, with emotions similar to those with which, when a child, he roamed through the wilderness created in Arabian tales, or the imaginary regions spread before him in a dream. He is not only separated from all human beings, but is every moment conscious of this separation. Whenever he ascends one of the superior elevations, he seems to stand above the rest of the globe. On every side he looks downward; and beholds a prospect with many vistas, opening indeed around him, but conducting his eye to no definite object, and losing it in confusion and obscurity. His view is confined by neither forests nor mountains: while yet trees in a thin dispersion partly interrupt it; but at the same time discover, through their various openings, that it has no other limitation than the skirts of the heavens.—While he wanders on through this bewildering scenery, he cannot fail to remember, that on these plains Indians have lived, and roved, and hunted, and fought, ever since their first arrival from the shores of Asia. Here, unless they molested each other, there was nothing to molest them. They were the sole lords, the undisturbed possessors of the country. Here, therefore, he will call up before his imagination the secret windings of the scout; the burst of the war-hoop; the fury of an Indian onset; the triumphant display of scalps; and the horrors of the war-dance before the tortured and expiring captive. Whether these thoughts will be excited in the mind of any future traveller, I know not: in my own they sprang up instinctively."

STAFFORD, taken from Batavia and Le Roy in 1820; from Albany 238 miles. Stafford Centre, 6 miles E. from Batavia, Morgansville 7, and Roanoke 9 miles, are small villages. Pop. 2,560.

GREENE COUNTY.

GREENE COUNTY, on the west side of the Hudson river, was taken from Ulster and Albany counties in 1800; greatest length 42 miles; greatest breadth on the Hudson 28 miles; centrally distant from New York 130, and from Albany 35 miles. The surface is everywhere hilly, and the larger portion mountainous. The Cattskill mountains, after following the southern boundary of the county in an easterly direction to the southeast angle, turn north and northwest, and pass nearly through the centre of the county into Schoharie. The general elevation of this range is from 2,000 to 2,500 feet above the adjacent country; while many of the peaks are elevated from 3,000 to 3,800 feet above the level of the Hudson. Round Top has an elevation of 3,718 feet, High Peak 3,804, and Pine Orchard 3,000 feet. The whole southwestern part of the county is hilly and mountainous, yet it affords a fine soil for pastures, with some arable land. The northeastern and eastern parts of the county are less hilly, and have many valleys, rich and extensive. Much attention is paid to agriculture, and more leather is manufactured in this than in any other county in the state. The county was originally settled by the Dutch. A large proportion, however, of the present inhabitants are of New England descent, and are noted for morality and industry. Pop. 30,446. The county is divided into eleven towns.

ATHENS was taken from Cattskill and Coxsackie in 1815. Athens village was incorporated in 1805. It lies on the west bank of the Hudson, opposite the city of Hudson; from New York 116, from Albany 29 miles. It is beautifully situated, extending along the shore about a mile and a half, and is viewed advantageously from the city of Hudson. [*See view of Hudson.*] The northern section of the village was laid out about 1790, by Edward Livingston, Brockholst Livingston, Elihu Chauncey Goodrich, and associates; the southern in 1801, by Isaac Northrop, Alexander Alexander, Patrick Hamilton, and others. The village now contains several churches, and about 150 dwellings. It is a place of much business, and its natural advantages are such, that in time it must be one of considerable importance. A ferry plies constantly between it and Hudson. Pop. 2,387.

The following account of the murder of Miss Hamilton, in 1813, is taken from a newspaper published at the time:

"*A most daring atrocity.—Hudson, August* 1, 1813.—On Saturday afternoon last, the body of Miss Sally Hamilton, the daughter of Samuel Hamilton, Esq., of Athens, (on the opposite bank of the North river,) was found in the creek which empties itself into the river, about one hundred rods north of the upper settlement of that village. The circumstances attending the daring deed which produced this young lady's death, are most agonizing, and such as at once exhibit a most wretched deterioration in the morals of society, The facts as we have been able to collect them are as follows:

"On Wednesday evening last, about 8 o'clock, Miss Hamilton left the house of her sister, in the lower settlement of the village of Athens, where she had been visiting, to return to her father's house in the upper settlement, 'the two settlements are towards half a mile apart,) accompanied by several of her acquaintances. On reaching the upper settlement, part of her company stopped at a store to make some purchases, and on being desired to go in, she also stopped at the door, but excused herself, urging that she had been from home all day and was anxious to return. When she left this store it was precisely half-past 8 o'clock. From here she was accompanied by two elderly ladies, and when she parted from them, was within twenty rods of her father's house. After she parted from these ladies no positive account of her can be traced, although the twenty rods she had to walk to reach her father's house is nearly as thickly settled as any part of the city of Hudson; and it was not until the next afternoon that her absence was discovered, when her sister, at whose house she had been the preceding day, visited her father's, and both parties missing the favorite of the family, mutual inquiries of her were made, which, on further inquiry among the neighbors, resulted in the distressing eclaircissement embraced by the preceding detail. The alarm was instantly given, and search made for her in every direction without effect.

"The only intelligence that could be obtained that in any way tended to elucidate her fate was, that between 8 and 9 o'clock in the evening in which she disappeared, a woman who was in the back part of the house at the opposite corner of the street to that to which she had to turn to go to her father's, came into the front part of the house, and inquired with some agitation if they had just then heard the stifled cries of a woman in distress. The reply being given in the negative, the inquiry was dropped. This corner of the street is within a stone's throw of the water side, and turning which, from the street she was last parted with in, to go to her father's house, she would leave the road that led direct to the creek beyond the village. About 9 o'clock, also, or a little after, the cries of a female in distress were heard by the people of a house about 80 rods beyond the creek; they were heard twice or thrice very distinctly, and afterward rather faintly; but imagining that they must be deceived, and that it was the noise of the boys in the village, they thought but little of it until the next day, when the absence of Miss Hamilton was ascertained; blood was found upon the timbers of the bridge that crosses the creek, where two of the plank were missing. The creek was now searched, but all to no purpose; and, in this state of painful incertitude, the search was renewed on Saturday, the third day of her absence, when the body was found about half a mile up the creek beyond the bridge, nearly as far as a boat could be pushed. The body was afterward placed in the charge of a jury summoned for the purpose, (on which were two physicians,) who conveyed it to her father's house; and after an examination of evidence, &c., they were unanimously of opinion that the young lady had been *wilfully murdered by some person or persons unknown.* From the coroner and several of the jury, we understand that the skull above the left eye was fractured, that the upper part of the cheek bone under the left eye was broken, that the hands were much lacerated, each arm near the shoulder bore the marks of having been seized there with violence, and on her breast there were marks of blows—but that lower down on her body there were no signs of violence having been offered her.

"The conclusion drawn from all these circumstances is, that at the time of her passing the corner into the street that led to her father's house, where the stifled cries of a woman were heard, she was forcibly seized by ruffians, and conveyed by land or water to some place in the vicinity of the creek before mentioned, where the alternative was probably offered her, of submitting to the hellish embraces of these murderers, or of instant death. At this time it most undoubtedly was, that she uttered those moving shrieks which were heard at the house north of the creek, and when, to stop her cries, and prevent, as they probably conceived, all possibility of detection, the blows were inflicted that terminated her existence. After this, it appears probable that the murderers took the body to the bridge, and from thence plunged it into the water and it drifted up the creek; or else that it was lowered down from the bridge into a boat, and conveyed to near the place where it was found; one of the planks of the bridge being found near the body, is in support of the former position, but the circumstance of there being little or no current in the creek from the tide, argues that the latter mode was adopted.

"Miss Hamilton was about 20 years of age, of a very respectable family, and possessed to the full an equal share of the attractions and accomplishments of her sex; superadded to which, she enjoyed a most irreproachable character. Her funeral was attended on Sunday, by a large concourse of citizens from this city, as well as from the village of Athens; and no occurrence has ever taken place in this vicinity, that has ever excited to an equal degree the sensibility of the community. Suspicion rests upon no person residing in this neighborhood; but to be more particular on this head at the present moment, might jeopardize the prospect there is of apprehending the perpetrators of this atrocious act, for we are not without the strongest hope of soon being able to announce to the public that the villians have been detected."

In 1815, Patrick Cavanagh confessed himself the murderer, and re lated in detail the manner in which it was committed; but on his trial it was ascertained that he was insane, and he was accordingly acquitted. Some time after, Lent, a soldier in the U. S. army, complained of a comrade by the name of Sickler, as being the author of the crime. At the trial, Lent testified that he was with Sickler at the time, and stood silently by and witnessed, although he did not participate in the transaction; and that previous to the murder, Sickler committed an outrage upon her person. In the course of the trial it became evident that the whole story was a fabrication on the part of Lent, for the purpose of obtaining the offered reward. Sickler was acquitted, and Lent arrested, tried, and condemned to the state prison for perjury, where he died some years since.

Nearly thirty years have elapsed since the murder, and as yet the transaction remains a mystery. The following inscription is from the monument in one of the burying grounds at Athens:

"Sacred to the memory of Sally Hamilton, who was murdered by unknown hands in the evening of the 25th of August, A.D., 1813, in the 20th year of her age. Parental affection erects this monument.

    "Does youth, does beauty read this line?
    Do sympathetic tears their breast alarm?
    Speak, Heavenly Spirit! breathe a strain divine,—
    Ee'n from the grave thou shalt have power to charm;
    Tell them them that tho' it is an awful thing to die,—
    'Twas e'en in thee,—yet the dread path once trod,
    Heaven lifts its everlasting portals high,
    And bids the pure in heart behold their God."

CAIRO, originally named Canton, was taken from Catskill, Coxsackie, and Freehold, (now Durham and Greenville,) in 1803. The surface of the town is mountainous and hilly. Pop. 2,862. Cairo, upon the Susquehannah turnpike, 10 miles NW. of Catskill, has 1 Presbyterian, 1 Episcopal, 1 Baptist, and 1 Methodist church, and 400 inhabitants. Acra, 14 miles NW. from Catskill, is a small settlement.

CATSKILL was organized in 1788 as part of Albany county; since modified. The town had a small annexation from Saugerties in 1822. The surface and soil are quite diversified. On the west are the Kaatsbergs, of a lofty mountain character, bordered by many hills of no inferior magnitude; and the intervening plain that extends towards the Hudson has a broken surface, especially in the southern part, whilst the northern has a high level plain of sand and clay. The Catskill creek runs through the northern part of the town, receiving in its course a number of fine mill streams, which, with the Catskill, are bordered with rich tracts of alluvial land. Pop. 5,339. Leeds and Jefferson are small villages.

The village of Catskill was incorporated in 1806, and is the seat of justice for the county. The village is principally built in the deep valley of the Catskill, between which and the Hudson is a bluff 150 feet in height. The annexed engraving is a NW. view of the village, as seen from an elevation called Ashley Hill, at its northern extremity. The drawbridge over the Catskill is seen on the right, and will

Northwestern view of Catskill.

admit the passage of sloops some distance above it. The mouth of the creek makes a good harbor for sloops; and a long and broad dyke, walled with stone, connects the shore with an island in the river, affording a place for buildings, and a commodious landing for steamboats. The principal street in the village is about half a mile in extent, having quite a business-like appearance. The steamboat landing is about 1 mile distant. There are in the village 1 Dutch Reformed, 1 Episcopal, 1 Presbyterian, 1 Baptist, and 1 Methodist church. There are 2 banks, 2 newspaper establishments, and about 300 dwellings. Distant 6 miles from Hudson, 111 from New York, and 33 from Albany.

"Although not in the town, yet as connected by name and many relations with Catskill, we may describe here the Pine Orchard and Mountain House, noted attractions to tourists. They are in Hunter, near its eastern boundary, 12 miles west from Catskill village. The road from the village to the foot of the mountain, 9 miles, has little of interest. The ascent of the mountain is by a good though circuitous road of 3 miles, but which, often running upon the brink of a deep ravine, or beneath frowning precipices, excites an unwelcome degree of terror. The hotel, erected by 'The Kaatskill Mountain Association,' at the cost of $22,000, is on a circular platform of rock, of uneven surface, having an area of about 6 acres. The building is 140 feet by 24, 4 stories high, with piazzas in front, and a wing for lodging rooms, and is duly fitted and furnished for the accommodation of its numerous guests.

"The prospect from this rock is more extensive and diversified than, perhaps, from any other point in the United States. Petty inequalities disappear, and the whole surrounding country is spread out as a plain. The eye roves, in endless gratification, over farms, villages, towns, and cities, stretching between the Green mountains of Vermont on the north and the Highlands. The Hudson river, with

Catskill Mountain House.

its green isles and thousand sheets of white canvass, becomes visible for 60 miles in a clear atmosphere. At times, a thick curtain of clouds of ever-changing form, veils the region of lower earth from sight; and in their respective seasons, storms of rain and snow spend their force in mid air, beneath the rays of a bright sun which gilds the mountain above them. The scene, when gradually unfolded with the day, is most enchanting.

"A few years since this delightful position was almost unknown and rarely visited; but the reports of the extent, beauty, and grandeur of its prospects, and the salubrity of its atmosphere, at length fixed public attention. The number of visiters at each successive season increased, until the temporary buildings at first erected gave place to the edifice we have described. The following heights on the mountain have been given by Capt. Partridge: Mountain house, 2,212 feet above the Hudson; 1,882 feet above Lawrence's tavern; 1,547 feet above the turnpike gate, at the foot of the mountain, and 947 above Green's bridge.

"Two miles from the hotel are the Kaaterskill Falls, upon a stream flowing from two lakes, each about a mile and a half in circumference, and about a half mile in the rear of the house. After a west course of a mile and a half, the waters fall perpendicularly 175 feet, and pausing, momentarily, upon the ledge of a rock, precipitate themselves 85 feet more, making the whole descent of the cataract 260 feet. Below this point, the current is lost in the dark ravine or clove through which it seeks the valley of the Catskill. The water-fall, with all its boldness, forms, however, but one of the interesting features of this scene. From the edge of the first falls is beheld a dreary chasm, whose steep sides, covered with dark ivy and thick summer foliage, seem like a green bed prepared for the waters. Making a circuit from this spot, and descending about midway of the first fall, the spectator enters an immense natural amphitheatre behind the cascade, roofed by a magnificent ceiling of rock, having in front the falling torrent, and beyond it the wild mountain dell, over which the clear blue sky is visible. The falls on the west branch of Kaaterskill have a perpendicular descent of more than 120 feet, and the stream descends in rapids and cascades 400 feet in 100 rods. The Kaaterskill has a devious and very rapid course of about 8 miles, to the Catskill, near the village. The falls are best seen from below; and the view from the Pine Orchard is better between 3 o'clock, P. M. and at sunset, than in the middle of the day."—*Gordon's Gaz.*

The following description of this view from the Catskill mountain house is given by Miss Martineau:

"After tea I went out upon the platform in front of the house, having been warned not to go too near the edge, so as to fall an unmeasured depth into the forest below. I sat upon the edge as a security against stepping over unawares. The stars were bright overhead, and had conquered half the sky, giving promise of what we ardently desired, a fine morrow. Over the other half, the mass of thunder-clouds was, I supposed, heaped together, for I could at first discern nothing of the champaign which I knew must be stretched below. Suddenly, and from that moment incessantly, gushes of red lightning poured out from the cloudy canopy, revealing not merely the horizon, but the course of the river, in all its windings through the valley. This thread of river, thus illuminated, looked like a flash of lightning caught by some strong hand and laid along in the valley. All the principal features of the landscape might, no doubt, have been discerned by this sulphurous light; but my whole attention was absorbed by the river, which seemed to come out of the darkness like an apparition at the summons of my impatient will. It could be borne only for a short time; this dazzling, bewildering alternation of glare and blackness, of vast reality and nothingness. I was soon glad to draw back from the precipice and seek the candlelight within.

"The next day was Sunday. I shall never forget, if I live to a hundred, how the world lay at my feet one Sunday morning. I rose very early, and looked abroad from my window, two stories above the platform. A dense fog, exactly level with my eyes, as it appeared, roofed in the whole plain of the earth; a dusky firmament in which the stars had hidden themselves for the day. Such is the account which an antediluvian spectator would probably have given of it. This solid firmament had spaces in it, however, through which gushes of sunlight were poured, lighting up the spires of white churches, and clusters of farm buildings too small to be otherwise distinguished; and especially the river, with its sloops floating like motes in the sunbeam. The firmament rose and melted, or parted off into the likeness of snowy sky mountains, and left the cool Sabbath to brood brightly over the land. What human interest sanctifies a bird's-eye view! I suppose this its peculiar charm, for its charm is found to deepen in proportion to the growth of mind. To an infant, a champaign of a hundred miles is not so much as a yard square of gay carpet. To the rustic it is less bewitching than a paddock with two cows. To the philosopher, what is it not? As he casts his eye over its glittering towns, its scattered hamlets, its secluded homes, its mountain ranges, church spires, and untrodden forests, it is a picture of life; an epitome of the human universe; the complete volume of moral philosophy, for which he has sought in vain in all libraries. On the left horizon are the Green mountains of Vermont, and at the right extremity sparkles the Atlantic. Beneath lies the forest where the deer are hiding and the birds rejoicing in song. Beyond the river he sees spread the rich plains of Connecticut; there, where a blue expanse lies beyond the triple range of hills, are the churches of religious Massachusetts, sending up their Sabbath psalms; praise which he is too high to hear, while God is not. The fields and waters seem to him to-day no more truly property than the skies which shine down upon them; and to think how some below are busying their thoughts this Sabbath-day about how they shall hedge in another field, or multiply their flocks on yonder meadows, gives him a taste of the same pity which Jesus felt in his solitude when his followers were contending about which should be greatest. It seems strange to him now that man should call any thing *his* but the power which is in him, and which can create somewhat more vast and beautiful than all that this horizon encloses. Here he gains the conviction, to be never again shaken, that all that is real is ideal; that the joys and sorrows of men do not spring up out of the ground, or fly abroad on the wings of the wind, or come showered down from the sky; that good cannot be hedged in, nor evil barred out; even that light does not reach the spirit through the eye alone, nor wisdom through the medium of sound or silence only. He becomes of one mind with the spiritual Berkeley, that the face of nature itself, the very picture of woods, and streams, and meadows, is a hieroglyphic writing in the spirit itself, of which the retina is no interpreter. The proof is just below him, (at least it came under my eye,) in the lady, (not American,) who, after glancing over the landscape, brings her chair into the piazza, and, turning her back to the champaign, and her face to the wooden walls of the hotel, begins the study, this Sunday morning, of her lapful of newspapers. What a sermon is thus preached to him at this moment from a very hackneyed text! To him that hath much, that hath the eye, and ear, and wealth of the spirit, shall more be given, even a replenishing of this spiritual life from that which to others is formless and dumb; while from him that hath little, who trusts in that which lies about him rather than in that which lives within him, shall be taken away, by natural decline, the power of perceiving and enjoying what is within his own domain. To him who is already enriched with large divine and human revelations this scene is, for all its stillness, musical with divine and human speech; while one who has been deafened by the din of worldly affairs can hear nothing in this mountain solitude."

The annexed anecdotes, extracted from the New York Commercial Advertiser, are from the well-known pen of the editor.

"Passing through the little village of Jefferson, we arrived at the still larger and more bustling one of Madison, 4 miles from Cattskill. . . . . . The principal house at this place, is an ancient stone edifice, and for a generation past occupied as a store and as a tavern. Its builder and late proprietor was the late M——g S——n, Esq., an ancient and somewhat eccentric Dutch denizen, who stood six feet six in his shoes, weighed 15 stone, and was in a way somewhat of a wag withal.—The valley of the Kaatskill was chiefly settled by the Dutch; and the house of mynheer was the principal place of resort for the Van Bokkelins, Van Ordens, and Van Der Speigles of the neighborhood to smoke their pipes, and crack their jokes of long winter evenings, before their peaceful country was overrun by the Yankees, who have swarmed over this once happy region like the locusts of Egypt, equally hungry and destructive. It was the worthy host of huge dimensions whom we have described, who was so grievously taken in, once on a time, in an encounter of *wits* with one of those keen-eyed, cunning Yankees, who prowl over the country, seated on tin carts, with bags of feathers, or some other "*notion*" for their cushions. After some sporting and bantering between mynheer and Jonathan, who had shown off some common slight of hand tricks, with cards, to the great astonishment of the "*spoons*" who were looking on, he, that is, the said Jonathan, declared that he could swallow his robustuous host! Notwithstanding that Jonathan had already played off several of his Yankee tricks which puzzled the good people exceedingly, yet this assertion was too great a mouthful for them to swallow, if the pedler could. A bet sufficient to moisten the throats of the whole company was the consequence between the principal parties, though the landlord in proposing it had no idea that his customer would accept, when, as he supposed, he must be certain of losing. Jonathan then directed that mynheer should be divested of his coat and boots, and be stretched longitudinally upon the old oaken table which had stood in the bar-room for half a century. These arrangements having been made, Jonathan voraciously seized upon the honest landlord's great toe, which he pressed rather violently between his teeth, giving the good man a twinge which caused a writhing movement and a groan. 'Dunder and blixem,' exclaimed Mynheer: 'Vat de tetul do ye pite me sho vor!' 'Why you darned great fool,' said Jonathan, 'you didn't think I was going to *swallow you whole*, did you?' A burst of laughter proclaimed Jonathan victor, and mynheer had to pay the toast and toddy.

" . . . . Before reaching Cairo, an ancient and spacious stone house was pointed out to us bearing date of 1705, in large iron figures. This venerable mansion stands in the midst of an extensive farm of about 1,000 acres, well cultivated, and presenting a scene which, for a single farm, is hardly anywhere to be equalled for the rich, picturesque, and beautiful. The cultivation denotes the hand of industry rather than taste. The practised horticulturist had not been there; but rank pastures, heavy waving fields, and luxuriant meadows, indicated rich returns to the husbandman. The small clumps of trees left here and there in the fields to afford fuel in the winter, and lend a grateful shade in summer, diversified the scene and rendered it still more delightful. We linger longer at this spot than our wonted manner is, in consequence of an interesting tale connected with it, which is no fiction. During a part of the 17th and nearly the whole of the 18th century, it belonged to a single owner! When young he was a man of violent passions. A servant girl having once run away, he pursued and overtook her, and, in his exasperation, tied her to his horse's tail to lead her home. By a fright, or some other cause, the horse ran off, and the unfortunate girl was dashed to pieces against some rocks and stones. The unhappy master was arrested, tried, and convicted of murder! He was rich, of a powerful family for the times, and through the combined means of wealth and family influence, it being on all hands allowed to be a hard case, he was sentenced to be executed at *ninety-nine years* old. He lived on; and generations passed away—and yet he lived! Death seemed to have no arrow barbed for him. At length the time approached. Ninety, ninety-five, ninety-eight years had rolled away since his birth. The ninety-ninth came on, and yet he lived! But generations had risen up and gone down to the tomb since his offence. Nay, the tale had almost become a forgotten tradition, although many years before the keen eyes of superstition had seen, and her tremulous tongue related, many tales of startling terror concerning the appearances at the fatal spot, pointed out to this day, where the poor girl had lost her life. The hopeless swain, who, in returning from visiting his rustic mistress, was so unlucky as to have been detained in the lap of bliss to the solemn hour of midnight, was sure to encounter a nocturnal appearance of some sort. Sometimes sighs and lamentations were heard in the air, like the plaintiveness of the soft whistling wind. At others, a white cow, which was said to have been a favorite when the deceased was alive, would stand lowing among the rocks, while again at others, a shagged white dog would stand pointing and howling towards the mansion. But they always vanished on approaching them, though perhaps it would be difficult to prove that the spectators approached very near. A white horse of gigantic size, with fiery eyeballs and distended nostrils, was often seen to run past the fatal spot, with the fleetness of wind, dragging a female behind, with tattered garment and streaming hair, screaming for help. At other times the horse would appear to drag a hideous skeleton, clattering after him, half enveloped in a winding sheet, with cries and dismal howlings; while again a female figure would at times appear sitting upon a huge fragment of rock, with a lighted candle upon each finger, singing wildly, or uttering a piercing cry, or an hysterical laugh. People, too, began to wonder that the murderer did not die, while many shook their heads and indicated that he could not,—that his soul was bound to earth till the time should come. But these things, too, passed away. And now the revolution had intervened,—a new government bore rule; and the old man was not molested. For 75 years he had led a quiet and inoffensive life, and who would rudely break in upon his repose? He died tranquilly at more than a hundred years old. Peace be to his ashes! Tradition has added to his sentence that he was to wear a cord continually upon his neck; and a few years ago, there were those living, who pretended that they had seen a neat silken string worn in compliance to the sentence, but to appearance as an ornament."

COXSACKIE was originally settled by the Dutch; it was a part of Albany county, and organized in 1788. Pop. 3,539. It derives its name from an Indian word, meaning " hooting of owls." Coxsackie village and landing, on the Hudson, lies 124 miles from New York, 20 from Albany, and 11 N. of Cattskill. The village is over a mile W. of the landing, and has about 100 dwellings. At the landing there is a large village, where there is a good deal of business transacted connected with the river.

DURHAM was originally named Freehold, and taken from Coxsackie in 1790; from Cattskill, NW., 24, from Albany, SW., 30, and from New York 134 miles. Durham, South Durham, Cornwallsville, Winansville, and Oak Hill, are small settlements. Pop. 2,813.

GREENVILLE, taken from Coxsackie and Freehold, and organized in 1803 by the name of Greenfield, afterward changed to Freehold, and finally to its present name; from New York 130 miles, and from Albany, S., 25 miles. Freehold, 15 miles NW., Greenville 16, Newry 18, Gayhead 13 miles from Cattskill, are small villages. Pop. 2,338.

HUNTER was taken from Windham in 1813, by the name of Greenland, and changed to its present one in 1814; from New York 130, and from Albany 58 miles. Pop. 2,019. Tannersville is a small village in the central part of the town, upon the main branch of Schoharie kill, 22 miles from Catskill. The surface of this town is mountainous, having on the north the main ridge of the Kaatsbergs. The *Mountain House*, on the Catskill mountains, so noted among tourists, is within the limits of this town. (See Catskill.)

LEXINGTON, taken from Windham in 1813. Lexington Heights, 30 miles W. from Catskill, and Lexington 34, are small settlements. E. Lexington and Westville are post-offices. Pop. 2,813.

NEW BALTIMORE, organized in 1811. Pop. 2,306. New Baltimore, upon the Hudson, 15 miles below Albany, and 19 N. of Catskill, has about 50 dwellings, and is a place of considerable trade. Four Corners, 16 miles from Catskill, and Stanton Hill, are small settlements.

PRATTSVILLE, taken from Windham in 1833; from Albany, SW., 50 miles, from Catskill, NW., 36. Pop. 1,613. The town lies between two great ridges of the Kaatsbergs. Prattsville, on the Schoharie kill, is a small village.

WINDHAM, taken from Woodstock in 1798; from Albany 39 miles, from Catskill centrally distant W. 26. Pop. 2,417. Windham, Osborneville, and Scienceville, are small villages. Union Society and Big Hollow are post-offices.

HAMILTON COUNTY.

HAMILTON COUNTY was provisionally erected, in 1816, from the N. end of Montgomery county, but not organized. It remained attached to Montgomery county until 1838; when, by the division of Montgomery, it became attached to Fulton county. It is not yet separately organized; though probably from its flourishing condition it will soon become detached from Fulton. It is 62 miles long N. and S., and with an average breadth, E. and W., of 30 miles; centrally distant from New York 250, and from Albany, westerly, 105 miles. This county contains 7 towns. Pop. 1,907.

The following remarks respecting this county, which is yet a wilderness and comparatively unknown, are extracted from the report of E. Emmons, Esq., one of the geologists employed by the state. "Contrary to the published accounts, and to common opinions, which are of course formed principally from those accounts, especially from Burr's and Gordon's statistics of this county, I have the pleasure of stating that it is far from being the *wet, cold, swampy,* and *barren* district which it has been represented to be. The soil is generally strong and productive; the mountains are not so elevated and steep but that the soil is preserved of sufficient thickness to their tops to secure their cultivation, and most of the marshy lands may be reclaimed by ditching; by this means they will become more valuable than the uplands for producing hay. In fine, it will be found an excellent country for grazing, raising stock, and producing butter and cheese. The strength of the soil is sufficiently tested by the heavy growth of timber, which is principally of hard wood, as beach, maple, yellow birch, butternut, and elm. The evergreens or pines, are confined mostly to the lower ranges of mountains. Some of them are of the largest growth of any in the state, and are suitable for the main shafts of the largest of the cotton mills. In the main, the county resembles the mountainous districts of New England, and like these produces the same intermixture of forest trees, and has about the same adaptations for the production of the different kinds of grain, as wheat, rye, oats, peas, barley, together with fine crops of potatoes.

"The face of the country varies from hilly to mountainous. A low range of mountains cross the county between the town of Wells and Lake Pleasant; the whole width is not far from six miles. This range, in its progress northeastwardly, increases in elevation until it constitutes the highest mountain group in the state, in the towns of Moriah and Keene, in Essex county.

"The most interesting physical features in this county arise from the number and beauty of the lakes which are sprinkled liberally and picturesquely over its surface. Much has been said of the clearness of the waters of Lake George, and not without reason; if, however, the traveller will extend his wanderings to Lake Pleasant, Round, Piseco, and Racket lakes, he will find them its equals, if not its rivals. The clearness of the waters in all these lakes is owing to the primitive character of the region in which they occur. The lakes of Hamilton form a beautiful addition to the scenery of our country. Although the mountains are not so high as those of Scotland, still it will be a matter which will occasion no surprise, (when Americans shall have acquired sufficient independence to admire a thing that is American,) if these lakes do not become objects of admiration, and shall be considered as vieing with those of Scotland. Settlements are now forming on the margin of those beautiful sheets of water, and were buildings erected suitable for the accommodation of travellers, in some central place among these lakes, (which we doubt not will be the case in a short time,) our pleasure-seeking community, of whatever cast, could spend a few days or weeks with as much zest as is afforded by any of the places of public resort which are so thronged during the heat of summer. As I have already intimated, the axe has been laid at the root of the tree, and ere long where nought now greets the eye but a dense, and to all appearance impassable forest, will be seen the golden grain waving with the gentle breeze, the sleek cattle browsing on the rich pastures, and the farmer with well-stored granaries enjoying the domestic hearth." While thousands are annually emigrating to the unsettled regions of the "far west," it should be remembered that here is a tract which perhaps offers as strong inducements as the former, with the additional advantages of a near market, and of becoming ere long possessed of all the blessings of an old country.

ARIETTA was erected in 1836, from Lake Pleasant. It is about 55 miles long, with an average breadth of 6½. Pop. 209. The site designated for the county seat is at Piseco, in this town, a flourishing village on the Piseco lake.

GILMAN was erected in 1839, from Wells. It is about 37 miles long, N. and S., and 5 broad, E. and W. Pop. 98.

HOPE, the SE. corner town, was taken from Wells in 1818. It is about 10 miles long, E. and W., and 7½ broad, N. and S. Hope, Hope Centre, and Benson, are post-offices. Pop. 711.

LAKE PLEASANT, taken from Johnstown in 1812; centrally distant from New York 255, from Albany 120, and from Johnstown 43 miles. It is about 50 miles long, N. and S., and 7 broad, E. and W. Pop. 296. Lake Pleasant is a small village, about 16 miles N. of Fulton county line.

LONG LAKE is E. and W. 28 miles long, by about 12 broad, and occupies the whole breadth of the northern portion of the county. It was erected in 1838, from Wells, Lake Pleasant, Arietta, and Morehouse. Pop. 59.

MOREHOUSE, the westernmost town of the county, was taken from Lake Pleasant in 1835. It is about 40 miles long, N. and S., by about 6½ broad, E. and W. Pop. 169. Morehouseville is a small village, in the southern part.

WELLS, the easternmost town of the county, is about 40 miles long, N. and S., with an average breadth, E. and W., of about 5 miles. Wells post-office is in the S. part. Pop. 365.

HERKIMER COUNTY.

HERKIMER COUNTY was originally constituted in 1791. Greatest length N. and S. 90, greatest breadth E. and W. 23 miles. Centrally distant from New York 260, from Albany 115 miles. This county has a broken and diversified aspect. South of the Mohawk, within this county, is the great dividing ridge separating the waters of the Mohawk from those of the Susquehannah. A high range of hills extend across the valley of the Mohawk at the Little Falls, and the whole county north of the Mohawk is of a mountainous character. Most of the county south of the Mohawk, and for many miles north of it, is under cultivation, which the greater portion of the hills will admit of to their summits. There is a variety of soil, but the greater part of the county is better adapted for grass than grain. The extensive alluvial valley of the Mohawk, and those of some of the smaller streams, are among the finest grain lands in the state. The northern part of the county is elevated, and covered with extensive forests of evergreens and marshes, and is of a cold and sterile soil. The Mohawk river runs across its whole width. The East and West Canada creeks, (large branches of the Mohawk,) form the former part of the eastern, and the latter part of the western boundary of the county. Black river of Lake Ontario, has its sources in the northern part, and also some of the branches of the Oswegatchie river. Several small streams running into the Mohawk, and some of the sources of the Susquehannah, have their rise in the southern part. The Erie canal and Utica railroad cross the county in the Mohawk valley. The long level of the canal, 69½ miles, extends from Syracuse, Onondaga county, to Frankfort, near the western boundary of this county. From thence across the county the canal has a descent of 97 feet by 12 locks; 5 of which are at the Little Falls, at which place there is an aqueduct over the Mohawk, built of 3 arches, one of 700, two of 50 feet each. The lands of this county were originally granted in large tracts; such were the "Royal Grant," to Sir William Johnson, embracing the country between the East and West Canada creeks; the "Jerserfield patent," covering a larger portion of the northern part of the county, made in 1770; the "German Flats patent," granted in 1725, and others. The county has 19 towns. Pop. 37,378.

COLUMBIA, taken from Warren in 1812; from Albany 75, from Herkimer S. 10 miles. Pop. 2,130. This town was settled previous to the revolution, by some Germans. Columbia and South Columbia are post-offices.

DANUBE was taken from Minden in 1817; from Albany 76, from Herkimer SE. 10 miles. Pop. 1,907. Near the mouth of the Nowadaga, a small stream in this town, formerly stood a Mohawk castle with a church and bell.

General Herkimer house, Danube.

The above is an eastern view of the Gen. Herkimer house, in Danube, now owned by Mr. Connor. This house is built of brick, and is upwards of 2 miles eastward of the village of Little Falls, just below the rocky pass of the Mohawk. It is situated but a few rods south from the Erie canal, fronting the beautiful interval of the Mohawk, at this place. This house was built by the general, who, after being wounded at the battle of Oriskany, was brought here, where he died. He was buried on a little knoll, a few rods in a southerly direction from his house, in the family burying ground, without a monument to tell where he lies.

The battle of Oriskany was fought on the 6th of Aug., 1777; and Gen. Herkimer did not long survive his wound. The following account of his last moments, and his character, is taken from Col. Stone's interesting account in his Life of Brant, vol. I.

"He was conveyed to his own house near the Mohawk river, a few miles below the Little Falls; where his leg, which had been shattered 5 or 6 inches below the knee, was amputated about 10 days after the battle, by a young French surgeon in the army of Gen. Arnold, and contrary to the advice of the general's own medical adviser, the late Dr. Petrie. But the operation was unskilfully performed, and it was found impossible by his attendants to stanch the blood. Col. Willet called to see the general soon after the operation. He was sitting up in his bed, with a pipe in his mouth, smoking, and talking in excellent spirits. He died the night following that visit. His friend, Col. John Roff, was present at the amputation, and affirmed that he bore the operation with uncommon fortitude. He was likewise with him at the time of his death. The blood continuing to flow—there being no physician in immediate attendance—and being himself satisfied that the time of his departure was nigh, the veteran directed the Holy Bible to be brought to him. He then opened it and read, in the presence of those who surrounded his bed, with all the composure which it was possible for any man to exhibit, the 38th psalm—applying it to his own situation. He soon afterward expired; and it may well be questioned whether the annals of man furnish a more striking example of Christian heroism—calm, deliberate, and firm in the hour of death—than is presented in this remarkable instance. Of the early history of Gen. Herkimer, but little is known. It has been already stated that his family was one of the first of the Germans who planted themselves in the Mohawk valley. And the massive stone mansion, yet standing at German Flatts, bespeaks its early opulence. He was an uneducated man—with, if possible, less skill in letters, even than Gen. Putnam, which is saying much. But he was, nevertheless, a man of strong and vigorous understanding—destitute of some of the essential requisites of generalship, but of the most cool and dauntless courage. These traits were all strikingly disclosed in the brief and bloody expedition to Oriskany. But he must have been well acquainted with that most important of all books—THE BIBLE. Nor could the most learned biblical scholar, lay or clerical, have selected a portion of the Sacred Scriptures more exactly appropriate to the situation of the dying soldier, than that to which he himself spontaneously turned. If Socrates died like a philosopher, and Rousseau like an unbelieving sentimentalist, Gen. Herkimer died like a CHRISTIAN HERO. Congress passed a resolution requesting the governor and council of New York to erect a monument, at the expense of the United States, to the memory of this brave man, of the value of five hundred dollars.

"Sixty years have since rolled away, and the journal of Congress is the only monument, and the resolution itself the only inscription, which as yet testify the gratitude of the republic to GENERAL NICHOLAS HERKIMER."

FAIRFIELD, taken from Norway in 1796; from Albany 76, from Herkimer NE. 10 miles. Pop. 1,836. The village of Fairfield is centrally situated, and contains 1 Methodist, 1 Episcopal, and 1 Presbyterian church, and about 50 dwellings.

The college of physicians and surgeons of the western district is located in this village, and numbers 6 professors and 105 students; also, a flourishing academy, under the charge of the Rev. Henry Bannister, and numbering 150 pupils, including males and females. In the following view, the two buildings shown on the right are the medical colleges, the structure with a steeple is the academy chapel, and the building partially seen on the left is the one appropriated for the male department of the academy. These buildings are favorably located on a fine green. The building for the females is not shown

Medical College, and Academy, at Fairfield.

in this view. Middleville, on West Canada creek, on the west line of the town, and partly in Newport, has 1 church and about 50 dwellings.

FRANKFORT was taken from German Flats in 1796; from Albany 86 miles. Frankfort, a manufacturing village upon the canal 4 miles NW. of Herkimer, has about 60 dwellings. Frankfort Hill is a post-office. Pop. 3,096.

GERMAN FLATS was organized in 1788. Its surface is undulating, rising from the Mohawk river on the northern boundary. The extensive alluvial flats in this town, as well as those in Herkimer, were settled at an early period by German families, and have now been known as the German Flats for more than a century. The soil of the township is uncommonly good, particularly the flats on the Mohawk, which are proverbially fertile. Centrally distant from Herkimer 5, and from Albany 75 miles. Pop. 3,245.

Mohawk, a small post village on the Mohawk river and Erie canal, is nearly 2 miles from Herkimer, the county seat; contains an ancient stone church, the westernmost of the line of those structures built under the auspices of Sir William Johnson. A short distance E. of the church stood the large and massive-built mansion of the Herkimer family, which, like the church itself, was used as a fort. Hence it was called Fort Herkimer. "It was at this place," says Col. Stone, "that the first liberty pole in the valley was reared in the spring of 1775." White, the sheriff of Tryon county at that time, came up the flats with a large body of militia from Johnstown, and cut it down. When the Mohawk valley was ravaged in 1778 by the tories and Indians, there were 34 dwellings on the south side of the Mohawk laid in ashes.

HERKIMER was organized in 1788. The surface of the township on the north is hilly; on the south, along the banks of the Mohawk, which forms its southern boundary, are the German flats, so noted for their fertility. This place was an early German settlement, "originally called Burnetsfield, from the circumstance that the patent had been granted by Gov. Burnet. This patent extended over the richest and most beautiful section of the Mohawk valley, comprehending the broad alluvial lands directly beyond the junction of the West Canada creek and river, and including about 10 miles of the valley from E. to W." Pop. 2,369.

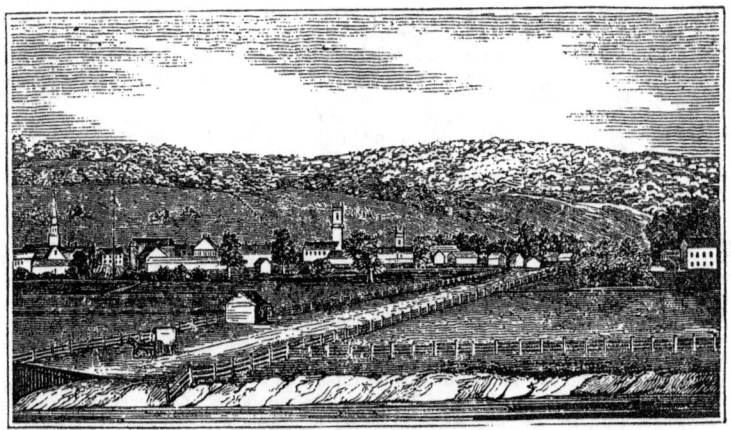

View of Herkimer, from the Erie canal.

The above shows the appearance of the village as seen from an elevation rising from the south bank of the Mohawk and the Erie canal, about a mile distant. The village was incorporated in 1807–1825, and is built on a gravelly plain elevated some 10 or 15 feet above the surrounding flats, occupying the site of the ancient Fort Dayton. The village consists of upwards of 100 dwellings, the county buildings, 1 Dutch Reformed and 1 Methodist church, a printing office, &c. The principal street runs N. and S., and is about half a mile in extent; the railroad passes through the village at its southern extremity.

The following account of the destruction of this place by the tories and Indians in 1778, is from Stone's Life of Brant.

"At the time of which we are writing, the settlement on the south side of the river numbered 34 dwelling-houses, and there were about an equal number upon the north side, together with as many barns and other outbuildings, and several mills. The population, for the number of houses, was numerous. The lands, rich by nature, and well cultivated, had that year brought forth by handfuls; so that the barns were amply stored with their products.

"It was at the close of August, or early in the month of September, that this fine district was laid waste by the Indians under the direction of Brant. Most providentially, however, the invasion was attended with the loss of but two lives—one man being killed outright, and another, named McGinnis, perished in the flames. The particulars of this hostile irruption were these:—Entertaining some suspicions of Brant, who was at Unadilla, a scout of four men had been despatched into that vicinity for observation. Three of these men were killed at the Edmeston settlement. The fourth, John Helmer, succeeding in making his escape, and returned to the Flats at half an hour before sun-down, just in time to announce that Brant, with a large body of Indians, was advancing, and would, in a few hours, be upon them. All was, of course, terror and alarm through the settlement; and the inhabitants,—men, women, and children—were gathered into forts Dayton and Herkimer for security. In flying to those defences, they gathered up the most valuable of their stuff, and by means of boats and canoes upon the river, succeeded, in the course of the evening, in collecting a large portion of their best articles of furniture. But they had no time to look after their flocks and herds.

"Early in the evening Brant arrived at the edge of the settlement, but as the night came on excessively dark and rainy, he halted with his forces in a ravine, near the house of his tory friend Shoemaker, where the younger Butler and his party were captured the preceding year. Here the chieftain lay with his warriors until the storm broke away towards morning —unconscious that his approach had been notified to the people by the scout in season to enable them to escape the blow of his uplifted arm. Before the dawn he was on foot, and his warriors were sweeping through the settlement; so that the torch might be almost simultaneously applied to every building it contained. Just as the day was breaking in the east, the fires were kindled, and the whole section of the valley was speedily illuminated by the flames of houses and barns, and all things else combustible. The spectacle, to the people in the forts, was one of melancholy grandeur. Every family saw the flames and smoke of its own domicil ascending to the skies, and every farmer the whole product of his labor for the season dissolving into ashes.

"Having no fire-arms larger than their rifles, the Indians avoided even a demonstration against the forts, notwithstanding their chagrin that neither scalps nor prisoners were to grace their triumph. But as the light of day advanced, their warriors were seen singly, or in small groups, scouring the fields, and driving away all the horses, sheep, and black cattle that could be found. Nothing upon which they could lay their hands was left; and the settlement, which, but the day before, for ten miles had smiled in plenty and in beauty, was now houseless and destitute. Happily, however, of human life there was no greater sacrifice than has already been mentioned. After the Indians had decamped with their booty, a force of between 300 and 400 militia-men collected, and went in pursuit—following as far as Edmeston's plantation on the Unadilla river, where the bodies of the three scouts were found and buried. But no other results attended this expedition."

LITCHFIELD was taken from German Flats in 1796; from Albany 88, centrally distant from Herkimer and Utica 11 miles. Cedarville, partly in the towns of Winfield and Columbia, has about 40 dwellings. Litchfield is a post-office. Pop. 1,672.

LITTLE FALLS was taken from Herkimer, Fairfield, and German Flats, in 1829. It has a hilly and broken surface, lying on both sides of the Mohawk. Pop. 3,881. The first settlement in the town appears to have been made at the falls of the Mohawk, by or under the direction of Alexander Ellis. This gentleman was a Scotch merchant, who, under the favor of Sir William Johnson, had obtained a patent of the wild mountain gorge, through which the Mohawk leaps from the upper into the lower section of the valley.

The engraving shows a southern view of part of the village as seen from a point about 20 rods below the aqueduct over the Mohawk. The village consists of upwards of 300 dwellings, 5 churches— viz, 1 Presbyterian, 1 Baptist, 1 Episcopal, 1 Methodist, and 1 Catholic—a bank, an academy, 2 newspaper printing offices, and various manufacturing establishments. The village is supplied with water brought from a spring in the granite mountain, 300 feet above the tops of the houses. The singular building with a spire, seen in the engraving on the left, on elevated ground, is the oldest church in the village, formerly used by the Scotch Presbyterians, but now occupied by the Catholics.

"This spot is remarkable for the passage of the Mohawk river through the mountain barrier; for its wild and picturesque scenery; and for the difficulties which have been overcome in constructing the Erie canal through the pass. It receives the name of the Little Falls, in contradistinction to the Great Falls at Cahoes. The falls extend

Southern view of part of the Village of Little Falls.

upon the river about three fourths of a mile, descending in that distance 42 feet, and consist of two long rapids, separated by a stretch of deep water, occupying each about the fourth of a mile. The upper rapids are most considerable. Above them, a dam across the stream renders it placid, over which the waters, separated by a small island, form beautiful low cascades, falling into a deep pool beneath, whence the current rushes, murmuring and foaming, over ridges and amorphous masses of granite and gneiss rock, flowing with comparative gentleness beneath the overarching bridge and aqueduct, and thence hurrying, with new impetuosity, over the stony bed below.

"This waterfall would be beautiful anywhere; but it acquires grandeur here, from the high hills which confine it, and which the slightest observation teaches us have been cut down by its ever enduring and irresistible force. The defile is two miles long, with a medial breadth of one hundred rods. On either bank, the hill, on which deciduous and evergreen trees are pleasingly intermingled, rises from 360 to 400 feet, and the fall, over which may have once poured the waters of Lake Ontario, may have had a very little inferior altitude. A mound, raised here to the height of 70 feet, would now cause the waters to overflow the Rome summit, and send them again by Wood creek and the Oneida lake to Ontario.

"That the hill has been so abraded is incontestibly demonstrated by the many cavities, basins, and channels, worn in the rock, at the bottom and sides of the defile, visible throughout its extent, and at an elevation of 60 feet. Below the Gulf Bridge, on the north side of the road, is an insulated rock, having a remarkable water-worn cavity or funnel; its top is between 30 and 40 feet above the low-water mark of the river, and the rock in which it is formed is 16 feet high. The funnel, 2½ feet diameter, descends perpendicularly fromt he top below the exposed part of the base. Near the base it is broken so that the sky may be seen as through a chimney. This funnel has doubtless been worn by the violent action of water upon loose stones within its cavity. Similar indications of like action are common here, and some have lately been disclosed by removal of the soil from other portions of rock.

"At the foot of the falls the river expands into a basin more than a hundred feet deep, into which the high cataract once poured its floods, and from whose depths rocky spires rise above the surface.

"A canal, with 5 locks, was constructed here by the Western Inland Navigation Company, in 1802, which now gives a valuable hydraulic power, and serves as a feeder for the Erie canal, with which it is connected by a noble aqueduct of marble, 214 feet long, 16 feet wide, confined by walls 14 feet high and 4 feet broad, sustained by three arches, the central one of 70, and the outer ones each of 50 feet span. The western parapet, guarded with an iron balustrade, forms an agreeable promenade, from which a great portion of this varied scenery is visible. This beautiful structure is best seen from a fine stone bridge immediately above it.

"This defile presented an obstacle to the Erie canal, inferior to none save the deep excavation at Lockport. Here, two miles of deep rock cutting were necessary; years were supposed requisite to accomplish the work; but the perseverance and skill of the contractors effected the most difficult portion in less than 90 days.

"The canal descends the pass by 5 locks, 40 feet in the distance of one mile, and the time of the passage permits the traveller in boats to view, leisurely, the natural scenery and artificial improvements.

"This place has much attraction for the student of natural science. The geologist will find the various formations curiously blended in its vicinity. The rocks, immediately at the falls, are granite, gneiss, and hornblende, with calciferous sand rock overlaid by transition limestone. Beautiful quartz crystals of unusual size, purity, and lustre, and fine specimens of tourmaline, may be obtained."—*Gordon's Gaz.*

In 1780, a party of tories and Indians made a descent upon the small settlement at Little Falls, for the purpose of destroying the mills, which were of much importance to the inhabitants in this section. This was easily accomplished—" the enemy having stolen upon the settlement unawares, and the flouring mill being garrisoned by not more than a dozen men. Only a few shots were exchanged, and but one man was killed—Daniel Petrie. As the Indians entered the mill, the occupants endeavored to escape as fast as they could—some leaping from the windows, and others endeavoring to conceal themselves below. It was night, and two of the number, Cox and Skinner, succeeded in ensconcing themselves in the race-way, beneath the water-wheel—Skinner having previously made fight hand to hand, and been wounded by a cut from a tomahawk. Two of their companions, Christian Edick and Frederick Getman, leaped into the race-way above the mill, and endeavored to conceal themselves by keeping as much under water as possible. But the application of the torch to the mills soon revealed the aquatic retreat, and they were taken. Not so with Cox and Skinner, who survived the storm of battle, and the mingled elements of fire and water; the showers of coals and burning brands being at once extinguished as they fell around them, while the water-wheel served as an effectual protection against the falling timbers. The enemy retired after accomplishing their object, carrying away five or six prisoners."—*Life of Brant.*

MANHEIM, taken from Palatine in 1797; from Albany 69 miles. Manheim, on the Utica turnpike and railroad, 14 miles east from Herkimer, is a small village. Manheim Centre is a post-office. This town was settled by Germans in 1770. During the revolution the inhabitants were driven from their possessions. Pop. 2,095.

NEWPORT, taken from Norway, Fairfield, and Schuyler in 1806; from Albany 95, from Herkimer N. centrally distant 13 miles. Pop. 2,020. Newport village has about 100 dwellings. Middleport is a small village, partly in the town of Fairfield.

NORWAY, taken from Herkimer in 1792; from Albany 90, from Herkimer N. centrally distant 18 miles. Pop. 1,046. Norway is a small village.

OHIO, erected from West Brunswick; from Herkimer centrally distant N. 22 miles. Pop. 692. West Brunswick is the post-office.

RUSSIA, originally named Union, and taken from Norway in 1806; from Albany 94, centrally distant NNW. from Herkimer 20 miles. Pop. 2,198. Russia and Poland are small villages; Cold Brook and Portville, post-offices.

SALISBURY, taken from Palatine in 1817; from Albany 76 miles. It has a mountainous surface, with broad valleys on the northeast. Salisbury 14 NE., Salisbury Centre 17 miles, and Winton, are small villages. Pop. 1,859,

SCHUYLER, taken from Herkimer in 1792; from Albany 86, centrally distant from Herkimer 8, and from Utica 6 miles. East Schuyler and West Schuyler are post-offices. Pop. 1,798.

STARK, taken from Danube in 1828; from Albany centrally distant 29, from Herkimer SE. 16 miles. Pop. 1,766. Vanhornsville is a small village, and Starkville a post-office. "The Otsquake creek in this town, flowing 9 miles to the Mohawk river, is remarkable for the number and extent of the calcareous incrustations and petrifactions along its banks and tributaries near its source. A fine example is presented of the former about half a mile above the first mill, where a tufaceous rock stretches across the dell from 60 to 70 yards, with a breadth of 16, and a height of 2 yards, enclosing masses of petrified wood. The most perfect petrification, in a ravine of a small stream descending to the creek, is the trunk of a hemlock tree, 2 feet in diameter, in which the concentric circles and color of the wood are admirably preserved. This curious laboratory of stone is still in action."—*Gordon's Gazeteer.*

WARREN, taken from German Flats in 1796; from Albany 68, from Herkimer centrally distant S. 10 miles. Subterranean streams burst forth here in large volumes sufficient for hydraulic purposes. Pages Corners and Crains Corners are post-offices, and Little Lakes a small village. Pop. 2,003.

WINFIELD, taken from Richfield and Plainfield of Otsego county, and Litchfield of Herkimer county, in 1816; from Albany 75, from Herkimer SW. 15 miles. Winfield and West Winfield are small villages. Pop. 1,652.

WILMURT comprises the whole northern and unsettled section of the county: in length about 50, and in breadth about 16 miles. Pop. 60.

JEFFERSON COUNTY.

JEFFERSON COUNTY, taken from Oneida in 1805, is situated at the E. end of Lake Ontario, and on the St. Lawrence river, comprising Chaumont bay, and most of the islets called the "Thousand Isles," and is a territory having as many natural advantages as any portion of the interior of the state. It is centrally distant NW. from New York 305, and from Albany 160 miles. Length N. and S. 48 miles; greatest breadth E. and W. 36. This county in its surface is either quite level or agreeably diversified, waving in gentle undulations. Generally, the soil is of a sandy loam of a superior quality, with some gravel and clay, and yields abundant crops. The natural growth of timber is luxuriant. Originally it was covered with trees of an enormous height. The many and very rapid streams of this county furnish an abundance of hydraulic power. The cattle sent to market from this county exceed 4,000 head per annum. Its horses are equal to any in the state, and their sale is a source of much revenue. The raising of sheep is a growing business. The roads in the county are numerous and good; among which may be noticed a turnpike from Brownville to Cape Vincent, 21 miles, the St. Lawrence and Ogdensburg turnpikes, and the great military road between Sacketts Harbor and Plattsburg, on Lake Champlain. About one half of the exports descend to Montreal. It is divided into 19 towns. Pop. 61,028.

Southern view of Adams, Jefferson County.

ADAMS, taken from Mexico, 1st April, 1802; NW. from Albany 149 miles. It was originally the property of Mr. Nicholas Low, of New York, and was settled in 1801, by New England emigrants. Among the early settlers were David Smith, Elihu Morton, a Mr. Brown, and the Salisbury family. Here have been found many of those ancient works so common in the western country. Pieces of coarse earthenware and pipes have frequently been met with, and old stone hearths, many feet under ground. There have also been discovered seven of the tumular remains, of moderate height, with the ditch encircling them, the area from a half to two acres each. Adams village, 14 miles south of Watertown, has 1 Presbyterian and 1 Methodist church, a select school, a seminary for young ladies, and 120 dwellings.

The preceding view of the central part of the village was taken a few rods south of the bridge, in the principal street. The academy steeple and the Presbyterian church are seen on the right, and the bridge in the centre of the engraving. Adams Centre contains a church belonging to the society of the Seven-day Baptists. Appling and Smithville are post villages. Pop. of the town, 2,941.

ALEXANDRIA, settled by New Englanders in 1817; taken from Brownville and Le Ray in 1821, including the islands in the St. Lawrence river fronting the town. Pop. 3,472. The river, from two to five miles in width, is speckled by the "Thousand Isles." Indian river flows across the east part of the town, having falls of 80 feet near Theresa. There are here many useful mill-streams, and 12 small lakes well stocked with fish. Alexandria village, on the St. Lawrence, 30 miles above Ogdensburg, has about 30 dwellings. Theresa, 25 miles from Ogdensburg, has about 25 dwellings. Plessis, Military Road, and Redwood, are post-offices.

ANTWERP, taken from Le Ray in 1810. Antwerp, upon Indian river, 164 miles from Albany, and 20 NE. of Watertown, has about 40 or 50 dwellings. Oxbow, on the Oxbow of the Oswegatchie river, 25 miles NE. from Watertown, has about 30 dwellings. One mile west of the village is a rock called "pulpit rock," in the form of a pulpit, where public worship has occasionally been performed. Pop. 3,108.

BROWNVILLE, taken from Leyden in 1802; surface level; soil marley loam on limestone, of excellent quality, and highly improved, and producing much wheat. The town has its name from Mr. John Brown, an early settler, and father of the late Gen. Brown. Brownville, on the right bank of the Black river, 3 miles from its mouth, and at the head of navigation, 4 miles below Watertown, is a large manufacturing village, containing about 100 dwellings, and 1 Presbyterian, 1 Episcopal, and 1 Methodist church. The fall of the river here is 24 feet. Dexter is a small but flourishing village, at the head of navigation, on Black river, a few miles below Brownville. Limerick and Perch River are post-offices. Pop. 3,972.

CHAMPION, settled principally by emigrants from Connecticut; taken from Mexico in 1800; from Albany 148 miles, from Watertown E. centrally distant 12 miles, and drained by the Black river. Champion and Great Bend are small post villages. Pop. 2,206.

CLAYTON, taken from Orleans and Lyme in 1832; from Albany 180 miles, from Watertown centrally distant N. 14 miles. Depauville and French Creek are small villages. Pop. 4,042.

ELLISBURG, settled in 1793, by Mr. Lyman Ellis, and taken from Mexico in 1803; from Watertown centrally distant SW. 17, from Albany 169 miles. Pop. 5,356. Bellville, Woodville, Ellisburg, and Mannsville, are small post villages. There are in the north part of the town some remains of ancient fortifications, consisting of seven mounds, surrounded by ditches, varying from a half to two acres in area. Stone instruments, as axes, wedges, knives, &c., are ploughed up from time to time in the adjacent fields.

HENDERSON, taken from Ellisburg in 1806; from Albany 173 miles. Pop. 2,478. Henderson is a post village and port, at the head of Hungry bay, where vessels of 100 tons may find safe harborage. At the dock there are about 15 or 20 dwellings. At the village, on Stony creek, three quarters of a mile from the dock, there are about 70 dwellings. Smithville, 12 miles SW. from Watertown, and 5 from Sacketts Harbor, has about 65 dwellings.

The following account of an action which took place in this town during the late war with Great Britain, is from a newspaper published at that time, entitled "The War."

"On the 30th ult., (May, 1814,) a number of boats coming from Oswego, with cannon and rigging for the new vessels, put into Sandy Creek, about 16 miles from the harbor,—being well manned with sailors, riflemen, and Indians, under the command of Capt. Woolsey of the navy; who, on entering the creek, despatched an express for reinforcements, which were immediately ordered on, but they did not arrive until the business was over. The captain apprehending an attack, placed the riflemen and Indians in the woods on each side of the creek, and sent a few raw militia, with the show of opposing the enemy's landing. The plan succeeded. The militia retreated on the first fire, pursued by the enemy; but as soon as they had passed the Indians and riflemen, who were in ambush, these last attacked them in the rear, while a battery of four field-pieces opened upon them in front. Thus cut off in their retreat, after a smart action of 20 minutes, in which they had 20 killed and 40 or 50 wounded, the whole force of the enemy, 137 in number, surrendered with their gun-boats, five in number.—One of these boats carried a 68lb. carronade; one, a long 32; one, a long 24; one, two long 12s.; and one, two brass pieces; one of which they threw overboard. Not a man escaped. There were among the enemy's killed, one Lieut. of marines, and one midshipman. Among the prisoners are two Post Captains, one the commander of the Wolf, 4 lieutenants, and 4 midshipmen. The British force consisted of sailors and marines. Our loss, is one Indian killed and three wounded. The prisoners were conducted to Sacketts Harbor by the militia.—Another gun-boat from the British fleet, with 36 men, went up the creek, where they were attacked and captured after a few shots."

HOUNSFIELD, taken from Watertown in 1806; drained west by Black river and some small creeks. This town was settled in 1801, by Augustus Sackett, agent for the owners. Pop. 4,143.

Sacketts Harbor, incorporated in 1821, on the SW. side of Black river bay, on Lake Ontario. The settlement of this town was commenced in 1802, by Augustus Sackett, Esq., agent for the owners, who came from New York and settled at the harbor which derives its name from him. The first house built here, erected by Judge Sackett, is now standing in Baird-street, and is occupied by Mrs. McGwinn. The progress of the settlement was slow until 1812. After the declaration of war this spot became an important military and naval position. The harbor is the best on the lake for shipbuilding and as a naval depot. The following view was taken from the military hospital. The small building on the point of the

JEFFERSON COUNTY.

Northern view of Sacketts Harbor, N. Y.

harbor, on the right of the engraving, is the old blockhouse which stands near, or on the site of old Fort Tompkins. The large building on a rocky island a few rods from the shore, is a ship-house, which covers the frame of the "New Orleans," a 110 gun ship commenced during the late war. The steeple on the left is that of the Presbyterian church. There is also an Episcopal and a Methodist church in the place, and about 1,800 inhabitants. A considerable trade is carried on here by the lake and St. Lawrence river, and by the Oswego, Erie, and Welland canals. After the late war, business very much decreased, but it has since grown with the general improvement of the country.

The troops destined for the attack upon York, (U. C.) embarked from this place. The following account of the expedition is from Thompson's History of the late war:

"On the 22d and 23d of April, 1813, agreeably to previous arrangement with Commodore Chauncey, who had the command of the fleet on Lake Ontario, General Dearborn and his suite, with a force of seventeen hundred men, embarked on this expedition, but the prevalence of a violent storm prevented the sailing of the squadron, until the 25th. On that day it moved into Lake Ontario, and having a favorable wind, arrived safely at 7 o'clock, on the morning of the 27th, about one mile to the westward of the ruins of Fort Toronto, and two and a half from the town of York. The execution of that part of the plan which applied immediately to the attack upon York, was confided to Colonel Pike, of the 15th regiment, who had then been promoted to the rank of a brigadier-general, and the position which had been fixed upon for landing the troops, was the site of the old fort. The approach of the fleet being discovered from the enemy's garrison, General Sheaffe, the British commandant, hastily collected his whole force, consisting of upwards of seven hundred and fifty regulars and militia, and one hundred Indians, and disposed them in the best manner to resist the landing of the American force. A body of British grenadiers were paraded on the shore, and the Glengary fencibles, a corps which had been disciplined with uncommon pains since the commencement of the war, were stationed at another point. Bodies of Indians were observed in groups in different directions, in and about the woods below the site of the fort, and numbers of horsemen were stationed in the clear ground surrounding it. These were seen moving into the town, where strong field works had been thrown up to oppose the assailants. The Indians were taking post at stations, which were pointed out to them by the British officers with great skill, from which they could annoy the Americans at the point where the water and the weather would compel them to land. Thus posted, they were to act as *tirrailleurs*. The regulars were discovered to be moving out of their works in open columns of platoons, and marching along the bank in that order into the woods.

"At 8 o'clock the debarkation commenced; at ten it was completed. Major Forsythe and his riflemen in several large batteaux, were in the advance. They pulled vigorously for the designated ground at the site, but were forced by a strong easterly wind a considerable distance above. The enemy being within a few feet of the water, and completely masked by the thickness of a copse, commenced a galling fire of musketry and rifle. To have fallen further from the clear ground at which he was first ordered to land, would have subjected, not only his own corps, but the whole body of the troops, to great disadvantages; and by landing at a greater distance from the town, the object of the expedition might be frustrated. Major Forsythe therefore determined upon making that part of the shore on which the enemy's principal strength was stationed, and desired his men to rest a moment on their oars, until his riflemen should return the shot. General Pike was at this moment hastening the debarkation of the infantry, when, as he was standing on the ship's deck, he observed the pause of the boats in advance, and springing into that which had been reserved for himself and his staff, he called to them to jump into the boat with him, ordered Major King of the 15th (the same who had distinguished himself in carrying the enemy's batteries opposite Black Rock,) to follow him instantly with three companies of that regiment, and pushed for the Canadian shore. Before he reached it, Forsythe had landed and was already engaged with the principal part of the British and Indian force, under the immediate command of General Sheaffe. He contended with them nearly half an hour. The infantry under Major King, the light artillery under Major Eustis, the volunteer corps commanded by Colonel M'Clure, and about thirty men, who had been selected from the 15th at Plattsburg, trained to the rifle, and designed to act as a small corps of observation, under Lieutenant Riddle, then landed in rapid succession, and formed in platoons. General Pike took command of the first, and ordering the whole body to prepare for a charge, led them on to the summit of the bank, from which the British grenadiers were pouring down a volley of musketry and rifle shot. The advance of the American infantry was not to be withstood, and the grenadiers yielded their position and retired in disorder. The signal of victory was at the same instant heard from Forsythe's bugles, and the sound had no sooner penetrated the ears of the Indians, than they gave a customary yell and fled in every direction. The Glengary corps then skirmished with Forsythe's, whilst a fresh body of Grenadiers, supposed to have been the 8th or King's regiment, made a formidable charge upon the American column, and partially compelled it to retire. But the officers instantly rallied the troops, who returned to the ground, and impetuously charged upon, and routed the grenadiers. A reinforcement of the remainder of the 15th then arrived, with Captain Steel's platoon and the standards of the regiment, and the Americans remained undisputed masters of the ground. A fresh front, however, was presented by the British at a distance, which gave way and retired to the garrison, as soon as the American troops were again formed by Major King, for the charge. The whole body of the troops being now landed, orders were given by General Pike to form in platoons, and to march in that order to the enemy's works. The first line was composed of Forsythe's riflemen, with front and flank guards; the regiments of the first brigade, with their pieces; and three platoons of reserve, under the orders of Major Swan; Major Eustis and his train of artillery were formed in the rear of this reserve, to act where circumstances might require. The second line was composed of the 21st regiment, in six platoons, flanked by Col. M'Clure's volunteers, divided equally as light troops, and all under command of Colonel Ripley. Thus formed, an injunction was given to each officer, to suffer no man to load; when within a short distance of the enemy, an entire reliance would be placed upon the bayonet; and the column moved on, with as much velocity as the streams and ravines which intersected the road along the lake would permit. One field-piece, and a howitzer, were with difficulty passed over one of these, the bridges of which had been destroyed, and placed at the head of the column, in charge of Lieutenant Fanning, of the 3d artillery. As the column emerged from the woods, and came immediately in front of the enemy's first battery, two or three 24 pounders were opened upon it, but without any kind of effect. The column moved on, and the enemy retreated to his second battery. The guns of the first were immediately taken, and Lieutenant Riddle, having at this moment come up with his corps to deliver the prisoners which he had made in the woods, was ordered to proceed to take possession of the second battery, about one hundred yards ahead, the guns of which, Lieutenant Fraser, aid-de-camp to the general, reported to have been spiked by the enemy, whom he discovered retreating to the garrison. General Pike then led the column up to the second battery, where he halted to receive the captured ammunition, and to learn the strength of the garrison. But as every appearance indicated the evacuation of the barracks, he suspected the enemy of an intention to draw him within range of the shot, and then suddenly to show himself in great force. Lieutenant Riddle was sent forward with his corps of observation, to discover if there were any, and what number of troops, within the garrison. The barracks were three hundred yards distant from the second battery, and whilst this corps was engaged in reconnoitering, General Pike, after removing a wounded prisoner from a dangerous situation, had seated himself upon a stump, and commenced an examination of a British sergeant, who had been taken in the woods. Riddle having discovered that the enemy had abandoned the garrison, was about to return with this information, when the magazine, which was situated outside the barrack yard, blew up, with a tremendous and awful explosion, passed over Riddle and his party, without injuring one of his men, and killed and wounded General Pike, and two hundred and sixty of the column. The severity of General Pike's wounds disabled him from further service, and the command of the troops devolved upon Colonel Pearce of the 16th regiment, who sent a demand to the town of York for an immediate surrender. The plan of the contemplated operations was known only to General Pike, and, as General Dearborn had not yet landed, the future movements of the troops would depend upon the will of their new commander. He ordered them immediately to form the column, and to march forward and occupy the barracks, which Major Forsythe, who had been scouring the adjoining wood, had already entered. Meanwhile the British regulars were retreating across the Don, and destroying the bridges in their rear. After the explosion, which killed about fifty of the enemy who had not retired in time from the garrison, Lieutenant Riddle with his party, then reinforced by thirty regulars under Lieutenant Horrel of the 16th, pursued the enemy's route, and annoyed his retreating guard from the wood. This was the only pursuit which was made. Had a more vigorous push followed the abandonment of the enemy's garrison, his whole regular force must have been captured, and the accession of military stores would have been extensively great. The majority of the officers were well aware of this, and as it was known that the stores were deposited at York, they urged the necessity of the immediate approach of the whole column, to prevent their removal. Colonel Pearce then marched towards the town, which was distant three-quarters of a mile. About half way between York and the garrison, the column was intercepted by several officers of the Canadian militia, who had come out with terms of capitulation. Whilst these were discussing, the enemy was engaged in destroying the military storehouse, and a large vessel of war then on the stocks, which in three days might have been launched, and added to the American squadron on Ontario. Forsythe, who was on the left in advance, being aware of this, despatched Lieutenant Riddle to inform Colonel Pearce. Colonel Ripley was at the same time urging a rapid march, and the troops again proceeded. Colonel Pearce enjoined the observance of General Pike's orders, that the property of the inhabitants of York should be held sacred, and that any soldier who should so far neglect the honor of his profession, as to be guilty of plundering, should, on conviction, be punished with death. At 4 o'clock in the afternoon, the Americans were in possession of the town, and terms of capitulation were agreed upon, by which, notwithstanding the severe loss which the army and the nation had sustained by the death of the general; the unwarrantable manner in which that loss was occasioned; and the subtlety with which the militia colonels offered to capitulate at a distance from the town, so that the column might be detained until General Sheaffe should escape, and the destruction of the public property be completed, although one of its articles stipulated for its delivery into the hands of the Americans; the militia and inhabitants were freed from all hardship, and not only their persons and property, but their legislative hall and other public buildings were protected. The terms of the capitulation were, 'that the troops, regular and militia, and the naval officers and seamen, should be surrendered prisoners of war. That all *public stores, naval and military, should be immediately* given up to the commanding officers of the army and navy of the United States, and that all private property should be guaranteed to the citizens of the town of York. That all papers belonging to the civil officers should be retained by them, and that such surgeons as might be procured to attend the wounded of the British regulars and Canadian militia, should not be considered prisoners of war.' Under this capitulation, one lieutenant-colonel, one major, thirteen captains, nine lieutenants, eleven ensigns, one deputy adjutant-general, and four naval officers, and two hundred and fifty-one non-commissioned officers and privates, were surrendered. The American infantry were then ordered to return to, and quarter in the barracks, while the riflemen were stationed in the town.

"When General Pike's wound was discovered to be mortal, he was removed from the field, and carried to the shipping with his wounded aids. As they conveyed him to the water's edge, a sudden exclamation was heard from the troops, which informed him of the American having supplanted the British standard in the garrison. He expressed his satisfaction by a feeble sigh, and after being transferred from the

Pert schooner to the commodore's ship, he made a sign for the British flag, which had then been brought to him, to be placed under his head, and expired without a groan. Thus perished in the arms of victory, by the ungenerous stratagem of a vanquished foe, a soldier of tried valor and invincible courage,—a general of illustrious virtues and distinguished talents.

"When the British general saw the American column advancing from the woods, he hastily drew up the articles of capitulation, and directed them to be delivered to a colonel of the York militia. This colonel was instructed to negotiate the terms, after the regulars should have retreated. General Sheaffe, therefore, considered the garrison to be as much surrendered, as if the articles had been actually agreed upon and signed. Yet he treacherously ordered a train to be laid, which was so calculated, that the explosion of the magazine should be caused at the time when the Americans would arrive at the barracks. Had not General Pike halted the troops at the enemy's second battery, the British plan would have attained its consummation, and the destruction of the whole column would have been the natural consequence. The train had been skilfully laid, and the combustibles arranged in a manner to produce the most dreadful effect. Five hundred barrels of powder, several cart loads of stone, and an immense quantity of iron, shells, and shot, were contained in the magazine. The calamity which followed the explosion, caused no discomfiture among the troops. A number of their officers of high rank, and of equal worth, were either killed or wounded, and they became actuated by a desire to revenge their fall. '*Push on, my brave fellows, and avenge your general*,' were the last words of their expiring commander. They instantly gave three cheers, formed the column, and marched on rapidly. Had they been led directly to York, the issue of the expedition would have been fruitful with advantages. As it was, however, the enemy's means were crippled, his resources cut off, and the military stores of the captors extensively multiplied. Most of the guns, munitions of war, and provisions, necessary to carry on the campaign by the enemy, had been deposited at York, and notwithstanding the firing of the principal storehouse, an immense quantity fell into the hands of the Americans. The baggage and private papers of General Sheaffe were left at York, in the precipitation of his flight, and proved to be a valuable acquisition to the American commander. These and the public stores were the only articles of capture. The conduct of the troops needed no restraint. Though their indignation was highly excited, by the circumstance of a scalp having been found suspended near the speaker's chair, in the legislative chamber, neither the ornaments of the chamber, the building itself, nor the public library, was molested. A large quantity of flour, deposited in the public stores, was distributed among the inhabitants, on condition that it should be used for their own consumption; and those whose circumstances were impoverished, were supplied with many other articles of the captured provisions. The balance was taken on board the fleet, with the naval stores, or destroyed upon the shore.

"Immediately after the fall of General Pike, the commander-in-chief landed with his staff, but he did not reach the troops until they had entered York. He there made arrangements to expedite their departure for the other objects of the expedition, and they were soon after re-embarked.

"The co-operation of the squadron was of the greatest importance in the attack upon the enemy's garrison. As soon as the debarkation was completed, Commodore Chauncey directed the schooners to take a position near the forts, in order that the attack of the army and navy might, if possible, be simultaneous. The larger vessels could not be brought up, and in consequence of the wind, the schooners were obliged to beat up to their intended position. This they did, under a very heavy fire from the enemy's batteries, and having taken their station within six hundred yards of the principal fort, opened a galling fire, and contributed very much to its destruction. The loss on board the squadron, was three killed and eleven wounded. Among the killed were midshipmen Thompson and Hatfield, the latter of whom, in his dying moments, had no other care than to know if he had performed his duty to his country.

"In the action the loss of the American army was trifling; but in consequence of the explosion, it was much greater than the enemy's loss in killed and wounded. Fourteen were killed and thirty-two wounded in battle, and thirty-eight were killed and two hundred and twenty-two wounded by the explosion, so that the total American loss amounted to 320 men. Among those who fell by the explosion, besides General Pike, were seven captains, seven subalterns, one aid-de-camp, one acting aid, and one volunteer aid. The enemy's loss in killed and wounded amounted to two hundred, and in prisoners to five hundred and fifty. His wounded were left in the houses on the road leading to and in the neighborhood of York, and were attended to by the American army and navy surgeons. The prisoners were all paroled, and the troops withdrawn from York immediately after its capture."

The following is an account of the attack on Sackett's Harbor by the British, May, 1813:

"Whilst the troops were preparing to embark at York, for the expedition against Fort George, the British at Kingston, having gained intelligence of their absence from Sackett's Harbor, of the batteries at that place having been principally dismantled, and of the smallness of the force which had been left for its protection, hastily collected all their disposables, and embarked on board their fleet, under the command of Sir George Prevost. The fleet was commanded by Sir James Yeo. On the night of the 27th day of May, five hours after the capture of Fort George, the British appeared off the entrance to the harbor. The American force consisted of two hundred invalids, and two hundred and fifty dragoons, then newly arrived from a long and fatiguing march. Two small vessels, under Lieutenant Chauncey, were stationed at its mouth, and gave instant signals of alarm, at the approach of the British squadron. Expresses were immediately forwarded to General Brown, then at his seat, eight miles from the harbor, and he immediately repaired thither, to take the command.

"The tour of duty of the militia of his brigade had expired many weeks before, but he had been requested by General Dearborn to take the command of the harbor, at any time when the enemy should approach it, and to provide for its defence. Immediately on his arrival, dispositions were made to that effect. The movements of the enemy indicated his intention to land on the peninsula, called Horse Island. General Brown, therefore, determined on resisting him at the water's edge, with the Albany volunteers, under Colonel Mills, and such militia as could be instantly collected. Alarm guns were therefore fired, and expresses sent out for that purpose. Lieutenant-colonel Backus, of the first regiment of United States dragoons, who commanded at Sackett's Harbor in the absence of the officers who had proceeded to Fort George, was to form a second line with the regulars. The regular artillerists were stationed in Fort Tompkins, and the defence of Navy Point was committed to Lieutenant Chauncey.

"On the 28th, the Wolfe, the Royal George, the Prince Regent, the Earl of Moira, and one brig, two schooners, and two gun-boats, with thirty-three flat-bottomed boats and barges, containing in all twelve hundred troops, appeared in the offing, at five miles distance. They were standing their course for the harbor, when, having discovered a fleet of American barges, coming round Stony Point with troops from Oswego, the whole of their boats were immediately despatched to cut them off. They succeeded in taking twelve of them, after they had been run on shore and abandoned by their crews, who arrived at the harbor in the night. The remainder, seven in number, escaped from their pursuers, and got safely in. The British commanders, being then under an impression that other barges would be sailing from Oswego, stood into South bay, and despatched their armed boats to waylay them. In this they were disappointed; and during the delay which was caused by this interruption of their intended operations, the militia from the neighboring counties collected at the harbor, and betrayed great eagerness to engage in the contest with the invading enemy. They were ordered to be stationed on the water side, near the island on which Colonel Mills was posted with his volunteers. The strength at that point was nearly five hundred men. But the whole force, including the regulars, effectives and invalids, did not exceed one thousand. The plan of defence had been conceived with great skill, and if the conduct of the militia had proved to be consistent with their promises, it would have been executed with equal ability. Disposed of as the forces were, in the event of General Brown's being driven from his position at Horse Island, Colonel Backus was to advance with his reserve of regulars, and meet the head of the enemy's column, whilst the general would rally his corps, and fall upon the British flanks. If resistance to the attack of the enemy should still fail, Lieutenant Chauncey was to destroy the stores at Navy Point, and to retire with his two schooners, and the prize schooner, the Duke of Gloucester, which had been a few weeks before captured from the enemy, to the south shore of the bay, and east of Fort Volunteer. In this fort the regulars and militia were to shut themselves up, and make a vigorous stand, as their only remaining resort. Every thing being thus ordered, General Brown directed his defensive army to lay upon their arms, whilst he continued personally to reconnoitre the shores of the harbor, during the whole night of the 28th. At the only favorable point of landing, he had caused a breast-work to be thrown up, and a battery *en barbette* to be erected. Behind this most of the militia were stationed.

"At the dawn of the 29th, the enemy was discovered with his vessels drawn up in line, between Horse Island and Stony Point; and in a few minutes, all his boats and barges approached the shore, under cover of his gun-boats, those being the heaviest of his vessels which, in consequence of the lightness of the winds, could be brought up. The troops with which the boats were filled, were commanded by Sir George Prevost, in person. Commodore Yeo directed the movements of the barges. General Brown instantly issued his orders, that the troops should lay close, and reserve their fire until the enemy should have approached so near, that every shot might take effect. This order was executed, and the fire was so destructive, that the enemy's advance boats were obliged to make a temporary pause, and numbers of their officers and men were seen to fall. Encouraged by the desired effect of the first fire, the militia loaded their pieces with the utmost quickness, and the artillery was ordered to be opened at the moment of their second. But, before the second round had been completely discharged, the whole body of the militia, none of whom had ever seen an enemy until now, and who were entirely unaccustomed to subordination, though they were well protected by the breastwork, rose from behind it, and abandoning those honorable promises of noble daring which they had made but a little while before, they fled with equal precipitation and disorder. A strange and unaccountable panic seized the whole line; and with the exception of a very few, terror and dismay were depicted in every countenance. Colonel Mills, vainly endeavoring to rally his men, was killed as he was reminding them of the solemn pledges which they had given; but the fall of this brave officer served rather to increase their confusion, than to actuate them to revenge it.

"General Brown seeing that his plan was already frustrated, and fearing his inability to execute any other without the vigorous co-operation of the militia, hastened to intercept their retreat; and, finding one company, of about one hundred men, who had been rallied by the active and zealous conduct of Capt. M'Nitt, of that corps, he brought them up, and ordered them to form in line with the regulars and volunteers, who had continued to keep their ground.

"In the interval which had thus elapsed, the enemy had effected his debarkation, with little opposition; and drawing up his whole force on Horse Island, he commenced his march for the village; on the road to which, he was met by a small party of infantry, under Major Aspinwall, and a few dismounted dragoons under Major Laval, who opposed him with much gallantry. Two of the gun-boats ranged up the shore, and covered the field with grape. This handful of troops then gradually retired in good order, from an immense superiority of numbers, and occupied the intervals between the barracks.

"Lieutenant-colonel Backus, with his reserve of regulars, first engaged the enemy, when the militia company of Captain M'Nitt was formed on his flank; and in the vigorous fight which then followed, this company behaved with as much gallantry as the bravest of the regulars. The whole force was compelled to fall back, however, by the superior strength of the enemy's column, and resorting to the barracks for what shelter they could afford, they posted themselves in the unprotected log houses, and kept up an incessant and effective fire. From these, the most violent assaults, and the repeated and varying efforts of the British, were incompetent to dislodge them. Colonel Gray, the quartermaster-general of the enemy's forces, advanced to the weakest part of the barracks, at the head of a column of regulars, and after exchanging shots with an inferior party of militia and regulars, led his men on to the assault. A small boy, who was a drummer in Major Aspinwall's corps, seized a musket, and levelling it at the colonel, immediately brought him to the ground. At that moment Lieutenant Fanning, of the artillery, who had been so severely wounded by the explosion at Little York, and was yet considered to be unable to do any kind of duty, leaned upon his piece whilst it was drawn up, and having given it the proper elevation, discharged three rounds of grape into the faces of the enemy, who immediately fell back in disorder. At this instant, Lieutenant-colonel Backus fell, severely wounded.

"Whilst the battle was raging with its greatest violence, information was brought to Lieutenant Chauncey, of the intention of the American forces to surrender. He therefore, in conformity to his previous orders, relating to such an event, fired the navy barracks, and destroyed all the property and public stores, which had previously belonged to the harbor, as well as the provisions and equipments which had been brought from York. The destruction of these buildings, and the conflagration which was thence produced, was thought to have been caused by the troops of the enemy, and although the undisciplined militia and volunteers, and the invalid regulars, were suspicious of being placed between the fire of two divisions of the enemy, they continued to fight on, regardless of their inferiority, or the consequences of their capture.

"General Brown was all this time actively superintending the operations of his little army. He now determined on making a diversion in its favor, which, if it should be successful, would be the only means of saving the place, or of relieving his exhausted troops. Having learned that the militia, who had fled from their stations in the early part of the engagement, had not yet entirely dispersed, and that they were still within a short distance of the scene of action, he hastened to exhort them to imitate the conduct of their brave brethren in arms. He reproached them with shameful timidity, and ordered them instantly to form and follow him, and threatened with instant death the first man who should refuse. His order was obeyed with alacrity. He then attempted a stratagem, by which to deceive the enemy, with regard to the forces against which he was contending. Silently passing through a distant wood, which led towards the place at which the enemy had landed, General Brown persuaded the British general of his intention to gain the rear of his forces, to take possession of the boats, and effectually to cut off their retreat.

"This was done with such effect, at the moment when the fire of Lieutenant Fanning's piece had caused the destruction in the British line, that General Sir George Prevost was well convinced of the vast superiority of the American force to his own. He gave up all thoughts of the capture of the place, and hurrying to his boats, put off immediately to the

British squadron. He was not pursued, because, if the real number of the American troops had been exposed to his view, he would have returned to the contest, might easily have outflanked, and in all human probability, would still have captured the army and the village.

"But the precipitation of his flight was such, that he left not only the wounded bodies of his ordinary men upon the field, but those of the dead and wounded of the most distinguished of his officers. Among these were Quartermaster-general Gray, Majors Moodie and Evans, and three captains. The return of his loss, as accurately as it has been ascertained, amounted to three field officers, one captain, and twenty-five rank and file, found dead on the field; two captains and twenty rank and file found wounded; and two captains, one ensign, and thirty-two rank and file made prisoners. In addition to which, many were killed in the boats, and numbers had been carried away previously to the retreat. The loss of the Americans was greater in proportion, as the number of their men engaged were less. One colonel of volunteers, twenty regulars, privates, and one volunteer private, were killed; one lieutenant-colonel, three lieutenants, and one ensign of the regulars, and seventy-nine non-commissioned officers and privates, were wounded; and twenty-six non-commissioned officers and privates were missing. Their aggregate loss was one hundred and ten regulars, twenty-one volunteers, and twenty-five militia; making a total of one hundred and fifty-six. It was severe, because of the worth, more than of the number of those who fell. The injury in public stores, sustained at Sackett's Harbor, though not by any act of the invading enemy, was extensive; but the gallantry of several individuals prevented its being more so. Lieutenant Chauncey was no sooner apprized of the error of the report which had been brought to him, than he made every exertion to save as much of the public property as it was possible to rescue from the increasing conflagration, and to that effect, he ran the Fair American and the Pert up the river. The new frigate, the General Pike, which was then on the stocks, was saved; and Lieutenant Talman, of the army, at the imminent risk of his life, boarded the prize schooner the Duke of Gloucester, which was then on fire, with a considerable quantity of powder in her hold, extinguished the fire, and brought her from under the flames of the storehouses.

"Notwithstanding this signal repulse, the British commanding officers attempted to play off the stratagem which Sir James Yeo afterward adopted at the Forty Mile Creek. They sent in a flag with a peremptory demand for the formal surrender of the post, which was as peremptorily refused."

The British colonel, Gray, fell near the present residence of Mr. John Hall, in Hill-street, and the stump against which he reposed his head, is still to be seen by the sidewalk. He was a noble-looking man, about six feet in height, and about forty years of age. Beside him was a Glengarian officer, mortally wounded. A private named David Johnson, from Berkshire county, Mass., lay near, wounded in a most horrible manner. This young man was a widow's only son. At the time of his enlistment at Greenbush, his mother requested the sergeant to take good care of him. His face was carried away by a side shot from below his forehead, downward, including his eyes, nose, upper jaw, tongue, and some of the teeth of the lower jaw. He notwithstanding had his reason. Being requested by the bystanders, if he wanted water to lift up his right hand, he did so. A soldier who was shot by a musket ball through the abdomen, informed his captain, who gave him permission to leave the ground, with the expectation that he would fall before he had got many rods distant. An hour or two after the battle, the officer was astonished to meet the man quietly walking in the streets of the village. He asked him where he had been? "*To get some milk,*" was the reply. It appears that he had not eaten any thing for thirty hours previous to the action, and the ball was thus enabled to pass through the intestines without mortal injury.

The following is a view of the barracks from the military hospital.

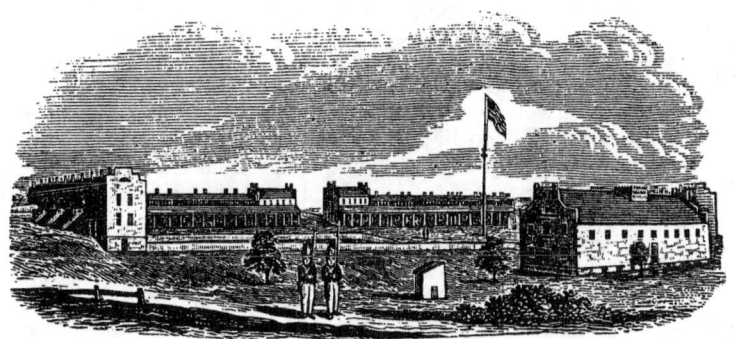

Northern view of Jefferson Barracks, Sacketts Harbor.

The two long ranges of buildings in the distance, facing the spectator, are the officers' quarters. The buildings at each end are the soldiers' barracks. These structures are of limestone, about 250 feet in length, two stories in height, with neat piazzas in front, forming three sides of a square, on which is the parade ground. The large building on the right is the commissary's department. The barracks were commenced in 1816, and finished in 1819. The grounds attached include about forty acres, and the whole is surrounded on three sides by a log picket fence, painted white, and about 9 feet in height. The fourth side is open to the water.

On a monument in the military burial place, which is included in the barrack grounds, are the following inscriptions:

South side.—" In memory of Gen. Z. M. Pike, killed at York, U. C., 27 April, 1813.—Capt. Joseph Nicholson, 14 infantry, aid-de-camp to Gen. Pike, do." *East side.*—" In memory of Lieut. Col. John Mills, volunteer; killed at Sacketts Harbor, 29 May, 1813.—Capt. A. Spencer, 29 infantry, aid-de-camp to Maj. Gen. Brown, killed at Lundy's Lane, 25 July, 1814." *North side.*—" In memory of Col. Tuttle, Lieut. Col. Dix, Maj. Johnson, Lieut. Vandeventer." *West side.*—" In memory of Brig. Gen. L. Covington, killed at Chry'rs Fields, U. C., 11 Nov. 1812. Lieut. Col. E. Backus, 1st dragoons, killed at S. Harbor, 29 May, 1813."

" Sacred to the memory of Frederick Augustus Leonard, son of James and Mercy Leonard, of New York, aged 23 years, 2 months and 12 days; a sailing-master in the American navy, who died on the 12th of May, 1813, by a violent illness brought on by fatigue in the attack of the American forces on York, in Upper Canada, April 27th, 1813.—This monument is erected by his brother, Capt. James T. Leonard of the navy."

LE RAY, settled in 1803 and organized in 1806; from Albany 156 miles. Evans Mills, 10 miles NE. from Watertown, and Le Raysville, are small but flourishing villages. Sandfords Corners and West Le Ray are post-offices. Pop. 3,722.

LORRAINE, originally named Malta, and taken from Mexico in 1804; from Albany 145, and from Watertown S. 16 miles. Lorraine is a post-office. Pop. 1,721.

LYME, taken from Brownville in 1817; from Albany 185 miles. Pop. 5,467. It includes several islands in Lake Ontario and one in the St. Lawrence river. Cape Vincent, port of entry of Cape Vincent district, at the fork of Lake Ontario and at the head of the St. Lawrence, 25 miles from Watertown, has about 70 dwellings. Chaumont, at the head of Chaumont bay, 14 miles from Watertown, has about 30 dwellings. At Tibbets point there is a lighthouse. Three Mile Bay, Mileno Bay, and Peninsula, are post-offices.

ORLEANS, taken from Brownville in 1821; from Albany 184 miles. Le Fargeville, named from John Le Farge, the original proprietor of the town, 16 miles N. from Watertown, and Stone Mill, in the SW. angle of the town, are small settlements with post-offices. Pop. 3,000.

PAMELIA, taken from Brownville in 1819; from Albany 166 miles. Williamstown has about 40 dwellings, and is on the bank of the river and connected with Watertown by a bridge. Pamelia and Pamelia Four Corners are post-offices. Pop. 2,119.

PHILADELPHIA, settled principally by Friends, and taken from Le Ray in 1821; from Watertown centrally distant NE. 16 miles. Pop. 1,888. The Friends settlement has about 60 dwellings.

RODMAN, originally named Harrison, taken from Adams in 1804, and settled in 1801, by New England emigrants; from Albany 154, centrally distant from Watertown S. 10 miles. Pop. 1,703. Rodman has about 40 dwellings. Whitesville is a small post village. Several Indian mounds are in this town, with ancient fortifications Pop. 1,700.

RUTLAND, formed in 1802; from Albany 154, from Watertown centrally distant E. 6 miles. There are here remains of ancient works. There is an old camp or fort near the Watertown and Rutland line, situated on a hill surrounded by a hollow that seems to have been a ditch enclosing about four acres of ground. Its form is an irregular oval. On one side is a triangular projection of 50 paces, terminating in an acute angle, surrounded, like the camp, by an intrenchment. On digging into this, many remains of human bones were found, and a part of a human skull imbedded in two or three quarts of Indian corn, which seems to have been parched to a dark chocolate-brown color, but was sound and well preserved. The place was lately covered with lofty trees, like the surrounding ground, which must have been some centuries in growing. South Rutland, Tylersville, Felts Mill, and Lockport, are small post villages. Rutland Centre is a post-office.

WATERTOWN was organized as part of Oneida county in 1800. Pop. 5,025. Watertown, incorporated village and seat of justice for the county, is from New York NW. 325 miles, from Albany 176, from Utica NNW. 81, from Sacketts Harbor E. 10 miles. It contains 2 Presbyterian, 1 Episcopal, 1 Methodist Episcopal, 1 Universalist, and 1 Catholic church, an incorporated academy, the Jefferson Company and Watertown banks, an insurance company, county buildings, and about 550 dwellings.

In March, 1800, this town was first settled by Henry Coffin, who originally came from New Hampshire, and built his log cabin on the brow of the hill about 3 rods easterly from the front door of the American Hotel. Soon after he was joined by Zechariah Butterfield, who built his cabin on the ground now occupied by Davenport's tavern. Both of these individuals brought with them their families. The unevenness and apparent unproductiveness of the soil were more than counterbalanced, in the discerning minds of these pioneers, by the immense hydraulic power appropriable, from the numerous falls and rapids of Black river at this point, which in the space of about a mile amount to nearly 100 feet descent. In this, as well as the richness and fertility of the adjacent country, they wisely believed that they discovered the elements of future prosperity and greatness.

Hart and Isaiah Massay, who came from Windsor, Vermont, joined them in the succeeding year. In 1802, the first tavern was opened by Isaiah Massay, and the first saw-mill erected on the present site of W. Pattridge's woollen factory. The high reputation of the Black river country now began to be sounded abroad, and the number of settlers rapidly augmented. Among the other earliest emigrants were Aaron Bacon, Jonathan Cowan, two brothers by the name of Thornton, Jesse Doolittle, M. Canfield, Aaron Keyes, D. Huntington, William Smith, John Paddock, Chauncey Calhoun, Philo Johnson, and John Hathway.

"An inventory of the entire effects of each settler, as he arrived upon the ground, would have been a short and easy matter. Those with families had possessed but small estates in the places from which they emigrated, and generally found their means exhausted when they had procured an outfit for their westward journey. The whole possession of many a young man who planted the germ of his fortune here, was comprised in the axe that he brought upon his shoulder, and in the nerves of the vigorous arm which wielded it. Very little money was brought into Watertown by its first inhabitants. They were all thrown upon their immediate exertions for subsistence. In these circumstances, want, with its horrors, might have visited them, had it not been the case that quick returns of fruitful harvests were made to their industry. It is a well-known fact, that throughout the whole of Western New York, the first harvest reaped from the soil is often more abundant than any succeeding one. The forests here are found to be unencumbered with the mass of dead leaves, and undecomposed vegetable matter, which, in many parts of our country, the farmer finds so prejudicial to the cultivation and production of his new land. There is that, either in the climate or the soil itself, which seems to effect the decomposition of vegetables very soon after they are deprived of life. From this circumstance, the deposition upon the ground of a great body of forest leaves, every season, instead of opposing an obstacle to immediate production, facilitates it, and contributes to the richness and fertility of the soil.

"The enterprising mechanics and agriculturists in Watertown did not long allow their hydraulic privileges to remain unimproved. In 1803, Jonathan Cowan built the first grist-mill. This was an invaluable acquisition to the place, as it relieved the inhabitants from the necessity of travelling to a great distance for the flouring of all their grain.

"In 1803, the first bridge across Black river, at Watertown, was built at the site of the lower bridge, on the Brownville road, by Henry Coffeen and Andrew Edmonds. The business of the little community increased as their number was augmented, and soon demanded some medium of disposing of the products of their industry. Accordingly, in 1805, a store was opened by J. Paddock and William Smith. The year 1807 brought with it the accession of a paper-mill, built by Gurden Caswell, and a brewery, by Gursham Tuttle.

"At this period, and for a considerable time after, the manufacture of potash was an object of much attention with those who had land in their possession. The high price which this article then commanded, and the fine adaptation of the timber and the soil to the production and the preservation of ashes, rendered it one of the most lucrative branches of business to which the settlers could devote themselves. As every barrel of potash yielded the manufacturer $25, the purchasers of lots, by their characteristic enterprise and prudence, were enabled to realize a sum fully equal to the first cost of their lands from this article alone.

"The principal commercial operations in the years 1806-7-8, consisted in the exchange of goods for potash, which took place between the agricultural portion of the community and the merchants before mentioned. The amount of exchanges thus effected during this period was not inconsiderable, when we consider the limited number of persons engaged in the transaction. In 1806, it was not less than $3,500; in 1807, about $6,000; and in 1808, it exceeded $9,000. A comparative view of the business of the place may be had, by stating in this connection, that the goods sold in Watertown during the year 1839, including those manufactured in it, amounted to about $500,000.

"The first cotton factory which reared its form in this village is still standing, and known as the 'Old Cotton Factory'—now under the proprietorship of the Watertown Cotton Mills Company. It was erected by a company, and went into operation in 1814. The machinery was manufactured by James Wild, of Hudson, much of which is still in use; and although cotton machinery has been much improved by 25 years' experience, few cotton factories do more or better work. This establishment was succeeded in 1827 by a similar one, erected by Levi Bebee, upon the island which bears his name. It was, however, on a much more extensive plan; being a building 250 feet in length, 50 in breadth, and 4 stories high, built of limestone, of the most substantial character. This building was designed to receive 10,000 spindles; and half that number, with 128 power looms, had been put into it, when it was destroyed by fire in 1832. It was erected, and thus far completed, at an expense of $120,000, employed a great number of hands, directly and indirectly, and its destruction gave a shock to the village of Watertown from which it has yet hardly recovered. The ruins still stand, frowning upon a majestic and beautiful cascade, whose waters leap past them, as if in terror, lest the columns of ragged stone should precipitate themselves upon their bosom; or, as if in haste to escape from the gloom and sadness of their presence. They also remain a monument of the enterprise and public spirit of their late proprietor.

"In the early settlement of the county, strenuous efforts were made to fix the county seat at Brownville. Gen. Jacob Brown was appointed one of the commissioners by the state, to lay out and open two roads; one from Utica, through Boonville, to some point on Black river; and one from Rome, through Redfield, to the same point. Brownville was fixed upon as this point. Every exertion was then put forth by those interested, and every argument pressed, which the circumstances of the case, policy, and ingenuity could supply, to effect the location of the county seat at that place. The commissioners, who were to designate the site of the courthouse, decided however upon placing it at Watertown. But by way of compromise they selected its present site, then quite remote from the village.

"The first courthouse was built in 1807, by William Rise and Joel Mix; its erection was superintended by William Smith. It being thus placed at a distance from the centre of the village, had a tendency to draw attention, and induce settlement in that direction. Another circumstance had a considerable influence in fixing the location of mills and manufactories remote from the common centre. Mr. Jonathan Cowan was the owner of all the hydraulic privileges here, at the point where his mills were situated. From a mistaken belief as to the best method of stimulating industry and enterprise, he refused, on all occasions, to sell, without limiting the purchaser to one kind of business. The spirited settlers would not brook this fetter upon their enterprise, and determined not to submit to the restriction, so long as the waters of Black river were free. This policy occasioned the erection of a dam further down the river in 1807, and another above in 1814. Although, for a time, this appeared to check the growth of the village, it ultimately operated to its advantage, by enlarging its sphere of action, and more fully developing its resources.

"It is generally the case, that in planting new settlements, a very early attention to the cultivation of the intellect and moral powers of the community, is prevented by the arduousness of the duties and the engrossment of mind incident upon their condition, as well as their remoteness from institutions of learning and the great centres of literary and moral influence. In Watertown, however, as early as the year 1811, efforts were made for the establishment of an academy. A piece of ground was given for this purpose, by Mr. P. Keyes, near where the first church now stands. A building was commenced the same year, and completed in the following, 1812, simultaneous with the commencement of the last hostilities between the United Sates and Great Britain. The declaration of war occasioned the stationing of a garrison of soldiers in Watertown; who finding the academy building conveniently situated for barracks, took possession of it and occupied it for that purpose.

"The proximity of Watertown to the Canadian frontier and the site of several battles, as also its exposed and unprotected condition, produced, during this conflict, a constant agitation and an intense excitement of the public mind, which forbade the inhabitants thinking of any thing but the 'war.' The project of the academy was in consequence abandoned. After the evacuation of the building by the troops, which took place in 1814, it was taken down, and the materials of which it was composed transferred to what is now known as Clinton-street, and erected into a schoolhouse. This, until recently, has been employed for the purposes designed. The land thus left vacant, according to a condition in the deed given by Mr. Keyes, could be sold by appraisal. A part of it was thus sold, and a part went into the possession of the First church.

"With this failure, however, the efforts for the accomplishment of the truly noble design did not cease. Another commodious academy building was erected a few years after, upon the street which has taken its name from this circumstance. This academy was opened under favorable auspices, and for a considerable time prospered flourishingly. But, although the noble stone edifice still stands in its beautiful and sequestered location, as an abode of learning it is now superseded by the Black River Literary and Religious Institute—a school most deservedly popular, an ornament to the place, and an honor to its conductors and patrons.

"The religious opportunities of the inhabitants of Watertown, for the first few years, were necessarily limited. For the purpose of public worship, they were accustomed often to assemble at the dwelling of some one of the little community, to hear read a sermon, from the pen of some excellent New England divine; and whence, no doubt, many a petition went up to Him who 'regards not the condition of men,' as fervent and acceptable, as if uttered in the stately temple embellished with cornice and damask. They were occasionally visited by an itinerant minister of the Methodist connection, but seldom by any others. The place was regarded as proper missionary ground, and the work of proclaiming to the inhabitants the 'Word of life,' as demanding the exercise of as much benevolence and self-denial as is now required in him who would carry the Bible into the savage regions west of the Rocky mountains. This is well illustrated by the remark of a benevolent-hearted herald of the cross, while on his way to the settlement here; being asked whither he was bound and what was the object of his mission, he replied, '*I am going to preach to the heathen.*' In 1803, a church was organized by the Rev. Ebenezer Lazel—Presbyterian in its confession of faith, and Congregational in its form of government. The Presbyterian clergymen located here, were, successively, the Rev. Messrs. Leavenworth, Porter, Cook, and, immediately after the war, Mr. Banks. As the population of the place increased, bringing together, of necessity, persons of various religious sentiments, churches of the different persuasions were organized, from time to time, until the village now embraces two churches of the Presbyterian denomination, (the 1st and the 2d,) 1 of the Baptist, 1 of the Methodist, 1 of the Roman Catholic, 1 of the Episcopal, and 1 of the Universalist; all occupying attractive and commodious houses of worship.

"In the early years of the village it was remarkable for nothing, perhaps, more than the union and harmony of its inhabitants. Common dangers, privations, and labors, begat a community of interests and feeling, and actuated to a mutual reciprocation of assistance and benefits. The prosperity and joys, as well as the griefs and misfortunes of one, were shared by all. Death never invaded their number, without throwing a gloom over the whole community, and touching every heart with the affliction. The melancholy circumstances attending the first instance of mortality, afforded great occasion for the exercise of these sympathetic feelings.

"Late at the close of a still, sultry day in summer, Mrs. Thornton, the wife of one of the young settlers, gave the alarm that her husband had not returned from the forest, whither he had gone in the afternoon to procure a piece of timber for a particular purpose. Immediately every man in the settlement answered to the call, and hastened to the place designated for meeting to concert a plan for search. Here all armed themselves with torches of lighted pine knots or birch bark, and calling every gun in the place into use for firing alarms and signals, started out, in small companies, into the forest in all directions. After a search of several hours, the preconcerted signal-gun announced that 'the lost was found.' All hurried to the spot; and upon the ground where now stands the Black River Institute, crushed beneath a tree which he had felled, lay the lifeless body of their companion. He was laid upon a bier, hastily prepared for the occasion, and conveyed through the gloom of midnight, by the light of their torches, back to his house. What must have been the emotions of the bereaved young widow, when the mangled corpse of her husband, so suddenly fallen a victim to death, was brought in and laid before her! She did not, however, mourn alone. As the remains were borne to their resting-place,—the first grave that was opened in Trinity churchyard,—it needed no sable emblems of mourning to tell of the grief which hung dark around every heart. Each one of the little company, as he returned from performing the last duties to his departed companion, *felt* as if from his own family one had been taken.

"A similar incident occurred, a short time after, in the death of a child, which was killed by the falling of a tree, on the present site of the courthouse; thus designating with blood, as one can imagine, the location of the halls of justice and science in our village, and consecrating the ground of each by a human sacrifice.

"Notwithstanding the general union and harmony which prevailed, clashing interests and individual enmities would sometimes show, that even the common dangers and hardships of the wilderness have not power to change the character of human passion, or to soften its malignity, when occasion arouses it. One incident will illustrate this.

"By some unfortunate circumstance, a feud was enkindled between one of the settlers in Watertown and his neighbor, 15 or 20 miles distant; for, be it known, distance was then no barrier to neighborship. Not long after the commencement of hostilities between the parties, it came to the ears of the one in Watertown, that his enemy had offered a reward of $5 for his head. Feeling rather uneasy under this summary outlawry—as it necessarily, he thought, rendered insecure the tenure by which he held his life,—and being unwilling to dispose of it except upon more reasonable terms, he determined to go and negotiate the matter, *propria persona*, with this dealer in *personal* estate, and, if possible, induce him to withdraw the reward. As there was no road practicable for travelling by horse, he was obliged to accomplish the whole distance on foot. This he did; and having arrived at the residence of his enemy, he found him in company with two or three of his nearer neighbors. Wishing to avoid publicity in the affair as much as possible, he requested a private interview. But he was tartly replied to, that there was nothing between them that required secrecy, and if he had any thing to say, he must 'speak out.' Being obliged thus to make known his errand publicly, rather disturbed his equanimity; but his situation was desperate. Here was his last hope of effecting a reconciliation; and he therefore commenced by saying, he had learned, with much regret, that their late difficulties had drawn from him the offer of a reward of $5 for his life; he hoped it was not the case. But he had come to learn the truth from his own lips; and if it were really so, if possible, to compromise the affair, and adjust their differences. His enemy quickly retorted, that it was a 'most rascally untruth—as great a lie as ever was told.' 'I never,' said he, 'have offered $5 for your head; never—not I. I may have said that I would give *twenty shillings;* but I never went over that.' With this very satisfactory information, he was obliged to return and await patiently the issue of the struggle which was to determine whether he could be allowed to retain his head, between the consciences of his fellow settlers, and their cupidity, so strongly appealed to by the twenty-shilling reward.

" Such circumstances were then, however, of rare occurrence. Unanimity of sentiment and feeling was the general law; these were but the exceptions. No doubt that amidst the dangers, the rugged toil, and the coarse fare of this new settlement, happiness was found to dwell with as much fulness and purity, as with the safety, the ease and the refinement of the town or city. Ask those venerable pioneers of the wilderness who still remain in our midst, and they will tell you, that they look with less complaisance and pleasure upon the last few years of their lives, than upon those in which the forests were falling beneath their axes; or, in their tow-frocks—the insignia of their priestly office—they performed the obsequies of the monarchs of the wood, at their funeral piles. They are now made to witness scenes of more wealth and action, but not of more tranquillity and purity. The affections then were warm, and confidence mutual. At their convivial assemblies, which, at the close of a day's toil, they sometimes found time to convene, the simplicity of their rude entertainments, served up as they often were upon an oak slab, elevated to its proper position by substantial wooden pegs, was more than compensated by the full flow of spirits, and the absence of rivalry and envy. The heart had not then lost its radiating power by the polish of excessive refinement, and the freedom of communication was unfettered by the stiff formality of modern etiquette.

" It is a fact worthy of remark, that almost every cent of the wealth in this village has been created upon the ground. But a small amount of capital has been brought into it from abroad; and this not for the purposes of speculation, but in obedience to the demands of established business. It has never stood in need of foreign assistance. Its resources have ever been, and are still inexhaustible. The secret of its commanding influence, however, is to be found in the immense hydraulic force of Black river at this point. By a pretty accurate computation, it has been ascertained that the quantity of water, at low-water mark, is seldom less than 60,000 cubic feet per minute. This, with economy, under 9 feet head and fall, would be sufficient to turn 150 runs of stone. Now, by considering that the water, in passing from the upper end of the village to the lower, a distance of about a mile, falls 88 feet, over 7 artificial dams and 5 natural cascades, and at each of these dams the whole body of water can be used, we have a force sufficient to turn more than a thousand runs of stone, or to apply to the driving of other machinery.

" With this great power before us, and reflecting that Watertown is surrounded by a rich and fertile country,—prosecuting a firmly established and well-balanced business—a business that has never been affected by the insane spirit of speculation which has often raged over our country—it is not difficult to account for its great prosperity, and to anticipate for it a still more vigorous end rapid progress."—*Hist. Sketch of Watertown, by J. P. Fitch.*

The following view was taken on the west bank of the river, a few rods below the bridge. The ruins seen in front are those of the Bebee manufactory, noticed in the foregoing sketch. Just beyond the bridge, the river descends in a perpendicular fall of 18 feet. The steeple on the left, is that of the 2d Presbyterian church, the one

View in Watertown, Jefferson county, New York.

further to the right, that of the Catholic, and that on the extreme right, the Institute. This is a wild and picturesque spot, and the ruins remind the spectator of some time-decayed structure of a former age. On the bank of the river, seen beyond the opening between the pines, is a place where the rite of baptism is administered by immersion. A traveller who here recently witnessed a scene of this kind, describes it as "unusually solemn and impressive." Amid the roar of the rapids ascended the prayer of the clergyman, and the music of the assembled worshippers was softened by the sound of the waterfall.

Well would the language of the poet have applied:

> "Ye headlong torrents, rapid and profound,
> Ye softer floods, that tread the humid maze,
> Sound his stupendous praise, ...
> And as each mingling flame increases each,
> In one united ardor rise to heaven."—

In the limestone rocks which bound the Black river at this point are numerous caves, two of which are very extensive, and have never been explored to their terminations. The first, called the "*old cave,*" is situated a few rods west of the bridge, at Bebee's island, in the town of Pamelia, and running up in an easterly direction, is supposed to go under the falls. The other, entitled the "*new or ice cave,*" is about 50 rods below the bridge on the eastern bank of the stream, and was discovered about two years since. It has been explored about ½ a mile. Some distance in it there is an extensive excavation, which forms a large room of about 20 feet square, and as regularly shaped as though effected by human agency. Columns of ice formed by the infiltration of water from the ceiling to the floor, resembling marble pillars neatly polished, are to be seen in this apartment even in the warmest of weather. Both of these caves have many branches, and are beautified with varied petrifactions, stalactites of all shapes, petrified bats, &c., &c. About 50 rods in a NE. direction from the Bebee ruins, back of the knoll, is a singular oval-shaped basin in the sand, of about 7 rods in its greatest diameter. It is about 100 feet in depth, and water never remains in it even during the most rainy weather.

WILNA, taken from Le Ray in this, and Leyden in Lewis county, in 1818; from Albany, NW., 151, from Watertown distant E. 17 miles. The place was settled by Irish and New England emigrants. The Count Survilliers, (Joseph Bonaparte,) brother of the Emperor Napoleon, purchased here 80,000 acres of land and erected a large mansion. Carthage, at the head of Long Falls, on the Black river, has about 75 dwellings. A large quantity of iron is manufactured here. The *Natural Bridge*, where there is a small settlement, is a curiosity. It is about 12 feet wide, and 6 above the water. Wilna and North Wilna are post-offices. Pop. 2,583.

KINGS COUNTY.

KINGS COUNTY was organized in 1683, by an act of the colonial assembly dividing the province, and abolishing the *ridings* which previously existed. Its greatest length is 12, and greatest breadth 7 miles. The county includes Coney and Barren islands, and all other islands south of the town of Gravesend. The surface on the NE. for three or four miles back from the river is hilly and ridgy. Upon the SE. a plain of sandy loam and sand extends to the ocean. The soil for the most part is light, warm, and when properly manured, fertile. It is generally well improved, and supplies a large portion of the vegetables sold in New York. The first settlement in the county was made at Brooklyn in 1625. In 1641, the Dutch government permitted some English settlers to locate themselves at Gravesend. All the other towns of the county appear to have been settled by the Dutch. The county courts were originally held at the village of Gravesend; they were removed in 1686 to Flatbush, where they were held till 1832, when they were removed to Brooklyn. The county contains six towns. Pop. 47,613.

BROOKLYN. This town, the whole of which is now included within the corporation of the city of Brooklyn, lies upon the extreme western part of Long Island, opposite the southern portion of the city of New York, and separated therefrom by the East river, which is here about three quarters of a mile in width. Its length from NE. to SW. is six, and its greatest breadth four miles; giving an area of 9,200 acres, most of which has been apportioned into city lots. "The surface is high, broken, and stony; and the more elevated points afford beautiful and romantic sites, many of which have been built upon, and are not excelled in elegance by any others in the country. The soil, in common with the whole county, was originally claimed by the Canarsee Indians, a numerous tribe inhabiting the more southern parts of the county, and from whom the title to the lands was procured by the Dutch government.

"The name conferred upon this town by the Dutch was Breucklen, (or broken land;) and in the act for dividing the province into counties and towns, passed November 1, 1685, it is called *Breucklyn;* nor does the present appellation appear to have been generally adopted until after the revolution. Many changes have doubtless taken place upon the shore, and it is believed that Governor's Island was formerly connected with Red Hook point. It is well known that a short period previous to the war of independence, cattle were driven across what is called Buttermilk Channel, now sufficiently deep to afford passage to vessels of the largest class. The alteration is no doubt in great measure attributable to the vast extension of the wharves on both sides of the river, thereby diverting the course, and increasing the force of the currents. The first European settler in this town is supposed to have been George Jansen de Rapelje, at the Waalboght, or Waaloons Bay, during the Directorship of Peter Minuit, under the charter of the West India Company. In a family record in the possession of Jeremiah Johnson, Esq., it is stated that the first child of Rapelje was Sarah, born in 1625, unquestionably the first white child born upon Long Island. Watson says she was born on the 9th of June, and honored as the first-born child of the Dutch settlers; also that, in consideration of such distinction, and of her widowhood, she was afterward presented with a tract of land at the Wallabout. She was twice married; first to Hans Hanse-Bergen, by whom she had six children, namely, Michael Hanse, Joris Hanse, Jan Hanse, Jacob Hanse, Breckje Hanse, and Marytje Hanse. Her second husband was Teunis Guisbertse Bogart, by whom also she had six children, namely, Aurtie, Antje, Neelje, Aultje, Catalyntje, and Guysbert. The account of this remarkable woman in the archives of the New York Historical Society contains the names of the persons to whom eleven of her children were married, and the places where they settled. The twelfth, Breckje Hanse, went to Holland. In the journal of the Dutch Council in 1656, it is related that " the widow Hans Hanson, the first-born Christian daughter in New Netherlands, burdened with seven children, petitions for a grant of a piece of meadow, in addition to the twenty morgen granted to her at the Waale-Boght.' There is a tradition in the family, that the Indians, induced by the circumstance of her being the first white child born here, gave to her father and his brethren, the other French who followed them, the lands adjacent to the bay; hence called (says Judge Benson) *Het-Waale Boght,* corrupted to *Wallabout Bay.* A few of the other associates of De Rapelje were Le Escuyer, Duryee, La Sillier, Cershow, Conscillaer, Musserol; these, with some changes in the mode of spelling, are still found among us. It appears by the Dutch records, that in 1634 a part of the land at Red Hook was the property of Wouter Van Twiller, being one of the oldest titles in the town. The earliest deed for land was from Governor Kieft to Abraham Rycken, in 1638. The oldest grant recorded is to Thomas Besker in 1639. This must be considered as the commencement of permanent Dutch settlements on Long Island, and there is no evidence of any direct and systematic efforts being made for the purpose till this period."— *Thompson's Hist. of Long Island.*

It seems to have been enjoined upon the overseers and constables to admonish the inhabitants to instruct their children and servants in matters of religion, and in the laws of the country. The inhabitants at first attended divine worship at New Amsterdam, (New York,) and at Flatbush. In 1659, the inhabitants of the town applied to Gov. Stuyvesant for permission to call a minister for their congregation. This request was granted, and the Rev. Henry Solinus, being approved by the classis of Amsterdam, was sent over from Holland, and installed their pastor in 1660. The first Dutch church was built in 1666, and stood about forty years; when another was erected on

NORTH WESTERN VIEW OF BROOKLYN, N. Y., FROM NEAR PECK SLIP, NEW YORK CITY.

The view shows the appearance of the most compact part of Brooklyn, as seen from New York city, opposite Fulton street, Brooklyn. The Collonade buildings on Brooklyn heights, appear on the right.

the same spot, which was taken down in 1810, and a new and substantial one built in Jerolemon street; this last has given place to a more splendid edifice on nearly the same site. An Episcopal society existed in this town as early as 1766. In 1795, St. Ann's church was occupied for the first time. The first Methodist church was incorporated in 1794; the first Presbyterian in 1822; the first Baptist in 1822; the first Catholic in 1822; and the first congregational in 1839. The first printing press established in this town, was by Thomas Kirk, in 1799, who issued a newspaper, entitled the "*Courier, and New York and Long Island Advertiser,*" which continued four years. The first number of the "Long Island Star" was also issued by Mr. Kirk, in 1809.

The most compact part of Brooklyn was incorporated into a village in 1816, which, although much opposed by a portion of the population, gave a new impulse to the spirit of improvement, which has resulted in raising it to be the second city in point of population in the state of New York. In April, 1834, the whole territory of the town was incorporated under the name of the "City of Brooklyn." It is divided into 9 wards; the powers of the corporation are vested in a mayor, and a board of aldermen, composed of two elected from each ward. Brooklyn contains 28 churches, viz: 6 Episcopalian, 2 Dutch Reformed, 7 Presbyterian, 2 Baptist, 4 Episcopal Methodist, 1 Centenary Episcopal Methodist, 1 Primitive Methodist, 1 Wesleyan Methodist, 2 Roman Catholic, 1 Unitarian Congregational Church, and 1 Friends Meeting-house. Population in 1820, 7,175; in 1825, 10,790; in 1830, 15,394; in 1835, 25,312; in 1840, 36,233.

Northern view of the Navy-yard at Brooklyn.

The above shows the appearance of the buildings, shipping, &c., at the navy-yard, at Brooklyn, as seen from Corlear's Hook. The United States possess about forty acres at this spot, including the old mill-pond. Here have been erected a spacious navy-yard, public stores, machine shops, and two immense edifices, in which the largest ships are protected from the weather, while building. On the east side of the *Wallabout* bay, opposite the navy-yard, stands the U. S. Naval Hospital, a magnificent structure. The Wallabout is rendered memorable in the revolutionary period, from having been the scene of the heart-rending sufferings of many thousand American prisoners confined in the prison ships stationed in the bay. The following, relating to these vessels, communicated to the editor of the "Naval Magazine," in 1836, was written by Jeremiah Johnson, Esq., of Brooklyn, a gentleman who has filled many public offices in this place.

"The subject of the naval prisoners, and of the British prison ships stationed at the Wallabout during the revolution, is one which cannot be passed by in silence. From printed journals published in New York at the close of the war, it appears that eleven thousand five hundred American prisoners had died on board the prison ships. Although the number is very great, still if the number who perished had been less, the commissary of naval prisoners, David Sprout, Esq., and his deputy, had it in their power, by an official return, to give the true number exchanged, escaped, and dead. Such a return has never appeared in the United States. This man returned to America after the war, and resided in Philadelphia, where he died. He could not have been ignorant of the statement published here on this interesting subject. We may therefore infer, that about that number perished in the prison ships. A large transport, named the *Whitby*, was the first prison ship anchored in the Wallabout. She was moored near 'Remsen's Mill,' about the 20th of October, 1776, and was crowded with prisoners. Many landsmen were prisoners on board this vessel; she was said to be the most sickly of *all* the prison ships. Bad provisions, bad water, and scanted rations were dealt to the prisoners. No medical men attended the sick. Disease reigned unrelieved, and hundreds died from pestilence, or were starved, on board this floating prison. I saw the sand-beach between a ravine in the hill and Mr. Remsen's dock become filled with graves in the course of two months; and before the 1st of May, 1777, the ravine alluded to was itself occupied in the same way. In the month of May of that year two large ships were anchored in the Wallabout, when the prisoners were transferred from the Whitby to them. These vessels were also very sickly, from the causes before stated. Although many prisoners were sent on board of them, and were exchanged, death made room for all. On a Sunday afternoon, about the middle of October, 1777, one of the prison ships was burnt; the prisoners, except a few, who, it was said, were burnt in the vessel, were removed to the remaining ship. It was reported at the time that the prisoners had fired their prison; which, if true, proves that they preferred death, even by fire, to the lingering sufferings of pestilence and starvation. In the month of February, 1778, the remaining prison ship was burnt at night; when the prisoners were removed from her to the ships then wintering in the Wallabout. In the month of April, 1778, the Old Jersey was moored in the Wallabout, and all the prisoners (except the sick) were transferred to her. The sick were carried to two hospital ships, named the Hope and Falmouth, anchored near each other about two hundred yards east from the Jersey. These ships remained in the Wallabout until New York was evacuated by the British. The Jersey was the receiving-ship—the others, truly, the *ships of Death!* It has been generally thought that all the prisoners died on board of the Jersey. This is not true; many may have died on board of her who were not reported as sick: but all the men who were placed on the sick-list were removed to the hospital ships, from which they were usually taken, sewed up in a blanket, to their *long home*.

"After the hospital ships were brought into the Wallabout, it was reported that the sick were attended by physicians; few, very few, however, recovered. It was no uncommon thing to see five or six dead bodies brought on shore in a single morning; when a small excavation would be made at the foot of the hill, the bodies be cast in, and a man with a shovel would cover them by shovelling sand down the hill upon them. Many were buried in a ravine on the hill; some on the farm. The whole shore from Rennie's Point to Mr. Remsen's dock-yard was a place of graves; as were also the slope of the hill near the house, the shore from Mr. Remsen's barn along the mill-pond to Rapelje's farm and the sandy island, between the flood-gates and the mill-dam; while a few were buried on the shore, the east side of the Wallabout. Thus did *Death* reign *here*, from 1776 until the peace. The whole Wallabout was a sickly place during the war. The atmosphere seemed to be charged with foul air from the prison ships, and with the effluvia of the dead bodies washed out of their graves by the tides. We have ourselves examined many of the *skulls* lying on the shore; from the teeth, they appear to be the remains of men in the prime of life. A singularly daring and successful escape was effected from the Jersey about 4 o'clock one afternoon, in December, 1780. The best boat of the ship had returned from New

York, was left fastened at the gangway, with the oars on board. It was stormy; the wind blew from the northeast, and the tide ran flood. A watchword was given, and a number of prisoners placed themselves between the ship's waist and the sentinel; at this juncture four eastern captains got on board the boat, which was cast off by their friends. The boat passed close under the bows of the ship, and was a considerable distance from her before the sentinel on the forecastle gave the alarm, and fired at her. The boat passed Hell-Gate, and arrived safe in Connecticut next morning."

The following additional account of the sufferings of these unfortunate men was obtained from the prisoners, and published in the Connecticut Journal of Jan. 30, 1777. It is painfully minute in its details.

"As soon as they were taken they were robbed of all their baggage, of whatever money they had, though it were of paper and could be of no advantage to the enemy, of their silver shoe-buckles, knee-buckles, &c., and many were stripped almost naked of their clothes. Especially those who had good clothes, were stripped at once, being told that *such clothes were too good for rebels.* Thus deprived of their clothes and baggage, they were unable to shift even their linen, and were obliged to wear the same shirts for even three or four months together, whereby they became extremely nasty and lousy; and this of itself has been sufficient to bring on them many mortal diseases.

"After they were taken, they were in the first place put on board the ships and thrust down into the hold where not a breath of fresh air could be obtained, and they were nearly suffocated for want of air. Particularly some who were taken at Fort Washington, were first in this manner thrust down into the holds of vessels in such numbers that even in the cold season of November, they could scarcely bear any clothes on them, being kept in a constant sweat. Yet these same persons, after lying in this situation awhile, till the pores of their bodies were as perfectly opened as possible, were of a sudden taken out and put into some of the churches in New York, without covering or a spark of fire, where they suffered as much by the cold as they did by the sweating stagnation of the air in the other situation; and the consequence was, that they took such colds as brought on the most fatal diseases, and swept them off almost beyond conception.

"Besides these things, they suffered extremely for want of provisions. The commissary pretended to allow half a pound of bread and four ounces of pork per day; but of this pittance they were much cut short. What was given them for three days was not enough for one day; and in some instances, they went for three days without a single mouthful of food of any sort. They were pinched to that degree that some on board the ships would pick up and eat the salt, which happened to be scattered there; others gathered up the bran which the lighthorse wasted, and ate that, mixed with dirt and filth as it was. Nor was this all, both the bread and pork which they did allow them was extremely bad. For the bread, some of it, was made out of the bran which they brought over to feed their lighthorse, and the rest of it was so muddy and the pork so damnified, being so soaked in bilge water in the transportation from Europe, that they were not fit to be eaten by human creatures; and when they were eaten, were very unwholesome. Such bread and pork as they would not pretend to give to their own countrymen, they gave to our poor, sick, dying prisoners.

"Nor were they in this doleful situation allowed a sufficiency of water. One would have thought that water was so cheap and plentiful an element, that they would not have grudged them that. But there are it seems no bounds to their cruelty. The water allowed them, was so brackish and withal nasty, that they could not drink it, till reduced to extremity. Nor did they let them have a sufficiency even of such water as this.

"When winter came on, our poor people suffered extremely for want of fire and clothes to keep them warm. They were confined in churches where there were no fireplaces, that they could make fires even if they had wood. But wood was only allowed them for cooking their pittance of victuals; and for that purpose very sparingly. They had none to keep them warm even in the extremest of weather, although they were almost naked, and the few clothes that were left them were their summer clothes. Nor had they a single blanket or any bedding, not even straw allowed them till a little before Christmas.

"At the time that those were taken on Long Island, a considerable part of them were sick of the dysentery, and, with this distemper on them, were first crowded on board of ships, afterward in the churches in New York, three, four, or five hundred together, without any blankets, or any thing for even the sick to lie upon, but the bare floors or pavements. In this situation that contagious distemper soon communicated from the sick to the well, and who would probably have remained so, had they not in this manner been thrust in together without regard to sick or well, or to the sultry, unwholesome season, it being then the heat of summer. Of this distemper numbers died daily, and many others, by their confinement and the sultry season, contracted fevers and died of them. During their sickness, with these and other diseases, they had no medicines, nothing soothing or comfortable for sick people, and were not so much as visited by the physician by the month together.

"Nor ought we to omit the insults which the humane Britons offered to our people, nor the artifices which they used to enlist them in their service and fight against their country. It seems that one end of their starving our people was to bring them, by dint of necessity, to turn rebels to their own country, their own consciences, and their God. For while thus famishing, they would come and say to them, 'This is the just punishment of your rebellion. Nay, you are 'treated too well for rebels; you have not yet received half you de-'serve or half you shall receive. But if you will enlist into His 'Majesty's service, you shall have victuals and clothes enough.'

"As to insults, the British officers, besides continually cursing and swearing at them as rebels, often threatened to hang them all; and at a particular time, ordered a number, each man to choose his halter out of a parcel offered, wherewith to be hanged; and even went so far as to cause a gallows to be erected before the prison, as if they were immediately to be executed. They further threatened to send them all into the East Indies, and sell them there for slaves. In these, and numberless other ways, did the British officers seem to rack their inventions, to insult, terrify, and vex the poor prisoners. The meanest upstart officers among them would insult and abuse our colonels and chief officers.

" In this situation, without clothes, without victuals or drink, and even water, or with those which were base and unwholesome, without fire, a number of them sick, first with a contagious and nauseous distemper; these with others crowded by hundreds into close confinement, at the most unwholesome season of the year, and continued there for four months without blankets, bedding or straw; without linen to shift or clothes to cover their bodies;—no wonder they all became sickly, and having at the same time no medicine, no help of physicians, nothing to refresh or support nature, died by scores in a night; and those who were so far gone as to be unable to help themselves, the workings of their distemper passing through them as they lay, could not be cleansed for want of change of clothes. So that many lay for six, seven, or eight days, in all the filth of nature and of dysentery, till Death. more kind than Britons, put an end to their misery.

" By these means and in this way, above 1,500 brave Americans, who had nobly gone forth in defence of their injured, oppressed country, but whom the chance of war had cast into the hands of our enemies, died in New York; many of whom were very amiable, promising youths of good families, the very flower of our land. And of those who lived to come out of prison, the greater part, as far as I can learn, are dead and dying. Their constitutions are broken, the stamina of nature worn out, they cannot recover, they die. Even the few that might have survived, are dying of the small-pox. For it seems that our enemies determined that even these, whom a good constitution and a kind Providence had carried through unexampled sufferings, should not at last escape death, just before their release from imprisonment infected them with that fatal distemper.

" To these circumstances, I shall subjoin the manner in which they buried those of our people who died. They dragged them out of their prisons by one leg or one arm, piled them up without doors, there let them lie till a sufficient number were dead to make a cart load; then loaded them up in a cart, drove the cart thus loaded out to the ditches made by our people, when fortifying New York; there they would tip the cart, tumble the corpses together into the ditch; and afterward slightly cover them with earth.

" . . . . While our poor prisoners have been thus treated by our foes, the prisoners we have taken have enjoyed the liberty of walking and riding about within large limits, at their pleasure; have been fully supplied with every necessary, and have even lived on the fat of the land; so none have been so well fed, so healthy, so plump, and so merry as they. And this generous treatment it is said they could not but remember. For when they were returned, in the exchange of prisoners, and saw the miserable, famished, dying state of our prisoners, conscious of the treatment they had received, they could not refrain from tears."

In 1808, a tomb was erected to the memory of these martyrs to liberty, on the corner of Jackson-street, nearly opposite the end of Front-street, in the vicinity of the navy-yard. Thirteen coffins were filled with their bleached bones, and interred in it with great veneration and respect. There was a grand civic and military procession on the occasion, at which fifteen thousand persons are said to have been present. "The tomb is a small square frame building, surmounted by an eagle on the point of the roof; the interior is an antechamber to the vault beneath, in which the coffins are deposited; there is a row of posts and rails in front of the tomb, on which the names of the 13 original states of the Union are inscribed; the area around the tomb is enclosed by a rail fence, over the entrance of which is the following inscription: '*Portal to the Tomb of* 11,500 *Patriot Prisoners, who died in dungeons and prison ships, in and about the city of New York during the revolution.*'"

The following account of the blowing up of the *steam-frigate Fulton* at the navy-yard in this place, June 4th, 1829, was written on the morning after the explosion:

"The Fulton has ever since the war been occupied as a receiving ship, and was moored within two hundred yards of the shore. The magazine was in the bow of the ship, and contained at the time of the explosion but three barrels of damaged powder. The explosion was not louder than that produced by the discharge of a single cannon; and many persons in the navy-yard supposed the report to have proceeded from such a source, until they saw the immense column of smoke arising from the vessel. Others about the yard saw the masts rising into the air before the explosion, and immediately after, the air was filled with fragments of the vessel. It is not a little remarkable, that a midshipman who was, at the time of the accident, asleep on board of the frigate United States, within two hundred yards of the Fulton, was not at all disturbed by the report of the explosion, and was not aware of the occurrence, until he was told of it after he awoke.

"The Fulton is a complete wreck; the bow being destroyed nearly to the water, and the whole of this immense vessel, whose sides were more than four feet thick, and all other parts of corresponding strength—is now lying an entire heap of ruins, burst asunder in all parts, and aground at the spot where she was moored. Although she was but 200 yards from the navy-yard, and many vessels near her, not one of them received the least damage; nor was the bridge which led from the shore to the Fulton at all injured. The sentinel upon the bridge received no wound whatever, and continued to perform his duty after the accident, as unconcerned as though nothing had happened. The sentinel on board the ship was less fortunate, and escaped with merely (a light accident on such occasions) a broken leg. There were attached to the Fulton, by the roll of the ship, 143 persons; and, at the time of the explosion, there were supposed to have been on board the vessel about sixty persons.

"It happened fortunately that sixty-two men, formerly attached to the frigate, were drafted on Tuesday, and had proceeded to Norfolk to form part of the crew of the frigate Constellation, then on the eve of departure for a foreign station. The band, 17 in number, were on shore. This dreadful accident was occasioned by the gunner's going into the magazine to procure powder to fire the evening gun. He was charged by one of the officers previously to his going below, to be careful; and soon after, the explosion took place. We understand that he was a man between fifty and sixty years of age, and had just been appointed to that office; the old gunner having been discharged the day before. He was desired by Lieutenant Breckenridge to be cautious with the light, and to place it in the location invariably provided for it, on such occasions, viz. behind a reflecting glass in the partition, through which the rays of light are thrown. It is supposed he had been careless in this particular, and that having carried the candle into the magazine, some of its sparks were communicated to the powder: but as he is among the dead, nothing certain on this point can ever be known. Lieutenant Mull states, that the necessary precautions had been taken for opening the magazine, and a sentinel placed at the hatch before he left the deck, and that after being in the ward room some twenty minutes the explosion took place.

"At the time of the explosion, the officers were dining in the ward room. The lady of Lieutenant Breckenridge, and the son of Lieutenant Platt, a lad about nine years old, were guests, and one account says both were slightly wounded. Another account says, Lieutenant Mull, who was sitting next to the son of Lieutenant Platt, with great presence of mind, caught hold of him and placed him in one of the port-holes, by which means he escaped uninjured. Lieutenant Platt had returned only yesterday morning, having been absent one month on leave. Commodore Chauncey, with the commander of the frigate, Captain Newton, left her only a few minutes before the explosion—the former having been on board on a visit of inspection.

"The escape of Midshipman Eckford seems to have been almost miraculous. When Commodore Chauncey (who was one of the first to reach the vessel) got on board, the first object he saw was young Eckford hanging by one of his legs between the gun-deck, whither he had been forced by the explosion. A jack-screw was immediately procured, by means of which the deck was raised and he was extricated from his perilous situation.

"The room in which the officers were dining was situated about midships. The whole company at the table were forced, by the concussion, against the transom with such violence as to break their limbs, and otherwise cut and bruise them in a shocking manner.

"The magazine was situated in the bows of the vessel. This part of the ship, as may well be imagined, is completely demolished. Indeed the ship remains as complete a wreck as probably was ever beheld. The timbers throughout appear to have been perfectly rotten. Many of the guns were thrown overboard, and some of them (of large dimensions) hung as it were by a hair.

"The bodies of the dead and wounded were brought on shore as soon as circumstances would permit. The former, after being recognised, were put into coffins. The latter were carried to the hospital of the navy-yard and every attention paid to them. The bodies of the dead were shockingly mangled; their features distorted, and so much blackened, that it was difficult to recognise them.

"Commodore Chauncey and the officers of the station were on board the wreck, after the explosion, giving directions to remove the scattered timber, in order that a search might take place for such bodies as might be buried in the ruins. The tide being at the ebb, immense quantities of the fragments of the ship floated down in front of the city, and hundreds of small boats were seen busily engaged in securing them.

"What is a very remarkable circumstance, although several of the persons at dinner in the ward room escaped with their lives, and some of them uninjured, not a vestige of the table, chairs, or any of the furniture in the room remains. Every thing was blown to atoms.

"The Fulton was built with two keels, or rather was in fact two boats, joined together by the upper works. The sides were of immense thickness, and the whole frame was, when built, probably the strongest of the kind ever constructed. But the timbers had now become very rotten, and the whole hulk was, as it were, kept together by its own weight. It is supposed that the rotten state of the vessel, making her timbers give way easily, rendered the destruction greater than if she had been new and sound.

"Midshipman Eckford was standing in the starboard gangway, and was strangely tumbled to the inside, instead of being blown out upon the platform. He was then caught under one of the beams, where he hung fast by one leg.

"While he hung in this painful condition, not a groan, nor a complaint, nor a word of supplication escaped him. His cheek was unblanched, and his features composed, while he held on to the beam with his arms to keep his head up.

"Attempts were made to raise the beam, but there was such a mass of materials above, that no muscular force could move it. In this emergency, Commodore Chauncey, with great promptness, ordered the jack-screw to be brought from the shore. This took time, and it was not then the work of a moment to apply it, and bring it into action. An hour went by, ere the youth was extricated; and yet not a single murmur of impatience was heard from his lips. His only words were in direction or encouragement to those who were aiding him—exclaiming from time to time, ' *Hurra my hearties!*' ' *There it moves!*' His only reproof was to the sailor, who, when the beam was raised, attempted, rather rudely, to withdraw the fractured limb. The sailor supported him whilst he performed the office himself.

" The whole number of killed was thirty-three, including Lieutenant Breckenridge and the three women. Twenty-nine were reported as wounded, but there were many more who were slightly injured. Nearly every person on board received at least a scratch.

" The greatest part of the mischief was done by the force of the fragments and splinters. These were driven into every part of the ship. Captain Newton, who commanded the ship, employed all the force he could spare, to clear the wreck, and find the bodies of the unfortunate sufferers. Twenty-four were taken out of the ruins at the time, but some of the others were not found till a considerable time after. One was found horribly mutilated, and drifted ashore on Staten Island. Another got fastened to a beam, and was picked up. Two were picked out of the water near the wreck."

Brooklyn is distinguished as being the scene of important military operations, and was for a long time in possession of the enemy during the revolutionary war. The most sanguinary part of the battle of Long Island, August 27th, 1776, took place in this town. The following account is from Thompson's History of Long Island.

" After the commencement of hostilities in 1776, New York being situated near the centre of the colonial sea-board, and readily accessible from the sea, was selected by the enemy as a principal point for their future operations. With this view, a first division of their army arrived at Staten Island in the latter part of June of that year, followed, about the middle of July, by the grand armament under Lord Howe, consisting of six ships of the line, thirty frigates, with smaller armed vessels, and a great number of transports, victuallers, and ships with ordinance.

" The Americans anticipating the invasion of Long Island, had fortified Brooklyn before the arrival of the British at Staten Island. A line of intrenchment was formed from a ditch near the late Toll-House of the Bridge Company at the navy-yard to Fort Green, then called Fort Putnam, and from thence to Freek's mill-pond. A strong work was erected on the lands of Johannis Debevoice and of Van Brunt; a redoubt was thrown up on Bæmus' Hill opposite Brown's mill, and another on the land of John Johnson, west of Fort Green. Ponkiesburg, now Fort Swift, was fortified, and a fort built on the land of Mr. Hicks on Brooklyn heights. Such were the defences of Brooklyn in 1776, while a *chevaux de frise* was sunk in the main channel of the river below New York. The troops of both divisions of the British army were landed on Staten Island after their arrival in the bay, to recruit their strength and prepare for the coming conflict. It was not till the middle of August, that a first landing on Long Island was made by them at New Utrecht. Here they were joined by many royalists from the neighborhood, who probably acted the infamous part of informers and guides to the enemy. General Sir Henry Clinton arrived about the same time, with the troops reconducted from the expedition to Charleston.

"Commodore Hotham already appeared there with the reinforcements under his escort; so that in a short time the hostile army amounted to about twenty-four thousand men,—English, Hessians, and Waldeckers. Several regiments of Hessian infantry were expected to arrive shortly, when the army would be swelled to the number of thirty-five thousand combatants, of the best troops of Europe, all abundantly supplied with arms and ammunition, and manifesting an extreme ardor for the service of their king. The plan was, first to get possession of New York, which was deemed of most essential importance.

"To resist this impending storm, Congress had ordained the construction of rafts, gunboats, galleys, and floating batteries, for the defence of the port of New York and the mouth of the Hudson. They had also decreed that thirteen thousand of the provincial militia should join the army of Washington, who, being seasonably apprized of the danger of New York, had made a movement into that quarter; they also directed the organization of a corps of ten thousand men, destined to serve as a reserve in the province of the centre. All the weakest posts had been carefully intrenched, and furnished with artillery. A strong detachment occupied Long Island, to prevent the English from landing there, or to repulse them if they should effect a debarkation. But the army of Congress was very far from having all the necessary means to support the burden of so terrible a war. It wanted arms, and it was wasted by diseases. The reiterated instances of the commander-in-chief had drawn into his camp the militia of the neighboring provinces, and some regular regiments from Maryland, from Pennsylvania, and from New England, which had swelled his army to the number of twenty-seven thousand men; but a fourth of these troops were composed of invalids, and scarcely was another fourth furnished with arms.

"The American army, such as it was, occupied the positions most suitable to cover the menaced points. The corps which had been stationed on Long Island, was commanded by Major-general Greene, who, on account of sickness, was afterward succeeded by General Sullivan. The main body of the army encamped on the island of New York, which, it appeared, was destined to receive the first blows of the English.

"Two feeble detachments guarded Governor's Island and the point of Paulus' Hook. The militia of the province, commanded by the American General Clinton, were posted upon the banks of the Sound, where they occupied the two Chesters, East and West, and New Rochelle. For it was to be feared that the enemy, landing in force upon the north shore of the Sound, might penetrate to Kingsbridge, and thus entirely lock up all the American troops on the island of New York. Lord Howe made some overtures of peace upon terms of submission to the royal clemency, which, resulting in nothing, decided the British general to attack Long Island. 'Accordingly,' says Botta, 'on the twenty-second of August, the fleet approached the *Narrows;* all the troops found an easy and secure landing-place between the villages of Gravesend and New Utrecht, where they debarked without meeting any resistance on the part of the Americans. A great part of the American army, under the command of General Putnam, encamped at Brooklyn in a part of the island which forms a sort of peninsula. He had strongly fortified the entrance of it with moats and intrenchments; his left wing rested upon the *Wallabout* bay, and his right was covered by a marsh contiguous to *Gowanus' Cove*. Behind him he had Governor's Island, and the arm of the sea which separates Long Island from the Island of New York, and which gave him a direct communication with the city, where the other part of the army was stationed under Washington himself. The commander-in-chief, perceiving the battle was approaching, continually exhorted his men to keep their ranks, and summon all their courage: he reminded them that in their valor rested the only hope that remained to American liberty ; that upon their resistance depended the preservation or the pillage of their property by barbarians; that they were about to combat in defence of their parents, their wives, and their children, from the outrages of a licentious soldiery ; that the eyes of America were fixed upon her champions, and expected from their success on this day either safety or total destruction.'

"The English having effected their landing, marched rapidly forward. The two armies were separated by a chain of hills, covered with woods, called the heights, and which, running from west to east, divide the island into two parts. They are only practicable upon three points : one of which is near the Narrows ; the road leading to that of the centre passes the village of *Flatbush ;* and the third is approached, far to the right, by the route of another village called *Flatlands.* Upon the summit of the hills is found a road, which follows the length of the range, and leads from Bedford to Jamaica, which is intersected by the two roads last described : these ways are all interrupted by precipices, and by excessively difficult and narrow defiles.

"The American general, wishing to arrest the enemy upon these heights, had carefully furnished them with troops ; so that, if all had done their duty, the English would not have been able to force the passages without extreme difficulty and danger. The posts were so frequent upon the road from Bedford to Jamaica, that it was easy to transmit, from one of these points to the other, the most prompt intelligence of what passed upon the three routes. Colonel Miles, with his battalion, was to guard the road of Flatland, and to scour it continually with his scouts, as well as that of Jamaica, in order to reconnoitre the movements of the enemy. Meanwhile the British army pressed forward, its left wing being to the north and its right to the south ; the village of Flatbush was found in its centre. The Hessians, commanded by General Heister, formed the main body ; the English, under Major-general Grant, the left ; and the other corps, conducted by General Clinton, and the two lords, Percy and Cornwallis, composed the right. In this wing the British generals had placed their principal hope of success ; they directed it upon Flatland. Their plan was, that while the corps of General Grant, and the Hessians of General Heister, should disquiet the enemy upon the two first defiles, the left wing, taking a circuit, should march through Flatland, and endeavor to seize the point of intersection of this road with that of Jamaica ; and then rapidly descending into the plain which extends at the foot of the heights upon the other side, should fall upon the Americans in flank and rear. The English hoped, that as this post was the most distant from the centre of the army, the advanced guards would be found more feeble there, and perhaps more negligent : finally, they calculated that, in all events, the Americans would not be able to defend it against a force so superior. This right wing of the English was the most numerous, and entirely composed of select troops.

"The evening of the twenty-sixth of August, General Clinton commanded the vanguard, which consisted in light infantry ; Lord Percy the centre, where were found the grenadiers, the artillery, and the cavalry ; and Cornwallis, the rear-guard, followed by the baggage some regiments of infantry and of heavy artillery; all this part of the English army put itself in motion with admirable order and silence, and leaving Flatland, traversed the country called New Lots. Colonel Miles, who this night performed his service with little exactness, did not perceive the approach of the enemy; so that two hours before day the English were already arrived within a half mile of the road to Jamaica, upon the heights. Then General Clinton halted, and prepared himself for the attack. He had met one of the enemy's patrols, and made him prisoner. General Sullivan, who commanded all the troops in advance of the camp of Brooklyn, had no advice of what passed in this quarter. He neglected to send out fresh scouts; perhaps he supposed the English would direct their principal efforts against his right wing, as being nearest to them.

"General Clinton, learning from his prisoners that the road to Jamaica was not guarded, hastened to avail himself of the circumstance, and occupied it by a rapid movement. Without loss of time he immediately bore to his left towards Bedford, and seized an important defile, which the American generals had left unguarded. From this moment the success of the day was decided in favor of the English. Lord Percy came up with his corps; and the entire column descended by the village of Bedford from the heights into the plain which lay between the hills and the camp of the Americans. During this time General Grant, in order to amuse the enemy, and divert his attention from the events which took place upon the route of Flatland, endeavored to disquiet him upon his right: accordingly, as if he intended to force the defile which led to it, he had put himself in motion about midnight, and had attacked the militia of New York and of Pennsylvania, who guarded it. They at first gave ground; but General Parsons being arrived, and having occupied an eminence, he renewed the combat, and maintained his position till Brigadier-general Lord Stirling came to his assistance with fifteen hundred men. The action became extremely animated, and fortune favored neither the one side nor the other. The Hessians, on their part, had attacked the centre at break of day; and the Americans, commanded by General Sullivan in person, valiantly sustained their efforts. At the same time the English ships, after having made several movements, opened a very brisk cannonade against a battery established in the little island of Red Hook, upon the right flank of the Americans, who combated against General Grant. This also was a diversion, the object of which was to prevent them from attending to what passed in the centre and on the left. The Americans defended themselves, however, with extreme gallantry, ignorant that so much valor was exerted in vain, since victory was already in the hands of the enemy. General Clinton being descended into the plain, fell upon the left flank of the centre, which was engaged with the Hessians. He had previously detached a small corps, in order to intercept the Americans.

"As soon as the appearance of the English light infantry apprized them of their danger, they sounded the retreat, and retired in good order towards their camp, bringing off their artillery. But they soon fell in with the party of royal troops which had occupied the ground on their rear, and who now charged them with fury; they were compelled to throw themselves into the neighboring woods, where they met again with the Hessians, who repulsed them upon the English; and thus the Americans were driven several times by the one against the other with great loss. They continued for some time in this desperate situation, till at length several regiments, animated by an heroic valor, opened their way through the midst of the enemy, and gained the camp of General Putnam; others escaped through the woods. The inequality of the ground, the great numbers of positions which it offered, and the disorder which prevailed throughout the line, were the cause that for several hours divers partial combats were maintained, in which many of the Americans fell.

"Their left wing and centre being discomfited, the English, desirous of a complete victory, made a rapid movement against the rear of the right wing, which, in ignorance of the misfortune which had befallen the other corps, was engaged with General Grant. Finally, having received the intelligence, they retired. But, encountering the English, who cut off their retreat, a part of the soldiers took shelter in the woods; others endeavored to make their way through the marshes of Gowan's Cove; but here many were drowned in the waters or perished in the mud; a very small number only escaped the hot pursuit of the victors, and reached the camp in safety. The total loss of the Americans, in this battle, was estimated at more than three thousand men in killed, wounded, and prisoners. Among the last were found General Sullivan, and Brigadier-general Lord Sterling. Almost the entire regiment of Maryland, consisting of young men of the best families in that province, was cut to pieces. Six pieces of cannon fell into the power of the victors. The loss of the English was very inconsiderable; in killed, wounded, and prisoners, it did not amount to four hundred men.

" The enemy encamped in front of the American lines; and on the succeeding night broke ground within six hundred yards of a redoubt on the left, and threw up a breast-work on the Wallabout heights, upon the Debevoice farm, commenced firing on Fort Putnam, and reconnoitred the American forces. The Americans were here prepared to receive them; and orders issued to the men to reserve their fire till they could see the eyes of the enemy. A few of the British officers reconnoitred the position, and one, on coming near, was shot by William Van Cotts, of Bushwick. The same afternoon Captain Rutgers, brother of the late Colonel Rutgers, also fell. Several other British troops were killed, and the column which had incautiously advanced, fell back beyond the range of the American fire. In this critical state of the American army on Long Island—in front a numerous and victorious enemy with a formidable train of artillery, the

*Washington's Quarters at Gowanus, Brooklyn.**

fleet indicating an intention of forcing a passage up the East river, the troops lying without shelter from heavy rains, fatigued and dispirited—General Washington determined to withdraw the army from

---

* This dwelling, the head-quarters of Washington when on Long Island, is now owned by Mr. Cortelyou, and is situated on the Gowanus road near the sea shore, a mile and a half distant from the south ferry.

the island; and this difficult movement was effected with great skill and judgment, and with complete success. The retreat was to have commenced at eight o'clock in the evening of the 29th, but a strong northeast wind and a rapid tide caused a delay of several hours; a southwest wind springing up at eleven, essentially facilitated its passage from the island to the city; and a thick fog hanging over Long Island towards morning, concealed its movements from the enemy, who were so near that the sound of their pick-axes and shovels were distinctly heard by the Americans.

"General Washington, as far as possible, inspected every thing from the commencement of the action on the morning of the 27th; till the troops were safely across the river, he never closed his eyes, and was almost constantly on horseback. After this the British and their allies, the tories and refugees, had possession of Long Island; and many distressing scenes occurred, which were never made public, and can therefore never be known. The whigs, who had been at all active in behalf of independence, were exiled from their homes, and their dwellings were objects of indiscriminate plunder. Such as could be taken, were incarcerated in the church of New Utrecht and Flatlands; while royalists, by wearing a red badge in their hats, were protected and encouraged. It is believed that had Lord Howe availed himself of the advantages he possessed by passing his ships up the river between Brooklyn and New York, the whole American army must have been almost inevitably captured or annihilated. General Washington saw but too plainly the policy which might have been pursued, and wisely resolved rather to abandon the island than attempt to retain it at the risk of sacrificing his army."

BUSHWICK is situated in the NE. extremity of Kings county. Population of the town, including Williamsburg, 6,389. The settlement of the town was commenced by the Dutch, who were joined many years after by a number of Huguenot families, whose descendants are numerous and respectable in this and the neighboring towns. The name is of Dutch origin, indicating that the territory was remarkable for the woods which covered its surface in early times. From the organization of the town till 1690, it was for certain civil purposes associated with the other towns in the county, except Gravesend, constituting a separate district under the appellation of the "*Five Dutch Towns*," and for which a secretary or register was specially commissioned by the governor to take proofs of wills, of marriage settlements, &c. These five towns formed but one ecclesiastical congregation. The population of Bushwick was inconsiderable at the time of the revolutionary war. The vicinity of its forests to the garrisons and barracks of New York and Brooklyn, led to the entire waste of the valuable timber, which abounded at the commencement of the contest.

"On the 12th of May, 1664, the magistrates of this town sentenced one John Van Ly den, convicted of publishing a libel, to be fastened to a stake, with a bridle in his mouth, eight rods under his arm, and a label on his breast with the words, '*writer of lampoons, false accuser, and defamer of magistrates*,' upon it, and then to be banished from the colony. An instance also occurred, of a clergyman, who had improperly married a couple, being sentenced to '*flogging and banishment*,' but which, on account of the *advanced age* of the delinquent, was mitigated by the governor to *banishment* only. Another person, convicted of theft, was compelled to stand for the space of three hours under a gallows, with a rope around his neck and an empty scabbard in his hands. In 1664 permission was given by the town to Abraham Janson to erect a mill on Maspeth Kill, which was probably the first water-mill built within the town, and for grinding of the *town's grain* he was to receive the '*customary duties*.' November 12, 1695, the court of sessions of Kings county made an order 'That Mad James should be kept at the expense of the county, and that the deacons of each towne within the same doe forthwith meet together, and consider about their *propercons* for maintainence of said James.'"

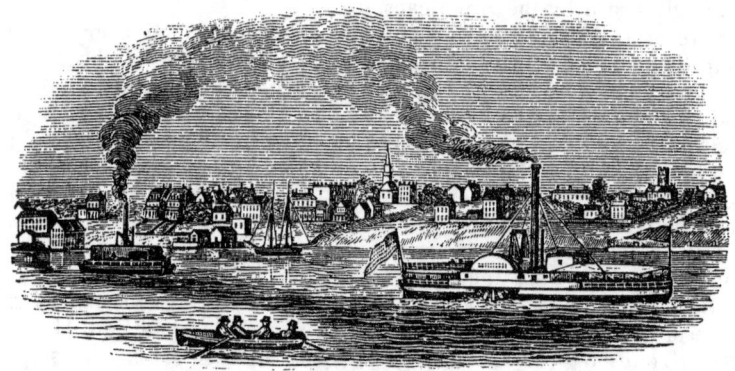

Western view of Williamsburg, New York.

The above shows the appearance of the central part of the village of Williamsburg,* as seen from the New York side of the East river. This flourishing village was till within a few years an inconsiderable place, although it was commenced by a few spirited individuals nearly thirty years ago, by erecting a few houses and establishing a ferry between it and the foot of Grand-street. In 1817, a ferry boat, impelled by horse power, gave Williamsburg a new impulse, and in 1827, an act of incorporation was obtained. The village has a bold water front upon the East river, one mile and a half in extent, and a sufficient depth of water for all commercial purposes. Several large and substantial wharves and docks have been constructed, affording safe and convenient moorings for vessels even of the largest class. Its ferry is the nearest approximation to the upper parts of the city of New York from the eastern towns of Long Island, by two lines of steam ferry boats. So great has been the progress of improvement that the ancient village of Bushwick can scarcely be identified, having been amalgamated with Williamsburg. The village has now upwards of 70 streets permanently laid out, about thirty of which have been graded and regulated, some paved, and one macadamized. There are upwards of six hundred dwellings, 5 churches— 3 Methodist, 1 Dutch Reformed, and 1 Episcopal—a newspaper printing office, and manufacturing establishments of various kinds. Population of the village 5,094.

---

* Williamsburg has recently been erected into a separate town.

FLATBUSH, called by the Dutch Midwout, or *Middle Woods*, was first settled in 1651. In Dec., 1654, Gov. Stuyvesant, who seems to have exercised ecclesiastical as well as civil and military authority, gave orders that a house of public worship should be erected in this town, "sixty feet long, thirty-eight wide, and fourteen feet in height below the beams." In 1655, he issued his commands that the people of Brooklyn and Amersfort should assist the people of Midwout in getting timber for the house. This building cost 4,637 guilders. This, it appears, was the first church erected on the island. The Rev. *Johannis Polhemus* was employed to preach soon after its erection, with a salary of 1,040 guilders, (about $460,) raised by assessment upon the towns in which he officiated. "He was required by the governor in 1656, to preach every Sunday morning at Midwout; and in the afternoon, alternately at Amersfort and Brooklyn.

The soil in this township is generally of a good quality, and by careful cultivation is made highly productive. The village of Flatbush is about four miles from the City Hall of New York, and has several splendid private residences finely situated. The courthouse of the county was erected here in 1685, and the courts continued to be held therein till it was destroyed by fire in 1832. *Erasmus Hall*, an academical institution, was incorporated in 1787, and has ever maintained a high reputation. Pop. 2,099.

FLATLANDS was originally called by the Dutch, New Amersfort. The settlement was commenced in 1636; and one of the first grants for land was that for Barren Island, which at that time was much larger than at present, and covered with cedar and other timber which has long since disappeared. Ex-governor Van Twiller had a farm in this town at the time of its first settlement. The village of Flatlands, situated about 8 miles from Brooklyn, is a pleasant spot, in the centre of which is the Dutch church, originally erected in 1661, and has been since twice rebuilt. Pop. 810.

"The surface of the town is, as its name indicates, a perfect level; the soil, a light sandy loam, warm and pleasant to till; and from the skill and industry of its farming population, yields a large amount over and above the wants of the inhabitants. The people, generally, are conspicuous for habits of economy; and modern fashions have not yet extinguished their love of simplicity and substantial comfort."

"An extraordinary interview took place on the 2d day of April, 1691, between the governor of New York and a sachem of Long Island, attended by his two sons and 20 other Indians. The sachem, on being introduced, congratulated Gov. Slaughter, in an eloquent manner, upon his arrival, and solicited his friendship and protection for himself and his people; observing that he had in his own mind, fancied his excellency was a *mighty tall tree, with wide spreading branches;* and therefore he prayed leave *to stoop under the shadow thereof.* Of old (said he) the Indians were *a great and mighty people*, but now they are reduced to *a mere handful.* He concluded his visit by presenting the governor with 30 fathoms of wampum, which he graciously accepted, and desired the sachem to visit him again in the afternoon. On taking their leave, the youngest son of the sachem handed a bundle of brooms to the officer in attendance, saying at the same time, 'that as Leisler and his party had left the house very foul, he had brought the brooms with him for the purpose of making it clean again.' In the afternoon the sachem and his party again visited the governor, who made a speech to them, and on receiving a few presents they departed."

GRAVESEND occupies the most southerly part of Kings county. Much of this town consists of salt marsh, not more than one third being under cultivation; the surface is generally level, but near the seashore there are some ridges of sand hills. Coney Island, which covers the town on the ocean, is about 5 miles long by 1 in breadth. The central part of the town is about 10 miles from the city of New York. Pop. 799. This place was settled by English emigrants from Massachusetts as early as 1640, who gave it the name of Gravesend, they having sailed from a place of that name in England, on their departure for America. They were soon after joined by Lady Deborah Moody, a woman of rank, education, and wealth, who, with her associates, were obliged to leave Lynn, and other places in Massachusetts, on account of their religious sentiments.

"Considering the situation of this town calculated it for the site of a commercial village, they proceeded almost immediately to lay out 10 acres of ground near the centre, into streets and squares, which they enclosed with a palisado defence. The plan of the village is still preserved in the clerk's office of the town, and is worthy admiration for its simplicity and beauty. It seems the project was soon after abandoned on discovering the insufficient depth of the water for the approach of large vessels. One of the original squares of the contemplated city was occupied by the courthouse of the county so long as the courts continued to be held here; another contained the first Dutch church; and a third has long been used for a public cemetery. On the same plot are a considerable number of graves of the first Quakers, the whole of which have been levelled by the plough, except that of Peter Sullivan and his wife, at the head of which is a large granite slab, containing only the names of the deceased. As this particular sect make no use of such memorials, it was probably placed here by some friend or relative who was not a Quaker."

In 1645, a general patent for this town, written in Dutch and English, was obtained from Gov. Kieft. The patentees named therein are *Lady Deborah Moody*, Sir Henry Moody, Baronet, Ensign George Baxter, and Sergeant James Hubbard with their associates. We find in Mr. Lewis's "History of Lynn," that Lady Moody came to that town in 1640; also,

"That in 1635, she went from one of the remote counties in England to London, where she remained in opposition to a statute which directed that no person should reside beyond a limited time from their own homes. On the 21st of April in that year, the court of star-chamber ordered that 'Dame Deborah Mowdie,' and others, should return to their hereditaments in 40 days, as a good example necessary for the poorer class. Soon after her arrival at Lynn, she united with the church of Salem; and on the 13th of May, the court granted her 400 acres of land. In 1641, she purchased the farm of the deputy-governor, John Humphry, called Swamscut, for which she paid £1,100. Some time after she became imbued with the erroneous idea that the baptism of infants was a sinful ordinance, and she was therefore excommunicated; and in 1643, she removed to Long Island. Governor Winthrop, in his journal says, that 'in 1643, Lady Moody was in the colony of Massachusetts, a wise and anciently religious woman; and being taken with the error of denying baptism to infants, was dealt with accordingly by many of the elders and others, and admonished by the church of Salem, whereof she was a member; but persisting still, and to avoid further trouble, &c., she removed to the Dutch settlements, against the advice of her friends.' 'After her arrival at Long Island, (says Mr. Lewis,) she experienced much trouble from the Indians, her house being assailed by them many times. Her wealth enabled her to render assistance to Gov. Stuyvesant, in some trouble with the neighboring settlers, in 1654; and so great was her influence over him, that he conceded, in part, the nomination of the magistrates to her. In the quarterly court records, her son is styled *Sir Henry Moody*.' 'At the same court, 14th December, 1642, the Lady Deborah Moody, Mrs. King, and the wife of John Tilton, were presented, for holding that the baptism of infants is no ordinance of God.' From these historical records we learn the reason why the Lady Moody, her son *Sir Henry Moody*, Ensign Baxter, Sergeant Hubbard, John Tilton, and others of her associates and friends, left New England, and located themselves at Gravesend, where they hoped to enjoy the most perfect freedom of opinion, unawed by the civil power, and be allowed unmolested to propagate those religious opinions which to them seemed most agreeable to their principles of reason and justice.

"On the first of January, 1643, a soldier was convicted before the court of sessions at Gravesend of having left his station while on guard, and was punished by being compelled to sit upon a wooden horse during the parade, with a pitcher in one hand, and a drawn sword in the other, to show that he liked beer better than his duty, and that his courage was always in proportion to the quantity of beer he consumed. 'At *a town meeting*, held September the 27th, 1644, it was *voted*, that those who have boweries, (farms,) should have 50 morgen of upland, with meadow proportionable to their stock; and it was further *ordered*, that if any did not build a habitable house upon it before the last day of May next, should be defaulted, and forfeit their land to the town.' The records of this town, which were uniformly kept in the English language, are still preserved almost entire. They commence with the year 1645 and for a series of years are chiefly occupied with the records of wills, inventories, letters of administration, and a variety of private contracts, bargains, sales, &c. In January, 1648, the town elected Sergeant James Hubbard, a man of respectability and influence, to execute the office of schout, or constable, which was considered as one of much importance. On the 14th of April, 1649, John Furman agreed with the town to keep their calves three months for 20 guilders a month, to be paid in *money, tobacco*, or *corn,* and *some bitters,* if desired."

"Coney Island, on the seaboard, is a place of great resort for strangers in the summer season, is constantly fanned by cool breezes, and affords an unlimited view of the ocean.

"It is separated from the main of Long Island by a narrow creek or inlet, over which a handsome bridge has been erected. There is a fine spacious hotel here, called the Ocean House, which is conducted in a superior manner; a railroad is attached to the establishment, and cars leave the hotel for the beach, a distance of 80 rods, at particular intervals during the day. The bathing at this place is not surpassed by any in the United States. The beach is a beautiful white sand. The island is about 5 miles long and 1 wide, and is entirely an alluvial formation. The destructive effect of ocean storms has long been very visible here, for much of what was once Coney Island has now disappeared. It has been conjectured by some persons that Coney Island proper, 200 years ago, lay at the entrance of Sandy Hook, and was separated from the present Coney Island by a channel of considerable width, which is supposed to have been entirely demolished by a storm about 1715. It is well ascertained that in 1643 there was a convenient harbor for vessels of a large size, which is now in a great measure filled up. The exposed situation of this island subjects it to great encroachments of the sea, and to the probability that at some future (though perhaps distant) period it will be entirely destroyed. In a terrible gale which occurred upon the coast on the 26th of January, 1839, the whole of Coney Island, with the exception of a few sand-hills, was completely inundated by the sea; the basement of the Ocean House was filled with water; the bridge was carried away, several small vessels were cast on shore, and one was driven a considerable distance towards Flatlands."

NEW UTRECHT is at the west end of Long Island, opposite the Narrows; 9 miles S. from Brooklyn. The soil of the township is mostly a light loam or sand. Pop. 1,283. Bath House and village are upon the margin of the bay, a mile and a half from the Narrows, having a full view of the military works at that place. It is quite a favorite place of resort during the warm season. It was near this delightful spot that the British army, under the command of Sir William Howe, effected a landing, August 22, 1776, a few days previous to the disastrous battle of Long Island. Fort Hamilton, at the Narrows, has become an important military station; several handsome buildings, with an Episcopal church, have been erected at this place, and few situations can boast of a finer prospect. The town appears to have been first settled in 1654, by about 20 families from Holland, and a few Palatines, who at first erected a blockhouse, as well for security against the natives, as from the hordes of wandering savages, robbers, and pirates, which for some time infested the country and this part of the coast.

"Some years ago, on digging a few feet below the surface at the Narrows, more than a wagon load of Indian stone arrow-heads were discovered lying together, under circumstances calculated to induce the belief, that a large manufactory of those indispensable articles of Indian warfare once existed at this place; they were of all sizes, from one to six inches in length, some perfect, others only partly finished. There was also a number of blocks of the same kind of stone found in the same rough state as when brought from the quarry; they had the appearance of ordinary flint, and were nearly as hard; not only arrow-heads, but axes, and other articles of domestic utility, were made from these stones. It will perhaps forever remain a matter of surprise and conjecture, how these native artificers, destitute, as they were, of iron tools, or even a knowledge of the use of them, could form and polish, with such exquisite art, so many various instruments from so hard a material."

LEWIS COUNTY.

Lewis county was taken from Oneida in 1805, and named in honor of Gov. Morgan Lewis. Centrally distant NW. from New York 275, and from Albany 130 miles. Greatest length N. and S. 54; greatest breadth E. and W. 35 miles. The whole of this county was included in the patent from the state to Alexander Macomb, and was sold by him to William Constable, and by the latter in parcels: the portion west of the Black river, to capitalists in New York city, among whom Nicholas Low, Richard Harrison, and Josiah Ogden Hoffman, were principal purchasers; and the portion on the east of the Black river, to a French company in Paris. From these sources the present possessors derived their title. . The first settlements commenced here in 1795, by pioneers from Massachusetts and Connecticut, who with characteristic enterprise and perseverance entered the wilderness with a determination to surmount the most formidable obstacles. There were at this time small settlements at Utica and Fort Stanwix, (now Rome,) whence the settlers made their way into this county, by a line of marked trees, to the High Falls, on Black river; and thence floated with the stream to the town of Lowville, where they established themselves. Their families followed in the succeeding winter, shod with snow shoes; mothers making their way with their infants in their arms, whilst their husbands and fathers trod paths through the snow for their cattle and teams. It was not unusual, some time after, for farmers to go forty miles to mill, and to carry the grist upon their shoulders.

The Black river divides the county into two not very unequal portions. Upon this river are broad alluvial flats, of easy cultivation and highly productive. Of the Black river we may observe here, that below the High Falls at Leyden, which are 63 feet in altitude, it has a tranquil course of nearly 40 miles through the country; in all which, it is navigable for steamboats. The Black river canal, the construction of which was authorized in May, 1836, commences at Rome in Oneida county.

The county is at present thinly inhabited, but it merits attention from the great forests of useful timber which incumber the soil, the beds of iron ore which lie beneath it, and the vast water-power which the streams supply. The staple products are wheat, rye, Indian corn, peas, beans, oats, and barley, and the whole country is adapted to grass. It is divided into 11 towns. Pop. 17,849.

DENMARK, taken from Harrisburg in 1807; NW. from Albany 143 miles. It is watered by the Deer river, which has at one place a fall of 175 feet, nearly perpendicular. Denmark, 14 miles N., and Copenhagen, 12 miles NW. of Martinsburg, are small villages. Pop. 2,398.

DIANA, taken from the northern part of Watson in 1830; from Albany 150, and NE. from Martinsburg 22 miles. Louisburg is a post-office. Pop. 883.

GREIG, taken from Watson in 1828, by the name of Brantingham; NW. from Albany 150, SE. from Martinsburg 18 miles. Brantingham and Lyonsdale are post-offices. Pop. 592.

HARRISBURG, taken from Turin as part of Oneida county in 1803, and settled that year; NW. from Albany 150, centrally distant NW. from Martinsburg 11 miles. Harrisburg post-office is on the Lowville and Whitesville road. Pop. 850.

LEYDEN, taken from Steuben when part of Herkimer county, in 1797; NW. from Albany 116, from Martinsburg, S., centrally distant 14 miles. Leyden Hill and Talcottville are small villages. Pop. 2,438.

LOWVILLE, taken from Mexico when part of Oneida county, in 1800; and named after Mr. Nicholas Low. Pop. 2,047. This place is distant from Albany 132 miles. The first settler was Jonathan Rogers, who emigrated from Branford, Ct., in the spring of 1795. At this time there were no settlements between here and the Canada line. Many others emigrated in the succeeding summer and fall, among whom were Moses Waters, James Bailey, Isaac Perry, William and Charles Davenport, Judge Kelly, Silas Stow, Esq., Moses Coffin, and David Cobb. Rev. Isaac Clinton, a Presbyterian, was the first settled clergyman. During the early settlement, a few hundred of the St. Regis Indians were accustomed to hunt in this vicinity, and were of much assistance to the settlers. This is one of the best towns in the county, being bounded on the east by the rich lowlands of the Black river. Lowville, on the great road from Utica to Sacketts Harbor, 3½ miles from Martinsburg, in a pleasant valley, handsomely laid out in squares, is the largest village in the county, and contains 1 Presbyterian, 1 Baptist, 1 Methodist church, and 1 Orthodox Friends meeting-house, a flourishing incorporated Academy, a printing office, publishing a weekly paper, 1 large grist and sawmill, and 60 neat dwellings. Stowe's Square has 1 Presbyterian church, and a few dwellings. There is a post-office called West Leyden.

LEWIS COUNTY.

Southeastern view of Lowville.

The above engraving is from a drawing taken on the road to Martinsburg in the SE. extremity of the village. The Presbyterian church is at the head of the street, and the spire of the Baptist at the left. The steeples of the Academy and Methodist church are seen on the right.

MARTINSBURG, taken from Lowville, Champion, and Mexico, as part of Oneida county, 22d of February, 1803; NW. from Albany 129, and N. from Utica 48 miles. The first settler was Elijah Baldwin, who came here with his family in July, 1801, from Washington county. The first week they encamped in the forest, and their midnight slumbers were disturbed by the howling of bears and other wild animals. Baldwin was in the employ of Gen. Walter Martin, who came shortly after him, and whose wealth and enterprise soon placed the settlement in a prosperous condition. Eherd Stevens and Nathan Cheney came about the same time with Gen. Martin, after whom the place was named. Rev. James Murdock, a Presbyterian, was the first settled clergyman. Martinsburg, post village and county town, is situated upon a high and commanding site, contains a courthouse and prison of wood, 1 cotton, and 1 woollen factory, 40 dwellings, the Lewis County Bank, and a printing office. West Martinsburg has about a dozen dwellings and a post-office. This town has 5 churches—viz: 2 Baptist, 2 Methodist, and 1 Presbyterian. Pop. 2,488.

About two miles in a southwesterly direction from the village of Martinsburg is a remarkable chasm, near the junction of two forks of the Whetstone creek, a tributary of the Black river. This chasm is about two hundred feet in depth, and of a bowl-like shape. On the north and west sides the rocks are nearly perpendicular, but on the south sloping and covered with lofty trees. It derives its name, that of *Chimney Point,* from the resemblance which a prominence in the slate rock bears to the termination of a conical pointed chimney, while the horizontal strata increase the likeness by their similarity to

Chimney Point Gulf, Martinsburg.

tiles. The above drawing was taken on the south side, part of the way down the chasm. The point opposite, about six or eight rods distant, is the one from which its name is derived, and the beautiful cascade of nearly one hundred feet fall is one of the forks of the creek, the valley of the other being seen in the distance. The two unite a few rods to the east of the Chimney Point. The visiter usually approaches this spot from the south. The surface of the ground in the vicinity is nearly level, and as he comes upon its brink suddenly, its wildness strikes him with awe. Opposite and on the left are dark, massy, perpendicular rocks; before him are lofty pines and hemlocks, and far, far below, as it were in the very bowels of the earth, through the openings in the foliage, indistinct glimpses are caught of the foaming rivulet, while the roar of the waterfall and the grandeur of the surrounding landscape add an interest to the scene rarely experienced. Although unknown to the fashionable tourist, this place is not without incident. About 20 rods below, and on the same side where the drawing was taken, is a rock called *Peebles Slide*, which derives its name from the following circumstance. In the spring of 1834, as Mr. Chillus L. D. Peebles, of Martinsburg, was drawing logs near the precipice, which here generally forms the boundary of the river, his foot slipped, and he fell. For the first twenty or thirty feet he slid, then descended from the precipice perpendicularly for nearly one hundred feet, when striking some loose rock and sand, he rolled the remainder of the distance to the bottom of the ravine. He was enabled to walk to a neighboring house, and although badly bruised, he soon recovered.

PINCKNEY, taken from Harrisburg and Harrison in 1808; NW. from Albany 153, and from Martinsburg centrally distant NW. 14 miles. The town was settled by William Henderson, Esq., the original proprietor. Pop. 907.

TURIN, organized as part of Oneida county in 1800; NW. from Albany 121, centrally distant SE. from Martinsburg 6 miles. Turin Four Corners and Houseville are small villages. Pop. 1,704.

WATSON, taken from Leyden in 1821; NW. from Albany 136 miles. Dayanville is a small village founded by Charles Dayan, Esq., on the falls of the Crystal creek, 9 miles N. of Martinsburg. Belfort and Carter are post-offices. Pop. 1,707.

WEST TURIN, taken from Turin in 1830; NW. from Albany 130, centrally distant SW. from Martinsburg 15 miles. Constableville and Collinsville are small post villages. Pop. 2,042.

LIVINGSTON COUNTY.

LIVINGSTON COUNTY was taken from Ontario and Genesee counties in 1821. Greatest length N. and S. 30; greatest breadth E. and W. 28 miles. Centrally distant NW. from New York 360, and from Albany W. 224 miles. The surface of the country is in some parts hilly, in others quite level, or but gently undulated. Flats of rich alluvion border the Genesee river in its course through the county from 1 to 2 miles in width, but a gravelly loam predominates on the upland. The great staples are wheat, pork, and cattle. Of the first, it is estimated that there is an annual surplus of over a million of bushels. The Genesee Valley canal enters the county at Caledonia, and following the valley of the Genesee, crosses the same near Mount Morris, and passing along the valley of the Cashqua creek, leaves the county in the southern portion of Mount Morris. Four miles south of Mount Morris village, a branch runs to Dansville. The county is part of the tract ceded to Massachusetts, and is divided into 12 towns. Pop. 35,710.

AVON, originally named Hartford, and organized by general sessions of Ontario county in 1789; from Albany 220 miles. This town was settled in 1790, by five families from Farmington in Connecticut. Avon is a village upon the upper bank of the Genesee, 10 miles NW. from Geneseo. It was laid out in 1826, by James Wadsworth, Esq., and contains an academy and about 70 neat dwellings. The river is navigable 20 miles for boats to the Erie canal, at Rochester, with which it is connected by a feeder. "The situation of the village in one of the most fertile and beautiful portions of western New York, and the valuable medicinal qualities of its springs, combine to render this one of the most attractive watering-places in the state. Three springs have already been discovered here, and as their chemical composition does not differ materially, it is probable that they exert similar effects on the animal economy. The first, called the New Avon Bath Spring, was discovered in 1835. Its depth is about 36 feet, and the formation through which the water passes is limey slate. Its water, when heated, assumes a beautiful green color. These waters were known to the Senecas, who, until within a few years, inhabited a village on the opposite bank of the river called Canawagus. The Indian chief, Red Jacket, held them in high estimation. These springs are rapidly rising in public favor, and the place ere long is destined to become a second Saratoga. Upon the flats there is a singular pond about 2 miles in diameter, in an irregular circular form; a neck of land runs into and expands within the circle occupying the centre, on which are remains of ancient Indian works." East Avon, 11 miles NE., and Littel's Mills, 8 miles N. from Geneseo, are small villages. South Avon is a post-office. Pop. 2,998.

The Genesee in the early French histories is called the Seneca river, probably from the circumstance that its rich valleys were studded with the villages of the Senecas. This tribe, one of the Five Nations, was on terms of friendship with the English, while the Indians of the upper lakes were strongly attached to the French. The subjects of these rival nations were exceedingly jealous of each other, particularly with respect to the Indian trade, which both endeavored to monopolize. Hence hostilities between these parties often occurred. In 1787, Monsieur De la Barre, the governor of Canada, having made an unsuccessful attempt against the Five Nations, the Marquis De Nonville, his successor, resolved to retrieve the fallen honor of his countrymen. For this purpose he sent messengers to the tribes around the northern lakes, and succeeded in collecting a considerable body of Indians to assist him in his enterprise against the Senecas.

"Preparatory to this expedition, De Nonville collected large supplies at Cadarackui, (now Kingston,) in anticipation of the march of his troops, and the Indians from the neighborhood of Quebec, to that post. The advance of his army, consisting of two or three hundred Canadians, were commanded by M. Campagnie, who surprised two villages of the Five Nations, in the neighborhood of Cadarackui, and put the inhabitants to death with great cruelty, to prevent them, as it was said, from conveying intelligence of the movements of the French to their own people, as it was supposed they had done in regard to the last expedition under M. De la Barre. These people, however, had settled there at the invitation of the French, and anticipating no harm, were the more easily surprised. 'They were carried in cold blood to the fort,' (says Dr. Colden,) 'and tied to stakes to be tormented by the French Indians, (Christians as they were called,) and during the torture continued singing in their country manner, and upbraiding the French with their perfidy and ingratitude'

"...... Several attempts of the English to sow dissensions among the upper lake Indians, and divert them from their purpose, having proved unavailing, and De Nonville's preparations for the expedition being completed, he departed from Cadarackui for the entrance of the Genesee river on the 23d of June, 1687, embarking his army in canoes, and sending one half thereof along the northern shore of the lake, while he, with the other half, passed coastwise by the southern shore, that no accidents by wind might altogether defeat the expedition. So punctually were the arrangements executed, that both divisions arrived at Irondequoit on the same day, where their Indian allies appear to have been already assembled. Immediately after landing, the canoes were hauled up, and a military defence was constructed, in which a guard of four hundred men was left, while the main body of the forces advanced upon the principal town of the Senecas—the site of which, at that time, was upon the Genesee river, within the territory now forming the town of Avon. Before departing from Irondequoit, however, a young Canadian Frenchman was shot for the crime of having conducted a party of Englishmen to the upper lakes. The charge was that of being a spy, although France and England were then at peace.

"During the march, the Indians, led by a party of Indian traders, formed the van, while the regular troops and Canadian militia composed the main body of the forces. They advanced four leagues on the first day, without discovering an enemy. On the morning of the second, scouts were despatched in advance, who approached the cornfields of the villages without making any discoveries—a circumstance not very creditable to the sagacity of De Nonville's Indians, since they passed within pistol shot of an ambuscade of five hundred Senecas. Supposing the warriors had all fled, De Nonville pushed rapidly forward, for the purpose at least of coming up with and capturing the women, children, and old men. But no sooner had the French reached the foot of the hill, (a short distance north of Comstock's hotel, between the present village of Avon and the river,) than the war-whoop of the ambuscade rang in their ears, while a well-directed volley of musketry brought many of them to the ground.

"The surprise was complete, and the panic so great that the divisions of the French separated in the woods, and in their confusion fired upon each other. Availing themselves of the advantage, the Senecas rushed in upon their foes with tomahawk in hand, and the battle was fierce and bloody until De Nonville's regulars had time to rally and move again in phalanx. The brave Senecas were then repulsed; but it was an empty victory to De Nonville. He was so dispirited by the surprise he had met, that even his Indians could not persuade him to a pursuit that day. On the following day he marched upon the villages, with a view of burning them; but that labor had been performed to his hands by the Senecas themselves. Two prisoners only were made by the invaders—old men, who were discovered in the castle—and who were cut to pieces and boiled into soup for De Nonville's allies. The invaders remained five or six days, traversing the valley of the river for a few miles, and destroying the growing corn in the fields. They then returned to their canoes, and back to Canada—stopping awhile at Niagara, where a small fort was erected, in which a garrison was left of one hundred men. The Indians from the upper lakes were gratified with the erection of this post, believing that it would be of essential service in their operations against the Five Nations, whom De Nonville promised yet to assist them in subduing. But that promise was never fulfilled. On the contrary, the fort at Niagara was so closely invested by the Five Nations, that eighty-eight of the hundred died of hunger, and but for the aid of a party of French Indians, the others would have shared the same fate. The Five Nations, moreover, afterward carried the war into Canada, even to Montreal and Quebec. The loss of the French, killed in the battle, was one hundred men and ten Indians. The Senecas had about eighty warriors slain. In the course of the expedition, De Nonville contrived to make thirteen captives, who were sent to France as trophies, and thence as slaves to the galleys."*

CALEDONIA, originally named Southampton, and organized as part of Genesee county in 1802; from Albany 228, from Geneseo centrally distant N. 12 miles. Pop. 1,985. Caledonia village has about 50 dwellings.

CONESUS, originally named Freeport, afterward changed to Bowersville, and finally to its present name, was taken from Livonia and

---

* The above account, and that relating to Geneseo, are extracted from a series of historical and descriptive letters, published in the New York Commercial Advertiser during the summer and autumn of 1840. They were written by the editor, William L. Stone, Esq.

Groveland in 1819; from Albany 221, centrally distant SE. from Geneseo 10 miles. Conesus and West Conesus are post-offices. Conesus Centre is a small village. Pop. 1,654.

Geneseo, from the residence of James Wadsworth, Esq.

GENESEO is a large township, having an area of 36 square miles. Pop. 2,892. The rich alluvial bottom-lands of the river are spread out in this section to their broadest expansion. The village of Geneseo, the seat of justice of Livingston county, about one mile from the river, was incorporated in 1832. It contains about 120 dwellings, the county buildings, 3 churches, the Livingston county high school, 2 newspaper printing offices, and a bank. Distant from Albany 226, from Washington 345, and from Rochester about 27 miles. " The village is pleasantly situated upon a site sloping to the west, and enjoys a delightful prospect, stretching across the valley, and including the town of Leicester. The landscape, embracing an area of perhaps fifteen miles in diameter, agreeably undulated with gentle hills and valleys—rich in the garniture of fields, agreeably interrupted by masses of woods, and enlivened by villas, bespeaking the comfortable circumstances of their owners—forms a prospect of matchless beauty. It is rendered still more picturesque by the river, which flows lazily through the valley, but disclosing only here and there a section of the stream, breaking through the bower of trees and clustering vines by which its bright waters are overarched.

" This town was first settled by William and James Wadsworth in 1790. Lands being cheap, and they being gentlemen of sagacity, who foresaw the rapid growth of the country in no distant prospective, they were enabled to accumulate splendid estates. The former, Gen. William Wadsworth, served with his militia command upon the Niagara frontier during the last war with England, and acquitted himself with gallantry. Mr. James Wadsworth yet survives in a green old age, the patriarch of the Genesee country. The whole valley of the Genesee was studded with Indian towns, when the white men made their advances thither, and the country was full of Indians when he planted himself down among them. His mansion, the abode of refinement and elegant hospitality, is finely situated at the southern extremity of the principal street of the village, embosomed in groves of ornamental trees, thickly sprinkled, among which are the elm, locust, and willow, and looking out upon a princely domain of his own, including a broad sweep of flats. . . . . Adjacent to the mansion is a large garden, rich with every description of fruit which the climate will allow, and adorned with flowers of every variety and class of beauty.

" . . . . It was at this point that the memorable campaign of General Sullivan in 1779 was brought to a close. In setting this expedition on foot, it was the intention of Washington that the American forces should pass through to the great Indian and loyalist rendezvous at Niagara; but having ravaged the most populous portions of the Indian country, Sullivan, for reasons never fully explained, proceeded no further than Genesee—sending a detachment across the river, however, to Little Beardstown, (now the town of Leicester.) The Indian town of Genesee, lying on the eastern side of the river, was the largest of their populous places, containing according to Sullivan's official report, 'one hundred and thirty-eight houses, most of them very elegant. It was beautifully situated, almost encircled with a clear flat, extending for a number of miles; on which extensive fields of corn were growing, together with every kind of vegetable that could be conceived.' This and the neighboring towns, together with thousands of acres of corn, were destroyed. The Indians were disposed to make a stand for the protection of their towns, but the numbers and discipline of Sullivan's army were too much for them. . . . . At no great distance south of the village a considerable stream, called Fall Brook, crosses the road, and descends into the river. Before it reaches the flats it plunges abruptly into a chasm one hundred feet deep. It is a tradition of the neighborhood that in one of the fights with Sullivan, many of the Indians were driven to the brink of this precipice, whence they leaped into the gulf, and were killed by the fall. There is no mention of any such incident in the official account of Sullivan, or in the other chronicles of the day." Sullivan's army encamped on or near this spot, and it is said that the initials of some of his soldiers are now plainly to be seen carved on the trees, to the left of the cataract.

GROVELAND, taken from Sparta in 1812; from Albany 237, from Geneseo S. 7 miles. Pop. 1,993. Groveland Hill and Groveland are hamlets.

LEICESTER, organized in 1802 as part of Genesee county; since changed; from Albany 232, from Geneseo W. 5 miles. Moscow is a village, Gibsonville a post-office. Pop. 2,419.

During Sullivan's expedition, Lieut. Boyd with a scouting party had a severe battle with a superior force of Indians in this vicinity. Boyd and a man named Parker were taken prisoners, and the former tortured in the most horrible manner. The following account is from Wilkinson's Annals of Binghamton:—

"From Canandaigua the army proceeded to Honeoye which they destroyed; and passing by Hemlock Lake, they came to the head of Connissius Lake, where the army encamped for the night, on the ground which is now called Henderson's Flats.

"Soon after the army had encamped, at the dusk of evening, a party of twenty-one men, under the command of Lieut. William Boyd, was detached from the rifle corps, which was commanded by the celebrated Morgan, and sent out for the purpose of reconnoitering the ground near the Genesee river, at a place now called Williamsburgh, at a distance from the place of encampment of about seven miles, and under the guidance of a faithful Indian pilot. The place was then the site of an Indian village; and it was apprehended that the Indians and rangers, as their allies were called, might be there, or in its vicinity.

"When the party arrived at Williamsburgh, they found that the Indians had very recently left the place, as the fires in their huts were still burning. The night was so far spent when they got to the place of their destination, that the gallant Boyd, considering the fatigue of his men, concluded to remain quietly where he was, near the village, sleeping upon their arms, till the next morning, and then to despatch two messengers with a report to the camp. Accordingly, a little before daybreak, he sent two men to the main body of the army with information that the enemy had not been discovered, but were supposed to be not far distant, from the fires they found burning the evening before.

"After daylight, Lieut. Boyd and his men cautiously crept from the place of their concealment, and upon getting a view of the village, discovered two Indians lurking about the settlement. One of whom was immediately shot and scalped by one of the riflemen, by the name of Murphy. Lieut. Boyd—supposing now that if there were Indians near they would be aroused by the report of the rifle, and possibly by a perception of what had just taken place, the scalping of the Indian—thought it most prudent to retire and make his best way back to the main army. They accordingly set out, and retraced the steps they had taken the evening before.

"On their arriving within about one mile and a half of the main army, they were surprised by the sudden appearance of a body of Indians, to the amount of five hundred, under the command of Brant, and the same number of rangers, commanded by the infamous Butler, who had secreted themselves in a ravine of considerable extent, which lay across the track that Lieut. Boyd had pursued. These two leaders of the enemy had not lost sight of the American army since their appalling defeat at the narrows above Newtown, though they had not shown themselves till now. With what dismay they must have witnessed the destruction of their towns and the fruits of their fields, that marked the progress of our army! They dare not, however, any more come in contact with the main army, whatever should be the consequence of their forbearance.

"Lieut. Boyd and his little heroic party, upon discovering the enemy, knowing that the only chance for their escape would be by breaking through their lines, an enterprise of most desperate undertaking, made the bold attempt. As extraordinary as it may seem, the first onset, though unsuccessful, was made without the loss of a man on the part of the heroic band, though several of the enemy were killed. Two attempts more were made, which were equally unsuccessful, and in which the whole party fell, excepting Lieut. Boyd and eight others. Boyd and a soldier by the name of Parker, were taken prisoners on the spot; a part of the remainder fled, and a part fell on the ground apparently dead, and were overlooked by the Indians, who were too much engaged in pursuing the fugitives to notice those who fell.

"When Lieut. Boyd found himself a prisoner, he solicited an interview with Brant, preferring, it seems, to throw himself upon the clemency and fidelity of the savage leader of the enemy, rather than trust to his civilized colleague. The chief, who was at that moment near, immediately presented himself, when Lieut. Boyd, by one of those appeals and tokens which are known only by those who have been initiated and instructed in certain mysteries, and which never fail to bring succor to a distressed brother, addressed him as the only source from which he could expect respite from cruel punishment or death. The appeal was recognised, and Brant immediately, and in the strongest language, assured him that his life should be spared.

"Boyd and his fellow-prisoner were conducted immediately by a party of the Indians to the Indian village called Beardstown, after a distinguished chief of that name, on the west side of the Genesee river, and in what is now called Leicester. After their arrival at Beardstown, Brant, being called on service which required a few hours' absence, left them in the care of Col. Butler. The latter, as soon as Brandt had left them, commenced an interrogation, to obtain from the prisoners a statement of the number, situation, and intentions of the army under Sullivan; and threatened them, in case they hesitated or prevaricated in their answers, to deliver them up immediately to be massacred by the Indians; who, in Brant's absence, and with the encouragement of their more savage commander, Butler, were ready to commit the greatest cruelties. Relying probably upon the promises which Brant had made them, and which he most likely intended to fulfil, they refused to give Butler the desired information. Upon this refusal, burning with revenge, Butler hastened to put his threat into execution. He delivered them to some of their most ferocious enemies, among which the Indian chief Little Beard was distinguished for his inventive ferocity. In this, that was about to take place, as well as in all the other scenes of cruelty that were perpetrated in his town, Little Beard was master of ceremonies. The stoutest heart quails under the apprehension of immediate and certain torture and death; where too, there is not an eye that pities, nor a heart that feels. The suffering lieutenant was first stripped of his clothing, and then tied to a sapling, when the Indians menaced his life by throwing their tomahawks at the tree directly over his head, brandishing their scalping-knives around him in the most frightful manner, and accompanying their ceremonies with terrific shouts of joy. Having punished him sufficiently in this way, they made a small opening in his abdomen, took out an intestine, which they tied to a sapling, and then unbound him from the tree, and by scourges, drove him around it till he had drawn out the whole of his intestines. He was then beheaded, and his head was stuck upon a pole, with a dog's head just above it, and his body left unburied upon the ground. Through out the whole of his sufferings, the brave Boyd neither asked for mercy, or uttered a word of complaint.

"Thus perished William Boyd, a young officer of heroic virtue and of rising talents; and in a manner that will touch the sympathies of all who read the story of his death. His fellow-soldier, and fellow-sufferer, Parker, was obliged to witness this moving and tragical scene, and in full expectation of passing the same ordeal. According, however, to our information, in relation to the death of these two men, which has been obtained incidentally from the Indian account of it, corroborated by the discovery of the two bodies by the American army, Parker was only beheaded.

"The main army, immediately after hearing of the situation of Lieutenant Boyd's detachment, moved towards Genesee river, and finding the bodies of those who were slain in the heroic attempt to penetrate the enemy's line, buried them in what is now the town of Groveland, near the bank of Beard's creek, under a bunch of wild plum-trees, where the graves are to be seen to this day."

LIMA, originally named Charleston, and organized by general sessions of Ontario county in 1789; from Albany 213 miles. Pop. 2,186. Lima village, centrally situated on the great western road, has about 100 dwellings, remarkable for their neatness. The Genesee Wesleyan University, a highly flourishing and well-endowed institution, is situated here.

LIVONIA, taken from Pittstown in 1808; from Albany 217 miles. Livonia Centre, Lakeville, 6 miles E. from Geneseo, Jacksonville, and South Livonia, are villages. Pop. 2,719.

MOUNT MORRIS, taken from Leicester in 1818; from Albany 236 miles. Pop. 4,547. "On the bank of the river in this town, an ancient mound was discovered and opened in 1835, in which were some human skeletons in a very decayed state, and uncommonly large, with some stone arrow-heads, stone knife and cleaver, and a copper skewer, about the size of a pipe shank, flattened at one end and slightly twisted. The knife was of fine hard stone of the thickness of a quire of paper, with sharpened edges. The cleaver was of slate. These articles were of the rudest workmanship." There was formerly an Indian village here called Allenshill. It was named after Ebenezer Allen, the first miller in Rochester, a monster in human shape. Many are the tales related of his wickedness, almost too painful for recital. One will suffice. "During the revolution he was a tory, and on one occasion, when on a scouting party with some Indians in the Susquehannah country, they entered a dwelling where they found a man, and his wife, and one child, in bed. As they entered, the man sprang upon the floor to defend himself, but Allen felled him at a blow, struck off his head, and tossed it bleeding into the bed with the hapless woman. He then snatched the infant from its mother's bosom, and dashed its head against the jamb of the fireplace." Allen died in 1814, on the river De Trench, in Upper Canada—three of his wives and their children surviving him.

Western view of Mount Morris village, Livingston county.

The Indians sold out this country to Messrs. Phelps & Gorham, making, however, the reservation known as the Gardeau reservation. This, commonly called the White Woman's* land, is partly in this town, and partly in Nunda, and in Castile, Wyoming county. Mr. Thomas Morris from Philadelphia, from whom the town is named, bought out Allen, and in 1804 the village was founded, mostly by families from Connecticut. Mount Morris village, incorporated in 1835, is at the head of the boat navigation on Genesee river, 36 miles S. of Rochester, and by the Genesee valley canal 38½, from Geneseo SW. 6 miles. The site is beautiful, being elevated above the fertile flats which border the river. The annexed view was taken near the residence of Mr. Joseph Starkey. The three churches seen in front are respectively the Episcopal, Baptist, and Methodist; the spire on the left is that of the Presbyterian church. The hills in the distance are on the opposite side of the Genesee flats. The village contains about 120 dwellings. The post-offices are River Road, River Road Forks, Tuscarora, at Brushville village, and Brooks Grove.

SPARTA, organized as part of Ontario county in 1789; area since reduced; from Albany 231 miles. Pop. 5,841. Dansville village, 18 miles SE. from Geneseo, is at the head of the Genesee valley, 45

---

* For a biographical sketch of Mary Jemison, or the "White Woman," the reader is referred to Castile, Wyoming county.

Western view in Dansville, Livingston county.

miles from Rochester. A side-cut connects this village and the valley of the Canascraga with the Olean and Rochester canal. The above is a central view in Dansville. There is a Lutheran and a Methodist church besides the one shown, which is a Presbyterian, and a flourishing Academy. This is a thriving place and rapidly increasing. Within the circle of 6 miles, there are no less than 60 saw-mills. There are now in the village about 200 dwellings. The first settler in the village was Amariah Hammond, originally from New London, Conn. He came here in 1795, and erected in June of that year the first log cabin, which stood a few rods south of his present residence. Shortly after came Samuel Stillwell, Alexander Fullerton, Frederick Covert, Richard Porter, and others. The village was laid out in 1796, by Daniel Faulkner from Dansville, Penn., after which it was named. He was a wealthy enterprising man, and making large purchases of land, held out inducements to emigrants. When Mr. Hammond came, there was no blacksmith nearer than 40 miles, at Bath. The usual price for laborers was $2, and some, by jobbing, would earn 4 or 5 a day. In the spring of 1796, the settlers were alarmed by a loud noise like the report of a cannon. It was immediately ascertained to be the bursting out of a stream on the hill east of the village. The water came with such force as to throw forth earth and stones weighing two or three hundred pounds. An oak two and a half feet in diameter was cast butt foremost down the hill. The stream is supposed to be the outlet of a pond one and a half mile distant, on the summit of the mountain. It continues to flow to the present day, and is used to turn the wheels of a tannery. Before the revolution, according to tradition, a battle took place on a hill, a few miles distant, between the Canisteo Indians and those living in this vicinity, during which a chief of the latter was killed. When the whites first settled here, the spot where he fell was marked by a large hole dug in the earth in the shape of a man with arms extended. An Indian trail led by the place, and the Indians, on passing, were always accustomed to clear away the dry leaves and brush which had blown in. This chief was buried in an old Indian burying ground which stood on the present site of the Lutheran church, and was thickly covered with graves to the extent of two or three acres. His monument consisted of a large pile of small stones gathered from time to time by the natives from a hill a mile distant; who, on passing, were accustomed to take one in their hand and add to the heap. His bones were afterward disinterred by the settlers, and judging from them, and the length of the hole on the hill, he must have been 7 feet or more in height. Scottsburg, Byersville, Kysorville, and Union Corners, are small villages. Sparta is a post-office.

SPRINGWATER, taken from Sparta and Naples in 1816; from Geneseo, SE., 18 miles. Springwater valley is a small village. Pop. 2,832.

YORK, taken from Caledonia and Leicester in 1819; from Albany 237 miles. Pop. 3,644. Fowlersville, on the Genesee, 10 miles N., Greggsville, 4 miles NW. from Geneseo, and York Centre, are small villages.

LONG ISLAND.*

" LONG ISLAND may be described as the southeasterly portion of the state of New York, and extending from about 40° 34' to 41° 10' north latitude, and from 2° 58' to 5° 3' east longitude from Washington city; being in length from Fort Hamilton, at the Narrows, to Montauk Point, nearly one hundred and forty miles, with a mean range north, 90° 44' east. Its breadth from the Narrows, as far east as the Peconic bay, varies from 12 to 20 miles in a distance of ninety miles." A ridge or chain of hills commences at New Utrecht, in Kings county, and extends with occasional interruptions to near Oyster Pond Point, in Suffolk county. The surface of the island north of the ridge is in general rough and broken, while the surface south of the range is almost a perfect plain, with scarce a stone exceeding in weight a few ounces.

On the south side of the island is the great South bay, extending from Hempstead to the eastern boundary of Brookhaven—a distance of more than seventy miles of uninterrupted inland navigation. It varies in width from two to five miles, communicating with the sea by a few openings in the beach, the principal of which is opposite the town of Islip, called Five Island Inlet. In this bay are very extensive tracts of salt marsh, and islands of meadow furnishing immense quantities of grass; while its waters contain great quantities of shell and scale fish. Wild-fowl of many kinds and in almost countless numbers are found here, and many hundreds of people are engaged in taking them for the New York market. The north shore

---

* A history of Long Island in an octavo volume of 536 pages, by B. F. Thompson, Esq., has been recently published; it is to this valuable and interesting work that the authors are deeply indebted for the account given of the various towns on Long Island.

of the island is very irregular, and where not protected by masses of rock and stone, has been worn away by the sea to a considerable extent. The soil on the north side generally consists of loam, on the south side it consists more of sand, while through the middle of the island it consists chiefly of sand and gravel. The soil on the high grounds is in most cases better than that upon the plains, yet that found upon the necks or points on both sides is better than either. The soil in the vicinity of New York is highly productive and valuable, but in the greater part of the island it is naturally light and poor. Much of the land in the central part of the island is covered with a vast pine forest, in which wild deer are still to be found.

" Long Island Sound is a bay, or inland sea, with two outlets. If considered as extending from the Battery, in New York, to Fisher's island, its length is the same as that of the island. Proceeding from the city, easterly, it has a tortuous course of 16 miles, in which it varies from half a mile to two miles in width. From the Battery to Harlaem river, the course is NNE. 8 miles, and thence to Throg's Point, nearly E., 8 more. This portion is known as the East river. At the bend, opposite to Harlaem river, is the noted pass of *Helle Gat* (Dutch) or the gut of hell, narrow, crooked, and to the inexperienced, dangerous. The water here, when the tide is rising or falling, forms cataracts and vortices, which may dash to pieces or swallow up the largest vessel coming within their influence. The best times for passing it are at high and low water.

" Above Throg's Point, the Sound, properly speaking, commences, and turns to the NE. 18 miles, between Lloyd's neck and Stamford, in Connecticut. Thus far the shores are rugged and the channel rocky, and much interrupted by small islets and projecting points; but beyond Lloyd's neck it opens into a noble elliptical expanse, from 8 to 20 miles wide, and with depth sufficient for the largest vessels of commerce or war; presenting, along its northern shore, a continued picture of gradually rising hills, bold promontories, and commodious havens, which is chased before the eye like a brilliant phantasmagoria, in the rapid passage of the steamboats."

Long Island was claimed by the Dutch and English nations respectively by right of discovery. The Dutch commenced their settlements as early as 1625, at the west end of the island. In 1623, the Plymouth company, by order of Charles I., issued letters patent to William Alexander, Earl of Stirling, for the whole of the island. The English made settlements at the east end of the island, but they were for a season resisted by the Dutch. The settlements, both at the E. and W. end, were nearly cotemporary. In the Dutch towns, the Indian title was bought by the governor, and the lands granted to individuals by him; in the English towns lands were obtained under the license of the agent of Lord Stirling, and after his death, by the people of the several towns for their common benefit. The line of *division* between the two nations was a source of much contention and many complaints. The several English towns united themselves with the colonies of Connecticut and New Haven. After

Connecticut received her royal charter, in 1662, she exercised jurisdiction, and gave each of the towns who united with her, permission to send a deputy to the general court. But before these measures could be fully completed they were frustrated by the grant of Long Island to the Duke of York.

The following account of the Indians on Long Island, is taken from "*Wood's History of Long Island,*" published in 1828.

"When the first settlements were made on the island by the Dutch and English, it appears, from the original Indian deeds, that the principal tribes that occupied it, were as follows:—

"The Canarse, the Rockaway, the Merikoke, the Marsapeague, the Secatague, and the Patchague, on the south side—the Matinecoc, the Nissaquague, the Satauket, and the Corchaug, on the north side; the Shinecoc, the Manhanset, and the Montauk, from the Canoe Place on Montauk Point.

"The Canarse appears to have been the only tribe, or the only tribe of any consequence, in Kings county. This tribe claimed the chief part of the lands in Kings county, and a part of the lands in Jamaica.

"The Rockaway tribe claimed the territory around Rockaway, and more or less of the lands in Newtown and Jamaica.

"The Merikoke and Marsapeague tribes extended from Rockaway through Queens county into Suffolk, on the south side of the island.

"The territory of the Matinecoc tribe extended from Flushing through Queens county to Fresh Pond in Suffolk, on the north side.

"The Nissaquague tribe extended from Fresh Pond to Stonybrook.

"The Satauket tribe claimed from Stonybrook to the Wading river.

"The Corchaug tribe extended from the Wading river through South Old on the north side.

"The territory of the Manhanset tribe was Shelter-Island.

"The territory of the Secataug tribe adjoined that of the Marsapeagues, and extended to Patchogue.

"The territory of the Patchogue tribe extended to South Hampton.

"The Shinecoc tribe extended from the Canoe Point to Montauk, and that peninsula was the seat of the Montauk tribe.

"There are one or two other tribes named in the old records, but the place they occupied cannot be ascertained, and it is evident from that circumstance, that they must have been very small, perhaps the mere remnants of tribes which had been destroyed in their wars.

"Those above enumerated are the principal tribes that occupied the island when the English and Dutch commenced their settlements there, and the original purchases of the several towns were made of these tribes.

"The Indian settlements were all on the bays, creeks, and harbors on the north and south sides of the island, and their territories were divided from each other by the middle of the island.

"At the time of the first settlement of the island, the whole Indian population was considerable, but by no means as great as the facilities of subsistence would have authorized us to expect, nor as great as it probably had formerly been.

"The shell banks which indicate the sites of their villages, on the western half of the island, are large and numerous, and beds of shells of some size or other are found at intervals of a few miles all around the margin of the island. From these it would seem that the population of some parts of the island was once very numerous, or must have been stationary there a long time.*

"The state of the Indian population must be ascribed to their perpetual wars, by which they had been diminished.

"All savage nations are addicted to war. The causes of war among them are numerous, and the mode of carrying it on destructive to their numbers.

---

* "The shell banks in the western towns of Suffolk county are much larger and more numerous than in the eastern towns, where shell fish are as abundant: which proves that the western part of the island had been the longest settled, and that the Indian emigration proceeded from west to east."

"It appears that Long Island had been overrun by hostile tribes, and many of the natives must have been destroyed by them.

"The confederacy of the Five Nations extended their conquests as far south as Manhattan Island, and had passed over to the west end of Long Island, and subdued the Canarse Indians.

"There is a tradition among the Dutch, that at the time of the first settlement of the island, the Canarse tribe paid the Mohawks an annual tribute of wampum and dried clams, and that they discontinued the payment of it on the persuasion of the whites, in consequence of which a party of the conquerors came and destroyed the whole tribe, except a few who happened to be from home.

"Some writers have supposed that the conquest of the Mohawks extended to the whole island, but there is no tradition to support it, and it is believed that the conquest never extended beyond the territories of the Canarse Indians. This may have been owing to the fact, that all the other Indians were in subjection to the Pequots. It is well known that this tribe never was subdued by the Five Nations, and it would have been a violation of their rules of warfare, to have turned their arms against a tributary people, when they had not subdued the power that held them in subjection.

"The Montauks had probably been the most warlike tribe on Long Island, had overrun the other tribes on the island east of the Canarse territory, and had reduced them to some kind of subjection. At the time of the first settlement of the island, the Montauk sachem claimed and exercised some kind of sovereignty over the whole territory, and it is stated that he justified his claim before the governor and council in virtue of a former conquest of the country. In 1659, he conveyed the territory which constitutes the town of Smithtown, then occupied by the Nissaquague Indians, to Lyon Gardiner.

"It was under a belief of his superiority over the chiefs of the other tribes, that the first settlers were anxious to have their purchase deeds signed by that chief, as well as by the sachem of the tribe of whom the land was purchased.

"The confirmation deed of Hempstead in 1657, the deed for Lloyd's neck, and others, are executed in this manner, and in some of the original deeds the Mantauk chief is styled the sachem of Long Island.

"The superiority ascribed to the chief of that tribe after the settlement of the country, might have arisen in part from the distinction conferred on him or recognised by the commissioners of the united colonies. In 1651 it is stated in some of our early records, that they constituted one, who is supposed to have been the Montauk chief, grand sachem of the Long Island Indians. It is probable that the commissioners only recognised or confirmed an authority with which they found him invested.

"It is evident from the early writers of New England, that the Pequots, who occupied the country around New London, and was the most warlike tribe in Connecticut, had subdued the Montauks with their tributaries, and that at the time of the first settlement of New England, the Long Island Indians were in subjection to the Pequots, and paid them a tribute. The victory over the Montauks involved the subjection of all the tribes that were under them, and the conquest of the Pequots must have embraced all the tribes on the island east of the Canarse territory.

"In 1637, the New England colonies made war on the Pequots, to avenge the murders and other hostile aggressions which they had committed on the whites, and subdued and dispersed the whole tribe. The Long Island Indians who had been subject to the Pequots, immediately repaired to the English to make their peace with them. Winthrop, in his journal, states that on the reduction of the Pequots in 1637, 'sachems from Long Island came voluntarily and brought a tribute to us of twenty fathom of wampum each of them.'

"From this time they seem to have considered themselves to be in subjection to the English, and to have paid them tribute, perhaps the same they had paid the Pequots. In 1644, they applied to the commissioners for some evidence of their relation to them, and the commissioners gave them a certificate in writing, in effect promising them security from injury by the English, and all others in friendship with them; at which time they assured the commissioners 'that they had been tributaries to the English ever since the Pequot war, and that they had never injured the English or Dutch, but had been friendly to both,' which implied that they had been subject to the Pequots and followed their fate. In 1650, the commissioners sent Captain Mason to Long Island to require payment of the tribute due from the Indians there, and to settle a way in which it might be punctually discharged in future.

"In 1656, the Montauk chief visited the commissioners at Boston, and in answer to an inquiry whether he had paid the tribute due from him, stated that he had paid it at Hartford for the space of ten years, and that it was in arrear for the four last years, which they remitted in consideration of his distressed condition by the late war in which he had been engaged with the Narragansetts. In 1653, Ninnigrate, the chief of the Nehantic Indians, who were either a tribe of the Narragansetts or closely connected with them, made war on the Long Island Indians, which lasted several years, and reduced them to great extremity. He invaded the territory of the Montauks, and would have extirpated the whole tribe, if they had not found protection in the humanity of the people of East Hampton.

"They were obliged to abandon their villages, and to flee for refuge to East Hampton, where they were kindly received, sustained, and protected. They continued to reside in that town for several years, before they deemed it safe to return to Montauk."

Long Island is divided into three counties, Kings, Queens, and Suffolk. An account of the various towns on the island, with historical notices, &c., is given under the head of these counties in their alphabetical order.

MADISON COUNTY.

MADISON COUNTY was taken from Chenango county in 1806, and named after James Madison, president of the United States. Greatest length N. and S. 33, greatest breadth E. and W. 32 miles. Centrally distant from New York 250, from Albany 108 miles. The surface of the county is much diversified. The middle and southern towns are more or less uneven and hilly; but the northern is more level. In the northern part much wheat is produced: the southern is better adapted to grass. The county is generally well watered. The route of the Chenango canal follows up the Oriskany, and crosses thence into the Chenango valley. The Erie canal runs westerly through the northern towns of Lenox and Sullivan. The county is divided into 14 towns. Pop. 40,032.

BROOKFIELD, taken from Paris when part of Herkimer county, in 1795; from Albany 90 miles. Pop. 3,695. Clarksville, incorporated in 1834, has about 60 dwellings. Leonardsville, on the Unadilla river, 22 miles SE. from Morristown, is a small settlement.

CAZENOVIA, taken from Whitestown and Paris when part of Herkimer county, in 1795; from Albany 113 miles. When erected, this town comprised an area nearly equal to that of the county. Pop. 4,153. It was first settled in 1793, by Col. John Linklaen, from Amsterdam, agent for a company in Holland, who were owners of large tracts in this and the adjacent towns, and sold them out in farms principally to New Englanders. Cazenovia village was founded by Col. Linklaen, about 1695, and incorporated in 1800.

It is situated upon the margin of Cazenovia lake and its outlet, and upon Chittenango creek, 8 miles S. of the Erie canal, 11 from Morrisville, 40 from Utica, and 113 from Albany. The following engraving is a SW. view of the village as seen from the bridge, at the outlet of the lake. The village contains upwards of 200 dwellings, 1 Presbyterian, 1 Methodist, 1 Baptist, and 1 Congregational church, a bank, 2 printing offices, and the "Oneida Conference Seminary," incorporated in 1825. This institution was established under the patronage

South Western view of Cazenovia.

of the Methodist denomination for the education of youth of both sexes. It has ever maintained a high standing. The number of pupils in 1840 was 327. Woodstock is a small village.

DE RUYTER, taken from Cazenovia in 1798; from Albany 123 miles. Pop. 1,799. De Ruyter village is 17 miles SW. from Morrisville, and was incorporated in 1833. It contains about 80 dwellings and the De Ruyter Institute, a flourishing literary seminary, established a few years since under the patronage of the Seventh-day Baptists. The annual catalogue for 1840 gives 162 as the number of pupils male and female. A newspaper entitled the "Seventh-day Baptist Register," is published in the village.

EATON, named in honor of General William Eaton, settled in 1794,

Northeast view of the public buildings in Morrisville.

and taken from Hamilton in 1807; from Albany 100 miles. Pop.

3,408. Morrisville, the county seat, on the three great western turnpikes, 102 miles from Albany, 15 S. of the Erie canal at Canastota, was founded in 1803 by Thomas Morris, and incorporated in 1833: settled principally by emigrants from Connecticut. The above view shows the county buildings and all the churches in the village excepting the Baptist. The first building on the left is the jail; the second, with a cupola, the county house; the third, the county clerk's office; the fourth, the Methodist church; and the two on the right, are respectively the academy and the Presbyterian church. There are in the village and vicinity about 100 buildings. Eaton village, sometimes called the Log City, 4 miles SE. from Morrisville, was founded in 1790 by Mr. Joseph Morse, and has about as many dwellings as Morrisville, and 1 Baptist and 1 Presbyterian church. Pratts Hollow, 3½ miles N. of Morrisville, is a small village.

In September, 1823, an Indian by the name of Abram Antone was executed at this place for murder. The following narration is drawn from a memoir published at that time.

Abram Antone was born in the year 1750, on the banks of the Susquehannah. When a boy, his parents removed to Chenango. During the revolution he took up arms in favor of the Americans, and besides being in several battles, it is said, was employed on a secret mission by Governor Clinton. Bold, adventurous, and revengeful, few dared to encounter his wrath. Years might elapse before the opportunity for revenge was afforded: but then, when perhaps the hapless offender least expected, he paid the price of his temerity with his life. " But the most atrocious deed of all, was one at which humanity starts with horror— the murder of an infant child, and that child his own ! The circumstances of this event are almost too horrible to relate. It appears from the account of his wife, that returning from an assembly of Indians one evening to his wigwam, he found his little child of four or five months old vociferously crying. Impatient at the noise, the monster snatched the child from its mother's arms, and raking open a hot bed of coals, buried the infant beneath them."

The following are the circumstances connected with the murder for which he was executed. —" In the year 1810, Mary, the daughter of Antone, formed a connection with a young Indian, it is said of the Stockbridge tribe; however, the connection was soon broke off, and the young savage left his former mistress for one more agreeable. This so enraged the heroine, that she determined to kill her rival, which she effected by stabbing her with an Indian knife. When arrested, and on her way to prison, she manifested a remarkable indifference as to her fate, justifying herself concerning the murder of the squaw, by observing *that she had got away her Indian, and deserved to die.* She was executed in Smithfield, in this county. John Jacobs was the principal evidence against her. He had also been very active in her arrest. In short, he was considered by Antone as the principal cause of his daughter's death, and both before and after her execution he openly threatened to kill him the first opportunity. Jacobs hearing of it, left the country, and did not return till Antone sent him word that he would not molest him, probably for the purpose of getting him into his power. The circumstances of the poor fellow's death are these: Relying on Antone's promise, he did not take all the precaution which seems to have been necessary. He was hoeing corn in a field, with a number of men, when Antone came up in a friendly way, shaking hands with each one until he came to Jacobs, and while grasping his hand in apparent friendship, slipt a long knife from out the frock sleeve of his left arm, pronouncing ' *How d'ye do, brother !*' and quicker than lightning plunged it into the body of Jacobs, striking him three times under the short ribs. He fell at the first blow. Antone giving a terrific yell, bounded off before any one had recovered presence of mind sufficient to pursue him.

" The same night, the Indians, learning where he had secreted himself, to the number of fifteen or twenty pursued him. He had encamped in a thick copse of underbrush, and had provided himself with dogs that might give the alarm in case he was discovered. He had also with much labor cut a path through the thicket, which was almost impassable. On the approach of the pursuers the dogs gave the alarm, and Antone, flying with the speed of a deer through the narrow path which he had cut, escaped. Shortly after, a company composed of about thirty white men and Indians, followed him to his hiding-place. They approached within twelve yards before they discovered him. Again by his agility he escaped, the night also favoring him. He went constantly armed with a rifle, two or three knives, and it has been said that he wore pistols in his belt; this, however is not certain. His two sons were almost constantly with him, well armed, and, as they declared, for the purpose of defending their father. One of the brothers, called Charles, was a most powerful and desperate fellow. He was said to be the strongest Indian of his tribe. He died some years since in Chenango county, having undertaken to drink a quart of rum on a wager.

"There was an attempt made to take Antone while encamped on a Mr. John Guthrie's land, in the town of Sherburne. Two large and resolute Indians having obtained information that Antone was alone in his camp, his two sons having left him for a few days on a hunting tour, went with the full determination of securing him. They approached his camp undiscovered. Antone was making a broom; but the ever watchful Indian hearing a rustling at the entrance of his camp, seized his rifle, and as they suddenly entered, pointing at the foremost, declared if he advanced a step further he would shoot him dead. His determined manner appalled the pursuers, and after parleying with him a short time, they withdrew, very much mortified at the result of their enterprise. But the most curious circumstance of all was that Antone's rifle was not loaded at the time. He has frequently boasted since of having scared two Indians with an empty rifle. He at length grew so fearless that he marched through our towns and villages in open day, without any fear of being taken. It is even said, that in the village of Sherburne he entered a store in which were about twenty men, and drank till he was completely intoxicated.

"There was nothing remarkably interesting in his trial. His honor Judge Williams, of Utica, presided. The prisoner was brought to the bar, and plead *not guilty*. The witnesses against him were principally uncultivated sons of the forest. But it was remarked that their testimony was given with a carefulness and precision scarcely to be expected. The testimony was clear and decisive. The court appointed Judge Platt and General Kirkland his counsel. They rested their defence altogether on this, that the state of New York had no jurisdiction over the Indian tribes within her territory. The court, however, overruled the objection, and Antone was sentenced to be hanged on Friday, the 12th of September, 1823. The prisoner has always objected to a trial, except by his own people. He says that he has paid two hundred and seventy dollars to the different tribes for a ransom, and thinks it hard that he should die when he has made his peace with the Indians. He particularly objects to the mode of execution, which he thinks is very degrading. '*No good way*,' said he, putting his hands around his neck—'*No good way*,' and then pointing to his heart, he observed that he should be willing to be shot.

"Two or three different tribes have sent petitions praying for his release; but the Oneida, of which tribe he is said by some to be a chief, have neglected it. This is said to be owing to the influence of the head chief, who is the enemy of Antone. Without doubt the Indians generally would be pleased with his release; though it is certainly a very singular circumstance that the same ones who volunteered in pursuit of him after the murder of John Jacobs, and to whom he was always a particular object both of dread and fear, should now turn and petition for him. The natives do not generally assent to our jurisdiction over them, and it may perhaps be thought that they petition for Antone on this principle.

"It may be interesting to some to know what ideas of religion are entertained by Antone. As is usual, pious people have talked with him and endeavored to explain the principles of the Christian religion. But he either cannot or will not understand them. He has no idea of a Saviour—indeed he appears to be utterly ignorant of every principle of Christianity. He mentioned through the interpreter that he put his trust in God, or more properly the Great Spirit. He was then asked whether it was the God of the Christians, or the Spirit which was worshipped by his fathers. The eye of the warrior sparkled as he readily replied, '*The God of my Fathers!*' Until within a short time he has nourished some hopes of being reprieved, but they seem to have failed him. He says that he is willing to die, and only complains of the *manner*. He is very anxious respecting his body, being fearful that it will be obtained for dissection.

"To look at the old warrior, one would scarcely suppose that he could be guilty of so enormous a crime. He has a noble countenance, in which there is not the least expression of malice. On the contrary, there is something placable, and bordering on serenity in his features. His eye is penetrating, but yet expresses no cruelty. His voice is somewhat broken by age, but pleasant and sonorous."

FENNER, taken from Cazenovia and Smithfield in 1823; from Albany 115 miles. Pop. 1,997. Perrysville, on the Sullivan line 15 miles

NW. from Morrisville, and Fenner centrally situated, are small settlements.

GEORGETOWN, taken from De Ruyter in 1815; from Albany 106 miles, and from Morrisville centrally distant SW. 12 miles. Georgetown is a small settlement, near the centre of the town. Pop. 1,130.

HAMILTON was originally taken from Paris, when part of Herkimer county in 1801. At the period of its incorporation it comprised townships No. 2, 3, 4, and 5, Eaton, Madison, Hamilton, and Lebanon. The surface of the township is hilly, but the soil is of a superior quality: it is drained on the south by the Chenango river and its branches. Pop. 3,738.

Northern view of Hamilton village, Madison county.

Hamilton village is 8 miles SW. of Morrisville, 28 from Utica, and 96 from Albany; it contains nearly 100 dwellings, 1 Baptist, 1 Presbyterian, and 1 Methodist church, and a newspaper printing office. The above engraving shows the appearance of the village as seen from a point near the burying ground. The buildings of the "Hamilton Literary and Theological Seminary" are seen on the elevated ground on the left. This institution was incorporated in 1819, and commenced operations in 1820. The principal building, which was erected in 1827, is of stone, 100 by 60 feet, 4 stories, containing 34 rooms for study, 34 lodging rooms, a reading room, library, and a large chapel. Another large stone edifice, 100 feet by 60, was erected in 1834. There is a boarding-house, a joiner's shop, and a farm of 130 acres belonging to the society. The regular course of studies is six years; four in the collegiate, and two in the theological department. This seminary was established under the patronage of the Baptists, and it is said to be the largest theological institution of that denomination in the world. "The institution is open to young men having the ministry in view from every denomination of evangelical Christians." Poolville, Hamilton Centre, and Colchester, are small settlements.

LEBANON, taken from Hamilton in 1807; from Albany 110, from Morrisville centrally distant S. 9 miles. Lebanon, Smith's Valley, and the "Centre," are small settlements. Pop. 1,794.

LENOX, taken from Sullivan in 1809; from Albany 118 miles. Pop. 5,441. Clockville, 10 miles NW. from Morrisville, has about 60 dwellings. Canastota, post village, on the line of the Erie canal and great Western railroad, 15 miles from Morrisville, has 1 Dutch Reformed and 1 Methodist church, 7 mercantile stores, and 750 inhabitants. The village takes its name from a cluster of pine trees that united their branches over the creek which passes through the centre of the village and bears its name, called in the native dialect of the Oneidas, *Kniste*. The tract on which the village is located was patented in 1810 by the state of New York to Capt. Reuben Perkins. its first, and now its oldest inhabitant. The present site of the village was a wheat field when the Erie canal was laid out and constructed. The first framed house was erected by Capt. Perkins on an eminence where it now stands, near the cluster of pines. The Rev. Mr. Young was the first settled minister. Wampsville, 13 miles from Morrisville, Lenox, and Lenox Basin, are small villages.

MADISON, taken from Hamilton in 1807; from Albany 94 miles. Madison, Bouckville, 6 miles E. from Morrisville, Madison Centre, and Solesville, are small settlements. Pop. 2,344.

NELSON, taken from Cazenovia in 1807; from Albany 109 miles. Erieville, 9 miles SW. from Morrisville, has about 45 dwellings. Nelson Flats is 7 miles W. from Morrisville. Pop. 2,100.

STOCKBRIDGE, recently taken from Smithfield; centrally distant 7 miles NE. from Morrisville. Cooks Corners and Munsonville are small settlements. Knoxville is a post-office. Pop. 2,344.

SMITHFIELD, taken from Cazenovia in 1807; from Albany 108, centrally distant N. from Morrisville 5 miles. Pop. 1,699. Peterboro, centrally situated, has about 60 dwellings, 2 churches, and a school for the education of colored persons. Siloam and Stockbridge are villages. The principal part of this town and Stockbridge was leased of the Oneida Indians by Peter Smith in 1794, and purchased by the state in 1795. These towns comprise the larger part of the New Petersburg tract, and a portion of the Oneida reservation and New Stockbridge tract.

SULLIVAN was first erected in 1803, then in Chenango county; and in 1809 the eastern and largest part was erected into the town of Lenox. Canaseraga and Bridgeport are villages. Joslin's Corners is a post-office. Pop. 4,390.

The above shows the appearance of Chittenango village as it is entered from the SE. The village consists of upwards of 100 dwellings, 3 churches—1 Dutch Reformed, 1 Methodist, and 1 Baptist—a large woollen factory, and several other manufacturing establishments. The Methodist church is seen in the central part of the engraving; the woollen factory, built of stone, is seen on the left; the spire of the Baptist church is seen towards the right, near which is the spire of the youths' Bethel. The Dutch Reformed church, a large stone structure, is a pro-

MADISON COUNTY.   261

Southeastern view of Chittenango.

nent object as the village is entered on the road from the Erie canal, but it could not be seen from the spot from whence the above view was taken. The site of the village was probably at a former period a lake; it is surrounded on almost every side by elevated grounds, in which are found numerous petrifactions of trees, branches, &c., in various stages of conversion. In the valley of the Chittenango creek, about a mile above the village, are two mineral springs, one mostly sulphur; the other has a large portion of magnesia: both have been found efficient in some diseases. The village is situated one mile S. of the Erie canal, 2 from the Utica and Syracuse railroad, 8 from Cazenovia, 16 from Morristown, 34 from Utica, and 15 from Syracuse. Canesaraga and Bridgeport are post villages. The latter is 20 miles from Morrisville, and has grown within a few years from a hamlet to a thriving village.

The murder of Robert Barber, by Lewis Wilber, on the line of the Erie canal in this town, August 30th, 1837, caused a great sensation in this part of the country. Robert Barber was from Coleraine, in the northern part of Massachusetts, and was a man of respectability, and in easy circumstances. He was a widower of upwards of fifty years of age, and had children and numerous respectable relatives in Coleraine. He left home on the 28th of August, for the purpose of marrying a lady residing at Onondaga, N. Y. On his journey to Utica he became acquainted with Wilber, who was about 21 years of age, a native of Saratoga, N. Y. This person was of a low and vicious character, and in the habit of thieving from his childhood. The following account of the murder is from a pamphlet published in Morrisville in 1839.

"At Utica, Wilber first entertained the thought of murdering the old man. For that object, or any similar one, he purchased a common shoe-knife, as he said,—but such a one as is often called a bread-knife, with a sharp point and a turned wooden handle; it cost eighteen pence. This he wrapped in a paper, and carried it in a pocket in the skirt of his coat.

"Sometime towards evening of the same day, (the 29th,) they both took a line boat to go west, of which Edwin H. Munger was captain; the name of the boat he could not recollect. Night coming on, they lodged together in the same berth. Little of interest occurred during the passage until morning, when they arrived very early at Burr's Tavern, on the canal, in Sullivan, about three miles east of the Chittenango Landing. There, the boat having stopped, Wilber and his companion (for they had by this time become considerably acquainted, and the old gentleman familiar with him) stepped off from the boat, went into the house, and drank something at the bar that they called for, which was handed to them by a woman.

"They then walked along the towpath to Lee's Bridge (so called,) about eighty rods west, and had some conversation about going on foot to Chittenango Landing; and at the suggestion of Wilber, they crossed over Lee's Bridge, and took a westerly direction in the highway leading to Chittenango Landing. They passed the crotch of the road that leads off towards Canesaraga, and turning west, went on beyond all the houses and buildings. When they reached the last open field on the right, before entering the woods, Wilber informed the old gentleman that it would lessen the distance to turn to the right from the road, and cross the woods in that direction. They accordingly got over the fence, and walked in the direction of the woods, which they soon reached and entered. In the direction they were travelling at the time, the woods, where they entered them, were about sixty rods from the highway, and the distance through the woods to the canal (towards which they were going at an angle of about forty-five degrees to the general course of the canal,) must be not far from a quarter of a mile.

"When they arrived at the place where the body of the old gentleman was subsequently found, (eighteen or twenty rods distant from the canal,) Wilber said he took from his pocket the knife before described, and a pistol that he carried, which at the time was not charged—and presenting the pistol to the old gentleman, demanded of him his money, at the same time showing him the knife. Here he said he became much agitated, and apparently more so than the old gentleman. The latter deliberately took his pocket-book from a side-pocket in his coat, and a purse from his pantaloons pocket—saying at the same time, 'I did not think that of you—I thought you was my friend.' Wilber then told him to throw down the pocket-book and purse, which he did. 'I was afraid to take them up,' said he, 'and told him to lie down and hide his face, and not look up for half an hour.' He then laid down in the same position in which he lay when found, according to the testimony of the witnesses. Here Wilber resolved to take the money and leave him. He took the pocket-book and purse, and secured them. Then, standing by the right side of the old gentleman, who lay on his face, with his right hand under his eyes and his hat on his head, a second thought warned Wilber of the danger of detection if the old gentleman should live; and throwing up the skirt of his coat, with a back-handed stroke he plunged the knife into his body, near the back-bone and below the ribs. This he repeated several times. He said that from the time he struck the first blow with the knife, no signs of life appeared. Indeed, he never moved from the original position in which he laid down.

"But this seemed not enough. He then stepped a few paces to the west, and thinking that by possibility his victim might survive, he picked up a large stone, and approaching him as he lay, threw it at him, and it struck his head. This he thought made the fracture in the skull above the left ear, on the back of the head, which appeared when the body was found, and also a similar corresponding hole in the hat.

"In describing this scene—which he did with a great deal of accuracy and minuteness—his feelings frequently overcame his utterance, and the burden of his thoughts choked him to silence. He would pause, and groan and weep; and when he spoke again, it would be by exclamations and ejaculations, accompanied by the most frightful writhings, manifesting the greatest mental suffering. He declared that if the old gentleman had made the least resistance or noise, he should have fled, and left him untouched."

Wilber after the murder proceeded on to Buffalo, and from thence to Cleaveland, Ohio, where he was arrested in April, 1838. After Mr. Barber was missed by the captain of the boat, from which he went with Wilber, his trunk was kept on board through to Buffalo and back again to Albany, where he saw a notice respecting the disappearance of Mr. B. His suspicions now rested on Wilber as his murderer. Search was made far and near on the north side of the canal; this was in October, and the winter passed away without any discovery. In March, 1838, the body was accidentally discovered, which immediately led to the apprehension of Wilber. He was executed at Morrisville, October 3d, 1839.

MONROE COUNTY.

MONROE COUNTY was taken from Ontario and Genesee in 1821. Distant from New York by way of Albany NW. 365, and from Albany W. 219 miles. Greatest length E. and W. 34, greatest breadth N. and S. 24 miles. The surface is level, or gently waving. The mountain ridge, a high terrace of land nearly parallel with Lake Ontario, extends across the county, as also the alluvial way, supposed to have been formed by the action of the waters of that lake at some former period. The soil is generally a rich mould and very productive. "It is said that an analysis of the Genesee wheat, for which this county is so celebrated, exhibits more saccharine than that of the southern states; whilst the latter combines with a larger portion of water in the composition of bread. This may explain why southern flour is more acceptable to the baker, and Genesee to the consumer. It is common for extensive farmers to sow from 50 to 200 acres with wheat, and to reap an average crop of 20 bushels to the acre. The product is sometimes 30, 40, and even 50 bushels to the acre." The long level of the Erie canal continues 2½ miles E. of the Genesee river. In the towns of Rochester, Mendon, and Gates, there are sulphur springs. "The towns of Parma, Ogden, Chili, Riga, Gates, and Greece, E. of the Triangle, belonged to the great tract of Phelps and Gorham, together with that portion of the county E. of the Genesee river. Clarkson and Sweden, part of the Triangle, and Wheatland, were of the tract purchased by Robert Morris from Massachusetts. Phelps and Gorham sold out Greece and Gates, in fractional parts to settlers; and Parma, Ogden, Riga, and Chili, in mass to Robert Morris. The lands on the east side of the river were sold by them in parcels, consisting of whole and parts of townships. The county was settled chiefly by emigrants from New England, with a few from Pennsylvania and the lower parts of New York." It contains the city of Rochester and 19 towns. Pop. 64,912.

BRIGHTON was taken from Smallwood and Penfield in 1814; NW. from Albany 216, from Rochester E. 3 miles. Pop. 2,337. Blossomsville, situated on the canal, is a small settlement.

CHILI was taken from Riga in 1802; NW. from Albany 230, from Rochester SW. 11 miles. Chili, North Chili, South Chili, and O'Connelsville, are post-offices; around which are small settlements. Pop. 2,174.

CLARKSON was taken from Murray in 1819; NW. from Albany 238 miles. Clarkson on the Ridge road, 18 miles W. of Rochester, is a small village. Pop. 3,486.

GATES, originally named Northampton, and organized in 1802; from Albany 225, from Rochester W. 6 miles. Pop. 1,728.

GREECE was taken from Gates in 1802; NW. from Albany 225 miles. Pop. 3,669. Port Genesee, formerly called Charlotte, at the mouth of the Genesee river, on Lake Ontario, 7 miles N. of Rochester, is a small village. It has a customhouse, a pier over half a mile in length, for the protection of the harbor, with a lighthouse built by the United States. Hanford's Landing, 3 miles N. of Rochester on the west bank of the Genesee, was formerly a place of considerable business. "It was the first landing on the river for lake navigation, and here in 1798 was built the first dwelling, and in 1810 the first store, on the river below Avon, on the west side of the Genesee river." Greece is a small settlement on the ridge road, 9 miles NW. from Rochester. North Greece is a post-office. The following relative to Hanford's landing is from Mr. O'Reilly's History of Rochester.

"A settlement was formed here in 1796. In 1800, the English traveller Maude mentions that, as he could not find any accommodations for refreshment—'not even a stable for his horse'—at the place where the city of Rochester has since sprung into existence, he 'was obliged to proceed to Gideon King's, at the Genesee Landing, where [he] got a good breakfast on wild pigeons. Mr. King is the only respectable settler in this township, (No. 1, short range,) in which there are at present twelve families, four of whom have established themselves at the Landing. King, though the proprietor of 3,000 acres, lives in an indifferent log house: one reason for this is, that he has not been able to procure boards. The Landing is the port from whence all the shipments of the Genesee river must be made; but further improvements are much checked in consequence of the titles to the lands being in dispute. The circumstances are as follow: Mr. Phelps sold 3,000 acres in this neighborhood to Zadok Granger for about $10,000, the payment being secured by a mortgage on the land. Granger died soon after his removal here; and having sold part of the land, the residue would not clear the mortgage, which prevented his heirs from administering on his estate. Phelps foreclosed the mortgage and entered on possession, even on that part which had been already sold and improved. Some settlers, in consequence, left their farms—others repaid the purchase money—and others again, are endeavoring to make some accommodation with Mr. Phelps. A son of Mr. Granger resides here, and Mr. Greaves, his nephew, became also a settler, erected the frame of a good house, and died. The Landing is at present an unhealthy residence, but when the woods get more opened it will no doubt become as healthy as any other part of the Genesee country. I went to see the new store and wharf. It is very difficult to get goods conveyed to and from the wharf, in consequence of the great height and steepness of the bank.'

"As illustrative of the condition of things in the way of roads as well as navigable facilities, we may note a remark of the traveller, that 'yesterday, August 18, 1800, a schooner of forty tons sailed from this Landing for Kingston, U. C., laden with potash, which had been sent from Canandarqua to Rundicut Bay, and from thence round about in boats to this (Genesee) Landing.'

"'This Landing,' adds Maude, 'is four miles from the mouth of the river, where two log huts are built at its entrance into Lake Ontario. At this Landing the channel runs close along shore, and has thirty feet depth; but upon the bar at the mouth of the river the water shoals to sixteen or eighteen feet. This place is about equally distant from the eastern and western limits of Lake Ontario, and opposite to its centre and widest parts, being here about eighty [sixty] miles across.'

"In January, 1810, Frederic Hanford opened a store of goods at what was called the Upper Landing or Falltown—the name of Genesee Landing was no longer strictly applicable, as another Landing had been established at the junction of the river and lake, at the village called Charlotte. Hanford's was the first merchant's store on the river between Avon and Lake Ontario—a distance of about twenty-five miles. Hence the place has since been termed 'Hanford's Landing.'

"In the same year Silas O. Smith opened a store at Hanford's Landing, but in 1813 removed to the new village of Rochester, where he built the first merchant's store; the plat of Rochester having been planned only the previous season.

"As at the present steamboat landing on the river at the north part of the city of Rochester, railways were used to facilitate the transit of freight between the top of the bank at Hanford's Landing and the warehouses or vessels on the margin of the river. The railway, the warehouses, and the wharves at Hanford's were burned in 1835."

HENRIETTA was taken from Pittsford, when part of Ontario county, in 1818; from Albany 228 miles. Henrietta Corners is a small post village 8 miles S. of Rochester. West Henrietta is a post-office. Pop. 2,085.

IRONDEQUOIT, recently taken from Brighton, of which it formed the northern part. It receives its name from Irondequoit bay, which extends through the eastern part of the town. Pop. 1,252.

"This bay, [Irondequoit,] well known in the early history of the country, is now wholly unfitted for navigation, owing to the sandbar formed at its junction with Lake Ontario. It is now much frequented by parties from Rochester, for gunning, fishing, &c. The geologist also has many attractions for a visit thither; for ' on the borders of the bay, and of the creek of the same name which discharges itself there, the surface of the earth presents a most extraordinary and picturesque appearance—a multitude of conical or irregular mounds of sand and light earth, sometimes insulated and sometimes united, rising to an average height of 200 feet, form a perfectly level meadow of the richest alluvial loam.'

"The history of Irondequoit is intimately connected with that of the Military and Trading Posts of western New York. A station was established there in 1726, to aid the British in securing the trade with the western Indians, to the exclusion of the French at the lower end of Lake Ontario.

"In connection with the fact that there was a city laid out at Irondequoit bay, it might be mentioned that formerly supplies from New York, destined for our western posts, were sent to the head of that bay, (instead of the Genesee river,) there freighted in batteaux, to proceed through Lake Ontario to Niagara river—thence to be taken across the portage to Fort Schlosser; and there re-embarked to proceed up the Niagara river, through Lake Erie, &c. The city was laid out at the head of the bay, near the route of the present road between Canandaigua and Rochester.

"It may amuse some readers to learn that Maude, a traveller in 1800, mentions that the cargo of a schooner which sailed from Genesee river for Kingston, U. C., had 'been sent from Canandarqua for Rundicut bay, and from thence in boats round about to Genesee river landing,' for shipment in the above schooner. [The cargo thus circuitously forwarded from Canandaigua was potash—and ' no potash was then made about Irondequoit or Genesee landings for want of kettles' in 1800.]

"The mouth of Irondequoit is about four miles eastward of Genesee river on Lake Ontario; and the bay extends southwardly about five miles, nearly to the present main-travelled route through Brighton between Rochester and Canandaigua.

"'The Teoronto bay of Lake Ontario,' says Spafford, 'merits more particular notice, if for no other purpose than to speak of Gerundegut, Irondequoit, and Rundicut—names by which it is also known. The Indians called it ' Teoronto'—a sonorous and purely Indian name, too good to be supplanted by such vulgarisms as Gerundegut or Irondequoit! The bay is about five miles long and one mile wide, communicating with the lake by a very narrow opening—or such it used to have—and Teoronto, or Tche-o-ron-tok, perhaps rather nearer the Indian pronunciation, is *the place where the waves breathe and die*, or *gasp and expire*. Let a person of as much discernment as these savages watch the motion of the waves in this bay, and he will admire the aptitude of its name, and never again pronounce Gerundegut, Irondequoit, or Rundicut.' "

MENDON was taken from Bloomfield in 1812; from Albany 209 miles. Pop. 3,435. Mendon, incorporated in 1833, is a small village near the eastern line of the town. West Mendon is 10 miles S. of the Erie canal, on the Honeoye creek, which has here a fall of 60 feet, on which are extensive manufacturing establishments. There are here upwards of 100 dwellings. North Mendon is a hamlet.

OGDEN, taken from Parma in 1817; from Rochester 10, and Albany 230 miles. Pop. 2,404. Adams and Spencers basins, on the canal, are post-offices, and small settlements. At Ogden, post-office, 2 miles S. from the canal, 10 W. from Rochester, are 1 Presbyterian and 1 Baptist church, and a small number of dwellings.

PARMA, organized as part of Genesee county in 1808, and taken from Northampton, the original name of Gates; from Albany 230 miles. Pop. 2,651. Parma village, on the ridge road, 12 miles W. from Rochester, is a small village. At Parma Centre, 15 miles from Rochester, there is a small collection of dwellings.

PENFIELD, taken from Boyle in 1810; NW. from Albany 211 miles. Pop. 2,842. Penfield village, on the Irondequoit creek, 8 miles SE. of Rochester, has about 30 dwellings. The creek in passing through the village has a descent of 90 feet, forming the high falls of the Irondequoit, affording a valuable water-power.

PERRINTON, taken from Boyle in 1812; NW. from Albany 209 miles. Pop. 2,513. Bushnells, Fulloms, and Fairport, are basins and settlements on the canal. At Bushnells basin, 11 miles SE. from Rochester, is the great embankment over the Irondequoit creek. This embankment is the greatest work on the canal; it is nearly a mile in length and from 40 to 76 feet in height. It is partly natural, partly artificial, and extending in a winding direction across the valley. The following is extracted from the journal of De Witt Clinton, while on his exploring tour with the canal commissioners in 1810.

" We arrived at the tavern at Perrin's, in the town of Boyle, [now Perrinton,] twenty-one miles from Canandaigua, four and a half from Gerundegut or Irondequoit landing, and fourteen from Charlottesburgh. A vessel of thirty tons can go to the head of this landing [from Lake Ontario; but the sandbar at the mouth of the bay now prevents all intercourse of that sort.] The sign of the tavern contains masonic emblems, and is by S. Felt & Co. Felt is a man in the landlord's employ; and the object of this masked sign is, as the landlord says, to prevent his debtors from avoiding his house. * * * We drew lots for the choice of beds; and it turning out in my favor, I chose the worst bed in the house. I was unable to sleep on account of the fleas, &c. * * * At this place we eat the celebrated whitefish, salted; it is better than shad, and cost at Irondequoit landing $12 per barrel.

" We departed from here at seven o'clock, after breakfast; and after a ride of eight and a half miles, arrived at a ford of the Genesee river about half a mile from the Great Falls, and seven and a half from Lake Ontario."

PITTSFORD was taken from Smallwood in 1814; NW. from Albany 215 miles. Pop. 1,983. Pittsford, a thriving village on the canal, 6 miles SE. from Rochester, was incorporated in 1827; it has about 100 dwellings.

RIGA was taken from Northampton in 1808; from Albany 230 miles. Pop. 1,983. Churchville and Riga are the post-offices. The pleasant little village of Churchville is on the Rochester and Batavia railroad, 15 miles SW. from Rochester.

ROCHESTER, one of the most remarkable instances of a rapid and vigorous growth as a village or city in this country, is situated in lat. N. 43°, long. W. 40'; distant from Albany 217 miles, Buffalo 73, Canandaigua 28, Batavia 35, S. from Lake Ontario 7, and 361 miles from Washington. In the year 1810 there was not a house where Rochester now stands. The first allotments for a village were made in 1812, when Nathaniel Rochester, Charles H. Carroll, and William Fitzhugh, surveyed the hundred-acre tract for a settlement, under the name of "*Rochester*," after the senior proprietor. This tract was a "mill lot," bestowed by Phelps and Gorham on a semi-savage called *Indian Allen*, as a bonus for building mills to grind corn and saw boards for the few settlers in this region at the time. The mills decayed, as the business of the country was insufficient to support them, and Allen sold the property to Sir William Pulteney, whose estate then included a large section of the "Genesee country." The sale to Rochester, Fitzhugh, and Carroll, took place in 1802, at the rate of $15.50 per acre, or $1,750 for the lot, with its "betterments." Some of the land on the east side of the Genesee in Rochester, (the hundred-acre tract being on the west side,) was sold by Phelps and Gorham in 1790, for *eighteen pence* an acre.

The last war with Great Britain, which produced much distress in this frontier region, impeded the progress of Rochester to such a degree that the population at the commencement of 1816 amounted to only 331. By the opening of the Erie canal, Rochester became the great thoroughfare between the seaboard and the inland waters. On the incorporation of the village in 1817, about 750 acres were included within its limits. The city charter, in 1834, extended the bounds so as to embrace upwards of 4,000 acres. The staple product of the fertile valley of the Genesee is wheat, remarkable for its quantity as well as its quality. Its celebrity is increased by the skill with which it is prepared for market. By the immense water-power formed by the falls of the Genesee, Rochester is the largest as well as the best flour manufactory in the world. There are now within the city 20 mills, (exclusive of grist-mills,) with nearly 100 runs of stone. These mills are capable of manufacturing 5,000 barrels of flour daily, and when in full operation, require about 20,000 bushels of wheat daily. About half a million barrels of flour are yearly manufactured. There are 12 saw-mills, and various other establishments that use the water-power, such as turning, stone-cutting, grinding dye-woods and bark. There are 1 cotton and 3 woollen mills. Carpets, edge tools, and various other articles are here manufactured. The business portion of the city is compactly built, and contains many splendid houses and stores four stories high. The east and west portions of the city are connected by several bridges, and by the great aqueduct of the Erie canal, upwards of 800 feet long. There are 3 banks, having an aggregate capital of about one million of dollars; 6 newspapers, and numerous religious, benevolent, and literary associations. Population in 1840 was 20,202.

The following is a list of the churches in Rochester, with the date of their organization.*

First Presbyterian,	1815	Brick, formerly second, (Presbyterian,)	1833
St. Luke's, (Episcopal,)	1817	Second Baptist,	1834
Friends,	1817	Zion church, (African,)	1835
First Baptist,	1818	German Evangelical Lutheran,	1835
First Methodist Episcopal,	1820	German Roman Catholic,	1836
St. Patrick's, (Catholic,)	1820	Second Methodist Episcopal,	1836
Third Presbyterian,	1827	Free Will Baptist,	1836
Orthodox Friends	1828	Bethel Free, (Presbyterian,)	1836
Reformed Presbyterian,	1831	Free Congregational,	1836
Free Presbyterian,	1832	Universalist,	1837
Grace, formerly St. Paul's, (Episcopal,)	1833	African Methodist Episcopal church,	1837

* For this and most other facts respecting this place, the authors are indebted to a work entitled "*Sketches of Rochester; with incidental Notices of Western New York*, &c., by Henry O'Reilly." This volume was published in 1838; it is a duodecimo of 416 pages, full of interesting historical details, and illustrated by 42 engravings.

No longer ago than 1813, pagan rites were performed on the spot where so many Christian temples have been since erected. The following account of the last sacrifice of the Senecas, near where the Bethel church now stands, is from Mr. O'Reilly's History.

"It may be premised that the Senecas, and probably others of the Six Nations, have five feasts annually; on which occasions it is customary to return thanks to Nauwanew for his blessings, or to deprecate his wrath. At these times also the chiefs conversed upon the affairs of the tribes, and generally urged upon the people the duty of demeaning themselves so as to ensure a continuance of the favor which had attended them in their pursuits of peace or war. These feasts followed the consummation of the matters usually watched with most interest by Indians in peaceful times—one of the ceremonies occurring after 'sugar-time;' another after planting; a third called the green-corn feast, when the maize first becomes fit for use; the fourth after the corn-harvest; and the fifth at the close of their year, late in January or early in February, according to the moon.

"The latter ceremonial was performed for the last time in Rochester in January, 1813. The concluding rites were seen by some of the few persons then settled in 'these parts.' From Mr. Edwin Scrantom, now a merchant of the city, who was among the spectators, we have had an account of the ceremonial, as far as he beheld it, which corresponds with the accounts given by the Rev. Mr. Kirkland, long a missionary among the Six Nations, and by the 'White Woman,' that remarkable associate of the Senecas. The latter personage related, that when the Indians returned from hunting, ten or twenty of their number were appointed to superintend the great 'sacrifice and thanksgiving.' Preparations were made at the council-house or other place of meeting for the accommodation of the tribe during the ceremonial. Nine days was the period, and two white dogs the number and kind of animals formerly required for the festival; though in these latter days of reform and retrenchment (for the prevailing spirit had reached even the wigwams and the altars of the Senecas) the time has been curtailed to seven or five days, and a single dog was made the scapegoat to bear away the sins of the tribe! Two dogs, as nearly white as could be procured, were usually selected from those belonging to the tribe, and were carefully killed at the door of the council-house by means of strangulation; for a wound on the animal or an effusion of blood would spoil the victim for the sacrificial purpose. The dogs were then fantastically painted with various colors, decorated with feathers, and suspended about twenty feet high at the council-house or near the centre of the camp. The ceremonial is then commenced, and the five, seven, or nine days of its continuance are marked by feasting and dancing, as well as by sacrifice and consultation. Two select bands, one of men and another of women, ornamented with trinkets and feathers, and each person furnished with an ear of corn in the right hand, dance in a circle around the council-fire, which is kindled for the occasion, and regulate their steps by rude music. Hence they proceed to every wigwam in the camp; and, in like manner, dance in a circle around each fire. Afterward, on another day, several men clothe themselves in the skins of wild beasts, cover their faces with hideous masks and their hands with the shell of the tortoise, and in this garb they go among the wigwams, making horrid noises, taking the fuel from the fire, and scattering the embers and ashes about the floor, for the purpose of driving away evil spirits. The persons performing these operations are supposed not only to drive off the evil spirit, but to concentrate within themselves all the sins of their tribe. These sins are afterward all transfused into one of their own number, who, by some magical dexterity or sleight-of-hand, works off from himself into the dogs the concentrated wickedness of the tribe! The scapegoat dogs are then placed on a pile of wood, to which fire is applied, while the surrounding crowd throw tobacco or other incense upon the flame, the scent of which is deemed to co-operate with the sacrifice of the animals in conciliating the favor of Nauwanew or the Great Spirit. When the dogs are partly consumed, one is taken off and put into a large kettle with vegetables of various kinds, and all around devour the contents of the 'reeking caldron.' After this the Indians perform the dances of war and peace, and smoke the calumet: then, free from wickedness, they repair to their respective places of abode, prepared for the events of the new year."

The following is a view of the middle or main falls, as seen from the east bank of the Genesee. The Rochester and Auburn railroad bridge is viewed a few rods north of the falls. The perpendicular fall of the water at this place is 96 feet; towards the right of the engraving is seen a small tabular projection from the general line of the

CENTRAL PART OF BUFFALO STREET, ROCHESTER, N. Y.

The view shows the central part of the city, near the junction of State and Exchange streets, with Buffalo street. The spire of the Court House is seen on the right; part of the Methodist church, and other public buildings, on the left.

Genesee Falls at Rochester.

verge of the precipice. From this projection, in the fall of 1829, Sam Patch took a last leap, and perished, not much unlike many others before him,

"seeking the bubble reputation, even in the cannon's mouth."

 The river below this fall is broad and deep, with occasional rapids for a mile and a half to the Lower Falls, the first 25, the other 84 feet, making a total descent of 109 feet in a few rods. Just below this place stood the celebrated *Carthage bridge*, remarkable in its fate as in its construction. It was completed in February, 1819; it consisted of an entire arch, the chord of which was 352 feet, and the versed sine 54 feet. Its entire length was 718 feet, and the width 30; the summit of the arch was 196 feet from the water. "The most lofty single arch at present in Europe, is 116 feet less in length than this was, and the arch not as high by 96 feet." This daring work stood but one year, and *one day;* which latter period saved the builders from loss, as they guarantied that the structure should endure for *one year*. It contained about 70,000 feet of timber, running measure, besides 64,620 feet of board measure. "The immense weight of timber pressing unequally upon the arch, threw up the centre from its equilibrium, and the whole tumbled into ruins." A port of entry was established at what is now known as the harbor of Rochester, in 1805; when Samuel Latta, residing at the junction of the river and lake, was appointed the first collector. The Rochester or Genesee revenue district has a frontier of about 70 miles on Lake Ontario, extending westward from Sodus bay, Wayne county. The port of Rochester, at the Ontario steamboat landing, is situated at the north line of the city, about five miles from the lake. The largest vessels on the lake can ascend the river to this point. There are three railways for facilitating the business between the vessels and the warehouses on the upper banks, which are here about 160 feet high.

"A serious alarm, attended by some amusing consequences, occurred in May, 1814, when Sir James Yeo, with a fleet of thirteen vessels of various sizes, appeared off the mouth of the Genesee, threatening the destruction of the rude improvements in and around Rochester. Messengers were despatched to arouse the people in the surrounding country for defence against the threatened attack. There were then but thirty-three people in Rochester capable of bearing arms. This little band threw up a breastwork called Fort Bender, near the Deep Hollow, beside the Lower Falls, and hurried down to the junction of the Genesee and Lake Ontario, five miles north of the present city limits, where the enemy threatened to land; leaving behind them two old men, with some young lads, to remove the women and children into the woods, in case the British should attempt to land for the capture of the provisions and destruction of the bridge at Rochester, &c. Francis Brown and Elisha Ely acted as captains, and Isaac W. Stone as major of the Rochester forces, which were strengthened by the additions that could be made from this thinly-settled region. Though the equipments and discipline of these troops would not form a brilliant picture for a warlike eye, their very awkwardness in those points, coupled as it was with their sagacity and courage, accomplished more perhaps than could have been effected by a larger force of regular troops bedizenned with the trappings of military pomp. The militia thus hastily collected, were marched and countermarched, disappearing in the woods at one point and suddenly emerging elsewhere, so as to impress the enemy with the belief that the force collected for defence was far greater than it actually was. (The circumstances here related are substantially as mentioned to the writer by one who was then and is now a resident of Rochester.) An officer with a flag of truce was sent from the British fleet. A militia officer marched down, with ten of the most soldierlike men, to receive him on Lighthouse Point. These militiamen carried their guns as nearly upright as might be consistent with their plan of being ready for action by keeping hold of the triggers! The British officer was astonished: he 'looked unutterable things.' 'Sir,' said he, 'do you receive a flag of truce under arms, with cocked triggers?' 'Excuse me, excuse me, sir; we backwoodsmen are not well versed in military tactics,' replied the American officer, who promptly sought to rectify his error by ordering his men to '*ground arms!*' The Briton was still more astonished; and, after delivering a brief message, immediately departed for the fleet, indicating by his countenance a suspicion that the ignorance of tactics which he had witnessed was all feigned for the occasion, so as to deceive the British commodore into a snare! Shortly afterward, on the same day, another officer came ashore with a flag of truce for further parley, as the British were evidently too suspicious of stratagem to attempt a hostile landing if there was any possibility of compromising for the spoils. Capt. Francis Brown was deputed with a guard to receive the last flag of truce. The British officer looked suspiciously upon him and upon his guard; and, after some conversation, familiarly grasped the pantaloons of Capt. B. about the knee, remarking, as he firmly handled it, 'Your cloth is too good to be spoiled by such a bungling tailor;' alluding to the width and clumsy aspect of that garment. Brown was quickwitted as well as resolute, and replied jocosely, that 'he was prevented from dressing fashionably by his haste that morning to salute such distinguished visiters!' The Briton obviously imagined that Brown was a regular officer of the American army, whose regimentals were masked by clumsy overclothes. The proposition was then made, that, if the Americans would deliver up the provisions and military stores which might be in and around Rochester or Charlotte, Sir James Yeo would spare the settlements from destruction. 'Will you comply with the offer?' '*Blood knee-deep first!*' was the emphatic reply of Francis Brown.

"While this parley was in progress, an American officer, with his staff, returning from the Niagara frontier, was accidentally seen passing from one wooded point to another; and this, with other circumstances, afforded to the British 'confirmation strong' that their suspicions were well founded; that there was a considerable American army collected; and that the Yankee officers shammed ignorance for the purpose of entrapping ashore the commodore and his forces! The return of the last flag to the fleet was followed by a vigorous attack in bombs and balls, while the compliment was spiritedly returned, not without some effect on at least one of the vessels, by a rusty old six-pounder, which had been furbished and mounted on a log for the important occasion. After a few hours spent in this unavailing manner, Admiral Yeo run down to Pulteneyville, about twenty miles eastward of Genesee river, where, on learning how they had been outwitted and deterred from landing by such a handful of militia, their mortification could scarcely restrain all hands from a hearty laugh at the 'Yankee trick.'"

Rush was taken from Avon in 1818; from Albany 229 miles. Pop. 1,929. Rush, 12 S., Sibley's Corners and Green's Corners, each 15 miles from Rochester, Hartwell's Corners and Davis' Corners, are small settlements.

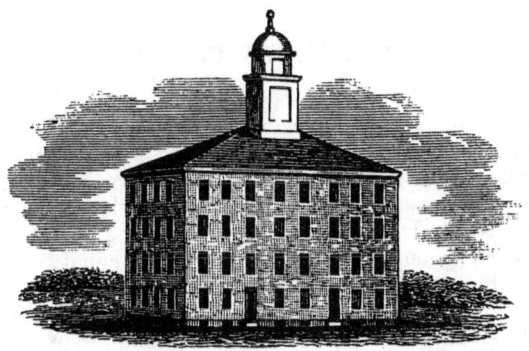

Collegiate building at Brockport.

SWEDEN, taken from Murray in 1813; from Albany 241 miles. Pop. 3,133. Brockport village was incorporated in 1829. It is situated on the Erie canal, 20 miles SE. from Rochester, and 239 from Albany. The village consists of about 300 dwellings, some of them three and four stories high, built of brick or freestone. The citizens have erected a noble stone building five stories high, for a collegiate institution, at an expense of $25,000, of which the above engraving is a representation. Large quantities of wheat have been purchased in this village for the Rochester mills; 451,000 bushels were bought here in 1835. The first buildings in the village were erected in 1820; the population is now upwards of 1,300.

WEBSTER, 14 miles NE. from Rochester, was recently taken from Penfield, of which it formed the northern part. The township is bounded on the north by Lake Ontario. Pop. 2,235.

WHEATLAND, originally named Inverness, and taken from Caledonia in 1821; from Albany 232 miles. Pop. 2,871. Scottsville, on Allens creek, 12 miles SW. from Rochester, near Genesee river, contains several churches, and upwards of 150 dwellings. The water-power here has been lately much improved by a canal one mile in length, taken from the creek to the Genesee river, by which a head of about 16 feet is obtained. Indian Allen, so called, was the first settler at the mouth of the creek which goes by his name. In the year 1800, Isaac Scott located himself where the village is now built. From this pioneer of the wilderness the village derives its name. There are within three miles of this place the remains of four ancient fortifications. Trees have grown on these mounds indicating a lapse of from four to five hundred years since they were constructed. Mumfordsville, also on Allens creek, 18 miles SW. from Rochester, is a small settlement. There is a small collection of dwellings in the vicinity of Wheatland post-office and at Garbetts mills.

MONTGOMERY COUNTY.

Montgomery county was named after the lamented Gen. Montgomery, who fell at the attack on Quebec, in the revolution. Its greatest length is 34 E. and W., greatest breadth N. and S. 13 miles. It was originally taken from Albany and named in honor of William Tryon, then governor of the province. Its name was changed in 1784. It embraced all that part of the state lying west of a line running north and south nearly through the centre of the present county of Schoharie. It was divided into five districts—subdivided into precincts. The Mohawk district included Fort Hunter, Caugnawaga, Johnstown, and Kingsboro'; Canajoharie district embraced the present town of that name, with all the country southward, comprehending Cherry Valley of Otsego, and Harpersfield of Delaware counties; Palatine district, north of the Mohawk, extended over the region so called, and Stone Arabia, &c.; German Flats district and Kingsland covered the most western settlements. The Erie canal crosses the county on the south side of the Mohawk, and the Schenectady and Utica railroad on the north side. The Erie canal passes the Schoharie creek through a pond formed by a dam across the stream below. Its fall within this county is 86 feet, by 12 locks. The county is divided into ten towns. Pop. 35,801.

Southern view of Sir Guy Johnson's house, Amsterdam.

Amsterdam, taken from Caugnawaga in 1793. It has a rolling surface and fertile soil. Pop. 5,329. Amsterdam village, incorporated in 1830, upon the Mohawk river and turnpike and Utica railroad, 16 miles W. of Schenectady, contains several churches, an academy, and about 700 inhabitants. The Erie canal is on the south side of the river, over which there is a commodious bridge.

The above shows the appearance of the mansion house of Colonel Guy Johnson, as seen from the opposite side of the river. It is built of stone, on the north bank of the Mohawk, about a mile from Amsterdam village. The western railroad now passes a few rods north, and in front. It is a beautiful situation, and was formerly called "Guy

[*Fac-simile of the signatures of the Johnsons, and of Colonel John Butler, and his son Walter.*]

Park." The house occupied by Sir John Johnson is further to the west, on the opposite side of the road. These men lived here essentially in the rank and splendor of noblemen, till their possessions were confiscated by the state for their adherence to the British cause. Sir John was not as popular as his father, Sir William Johnson, being less social and less acquainted with human nature. He accompanied his father on some of his military expeditions, and probably saw considerable service. After his flight from Johnstown to Canada, he in the month of January, 1777, found his way into New York, then in possession of the British troops. "From that period he became not only one of the most active, but one of the bitterest foes of his own countrymen of any who were engaged in the war, and repeatedly the scourge of his own former neighbors. He was unquestionably a loyalist from principle, else he would scarcely have hazarded, as he did, and ultimately lost, domains larger and fairer than probably ever belonged to a single proprietor in America, William Penn only excepted.

After the flight of Sir John from Johnson Hall, [*see Johnstown*] lady Johnson, his wife, was removed to Albany, where she was retained as a kind of hostage for the good conduct of her husband. "She wrote to Gen. Washington complaining of this detention, and asking his interference for her release; but the commander-in-chief left the matter with Gen. Schuyler and the Albany committee. After the confiscation of the property of Sir John, the furniture of the hall was sold at auction at Fort Hunter. The late lieutenant-governor of New York, John Taylor, purchased several articles of the furniture; and among other things, the bible mentioned in the text. Perceiving that it contained the family record, which might be of great value to Sir John, Mr. Taylor wrote a civil note to Sir John, offering its restoration. Some time afterward a messenger from the baronet called for the bible, whose conduct was so rude as to give offence. 'I have come for Sir William's bible,' said he, 'and there are four guineas which it cost.' The bible was delivered, and the runner was asked what message Sir John had sent. The reply was, 'Pay four guineas and take the book!'"—*Stone's Life of Brant.*

"About a mile and a half above the village of Amsterdam under a jutting rock, on the north side of the Mohawk river, are still to be seen the remains of an Indian painting. It was the custom of the Mohawks, and doubtless of all the different tribes of the Iroquois, when they contemplated a military expedition, to make a representation thereof, by painting on trees or rocks the figures of the warriors, with hieroglyphics designating the design of the expedition. When they went by water, canoes were painted, and as many figures placed in them as there were men constituting the party—their faces looking towards the place whither they were bound. The painting in question was executed to commemorate an expedition undertaken by a party of Mohawks, against the French Indians, about the year 1720. We know five or six individuals, who saw the painting fifty years ago, when the outlines were very distinctly to be seen. It was done with red chalk, and represented five or six canoes, with six or seven men in each."—*Schenectady Reflector,* Oct. 9*th,* 1835.

Eastern view of Canajoharie.

CANAJOHARIE* was organized in 1788. The surface of the township is considerably uneven, but the hills are generally arable and have a strong soil. The early inhabitants were Germans. Pop. 5,150. The village of Canajoharie was incorporated in 1829. It is situated at the confluence of Bowman's creek with the Mohawk, and on the Erie canal, 55 miles from Albany. It consists of about 100 houses, a Lutheran church, and an academy. The Radii, a newspaper, edited and printed by Mr. L. S. Backus, a deaf and dumb person, is published in this place. "The Canajoharie and Palatine manufacturing company" was incorporated in 1833. The accompanying engraving shows the appearance of the village as viewed from the elevated bank of the Mohawk, a few rods from the bridge seen passing

---

"* This name is of Indian origin; and Cana-jo-harie, as spoken by the Mohawks, signifies the pot or kettle that washes itself. This name was given by the Mohawk Indians to a deep hole of foaming water, at the foot of one of the falls of Canajoharie creek; from which it became the common name of that stream, and an extensive tract of country around it."—*Spafford's Gazetteer.*

over the river, connecting the village of Palatine Bridge with Canajoharie. Central Canajoharie, Ames, and Freysbush, are post-offices in this town.

In the spring of 1780, the Indians again made their appearance in the Mohawk valley. Gen. Clinton hearing of their movements, sent orders to Col. Gansevoort on the 6th of June, to repair to Fort Plank with his regiment, to take charge of a quantity of stores destined for Fort Schuyler. These stores were to be transported in batteaux, and carefully guarded the whole distance. Joseph Brant, the celebrated chieftain, at the head of four or five hundred Indians, was in the vicinity, and he artfully caused a rumor to be circulated that he intended to capture the batteaux, in order to divert attention from other points of attack. This artifice proved too successful; the militia of the lower section of the county were drawn off to guard the convoy. Brant now made a circuit through the woods, and coming in the rear of them, laid waste the whole country around Canajoharie. On the first approach of Brant in Canajoharie a few miles eastwardly of the fort, the alarm was given by a woman, who fired a cannon for that purpose. The following account of this incursion is given by Col. Samuel Clyde, in a letter to Gov. George Clinton, dated at Canajoharie, Aug. 6, 1780:—

"I here send you an account of the fate of our district. On the second day of this instant, Joseph Brant, at the head of about four or five hundred Indians and tories, broke in upon the settlements, and laid the best part of the district in ashes, and killed sixteen of the inhabitants that we have found; took between fifty and sixty prisoners, mostly women and children, twelve of whom they have sent back. They have killed and drove away with them upwards of three hundred head of cattle and horses; have burnt fifty-three dwelling-houses, besides some out-houses, and as many barns, one very elegant church, and one grist-mill, and two small forts that the women fled out of. They have burnt all the inhabitants' weapons and implements for husbandry, so that they are left in a miserable condition. They have nothing left to support themselves but what grain they have growing, and that they cannot get saved for want of tools to work with, and very few to be got here.

"This affair happened at a very unfortunate hour, when all the militia of the county were called up to Fort Schuyler to guard nine batteaux about half laden. It was said the enemy intended to take them on their passing to Fort Schuyler. There was scarce a man left that was able to go. It seems that every thing conspired for our destruction in this quarter; one whole district almost destroyed, and the best regiment of militia in the county rendered unable to help themselves or the public. This I refer you to Gen. Rensselaer for the truth of.

"This spring, when we found that we were not likely to get any assistance, and knew that we were not able to withstand the enemy, we were obliged to work and build ourselves forts for our defence, which we had nearly completed, and could have had our lives and effects secure, had we got liberty to have made use of them. But that must not be, we must turn out of them; not that we have any thing against assisting the general to open the communication to Fort Schuyler, but still doubted what has happened while we were gone. But it was still insisted on, that there was no danger when we were all out; that in my opinion there never has been such a blunder committed in the county since the war commenced, nor the militia so much put out; and to send generals here without men, is like sending a man to the woods to chop without an axe. I am sensible had the general had sufficient men, that he would have been able to have given satisfaction both to the public and inhabitants here."

The parents of Joseph Brant, the celebrated Mohawk chieftain, resided at the Canajoharie castle, the central of the three castles of the Mohawks, in their native valley. He appears to have been born in the year 1742, on the banks of the Ohio, while his parents

Fac-simile of Brant's signature.

were on a hunting excursion in that part of the country.* "In July, 1761, he was sent, by Sir William Johnson, to the 'Moor's Charity school,' at Lebanon, Connecticut, established by the Rev. Dr. Wheelock, which was afterward removed to Dartmouth, and became the foundation of Dartmouth College. The following mention of him is made in the memoirs of that gentleman:—

"Sir William Johnson, superintendent of Indian Affairs in North America, was very friendly to the design of Mr. Wheelock, and, at his request, sent to the school, at various times, several boys of the Mohawks to be instructed. One of them was the since celebrated Joseph Brant; who, after receiving his education, was particularly noticed by Sir William Johnson, and employed by him in public business. He has been very useful in advancing the civilization of his countrymen, and for a long time past has been a military officer of extensive influence among the Indians in Upper Canada."

In confirmation of these statements it may be added, that he translated into the Mohawk language the gospel of St. Mark, and assisted the Rev. Mr. Stewart, the episcopal missionary, in translating a number of religious works into the Indian tongue. Brant being a neighbor, and under the influence of the Johnson family, he took up arms against the Americans in the revolutionary contest. "Combining the natural sagacity of the Indian, with the skill and science of the civilized man, he was a formidable foe. He was a dreadful terror to the frontiers. His passions were strong. In his intercourse he was affable and polite, and communicated freely relative to his conduct. He often said that during the war he had killed but one man in cold blood, and that act he ever after regretted. He said, he had taken a man prisoner, and was examining him; the prisoner hesitated, and as he thought equivocated. Enraged at what he considered obstinacy, he struck him down. It turned out that the man's apparent obstinacy arose from a natural hesitancy of speech.

"In person, Brant was about the middling size, of a square, stout build, fitted rather for enduring hardships than for quick movements. His complexion was lighter than that of most of the Indians, which resulted, perhaps, from his less exposed manner of living. This circumstance, probably, gave rise to a statement, which has been often repeated, that he was of mixed origin. He was married in the winter of 1779 to a daughter of Col. Croghan by an Indian woman. The circumstances of his marriage are somewhat singular. He was

---

* The Indian name of Brant was *Thayendanegea*, a word signifying, it is said, *two-sticks-of-wood-bound-together*, denoting strength. The life of Brant, in two octavo volumes, has been recently written by William L. Stone, Esq., editor of the Commercial Advertiser, New York. This valuable and highly interesting work is one of great research, and embraces a full history of the border wars of the revolution, and much other matter connected with Indian history.

present at the wedding of Miss Moore from Cherry Valley, who had been carried away a prisoner, and who married an officer of the garrison at Fort Niagara.

Brant had lived with his wife for some time previous, according to the Indian custom, without marriage; but now insisted that the marriage ceremony should be performed. This was accordingly done by Col. Butler, who was still considered a magistrate. After the war he removed, with his nation, to Canada. There he was employed in transacting important business for his tribe. He went out to England after the war, and was honorably received there. He died about ten or fifteen years since, at Brantford, Haldiman county, Upper Canada, where his family now reside. One of his sons, a very intelligent man, has been returned to the Colonial Assembly."

The following is an account of the taking of the three Mohawk castles, which were situated in this vicinity, by the French and Indians, in the early settlement of the country. It is drawn from Colden's History of the Six Nations.

In January, 1692-3, a large body of French and Indians, amounting to six or seven hundred, started on an expedition from Canada, for the purpose of punishing the Five Nations, who had the previous summer carried the war into Canada, and in small parties had ravaged the whole country. Count de Frontenac chose the winter season for this incursion, when the enemy could not, without great hardship, keep scouts abroad to discover them, or their allies, the English, give assistance.

On the 15th of January, they set out from *la Prairie de Magdaleine*, and endured innumerable hardships. The ground was at that time covered with a deep snow, and the foremost, marching on snowshoes, beat a track for those which followed. At night the army was accustomed to divide itself into small groups, and each party to dig a hole in the snow, throwing up the snow all around, but highest towards that side from whence the wind blew. The ground was then covered with the small branches of fir-trees, and each man wrapped in his cloak with his feet pointed towards a fire in the centre, would thus pass the night.

They passed by Schenectady on the 8th of February. The two first forts of the Mohawks being in the neighborhood of the English settlements, were not fortified, and were therefore easily taken. At the last Mohawk fort, which was strongly garrisoned, they met with considerable resistance, and the French lost thirty men before the Indians submitted. The Indians at Schenectady having obtained information of the capture of their castles, sent to Albany for assistance to pursue the enemy. Col. Peter Schuyler, with a body of militia, regulars, and Indians, pursued the enemy on their retreat, and had a severe skirmish with them. On the 20th, Col. Schuyler was obliged to give up the pursuit, the weather being very cold and provisions scarce. Schuyler lost only 8 men killed and 14 wounded. The French lost 59 men in killed and wounded, besides several by desertion. Schuyler's Indians ate the bodies of the French whom they found. The colonel was invited to partake of broth with them: he ate quite hearty until, putting the ladle into the kettle to draw out more, he brought up a Frenchman's hand, which put an end to his appetite.

The French arrived at their settlements in a state of starvation, having been obliged to eat their shoes on their march.

CHARLESTON, organized in 1788, by the name of Mohawk; part erected into a separate town, and the residue called Charleston, in 1793; from Fonda S. 8 miles, from Albany 40. Charleston, Charleston Four Corners, and Bensonville, are post-offices. Pop. 2,103.

FLORIDA, taken from Mohawk in 1793; from Albany 35 miles. Pop. 5,162. The town was settled by some Dutch families from Schenectady, who in 1750 were joined by some Germans, subsequently by Irish and Dutch, and lastly by New Englanders. Fort Hunter, 5 miles SE. of Fonda, is a small settlement. Port Jackson, on the Erie canal, is a flourishing village. Minaville, 4 miles S. of the canal, is a village of about 40 dwellings. Fort Hunter, which formerly stood on the line of the canal in this town, was a place of some importance in colonial history. At this place also stood *Queen Anne's Chapel*, a stone structure, built by Queen Anne of England for the use of the Mohawk Indians. The English Episcopal missions to the Mohawks appear to have been commenced as early as 1702, and continued down to the beginning of the revolutionary war.

GLEN, taken from Charleston in 1823; from Albany 43 miles. Pop. 3,697. This town was originally settled by the Dutch. Fultonville, on the canal, 1 mile S. from Fonda, 57 from Albany, and 53 from Utica, has about 50 dwellings, and a Dutch Reformed church. Auriesville or Smithtown, on the canal, 3 miles E. of Fultonville, and Voorheesville, are small settlements.

"Somewhere between this [Schoharie] creek and Caughnawaga, commenced an Indian road or foot-path, which led to Schoharie. Near this road, and within the northern bounds of Schoharie county, has been seen from time immemorial a large pile of stones, which has given the name 'stone heap patent' to the tract on which it occurs, as may be seen from ancient deeds. Indian tradition saith that a Mohawk murdered a brother (or two of them) on this spot, and that this tumulus was erected to commemorate the event. A similar practice is supposed to have been in vogue among the Hebrews; in Scotland and in Wales, many heaps of stones, called ' cairns,' are to be found, probably constructed for a similar purpose. May not the bones of this Indian Abel be found here sepulchred? Every individual passing this way made an offering to propitiate the manes of the deceased, or the Minetto of the place; which was performed by the act of adding another stone to the pile; and a person was but a few years since living, who had witnessed this ceremony. It was confidently believed by the Indians that those who neglected to do it would meet with some misfortune. . . . . . In the early settlement of the province, *Benoni Van Corlear*, a great favorite and friend of the Indians, on a certain occasion, passed this stone heap in company with a party of Mohawks on their way to Canada. They all cast a stone upon the pile except Van Corlear, who refused, alleging that it would be folly for him to comply with an idle superstition. His Indian companions considered the matter in a more serious light, and expressed great alarm lest some mishap might befall him or the party. These presages were not unreal, for by one of those coincidences which the Almighty sometimes permits, Van Corlear lost his life before he arrived at the end of his journey. He was drowned in the lake now called Lake Champlain. The Indians in memory of this event called it Van Corlear's Lake, which name it retained for some time, until called by the Canadian Catholic priests 'Lac Sacrement,' for the reason they had selected, and used its waters for sacramental purposes."

MINDEN was taken from Canajoharie in 1798. The town was settled at an early period by Germans, who suffered severely from the incursions of the Indians and tories during the revolutionary war. The surface of the township is agreeably diversified by gentle hills and fertile valleys on Mohawk river and Otsquake creek. Pop. 3,507. The village of Fort Plain is situated on the Mohawk river and Erie canal, 15 miles from Fonda, 12 miles from Cherry Valley, 22 from Cooperstown, and 60 from Albany: it consists of about 80 houses, 2 churches—1 Presbyterian, 1 Universalist—a printing office, and a number of mills.

Ancient Blockhouse, Fort Plain.

The above is said to be a correct representation of Fort Plain, from which the village derives its name.

"The fort was situated on the brow of the hill, about half a mile northwest of the village, so as to command a full view of the valley, and the rise of the ground, for several miles in any direction; and hence it doubtless derived its name, because its beautiful location commanded a '*plain*' view of the surrounding country. It was erected by the government, as a fortress, and place of retreat and safety for the inhabitants and families in case of incursions from the Indians, who were then, and, indeed, more or less during the whole revolutionary war, infesting the settlements of this whole region. Its form was an octagon, having port-holes for heavy ordnance and muskets on every side. It contained three stories or apartments. The first story was thirty feet in diameter; the second, forty feet; the third, fifty feet; the last two stories projecting five feet, as represented by the drawing aforesaid. It was constructed throughout of hewn timber about fifteen inches square; and, besides the port-holes aforesaid, the second and third stories had perpendicular port-holes through those parts that projected, so as to afford the regulars and militia, or settlers garrisoned in the fort, annoying facilities of defence for themselves, wives, and children, in case of close assault from the relentless savage. Whenever scouts came in with tidings that a hostile party was approaching, a cannon was fired from the fort as a signal to flee to it for safety.

"In the early part of the war there was built, by the inhabitants probably, at or near the site of the one above described, a fortification, of materials and construction that ill comported with the use and purposes for which it was intended. This induced government to erect another, (Fort Plain,) under the superintendence of an experienced French engineer. As a piece of architecture, it was well wrought and neatly finished, and surpassed all the forts in that region. After the termination of the revolutionary war, Fort Plain was used for some years as a deposit of military stores, under the direction of Captain B. Hudson. These stores were finally ordered by the United States government to be removed to Albany. The fort is demolished. Nothing of it remains except a circumvallation or trench, which, although nearly obliterated by the plough, still indicates to the curious traveller sufficient evidence of a fortification in days by-gone."—*Fort Plain Journal, Dec.* 26, 1837.

Hendrick, a celebrated Indian chieftain, lived in this town. He is sometimes called old King Hendrick, and the great Hendrick.

"'The site of his house,' says Dr. Dwight, 'is a handsome elevation, commanding a considerable prospect of the neighboring country. It will be sufficient to observe here, that for capacity, bravery, vigor of mind, and immoveable integrity united, he excelled all the aboriginal inhabitants of the United States of whom any knowledge has come down to the present time. A gentleman of very respectable character, who was present at a council held with the Six Nations, by the governor of New York, and several agents of distinction from New England, informed me that his figure and countenance were singularly impressive and commanding; that his eloquence was of the same superior character, and that he appeared as if born to control other men, and possessed an air of majesty unrivalled within his knowledge.' In the French wars he led forth his Mohawk warriors and fought side by side with Sir William Johnson. Through all the intrigues of the French he remained faithful to his alliance. He was also highly esteemed by the white inhabitants. During some of the negotiations with the Indians of Pennsylvania and the inhabitants of that state, Hendrick was present at Philadelphia. His likeness was taken, and a wax figure afterward made which was a very good imitation. After the death of Hendrick, an old friend, a white man, visited Philadelphia, and among other things was shown this wax figure. It occupied a niche, and was not observed by him until he had approached within a few feet. The friendship of former days came fresh over his memory, and forgetting for the moment Hendrick's death, he rushed forward and clasped in his arms the frail, icy image of the chieftain."

MOHAWK, the ancient Caughnawaga, recently organized, was formerly the southern section of the town of Johnstown, from which it was taken in 1837. Pop. 3,106. Since the formation of the new county of Fulton, the seat of justice for Montgomery county has been

East view of the Courthouse and Hotel in Fonda.

located in this town. The above is an engraving of the courthouse and hotel recently erected in the new village of Fonda. The railroad passes between these two buildings. The central part of the village of Caughnawaga is about half a mile eastward of the courthouse, and consists of about 30 dwelling-houses, on the north side of the Mohawk, 40 miles from Albany, and 4 miles S. from Johnstown. The village occupies the site of an ancient Indian village, one of the principal towns of the Mohawk tribe. Its name, Caughnawaga, is said to signify " *a coffin,*" which it received from the circumstance of there being, in the river opposite the place, a large black stone, (still to be seen,) resembling a coffin, and projecting above the surface at low water.

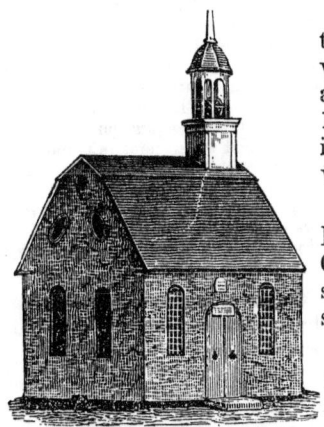

Ancient Church, Mohawk.

The annexed is a representation of the ancient Dutch church in Caughnawaga. It is a massive stone structure, and is believed to have been erected in 1763. The following is a copy of the inscription on the stone tablet which was formerly placed over the door.

"Komt laett ons op gaen tot den Bergh des Heeren, to den huyse des Godes Jacobs, op dat hy ons leere van syne wegen, en dat wy wandele in syne paden."

[" Come ye, and let us go up to the mountain of the Lord; to the house of the God of Jacob, and he will teach us his ways, and we will walk in his paths."]

The following, relating to the history of this town, is taken from a newspaper published in Schenectady a few years since.

"The Caughnawaga flats extend from the western base of Tripe's Hill to the Cayadutta creek, a distance of four miles. A patent for 2,500 acres of these flats, was granted in the year 1713, to John, Edward, and Margaret Collins. These individuals aliened to Myndert Wemple, Douw Fonda, and Hendrick A. Vrooman; and many of their descendants are proprietors at the present day.

"Until 1695, there were no buildings on the site where Caughnawaga now stands, except a Dutch church edifice and a parsonage. This church was founded in 1762, by the patronage of Sir William Johnson. Its principal benefactors were the Fonda, Vrooman, Wemple, and Veeder families. The church edifice is still standing, but in a dilapidated condition. Its first pastor was the Rev. Thomas Romeyn, who died in 1794. He was succeeded by the Rev. Abraham Van Horne, of New Jersey, who continued his pastoral duties until a few years since.

"Caughnawaga hardly deserved to be called a hamlet until 1795, when Messrs. Douw and Henry Fonda, of Albany, erected several buildings.

"This place suffered much during the revolution. At the western extremity of the flats, is a small hill called by the Dutch '*Teaburg*' or Teahill. It was a place of resort, during the time of the French war, by the Caughnawaga ladies during the absence of their husbands, to indulge in their delicious beverage of *tea*. It was considered a good place of retreat from danger, and from which the approach of the enemy might be seen. The Mohawk name of this elevation is '*Kaheka-nunda*,' or 'hill of berries;' probably because many berries are found there. The ancient Mohawks required their male papooses to run up and down this hill, and those who flagged under the exercise, were deemed unqualified to endure the fatigues of war.

"The first settlers of Tripe's Hill, were respectable yeomen. Nicholas Hanson's family emigrated thither about 1725, from Albany. His son Hendrick was the first white child born in the Mohawk valley west of Schenectady, on the north side of the river. About 1728, a New Englander by the name of Bowen, and a Mr. Putnam from Schenectady, took up their residence here. The descendants of the Hansons and Putnams are to found to this day in this region, and the creek on the eastern side of Tripe's Hill received its name from the circumstance of the Putnam family owning the land through which it passes.

"About the time the colonies declared their independence, the Bowen, with several other families, took part with the mother country and moved to Canada. They were induced to take this course in consequence of their attachment to Sir William Johnson, who, whatever his faults might have been, possessed much warm-heartedness and benevolence.

Had he lived during the revolutionary contest, it is generally believed he would have done much towards restraining the ferocity of the bloodthirsty tories and their savage allies, whose murderous attacks on the defenceless inhabitants of 'the valley,' are so famous in tradition. But the mantle of Sir William did not descend on his son Sir John Johnson. The latter with a party of tories, most of whom had formerly resided at Tripe's Hill, and among whom Henry and William Bowen held conspicuous stations, made an arrangement for a descent on this settlement. The most zealous whig at the 'Hill' was Garret Putnam, captain of a company of rangers. He had rendered himself particularly obnoxious to the British in consequence of the fearless and zealous stand which he had taken against them. On the 18th of May, 1780, he received orders to repair to Fort Hunter; which he did, taking his family along with him. He leased his house to William Gort and James Plateau, two Englishmen, who, although tories, took no active part and were therefore unmolested by the whigs. About midnight on the 20th of May, Sir John's party reached the 'Hill,' and stealthily entering Mr. Putnam's house, instantly killed and scalped its inmates. The hapless victims had not an opportunity to reveal themselves. The enemy supposed they had the scalps of Captain Putnam and his son, and were not undeceived until the morning light revealed to them the corpses of their two brother tories, Gort and Plateau. The same night Henry Hanson, a zealous whig, was also murdered."

Butler's House, Mohawk.

The annexed is a representation of the house of Col. Butler the loyalist, and is probably the oldest dwelling in the town; it is now owned and occupied by Mr. Wilson. It is situated on a commanding eminence about one mile in a NE. direction from the courthouse, in Fonda, overlooking the beautiful Mohawk valley at this place. At the breaking out of the revolutionary war, John Butler was lieutenant-colonel of a regiment of the Tryon county militia, of which Guy Johnson was the colonel, and Jelles Fonda the major. Sir John Johnson had been commissioned a general after the decease of his father. "Colonel John Butler," says Mr. Tryon, in his Annals, "had some good traits of character, and in his calmer moments would regret the ravages committed by the Indians and tories; but Walter Butler was distinguished from youth for his severe acrimonious disposition. After the massacre at Cherry Valley he went to Quebec; but Gen. Haldiman, governor of Canada, gave out that he did not wish to see him."

PALATINE, organized in 1782; from Fonda, W., 14 miles. This town was first settled by the Dutch, in 1724, and though constantly under cultivation, ever since that time its choice lands can hardly be said to have lost any of their original fertility! Palatine is 13 miles W. of Johnstown, on the river, turnpike, and Utica railroad. *Palatine Bridge* is also on the river, turnpike, and railroad, immediately opposite Canajoharie village, with which it is connected by a bridge. (See view of Canajoharie.) Stone Arabia is 3 miles N. from Canajoharie. The above are all small villages. Pop. 2,845. During the revolutionary war there was a small stockade erected in this town, at Stone Arabia, called Fort Paris. When Sir John Johnson was ravaging the valley of the Mohawk, in 1780, this fort was in command of Col. Brown, with a garrison of one hundred and thirty men. Gen. Van Rensselaer, who was pursuing Sir John up the valley, having received information that he intended to attack Fort Paris on the

19th of Oct., despatched orders to Col. Brown to march out and check his advance, while he fell upon his rear. Col. Brown accordingly sallied forth, and gave Sir John battle near the site of a former work, called Fort Keyser. Van Rensselaer having failed to advance at the appointed time, Brown's force was too feeble to check the progress of the enemy. Col. Brown fell gallantly at the head of his little division, of which from forty to forty-five were also slain, and the remainder sought safety in flight.*

Root, taken from Canajoharie and Charleston in 1823; from Albany 51 miles. *Sprackers Basin*, on the canal, 9 miles W. of Fonda, and Currytown, are small villages. "In the rocky cliffs of the *Nose*, near the river, is a remarkable cavern known as Mitchell's Cave. Fourteen apartments, some it is said at the depth of 500 feet, have been visited. The ceilings are ornamented with stalactites, the walls with incrustations, and the floors with stalagmites. On the Plattekill, a mile from the river, there is a waterfall of about 80 feet in 10 rods, with a perpendicular pitch of 50 feet." Pop. 2,000.

St. Johnsville, recently taken from Oppenheim of Fulton county. The township is small in its territorial limits, being a narrow strip of land on the north bank of the Mohawk. Pop. 1,923. The village of St. Johnsville is about 20 miles from Fonda, and 77 from Albany.

In the fall of 1780, when Sir John Johnson ravaged the Mohawk valley, he made a stand near the western line of this town, when pursued by Gen. Van Rensselaer. This was at Fox's mills, about eight miles above Fort Plank, (or as it is now called, Fort Plain,) and two miles below the upper Mohawk castle.

"On the north side and on a flat, partly surrounded by a bend of the river, he posted his regiment of regulars and tories. A small breastwork was thrown across the neck of land. The Indians occupied a tract of elevated land to the north, and in the immediate vicinity, which was covered with a thick growth of shrub oak. In

---

* Colonel Brown was a brave soldier of high moral worth. He was early in the service, and was engaged in the disastrous campaign in Canada. Col. Stone, in his Life of Brant, states that Col. Brown detected, or believed he detected, a design on the part of Gen. Arnold to play the traitor when the American army was at Sorel, by an attempt to run off with the American flotilla and sell out to Sir Guy Carleton. During the winter of 1776-7, while Arnold and many other officers were quartered in Albany, a difficulty arose between him and Col. Brown. The latter published a handbill severely reflecting on Arnold, and concluded with these remarkable words—"*Money is this man's God, and to get enough of it he would sacrifice his country.*" This publication produced quite a sensation among the officers. Arnold was greatly excited; he applied a variety of course and harsh epithets to Col. Brown, calling him a scoundrel, and threatened to kick him wherever he should meet him. This coming to the ears of the latter, he proceeded to the dining place of Arnold, where a company of officers were assembled; going directly up to Arnold he stopped, and looked him in the eye. After a pause of a moment, he observed: "*I understand, sir, that you have said you would kick me: I now present myself to give you an opportunity to put your threat into execution!*" Another brief pause ensued. Arnold opened not his lips. Brown then said to him—"*Sir, you are a dirty scoundrel!*" Arnold still remained silent. Col. Brown, after apologizing to the gentlemen present for his intrusion, left the room. Arnold appears to have kept an unbroken silence on this occasion, which can only be accounted for on the supposition that he feared to provoke inquiry on the charges of Col. Brown. A monument to the memory of Col. Brown has recently been erected by his son, at Stone Arabia.

this position Sir John awaited the approach of Gen. Van Rensselaer, who was joined by the Canajoharie militia and the tories from Fort Plain under Col. Du Bois. After a slight skirmish, the Indians were driven from their position, and fled up the river to the fording place, near the castle, where they crossed, and directed their course towards the Susquehannah. Sir John's troops made a more effective resistance, though they were almost exhausted by the forced marches which they had made and the labors they had performed. The attack had been commenced late in the day. Though it was conducted with considerable spirit, night came on before the works of Sir John were carried. In this situation Gen. Van Rensselaer ordered his troops to fall back a mile and encamp. Many of the militia were enraged on account of this order, and refused to obey it. They remained during most of the night, and took several prisoners, who informed them that the enemy were on the point of offering to capitulate, when Gen. Van Rensselaer ordered his troops to fall back. A detachment of the Canajoharie militia under Col. Clyde took one of their field-pieces during the night.

"On the following morning, when Gen. Van Rensselaer advanced with his troops, the enemy had entirely disappeared. They had left their ground, and retreated up the river a short distance, and then crossed to the south. The river was deep and rapid where it formed the bend, which would have ensured Gen. Van Rensselaer a complete victory had he prosecuted his attack with more vigor. A detachment was sent in pursuit, who discovered in the trail of the enemy evidence of the extreme state to which they were reduced by hunger and fatigue. The whole country on the north side of the river, from Caughnawaga to Stone Arabia and Palatine, had been devastated—which, with the ravages of Brant on the south side of the river, in the previous August, almost completed the destruction of the Mohawk settlements.

"If here and there a little settlement escaped their ravages, each were like an oasis in the desert, affording temporary shelter and protection, and, like them, liable to be destroyed or buried up by the next whirlwind which should sweep over the land."

NEW YORK COUNTY.

THE county and city of New York are of the same extent, comprising the whole of New York, or Manhattan Island, about $14\frac{1}{2}$ miles long, varying from half a mile to two miles in width; area $21\frac{3}{4}$ square miles, or 13,920 acres. It is bounded on the north and east by Haerlem and East rivers, south and west by the Hudson, or by New York bay and the state of New Jersey. The legal subdivisions of the county and city are the wards, 17 in number, of various extent, ac-

S.W. VIEW OF NEW YORK FROM BEDLOW'S I.

Ellis Island, with Hudson River beyond, as seen on the left. Governors Island and East River on the right. New York with the river of shipping on the East River (Castle Garden and Battery in front) appears in the distance, in the central part of the engraving.

cording to local convenience. Agreeable to the charter of New York its jurisdiction extends to the lands under the adjoining waters as far as to low-water mark on the opposite sides. The compact part of the city is at the southern part of the island, and covers about one sixth part of its surface. Its latitude and longitude, reckoned from the City Hall, were determined in 1817, by order of the corporation, as follows: N. lat. 40° 42' 43''; W. long. from Greenwich, England, 73° 59' 46'', and E. long. from the city of Washington 3° 1' 13''.

A table of the population of the city of New York, of the state of New York, and of the United States, at various periods.

Years.	City.	State.	United States.
1656	1,000		
1697	4,302		
1731	8,622	49,819	
1750	10,000	100,000	1,000,000
1774	22,750	250,000	3,000,000
1800	60,489	586,000	5,309,750
1810	96,373	959,220	7,238,903
1820	123,706	1,372,812	9,638,226
1830	202,589	1,918,608	12,852,858
1835	270,089	2,174,517	
1840	312,932	2,429,481	17,068,112

The relative proportion of the population of the *city* to that of the whole *state*, has generally been from *one-eight* to *one-tenth;* and the *state of New York* has borne the same relative proportion also to the whole United States.

"The number of buildings in the compact part of the city of New York is 32,116; of which there are used as breweries, distilleries, tanneries, and the like 46; as dwelling houses exclusively, 16,458; as dwellings with shops 6,614; as stores and offices exclusively 3,855; as taverns and private boarding-houses 736; as baths 9; as factories, with engines equal to 1100 horse power, 74; as large factories, with labor-saving power, 172; as private stables 2,603; as livery stables 137; as dairy stables 57; miscellaneous 1,355.

"The valuation of real estate in the city, as corrected by the board of supervisors in 1840, is $187,222,714; and of personal estate $65,013,801. Aggregate $252,235,515.

"From 1810 to 1841, the corporation has expended for opening, widening, and improving streets, &c., $6,275,317.

"The total amount derived from the city, by the state, from auction duties, from 1816 to 1840 inclusive, is $4,249,527.

"The receipts into the general Treasury during the year 1840, from the ordinary revenues of the city, from the negotiation of its stocks, and from the management of its 'trust accounts,' including the cash on hand at the commencement of the year, amounted to $6,004,610 12.

"The amount of warrants drawn upon the Treasurer, for the ordinary expenses of the city government, the payment of its pre-existing debts, for its disbursements on the public works, and on its 'trust accounts,' including the warrants outstanding at the commencement of the year, amounted to $6,007,260 54; from which is to be deducted the warrants outstanding and unclaimed at the close of the year, amounting to $176,829 50. The result showing the actual amount paid by the Treasurer, during the year to be $5,830,431 04; and the cash balance in the treasury January 1st, 1841, to be $174,179 08."

Population of the several Wards in New York.

1st ward	10,629	10th ward	29,093
2d ward	6,408	11th ward	17,052
3d ward	11,581	12th ward	11,678
4th ward	15,770	13th ward	18,516
5th ward	19,159	14th ward	20,230
6th ward	17,199	15th ward	17,769
7th ward	22,985	16th ward	22,275
8th ward	29,173	17th ward	18,622
9th ward	24,795		

The bay of New York spreads to the southward, and is about 8 miles long, and from 1½ to 5½ broad. It is one of the finest harbors in the world, generally open for vessels at all seasons of the year, but is, at rare intervals, obstructed for a few days in very severe winters by ice. The currents in the bay are rapid and strong, circumstances that are of great importance in keeping the port of New York open, while others further to the south are obstructed by frost. The usual tides at New York are about six feet, and the depth of water sufficient for the largest ships. The bay contains Governor's, Bedlow's, and Ellis' islands, upon which are strong fortifications guarding the approach to the city. There are also fortifications on Long and Staten islands, commanding the narrows.

Stadt Huys, built 1642—*razed* 1700.

New York derives its origin from the colonizing and commercial spirit of the Hollanders, and the general spirit of adventure which prevailed among the maritime nations of Europe after the discovery of the western continent by Columbus. The Dutch immediately after the discovery of Hudson in 1609, began to avail themselves of the advantages which his discoveries presented to their view. In 1614 or 1615, a kind of fort and trading-house was erected on the southwest point of Manhattan or New York Island, which was named New Amsterdam. In 1614, an expedition from South Virginia, under Capt. Argal, was sent out by Sir Thomas Dale, and took possession of New Amsterdam. At that time there were only *four houses* outside of the fort. But an arrangement was soon after made with the English government, by which the Dutch remained in possession of Manhattan Island, and of the trade of the neighboring country for fifty years.

The above is a representation of the ancient "*Stadt Huys*," or City Hall, which was built early in the Dutch dynasty, in 1642. It was built of stone at the head of Coenties slip, facing Pearl-street. About the year 1700, it became so weakened and impaired, that it was sold, and a new one erected by the head of Broad-street, which was afterward the Congress Hall, on the corner of Wall-street.

The city was laid out in streets, some of them crooked enough, in 1656. It then contained by enumeration ' 120 houses, with extensive garden lots,' and 1000 inhabitants. In 1677 another estimate of the city was made, and ascertained to contain 368 houses. In the year 1674, an assessment of ' the most wealthy inhabitants' having been made, it was found that the sum total of 134 estates amounted to £95,000.

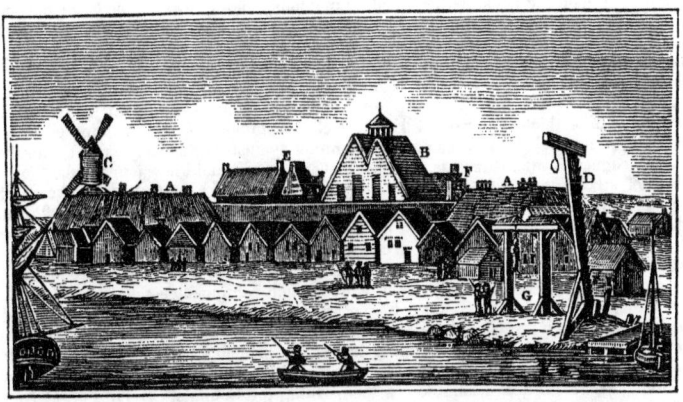

Nieuw Amsterdam, in 1659.

[A, the fort. B, the church. C, the wind-mill. D, the flag, which is hoisted when vessels arrive in port. E, the prison. F, the house of the general. G, the place of execution. H, the place of expose or pillory.]

During the military rule of Governor Colve, who held the city for one year for the states of Holland, after its re-capture from the British, every thing partook of a military character, and the laws still in preservation at Albany show the energy of a rigorous discipline. Then the Dutch mayor, at the head of the city militia, held his daily parades before the City Hall, (Stadt Huys,) then at Coenties slip; and every evening at sunset, he received from the principal guard of the fort, called the *hoofd-wagt*, the keys of the city, and thereupon proceeded with a guard of six to lock the city gates; then to place a *Burger-wagt*—a citizen-guard—as night-watches at assigned places. The same mayors also went the rounds at sunrise to open the gates, and to restore the keys to the officer of the fort. All this was surely a toilsome service for the domestic habits of the peaceful citizens of that day, and must have presented an irksome honor to any mayor who loved his comfort and repose.

" It may amuse some of the present generation, so little used to Dutch names, to learn some of the titles once so familiar in New York, and now so little understood. Such as— *De Heer Officier,* or *Hoofd-Schout*—High-Sheriff. *De Fiscaal,* or *Procureur Gen.*—Attorney General. *Wees-Meesters*—Guardians of orphans. *Roy-Meesters*—Regulators of fences. *Groot Burgerrecht and Klein Burgerrecht*—The great and small citizenship, which then marked the two orders of society. *Eyck-Meester*—The Weigh Master. *The Schout,* (the Sheriff.) *Bourgomasters and Schepens* then ruled the city ' as in all cities of the Fatherland.' *Geheim Schryver*—Recorder of secrets."—*Watson's Olden Times, New York.*

The preceding cut shows the principal buildings standing on the present site of the city of New York in 1659. The following description of New York at about that period, is copied from "*Ogilby's America*," a large folio volume illustrated by engravings, published in London in 1671. This work contains a view of *Novum Amsterodamum*, (as it is called,) similar to the engraving from which the annexed cut is copied.

"It is placed upon the neck of the Island Manhatans looking towards the Sea; encompass'd with Hudson's River, which is six Miles broad, the town is compact and oval, with very fair streets and several good Houses; the rest are built much after the manner of Holland, to the number of about four hundred Houses, which in those parts are held considerable: Upon one side of the Town is James-Fort, capable to lodge three hundred souldiers and Officers; it hath four bastions, forty Pieces of Cannon mounted; the Walls of Stone, lined with a thick Rampart of Earth, well accommodated with a spring of Fresh Water, always furnish'd with Arms and Ammunition against Accidents: Distant from the Sea seven Leagues, it affords a safe entrance, even to unskilful Pilots; under the Town side, ships of any burthen may ride secure against any Storms; the Current of the River being broken by the interposition of a small Island, which lies a mile distant from the Town.

"About ten Miles from New York is a place call'd Hell Gate, which being a narrow passage, there runneth a violent Stream both upon Flood and Ebb; and in the middle lie some Rocky Islands, which the Current sets so violently upon, that it threatens present Shipwrack; and upon the Flood is a large Whirlwind, which continually sends forth a hideous roaring; enough to affright any Stranger from passing farther; and to wait for some Charon to conduct him through; yet to those who are acquainted little or no danger: It is a place of great Defence against any Enemy coming in that way, which a small Fortification would absolutely prevent, and necessitate them to come in at the West End of Long Island by Sandy Hook, where Statten Island forces them within the Command of the Fort at New York, which is one of the best Pieces of Defence in the North parts of America. It is built most of Brick and Stone and cover'd with Red and Black Tyle, and the Land being high, it gives at a distance a most pleasing prospect to the Spectators. The inhabitants consist most of English and Dutch, and have a considerable trade with Indians for Beaver, Otter and Rackoon Skins with other Furrs; as also for Bear, Deer, and Elke-Skins; and are supply'd with Venison and Fowl in the winter, and Fish in the Summer by the Indians, which they buy at an easie Rate; and having the Countrey round about them, and are continually furnish'd with all such provisions as are needful for the Life of Man, not onely by the English and Dutch within their own, but likewise by the adjacent Colonies.

"The Manhattans, or Great River being the chiefest, having with two wide Mouths wash'd the mighty Island Watonwaks, falls into the Ocean. The Southern Mouth is call'd Port May, or Godyns Bay. In the middle thereof lies an Island call'd 'The States Island; and a little higher the Manhattans, so call'd from the Natives which on the East side of the River dwell on the Main Continent. They are a cruel people, and enemies to the Hollanders, as also of the Sarhians which reside on the Western Shore. Farther up are the Mackwaes and Mahikans which continually War, one against another. In like manner all the Inhabitants on the West Side of the River Manhattan, are commonly at enmity with those that possess the Eastern Shore; who also us'd to be at variance with the Hollanders, when as the other People at the Westward kept good correspondency with them. On a small Island near the Shore of the Mackwaes, lay formerly a Fort, provided with two Drakes and eleven Stone Guns, yet was at last deserted."

"The settlement and fort continued to bear the name of Nieuw Amsterdam, by the Dutch, down to the time of the surrender by Governor Stuyvesant to the English, in 1664. Then for ten years under the rule of Cols. Nicolls and Lovelace, acting for the Duke of York, it was called *New York*; but in August, 1673, a Dutch fleet, in time of war, re-captured it from the British, and while exercising their rule for their High Mightinesses of Holland, to the time of the peace in 1674, they called the place *New Orange*, in compliment to the prince of Orange, and the fort they called Willem Hendrick.

"The city being restored to the British by the treaty, was re-delivered to the British in October, 1674. The fort then took the name of Fort James, being built of quadrangular form, having four bastions, two gates, and 42 cannon. The city again took the name of New York, once and forever.

The following extracts are from a pamphlet publication by J. W. Moulton, Esq., entitled "View of the city of New Orange (now New York) as it was in the year 1673."

"*Fort Amsterdam, genaamt James-Fort by de Engelsche.* Fort Amsterdam, otherwise called James-Fort by the English. The name officially given to the fort in 1673, was 'fort Willem Hendrick.' It was first erected and finished in 1635, by Gov. Van Twiller, neglected by Governor Kieft, repaired and surrounded by a stone wall by Governor Stuyvesant, and demolished, and the ground levelled in 1790 and '91. It was situated directly south of the Bowling green, on high ground, was in shape of a regular square, with four bastions, had two gates, and mounted forty-two cannon.

"*Gereformeerde Kerck.* The reformed Dutch church was erected within the fort, by Governor Kieft, in 1642. It was of stone, and covered with oak shingles, which exposed to the weather, soon resembled slate. The motives that induced Governor Kieft to become the founder of the first church in this city, may be best related in the words of captain David Pietersz de Vriez 'artillery meester van 't noorder Quartier,' who performed three voyages to New Netherlands, associated with Killiaen Van Rensalaer and others, in 1630, to colonize this region, attempted a colony at the Hore-Kill on the Delaware, in the time of Van Twiller, and another on 'Staaten Eylandt,' which he sustained till the troubles with the Indians in the latter time of Kieft drove him to abandon the country. De Vriez observes: 'As I was every day with Commander Kieft, dining generally at his house when I happened to be at the fort, he told me one day that he had now made a fine tavern, *built with stone*, for the English, by whom, as they passed continually with their vessels from New England to Virginia, had much suffered, and who now might take lodgings there. I told him this was very good for travellers, but that we wanted very badly for our people a church. It was a shame that when the English passed, they should see nothing but a *mean barn*, in which we performed our worship; on the contrary, the first thing that they in New England did, when they had built fine dwellings, was to erect a fine church: we ought to do the same, it being supposed that the West India Company were very zealous in protecting the Reformed church (Calvinist) against the Spanish tyranny, that we had good materials for it, fine oak wood, fine building stone, good lime made of oyster shells, being better than our lime in Holland. Kieft asked me then who would like to attend to this building? I replied the lovers of the reformed religion, as certainly some of them could be found. He told me that he supposed I myself was one of them, as I made the proposition, and he supposed I would contribute a hundred guilders! I replied that I agreed to do so, and that as he was Governor, he should be the first. We then elected Jochem Pietersz Kuyter, who having a set of good hands, would soon procure good timber, he being also a devout Calvinist. We elected also Jan Claesz Damen, because he lived near the fort, and thus we four "Kerk meesters" formed the first consistory to superintent the building of the church. The governor should furnish a few thousand guilders of the company's money, and would try to raise the remainder by subscription. The church should be built in the fort, where it would be free from the depredations of the Indians. The building was soon started of stone, and was covered by English carpenters with slate, split of oakwood,' (that is, with oak shingles, which by rain and wind soon became blue, and resembled slate.)

"The contract for the erection of this church is upon record. It was made in May, 1642, before the secretary of the New Netherlands, between 'William Kieft, church-warden, at the request of his brethren, the church-wardens of the church in New Netherland, and John Ogden of Stanford, and Richard Ogden, who contracted to build the church of rock-stone, 72 feet long, 52 broad, and 16 feet high above the soil, for 2,500 guilders (£416 13 4) "in beaver, cash or merchandize, to wit, if the church-wardens are satisfied with the work, so that, in their judgment, the 2,500 guilders shall have been earned—then said church-wardens will reward them with one hundred guilders (£16 13 4) more," in the mean time assist them whenever it is in their power, and allow them the use, for a month or six weeks, of the Company's boat, to facilitate the carrying of the stone thither.'

"The church was not completely finished until the first year of Governor Stuyvesant's administration. In July, 1647, he and two others were appointed kerk-meesters, (church-wardens,) to superintend the work, and complete it the ensuing winter.

"The town bell was removed to this church. Besides the office of calling the devout to meeting, and announcing the hour of retirement at night, the bell was appropriated fo. various singular uses. In October, 1638, a female, for slandering the Rev. E. Bogardus, was condemned to appear at fort Amsterdam, and before the governor and council, 'to declare in public, *at the sounding of the bell*, that she knew the minister was an honest and pious man, and that she lied falsely.'

"In 1639, all mechanics and laborers in the service of the Company commenced and left work at the *ringing of the bell*, and for every neglect forfeited double the amount of their wages, to the use of the attorney-general.

"In 1647, all tavern keepers were prohibited, by the placards of Governor Stuyvesant and council, from accommodating any clubs, or selling any ardent liquor, *after the ringing of the bell*, at nine o'clock in the evening.

In 1648, two runaways were summoned into court by the *ringing of the bell*, to defend themselves. And in 1677, an ordinance was passed by the common council of New York, imposing a fine of six shillings on any members of the corporation and jurymen, who should neglect to appear in court at the *third ringing of the bell*. The bell-ringer was anciently the court messenger. In 1661, amid his multifarious official duties, he was to 'assist in burying the dead and attend to *toll the bell*.'

"The proclamation of governor Lovelace, issued December 10, 1672, is a document too curious to be omitted. It was in the following words:—

"'Whereas it is thought convenient and necessary, in obedience to his Sacred Majesty's Commands, who enjoynes all his subjects, in their distinct colonyes, to enter into a strict Allyance and Correspondency with each other, as likewise for the advancement of Negotiation, Trade and Civill Commerce, and for a more speedy Intelligence and Dispatch of affayres, that a messenger or Post bee authorised to sett forth from this City of New-Yorke, *monthly*, and thence to travaile to Boston, from whence within that month hee shall returne againe to this City: These are therefore to give notice to all persons concerned, That on the first day of January next (1673) the messenger appointed shall proceed on his Journey to Boston: If any therefore have any letters or small portable goods to bee conveyed to Hartford, Connecticott, Boston, or any other parts in the Road, they shall bee carefully delivered according to the Directions by a sworne Messenger and Post, who is purposely imployed in that Affayre; In the Interim those that bee dispos'd to send Letters, lett them bring them to the *Secretary's office*, where in a lockt Box they shall bee preserv'd till the Messenger calls for them. All persons paying the Post before the Bagg bee seald up. Dated at New Yorke this 10th day of December 1672.'

"*Stuyvesant Huys*. Governor Stuyvesant's house or dwelling was built about four years before he surrendered his government to the English. It fronted the public wharf and stood on the west side of the present Whitehall-street, nearly opposite the commencement of the present Water-street.

"The public wharf and harbor or dock, were built by the burgomasters of the city about the year 1658. Here vessels loaded and unloaded, and a wharfage duty was exacted at first of eight stivers per last. The harbor was constructed to accommodate vessels and yachts, in which, during winter, the barques stationed there might be secured against the floating ice; for which large vessels paid annually ' one beaver, and smaller in proportion, to the city, to keep it in order.' This wharf and harbor are now a part of Whitehall-street, Whitehall slip having since been formed into the river.

"*De Waegh*. The weigh, or balance. This was erected in 1653, by Governor Stuyvesant, and the standard weight and measure kept in the balance-house, was according to those of the city of Amsterdam. To this standard merchants were obliged to conform, and to pay the *eyck-meester* for marking their weights and measures. Goods were here also brought in bulk and weighed, before they were stored in the public store-houses.

"In front of the City-Hall were also the stocks and whipping-post. The ducking-stool, or rather cucking-stool, was not yet erected, notwithstanding the Lutheran minister in 1673 pleaded in bar to a public prosecution against him for striking a female that she 'provoked him to it *by scolding*.' The Dutch had the credit of introducing the wooden-horse, but the cucking-stool was reserved for the superior ingenuity of the English, who deriving a sanction for their want of gallantry from the immemorial authority of their Common Law, ordered in February, 1692, 'at a meeting of a grand Committee of the Common Council, a pillory, cage and ducking-stool to be forthwith built.'"

The following relation from Knickerbocker's New York, of the manners and customs of the early Dutch inhabitants of this city, although humorously exaggerated, is by no means devoid of historical truth.

"I will not grieve their patience, however, by describing minutely the increase and improvement of New Amsterdam. Their own imaginations will doubtless present to them the good burghers, like so many pains-taking and persevering beavers, slowly and surely pursuing their labors—they will behold the prosperous transformation from the rude log-hut to the stately Dutch mansion, with brick front, glazed windows, and tiled roof—from the tangled thicket to the luxuriant cabbage garden; and from the skulking Indian to the ponderous burgomaster. In a word, they will picture to themselves the steady, silent, and undeviating march to prosperity, incident to a city destitute of pride or ambition, cherished by a fat government, and whose citizens do nothing in a hurry.

"The sage council, as has been mentioned in a preceding chapter, not being able to determine upon any plan for the building of their city—the cows, in a laudable fit of patriotism, took it under their peculiar charge, and as they went to and from pasture, established paths through the bushes, on each side of which the good folks built their houses; which is one cause of the rambling and picturesque turns and labyrinths, which distinguish certain streets of New York at this very day.

"The houses of the higher class were generally constructed of wood, excepting the gable end, which was of small black and yellow Dutch bricks, and always faced on the street, as our ancestors, like their descendants, were very much given to outward show, and were noted for putting the best leg foremost. The house was always furnished with abundance of large doors and small windows on every floor; the date of its erection was curiously designated by iron figures on the front, and on the top of the roof was perched a fierce little weathercock, to let the family into the important secret, which way the wind blew. These, like the weathercocks on the tops of our steeples, pointed so many different ways, that every man could have a wind to his mind;—the most stanch and loyal citizens, however, always went according to the weathercock on the top of the governor's house, which was certainly the most correct, as he had a trusty servant employed every morning to climb up and set it to the right quarter.

"In those good days of simplicity and sunshine, a passion for cleanliness was the leading principle in domestic economy, and the universal test of an able housewife,—a character which formed the utmost ambition of our unenlightened grandmothers. The front door was never opened except on marriages, funerals, new year's days, the festival of St. Nicholas, or some such great occasion. It was ornamented with a gorgeous brass knocker, curiously wrought, sometimes in the device of a dog, and sometimes of a lion's head, and was daily burnished with such religious zeal, that it was ofttimes worn out by the very precautions taken for its preservation. The whole house was constantly in a state of inundation, under the discipline of mops and brooms and scrubbing brushes; and the good housewives of those days were a kind of amphibious animal, delighting exceedingly to be dabbling in water—insomuch than an historian of the day gravely tells us, that many of his townswomen grew to have webbed fingers like unto a duck; and some of them, he had little doubt, could the matter be examined into, would be found to have the tails of mermaids—but this I look upon to be a mere sport of fancy, or what is worse, a wilful misrepresentation.

"The grand parlor was the sanctum sanctorum, where the passion for cleaning was indulged without control. In this sacred apartment no one was permitted to enter, excepting the mistress and her confidential maid, who visited it once a week, for the purpose of giving it a thorough cleaning, and putting things to rights—always taking the precaution of leaving their shoes at the door, and entering devoutly on their stocking feet. After scrubbing the floor, sprinkling it with fine white sand, which was curiously stroked into angles, and curves, and rhomboids with a broom—after washing the windows, rubbing and polishing the furniture, and putting a new bunch of evergreens in the fireplace—the window shutters were again closed to keep out the flies, and the room carefully locked up until the revolution of time brought round the weekly cleaning day.

"As to the family, they always entered in at the gate, and most generally lived in the kitchen. To have seen a numerous household assembled around the fire, one would have imagined that he was transported back to those happy days of primeval simplicity, which float before our imaginations like golden visions. The fireplaces were of a truly patriarchal magnitude, where the whole family, old and young, master and servant, black and white, nay, even the very cat and dog, enjoyed a community of privilege, and had each a right to a corner. Here the old burgher would sit in perfect silence, puffing his pipe, looking in the fire with half-shut eyes, and thinking of nothing for hours together; the goede vrouw on the opposite side would employ herself diligently in spinning yarn, or knitting stockings. The young folks would crowd around the hearth, listening with breathless attention to some old crone of a negro, who was the oracle of the family, and who, perched like a raven in a corner of the chimney, would croak forth for a long winter afternoon a string of incredible stories about New England witches—grisly ghosts—horses without heads—and hairbreadth escapes and bloody encounters among the Indians.

"In those happy days a well-regulated family always rose with the dawn, dined at eleven, and went to bed at sundown. Dinner was invariably a private meal, and the fat old burghers showed incontestible symptoms of disapprobation and uneasiness at being surprised by a visit from a neighbor on such occasions. But though our worthy ancestors were thus singularly averse to giving dinners, yet they kept up the social bands of intimacy by occasional banquetings, called tea parties.

"These fashionable parties were generally confined to the higher classes, or noblesse, that is to say, such as kept their own cows, and drove their own wagons. The company commonly assembled at three o'clock, and went away about six, unless it was in winter time, when the fashionable hours were a little earlier, that the ladies might get home before dark. The tea table was crowned with a huge earthen dish, well stored with slices of fat pork, fried brown, cut up into morsels, and swimming in gravy. The company being seated around the genial board, and each furnished with a fork, evinced their dexterity in launching at the fattest pieces in this mighty dish—in much the same manner as sailors harpoon porpoises at sea, or our Indians spear salmon in the lakes. Sometimes the table was graced with immense apple pies, or saucers full of preserved peaches and pears; but it was always sure to boast an enormous dish of balls of sweetened dough, fried in hog's fat, and called doughnuts, or oly koeks—a delicious kind of cake, at present scarce known in this city, excepting in genuine Dutch families.

"The tea was served out of a majestic delft teapot, ornamented with paintings of fat little Dutch shepherds and shepherdesses tending pigs—with boats sailing in the air, and houses built in the clouds, and sundry other ingenious Dutch fantasies. The beaux distinguished themselves by their adroitness in replenishing this pot from a huge copper tea-kettle, which would have made the pigmy macaronies of these degenerate days sweat merely to look at it. To sweeten the beverage, a lump of sugar was laid beside each cup—and the company alternately nibbled and sipped with great decorum, until an improvement was introduced by a shrewd and economic old lady, which was to suspend a large lump directly over the tea table, by a string from the ceiling, so that it could be swung from mouth to mouth—an ingenious expedient, which is still kept up by some families in Albany; but which prevails without exception in Communipaw, Bergen, Flat Bush, and all our uncontaminated Dutch villages.

"At these primitive tea parties the utmost propriety and dignity of deportment prevailed. No flirting nor coquetting—no gambolling of old ladies nor hoyden chattering and romping of young ones—no self-satisfied struttings of wealthy gentlemen, with their brains in their pockets—nor amusing conceits, and monkey divertisements, of smart young gentlemen, with no brains at all. On the contrary, the young ladies seated themselves demurely in their rush-bottomed chairs, and knit their own woollen stockings; nor ever opened their lips, excepting to say, *yah Mynher*, or *yah ya Vrouw*, to any question that was asked them; behaving, in all things, like decent, well-educated damsels. As to the gentlemen, each of them tranquilly smoked his pipe, and seemed lost in contemplation of the blue and white tiles with which the fireplaces were decorated; wherein sundry passages of scripture were piously portrayed—Tobit and his dog figured to great advantage; Haman swung conspicuously on his gibbet, and Jonah appeared most manfully bouncing out of the whale, like Harlequin through a barrel of fire.

"The parties broke up without noise and without confusion. They were carried home by their own carriages, that is to say, by the vehicles nature had provided them, excepting such of the wealthy as could afford to keep a wagon. The gentlemen gallantly attended their fair ones to their respective abodes, and took leave of them with a hearty smack at the door; which, as it was an established piece of etiquette, done in perfect simplicity and honesty of heart, occasioned no scandal at that time, nor should it at the present—if our great grandfathers approved of the custom, it would argue a great want of reverence in their descendants to say a word against it.

"In this dulcet period of my history, when the beauteous island of Manna-hatta presented a scene, the very counterpart of those glowing pictures drawn of the golden reign of Saturn, there was, as I have before observed, a happy ignorance, an honest simplicity prevalent among its inhabitants, which, were I even able to depict, would be but little understood by the degenerate age for which I am doomed to write. Even the female sex, those arch innovators upon the tranquillity, the honesty, and greybeard customs of society, seemed for a while to conduct themselves with incredible sobriety and comeliness.

"Their hair, untortured by the abominations of art, was scrupulously pomatomed back from their foreheads with a candle, and covered with a little cap of quilted calico, which fitted exactly to their heads. Their petticoats of linsey woolsey were striped with a variety of gorgeous dyes—though I must confess these gallant garments were rather short, scarce reaching below the knee; but then they made up in the number, which generally equalled that of the gentlemen's small-clothes; and what is still more praiseworthy, they were all of their own manufacture—of which circumstance, as may well be supposed, they were not a little vain.

"These were the honest days, in which every woman staid at home, read the Bible, and wore pockets—ay, and that too of a goodly size, fashioned with patch-work into many curious devices, and ostentatiously worn on the outside. These, in fact, were convenient receptacles, where all good housewives carefully stored away such things as they wished to have at hand; by which means they often came to be incredibly crammed—and I remember there was a story current when I was a boy, that the lady of Wouter Van Twiller once had occasion to empty her right pocket in search of a wooden ladle, and the utensil was discovered lying among some rubbish in one corner—but we must not give too much faith to all these stories; the anecdotes of those remote periods being very subject to exaggeration.

"Besides these notable pockets, they likewise wore scissors and pincushions suspended from their girdles by red ribands, or among the more opulent and showy classes, by brass, and even silver chains —indubitable tokens of thrifty housewives and industrious spinsters. I cannot say much in vindication of the shortness of the petticoats; it doubtless was introduced for the purpose of giving the stockings a chance to be seen, which were generally of blue worsted with magnificent red clocks—or perhaps to display a well-turned ankle, and a neat, though serviceable, foot, set off by a high-heeled leathern shoe, with a large and splendid silver buckle. Thus we find that the gentle sex in all ages have shown the same disposition to infringe a little upon the laws of decorum, in order to betray a lurking beauty, or gratify an innocent love of finery.

"From the sketch here given, it will be seen that our good grandmothers differed considerably in their ideas of a fine figure from their scantily dressed descendants of the present day. A fine lady, in those times, waddled under more clothes, even on a fair summer's day, than would have clad the whole bevy of a modern ball-room. Nor were they the less admired by the gentlemen in consequence thereof. On the contrary, the greatness of a lover's passion seemed to increase in proportion to the magnitude of its object—and a voluminous damsel, arrayed in a dozen of petticoats, was declared by a Low Dutch sonnetteer of the province to be radiant as a sunflower, and luxuriant as a full blown cabbage. Certain it is, that in those days, the heart of a lover could not contain more than one lady at a time; whereas the heart of a modern gallant has often room enough to accommodate half a dozen. The reason of which I conclude to be, that either the hearts of the gentlemen have grown larger, or the persons of the ladies smaller—this, however, is a question for physiologists to determine.

"But there was a secret charm in these petticoats, which no doubt entered into the consideration of the prudent gallants. The wardrobe of a lady was in those days her only fortune; and she who had a good stock of petticoats and stockings, was as absolutely an heiress as is a Kamschatka damsel with a store of bear skins, or a Lapland belle with a plenty of reindeer. The ladies, therefore, were very anxious to display these powerful attractions to the greatest advantage; and the best rooms in the house, instead of being adorned with caricatures of dame nature, in water colors and needle-work, were always hung round with abundance of homespun garments, the manufacture and the property of the females—a piece of laudable ostentation that still prevails among the heiresses of our Dutch villages.

"The gentlemen, in fact, who figured in the circles of the gay world in these ancient times, corresponded, in most particulars, with the beauteous damsels whose smiles they were ambitious to deserve. True it is, their merits would make but a very inconsiderable impression upon the heart of a modern fair; they neither drove their curricles nor sported their tandems, for as yet those gaudy vehicles were not even dreamt of—neither did they distinguish themselves by their brilliancy at the table, and their consequent rencontres with watchmen, for our forefathers were of too pacific a disposition to need those guardians of the night, every soul throughout the town being sound asleep before nine o'clock. Neither did they establish their claims to gentility at the expense of their tailors—for as yet those offenders against the pockets of society, and the tranquillity of all aspiring young gentlemen, were unknown in New Amsterdam; every good housewife made the clothes of her husband and family, and even the goede vrouw of Van Twiller himself thought it no disparagement to cut out her husband's linsey woolsey galligaskins.

"Not but what there were some two or three youngsters who manifested the first dawnings of what is called fire and spirit. Who held all labor in contempt; skulked about docks and market places; loitered in the sunshine; squandered what little money they could procure at hustle-cap and chuck-farthing, swore, boxed, fought cocks, and raced their neighbor's horses—in short, who promised to be the wonder, the talk, and abomination of the town, had not their stylish career been unfortunately cut short by an affair of honor with a whipping-post.

"Far other, however, was the truly fashionable gentleman of those days—his dress, which served for both morning and evening, street and drawing-room, was a linsey woolsey coat, made, perhaps, by the fair hands of the mistress of his affections, and gallantly bedecked with abundance of large brass buttons.—Half a score of breeches heightened the proportions of his figure—his shoes were decorated by enormous copper buckles—a low-crowned broad-brimmed hat overshadowed his burly visage, and his hair dangled down his back in a prodigious queue of eel skin.

"Thus equipped, he would manfully sally forth with pipe in mouth to besiege some fair damsel's obdurate heart—not such a pipe, good reader, as that which Acis did sweetly tune in praise of his Galatea, but of one of true delft manufacture, and furnished with a charge of fragrant tobacco. With this would he resolutely set himself down before the fortress, and rarely failed, in the process of time, to smoke the fair enemy into a surrender, upon honorable terms.

"Such was the happy reign of Wouter Van Twiller, celebrated in many a long-forgotten song as the real golden age, the rest being nothing but counterfeit copper-washed coin. In that delightful period, a sweet and holy calm reigned over the whole province. The burgomaster smoked his pipe in peace—the substantial solace of his domestic cares, after her daily toils were done, sat soberly at the door, with her arms crossed over her apron of snowy white, without being insulted by ribald street walkers or vagabond boys—those unlucky urchins, who do so infest our streets, displaying under the roses of youth the thorns and briers of iniquity. Then it was that the lover with ten breeches, and the damsel with petticoats of half a score, indulged in all the innocent endearments of virtuous love without fear and without reproach; for what had that virtue to fear, which was defended by a shield of good linsey woolseys, equal at least to the seven bull hides of the invincible Ajax.

"Ah, blissful, and never to be forgotten age! when every thing was better than it has ever been since, or ever will be again—when Buttermilk Channel* was quite dry at low water—when the shad in the Hudson were all salmon, and when the moon shone with a pure and resplendent whiteness, instead of that melancholy yellow light which is the consequence of her sickening at the abominations she every night witnesses in this degenerate city!

"Happy would it have been for New Amsterdam could it always have existed in this state of blissful ignorance and lowly simplicity; but alas! the days of childhood are too sweet to last! Cities, like men, grow out of them in time, and are doomed alike to grow into the bustle, the cares, and miseries of the world. Let no man congratulate himself, when he beholds the child of his bosom or the city of his birth increasing in magnitude and importance—let the history of his own life teach him the dangers of the one, and this excellent little history of Mannahatta convince him of the calamities of the other."

THE NEGRO PLOT.

The celebrated Negro Plot, 1741, occurred when there were about ten thousand inhabitants in this city, of which one sixth part were negro slaves.

"After a lapse of a century, we look back with astonishment on the panic occasioned by the Negro Plot, and the rancorous hatred that prevailed here against the Roman Catholics. To judge from tradition, and the journal of the proceedings against the conspirators, no doubt can be had of the actual existence of a plot; but its extent could never have been so great as the terror of those times depicted. The very mode adopted to discover abettors by mutual criminations and confessions, tended in the progress of the trials to inculpate every negro slave in the city. We accordingly find, that the number of conspirators daily increased. As it was impossible to prove all equally guilty, the ringleaders only were executed; and those who, to save their lives, plead guilty, and threw themselves on the mercy of the court, were transported.

"Insurrections and conspiracies were at this juncture frequent in the West India islands, and great apprehensions were entertained of an invasion by the French and Spaniards. These circumstances aggravated the horror of a domestic plot to such a degree, that the white inhabitants, regarding every negro slave as an incendiary and an assassin, carried their apprehensions and resentment beyond all bounds.

"A holy hatred of the Roman Catholics was at that period inculcated by church and state. Our Dutch forefathers, glowing with all the zeal of the early reformers, emigrated to this country shortly after the emancipation of the United Netherlands from the Spanish yoke, and fostered all the rancor of their race against Papists and Spaniards. It was the policy of the English government, after the conquest, to cherish this animosity, and those of our readers who were born and educated before the American revolution, will recollect how religiously they were taught to abhor the Pope, Devil, and Pretender. The act of our Provincial Assembly, against Jesuits and Papist priests, passed 2d William and Mary, and which continued in full force until our independence, was owing, not only to these prejudices, but to the exposed situation of the colony, the northern frontier of which was bounded by Canada, at that time in possession of France, the natural and ever-daring enemy to England. The intolerant spirit of this act shows the horror and detestation in which the Roman Catholics were held, and will account why so few of this profession existed in this city and colony before the revolution.

---

* In olden times the channel was but a little creek which separated the mainland from Governors Island.

"In estimating this singular event in our colonial history, the circumstances of the times should be duly considered, before we too hastily condemn the bigotry and cruelty of our predecessors. The advantages of a liberal, indeed of the plainest education, was the happy lot of very few. Intercourse between the colonies and the mother country, and between province and province, was very rare. Ignorance and illiberal prejudices universally prevailed. Their more favored and enlightened posterity will therefore draw a veil of filial affection over the involuntary errors of their forefathers, and emulating their simple virtues, endeavor to transmit a brighter example to their successors."—*Hist. of Negro Plot*, 8vo. *New York*, 1810.

"The first suspicion of a plot among the negroes, and which subsequently led to a full investigation and discovery, was caused by frequent alarms of fire, and a robbery committed at a Mr. Hogg's, 'from whence were taken divers pieces of linen, and other goods, and several silver coins, chiefly Spanish, and medals, and wrought silver, &c., to the value, in the whole, of sixty pounds and upwards.' The scene of this famous robbery was in a house in Broad street. On Wednesday, the 18th March, 1740, about 1 o'clock, a fire broke out of the roof of His Majesty's house, at Fort George, within this city, near the chapel, on the east side, and the wind blowing a violent gale at southeast, it soon became impossible to stop its progress. The citizens and engines assembled promptly on the ringing of the chapel bell, and assisted in saving the records and papers in the office of the Secretary of State, over the fort gate, which fortunately were preserved, although in the hurry they were tossed out at the windows, and the papers blown and scattered. An alarm being given, the people were soon after fearful of an explosion, and stood aloof, although assured by the Governor that it was groundless. In one hour and a quarter, the Governor's house, and the venerable old Dutch Church, were thus consumed. A plumber had that morning been at work, with his pot of coals and soldering iron, to mend a leak in the gutter, between the house and the chapel, and the high wind had no doubt blown some sparks on the dry shingles, or under the eaves. On the 25th of March, a week after the fire at the fort, another broke out at the southwest end of the town, and on the 1st of April, another at the east end of the town, at Van Zandt's, corner of Burling's slip and Water-street. On the 4th of April, two other alarms were made, and fire discovered; and on the 5th, being Sunday, Mr. Murray's haystack, standing near some stables and houses in Broadway, had some live coals put under it, which went out of themselves. On Monday, three more fires occurred, and the panic commenced. Many negroes were arrested, and the investigations were long and intricate. By the course of the evidence, it appeared that the city was destined to be fired, and the inhabitants massacred on coming out of the English Church in Broadway.

"St. Patrick's night was selected to begin the bloody scene, and many Irish Catholics, lately arrived, enlisted in the gang, were even detected as being concerned. The negroes were led on by a villian named Hughson, at whose house they were freely entertained, and brought their stolen goods, and were sworn to secrecy. Ury, a priest, was also deeply concerned.

"It is somewhat remarkable, that London has had its Popish Plot and fire; Boston and Salem its delusions of witchcraft, and New York its Negro Plot: and there can be no doubt that some innocent persons were at those times accused, and suffered.

"One hundred and fifty-four negroes, and twenty white persons, were committed to prison, of which fifty-five were convicted, and seventy-eight confessed. Thirteen negroes were burnt at the stake, at a place then out of town, but situated near the present intersection of Pearl and Chatham streets, where there formerly was a hollow place, as recollected by one of our oldest citizens, who was present at the execution, and declares that the horrible shrieks and cries of the miserable victims still dwell on his memory. Twenty were hung, (one in chains, 'on the island, by the powder-house,' where the Arsenal now is, in Elm street.) Seventy were transported to foreign parts, viz. Newfoundland, Madeira, Hispaniola, Cape François, Curraçoa, Surinam, &c., &c., and fifty were discharged.

"Although the black population has increased from that period to the present, in this city, yet the proportion they *now* bear to the whites is much *less* than at that time, being only one-twelfth part; then they were one-sixth."

The following extracts are from newspapers published previous to and during the revolution: they will serve to throw light on the history of the times.

"*New York, November* 4, 1765.—The late extraordinary and unprecedented preparations in Fort George, and the securing of the Stamped Paper in that garrison, having greatly alarmed and displeased the inhabitants of this city, a vast number of them assembled last Friday evening in the commons, from whence they marched down the Fly, preceded by a number of lights, and having stopped a few minutes at the Coffee House, proceeded to the Fort Walls, where they broke open the stable of the L—t G——r, took out his coach, and after carrying the same through the principal streets of the city, in triumph marched to the commons, where a gallows was erected; on one end of which was suspended the effigy of the person whose property the coach was. In his right hand he held a stamped Bill of Lading, and on his breast was affixed a paper with the following inscription, ' *The Rebel Drummer in the year* 1715 :' at his back was affixed a drum, the badge of his profession; at the other end of the gallows hung the figure of the devil, a proper companion for the other, as 'tis supposed it was entirely at his instigation he acted: after they had hung there a considerable time, they carried the effigies, with the gallows entire, being preceded by the coach, in a grand procession to the gate of the fort, where it remained for some time, from whence it was removed to the Bowling Green, under the muzzles of the fort guns, where a bon-fire was immediately made, and the *drummer, devil, and coach*, &c., were consumed amidst the acclamations of some thousand spectators, and we make no doubt, but the L—t G——r, and his friends, had the mortification of viewing the whole proceeding from the ramparts of the fort: But the business of the night not being yet concluded, the whole body proceeded with the greatest decency and good order to Vauxhall, the house of M—r J——s, who, it was reported, was a friend to the Stamp Act, and had been over officious in his duty, from whence they took every individual article to a very considerable amount; and having made another bon-fire, the whole was consumed in the flames, to the great satisfaction of every person present; after which they dispersed, and every man went to his respective habitation. The whole affair was conducted with such decorum, that not the least accident happened.

"The next evening another very considerable body assembled at the same place, having been informed that the L—t G——r had qualified himself for the distribution of the Stamped paper, were determined to march to the fort, in order to insist upon his delivering into their hands, or to declare that he would not undertake to distribute the same; but before this resolution could be executed, the minds of the people were eased by the L—t G——r's sending the following declaration from the fort, viz:—

"'THE Lieut. Governor declares he will do nothing in Relation to the Stamps, but leave it to Sir Henry Moore, to do as he pleases on his arrival. *Council Chamber, New York, Nov.* 2, 1765. *By Order of His Honor.* Ww. BANYAR D. Cl. Con.

"' We can assure the Gentlemen of the neighboring Provinces, That every Importer of European Goods in this City, have agreed not to Import any Goods from England next Spring, unless the Sugar Act, and the Oppressive and Unconstitutional Stamp Act are repealed.' "

"*New York, Jan.* 8th, 1763.—Thursday next is appointed to celebrate the birth of the Prince of Wales, when there is to be a treble discharge of all the artillery in this place, and the evening is to be concluded with the play of the Fair Penitent, by the officers of the army, in a theatre built for that purpose."

"*New York, Dec.* 13, 1765.—We are credibly informed that there were married last Sunday evening, by the Rev. Mr. Auchmuty, a very respectable couple, that had been published at three different times in Trinity church. A laudable example and worthy to be followed. If this decent, and for many reasons, proper method of publication was once generally to take place, we should hear no more of clandestine marriages, and save the expense of licenses, no inconsiderable sum these hard and distressing times."

"*New York, March* 13th, 1766.—Upon a supposition that the cannon upon the Battery in this city were spiked by order of Lieutenant-governor Colden, his effigy was exhibited last Thursday, sitting upon a piece of ordnance, properly mounted with a drill constructed in such a manner as to be continually working; at his back hung a drum as a badge of his former profession: On his breast was fixed a paper on which were the following lines:

' I'm deceived by the devil and left in the lurch ;
And am forced to do penance, tho' not in the church.'

"After it had appeared in the principal streets of the city attended by many thousand spectators, (although it rained great part of the time,) it was carried to the common, where a fire was immediately made, and the whole consumed by 5 o'clock in the afternoon, amidst the acclamations of the multitude, who dispersed directly thereafter. . . . . The affair was conducted with such order and decorum, that no person sustained the least damage.

"N. B. The public are desired to take notice, that the cannon still remain spiked; and it is expected that no further hint will be necessary."

"*New York, May* 3, 1766.—The play advertised to be acted last Monday evening, having given offence to many of the inhabitants of this city, who thought it highly improper that such entertainments should be exhibited at this time of public distress, when great numbers of poor people can scarce find means of subsistence, whereby many persons might be tempted to neglect their business, and squander that money which is necessary to the payment of their debts and support of their families, a rumour was spread about the town on Monday, that if the play went on, the audience would meet with some disturbance from the multitude. This prevented the greatest part of those who intended to have been there from going; however, many people came and the play was begun: but soon interrupted by the multitude, who burst open the doors, and entered with noise and tumult. The audience escaped in the best manner they could; many lost their hats and other parts of dress. A boy had his skull fractured, and was yesterday trepanned; his recovery is doubtful: several others were dangerously hurt, but we heard of no lives lost. The multitude immediately demolished the house, carried the pieces to the common, where they consumed them in a bonfire."

From the New York Gazette of August 3, 1769.

"Extract of a letter to a gentleman in the city from a correspondent in the country, dated July 20,—'Sir: As a sincere friend I give you a caution now to be particularly on your guard against the importation of English goods; for I fear you will not get them sold at any rate, as it appears quite plain from this hint of facts, you may depend upon. Within these few weeks I happened to be present at several meetings of some towns here, when among other things, they took into their most serious consideration the affair of buying English goods from your merchants, and it was strongly reasoned thus: We have gone (said they) these several years past clearing new lands and raising grain only, and have foolishly neglected the raising of sheep and flax, because we vainly thought we could buy them cheaper at the stores than make them at our houses; until now our cash is wholly carried to England for their fineries, and here it has got so scarce, that in a whole town one guinea is scarcely seen in a year's time: so that when a man goeth to buy any necessaries at a merchant's shop, instead of his purse, he must take a wagon load of grain, and sell it to the merchant's and take his English goods at whatever price he pleases to ask.

"Wherefore they unanimously and firmly resolved, 1st. That for them to buy any more Scotch or English goods from merchants, was in fact a sure wicked way to qualify Britain tyrannically and inflexibly, from time to time to impose upon Americans whatsoever new laws, new admiralty courts, or bishop's courts they pleased, to take away our civil and religious liberties piecemeal, until we and our posterity were finally enslaved as deep as any Spaniard or African.

"2d. That therefore, whosoever of their town, durst presume to buy any more of said British goods, before the restoring of our liberty, should be held, reputed, deemed, and treated by all his neighbors as an open enemy to all the civil and religious interests of their country, &c. &c.

"I have heard that a great many towns, through the inland parts of this, and the other provinces, are beginning to be greatly alarmed with the fears of their new admiralty courts, and bishop's courts, &c., and therefore are forming *resolves* of the same nature. Now if you do in these circumstances import goods, you will be ruined. Look round and see how many merchants have been sent to jail, and their families ruined by importing English goods, and not getting them sold to any advantage. Yours, &c."

From the New York Gazette, March 29, 1770.

"Last Saturday night about 11 o'clock, 14 or 15 soldiers were seen about the liberty-pole in this city, which one of them had ascended, with an intent to take off and carry away the topmast and vane; as soon as they were discovered, five or six young men who were accidentally crossing the green at that time made up towards the pole, to see what they were about, but they were immediately attacked and driven off the green by the soldiers; who, finding that they were discovered, and being apprehensive that the inhabitants would be alarmed, they made off. Soon after some persons went into town and acquainted their friends with the proceedings of the soldiers, upon which 14 or 15 persons came up to the green, and going to the pole were there surrounded by 40 or 50 soldiers, with their cutlasses drawn; upon which 4 or 5 of them retreated to the house of Mr. Bicker, and were followed by part of the soldiers, who immediately called out for the soldiers from the barracks; upon which they were joined by a very considerable body who came over the barrack fence. Mr. Bicker seeing himself and family in danger, and exposed to the insults of a licentious and brutal soldiery, stood with his bayonet fixed, determined to defend himself to the last extremity, and declared that he would shoot the first man that should attempt to enter; they several times attempted to force the under door, the upper door being open, which Mr. Bicker kept shut by fixing the point of his bayonet against it, while they kept cutting and hacking the barrel of his gun, in attempting to cut him down with their cutlasses,—but he soon after got the upper door shut and barred; upon which they strove to break open the front windows, which were also shut, one of which they forced open, broke the panes of glass, and cut all the frame to pieces, in order to get into the house. Some people who were in the house seeing the imminent danger to which Mr. Bicker and his family were exposed, got out the back way and ran to alarm the citizens. The chapel bell was immediately rung, upon the hearing of which, the soldiers retreated precipitately. A number of the citizens were up all night and under arms, which probably prevented any mischief being done, as they repeatedly swore that they would set fire to the house, and burn or destroy every person in it. Col. Robertson, the commanding officer of the regiment, repaired to the barracks, as soon as he had notice of the disturbance; he immediately ordered the centinels to be confined, and remained up all night to prevent any further mischief being done; and as a number of inhabitants nightly guarded the pole, till the Transports with the soldiers were sailed, they were disappointed in effecting their designs against it, although they positively swore that they would carry off some part of it with them."

From the same, December 24, 1767

"To be disposed of—the remaining time, being about three years, of three German servants, one a baker by trade, one a butcher, and the other a laborer. They are very industrious good men, whose honesty has been tried, and may be had on reasonable terms. Inquire of the printer hereof."

"Last Thursday being the anniversary of His Majesty's birth-day, when he entered his 30th year, the same was observed here with great solemnity. About 11 o'clock the detachment of the train, with the 17th and 46th regiments, were paraded on the battery, and marched in order by, and saluted his Excellency, General Gage; at the same time his Excellency, Sir Henry Moore, the members of His Majesty's council for this province, his worship the mayor, and the rest of the corporation, and most of the other gentlemen of the city, were assembled in FORT GEORGE, where his Majesty's and many other loyal healths were drank, under the discharge of a Royal Salute from the Fort, which was immediately followed by a salute of 21 guns from the LIBERTY POLE, on which was suspended a UNION; these were answered by three vollies from the troops, five of His Majesty's ships, and many other vessels in our harbor, which with their colors displayed made a very grand and beautiful appearance; the two regiments then returned to their barracks and the train to the GREEN, and there grounded their arms. Elegant entertainments were given at Fort George, and Head Quarters, by their Excellencies Sir Henry Moore and General Gage, at which were present all the gentlemen of the army and navy, and most of the principal gentlemen of this place. In the evening the most magnificent fire-works ever seen in America were played off before a very great number of spectators. Over the gate of FORT GEORGE a number of lamps were disposed in such a manner as to represent a REGAL CROWN with a LAUREL TREE on each side, and before the door of his Excellency Gen. Gage, was exhibited, by lamps properly placed, a large and elegant appearance of the ROYAL ARMS; there being a general illumination throughout the city. The fire-works were conducted in such a manner as showed great skill and judgment in the projectors and operators, every part being played off with the greatest ease imaginable, in the following order, viz :—

First Set.—Two signal rockets, royal salutes of 21 marons, 12 sky rockets, a single vertical wheel, a Chinese fountain, a line rocket of three changes and a swarm box, 2 gerbs, 2 air balloons of crackers and serpents, a Chinese piece with a horizontal wheel, a yew tree with a brilliant fire, a nest of serpents.

"*Second Set.*—Two signal rockets, a salute of 19 marons, 12 sky rockets, a double vertical wheel, an illuminated globe, a fire tree and swarm box, 2 air balloons with crackers and stars, 3 fixed pieces with double vertical wheels, a range of fountains, a yew tree of brilliant fire, 2 nests of serpents.

"*Third Set.*—Two signal rockets, a salute of 17 marons, 12 sky rockets, 2 signal vertical wheels, a cascade of brilliant fire, a line rocket of three changes and swarm box, a range of fountains, two air balloons with serpents and stars, a Chinese piece with a horizontal wheel, an illuminated yew tree, a star with brilliant rays and glory. *Conclusion.*— A flight of rockets."

From the same, January 29th, 1767.

"Wednesday last several gentlemen arrived here from Quebec, in Canada, in 12 days. They came over the mountains on snow-shoes to Crown Point, and from thence down Lake George on the ice. The river St. Lawrence was not frozen over at Quebec when they came away; and we are told in the hardest weather it seldom is frozen there before the month of February."

"*New York, May* 7, 1772.—On Saturday last Mr. Montanny's negro man who had misbehaved, and was a remarkable drunkard, was sent to Bridewell, and underwent the *usual discipline of the house for such offences,* viz. a plentiful dose of warm water and salt to operate as an *emetic*, and of lamp oyl as a *purge*, in proportion to the constitution of the patient. Of these he took about 3 quarts of the one, and 2½ spoonfuls of the other, also a gill of *New England rum*, which operated very powerfully, attended with a violent sickness which obliged him to lye down, and between 8 and 9 at night he was discovered to be dead. He had been drunk three times that day before he was brought to Bridewell, and was not sober when the discipline began. Several physicians and surgeons attended, the body of the negro was opened and no marks of violence external or internal appeared: the coroner's inquest brought in their verdict that he died of excessive drinking, co-operating with the effects of the medicine he had taken. But that Mr. Dobbs, (the operator,) was innocent of his death."

"*New York, December* 24, 1773.—His Excellency the Governor having sent to Whitehead Hicks, Esq., Mayor of this city, the sum of two hundred pounds, which he most munificently ordered to be applied in relieving the properest objects of distress confined in the city gaol. We have the pleasure to inform the public that near thirty persons have been entirely released from imprisonment, and those whose debts were too large to be cleared by this gracious bounty have had a very comfortable provision made in wood, &c., to carry them through the winter."

"We hear from Dutchess County that the High Sheriff, having received the sum of fifty pounds from his Excellency Governor Tryon, to be distributed for the relief of debtors confined in his gaol, has applied that money in the manner prescribed, and cheered many indigent men whose misfortunes had reduced them to melancholy durance. The gratitude of these unhappy persons on this gracious attention to them cannot be described."

By His Excellency *William Cosby, Esq.*, Captain General and Governour in Chief of the Provinces of New York, New Jersey, and Territories thereon depending, in America, Vice Admiral of the same, and Colonel in His Majesty's Army, &c.

To any Protestant Minister.

Whereas there is a Mutual Purpose of Marriage between Jacob Glenn, of the City of Albany, Merchant, of the One Party, and Elizabeth Cuyler of the same City, Spinster, of the other party, for which they have desired my Licence, and have given Bond upon Conditions, That neither of them have any Lawful Let or Impediment of Pre-Contract, Affinity or Consanguinity to hinder their being joyned in the Holy Bands of Matrimony: these are therefore, to Authorize and Impower you to Joyn the said Jacob Glenn and Elizabeth Cuyler in the Holy Bands of Matrimony, and them to Pronounce Man and Wife.

Given under my Hand and Perogative Seal, at Fort George, in New York, the Sixteenth Day of October, in the Sixth Year of the Reign of our Sovereign Lord GEORGE *the Second, by the Grace of God, of Great Britain, France and Ireland,* KING, *Defender of the Faith.* Annoq: Domini 1732.

W. COSBY.

HENDK. MORRIS, D. Secry.

From the Connecticut Journal, Nov. 20, 1775.

"On the 20th of this month sixteen respectable inhabitants of this town, (New Haven,) in company with Capt. Sears, set out from this place for East and West Chester, in the Province of New York, to disarm the principal tories there, and secure the persons or Parson Seabury, Judge Fowler, and Lord Underhill. On their way thither they were joined by Captains Scillick, Richards, and Mead, with about 80 men. At Marrineck they burnt a small sloop, which was purchased by government for the purpose of carrying provisions on board the Asia. At East Chester they seized Judge Fowler, and then repaired to West Chester and secured Seabury and Underhill. Having possessed themselves of these caitiffs, they sent them to Connecticut under a strong guard. The main body, consisting of 75, then proceeded to New York, which they entered at noon-day on horseback, with bayonets fixed, in the greatest regularity went down the main street, and drew up in close order before the printing office of the infamous James RIVINGTON. A small detachment entered it, and in about three quarters of an hour brought off the principal part of his types, for which they offered to give an order on Lord Dunmore. They then faced and wheeled to the left and marched out of the town to the tune of YANKEE DOODLE. A vast concourse of people assembled at the coffee-house bridge, on their leaving the ground, gave them three hearty cheers.

"On their way home, they disarmed all the tories that lay on their route, and yesterday arrived here escorted by great number of gentlemen from the westward, the whole making a very grand procession. Upon their entrance into town they were saluted with the discharge of two cannon, and received by the inhabitants with every mark of approbation and respect. The company divided into two parties, and concluded the day in festivity and innocent mirth. Captain Sears returned in company with the other gentlemen, and proposed to spend the winter here unless public business should require his presence in New York. Seabury, Underhill, and Fowler, three of the dastardly protesters against the proceedings of the Continental Congress, and who it is believed had concerted a plan for kidnapping Capt. Sears, and conveying him on board of the Asia man-of-war, are (with the types and arms) safely lodged in this town : where it is expected Lord Underhill will have leisure to form the scheme of a lucrative lottery, the tickets of which cannot be counterfeited ; and Parson Seabury sufficient time and opportunity to compose sermons for the next Continental Fast."

After the Americans were defeated on Long Island, August 26, 1776, New York fell into the hands of the British troops, who kept possession of it during the revolutionary war. The annexed account of the military movements on New York island is from Colonel Humphrey's Life of General Putnam.

"The unfortunate battle of Long Island, the masterly retreat from thence, and the actual passage of part of the hostile fleet in the East river, above the town, preceded the evacuation of New York. A promotion of four major-generals, and six brigadiers, had previously been made by congress. After the retreat from Long Island, the main army, consisting, for the moment, of sixty battalions, of which twenty were continental, the residue levies and militia, was, conformably to the exigencies of the service, rather than to the rules of war, formed into fourteen brigades. Major-general Putnam commanded the right grand division of five brigades, the Majors-general Spencer and Greene the centre of six brigades, and Major-general Heath the left, which was posted near Kingsbridge, and composed of two brigades. The whole never amounted to twenty thousand effective men ; while the British and German forces, under Sir William Howe, exceeded twenty-two thousand ; indeed, the minister had asserted in parliament that they would consist of more than thirty thousand. Our two centre divisions, both commanded by General Spencer, in the sickness of General Greene, moved towards Mount Washington, Harlaem heights, and Horn's hook, as soon as the final resolution was taken in a council of war, on the 12th of September, to abandon the city. That event, thus circumstanced, took effect a few days after.

"On Sunday, the 15th, the British, after sending three ships of war up the North river, to Bloomingdale, and keeping up, for some hours, a severe cannonade on our lines, from those already in the East river, landed in force at Turtle bay. Our new levies, commanded by a state brigadier-general, fled without making resistance. Two brigades of General Putnam's division, ordered to their support, notwithstanding the exertion of their brigadiers, and of the commander-in-chief himself who came up at the instant, conducted themselves in the same shameful manner. His excellency then ordered the heights of Harlaem, a strong position, to be occupied. Thither the forces in the vicinity, as well as the fugitives, repaired. In the mean time, General Putnam, with the remainder of his command, and the ordinary outposts, was in the city. After having caused the brigades to begin their retreat by the route of Bloomingdale, in order to avoid the enemy, who were then in the possession of the main road leading to Kingsbridge, he galloped to call off the pickets and guards. Having myself been a volunteer in his division, and acting adjutant to the last regiment that left the city, I had frequent opportunities, that day, of beholding him, for the purpose of issuing orders, and encouraging the troops, flying, on his horse covered with foam, wherever his presence was most necessary. Without his extraordinary exertions, the guards must have been inevitably lost, and it is probable the entire corps would have been cut in pieces. When we were not far from Bloomingdale, an aid-de-camp came from him at full speed, to inform that a column of British infantry was descending upon our right. Our rear was soon fired upon, and the colonel of our regiment, whose order was just communicated for the front to file off to the left, was killed on the spot. With no other loss we joined the army, after dark, on the heights of Harlaem.

"Before our brigades came in, we were given up for lost by all our friends. So critical indeed was our situation, and so narrow the gap by which we escaped, that the instant we had passed, the enemy closed it by extending their line from river to river. Our men, who had been fifteen hours under arms, harassed by marching and countermarching, in consequence of incessant alarms, exhausted as they were by heat and thirst, (for the day proved insupportably hot, and few or none had canteens, insomuch, that some died at the brooks where they drank,) if attacked, could have made but feeble resistance.

"... That night our soldiers, excessively fatigued by the sultry march of the day, their clothes wet by a severe shower of rain that succeeded towards the evening, their blood chilled by the cold wind that produced a sudden change in the temperature of the air, and their hearts sunk within them by the loss of baggage, artillery, and works in which they had been taught to put great confidence, lay upon their arms, covered only by the clouds of an uncomfortable sky.

"... Next morning several parties of the enemy appeared upon the plains in our front. On receiving this intelligence, General Washington rode quickly to the outposts, for the purpose of preparing against an attack, if the enemy should advance with that design.

Lieutenant-colonel Knowlton's rangers, a fine selection from the eastern regiments, who had been skirmishing with an advanced party, came in, and informed the general that a body of British were under cover of a small eminence at no considerable distance. His excellency, willing to raise our men from their dejection by the splendor of some little success, ordered Lieutenant-colonel Knowlton, with his rangers, and Major Leitch, with three companies of Weedon's regiment of Virginians, to gain their rear; while appearances should be made of an attack in front. As soon as the enemy saw the party sent to decoy them, they ran precipitately down the hill, took possession of some fences and bushes, and commenced a brisk firing at long-shot. Unfortunately, Knowlton and Leitch made their onset rather in flank than in rear. The enemy changed their front, and the skirmish at once became close and warm. Major Leitch having received three balls through his side, was soon borne from the field; and Colonel Knowlton, who had distinguished himself so gallantly at the battle of Bunkerhill, was mortally wounded immediately after. Their men, however, undaunted by these disasters, stimulated with the thirst of revenge for the loss of their leaders, and conscious of acting under the eye of the commander-in-chief, maintained the conflict with uncommon spirit and perseverance. But the general, seeing them in need of support, advanced part of the Maryland regiments of Griffith and Richardson, together with some detachments from such eastern corps as chanced to be most contiguous to the place of action. Our troops this day, without exception, behaved with the greatest intrepidity. So bravely did they repulse the British, that Sir William Howe moved his *reserve*, with two field-pieces, a battalion of Hessian grenadiers, and a company of Chasseurs, to succor his retreating troops. General Washington, not willing to draw on a general action, declined pressing the pursuit. In this engagement were the second and third battalions of light infantry, the forty-second British regiment, and the German Chasseurs, of whom eight officers, and upwards of seventy privates were wounded, and our people buried nearly twenty, who were left dead on the field. We had about forty wounded; our loss in killed, except of two valuable officers, was very inconsiderable.

"An advantage so trivial in itself produced, in event, a surprising and almost incredible effect upon the whole army. Amongst the troops not engaged, who, during the action, were throwing earth from the new trenches, with an alacrity that indicated a determination to defend them, every visage was seen to brighten, and to assume, instead of the gloom of despair, the glow of animation. This change, no less sudden than happy, left little room to doubt that the men, who ran the day before at the sight of an enemy, would now, to wipe away the stain of that disgrace, and to recover the confidence of their general, have conducted themselves in a very different manner."

The following is Mr. Grim's account of the great fire, 21st of September, 1776.

"The fire of 1776 commenced in a small wooden house, on the wharf, near the Whitehall slip. It was then occupied by a number of men and women, of a bad character. The fire began late at night. There being but a very few inhabitants in the city, in a short time, it raged tremendously. It burned all the houses on the east side of Whitehall slip, and the west side of Broad-street to Beaver-street. A providential and happy circumstance occurred at this time; the wind was then southwesterly. About two o'clock that morning, the wind veered to the southeast; this carried the flames of the fire to the northwestward, and burned both sides of Beaver-street to the east side of Broadway, then crossed Broadway to Beaver-lane, and burning all the houses on both sides of Broadway, with some few houses in New-street, to Rector-street, and to John Harrison, Esq.'s three story brick house, which house stopped the fire on the east side of Broadway; from thence it continued burning all the houses in Lumber-street, and those in the rear of the houses on the west side of Broadway to St. Paul's church, then continued burning the houses on both sides of Partition-street, and all the houses in the rear (again) of the west side of Broadway to the North river. The fire did not stop until it got into Mortkile-street, now Barclay-street. The college yard and the vacant ground in the rear of the same, put an end to this awful and tremendous fire. Trinity church being burned, was occasioned by the flakes of fire that fell on the south side of the roof. The southerly wind fanned those flakes of fire in a short time to an amazing blaze, and it soon became out of human power to extinguish the same, the roof of this noble edifice being so steep that no person could go on it. St. Paul's church was in the like perilous situation. The roof being flat, with a balustrade on the eaves, a number of the citizens went on the same, and extinguished the flakes of fire as they fell on the roof. Thus happily was this beautiful church saved from the destruction of this dreadful fire, which threatened the ruin thereof, and that of the whole city. The Lutheran church being contiguous to houses adjoining the same fire, it was impossible to save it from destruction. This fire was so furious and violently hot, that no person could go near it, and there were no fire engines to be had at that time in the city.

"The number of houses that were burned and destroyed in this city at that awful conflagration, were thus, viz.—From Mortkile-street to Courtlandt-street, 167; from Courtlandt-street to Beaver-street, 175; from Beaver-street to the East river, 151. Total, 493. There being very few inhabitants in the city at the time, and many of those were afraid to venture at night in the streets, for fear of being taken up as suspicious persons. An instance to my knowledge occurred. A Mr. White, a decent citizen and house-carpenter, rather too violent a loyalist, and latterly, had addicted himself to liquor, was, on the night of the fire, hanged on a tavern signpost, at the corner of Cherry and Roosevelt-street. Several of the citizens were sent to the provost guard for examination, and some of them remained there two and three days, until they could give satisfactory evidence of their loyalty.

"Mr. Hugh Gain, in his Universal Register for the year 1787, page 119, says, New York is about a mile and a half in length, and half a mile broad, containing, before the fires on the 21st of September, 1776, and 3d of August, 1778, about 4,200 houses, and 30,000 inhabitants."

The following annexed account of the incidents of the revolutionary war in New York, is from Watson's Sketches of Olden Times in New York city.

"After the war had commenced and New York was expected to be captured, almost all the Whig families, who could sustain the expense, left their houses and homes to seek precarious refuge where they could in the country. On the other hand, after the city was possessed by the British, all the Tory families who felt unsafe in the country made their escape into New York for British protection. Painfully, family relations were broken; families as well as the rulers took different sides, and 'Greek met Greek' in fierce encounter.

"Mr. Brower, who saw the British force land in Kip's bay as he stood on the Long Island heights, says it was the most imposing sight his eyes ever beheld. The army crossed the East river, in open flat boats, filled with soldiers standing erect; their arms all glittering in the sunbeams. They approached the British fleet in Kip's bay, in the form of a crescent, caused by the force of the tide breaking the intended line of boat after boat. They all closed up in the rear of the fleet, when all the vessels opened a heavy cannonade.

"All the Presbyterian churches in New York were used for military purposes in some form or other. I suspect they were deemed more whiggish in general than some of the other churches. The clergymen of that order were in general, throughout the war, said to be zealous to promote the cause of the revolution. The Methodists, on the contrary, then few in number, were deemed loyalists. chiefly from the known loyalism of their founder,

Mr. Wesley. Perhaps to this cause it was that the society in John street enjoyed so much indulgence as to occupy their church for Sunday night service, while the Hessians had it in the morning service for their own chaplains and people.

"The British troops were quartered in any empty houses of the Whigs which might be found. Wherever men were billeted, they marked it.

"The middle Dutch church in Nassau-street, was used to imprison 3,000 Americans. The pews were all gutted out and used as fuel. Afterward they used it for the British cavalry, wherein they exercised their men, as a riding school; making them leap over raised windlasses. At the same place they often picketed their men, as a punishment, making them bear their weight on their toe on a sharp goad. At the same place, while the prisoners remained there, Mr. Andrew Mercein told me he used to see the '*dead cart*' come every morning, to bear off six or eight of the dead. The old sugar-house, which also adjoined to this church, was filled with the prisoners taken at Long Island; there they suffered much, they being kept in an almost starved condition. This starving proceeded from different motives; they wished to break the spirit of the prisoners, and to cause their desertion, or to make the war unwelcome to their friends at home. On some occasions, as I shall herein show, the British themselves were pinched for supplies; and on other occasions the commissaries had their own gain to answer, by withholding what they could from the prisoners. I could not find, on inquiry, that Americans in New York were allowed to help their countrymen unless by stealth. I was told by eye-witnesses of cases, where the wounded came crawling to the openings in the wall, and begging only for one cup of water, and could not be indulged, the sentinels saying, we are sorry too, but our orders have been, 'suffer no communication in the absence of your officer.'

"The north Dutch church in William-street was entirely gutted of its pews, and made to hold 2,000 prisoners. The Quaker meeting in Pearl-street was converted into an hospital. The old French church was used as a prison. Mr. Thomas Swords told me they used to bury the prisoners on the mount, then on the corner of Grace and Lumber streets. It was an old redoubt.

"Cunningham was infamous for his cruelty to the prisoners, even depriving them of life, it is said, for the sake of cheating his king and country by continuing for a time to draw their nominal rations! The prisoners at the Provost, (the present debtors' prison in the Park,) were chiefly under his severity, (my father among the number for a time.) It was said he was only restrained from putting them to death, (five or six of them of a night, back of the prison-yard, where were also their graves,) by the distress of certain women in the neighborhood, who, pained by the cries for mercy which they heard, went to the commander-in-chief, and made the case known, with entreaties to spare their lives in future. This unfeeling wretch, it is said, came afterward to an ignominious end, being executed in England, as was published in Hall and Sellers' paper in Philadelphia. It was there said, that it came out on the trial that he boasted of having killed more of the king's enemies by the use of his *own* means than had been effected by the king's arms!—he having, as it was there stated, used a preparation of arsenic in their flour!

"Loring, another commissary of prisoners, was quite another man, and had a pretty good name. Mr. Lennox, the other, being now a resident of New York, I forbear any remarks.

"There was much robbing in the city by the soldiery at times. In this, Lord Rawdon's corps and the king's guards were said to have been pre-eminent.

"The British cast up a line of intrenchments quite across from Corlear's hook to Bunker's hill, on the Bowery road, and placed gates across the road there. The Hessians, under Knyphausen, were encamped on a mount not far from Corlear's hook.

"Mr. Andrew Mercein, who was present in New York when most of the above-mentioned things occurred, has told me several facts. He was an apprentice with a baker who made bread for the army, and states, that there was a time when provisions, even to their own soldiery, was very limited. For instance, on the occasion of the Cork provision fleet over-staying their time, he has dealt out six penny loaves, as fast as he could hand them, for 'a hard half dollar a-piece!' The baker then gave $20 a cwt. for his flour. They had to make oatmeal bread for the navy. Often he has seen 7s. a pound given for butter, when before the war it was but 2d.

"When Cornwallis was in difficulties at Yorktown, and it became necessary to send him out all possible help, they took the citizens by constraint and enrolled them as a militia. In this service Mr. Mercein was also compelled, and had to take his turns at the fort. There they mounted guard, &c. in military attire, just lent to them for the time and required to be returned. The non-commissioned officers were generally chosen as Tories, but often without that condition. Mr. Mercein's sergeant was whiggish enough to have surrendered if he had had the proper chance. There were some independent companies of Tories there.

"It was really an affecting sight to see the operations of the final departure of all the king's embarkation; the royal band beat a farewell march. Then to see so many of our countrymen, with their women and children, leaving the lands of their fathers because they took the king's side, going thence to the bleak and barren soil of Nova Scotia, was at least affecting to them. Their hearts said, 'My country, with all thy faults I love thee still.'

"In contrast to this, there followed the entry of our tattered and weather-beaten troops, followed by all the citizens in regular platoons.

"'Oh! one day of such a welcome sight,
Were worth a whole eternity of lesser years.'

"Then crowded *home* to their own city, all those who had been abroad, reluctant exiles from British rule; now fondly cherishing in their hearts, 'this is *my own,* my native land.'

"The Hessian troops were peculiarly desirous to desert so as to remain in our country, and hid themselves in every family where they could possibly secure a friend to help their escape.

"... Captain Graydon of Philadelphia, who has left us amusing and instructive memoirs of sixty years of his observing life, having been among the officers and men (2,000) captured at Fort Washington near New York, and held prisoners, has left us many instructive pages concerning the incidents at New York while held by the British, which ought to be read by all those who can feel any interest in such domestic history as I have herein endeavored to preserve.

"After our capture, (says he,) we were committed, men and officers, to the custody of young and insolent officers; we were again and again taunted as 'cursed rebels,' and that we should all be hanged. Repeatedly we were paraded, and every now and then one and another of us was challenged among our *officers* as *deserters;* affecting thereby to consider their common men as good enough for our ordinary subaltern officers. Unfortunately for our pride and self-importance, among those so challenged was here and there a subject fitted to their jibes and jeers. A little squat militia officer, from York county, with dingy clothes the worse for wear, was questioned with ' What, sir, is your rank ?' when he answered in a chuff and firm tone, ' a *keppun, sir ;'* an answer producing an immoderate laugh among 'the haughty Britons.' There was also an unlucky militia trooper of the same school, with whom the officers were equally merry, obliging him to amble about for their entertainment on his old jade, with his odd garb and accoutrements. On being asked what were his duties, he simply answered, '*it was to flank a little and bear tidings.*'

" At this beginning period of the war, most things on the American side were coarse and rough. Maryland and Philadelphia county put forward young gentlemen as officers of gallant bearing and demeanor; but New England, and this, then seat of war, was very deficient in such material. In many cases subaltern officers at least could scarcely be distinguished from their men other than by their cockades. It was not uncommon for colonels to make drummers and fifers of their sons. Among such the eye looked around in vain for the leading gentry of the country. General Putnam could be seen riding about in his shirt sleeves, with his hanger over his open vest: and Colonel Putnam, his nephew, did not disdain to carry his own piece of meat, saying, as his excuse, 'it will show our officers a good lesson of humility.'

"... The American officers took full latitude of their parole, in traversing the streets in all directions with a good deal of purposed assurance. One of them, on one occasion, wearing his best uniform, to the great gaze and wonderment of many, actually ventured disdainfully to pass the coffee house, then the general resort of the British officers. At other times, when the Kolch water was frozen over, and was covered with British officers, who thought themselves proficients in skating, it was the malicious pleasure of some of our officers to appear and eclipse them all. The officers occasionally met with cordial civilities and genteel entertainment from British officers with whom they came in contact; for, in truth, the latter valued their personal gentility too much to seem to be in any degree deficient in politeness and courtesy when they met with those whom they thought sufficiently polished to appreciate their demeanor.

"... The residence of Admiral Digby, and indeed of all naval officers of distinction arriving on the station, was Beekman's house, on the northwest corner of Sloate-lane and Hanover square. There dwelt, under the guardianship of Admiral Digby, *Prince Willaim Henry*, the late king of England. What associations of idea must be produced in the minds of those who can still remember when he walked the streets of New York in the common garb of a midshipman's 'roundabout,' or when they saw him a knocked-kneed lad, joining the boys in skating on the Kolch pond!"

The annexed is a description of some of the principal British officers. "Sir William Howe was a fine figure, full six feet high, and admirably well proportioned. In person he a good deal resembled Washington, and might have been mistaken for him at a distance. His features, though good, were more pointed, and the expression of his countenance was less benignant. His manners were polished, graceful, and dignified. He lived at N. Prime's house, at the south end of Broadway, near the battery.

"Sir Henry Clinton was short and fat, with a full face, prominent nose, and animated intelligent countenance. In his manners he was polite and courtly, but more formal and distant than Howe; and in his intercourse with his officers, was rather punctilious and not inclined to intimacy.

"Lord Cornwallis in person was short and thick set, but not so corpulent as Sir Henry. He had a handsome aquiline nose, and hair, when young, light and rather inclined to sandy; but at the time of his leaving here it had become somewhat gray. His face was well formed and agreeable, and would have been altogether fine had he not blinked badly with his left eye. He was uncommonly easy and affable in his manners, and always accessible to the lowest of his soldiers, by whom he was greatly beloved. With his officers he used the utmost cordiality.

"General Knyphausen, who commanded the Germans, was a fine-looking German, of about five feet eleven, straight and slender. His features were sharp, and his appearance martial.

"Tarleton was below the middle size, stout, strong, heavily made, with large legs, but uncommonly active. His eye was small, black, and piercing; his face smooth, and his complexion dark; he was quite young, probably about twenty-five.

"Colonel Abercrombie, who afterward gained so much eclat in Egypt, where he fell, was one of the finest built men in the army; straight and elegantly proportioned. His countenance was strong and manly, but his face was much pitted by the small-pox. When here he appeared to be about forty."

CAPTAIN DAVID HALE.

"This eminent martyr to American liberty was the son of Deacon Richard Hale, of Coventry, Connecticut, where he was born June 6, 1755; and graduated at Yale College in 1773. Possessed of genius, taste, and ardor, he early became distinguished as a scholar, and being endowed in an eminent degree with those gifts and graces which always add a new charm to youthful excellence, he gained the respect and confidence of all that knew him. Being a patriot from principle, and enthusiastic in a cause which appealed equally to his sense of justice and his love of liberty, he was among the first to take up arms in defence of his country, whose soil had been invaded by a hostile force, and its citizens subjected to the alternative of *determined resistance* or *humiliating submission*. The life of Captain Hale was short, but eventful. Its termination was under rare circumstances of intrepidity and cruelty. His case has been deemed parallel with that of Major Andre, and in some respects it was so—the nature of the service was identical. Both were young, well educated, ardent and brave; one for his king, the other for his country; and each fell a victim to the rigor of military law. The news of the battle of Lexington roused his martial spirit, and summoned him to the tented field. Before arriving at the age of twenty-one, a captain's commission was tendered him, and he soon became an efficient officer in the continental army; where his activity, zeal, and patriotism, obtained universal approbation. The company under his command, participating in the same spirit, submitted to a system of discipline before unknown to the army; and which produced very beneficial results. He entered as a captain in the light infantry regiment commanded by Colonel Knowlton, of Ashford, and was with the army on its retreat from Long Island, in August, 1776. The American forces took refuge in the city of New York, and afterward at the heights at Harlaem; and it became a matter of the utmost importance, in the opinion of the commander in-chief, to ascertain the numerical force and contemplated operations of the enemy; for on that knowledge depended the safety of the American army, and perhaps the nation also. A council of officers was assembled, and resulted in a determination to send some one competent to the task into the heart of the enemy's camp, and Colonel Knowlton was charged with the selection of an individual to perform the delicate and hazardous service. On being informed of the views and wishes of Washington, Hale, without hesitation, volunteered his services, saying that he did not accept a commission for fame alone; that he had been sometime in the army without being able thus far to render any signal aid to his country; and that he now felt impelled, by high considerations of duty, to peril his life in a cause of so vital importance when an opportunity presented itself of being useful. The arguments of his friends were unavailing to dissuade him from the undertaking; and having disguised himself as well as he could, he left his quarters at Harlaem Heights, and having an order from the commander-in-chief to all the American armed vessels to convey him to any point which he should designate, he was enabled to cross the sound from Fairfield to Long Island, and arrived at Huntington about the middle of September, 1776. When he reached Brooklyn, the British army had taken possession of New York. He examined with the utmost caution the fortifications of the enemy, and ascertained as far as possible their number, position, and future intentions; and having satisfactorily accomplished the objects of his mission, he again reached Huntington for the purpose of re-crossing the sound. While waiting for a passage, a boat came on shore, which he at first supposed to be from Connecticut, but proved to be from a British vessel, the Cerberus, lying in the sound; and on board this boat, it is said, was a relative of Capt. Hale, a tory refugee, who recognised and betrayed him. He had assumed a character which did not belong to him, that of pretending to be what he was not. That he was a *spy*, could no longer be concealed, and he was immediately sent to General Howe at New York. Here the parallel between *his* case and that of *Andre* ceases. The latter was allowed time and an impartial trial before officers of honorable rank and character, and his last moments were soothed by tenderness and sympathy. Not so with the former; he was delivered into the possession of the infamous provost-marshal, Cunningham, and ordered immediately for execution, without even the formality of a trial. The order was performed in a brutal manner on the twenty-first of September, 1776, and his body was buried on the spot where he breathed his last. He was, indeed, permitted to consecrate a few previous moments in writing to his family; but as soon as the work of death was done, even this testimony of affection and patriotism was destroyed, assigning as the cause, '*that the rebels should never know they had a man in their army who could die with such firmness.*' In this t.ying hour the use of a bible and the attendance of a minister, which he desired, were also denied him. Thus unknown to those around him, with no eye to pity, or a voice to administer consolation, fell one of the most noble and amiable youths which America could boast; with this his dying observation, '*that he only lamented he had but one life to lose for his country.*' Though the manner of his execution will be abhorred by every friend of humanity, yet there cannot be a question but that the sentence of death was conformable to the practice of all civilized nations. It is, however, but common justice to the character of Captain Hale to state, that his motives for engaging in this service were entirely different from those which sometimes influence o'hers in like cases. Neither expectation of promotion or pecuniary reward induced the attempt. A high sense of public duty, and a hope of being in this way useful to his country, and the opinion which he had adopted, that every kind of service became honorable by being necessary, were the motives which prompted him to this hazardous, and, to him, fatal enterprise. To see such an one, in the bloom of youth, influenced by the purest intentions, and emulous of doing good to his beloved country, fall a victim to the policy of nations, must have been wounding even to the feelings of his enemies.

"Among other causes of distress in 1776, the want of provisions and clothing was severely felt by the American army. Just previous to the battle of Long Island it was ascertained that an *English sloop*, with supplies of these essential articles, had arrived in the East river, and lay there under the protection of the ship Asia, of ninety guns. Captain Hale conceived the bold project of capturing this sloop, and bringing her into the port of New York, and found a sufficient number of bold hearts and stout hands to make the attempt. At an hour concerted, they passed in a boat to a point of land nearest the sloop, where they lay till the moon was down; and when all was quiet, except the voice of the watchman on the quarter-deck of the Asia, they pulled for the sloop, and in a few minutes were on board. She became their prize, and the goods were distributed to those who needed them in our army.

"A meeting of the citizens of Coventry and the neighboring towns was held on the 25th of November, 1836, at which a society was formed called the HALE MONUMENT ASSOCIATION, for the purpose of taking measures to erect a suitable memorial to the memory of the subject of this notice. An eloquent address was delivered on the occasion, by Andrew T. Judson, Esq., to whom we are indebted for much of the information contained in this brief memoir.

"The following poetical tribute to the lamented Hale, is from the pen of the late President Dwight:—

> ' Thus, while fond virtue wished in vain to save,
> HALE, bright and generous, found a hapless grave;
> With *genius*' living flame his bosom glow'd,
> And *science* charmed him to her sweet abode;
> In *worth's* fair path, adventured far,
> The *pride* of peace, and rising *grace* of war.'

"As yet no monument has been erected, nor have his ashes ever been recovered. A select committee of congress, on the 19th of January, 1836, recommended an appropriation of one thousand dollars from the treasury of the United States towards carrying the object into effect; but no action was ever had upon it afterward, and it is much to be feared so praiseworthy a design will be suffered to sleep, perhaps forever."—*Thompson's History of Long Island.*

The annexed account of the evacuation of New York by the British, and the entrance of the American troops, under Washington, is extracted from Thatcher's Military Journal.

"*November 25th*, 1783.—The British army evacuated New York, and the American troops under General Knox, took possession of the city. Soon after, General Washington and Governor Clinton, with their suite, made their public entry into the city on horseback, followed by the lieutenant-governor and the members of council, for the temporary government of the southern district, four abreast; General Knox and the officers of the army, eight abreast; citizens on horseback, eight abreast; the speaker of the assembly and citizens on foot, eight abreast. The governor gave a public dinner, at which the commander-in-chief, and other general officers were present. The arrangements for the whole business were so well made and executed, that the most admirable tranquillity succeeded through the day and night. On Monday the governor gave an elegant entertainment to the French ambassador, the Chevalier de la Luzerne; General Washington, the principal officers of New York state, and of the army, and upwards of a hundred gentlemen were present. Magnificent fireworks, infinitely exceeding every thing of the kind before seen in the United States, were exhibited at the Bowling Green, in Broadway, on the evening of Tuesday, in celebration of the definitive treaty of peace. They commenced by a dove descending with the *olive branch*, and setting fire to a marron battery. On Tuesday noon, December 4th, the principal officers of the army assembled at Francis' tavern, to take a final leave of their much loved commander-in-chief. Soon after, his excellency entered the room. His emotions were too strong to be concealed. Filling a glass, he turned to them and said, ' With a heart full of love and gratitude, I now take leave of you. I most devoutly wish that your latter days may be as prosperous and happy as your former ones have been glorious and honorable.' Having drank, he added, ' I cannot come to each of you to take my leave, but shall be obliged to you, if each of you will come and take me by the hand.' General Knox being nearest, turned to him. Incapable of utterance, Washington, *in tears*, grasped his hand, embraced and kissed him. In the same affectionate manner he took leave of each succeeding officer. In every eye was the tear of dignified sensibility; and not a word was articulated to interrupt the eloquent silence and tenderness of the scene. Leaving the room, he passed through the corps of light infantry, and walked to Whitehall, where a barge waited to convey him to Paulus' Hook. The whole company followed in mute and solemn procession, with dejected countenances, testifying feelings of delicious melancholy which no language can describe. Having entered the barge he turned to the company, and waving his hat, bid them a silent adieu. They paid him the same affectionate compliment, and after the barge had left them, returned in the same solemn manner to the place where they had assembled. The passions of human nature were never more tenderly agitated than in this interesting and distressful scene."

The following, respecting the prevalence of the yellow fever at various times in New York, is from a publication written by James Hardie, A. M., printed in New York in 1822.

"The yellow fever, in our times, was first observed in this city in the year 1791, when General Malcolm and some other very respectable citizens fell victims to its fury. The late respectable Dr. James Tillary, at a meeting of a number of physicians, explained the symptoms of the disease, described its character, and gave it its true name. To all present, excepting two, the doctor spoke in a language which was past their comprehension, as he had described a disease which they had never seen, and of which they had not the most distant conception. But it was well remembered by the late venerable Dr. John Carleton and Dr. Samuel Bard, who had seen the same fell destroyer, spreading havoc and destruction in this city, about forty years before that period. Since that time, it has repeatedly made its appearance amongst us, and every physician in this city as well as in most other maritime cities in the United States has had repeated opportunities of seeing it and of devising, in his own mind, what he might deem the most effectual means of its prevention and cure.

"As the sickness, which occurred in the year 1798, was by far more fatal than any which has happened since that time, I shall endeavor to give as brief an account as possible of its origin, progress, and termination.

"Its first victim, in all probability, was Mr. Melancton Smith, who died on the 28th or 29th of July, after an illness of a few days. His case was said to have been attended with the most malignant symptoms; but such was the general opinion of the inhabitants with respect to the healthiness of our city, that his death excited little or no alarm. It was believed that Mr. Smith had been taken sick at his store, in Front-street, near Coenties-slip, and a few days after his death, several persons were attacked with sickness in that vicinity. The symptoms of their disorders, however, appeared to be similar to that of a *common cold*. They were, therefore, negligent in obtaining medical aid; hence the disease got the ascendancy before they were aware of their danger, and the assistance of physicians was called for when it was too late.

"Whether any case of pestilential fever existed in the earlier part of August, remote from the place where it was believed to have originated, was not, at the time, ascertained to a certainty; but of this there was no doubt, viz. that about the 20th of the month, cases of a highly malignant nature appeared in different parts of the city on the same day, and in the course of six or eight days in different streets very remote from one another. In particular, it began to rage with great violence at the New-slip; in Cliff-street and John-street: but more especially in Rider-street and Eden's-alley, where not a family escaped it, nor was there a house, except two, in which it did not terminate fatally to one or more individuals.

"The Health Commissioners began to be apprehensive respecting the appearance of this pestilence so early as the 6th of August, on which day they addressed a letter to the Mayor. It was to the following purport, viz. that 'the unfinished state of the docks in Front-street, between Coenties and the Old slips, generally, had been, in their opinion, a source of disease, in that neighborhood, last year, and had occasioned the death of several valuable citizens. That they cannot sufficiently regret that they had reason to renew their remonstrances on this subject, and that its present situation was likely to be productive of still greater evils than those of last year.' They added, that several persons had sickened in the neighborhood of these unfinished grounds within a week, and with symptoms strikingly characteristic of yellow fever; and they recommended that the common council would appoint two of their members, with whom they (the commissioners) would meet, at an early hour on the ensuing morning, to concert measures adapted to the emergency of the case. The board very cheerfully complied with this recommendation, and such measures were immediately adopted as were deemed most likely to check the progress of the growing malady; but it had now taking so deep root, that it could neither be eradicated nor checked by human means.

"On the same day (6th August) the commissioners issued an advertisement, notifying their determination to put the laws in force against those who should neglect to keep the streets clean before their respective doors, &c., adding that the street inspectors were directed to report all offences of this nature to the police, and that the penalty against offenders would be rigidly exacted.

"On the 12th, 13th and 14th of August, there were heavy showers of rain; that on the 14th commenced at four in the morning, and continued without intermission until nine, with considerable thunder. The quantity which fell during these five hours, was supposed to have been greater than had at any time fallen, during the same space of time, for many years. The streets were covered with water in many places knee-deep, and a vast number of cellars were filled with it.

"It was at the time generally believed, that this excessive rain and thunder would have so purified the air, that the city would, in a few days, be totally exempt from any cases of this disorder; but, alas! our expectations were dreadfully disappointed. It is well known, that stagnant water in confined places, during hot weather, will, in a few days, exhale a pestilential vapor, which, if it does not generate, will certainly propagate or throw into more extensive circulation dangerous diseases which have already made their appearance. To prevent an occurrence of this kind, the citizens were repeatedly and most earnestly entreated by the Health Commissioners to cause the water to be removed, and lime afterward to be liberally scattered in their cellars. Although it might have been reasonably expected, that a regard to self-preservation would have produced a prompt compliance with this recommendation, it is well known that many neglected it, and of those not a few were amongst the first victims to the disease. From this time, the number of deaths almost daily increased.

"About the 24th of August, numbers began to leave the city, and many of those who had offices for the transaction of business towards the East river, moved to Broadway, which was deemed more healthy. The customhouse, in Mill-street, and the Insurance Office, in Water-street, were fixed, for the time, in the Tontine City Tavern, in Broadway.

"During the whole month of August, the number of deaths amounted to three hundred and twenty-nine. As particular attention was not paid by the sextons, during this month, to distinguish those who fell victims to the fever from those who had died of other disorders, it was difficult to ascertain their precise numbers. It was believed, however, that by fixing it at one hundred, it would not be far from the truth. On the 15th of August, the deaths were 14—from which day the number continued to progress, so that on the 1st of September they amounted to 23. The daily averages during August was about 12.

"On the 15th of September the number of funerals was 38, on the 19th they were no less than 63, and on each of the two following days they were reduced to 40—from which circumstance hopes were entertained that our mortal foe was about to leave us; but we were again disappointed, for the next four days it kept fluctuating between 41 and 50, and on the 26th rose up to 60. The total number of deaths during this month was eleven hundred and fifty-two, of whom nine hundred and fifty-four died of fever. The daily average through the month was about 38.

"The number of the dead on the 1st of October was 43, and this was the greatest number during the whole month. On the 18th it was reduced to 16, and on the 21st it only amounted to 9. After this the number of deaths on any one day, during the existence of the calamity, did not exceed 15; and it is almost certain, that had our absent citizens attended to the advice of the Health Committee, dissuading them from a premature return, the death warrant of the disorder might have been dated from that day. The whole number of funerals in October was five hundred and twenty-two, of whom four hundred and thirty-one died of fever. The average of the deaths, during this month, was about 17.

"On the 10th of November the deaths were 5, and on each of the preceding days they were only 4. The total number during these ten days were 83, of whom thirty-nine died of yellow fever. The following address of the Committee to the public now made its appearance.

" 'The Health Committee for the relief of the sick and indigent in the city of New York, beg leave to congratulate their fellow-citizens, that under Divine Providence, this long afflicted city is once more restored to its usual state of general health, and, with the most heartfelt pleasure, inform those who yet remain in exile, that although a few cases of the pestilential fever exist, yet that by the *late cold weather and frost*, the contagion is so far destroyed, as to render the return of their families to the city perfectly safe, provided they take the necessary previous measures of cleansing and ventilating their long unaired dwellings, and purifying the bedding and clothing, which may have been left therein during the prevalence of the fever.

" ' It would have afforded the Committee much satisfaction, could they have given this invitation at an earlier period, but they did not conceive themselves warranted by the then existing circumstances. There have, until the present moment, been several new cases of fever, *particularly among those citizens who returned earlier than the committee thought prudent, many of whom have fallen victims to the devouring pestilence.* This, among other circumstances, has induced the committee, to withhold this invitation until the present time, &c.'

" The whole number of deaths during this awful calamity, was two thousand and eighty-six, viz. eleven hundred and ten men, five hundred and eighty-nine women, and eight hundred and eighty-five children. Of these, if we admit that one hundred died of the fever in August, its victims would amount to one thousand five hundred and twenty-four. A great many of our citizens, too, who fled, were likewise cut off by it. Hence it is probable, that the whole number of deaths would be between 2,400 and 2,500. An awful number indeed; particularly if we consider that more than one third, some suppose that one half, of the inhabitants had left the city.

" An opinion generally prevailed, that the progress of the disease varied according to the state of the atmosphere; but from my observations on this subject, in the years 1798, 1799, 1800, 1803, 1805, and also in the present year, I am much inclined to doubt its accuracy. *The pestilence walketh in darkness*, and the wisest of men, as yet, know very little of the nature of its progress. Of this, however, we may be certain, that cool mornings and evenings, accompanied by hot days, contribute greatly to spread infection; that in case of yellow fever having for some time existed in a city, it is extremely dangerous for those who have fled to return to their houses till the hard frost shall set in, and that a *keen black frost* has uniformly and almost instantaneously put an end to the further progress of the disorder."

The following is an account of the yellow fever in 1803, as given in an official letter by Dr. Miller.

" The commencement of the disease took place about the 20th of July, and from that time, it continued to prevail, in a greater or less degree, till the end of October. The number of deaths, in this city, amounted to five hundred and three; those at the Hospital of Bellevue, to one hundred and three, and those at the Marine Hospital on Staten Island, to sixty-eight, making a total of six hundred and seventy-four. To this should be added an indefinite number, about fifty or sixty, who fled from the city, and died of this disease in the neighboring country and villages.

" The first public alarm arose from some fatal cases at the Coffee-House Slip, and in that neighborhood. About the same time, the disease was discovered in many other parts of the city, without any known intercourse or communication between the persons who fell sick. Although the number of cases, even at the worst periods of the epidemic, could not be pronounced to be great, especially if compared with some preceding seasons, they were certainly more generally diffused, and left fewer parts of the city exempt than on any former occasions. Broadway and some of the adjacent parts of the town retained their healthy character. The streets lying near the margins of the two rivers, and some of those in the upper part of the city, which are principally inhabited by indigent, uncleanly, and dissolute classes of the community, suffered the worst ravages of the disease. The alarm of the inhabitants was very suddenly produced, and the suspension of business and the desertion of the city far exceeded what had been ever experienced in former seasons."

The following respecting the yellow fever in 1805, is extracted from a letter from Dr. E. Miller to Gov. Lewis.

" In former seasons, it has been usual to observe sporadic cases of this disease, for several weeks, before the commencement of the epidemic. This was remarkably verified in the late season; and such cases deserve the more attention, as they furnish the best means of calculating the probability of approaching pestilence. Accordingly, one case of a decidedly malignant character was observed in the month of June; several took place in July; a still greater number in August: and at the beginning of September, they had become so nu merous as to ascertain the existence of the epidemic. Throughout September and October, the disease continued to prevail with more or less severity, according to the fluctuating state of the weather; but towards the close of the latter month, the coldness of the season had evidently checked its progress; and at the beginning of November, the city was nearly restored to its usual health.

" During the early period of the epidemic, nearly all the cases took place on the eastern side of the city, in Front, Water, and Pearl streets, and principally below Burling-Slip. They afterward became more generally diffused. About the 20th of September, they began to prevail near the North river. On the whole, the *low* grounds on the margin of the two rivers certainly produced a chief part of the cases. The number of deaths in the city amounted to about two hundred; those at the Bellevue Hospital to 52, and those in the Marine Hospital, sent from the city, to twenty-eight. The number of cases of malignant fever reported to the Board of Health, amounted to six hundred. It is proper, likewise, in estimating the extent of the epidemic, to notice an unascertained number, probably about forty, who after their flight from the city died in various parts of the country.

" The source of this disease forms a most interesting subject of inquiry; on the success of which must depend all rational and adequate means of preventing and eradicating the evil. After a long and careful investigation of the subject, I cannot hesitate to conclude, that *a pernicious exhalation or vapour floating in the atmosphere, is the primary and essential cause of this disease.*"

The yellow fever in 1822, made its appearance in a different quarter from that in which it had commenced its depredations in former years. It had uniformly begun somewhere on the East river; but now it was first seen in Rector-street towards the North river, a part of the city which had been heretofore deemed peculiarly unhealthy. The disease was first formerly noticed by the Board of Health on the 31st of July. The Board again met at 12 o'clock, having agreed to meet every day at that hour during the prevalence of fever. From the 13th of July to the 2d of November, twelve hundred and thirty-six persons died.

" On the same day, Saturday, the 24th August, our city presented the appearance of a town besieged. From daybreak till night, one line of carts, containing boxes, merchandise, and effects, were seen moving towards Greenwich Village and the upper parts of the city. Carriages and hacks, wagons and horsemen, were scouring the streets and filling the roads; persons with anxiety strongly marked on their countenances and with hurried gait were bustling through the streets. Temporary stores and offices were erecting, and even on the ensuing day (Sunday) carts were in motion and the saw and hammer busily at work. Within a few days thereafter, the Customhouse, the Post-office, the Banks, the Insurance offices, and the printers of newspapers, located themselves in the village or in the upper part of Broadway, where they were free from the impending danger, and these places almost instantaneously became the seat of the immense business usually carried on in this great metropolis.

Friday, the 11th of October, was observed as a day of public humiliation and prayer on account of the pestilence.

" Immediately after the address of the Board to their fellow-citizens on the 26th October, the absentees began to return to their respective abodes with a precipitation almost unparalleled. Forty or fifty carts and wagons could be seen in a line transporting goods, wares, merchandise, and household furniture from the village of Greenwich and places in the outskirts of the city, to the stores and houses from which they had been taken several weeks before. On the 5th November, the Customhouse, Post-office, Banks, Insurance offices, Printing offices, Vendue Masters, Merchants, &c., returned to their former habitations. About this time, the places of worship, which had been so long shut, in the lower part of the city, were re-opened, vessels came to our docks as usual, and a bustle again became visible at the former places of trade and commerce."

In July, 1832, the asiatic cholera made its appearance in this city. The following table is extracted from the New York Observer. It includes all the deaths from July 2d, at about the time of its commencement, until Oct. 19th, when the pestilence had almost ceased.

NEW YORK COUNTY.

Week ending	City Inspector's Report.		Our Estimate.	
	Burials.	Of Cholera.	Deaths by pestilence.	Average per day.
July 7	191	56	81	11
" 14	510	336	400	57
" 21	887	716	777	111
" 28	879	686	769	110
Aug. 4	580	383	470	67
" 11	467	281	357	51
" 18	444	222	334	48
" 25	391	178	281	40
Sept. 1	324	138	214	30
" 8	355	201	245	35
" 15	291	128	181	26
" 22	238	72	128	18
" 29	180	50	70	10
Oct. 5	137	24	27	4
" 12	129	14	19	2
" 19	94	11	11	2
Total	6,097	3,496	4,364	

The annexed description of New York in 1800, was taken from a series of historical articles relating to the city, now being published in the New York Express, ... commenced two years since.

"The fashionable part of the city, *or west end of the town,* was in Wall and Pine streets, between Broadway and Pearl,—Pearl from Hanover square, (now part of Old slip,) to John-street, along State-street and a part of Broadway, below Wall-street. Then the city hall was not built, and on the site where it now stands was the rear of the almshouse—the hog-pen of which enclosed the ground now the most beautiful part of the Park. The change is truly astonishing. In Wall-street, for example, there now is but one family residing in the whole street, and that is over a bank. Hardly an old building remains, and not one that is not so altered as to be totally different from what it was then. At the corner of Nassau-street, stood the venerable Federal hall, since torn down—a splendid row of dwellings was afterward put up, which were subsequently torn down to give place to the new customhouse, now building. Next below stood the elegant mansion of Mr. Verplanck, the brick of which were brought from Holland, and in its stead is the Bank of the State of New York. Next was the residence of John Keese, now the Union Bank—less changed than any other building. This, however, on the first of May, is to be levelled with the ground, and a new banking-house to be put up. Between it and William-street were the residences of Francis B. Winthrop and Charles Wilkes—in the place of which are the Dry Dock Bank, and Bank of America. On the lot where the United States Bank now stands was the elegant mansion of Gen. John Lamb, first collector of the port, and father of Alderman Lamb. This was considered not only the finest house, but was believed to be the grandest house that could be built. On the opposite side, where is now going up the massive new Merchants' Exchange, stood the residence of Thomas Buchanan, Mrs. White, and William C. Leffingwell. Mr. Jauncey, an English gentleman who lived in great style, occupied the building now rented by Messrs. Dykers & Alstyne—his stable is the same building now used by the Board of Brokers. The very room in which millions of stock are sold every week was then a hay-loft.

"The watch-house was kept at the corner of Broad-street, now used by Robinson for the sale of his caricatures. Baker's tavern, one of the most noted public houses, was at the corner of New-street—a club met there nightly for more than half a century. Pine-street has undergone still greater changes,—from Water-street to Broadway, every house has been demolished. Then not a store was to be seen. The old French church, the sanctuary of the Huguenots, stood at the corner of Nassau,—its surrounding burying yard contained the ashes of many of the most valued citizens. The Walcotts, Jays, Waddingtons, Radcliffs, Brinkerhoffs, Wells, and a host of others, resided in this street, without a thought that in less than 40, and even 30 years, not one brick then standing, would remain on another. In Pearl-street were the fashionable residences of Samuel Denton, John Ellis, John J. Glover, John Mowett, Robert Lenox, Thomas Cadle, John Glendenning, John B. Murray, Governor Broome, Andrew Ogden, Governor George Clinton, Richard Varick, and a great number of others. Nearly all of these gentlemen are deceased. We noticed a few days since, one of the number, Mr. Denton, for a long time past a resident of Tennessee. He remarked that he was absolutely a stranger; knew no one, and could hardly identify a single spot. In Hanover square, stood a block of buildings fronting Old slip and Pearl-street. They have all been removed. The city consisted of seven wards, now increased to seventeen."

View of the City Hall, New York.

The city hall* is one of the most prominent buildings in New York, standing near the centre of the park, an area of about four acres. Situated in this spacious area, it is seen to great advantage in every direction.

"The building is of a square form, two stories in height, besides a basement story. It has a wing at each end, projecting from the front, and in the centre the roof is elevated to form an attic story. The whole length of the building is 216 feet, the breadth 105, and the height 51 feet. Including the attic story, it is 65 feet in height. The front and both ends, above the basement story, are built of native white marble, from Stockbridge, Massachusetts; and the rest of the building is constructed of brown freestone. The roof is covered with copper, and there is a balustrade of marble entirely round the top. Rising from the middle of the roof, is a cupola, on which is placed a colossal figure of JUSTICE, holding in her right hand, which rests on her forehead, a balance, and in her left, a sword pointing to the ground. Justice is not blindfold, as she is represented in Europe.

"There are four entrances to the building; one in front, one in the

---

* The above engraving was copied from a drawing taken some years ago. Since then, the cupola has been slightly altered, and a clock placed in it. A small cupola has also been added in the rear, on which hangs the city fire-bell. The city is divided into five fire districts, and when there is a fire the particular district in which it is located is indicated by the number of times which the bell tolls. For instance, when it is in the first it tolls once, in the second, twice in succession, and so on, excepting in the fifth, which is indicated by a continual tolling.

rear, and one in each end. The front, which is the principal, is on the first story, to which there is access by a flight of 12 marble steps, rising from which there are 16 columns supporting a portico immediately over the entrance, also composed of marble. In the centre of the rear of the building, there is a projecting pediment. The entrance in this quarter is also on the first story, by a flight of freestone steps. The first story, including the portico, is of the Ionic, the second of the Corinthian, the attic of the Fancy, and the cupola of the Composite orders.

"The foundation stone of this building was laid on 26th September, 1803, during the mayoralty of Edward Livingston, Esq., and at a time when the yellow fever prevailed in the city. It was finished in 1812, and the expense, exclusive of the furniture, amounted to half a million of dollars."

"Fifty dollars," says the New York Express, "were appropriated to defray the expenses of the ceremony of laying the corner-stone. These were the times when expenses of this sort were dealt out with a most sparing hand. No corporation dinners were allowed and two to three thousand dollars expended. When the corner-stone was laid, and long after, the long building now standing on Chamber-street, and in which various courts are held, was the almshouse. The paupers of that day numbered less than four hundred; now, our Bellvue establishment has more inmates than the number of many of our most flourishing cities. Three to four thousand are the permanent inhabitants of the almshouse, besides quadruple that number who receive temporary relief from the commissioners. The space between the almshouse and city hall, was then a pig-pen, and contained hundreds of pigs, fattened by the wash of the almshouse, debtor's prison, and bridewell. It will be seen that the hall is mainly built of marble; the first design was that the whole should be built of that material. At that time, marble was high, and it was desirable to make a saving. It was maintained that the population would never, to any extent, settle above Chamber-street, and therefore, as the rear of the hall would not be seen, it was concluded to build the same of red freestone. This accounts for the difference between the front and rear."

The following shows the Egyptian building, embracing the halls of justice, as it appears fronting Centre-street. The police courts are held here at all hours of the day; the justices relieving each other in their sittings. This place may be considered as the head-quarters of the police officers or constables, who are constantly seen going after, and returning with criminals of every grade, from the genteel and accomplished rascal, to his brother in crime, the coarse and brutal villain. Perhaps in no other part of the country are seen such degraded and disgusting exhibitions of fallen humanity, as in this place. Here many culprits of both sexes are literally *dragged* up to the tribunal of justice. While some are making complaints, others are being "examined," "sentenced," "bound over," or "reprimanded," as the case may be. While this is going on, the officers may

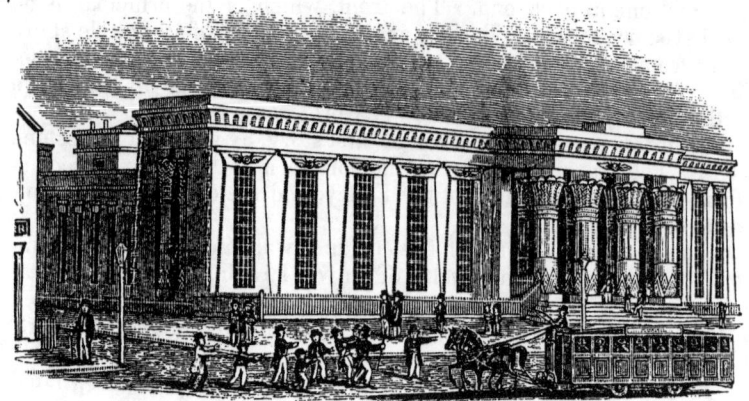

Southern view of the Halls of Justice, Centre-street.

be seen leading off some to the prisons, or *tombs*, (as they are familiarly called,) in another part of the building. The court of sessions is held in an adjoining part of the building, at which the recorder presides.

"This edifice now occupies the whole of the block bounded by Leonard, Elm, Franklin, and Centre streets, (formerly the corporation yard,) and is 253 feet 3 inches in length, by 200 feet 5 inches in width.

"The interior combines accommodations for the courts of sessions, police, grand jury, house of detention, records, city watch, district attorney, sheriff, clerk of the court, and other officers belonging to the different branches of the institution, together with the necessary offices for cooking, washing, watering, warming, &c. The whole designed by Mr. John Haviland.

"The four facades, as well as the entrance hall, are executed in the Egyptian style of architecture, with Hallowell granite.

"The principal front has a distyle portico of four columns, with palm-leaved capitals. Above the capitals are square dies, upon which rests the architrave, ornamented with a large winged globe encircled by serpents. The architrave is surmounted by a cornice, composed of a bold Scotia, enriched with reeded Triglyphs and a banded Torus; and which, being of the same height with that of the similarly embellished wings, forms with them one continued line. Moreover, the banded moulding of the cornice descends in the form of a roller on all the external angles of the edifice. Both the wings are perforated with five lofty windows, extending the height of two stories, and finished with diminished pilasters, which support a cornice over each, composed simply of a bold Scotia, enriched with a winged globe and serpents.

"The lateral fronts on Leonard and Franklin streets have each two projecting pylones or porches, with two columns; the one on Leonard-street adjoining the principal front, is the entrance to the debtors' ward, and the opposite one on Franklin-street is the entrance to the police ward; the other two corresponding porches next to Elm-street, form the carriage entrance to the house of detention. These porches are 54 feet wide, and their columns and entablatures correspond with those of the principal front, but the caps and shafts of the columns are less enriched. The recess in both these lateral fronts is six feet, and is relieved by five windows corresponding in character with those of the principal front, but of less proportion and enrichment, the Scotia being finished with reeded Triglyphs only, instead of the winged globe and serpents. The approach to the windows on these fronts is guarded against by a neat railing in keeping with the architecture. The rear or front on Elm-street having no entrance or windows, is simply relieved by seven narrow recesses in imitation of embrasures, and a railing in the same style as those on the lateral fronts.

"A terrace surrounds the whole enclosure, raised ten feet above the level of Centre-street, from which you ascend eight steps of a truncated and pyramidal form, to the platform of the portico, from which you ascend also twelve steps, between the intercolumniation of the rear columns to the entrance hall. This hall is 50 feet square and 25 feet high, supported by eight columns, ranged between two rows with their antæ placed on the opposite walls. These columns bear the character or an order taken from the colonnade of the temple of Medynet Abou. Attached to the antes opposite these columns, the architect originally designed to place the Egyptian caviatides, so highly spoken of by the French artists in Napoleon's great work on Egypt, published by Pauckonche; and he feels assured that the Board will yet be of his opinion, and finally adopt these splendid and imposing figures in this entrance hall, as nothing else will be wanting to perfect the edifice; their capitals are ornamented with the leaves and flowers of the Lotus. The floors are arched and laid in mosaic of an Egyptian character, governed in form by the compartments in the ceiling to which each belongs.

"The principal courts, jury, witness, and other business rooms, are connected with, and lead into the entrance hall. On the left side are doors and passages communicating with the grand jury room, offices for register, clerk of the court, district attorney, and sheriff, debtors' ward and witness' rooms; and on the right side are disposed the magistrates' offices, court, and witness' rooms, watchmen's dormitories, police court, officers' rooms, and cells for nightly commitments. The centre leads to the court of sessions, (including two jury rooms, and separate gallery capable of containing an audience of 300 persons;) the whole well ventilated and lighted, and in a situation the least liable to be disturbed by the noise of the adjoining streets.

"The house of detention is a distinct and isolated building, 142 feet in length by 45 in width. It contains 148 cells, divided into four distinct classes for prisoners, including baths, and rooms for male and female, white and black vagrants. The lower cells are 6 feet 9 inches wide, 11 feet high, and 15 feet long, diminishing 18 inches in length in each story; they are provided with cast-iron water closets, hydrant, water cock, ventilators, and are warmed by Perkins' hot water pipes, (introduced and now in successful operation in the new penitentiaries at Philadelphia and Trenton, by J. Haviland, architect.) The floors, and ceilings, and galleries are formed of slabs from the North river flagging; the doors and window jambs of iron; and the entire cells are otherwise finished on the most approved plan for security, seclusion, ventilation, economy of supervision and watching. The corridors are ten feet wide below, and widen at each story to 19 feet at the summit, affording a free ventilation and uninterrupted view of every cell door, from the observatory. A bridge leads across from the house of detention to the prisoners' seat in the courthouse. By reference to the specifications and drawings, it will be seen that every part of the building is calculated to be executed in the most substantial and approved manner, with the best materials of their kind: and that no pains or expense is spared to effect all the desired objects of the institution, with the aid, experience, and best talent that the country affords.

"The building is generally fire-proof by ceilings and floors of arched masonry.

"The site on which the building is erected, is formed of made ground, every precaution having been used to render the foundation secure by the introduction of iron ties, inverted arches, and heavy timbering. The whole area was excavated several feet below the water level, large timbers were placed together, and range timbers at right angles with these laid several feet wider than the respective walls.

"This edifice was commenced in 1836, and finished during the summer of 1838."—*New York in* 1840.

View of the Penitentiary on Blackwell's island.

The above is a view of the penitentiary on Blackwell's island, about four miles NE. of the city hall. It is an immense stone edifice, recently erected, partly by convicts. The main building is four stories high, surmounted by a square tower; the two wings, each extending upwards of 200 feet from the centre building, are also four stories high. The interior is fitted up with rooms for the accommodation of the keepers, workshops in which the prisoners are obliged to labor, and numerous cells; the whole being constructed in the most substantial and secure manner. Bridewell is situated at Bellvue, being part of the building now used as the female penitentiary. Criminals convicted of petit larceny, &c., are confined here; also prisoners before trial. The house of refuge is situated about 2½ miles N. of the city hall, and is under the control of the 'Society for the Reformation of Juvenile Delinquents.' It was incorporated in 1825.

"BANKS.—There are now in the city of New York twenty-three incorporated banks, with an aggregate capital of $20,361,200. There are also incorporated in the state of New York seventy-five other banks, with an aggregate capital of $16,740,260, making in all ninety-eight banks, with a total capital of $37,101,468. All but eight of the above banks are subject to the Safety Fund Act; the exceptions are the Manhattan, Dry Dock, Fulton, North River, and Chemical banks, in the city of New York; the Long Island Bank, Brooklyn; Commercial Bank, Albany; and Bank of Rochester, in the city of Rochester. The Safety Fund now amounts to $500,000, which is the maximum provided by law. This fund was created by an annual tax upon the *Safety Fund Banks*, and in case of the failure of any one or more of them, it is liable to be drawn on for the deficit.

"The banks are open every day in the year, from 10 A. M. to 3 P. M., except Sundays, Christmas day, New Year's day, the Fourth of July, and general holidays appointed by legal authority, and the Bank of New York on Good Fridays.

"The rate of discount is 6 per cent. per annum, (calculating 360 days to the year,) excepting when notes have over 60 days to run. Three days' grace are allowed on all notes, and the discount taken for the same. When notes have over 60 days to run, the banks have the privilege of charging 7 per cent."

The following is an account of the great fire in 1835, by which it is estimated that about twenty millions worth of property was destroyed.

"One of the most alarming and destructive fires ever known in this hemisphere, broke out on Wednesday evening, December 16th, 1835, in the premises of Messrs. Crawford & Andrews, situate No. 25 Merchant-street, in this city, which in a short time raged with such intensity as to defy the exertions of the firemen, and others, who with equal zeal and promptitude were quickly on the spot for the purpose of stopping its ravages. The inutility of all aid was, however, soon perceptible, and all that could be done, was to remove what could in haste be got together, to such places as were deemed beyond the reach of the devouring element. With this impression, an immense quantity of goods were placed, for safety from buildings in the immediate vicinity of the fire, in the Merchants' Exchange and Reformed Dutch Church, where it was presumed they would remain free from danger: alas! the futility of human speculation; but a short time had elapsed from the time of such deposit to the whole being enveloped in flames, and these splendid buildings were soon reduced to a heap of ashes. The power of man was fruitlessly employed in attempts to stay its impetuosity, which every minute increased in the most alarming manner, spreading in all directions, and causing the utmost dismay and consternation through the whole city Any attempt to convey to the mind a faithful description of the awfully grand scene that presented itself to the view of those who were witnesses of this dreadful catastrophe, must of necessity be very feeble.

"The morning of the 17th of December, 1835, opened upon New York with a scene of devastation around, sufficient to dismay the stoutest heart. The fine range of buildings and splendid stores in Exchange place, Merchant-street, and all the adjoining streets down to the river, lay literally levelled to the earth, with their contents consumed; the Merchants' Exchange and Post-office entirely destroyed—the whole one heap of smoking ruins.

"A tolerably correct idea of the extent of the devastation may be formed from the following account, which appeared the next morning in the Courier and Enquirer.

"South-street is burned down from Wall-street to Coenties slip. Front-street is burned down from Wall-street to Coenties slip. Pearl-street is burned down from Wall-street to Coenties alley, and was there stopped by blowing up a building. Stone-street is burned down from William-street to No. 32 on the one side and No. 39 on the other. Beaver-street is burned down half way to Broad-street. Exchange place is burned down from Hanover-street to within three doors of Broad-street; here the flames were stopped by blowing up a house. William-street is burned down from Wall-street to South-street, both sides of the way. Market-house down. Wall-street is burned down on the south side, from William-street to South-street, with the exception of 51, 53, 65, 57, 59, 61, opposite this office. All the streets and alleys within the above limits are destroyed.

"The following will be found a tolerably accurate statement of the number of houses and stores now levelled with the ground: 26 on Water-street, 37 on South-street, 80 on Front-street, 62 on Exchange place, 44 on William-street, 16 on Coenties slip, 3 on Hanover square, 20 on Gouverneur's lane, 20 on Cuyler's alley, 79 on Pearl-street, 76 on Water-street, 16 on Hanover-street, 31 on Exchange-street, 33 on Old slip, 40 on Stone-street, 23 on Beaver-street, 10 on Jones' lane, 38 on Mill-street;—Total, 674.

"Six hundred and seventy-four tenements. By far the greater part in the occupancy of our largest shipping and wholesale drygoods merchants, and filled with the richest products of every portion of the globe. How estimate the immense loss sustained, or the fearful consequences to the general prosperity?

"Of the Merchants' Exchange nothing but its marble walls remain standing.

"Three or four vessels lying at the wharves on South-street were slightly injured in their yards and rigging. They were all hauled out into the river as soon as practicable.

"A detachment of marines from the navy-yard under Lieut. Reynolds, and of sailors under Capt. Mix of the navy, arrived on the spot at two o'clock in the morning. They rendered most valuable service. The gunpowder brought from the magazine at Red hook was partly under their charge.

"The cold during the whole time was excessive; the thermometer at zero. It may be easily supposed that this greatly paralyzed the exertion of the firemen. One sank under its effects, and was with difficulty resuscitated.

"Two companies, with their engines, arrived here from Newark, and rendered very material assistance.

"The passengers in the steamboat coming down the river, saw the flames from the Highlands, forty-five miles distant, and such was the violence of the gale, during the prevalence of the fire, that burning embers were carried across the East river to Brooklyn and set fire to the roof of a house there, which was however speedily extinguished.

"Strong bodies of cavalry and volunteer infantry were patrolling the streets near the fire, and preserved perfect order for the purpose of preventing depredations."

Columbia college, (formerly King's college,) is situated on a beautiful square between Murray, Barclay, Church, and Chapel streets, in the city of New York. It was established under a royal charter in 1754, which has been confirmed by various acts of the legislature since the revolution.

"There are two literary societies connected with the college, composed of students and graduates—viz, the *Peithologian* and the *Philolexian* societies.

"There is also connected with the college, a grammar school, subject to the control of the trustees, and under the direction of Professor Anthon, as rector. The school is composed of upwards of 200 hundred scholars, and instruction is given in all branches necessary for admission into any college, or for the counting-house.

"Eight instructers are constantly employed, besides one teacher in French, one in Spanish, and one in German and Italian. There is also a primary school attached to this institution, in which boys from five to ten years are prepared for the more advanced classes.

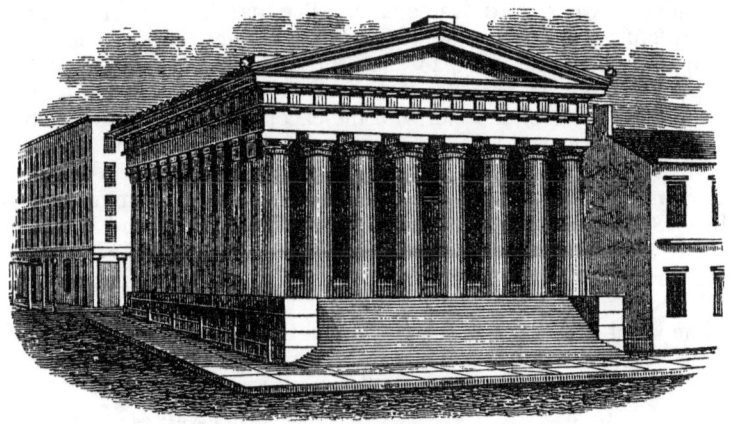

View of the Customhouse, Wall-street.

"By a statute of Columbia college, the corporation of the city of New York, the trustees of the New York Public School Society, the trustees or directors of the Clinton Hall Association, of the Mercantile Library Association, and of the Mechanic and Scientific Institutions, the General Society of Mechanics and Tradesmen, and such other societies as the board of trustees may from time to time designate, are each entitled to have always two students educated in the college free of all charges of tuition. Every religious denomination in the city is also entitled to have one student, who may be designed for the ministry, educated free of all charges. And every school, from which there shall be admitted in any one year into the college four students, have the privilege of sending one scholar, to be educated gratuitously. In order to give effect to the privilege in regard to the common schools in the city, twelve scholars at one time receive gratuitous instruction in the grammar school preparatory to their entering the college."

The above is a view of the new customhouse as seen from Wall-street. This structure surpasses any building of its size in the world, both in the beauty of its design and the durability of its construction. It is in the form of a parallelogram, 200 feet long, by 90 wide; and about 80 feet in height from the bottom of the foundation wall to the top. Brick, granite, and marble are used in the construction; all the inside walls are of brick, with the exception of those in the rotunda, which are of marble. The steps and stairs throughout are of a light-colored granite, employed for the sake of durability. At the extremity of the entrance hall is the rotunda, or large circular apartment to be used as the collector's office. This is a most splendid room; the roof is supported by 16 beautiful marble columns, highly polished with Corinthian capitals, 30 feet high, and 2 feet 8 inches in diameter. The diameter of the rotunda is 60 feet in the clear, and 80 feet in the recesses. The largest blocks of marble used in the building weigh thirty-three tons. The marble slabs for the roof weigh 300 or 400 pounds, and lap over each other eight inches with an upper and an under lip, to allow of the expansive power, and to keep out the least particle of water. The entire outside of this splendid edifice is of marble, with the exception of the granite steps. There is not a particle of wood work in any part of the building, and it is probably the only structure in the world that has been erected so entirely fire-proof. This elegant edifice was commenced in May, 1834, and finished in May, 1841. The cost, ground inclusive, was $1,175,000—building alone, $950,000. The architect is Mr. John Frazee, and it will probably remain for ages a monument of his skill.

The number of officers employed in the customhouse is 354, of whom nearly 200 are inspectors. The amount of duties received for the last three years has been as follows, viz:—

<pre>
1838..$10,494,055 34
1839.. 13,970,332 49
1840.. 7,557,441 36
</pre>

The old city or Federal Hall stood on the present site of the Customhouse. It was in its gallery on Wall-street, on April 30th, 1789, that George Washington was inaugurated the first President of the United States. The annexed account of this ceremony is from Sparks' Life of Washington:—

"A committee of congress, consisting of three members of the Senate and five of the House of Representatives, was appointed to meet him in New Jersey and attend him to the city of New York. To Elizabethtown Point came many other persons of distinction, and the heads of the several departments of government. He was there received in a barge, splendidly fitted up for the occasion, and rowed by thirteen pilots in white uniforms. This was followed by vessels and boats, fancifully decorated, and crowded with spectators. When the President's barge came near to the city, a salute of thirteen guns was fired from the vessels in the harbor, and from the battery. At the landing he was again saluted by a discharge of artillery, and was joined by the governor and other officers of the state, and the corporation of the city. A procession was then formed, headed by a long military train, which was followed by the principal officers of the state and city, the clergy, foreign ministers, and a great concourse of citizens. The procession advanced to the house prepared for the reception of the President. The day was passed in festivity and joy, and in the evening the city was brilliantly illuminated.

"The first public act of the President was that of taking the oath of office. It was decided by congress, that this should be done with some ceremony. In the morning of the day appointed, April 30th, at 9 o'clock, religious services suited to the occasion were performed in all the churches of the city. At twelve the troops paraded before the President's door, and soon afterward came the committees of congress and the heads of departments in carriages, to attend him to the Federal Hall, where the two houses of congress were assembled.

The procession moved forward with the troops in front, next the committees and heads of departments, then the President in a coach alone, followed by the foreign ministers, civil officers of the state, and citizens. Arrived at the hall, he ascended to the senate chamber, and passed thence to a balcony in front of the house, where the oath was administered to him in presence of the people by Chancellor Livingston. The President returned to the senate chamber, in the midst of loud acclamations from the surrounding throng of spectators, and delivered to the two branches of congress his inaugural speech. He then went on foot to St. Paul's church, where prayers were read by the bishop, and the ceremonies were closed. Tokens of joy were everywhere exhibited, as on the day of his arrival, and at night there was a display of illuminations and fire-works."

Merchant's Exchange, Wall-street.

This structure, now erecting and nearly completed, is in part on the site of the Exchange building destroyed by the great fire of December, 1835, and embraces all the ground between William and Wall streets, Exchange place, and Hanover-street, covering the entire block. The dimensions are 198 feet on Wall-street, 171 on William-street, 144 on Hanover-street, and 196 feet on Exchange place. It is 77 feet high to the top of the cornice, and 124 feet from the foundation wall to the top of the dome.

The building when finished will be of the Grecian Ionic style of architecture, the exterior of which will be constructed of blue Quincy granite, in the most chaste and durable manner. In front, on Wall-street, will be a recessed portico, with 18 massive columns, 38 feet in height. The process of quarrying is curious. The quarry is in in the side of a hill; the ends of a block of granite are cleared, a row of holes are drilled in a straight line, wedges are inserted, and an enormous piece of stone weighing from 300 to 400 tons is thus wedged off with ease. Each of the columns for the portico weigh about 90 tons in the rough, and five men with a simple apparatus draw it out of the quarry in two or three days to the place where the workmen stand

View of the New York University.

ready to hammer-dress it. The fair market price of one of these columns is $6,000; but the Exchange company pay only $3,000 for them, delivered in New York. These columns with but one exception, (that of a church at St. Petersburg,) are the largest in the world, being 38 feet in height, and 4 feet 4 inches in diameter; and each of the columns, including the base, cap, and shaft, weighs 43 tons. The exchange room or rotunda is a most magnificent apartment, in the centre of the building. The height of it to the spring of the dome is 51 feet, and above this the dome is 30 feet high; the whole to be surmounted by a lantern sky-light 37 feet diameter, and 6 feet high. The floor is to be of fine marble—its diameter is 80 feet in the clear, and 100 feet in the recesses, forming an area of 7000 square feet, which it is estimated will hold 3000 persons. The dome is partly supported by eight polished Italian marble columns with Corinthian capitals, executed in Italy; these are 41 feet in height, including the cap and base, and 4 feet 8 inches in diameter. There will also be many rooms for the accommodation of public and private offices, so constructed as to be entirely fire-proof, under the superintendence of Mr. Isaiah Rogers, the architect of the building. The cost of the structure will be about $2,000,000.

The above is a view of the New York University, built in the collegiate gothic style, situated on the east side of Washington square. This institution was chartered in 1831, and opened for the reception of students in 1832. The number of students in 1840 was 364.

" This building has just been completed, after a labor of several years; it is one hundred feet wide, and one hundred and eighty feet long. In front this oblong is divided into five parts—a central building, with wings flanked by towers, one rising on each of the four corners of the edifice. This central building or chapel is superior to the rest in breadth, height, and character; and is somewhat similar to that of King's college, Cambridge, England; a masterpiece of pointed architecture, and the model for succeeding ages. It is fifty-five feet broad, and eighty-five feet deep, including the octangular turrets, one of which rises at each of the four corners. The two ends are gabled, and are, as well as the sides, crowned with an embattled parapet. The chapel will receive its principal light from a window in the western end. This window is twenty-four feet wide, and fifty high. It has eight lights and two embattled transoms. The heads of the lights are cinque-foiled in a plain arch, and the divisions above are quatre-foiled. Over the head of the window is a dripstone, with plain returns. From the central building, or chapel, wings project right and left, and are four stories in height, flanked by towers of five, supported by angular buttresses of two stages, running above an embattled parapet, and are at the top themselves embattled. The

New York Institution for the Deaf and Dumb.

windows in the wings have square heads, with two lights, a plain transom, and the upper division tre-foiled. The heads of the windows are labelled, and have plain returns. The lower range of windows is set on a tablet, which serves as a base, and the two ranges above are set on strings, which return around the turrets, and stop against the buttresses. The principal entrance is under the great western window, through a richly moulded and deeply recessed portal, flanked by buttresses of two stages, the upper stage set diagonally, and rising above an embattled parapet. The doors are of oak, richly pannelled, and filled with tracery of open work, closely studded with bronze."

" *The New York Institution for the instruction of the deaf and dumb*, was incorporated in 1817, and commenced operations under its charter, by opening a school for the reception of pupils on the 12th day of May, 1818. Until the spring of 1829, the school was held in the building now called the new City Hall. At that time the pupils were transferred to a large building erected for the purposes of the institution, on Fiftieth-street and the Fourth Avenue, three and a half miles from the City Hall. Communication between the institution and the city is rendered very easy, by the cars which pass on the Harlæm railroad, (Fourth Avenue,) every fifteen or twenty minutes in both directions.

"The principal building occupied for the purposes of the institution, is one hundred and ten feet by sixty, in the dimensions of its plan, and five stories in height, including the basement. It accommodates, with some inconvenience, the number of pupils which the institution embraces at present, with the teachers, the family of the principal, and such other persons as are needed to assist in conducting the affairs of the establishment.

"The original charter of the institution being about to expire by limitation on the first day of April, 1837, it was extended by the le gislature, in the spring of 1836, for a period of twenty-five years.

"The number of pupils who were members of the institution in 1840, was one hundred and fifty-two. One hundred and fourteen of these are supported at the expense of the state of New York, six at the expense of the state of New Jersey, twelve by the city authorities, one by the supervisors of the county of Dutchess, twelve by the funds of the institution, and the rest by their parents or friends."

The New York institution for the blind.—This institution contains about fifty blind pupils, who, in addition to the school exercises, are employed in making baskets, mats, rugs, carpeting, and in braiding palm-leaf hats. They are also taught instrumental and vocal music.

The New York Historical Society, established in 1809, by private contribution and legislative assistance, possesses a library of about 10,000 volumes, valuable manuscripts, coins, &c. The *Stuyvesant Institute* was organized in 1834, for the diffusion of knowledge by means of popular lectures, to establish a cabinet of natural history, library, &c. The *American Lyceum*, for the promotion of education, was founded in 1831. The *New York Society Library* was established in 1754, and has 35,000 volumes. The *Apprentices' Library* was established by the General Society of Mechanics and Tradesmen in 1821, and has about 12,000 volumes.

The *Mercantile Library Association.*—This noble institution was established in 1821, since which time it has gone on gradually and steadily increasing, until it now numbers 3,500 members, and a splendid library of 22,500 volumes, with an annual income of about $8,000. Connected with the library are extensive reading-rooms, which are supplied with all the principal American and foreign periodicals. Lectures are regularly given by those distinguished in the various departments of science or literature. Classes are also formed for instruction, and the facilities here given at a trifling expense to the clerk for acquiring a finished mercantile education, are unequalled perhaps by any similar institution in the world.

The *College of Physicians and Surgeons* was formed in 1807, by the legislature of New York, at the recommendation of the regents of the University, by whose immediate government it is controlled. The *New York Eye Infirmary* was founded in 1820; since this period about 17,000 persons have for a longer or shorter period been under the care of the surgeons of this institution. The *New York Hospital* was founded in 1771, by the earl of Dunmore, the governor of the colony. This institution has an annual revenue from various sources of about $68,000, the larger portion of which is annually expended. The *Bloomingdale Asylum* for the insane is pleasantly situated near the banks of the Hudson river, distant 7 miles from the city, and has attached to it 40 acres of land, laid out in gardens, pleasure grounds, &c., well adapted for the unfortunate inmates.

The *American Academy of Fine Arts*, in Barclay-street, was incorporated in 1808. Napoleon, while first consul, presented Mr. Livingston, our ambassador to France, with a valuable collection of casts, engravings, &c., for this institution, which may be seen by the public during the season of exhibition. The *National Academy of Design* was instituted in 1826. It is enriched with many productions of American art. It has professorships of Painting, Anatomy, Sculpture, and Mythology.

The number of churches in the city is one hundred and fifty, comprised in the annexed list.

Presbyterian............34	Methodist..............20	Unitarian...............2
Congregationalist...... 4	Catholic................7	Jews....................3
Dutch Reformed........14	Friends.................4	New Jerusalem........1
Episcopalian............28	Lutheran...............2	Moravian...............1
Baptist..................19	Universalist..........3	Miscellaneous.........6

Gothic (late Masonic) Hall, Broadway.

This building, lately the head-quarters of the Whig party in this city, is situated on the east side of Broadway, about 60 rods north of the Park. The foundation was commenced on St. John's day, 24th June, 1826; when the corner-stone was laid with all due ceremony by the craft, in presence of thousands of citizens. It was finished in the subsequent year; the whole cost being $50,000. The building has lately undergone some alterations internally, and the name been changed to that of Gothic Hall.

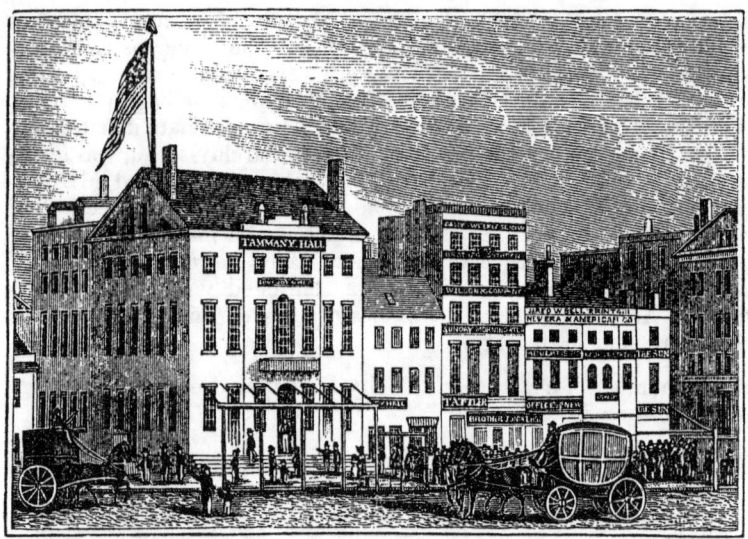

View of Tammany Hall* and the adjoining buildings.

The above shows the appearance of Tammany Hall and the adjacent buildings as they appear from the southern wing of the City Hall. Tammany Hall has acquired considerable celebrity from being the head-quarters of the democratic party. The other buildings seen on this block are mostly newspaper establishments: "The Sun," "New Era," "Brother Jonathan," the "Tattler," and some others are published here. The office of the Sun, a daily paper, is on the corner of the block. This is the oldest penny paper in the city, having been commenced towards the close of 1833, on a medium sheet, by Day and Wisner. Two or three months afterward the Transcript was begun of the same size, by Hayward, Lynde, and Stanley. The Herald, by J. G. Bennet, was the next living penny publication: it was started in 1835. The New Era, by Locke and Price, followed in 1836. From 5,000 to 30,000 copies of some of the penny papers are sold daily. A large proportion of these go into the hands of those who take no other paper; and who, were it not for their

---

* This name is derived from an Indian chief or saint, who is supposed to have been alive as late as the year 1680. Mr. Heckwelder, in his History, says that all that is known of him is "that he was a Delaware chief, who never had his equal. The fame of this great man extended even among the whites, who fabricated numerous legends respecting him, which I never heard, however, from the mouth of an Indian, and therefore believe to be fabulous. In the revolutionary war, his enthusiastic admirers dubbed him a saint, and he was established, under the name of *St. Tammany*, the patron saint of America. His name was inserted in some calendars, and his festival celebrated on the first day of May in every year. On that day a numerous society of his votaries walked together in procession through the streets of Philadelphia, their hats decorated with bucks' tails, and proceeded to a handsome rural place out of town, which they called the *wigwam;* where, after a *long talk*, or Indian speech had been delivered, and the calumet of peace and friendship had been duly smoked, they spent the day in festivity and mirth."

cheapness, would be destitute, in a great measure, of correct information respecting public events. It is estimated that about 620,000 newspapers are issued in the city every week, and in the course of the year upwards of thirty-two millions.

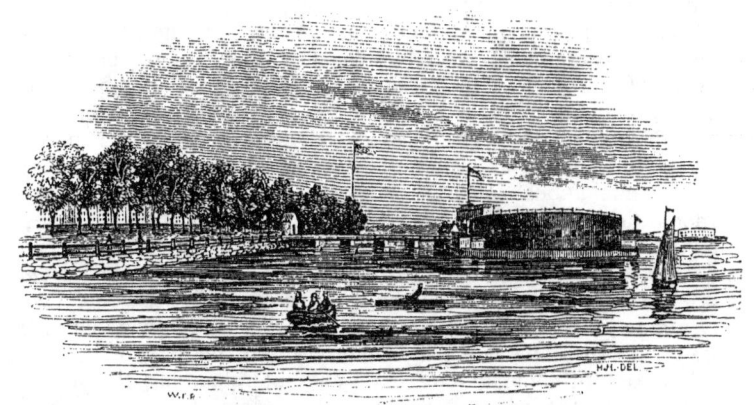

The Battery, and Castle Garden.

"THE BATTERY.—This beautiful promenade is situated at the southwest end of the island, and junction of the North and East rivers, and possesses attractions unsurpassed, perhaps, by any other similar place of resort in the world, justly commanding the admiration of every visiter. It is in full view of the bay and surrounding scenery of Long Island, Staten Island, New Jersey, and the islands in the harbor. From no one point can a better idea be formed of the magnitude of the commerce of the city; the numerous ships, steamboats, and small vessels, that are constantly entering and departing from the port, forming a scene of stirring interest. Of the bay itself, we deem it appropriate in this place to quote the language of a late English tourist.

"'I have never seen the bay of Naples, I can therefore make no comparison; but my imagination is incapable of conceiving any thing more beautiful than the harbor of New York. Various and lovely are the objects which meet the eye on every side; but the naming them would only be to give a list of words, without conveying the faintest idea of the scene. I doubt if even the pencil of Turner could do it justice, bright and glorious as it rose upon us. We seemed to enter the harbor of New York upon waves of liquid gold; and as we dashed past the green isles which rise from its bosom like guardian sentinels of the fair city, the setting sun stretched his horizontal beams further and further, at each moment, as if to point out to us some new glory in the landscape.'

"The Battery extends somewhat in the form of a crescent, from the termination of Broadway, Greenwich, and Washington streets, on the northwest, to Whitehall-street, on the east, covering an area of nearly 11 acres, and laid out in grass-plots and gravel walks, shaded with trees. The exterior, fronting the harbor, is built up with hewn stone; and on this side is a paved walk, with stone posts connected with a neat open railing. An expensive iron railing, with gateways. extends along the interior front."

"Originally this point of land was fortified by the Dutch, who threw up embankments, upon which they placed some pieces of cannon. 'In process of time,' says Knickerbocker, 'it came to be pleasantly overrun by a verdant carpet of grass and clover, and their high embankments overshaded by wide-spreading sycamores, among whose foliage the little birds sported about, rejoicing the ear with their melodious notes. The old burghers would repair of an afternoon to smoke their pipes under the shade of their branches, contemplating the golden sun, as he gradually sunk in the west, an emblem of that tranquil end towards which themselves were hastening; while the young men and the damsels of the town would take many a moonlight stroll among these favorite haunts, watching the chaste Cynthia tremble along the calm bosom of the bay, or light up the white sail of some gliding bark, and interchanging the honest vows of constant affection. Such was the origin of that renowned walk, *the Battery*, which though ostensibly devoted to the purposes of war, has ever been consecrated to the sweet delights of peace: The favorite walk of declining age; the healthful resort of the feeble invalid; the Sunday refreshment of the dusty tradesman; the scene of many a boyish gambol; the rendezvous of many a tender assignation; the comfort of the citizen; the ornament of New York, and the pride of the lovely island of Mannahatta.'"

"Castle Garden.—On a mole, connected with the Battery by a bridge, is situated Castle Garden, originally erected for a fortification, and used for that purpose until 1823, when it was ceded by the United States to the corporation of this city, since which it has been leased for a place of public amusement or recreation. On the top of the walls, a walk, covered by an awning, has been constructed, from whence a fine view of the harbor and adjacent scenery is obtained. Within the walls over ten thousand people may be accommodated, and concerts and fireworks are occasionally given."

"Vauxhall Garden—Is situated near the junction of the Bowery and Broadway, fronting on the former, and is at present a place of great resort in summer. On the evenings of public days, fireworks and other entertainments are exhibited; but by the late improvements in that part of the city, particularly by the extension of Lafayette place through the garden, its dimensions have been much lessened.

Niblo's Garden—Is one of the most fashionable places of resort in the city, during the summer months. It has been laid out with great taste, and when open to the public, is handsomely lighted, and decorated with paintings, mirrors, &c. The walks are bordered with shrubbery and flowers in great variety. Fireworks are occasionally exhibited; and in the saloon, which is a very tasteful and airy building, theatrical and musical entertainments are given."

"AMERICAN MUSEUM.—This excellent institution was founded in 1810, by the late John Scudder, by whose arduous efforts, and the persevering exertions of its more recent proprietors, it has arose to its present high standing. It continues daily to improve in every department, by extensive and valuable additions of the works of nature and artificial curiosities, from all parts of the world. Its immense collections are well arranged and beautifully displayed in four spacious saloons, each one hundred feet in length; in addition to which another apartment has recently been added of still larger dimensions. The Grand Cosmorama of this establishment is truly a most splendid affair, which for extent of glasses and magnificence of views, is not surpassed in this or any other country. The views embrace a great variety of subjects, and were all executed expressly by Italian artists of eminence in their profession. No labor or expense has been spared to render this establishment well deserving a continuance of that liberal and distinguished patronage it has always received. The building is very high, and from its observatory may be enjoyed some of the finest views in the city, and of the beautiful bay and surrounding country. The halls are well warmed and ventilated, and at evening brilliantly lighted with gas, altogether forming a very inviting, agreeable lounge, and at the same time, a place for serious contemplation and amusement, to those who delight in the study of the wonderful works of nature.

"PEALE'S MUSEUM AND GALLERY OF FINE ARTS.—This establishment was founded in the year 1825, and has increased with astonishing rapidity. It contains four spacious apartments, which are arranged in the following order: The 1st contains specimens of Natural History in all its branches, and its beauty of arrangement, and the exquisite style in which the articles are mounted, renders it one of the most interesting places of public amusement in the country. The 2d is a large and valuable collection of Paintings, by eminent artists, amongst which may be particularly mentioned a Portrait of Napoleon, by Le Fevre; a Magdalen, by Le Bron, together with Portraits of at least 150 celebrated citizens and foreigners. The 3d contains a very superior Cosmorama, several Wax Figures of good workmanship, Fossils, Shells, Minerals, and Miscellaneous Curiosities."

There are five theatres in the city, viz: Park Theatre, Bowery, Chatham, Little Drury, and Olympic. The National Theatre was burnt down the present year, (1841.)

The following is a list of the periodical publications issued in the city of New York.

"QUARTERLY PUBLICATIONS.—Literary and Theological Review, Naval Magazine, New York Review and Quarterly Church Journal, New York Quarterly Magazine, Quarterly Anti-Slavery Magazine, Quarterly Christian Spectator, Tailors' Magazine, United Brethren's Missionary Intelligencer.

"MONTHLY PUBLICATIONS.—American Monthly Magazine, Anti-Slavery Record, Children's Magazine, Home Missionary and Pastor's Journal, Human Rights, Journal of the American Institute, Knickerbocker Magazine, Ladies' Companion, La Revue Francais, (French) Mechanics' Magazine, Missionary Herald, Mothers' Magazine, Merchants' Magazine, National Preacher, New York Farmer and American Gardner's Magazine, Parley's Magazine, Sailor's Magazine, Sunday School Visiter, Tract Magazine, Youth's Friend, Family Magazine.

View of the Astor House, Broadway.

This splendid hotel, furnished with magnificence and taste, corresponding to its grandeur and simplicity, is the largest in the country, if not in the world. It was erected by John Jacob Astor, at an expense of about a million of dollars, and opened May 31st, 1836. It is built of Quincy granite, in a style remarkably massive, simple, and chaste, fronts 201 feet on Broadway, directly opposite the park, 154 on Barclay-street, and 146½ on Vesey-street. It is 77 feet in height. The dining-room on Barclay-street is 100 feet by 40, and 19½ high. The house contains at times about 500 persons, and the basement is distributed into stores; and thus the establishment forms of itself, like the Palais Royal of Paris, an almost independent colony.

The annexed account of the completion of the Erie Canal, October 20th, 1825, and the celebration of the event in New York city, is extracted from newspapers published at the time.

" The canal connecting the great lakes of North America with the Atlantic Ocean, is finished. On Wednesday, at 10 o'clock, A. M., the waters of Lake Erie were admitted at Buffalo, and the first boat from the lake commenced its voyage to New York. This joyful event was announced to the citizens of the state by the roar of cannon planted in a continued line along the banks of the canal and of the Hudson, at intervals of about eight miles, and extending from Buffalo to Sandy Hook, a distance of about 544 miles. The cannon were fired in succession, commencing at Buffalo at the moment of the entrance of the boat into the canal, and the intelligence thus communicated, reached this city precisely at twenty minutes past eleven o'clock, at which time a national salute was fired from the battery, and this acknowledgement that we had received the intelligence was then immediately returned by the same line of cannon to Buffalo. Thus the work is finished; the longest canal in the world is completed, and completed in the short space of eight years, by the single state of New York, a state which seventy years ago was a wilderness, thinly peopled by a little more than 100,000 souls."

CANAL CELEBRATION.

" The splendid exhibition in honor of the completion of the Erie Canal took place on Friday of last week, Nov. 4th. For several days previous, strangers from every part of the surrounding country had been crowding into the city to witness the interesting event. The day was remarkably pleasant, and favorable for the display. The following account of the ceremonies which took place is from the Daily Advertiser :—

" *The Societies.*—The procession formed agreeably to arrangement, and about half-past ten, moved down the west side of Greenwich-street to the battery, where it wheeled and passed up the east side of Greenwich-street, &c., in the following order :

" At the head were four buglemen on horseback, who preceded the—Agricultural and Horticultural Societies, many of whose members wore nosegays.—The Journeymen Tailors.—The Butchers, mounted and wearing aprons, with the banners of their society, and 2 cars, each drawn by 4 horses. The first was covered with a roof, decorated, and contained a calf and a sheep; the other a fine white ox and 4 large sheep, and over it, on a second stage, a stuffed ox, with several butchers' boys.—The Tanners' boys.—The Tanners had a car drawn by four horses, in which were several men at work tanning and currying leather, with hides hanging overhead. The Skinners followed with a banner, and then came another banner with four horses, where a number of morocco dressers were at work on skins of all colors.—The Cordwainers had also a car drawn by 4 horses, on which were 6 or 8 men seated at their benches, making shoes.—The Hatters' Society had a large banner with a portrait of St. Clement, and a car drawn by six horses, containing a shop, in which eight men were at work at the kettle, and others employed in the different operations of hat-making. A great number of small banners succeeded, bearing the names of the western Lakes, great and small, and those of the principal towns in the western part of the state and country; 24 boys marching under the banners bearing ' Washington,' the ' United States of America,' and a portrait of Gov. Clinton, represented the states of the Union. In a barouche rode the two oldest hatters and journeymen hatters in the city. Banner— ' The *heart* is devoted to our country.'—The Bakers, with white hats.—The Journeymen Masons came next, and then the Coopers, with a car in which men were at work on barrels, &c.—The Chairmakers had a large chair over their banner, with two eagles following, one large and gilt, with a miniature chair in his mouth.—The Potters came next, and then the Saddlers, with a pair of horses in harness, and 3 fine white ones with ladies', gentlemen's, and military saddles, all of the most superb workmanship. The horses were led by blacks in rich Moorish costumes—the insignia, implements, &c., followed, with a rocking-horse saddled and bridled.—The Shipwrights had the model of a line of battle ship, mounted on wheels, and drawn by eight horses. The officers and crew were represented by boys in gay dresses, and flags and ensigns were hoisted on board. A banner bore ' *Commerce is ours*;' and a great number of others succeeded, on which were the names of our distinguished naval commanders.—The Boat-builder's Association had a model of a boat borne by a carrier, and another drawn by horses. A car drawn by four horses, contained two half-finished boats of considerable size, at which the workmen were employed, while smoke was coming from the chimney where they warped their plank and timber.—The Rope-makers had a ropewalk, in which a number of men and boys were employed in spinning and laying, all drawn by four horses.—The Comb-makers had also a shop, and men at work, &c., and after them came the General Society of Mechanics; the Cabinet-makers with specimens of furniture, and the Apprentices' Library Association.—The New York Fire Department was represented by eight companies, Nos. 20, 42, 15, 13, 41, 32, 7, and 4, with their engines, and several hook and ladder companies, with their implements raised aloft, and handsomely decorated.—The Printers' Society had a car drawn by horses, on which were mounted two presses. These were kept in operation, striking off copies of an Ode, which were distributed to the people from the car.—The Book-binders had a large volume bound in red morocco and gilt, labelled ' Erie Canal Statistics.'—After a full band of musicians in dresses of scarlet and gold, came the members of Columbia College, dressed in their Academic gowns; and then a great number of military officers, and soldiers from the different city companies, followed by the Society of Free Masons.—The Tin Plate Workers had a car drawn by four gray horses, with a model of some of the locks on the canal,—a Canal boat, barge, &c., made of tin.

" *Aquatic Procession.*—At eight o'clock the citizens were seen crowding in all directions on board the various steamboats which were announced to compose the fleet which was to proceed to the ocean. The steamboat Washington, under the command of Capt. Bunker, took the lead, on board of which the Hon. the Corporation, with the society of Cincinnati, the Rev. Clergy, of all denominations, the Army and Naval officers—all the consuls of Foreign nations—the judges of all our courts and many other citizens and strangers were guests. The steamboats Fulton, James Kent, Chancellor Livingston, and several others were also employed by the corporation to receive other guests, all which were filled with our most distinguished citizens—The safety barges Lady Clinton and Lady Van Rensselaer, were most tastefully festooned with evergreens and flowers, and were exclusively appropriated to the ladies. At about 10 o'clock the signal was given for departure, and the boats all proceeded up the East river, and formed in a line, accompanied by the canal boats, when they wore round and proceeded down the bay. As the fleet passed the Battery they were saluted by the military, the revenue cutter, and the castle on Governor's Island. As they proceeded, they were joined by the ship Hamlet, which had previously been dressed for the occasion with the flags of all nations, and on board of which were the Marine and Nautical societies, composed of all our most respectable shipmasters. As the fleet passed the Narrows, they were saluted by Forts Lafayette and Tompkins. They then proceeded to the United States schooner Dolphin, moored within Sandy Hook, where Gov. Clinton went through the ceremony of uniting the waters, by pouring that of Lake Erie into the Atlantic; upon which he delivered the following address:—

"'This solemnity at this place on the first arrival of vessels from Lake Erie, is intended to indicate and commemorate the navigable communication, which has been accomplished between our Mediterranean seas and the Atlantic Ocean, in eight years, to the extent of more than four hundred and twenty-five miles, by the wisdom, public spirit, and energy of the people of the state of New York; and may the God of the Heavens and the earth smile most propitiously on the work, and render it subservient to the best interests of the human race.' Dr. Mitchell then poured the contents of several vials, which he stated contained the waters of the Elbe, &c. &c., and delivered a long address, but the crowd was so great that but few were able to hear any part of it. The Hon. Mr. Colden presented to his honor the Mayor, a memoir which contains a brief history of the canal from its commencement to the present day. Salutes were then fired from the revenue cutter, the pilot boats, and several of the steamboats, and the procession returned to the city.

"On the return from the excursion to Sandy Hook, the atmosphere was nearly clear, and the appearance of the steamboats was truly magnificent. Here were 26 of these vessels, splendidly equipped and decorated, moving in the most majestic manner, all crowded with passengers, and arranged in the most striking order. The packet ship Hamlet, which was generously offered by Capt. Chandler for the use of the Marine and Nautical societies, made a splendid appearance, towed along in the line by steamboats, with her masts and rigging decorated by a fine display of flags of all nations.

"Persons abroad may judge of the splendor of the celebration, when it is stated that there were displayed among the different societies, upwards of 200 banners and standards—many of them extremely splendid, and a large number painted expressly for the occasion.

"It is with pleasure we state that the two British packets now at anchor in our port, saluted and cheered the line of steamboats as they passed; instances of good feeling of this description should not be omitted to be recorded. The band in return played 'God save the king.' The whole line of steamboats landed their passengers at 3 o'clock, in time for them to form and join the procession of their fellow-citizens.

"The festivities were concluded by fireworks in the evening, at the Battery, City Hall, and Vauxhall Garden, and by illuminations of some of the principal buildings in the city,—the City Hall, City Hotel, Theatre, Sikes' Hotel, &c. A large transparency was exhibited at the City Hall, representing the introduction of Neptune to the Lady of the Lakes by the Genius of America.

"We cannot help expressing our gratification, at observing among the thousands we saw in the streets during the day and evening, hardly a single instance of intoxication, and not one of unpleasant disturbance; and so far as we could learn, no accident happened to mar the festivities of the day."

CROTON AQUEDUCT.—This great work, designed for the supply of the city of New York with pure and wholesome water, is at present constructing. Its whole length is $40\frac{1}{2}$ miles. It is a long brick vault stretching from Croton to New York, descending at the rate of nearly 14 inches to the mile. Its dimensions are about 6 feet at bottom, 7 feet at top, and from 8 to 10 feet in height. The foundation is of stone, well laid, and the interstices filled up with rubble, and over this a bed of concrete composed of cement, broken stone and gravel, in due proportions, well mixed and combined together, except where the earth is of a compact and dry consistence, when the stone foundation is omitted, and the bed of concrete laid on the earth foundation. The side walls are of good building stone, inches thick at bottom, and 27 inches at top. These walls are laid in regular courses. The bottom of the aqueduct is an inverted arch, and the roof a semicircle; both arches are formed of brick. All the materials used are the most perfect of their kind, and every possible pains taken in the construction.

The work commences at Croton, about 5 miles above the mouth of the river. Here is to be the dam which will back the river for several miles, and will cover, exclusive of its present bed, 5 or 600 acres, and thus form the great reservoir, which will contain 100,000,000 of gallons for each foot in depth from the surface. Inasmuch as the aqueduct is to maintain a uniform descent, extensive excavations or tunnels in passing through hills and heavy embankments, with culverts in crossing valleys, are required. Several of the tunnels are cut through solid rock at an enormous expense. The longest tunnel is the Manhattan hill tunnel near the village of Manhattanville, on New York Island; it is 1,215 feet in length.

In crossing the Harlaem river the aqueduct encounters its most formidable impediment. "Owing to the great depression of the stream below the grade line, and the peculiar inclinations of its banks, the length of the aqueduct bridge will greatly exceed the width of the strait at its surface, (620 feet.) The bridge will be 1,420 feet in length, between the pipe chambers at either end; 18 feet in width, inside of the parapet walls; and 27 feet between the outer edges of the coping; 16 piers, built of stone laid in courses of uniform thickness. Of these, 6 will be in the river, and 10 on the land, (8 of which will be on the Westchester side of the strait.) The river piers will be 20 by 40 feet at base, and 84 feet in height, to the spring of the arch; diminishing as they rise in height. The arches will have a span of 80 feet. The land piers will be proportionally less in size, their height varying according to the slope of the banks, and the span of these arches will be 50 feet each.

"The central height of the arches over the stream is to be 100 feet above high-water level, in the clear; and the distance from high tide to the top of the parapet walls will be 116 feet. The total elevation of the structure, from its base at the bottom of the strait to the top of the parapet, will be about 138 feet. The piers and abutments will be carried up with pilasters to the top of the parapet, with a projection of two feet beyond the face of the work. Those piers to be erected in the water, will commence with solid rock, upon which the earthy bed of the stream reposes. The estimated cost of this structure is $755,130.

"The bridge is intended for the support of iron pipes; and these will be laid down, in the first instance, two or three feet diameter, which it is supposed will be adequate for the supply of water to the city, for many years to come. The work however will be so arranged, as to admit the introduction, at any time hereafter, of two four-feet pipes, whose capacity will be equal to that of the grand trunk. The pipes will be protected from the action of the frost, by a covering of earth four feet in depth, well sodded on the surface. The aqueduct will discharge its water into the northern pipe chamber, whence it will pass over the bridge into the southern chamber, where the aqueduct resumes its course towards the city. At the distance of half a mile, the line crosses a ravine of 30 feet to the top line of the embankment; and at a short distance beyond, it enters the Jumel tunnel, 234 feet in length; and 6½ miles from the city. A ravine is passed soon after leaving the tunnel, 25 feet below the grade line; and soon after, another, still more formidable, presents itself; which required a foundation of 30 feet to elevate it to the grade.

"The water will be conducted over the Manhattan valley by means of iron pipes or inverted syphons. The depression of the valley is 105 feet below the grade line, and arrangements of pipe chambers, on each side of the valley, similar to that at Harlaem strait, will be adopted here. The pipes are to be laid on a foundation of stone, covered with a course of concrete masonry, six inches thick. After the pipes are laid, concrete is to be worked under them, as a support, 18 inches wide, and 12 high; and the whole is to be protected with a covering of earth, to guard against frost and other injury. The aqueduct having terminated at one pipe chamber, on Manhattan hills, it re-commences at another on the Asylum Hill; and after proceeding a short distance southward, enters the Asylum Hill tunnel 640 feet in length, which is the last. About three miles from the southern terminus of this Herculean work, the aqueduct commences its passage over several streets, the grading of which has a mean depression below that of the aqueduct, of about 40 feet; this vale is to be passed by a bridge of a corresponding height. The line of aqueduct runs 100 feet east of the Ninth avenue; and on the land, extending from one street to the other, a foundation wall is to be built of sufficient width and height to support the aqueduct. Over the carriage way and side-walks of each street, there will be circular arches turned. Ninety-sixth street, being 100 feet wide, will have two arches of 27 feet span, for the carriage way; and one arch of 14 feet span, on each side, for the side-walks. The other streets being only 60 feet in width, will each have an arch of 30 feet span for the carriage way, and one on each side of 10 feet span. The breadth over the arches to be 24 feet.

"On the whole line there will be ventilators placed at intervals of one mile apart; and between each, triangular cavities, designed for the erection of additional ventilators, are left, covered with flag stone, and their location indicated by marble slabs. Some of the ventilators can be used as waste weirs and as entrances into the aqueduct. The next important work is the receiving reservoir, 38 miles by the line of the aqueduct from its northern terminus. It covers 35 acres of ground, divided into two sections. The north section to have 20 feet of water when full, and the south 25 feet; the whole reservoir will contain about 160,000,000 of gallons. From this reservoir the water will be conveyed through the Fifth avenue to the distributing basin, of about 5 acres, holding 20,000,000 of gallons, at Murray Hill, in Forty-second street, by means of pipes 30 inches in diameter. From Murray Hill the water will be conveyed to the city by the ordinary distributing pipes. The difference of level between the basin at Murray Hill and the pool at Croton, is about 46 feet, being a fraction less than 14 inches to the mile.

"About 26 miles of the aqueduct are now (April, 1840,) completed, and several other detached sections are nearly so. It must not, however, be inferred that the work still to be done is of but small amount; on the contrary, the most difficult and expensive portions of it remain to be performed. According to the engineer's report, the whole work, with the exception of the bridge over Harlaem strait, will be completed and ready for use in the spring of 1842. The completion of the bridge cannot be expected before the close of 1843; and it may and will probably be still further delayed. To diminish this delay, it is proposed to erect a temporary conduit pipe of suitable dimensions, as soon as the coffer dams at Harlaem will admit of it, by which means the city may have the benefit of the water, two or three years before a supply could be had by the Harlaem aqueduct bridge.

"The original estimate of cost of this great work, was $4,718,197; but it will not fall short of $10,000,000;—$3,924,650 08 having been expended at the date of the last report, January 1st, 1840."

Northern view of Harlem Tunnel.

Harlem 8, **Yorkville** 5, and **Manhattanville** 9 miles from the City Hall, are small villages on Manhattan Island, and included within the city limits. *The New York and Harlem railroad* commences at the City Hall and extends to Fordham in Westchester county, 12½ miles from the city. By a late act of the legislature, (May 7, 1841,) the company have the privilege of extending it to the north line of Westchester county. "The road is laid with a double track, and is traversed for nearly three-fourths of its length, by steam power. Owing to the peculiar nature of the ground and the necessity for maintaining a nearly level grade, for a considerable part of the line, long and heavy cuts and embankments were required, which augmented the cost of construction far beyond that of any other similar work in this country. The whole cost of the work, including depots, motive and other power, &c., amounted to $1,100,000 or $137,500 per mile. The receipts for fare by the company, during the year ending December 31st, 1839, were $99,811. Notwithstanding the great number of persons conveyed on this road, about 1,200,000 annually, the directors have not as yet declared a dividend, and up to the 1st of January, 1840, the stockholders had not received a dollar from the work. The tunnel through which the line passes, is the most costly portion, as well as the most attractive feature of the road. Among the thousands who are almost daily conveyed through it, a vast majority is impelled by a desire to examine the '*tunnel*,' which, though excavated at an immense cost, ($90,000,) contributes, in no small degree, to increase the revenues of the company. The tunnel is cut through solid rock, which chiefly consists of quartz and hornblende of such a compact texture, that masonry is entirely dispensed with, even at the ends. It extends along the Fourth Avenue from 91st to 94th streets, and is 595 feet in length, 24 in width, and 21 in depth from the crown of the arch. The fare on this road is as follows: to 27th street, $6\frac{1}{4}$ cents; to Yorkville, 5 miles, $12\frac{1}{2}$ cents; to Harlem, 8 miles, $18\frac{3}{4}$ cents; and to Fordham, $12\frac{1}{2}$ miles, 25 cents."

Fac-simile of Peter Stuyvesant's signature.

"PETER STUYVESANT, the last of the Dutch governors in New York, deserves to be kept in remembrance. He began his administration in 1647; and he exerted all his energies to prevent the encroachments of the English and Swedes, on the territory under his command. He was more successful with the latter than the former. In 1655, he obliged the Swedes, at a place in Delaware bay, now called New Castle, to swear allegiance to the Dutch authority. But in 1664, Colonel Nichols, with an English fleet, arrived at New York, then called New Amsterdam, and compelled Governor Stuyvesant and his whole colony to surrender to their invaders. He however remained in the country until his death."—*Blake's Biographical Dictionary.*

"His remains 'rest in hope' near by, in the family vault, once constructed within the walls of the second built Reformed Dutch church, which, for pious purposes, he had built at his personal expense on his own farm. The church is gone, but the place is occupied by the present church of St. Mark. On the outside wall of this latter church is the original stone designating the body of him whose rank and titles stood thus described, to wit:

'In this vault, lies buried
PETRUS STUYVESANT,
late Captain General and Commander-in-chief of Amsterdam,
in New Netherland, now called New York, and the
Dutch West India Islands.
Died in August, A.D. 1682, aged eighty years.'"

"PHILIP LIVINGSTON was born at Albany, in January, 1716. He was educated at Yale College, in Connecticut, where he graduated in 1737. He then directed his attention to commercial pursuits; and, by his integrity, sagacity, and comprehensive views, laid the foundation, and erected the superstructure of extraordinary prosperity.

"He commenced his career in public life in 1754, as an alderman of the east ward of the city of New York; and, in 1759, was returned by the freeholders of this city as a member of the assembly. In this body, he soon became conspicuous for his talents and devotedness to the interests of the people. In 1769, he declined an election for New York, and was returned a member of the house for the manor of Livingston. His liberal views, and powerful exertions in defending the rights of the citizens, soon after rendered him obnoxious to the governor; and, as a majority of the assembly were now under the influence of the crown, his seat in the house was vacated, by a vote of that body, on the plea of non-residence.

"Mr. Livingston was chosen a member of the first congress, which met at Philadelphia, 1774. He was, the following year, appointed president of the provincial congress, assembled at New York. In 1776, in conjunction with his colleagues, he affixed his signature to the Declaration of Independence, in behalf of the state of New York.

"During the recesses of the general congress, he rendered important services in the organization of the state government. In May, 1778, he took his seat in congress for the last time. Although feeble in body, and low in health, he consented to forego all considerations but those of patriotism; and, at a distance from his family, willingly devoted to his country the last hours of his life. He expired on the 12th of June, at the age of sixty-two years."

Fac-simile of William Livingston's signature.

"WILLIAM LIVINGSTON, L L. D., governor of New Jersey, was born in the city of New York about the year 1723, and was graduated at Yale College, in 1741. He studied law, and possessing an understanding of great energy, a brilliant imagination, and a retentive memory, and devoting himself assiduously to the cultivation of his mind, he soon rose to distinction in the profession. He early exhibited himself an able and zealous advocate of civil and religious liberty, and employed his pen in vindicating the rights of the colonies against the arbitrary claims of the British. After enjoying several important offices in New York, he removed to New Jersey, and as a representative of that state was one of the most distinguished of the congress of 1774. On the formation of a new constitution for that state in 1776, he was appointed the first governor, and was annually re-elected to the office till his death in 1790. He was characterized by simplicity in his manners, and ease, amiableness, and wit in his social intercourse. His writings display uncommon vigor, keenness, and refinement, and are often eloquent. He devoted himself, during the revolution, ardently to the cause of his country, and did much by the shrewdness and severity of his writings both to encourage his countrymen and exasperate the British.

Fac-simile of Robert Fulton's signature.

"ROBERT FULTON, eminent as the inventor of steamboats, was born in the town of Little Britain, Lancaster county, Pennsylvania, 1765. His parents, who were Irish, were respectable, and gave him a common English education at Lancaster. He early exhibited a superior talent for mechanism and painting, and in his eighteenth year established himself in the latter employment in Philadelphia, and obtained much credit and emolument by his portraits and landscapes. On entering his 22d year he went to England, for the purpose of improving his knowledge of that art, and was received into the family of Mr. West, with whom he spent several years, and cultivated a warm friendship. After leaving that family, he employed two years in Devonshire as a painter, and there became acquainted with the duke of Bridgewater and Lord Stanhope, the former famous for his canals, and the latter for his love of the mechanic arts. He soon turned his attention to mechanics, particularly to the improvement of inland navigation by canals, and the use of steam for the propelling of boats; and in 1794 obtained patents for a double inclined plane, to be used for transportation, and an instrument to be employed in excavating canals. He at this time professed himself a civil engineer, and published a treatise on canal navigation. He soon after went to France, and obtained a patent from the government for the improvements he had invented. He spent the succeeding seven years in Paris, in the family of Mr. Joel Barlow, during which period he made himself acquainted with the French, Italian, and German languages, and soon acquired a knowledge of the high mathematics, physics, chemistry, and perspective. He soon turned his attention to submarine navigation and explosion, and in 1801, under the patronage of the first consul, constructed a plunging boat, and torpedoes, (differing materially from Bushnel's invention, with which he was acquainted,) with which he performed many experiments in the harbor of Brest, demonstrating the practicability of employing subaquatic explosion and navigation for the destruction of vessels. These inventions attracted the attention of the British government, and overtures were made to him by the ministry which induced him to go to London, with the hope that they would avail themselves of his machines; but a demonstration of their efficacy which he gave the ministry, by blowing up a vessel in their presence, led them to wish to suppress the invention rather than encourage it; and accordingly they declined patronising him. During this period he also made many efforts to discover a method of successfully using the steam engine for the propelling of boats, and as early as 1793, made such experiments as inspired him with great confidence in its practicability. Robert R. Livingston, Esq., chancellor of New York, and minister of the United States to the French court, on his arrival in France, induced him to renew his attention to this subject, and embarked with him in making experiments for the purpose of satisfying themselves of the possibility of employing steam in navigation. Mr. Fulton engaged with intense interest in the trial, and in 1803, constructed a boat on the river Seine, at their joint expense, by which he fully evinced the practicability of propelling boats by that agent. He immediately resolved to enrich his country with this invaluable discovery, and on returning to New York in 1806, commenced, in conjunction with Mr. Livingston, the construction of the first Fulton boat, which was launched in the spring of 1807 from the ship-yard of Charles Browne, New York, and completed in August. This boat, which was called the Clermont,* demonstrated on the first experiment, to a host of, at first incredulous, but at length astonished spectators, the correctness of his expectations, and the value of his invention. Between this period and his death he superintended the erection of fourteen other steam vessels, and made great improvements in their construction."

"I myself," says Judge Story, "have heard the illustrious inventor *relate*, in an animated and affecting manner, the history of his labors and discouragements:—' When,' said he, ' I was building my first steamboat at New York, the project was viewed by the public either with indifference or with contempt as a visionary scheme. My friends indeed were civil, but they were shy. They listened with patience to my explanations, but with a settled cast of incredulity on their countenances. I felt the full force of the lamentation of the poet,—

"Truths would you teach, to save a sinking land,
All shun, none aid you, and few understand."

As I had occasion to pass daily to and from the building yard while my boat was in progress, I have often loitered unknown near the idle groups of strangers gathering in little circles, and heard various inquiries as to the object of this new vehicle. The language was uniformly that of scorn, sneer, or ridicule. The loud laugh rose at my expense, the dry jest, the wise calculation of losses and expenditures; the dull but endless repetition of the *Fulton folly*. Never did a single encouraging remark, a bright hope, or a warm wish, cross my path. Silence itself was but politeness veiling its doubts or hiding its reproaches. At length the day arrived when the experiment was to be got into operation. *To me it was a most trying and interesting occasion.* I invited many friends to go on board to witness the first successful trip. Many of them did me the favor to attend as a matter of personal respect; but it was manifest they did it with reluctance, fearing to be partners of my mortification and not of my triumph. I was well aware that in my case there were many reasons to doubt of my own success. The machinery (like Fitch's before him) was new and ill made; and many parts of it were constructed by mechanics unacquainted with such work, and unexpected difficulties might reasonably be presumed to present themselves from other causes. The moment arrived in which the word was to be given for the vessel to move. My friends were in groups on the deck. There was anxiety mixed with fear among them. They were silent, sad, and weary. I read in their looks nothing but disaster, and almost repented of my efforts. The signal was given, and the boat moved on a short distance and then stopped, and became immovable. To the silence of the preceding moment now succeeded murmurs of discontent, and agitations, and whispers, and shrugs. I could hear distinctly repeated, "*I told you it was so; it is a foolish scheme; I wish we were well out of it.*" I elevated myself upon a platform and addressed the assembly. I stated that I knew not what was the matter; but if they would be quiet, and indulge me

---

* So named from the seat of the Livingston family. (See Clermont, Columbia county.)

for half an hour, I would either go on or abandon the voyage for that time. This short respite was conceded without objection. I went below and examined the machinery, and discovered that the cause was a slight maladjustment of some of the work. In a short period it was obviated. The boat was again put in motion. She continued to move on. All were still incredulous. None seemed willing to trust the evidence of their own senses. We left the fair city of New York; we passed through the romantic and ever-varying scenery of the Highlands; we descried the clustering houses of Albany; we reached its shores; and then, even then, when all seemed achieved, I was the victim of disappointment. Imagination superseded the influence of fact. It was then doubted if it could be done again; or if done, it was doubted if it could be made of any great value.'"

"*The Clermont,*" *Fulton's first American Steamboat.*

"Fulton obtained a patent for his inventions in navigation by steam in February, 1809, and another for some improvements in 1811. In the latter year he was appointed by the legislature of New York, one of the commissioners to explore a route for a canal from the great lakes to the Hudson, and engaged with zeal in the promotion of that great work. On the commencement of hostilities between the United States and Great Britain in 1812, he renewed his attention to submarine warfare, and contrived a method of discharging guns under water, for which he obtained a patent. In 1814 he contrived an armed steam-ship for the defence of the harbor of New York, and also a submarine vessel, or plunging boat, of such dimensions as to carry 100 men, the plans of which being approved by government, he was authorized to construct them at the public expense. But before completing either of those works, he died suddenly, February 24th, 1815. His person was tall, slender, and well formed, his manners graceful and dignified, and his disposition generous. His attainments and inventions bespeak the high superiority of his talents. He was an accomplished painter, was profoundly versed in mechanics, and possessed an invention of great fertility, and which was always directed by an eminent share of good sense. His style as a writer was perspicuous and energetic. To him is to be ascribed the honor of inventing a method of successfully employing the steam engine in navigation, an invention justly considered one of the most important which has been made in modern ages, and by which he rendered himself both a perpetual and one of the greatest benefactors of mankind. He was not indeed the first who conceived it to be possible; others had believed its practicability, and made many attempts to propel boats by steam, but having neither his genius, his knowledge, nor his perseverance, they were totally unsuccessful. Mr. Fulton was familiarly acquainted with many of the most distinguished literary and political characters both of the United States and of Europe, was a director of the American academy of fine arts, and a member of several literary and philosophical societies."

"Brockholst Livingston, judge of the supreme court of the United States, was the son of William Livingston, governor of New Jersey, and was born in the city of New York, November 25th, 1757. He entered Princeton college, but in 1776 left it for the field, and became one of the family of General Schuyler, commander of the northern army. He was afterward attached to the suite of general Arnold, with the rank of major, and shared in the honors of the conquest of Burgoyne. In 1779 he accompanied Mr. Jay to the court of Spain as his private secretary, and remained abroad about three years. On his return he devoted himself to law, and was admitted to practice in April, 1783. His talents were happily adapted to the profession, and soon raised him into notice, and ultimately to eminence. He was called to the bench of the supreme court of the state of New York, January 8th, 1802, and in November, 1806, was transferred to that of the supreme court of the United States, the duties of which station he discharged with distinguished faithfulness and ability until his death, which took place during the sittings of the court at Washington, March 18th, 1823, in the 66th year of his age. He possessed a mind of uncommon acuteness and energy, and enjoyed the reputation of an accomplished scholar, an able pleader and jurist, an upright judge, and a liberal patron of learning.

Fac-simile of Richard Montgomery's signature.

"RICHARD MONTGOMERY, a major-general in the army of the United States, was born in the north of Ireland, in 1737. He possessed an excellent genius, which was matured by a fine education. Entering the army of Great Britain, he successfully fought her battles, with Wolfe, at Quebec, in 1759; and on the very spot where he was, afterward, doomed to fall, when fighting against her, under the banners of freedom.

"He early imbibed an attachment to America; and, after his arrival in New York, purchased an estate, about one hundred miles from the city, and married a daughter of Judge Livingston. When the struggle with Great Britain commenced, as he was known to have an ardent attachment to liberty, and had expressed his readiness to draw his sword on the side of the colonies, the command of the continental forces, in the northern department, was intrusted to him and Gen. Schuyler, in the fall of 1775.

"By the indisposition of Schuyler, the chief command devolved upon him in October. After a succession of splendid and important victories, he appeared before Quebec. In an attempt to storm the city, on the last of December, this brave commander fell, by a discharge of grape-shot, both of his aids being killed at the same time. In his fall, there was every circumstance united, that could impart fame and glory to the death of a soldier."

"General Montgomery was gifted with fine abilities and had received an excellent education. His military talents especially were great; his measures were taken with judgment and executed with vigor. The sorrow for his loss was heightened by the esteem which his amiable character had gained him. At the period of his death he was only thirty-eight years of age."

Fac-simile of Lord Stirling's signature.

"WILLIAM ALEXANDER, LORD STIRLING, a major-general in the service of the United States during the revolutionary war, was born in the city of New York, but passed a portion of his life in New Jersey. He was generally styled through courtesy *Lord Stirling*, in consequence of being considered by many as the rightful heir to the title and estates of an earldom in Scotland, from which country his father came, though the government refused to acknowledge the son's claim when he repaired to Great Britain in pursuit of this inheritance. He was early remarkable for his fondness for mathematics and astronomy, in which sciences he made considerable progress.—Throughout the revolution he acted an important part, and distinguished himself particularly in the battles of Long Island, Germantown, and Monmouth. In the first, he was taken prisoner, after having, by a bold attack upon a corps commanded by Cornwallis, effected the escape of a large part of his detachment. In the second, his division, with the brigades of Generals Nash and Maxwell, formed the *corps de reserve;* and in the last he commanded the left wing of the American army. He was always warmly attached to General Washington, and the cause which he had espoused. He died at Albany, Jan. 15th, 1783, aged 57 years, leaving behind him the repu-

tation of a brave, discerning, and intrepid officer, and an honest and a learned man."—
Enclyclopedia Americana.

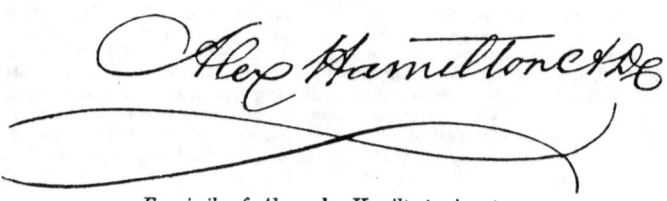

Fac-simile of Alexander Hamilton's signature.

"ALEXANDER HAMILTON was born in 1757, in the island of Nevis, West Indies. His father was a native of England, and his mother of the island. At the age of sixteen, he became a student of Columbia college, his mother having emigrated to New York. He had not been in that institution more than a year, before he gave a brilliant manifestation of the powers of his mind in the discussion concerning the rights of the colonies. In support of these he published several essays, which were marked by such vigor and maturity of style, strength of argument, and wisdom and compass of views, that Mr. Jay, at that time in the meridian of life, was supposed to be the author. When it had become necessary to unsheath the sword, the ardent spirit of young Hamilton would no longer allow him to remain in academic retirement; and before the age of nineteen he entered the American army in the rank of captain of artillery. In this capacity he soon attracted the attention of the commander-in-chief, who appoin'ed him his aid-de-camp, with the rank of lieutenant-colonel. This occurred in 1777, when he was not more than twenty years of age. From this time he continued the inseparable companion of Washington during the war, and was always consulted by him, and frequently by other public functionaries, on the most important occasions. He acted as his first aid-de-camp at the battles of Brandywine, Germantown, and Monmouth, and at the siege of Yorktown he led, at his own request, the detachment that carried by assault one of the enemy's outworks, October 14, 1781. In this affair he displayed the most brilliant valor.

"After the war, Col. Hamilton, then about twenty-four, commenced the study of the law, as he had at that time a wife and family depending upon him for support. He was soon admitted to the bar. In 1782, he was chosen a member of congress from the state of New York, where he quickly acquired the greatest influence and distinction, and was always a member and sometimes chairman of those committees to which were confided such subjects as were deemed of vital interest to the nation. The reports which he prepared are remarkable for the correctness and power which characterize every effort of his pen. At the end of the session he returned to the practice of his profession in the city of New York, and became eminent at the bar. In 1786, he was chosen a member of the legislature of his state, and was mainly instrumental in preventing a serious collision between Vermont and New York, in consequence of a dispute concerning territorial jurisdiction. He was elected a delegate from New York to the convention which was to meet at Philadelphia, in order to form a constitution for the United States. As the doors of the convention were closed during its sitting, and its records were never given to the world, it is not possible to state the precise part which he acted in that body. It is well ascertained, however, that the country is at least as much indebted to him for the excellences of the constitution as to any other member of the illustrious assembly. Hamilton and Madison were the chief oracles and artificers. After the adoption of the constitution by the convention, he associated himself with Mr. Madison and Mr. Jay, for the purpose of disposing the public to receive it with favor. The essays which they wrote with that design, addressed to the people of New York during the years 1787 and 1788, are well known under the name of the Federalist, and contributed powerfully to produce the effect for which they were composed. The larger portion of them was written by Hamilton. In 1788, he was a member of the State convention of New York, which met to deliberate on the adoption of the federal constitution, and it was chiefly in consequence of his efforts that it was accepted. On the organization of the federal government in 1789, he was appointed to the office of secretary of the treasury. This was a situation which required the exercise of all the great powers of his mind, for the public credit was at that time at the lowest state of depression; and as no statistical account of the country had ever been attempted, its fiscal resources were wholly unknown. But before Hamilton retired from the post, which he did after filling it somewhat more than five years, he had raised the public credit to a height altogether unprecedented in the history of the country; and by the admirable system of finance which he established, had acquired the reputation of one of the greatest financiers of the age. His official reports to congress are considered as masterpieces, and the principles which he advocated in them still continue to exercise a great influence in the revenue department of the American government. Whilst secretary of the treasury, he was *ex officio* one of the cabinet counsellors of President Washington; and such was the confidence reposed by that great man in his integrity and ability, that he rarely ventured upon any executive act of moment without his concurrence. He was one of the principal advisers of the proclamation of neutrality issued by Washington in 1793, in consequence of the attempt made by the minister of France to cause the United States to take part with his country in the war then raging between it and England. This measure he defended in a series of essays, under the signature of *Pacificus*, which were successful in giving it popularity. In 1795, Hamilton resigned his office and retired to private life, in order to be better able to support a numerous family by the practice of his profession. In 1798, however, when an invasion was apprehended from the French, and a provisional army had been called into the field, his public services were again required. President Adams had offered the chief command of the provisional army to Washington, who consented to accept in case Hamilton should be chosen second in command, with the title of inspector-general. This was accordingly done, and in a short time he succeeded in bringing the organization and discipline of the army to a high degree of excellence. On the death of Washington in 1799, he succeeded of course to the chief command. The title of lieutenant-general, however, to which he was then entitled, was from some unexplained cause never conferred on him.

"When the army was disbanded after the cessation of hostilities between the United States and France, General Hamilton returned again to the bar, and continued to practise with increased reputation and success until 1804. In June of that year he received a note from Col. Burr,—between whom and himself a political had become a personal enmity,—in which he was required, in offensive language, to acknowledge or disavow certain expressions derogatory to the latter. The tone of the note was such as to cause him to refuse to do either, and a challenge was the consequence. July 11, the parties met at Hoboken, opposite New York, on the Jersey side of the Hudson, and on the first fire Hamilton fell mortally wounded, on the same spot where, a short time previously, his eldest son had been killed in a duel. He lingered until the afternoon of the following day, when he expired. The sensation which this excited throughout the United States had never been exceeded on this continent. Men of all parties felt that the nation was deprived of its greatest ornament. His transcendent abilities were universally acknowledged. Every citizen was ready to express confidence in his spirit of honor and his capacity for public service. Of all the coadjutors and advisers of Washington, Hamilton was undoubtedly the one in whose sagacity and judgment he reposed the greatest confidence, whether in the military or in the civil career; and of all the American statesmen he displayed the most comprehensive understanding, and the most varied ability, whether applied to subjects practical or speculative. A collection of his works was issued in New York in three octavo volumes, some years after his death. His style is nervous, lucid, and elevated; he excels in reasoning founded on general principles and historical experience. General Hamilton was regarded as the head of the Federalists in the party divisions of the American republic. He was accused of having preferred in the convention that framed the Federal constitution, a government more akin to the monarchical; he weakened the federal party by denouncing President Adams, whose administration he disapproved, and whose fitness for office he questioned. But his general course and his confidential correspondence, show that he earnestly desired to preserve the constitution, when it was adopted, and that his motives were patriotic in his proceedings towards Mr. Adams. Certain it is, that no man labored more faithfully, skilfully, and efficiently in organizing and putting into operation the federal government."—*Encyclopedia Americana.*

The annexed inscriptions are copied from monuments in this city. The monument of Emmet is in St. Paul's churchyard, that of Montgomery is placed in front of the church itself. The monuments of Alexander Hamilton and Captain James Lawrence, are in the old Trinity churchyard; and the one of the Rev. Mr. Kunze, is in the Lutheran graveyard adjoining the Episcopal burying-ground in Hudson-street.

The monument erected to the memory of Thomas Addis Emmet, consists of one entire block of white marble, about thirty feet in height. On its face fronting Broadway is a medallion likeness of Emmet, in bas-relief, below which is the following inscription.

Emmet's Monument.

"In memory of THOMAS ADDIS EMMET, who exemplified in his conduct, and adorned by his integrity, the policy and the principles of the United Irishmen—' To forward a brotherhood of affection, a community of rights, an identity of interests, and a union of power among Irishmen of every religious persuasion, as the only means of Ireland's chief good, an impartial and adequate representation in an Irish parliament.' For this (mysterious fate of virtue!) exiled from his native land, in America, the land of freedom, he found a second country, which paid his love, by reverencing his genius. Learned in our laws, and the laws of Europe, in the literature of our times, and in that of antiquity, all knowledge seemed subject to his use. An orator of the first order ; clear, copious, fervid, alike powerful to kindle the imagination, touch the affections, and sway the reason and the will; simple in his tastes, unassuming in his manners, frank, generous, kind-hearted, and honorable ; his private life was beautiful, as his public career was brilliant.—Anxious to perpetuate the name and example of such a man, alike by his genius, his virtues, and his fate ; consecrated to their affections by his perils, his sacrifices, and the deeper calamities of his kindred, in a just and holy cause ; his sympathizing countrymen erected this monument and cenotaph. Born at Cork, April twenty-fourth, 1764; he died in this city, November fourteenth, 1827."

A figure of an American eagle is seen beneath this inscription resting on the Irish harp, which, as an emblem of the condition of Ireland, is represented as unstrung ; and surmounting these are two hands clasped together, on the bracelet of one of which, are the stars of our Union, on that of the other a wreath of shamrock. The following Latin inscription is on the face towards the church.

" M + S. THOMAS ADDIS EMMET, qui ingenio illustri, studiis altioribus, moribus integris, dignum se præstabat laudibus illis, illâ reverentiâ, illo amore quæ semper eum viventem prosequebantur ; et subitâ illo erepto morte, universæ in luctum civitatis se effuderunt. Quum raro extiterit vir naturæve dotibus, doctrinæve subsidiis omnibus illo instructior ; tum eloquentiâ altâ illâ et verâ qualem olim mirabantur Roma Athenæque, præcipue alios anteibat ; gravis, rarius, vehemens, fervidus, omnes, animi motus sic regere norit, uti eos qui audirent quo vellet et invitos impelleret. Hiberniâ natus, dilectam sibi patriam diu subjectam alieno, servis tantum ferendo jugo ad libertatem, ad sua jura vocare magno est a usus animo ; at præclara et consilia et vota fefellere fata. Spe, non animo, dejectus nobilis exul ; et hæc Americana libens respublica illum excepit, civemque, sibi gratulans adscivit ; dein hæc civitas illi domus, hæc patria fuit, hæc gloriam illi auxit, hæc spiritus ultimos recepit. Mærentium civium voluntas hoc exegit monumentum."

The following inscription in the ancient Irish character and language faces Fulton-street.

"He contemplated invaluable benefits for the land of his birth ; he gave eclat to the land of his death ; and received, in return, her love and admiration."

"This monument is erected by the order of congress, 25th Jan., 1776, to transmit to posterity a grateful remembrance of the patriotism, conduct, enterprise, and perseverance, of MAJ. GEN. RICHARD MONTGOMERY, who after a series of successes amid the most discouraging difficulties, fell in the attack on QUEBEC, 31st Dec., 1775, aged 37 years.—The State of New York caused the remains of Maj. Gen. Richard Montgomery to be conveyed from Quebec and deposited beneath this monument the 8th day of July, 1818."

"In memory of CAPTAIN JAMES LAWRENCE, of the United States navy, who fell on the 1st day of June, 1813, in the 32d year of his age, in the action between the frigates Chesapeake and Shannon. He had distinguished himself on various occasions, but particularly when commanding the sloop of war Hornet, by capturing and sinking his Britannic Majesty's sloop of war Peacock, after a desperate action of 14 minutes. His bravery in action was only equalled by his modesty in triumph and his magnanimity to the vanquished. In private life, he was a gentleman of the most generous and endearing qualities, and so acknowledged was his public worth that the whole nation mourned his loss, and the enemy contended with his countrymen who most should honor his remains.—The HERO, whose remains are here deposited, with his expiring breath expressed his devotion to his country. Neither the fury of battle, the anguish of a mortal wound, nor the horrors of approaching death, could subdue his gallant spirit. His dying words were, 'DON'T GIVE UP THE SHIP!'"

"Dan. 12, 3. Die lehrer aber werden leuchten wie des himmels glanz; und die, so viele zur gerechtigkeit weisen, wie die sterne immer und ewiglich. Dem andenken ihres unvergeslichen lehrers des herrn JOHANN CHRISTOPH KUNZE, doctor der theologie, professor der oriental sprachen, senior der Lutherischen geistlichkeit im New Yorker staat, und seit 23 jahren prediger der Deutsch Lutherischen gemeine in New York, die ihm diesen grabstein als ein zeichen widmet ihrer verehrung und liebe. Er wurde gebohren im jahr, 1744, entschlief den 24 July, 1807, so das sich sein alter auf 64 jahre belaüst.

"Hier liegt ein knecht des herrn der seinen Jesum liebte
Ihm treu war bis in's grab, und manche seel gewan
Dr'um denkt zu euren trost, die euch sein todt betrubte
Wie trefen ihm einst dort hey unserm Jesus an."

Translation.—Dan. 12, 3. And they that be wise shall shine as the brightness of the firmament, and they that turn many to righteousness, as the stars, forever and forever. To the memory of their never to be forgotten pastor, JOHN CHRISTOPHER KUNZE, D. D., professor of the oriental languages, senior of the Lutheran clergy in the State of New York, and for 23 years pastor of the German Lutheran congregation in the city of New York, this stone is dedicated by the people of his late charge, in testimony of their veneration and love. He was born in the year 1744, and fell asleep 24 July, 1807, in the 64 year of his age.

Here lies a servant of the Lord, who loved his Saviour, was faithful to the grave, and gathered many souls. Think, therefore, to your solace, ye who mourn his death, we shall find him with our Jesus.

"To the memory of ALEXANDER HAMILTON. The corporation of Trinity church has erected this monument in testimony of their respect for the patriot of incorruptible integrity, the soldier of approved valor, the statesman of consummate wisdom, whose talents and virtues will be admired by grateful posterity long after this marble shall have mouldered into dust. He died July 12th, 1804, aged 47."

NIAGARA COUNTY.

NIAGARA COUNTY was taken from Genesee in 1808. Greatest length E. and W. 30; breadth N. and S. 21 miles. The word *Niagara* is of Indian origin, and signifies across the neck or strait. The streams are few, and with the exception of Eighteen Mile, Johnson's, and Tonawanta creeks, and Niagara river, are inconsiderable. In 1796, exclusive of the occupants of Forts Niagara and Schlosser, there was but one white family in the territory now forming this county. The proposed line for a ship canal, from the Niagara river above the Falls to Lewiston, lies wholly within the county, commencing near Gill creek and the site of old Fort Schlosser. A railroad runs from Lockport and another from Buffalo to the Niagara Falls. A branch has been made from Lewiston to intersect the Lockport and Niagara Falls railroad, a distance of about 2 miles. The Erie canal enters the Tonawanta creek near its mouth. The creek is used for 12 miles as a canal by a tow-path on its bank. At Pendleton village, the canal leaves the creek and turns in a northeasterly direction across the mountain ridge, with a deep cut of about three miles through rock averaging 20 feet; and then descending 60 feet, by five double combined locks of 12 feet each, it passes out of the county south of the Ridge road. The county is divided into 12 towns. Pop. 31,114.

CAMBRIA, organized in 1808, as part of Genesee county, and then embracing the whole country now forming Niagara county; from Albany 288 miles. Pekin, 10 miles W. from Lockport, is a small settlement on the route of the railroad, on elevated ground, having a fine prospect to the northward. Pop. 2,100.

HARTLAND, organized in 1812; bounds since changed; from Albany 270 miles. Hartland, 10 miles NE. from Lockport, and Johnson Creek 14 miles, are small villages on the Ridge road. Pop. 2,301.

LEWISTON, taken from Cambria in 1813; from Albany 293 miles. Lewiston village, upon the river, was surveyed in 1813; it is 7 miles N. of Niagara Falls, 27 from Buffalo, 7 S. of Lake Ontario, 18 W. of Lockport, 80 from Rochester. Pop. 2,543. It lies opposite Queenston, U. C. It is the port of entry for the Niagara collection district, and is on the Ridge road, elevated about a hundred feet above the river, at the foot of the mountain ridge portage, and at the head of the navigation, and contains about 70 dwellings. The chief export is lumber. Steamboats from the lake touch daily at the landing. There is a ferry across the river at Queenston, the passage of which, though safe, is somewhat appalling by reason of the rapidity and eddies of the stream. In the central part of this town, now intersected by the Niagara Falls and Lockport railroad, "8 miles below the falls and 3 miles back from the river, is the reservation of the Tuscarora Indians, containing 2 miles in width by 4 in length, (about 5,000 acres,) of very excellent land. They consist of about 300 souls; have a Presbyterian church of 50 members, a resident clergyman, and a school teacher, and a temperance society of more than 100 members. They are under the care of the American Board of Foreign Missions. Their village is delightfully situated on a high bank, commanding an extensive prospect of the surrounding country and of Lake Ontario. These Indians came from North Carolina about the year 1712, and joined the confederacy of the Five Nations, themselves making the sixth. They formerly held a very valuable interest in land in North Carolina, but have recently sold it and divided the proceeds equally among themselves. Many of them are in very prosperous circumstances; in 1834, one man raised and gathered 50 acres of wheat. Visiters at the falls have been in the habit of going, sometimes in crowds, to this village on the Sabbath; but the Indians, with their missionary, have often expressed their desire that visiters would not interrupt them at that time."

The following is a northern view taken near the steamboat landing at Lewiston, showing in the distance Queenston Heights, distinguished as the battle-ground during the war of 1812. On the summit of the

Lewiston Landing, and Queenston Heights, U. C.

elevated ground, 370 feet above the river, is seen Gen. Brock's monument, constructed of freestone, at the expense of the provincial government. The base is 20 feet square, and the shaft rises 126 feet from the ground; from this eminence the country around, including the picturesque lake and river scenery, may be seen for fifty miles. The following is the inscription on the monument.

"The legislature of Upper Canada has dedicated this monument to the many civil and military services of the late SIR JAMES BROCK, Knight commander of the Most Honorable Order of the Bath, Provincial Lieutenant Governor and Major-general, commanding His Majesty's forces therein. He fell in action, on the 13th of October, 1812, honored and beloved by those whom he governed, and deplored by his Sovereign, to whose services his life had been devoted. His remains are deposited in this vault, as also his Aid-de-camp, Lieutenant-colonel John McDonald, who died of his wounds the 14 of October, 1812, received the day before in action."

Gen. Brock was killed at a spot about 80 rods down the hill, in a northwestern direction from the monument, near a cherry-tree. He was a brave officer, and fell at the head of his men while cheering them on to action. It is stated that when leading on his men, he laid his hand on his breast, exclaiming, "*Here is a breast for your yankee balls—shoot me if you can;*" when mortally wounded, soon after, he took off his cravat and told one of his aids to deliver it to his sister. He was at first interred in the northeastern bastion of Fort George, and a 24 pound American cannon, captured with Hull, placed at his head. His remains were removed to Queenston Heights, on one of the anniversaries of the battle.—On the night of the 17th of April, 1840, some evil-minded and unknown persons endeavored to blow up the monument by gunpowder. This disgraceful attempt was partially successful; the keystone over the door was thrown out, and the structure itself was cracked up to nearly two thirds of its height.—The following account of the battle of Queenston is from the Albany Gazette, Oct. 20th, 1812.

"At four o'clock in the morning of the 13th inst. Col. Solomon Van Rensselaer, at the head of 300 militia, and Lieut. Col. Christie, at the head of 300 regulars of the 13th regiment, embarked in boats to dislodge the British from the heights of Queenston. They crossed under cover of a battery of two eighteen and two six pounders. Their movement was discovered almost at the instant of their departure from the American shore. The detachments landed under a heavy fire of artillery and musketry. Col. Van Rensselaer received a wound through his right thigh soon after landing, but proceeded on until he received two other flesh wounds in his thigh and the calf of one of his legs, and a severe contusion on one of his heels, when he ordered the detachments to march on and storm the first battery, and was himself carried off the field. The order for storming was gallantly executed, and a severe conflict ensued. Lieut. Col. Christie received a severe wound in his hand, but got over the works. At this time both parties were reinforced. The enemy soon gave way and fled in every direction. Maj. Gen. Van Rensselaer crossed over to sustain the attack, and ascended the heights of Queenston, where he was attacked with great fury by several hundred Indians, who however were soon routed and driven into the woods. The reinforcements ordered over from the American side began to move tardily, and finally stopped. This induced the major-general to return, in order to accelerate their movements. He mounted a horse and used every exertion in his power to urge on the reinforcements, but in vain; whereupon the general perceiving that a strong reinforcement was advancing to support the British, ordered a retreat, but before the order reached Brig. Gen. Wadsworth, the battle was renewed by the enemy with great vigor and increased numbers, which compelled the Americans, whose strength and ammunition were nearly exhausted by hard fighting for eleven hours, and with very little intermission, to give way. The number of killed is considerable on both sides, but the Americans have lost many prisoners, including about 60 officers, most of whom are wounded. Among the prisoners are Lieut. Cols. Scott, Christie, and Fenwick, of the United States troops; Gen. Wadsworth and Col. Stranahan of the militia. Maj. Gen. Brock, of the British, is among the slain, and his aid-de-camp mortally wounded. The whole number of Americans said to have been engaged, is about 1,600, of which 900 were regular troops and 700 militia.— On the 14th, an arrangement was made between Maj. Gen. Van Rensselaer and Gen. Sheafe for the liberation of all the militia prisoners on parole, not to serve during the war."

The following, from the Albany Register, *Extra*, contains some additional particulars.

" A large body of the enemy got behind a stone guard-house, in which was mounted a pair of heavy ordnance. Two eighteen pounders were directed against it, which raked them severely; and at the 8th shot tumbled up a heap of men and dismounted one gun. They fled behind Judge Hamilton's store-house; but our eighteens raked them from thence and they fled. By this time, about ten o'clock, the enemy's fire, except one gun out of reach, was silenced, and victory seemed complete. The general had passed over to the heights, but sent back to urge on the troops which were passing over to head the columns. At this time, however, the enemy received a reinforcement of several hundred of Chippeway Indians, and commenced an attack with great fury. The rifle and the bayonet had scarcely put them to route, and drove them to the woods, when they were joined by a large reinforcement of regulars from Fort George. They renewed the attack, and the conflict became tremendous. It lasted about half an hour, when our valiant Spartan band, who had waded through blood anticipating victory, being exhausted in strength and ammunition, were obliged to yield the day. They had fought eleven hours without intermission."

The loss of the Americans in this affair in killed, wounded, and missing, was estimated at 1,000; of this number about 90 are supposed to have been killed. The militia, previous to the action, insisted on being led on against the enemy to drive them from the Niagara peninsula, so that they could return home. Many of them threatened to leave the camp unless led to immediate action. After the commencement of the battle, the sight of the wounded, as they were brought across the river covered with blood, and the groans of the dying, cooled their military ardor. They now appeared to have made the discovery that the constitution did not require them to go beyond the limits of the United States. Rather than cross over to an enemy's country, be shot at, with a chance of being killed, or made cripples for life, they determined to forego their chance of obtaining military honors. It is said that several hundred of the militia, after they had crossed over to the Canadian shore, availed themselves of the darkness and other facilities to hide themselves in the clefts of the rocks, where they remained in concealment during the day, and were only dragged by the legs from their lurking places by the British troops, after the surrender of the fighting part of the Americans.

LOCKPORT, formed from Royalton and Cambria in 1824; centrally distant from Albany by canal 333, from Rochester W. 63, from Buffalo E. 30 miles, by road 24, and from Niagara Falls 20 miles. Pop. of the town, 9,162. Lockport village, incorporated in 1829 was founded in the spring of 1821, by Mr. Sherard Comstock, deceased, who surveyed his farm of 100 acres into town lots. The first house was erected by Joseph Langdon, additions were soon made to the village plat, and in 1822 it became the county town.

Northeastern view of the locks at Lockport.

The above is a view of the *five double locks* on the Erie canal, (from which the village derives its name,) and part of the buildings in the vicinity. A new set of locks by the side of those represented in the engraving are now constructing, which will give increased facility to the passage of boats. The village contains about 500 houses, 9 churches, and, according to the census of 1840, 5,711 inhabitants. Its buildings, both public and private, are mostly built of the excellent stone which is here quarried. There is a bank and two newspaper establishments. The manufacture of flour is an important branch of business in this place. The great abundance of water derived from Lake Erie, which is brought through the deep cut to the brow of the ridge, and all around the basin, is used for various mills and factories. The waste water of these mills, and of the locks of the sixty feet mountain ridge, after it has fulfilled its hydraulic operations in its descent to the basin, is there retained by a dam across the ravine, and forms the head or fountain to fill the long, or sixty-five mile level, and as such is chiefly relied on, though the Oak orchard, the Genesee, and other feeders are useful in their place.

" The upper part of the village is about 80 feet above the level of the basin and long level of the canal. In moving up in a boat to the head of the basin to enter the chain of double locks, which are arranged in the most massive style side by side, in huge chambers, with stone steps in the centre, guarded by iron railings for safety and convenience, the gates of the lock are closed after the boat is in the chamber, and the roaring and sudden influx of the water from the lock above, in three or four minutes raises the boat to the level of the lock above; and this is repeated five times, the adjoining side lock being, perhaps, employed in letting a boat pass down the lock to the basin and canal. The boat having in this manner risen up 60 feet in five lifts, the passenger finds before him a vista of several miles, bounded on either hand by walls of the solid limestone rock, 25 to 30 feet high, and very appropriately called the '*Deep rock cutting at Lockport.*'"

NEW FANE, taken from Wilson, Hartland, and Somerset in 1824; from Albany 276 miles. Kempsville, a small village on Lake Ontario, 12 miles N. of Lockport, is a place of considerable trade for lumber, wheat, &c. Charlotte, or New Fane Centre, is 7 miles from Lockport. New Fane is a post-office. Pop. 2,375.

NIAGARA was taken from Cambria in 1812, by the name of Schlosser; it was changed in 1816. The village of Niagara Falls is situated at the celebrated Falls of Niagara river, lat. 43° 6' N., long. 2° 6' W. The village was laid out by Augustus Porter, Esq., and others, in 1805. It was at first called Manchester, afterward Niagara Falls. The village contains 2 churches, 2 splendid hotels, and 3 other public houses, 2 public schools, 80 dwellings of all kinds, and 500 inhabitants. Distance from Albany 290 miles, New York 440, Buffalo 22, Lockport 18, Chillicothe, Ohio, 403, Kingston, U. C., 200, Montreal 388, Quebec 568, Detroit 332, Cincinnati 468, and Washington 703 miles. Pop. 1,261.

" The river Niagara is 35 miles in length, and flows northerly; about midway between the two lakes it separates into two channels, forming Grand Island. A short distance below the union of these channels are the falls of Niagara, the grandest cataract in the world. Half a mile above the falls the river is a furious rapid, which sweeps away to certain destruction every thing involved in it. The river is here three quarters of a mile broad, and from this point it rushes down with increased velocity to the fall, where it leaps in an immense mass down a perpendicular precipice 160 feet in depth, with a roar heard in favorable states of the wind and atmosphere, 5, 10, 20 or even 30 miles. The cataract forms an irregular semicircle, the deepest hollow of which is called Horse-shoe Fall, and is on the

View of Niagara Falls from the American side.

Canada side. At the brink of the fall stands a small island, called Goat Island, which separates the Canada from the American fall. A bridge is thrown across the falls from the American side to the island. On the British side, a few yards below, is a projection called Table Rock, commanding a magnificent view of the falls. From this rock a spiral staircase leads down to the foot of the cataract, where visiters may pass under the fall between the sheet of water and the rock. The path leads far under the excavated bank of the river, which in some places forms a roof overhanging 30 or 40 feet. The fall of such an immense mass of water produces violent whirls in the air, and the spray is driven out with such force that no one can approach the edge of the cataract without being drenched to the skin. It is difficult even to draw a breath here, and in entering this tremendous cavern, there is danger of being blinded by the strong driving showers of spray. The greatest distance to which it is possible to pass within this sheet of water is about 150 feet. The banks of the river for several miles below the falls are perpendicular precipices of rock, and there is every reason to believe that the cataract was formerly much further down the river, the rock having gradually worn away to the present spot. A cloud of spray is continually rising from the foam of water, and exhibiting in the sunshine a brilliant rainbow."

The above view of the falls was taken from the ferry, and shows on the left of Goat Island, and near to the spectator, the American fall, and to the right of the island and in the distance, the Crescent or Horse-shoe fall. The cataract on the American side is 164, and on the Canada side 158 feet in height. The stone tower seen in the view is connected with Goat Island by the Terrapin bridge, a structure 300 feet in length, and projecting 10 feet over the falls. This tower, 45 feet in height, with winding steps to the top, was erected in 1833, from which, or from the end of the bridge, the view is awfully sublime. Apart from the falls, this whole region is one of deep interest, from the other natural curiosities and the historical reminiscences with which it is connected. The visiter should not fail to visit the *whirlpool* in the Niagara river, 3 miles below the village. " A mile from the whirlpool, the road runs within a few feet of the river's bank, where a deep and gloomy chasm is rent or worn out of the rock. This is called the *Devil's Hole*, and the small stream which crosses the road and falls into the chasm, is the Bloody Run." In 1759, during the old French and Indian war, a detachment of 100 British regulars, who were conveying provisions, in wagons, to Fort Schlosser, were here surprised by a party of Indians in ambuscade. "Many of the soldiers were killed at the first discharge, and the others were thrown into hopeless confusion. The Indians fell like tigers upon the drivers, tomahawked them in their seats, and threw them under foot. The wagons were backed off the precipice, and men and cattle fell with their loading in one dismembered and mutilated mass below. Some threw themselves from the bank, and fell mangled and dying on the rocks; others lodged in the branches of the trees, where they remained, disabled, until the affray was over, when the savages, at their leisure, despatched them." The brook that courses the bank ran red with the blood of the slain. Only four escaped to relate the horrible fate of their companions. Pieces of wagons and other relics of this bloody affray remained in this vicinity until within a few years, but have now mouldered away.

The immediate vicinity of the falls is rendered memorable on account of its being the place where a number of bloody battles were fought during the last war. The battle of Chippewa was fought on the 6th of July, 1814, at the village of that name, on the Canada side, about two miles from the falls. In July, the British and American forces being near each other, Gen. Ripley ordered Gen. Scott to make an advance on Chippewa.

" On the morning of the fourth, General Scott advanced with his brigade and corps of artillery, and took a position on the Chippewa plain, half a mile in front of the village, his right resting on the river, and his front protected by a ravine. The British were encamped in force at the village. In the evening General Brown joined him with the reserve under General Ripley, and the artillery commanded by Major Hindman. General Porter arrived the next morning, with the New York and Pennsylvania volunteers, and a number of Indians of the Six Nations. Early in the morning of the 5th, the British commenced a firing on the pickets. Captain Trott, who commanded one of them, hastily retreated, leaving one of his men wounded on the ground. General Brown instantly ordered him to retire from the army, and directed Captain Biddle to assume the command of the picket, lead it back to the ground, and bring off the wounded man; which he accomplished without loss. At four in the afternoon, General Porter advanced, taking the woods in order to conceal his approach, and in the hope of bringing their pickets and scouting parties between his line of march and the American camp. In half an hour his advance met the light parties of the British in the woods on the left. These were driven in, and Porter, advancing near Chippewa, met the whole British force approaching in order of battle. General Scott, with his brigade and Towson's artillery, met them on the plain, in front of the American encampment, and was directly engaged in close action with the main body. General Porter's command gave way, and fled in every direction, by which Scott's left flank was entirely uncovered. Captain Harris, with his dragoons, was ordered to stop the fugitives, at the ravine, and form them in front of the camp. The reserve were now ordered up, and General Ripley passed to the woods in left of the line to gain the rear of the enemy; but before this was effected, General Scott had compelled the British to retire. Their whole line now fell back, and were eagerly pursued by the Americans. As soon as they reached the sloping ground descending towards the village, their lines broke, and they regained their works in disorder. The American troops pursued until within reach of the guns from the works; when they desisted and returned to their camp. The British left two hundred dead on the ground, ninety-four wounded, beside those in the early part of the action, who were removed back to the camp, and fourteen prisoners. The American loss was sixty killed, and two hundred and sixty-eight wounded and missing."—*Perkin's Hist. of the Late War.*

The battle of *Bridgewater* or *Lundy's Lane*, was fought on the 25th of July. The principal scene of this bloody action, was at an obscure road, called Lundy's Lane, about half a mile westward from the Niagara cataract. "The thunder of the cannon, the roaring of the falls, the incessant discharge of musketry, the groans of the dying and wounded, during the six hours in which the parties were engaged in close combat, heightened by the circumstances of its being in the night, afforded such a scene as is rarely to be met with in the annals of slaughter. The evening was calm, and the moon shone with lustre when not enveloped in clouds of smoke from the firing of the contending armies." Since the retreat of the enemy from Chippewa, they had received reinforcements of troops from Lord Wellington's army in Spain; and on the 25th of July, encamped on a hill, with the design of attacking the Americans the next morning.

"On the 25th ult., the army under the command of Major Gen. Brown encamped above Chippewa, near the battle ground of the 5th. At 4 P. M., information was received that the enemy had thrown a body of troops across the Niagara, at the five-mile meadows; but our commanding general was not diverted by this movement. The 1st brigade, under Brig. Gen. Scott, moved past Chippewa and halted at Bridgewater, a mile below Chippewa, in plain view of Niagara Falls. Gen. Scott learnt that the enemy, under Gen. Riall, was approaching him. Battle was immediately given the enemy, near Mr. Wilson's, at half past 4 P. M.; their cannon were planted about 200 rods from this position on an eminence. The enemy's numerical force was much superior to Gen. Scott's; his line was far extended, and he showed a disposition to flank.—In order to counteract these views of Gen. Riall, he was *fought in detachments—he was charged in column;* Gen. Scott being at the head of his troops in almost every charge.—Capt. Towson, with his company of artillery, attached to Scott's brigade, kept up his fire with great vigor and effect. The action was continued, and the ground maintained by Gen. Scott, for more than an hour, before the reserve under Gen. Ripley, and the volunteers under Gen. Porter, were successfully brought into action.

"The ground was obstinately contested until past 9 o'clock, in the evening, when Gen. Brown perceiving that the enemy's artillery was most destructive, decided to storm the battery. Col. Miller,* the hero of Magagua, was ordered to this enterprise; he approached

---

* On receiving this order from Gen. Brown, Col. Miller calmly surveyed the position, and

the enemy's cannon with a quick step, and delivered his fire within a few paces of the enemy's line; who, after receiving two or three rounds and a vigorous charge, retired to the bottom of the hill, and abandoned his cannon. Only one piece was brought off the field for want of horses. The enemy now gave way and retreated; they were followed some distance. Our army was now employed in securing the prisoners and bringing off the wounded.—The cessation however was short: Lieut. General Drummond is supposed to have arrived at this interval with a reinforcement. The enemy renewed the action, whilst our troops were busily employed in clearing the ground of the wounded; but the gallant Americans formed with alacrity, and after a close engagement of 20 minutes, the enemy were repulsed. The army now effected the removal of nearly if not all of the wounded, and retired from the ground, it being nearly 12 o'clock at night; they returned to their encampment in good order. On the morning of the 28th, our forces under Generals Ripley and Porter, reconnoitred the enemy near the battle ground, returned and burnt the Bridgewater mills, and all the enemy's barracks, and the bridge at Chippewa, and passed up the river to Fort Erie, where they made a stand. The enemy's force engaged must have been nearly 5,000; ours short of that number. Major-Gen. Riall was wounded, and taken in the rear of his army by Capt. Ketchum, together with one of his aids, the other being killed.

"Major-Gen. Brown was severely wounded in the thigh (besides a contusion on his body) in the hottest of the action, but continued to command until the enemy retreated. Brig. Gen. Scott was also severely wounded by a grape in the shoulder, besides a severe bruise occasioned by a shell or cannon shot, having lost 2 horses, killed. Col. Brady 22d infantry; Majors Jessup 25th, Leavenworth 9th, M'Niel 11th; Brigade-major Smith; Lieuts. Campbell and Smouck, artillery; Lieut. Worth, aid to Gen. Scott; Lieut. Camp 11th; together with many others, whose names we have not learnt, were wounded, some badly.—The loss of the enemy in killed and wounded, was rising 800, exclusive of 200 regulars and 20 officers prisoners. Our loss in killed, wounded, and missing, is from 6 to 700. Major M'Farland 23d, Capt. Ritchie, artillery, Capts. Kinney and Goodrich, Lieut. Bigelow, infantry, and several other officers, killed; Capt. Spencer, aid to Major-Gen. Brown, supposed to be mortally wounded; Major Stanton, of the New York volunteers, Adj. Pew, of the Pennsylvania volunteers, killed. Major Camp, of the staff, lost two horses on the field, but escaped a wound. The 9th, 11th, and 25th, suffered very severely."

View of Schlosser Landing, Niagara.

The above is a northern view of the steamboat landing at Porter's storehouse, commonly called Schlosser Landing, upwards of two

---

answered, "*I will try, sir!*" which expression was afterward the motto of his regiment. During the battle in the evening, Capt. Ambrose Spencer, son of the chief-justice of New York, and aid to Gen. Brown, was despatched with orders to one of the regiments; when about to deliver them, he suddenly found himself in contact with a British corps; with great coolness and a firm air, he inquired what regiment is this? On being answered, *the Royal Scots,* he immediately replied, "*Royal Scots, remain as you are.*" The commandant of the corps, supposing the orders came from his commanding general, immediately halted his regiment, and Captain Spencer rode off. Captain Spencer was afterward mortally wounded, and taken prisoner. Capt. Loring, the aid of Gen. Drummond, was also taken prisoner He was exchanged for the *corpse* of Capt. Spencer.

miles from the falls. The site of old Fort Schlosser is nearly a mile below the landing: it was anciently a stoccade built upon banks slightly raised above the plain. The steamboat Caroline, the burning of which has caused so much sensation on the frontiers, lay beside the store-house represented in the engraving. Part of the village of Chippewa, on the opposite side of the Niagara river, is seen on the right in the extreme distance. Navy Island, so celebrated as a place of resort for the Canadian patriots, or rebels, as they are alternately called, is seen to the left beyond the store-house. The following is extracted from "De Veaux's Falls of Niagara."

"About the middle of the month of December, 1837, twenty-eight men, principally Canadians, with Rensselaer Van Rensselaer and William Lyon Mackenzie, went on Navy Island. They called to them the patriots of Canada, and all others the friends of that cause. In the space of three weeks, between three and four hundred responded to the call: some from the United States, and some from Canada. They brought with them arms and provisions. They staid on the island for one month, and then, at their own choice, left it, and not in fear of their opponents. Opposite to them, were assembled five thousand men, consisting of British regulars, incorporated militia, and a body of Indians and Negroes. Batteries were erected, and balls and shells were, at intervals, cast upon the island. The islanders were incessantly in a state of danger and alarm; yet they would, at times, provokingly return the fire; still they remained unattacked. For a month, a raw, undisciplined band of men, in the severity of winter, with no shelter but such as they then constructed, and miserably clad, set at defiance and laughed at the overwhelming force, which lay so near to them that they frequently conversed together.

"The steamboat Caroline came from Buffalo, on the 29th of December, it was said, to ply as a ferry-boat between Schlosser and Navy Island. It passed, that day, forth and back several times, and before sun-down was brought to at the wharf, at Schlosser, and moored for the night. At that place, there was but one house, and that a tavern. The warlike movements between the patriots and British, had drawn to the frontier, through motives of curiosity, a great number of persons. The tavern was crowded—lodgings could not be obtained—and several persons, observing the steamboat, sought for accommodations on board, and were received. In the middle of the night, the watch, for a watch on board steamboats is usually kept, saw something advancing on the water. He hailed, but before he could give the alarm, a body of armed men rushed on board, shot at the sentinel and all they met, crying—' Cut them down !' ' Give no quarter !' No arms were on board of the boat; no attack was expected; and no resistance was made. Some got on shore uninjured; others were severely cut and dangerously wounded. One man was shot dead on the wharf, and twelve were missing, either killed, or burnt and sunk with the boat. They towed the boat out in the river, and set it on fire; the flames burst forth; it drifted slowly, and its blaze shone far and wide over the water and adjacent shores. On the Canada side, at a distance above Chippewa, was burning a large light, as a signal to those engaged in the expedition. In a short time, an astounding shout came booming over the water: it was for the success and return of those who had performed this deed. The beacon was extinguished. The Caroline still moved on, and cast its lurid light far and wide, clothing the scene in gloom and horror; and just below the point of Iris Island, suddenly disappeared. Many of the wrecked and charred remains were, the next morning, floating in the current and eddies below the falls."

PENDLETON, taken from Niagara in 1827; from Albany 284 miles. Pendleton is a small village, 7 miles SW. from Lockport, at the junction of the Erie canal with the Tonawanta creek. Pop. 1,098.

PORTER, taken from Cambria in 1812; from Albany 304 miles. Pop. 2,175. Youngstown, port of delivery on the Niagara river, 1 mile above Lake Ontario, 19 miles NW. from Lockport, has about 40 dwellings.

The following is a distant view of Fort Niagara as seen from near the lighthouse on the British side. The engraving from which the above was copied, was published during the last war, and shows its

Distant view of Fort Niagara.

appearance at that period. On the 19th of Dec., 1813, a British force of more than 1,200 men crossed over and took the fort by surprise. The garrison consisted of but 370, and the commander was absent, and the gates of the fort were open and unguarded. The result of the attack was as might have been expected—sixty-five of the garrison were killed ; twenty-seven pieces of ordnance and large quantities of military stores were taken. The following interesting historical account of this place, is taken from " De Veaux's Falls of Niagara," published in 1839.

" This fortress is in latitude 43 deg. 14 sec. N. In 1679, a small spot was enclosed by palisades, by M. De Salle, an officer in the service of France. In 1725, the fort was built. In 1759, it was taken by the British, under Sir William Johnson. The capture has been ascribed to treachery, though there is not known to be any existing authority to prove the charge. In 1796, it was surrendered to the United States. On the 19th of December, 1813, it was again taken by the British, by surprise ; and in March, 1815, again surrendered to the Americans. This old fort is as much noted for enormity and crime, as for any good ever derived from it by the nation in occupation. While in the hands of the French, there is no doubt of its having been, at times, used as a prison ; its close and impregnable dungeons, where light was not admitted, and where remained, for many years after, clear traces, and a part of the ready instruments for execution, or for murder. During the American revolution, it was the head-quarters of all that was barbarous, unrelenting, and cruel. There, were congregated the leaders and chiefs of those bands of murderers and miscreants, that carried death and destruction into the remote American settlements. There, civilized Europe revelled with savage America ; and ladies of education and refinement mingled in the society of those whose only distinction was to wield the bloody tomahawk and scalping-knife. There, the squaws of the forest were raised to eminence, and the most unholy unions between them and officers of the highest rank, smiled upon and countenanced. There, in their stronghold, like a nest of vultures, securely, for seven years, they sallied forth and preyed upon the distant settlements of the Mohawks and Susquehannahs. It was the depot of their plunder ; there they planned their forays, and there they returned to feast, until the hour of action came again.

" Fort Niagara is in the state of New York, and stands on a point of land at the mouth of the Niagara river. It is a traditionary story, that the mess-house, which is a very strong building and the largest in the fort, was erected by stratagem. A considerable, though not powerful body of French troops, had arrived at the point. Their force was inferior to the surrounding Indians, of whom they were under some apprehensions. They obtained consent of the Indians to build a wigwam, and induced them, with some of their officers, to engage in an extensive hunt. The materials had been made ready, and, while the Indians were absent, the French built. When the parties returned, at night, they had advanced so far with the work, as to cover their faces, and to defend themselves against the savages, in case of an attack. In progress of time, it became a place of considerable strength. It had its bastions, ravines; its ditch and pickets; its curtains and counterscarp; its covered way, drawbridge, raking-batteries; its stone towers, laboratory, and magazine; its mess-house, barracks, bakery, and blacksmith shop; and, for worship, a chapel, with a large ancient dial over the door, to mark the hourly course of the sun. It was, indeed, a little city of itself, and for a long period the greatest place south of Montreal, or west of Albany. The fortifications originally covered a space of about eight acres. At a few rods from the barrier gate, was the burying ground; it was filled with memorials of the mutability of human life; and over the portals of the entrance was painted, in large and emphatic characters, the word 'REST.'

"It is generally believed, that some of the distant fortresses of France were often converted into state prisons, as well as for defensive purposes. There was much about Fort Niagara, to establish the belief that it had been used as such. The dungeon of the mess-house, called the black-hole, was a strong, dark, and dismal place; and in one corner of the room was fixed the apparatus for strangling such unhappy wretches as fell under the displeasure of the despotic rulers of those days. The walls of this dungeon, from top to bottom, had engraved upon them French names, and mementos in that language. That the prisoners were no common persons was clear, as the letters and emblems were chiselled out in good style. In June, 1812, when an attack was momentarily expected upon the fort by a superior British force, a merchant, resident at Fort Niagara, deposited some valuable articles in this dungeon. He took occasion, one night, to visit it with a light; he examined the walls, and there, among hundreds of French names, he saw his own family name engraved in large let'ers. He took no notes, and has no recollection of the other names and memorials; he intended to repeat his visit, and to extend his examination, but other avocations caused the subject to be neglected; and it was not brought to mind again until of late years, when all was changed. In further corroboration that Fort Niagara had witnessed scenes of guilt and foul murder, was the fact that, in 1805, it became necessary to clear out an old sink attached to the mess-house. The bones of a female were found therein, evidently, from the place where discovered, the victim of some atrocious crime.

"There were many legendary stories about the fort. In the centre of the mess-house was a well of water, but, it having been poisoned by some of the former occupants, in latter years the water was not used; and it was a story with the soldiers, and believed by the superstitious, that at midnight the headless trunk of a French general officer was often seen sitting on the curb of the old well, where he had been murdered, and his body thrown in; and, according to dreamers and money-diggers, large treasures, both in gold and silver, have been buried in many of the nooks and corners of the old fort. Many applications used to be made to the American officers, to dig for money, and persons have been known to come from a considerable distance for that purpose. The requests were, of course, refused."

ROYALTON, taken from Hartland in 1817; from Albany 268 miles. Middleport 12, Gasport 6, and Reynales Basin 7½ miles E. from Lockport, are all small villages on the canal. Royalton Centre is a small village centrally located. Pop. 3,557.

SOMERSET, taken from Hartland in 1823; from Albany 280, from Lockport, NE., 14 miles. Somerset is a small settlement near the lake shore. Pop. 1,741.

WHEATFIELD, recently taken from Niagara. The village of Tonawanda, in Erie county, is partially on the SW. angle of the town on both sides of the Tonawanda creek, and on the lines of the Buffalo and Niagara Falls railroad and Erie canal. Pop. 1,048.

WILSON, taken from Porter in 1818; from Albany 294 miles. Wilson is a small village, 13 miles NW. from Lockport, and 1½ miles from Lake Ontario, upon the lake road. Pop. 1,753.

ONEIDA COUNTY.

ONEIDA COUNTY was taken from Herkimer in 1789; since much reduced by the formation of other counties. Oneida is a corruption of the Indian word *Oneiyuta*, signifying upright or standing stone. Greatest length N. and S. 47, greatest breadth E. and W. 40 miles. From New York NW. 252, from Albany 107 miles. The surface has just diversity and unevenness enough to form a pleasing variety, and to supply brisk streams of pure water, and a salubrious atmosphere. Hardly a farm is without perpetual streams and brooks. The northeast and southern parts approach a hilly character, a waving surface with an easy swell; the northwest part is tolerably level, and the central richly variegated with easy undulations. The soil is of various qualities, but everywhere rich and productive. The cotton and woollen manufactures are carried on here more extensively than in any other county in the state. The Erie canal crosses this county, following the south side of the Mohawk river to Rome, and there turns southwestward into Madison county. This section of the canal is part of the long level $69\frac{1}{2}$ miles in length, extending from Frankfort in Herkimer county to Syracuse in Onondaga. The route of the Chenango canal, which unites the Susquehannah river with the Erie canal, leaves the latter at Utica, passing thence into the valley of the Oriskany, and thence follows the same into the county of Madison. Another canal is also commenced, uniting the Black river with the Erie canal; it leaves the latter at Rome, and follows thence up the valley of the Mohawk, and crosses the dividing ridge between the waters of the same and the Black river in the town of Boonville. Parts of the Utica and Schenectady, and Utica and Syracuse railroads, are in this county. The county buildings are located at Whitesborough, Utica, and Rome. The county is divided into 25 towns and the city of Utica. Pop. 85,345.

ANNSVILLE, taken from Lee, Florence, Camden, and Vienna, in 1823; from Albany 112, from Rome NW. 10 miles. Pop. 1,765. Taberg is a small post village.

AUGUSTA, organized in 1798, and settled in 1794; Oriskany Falls or Casety Hollow, 21 miles, and Augusta 18 miles SW. from Utica, are small villages. The Oriskany Falls, a cascade of 50 or 60 feet, are at Casety Hollow. The Chenango canal passes through the village. Knox's Corners is a small settlement. Pop. 2,175.

BOONVILLE, taken from Leyden of Lewis county in 1805; NW. from Albany 110 miles. Boonville, in the northern part of the town on the Black river road, 26 miles N. from Utica, contains about 40 dwellings. Ava is a post-office. Pop. 5,519.

BRIDGEWATER, organized in 1797 as part of Herkimer county; from Albany 81 miles. Bridgewater, an incorporated village upon the Unadilla river, 18 miles S. from Utica, has about 40 dwellings. Pop. 1,418.

CAMDEN, taken from Mexico in Oswego county in 1799; from Albany 127 miles. This town was settled about 1808 by New England farmers. Camden, 17 miles NW. of Rome, was incorporated in 1834, and contains about 50 dwellings. West Camden is a post-office. Pop. 2,329.

DEERFIELD, organized in 1798; from Albany 100 miles. Deerfield village is connected with Utica by a causeway a mile in length, and a bridge across the Mohawk. North Gage is a post-office. Pop. 3,120. The soil on the river flats in this town is of great fertility.

FLORENCE, the NW. town of the county, was taken from Camden in 1805; from Albany 121, from Rome 28, and from Utica 43 miles. Pop. 1,259.

FLOYD, taken from Steuben as part of Herkimer county in 1796; from Albany 100 miles. Floyd's Corners is a small settlement 12 miles NW. from Utica. This town was named after William Floyd, one of the signers of the Declaration of Independence. Pop. 1,741.

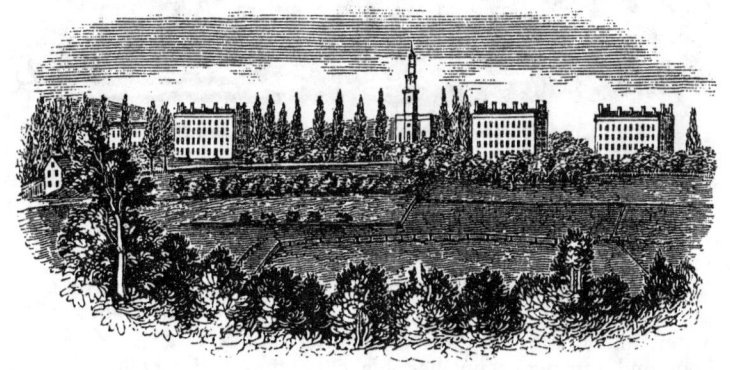

Distant view of Hamilton College, Kirkland.

KIRKLAND was taken from Paris in 1827. It was settled by Moses Foote, Esq., in company with ten families, in 1787. It has a fertile soil, and its surface is diversified with hills and valleys. Pop. 2,984. Clinton, the principal settlement in this town, is 9 miles from Utica, on the Chenango canal. The village consists of about 50 dwellings, 1 Congregational, 1 Baptist, and 1 Universalist church, 2 academies, and 2 seminaries for females. The annexed engraving shows the appearance of the Hamilton college buildings as seen from the canal in Clinton village, about one mile and a half distant, beautifully situated on a commanding eminence westward of the Oriskany valley, overlooking the village, having a delightful distant prospect. The college buildings consist of three stone buildings four stories high, for study, lodging-rooms, a chapel, President's dwelling-house, boarding and servants' house, and 41 acres of land. This institution was established in 1812. The original cost of the college grounds and buildings was about $80,000. " The college in 1834 raised by subscription the sum of $50,000; forming a fund for the payment of the salaries of the officers. William H. Maynard, who died in Sept. 1832, bequeathed to it $20,000, to endow a professorship of law; and S. N. Dexter, Esq., of Whitestown, in 1836, gave $15,000 for endowing a professorship."

The annexed is a view of the "Clinton Liberal Institute" in the village of Clinton. This building is built of gray stone 96 by 52 feet,

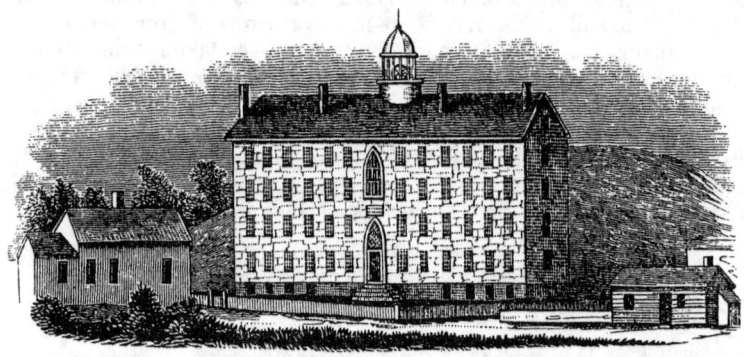

Clinton Liberal Institute, Kirkland.

four stories in height besides the basement. The building for the female department is of wood, 40 by 25 feet, 2 stories. This institution was incorporated in 1834, and placed under the visitation of the Regents of the University in 1836.

The Rev. Samuel Kirkland, from whom this town derives its name, was the son of Rev. Mr. Kirkland, of Norwich, Connecticut. This devoted missionary was for a time a member of Mr. Wheelock's school, and afterward finished his education at the college in New Jersey, where he graduated in 1765. The next year, (1766,) he commenced his mission among the Oneidas, laboring and living with them and endearing himself to them by his attention and efforts to do them good. Upon the breaking out of the revolutionary war, the Six Nations, with the exception of the Oneidas, who were mostly under the influence of Mr. Kirkland, joined the British cause. The intestine war which now took place forced Mr. Kirkland to remove his family from this region, but he himself continued his labors among the Oneidas as opportunities offered, and by his influence a firm friendship was maintained between them and the Americans. During a portion of the war he officiated as chaplain to the American forces in the vicinity; he also accompanied the expedition of Gen. Sullivan, in 1779, through the western part of the state.

After the conclusion of the war, the state of New York, in consideration of his valuable services during the revolution, granted to him the lands lying in the town of Kirkland, known as Kirkland's patent, upon a portion of which, Hamilton College stands. To these lands he removed his family in 1792, and fixed his residence near the village of Clinton, where he continued till his death, March 28th, 1808, in the sixty-seventh year of his age. The labors of Mr. Kirkland among the Oneidas, were in many instances attended with happy consequences; a large portion of the nation ultimately professed to believe in the Christian religion, and many of them appeared devoted Christians, among whom was the venerable chief Skenandoa. About the year 1791, Mr. Kirkland conceived the project of establishing a seminary which should be accessible to the Indian youth as well as the whites. Through his exertions a charter of incorporation was obtained for the institution in 1793, under the name of "Hamilton Oneida Academy." In 1794 a building was erected, which for many years afterward continued to be known as *Oneida Hall*, till the seminary was raised to the rank of a college, with the style of Hamilton college. Mr. Kirkland was a generous benefactor of this institution, and expended much of his time and means in promoting its interests.

The following account of the death of Skenandoa, the Oneida chief, and the "white man's friend," was published in the Utica Patriot, March 19th, 1816. In a few particulars it is abridged.

"Died at his residence, near Oneida Castle, on Monday, 11th inst., Skenandoa, the celebrated Oneida chief, aged 110 years: well known in the wars which occurred while we were British colonies, and in the contest which issued in our independence, as the undeviating friend of the people of the United States. He was very savage and addicted to drunkenness* in his youth, but by his own reflections and the benevolent instruction of the late Rev. Mr. Kirkland, missionary to his tribe, he lived a reformed man for more than sixty years, and died in Christian hope. From attachment to Mr. Kirkland he had always expressed a strong desire to be buried near his minister and father, that he might (to use his own expression,) '*Go up with him at the great resurrection.*' At the approach of death, after listening to the prayers which were read at his bed-side by his great-granddaughter, he again repeated the request. Accordingly, the family of Mr. Kirkland having received information by a runner that Skenandoa was dead, in compliance with a previous promise, sent assistance to the Indians that the corpse might be carried to the village of Clinton for burial. Divine service was attended at the meeting-house in Clinton on Wednesday at 2 o'clock, P. M. An address was made to the Indians by the Rev. Dr. Backus, President of Hamilton college, which was interpreted by Judge Deane, of Westmoreland. Prayer was then offered and appropriate psalms sung. After service, the concourse which had assembled from respect to the deceased chief, or from the singularity of the occasion, moved to the grave in the following order:—

Students of Hamilton College,
CORPSE,
Indians,
Mrs. Kirkland and family,
Judge Deane,—Rev. Dr. Norton—Rev. Mr. Ayre,
Officers of Hamilton College,
Citizens.

"After interment, the only surviving son of the deceased, self-moved, returned thanks, through Judge Deane as interpreter, to the people for the respect shown to his father on the occasion, and to Mrs. Kirkland and family for their kind and friendly attention.

"Skenandoa's person was tall, well made, and robust. His countenance was intelligent,

---

* In the year 1755 Skenandoa was present at a treaty made in Albany. At night he was excessively drunk, and in the morning found himself in the street, stripped of all his ornaments and every article of clothing. His pride revolted at his self-degradation, and he resolved that he would never again deliver himself over to the power of *strong water*.

and displayed all the peculiar dignity of an Indian chief. In his youth he was a brave and intrepid warrior, and in his riper years one of the noblest counsellors among the North American tribes; he possessed a vigorous mind, and was alike sagacious, active, and persevering. As an enemy, he was terrible. As a friend and ally, he was mild and gentle in his disposition, and faithful to his engagements. His vigilance once preserved from massacre the inhabitants of the little settlement at German Flats. In the revolutionary war his influence induced the Oneidas to take up arms in favor of the Americans. Among the Indians he was distinguished by the appellation of the 'white man's friend.'

"Although he could speak but little English, and in his extreme old age was blind, yet his company was sought. In conversation he was highly decorous; evincing that he had profited by seeing civilized and polished society, and by mingling with good company in his better days.

"To a friend who called on him a short time since, he thus expressed himself by an interpreter: 'I am an aged hemlock. The winds of an hundred winters have whistled through my branches; I am dead at the top. The generation to which I belonged have run away and left me : why I live, the Great Good Spirit only knows. Pray to my Jesus that I may have patience to wait for my appointed time to die.'

"Honored Chief! His prayer was answered; he was cheerful and resigned to the last. For several years he kept his dress for the grave prepared. Once and again, and again, he came to Clinton to die : longing that his soul might be with Christ, and his body in the narrow house near his beloved Christian teacher. While the ambitious but vulgar great, look principally to sculptured monuments and to riches in the temple of earthly fame; Skenandoa, in the spirit of the only real nobility, stood with his loins girded, waiting the coming of the Lord."

The following inscriptions are copied from monuments in the Hamilton College grave-yard :—

"SKENANDOA. This monument is erected by the NORTHERN MISSIONARY SOCIETY, in testimony of their respect for the memory of Skenandoa, who died in the peace and hope of the gospel, on the 11th of March, 1816. Wise, eloquent, and brave, he long swayed the councils of his tribe, whose confidence and affection he eminently enjoyed. In the war which placed the Canadas under the crown of Great Britain he was actively engaged against the French : in that of the revolution, he espoused that of the colonies, and ever afterward remained a firm friend to the United States. Under the ministry of the Rev. Mr. Kirkland he embraced the doctrines of the gospel, and having exhibited their power in a long life adorned by every Christian virtue, he fell asleep in Jesus at the advanced age of one hundred years."

"H. S. E. Azel Backus, STD., vir pietate insignis omni doctrina excultus, Evangelii minister fervidus et præclarus Collegii Hamiltonensis fuit Præses semper dilligentissimus et alumnis carissimus. In eo, summa in homines benevolentia, misericordia incorrupta fides, nudaque veritas: conjux superstes dolet. Et omnes quibus vivens ille fuit natus. Lugent et plorant.—Memoriæ Præsidis dilectissimi et venerandi, curatores Collegii Hamiltonensis : Hoc monumentum prosuerunt.—Ecclesiæ apud Bethlem, Conn., Pastor Annos xxii, Coll. Ham. Præses iv.—De vita decessit Die Dec. duodetricesimo, Anno Domini, MDCCCXVI. Æt. LII."

"[Here lies buried, Azel Backus, DD., a man of remarkable piety and learning, a zealous minister of the gospel, a distinguished President of Hamilton College ; a man of extraordinary diligence, and greatly endeared to the members of the institution. In him were conspicuous the highest benevolence towards his fellow men, uncorruptible integrity, and uncompromising truth. His wife survives to lament his loss : and all who knew him mourn also. The corporation of Hamilton College have erected this monument to the memory of their beloved and venerated President. He was pastor of the church in Bethlem, Conn., 22 years, President of Hamilton College, 4. He departed this life December 28th, AD. 1816, aged 52 years.]

"H. S. Quod potuit mori Sethi Norton, A.M., Linguarum Professoris in Collegio Hamiltonensi; Sui brevem vitæ cursum Literis deditus cum magno studio Præceptoris Peritissimus et carissimus cucurrit. Et in mediis laboribus maximo sui desiderio subitæ morti succubuit Dec. 7th, 1818, Ætatis Anno 40. Linguarum fuit Professor Annos 6. Curatores Collegii Hamiltonensis Hoc monumentum ponendum curaverunt."

["Here is buried all that was mortal of Seth Norton, M.A., Professor of Languages in Hamilton College. Devoted to learning, he ran his brief career with great zeal as an instructor, skilful and endeared to all. In the midst of his labors, he was overtaken by sudden death, to the great lamentation of those who knew him. He died December 7, 1818, in the 40th year of his age. He was Professor of Languages during six years. The corporation of Hamilton College have erected this monument."]

LEE, taken from Western in 1811; from Albany 115, from Rome N. 8 miles. Stokes or Nisbet's Corners and Portage are villages, Lee and Delta post-offices. Pop. 2,936.

MARCY, taken from Deerfield in 1832; from Utica NW. centrally distant 7 miles. Pop. 1,799.

MARSHALL, taken from Kirkland in 1819; from Albany 110, from Rome S. 16 miles. Marshall, Canning, and Deansville are post villages. The Waterville branch of the Oriskany falls here within half a mile 50 feet. There is in the valley a remnant of the Brothertown Indians, some of whom are comparatively civilized and wealthy. Pop. 2,251.

NEW HARTFORD, taken from Whitestown in 1827; from Albany 100 miles. New Hartford, a substantial village near the line of the Chenango canal, 4 miles SW. from Utica, contains about 100 dwellings, a number of mills and manufacturing establishments. Middle Settlement, 6½ miles from Utica, is a small settlement. Pop. 3,819.

Jedediah Sanger, Esq., was one of the first settlers of the village of New Hartford. "He possessed an active, vigorous, and enterprising mind, governed and controlled by unimpeachable integrity, and a high sense of moral obligation, placed him at once in a conspicuous station among the inhabitants of the vicinity. Immediately after his establishment, he erected a grist-mill on the site of the present paper-mill in the village of New Hartford, then the second mill established in the vicinity. By a judicious and liberal encouragement to emigrants, and particularly mechanics, he succeeded in building up a village, which, for many years, contested the palm of superiority and importance with any of her neighbors. The office of first judge of Oneida county he continued to hold from its organization until the year 1810. He several times occupied a seat in the legislature, and in the various offices in which he was called to act, served with equal credit to himself and usefulness to the community. To his beneficence the Episcopal church in New Hartford is indebted for a valuable permanent fund to aid in the support of its minister."

The Rev. Dan Bradley was settled as a pastor in this place in 1791, and continued his care of the church for several years. He was succeeded by the Rev. Mr. Johnson; and in honor of the occasion of his induction to the pastoral office, according to a custom which sounds singular in our ears, but which was introduced from New England, the exercises were concluded by an *ordination ball.*

The following anecdote, having a connection with the first court held in this county, is taken from a publication in a pamphlet form by William Tracy, Esq., entitled "Notices of Men and Events, connected with the early history of Oneida county:"—

"On the 19th of January, 1793, an act was passed authorizing every alternate term of the court of common pleas of Herkimer county to be held at such place in Whitestown, as should by the courts be directed by orders to be entered in the minutes. The first court held in this county under this provision was held in a barn, in New Hartford, belonging to the late Judge Sanger, (New Hartford then forming a part of the town of Whitestown,) in the month of October, in the year 1793, Judge Staring presiding, and the late Judge Platt, then clerk of the county of Oneida, officiating as clerk. The sheriff of Herkimer county at that day was a Colonel Colbraith—an Irishman, who, in the war, had done some service to his adopted country, and had acquired his title as a militia officer since the peace. His education had not been conducted with especial reference to the usages of what is technically called good society; and indeed, his manners bore unequivocal evidence that they originated from a native mind of genuine good humor and a most capacious soul, rather than from the arbitrary rules of a professor of polite breeding. A gentleman who attended the court as a spectator informed me that the day was one of the damp, chilly days we frequently have in October, and that in the afternoon and when it was nearly night, in order to comfort themselves in their by no means very well appointed court-room, and to keep their vital blood at a temperature at which it would continue to circulate, some of the gentlemen of the bar had induced the sheriff to procure from a neighboring inn a jug of spirits. This, it must be remembered, was before the invention of temperance societies, and we may not, therefore, pass too hasty an opinion upon the propriety of the measure. Upon the jug appearing in court, it was passed around the bar table, and each of the learned counsellors in his turn upraised the elegant vessel and decanted into his mouth, by the simplest process imaginable, so much as he deemed a sufficient dose of the delicious fluid. While the operation was going on, the dignitaries on the bench, who were no doubt suffering quite as much from the chilliness of the weather as their brethren of the bar, had a little consultation, when the first Judge announced to the audience that the court saw no reason why they should continue to hold open there any longer and freeze to death, and desired the crier forthwith to adjourn the court. Before, however, this functionary could commence with a single, 'Hear ye,' Colonel Colbraith jumped up, catching, as he rose, the jug from the lawyer who was complimenting its contents, and holding it up towards the bench, hastily ejaculated—' Oh no, no, no, Judge—don't adjourn yet—take a little gin, Judge—that will keep you warm—'tant time to adjourn yet;' and suiting the action to the word, he handed his Honor the jug. It appeared that there was force in the Sheriff's advice; for the order to adjourn was revoked, and the business went on."

PARIS was taken from Whitestown in 1792; from Albany 85 miles. This town was named by the inhabitants in grateful acknowledgment of the kindness of Mr. Isaac Paris, a merchant of Fort Plain, who in the year of scarcity, 1789, supplied them with Virginia corn on a liberal credit, and finally accepted payment in such produce as they were enabled to supply. Famine is now the least dreaded here of all evils. Paris Hill has about 30 dwellings. Paris Furnace and Paris Hollow are small villages. Sauquoit, on the creek 9 miles south from Utica, is a manufacturing village, containing about 100 dwellings. Near this village is a burning spring. Large quantities of limestone are obtained here, and used for building materials at Utica and elsewhere. Pop. 2,844.

REMSEN, taken from Norway in 1798; bounds since altered; from Albany 100 miles. Settlements were made in this town in 1798 by 22 families. Remsen village, in the southern part of the town, is 17 miles north from Utica. Pop. 1,648.

ROME, one of the shiretowns of Oneida county, was incorporated in 1796. The surface of the township is level or gently undulating, and watered by the Mohawk river, and by Wood and Fish creeks. The village of Rome, occupying the site of old Fort Stanwix, was incorporated in 1819. The two first white families who located themselves at this spot, were those of two men from German Flats, named Roof and Brodock, who settled at the landing place on the Mohawk in the vicinity of Fort Stanwix, to gain a livelihood by assisting in the transportation of goods destined for the Indian trade, across the carrying place from the river to Wood creek. They held no title to their lands, but occupied them under a contract for their purchase from Oliver Delancy, one of the proprietors of the Oriskany patent, who was afterward attainted of treason. This little outpost, however, was broken up during the revolutionary war. The first regular settlement of Rome was by emigrants from the New England states.

Southern view of Rome.

The above is a southern view of part of the village as viewed from the railroad track. The building seen on the right having four chimneys is but a few yards distant from the central part of the fortifications of the old fort, the cellar of which is still to be seen. The Black river canal passes a few rods this side of the buildings seen in the engraving; the Erie canal is about half a mile westward of the village. Mohawk river and Wood creek, at this place, approach within a mile of each other; in 1797, a canal was completed between the two streams, thus connecting the waters of the Mohawk with those of Lake Ontario. The village consists of upwards of 300 dwellings, 2 Presbyterian, 2 Baptist, 1 Episcopal, and 1 Methodist church, an academy incorporated in 1835, a bank, printing office and a number of select schools. The United States arsenal and barracks, sufficient for a regiment, were erected here in 1813, under the direction of Maj. James Dalliba. Rome is situated on the summit level between the ocean and Lake Ontario, four hundred and thirty-five feet above tide at Albany; lat. 43° 12′; long. 1° 27′ W. from New York. Distant from Albany 112, from Utica 12 miles. Pop. 5,680.

Fort Stanwix, named from Gen. Stanwix, was originally erected in the year 1758, during the French war. It occupied a position commanding the carrying place between the navigable waters of the Mohawk and Wood creek, and was regarded as the key to the communication between Canada and the settlements on the Mohawk. "It was originally a square fort, having four bastions surmounted by a broad and deep ditch, with a covert way and glacis. In the centre of the ditch a row of perpendicular pickets was planted, and another horizontal row fixed around the ramparts. But although the principal fortress had been erected at the enormous expense for those times of $266,400, yet at the commencement of the revolutionary war the whole was in ruins. On the incursion of Burgoyne from Montreal towards Albany, a detachment of the invading forces, under the command of Col. St. Leger, consisting of 200 British troops, a regiment of loyalists, and a large body of Indians under Brant, the great captain of the Six Nations, went up the St. Lawrence, then to Oswego, and from thence to Fort Stanwix. From this point it was intended to pass down the Mohawk and join the forces of Burgoyne at Albany. Gen. Schuyler, who had the command of the northwestern frontier, sent Col. Dayton to repair the works at Fort Stanwix. He seems to have done little towards effecting this object; he however thought proper to change its name to Fort Schuyler, which name it retained during the war. Gen. Peter Gansevoort was afterward sent to supply his place. On the 3d of August, Col. St. Leger arrived before the fort with his whole force, consisting of a motley collection of British regulars, Hessians, Tories, and about one thousand Indians. The garrison, under Col. Gansevoort, consisted of about 750 men. Soon after his arrival, St. Leger sent a flag into the fort with a manifesto, advising submission to the mercy of the king, and denouncing severe vengeance against those who should continue in their 'unnatural rebellion.' This manifesto produced no effect on the brave garrison, who had determined to defend the fortress to the last extremity. At the time of the battle of Oriskany, [see Whitestown,] when Gen. Herkimer was advancing to the relief of the fort, a diversion was made in his favor, by a sortie of 250 men, under the command of Col. Willet. Such was the impetuosity of Willet's movements, that Sir John Johnson and his regiment, who lay near the fort with his Indian allies, sought safety in flight. The amount of spoil found in the enemy's camp was so great that Willet sent hastily for wagons to convey it away. The spoil thus captured, twenty wagon loads, consisted of camp equipage, clothing, blankets, stores, &c., five British standards, and the baggage and papers of most of the officers. For this brilliant exploit, congress directed that Col. Willet should be presented with an elegant sword in the name of the United States.

The siege of the fort still continued, and the situation of the garrison, though not desperate, began to be somewhat critical. Col. Willet and Maj. Stockwell readily undertook the hazardous mission of passing through the enemy's lines to arouse their countrymen to their relief. After creeping on their hands and knees through the enemy's encampment, and adopting various arts of concealment, they pursued their way through swamps and pathless woods, until they arrived safely at German Flats, and from thence to the head-quarters of Gen. Schuyler, then commanding the American army at Stillwater

Gen. Arnold was immediately despatched with a body of troops to the relief of Col. Gansevoort.* As he was advancing up the Mohawk, he captured a tory by the name of Hon-yost Schuyler, who being a spy, was condemned to death. Hon-yost " was one of the coarsest and most ignorant men in the valley, appearing scarce half removed from idiocy; and yet there was no small share of shrewdness in his character." He was promised his life if he would go to the enemy, particularly the Indians, and alarm them by announcing that a large army of the Americans was in full march to destroy them, &c. Hon-yost being acquainted with many of the Indians, gladly accepted the offer; one of his brothers was detained as a hostage for his fidelity, and was to be hung if he proved treacherous. A friendly Oneida Indian was let into the secret, and cheerfully embarked in the design. Upon Hon-yost's arrival, he told a lamentable story of his being taken by Arnold, and of his escape from being hanged. He showed them also several shot-holes in his coat, which he said were made by bullets fired at him when making his escape. Knowing the character of the Indians, he communicated his intelligence to them in a mysterious and imposing manner. When asked the number of men which Arnold had, he shook his head mysteriously and pointed upward to the leaves of the trees. These reports spread rapidly through the camps. Meantime the friendly Oneida arrived with a belt and confirmed what Hon-yost had said, hinting that a bird had brought him intelligence of great moment. On his way to the camp of the besiegers he had fallen in with two or three Indians of his acquaintance, who readily engaged in furthering his design. These sagacious fellows dropped into the camp as if by accident: they spoke of warriors in great numbers rapidly advancing against them. The Americans, it was stated, did not wish to injure the Indians, but if they continued with the

---

* A short time previous to the investment of the fortress the following singular incident occurred.—" Capt. Greg went with two of his soldiers into the woods a short distance to shoot pigeons; a party of Indians started suddenly from concealment in the bushes, shot them all down, tomahawked and scalped them, and left them for dead. The captain, after some time revived, and perceiving his men were killed, himself robbed of his scalp, and suffering extreme agony from his numerous wounds, made an effort to move and lay his bleeding head on one of the dead bodies, expecting soon to expire. A faithful dog who accompanied him manifested great agitation, and in the tenderest manner licked his wounds, which afforded him great relief from exquisite distress. He then directed the dog, as if a human being, to go in search of some person to come to his relief. The animal, with every appearance of anxiety, ran about a mile, when he met with two men fishing in the river, and endeavored in the most moving manner, by whining and piteous cries, to prevail on them to follow him into the woods. Struck with the singular conduct of the dog, they were induced to follow him part of the way, but fearing some decoy, or danger, they were about to return, when the dog, fixing his eyes on them, renewed his entreaties by his cries, and taking hold of their clothes with his teeth, prevailed on them to follow him to the fatal spot. Such was the remarkable fidelity and sagacity of this animal. Capt. Greg was immediately carried to the fort, where his wounds were dressed; he was afterward removed to our hospital, and put under my care. He was a most frightful spectacle, the whole of his scalp was removed; in two places on the fore part of his head, the tomahawk had penetrated through the skull; there was a wound on his back with the same instrument, besides a wound in his side and another through his arm by a musket ball. This unfortunate man, after suffering extremely for a long time, finally recovered, and appeared to be well satisfied in having his scalp restored to him, though uncovered with hair."—*Thacher's Military Journal.*

British they must all share one common fate. The Indians were thoroughly alarmed, and determined on an immediate flight, being already disgusted with the British service. Col. St. Leger exhorted, argued, and made enticing offers to the Indians to remain, but all in vain. He attempted to get them drunk, but they refused to drink. When he found them determined to go, he urged them to move in the rear of his army; but they charged him with a design to sacrifice them to his safety. In a mixture of rage and despair, he broke up his encampment with such haste, that he left his tents, cannon, and stores to the besieged. The friendly Oneida accompanied the flying army, and being naturally a wag, he engaged his companions who were in the secret, to repeat at proper intervals the cry, "*They are coming! they are coming!*" This appalling cry quickened the flight of the fugitives wherever it was heard. The soldiers threw away their packs; and the commanders took care not to be in the rear. After much fatigue and mortification, they finally reached Oneida Lake; and there probably, for the first time, felt secure from the pursuit of their enemies. From this place St. Leger hastened with his scattered forces back to Oswego, and thence to Montreal.

Hon-yost, after accompanying the flying army as far as the estuary of Wood creek, left them and returned to Fort Schuyler, and gave the first information to Colonel Gansevoort of the approach of Arnold. From thence he proceeded to German Flats, and on presenting himself at Fort Dayton his brother was discharged. He soon after rejoined the British standard, attaching himself to the forces under Sir John Johnson.

The following inscriptions are copied from monuments in the village graveyard.

"In memory of the Hon. JOSHUA HATHAWAY, more than 40 years a resident of this town. He was born at Suffield, Ct., Aug. 13, 1761; graduated at Yale college in 1787, and died at Rome, Dec. 8, 1836.—' Requiescat in pace.'—As a husband and father, ever worthy, loved, and venerated. As a man and Christian, upright and exemplary; a friend to the needy and the injured; and a father in the church. As a magistrate and judge, by the grace of God, an executor of justice, and maintainer of the truth, ' a terror to evil-doers, and praise to such as did well.' As a patriot, he bore arms in two wars for his country; and sustained at all times the cause of the people with zeal and fidelity. As a citizen, ever active and enterprising for the benefit of our common country, and among the foremost for the improvement of this favored portion of it; to him was assigned the honor of breaking ground on commencing that great and beneficial work, the Erie canal, July 4th, 1817. In the various relations of life, he fulfilled its duties as in the fear of God, with faithfulness, ability, and honesty of purpose. He died lamented—' the memory of the just is blessed.'"

"To the memory of CAPT. SAMUEL PERKINS, who departed this life at the United States arsenal, Rome, Dec. 30, 1837, in the 75th year of his age. He entered the service of his country during the war of the revolution, when he was but 14 years old, and served till its independence was gained. He was actively engaged in the Indian campaign of 1795, *under Gen. Wayne.* He also participated in, and rendered valuable services during the late war with Great Britain. After which, retiring from active duties, he held for 18 years the station of ordnance storekeeper, and died in the public service. In every situation of his life was remarkably exemplified that just sentiment, ' an honest man is the noblest work of God.'"

SANGERFIELD, taken from Paris in 1795; from Albany 94, SW. from Utica 18 miles. It was settled in 1793, and named after Judge Jedediah Sanger, one of the primitive settlers in this part of the country. In 1804, it was annexed to Oneida county. Waterville, in the north part of the town, contains about 70 dwellings, and is adorned by a handsome public square. Sangerfield is a small settlement. Pop. 2,251.

STEUBEN, principally settled by Welsh emigrants, and taken from Whitestown when part of Herkimer county; NW. from Albany 110, from Utica N. 20, and from Rome NE. 15 miles. Pop. 1,993.

The principal part of this town was granted by the state to Baron Steuben, for his services during the revolutionary war. He resided here on his farm until his death. He was buried beneath an evergreen he had selected to overshadow his grave. Afterward a new road was laid over the spot, and his remains were removed to a neighboring grove in this town, situated about 7 miles NW. of the Trenton Falls.

Grave of Baron Steuben.

His grave is protected by a neat monument erected in 1826 by private subscription, and shown in the above engraving. On it is the brief inscription, MAJOR GENERAL FREDERICK WILLIAM AUGUSTUS BARON DE STEUBEN. Baron Steuben resided in a log house about a quarter of a mile south of his burial place. He lived there during the summers and cultivated his farm, but in the winters resided in New York. The following sketch is from Allen's Biographical Dictionary.

"FREDERICK WILLIAM BARON DE STEUBEN, a major-general in the American army, was a Prussian officer, who served many years in the armies of Frederick the Great, was one of his aids, and had held the rank of lieutenant-general. He arrived in New Hampshire from Marseilles in November, 1777, with strong recommendations to congress. He claimed no rank, and only requested permission to render as a volunteer what services he could to the American army. He was soon appointed to the office of inspector-general, with the rank of major-general. He established an uniform system of manœuvres, and by his skill and persevering industry effected, during the continuance of the troops at Valley Forge, a most important improvement in all ranks of the army. He was a volunteer in the action at Monmouth, and commanded in the trenches of Yorktown on the day which concluded the struggle with Great Britain. He died at Steuben, New York, November 28, 1795. He was an accomplished gentleman and a virtuous citizen, of extensive knowledge and sound judgment. An abstract of his system of discipline was published in 1779, and in 1784 he published a letter on the subject of an established militia and military arrangements."

The annexed inscription to the memory of Baron Steuben, adorns an elegant tablet on the wall of the German Lutheran church in the city of New York.

"Sacred to the memory of FREDERICK WILLIAM AUGUSTUS BARON STEUBEN, a German; knight of the order of Fidelity; aid-de-camp to Frederick the Great, king of Prussia; major-general and inspector-general in the revolutionary war; esteemed, respected, and supported by Washington. He gave military skill and discipline to the citizen soldiers, who, fulfilling the decrees of heaven, achieved the independence of the United States. The highly polished manners of the baron were graced by the most noble feelings of the heart. His hand, open as day for melting charity, closed only in the strong grasp of death. This memorial is inscribed by an American, who had the honor to be his aid-de-camp, the happiness to be his friend. Ob. 1795.

The baron was a man of strong feelings, subject to sudden bursts of passion, but ever ready to atone for an injury. The following anecdotes are illustrative of the generosity of his disposition. At a review, he directed an officer to be arrested for a fault which he thought he had been guilty of. On being informed of his innocence, he directed him to be brought forward, and in the presence of all the troops, and with the rain pouring upon his uncovered head, asked his forgiveness in the following words. "Sir, the mistake which was made, might, by throwing the line into confusion, have been fatal in the presence of an enemy. I arrested you as its author, but I have reason to believe I was mistaken; and that in this instance you were blameless. I ask your pardon. Return to your command; I would not deal unjustly by any; much less by one whose character as an officer is so respectable."—"After the capture at Yorktown, the superior officers of the American army, together with their allies, vied with each other in acts of civility and attention to the captive Britons. Entertainments were given by all the major-generals, except Baron Steuben. He was above prejudice or meanness, but poverty prevented him from displaying that liberality towards them which had been shown by others. Such was his situation, when, calling on Col. Stewart, and informing him of his intention to entertain Lord Cornwallis, he requested that he would advance a sum of money, as the price of his favorite charger. ''Tis a good beast,' said the baron, 'and has proved a faithful servant through all the dangers of the war; but, though painful to my heart, we must part. Col. Stewart immediately tendered his purse, recommending the sale or pledge of his watch, should the sum it contained prove insufficient. 'My dear friend,' replied the baron, ''tis already sold. Poor North was sick, and wanted necessaries. He is a brave fellow, and possesses the best of hearts. The trifle it brought is set apart for his use. My horse must go—so no more. I beseech you not to turn me from my purpose. I am a major-general in the service of the United States; and my private convenience must not be put in a scale with the duty which my rank imperiously calls upon me to perform.'"

TRENTON was organized in 1797, as part of Herkimer county; NW. from New York 238, from Albany 93, from Utica N. 13, from Rome 20 miles. The inhabitants are principally of New England descent, though there are some of the ancient Dutch from Holland,

GENESEE AND WASHINGTON STREETS, UTICA, N. Y.

Washington street, with the Presbyterian Church, is seen on the left; the bridge across the Erie Canal is seen on the right, down Genesee street, and at its extremity the depot of the Utica and Schenectady Railroad.

the original purchasers from the state. Trenton, an incorporated village on the road to Martinsburg, and 2 miles SW. from the falls, South Trenton, 9 miles from Utica, Holland Patent, and Prospect, 16 miles from Utica, are all small villages. Pop. 3,178.

Trenton Falls, at Trenton.

The Trenton Falls on the West Canada creek, on the east line of the town and county, are highly picturesque and sublime. The river descends in a high, narrow, and rocky dell by a succession of cataracts, the most magnificent of which are the High Falls, 2 miles NW. from the village of Trenton. This cataract is one hundred and nine feet in height, descending by three different sheets, respectively thirty-seven, eleven, and forty-eight feet fall, besides a connecting slope or rapids between. The rocks that bind the stream below, rise perpendicularly from 100 to 130 feet, capped by evergreens of spruce, fir, hemlock, and sublimely finish a landscape of uncommon beauties. The rocks are of a dark limestone, and contain large quantities of petrified marine shells, &c. &c. These falls are much visited, being within two or three hours' ride from the city of Utica, and there is here a hotel for the accommodation of visiters.

UTICA CITY comprehends the former town and village of that name, taken from Whitestown in 1817. It was incorporated a city in 1832, and divided into four wards. Its population in 1830, was 8,323; in 1840, 12,810. The land on which the city is situated is a rich alluvion, rising gently from the south side of the Mohawk river, and was formerly covered with a gigantic growth of forest trees. It is quite a central point for roads, canals, &c., to various parts of the state. Distance from Albany 96 miles, from New

York 241, from Buffalo 202, from Rochester 140, from Oswego 76, from Sacketts Harbor 94, from Ithaca 96, and from Ogdensburg 145 miles. It contains 14 churches—3 Presbyterian, 2 Methodist, 2 Baptist, 1 Episcopal, 1 Dutch Reformed, 1 Welsh Presbyterian, 1 Catholic, 1 Friends, 1 Bethel, and 1 Universalist. There are 3 banks, with an aggregate capital of one million and a half of dollars. The buildings are generally very good, the stores large and splendid. There are nine periodical publications, including newspapers, 4 academies or high schools, and numerous moral, religious, benevolent, and scientific associations.

The first building erected within the limits of Utica was a mud fort, constructed during the old French war. It was situated between Main-street and the banks of the river, a little eastward of Second-street, and named Fort Schuyler,* in honor of Col. Schuyler, an uncle of Gen. Philip Schuyler of the revolution.

" The settlement of Utica commenced at an early period, but was not prosecuted with the vigor that the neighboring settlements were. Whitestown was regarded as the great central point of the whole region up to the years 1793 or 1794. At this period quite a village had grown up there, while Utica, or old Fort Schuyler, as its site was then called, could boast of but three houses. About this time the public attention was directed to Rome, as the probable future metropolis of the state. Its local position favored the idea. It occupied the portage or carrying place between the Mohawk and Wood creek, which discharging through Oneida lake into Lake Ontario, formed a channel of communication between the Hudson and the whole chain of western lakes. The connecting the two streams by a navigable canal, which was projected at a very early day, and was accomplished by the Western Inland Lock Navigation Company, which was chartered in 1792, encouraged the belief, that that site must become the focus of the business of the country. And for several years the growth of Rome warranted the expectation. The location of the Seneca turnpike road first operated to change the current of business and divert it to this location. This event took place in the year 1800, and the crossing of the river at this point rendered it immediately important as a place of deposit and of trade. A steady and healthful growth ensued, and the aid and influence of enlightened and enterprising men in the various walks of life, contributed very shortly to render it the leading place of business in the neighborhood. Its present name was given to it in 1798, when it was incorporated as a village, and it has since then continued its municipal capacity until the present day. The first church gathered in this city was organized under the care of the Rev. Bethuel Dodd, as a branch of the church at Whitestown, in the year 1794. The style of the corporation was—" The United Presbyterian Societies of Whitestown and old Fort Schuyler." Previous to that time, although

---

* Fort Stanwix, at Rome, during the revolutionary war had its name changed to Fort Schuyler; these two are sometimes confounded in history.

the people of Whitestown had employed a clergyman, the Rev. Dr. Hillyer, whom I have already mentioned, they had not settled a pastor. Mr. Dodd was ordained pastor of the United Societies. The union of the two churches continued for more than twenty years, under the pastorates of Mr. Dodd and his successor, the Rev. Dr. Carnahan. They were the first Presbyterian churches organized west of the city of Albany, those at Clinton and New Hartford being Congregational in their forms of government. The Episcopal church in this city was gathered in 1798, and its present church edifice erected in 1803."—*Tracy's Lectures.*

The following inscriptions are copied from monuments in the graveyard at Utica.

"Erected by the Utica lodge, Oneida chapter, and Utica encampment, in memory of EZRA S. COZIER, ESQ. An upright magistrate, a kind-hearted friend, an honest man. He fell a victim to his exertions in the cause of benevolence during the epidemic cholera, 17th August, 1832, aged 47 years."

"Here lie the bodies of DR. JOHN COCHRANE, director-general of the military hospitals of the United States in the revolutionary war, and GERTRUDE, his wife. The former died in April, in the year 1807, in the 77th year of his age, and the latter in March, in the year 1813, in the 89th year of her age.—This monument is erected by their sons, James and Walter L. Cochran."

"In memory of JOHN HUGHES, a native of South Wales, who departed this life September 3d, A. D. 1831, Æ. 62.

Mewn rhyfel bu'fe yma'n hir
Yn colli ac yn ennill tir;
Ond' nawr gorphenodd ar ei waith,
Acaeth yn deg i ben ei daith."

VERNON, taken from Westmoreland in 1802; from Albany 116 miles. This town was settled in 1797.* About one fifth of the town belongs to the Oneida Indians, forming part of their reservation, and comprising their principal settlements near the Oneida village on the Oneida creek. Oneida Castleton, 22 miles SW. from Utica and 16 from Rome, has about 25 dwellings, and a church belonging to the Indians, who number about 200. On the south side of the turnpike road, at the entrance of the village, is the ancient council grove of the Six Nations, consisting of about 50 large white walnut-trees, still in full vigor. Vernon, upon the Skanandoa creek, 17 miles SW. from Utica, contains an academy, a female seminary, and about 80 dwellings. Vernon Centre, 2 miles S. from Vernon, has about 25 dwellings. Pop. 3,043.

VERONA, taken from Westmoreland and Augusta in 1802; from Albany 113, from Rome centrally distant SW. 9 miles. The town formed part of the Oneida reservation, but was purchased in 1796, by the state from the Indians. Pop. 4,504. Durhamville, New London, Verona, Verona Centre, Skanandoa, and Andover, are villages. The sulphur springs near Andover are in high repute.

VIENNA, originally named Orange, afterward changed to Bengal, and finally to Vienna; taken from Camden in 1807; from Albany

125, from Rome W. 17 miles. Settled in 1802, by New Englanders Vienna, McConnelsville, and Pine, are post-offices. Pop. 2,530.

WESTERN, taken from Steuben, as part of Herkimer county in 1797; from Albany 109, from Rome NE. 8 miles. Western and Big Brook are post-offices. Pop. 3,488.

WESTMORELAND, taken from Whitestown in 1792; from Albany 105 miles. Rock iron ore is here found in abundance, and is extensively wrought. Hampton, 9 miles W. from Utica and 7 S. from Rome, contains about 30 dwellings. Lairdsville is a small village, and Republican the name of a post-office. Pop. 3,105.

The first settlement of this town was commenced in 1786, by James Dean, Esq., a name distinguished in the history of Oneida county. He was a native of New England, the child of religious parents, who educated him for the purpose of being a missionary among the Indians. At the age of eleven he was sent among the Indians on the Susquehannah, in order to acquire their language, and gain a knowledge of their habits and manners: he afterward was a student in Dartmouth college. On the breaking out of hostilities in 1775, Mr. Dean was appointed to the office of Indian agent, with the rank of a major in the army, and during the revolutionary war continued his services. For most of the time, his duties were performed in the neighborhood of Oneida. At the close of the war the Oneidas granted him a tract of land, two miles square, near Rome, where he removed in 1784 and commenced its improvement. He afterward effected an exchange with the nation for a tract in Westmoreland, where he removed in 1786, and resided till his death, in 1832. He was appointed a judge in the county courts, and filled various other public offices. Two or three years after the removal of Mr. Dean to Westmoreland, an incident occurred, which furnishes a parallel to the rescue of Capt. Smith by Pocahontas in the early days of Virginia.

"An institution existed among the Indians for the punishment of a murderer, answering in some respects to the Jewish code. It became the duty of the nearest relative of the deceased to pursue him, and avenge his brother's death. In case the murder was perpetrated by a member of a different tribe, the offence demanded that the tribe of the murdered man should require the blood of some member of the offending tribe. This was regarded as a necessary atonement, and as absolutely requisite to the happiness of the deceased in the world of spirits, and a religious duty, and not as a mere matter of vengeful gratification. At the period to which I have referred, an Indian had been murdered by some unknown white man, who had escaped. The chiefs thereupon held a consultation at Oneida to determine what was to be done. Their deliberations were held in secret, but through the friendship of one of the number, Mr. Dean was advised of what was going on. From the office that he had held, and the high standing he maintained among the white men, it was urged in the council that he was the proper person to sacrifice in atonement for the offence committed. The question was, however, a very difficult one to dispose of. He had been adopted into the tribe, and was held to be a son, and it was argued by many of the chiefs that he could now be no more responsible for the offence than one of the natives of the tribe, and that his sacrifice would not furnish the proper atonement. For several days the matter was debated and no decision was arrived at. While it was undetermined, he continued to hope for the best, and his friendly informant kept him constantly advised of all that was done. At first he reflected upon the propriety of his leaving the country and escaping from the danger. But his circumstances, together with the hope of a favorable issue of the question in the council, induced him to remain. He had erected a small house which he was occupying with his wife and two children, one an infant, and it was idle to think of removing them without exciting observation and perhaps causing a sacrifice of all. As the council continued its session for several days, his hopes of a favorable decision brightened. He however kept the whole matter to himself, not even mentioning it to his wife, and prepared himself for any emergency which might befall him. One night after he had retired to bed, he was awoke by the sound of the death whoop, at a short distance from his house. He then for the first time communicated to his wife his fears that a party were approaching to take his life. He enjoined it upon her to remain quiet with her children in the room where they slept, while he would receive the council in an adjoining one and endeavor to avert their determination, trusting to Providence for the result. He met the Indians at the door, and seated them in the outer room. There were eighteen, and all chiefs or head men of the nation. The senior chief informed him that they had come to sacrifice him for the murder of their brother, and that he must now prepare to die. He replied to them at length, claiming that he was an adopted son of the Oneidas; that it was unjust to require his blood for the wrong committed by a wicked white man; that he was not ready to die, and that he could not leave his wife and children unprovided for. The council listened to him with profound gravity and attention, and when he sat down, one of the chiefs replied to him. He rejoined, and used every argument his ingenuity could devise in order to reverse their sentence. The debate continued a long time, and the hope of escape grew fainter and fainter as it proceeded. At length he had nearly abandoned himself to the doom they had resolved upon, when he heard the pattering of a footstep without the door. All eyes were fixed upon the door. It opened and a squaw entered. She was the wife of the senior chief, and at the time of Mr. Dean's adoption into the tribe in his boyhood, she had taken him as her son. The entrance of a woman into a solemn council, was, by Indian etiquette, at war with all propriety. She, however, took her place near the door, and all looked on in silence. A moment after, another footstep was heard, and another Indian woman entered the council. This was a sister of the former, and she too was the wife of a chief then present. Another pause ensued, and a third entered. Each of the three stood wrapped closely in her blanket, but said nothing. At length the presiding chief addressed them, telling them to begone and leave the chiefs to go on with their business. The wife replied, that the council must change their determination and let the good white man—their friend—her own adopted son, alone. The command to be gone was repeated, when each of the Indian women threw off her blanket and showed a knife in her extended hand, and declared that if one hair of the white man's head was touched, they would each bury their knives in their own heart's blood. The strangeness of the whole scene overwhelmed with amazement each member of the council, and regarding the unheard-of resolution of the women to interfere in the matter as a sort of manifestation of the will of the Great Spirit that the white man's life should not be taken, their previous decree was reversed on the spot, and the life of their victim preserved."—*Tracy's Lectures.*

WHITESTOWN was organized in 1788. It lies on the west side of the Mohawk, having an undulating surface with broad and fertile valleys. It is drained by the Oriskany and Sauquoit creeks, on which are numerous mills of various kinds. Oriskany, Whitesborough, and Yorkville are post villages. Pop. 5,156. Whitesborough, the principal village, is near the confluence of Sadaquada or Sauquoit creek with the Mohawk, contains about 100 dwelling-houses, 2 churches, an academy, and the Oneida Institute. Distant 100 miles from Albany; 4 from Utica, and 12 from Rome.

The following is a SW. view of the Oneida Institute, as seen from the Erie canal, which passes a short distance from these buildings. The "Oneida Institute of Science and Industry," was founded in 1827; incorporated in 1829. "The design of this Seminary is to furnish means to obviate the evils resulting to students from the usual application to a course of professional study, and the attendant deprivation of bodily exercise. The plan that the Seminary has established to effect this, is to blend productive manual labor with the course of study. Three hours labor per day is required of each student in the young men's department, and somewhat less of each in the juvenile department. The farm consists of the flat on the left bank of the

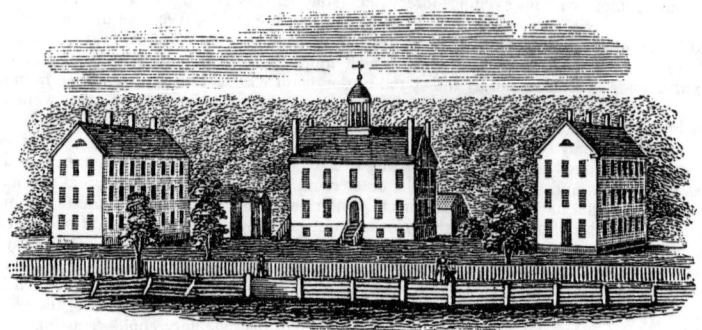

Southwest view of Oneida Institute, Whitestown.

Sauquoit, and contains 114 acres. The chief building upon it when purchased, was a large two story wood house to which a wing has been appended, and which is now occupied by the juvenile department. The other principal buildings, which are all of wood, with stone basements, are as follows: two of 82 by 32 feet, and one 48 by 48 feet, all of three stories, including the basements. The latter includes the chapel, with seats for 250 persons. The library contains upwards of 1,000 volumes; and in the reading-room are files of newspapers from various parts of the United States. The expense for instruction, room rent, fuel, and contingences per year, $28. Board at $1,05 per week, $54,60 per year. Total $82,60.

Immediately after the revolutionary war, Hugh White, a native of Middletown, Conn., Zephaniah Platt, Ezra L'Hommedieu, and Melancthon Smith, became joint proprietors of Sadaquada Patent. It was agreed among the proprietors, that they should meet on the land in the summer of 1784, and make a survey and partition of it. Judge White, having determined to make this place his home, he accordingly, in the month of May in that year, left his native place, accompanied by his four sons, all of whom had arrived at manhood, a daughter, and daughter-in-law. The party sailed to Albany, there crossed the carrying place to Schenectady, and procuring a batteau, ascended the Mohawk, and arrived in June at the mouth of the Sauquoit creek. They there erected a shanty for their temporary accommodation, while surveying and dividing the lands. Upon obtaining the partition Judge White proceeded to the erection of a log house: the site fixed upon was upon the bank which forms the eastern boundary of the village green in Whitesborough, just on the right of the Indian path which led from old Fort Schuyler to Fort Stanwix. He remained at this house with his sons until winter, cutting away the forest and making preparations for the ensuing season. In January, he returned to Connecticut, and brought his wife and the remainder of his family. Four years after this, he erected the house still standing on the southeastern corner of the village green of which the annexed is a representation. He continued to occupy it until a year or two

House of Judge White, Whitestown.

previous to his death, when he removed to the dwelling owned by him upon the hill, where he died April 16th, 1812. At the organization of Herkimer county, he was appointed a judge, and afterward performed the duties of the same office in Oneida county.

For the first two years of Judge White's residence at Whitesborough, the nearest mill was situated at Palatine, a distance of about forty miles. This distance was traversed by an Indian path impassable to a wheel-carriage. The want of animal food induced the first settlers to salt down a barrel or two of the breasts of pigeons, which they separated from the remainder of these birds, which were here caught in great numbers. In the year 1786, the settlement of Whitestown had so far increased, that its inhabitants formed a religious society, and employed as a minister the Rev. Dr. Hillyer, of Orange, New Jersey, and organized the first Presbyterian church formed in the state west of Albany. In 1788, when Whitestown was organized, its limits were laid off by a line crossing the Mohawk at a small log cabin which stood upon the site occupied by the railroad depot in Utica, and running north and south to the boundaries of the state, and comprehending all the state lying westward—a territory which at present is inhabited by more than a million of inhabitants. The first town meeting was held in a barn owned by Needham Maynard, Esq., on the road leading from Whitesborough to Middle Settlement.

For a number of years after Judge White's arrival quite a number of the Oneida Indians resided in his vicinity. The following interesting incident, which took place during this period, is copied from Tracy's Lectures.

"An old chief, named Han Yerry, who, during the war, had acted with the royal party, and now resided at Oriskany in a log wigwam which stood on this side of the creek, just back of the house, until recently, occupied by Mr. Charles Green, one day called at Judge White's with his wife and a mulatto woman who belonged to him, and who acted as his interpreter. After conversing with him a little while, the Indian asked him—Are you my friend? Yes, said he. Well, then, said the Indian, do you believe I am your friend? Yes, Han Yerry, replied he; I believe you are. The Indian then rejoined—Well, if you are my friend, and you believe I am your friend, I will tell you what I want, and then I shall know whether you speak true words. And what is it that you want? said Mr. White.

The Indian then pointed to a little grandchild, the daughter of one of his sons, then between two and three years old, and said,—My squaw wants to take this pappoose home with us to stay one night, and bring her home to-morrow: if you are my friend, you will now show me. The feelings of the grandfather at once uprose in his bosom, and the child's mother started with horror and alarm at the thought of intrusting her darling prattler with the rude tenants of the forest. The question was full of interest. On the one hand, the necessity of placing unlimited confidence in the savage, and intrusting the welfare and the life of his grandchild with him; on the other, the certain enmity of a man of influence and consequence in his nation, and one who had been the open enemy of his countrymen in their recent struggle. But he made the decision with a sagacity that showed that he properly estimated the character of the person he was dealing with. He believed that by placing implicit confidence in him, he should command the sense of honor which seems peculiar to the uncontaminated Indian. He told him to take the child; and as the mother, scarcely suffering it to be parted from her, relinquished it into the hands of the old man's wife, he soothed her fears with his assurances of confidence in their promises. That night, however, was a long one; and during the whole of the next morning many and often were the anxious glances cast up the pathway leading from Oriskany, if possible to discover the Indians and their little charge, upon their return to its home. But no Indians came in sight. It at length became high noon: all a mother's fears were aroused: she could scarcely be restrained from rushing in pursuit of her loved one. But her father represented to her the gross indignity which a suspicion of their intentions would arouse in the breast of the chief; and half frantic though she was, she was restrained. The afternoon slowly wore away, and still nothing was seen of her child. The sun had nearly reached the horizon, and the mother's heart had swollen beyond further endurance, when the forms of the friendly chief and his wife, bearing upon her shoulders their little visiter, greeted its mother's vision. The dress which the child had worn from home had been removed, and in its place its Indian friends had substituted a complete suit of Indian garments, so as completely to metamorphose it into a little squaw. The sequel of this adventure was the establishment of a most ardent attachment and regard on the part of the Indian and his friends for the white settlers. The child, now Mrs. Eells of Missouri, the widow of the late Nathaniel Eells of Whitesboro, still remembers some incidents occurring on the night of her stay in the wigwam, and the kindness of her Indian hostess."

Oriskany village is about 3 miles NE. from Whitesborough, at the confluence of Oriskany creek with the Mohawk: it has about 60 dwellings, a number of mills, and 2 woollen factories, viz. the Oriskany, first incorporated in 1804, and the Dexter. The Erie canal and the railroad between Utica and Syracuse pass through this village. The battle of Oriskany, in which Gen. Herkimer received a mortal wound, was fought about two miles in a western direction from the village.

On the advance of the British forces under Lieut. Col. St. Leger to the siege of Fort Schuyler, (Stanwix,) at Rome, General Herkimer summoned the militia of Tryon county to the field to march to the succor of the garrison. On the 5th of Aug., 1777, he arrived near Oriskany with a body of upwards of 800 men, all eager to meet the enemy. On the morning of the 6th of August, Gen. Herkimer determined to halt till he had received reinforcements, or at least until the signal of a sortie should be received from the fort. His officers, however, were eager to press forward; high words ensued: during which his two colonels and other officers denounced their commander to his face as a tory and a coward. "The brave old man calmly replied that he considered himself placed over them as a father, and that it was not his wish to lead them into any difficulty from which he could not extricate them. Burning as they now seemed to meet the enemy, he told them roundly that they would run at his first appearance. But his remonstrances were unavailing. Their clamor increased, and their reproaches were repeated, until, stung by imputations of cowardice and a want of fidelity to the cause, and somewhat irritated withal, the general immediately gave the order—'march on!' The words were no sooner heard than the troops gave a shout, and moved, or rather rushed forward." Col. St. Leger having heard of the advance of Gen. Herkimer, determined to attack him in an ambuscade. The spot chosen favored the design. There was a deep ravine crossing the path which Herkimer was traversing, "sweeping towards the east in a semi-circular form, and bearing a northern and southern direction. The bottom of this ravine was marshy, and the road crossed it by means of a causeway. The ground, thus partly enclosed by the ravine, was elevated and level. The ambuscade was laid upon the high ground west of the ravine."

The British troops, with a large body of Indians under Brant, disposed themselves in a circle, leaving only a narrow segment open for the admission of Herkimer's troops. Unconscious of the presence of the enemy, Gen. Herkimer with his whole force, with the exception of the rear-guard, found themselves encompassed at the onset—the foe closing up the gap on their first fire. Those on the outside fled as their commander had predicted; those within the circle were thrown into disorder by the sudden and murderous fire now poured in upon them on all sides. Gen. Herkimer fell wounded in the early part of the action, and was placed on his saddle against the trunk of a tree for his support, and thus continued to order the battle. The action having lasted more than half an hour, in great disorder, Herkimer's men formed themselves into circles to repel the attacks of the enemy, who were now closing in upon them from all sides. From this moment their resistance was more effective. The firing in a great measure ceased; and the conflict was carried on with knives, bayonets, and the butt-ends of muskets. A heavy shower of rain now arrested the work of death; the storm raged for an hour, and the enemy retired among the trees, at a respectful distance, having suffered severely, notwithstanding the advantages in their favor. During this suspension of the conflict, Gen. Herkimer's men, by his direction, formed themselves into a circle and awaited the movements of the enemy. In the early part of the battle, whenever a gun was fired by a militiaman from behind a tree, an Indian rushed up and tomahawked him before he could reload. To counteract this, *two men were stationed behind a single tree, one only to fire at a time—the other to reserve his fire till the Indian ran up as before* The fight was soon renewed, but by this new arrangement the Indians suffered so severely that they began to give way. A reinforcement of the enemy now came up, called Johnson's Greens. These men were mostly royalist, who having fled from Tryon county, now returned in arms against their former neighbors. Many of the militia and the Greens knew each other, and as soon as they advanced near enough for recognition, mutual feelings of hate and revenge raged in their bosoms. The militia fired upon them as they advanced, and then springing like tigers from their covers, attacked them with their bayonets and butts of their muskets; or both parties in closer contact throttled each other and drew their knives—stabbing, and sometimes literally dying in each other's embrace."

This murderous conflict did not continue long: the Indians seeing with what resolution the militia continued the fight, and finding their own numbers greatly diminished, now raised the retreating cry of "*Oonah !*" and fled in every direction under the shouts of the surviving militia, and a shower of bullets. A firing was heard in the distance from the fort: the Greens and Rangers now deemed that their presence was necessary elsewhere, and retreated precipitately, leaving the victorious militia of Tryon county masters of the field.— "Thus ended," (says Col. Stone in his Life of Brant,) "one of the severest, and, for the numbers engaged, one of the most bloody battles of the revolutionary war." The loss of the militia, according to the American account, was two hundred killed, exclusive of wounded and prisoners. The British claimed that four hundred of the Americans were killed and two hundred taken prisoners. "The loss of the enemy was equally if not more severe, than that of the Americans." Gen. Herkimer, though wounded in the onset, bore himself during the six hours of conflict, under the most trying circumstances, with a degree of fortitude and composure worthy of admiration. "At one time during the battle, while sitting upon his saddle, raised upon a little hillock, being advised to select a less exposed situation, he replied—'I will face the enemy.' Thus surrounded by a few men, he continued to issue his orders with firmness. In this situation, and in the heat of the onslaught, he deliberately took his tinder box from his pocket, lit his pipe, and smoked with great composure." After the battle was over, he was removed from the field on a litter, and was conveyed to his house, below the Little Falls on the Mohawk.

The following inscriptions are copied from monuments in the Whitesborough grave-yard.

"Here sleep the mortal remains of *Hugh White*, who was born 5th February, 1733, at Middletown, Connecticut, and died 16th April, 1812. In the year 1784, he removed to Sedaghquate, now Whitesborough: where he was the first white inhabitant in the state of New York west of the German settlers on the Mohawk. He was distinguished for energy and decision of character; and may justly be regarded as a *Patriarch* who led the children of New England into the wilderness. As a magistrate, a citizen, and a man, his character for truth and integrity was proverbial. This humble monument is reared and inscribed by the affectionate partner of his joys and his sorrows, May 15, 1826."

"To the memory of the Rev. Bethuel Dodd, first pastor of the United Presbyterian Society of Whitestown and Utica. Born 1767, died 1804; and of Sarah his wife, born 1768, died 1828. In the year 1794, they emigrated from Orange, New Jersey, to this village. Mr. Dodd assisted in forming the first Presbyterian church west of Albany, and spent the remainder of a short but useful career in the upbuilding of this branch of his Master's kingdom."

ONONDAGA COUNTY.

ONONDAGA COUNTY was taken from Herkimer in 1794; bounds since altered by the formation of other counties from it. Greatest length N. and S. 36, greatest breadth E. and W. 28 miles. Centrally distant from New York 280 miles, from Albany 135 miles. This county, though not extensive, embraces a most important portion of the territory of this state. Here are the salt springs, an inexhaustible source of immense wealth; beds of gypsum or plaster, of vast extent, hydraulic lime and common limestone. Surface is diversified. The northern portion of the county is level; the centre and southern rolling, and rising in some places into hills. The soil is generally good, and in some portions excellent, and under high cultivation. Large crops of wheat and Indian corn are annually raised. Both are greatly aided by the use of plaster. The principal lakes are Oneida, Skaneateles, Onondaga, and Otisco. The Rome summit, or long level of the Erie canal, 69½ miles in length, has its western extremity near Syracuse. The county forms part of the military tract, and settlements were first made here in the spring of 1788, whilst composing part of Whitestown, Oneida county. The county is divided into 18 towns, of which Lysander, Manlius, Marcellus, Onondaga, and Pompey were organized by general sessions in 1789. Pop. 67,915.

CAMILLUS, organized in 1789: from Albany 141 miles. Camillus has about 60 dwellings. This village is connected with the Erie canal by a feeder. Belleisle, on the canal 6 miles W., and Amboy 7 miles W. from Syracuse, are small settlements. Pop. 3,957.

CICERO, organized in 1807; from Albany 143, from Syracuse NE. 10 miles. Cicero is a small village. On the bank of the Seneca river, opposite Brewerton post-office, in the north part of the town, are the remains of an old French fort. Pop. 2,464.

CLAY, taken from Cicero in 1827; from Albany 151, from Syracuse N. 11 miles. Clay and Euclid are names of post-offices. Pop. 2,852.

DE WITT, taken from Manlius in 1835; from Albany 128 miles. Jamesville, 7 miles SE. from Syracuse, has about 45 dwellings. Orville is a small village. Pop. 2,802.

ELBRIDGE, taken from Camillus in 1829; from Albany 169 miles. Elbridge, 15 miles W. from Syracuse, has about 60 dwellings. Near this village are Indian remains, the largest of which, upon a hill, has an area of about three acres, surrounded by a ditch and wall of earth. It is said that a large limestone was found here, having writing upon it in an unknown character, and that from a well within the wall, many mouldering human bones have been taken. Jordan, on the canal, 12 miles W. from Syracuse, is an incorporated village having about 150 dwellings. Elbridge has about 60 dwellings. Peru and Wellington are small settlements. Pop. 4,647.

FABIUS, organized in 1798; from Albany 125, from Syracuse SE. 18 miles. The remains of anŧient forts are found here, and beneath the earth human bones. Franklinville is a large village, and Apulia has about 40 dwellings. Pop. 2,562.

LAFAYETTE, taken from Pompey and Onondaga in 1825; from Albany 134, from Syracuse S. 11 miles. Lafayette and Cardiff are small post villages. Pop. 2,600.

LYSANDER, from Albany 152 miles. Baldwinsville, on the Seneca river, 12 miles NW. from Syracuse, is a manufacturing village containing 80 or 100 dwellings. Plainville, Lysander, Betts Corners, and Little Utica, are villages. Pop. 4,036.

MANLIUS,* in common with many other towns in this section, was originally divided by the surveyor-general into lots one mile square, which were drawn as bounty lands by revolutionary soldiers; and hence its name, after a celebrated Roman general, is very appropriate. The town throughout is fertile, the southern part being uneven, the northern level; and is crossed both by the canal and railroad. It is well watered by the Limestone and Butternut creeks, the former of which runs through nearly its whole length. Its principal exports are grain, plaster of Paris, and water lime. Pop. 5,509.

About 100 rods south, and about a mile NW. of the village of Manlius, are found mineral springs, which are much resorted to by people living near them. At the latter place there are three fountains, within a few feet of each other, the waters of which differ very decidedly in their sensible properties. A boarding-house for the reception of guests was kept here by its former proprietor, connected with which were bathing places, swings, &c. At both these springs, but more particularly than at either, upon the bank of the Limestone creek about 100 rods NW. of the latter, are found specimens of calcareous tufa, petrified leaves, and fragments of wood, some of which, for their perfection, have been deposited in the cabinet of Yale college, New Haven, Connecticut.

The first white inhabitant of this town was David Tripp, who moved here with his family about the year 1790. He lived in a log cabin nearly a mile NW. of the present village of Manlius, his nearest neighbor being probably Gen. A. Danforth, at Onondaga, 10 miles distant. When he settled here, being surrounded with wilderness, it was with great difficulty that he could procure the food necessary for the subsistence of his family, until he could raise it from the soil by his own labor. At one time, the only article of food which they had for three months, with the exception of wild roots and milk, was a bushel of corn, which he brought from Herkimer, 55 miles, on his back. Soon after Mr. Tripp became located in this town, several persons formed a settlement at Eagle village, a mile E. of the present village of Manlius. The first wedding in town was celebrated about the 1st of July, 1794, in the open yard in front of Mr. Foster's tavern in this settlement. It was on "a training day,"

---

* For the account of this town the authors are indebted to Azariah Smith, M. D.

and the soldiers of the company who met there for parade, formed a hollow square, in the centre of which Cyrus Kinne, Esq., united in "wedlock's holy bonds" Mr. Billy McKee to Miss Jenny Mulholland. It is somewhat remarkable that this couple met with violent deaths about twelve years ago, and but a few months from each other.

The first frame dwelling erected in town was built near Mr. Tripp's, by Conrad Lower, in 1792. He brought the floor boards from Palatine, and the other boards from Danforth's mill, which was erected on Butternut creek the same season. Not having a sufficient quantity of nails, his son was sent to Oriskany, 33 miles, after some, and returned with 46 pounds on his back. The house built by him constitutes part of the dwelling now occupied by Salmon Sherwood. The first saw-mill in the present town was erected at the eastern Limestone falls, by Phineas Stevens in 1793, and the first grist-mill by William Ward, near the western extremity of the present village of Manlius, in the summer and fall of 1794.

View in the central part of Manlius.

The lot assigned, at the time of the original division of this town by the surveyor-general, for the support of the gospel and of common schools, was set apart by the town for the latter object, and was sold May 2, 1814, for $12,114.42. When De Witt was set off from Manlius, this fund was divided, and the present town of Manlius received for its share $7,752.42. This fund is invested in bonds and mortgages paying 7 per cent. interest; and the annual income, $542.67, is divided among the school districts, in addition to the proper share of money which the town receives from the state.

The principal village, called Manlius after the name of the town, is situated 3 miles S. of the Erie canal at Hulls landing, and about 5 miles from the railroad. It is 10 miles from Syracuse, and 134 from Albany, and contained, in 1830, 472 male, and 517 female inhabitants. Its present population is estimated at between 11 and 12 hundred. Annexed is a cut of the village; the building with an attic and cupola is the academy, the church to the right of it is the Presbyterian, and the one on the opposite side of the street the Episcopa-

49

lian. This church is the oldest in the place, and formerly stood on the top of the steep hill east of the academy, (not seen in the view,) from whence it was removed on wheels to its present location a few years since, with its steeple, bell, organ, &c., without jarring it so much as to remove a square foot of plastering. The Baptist and Methodist churches are not seen from this point. The latter was originally ornamented with a spire, but as it was thought by some of the congregation to betoken spiritual pride, it was torn down soon after it was built, and in its place was substituted the present low tower. The two story and a half building near and to the right of the academy, was formerly a tavern, and is made up in part of the oldest frame in the village. The cupolas in the distance belong to cotton mills, of which there are 3 in the place, known as the Limestone, Manlius, (carried on by an incorporated company,) and Cold Spring factories. The first of them—owned by Azariah Smith, who moved to this place from Middlefield, Mass., June 2, 1807, and has traded in the three story building on the right side of the street in the above cut since July 4, 1816—is the largest, having 2,004 spindles, and manufactures annually about 500,000 yards of brown sheetings and shirtings. There are also in this village 3 flouring mills, 3 coach factories, 2 furnaces, &c.

The Manlius academy was incorporated April 13, 1835, with nine trustees, who are authorized to fill vacancies in their number. It has already attained the rank of fifth in the literary institutions of this senate district, and received in 1840 from the regents of the university $316.65, as its portion of the state literature fund. The number of students during that year was 274, 62 of whom studied languages.

The following ministers have filled the pulpits in this place in order, viz: Rev. Messrs. Clark, Davis, Pardee, Wm. J. Bulkeley, Dyer, Burton, H. Hickox, James Selkrigg, A. S. Hollister, Jesse Pound, Appleton, and Davis, the Episcopalian; Rev. Messrs. Reed, Olds, Samuel Hopkins, Hezekiah Woodruff, Ralph Cushman, Hiram Kellogg, John Ingersoll, Talcott Bates, Carlos Smith, Amzi Benedict, and John J. Slocum, the Presbyterian; Rev. Messrs. Charles Morton, D. Bellamy and McCarthy, the Baptist. The Methodist ministers, as they biennially change, are not mentioned.

The first newspaper printed in the county of Onondaga, was published in this village by Mr. Abraham Romain, under the title of the "Derne Gazette." The first number was issued in the spring of 1806, and a contemporaneous effort was made to change the name of the village to Derne; this effort however failed, and the paper was discontinued after a little more than a year, for want of sufficient support. Since that time there have been published here several newspapers, The Manlius Times, Manlius Republican, Onondaga Republican, Manlius Repository, and Onondaga Flagg. The Manlius Repository commenced in 1830, and reached its fifth volume.

James O. Rockwell, a young man of considerable reputation, author of a prize poem, in one of the annuals, formerly associate editor of a newspaper in Boston, and afterward of one in Providence, in which city he died, was a native of this place. His parents being in indigent circumstances, he was employed when a small lad in the Manlius factory, at which time his happy genius for rhyming was first observed. While employed in tending a picking machine, he made a small book, on each right hand page of which was a picture of different parts of the factory, and on the opposite page a verse describing it. On the outside was a front view of the factory with an overseer on the foreground, dragging a boy towards the door, and under it this verse—

The factory life	And every boy
Is full of strife:	That they employ
I own I hate it dearly;	Will own the same, or nearly.

Fayetteville, 2½ miles N. of Manlius village, is situated on a feeder to the Erie canal, and contains about 100 houses. It has 4 churches, 1 Presbyterian, 1 Baptist, 1 Methodist, and 1 Episcopalian. It has an incorporated academy, which received from the literature fund of the state in 1840, $183.39. The principal business men are engaged in the purchase and forwarding of produce brought from the country south of the canal to this place.

The other settlements are Kirkville and Manlius Centre, on the canal, Eagle village, referred to in the above history of the town, Hartsville, and Matthews Mills.

MARCELLUS has a hilly surface with a soil of fertile loam; centrally situated from Albany 157, and from Syracuse SW.14 miles. The village of Marcellus has about 75 dwellings, 3 churches, and a number of mills of various kinds. Clintonville is a post-office. Pop. 2,727.

Perhaps the most remarkable case on record of *devotional somnium*, so called, is that of Miss Rachel Baker of this town. A full history of her case may be found in the Transactions of the Physico-Medical Society of New York, vol. I. p. 395. Rachel Baker was born at Pelham, Massachusetts, May 29, 1794. Her parents were pious persons, and early taught her the importance of religion. From childhood she appeared to possess a contemplative disposition; but her mind was not vigorous, nor was she much disposed to improve it by reading. At the age of nine years she removed with her parents to the town of Marcellus in the state of New York. From that time she said " she had frequently strong convictions of the importance of eternal things, and the thoughts of God and eternity would make her tremble."—In June, 1811, while on a visit to the town of Scipio, she was deeply affected in witnessing the baptism of a young lady, and from that period was impressed with a stronger conviction of her own sinfulness. On her return to Marcellus, she endeavored to suppress her religious anxiety, but in vain; her anguish of mind was fully depicted in her countenance.

On the evening of the 28th of November, while she was sitting in a chair, apparently asleep, she began to sigh and groan as if in excessive pain. She had said a short time before that she would live only a little while, and as she now repeated the expression, her parents were apprehensive that she was dying. This evening she talked incoherently; but manifested in what she said much religious concern. She continued almost every night talking in her sleep till the 27 Jan., 1812. On that evening, soon after she had fallen asleep, she was seized with a fit of trembling, shrieked aloud and awoke in great terror. Horror and despondency overwhelmed her with the dread of a miserable eternity, and of her speedy and inevitable doom. But these agonizing feelings were soon succeeded by a calm; her mind became tranquil, and in her nightly devotions, which were now regular and coherent, she poured forth a spirit of meekness, gratitude, and love. From this time the whole tenor of her soul seemed to be changed. She was incapable of expressing her sentiments clearly when awake; but her sleeping exercises were so solemn and impressive, that few who heard them doubted that they were the genuine fruits of repentance, piety, and peace.

Dr. Mitchell, in describing Miss Baker's case, says, " the latter of these remarkable affections of the human mind, (*Somnium cum religione*,) i. e. sleep with religion, belongs to Miss Rachel Baker, who for several years has been seized with somnium of a religious kind once a day with great regularity. These daily paroxysms recur with wonderful exactness, and from long prevalence have now become habitual. They invade her at early bedtime, and a fit usually lasts about three quarters of an hour. A paroxysm has been known to end in 35 minutes, and to continue 98. The transition from the waking state to that of somnium is very quick, frequently in quarter of an hour, and sometimes even less. After she retires from company in the parlor, she is discovered to be occupied in praising God with a distinct and sonorous voice. Her discourses are usually pronounced in a private chamber, for the purpose of delivering them with more decorum on her own part and with greater satisfaction to her hearers. She has been advised to take the recumbent posture. Her face being turned towards the heavens, she performs her nightly devotions with a consistency and fervor wholly unexampled in a human being in a state of somnium. Her body and limbs are motionless, they stir no more than the trunk and extremities of a statue: the only motion the spectator perceives is that of her organs of speech, and an oratorical inclination of the head and neck, as if she was intently engaged in performing an academic or theological exercise. According to the tenor and solemnity of the address, the attendants are affected with seriousness. She commences and ends with an address to the throne of grace, consisting of proper topics of submission and reverence, of praise and thanksgiving, and of prayer for herself, her friends, the church, the nation, for enemies, and the human race in general. Between these is her sermon or exhortation. She begins without a text, and proceeds with an even course to the end, embellishing it sometimes with fine metaphors, vivid descriptions, and poetical quotations. There is a state of the body felt like groaning, sobbing, or moaning, and the distressful sound continues from two minutes to quarter of an hour. This agitation, however, does not wake her; it gradually subsides, and she passes into a sound and natural sleep, which continues during the remainder of the night. In the morning she wakes as if nothing had happened, and entirely ignorant of the scenes in which she has acted. She declares she knows nothing of her nightly exercises except from the information of others. With the exception of the before-mentioned agitation of body and exercise of mind, she enjoys perfect health. In October, 1814, Miss Baker was brought to New York by her friends, in hopes that her somnial exercises, (which were considered by some of them as owing to disease,) might by the exercise of a journey and the novelty of a large city be removed. But none of these means produced the desired effect. Her acquaintances stated that her somnial exercises took place every night regularly, except in a few instances when interrupted by severe sickness, from the time they commenced in 1812. In September, 1816, Dr. Sears, by a course of medical treatment, particularly by the use of opium, prevented a recurrence of her nightly exercises.

ONONDAGA is from Albany 135 miles. Onondaga West Hill, a village and formerly the county seat, 4 miles SW. of Syracuse, contains about 50 dwellings. Onondaga* Hollow, an incorporated village, has about 60 dwellings. South Onondaga and Navarino are small villages. Pop. 5,662. The Onondaga castle, or the council-house of the remnant of the Onondagas, is in a rich tract in

Council-house of the Onondagas.

the Hollow, 3 miles S. of the village of Onondaga Hollow, on a small reservation of theirs, and contains about 50 houses on a street of a mile or more in length. Their dwellings are built of hewn logs, the spaces of which are filled with masoned mortar work, and are quite comfortable. The above view represents a portion of their village with their new council-house, which is the building seen on the right with three chimneys. The old council-house, now in ruins, is seen on the left. There are at present remaining not far from 300 souls. The first white settler in this county was a Mr. Webster, who came here in 1786, and settled in the Hollow among the Indians. They gave him a tract of a mile square. He then opened a small shop, married a squaw, and became domesticated among the savages. In 1788, he obtained permission of the Onondagas for Messrs. Asa Danforth and Comfort Tyler to establish themselves at Onondaga Hollow.

" It was in this 'hollow' that the principal town and castle of the Onondaga Indians, in the prouder days of that nation stood ; and the poor remains of that once warlike and haughty member of the Oquanuschioni, or the amphyctionic league of the Five Nations, numbering a few hundred souls, are yet dragging out their lingering existence in the same valley a short distance to the south of the village I have just mentioned.

" The history of the Onondaga nation, to say nothing of their own legends antecedent to the discovery and settlement of the country by the ' pale faces,' is full of interest. It was the central nation of the great confederacy, the terror of whose arms was almost co-exten-

* *Onon-laga* is an Indian word, signifying a swamp under or at the foot of a hill or mountain.

sive with the northern and eastern division of the continent, and whose actual domain at one time extended from the Sorel, south of the great lakes, to the Mississippi west, thence east to the Santee, and coastwise back to the Hudson. The great council-fire of the confederacy was in the special keeping of the Onondagas, and by them was always kept burning. The territory proper of the confederacy extended from Albany to Lake Erie, and was called the Long House. The Mohawks kept the eastern door, and the Senecas the western. On the arrival of ambassadors from either direction, the keepers of the doors demanded their business. If of minor or trifling consequence, a council of the tribe, by whom the ambassadors were received, disposed of the matter. But if by such council judged to be of sufficient weight and importance to demand the consideration of a national council, the messengers were conducted to the great council-fire at Onondaga, where the Congress of the confederacy was convoked.

"The Onondagas have been distinguished both as orators and warriors. In their early intercourse with the 'pale faces,' they brought forward orators of great ability; and some of the finest passages that have been preserved of Indian eloquence, fell from the lips of Garangula, Thurensera, Decanesora, and Sadekanaghtie, all chiefs of the Onondaga nation. Indeed, during more than a century subsequent to the invasion of Onondaga by the French in 1696, Red Jacket and Farmer's Brother only have equalled the oratorical efforts of the more ancient chiefs whom I have named. By the ancient unwritten constitution of the confederacy, the Onondagas were entitled to furnish the grand sachem, or principal civil chief, while the principal war chiefs were to be supplied by the Mohawks. But the great warrior of the confederacy, towards the close of the 17th century, was an Onondaga named *Black Kettle*, called by the French historians La Chaudiere Noire. He led his Indians with Colonel Schuyler in 1690, against the French settlements on the north of Lake Champlain, and repulsed De Calheres, the governor of Montreal, who came against him with a superior force. He next attacked and defeated a French expedition sent against the Indians at Niagara, and subsequently carried the war into Canada, with immense loss and damage to the French settlements. Enraged at the success of Black Kettle, the French governor, having made prisoner of one of his warriors, put him to death by the most horrible tortures But the captive withstood the most exquisite tortures with the utmost firmness—singing his achievements while they broiled his feet, burnt his hands with red hot irons, cut and wrung off his joints, and pulled out the sinews; and to close all, his scalp was torn off, and red hot sand poured upon his head!

"This atrocious deed by civilized men again re-awakened the vengeance of Black Kettle, and the French had speedy cause to lament with the deepest bitterness their own atrocity. A detachment of Senecas being soon afterward in the neighborhood of Quebec, Black Kettle, with a company of Onondagas, placed himself at their head. In 1692 he fell upon the island of Montreal, carrying his arms to the gates of the citadel. This brave chief continued the war until the year 1697, when, being decoyed into Canada under the pretext of a desire to negotiate a peace, he was treacherously murdered by a party of Algonkins engaged for that purpose. His country, however, had been ravaged by the French the year before his death; and as the history of this first known invasion of Onondaga Hollow is interesting, I will give it in detail. In the year 1696, Count Frontenac, one of the most efficient and politic, as well perhaps as the most cruel of the French governors in Canada, attempted to detach the Five Nations from the friendship of the English colony and negotiate a separate peace.

"With this view, through the agency of the Jesuits, the count succeeded in persuading the Indians to call a grand council of their chiefs at the old council-fire in Onondaga, to which he despatched messengers with his proposals. There were eighty sachems present, and the council was opened by Sagdekanaghtie. The French commissioners labored assiduously to accomplish their purpose, and the conference continued several days. But a messenger from Albany informed the chiefs that a separate peace would displease the English, and the proposals were thereupon promptly rejected. Shortly afterward, the count determined to avenge himself upon the Five Nations, for having preferred the preservation of their good faith and honor to the peace which he had proffered. For this purpose he assembled all his disposable troops, amounting to four battalions, with the Indians in his service and under his control, and departed from Montreal on the 9th of July, 1696. In addition to small-arms, they took with them two light pieces of cannon, two mortars, a supply of grenades, &c. After a wearisome march of twelve days, during which the utmost circumspection was necessary to avoid ambuscades, the count reached the foot of Lake Cadarackui, (now called Ontario,) and crossed thence in canoes to the estuary of the Oshwego river, which flows from the northern extremity of the Onondaga, or Salt Lake—the Onondaga flowing into the southern end near the great salt licks. The expedition cautiously ascended the Oshwego, and crossed the Salt Lake, keeping strong scouts on the flanks, to prevent any surprise that might be attempted by a crafty enemy. This precautionary measure was the more necessary, inasmuch as the Indians, against whom they were marching, with their wonted chivalry, had given the French notice that they were apprized of their hostile approach. A tree had been discovered by one of the scouts, on the trunk of which, the savages had painted a representation of the French army on its march, and at the foot of the tree two bundles of rushes had been deposited, serving at once as a note of defiance, and giving the invader to understand that he would be compelled to encounter as many warriors as there were rushes in the bundles. These, being counted, were found to number fourteen hundred and forty-four.

"The castle of the Onondagas was situated in the midst of the deep and beautiful valley to which we have already referred, and through which the Onondaga river winds its way to the lake. Count Frontenac, with his motley forces, had made a halt near the licks, and thrown up some temporary defences. The site of the castle was but five or six miles removed from the French camp. It was a sacred spot in the eyes of the Indians, as the seat of the grand councils which had for ages regulated the affairs of the fierce and wild democracy of the Five Nations. They had, therefore, resolved to defend it to the last; and their women and children had been sent from the rude village deeper into the shades of the forest. Circumstances, however, changed this determination on the morning of the day upon which Count Frontenac intended to advance. Two of the Hurons deserted from the forces of the count, and gave the Onondagas, to whose assistance neither of their associate tribes had yet arrived, such an appalling description of the French, that they dared not remain and give battle.

"Yonnondio's* army, they said, was like the leaves on the trees—more numerous than the pigeons that fly to the north after the season of the snows. They were armed, they said, with great guns that threw up huge balls towards the sun; and when these balls fell into their castle, they would explode and scatter fire and death everywhere."

The Onondagas, having applied the brand to their dwellings, retreated into the wilderness. The Count Frontenac, astonished at the sight of the ascending columns of smoke, as they rose in curling folds towards the sky, moved rapidly forward. But it was to obtain an empty conquest. The huts and rude works of the Indians were already in ashes. An old venerable-looking chief, whose head had been whitened by the snows of more than a hundred winters, by his own desire was left behind. He was found seated by the trunk of a sycamore, and was tortured in a horrible manner by Frontenac's Indians. He bore their inflictions with stoical indifference, and died as became an Indian warrior.

"With the retreat of the French, the Onondagas repossessed themselves of their beautiful valley and rebuilt their town and castle. They moreover maintained their rank and position down to the breaking out of the war of the revolution. During the old French war, which resulted in the conquest of Canada by the English and provincials, the Onondagas sustained their part under the influence and conduct of Sir William Johnson; and when the war came on, they with the family of the deceased baronet espoused the cause of the crown.

"In the year 1779, their country was invaded and ravaged by the direction of General James Clinton, by a detachment of regular troops under the immediate command of Colonel Van Schaick. As in the case of the former invasion, the Indians retired before superior numbers, and their town and castle were again destroyed by fire. But little blood was shed, one Indian only being killed; and that little was sorely avenged by the Onondaga warriors, who fell upon the settlement of Cobleskill, in a few weeks thereafter. With the return of peace, however, the Onondagas became the friends of the United States, and during the late war with England, some of their warriors were engaged on the side of the Americans, in the Niagara campaign. Their principal warrior, Le Fort, was the leader of the Indians in the battle of Chippewa. His son, an educated and respectable man, yet resides with the remains of his people in their native valley."—*New York Commercial Advertiser.*

---

* The name by which the Five Nations designated the French governor.

OTISCO, taken from Pompey, Tully, and Marcellus in 1806; from Albany 140, from Syracuse SW. 14 miles. Otisco Lake in this town derives its name from the Indian word Otisco, signifying "decreased waters." Amber and Otisco Centre are post villages. Population, 1,906.

POMPEY has a hilly surface and a fertile sandy clay loam; it is centrally situated from Albany 146, and SE. from Syracuse 14 miles. Pop. 4,371. Pompey, Pompey Hill, Oran, and Delphi, are post villages. Pompey Hill, on an eminence which overlooks the country for a great distance, contains about 70 dwellings, a Baptist and Presbyterian church, and an academy. "About two miles south of Manlius square in the town of Pompey, are the remains of a town, which extended three quarters of a mile from north to south, and half a mile from east to west. Large spots of black mould in regular intervals, and a few paces apart in which are ashes, mark out the sites of the houses." Here were three forts of circular or elliptical forms, forming a triangle which protected the approaches. Near Delphi, in the southeast part of the town, are two falls 70 feet perpendicular; near this place are the remains of three ancient works. The largest contains six acres, and has a triangular form. It had a ditch, rampart, and gateway; the others also have ramparts, ditches, and entrances. There were many graves within the largest fort, over and around which were trees 200 years old. With human bones were found axes, brass kettles, gun-barrels, Spanish coins, &c.

The following account of a French colony located in this town in the year 1666, is from a memoir by De Witt Clinton, on the antiquities of western New York. He derived the account partly from a manuscript journal of one of the Jesuits, and partly from the sachems of the Six Nations:—

"From the Jesuit's journal it appears that in the year 1666, at the request of Karakontie, an Onondaga chieftain, a French colony was directed to repair to his village for the purpose of teaching the Indians the arts and sciences, and endeavor if practicable to civilize and Christianize them. We learn from the sachems that at this time the Indians had a fort, a short distance above the village of Jamesville, on the banks of a small stream near; a little above which, it seems the Chief Karakontie would have his new friends *set down*. Accordingly they repaired thither, and commenced the labor, in which being greatly aided by the savages, a few months only were necessary to the building of a small village.

"This little colony remained for three years in a very peaceable and flourishing situation, during which time much addition was made to the establishment, and among others a small chapel, in which the Jesuit used to collect the barbarians and perform the rites and ceremonies of his church. About this time, (1669,) a party of Spaniards, consisting of twenty-three persons, arrived at the village, having for guides some of the Iroquois, who had been taken captives by some of the southern tribes. It appears evident that this party came up the Mississippi, passed Pittsburg, and on to Olean Point, where, leaving their canoes, they travelled by land. They had been informed that there was a lake to the north whose bottom was covered with a substance shining and white, which they took from the Indians' description to be silver.

"Having arrived at Onondaga Lake and the French village, and finding no silver, they seemed bent on a quarrel with the French, whom they charged with having bribed the Indians, so that they would not tell them where the silver might be found. A compromise was finally effected, they agreed that an equal number of Spaniards and French should be sent on an exploring expedition. The Indians seeing these strangers prowling the woods, with various instruments, suspected some design to be in operation to deprive them of their country. This jealousy was much increased by the accusation of the Europeans themselves.

The Spaniards told the Indians that the only object of the French was to tyrannize over them. The French, on the other hand, asserted that the Spaniards were laying a plan to rob them of their lands.

" The Indians by this time becoming jealous of both, determined in private council to rid themselves of these intruders. Having privately obtained the assistance of the Oneidas and Cayugas, they agreed upon the time and manner of attack. A little before daybreak on *All-Saints' Day*, 1669, the little colony, together with the Spaniards, were aroused from their slumbers by the discharge of fire-arms and the war-whoop of the savages. Every house was immediately fired or broken open, and such as attempted to escape from the flames were killed by the tomahawk; and not one of the colonists or Spaniards were left alive to relate the sad disaster."

This history accounts, in the opinion of its author, for the appearance at this place of a small village, the evident remains of a blacksmith's shop. In several other places in the county, says the Rev. Mr. Adams, in his manuscript history, the remains of blacksmiths' shops have been discovered, and in some instances the tools used by the trade. A blacksmith's vice was found buried deep in the ground on a farm in Onondaga Hollow, about three-fourths of a mile south of the turnpike. But the existence of a fort near this spot, every vestige of which is nearly obliterated, readily accounts for these relics of civilization. In the cultivation of the lands lying upon the Onondaga creek, innumerable implements of war and of husbandry have been found, scattered over a territory of four or five miles in length. Swords, gun-barrels, gun-locks, bayonets, balls, axes, hoes, &c., have been found. A stone was found in the town of Pompey, (now in the Albany museum,) about fourteen inches long by twelve broad and eight inches in thickness. It has in the centre a figure of a tree with a serpent climbing it, with the following inscription on each side :—

Leo X De $\overset{\text{\tiny{\&c.}}}{\underset{\text{\tiny{tree,}}}{}}$ LS
VIx 1520   †   ∩

We have here the true chronology of the Pontificate of Leo X., and probably the year in which the inscriptions were made. The inscription may be thus translated, " Leo X., by the grace of God; sixth year of his Pontificate, 1520." The stone was doubtless designed as a sepulchral monument. LS., signified the initials of the name of the person buried; the cross, that he was a Catholic; and the inverted ∩, some other emblem which is now in a great measure effaced. Mr. Adams considers that it is not incredible that this stone was carved by a Spaniard, on or near the spot where it was found. Florida was discovered by the Spaniards as early as 1502. Possibly some adventurers of this nation, allured by the story of a lake at the north whose bottom was lined with silver [the salt at Salina springs,] traversed this region in pursuit of their darling object; one of the number dying here, the survivor or survivors may have placed this monument over his remains.

SALINA was taken from Manlius and Onondaga in 1809. The township consists of the land reserved by the law of the state for the use of the salt springs, and 8 or 9 lots of the original township of Manlius. Onondaga Lake. 6 miles long, with an average width of one mile, extends into the central part of this town. The water from which the salt is made rises in the marshes around its borders, or in the margin of the lake. The population of the town, including Syracuse and the other villages in its vicinity, is 11,012.

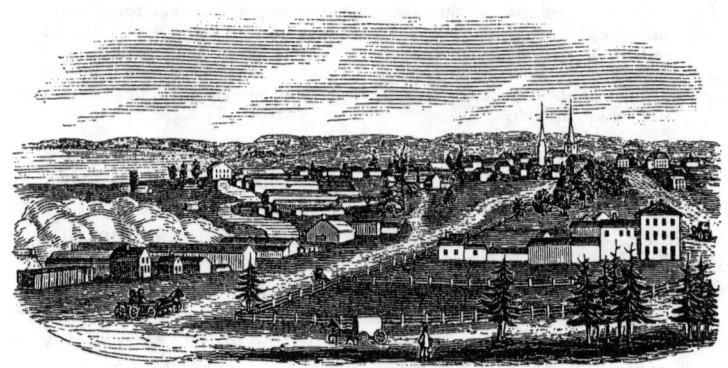

Southeastern view of Salina village.

The above is a southeastern view of the village of Salina and saltworks, as viewed from an elevation called Prospect Hill, which rises on the eastern side of Syracuse village. The Oswego canal, which forms a junction with the Erie canal at Syracuse, is seen on the left. The lake is seen in the distance. The central part of Salina is one and a half miles north of Syracuse. It is probable that the two villages in the course of a few years, by the increase of population, will be blended into one. Salina village lies upon a plain rising near the centre of the marsh. It contains 3 churches, a bank, and 86 salt manufactories. In 1839 the amount of salt inspected in this village was 1,283,204 bushels. The village of Liverpool is about 4½ miles north of Syracuse, on the lake and Oswego canal, consisting of about 60 dwellings; the amount of salt inspected here in 1839, was 859,733 bushels. Geddes village was incorporated in 1832; it is pleasantly situated 2 miles west from Syracuse, at the head of the lake. The amount of salt inspected here in 1839, was 249,245 bushels. The amount inspected at Syracuse, was 472,558 bushels.

The annexed is a western view in the central part of Syracuse,*

---

* Syracuse is a remarkable instance of the rapidity of growth of some of our western villages. The following, from the pen of the editor of the N. Y. Commercial Advertiser, who visited the place in 1820, and again in 1840, is well worthy of perusal :—

"It was only in the autumn of 1820, the year in which the middle and first-constructed section of the Erie canal was opened for navigation, that your humble servant made the passage from Utica to this place, in a rude boat, alone with Mr. Forman, a distance of sixty miles. The country at that time, from Rome to Salina, was wild. The canal pierced the wilderness at Rome only to emerge therefrom at this place. The land almost the entire distance was low, marshy, and cold. The forests, most of the distance evergreen, were deep and dank; and the advancing settlers had eschewed the region as unfit for cultivation. But the clearing for the canal let in a stretch of daylight, which enabled people to see more distinctly. The marshes and swamps were to a considerable extent drained by the canal; and its banks, instead of the shades of a gloomy forest, now for the most

Western view in the central part of Syracuse.

showing the Erie canal, the Syracuse House, and some other buildings in the vicinity. This village, which now has a city-like appearance, was incorporated in 1825, contains about 700 houses, the county buildings, 1 Episcopal, 1 Presbyterian, 1 Methodist, and 1 Baptist church, a bank, and 2 newspaper establishments. The Syracuse

part refresh the sight by the prospect of a well-settled country, smiling under the hand of well-rewarded industry.

" Mr. Forman was in one sense the father of the canal. That is, being a member of the legislature in 1807, (I think that was the year, but have not the journals by me,) he moved the first resolution of inquiry upon the subject of opening a channel of artificial navigation from the Hudson river to the great lakes. And from that day until the completion of that stupendous work, in 1825, his exertions were unremitting and powerful in the cause. Passing as the canal does, close by the head of Onondaga lake, within the toss of a biscuit of some of the salt springs, and within two miles of the principal and strongest fountain, at Salina, Mr. Forman saw the immense advantages which the site of this place presented for a town; with the completion of the middle section of the canal, Syracuse was begun. At the period of my first visit, but a few scattered and indifferent wooden houses had been erected, amid the stumps of the recently felled trees. I lodged for a night at a miserable tavern, thronged by a company of salt-boilers from Salina, forming a group of about as rough-looking specimens of humanity as I had ever seen. Their wild visages, beards thick and long, and matted hair, even now rise up in dark, distant, and picturesque perspective before me. I passed a restless night, disturbed by strange fancies, as I yet well remember. It was in October, and a flurry of snow during the night had rendered the morning aspect of the country more dreary than the evening before. The few houses I have already described, standing upon low and almost marshy ground, and surrounded by trees and entangled thickets, presented a very uninviting scene. 'Mr. Forman,' said I, '*do you call this a village? It would make an owl weep to fly over it!*' 'Never mind,' said he in reply, '*you will live to see it a city yet.*'

" These words were prophetical. The contrast between the appearance of the town then and now, is wonderful. A city it now is, in extent, and the magnitude and durability of its buildings, albeit it may not boast of a mayor and common council to oppress the people by insupportable assessments, and partake of turtle and champagne for the benefit of the poor. But as I glanced upward, and around, upon splendid hotels, and rows of massive buildings in all directions, and the lofty spires of churches glittering in the sun, and traversed the extended and well-built streets, thronged with people full of life and activity— the canal basins crowded with boats lading and unlading at the large and lofty stone warehouses upon the wharves—the change seemed like one of enchantment."

academy is a fine brick edifice 4 stories high, with an observatory, spacious grounds, &c. The Syracuse House is of brick, 4 stories high, and is one of the most splendid establishments of the kind in the state. Syracuse is 133 miles from Albany, by the canal 171, 278 from New York, 99 from Rochester, and from Utica 61 miles. This town embraces the principal salt springs and salt-works of the state, with the Onondaga or salt lake. "These salt springs were known to the aboriginal inhabitants, who communicated their knowledge to the white settlers. One of the latter about 50 years since, with an Indian guide in a canoe, descended the Onondaga creek, and by the lake approached the spring on mud creek. Salt water was at that time obtained by lowering to the bottom, four or five feet below the surface of the fresh water of the lake, an iron vessel; which filling instantly with the heavier fluid, was then drawn up. In this way, by boiling the brine, a small quantity of brownish-colored and very impure salt was obtained. With the settlement of the country the vicinity was explored and many other sources of brine discovered. Wells were then sunk, generally to the depth of 18 feet. There was a great difference in the strength of water which they afforded, varying with seasons, and diminishing in draught nearly one third. With the introduction of hydraulic machinery for pumping in 1822, a more rapid influx of brine was produced, and a new era in the manufacture. A difference of opinion prevails as to the source of the brine. The general opinion is, that *beds* of rock salt exist here as at other salt springs. Borings have been made at several points; in one instance to the depth of 250 feet, without finding fossil salt. But the very important fact was elicited, that the strength of the brine increased with the depth of the well. The salt beds in Cheshire, England, were discovered about 160 years since, in boring for coal at about 125 feet below the surface; and since have been penetrated to twice that depth. But the salt mines of Wilielska, near Cravocia, in Poland, are worked at the depth of 750 feet; and those at Eperies at 950 feet. The failure therefore to discover salt beds here should not discourage further efforts. Should beds of rock salt be discovered and rendered accessible, this source of wealth must be greatly enlarged. The salt beds near Norwich, England, produce more than 150,000 tons annually—nearly three times as much as the annual products of the Onondaga springs. The salt at Salina is manufactured by evaporation by the sun, or artificially. By the slower process of the former, the coarse salt is made, and the fine by the rapid evaporation produced by fire."

The following cut is a representation of a field of salt vats near Syracuse for the manufacture of coarse salt. In the distance is seen a pump house, from which the brine is conducted to each of the vats by a succession of bored logs. The vats are about 16 feet in length, by 7 in width, and are arranged in continuous rows for a great distance, as above represented. Between the rows alleys run sufficiently wide to admit the passage of a horse and cart. On each side and parallel with the vats, there is a line of light roofs which can be shoved off and on at pleasure, to permit the rays of the sun to act upon the waters or to avert the rain. As the salt precipitates, it assumes the form of beautiful crystals, like the various trinkets frequently made for the ladies' fairs, &c.; the action of shovelling the salt into carts destroys the crystals, when of course the elegance of form vanishes. These vats with their sheds cover enough ground in the vicinity to make several moderate sized farms, and the beams of the sun reflecting from their roofs cause them to appear in the distance not unlike the surface of a lake.

The fine salt requires more skill in the manufacture. For this purpose rough wooden structures are erected about 70 feet in length, and 25 feet in breadth. The annexed view of the inside of one of these salt manufactories was taken at the entrance, and shows imme-

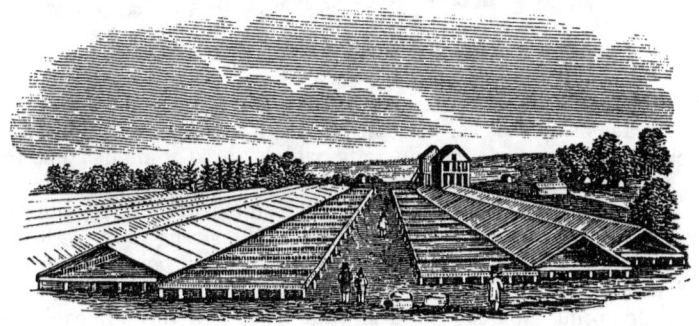

View of a field of salt-vats, Salina.

diately in front the commencement of the oven which runs the remaining length of the building. On top of it are the boilers, arranged in two parallel rows, generally numbering from 15 to 25 boilers in each row, which are supplied with the brine by a cylindrical hollow log with faucets. This log leads from a reservoir in the rear of the building, which in its turn is filled by tubular logs, connecting with the pump house, which in some cases is a mile or more distant. There are in the whole many miles of aqueduct logs, which are generally constructed of pine. On entering one of these works at night the view is interesting. Clouds of vapor are continually ascending from the numerous boilers, and partially obscuring the forms of the attendants. Huge piles of salt of snowy whiteness in the bins each side of the building are beheld laying in contact with the rough, dingy walls, while the fire from the furnace, shedding a partial light over the whole, renders it a striking scene.

"There are, however, various modes of applying artificial heat in the manufacture of salt, other than that employed in the ordinary process of boiling in kettles. In one arrangement, tubes heated by steam pass through a vat or vats of considerable extent, the brine having been previously freed from its insoluble impurities, by being

Internal view of a salt manufactory, Salina.

allowed to remain for some time in the cistern, or by the addition of lime. This furnishes salt in fine cubic crystals of great purity, especially in those parts of the vats which are at some distance from the immediate source of heat."

The springs from which the works are supplied are pierced through the alluvial and terminate on gravel. The strength of the brine is graduated on the following standard: fresh water being placed at 0°, and water perfectly saturated with salt at 100°. According to this, the "old spring" stands at 50°, and the "new" at 70°. In each cubic foot of water there is about 2½ ounces of "bitters," or impure deposit composed of lime, iron, &c. Fourteen pounds of salt are manufactured from a cubic foot of the water from the strongest spring.

The salt-works are quite a source of revenue to the state, as it receives 2 mills a bushel for pumping the water, and 6 cents duty on the salt made. The amount annually manufactured is three millions of bushels; and the number of men employed in the four villages of Geddes, Liverpool, Salina, and Syracuse, about three thousand.

Account of a French Colony established at Onondaga, in 1656, under the auspices of Le Sieur Dupuys.*

"The Jesuit Dablon had established himself at Onondaga in the character of a missionary. He arrived here in the month of September, 1655. In March of the following year, he in company with a numerous escort of savages, made the voyage to Quebec for the purpose of persuading M. de Lauson to establish a French colony at Onondaga. He arrived there in the beginning of April, and had no difficulty in getting M. De Lauson to enter into his views. Fifty Frenchmen were selected to go and form the proposed establishment, and the Sieur Dupuys, an officer of the garrison, was appointed their commandant. Father Francis Le Mercier, Superior General of the Catholic Missions, was desirous of conducting in person those whom he had destined to establish the first Iroquois church, who were Fathers Freemen, Mesnrard, and Dablon. Their departure was fixed for the 7th of May, and although the crop had been lighter than usual, they gave Dupuys provisions sufficient to last him a whole year, with grain enough to enable him to sow the land.

"The news of this enterprise being spread all around, gave the Mohawks much concern,

---

* Copied from a MS. History, by the Rev. J. W. Adams, of Syracuse.

and revived their jealousy towards the Onondagas. A general council of all the tribe was called to deliberate upon this affair, which seemed to them of great importance, and the conclusion was, that all their resources must be put in requisition to oppose the new establishment. A party of 400 men was immediately raised, and orders were given them either to disperse or cut to pieces the company of M. Dupuys. They failed, however, to accomplish their object, and only revenged themselves upon some straggling canoes, which were pillaged, and a part of those who conducted them were wounded. After a short stay at Three Rivers and at Montreal, M. Dupuys left the latter place on the 8th of June, and the same day fell in with a party of Mohawks, whom he pillaged as a reprisal for the outrage related above.

"On the 29th of the same month, towards 9 o'clock in the evening, they heard in the camp the voice of a man groaning. The commandant ordered the drum to be beat, and immediately they perceived a savage approaching in great distress. He was a Huron, who had escaped after the expedition of the isle of Orleans. The skin of his body was half roasted, and for seventeen days he had taken no nourishment, except some wild fruits which he had gathered. The Onondagas who accompanied the French, made him a drink which soon restored the tone of his stomach. They then gave him some provisions and sent him on to Quebec.

"The remainder of the voyage was prosperous, except that they suffered from a scarcity of provisions, which had been very badly managed. They had calculated as usual upon finding an abundance of fish and game. Both however failed, and the French, who were unaccustomed to fasting like the Indians, would have perished with hunger, had not the Onondaga sachems sent to meet them some canoes loaded with provisions. They learnt from these Indians, that a great number of the Iroquois of all the tribes, were awaiting their arrival on the shores of the Lake Gannentaha. M. Dupuys, therefore, prepared himself to make his entrance into the lake as imposing as possible. Before arriving at the place where the savages were stationed, he put ashore 5 small pieces of ordnance, and had them discharged. He then re-embarked, and rowing in beautiful order, entered the lake, where in less than an hour he made two discharges of all his musketry. He was received by the sachems and such as were with them awaiting his arrival with the greatest apparent cordiality and respect. They were welcomed with harangues, feasts, songs, and dances, and with every demonstration of joy which the savages were capable of giving. On the following day, which was the 12th of July, a solemn mass was offered and the Te Deum sung. The sachems then made presents, as they were accustomed to do in treaties of alliance, and on the 16th the French all united in celebrating the Eucharist. On the day following they commenced building huts, and Father Mercier went to visit the village of the Onondagas, where he was received with great ceremony. On the 24th a general council was held, at which the jesuits, Mercier and Chaumont, explained the views of the French and solicited their kind regards to their new neighbors. They also endeavored to enlighten their minds on the subject of religion, and produced so great an impression as to render it necessary to enlarge the chapel which had been built nearly a year before, more than one half. They experienced in the month of August excessive heat, which produced much sickness; but by the kind attention of the savages all the disorders were eased in a short time.

"This last mark of affection from these people persuaded the more credulous of them to believe that they might rely upon them in all cases; but the more prudent of them thought it necessary to make use of precaution at least against their inconstancy; and these were found in the end to have pursued the wisest course, for two years had not elapsed before they were compelled by the perfidy of the savages to abandon their settlement and return to Montreal. A conspiracy which extended itself through the Iroquois cantons was formed against them, and unequivocal indications of hostility were soon given. Three Frenchmen were scalped near Montreal by the confederates, and other hostilities committed, which left no doubt in the minds of the French of their intention to destroy the new colony. In the month of Feb., 1658, numerous bands of Mohawks, Oneidas, and Onondagas, had taken the field equipped for war. Dupuys was informed of all that transpired by a converted Indian. He found himself greatly embarrassed, and indeed saw no means of extricating himself from the difficulty without much trouble and at great hazard. To fortify himself and sustain a siege would be only to put off his ruin and not prevent it, for he had no succor to hope for from Quebec, or it would not be able to reach him in time. It would become necessary sooner or later to yield or die fighting, or at length to perish of hunger and misery.

"To effect his escape M. Dupuys required first to construct some canoes, for they had not taken the precaution to reserve any. But to work at them publicly would be to announce his retreat, and thereby render it impossible. Something must be resolved on immediately, and the commandant adopted the following plan. He immediately sent an express to M. D'Aillebout to inform him of the conspiracy. He then gave orders for the construction of some small light batteaux; and to prevent the Iroquois from getting wind of it, he made his people work in the garret of the Jesuit's house, which was larger and more retired than the others.

"This done, he warned all his people to hold themselves in readiness to depart on the day which he named to them, and he supplied each one with provisions sufficient for the voyage, and charged them to do nothing in the mean time to excite the suspicions of the Iroquois. It only remained now to concert measures for embarking so secretly that the savages should have no knowledge of their retreat until they should have advanced so far as not to fear pursuit, and this they accomplished by a stratagem singular enough.

"A certain young Frenchman who had acquired great influence with the Indians, had been adopted into one of their most respectable families. According to the custom of the Indians, whoever was adopted by them became entitled to all the privileges that belonged to native members of the family. This young man went one day to his adopted father, and told him that he had on the night before dreamed of one of those feasts where the guests eat every thing that is served, and that he desired to have one of the kind made for the village; and he added, that it was deeply impressed upon his mind he should die if a single thing were wanting to render the feast just such a one as he described. The Indian gravely replied that he should be exceedingly sorry to have him die, and would therefore order the repast himself and take care to make the invitations, and he assured him that nothing should be wanting to render the entertainment every way such an one as he wished. The young man having obtained these assurances, appointed for his feast the 19th of March, which was the day fixed upon for the departure of the French. All the provisions which the families through the village could spare were contributed for the feast, and all the Indians were invited to attend.

"The entertainment began in the evening, and to give the French an opportunity to put their boats into the water and to load them for the voyage without being observed, the drums and trumpets ceased not to sound around the scene of festivity.

"The boats having now been launched and every thing put in readiness for a departure, the young man, at the signal agreed upon, went to his adopted father and said to him, that he pitied the guests, who had for the most part asked quarter, that they might cease eating, and give themselves to repose, and adding, that he meant to procure for every one a good night's sleep. He began playing on the guitar, and in less than a quarter of an hour every Indian was laid soundly to sleep. The young Frenchman immediately sallied forth to join his companions, who were ready at the instant to push from the shore.

"The next morning a number of the Indians went, according to their custom on awaking, to see the French, and found all the doors of their houses shut and locked. This strange circumstance, joined to the profound silence which everywhere reigned through the French settlement, surprised them. They imagined at first that the French were saying mass, or that they were in secret council; but after having in vain waited for many hours to have the mystery solved, they went and knocked at some of the doors. The dogs who had been left in the houses replied to them by barking. They perceived some fowls also through the palings, but no person could be seen or heard. At length, having waited until evening, they forced open the doors, and to their utter astonishment found every house empty.

"The savages could not explain this movement. They could not comprehend how the French, whom they knew to have no canoes, had got away, and there was no idle fancy that did not enter into their heads rather than imagine in what manner the thing had happened. This was the first time in which boats had been used for such voyages. But had the French possessed canoes, it would not have been possible to use them, as the rivers were still covered with ice, and from this cause the Indians were prevented from successfully pursuing them. M. Dupuys took care however to leave nothing to fear from a pursuit. He used such diligence, that in spite of contrary winds which detained him a long time on Lake Ontario, he arrived at Montreal in fifteen days. The pleasure of finding himself delivered from such imminent danger, could not however prevent him from feeling sensibly, that so precipitate a flight was disgraceful to his nation, and from regretting that for the want of a trifling aid, he had been unable to sustain an establishment of so much importance, and of giving law to a people who drew their strength and the right of insulting them from their weakness.

"The Iroquois after this carried war into Canada, and in 1660, the colony was reduced to extreme distress by sickness and the incursions of the savages. In the year following it was ascertained that there was not less than twenty Frenchmen in Onondaga. They had been taken prisoners, but were suffered to enjoy a considerable degree of liberty. These men had converted a wigwam into a chapel, where, in connection with many of the Hurons and some of the Onondagas, they regularly assembled to say mass. It was reported also that the matrons of the Onondaga village, who are the principal *corps d'Etat*, had taken no part in the conspiracy which had obliged Dupuys to retire, and that for seven days successively they had wept with their children for the loss of the French priests. This report however had no foundation in truth. The credulity of the Jesuit could not distinguish, in matters of religion, between things which he only desired might be true and those which were really so."

Location of the colonies of Dupuys.—It will be very natural to conclude from the account which we have now given of the colony of Dupuys, that its location was contiguous to the Onondaga village. Such however was not the fact, if by the village of Onondaga be meant their principal village. From some incidental allusions made in history to the relative position of this colony, it is to be inferred that it was established upon grounds now occupied by the village of Salina. In a passage of the history written by Francis Creuxius, which we have already had occasion to quote, it is stated that the place agreed upon for the residence of the French was distant from the Indian village about four French leagues, and that this place was distinguished for two remarkable springs, issuing from the same hill, the one affording an abundance of salt water, the other of fresh. He states, also, that at this place there was an extensive meadow, or spacious open grounds which reached down to the bank of the Lake Gannentaha. It appears also from the circumstances connected with the departure of the colony, that they must have been in the immediate vicinity of the lake, as their batteaux were constructed in the Jesuit's house, and launched and freighted without any allusion from the historians to the time that must have been occupied or the difficulties that must have been encountered in transporting them to the place of debarkation. The reason why the narrative proceeds as though the Onondaga village and the French settlement occupied the same grounds, or were in (adjacent juxtaposition) to each other, is this—that the Indians were distributed into different villages or encampments, one of which was in the immediate vicinity of the place where Salina now stands. The main village was at Onondaga, but a constant intercourse was kept up between the different encampments, and the French settlement was now a point of attraction around which the Indians rallied; and this explains the facility of intercourse which existed between the French at Salina and the Indians at Onondaga.

SKANEATELES was taken from Marcellus in 1830. Pop. 3,981. The village of Skaneateles is situated at the outlet or northern termination of the lake of that name, 18 miles SW. from Syracuse, and has about 1,500 inhabitants. It is one of the most delightful and picturesque villages in western New York. The following shows the appearance of the village of Skaneateles as viewed from the residence of Mr. Joseph Barber, on the western Lake road in the vicinity of the outlet of the lake, seen on the left; the Episcopal and Presbyterian churches are seen on the right. From this village the eye measures about half the distance of the lake, which is 16 miles in length by an average width of one mile. There is no marshy land on either shore of this lake. The soil is of the best limestone quality, and the finely

Southwestern view of Skaneateles.

cultivated fields (mostly fenced with cedar posts and hemlock boards) make a gradual descent for a considerable distance to the margin of the lake. A railroad, 5 miles in length, has lately been constructed from this village north to Elbridge, where it intersects the railroad from Albany to Buffalo. A charter was obtained during the session of the legislature in 1841, for extending this lateral road 3 miles further north to the village of Jordan, on the Erie canal, where that canal receives a feeder from the Skaneateles lake, after its waters have afforded an immense power for milling and manufacturing purposes, the descent of the 8 miles from Skaneateles to Jordan being about 500 feet. The railroad between these two villages will run near the margin of this stream, affording important facilities to flouring mills and manufacturers. Goods will hereafter be carried on this road from Jordan to Skaneateles, and thence through the lake to Cortland county. Should a railroad be constructed from the head of the lake through Homer south to the Susquehannah, (and such an enterprise is much talked of,) Skaneateles and Jordan will become places of extensive business. Among the important items of transportation, will be that of coal from Pennsylvania, to be more particularly distributed at Jordan to various points. Previous to the making of the Erie canal, the great thoroughfare for merchandise and emigration to the west was through Skaneateles. Since the completion of that work, this village has not kept pace with some new towns which have grown into large cities in a few years, under the peculiar advantages afforded by the great internal improvements; but from its unsurpassed beauty of location, and its great facilities for manufacturing purposes, it cannot but experience a steady and healthful growth, until at some future day it will become a place of no ordinary importance. The stranger who visits this beautiful village, often expresses surprise that it has not long since been selected as the site of an extensive seminary of learning, or some public benevolent institution. In the village are 9 or 10 stores, three carriage-making establishments, an extensive woollen factory, flouring mill, iron foundry, machine shop, and various mechanics. The first grist-mill was erected in the village in 1795. About the same time the first merchant, Winston Day, established himself here. Bricks were first made here in 1797; the first tavern was erected the same year, and only two houses besides (of logs) in what is now called the village. The town had been first settled a few years earlier on the old Genesee road. The first bridge across near the outlet of the lake, was built about 1800. The first church in the place was organized July 20th, 1801, and then styled "The First Church of Christ in Marcellus." It was organized a Congregational church, but subsequently changed to the Presbyterian form of government. At its organization it consisted of but six members. In the course of about three months it increased to 19. It is believed to be the first church of any denomination that was formed in the old and formerly extensive town of Marcellus. There have been for many years past in the village a Baptist, Episcopal, and Methodist church, now flourishing societies.

SPAFFORD was named after Horatio Gates Spafford, LL. D., author of the Gazetteer of New York. It was taken from Tully, in 1811; since which a portion has been added from Marcellus; from Albany 157 miles. It was settled in 1806, by New England farmers. It is bounded on the W. by the Skaneateles lake. Spafford, 20 miles SW. from Syracuse, and Borodino, are small settlements. Pop. 1,873.

TULLY, taken from Fabius in 1803; bounds since altered; from Albany 128 miles. Tully, 18 miles S. of Syracuse, contains about 30 dwellings. Tulley, Tulley Valley, and Vesper, are villages. Pop. 1,663.

VAN BUREN, taken from Camillus in 1829; from Syracuse, NW. 14 miles. Macksville and Canton are small villages. Pop. 3,021.

ONTARIO COUNTY.

ONTARIO COUNTY was taken from Montgomery in 1789, and included all the land of which the pre-emptive right had been ceded to the state of Massachusetts, which that state afterward sold to Phelps and Gorham, and which afterward chiefly passed into the possession of the Holland Land Company and the Pulteney estate. Ontario county then extended from the pre-emption line a mile eastward of Geneva, so as to include within its limits all the territory within the bounds of this state west of that line. This was commonly known as the "Genesee country," although the title was occasionally more extensively applied, and from it has been formed the counties of Steuben, Allegany, Cattaraugus, Chatauque, Erie, Niagara, Genesee, Wyoming, Orleans, Monroe, Livingston, Yates, Wayne, in part, leaving to a tract around the former chief town, (Canandaigua,) the name of Ontario. In 1790, this extensive territory had only 1,075 inhabitants. The surface is agreeably diversified, waving in gentle swells and valleys of ample area, with tracts of champaign, and in the southern part more or less hilly. The soil partakes of a considerable variety, but a warm and rich mould forms the greater proportion, while along the borders of Lake Ontario there are tracts of clayey loam, with but a slight admixture of mould. The principal streams are Flint creek, Canandaigua outlet, and Mud creek. The lakes are Canandaigua, Honeoye, Caneadea, and Hemlock. The county has 15 towns, all of which, not otherwise noted, were organized in 1789. Pop. 43,501.

BRISTOL, from Albany 203 miles. North Bristol, 8 miles SW. from Canandaigua, and Bristol Centre, are small villages. Pop. 1,953.

CANADICE, taken from Richmond in 1829; from Albany 216, from Canandaigua SW. 24 miles. Canadice and Coyken Falls Corners are post-offices. Pop. 1,341.

Southwest view of the central part of Canandaigua.

CANANDAIGUA lies principally on the western side of Canandaigua lake; it has a fertile soil, and its surface is diversified with gentle undulations and fine level tracts. Pop. 5,652. Canandaigua village, the capital of Ontario county, is situated in N. lat. 42° 48' 41", and 3° 20' W. long. from New York. Distant from Albany 195 miles, from Buffalo 88, from Rochester 28, from Utica 111, from Sodus Bay on Lake Ontario 30, from the Erie canal at Palmyra 12, and from Washington city 365 miles. The principal part of the village is built on a single street upwards of a mile in length, rising by a gentle ascent from the lake. The annexed engraving shows the appearance of the central part of the village as seen from the Genesee road, about half a mile to the southwest. In the central part of the street, (north and south,) is an open square, on the western side of which are seen the courthouse, town-house and post-office. Blossom's hotel stands on the opposite side. The railroad passes a few yards westward of the courthouse. There are 4 churches—1 Presbyterian, 1 Baptist, 1 Methodist, and 1 Episcopal—2 banks, 2 printing offices, a state arsenal and academy, and a female seminary.

The residences of the inhabitants, and the tasteful manner in which their grounds are laid out, are, it is believed, not exceeded in beauty in any village in this country. Many of their mansions are large, splendidly furnished, surrounded by trees, commodious walks, odoriferous shrubberies, beautiful gardens and orchards adorned with flowers and fruits of various kinds, giving an air of wealth and refinement to this village rarely elsewhere to be found. The Ontario Female Seminary, founded by the subscriptions of the inhabitants, and incorporated in 1825, is an institution of high reputation. The number of pupils in 1839 was 174. The Canandaigua academy was founded by the liberal donations of Messrs. Gorham and Phelps. " The plan of this school embraces a thorough and extended course of English and mathematical study, instruction in the Latin and Greek classics, to an advanced standing of one or two years in our colleges, the teaching of the French language, and a department for the education of common school teachers. A course of mathematical study, as extensive and as practical as is usually pursued in our colleges, is taught in this academy. Surveying and civil engineering are ably and practically taught."

South view of Canandaigua academy.

The academy building, of which the annexed is a representation, is 130 feet long; it has 3 schoolrooms, 2 recitation, and 42 rooms for students, and apartments for the principal and his family. This institution has been selected by the regents of the university as one of the academies for the education of school teachers, and a department for this purpose has been organized. The course adopted will probably require three years, allowing the student to teach school four months each year. The annual expenses of a student, for board, tuition, room rent, and washing, are about $100. Many pupils, by adopting an economical mode of board, reduce their expenses to $60 a year. The principal of the institution is HENRY HOWE, A. M.

In the summer of 1788, the year after the purchase of western New York by Messrs. Phelps and Gorham, Oliver Phelps left Granville, Mass., with men and means for the purpose of exploring and surveying this extensive territory. The wilderness was penetrated as far as Canandaigua, about 130 miles west of the German Flats, then considered on the frontiers of civilization. By the assistance of the Rev. Mr. Kirkland, the missionary among the Six Nations, and a commissioner on behalf of Massachusetts, Mr. Phelps succeeded in collecting the chiefs and warriors of those tribes whose warlike spirit still rankled, on account of the chastisement inflicted by Sullivan's expedition. This conference with the Indians was held on a beautiful elevation overlooking Canandaigua lake.

"Two days had passed away in negotiation with the Indians for a cession of their lands. The contract was supposed to be nearly completed, when Red Jacket arose. With the grace and dignity of a Roman senator, he drew his blanket around him, and with a piercing eye surveyed the multitude. All was hushed. Nothing interposed to break the silence, save the rustling of the tree-tops, under whose shade they were gathered. After a long and solemn, but not unmeaning pause, he commenced his speech in a low voice and sententious style. Rising gradually with his subject, he depicted the primitive simplicity and happiness of his nation, and the wrongs they had sustained from the usurpations of the white man, with such a bold but faithful pencil, that the Indian auditors were soon roused to vengeance or melted into tears.

"The effect was inexpressible. But, ere the emotions of admiration and sympathy had subsided, the white men became alarmed. They were in the heart of an Indian country, surrounded by more than ten times their number, who were inflamed by the remembrance of their injuries, and excited to indignation by the eloquence of a favorite chief. Appalled and terrified, the white men cast a cheerless gaze upon the hordes around them. A nod from the chiefs might be the onset of destruction. At that portentous moment, Farmer's Brother interposed. He replied not to his brother chief; but, with the sagacity truly aboriginal, he caused a cessation of the council, introduced good cheer, commended the eloquence of Red Jacket, and, before the meeting had reassembled, with the aid of other prudent chiefs, he had moderated the fury of his nation to a more salutary review of the question before them."

The reassemblage of the council in cooler blood was followed by the satisfactory arrangement of the treaty, whereby the Indian title to more than two millions of acres was extinguished. The following account of facts connected with the operations of Phelps and Gorham, are from the Rochester Directory, published in 1827.

"After the treaty, Mr. Phelps surveyed the land into tracts, denominated *Ranges*, running north and south, and subdivided the ranges into tracts of six miles square, denominated *Townships*, and designated each by numbers, beginning to number both ranges and townships at the 82d mile-stone, in the southeast corner of the tract, [now the southeast corner of Steuben county,] numbering the townships northwardly to the lake from one to fourteen, and the ranges westwardly from one to seven. Thus, Bath is designated as township number four, in the third range; Canandaigua as township number ten, in the third range; Pittsford as number twelve, in the fifth range; and Brighton as number thirteen, in the seventh range of townships, in Gorham and Phelps' purchase.

"As the Genesee river runs about twenty-four degrees east of north below Avon, and Mr. Phelps continued his seventh range of townships to the lake, the fifth range was left to contain but twelve, and the sixth range but ten townships; and, in order to square the tract lying west of Genesee river, he set off two townships near the lake, which he called the *Short Range*, now comprising the towns of Gates and Greece, [and part of Rochester;] and the present towns of Caledonia, Wheatland, Chili, Riga, Ogden, and Parma, being then four townships, he called the first range of townships *west of Genesee river*, in Gorham and Phelps' purchase.

"This tract formed the counties of Ontario and Steuben for many years, until 1821, when Monroe and Livingston counties were formed, except that part of it lying west of the river, which was annexed to the county of Genesee at its organization in 1802, and the south part of the seventh range set off from Steuben to Allegany.

"In 1789, Oliver Phelps opened a land-office in Canandaigua—this was the first land-office in America for the sale of her forest-lands to settlers; and the system which he adopted for the survey of his lands, by *townships* and *ranges* became a model for the manner of surveying all the new lands in the United States; and the method of making his retail sales to settlers by *articles* has also been adopted by all the other land-offices of individual proprietorships that have followed after him.

"The *Article* was a new device, of American origin, unknown in the English system of conveyancing; granting the possession, but not the fee of the land; facilitating the frequent changes among new settlers, enabling them to sell out their improvements and transfer their possession by assignment, and securing the reversion of the possession to the proprietor where they abandoned the premises. His land-sales were allodial; and the other land-offices following his example, have rendered the Genesee farmers all fee-simple landholders, which has increased the value of the soil and the enterprise of the people.

"Oliver Phelps may be considered the *Cecrops* of the Genesee country. Its inhabitants owe a mausoleum to his memory, in gratitude for his having pioneered for them the wilderness of this CANAAN of the West."

Mr. Maude, who travelled through this part of the country in 1800, says: "Canandaigua, in 1792, was not further advanced in improvement than Geneva, as it then consisted of only two frame houses, and a few log houses. It is now one third larger than Geneva, containing 90 families, and is the county town. Canandaigua consists of one street; from this street are laid off sixty lots, thirty on each side. Each lot contains forty acres, having only 22 perches, or 121 yards in front; thirty lots consequently extend the town upwards of two miles; but the extremities of the present town are not more than a mile and half apart. These lots are valued in their unimproved state at $600 or $1,000 each.—The principal inhabitants of Canandaigua are, Thomas Morris, Esq., Mr. Phelps, Mr. Gorham, (who are the greatest land-owners in Canandaigua and its neighborhood,) and Judge Atwater. I was introduced also to Mr. Greig, from Morpeth, in England—a gentleman *reading law* with Mr. Morris."

"The settlement of this town," (Canandaigua,) says Mr. Spafford in his Gazetteer, "commenced in 1790, and in 1797 I found it but feeble, contending with innumerable embarrassments and difficulties. The spring of that year was uncommonly wet and cold. Besides a good deal of sickness, mud knee-deep, musquitoes and gnats so thick that you could hardly breathe without swallowing them, rattle-snakes, and the ten thousand discouragements everywhere incident to new settlements,—surrounded by these, in June of that year I saw with wonder that these people, all Yankees from Massachusetts, Connecticut, and Vermont, were perfectly undismayed, 'looking forward in hope, sure and steadfast.' They talked to me of what the country would be, by and by, as it were history, and I received it as all *fable*. In order to see the whole power of the county, a militia muster of all the men capable of bearing arms, I waited a day or two to attend the training. Major Wadsworth was the commanding officer, and, including the men who *had guns* and those who *had not*, the boys, women, and children, it was supposed that near 200 persons were collected. This training, one of the first, was held at Capt. Pitts's, on the Honeoye, and lasted all day and all night."

The following inscriptions are copied from monuments in the graveyard in this place.

"GIDEON GRANGER, died Dec. 31, 1822, aged 55 years. Mr. Granger was born at Suffield, Connecticut, on the 19th of July, 1767. Having completed his education at Yale college, he soon appeared at the bar, where he sustained a high character. He early mingled in the political conflicts of his country, in whose service he was engaged until a short time before his death. His native state will long remember him as one of the earliest and ablest advocates of her school fund system. For thirteen years he presided over the general post-office department, with zeal and usefulness. Bold in design and ardent in execution, true to his friends and liberal to his adversaries, warm in his attachments and social in his habits, his life was endeared to his associates and valuable to mankind.

"In memory of NATHANIEL GORHAM, who died Oct. 21st, 1826, aged 63 years."

"This is erected to the memory of the HON. OLIVER PHELPS, ESQ., who died 21st of Feb. 1809, in the 60th year of his age. He was born in the town of Windsor, in the State of Connecticut, and at the age of 7 years he removed to Suffield. And at the age of 22 years he removed from thence to Granville, in the State of Massachusetts, where he was honored with many important trusts under the government of that commonwealth. At the commencement of the revolutionary war, he took an active part in the defence of his country, and in various offices and relations, remained with the American army until Great Britain was compelled to acknowledge the Independence of the United States. On the 1st of April, 1788, the deceased, in company with the Hon. Nathaniel Gorham, Esq., purchased of the Commonwealth of Massachusetts, its pre-emptive right to the lands now comprised in the counties of Ontario, Steuben, Genesee, Niagara, Cattaraugus, Chatauque, and Allegany. In July of the same year he extinguished the Indian title in that part of it comprehended in the counties of Ontario and Steuben, and immediately thereafter opened the settlement of the country which has been generally known by the appellation of the GENESEE COUNTRY. In March, 1802, he removed with his family to this place, where he resided till his death. He was appointed the first Judge of the county of Ontario, and elected a representative in congress for the district.—Enterprise, Industry, and Temperance, cannot always ensure success, but the fruit of these virtues will be felt by society."

EAST BLOOMFIELD; from Albany 203 miles. East Bloomfield, 9 miles NW. from Canandaigua, has about 35 dwellings. Pop. 1,986.

FARMINGTON, from Albany 205, from Canandaigua N. 8 miles. This town is inhabited by Friends, noted, like all that sect, for their honesty, industry, and neatness. Pop. 2,122. New Salem 12, Brownsville 14 miles NW. of Canandaigua, and Farmington, are small villages.

GORHAM; from Albany W. 189 miles. Bethel, 10 miles SE. from Canandaigua, has about 40 dwellings. Rushville, 10 miles SE. from Canandaigua, partly in Yates county, has about 70 dwellings. Centre Gorham, is the name of a post-office, and Swarts Corners a small settlement. Pop. 2,779.

HOPEWELL, taken from Gorham in 1822; W. from Albany 190 miles. Chapinsville, on the outlet of Canandaigua lake, 3 miles NE., Hopewell 7 W. of Canandaigua, and Hopewell Centre, are small villages. Pop. 1,976.

MANCHESTER, originally named Burt, and taken from Farmington in 1821; from Albany 201 miles. Manchester, 7 miles NE. from Canandaigua, has about 45 dwellings. Port Gibson, on the Erie canal, 12 miles NE. from Canandaigua, has from 40 to 50 dwellings. Shortsville 6, and Coonsville 9 miles NE. from Canandaigua, are smaller villages. Pop. 2,912.

NAPLES, settled in 1791, and originally named Middletown; from Albany 211 miles. Naples, near the head of Canandaigua lake, on the Bath road, 22 miles SW. from Canandaigua, has about 45 dwellings. Pop. 2,345.

Phelps, 185 miles W. from Albany, is one of the best wheat-growing towns in the state. Pop. 5,563. The village of Vienna is beautifully situated at the junction of Flint creek and the outlet of Canandaigua lake, on the line of the Auburn and Rochester railroad, 6 miles S. of the Erie canal and 14 from Canandaigua. It is the principal produce market for the surrounding country. There are here 2 Presbyterian, 1 Methodist, and 1 Episcopal church, an Episcopal Female Seminary, 15 stores, 1 printing office, 5 flouring mills, which manufacture 37,300 barrels of flour annually, 2 grist-mills, 5 saw-mills, 5 plaster-mills, 1 clover-mill, 1 furnace, and many other manufacturing establishments. Vienna has a population of 1,400. In the vicinity are inexhaustible beds of gypsum, water and quick lime. Phelps and Orleans are small settlements.

Richmond, originally named Pittstown; from Albany 211 miles. Allens Hill, 14 miles W. from Canandaigua, West Richmond, Richmond Centre, and Pitts Flats, are small villages. Pop. 1,937.

Northeastern view of Geneva.

Seneca has an undulating surface and good soil. Pop. 7,073. The village of Geneva in this town, one of the most beautifully situated places in the state, was founded in 1794, by Messrs. Annin and Barton, and incorporated in 1812. Distant from Albany 179 miles, 98 from Utica, 23 from Auburn, 106 from Buffalo, 16 from Canandaigua, and 58 N. of Elmira. The Cayuga and Seneca canal connects Geneva with the Erie canal at Montezuma, a distance of 20 miles, one half canal and one half slack-water navigation. The village is situated at the NW. corner of Seneca lake, on the side and summit of an eminence 120 feet above the surface of the lake. The principal street runs parallel with the lake shore; the mansion houses on the eastern side in the southern part of the village have terraced gardens reaching down to the lake. Few, if any places in this country, can be selected, which present more attractions for persons retiring from business, who wish the enjoyments of a country life, combined with the advantages of social intercourse. The village contains about 480 dwellings, 1 Episcopal, 1 Presbyterian, 2 Methodist, 1 Baptist, 1 Associate Reformed, 1 Reformed Dutch, 1 Catholic, and 1 Universalist church, a bank, with a capital of $400,000, and 2 newspaper printing offices.

The Geneva college, in this place, was founded by the inhabitants and incorporated in 1825, having a president, a professor of mathematics and natural philosophy, a professor of the Latin and Greek languages and literature, a professor of statistics and civil engineering, a professor of modern languages, history, and belle-letters, a professor of chemistry and mineralogy. There is also a medical department, having four professors. "This college was one of the first, if not the very first, to adopt those liberal improvements which afford the advantages of a scientific and literary education to young men, who, from the want of time or inclination, are averse to entering on the study of the classics, and who, were no provision made to meet the exigency, would be deprived of many advantages to be derived from collegiate instruction." The college buildings are situated on the summit of the elevation which rises from the lake at the southern extremity of Main-street, a site rarely, if ever, surpassed for beauty and salubrity.

The following, relative to the early history of Geneva, is from Maude's Travels through this part of the country in 1800.

"Geneva is situate at the northwest extremity of Seneca lake. It is divided into Upper and Lower Town. The first establishments were on the margin of the lake, as best adapted to business; but Capt. Williamson, struck with the peculiar beauty of the elevated plain which crowns the high bank of the lake, and the many advantages which it possessed as a site for a town, began here to lay out his building-lots parallel with and facing the lake. These lots are three quarters of an acre deep, and half an acre in front, and valued (in 1800) at $375 per lot. One article in the agreement with Capt. Williamson is, that no buildings shall be erected on the east side of the street, that the view of the lake may be kept open. Those who purchase a lot have also the option of purchasing such land as lays between their lot and the lake—a convenience and advantage which I suppose few will forego—the quantity not being great, and consisting principally of the declivity of the bank, which, for the most part, is not so steep as to unfit it for pasturage or gardens.

"To give encouragement to this settlement, Capt. Williamson built a very large and handsome hotel, and invited an Englishman of the name of Powell to take the superintendence of it. Capt. Williamson has two rooms in this hotel appropriated to himself; and as he resides here the greater part of the year, he takes care that Powell does justice to the establishment and to his guests. From this cause it is, that, as it respects provisions, liquors, beds, and stabling, there are few inns in America equal to the hotel at Geneva. That part of the town where the hotel is situated is intended for a public square. At Mile-point, a mile south of the hotel, Capt. Williamson has built a handsome brick house, intended for the residence of his brother, who had an intention of establishing at Geneva.

"In 1792, Geneva did not contain more than three or four families; but such is the beauty, salubrity, and convenience of the situation, that it now consists of at least sixty families, and is rapidly receiving accessions as the new buildings get finished for their reception. There were at this time, (1800,) settled at Geneva, Mr. and Mrs. Colt, Messrs. Johnstone, Hallet, Rees, Bogart, and Beekman; three of these gentlemen were lawyers. Here were also two doctors, two storekeepers, a blacksmith, shoemaker, tailor, hatter, hairdresser, saddler, brewer, printer, watchmaker, and cabinet-maker. A hat made *entirely* of beaver is sold here for $10.

"Geneva is supplied with water conveyed in pipes from a neighboring spring, and also by wells. From the lake, the town is plentifully supplied with a great variety of excellent fish. Seneca lake is forty-four miles long, and from four to six miles wide. Its greatest depth is not known; the water is very clear and wholesome; the bottom is sand and gravel, with a clear sandy beach, like the seashore, and, consequently, not infested with musquitoes, &c. This lake is navigated by a sloop of forty tons, which runs as a packet, and carries on a trade between Geneva and Catherinetown, at the head of the lake."

SOUTH BRISTOL is centrally distant 15 miles SW. from Canandaigua. South Bristol is a small village. Pop. 1,375.

VICTOR, taken from Bloomfield in 1812; from Albany 203, from Canandaigua NW. 11 miles. Victor and East Victor are small villages. Pop. 2,393.

WEST BLOOMFIELD was formed in 1833; from Canandaigua W. 16 miles. West Bloomfield, on the outlet of the Honeoye lake, 16 miles W. from Canandaigua, has 2 Presbyterian, 1 Methodist church, an academy, and about 50 dwellings. Pop. 2,094. North Bloomfield and Bloomfield Centre are post-offices.

ORANGE COUNTY.

ORANGE, an original county, was organized in 1683; since modified by the subtraction of Rockland county and additions from Ulster county. Greatest length E. and W. 37; greatest breadth N. and S. 30 miles. Centrally distant NW. from New York 65, from Albany SE. 85 miles. On the east it is bounded by the Hudson, along whose banks are some of the highest mountains of the Highlands. Bear mountain is 1,350 feet in height, the Crow's Nest 1,418, and Butter Hill 1,530 feet above tide. The county is exceedingly fertile, and agriculture is conducted with great skill. Large quantities of sheep and cattle are raised. Its butter is celebrated. The New York and Erie railroad enters the SE. portion of the county and passes through the towns of Monroe, Blooming Grove, Goshen, Minisink, Wallkill, Mount Hope, and Deer Park. It is divided into 14 towns. Pop. 50,733.

BLOOMING GROVE, taken from Cornwall in 1799; NW. from New York 55, from Albany S., 96 miles. Salisbury, 9 miles SW. from Newburg, and 11 E. from Goshen, has about 40 dwellings. Washingtonville, 11 miles from Newburg, has about 45 dwellings. Blooming Grove, 2 miles SW. of Washingtonville, Craigsville, 15 miles from Newburg, and Oxford, 16 from Newburg and 8 from Goshen, are small settlements. Pop. 2,396.

CORNWALL was organized in 1788. It has a mountainous and rugged surface, being chiefly within the limits of the Highlands. The noted summits of the Crow's Nest, 1,418 feet, and Bears mountain, 1,350 feet in height, are on the Hudson. Pop. 3,919. Canterbury, about 5 miles SW. of Newburg, is a village containing about 1,000 inhabitants. Cornwall is a small village on the Hudson, 4 miles S. of Newburg.

West Point, the site of the U. S. Military Academy, is 8 miles S. of Newburg, 51 from New York, and 94 from Albany.

Northern view of West Point.

" West Point is a spot of peculiar interest. It has been hallowed by the footsteps of a Washington, a Kosciusko, and a Lafayette; it is consecrated by a nation to the Spartan-like training of a few devoted sons from every state of our wide-spread union: nor less sacredly secluded by nature as the scene of retirement and study; it seems alike calculated to please the pensive sage and the aspiring youthful soldier; while even female loveliness vouchsafes to paint its memories in lines of hope and brightness, as ' *the boast of a glory hallowed land:*'

> ' Bright are the moments link'd with thee,
> Boast of a glory hallowed land;
> Hope of the valiant and the free,
> Home of their youthful soldier band.'

" The view of West Point as you enter the Mountain Gap, after you leave Newburg, is delightful. On the left is Cozzens' hotel; beyond it are the academic halls, barracks, chapel, &c., appropriated to the cadets; and on the right, are the comfortable dwellings occupied by the officers of the academy. On the left, at the angle of the plain, are traces of Fort Clinton; and on the right, towering far above Camptown, (the suburb occupied by soldiers and citizens,) stands Fort Putnam, on mount Independence, venerable in its ruins—' stern monument of a sterner age,' which survived the attempts of treason and the assaults of bravery, only to yield its hallowed materials to the desecration of a rapacious owner. Of the three monuments which now meet your eye, the one on the right and nearest to you, on a projecting tongue of land bordered with thick groves, is the Cadet's Monument, erected to the memory of the deceased officers and cadets of the academy. It cost $12,000. The centre one, near the flag-staff, is a cenotaph, erected by Gen. Brown to the memory of

Colonel Eleazer D. Wood, an early and distinguished graduate of the academy, who fell at the sortie of Fort Erie, in 1814. And the monument on the left, over the levelled redoubt or citadel of Fort Clinton, is sacred to Kosciusko."

The military academy was established by act of congress, in 1802. It was not however until 1812, that it was placed on an efficient basis, sufficient to meet the wants of the country. The number of applicants for cadet appointments is very great. In selecting these, the descendants of revolutionary officers are considered as having peculiar claims to notice. The ratio of appointments is about three for each congressional district in four years, and on an average only about one third of those who enter graduate. The age of admission is limited from sixteen to twenty-one years; and the acquirements necessary are an acquaintance with reading, writing, and the elementary *principles* of arithmetic. There are generally here about 250 cadets who are instructed by no less than 34 gentlemen, themselves graduates of the institution.

" The months of July and August in each year are devoted solely to military exercises; for which purpose the cadets leave the barracks and encamp in tents on the plain, under the regular police and discipline of an army in time of war. For this purpose, the cadets are organized in a battalion of four companies, under the command of the chief instructor of tactics and his assistants. The corporals are chosen from the third class, or cadets who have been present one year; the sergeants from the second class, who have been present two years; and the commissioned officers, or captains, lieutenants, &c., are selected from the first class, or highest at the academy. All the other cadets fill the ranks as private soldiers, though necessarily acquainted with the duties of officers. In rotation they have to perform the duty of sentinels, at all times, day or night, storm or sunshine, in camp, and evenings and meal-times, in barracks. Cadets who have been present two encampments, are allowed, if their conduct has been correct, to be absent the third, on furlough. The drills or military exercises, consist in the use of the musket, rifle, cannon, mortar, howitzer, sabre, and rapier, or broad and small sword; fencing, firing at targets, &c., evolutions of troops, including those of the line; and the preparation and preservation of all kinds of ammunition and materials for war. The personal appearance of the corps of cadets cannot fail to attract admiration; especially on parade or review. The uniform is a gray coatee, with gray pantaloons in winter, and white linen in summer. The dress cap is black, with dark pompoon. The splendid band of music, which, under Willis, made hill and valley ring with notes of 'linked harmony long drawn out,' though changed, still pleases; and under its new leader, promises soon to deserve its former renown, as the best in our country.

" The cadets return from camp to barracks on the last of August, and the remaining ten months of the academic year are devoted to their arduous studies. The ceremony of striking the tents and marching out of camp is so imposing, as to be well worth an effort of the visiter to be present on that occasion. On the previous evening, the camp is brilliantly illuminated; and being enlivened with music, dancing, and bevies of beautiful strangers, presents quite a fairy scene.

"For the sake of more full instruction, each class is divided into several sections, each having a separate instructor. Thus each cadet is called upon, at almost every recitation, to explain a considerable portion of the lesson; for the morning recitations generally occupy two hours each. The written or delineated demonstrations, are explained on a black-board in the presence of the whole section.

"The studies of the first year are algebra, geometry, descriptive geometry, trigonometry, and the French language. All the mathematical studies are practically taught and applied to numerous problems not in the books; on the resolution of which greatly depends the reputation and standing of each rival candidate for pre-eminence. The studies of the second year, are the theory of shades, shadows, and perspective, practically illustrated; analytic geometry, with its application to conic sections; the integral and differential calculus, or science of fluxions; surveying and mensuration; the French language, and the elements of drawing, rhetoric, grammar, geography, and topography with the pen. This completes the course of mathematics, and also of French, which the cadets learn to translate freely as a key to military science, but which few of them speak fluently.

"The third year is devoted to a course of natural philosophy, including mechanics, optics, electricity, magnetism, and astronomy; together with chemistry, and sketching landscapes with the pencil.

"The fourth and last year is appropriated to the study of artillery and infantry tactics; the science of war, and fortification, or military engineering; a complete course of civil engineering, embracing the construction of roads and bridges, railroads and canals, with the improvement of rivers and harbors, &c. &.; a course of mineralogy, geology, and military pyrotechny; together with moral philosophy, and national and constitutional law.

"To test the progress of the cadets in these studies, semi-annual examinations are held, commencing on the first Mondays of January and June; at the latter of which a board of visiters, appointed by the secretary of war, is present, to make a critical official report of the state of the academy. The examination of all the classes usually occupies about a fortnight, and is very severe; but still is not considered the full test of individual proficiency. Each instructor makes a weekly class report, on which is recorded the daily performance of each cadet; those who excel being credited 3, and those who fail entirely marked 0. These marks are accessible to the cadets from week to week, and stimulate their exertions: finally, they are summed up at the end of the term, and laid before the academic staff and visiters; so that the standing of each cadet is influenced not only by his examination, but by all his previous recitations. A certain prescriptive proficiency being required of the cadets in each branch, those who fall below this limit are necessarily discharged from the service. Averaging the last ten years, where a class of one hundred enters the academy, it is reduced to about seventy at the end of six months, sixty at the end of one year, fifty at the end of two years, and forty at the end of three years; not more than about thirty-five graduating.

"There is a general merit-roll of every class, made out at the end of each academic year; the merit of each cadet being expressed by a number denoting his proficiency or acquirements. But the final standing of each cadet, on which depends his rank in the army, is determined by the sum of his merit in all the different branches; and this depends not only on his actual proficiency in any branch, but also on its relative importance. This latter is thus estimated at present by the academic staff, viz: Conduct 300; engineering 300; mathematics 300; natural philosophy 300; chemistry and mineralogy 200; rhetoric, ethics, and law 200; infantry tactics 200; artillery 100; French 100; and drawing 100. Hence the individual who should excel in all the branches, would be credited with 2,100 on the final merit-roll; but no more than three or four such instances have ever occurred at the academy. The cadet in each class having the greatest sum of merit is placed first on the roll, and so onward; and he who is deficient in only one single branch is discharged, or else turned back another year to receive a second probation."—*Hunt's Letters about the Hudson.*

The graduates of the military academy are entitled by law to a preference over other applicants for commissions in the army. On graduating they receive the commissions of brevet, second lieutenants, and are subsequently promoted on the occurrence of vacancies.

Kosciusko's Monument.

On the river bank at the point where the Hudson turns suddenly to the south, about 30 rods east of Cozzens' hotel, (seen in the drawing,) stands the monument of Kosciusko. It was completed in 1829, by the corps of cadets, at an expense of about $5,000. In the vicinity of the monument is Kosciusko's garden, "whither the Polish chieftain was accustomed to retire for study and reflection. Marks of cultivation are perceptible in the disposition of the walks and trees, and the beautiful seclusion of the spot still invite to thought and repose."

"THADDEUS KOSCIUSKO, an officer in the American revolutionary war, was born in Lithuania, in 1756, of an ancient and noble family, and educated at the military school of Warsaw. He afterward studied in France. He came to America, recommended by Franklin to Washington, by whom he was appointed an aid. He was also appointed an engineer with the rank of colonel, in Oct., 1776. He fortified the camp of Gen. Gates in his campaign against Burgoyne, and was afterward sent to West Point, to erect the works there. He was highly esteemed both by American and French officers. He was admitted a member of the Cincinnati, and received the thanks of congress for his services. At the close of the revolutionary war, he returned to his native country, and was made major-general under Poniatowski. He fought several battles with great bravery, but all his efforts were destroyed by the miserable conduct of the Polish diet. In the month of April, 1794, on the breaking out of a new revolution, he was made generalissimo, with the power of a dictator. He managed with great address and bravery, until the 10th of October, when being overpowered and wounded, he was made prisoner, and carried to St. Petersburg. He was kept in confinement until the death of Catherine, when he was relieved by Paul, loaded with honors, and offered employment in the Russian service, which he declined. It is said that when the emperor presented him with his own sword, Kosciusko told him, ' I no longer need a sword—I have no longer a country.' In 1797, he visited the United States, and received a grant from congress for his services. In the latter part of his life he retired to Switzerland, where he died in Oct. 16, 1817. His remains were taken to Cracow, and a public funeral made for him at Warsaw, where almost divine honors were paid him."—*Encyclopedia Americana.*

Ancient view of West Point.

[The above view of West Point as it appeared during the revolution, is copied from a plate in the New York Magazine, published in 1790. *Explanation.* A, Constitution Island, on the east side of the river. B, A chain, 450 yards in length, reaching across the Hudson. C, Fort Clinton, the principal fort, and intended for the defence of the river against any naval force.]

" After the capture of forts Washington and Lee, during the revolution, the British ascended the river freely in their armed ships. But in the execution of Washington's design of shutting up the enemy in New York, by the assistance of the French naval and military forces, it became necessary to exclude him from the Hudson. Skilful engineers sent out by the French monarch, selected West Point as the most advantageous position for commanding the river. The hill, composed of huge crags and blocks of stone, fantastically heaped by nature, protrudes to the middle of the river, impelling its waters to the opposite bank, and narrowing the channel to less than half a mile in width.

" The cliff selected for the fortress, rests against a lofty ridge broken into small eminences, that form a species of amphitheatre, washed below by the river. It rises in terraces, the first of which is very narrow, and nearly level with the river; the second, approachable by a steep ascent of 80 or 90 feet, and the third, rising 188 feet above the water, spreads into a *plateau* of more than a mile in circumference, on which the principal works were constructed; the chief of which, was Fort Clinton. The declivity is exceedingly steep nearly all around, and the only side on which the enceinte was accessible, was thickly palisaded, and defended by batteries. An escalade, the sole mode of carrying the works, was subjected to extreme hazard. There were several redoubts upon the eminences, which commanded Fort Clinton, of which Fort Putnam was the most important. These covered each other, and the garrison and ammunition stores were under bomb proof casements. The works partly hewn in the rock, and partly constructed of enormous trunks of trees, felled on the spot, communicating by defiles, formed a group of strongholds, connected by a common system of defence. The upper forts were secured from assault by the ruggedness of the ground, thick woods, and numerous *abatis*, which made the transport of artillery impracticable, whilst they gave full protection to the lower ones.

"But, another work besides these impregnable fortifications, was necessary to the command of the river. Constitution Island divides the bed of the Hudson unequally, at the bend round the Point; the western branch being a marshy shallow. The island, a mass of rock, was defended by batteries on a level with the water, and the glacis formed in the rock, bade defiance to trenches. A heavy chain cramped into the rocks at either end, supported by buoys, stretched across the angle made by the river, and formed an effectual bar.

"The great object of the works on both sides, was to protect this chain. Twenty pieces of heavy ordnance, discharging grape, menaced those who should attempt to cut a link, and would have inevitably sunk their boats. If a vessel, iron beaked, impelled by wind and tide, should attempt it, the chain moving on a roller would grow slack, and the shock thus broken, would be again strained to its due tension, and the vessel turned aside, must be stranded on one or the other shore, and remain exposed to the fire of the batteries, which might be poured upon all points of the Strait. These forts, provided with necessary munitions, were defended by four thousand men. They had been built in the course of a single year, almost without cost; the soldiers who labored at them received no pay, and the French engineers superintending, in the minutest detail, the execution of their own plans, had no emolument whatever. This post was much desired by the British commanders, and its surrender was to have been the first fruit of Arnold's treason."—*Gordon's Gazetteer.*

CRAWFORD, taken from Montgomery in 1823; from Albany 92 miles. Crawford, 14 N., Hopewell 11, Bullville 9, and Searsburg 11 miles from Goshen, are small settlements. Pop. 2,075.

DEERPARK, taken from Mamakating in 1798; from New York, NW., 77, from Albany, SW., 110 miles. Pop. 1,607. The settlements here, are among the oldest of the county, and were made by the Huguenots from Holland, among whom were the ancestors of the De Witts and other distinguished families. Cuddebackville, 25 miles NW. from Goshen, is an agricultural settlement extending from 3 to 4 miles, and has a post-office, in the vicinity of which are 20 or 30 dwellings. Port Jarvis, on the Delaware and Hudson canal, 24 miles W. from Goshen, has within the compass of a square mile about 60 dwellings. Honesville is a small settlement.

GOSHEN was organized in 1788. It has a hilly surface on the E.; in the western part it is flat and marshy. A large portion of the "drowned lands" on the Wallkill creek are in this town. The soil is highly productive in grass: much butter is made here, which is widely celebrated for its superior quality. The town was first settled in 1703, and then embraced all the county SE. of the Wallkill, now included in the towns of Minisink, Warwick, part of Wallkill, Blooming Grove, and part of Cornwall. Pop. 3,889. Chester, on the road from Goshen to New York, is a considerable village about 4 miles SE. from Goshen; it is divided into two sections known as E. and W. Chester. Goshen, the half-shire village of Orange county, was founded in 1722, and incorporated in 1809; the first court was holden in 1727. It is 20 miles W. from Newburg, 60 from New York, and 100 S. from Albany. It contains a bank, 2 newspaper printing offices, 2 academies (1 for males and 1 for females,) and about 60 or 70 dwellings. In the annexed engraving, the old stone courthouse, which was built about the commencement of the revolutionary war, is seen on the left: about the time of its erection the king's arms were affixed over the door, but the revolutionary excitement was so great at this place that these royal emblems were destroyed the first night after they were set up. The Episcopal church and the female academy are seen on the unit. The Presbyterian church is seen near the central part of the engraving.

Western view of the public buildings at Goshen.

The following inscriptions are copied from monuments standing in the enclosed ground near the Presbyterian church.

"Erected by the inhabitants of Orange county, 22d July, 1822. Sacred to the memory of 44 of their fellow-citizens, who fell at the battle of MINISINK, July 22d, 1779.

Benj. Tusten, Col.	Roger Townsend,	John Carpenter,
Bezaleel Tyler, Capt.	Samuel Knapp,	David Barney,
Samuel Jones, "	James Knapp,	Jonathan Haskell
John Little, "	Benjamin Bennet,	Abm. Williams,
John Duncan, "	William Barker,	James Mosher,
Benjamin Vail, "	Jonathan Pierce,	Isaac Ward,
John Wood, Lieut.	James Little,	Baltus Nierpos,
Nathaniel Finch, Adj.	Joseph Norris,	Galmatiel Bailey,
Ephm. Mastin, Ens.	Gilbert Vail,	Moses Thomas,
Ephm. Middaugh, Ens.	Abm. Shepherd,	Eleazer Owens,
Gabriel Wisner, Esq.	Joel Decker,	Adam Embler,
Stephen Mead,	Nathan Wade,	Samuel Little,
Maths. Terwilliger,	Simon Wait,	Benjamin Dunning,
Joshua Lockwood,	—— Talmadge,	Daniel Reed.
Ephraim Forgerson,	Jacob Dunning,	

"Here lie the remains of the Rev. John Bradner, a native of Scotland, the first pastor of the Presbyterian church in Goshen. Settled A. D. 1721 and died 1732; also of Rev. Nathan Ker, his successor, who preached the gospel in this place for 38 years. Died Dec. 14, 1804, aged 69 years. Also of his successor, Rev. Ezra Fisk, DD., who was born Jan. 10, 1785, at Sherburn, Mass. Settled as pastor of the Goshen church, Aug. 13, 1813; died Dec. 5, 1833, aged 49 years.

HAMPTONBURG, taken from Goshen, Blooming Grove, New Windsor, Montgomery, and Wallkill, in 1830; from Albany, S., 94, from Goshen centrally distant NE. 6 miles. Hamptonburg, Horace, and Little Britain, are post-offices. The name of Little Britain is given to a district of about 4 miles square, in Hamptonburg and New Windsor, settled in 1722 by Col. Charles Clinton, (the progenitor of the distinguished family of Clinton,) and his associate emigrants from Ireland. Pop. 1,379.

Fac-simile of George Clinton's signature.

"GEORGE CLINTON, the youngest son of Col. Charles Clinton, was born in Orange county, July 15, 1739. His education was superintended by his father, a gentleman of a highly cultivated mind, assisted by a minister of the gospel, named Daniel Thain, who had been educated at the university of Aberdeen. He evinced at an early age that spirit of activity and enterprise which marked his after life. During what was called the *French war*, he left his father's house and entered on board of a privateer, which sailed from the port of New York; and after encountering great hardships and perils, returned home, and immediately accepted a lieutenancy in a company commanded by his brother James. He was present at the capture of Fort Frontenac, now Kingston, where the company to which he belonged behaved with great gallantry. After the usual time of study he was admitted to the bar, and practised with much success in his native county, until his election to the colonial assembly, where he became the head of the whig party, or minority, and uniformly opposed the arbitrary course of the government. He was chosen, April 22d, 1775, a delegate to the continental congress; and in 1776, he was also appointed brigadier general of Ulster county, and some time after, a brigadier in the army of the United States. At the first election under the constitution of the state, which was adopted April 20, 1777, he was chosen both governor and lieutenant-governor. Having accepted the former office, the latter was filled by Pierre Van Cortlandt. He continued in the chief magistracy of the state during six terms, or 18 years, when he declined a re-election. In consequence of the great number of tories who resided in the state of New York, and its distracted condition, the situation of Governor Clinton was more arduous and important than any other in the Union, save that of the commander-in-chief. He, however, behaved with the greatest energy, not only as chief magistrate, but as an actual head of the militia; and for a long time resisted the attacks of the whole British army, commanded by Sir Henry Clinton. By a vigorous exertion of authority, in the impressment of flour on an important occasion, he preserved the army from dissolution. His conduct at the storming of the forts Montgomery and Clinton, in October, 1777, was particularly praiseworthy. He was greatly instrumental in crushing the insurrection under Shays, which took place in Massachusetts, in 1787.

"Governor Clinton was unanimously chosen president of the convention which assembled at Poughkeepsie June 17, 1788, to deliberate on the new federal constitution. After remaining five years in private life, he was elected a member of the state legislature, at a time when the country was in an agitated and critical condition, and it is affirmed that his influence was the principal cause of the great political revolution which took place in 1801. At that period he was also induced again to accept the station of governor, and after continuing in that capacity for three years, he was elevated to the vice-presidency of the U. States, a dignity which he continued until his demise at Washington, April 20, 1812. He married Cornelia Tappan, of Kingston, Ulster county, by whom he had one son and five daughters.

"The following anecdotes are related of his energy and decision:—At the conclusion of the revolutionary war, when violence against the tories was the order of the day, a British officer was placed on a cart in the city of New York, to be tarred and feathered. This was the signal of violence and assassination. Governor Clinton, at this moment, rushed in among the mob with a drawn sword, and rescued the victim at the risk of his life.' 'Some years after, a furious assemblage of people collected, called the *doctors' mob*, and raged through New York, with the intention of killing the citizens of that city, and pulling down their houses, on account of their having dug up bodies for dissection. The violence of this mob intimidated the local magistrates. Governor Clinton fortunately appeared in person, called out the militia, and restored peace to the city.' He discharged the functions of vice-president with great dignity. It was by his casting vote while in that station, that the renewal of the bank charter was negatived. In private life, he was kind and amiable, and warm in his friendships; as a public man, he is entitled to respectful remembrance."

Minisink was organized in 1788. It has a hilly surface on the W.; on the E. it is bounded by the Wallkill, on the borders of which are the "drowned lands." It is centrally situated W. from Goshen 15 miles, and 114 SW. from Albany. Pop. 5,093. Minisink, Ridgebury, Slate Hill, Unionville, Wells Corners, Graham, and Dollenstown are post-offices. This town was settled at an early period. In the colonial records of 1659, there is a notice of the discovery of a copper mine, which is reported to have been extensively wrought. In 1669, a severe battle was fought between the settlers and Indians, " the bloody horrors of which yet live in the traditions of that neighborhood." In July, 1779, a party of Indians and tories under Brant made an invasion on Minisink. It appears that Count Pulaski had been stationed at this place with a battalion of cavalry the preceding winter, but in February he was ordered to South Carolina, and the place was left unprotected. The following account of the invasion and battle, is taken from Stone's Life of Brant, vol. i.

" On the 20th of July, or rather during the night of the 19th, the crafty Mohawk stole upon the slumbering town, at the head of sixty Indians and twenty-seven tory warriors, disguised as Indians—which was a very common practice with the loyalists when acting with the savages. Such was the silence of their approach, that several houses were already in flames when the inhabitants awoke to their situation. Thus surprised, and wholly unprepared, all who could escape fled in consternation, leaving the invaders to riot upon the spoil. Ten houses and twelve barns were burnt, together with a small stockade fort and two mills. Several persons were killed, and others taken prisoners. The farms of the settlement were laid waste, the cattle driven away, and all the booty carried off which the invaders could remove. Having thus succeeded in his immediate object, Brant lost no time in leading his party back to the main body of his warriors, whom he had left at Grassy Brook.

" No sooner had the fugitives from Minisink arrived at Goshen with the intelligence, than Dr. Tusten, the colonel of the local militia, issued orders to the officers of his command to meet him at Minisink on the following day, with as many volunteers as they could raise. The order was promptly obeyed, and a body of one hundred and forty-nine men met their colonel at the designated rendezvous, at the time appointed—including many of the principal gentlemen of the county. A council of war was held, to determine upon the expediency of a pursuit. Colonel Tusten was himself opposed to the proposition, with so feeble a command, and with the certainty, if they overtook the enemy, of being obliged to encounter an officer combining, with his acknowledged prowess, so much of subtlety as characterized the movements of the Mohawk chief. His force, moreover, was believed to be greatly superior to theirs in numbers, and to include many tories as well acquainted with the country as themselves. The colonel, therefore, preferred waiting for the reinforcements which would be sure soon to arrive, the more especially as the volunteers already with him were but ill-provided with arms and ammunition. Others, however, were for immediate pursuit. They affected to hold the Indians in contempt, insisted that they would not fight, and maintained that a recapture of the plunder they had taken would be an easy achievement. Town-meeting counsels, in the conduct of war, are not usually the wisest, as will appear in the sequel. The majority of Tusten's command were evidently determined to pursue the enemy; but their deliberations were cut short by Major Meeker, who mounted his horse, flourished his sword, and vauntingly called out—' Let the brave men follow me; the cowards may stay behind !' It may readily be supposed that such an appeal to an excited multitude would decide the question, as it did. The line of march was immediately taken up, and after proceeding seventeen miles the same evening, they encamped for the night. On the morning of the 22d, they were joined by a small reinforcement under Col. Hathorn, of the Warwick regiment, who, as the senior of Col. Tusten, took the command. When they had advanced a few miles, to Halfway Brook, they came upon the Indian encampment of the preceding night, and another council was held there. Cols. Hathorn, Tusten, and others, whose valor was governed by prudence, were opposed to advancing further, as the number of Indian fires, and the extent of ground they had occupied, removed all doubt as to the superiority of their numbers. A scene similar to that which had broken up the former council was acted at this place, and with the same result. The voice of prudence was compelled to yield to that of bravado.

" Capt. Tyler, who had some knowledge of the woods, was sent forward at the head of a small scouting party, to follow the trail of the Indians, and to ascertain, if possible, their movements; since it was evident that they could not be far in advance. The captain had proceeded but a short distance before he fell from the fire of an unseen enemy. This circumstance occasioned considerable alarm; but the volunteers, nevertheless, pressed eagerly forward, and it was not long before they emerged upon the hills of the Delaware, in full view of that river, upon the eastern bank of which, at the distance of three fourths of a mile, the Indians were seen deliberately marching in the direction of a fording-place near the mouth of the Lackawaxen. This discovery was made at about nine o'clock in the morning. The intention of Brant to cross at the fording-place was evident; and it was afterward ascertained that his booty had already been sent thither in advance.

"The determination was immediately formed by Col. Hathorn, to intercept the enemy at the fording-place, for which purpose instant dispositions were made. But, owing to intervening woods and hills, the opposing bodies soon lost sight of each other, and an adroit movement on the part of Brant gave him an advantage which it was impossible for the Americans to regain. Anticipating the design of Hathorn, the moment the Americans were out of sight, Brant wheeled to the right, and by threading a ravine across which Hathorn had passed, threw himself into his rear, by which means he was enabled deliberately to select his ground for a battle and form an ambuscade. Disappointed in not finding the enemy, the Americans were brought to a stand, when the enemy disclosed himself partially, in a quarter altogether unexpected. According to the American account, the first shot was fired upon an Indian, who was known, and who was mounted upon a horse stolen at Minisink. The Indian fell, and the firing soon became general—the enemy contriving, in the early part of the engagement, to cut off from the main body of Hathorn's troops a detachment comprising one third of his whole number. The conflict was long and obstinate. The number of the enemy being several times greater than that of the Goshen militia, the latter were surrounded, and ultimately hemmed within the circumference of an acre of ground. Being short of ammunition, Hathorn's orders, in imitation of those of Putnam at Bunker Hill, were strict that no man should fire until very sure that his powder would not be lost. The battle commenced about eleven o'clock in the morning, and was maintained until the going down of the sun; both parties fighting after the Indian fashion, every man for himself, and the whole keeping up an irregular fire from behind rocks and trees as best they could. About sunset the ammunition of the militia was expended, and the survivors attempted to retreat, but many of them were cut down. Doctor Tusten was engaged behind a cliff of rocks in dressing the wounded when the retreat commenced. There were seventeen disabled men under his care at the moment, whose cries for protection and mercy were of the most moving description. The Indians fell upon them, however, and they all, together with the doctor, perished under the tomahawk. Among the slain were many of the first citizens of Goshen; and of the whole number that went forth, only about thirty returned to tell the melancholy story. Several of the fugitives were shot while attempting to escape by swimming the Delaware.

.... "There was one, (Major Wood,) who during the battle saved himself by means which Brant said were dishonorable. By some process or other, though not a freemason, he had acquired a knowledge of the master mason's grand hailing signal of distress; and having been informed that Brant was a member of the brotherhood, he gave the mystic sign. Faithful to his pledge, the chieftain interposed and saved his life. Discovering the imposture afterward, he was very indignant. Still, he spared his life, and the prisoner ultimately returned to his friends after a long captivity."

MONROE was taken from Cornwall, and organized in 1799. Its original name was Cheesecocks, afterward Southfield, then Monroe. It is 19 miles S. of Newburg and 115 from Albany: being in the Highland region, the surface of the township is broken and hilly. Pop. 3,914. At the extreme easterly point of this town upon the Hudson river, on the S. side of Poplopen's kill, stood Fort Clinton, and upon the opposite bank of the creek, in Cornwall, stood Fort Montgomery. These forts were erected for the defence of the passage of the river. At this place, the channel of the Hudson was obstructed by a chevaux-de-frize, boom and chains, and guarded by a number of armed vessels, stationed above them. On the 6th October, 1777, Sir Henry Clinton, with a force of about 3,000 men, took these forts by storm. The garrison consisted of but about 600 men. Their loss was about 250; that of the British was not less. The annexed account relative to their capture was written at Kingston, 3 days afterward, by a gentleman who was in Fort Montgomery when it was taken.

"On Saturday night the 5th inst., we had advice that a large number of ships, brigs, armed vessels, &c., had arrived at Tarrytown, where they had landed a considerable body of men, supposed to be 900 or 1,000, and had advanced towards the plains. Col. Luttington being posted there with about 500 militia, they sent in a flag to him requiring him to lay down his arms, and surrender himself and men prisoners of war; whilst he was parleying with the flag they endeavored to surround him, which he perceiving, ordered his men to retreat, whereupon they returned to their shipping, and next morning we had advice of their being under sail, and coming up as far as Kings Ferry. In the afternoon they landed a large body of men on the east side of the river, to draw our attention that way, but they re-embarked in the night, and next morning landed on the west side.

"On Sunday night his Excellency, Gov. Clinton, who then commanded at Fort Montgomery, sent out a party of about 100 men under the command of Major Logan, across the Dunderbergh, (Thunder Mountain,) to watch the motion of the enemy. The party returned in the morning and reported that they had seen about forty boats full of men land below the Dunderbergh. The governor sent out another small party of about 28 men, under the command of Lieut. Jackson. On the road that leads to Haverstraw, two or three miles below Fort Clinton, they fell in with a concealed party of the enemy, who ordered them to club their muskets, and surrender themselves prisoners. They made no answer, but fired upon the enemy and hastily retreated; they returned the fire and pursued our people half a mile; but they all got back to the fort without losing a man, though within five rods of the enemy before they were discovered. Upon this intelligence, one hundred men were immediately sent off under Col. Brown, who fell in with them two miles from the fort, about two o'clock in the afternoon, when a smart engagement ensued; but the enemy being of much superior force, our people were forced to retreat.

"At the same time it was thought proper to send some artillery with a field-piece to occupy an eminence that commands the road that leads to Orange Furnace, with a party of men to defend it; they were attacked soon after, and our field-piece did great execution. The field-piece bursting, our men in their retreat kept up the engagement for some time with small-arms. Most of our people got within the breastwork, and the attack became general on both forts. At the same time the enemy's shipping came in sight, but the wind being light, and the tide against them, none of their vessels came up except the galleys and armed sloops, which fired upon us, but did no execution; we in return fired upon them, and believe did them some damage.

"The enemy continued a vigorous and incessant attack upon the forts; but notwithstanding their utmost efforts, they were many times repulsed and beaten back from our breastworks with great slaughter. But the smallness of our number (being in both forts but about five hundred,) which required every man to be upon continual duty and obliged them to unremitted exertion, fatigued our people greatly, while the enemy, whose number was supposed to be at least four thousand, continued to press us with troops.

"About 4 o'clock they sent in a flag, demanding in 5 minutes a surrender of the fort and ourselves prisoners of war,—or they would put us all to the sword. An answer was returned by Col. Livingston, acquainting them that we were determined to defend the fort to the last extremity. The action was renewed with fresh vigor on both sides, and continued until the dusk of the evening, when they stormed our upper redoubt which commands the fort, which after a severe struggle and overpowering us with numbers they got possession of; and we were obliged to give way. At the same time they stormed and got possession of Fort Clinton, in which were none but militia, who nobly defended it till they, like the garrison at Fort Montgomery, were obliged to give way to superior force.

"The darkness of the evening much favored the escape of our people, the greatest part of whom, with almost all the officers, got off, and have since joined our army or returned to their places of residence. . . . . . We are told that the reinforcement from Peekskill, which had been twice urged* during the day, arrived only in time on the opposite side of the river to see the fort taken, but could give them no manner of assistance, and even a small reinforcement would have enabled the garrison to maintain it until efficient succor had arrived. Under this misfortune, we have the satisfaction to be assured, that all the officers of the garrison fought like heroes, distinguished themselves both by their courage and con-

---

* Waterbury, the express who was sent from Fort Montgomery, purposely delayed, and the next day deserted to the enemy.

duct, and that all the privates, as well militia as continental, fought with the utmost bravery.*
The quantity of provisions in the fort was not great, but the ammunition and stores which
fell into the enemy's hands were considerable.

Dr. Dwight, then a chaplain in the army, thus speaks of the appearances about these forts a few months after they were taken.

"I went down the river in company with several officers, to examine the forts Clinton and Montgomery, built on a point six or eight miles below West Point, for the defence of the river. The first object which met our eyes, after we left our barge and ascended the bank, was the remains of a fire kindled by the cottagers of this solitude, for the purpose of consuming the bones of some of the Americans who had fallen at this place, and had been left unburied. Some of these bones were lying partially consumed round the spot where the fire had been kindled; and some had evidently been converted into ashes. As we went onward, we were distressed by the fœtor of decayed human bodies. To me this was a novelty; and more overwhelming and dispiriting than I am able to describe. As we were attempting to discover the source from which it proceeded, we found, at a small distance from Fort Montgomery, a pond of a moderate size, in which we saw the bodies of several men, who had been killed in the assault upon the fort. They were thrown into this pond, the preceding autumn, by the British, when probably the water was sufficiently deep to cover them. Some of them were covered at this time; but a depth so small, as to leave them distinctly visible. Others had an arm, a leg, and a part of the body above the surface. The clothes which they wore when they were killed, were still on them; and proved that they were militia; being the ordinary dress of farmers. Their faces were bloated and monstrous; and their postures were uncouth, distorted, and in the highest degree afflictive. My companions had been accustomed to the horrors of war, and sustained the prospect with some degree of firmness. To me, a novice in scenes of this nature, it was overwhelming. I surveyed it for a moment and hastened away. From this combination of painful objects we proceeded to Fort Clinton, built on a rising ground, at a small distance further down the river. The ruins of this fortress were a mere counterpart of those of Fort Montgomery. Every combustible in both had been burnt; and what was not, was extensively thrown down. Every thing which remained was a melancholy picture of destruction. From this place we proceeded to find the grave of Count Grabouski, a Polish nobleman, who was killed in the assault, while acting as aid-de-camp to the British commander. The spot was pointed out to us by Lieut. Col. Livingston, who saw him fall, and informed us that he was buried in the place where he was killed. Here we found a grave—in all probability, that in which he was buried—without a 'stone' to 'tell where he lay,' and now forgotten and undiscoverable: a humiliating termination of a restless, vain, ambitious life."

MONTGOMERY, originally organized as part of Ulster county in 1788; from Albany, S., 100, from Newburg, W., 12, and from Goshen, NE., 10 miles. Pop. 4,100. A tamarac swamp near Montgomery village, is noted as a spot in which the bones of the mammoth were first discovered in this state. Montgomery village, incorporated in 1810, on the right bank of the Wallkill, on the Newburg and Cohecton turnpike, and having the relative distances above stated, contains about 160 dwellings, 2 or 3 churches, an academy, and a seminary for young ladies. Walden is a large manufacturing village on the Wallkill, 12 miles NW. from Newburg, 14 NE. from Goshen, and 4 from Montgomery, at the falls of the river, where there is great hydraulic power.

MOUNT HOPE, originally named Calhoun, and taken from Wallkill, Minisink, and Deer Park, in 1825; from Albany, SW., 121 miles. Mount Hope, 12 miles NW. from Goshen, Finchville 15, and Otisville 14, are small villages. Pop. 1,565.

---

* The late Lieutenant Timothy Mix, who died at New Haven, Conn., in 1824, was one of the defenders of Fort Montgomery. While in the act of firing a piece, his right hand was carried away by a shot. Instantly seizing the match with his left, he touched off the cannon; by which discharge *it is said forty of the enemy were killed.*

NEWBURG was organized in 1788. The township has a hilly and broken surface, and a good soil, much of which is under high cultivation. Pop. 8,933.

South View of Newburg.

Newburg, the half-shire village of Orange county, was originally settled by the Palatines from Germany in 1708: it was incorporated in 1800. It lies upon the steep acclivity of a hill rising from the

Washington's Head-quarters, Newburg.

river to the height of about 300 feet. Being thus situated, the village makes a fine appearance when seen from the river. The river margin, about 600 feet wide, affords space for convenient quays and docks. A large business centres here from the neighboring counties. There are 3 banks, 3 newspaper printing offices, an incorporated academy, 8 churches, and about 800 dwellings. The village is 84 miles from Albany, 61 from New York, 8 from West Point, 10 from Poughkeepsie, and 20 miles from Goshen, the other half-shire town.

From the upper terrace of the village there is a fine prospect to the S. of West Point, the Crow's Nest, Butter Hill, and the two Beacon mountains; on the SE. Pollopel's Island; on the E. the picturesque valleys of the Matteawan and Wappinger's creeks, and the village of Fiskhill Landing.

The preceding is a northern view of the old stone house in the south part of Newburg village, formerly the quarters of Washington when the American army were in cantonment in the vicinity, at the close of the revolutionary war. In the spring of 1783, when the troops were about to be disbanded without their pay, there was great discontent among them. At this time an anonymous letter was addressed to the officers, artfully calculated to excite passion. It was dated March 10th, 1783. It was subsequently ascertained, (says Mr. Dunlap,) to have been written by Major Armstrong, afterward secretary of war.

" The author assumes the character of a veteran who had suffered with those he addressed. He tells them that to be tame in their present situation would be more than weakness, and must ruin them forever. He bids them 'suspect the man who would advise to more moderation, and longer forbearance.' He then describes the high state in which the country has been placed by their services. And says, ' does this country reward you with tears of gratitude and smiles of admiration, or does she trample on your rights, disdain your cries, and insult your distresses?' He advised them to carry their appeal from the justice, to the fears of government. 'Assume a bolder tone—say, that the slightest indignity from congress now must operate like the grave, and part you from them forever.' That if peace takes place, 'nothing shall separate you from your *arms* but death: if war continues, that you will retire to some unsettled country, with Washington at your head, and mock at the distresses of government.' The insidious expression of ' courting the auspices, and inviting the direction of their illustrious leader,' was calculated to make the army believe that Washington would join them in rebellion against his country, and was certainly a bold artifice, coming, as it did, from one in constant correspondence with General Gates, and attached to him both by inclination and office.

" The commander-in-chief noticed the anonymous address in orders, with pointed disapprobation, and requested that the general and field officers, with a proper representation from the staff of the army, would assemble on the 15th instant, to hear the report of the committee deputed by the army to congress. This request was seized upon, and represented in a second paper as giving sanction to the proceedings of the officers, and they were called upon to act with energy. On the 15th of March, the commander-in-chief addressed the convention of officers, (General Gates being the chairman,) in the language of truth, feeling, and affection. He overthrew all the artifices of the anonymous writer and his friends, one of the principal of whom sat in the chair. Washington noticed the advice to *mark for suspicion the man who should recommend moderation*. He feelingly spoke of his own constant attention, from the commencement of the war, to the wants and sufferings of the army, and then pointed out the dreadful consequences of following the advice of the anonymous writer, *either to draw their swords against their country, or retire, if war continues, from the defence of all they hold dear*. He calls to mind the scenes in which they had acted together, and pledges himself to the utmost exertion for obtaining justice to his fellows in arms. He requests them to rely on the promise of congress. He said, ' I conjure you, in the name of our common country, as you value your own sacred honor, as you respect the rights of humanity, to express your utmost horror and detestation of the man who wishes, under any specious pretences, to overturn the liberties of your country; and who wickedly attempts to open the floodgates of civil discord, and deluge our rising empire in blood.''

" The convention resolved, unanimously, among other things, that 'the army have unshaken confidence in congress, and view with abhorrence, and reject with disdain, the *infamous propositions* contained in a late anonymous address to the officers of the army.' ''—*Dunlap's Hist. of New York.*

NEW WINDSOR was organized in 1788. It has an uneven surface, generally fertile and well cultivated. Pop. 2,482. The village of New Windsor, said to be the oldest village in the county, is situated about

2 miles south from Newburg, and lies at the confluence of Chambers' creek with the Hudson. The head-quarters of Washington was for a time here, in an humble Dutch-like mansion.

Birthplace of De Witt Clinton, New Windsor.

"DE WITT CLINTON was born in the village of New Windsor, March 2d, 1769. His paternal ancestors were of Norman origin. His grandfather, Mr. Charles Clinton, at the head of a company of associates, emigrated from Ireland in 1729, and settled in this town. His father, General James Clinton, was a brave and useful officer in the French and Indian wars, and in the revolutionary struggle. A short time previous to the revolution he married Miss Mary De Witt, a lady of Dutch descent. The fruit of this union were four sons, of whom De Witt was the second. His early education was intrusted to the care of the Rev. Mr. Moffat, the pastor of the Presbyterian church in Little Britain. At the age of thirteen he was transferred to an academy at Kingston, then conducted by Mr. John Addison. Here he remained two years, when he entered the junior class of Columbia col-

Fac-simile of De Witt Clinton's signature.

lege. At this institution he distinguished himself as a scholar, and closed his academic career in 1786, when he received the usual degree of bachelor of arts, taking, at the commencement, the highest honor which the institution could bestow. He thereupon commenced the study of the law under Samuel Jones, Esq., a celebrated counsellor. After receiving the usual licences or degrees in his profession, he was abruptly called from the further cultivation of the pursuit by circumstances arising from the situation of political affairs in the state. "The germs of the two great parties which have since divided the country, were at that time beginning to appear. His uncle, George Clinton, then governor of the state, was assailed by a combination of almost all the talents of that section of the country, and pamphlets and newspaper essays were poured upon the public with unrestrained profusion. Mr. Clinton, relinquishing every other pursuit, entered warmly and exclusively into the vindication of the conduct and principles of his uncle; and it is believed that the greater part of the controversial politics on the anti-federal or democratic side was managed by him during this period of turbulence. He continued with his uncle as his secretary during his administration, which ended in 1795. Mr. Clinton had been honored while with his uncle with the office of secretary of the University, and of the Board of Fortifications of New York. Upon the retirement of the governor he also withdrew from public life. But his efforts as an individual, in rallying and supporting the party of which he might then have been considered the leader, were not for a moment remitted. To do this with effect, however, it seemed necessary that he should be placed in a public station; and accordingly, in 1798, he was elected a member of the assembly from the city of New York, and in 1800 was chosen a senator from the southern district, and a member of the council

ORANGE COUNTY. 427

of appointment. From the senate of this state, by a joint ballot of both branches of the legislature, he was elected to a seat in the senate of the United States, where he took an active interest in the concerns of the country, in relation to the differences then existing with the Spanish authorities at New Orleans. His continuance in that august body, however, was short, as on receiving the appointment of mayor of New York in October, 1803, it became necessary that he should resign it, the duties of the two offices being by law incompatible. This office he held by successive appointment, with the exception of twenty-two months, until 1815. Notwithstanding the political change in the state in 1813, such was the public confidence in him, that he was continued in office during the exciting period of the late war. When President Madison received a nomination for a second term, Clinton was put in opposition, and received 89 electoral votes; while Madison was elected by 128. Clinton early became a strong partisan in favor of the Erie canal, and it is owing to the bold stand which he took in favor of this great enterprise that his popularity in a measure was owing. In the summer of 1810, he went on a tour with other commissioners for exploring the route of this work. This country was then comparatively a wilderness, and there was not a house where the city of Rochester now stands. In the spring of 1815 he was superseded in his office of mayor, and deprived of all his public employments except that of canal commissioner. In 1817, he was elected governor of the state, which station he held until the commencement of the year 1823. In the autumn of 1822, he declined another nomination, and returned to the pursuits of private life, holding only the office of canal commissioner; from which he was removed in the spring of 1824 by an overwhelming vote of the legislature. At the time of this vote, he had for fourteen years been steadily engaged in promoting the cause of the internal navigation of the state, and whether in or out of office, had received no compensation for these services. The news of his removal had no sooner reached the principal towns in the state, than large meetings were held to express the popular indignation at this measure. In the city of New York, not less than 10,000 persons assembled at the call, among whom were some of his strong political opponents. The consequence was, that the people rebuked this vote in a most emphatic manner six months afterward by electing him their governor, and by the largest majority ever previously known in the state, in a contested election; which office he held until his death. When the success of the canal policy was made apparent, other states eagerly embarked in similar enterprises, and he was invited to visit Pennsylvania and Ohio, to give the aid of his high authority to their projects of internal improvement. When the canal connecting the Ohio with Lake Erie was commenced, to him was assigned the compliment of removing the first earth of the excavation. His journey through that state, like the progress of Lafayette, was one continued triumph. His popularity extended to all classes. The merchants of New York of all political parties, grateful for his exertions in behalf of the canal, and sensible of its influence upon their prosperity, presented him with two large and rich silver vases. De Witt Clinton died suddenly on the 11th of February, 1828, aged 59 years. This event cast a gloom throughout the state, and in public meetings expressions were sent forth of heartfelt sorrow. Although placed in circumstances where most men would have accumulated unbounded riches, he manifested an utter indifference to money, and died in honorable poverty. Even the plate presented to him by the merchants of New York was exposed to sale after his death.

"Clinton was possessed of the sterner virtues, and would not sacrifice feeling to principle. Although a prominent mason, his stand in relation to the abduction of Morgan is in character. "The sheriff of one of the frontier counties was accused of participation in this abduction. The governor forthwith propounded a series of written interrogatories relative to his agency in the transaction, and on his refusal to answer, issued a proclamation removing him from office. This person, it is to be recollected, was his steadfast friend and political supporter; but he would not allow any personal considerations to weigh against the public interest. In an interview which the removed sheriff sought, he said, 'Strong as is my attachment to you, I will, if you are guilty, exert myself to have you punished to the extent of the laws.' To which the trembling culprit replied in faltering tones, 'I have done nothing worthy of chains or death.' Unlike most American statesmen, Clinton was devoted to literary and scientific pursuits, and was an efficient patron of learning. His writings place him high in the ranks of science.

"Clinton's person, in his youth and early manhood, was remarkable for its masculine beauty, and as years advanced assumed a majestic character. His stature was upwards of six feet, straight and finely proportioned. His eyes were a dark hazel, approaching to black, and highly expressive; his hair brown; his complexion clear, and more florid than usual among Americans; his teeth fine, giving a peculiar grace to his smile; his nose slightly aquiline. His habits of reflection and close study were marked in the ordinary expression of his countenance, which, controlled at an early period of his life to the gravity becoming the magistrate and the senator, presented an appearance of seriousness almost approaching to austerity. When speaking in public, however, his face expressed, with the utmost flexibility, the varying emotions to which his words gave vent; while in the intercourse of private life and in familiar conversation, the gravity which rested on his features when not excited, gave way on occasion to playfulness and mirth.' He truly exhibited the picture of a 'great man, an elegant and profound scholar, and a practical citizen—a man of letters and the world, and a character of active worth to the present generation, and of solid and permanent advantage to posterity.'"

WALLKILL, organized in 1788; from Albany S. 100 miles. Middletown, 7 miles NW. from Goshen, is a very thriving village on the New York and Erie railroad, and contains about 80 or 100 dwellings. Philipsburg, on the Wallkill, 4 miles NW. from Goshen, at the outlet of the "drowned lands," and Scotchtown, 6 miles N., are small settlements. Pop. 4,268.

WARWICK, organized in 1788; from Albany SW. 110, and from New York N. 54 miles. On the western border lie a portion of the "drowned lands."* The famous "Sterling iron works" have been in operation here about 80 years. Warwick, Amity, Florida, Bellville, Sugar Loaf, and Edenville are small villages. Pop. 5,113.

The following extract from a newspaper printed April 28th, 1779, will serve to show the ferocity of civil war:

"We hear from Goshen that a horrible murder was committed near the Sterling iron-works on the night of Saturday the 26th of March, by a party of villains five or six in number, the principal of whom was Richard Smith, oldest surviving son of the late Claudius Smith, of infamous memory, his eldest having been shot last fall at Smith's cove, in company with several other villains, by one of our scouting parties sent out in search of them. These bloody miscreants it seems that night intended to murder two men who had shown some activity and resolution in apprehending these robbers and murderers who infested the neighborhood.

"They first went to the house of John Clark, near the iron-works, whom they dragged from his house and then shot him; and observing some remains of life in him, one of them saying '*he is not dead enough yet*,' shot him through the arm again, &c., and left him. He lived some hours after, and gave an account of their names and behavior. They then went to the house of ———, who hearing some noise they made in approaching, got up and stood on his defence, with his gun and bayonet fixed, in a corner of his little log cabin. They burst open the door, but seeing him stand with his gun, were afraid to enter, and thought proper to march off. The following was pinned to Clark's coat:—

A WARNING TO THE REBELS.

"YOU are hereby warned at your peril to desist from hanging any more friends to government as you did Claudius Smith. You are warned likewise to use James Smith, James Fluelling, and William Cole, well, and ease them of their irons, for we are determined to hang six for one, for the blood of the innocent cries aloud for vengeance. Your noted friend Capt. Williams and his crew of robbers and murderers we have got in our power, and the blood of Claudius Smith shall be repaid. There are particular companies of us that belong to Col. Butler's army, Indians as well as white men, and particularly numbers from New York, that are resolved to be avenged on you for your cruelty and murder. We are to remind you that you are the beginners and aggressors, for by your cruel oppressions and bloody actions you drive us to it. This is the first, and we are determined to pursue it on your heads and leaders to the last—*till the whole of you are murdered.*"

---

* "The drowned lands" of Orange county lie along the Wallkill creek, in the towns of Minisink, Warwick, and Goshen. When drained of the waters, they have a deep soil of rich vegetable mould, which produces good crops of hemp, and are found to be productive and valuable. The tract so called, extends in length along each side of this creek about 10 miles, being from 3 to 5 miles in width.

ORLEANS COUNTY.

ORLEANS COUNTY was taken from Genesee in 1824. It is 24 miles long E. and W., and 18 miles broad N. and S. It is centrally distant from Albany 257, and from New York 302 miles. The summit of the mountain ridge extends across the county at an elevation of about 340 feet above Lake Ontario. Parallel with this, on the alluvial way, runs the ridge road. With these exceptions, the face of the country is generally level. The soil, mostly clay and argillaceous loam, is highly fertile. Grain is raised in considerable quantities. The Erie canal passes centrally through the county. The whole county was included in the grant to Massachusetts. The towns of Barre, Carlton, Gaines, Ridgeway, Shelby, and Yates, belonged to the Holland Land Company; whilst Murray, Clarendon, and Kendall, belonged to the Pulteney estate. The county was chiefly settled by New Englanders, and is divided into 9 towns. Pop. 24,995.

View of the public buildings in Albion.

BARRE, taken from Gaines in 1818; from Albany 260 miles. Albion, founded in 1823 by Nehemiah Ingersoll and George Standart, Jr., the county seat of justice, incorporated in 1828, lies near the centre of the county upon the Erie canal; from Albany, by the canal, 305, from Rochester 35, from Buffalo 58, from Lockport 28 miles. The annexed view was taken from the door of the Baptist church. The first building on the right, a large brick structure, is the Albion Female Seminary;* the small building in the centre of the engraving,

---

* Under the charge of Mrs. Caroline Achilles and Miss Sophronia Phipps, principals, and numbering about two hundred pupils.

is the county clerk's office. The building with a cupola is the courthouse, and the one partially seen in the rear, the jail. There are in the village 1 Presbyterian, 1 Baptist, and 1 Methodist church, the Orleans county bank, 2 weekly newspaper offices, and about 220 dwellings, many of them large, neat, and commodious. The surrounding country abounds in fruit. South Barre, 6 miles, and Barre Centre, 3 miles S. of Albion, are both small villages. Pop. 5,499.

CARLTON, originally named Oak Orchard, and taken from Gaines and Ridgeway in 1822; from Albany 265, from Albion centrally distant N. 8 miles. Carlton is a small post village, and West Carlton a post-office. Pop. 2,242.

CLARENDON, taken from Sweden in 1821; from Albany 251 miles. Clarendon is a small village 9 miles SE. from Albion. Pop. 2,261.

GAINES, taken from Ridgeway in 1816; bounds since altered; from Albany 260 miles. Pop. 2,431. Gaines, 3 miles NW. from Albion, incorporated in 1832, has about 60 dwellings. Eagle Harbor, 3 miles west of Albion, and Gaines Basin, 1½ miles north, both on the canal, are small villages. Fairhaven is 2½ miles north of Albion. West Gaines is a post-office.

KENDALL, the NE. corner town, was recently formed from Murray; centrally distant NE. from Albion 10 miles. Pop. 1,682.

MURRAY, taken from Gates in 1808; from Albany 245 miles. Pop. 2,678. Holley, 10 miles east of Albion and 25 west of Rochester, was founded in 1823 by Elisha Johnson. It has about 350 inhabitants. A short distance east of the village is the Holley embankment, one of the greatest on the Erie canal, elevated 76 feet above the creek. North Murray, Scio, and Sandy Creek, are small villages.

RIDGEWAY, taken from Batavia in 1812; bounds since much altered; from Albany 267 miles. Pop. 3,257. Medina, situated in a flourishing country on the canal, incorporated in 1832, 10 miles west of Albion, is a thriving place. There are here 1 Baptist, 1 Methodist, 1 Presbyterian, 1 Episcopal, and 1 Catholic church, and about 1,000 inhabitants. A railroad connects this place with Richfield, 12 miles distant. Knowlesville village, on the canal, 6 miles west of Albion, has 1 Presbyterian, 1 Methodist, and 1 Baptist church, and about 80 or 100 dwellings. Oak Orchard, 9 miles NW. from Albion, and Ridgeway Corners, 13 miles NW. from Albion, are small villages.

SHELBY, taken from Ridgeway in 1818; from Albany 260 miles. Ellicott's Mills, 13 miles SE., Shelby's Basin, on the canal 13 miles W., and Millville, 10 miles SW. from Albion, are small villages. Pop. 2,697.

YATES, originally named Northton, and taken from Ridgeway in 1822; from Albany 270 miles. Lindon, 14 miles NW. from Albion, and Yates Centre, are small villages. Pop. 2,248.

OSWEGO COUNTY.

OSWEGO COUNTY was taken from Oneida and Onondaga counties in 1816; centrally distant from New York NW. 235, and from Albany 150 miles. Greatest length E. and W. 37 miles, greatest breadth N. and S. 30 miles. The surface is level upon the west, south, and southeast; in the interior rolling, and in the north rising into hills. The soil generally is of a medium quality, some of it highly fertile, better adapted to grass than grain. With the exception of the Oswego river, there are no large streams. "The towns west of the Oswego river constituted a part of the military tract. The towns east of the river constitute a part of 'Scriba's patent.' These lands were originally granted to Nicholas Roosevelt, of New York, who not complying with the terms of sale, they were sold to George Scriba, a native of Germany, and at that time a merchant in New York. The town of Richland, a large part of Volney, about one half of Scriba, and the town of Vienna, in the county of Oneida, upon a sale of part of Mr. Roosevelt's interest by process from chancery, were jointly purchased by Gen. Alexander Hamilton, John Lawrence, and John B. Church." The county has 20 towns. Pop. 43,820.

ALBION, taken from Richland in 1825; from Albany 150, centrally distant from Pulaski SE. 8 miles. Sandbank, Salmon, and Spruce are post-offices. Pop. 1,499.

AMBOY, taken from Williamstown in 1830; from Albany 130, from Pulaski centrally distant SE. 22 miles. Amboy is a small post village. Pop. 1,084.

BOYLSTON, taken from Orwell in 1828; from Albany 140, from Pulaski NE. 10 miles. Pop. 481. The greater part of the town is still covered with a forest.

CONSTANTIA, taken from Mexico in 1808; from Albany 145 miles. Pop. 1,494. Constantia or Rotterdam, on the Oneida lake, 36 miles E. from Oswego, has about 30 dwellings. Here is one of the most extensive iron foundries in the state. Cleaveland village has about 25 dwellings.

GRANBY, taken from Hannibal in 1818; from Albany W. 158, centrally distant from Oswego S. 12 miles. Pop. 2,386. Phillips village is a small settlement on the Oswego river at the Oswego Falls, which are 800 feet in width, and can be made to furnish great hydraulic power. Six Mile Creek is a post-office.

HANNIBAL, originally taken from Lysander as part of Onondaga county in 1806; from Albany 168 miles. Pop. 2,275. Hannibalville, 11 miles S. of Oswego, and Kinney's Corners, 6 miles from Oswego, are small villages.

HASTINGS, taken from Constantia in 1825; from Albany 150, centrally distant from Pulaski S. 17 miles. Pop. 1,989. Opposite to Brewerton village, at the head of Oneida river, are the remains of Fort Brewerton. Central Square and Hastings are post-offices.

OSWEGO COUNTY.

MEXICO, originally taken from Whitestown, and organized as part of Herkimer county in 1792; from Albany 154 miles. Pop. 3,799. Mexico village, 10 miles S. from Pulaski, 16 from Oswego, has about 70 or 80 dwellings, and an academy—1 Presbyterian, 1 Baptist, and 1 Methodist church. Prattsville 9 miles, Colosse 10, and Union Square 8 from Pulaski, are small settlements.

NEW HAVEN, taken from Mexico in 1813; from Albany 157 miles. Pop. 1,735. New Haven, 10 miles E. from Oswego, and 12 SW. from Pulaski, has about 20 dwellings. Butterfly is a post-office.

ORWELL, taken from Richland in 1817; from Albany 139, and from Pulaski centrally distant E. 9 miles. Pop. 809. The falls of the Salmon river here are 107 feet perpendicular, and with a width during freshets of 250 feet. Above them the rocky banks rise 80 feet—below, 200 above the water.

OSWEGO was taken from Hannibal in 1818. It has a level surface and a soil of sandy loam. Pop. 4,673. Oswego village, post and half-shire town, port of entry and delivery for Oswego district, is 45 miles W. from Sacketts harbor, 60 from Kingston, Upper Canada, 60 from the mouth of Genesee river, 140 from the mouth of Niagara river, and 150 from Toronto in a straight line, and 38 from Syracuse on the Erie canal. The village lies on both sides of the Oswego river, with which it is connected by a bridge 700 feet in length. The portion on the eastern side is within the limits of the town of Scriba. The facilities which its situation gives for commerce and manufactures are great, commanding the markets of the lakes and the St. Lawrence river, and connected with the interior of the state by the Oswego and Erie canals. The water-power afforded by the canal* and river is very extensive, and upon them are many large manufacturing establishments. The harbor is formed at the mouth of the river by a pier of wood, 30 feet broad, filled with stone, and built by the general government, extending on the west side 1,250 feet, and on the east 250, between which there is an opening for vessels. Within the pier the water is from 10 to 20 feet deep. The cost of this work was $93,000. There is here an excellent marine railway constructed at considerable expense. The village is laid out on streets 100 feet wide, running at right angles. The courthouse is of wood, on the east side of the river. There is also 1 Presbyterian, 1 Episcopal, 1 Methodist, 1 Baptist, 1 Congregationalist, and 1 Catholic church, an incorporated academy, the Bank of Oswego, capital $150,000, the Commercial Bank of Oswego, incorporated in 1836, capital $150,000, and about 600 dwellings.

---

* "About three quarters of a mile from the mouth of the river was a rapid, on which the state has erected a feeder dam seven and half feet high for supplying the canal with water. On the east side of the stream, the Oswego Canal Company, pursuant to agreement with the commonwealth, have a right to the full use of the waters of the river from the canal, and have, by a subsidiary canal, conducted them to the village, where they have a fall of nineteen feet. Mr. Abraham Varick has constructed on the west side, under the direction of Mr. John McNair, civil engineer, (1835,) on the margin of the river, a wall eighteen feet high, forming a canal along the bank seven feet deep, sixty-two feet wide, at an estimated cost of $75,000, giving also a fall of nineteen feet at the village."—*Gordon's Gaz.*

SOUTHERN VIEW OF OSWEGO

The Oswego canal is seen on the right of the engraving; on the left, the Oswego river, with the bridge connecting the two parts of the village. A small portion of Lake Ontario is seen in the extreme distance.

"The fort here was of great military importance during the colonial wars. A factory was established by the New York government in 1722; and a fort erected on the west side of the river in 1727, and enlarged in 1755; which, with Fort Ontario, built on an eminence on the east in the latter year, were on the 14th of August, 1756, reduced by the French, under Gen. Montcalm." The following account of the investment and surrender of these forts is taken from the 26th number of the London Magazine, for the year 1757.

"The works at Oswego at this time consisted of three forts—viz, the old fort on the west side of the river, and two forts on the east side, situated on two eminences, which latter were commenced the year previous, and were in an unfinished state. These works were very weak, and the walls of insufficient strength to resist heavy artillery. The English relied for a defence upon having a superior naval force upon the lake. Unfortunately, the naval armament at that time fitting out was incomplete. On the 6th of August, Colonel Mercer, commanding officer of the garrison, which consisted of about 1,600 men, having received intelligence of a large encampment of French and Indians about twelve miles distant, despatched a schooner with an account of it to Capt. Broadley, who was then on a cruise with a large brigantine and two sloops, at the same time desiring him to sail as far eastward as he could, and to endeavor to prevent the approach of the French on the lake. The next day a violent gale of wind drove the brigantine ashore while attempting to get into the harbor. The French seized this opportunity to transport their heavy cannon within a mile and a half of the fort, which he would not have been enabled to have done had it not been for this disaster. On the morning of the 11th, some canoes were seen to the eastward, and the schooner was sent out to make a discovery of what they were; she was scarce half a mile distant before she hoisted a jack at mast head, fired a gun to leeward, and stood in again for the harbor, and brought intelligence that they had discovered a very large encampment, close round the opposite point; on which the two sloops, (the large brigantine being still on shore,) were sent out with orders if possible to annoy the enemy. They proceeded to within gun-shot of the enemy's camp, when they were fired upon from a battery of four twelve pounders. This fire was briskly returned from both vessels, but to no purpose, as their shot fell short of the shore, and the enemy's cannon being large and well managed, hulled the vessels almost every shot. After firing several broadsides the vessels returned.

"The same day the French invested the place with about 32 pieces of cannon, from 12 to 18 pounders, besides several large brass mortars and hoyets, (among which artillery was included that taken from Gen. Braddock,) and about 5,000 men. About noon they began the attack of Fort Ontario with small-arms, which was briskly returned with small-arms and 8 cannon of that fort, and shells from the opposite side of the river. The garrison on the west side of the river was this day employed in repairing the battery on the south side of the old fort. That night the enemy were engaged in approaching Fort Ontario, and bringing up their cannon against it. On the 12th, the enemy renewed their fire of small-arms on Fort Ontario, which was briskly returned. The garrison on the west side were employed as the day previous.

"The French on the east side continued their approaches to Fort Ontario. Notwithstanding the continued fire upon the enemy and the death of their chief engineer, by 10 o'clock next morning they opened a battery of cannon within 60 yards of the fort. At 12 o'clock, Col. Mercer sent the garrison word to destroy their cannon, ammunition, and provisions, and to evacuate the fort. About 3 P. M., the garrison, consisting of about 370 men, effected their retreat to the west side of the river without the loss of a man, and were employed on the night of the 12th in completing the works at the fort at the West hill. On this night as well as the night before, parties of the enemy's irregulars made several unsuccessful attempts to surprise the advanced guards and sentries on the west side of the river. On the night of the 13th, the enemy were employed on the east side of the river in bringing up their cannon and raising a battery against the old fort. A constant fire was kept upon them from the west side. The cannon which most annoyed the enemy were four pieces, which were reversed on the platform of an earthen work which surrounded the old fort, and which was entirely enfiladed by the enemy's battery on the opposite shore. In this situation, without the least cover, the train, assisted by a detachment of 50 of Shirley's regiment, behaved remarkably well. At daybreak, the 14th, the English renewed the fire of their cannon on that part of the shore where they had the evening previous observed the enemy erecting a battery. This was returned from a battery of ten 12 pounders. About

9 A. M., 2,500 of the enemy crossed the river in three columns. At this time Lieut. Col. Mercer was killed by a cannon ball. About 10 o'clock, the enemy had in readiness a battery of mortars. All the places of defence were either enfiladed or ruined by the constant fire of the enemy's cannon; 2,500 French and Indians were in the rear of the works ready to storm, and 2,000 regulars were ready to land in front under cover of their cannon. At this juncture, Col. Littlehales, upon whom the command now devolved, called a council of war, who were, with the engineers, unanimously of opinion, that the works were no longer tenable, and that it was by no means prudent to risk a storm with such unequal numbers. The 'chamade' was accordingly ordered to be beat. The soldiers throughout the siege showed great bravery, and it was with difficulty that they could now be restrained from continuing their resistance. On beating the 'chamade,' the firing ceased on both sides, and two officers were sent to the French general, to know upon what terms he would accept a surrender. Upon which Montcalm replied, that the English were an enemy he esteemed; that none but a brave nation would have thought of defending so weak a place so long, against such a strong train of artillery and superior numbers; that they might expect whatever terms were consistent with the service of His Most Christian Majesty; he accordingly sent the following proposals, viz:—

"'The Marquis of Moncalm, army and field marshal, commander-in-chief of His Most Christian Majesty's troops, is ready to receive a capitulation upon the most honorable conditions, surrendering to him all the forts. They shall be shown all the regard the politest nations can show; I send an aid-de-camp on my part—viz, Mons. De Bougainville, captain of dragoons; they need only send the capitulation to be signed; I require an answer by noon; I have kept Mr. Drake for an hostage.   MONTCALM.
"'Aug. 14, 1756.'"

"The terms required by the English were honorably granted. The victors immediately dismantled the forts and carried off the garrison, 121 pieces of cannon, 14 mortars, great quantities of ammunition and warlike stores, two sloops of war, and 200 boats and batteaux."

West view of Fort Oswego.

The following is the American official account of the attack upon this place during the late war, taken from a newspaper published at the time. Copy of a letter from Maj. Gen. Brown to the secretary of war, dated

"*H. Q., Sacketts Harbor, May* 12, 1814.

"SIR,—Enclosed is an abstract from the report of Lieut. Col. Mitchell, of the affair at Oswego. Being well satisfied with the manner in which the colonel executed my orders, and with the evidence given of steady discipline and gallant conduct on the part of the troops, I have noticed them in the general order, a copy of which is enclosed.—The enemy's object was the naval and military stores deposited at the falls, 10 miles in the rear of

the fort. These were protected. The stores at the fort and village were not important. I am, &c.
JACOB BROWN, Maj. Gen.

"*Hon. Secretary at War.*"

"REPORT.—I informed you of my arrival at Fort Oswego on the 30th ult. This post being but occasionally and not recently occupied by regular troops, was in a bad state of defence. Of cannon, we had but five old guns, three of which had lost their trunnions. What could be done in the way of repair was effected—new platforms were laid, the gun carriages put in order, and decayed pickets replaced. On the 5th inst. the British naval force, consisting of 4 large ships, 3 brigs, and a number of gun and other boats were descried at reveille—beating about 7 miles from the fort. Information was immediately given to Capt. Woolsey of the navy (who was at Oswego village) and to the neighboring militia. It being doubtful on what side of the river the enemy would attempt to land, and my force (290 effectives) being too small to bear division, I ordered the tents in store to be pitched on the village side, while I occupied the other with my whole force. It is probable that this artifice had its effect and determined the enemy to attack where from appearances they expected the least opposition. About 1 o'clock, the fleet approached. Fifteen boats, large and crowded with troops, at a given signal moved slowly to the shore. These were preceded by gun-boats sent to rake the woods and cover the landing, while the larger vessels opened a fire upon the fort. Capt. Boyle and Lieut. Legate, (so soon as the debarking boats got within the range of our shot,) opened upon them a very successful fire from the shore battery, and compelled them twice to retire. They at length returned to the ships, and the whole stood off from the shore for better anchorage. One of the enemy's boats which had been deserted, was taken up by us, and some others by the militia. The first mentioned was 60 feet long, and carried 36 oars and 3 sails, and could accommodate 150 men. She had received a ball through her bow, and was nearly filled with water.—Piquet guards were stationed at different points, as we lay on our arms during the night.—At daybreak on the 6th, the fleet appeared bearing up under easy sail. The Wolfe, &c., took a position directly against the fort and batteries, and for 3 hours kept up a heavy fire of grape, &c. Finding that the enemy had effected a landing, I withdrew my small disposable force into the rear of the fort, and with two companies (Romayne's and Melvin's) met their advancing columns, while the other companies engaged the flanks of the enemy. Lieut. Pearce of the navy, and some seamen, joined in the attack, and fought with their characteristic bravery. We maintained our ground about 30 minutes, and as long as consisted with my further duty of defending the public stores deposited at the falls, which no doubt formed the principal object of the expedition on the part of the enemy. Nor was this movement made precipitately. I halted within 400 yards of the fort. Capt. Romayne's company formed the rear-guard, and remaining with it, I marched to this place in good order, destroying the bridges in my rear. The enemy landed 600 of De Wattevilles regiment, 600 marines, two companies of the Glengary corps, and 350 seamen.—Gen. Drummond and Com. Yeo, were the land and naval commanders. They burned the old barracks and evacuated the fort about 3 o'clock in the morning of the 7th.—Our loss in killed is 6, in wounded 38, and in missing 25. That of the enemy is much greater. Deserters and citizens of ours taken prisoners and afterward released, state their killed at 64, and wounded in proportion—among these are several land and naval officers of merit.[*]—I cannot close this despatch without speaking of the dead and the living of my detachment. Lieut. Blaney, a young man of much promise, was unfortunately killed. His conduct was highly meritorious. Capt. Boyle and Lieut. Legate merit my highest approbation, and indeed I want language to express my admiration of their gallant conduct. The subalterns, M. Comb, Ansart, Ring, Robb, Earl, McClintock, and Newkirk, performed well their several parts.—It would be injustice were I not to acknowledge and report the zeal and patriotism evinced by the militia, who arrived at short notice, and were anxious to be useful.

"*H. Q., Sacketts Harbor,* 12 *May,* 1814.*

"GENERAL ORDERS.—Maj. Gen. Brown has the satisfaction of announcing to the troops of his division, that the detachment under the command of Lieut. Col. Mitchell of the corps

---

[*] Commodore Chauncey, in a letter about this date to the secretary of the navy, states—"The enemy has paid dearly for the little booty he obtained at Oswego. From the best information which I can collect, both from deserters and my agents, the enemy lost 70 men killed, and 165 wounded, drowned and missing—in all 235; nearly as many as were opposed to them. Capt. Mulcaster is certainly mortally wounded; a captain of marines killed, and a number of other officers killed and wounded."

of artillery, have by their gallant and highly military conduct on the 5th and 6th inst., gained a name in arms worthy of the nation they serve and the cause they support. For nearly two days they maintained an unequal contest against ten times their number, and but yielded their post when the interest of their country made that measure necessary. The companies composing this gallant detachment were Boyle's, Romayne's, McIntire's, and Pierce's, of the heavy artillery, and a few seamen under the command of Lieut. Pearce of the navy,—in all less than *three hundred men.* The enemy's force by land and water exceeded *three thousand men.*"

The following additional particulars are from Thomson's History of the Late War.—" On the morning of the 7th, the enemy finding that the object of the expedition, though prosecuted with a force, including the ship's crew, of 3,000 men, had not been achieved, evacuated the place after firing the barracks, spiking some and carrying off others of the guns.— On the 9th, they returned to Oswego, and sent a flag into the village, informing the inhabitants of their intention of landing a large force, to proceed to the falls for the execution of their original plan; but on being assured by the people that the stores had been removed from that place, and that the communication was cut off by the destruction of the bridges, they quitted Oswego and stood for Kingston."

PALERMO, taken from Volney in 1832; from Oswego centrally distant SE. 14 miles. Pop. 1,928. Palermo is a small post village.

PARISH, taken from Mexico in 1828; NW. from Albany 149, from Pulaski centrally distant S. 12 miles. Pop. 1,543.

REDFIELD, taken from Mexico in 1800; from Pulaski centrally distant E. 15 miles. Redfield village is in the southern part. Pop. 507.

View of Pulaski.

RICHLAND, taken from Williamstown in 1807; NW. from Albany 153 miles. Pop. 4,046. Pulaski village, half-shire town, was incorporated in 1833. Centrally situated on Salmon river, 4 miles from its confluence with Lake Ontario, 36 N. of Salina, and 60 from Utica. The river at this place affords considerable water-power, on which are a number of grist and saw mills, and several manufacturing establishments. There are about 80 dwellings, a number of churches, a courthouse and prison. The spires or cupolas of the courthouse, the Presbyterian and Baptist churches, and the academy, are seen on the left of the annexed engraving.

SANDY CREEK, taken from Richland in 1825; from Albany 159

miles. Washingtonville, 6 miles N. of Pulaski, is a small village. Pop. 2,431.

SCHROEPPEL, taken from Volney in 1832; from Oswego centrally distant SE. 21 miles. Phœnix, about 18 miles from Oswego, is a thriving village recently built, having 2 churches and about 50 dwellings, on the Oswego river and canal. Rosevelt is a post-office. Pop. 2,198.

SCRIBA, taken from Fredricksburg, the original name of Volney, in 1811; from Albany 167 miles. Pop. 4,051. That part of Oswego village which lies on the right or NE. bank of the Oswego river is in this town, and is called East Oswego.

VOLNEY, taken from Mexico in 1806, by the name of Fredricksburg; from Albany 160 miles. Pop. 3,154. Fulton, incorporated in 1835, is a flourishing place at the Oswego Falls, 10 miles from Oswego. It has 4 churches, an academy, about 200 dwellings, and 1,400 inhabitants. The centre of the village is half a mile below, or north of the Oswego Falls, on the east bank of the Oswego river, at a point where a dam is constructed for the use of the Oswego canal. The village limits extend above the falls, and include the state reservation, which has been laid out as a village and partly sold, called "Oswego Falls." The water-power is extensive and can be used on both sides of the river at the dam, and also at the natural falls. The fall is about 12 feet at each place.

WILLIAMSTOWN, taken from Mexico in 1804; from Albany 137, centrally distant from Oswego E. 31 miles. Williamstown is a small post village. Pop. 830. The greater part of the town is unsettled.

OTSEGO COUNTY.

OTSEGO COUNTY was taken from Montgomery in 1791. Centrally distant from New York city NW. 200, and from Albany W. 66 miles. Its form is very irregular. Greatest length N. and S. about 40; greatest breadth E. and W. 35 miles.

This county is considerably elevated, though there are no distinct ranges of mountains of much height. A larger portion of the soil of the county, is rich and productive. A large amount of capital is invested in agriculture and manufactures. The Susquehannah river, rising in the Otsego lake, flows southerly to the bounds of the county; then turning southwesterly, forms a part of the southern boundary. The Unadilla bounds the county on the west. Otsego lake, 9 miles long and from 1 to 3 wide, and Schuyler's lake, 5 miles long and from 1 to 2 wide, are beautiful sheets of water. Portions of this county were settled as early as 1739. The mass of the settlers were emigrants from the eastern states. The county is divided into 22 towns. Pop. 49,403.

BURLINGTON, taken from Otsego in 1792; from Albany 78, from Cooperstown W. 12 miles. Burlington Flats, Burlington, and West Burlington, are post villages; the first contains about 30, the second 25, and the last 15 or 20 dwellings. Pop. 2,144.

BUTTERNUTS, taken from Unadilla in 1796; from Albany 87 miles. Louisville or Butternuts, and Gilbertsville, each 30 miles SW. from Cooperstown, are small villages. Maple Grove is a post-office. Pop. 4,017.

CHERRY VALLEY, so called by the first settlers from its abundance of wild cherries, was taken from Canajoharie in 1791. Pop. 3,813. Cherry Valley village, upon the Cherry Valley creek, incorporated in 1812, lies 13 miles NE. from Cooperstown, 13 S. from the canal at Canajoharie, and 53 from Albany. The following view was taken from the residence of Joseph Phelon, Esq. The Presbyterian church is

Southwest view of Cherry Valley.

seen on the left, and the Episcopal and Methodist churches on the right. There is here a bank, a weekly newspaper office, an incorporated academy, and about 130 dwellings. The following interesting account of the first settlement of this place is from the valuable work of Wm. W. Campbell, Esq., entitled "Annals of Tryon County."

" Mr. Lindesay, having obtained an assignment from the three other patentees to himself and Gov. Clark, in 1739 caused the patent to be surveyed and subdivided into lots, and chose for himself the farm afterward successively owned by Mr. John Wells and Judge Hudson, and gave to it the name of Lindesay's Bush. In the following summer he left New York with his family, consisting of his wife and father-in-law, Mr. Congreve, a lieutenant in the British army, and a few domestics, and settled upon his farm. He was a Scotch gentleman of some fortune and distinction, having held several offices under government, and anticipated much pleasure from a residence in this high and rolling country, whose valleys, and hills, and lakes, would constantly remind him of the wild and romantic scenery of his native land. A luxuriant growth of beech and maple, interspersed with the wild cherry, covered the valley, and extended along up the sides of the hills, whose tops were crowned with clusters of evergreen; elk and deer were found here in great numbers, as were bears, wolves, beavers, and foxes; it was a favorite hunting ground of the Mohawks, who erected their cabins near some little spring, and hunted their game upon the mountains. Mr. Lindesay, as well as all the early settlers, found it important to cultivate their friendship; he received them into his house, and treated them with such hospitality as circumstances would permit: this kindness was not lost upon the high-minded savages, one of whom gave proof of no ordinary friendship during the first winter after his removal to Lindesay's Bush. Whatever of happiness and independence Mr. Lindesay may have looked forward to, he knew little of the privations of the settlers of a new country, especially such a country as he had selected; his farm was 15 miles from any settlement, difficult of access from that settlement, which was on the Mohawk river, by reason of its elevation above it; and the intervening country was traversed only by an Indian footpath.

"In the winter of 1740, the snow fell to a great depth; the paths were filled up; all communication with the settlers upon the Mohawk was stopped; Mr. Lindesay had not made sufficient preparation for such a winter; he had but a scanty supply of provisions; these were almost consumed long before spring: a wretched and lingering death was in prospect for him and his family. At this critical time, an Indian came to his house, having travelled upon the snow with snow-shoes; when informed of their situation, he readily undertook to relieve them; he went to the settlements upon the Mohawk, and having procured provisions, returned with them upon his back, and during the remainder of the winter, this faithful child of the forest thus continued to relieve them, and thus preserved the lives of the first inhabitants of our town and county.

"In New York, Mr. Lindesay became acquainted with the Rev. Samuel Dunlop, and prevailed upon him to visit his patent, offering him a tract of land of several hundred acres, on condition that he would settle upon it, and would use his influence with his friends, and persuade them to accompany him. Pleased with the situation, and the generous proprietor of the patent, he accepted of the proposal; he was an Irishman by birth, but had been educated in Edinburgh; had spent several years in the provinces, having travelled over most of those at the south; and at the time of his first acquaintance with Mr. Lindesay, was on a tour through those at the north. He went to Londonderry, in New Hampshire, where several of his countrymen were settled, whom he persuaded to remove, and in 1741, David Ramsay, William Gallt, James Campbell, William Dickson, and one or two others, with their families, in all about 30 persons, came and purchased farms, and immediately commenced making improvements upon them. They had emigrated from the north of Ireland several years anterior to their removal here; some of them were originally from Scotland; they were called Scotch Irish—a general name given to the inhabitants of the north of Ireland, many of whom are of Scotch descent; hardy and industrious, inured to toil from their infancy, they were well calculated to sustain the labors necessary in clearing the forest, and fitting it for the abode of civilized man.

"The following circumstance gave rise to its name. Mr. Dunlop, engaged in writing some letters, inquired of Mr. Lindesay where he should date them, who proposed the name of a town in Scotland; Mr. Dunlop, pointing to some fine wild cherry-trees, and to the valley, replied, 'Let us give our place an appropriate name, and call it Cherry Valley,' which was readily agreed to; it was for a long time the distinguishing name of a large section of country, south and west. Soon after the arrival of these settlers, measures were taken for the erection of a grist-mill and saw-mill, and a building for a school-house and church. Mr. Dunlop left Ireland under an engagement of marriage with a young lady of that country, and having made the necessary arrangements for his future residence in Cherry Valley, returned to fulfil it. This engagement was conditional; if he did not return in seven years from the time of his departure, it should be optional with her to abide by or put an end to the contract; the time had almost expired; she had heard nothing from him for some time, and supposed him either dead or unfaithful; another offered, was accepted, and the day appointed for the marriage. In the mean time Mr. Dunlop had been driven off the coast of Scotland by a storm: after a detention of several days, he finally made port in Ireland, and hastening on his journey, arrived the day previous, his arrival was as joyful as it was unexpected; he was married, and returned immediately with his wife to Cherry Valley, and entered upon his duties as the first pastor of its little church. A log-house had been erected to the north of Mr. Lindesay's, on the declivity of the little hill upon which his house was situated; where, though possessing little of this world's wealth, they offered up the homage of devout and grateful hearts. Most of the adult inhabitants were members of the church; the clergyman was to receive ten shillings on the hundred acres of land; a mere pittance, by reason of the small number of inhabitants; but he lived frugally; they made presents to him of the productions of their farms, which, with the avails of his own, afforded him a competent support. In these early days, an excellent state of feeling towards each other prevailed; common danger, and common interest, united them. In their worship and observances they were very strict. During the ten subsequent years, not more than three or four families had come into the settlement. Among them was Mr. John

Wells, grandfather of the late John Wells of New York city. He also was an Irishman, and became a resident in 1743, and in '44 purchased the farm, which Mr. Lindesay had selected for himself, and upon which he resided.

"Mr. Lindesay was unacquainted with practical farming, and his property had been expended to little advantage; after struggling several years, he was compelled to abandon his enterprise. The war between France and Great Britain had been, in part, transferred to America, and in 1744, our northern frontier was threatened with an attack by the French and Indians. Reinforcements were ordered to Oswego, and among them, the company of Independent Greens, in which Mr. Congreve was a lieutenant; he resigned his commission in favor of his son-in-law, Mr. Lindesay, who, having spent several years in the service, died in New York, leaving no children. Mr. Wells, a man of amiable disposition, and of great integrity, before there was any officer of justice, was frequently appealed to as the arbiter of any little difference; he was afterward appointed the first justice of the peace for the town, and one of the judges of Tryon county, which offices he continued to exercise until the time of his death, a little before the breaking out of the revolution.

"Mr. Dunlop, having received a classical education, opened a school for the instruction of boys, who came from the settlements upon the Mohawk, and from Schenectady and Albany. It is worthy of remark, that this was the first grammar school in the state west of Albany. The boys were received into his house, and constituted a part of his family. The extreme simplicity of the times may be learned from the fact, that they often went into the fields, and there recited their lessons as they followed their instructor about, while engaged in his usual avocations upon his farm; several individuals along the Mohawk, who were afterward conspicuous in the revolution, thus received the first rudiments of their education."

On the 11th of Nov., 1778, the Indians and tories, about 700 in number, under the command of Joseph Brant and Walter Butler, made a descent upon this beautiful valley, laid the settlement in ashes, and massacred 32 of the inhabitants, mostly women and children. During the day they made several attacks on the fort, but without success. The following is extracted from the "Annals of Tryon county."

"The inhabitants, many of whom had left in the summer, in consequence of the repeated attacks of the Indians upon the frontiers, had now returned to their homes, thinking the season so far advanced, that no danger need be apprehended. On the information above being given to Col. Alden, they requested permission to remove into the fort, or at least to deposit their most valuable property there. Both requests were denied by Col. Alden. He replied, that it would be a temptation to his soldiers to plunder; that the report was probably unfounded; that it was only an Indian story, and that he would keep out scouts, who would apprise them in season to secure themselves, in case of real danger. Scouts were accordingly sent out, to traverse the country in every direction. The scout sent down the Susquehannah kindled up a fire on the night of the 9th, and all very foolishly lay down to sleep. The fire was discovered by the enemy, and a little before daylight on the morning of the 10th, they were all surrounded and taken.

"On the night of the 10th, the enemy encamped on the top of a hill thickly covered with evergreens, about a mile southwest from the fort. On the morning of the 11th, the enemy moved from his encampment towards the fort. They had learned from the scout which they had taken, that the officers of the garrison lodged in different private houses out of the fort; their forces were so disposed that a party should surround every house in which an officer lodged nearly at the same time, while the main body would attack the fort. During the night the snow fell several inches. In the morning it turned to rain, and the atmosphere was thick and hazy. The whole settlement thought themselves secure. The assurances of Col. Alden had in a considerable degree quieted their fears. Every thing favored the approach of the enemy undiscovered. Col. Alden and Lieut. Col. Stacia, with a small guard, lodged at Mr. Wells's. A Mr. Hamble was coming up that morning from his house several miles below, on horseback; when a short distance from Mr. Wells's house he was fired upon and wounded by the Indians. He rode in great haste to inform Col. Alden of their approach, and then hastened to the fort. Still incredulous, and believing them to be only a straggling party, he ordered the guard to be called in. The delay of a few minutes gave the Indians time to arrive. The rangers had stopped to examine their firelocks, the powder in which having been wet with the rain. The Indians improving this opportunity, rushed by. The advance body was composed principally of Senecas, at that time the wildest and most ferocious of the Six Nations. Col. Alden made his escape from the house, and was pursued down the hill, towards the fort, by an Indian; when challenged to surrender, he peremptorily refused so to do; several times he turned round and snapped his pistol at the Indian; the latter, after pursuing some distance, threw his tomahawk, and struck him on the head, and then rushing up, scalped him. He thus 'was one of the first victims of this most criminal neglect of duty.' Lieut. Col. Stacia was taken prisoner. The guard were all killed or taken.

"The Senecas, who first arrived at the house, with some tories, commenced an indiscriminate massacre of the family, and before the rangers arrived, had barbarously murdered them all, including Robert Wells, his mother, and wife, and four children, his brother and sister, John and Jane, with three domestics. Of this interesting and excellent family, not one escaped, except the late John Wells of New York city. His father had left him in Schenectady the previous summer with an aunt, that he might attend the grammar-school there. He might almost have exclaimed with Logan, that not a drop of his blood ran in the veins of any human being; or as it has been beautifully expressed by an eminent English poet,

"They 'left of all my tribe
Nor man, nor child, nor thing of living birth,
No! not the dog that watched my household hearth
Escaped,—that 'morn' of blood upon our plains
All perished! I alone am left on earth!
To whom nor relative nor blood remains,
No! not a kindred drop that runs in human veins.'

"A tory boasted that he killed Mr. Wells while at prayer. The melancholy fate of Jane Wells deserves a more particular notice. She was a young lady, not distinguished for her personal beauty, but endeared to her friends by her amiable disposition, and her Christian charities. One 'in whom the friendless found a friend,' and to whom the poor would always say, ' God speed thee.' She fled from the house to a pile of wood near by, behind which she endeavored to screen herself. Here she was pursued by an Indian, who, as he approached, deliberately wiped his bloody knife upon his leggins, and then placed it in its sheath : then drawing his tomahawk, he seized her by the arm; she possessed some knowledge of the Indian language, and remonstrated and supplicated, though in vain. Peter Smith, a tory, who had formerly been a domestic in Mr. Wells's family, now interposed, saying she was his sister, and desiring him to spare her life. He shook his tomahawk at him in defiance, and then turning round, with one blow smote her to the earth. John Wells, Esq., at this time deceased, and the father of Robert Wells, had been one of the judges of the courts of Tryon county; in that capacity, and as one of the justices of the quorum, he had been on intimate terms with Sir William Johnson and family, who frequently visited at his house, and also with Col. John Butler, likewise a judge. The family were not active either for or against the country; they wished to remain neutral, so far as they could, in such turbulent times; they always performed military duty, when called out to defend the country. Col. John Butler, in a conversation relative to them, remarked—'I would have gone miles on my hands and knees to have saved that family, and why my son did not do it, God only knows.'

"Another party of Indians surrounded the house of the Rev. Samuel Dunlop, whom we have frequently had occasion to mention, as the pioneer in education in western New York. His wife was immediately killed. The old gentleman and his daughter were preserved by Little Aaron, a chief of the Oquago branch of the Mohawks. Mrs. Wells was also a daughter of Mr. Dunlop; Little Aaron led him out from the house, tottering with age, and stood beside him to protect him. An Indian passing by, pulled his hat from his head, and ran away with it; the chief pursued him, and regained it; on his return, another Indian had carried away his wig : the rain was falling upon his bare head, while his whole system shook like an aspen, under the combined influence of age, fear, and cold. He was released a few days after; but the shock was too violent; he died about a year after: his death was hastened by his misfortunes, though he could have borne up but a few years longer under the increasing infirmities of old age.

"A Mr. Mitchell, who was in his field, beheld a party of Indians approaching; he could not gain his house, and was obliged to flee to the woods. Here he evaded pursuit and escaped. A melancholy spectacle presented itself on his return—it was the corpses of his wife and four children. His house had been plundered and set on fire. He extinguished the fire, and by examination found life still existing in one of his children, a little girl ten or twelve years of age. He raised her up and placed her in the door, and was bending over her when he saw another party approaching. He had barely time to hide himself behind a log-fence near by, before they were at the house. From this hiding-place, he beheld an infamous tory by the name of Newbury, extinguish the little spark of life which remained in his child, with a blow of his hatchet. The next day, without a single human being to assist him, he carried the remains of his family down to the fort on a sled, and there the soldiers aided him in depositing them in a common grave. Retributive justice sometimes follows close upon the heels of crime. This tory was arrested, as a spy, the following summer, by order of Gen. James Clinton, when he lay with his army at Canajoharie, on the Mohawk river. Mr. Mitchell was called to prove this act. He was found guilty by a court-martial, and with a companion suffered an ignominious death.

"The party which surrounded the house of Col. Campbell, took Mrs. Campbell and four children prisoners. Mr. Campbell was absent from home, but hastened there on the first alarm, which was a cannon fired at the fort. He arrived only in time to witness the destruction of his property, and not even to learn the fate of his family; their lives were spared, but spared for a long and dreadful captivity.

"Many others were killed; some few escaped to the Mohawk river, and the remainder were made prisoners. Thirty-two of the inhabitants, principally women and children, were killed, and sixteen continental soldiers. The terror of the scene was increased by the conflagration of all the houses and out-houses in the settlement; the barns were many of them filled with hay and grain. He who fled to the mountains, saw as he looked back the destruction of his home, and of that little all which he had labored for years to accumulate.

".... The whole settlement exhibited an aspect of entire and complete desolation. The cocks crew from the tops of the forest trees, and the dogs howled through the fields and woods. The inhabitants who escaped, with the prisoners who were set at liberty, abandoned the settlement."

DECATUR, taken from Worcester in 1808; from Albany 64, from Cooperstown SE. 12 miles. Pop. 1,071.

EDMESTON, named after an extensive landholder, was taken from Burlington in 1808; from Cooperstown W. 18 miles. Pop. 1,907.

EXETER, taken from Richfield in 1799; from Albany W. 73, from Cooperstown NW. 10 miles. Le Roy, West Exeter, and Exeter, are small post villages. Pop. 1,423.

HARTWICK, taken from Otsego in 1802; from Albany 70 miles. Pop. 2,475. The Hartwick Lutheran Theological and Classical Seminary, is pleasantly situated on the bank of the river. West Hartwick, 9 miles W. from Cooperstown, and Hartwick, are small post villages.

LAURENS, taken from Otego in 1810; from Albany W. 78 miles. Pop. 2,173. Laurensville, an incorporated village, 18 miles SW. from Cooperstown, contains about 40 dwellings. Jackson, 14 miles from Cooperstown, has about 20 dwellings.

MARYLAND, taken from Worcester in 1808; from Albany 66 miles. Maryland, 14 miles S. of Cooperstown, Jacksonborough, and Maryland Centre, are small post villages. 2,050.

MIDDLEFIELD, taken from Cherry Valley in 1797; from Albany, W., 63 miles. Middlefield, 5 miles E., Middlefield Centre, 7 miles NE., and Phœnix, 3 miles S. from Cooperstown, are small villages. Pop. 3,318.

MILFORD, originally named Suffrage, taken from Unadilla in 1796; from Albany 76 miles. Milford, on the Susquehannah, 8 miles S. of Cooperstown, and Collierville, are small villages. Milford Centre and Portlandville are post-offices. Pop. 2,075.

NEW LISBON, taken from Pittsfield in 1806; from Albany, W., 76 miles. Garretsville 16 miles, New Lisbon 18 miles SW. from Cooperstown, and Nobleville, are small settlements. Pop. 1,909.

ONEONTA, formerly Otego, taken from Unadilla in 1796; from

Albany 80 miles. Oneonta village, 22 miles S. from Cooperstown, has about 60 dwellings. West Oneonta is a post-office. Pop. 1,936.

OTEGO, formerly Huntsville, taken from Unadilla and Franklin in 1822; from Albany 86 miles. Otego village, 31 miles SW. from Cooperstown, has about 40 dwellings. Otsdawa is a post-office. Pop. 1,919.

OTSEGO, originally organized as part of Montgomery county in 1788; since altered. Cooperstown and Oaksville are post villages. Pop. 4,118.

Cooperstown, the county seat, distant from New York by way of Catskill 200 miles, of Albany 211; from Albany 66, and from Utica, SE., 36 miles, is beautifully situated at the southern end of Otsego lake, at the head of the Susquehannah river.

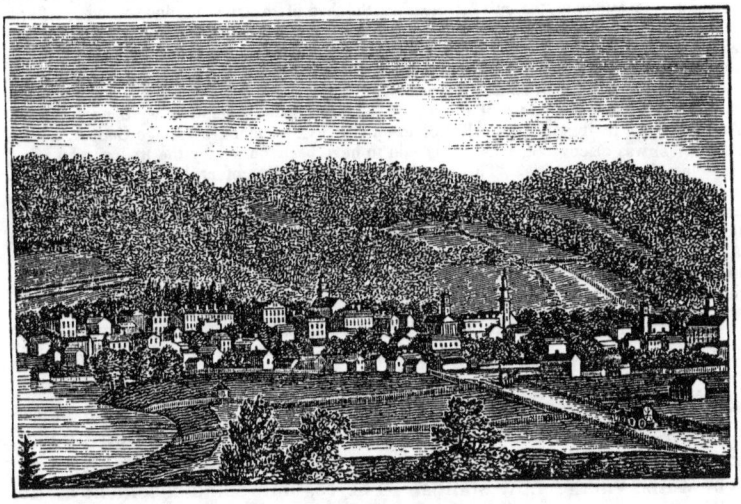

Western view of Cooperstown.

The site of the present village is said to have been a favorite place of resort with the savages from a remote period, for the purpose of hunting and fishing. The word "Otsego" is thought to be a compound which conveys the idea of a spot at which meetings of the Indians were held. There is a small rock near the outlet of the lake, called the "Otsego Rock," at which precise point the savages, according to an early tradition, were accustomed to give each other the rendezvous.

"It should also be stated, that the present site of Cooperstown is connected with an event of some interest that occurred during the war of the revolution. An expedition having been commanded to proceed under the orders of Major-general Sullivan, against the Indians who then dwelt in the vicinity of the Seneca lake, a brigade employed in the duty, under Brigadier-general James Clinton, (the father of the celebrated De Witt Clinton,) marched from Albany for that purpose. After ascending the Mohawk as far as Fort Plain, this brigade cut a road through the forest to the head of Lake Otsego, whither it transported its boats. Traces of this road exist, and it is still known by the name of the Continental Road. Embarking at the head of the lake, the troops descended to the outlet, where they encamped on the site of the present village. General Clinton's quarters are said to have been in a small building of hewn logs, which then stood in what are now the grounds of the 'Hall,' and which it is thought was erected by Col. Croghan, as a place in which he might hold his negotiations with the Indians, as well as for a commencement of a settlement.

"This building, which was about fifteen feet square and intended for a sort of block-house, was undoubtedly the first ever erected on this spot. It was subsequently used by some of the first settlers as a residence, and by Judge Cooper as a smoke-house, and it was standing in 1797, if not a year later. It was then taken down, and removed by Henry Pace Eaton to his residence on the road to Pier's, where it was set up again as an out-house.

"There were found the graves of two white men in the same grounds, which were believed to contain the bodies of deserters, who were shot during the time the troops were here encamped. These graves are supposed to be the first of any civilized man in the township of Otsego. All traces of them have now disappeared.

"As soon as encamped, the troops of Gen. Clinton commenced the construction of a dam at the outlet, and when the water had risen to a sufficient height in the lake, the obstruction was removed, the current clearing the bed of the river of flood-wood. After a short delay, for this purpose, the troops embarked and descended as far as the junction with the Tioga, where they were met by another brigade, commanded by General Sullivan in person. On this occasion, the Susquehannah, below the dam, was said to be so much reduced that a man could jump across it.

"Traces of the dam are still to be seen, and for many years they were very obvious. At a later day, in digging the cellar of the house first occupied by Judge Cooper, a large iron swivel was discovered, which was said to have been buried by the troops, who found it useless for their service. This swivel was the only piece of artillery used for the purposes of salutes and merry-makings in the vicinity of Cooperstown, for ten or twelve years after the settlement of the place. It is well and affectionately remembered by the name of the 'cricket,' and was bursted lately in the same good cause of rejoicing on the 4th of July. At the time of its final disaster, (for it had met with many vicissitudes by field and flood, having actually been once thrown into the lake,) it is said there was no very perceptible difference in size between its touch-hole and its muzzle."—*Chronicles of Cooperstown.*

An attempt was made to settle Cooperstown about 10 years before the revolution, by Mr. John Christopher Hartwick, which however proved abortive; and between the years 1761 and 1770, Col. Croghan with his family resided for a short time on the spot. A final settlement was commenced in 1786, under the auspices William Cooper, Esq., from Burlington, New Jersey, who purchased the tract on which the village now stands. The regular commencement of the village dates more properly from 1788, as at this time it was regularly laid out. At the formation of the county, in 1791, Cooperstown was designated as the county seat, Mr. Cooper being appointed the first judge of the county court.

Among the incidents of this early day, the following anecdote is related of an ex-officer of the French army, a Monsieur Ebbal, who kept "bachelor's hall" on the western bank of the lake. "Some wags told Monsieur Ebbal, that if chased by a bear, the most certain mode of escape, was to throw away his hat, or his coat, to induce the animal to stop and smell at it, and then to profit by the occasion, and climb a sapling that was too small to enable his enemy to fasten its claws in it, in the way it is known to ascend a tree. The advice was well enough, but the advised having actually an occasion to follow it the succeeding autumn, scrambled up a sapling first, and began to throw away his clothes afterward. The bear, a she one with cubs, tore to pieces garment after garment, without quitting the spot, keeping poor Ebbal treed, throughout a cool autumnal night."

As an indication of the intelligence of the inhabitants, a newspaper, the "Otsego Herald," was issued here as early as 1795. The first edifice constructed for religious worship was the Presbyterian, erected on the east side of West-street, in 1805, and is still occupied by that denomination. There are now in the village 169 dwellings, 20 stores,

42 shops, 14 offices, 5 churches, 2 weekly newspaper offices, a very extensive book publishing establishment, 2 female boarding schools, and a bank. Its present population is about 1,300. The private dwellings of this place are many of them substantial structures of stone and brick, some of which are elegant. The society is refined and intelligent. This, with the uncommon beauty of the surrounding scenery and healthiness of the climate, will ere long render it a summer resort for the *elite* of our large cities. Oaksville, 4 miles N. of Cooperstown, is a small manufacturing village.

PITTSFIELD, taken from Burlington in 1797; from Albany, W., 81, from Cooperstown, SW., 18 miles. Pop. 1,395.

PLAINFIELD, taken from Richfield in 1799; from Albany, NW., 77 miles; centrally distant NW. from Cooperstown 16 miles. Unadilla Forks and Lloydsville are small villages. Pop. 1,448.

RICHFIELD, taken from Otsego in 1792; since altered; from Albany, NW., 72, centrally distant N. from Cooperstown 16 miles. Canaderaga Springs, Brighton, and Monticello, are small villages. Pop. 1,670.

SPRINGFIELD, named from a large deep spring; taken from Cherry Valley in 1797; from Albany, W., 58 miles, centrally distant 11 miles N. of Cooperstown. Some few Dutch who had settled here, were driven off during the revolution. Springfield and East Springfield are small post villages. Pop. 2,382.

UNADILLA, taken from Otsego in 1792; from Albany, W., 100 miles, from Cooperstown, SW., 40 miles. Pop. 2,272. Unadilla, pleasantly situated on the Susquehannah, has about eighty dwellings. An *Indian monument* stood in this town about twenty rods west of the residence of Levi Bigelow, Esq. It was about 20 feet in diameter, 10 feet in height, and of a conical form. It was a landmark for the early travellers in this region. An Indian trail passed by it. Unadilla Centre is a small village.

In July, 1777, a conference was held in this place between Gen. Herkimer and Joseph Brant, the celebrated Indian chieftain, who complained of being threatened by Gen. Schuyler; and also, that the Mohawks did not have liberty to pass and repass as formerly, &c., &c. The following account of this meeting is given in the Annals of Tryon county.

"Information having been given, Gen. Herkimer in July marched to Unadilla with 380 militia. He was met here by Brant at the head of 130 warriors. Brant complained of the same grievances as above set forth. To the question whether he would remain at peace if these things were rectified, he replied; 'The Indians were in concert with the king, as their fathers and grandfathers had been. That the king's belts were yet lodged with them, and they could not falsify their pledge—That Gen. Herkimer and the rest had joined the Boston people against their king—That Boston people were resolute, but the king would humble them—That Mr. Schuyler, or General, or what you please to call him, was very smart on the Indians at the treaty at German Flats; but was not at the same time able to afford them the smallest article of clothing—That the Indians had formerly made war on the white people all united; and now they were divided, the Indians were not frightened.'

"After Brant had declared his determination to espouse the cause of the king, Col. Cox said, if such was his resolution the matter was ended. Brant turned and spoke to his warriors, who shouted and ran to their camp about a mile distant, when seizing their arms, they fired a number of guns, and raised the Indian war-whoop. They returned immediately, when Gen. Herkimer addressing Brant, told him he had not come to fight. Brant motioned to his followers to remain in their places. Then assuming a threatening attitude, he said, if their purpose was war, he was ready for them. He then proposed that Mr. Stewart, the missionary among the Mohawks, (who was supposed friendly to the English,) and the wife of Col. Butler, should be permitted to pass from the lower to the upper Mohawk castle.

"Gen. Herkimer assented, but demanded that the tories and deserters should be given up to him. This was refused by Brant, who after some further remarks, added that he would go to Oswego, and hold a treaty with Col. Butler. This singular conference was singularly terminated. It was early in July, and the sun shone forth without a cloud to obscure it, and as its rays gilded the tops of the forest trees, or were reflected from the waters of the Susquehannah, imparted a rich tint to the wild scenery with which they were surrounded. The echo of the war-whoop had scarcely died away before the heavens became black, and a violent storm of hail and rain obliged each party to withdraw and seek the nearest shelter. Men less superstitious than many of the unlettered yeomen who, leaning upon their arms, were witnesses of the events of this day, could not have failed in after times to have looked back upon them, if not as an omen, at least as an emblem of those dreadful massacres with which these Indians and their associates afterward visited the inhabitants of this unfortunate frontier.

"Gen. Herkimer appears to have been unwilling to urge matters to extreme, though he had sufficient power to have defeated the Indians. He no doubt entertained hopes that some amicable arrangement would eventually be made with them.

"This is believed to have been the last conference held with any of the Six Nations, except the Oneidas, in which an effort was made to prevent the Indians engaging in the war."

WESTFORD, taken from Worcester in 1808; from Albany 56 miles. Pop. 1,468. Westford and Westville are small post villages.

WORCESTER, taken from Cherry Valley in 1797; area since altered; from Albany, W., 56 miles. Pop. 2,420. Worcester and East Worcester are post-offices,—the first 16 miles SE., and the last 20 from Cooperstown.

PUTNAM COUNTY.

PUTNAM COUNTY was taken from Dutchess in 1812; greatest length 21, greatest breadth 12 miles. The Highlands extend across the western part. The highest point is about 1,580 feet above the Hudson. The remainder of the county, though generally uneven, has some handsome plains, with a soil various, and some of it fertile. The mountains abound with iron ore of good quality. Butter, beef, wool, calves, lambs, sheep, fowls, and the many other species of "marketing" are produced here in great quantities for the New York market, and their returns are rapidly enriching the producer. The evidences of prosperity are everywhere visible. Within a few years the lands have doubled in value and price. The county is watered easterly and centrally by the main branches of the Croton. It is divided into six towns. Pop. 12,825.

CARMEL, taken from Fredrickstown (now Kent) in 1795; centrally distant 106 miles from New York, 55 from Albany, 16 E. of the Hudson river at West Point, and 18 from Peekskill. Pop. 2,263. Carmel, the county seat, is a small village beautifully situated upon Shaws lake. Red Mills is a small village on the Muscoot river, 8 miles SW. of Carmel.

KENT, originally named Fredricktown and organized in 1788; from New York 60, and from Albany 101 miles. Pop. 1,830. Milltown, 7 miles NW., and Coles Mills, 3 miles N. from Carmel, are small settlements on a branch of the Croton.

PATTERSON, originally named Franklin, and organized in 1795. Pop. 1,349. Patterson or The City, formerly named Fredricksburg, in the valley of the Croton, is a small village. Towners and Haviland's Hollow are names of post-offices.

View of the West Point Foundry at Cold Spring.

PHILIPSTOWN was organized in 1788; centrally distant from New York 53, from Albany 95 miles. Pop. 3,814. This town extends the whole length of the west end of Putnam county on the Hudson. Some of the most prominent peaks of the Highlands are in this town, viz: Sugar Loaf, Bull Hill, Break Neck, and Anthony's Nose. This last is situated at the entrance of the Highlands, and is about 1,000 feet in height. During the revolution, a large boom and chain extended across from the foot of this peak to Fort Montgomery, on the opposite bank of the Hudson. The village of Cold Spring is situated 20 miles west of Carmel, on the bank of the Hudson, about one mile and a half above West Point. It is principally inhabited by the families of the officers and workmen of the West Point foundry. There is here 1 Presbyterian, 1 Baptist, 1 Episcopal, 1 Methodist, and 1 Catholic church, 171 dwellings, 11 mercantile stores, and 1,250 inhabitants.

The West Point foundry is situated about three fourths of a mile SE. from the village of Cold Spring. It was established in 1816, and is at present the largest establishment of the kind in the Union.

The establishment employs 400 men, and is divided into the following branches, with a foreman at the head of each branch, viz: an iron foundry, a brass foundry, pattern, smiths', machine, and boiler shops. There are attached to the foundry, 3 air furnaces, 3 cupolas. In the smiths' shop there is 1 trip-hammer of seven tons weight, and 2 tilt-hammers,—one of 1,000, and the other of 500 lbs. Shafts of 19 inches diameter have been forged here, weighing 12 tons, and they are prepared to forge shafts of 2 feet diameter. The machine shop contains 28 turning lathes, and 3 planing machines for iron. The consumption of the principal materials was as follows during the year 1840. Pig iron, $140,000; coal, $33,000; bar iron, $29,000; boiler iron plate, $14,500; copper, $44,640; total $261,140. The principal articles manufactured during that time were water pipes for the Croton water works; steam engines and sugar mills for the West Indies; steam engines and cotton presses for the southern states; flour mill, with 2 water wheels and 8 run of burr stones, for Austria; flour mill and 3 run of stones for Halifax, N. B.; engines, boilers, &c., for the steam frigate Missouri; heavy wrought iron work for the steam frigate Mississippi. Steam engines and boilers, both high and low pressure, are manufactured likewise; flour, rice, sugar, oil, and saw-mills, sugar kettles, cotton presses, hydrostatic cylinders, brass and iron cannon, bells, shot and shells, heavy and light forged work; castings of all sizes, either of composition or iron.

The Robinson House.

This dwelling, named after the unfortunate owner, Col. Beverly Robinson, is romantically situated on the east bank of the Hudson, about two miles below West Point, near the base of the "Sugar Loaf," one of the lofty peaks of the Highlands. Dr. Dwight, who in the year 1778 spent several months at West Point, has given the annexed account of this dwelling and its original possessor.

" A part of this time I resided at the head-quarters of General Putnam, then commanding at this post; and afterward of General Parsons, who succeeded him in the command. These gentlemen lodged in the house of Col. Beverly Robinson; a respectable native of Scotland, who married a lady of the Phillips family, one of the wealthiest, and most respectable of the province of New York. With this lady Col. Robinson acquired a large landed estate lying in Phillipstown, Fredericktown, and Franklin, as they are now called; and for the more convenient management of it planted himself in this spot. Here he had a spacious and convenient mansion, surrounded by valuable gardens, fields, and orchards, yielding every thing which will grow in this climate. The rents of his estate were sufficient to make life as agreeable as from this source it can be. Mrs. Robinson was a fine woman; and their children promised every thing which can be expected from a very hopeful family. His immediate friends were, at the same time, persons of the first consequence in the province.

" When the revolutionary war broke out, Col. Robinson was induced, contrary as I have been informed to his own judgment and inclination, by the importunity of some of his connections to take the British side of the question. To him it appeared wiser and safer to act a neutral part, and remain quietly on his estate. The pressure, however, from various sources was so strong against him, that he finally yielded, and carried his family with him to New York, and thence to Great Britain. His property was confiscated by the legislature of New York, and his family banished from their native country. It was impossible for any person, who finds an interest in the affairs of his fellow-men, and particularly while residing in the very mansion where they had so lately enjoyed all which this world can give, not to feel deeply the misfortunes of this family. Few events in human life strike the mind more painfully than banishment; a calamity sufficiently disastrous in the most ordinary circumstances, but peculiarly affecting when the banished are brought before us in the narrow circle of a family; a circle, the whole of which the eye can see, and whose sufferings the heart can perfectly realize. Peculiarly is this true, when the family in question is enlightened, polished, amply possessed of enjoyments, tasting them with moderation, and sharing them cheerfully with their friends and neighbors, the stranger and the poor."

When Arnold had obtained the command of West Point in Aug., 1780, he established his head-quarters at "Beverly," where was meditated that act of treachery which has stamped his memory with everlasting infamy. At the time the news of the capture of Andre was received by Arnold, General Washington s a his officers, together with the traitor, were seated at breakfast, in the lower room, to the left of the small tree seen near the centre of the engraving.

The annexed, from the pen of a late visiter, is extracted from the Knickerbocker for Sept., 1840.

"The commander-in-chief, at the time of the capture, was on his way from Hartford, and changing the route which he had first proposed, came by the way of West Point. At Fishkill he met the French minister, M. de la Luzerne, who had been to visit Count Rochambeau at Newport, and he remained that night with the minister. Very early next morning he sent off his luggage, with orders to the men to go with it as quickly as possible to 'Beverly,' and give Mrs. Arnold notice that he would be there at breakfast. When the general and his suite arrived opposite West Point, he was observed to turn his horse into a narrow road that led to the river. La Fayette remarked, 'General, you are going in a wrong direction; you know Mrs. Arnold is waiting breakfast for us.' Washington goodnaturedly remarked: 'Ah, I know you young men are all in love with Mrs. Arnold, and wish to get where she is as soon as possible. You may go and take your breakfast with her, and tell her not to wait for me: I must ride down and examine the redoubts on this side of the river.' The officers, however, with the exception of two of the aids, remained. When the aids arrived at 'Beverly,'* they found the family waiting; and having communicated the message of General Washington, Arnold, with his family and the two aids, sat down to breakfast. Before they had finished, a messenger arrived in great haste, and handed General Arnold a letter, which he read with deep and evident emotion.

"The self-control of the soldier enabled Arnold to suppress the agony he endured after reading this letter. He rose hastily from the table; told the aids that his immediate presence was required at West Point; and desired them so to inform General Washington, when he arrived. Having first ordered a horse to be ready, he hastened to Mrs. Arnold's chamber, and there, with a bursting heart, disclosed to her his dreadful position, and that they must part, perhaps for ever.† Struck with horror at the painful intelligence, this fond and devoted wife swooned, and fell senseless at his feet. In this state he left her, hurried down stairs, and mounting his horse, rode with all possible speed to the river. In doing so, Arnold did not keep the main road, but passed down the mountain, pursuing a by-path through the woods, which Lieutenant Arden pointed out, and which is now called '*Arnold's Path.*' Near the foot of the mountain, where the path approaches the main road, a weeping willow, planted there no doubt by some patriot hand, stands, in marked contrast with the forest trees which encircle and surround it, to point out to the inquiring tourist the very pathway of the traitor.

---

* The property now belongs to Richard D. Arden, Esq., and adjoins his own romantic and beautiful "Ardenia," whence no "visiter" departs, who can ever forget the generous "Highland welcome." Mr. Arden, with a true patriotism that does him honor, has permitted no alteration of the interior of the house. The same low ceiling, large and uncovered joists, the same polished tiles around the fire-places, and the absence of all ornament which marks the progress of modern architecture, preserve complete the interest which the stirring incidents of that period have flung around the "Robinson House."

† We also visited this chamber, which remains unaltered. Over the mantel is carved in the wood work: "G. WALLIS, *Lieut. VI. Mass. Regt.*"

"In our interesting visit, we were accompanied by the superintendent, Major Delafield, and in the barges kindly ordered for our accommodation, we were rowed to 'Beverly Dock,' and landed at the spot where Arnold took boat to aid his escape. He was rowed to the 'Vulture,' and using a white handkerchief, created the impression that it was a flag-boat: it was therefore suffered to pass. He made himself known to Captain Sutherland, of the Vulture, and then calling on board the leader of the boatmen who had rowed him off, informed him that he and his crew were all prisoners of war. This disgraceful and most unmanly appendix to his treason, was considered so contemptible by the captain, that he permitted the man to go on shore, on his parol of honor, to procure clothes for himself and comrades. This he did, and returned the same day. When they arrived in New York, Sir Henry Clinton, holding in just contempt such a wanton act of meanness, set them all at liberty.

"When General Washington reached 'Beverly,' and was informed that Arnold had departed for West Point, he crossed directly over, expecting to find him. Surprised to learn that he had not been there, after examining the works he returned. General Hamilton had remained at 'Beverly,' and as Washington and his suite were walking up the mountain road, from 'Beverly Dock,' they met General Hamilton, with anxious face and hurried step, coming towards them. A brief and suppressed conversation took place between Washington and himself, and they passed on rapidly to the house, where the papers that Washington's change of route had prevented his receiving, had been delivered that morning; and being represented to Hamilton as of great and pressing importance, were by him opened, and the dreadful secret disclosed. Instant measures were adopted to intercept Arnold, and prevent his escape, but in vain. General Washington then communicated the facts to La Fayette and Knox, and said to the former, 'more in sorrow than in anger,' ' *Whom can we trust now ?*' He also went up to see Mrs. Arnold; but even Washington could carry to her no consolation. Her grief was almost frenzied; and in its wildest moods, she spoke of General Washington as the murderer of her child. It seemed that she had not the remotest idea of her husband's treason; and she had even schooled her heart to feel more for the cause of America, from her regard for those who professed to love it. Her husband's glory was her dream of bliss—the requiem chant for her infant's repose; and she was found, alas! as many a confiding heart has oft been found,

'To cling like ivy round a worthless thing.' "

PUTNAM VALLEY, recently erected from Phillipstown, is situated in the mountainous region of the Highlands; from Carmel centrally distant W. 9 miles. Iron ore is found here. Pop. 1,659.

SOUTHEAST, organized in 1795; from Albany 113 miles. Joes Hill is a beautiful and romantic eminence extending W. from Connecticut into this town. Pop. 1,910. Milltown, 8 miles E. of Carmel, and Hatsville, are small settlements.

QUEENS COUNTY.

QUEENS COUNTY, an original county, was organized in 1683, and now contains all that part of Long Island which is bounded easterly by Suffolk county, southerly by the Atlantic ocean, northerly by Long Island sound, and westerly by Kings county, including Lloyds Neck or Queens Village, the islands called North and South Brother, Riker's Island, and some other islands lying in the sound opposite the said bounds and southerly of the main channel. The courts of the county were originally holden for the most part at Hempstead, at which place the governor on various occasions ordered meetings of the delegates from the different towns. By the act of the Assembly in 1683, by which the counties and towns upon Long Island were organized and established, the county courts were required thereafter to be held at the village of Jamaica. They were held there for about seven years in the old stone church which stood in the middle of the present Fulton street, opposite Union Hall street. In the year 1690, a courthouse and jail were erected upon the site now occupied by the female academy, and continued to be used for the purpose of holding the courts of the county until the present courthouse was built upon the north side of Hempstead plains, in the town of North Hempstead, in the year 1788. The county is divided into six towns. Pop. 30,324.

FLUSHING has for the most part a level surface and good soil. Pop. 4,124. The settlement of this town was commenced in 1644, principally by a company of Englishmen, who had been residents of Vlissengen, or Flushing, in Holland. They came to this place on account of the inducements held out to them by the government of the Netherlands. At the revocation of the edict of Nantes a number of French protestants fled from their native country, and several families came and settled in Flushing, most of whose posterity are now extinct. About the only memorial of them now existing are a number of the *lady apple* and *bell pear* trees which they planted in different places. They also introduced a variety of other fruits. From that time to this, Flushing has had a high reputation for the excellence and variety of its fruit. The well-known *Linnean Botanic Garden* was commenced here as early as 1750, by William Prince. Whitestone and Clintonville are small settlements in this town.

Flushing village, recently incorporated, contains about 2,000 inhabitants in a square mile. Its various attractions, with great facility of communication with New York, have induced many wealthy citizens to locate in its immediate neighborhood. Some of the private residences are among the most imposing and splendid edifices in the state. The village of Flushing lies at the head of Flushing bay, 5 miles from the sound, by water, 9 miles from the centre of New York, and 11 west from North Hempstead. *St. Paul's college*, under the direction of the Rev. Wm. A. Muhlenberg, is a flourishing institution on College point, about 3 miles north of Flushing village. *St. Thomas' Hall*, a literary institution for young men, has lately been established at Flushing, under the direction of Rev. Francis L. Hawks, D. D., principal and proprietor. *St. Ann's Hall* is a female institute, of which Rev. John F. Schroeder, D. D., is the principal.

On the right in the annexed view is the Bowne mansion-house, situated upon the elevated ground about half a mile eastward of the steamboat landing in Flushing. It is believed to be the oldest house now standing on Long Island, having been erected in 1661, by John Bowne, of the society of Friends. Besides the antiquity of the building, it is one of much historic interest. The celebrated George Fox, the founder of the society of Friends, has lodged within the walls of this house, which was the place for the yearly meeting for the whole body of Friends in the province of New York, previous to 1690. On the left of the engraving, on the opposite side of the street from

Bowne Mansion-house, Flushing, L. I.

the house, are seen two ancient oaks, under which Fox preached when in this country in 1672. Although differing in some of his tenets from the majority of those professing the Christian name, George Fox had the martyr spirit within, and, had he been called to the trial, would doubtless have sealed his testimony with his blood. His sufferings in the cause of religious freedom entitle him to the gratitude of mankind. Men of his stamp are the true patriots and genuine nobility of the human race. "A nobler object," says an eloquent writer, "no human or angelic mind could ever propose to itself, than to promote the glory of the great governor of the Universe, in studying and laboring to diffuse purity and happiness among his unholy and miserable creatures." Compared to a spirit like this, how fiendlike is the mere warrior or conqueror,

"Who wades through slaughter to a throne,
And shuts the gates of mercy on mankind."

The farm on which the Bowne house is situated is now owned by Mr. Samuel Parsons, and has ever been in the possession of some one of the Bowne family. The large and flourishing nursery establishment of Messrs. Parsons & Co. for fruit and ornamental trees, is on this farm.

Fac-simile of Cadwallader Colden's signature.

CADWALLADER COLDEN was for many years a resident of Flushing. He was the son of the Rev. Alexander Colden, of Dunse, in Scotland, where he was born Feb. 17, 1688. He studied medicine at Edinburgh, and in 1708 came to Philadelphia, and established himself as a physician. In 1718, he removed to New York, and was soon appointed surveyor-general, and afterward master in chancery. In 1720, he was advanced to a place in the king's council of the province, and was for a long time one of the most conspicuous members of that body. In 1761, he was appointed lieutenant-governor, and held the office till his death in 1776. He was a distinguished scholar as well as a civilian; was thoroughly versed in the knowledge of medicine, botany, and astronomy; and corresponded with many of the most eminent scholars both in America and Europe. Besides his publications relating to mathematics, botany, and medicine, he wrote a valuable history of the Five Indian Nations. While holding the office of lieutenant-governor, he resided most of the time at his farm in Flushing, called Spring Hill. He died Sept. 26, 1776, and was buried in a private cemetery on the Spring Hill farm. He had five sons and five daughters, a part of whom only survived him. Three of his sons, Alexander, Cadwallader, and David, were prominent men in the colony. *Cadwallader D. Colden*, the only son of David Colden, was born at Spring Hill in Flushing, April 4, 1769. He commenced his education in the town of Jamaica, and completed it in London. In 1785, he returned to the United States and commenced the study of law. He entered upon the practice of his profession at Poughkeepsie, in 1793, where he was soon made district attorney, and laid the foundation of his future fame. In a few years he stood, as a commercial lawyer, at the head of his profession, and in the other branches, among the first. In 1818 he was elected to the New York assembly, and the same year appointed mayor of New York. In 1822 he was chosen a representative in Congress. In 1824 he was elected to the state senate, and held the office three years in succession. The most untiring industry and patient research were peculiar traits in his professional character, and marked his proceedings in every thing he undertook. He was among the earliest and most efficient promoters, in connection with De Witt Clinton, of the system of internal improvements. At the completion of the Erie canal, he wrote and published the memoir upon the subject. He wrote also the Life of Robert Fulton. He died universally esteemed at Jersey City, Feb. 7, 1834.

Northern view of Hempstead, Long Island.

HEMPSTEAD, incorporated in 1784, was originally the south part of the ancient town of Hempstead. It has a level surface and a soil of sandy loam, much of which is rendered quite productive by a judicious cultivation. Pop. 7,619. The first permanent settlement in the town is supposed to have been commenced on the site of the present village of Hempstead, in 1643, by a few emigrants from New England, who obtained a patent from the Dutch governor Kieft. These emigrants came originally from a place commonly called *Hemel*-Hempstead, 23 miles from London. The annexed engraving shows the appearance of Hempstead village as it is entered from the north by the branch railroad, two miles in length, which connects the village with the Long Island railroad. It is pleasantly situated on the southern margin of the great "*Hempstead plains*," 21 miles from New York, and three from the courthouse in North Hempstead. These plains consist of about 17,000 acres of unenclosed lands, which the inhabitants of the town own in common. The village has within a square mile 200 dwellings, and about 1,400 inhabitants; there are three churches, 1 Presbyterian, 1 Episcopal, and 1 Methodist, and the Hempstead Seminary, a fine specimen of modern architecture. There is a newspaper printing office in the village. The village of Jerusalem, upon the eastern border of the town, contains about 150 inhabitants. The village of Near Rockaway is about 5 miles SW. of Hempstead village, at the head of Rockaway bay, which can be approached by vessels of 60 or 80 tons. It is a place of some business: here are several stores, a lumber and ship yard, &c. Far Rockaway, about 29 miles from New York, has grown into importance as a fashionable watering place. The "Marine Pavilion," a splendid hotel, was erected here in 1834, near the beach, 70 rods from the ocean. Raynortown is a small village 5 miles SE. from Hempstead village.

The annexed engraving is a representation of the monument erected to commemorate the terrible loss of life by the wreck of the Bristol and Mexico, on the south shore of this town in 1836-7. The grave is about 3 feet high, 9 wide, and 100 feet long, and contains the bodies of nearly 100 individuals. It is situated adjoining the Methodist burial ground at Near Rockaway, in this town, 4 miles southwest of Hempstead village. This monument is 18 feet in height from the bottom of the mound, and is constructed of white marble from the quarries of Westchester county. The following are the inscriptions:

Monument at Near Rockaway to the memory of 139 persons who perished in the wrecks of the Bristol and Mexico.

South side.—To the memory of 77 persons, chiefly emigrants from England and Ireland, being the only remains of 100 souls, comprising the passengers and crew of the American ship *Bristol*, Captain McKown, wrecked on Far Rockaway beach, November 21, 1836.

West side.—All the bodies of the *Bristol* and *Mexico*, recovered from the ocean, and decently interred near this spot, were followed to the grave by a large concourse of citizens and strangers, and an address delivered suited to the occasion.

North side.—To the memory of sixty-two persons, chiefly emigrants from England and Ireland; being the only remains of 115 souls, forming the passengers and crew of the American barque *Mexico*, Capt. Winslow, wrecked on Hempstead beach, Jan. 2d, 1837.

East side.—To commemorate the melancholy fate of the unfortunate sufferers belonging to the *Bristol* and *Mexico*, this monument was erected; partly by the money found upon their persons, and partly by the contributions of the benevolent and humane in the county of Queens

"The ship *Bristol* sailed from Liverpool Oct. 15, having on board a crew of sixteen men, including officers, and about one hundred passengers, chiefly emigrants. She had a fair passage across the Atlantic, and was off Sandy Hook at 9 o'clock on Saturday night, Nov. 20, with her lanterns out as a signal for a pilot; at which time the gale had just commenced. No pilots, however, were out, and the ship was obliged to stand off. About four o'clock on Sunday morning, she struck on Far Rockaway, and at daylight, though within half a mile of the shore, owing to the heavy sea, no relief could be afforded to the distressed passengers and crew, who were clinging to the shrouds and other parts of the rigging; in this situation they remained through the day. About 11 o'clock at night, the sea somewhat abating, some boats went to her relief, and succeeded in taking off the captain, a portion of the crew, and some of the passengers. All were rescued who remained on the wreck when the boats reached it, but during the day the ship went to pieces, and the next morning her stern-post was all that remained.

"Among the passengers lost was Mr. Donnelly, of New York, who died a victim to his own philanthropy; and Mrs. Hogan and two daughters. Mrs. Donnelly, her nurse and children were saved, and, with other women and children, landed by the first boat. Twice the boats returned to the wreck, and twice Mr. Donnelly yielded his place to others. In the third attempt to go off, the boats were swamped, and the crew became discouraged, and would not go back. In the mean time the storm increased, and Mr. Donnelly, with the two Mr. Carletons, took to the foremast, where the crew and many steerage passengers had sought temporary safety. Unhappily, this mast soon went by the board, and of about twenty persons on it, the only one saved was Mr. Briscoe, a cabin passenger, which was effected by his catching at the bowsprit rigging, whence he was taken by the boats. The captain, and a number of the cabin and steerage passengers, were on the mizenmast; and when that fell, they lashed themselves to the taffrail, where for four hours the sea broke over them.

"Some twenty of the steerage passengers, principally women and children, perished almost immediately after the ship struck. Even before they could leave their berths the ship bilged, filled, and all below were drowned. Not a groan was heard to denote the catastrophe—so awfully sudden was it.

"And to those whom the waves and the mercy of God had spared, what was the conduct of their brother man? Their persons, their trunks, were searched and robbed by the fiends that gathered around the wreck. One hapless being, thrown senseless but yet alive on the shore, and having about him his all—ten sovereigns—was plundered of them!"

Distressing as was the fate of the Bristol, the wreck of the Mexico was still more terrible. This occurred in the dead of winter, and the sufferings of the unhappy crew and passengers from the cold were intense. The annexed affecting description of the appearance after death of the unfortunate individuals who perished in her, is given by an eye-witness:—

"On reaching Hempstead, I concluded to go somewhat off the road, to look at the place where the ship Mexico was cast away. In half an hour, we came to Lott's tavern, some four or five miles this side of the beach, where the ship lay; and there, in his barn, had been deposited the bodies of the ill-fated passengers, which had been thrown upon the shore. I went out to the barn. The doors were open, and such a scene as presented itself to my view, I certainly never could have contemplated. It was a dreadful, a frightful scene of horror.

"Forty or fifty bodies, of all ages and sexes, were lying promiscuously before me over the floor, all frozen and as solid as marble—and all, except a few, in the very dresses in which they perished. Some with their hands clenched, as if for warmth, and almost every one with an arm crooked and bent, as it would be in clinging to the rigging.

"There were scattered about among the number, four or five beautiful little girls, from six to sixteen years of age, their cheeks and lips as red as roses, with their calm blue eyes open, looking you in the face, as if they would speak. I could hardly realize that they were dead. I touched their cheeks, and they were frozen as hard and as solid as a rock, and not the least indentation could be made by any pressure of the hand. I could perceive a resemblance to each other, and supposed them to be the daughters of a passenger named Pepper, who perished, together with his wife and all the family.

"On the arms of some, were seen the impressions of the rope which they had clung to, the mark of the twist deeply sunk into the flesh. I saw one poor negro sailor, a tall man, with his head thrown back, his lips parted, and his now sightless eye-balls turned upwards, and his arms crossed over his breast, as if imploring heaven for aid. This poor fellow evidently had frozen while in the act of fervent prayer.

"One female had a rope tied to her leg, which had bound her to the rigging; and another little fellow had been crying, and was thus frozen, with the muscles of the face just as we see children when crying. There were a brother and a sister dashed upon the beach, locked in each other's arms; but they had been separated in the barn. All the men had their lips firmly compressed together, and with the most agonizing expression on their countenances I ever beheld.

"One little girl had raised herself on tiptoe, and thus was frozen, just in that position. It was an awful sight; and such a picture of horror was before me, that I became unconsciously fixed to the spot, and found myself trying to suppress my ordinary breathing, lest I should disturb the repose of those around me. I was aroused from the revery by the entrance of a man—a coroner.

"As I was about to leave, my attention became directed to a girl, who, I afterward learned, had come that morning from the city to search for her sister. She had sent for her to come over from England, and had received intelligence that she was in this ship. She came into the barn, and the second body she cast her eyes upon, was hers. She gave way to such a burst of impassioned grief and anguish, that I could not behold her without sharing in her feelings. She threw herself upon the cold and icy face and neck of the lifeless body, and thus, with her arms around her, remained wailing, mourning, and sobbing, till I came away; and when some distance off, I could hear her calling her by name in the most frantic manner.

"So little time, it appears, had they to prepare for their fate, that I perceived a bunch of keys, and a half eaten cake, fall from the bosom of a girl whom the coroner was removing. The cake appeared as if part of it had just been bitten, and hastily thrust into her bosom, and round her neck was a riband, with a pair of scissors.

"And to observe the stout, rugged sailors, too, whose iron frames could endure so much hardship—here they lay masses of ice. Such scenes show us, indeed, how powerless and feeble are all human efforts, when contending against the storms and tempests, which sweep with resistless violence over the face of the deep. And yet the vessel was so near the shore, that the shrieks and moans of the poor creatures were heard through that bitter, dreadful night, till towards morning, when the last groan died away, and all was hushed in death, and the murmur of the raging billows was all the sound that then met the ear."

JAMAICA is in the southwestern part of the county. Pop. 3,782. Its name is derived from a small tribe or family of Indians, who it is believed dwelt upon the shore of the creek putting up from the bay south of the present village of Jamaica, and called the "*Jamaco*" tribe. In 1656 some individuals from Milford united with a few of the inhabitants from Hempstead, and obtained from Governor Stuyvesant permission to settle the town. A more formal and extensive patent was granted to the town in 1660, in which year it was incorporated by the name of *Rusdorpe*, from a town of that name in Holland, and which it retained until the conquest, when the present appellation was adopted. The first house for religious worship was erected in 1662, and the town by a public vote agreed to give the Rev. Zachariah Walker, as their minister, a salary of sixty pounds a year, payable in wheat and Indian corn at current prices; he was accordingly settled here in 1663.

The village of Jamaica is a beautiful place. It is located upon the Long Island railroad, 13 miles from New York, also upon the great thoroughfare from Brooklyn to the east end of Long Island, and enjoys every desirable facility of intercourse with the surrounding country. Here are concentrated the different roads leading to Brooklyn, Williamsburgh, Rockaway, Flushing, Jericho, and Hempstead. This village was made the seat of justice for the north-riding of Yorkshire, at its organization in 1665; and so continued after the division

Central part of Jamaica Village, Long Island.

of Long Island into counties in 1683, until the erection of the court-house on Hempstead plains in 1788. The offices of surrogate and county clerk are still required to be kept here, and for which a suitable building has been erected. The village was incorporated April 15, 1814, and has been gradually increasing in buildings and population, till it now contains about two hundred dwellings and fifteen hundred inhabitants. It has, besides the academies, five places for public worship, two newspaper printing offices, two drug-stores, eight drygoods and grocery stores, two book and stationary stores, circulating library, bindery, three carriage-makers, blind and sash manufactory, cabinet-maker, locksmith, pianoforte manufacturer, and many other mechanics and artisans. There are several splendid private residences in the village and its immediate vicinity, erected by gentlemen of the city, who find it both convenient and agreeable. Here is the depot of the Brooklyn and Jamaica railroad company, with their large and commodious car-house, engine-house, and machine-shops. This company was incorporated April 25, 1832, to continue for fifty years, with a capital of $300,000. In 1836 it was leased for a term of years to the Long Island railroad company at an annual rent, and has since been under the direction of that incorporation. The latter company commenced running cars upon their road as far as Hicksville on the 1st of March, 1837, from which time it has been in constant operation.

"*Union Course*, where thousands congregate at stated periods to witness the sports of the turf, is located upon the western limits of the town. This beautiful course is a few feet over a mile in length, on a perfectly level surface, with a good track; and is universally considered one of the best in the United States. Better time has been *made* upon it, and more frequently, than on any other course in the country. Connected with it is a Jockey Club of about two hundred and fifty members, who contribute annually twenty dollars each towards the Jockey Club purses. There was run over this course, the 27th of May, 1823, one of the most remarkable and best-contested races that ever took place in America; being a match race of four mile heats, for twenty thousand dollars aside, between the North and the South, upon their respective champions, *Eclipse* and *Henry*; and which was won in three heats by Eclipse. The time was as follows: first heat, 7' 37''—second heat, 7' 49''—and the third heat, 8' 24''; whole time, twenty-three minutes and fifty seconds."

Col. MARINUS WILLETT was born of a respectable family at Jamaica, July 31st, (old style,) 1740. He commenced his military career as a lieutenant, at the early age of 17, in the

Fac-simile of Col. Marinus Willett's signature.

French war, and was with Abercrombie in his unfortunate expedition against Ticonderoga. He was also at the capture of Fort Frontenac. In 1775, he served as a captain under Montgomery, in the earlier portion of his campaign in Canada. In November, 1776, he received the commission of lieutenant-colonel. During the investment of Fort Stanwix in August, 1777, by St. Leger with a body of regulars, Indians, and tories, he was second in command. (See p. 367.) For his skill and bravery on this occasion, congress voted him an elegant sword. He was a volunteer at the battle of Monmouth, 28th of June, 1788. From towards the close of 1780, until the end of the war, he had charge of the troops defending the northwestern frontier of New York. While on this duty he commanded at the battle of Johnstown. (See p. 172.) In private life, he was one of the most amiable of men, and after the war, held several civil offices, the last of which was the mayoralty of New York. He died universally regretted in the city of New York, August 3d, 1830, in the 91st year of his age, and was buried with military honors.

" RUFUS KING, minister of the United States to Great Britain, graduated at Harvard college in 1777. In 1778, he was an aid to Sullivan in an expedition against the British in Rhode Island. He studied law with Mr. Parsons, at Newburyport, and was admitted to practice in 1780. He was a representative from Newburyport in the legislature. In 1784, the legislature appointed him a delegate in congress. In 1787, he was selected as a delegate from Massachusetts to the convention called for devising a constitution for the United States. He afterward was a member of the convention of Massachusetts for adopting the constitution. Having removed to New York, he was elected a senator from that state in 1789. During the violent discussions respecting the British treaty in 1794, he co-operated with others in its defence. Of the paper concerning this treaty, with the signature of Camillus, usually ascribed to Gen. Hamilton, all the numbers excepting the ten first were written by him. He was one of those who opposed with success Mr. Gallatin's right to a seat in the senate. In 1796, he was appointed by Washington minister plenipotentiary to Great Britain. He returned to America in 1803. In May, 1806, he removed permanently with his family to Jamaica. In 1813, he was again chosen a senator in congress, and although personally opposed to the declaration of war in 1812 as impolitic, yet no one exhibited a higher degree of patriotism in supporting it. In 1816, he was the unsuccessful candidate of the anti-administration party for governor of the state. In 1820, he was re-elected again to the senate, where he continued until 1825. In 1825, he was again appointed minister to England, where after remaining one year he returned to the United States. He died April 27, 1827. In person, Mr. King was above the common size, and somewhat athletic; with a countenance, manly, dignified, and bespeaking high intelligence. His manners were courteous, his disposition affable, and his conversation and writings remarkable for conciseness and force."

" THOMAS TRUXTON, whose achievements shed lustre on the infant navy of this country, was the son of an eminent English lawyer, and was born at Jamaica, Feb. 17th, 1755." At the age of twelve, he made the choice of the profession of a sailor. " In 1775, he commanded a vessel, and distinguished himself by his depredations on British commerce during the revolution. He subsequently engaged in commerce, till the year 1794, when he was appointed to the frigate Constitution. In 1799, he captured the French frigate L'Insurgente; and in the following year he obtained a victory over the La Vengeance. On the close of the French war he retired from the navy, and died at Philadelphia in 1822, in his 67th year."

NEWTOWN, originally named Middleburgh, includes Ricker's and two other islands of the sound opposite the town; distant from

New York about 8 miles. Pop. 5,054. The first white emigrants of the town were English, who came here in 1651. They were allowed many privileges by the Dutch appertaining to an independent community. The village of Newtown is situated on the Flushing turnpike, 7 miles from Brooklyn. It contains 1 Dutch Reformed, 1 Episcopal, and 1 Presbyterian church, and about 80 dwellings. In the vicinity of Ravenswood are the valuable farms of the Corporation of New York, upon which buildings have been constructed for the accommodation of more than 500 children, maintained at the public expense.

"The first church was erected in the present village of Newtown, in the year 1670, on the arrival of the Rev. William Leverich, (sometimes spelled Leveridge.) He had been the first Presbyterian minister of Huntington, and was likewise one of the original purchasers of the town of Oyster Bay in 1653. Mr. Leverich remained here till his death in 1692, and was a highly useful man, being well acquainted with public business, and distinguished for great industry and enterprise. The most ancient volume of records in the clerk's office of this town is prefaced by about one hundred pages, in the hand-writing of this gentleman, but in abbreviated characters; purporting to be a commentary upon a portion of the Old Testament, affording conclusive evidence of his learning, patience, and industry. He is characterized by Hubbard, in his history of New England, as 'an able and worthy minister.' Many of his descendants are at this time residents of the town." St. James' Episcopal church in this town was built in 1734, and a Dutch Reformed church has been erected here for more than a century.

Besides Newtown village, there are several other smaller settlements; none of which are of much note except Hallet's Cove, lately incorporated under the name of Astoria. It is the most important place in the town, and is eligibly situated on East river, a short distance above Blackwell's Island, and opposite 86th street, New York city, where there is a convenient steam ferry. Two handsome churches and several splendid private mansions have lately been erected here. The village itself is compactly built, and well calculated for commercial and manufacturing purposes. Of this remarkable spot, the tradition is, that an English adventurer, whose name was Hallet, about the year 1640, for a barrel of beef and a few trinkets, purchased from the Indians this tract of land. Having taken to himself in marriage a sturdy Dutch lass, they settled down here, and in the process of some twenty years, by their united exertions became not only independent, but the parents of a numerous race, many of whom are still respectable in character and connections. There is here an extensive manufactory of carpets, chair factory, wool card factory, bellows factory, one for chemical preparations, and several gardens and nurseries for the rearing of fruit and ornamental trees. The celebrated Hell or Hurl gate is in this vicinity, where those, says a certain writer, who love to witness the impetuous stride of angry currents, with cragged and zigzag courses among the rocks, can hardly find a better place for full gratification. Vessels are sometimes wrecked at this spot. During the revolution the English frigate Huzza, in attempting to pass Hell Gate to get to sea by the sound, struck a rock, soon filled, and sunk in deep water. Under an impression that there was a rich military chest on board, unsuccessful attempts were made to recover the treasure by means of diving bells.

NORTH HEMPSTEAD, the county town, was formed from Hempstead in 1784. This town has produced several eminent men, among whom was the late Samuel L. Mitchell, Professor of Natural History, &c., in Columbia college. He was born August 20, 1764, and died September 7, 1831. Manhasset is the name lately substituted for Cow Neck, and designates a rich and fertile tract in this town. Situated on this tract, on the North Hempstead turnpike, is a small cluster of buildings, consisting of three houses of public worship, a tavern, academy, and a few private dwellings. At the most northerly part of Manhasset is the Sands' point lighthouse, in the vicinity of which formerly was the celebrated *Kidd's Rock*, near which it is generally believed that notorious freebooter made valuable deposits. During the revolution bands of marauders were accustomed to land upon these shores in the night, and rob and cruelly treat the inhabitants. In one instance a Mr. Jarvis, aided by an old lady living in the same house, succeeded in beating off one of these gangs, killing and wounding several of the assailants. Three miles easterly of the Manhasset churches, beautifully located at the head of the bay, is the village of Hempstead Harbor, containing about 40 dwellings. North Hempstead and Lakeville are small settlements; at the former are the county buildings. The first paper-mill erected in the state was established here about a century since by Andrew Onderdonk, ancestor of Bishop Onderdonk of the Episcopal church. Pop. 3,891.

OYSTER BAY embraces a larger extent of territory than any other town in the county, and includes Lloyds Neck or Queens village, and Hog island. Pop. 5,864. In 1640, an attempt was made by some persons from Lynn, Mass., to form a settlement upon the present site of the village of Oyster Bay; but meeting with opposition from the Dutch, the settlement was abandoned. The first permanent settlement was made in 1653, by the English, on the site of this village. Oyster Bay village, on the south side of the harbor, is 28 miles NE. from New York and contains about 350 inhabitants. On the high ground, near the Baptist church, are the remains of a fortification erected during the revolution, to prevent any hostile American force from entering the bay.

In the year 1660, Mary Wright, a very poor and ignorant woman of Oyster Bay was suspected of having a secret correspondence with the author of evil. She was arrested, but as there existed no tribunal here which the people considered competent to try her case, she was sent to Massachusetts, to stand her trial for *witchcraft*. She was acquitted of this crime, but nevertheless was convicted of being a Quaker, and sentenced to be banished out of the jurisdiction.

The first Baptist church in this village was erected in 1724, and still remains a curious relic of that age. It is about 20 feet square, with a quadrangular pointed roof, and no longer used "*for lodging folk disposed to sleep;*" having lately been converted into a stable. The present church was built in 1801. Glen Cove is a considerable village on the east side of Hempstead harbor. The Dutch church at Wolver Hollow was built in 1732, and having stood just 100 years, was followed by the present church in 1832. The village of Jericho contains about 250 inhabitants. The Friends meeting-house was first erected at this place in 1689, at which time several families of Friends took up their residence here, and soon after on the neighboring lands about Westbury. This place was for a considerable period the residence of Elias Hicks, the founder of the sect of Hicksite Quakers, so called in distinction from the orthodox Friends; he settled here in 1771, and died in 1830. He was born in the town of North Hempstead, on the 19th of March, 1748. His education was extremely limited. At the age of 17, he was apprenticed to a carpenter. He began his public labors in the society of Friends in 1795, and travelled at different periods over a great portion of the United States, from Maine to Ohio, and in the province of Canada. It is supposed that during his public ministry he travelled over 10,000 miles, and that he pronounced at least 1,000 public discourses. He likewise found time to write and publish much upon religious subjects, upon war and the practice of negro slavery. " He was a person of rough exterior, but of vigorous intellect; and making no pretensions to elegance of style, he reasoned with much force, and addressed himself to the every-day common sense, rather than the imagination of his auditors."

Norwich is a small village, 3 miles S. of Oyster Bay. Hicksville, 2 miles S. of Jericho, is located upon the eastern part of the great plains at the present termination of the Long Island railroad. In the vicinity of Bethpage is Fort Neck, so called on account of two old Indian forts, the remains of which are still very conspicuous. The village of Cold Spring is situated at the head and upon both sides of Cold Spring harbor, and partly in the town of Huntington. It contains about 500 inhabitants and several large manufacturing establishments, and is possessed likewise of considerable shipping.

In May, 1779, Maj. Gen. Silliman, superintendent of the coast of Fairfield, in Connecticut, was taken prisoner in the night, by a party of refugees who crossed over the sound from Lloyds Neck in a whale boat. The boat returned here with their prisoner, and he was soon after conveyed to New York. At that time there was no prisoner in possession of the Americans whom the British would accept for the general. After some consideration it was determined to procure one. The person selected was Hon. Thomas Jones, of Fort Neck, Long Island, at that time a justice of the supreme court of the province of New York. On the evening of the 4th of November, he was captured by a party of volunteers under Capt. Hawley, who had crossed over the sound for the purpose. The judge was conveyed to Connecticut, and became an inmate in the family of Mrs. Silliman; and during the several days that he remained in her house, she used every means in her power to make his situation agreeable. But although few ladies could contribute more effectually to this purpose, the judge was distant, reserved, and sullen. An exchange was effected sometime afterward. The grave of Capt. John Underhill, who was so celebrated in the Indian wars in New England, is in this town. He lived here for a number of years, and died upon his farm in 1672.

RENSSELAER COUNTY.

RENSSELAER COUNTY was taken from Albany in 1791. Greatest length 30, greatest breadth 22 miles; centrally distant from New York N. 156, and from Albany E. 10 miles. The eastern portion of the county is broken and hilly, and in some places rather mountainous and interspersed with fertile valleys. The central and western part is diversified with hills, and a gently undulating surface. It has extensive valleys and flats of alluvion, with a warm rich soil; and the uplands have an easy soil, well adapted to the various purposes of agriculture. There are an abundance of mill sites, and the numerous streams irrigate every portion of the county. This county had partial settlements at a very early period of our history, and has long sustained a very considerable population. The whole of the county, except the towns of Schaghticoke, Pittstown, Hoosick, and north part of Lansingburg and part of Troy, is comprised within the Rensselaerwyck patent, leased under the ordinary rent, in farms, at ten bushels of wheat the hundred acres. The county contains 13 towns and the city of Troy. Pop. 60,303.

BERLIN, taken from Petersburg, Stephentown, and Schodack, in 1806; centrally distant from Albany and Troy E. 20 miles. Pop. 1,794. A few German families settled in " the Hollow," about 1764. Berlin and Berlin Centre are small villages.

BRUNSWICK, taken from Troy in 1807; from Albany NE. 12 miles. Pop. 3,051. Ramerton and Millville are small villages.

GRAFTON, taken from Troy and Petersburg in 1807; from Troy E. 14 miles. Pop. 2,019. Patroons Mills is a small village.

GREENBUSH, taken from Rensselaerwyck in 1792 and 1795. Pop. 3,701. Bath, Defriestville, and Wynants Kill, are small settlements. Greenbush village, on the bank of the Hudson, opposite Albany, was incorporated in 1815, and has about 100 dwellings.

Remains of the Barracks at Greenbush, 1840.

The United States cantonment, now in ruins, was erected here during the late war, on a commanding eminence 2 miles SSE. of Albany. It consisted of very extensive wooden barracks for soldiers, officers' quarters, &c., &c., calculated for the accommodation in winter quarters of 5,000 men.

The annexed account of the execution of a deserter at this place during the late war, was written by an officer of the United States army. It is shockingly minute in its details.

" In 1814, I was stationed with a detachment of United States troops at Greenbush, in the state of New York. One morning several prisoners, confined in the provost guard-house, were brought out to hear the sentence which a court-martial had annexed to their delinquencies read on parade. Their appearance indicated that their lot had already been sufficiently hard. Some wore marks of long confinement, and on all, the severity of the prison-house had enstamped its impression. They looked dejected at this public exposure, and anxious to learn their fate. I had never seen the face of any of them before, and only knew that a single one of them had been adjudged to death. Soon as their names were called and their sentences announced, I discerned by his agony and gestures the miserable man on whom that sentence was to fall; a man in the bloom of youth and the fulness of health and vigor.

"Prompted by feelings of sympathy, I called next morning to see him in prison. There, chained by the leg to the beam of the guard-house, he was reading the bible, trying to prepare himself, as he said, for the fatal hour. I learned from him the circumstances of his case. He was the father of a family; having a wife and three young children, thirty or forty miles distant from the camp. His crime was desertion, of which he had been three times guilty. His only object in leaving the camp, in the last instance, was to visit his wife and children. Having seen that all was well with them, it was his intention to return. But whatever was his intention, he was a deserter, and as such taken and brought into the camp; manacled, and under the guard of his fellow-soldiers. The time between the sentence and its execution was brief; the authority in whom alone was vested the power of reprieve or pardon, distant. Thus he had no hope, and only requested the attendance of a minister of the gospel, and permission to see his wife and children. The first part of his request was granted, but whether he was permitted or not to see his family, I do not now remember.

"Dreading the hour of his execution, I resolved, if possible, to avoid being present at the scene. But the commander of the post, Col. L——, sent me an express order to attend, that agreeably to the usages of the army I might, in my official capacity of surgeon, see the sentence fully executed.

"The poor fellow was taken from the guard-house to be escorted to the fatal spot. Before him was his coffin; a box of rough pine boards—borne on the shoulders of two men. The prisoner stood with his arms pinioned, between two clergymen; a white cotton gown, or winding-sheet, reached to his feet. It was trimmed with black, and had attached to it over the place of the real heart, the black image of a heart; the mark at which the executioners were to aim. On his head was a cap of white, also trimmed with black. His countenance was blanched to the hue of his winding-sheet, and his frame trembled with agony. He seemed resolved, however, to suffer like a soldier. Behind him were a number of prisoners, confined for various offences; next to them was a strong guard of soldiers, with fixed bayonets and loaded muskets. My station was in the rear of the whole.

"Our procession thus formed, and with much feeling and in low voices on the part of the officers, we moved forward with slow and measured steps to the tune of the *death march*, (Roslin Castle,) played with muffled drums and mourning fifes. The scene was solemn beyond the powers of description. A man in the vigor of life *walking* to his grave; to the tune of his own death-march, clothed in his burial robes, surrounded by friends assembled to perform the last sad offices of affection, and to weep over him in the last sad hour: no, not by these, but by soldiers with bristling bayonets and loaded muskets, urged by stern command to do the violence of death to a fellow-soldier; as he surveys the multitude, he beholds no look of tenderness, no tear of sensibility; he hears no plaint of grief; all, all is stern as the iron rigor of the law which decrees his death.

".... Amid reflections like these, we arrived at the place of execution, a large open field, in whose centre a heap of earth, freshly thrown up, marked the spot of the deserter's grave. On this field the whole force then at the cantonment, amounting to many hundred men, was drawn up in the form of a hollow square, with the side beyond the grave vacant. The executioners, eight in number, had been drawn by lot. No soldier would volunteer for such a duty. Their muskets had been charged by the officer of the day; seven of them with ball, the eighth with powder alone. Thus prepared they were placed together, and each executioner takes his choice. Thus each may believe that he has the blank cartridge, and therefore has no hand in the death of his brother soldier; striking indications of the nature of the service.

"The coffin was placed parallel with the grave, and about two feet distant. In the intervening space the prisoner was directed to stand. He desired permission to say a word to his fellow-soldiers; and thus standing between his coffin and his grave, warned them against desertion, continuing to speak until the officer on duty, with his watch in his hand, announced to him in a low voice, 'Two o'clock, your last moment is at hand; you must kneel upon your coffin.' This done, the officer drew down the white cap, so as to cover the eyes and most of the face of the prisoner—still continuing to speak in a hurried, loud, and agitated voice. The kneeling was the signal for the executioners to advance. They had before, to avoid being distinguished by the prisoner, stood intermingled with the soldiers who formed the line. They now came forward, marching abreast, and took their stand a little to the left, about two rods distant from their living mark. The officer raised his sword. At this signal, the executioners took aim. He then gave a blow on a drum which was at hand; the executioners all fired at the same instant. The miserable man, with a horrid scream, leaped from the earth, and fell between his coffin and his grave. The sergeant of the guard, a moment after, shot him through the head with a musket reserved for this purpose in case the executioners failed to produce instant death. The sergeant, from motives of humanity, held the muzzle of his musket near the head; so near that the cap took fire; and there the body lay upon the face; the head emitting the mingled fumes of burning cotton and burning hair. O war, dreadful even in thy tenderness; horrible even in thy compassion!

"I was desired to perform my part of the ceremony; and placing my hand where just before the pulse beat full, and the life flowed warm, and finding no symptom of either, I affirmed, he is dead. The line then marched by the body, as it lay upon the earth, the head still smoking; that every man might behold for himself the fate of a deserter.

"Thus far, all had been dreadful indeed, but solemn, as it became the sending of a spirit to its dread account; but now the scene changes. The whole band struck up, and with uncommon animation, our national air, (Yankee Doodle,) and to its lively measures we were hurried back to our parade ground. Having been dismissed, the commander of the post sent an invitation to all the officers to meet at his quarters, whither we repaired, and were treated to a glass of gin and water. Thus this melancholy tragedy ended in what seemed little better than a farce; a fair specimen, the former of the dread severity—the latter of the moral sensibilities which prevail in the camp."

HOOSICK was originally organized as part of Albany county. Pop. 3,540. Hoosick Falls, 24 miles NE. of Troy, is a manufacturing village, containing about 70 or 100 dwellings. The Hoosick river here falls 40 feet. Buskirk's bridge, which is partly in Washington county, Barker's Mills, and Macnamara, or North Hoosick, are small villages.

Within the limits of this town a portion of the battle of Bennington was fought, August 16th, 1777.

The progress of Burgoyne thoroughly alarmed the American states, it being well known that the American forces under Gen. Schuyler were not sufficient to prevent the capture of Albany, whenever it was reached by the enemy. Instead of thinking of submission, the Americans met this alarming crisis with firmness and resolution, and great exertions were made to reinforce the army. Gen. Lincoln was directed to raise and take the command of the New England militia. Gen. Arnold, and Col. Morgan with his riflemen, were detached to the northern army, and congress elected Gen. Gates as commander.

"While the American army was thus assuming a more respectable appearance, Gen. Burgoyne was making very slow advances towards Albany. From the 28th of July to the 15th of August, (1777,) the British army was continually employed in bringing forward batteaux, provisions, and ammunition from Fort George, to the first navigable part of Hudson's river; a distance of not more than 18 miles. The labor was excessive, the Europeans were but little acquainted with the methods of performing it to advantage, and the effect was in no degree equivalent to the expense of labor and time. With all the efforts that Burgoyne could make, encumbered with his artillery and baggage, his labors were inadequate to the purpose of supplying the army with provisions for its daily consumption, and the establishment of the necessary magazines. And after his utmost exertions for 15 days, there were not above 4 days' provisions in the store, nor above 10 batteaux in Hudson's river.

"In such circumstances the British general found that it would be impossible to procure sufficient supplies of provision by the way of Fort George, and determined to replenish his own magazines at the expense of those of the Americans. Having received information that a large quantity of stores were laid up at Bennington, and guarded only by the militia, he formed the design of surprising that place; and was made to believe that as soon as a detachment of the royal army should appear in that quarter, it would receive effectual assistance from a large body of loyalists, who only waited for the appearance of a support, and would in that event come forward and aid the royal cause. Full of these expectations, he detached Col. Baum, a German officer, with a select body of troops, to surprise the place. His force consisted of about 500 regular troops, some Canadians, and more than 100 Indians, with two light pieces of artillery. To facilitate their operations, and to be ready to take advantage of the success of the detachment, the royal army moved along the east bank of Hudson's river, and encamped nearly opposite to Saratoga; having at the same time thrown a bridge of rafts over the river, by which the army passed to that place. With a view to support Baum, if it should be found necessary, Lieut. Col. Breyman's corps, consisting of the Brunswick grenadiers, light infantry and chasseurs, were posted at Battenkill.

"Gen. Stark having received information that a party of Indians were at Cambridge, sent Lieut. Col. Greg, on August the 13th, with a party of 200 men to stop their progress. Towards night he was informed by express, that a large body of regulars was in the rear of the Indians, and advancing towards Bennington. On this intelligence, Stark drew together his brigade, and the militia that were at hand, and sent on to Manchester to Col. Warner to bring on his regiment; he sent expresses at the same time to the neighboring militia, to join him with the utmost speed. On the morning of the 14th, he marched with his troops, and at the distance of 7 miles he met Greg on the retreat, and the enemy within a mile of him. Stark drew up his troops in order of battle; but the enemy coming in sight, halted upon a very advantageous piece of ground. Baum perceived the Americans were too strong to be attacked with his present force, and sent an express to Burgoyne with an account of his situation, and to have Breyman march immediately to support him. In the mean time small parties of the Americans kept up a skirmish with the enemy, killed and wounded 30 of them, with two of their Indian chiefs, without any loss to themselves. The ground the Americans had taken was unfavorable for a general action, and Stark retreated about a mile and encamped. A council of war was held, and it was agreed to send two detachments upon the enemy's rear, while the rest of the troops should make an attack upon their front. The next day the weather was rainy, and though it prevented a general action, there were frequent skirmishings in small parties, which proved favorable and encouraging to the Americans.

"On August the 16th, in the morning, Stark was joined by Col. Symonds and a body of militia from Berkshire, and proceeded to attack the enemy, agreeably to the plan which had been concerted. Col. Baum in the mean time had entrenched, on an advantageous piece of ground near St. Koicks mills, on a branch of Hoosick river, and rendered his post as strong as his circumstances and situation would admit. Col. Nichols was detached with 200 men to the rear of his left, Col. Herrick, with 300 men to the rear of his right; both were to join and then make the attack. Cols. Hubbard and Stickney, with 200 more, were ordered on the right, and 100 were advanced towards the front to draw the attention of the enemy that way. About 3 o'clock in the afternoon the troops had taken their situation, and were ready to commence the action. While Nichols and Herrick were bringing their troops together, the Indians were alarmed at the prospect, and pushed off between the two corps; but received a fire as they were passing, by which three of them were killed, and two wounded. Nichols then began the attack, and was followed by all the other divisions; those in the front immediately advanced, and in a few minutes the action became general. It lasted about two hours, and was like one continued peal of thunder. Baum made a brave defence; and the German dragoons, after they had expended their ammunition, led by their colonel, charged with their swords, but they were soon overpowered. Their works were carried on all sides, their two pieces of cannon were taken, Col. Baum himself was mortally wounded and taken prisoner, and all his men, except a few who had escaped into the woods, were either killed or taken prisoners. Having completed the business by taking the whole party, the militia began to disperse, and look out for plunder. But in a few minutes Stark received information that a large reinforcement was on their march, and within two miles of him. Fortunately at that moment Col. Warner came up with his regiment from Manchester. This brave and experienced officer commanded a regiment of continental troops, which had been raised in Vermont. Mortified that he had not been in the former engagement, he instantly led on his men against Breyman, and began the second engagement. Stark collected the militia as soon as possible, and pushed on to his assistance. The action became general, and the battle continued obstinate on both sides till sunset, when the Germans were forced to give way, and were pursued till dark. They left their two field-pieces behind, and a considerable number were made prisoners. They retreated in the best manner they could, improving the advantages of the evening and night, to which alone their escape was ascribed.

"In these actions the Americans took 4 brass field-pieces, 12 brass drums, 250 dragoon swords, 4 ammunition wagons, and about 700 prisoners, with their arms and accoutrements;—207 men were found dead upon the spot, the numbers of wounded were unknown. The loss of the Americans was but small; 30 were slain, and about 40 were wounded."

LANSINGBURG was taken from Troy and Brunswick in 1807, afterward enlarged by a portion from Schaghticoke. Pop. 3,330. Speigletown and Batestown are small villages, the former 3 miles N. from Lansingburg village, and the latter 1 mile S. The annexed engraving is from a view taken near the bridge, a short distance above the village, connecting it with Waterford. In the extreme distance on the right, the bridge over the Hudson at Troy is visible.

Northwestern view of Lansingburg.

Lansingburg was incorporated in 1801. It is beautifully situated on the Hudson, 3 miles N. of Troy, 9 N. from Albany, and 1 S. from Waterford. Formerly it was called the "New City," and the rapidity of its growth at that time excited wonder.* The village is regularly laid out with capacious streets in squares of 400 by 260 feet, and is a place of considerable manufacturing and commercial business. There is here 1 Presbyterian, 1 Methodist, 1 Episcopal, and 1 Universalist church, an academy in high repute, 2 printing offices, a bank, many mercantile stores, &c., and about 400 houses. Three of the sprouts of the Mohawk enter the Hudson opposite the village, and the Cahoos Falls are often distinctly heard in the stillness of the night.

NASSAU, originally named Philipstown, and taken from Petersburg, Stephentown, and Schodack, in 1806. Pop. 3,237. Nassau, 11½

---

* This was the time of the revolutionary period in France. Mr. A Reed, of East Windsor, Conn., commenced teaching a school in this village in 1793, and continued it for five years. He states that about the time Louis XVI. the French king was beheaded, in 1793, wheat, which had previously been sold in the village in the early part of the winter for 75 cents, rose to *four dollars* a bushel. On the opening of the river in the spring, the price fell back to $1.75. Mr. Reed taught school in a gambrel-roof building, which was used as the first meeting-house in the place. The lower story was divided by a swing partition. While Mr. R. was here, the Rev. Dr. Lee, of Connecticut, taught the languages in a chamber above. At this period the minister of the place was the Rev. Jonas Coe, who preached alternately at Lansingburg and Troy.

miles SE. of Albany, and East Nassau 16, are considerable villages. Brainards Bridge, Alps, and Hoags Corners, are names of post-offices.

PETERSBURG, taken from Stephentown in 1791. Pop. 1,901. Rensselaers Mills, 20 miles E. of Troy, and Petersburg Corners 27, are small villages.

PITTSTOWN, organized in 1788. The first settlements were commenced here in 1650. Pop. 3,785. Pittstown 13, Tomhenick 13 NE., Johnsonville 19, and Shermans Mills 13 miles from Troy, are small villages.

SANDLAKE, taken from Greenbush and Berlin in 1812. Pop. 4,305. Poestenkill 8 miles SE., Rensselaer 12, Sand Lake 10, Ulines 7 miles from Troy, are small villages.

SCHAGHTICOKE was organized in 1788. Pop. 3,389. About the year 1600, some Dutch and German families settled on the rich alluvial lands of this town, then occupied by a clan of the Mohawk Indians. Schaghticoke Point, on the Hoosick river, 13 miles NE. from Troy, is a large manufacturing village having about 150 dwellings. The Valley village, on both sides of the Hoosick, and partly in Pittstown, has about 45 dwellings.

SCHODACK, taken from Rensselaerwyck in 1795. Pop. 4,125. Schodack Landing 9 miles below Albany, Schodack Centre 7 miles SE. from Albany, Castleton, and South Schodack, are small settlements.

STEPHENTOWN, so called from the Christian name of the late patroon, was organized in 1788. Pop. 2,753. Stephentown Hollow or Centre, 21 miles SE. from Troy, North Stephentown 20, and South Stephentown 24, are small villages.

TROY CITY, seat of justice for the county, lies on the east side of the Hudson, 6 miles north of Albany, at the junction of the Hudson and Mohawk valleys. There is some reason to believe that its present site was visited by Hudson, the first navigator of Hudson river, in 1609. In the record of his voyage, it is stated he "went sounding his way above the highlands, till at last the Crescent, (the ship in which he made his voyage,) had sailed beyond the city of Hudson, and a boat had advanced a little beyond Albany." Probably this boat ascended to the rifts which lay at the northerly part of the city, where the ordinary tides spent their force, and the navigation was interrupted.

For more than a century after Hudson's voyage, the territory now comprising the site of Troy, (although within the limits of the grant made to the patroon,) probably remained part of the hunting ground of the Mohawk Indians. In 1720, a grant of 490 acres, extending along the Hudson between the Poestenkill and Meadow creek, comprehending the original allotments on which the city was erected, was made in fee by the proprietor of the manor of Rensselaerwyck to Derick Van Derheyden, at the small rent of three bushels and three pecks of wheat and four fat fowls annually. From the date of the grant, and possibly from a period a little earlier, this plain and the first range of hills adjoining, was possessed by the grantee and his descendants, and small portions of it cultivated as a farm.*

After the revolution, emigrants from New England, seeing the advantageous situation of Van Derheyden, as it was then called, induced the proprietors to lay it out into town lots. At this period Lansingburg, then called the "New City," was a village of considerable size and commercial importance; the city of Albany lay a few miles to the south, and had for many generations been the centre of trade for the entire country around. These circumstances at the first appeared unpropitious to the growth of this place. The establishment of the Federal government in 1789, and the settlement of the "new state" of Vermont, gave an impulse to the spirit of enterprise. The village of Van Derheyden being at the head of the natural navigation of the Hudson, after some struggle began to outstrip the "New City," which had been unwisely located above the rifts. The earliest surveys of the three allotments into which the site was originally divided, were made between the years 1786 and 1790; one or two slight buildings in 1786, and a small number the two years following. It is stated that by the spring of 1789, five small stores and about a dozen dwelling-houses had been erected. The appellation of Van Derheyden's Ferry was now changed into the more classic name of Troy.

In 1791, the county of Rensselaer was detached from Albany, and Troy was selected as the county seat. In 1793 the first courthouse was erected, and the jail the following year. The influential men among the first settlers were the friends of order, and supporters of the institutions of religion. When they were too few to support a clergyman, they were accustomed to assemble in a store at the sound of a conch-horn, and afterward in a school-house. Here they usually listened to a sermon read by Dr. Samuel Gall, or the late Col. Pawling, a revolutionary officer. In 1791, the inhabitants, too few to consult their denominational preferences, by an united effort erected a frame for a house of public worship, which was covered the following year, and although unfinished, was used as a place for public worship. This building became the first edifice of the Presbyterian congregation. The Rev. Dr. Jonas Coe was their first minister. His services at this period were divided between Troy and Lansingburg, his residence being in the latter place. An Episcopal church, an edifice of small dimension of brick, was erected in 1804, which was enlarged some years afterward, and is now known as St. John's church. In 1805, the Baptist congregation erected a house of worship in Third-street, which was afterward enlarged. The

---

* Mr. Elijah Adams, now (1840) 77 years of age, who has resided here about 60 years, states that when he first knew the Van Derheyden lands, there were patches or strips within the present site of the city, known as the *corn grounds* of the native Indians. Sometime after he had taken up his residence here, a full grown bear swam across the Hudson, landed near the upper ferry, and on being pursued ran across the low land among the small oaks, and at length ascended a pine tree near the present location of the Rensselaer Institute, and was there brought to the ground by a shot from his rifle.

Methodist Episcopal congregation erected their first house of worship in State-street in 1809.

Northwestern view of the Troy Female Seminary.

The Troy Female Seminary, located in this place, holds a high rank among the institutions of learning in our country. John H. and Sarah L. Willard are the principals, and Nancy Hinsdale the vice-principal: there are besides 21 teachers and officers. The following account and historical sketch has been kindly furnished by an individual well acquainted with it.

The school of which the Troy Seminary is a continuation, was begun in Middlebury, Vermont, in 1814, by Mrs. Emma Willard. It there obtained considerable celebrity, and the Principal was solicited to remove it to Waterford, in this state. She consented on the condition that the most influential gentlemen of that place should unite in carrying before the legislature a petition for incorporating and endowing a public institution for females. Their approbation of this measure was made to depend on that of De Witt Clinton, then governor of the state. On being presented with the plan, he expressed his high approval, and introduced the subject into his message.

In the winter of 1818–19, the petition was, under his auspices, presented to the legislature, and for the first time the rights of woman in regard to education, were plead in a legislative hall. Among its supporters were Mr. Van Buren, and Mr. John C. Spencer. The justice of the claim was acknowledged, an institution on the proposed plan incorporated, and a bill for endowment brought in, but the adjournment of the legislature prevented its passage.

In the spring of 1819, the proposed school went into operation in Waterford, in the large building now occupied as a hotel, that having been hired for two years. The next winter-session of the legislature defeated the hopes which had been excited of an endowment, but in the mean time private patronage was abundant.

In 1821, the school being large, and no place being provided in Waterford for its accommodation, it was removed to Troy, the corporation of that city having voted $4,000 for a building. Since that period, the rents of the building have been made to meet the interest and almost all the principal of the moneys expended in its several enlargements and in the additions to its grounds. Since 1837 this institution has received from the state a share of the literature fund, by which the library, apparatus, &c., previously furnished by the Principal, have been made more complete. This school has educated at least five thousand pupils; of whom about one tenth have been teachers, and it has furnished Principals for many of the most distinguished female schools in every part of the Union. The present Principal of this seminary, Mrs. Sarah L. Willard, spent nineteen years in the institution as pupil, teacher, and vice-principal, before assuming its government. But the larger number of the young ladies here educated have married, and are now, many of them, standing in the first circles and among the first women of our country in regard to piety and moral worth, domestic usefulness, and intellectual and social accomplishments. Several of the pupils have been distinguished as authors. About twenty teachers are constantly employed. The number of pupils being about two hundred, gives an average of one teacher to ten pupils. The objects of education as stated in the original plan are considered to be, first, religious and moral; second, literary; third, domestic; and fourth, ornamental. But to obtain these ends, the physical and mental powers must be developed and strengthened in due order and proportion. Great care has been bestowed on health, and but one death of a pupil, and that a sudden one from organic affection of the heart, has occurred.

The Rensselaer Institute is an excellent institution under the charge of Professor Eaton. Many young men are here fitted for the profession of civil engineering. The system of teaching is thorough and *practical*.

The city of Troy is regularly laid out, on a plan similar to that of Philadelphia. The principal street is River-street, which extends along the Hudson the whole length of the city, and is ornamented with many splendid and spacious stores. It is the theatre of a very extensive business. The remaining portion of the place generally exhibits the quiet aspect of the country. Many of the buildings, both public and private, are spacious and elegant. The courthouse, built of Sing Sing marble, is a splendid edifice, after the Grecian model. St. Paul's church is a noble Gothic edifice, erected at an expense of about 50,000 dollars. There are in Troy twelve places of public worship—viz, 3 Presbyterian, 2 Episcopal, 2 Methodist, 1 Scotch Presbyterian, 1 Roman Catholic, 1 African church, and 2 Friends meeting-houses. On the Wynant and Poestens kills, which here empty into the Hudson, are several extensive manufacturing establishments. The city is abundantly supplied with excellent water from the neighboring hills. Hydrants are placed at the corners of the streets with hose attached, which in case of fire, as the natural head of the water is 75 feet above the city level, supersedes the use of fire-engines. Troy is indebted in a great measure for its prosperity to its advantageous situation, and the enterprise and industry of her inhabitants. She has extensively availed herself of the facilities afforded by the river and the Erie and Champlain canals. The tides of the Hudson frequently ascend to a dam thrown across the river about a mile and a half above the centre of the city. By means of a lock, sloop navigation is thus afforded to the village of Waterford. Within the last few years Troy has increased rapidly in wealth and population. In 1820 her population was 5,268; in 1830, 11,566; in 1840, 19,373. The Rensselaer and Saratoga railroad, 24 miles to Ballston Spa, crosses the Hudson at this place by a bridge 1,600 feet in length.

Rensselaerwyck, or the *manor of Rensselaer*, includes a very extensive tract on both sides of the Hudson, in nearly the centre of which is the city of Albany. It is 24 miles wide on the river, and about 42 miles long, east and west. It includes in its area all of Rensselaer county, excepting the towns of Schaghticoke, Hoosick, and Pittstown, and the greater part of Albany county. The title to this patent is derived from several successive grants by the government of Holland, dating as far back as 1641, when the first grant was made to Killian Van Rensselaer, who had purchased the native right to the soil, under conditions stipulated by the government of Holland. "When this country changed masters, passing from the Dutch to the English, again for a short time to the Dutch, and finally again to the English, some controversies arose about indemnities, but the private right of the original

NORTHERN VIEW OF TROY, N. Y., FROM MOUNT OLYMPUS.

Mt. Olympus, from which the view was taken, is an elevation 120 feet in height, a short distance north of the city. The bridge across the Hudson, 1600 feet in length, with part of the flourishing village of West Troy, are seen on the right.

proprietor of the colony of Rensselaerwyck was never questioned. And on the 4th of March, 1685, the whole was confirmed by letters patent, under the great seal of the province of New York, by Thomas Dongan, lieutenant-governor of the same. The original design of the Dutch government extended only to the founding of colonies in this country by citizens of Holland, who should amicably acquire the Indian title to the lands; and the founder of a colony was therefore styled its patroon by the bill of privileges and the deed of conveyance, the latter of which was only granted when the native right had been acquired by purchase." A great portion of the land is permanently leased, and rent annually paid in the products of the soil to the patroon at Albany.

RICHMOND COUNTY.

Richmond, an original county, was organized November 1, 1683. and comprises Staten Island, Shooter's Island, and the islands of meadow on the west side of Staten Island. It is about 14 miles long, and its greatest breath is 8; mean breadth 5 miles. It is divided into 4 towns, all of which were organized in 1788. Pop. 10,985.

The higher and naked points of the island, (says Gordon in his Gazetteer,) afford varied and delightful prospects. Hence, in a clear day, may be seen the ever-growing city with its painted steeples and gilded spires hemmed in by a forest of masts; the broad bay studded with fairy islands, and whitened by the canvass of a hundred ships, overhung by small dark clouds, strongly relieved against the deep blue sky, which proceed from the many steamboats moving upon the waters, like things of life. Long Island, with its swelling hills and richly cultivated farms; the coast of New Jersey in a circular sweep of 40 miles, from Paulus Hook to the Neversink hills and Sandy Hook lighthouse; and last, but not least, the wide Atlantic, opening between the Hook and Long Island. From the point at New York Bay along the Kills, to a point nearly opposite to Elizabethtown landing, a distance of 5 miles, the shore has an almost unbroken street, in which neat country seats, and snug boxes of the citizens blend with the cottages of farmers, mechanics, fishermen, and watermen, who are the permanent inhabitants. This settlement, containing about 400 houses, is divided into 3 portions having separate names, viz: Northfield, Factoryville, and New Brighton. From landings along the sound, communication may be had almost hourly by steamboats with New York. The soil of the island consists of clay and sandy loam, and with good husbandry produces fine crops of oats, corn, and grass. Many of the inhabitants subsist by the fisheries. The muddy bottom of Staten Island sound produces an inexhaustible supply of oysters; which though not originally of good quality, on being transported to the beds in Raritan Bay, soon grow large and acquire an excellent flavor. The Raritan Bay affords also excellent clams, and those from the Great Kills are in high repute. The shad and herring fisheries are productive. In a military point of view, the island is one of the most important positions on the coast; its possessor having command of New York bay and the adjacent country. It was so deemed by the British, in the revolutionary war, and was the first place seized by Sir William Howe, (July 4th, 1776.) It was retained by the royal forces during the whole contest. Preparatory to the war of 1812, there were erected very efficient and extensive fortifications, known as forts Tompkins, Richmond, and Hudson, at the Narrows, opposite to Fort Fayette, on Long Island. These forts completely protect the strait, which is but one mile wide. Upon Signal Hill, back of the forts, overlooking the harbor, Sandy Hook, and a great extent of sea, is a telegraph communicating with the city. Staten Island was purchased from the Indians for Michael Pauw, one of the directors of the West India Company, together with an extensive tract in Bergen county in New Jersey, by deed dated August 10, 1630, and the whole tract received the name of Pavonia. It was a very desirable spot with the primitive Dutch settlers; and the Indians, who seem never to have considered themselves to lose right of possession by sale, and were always willing to convey for a consideration, sold the island, about the year 1638, to the Heer Melyn with the permission of Gov. Kieft; and subsequently in 1657, to the Baron Van Cappellan. Melyn and Van Cappellan, both made improvements; but the colony settled by the latter, was broken up by the savages from the Raritan, who murdered his people. Melyn subsequently obtained the exclusive title, and claiming to be independent of New Amsterdam, gave Gov. Stuyvesant much trouble. On the 14 June, 1659, he conveyed his rights to the company. This island was again purchased from the Indians by Gov. Lovelace, April 18, 1670.

Sailor's Snug Harbor.

CASTLETON, upon the Kills and New York bay, is the northeastern town of the county. Pop. 4,286. Tompkinsville, beautifully situated upon the bay, 5½ miles from New York city, and 7 from Richmond the county seat, was named after Vice-president Tompkins, whose seat was upon the summit of the hill. This is the largest village in the county, and, including Stapleton, contains 3,000 inhabitants, 500 dwellings, and 1 Episcopal, 1 Dutch Reformed, and 1 Methodist church. The Quarantine ground for the port of New York is situated here. Factoryville is a manufacturing village of about 100 dwellings in the NW. portion of the town, upon the Kill Van Kull. The far-famed village of New Brighton is situated about a mile N. of Tompkinsville, at the NE. point of the island. It was founded in 1834, by Thomas E. Davis, Esq., of New York. It is intended for residences of business men from the city. Nowhere, perhaps, in our country can be found such an assemblage of beautiful villas, and so favorably located as at this spot, both as regards health and beauty of scenery. With this, and the places in the vicinity, hourly communication by steamers is kept up with the city. The New Brighton Pavilion is in all respects one of the most splendid hotels in the Union—every lodging-room is equal to a gentleman's parlor. There are here superior facilities for sea-bathing.

The "Sailor's Snug Harbor," is a charitable institution for aged or infirm seamen, pleasantly located about a mile W. of New Brighton. The buildings are in the Grecian style, with marble fronts; the main building, 65 by 100 feet, has marble pillars in front, and is connected by corridors with wings of 53 by 100 feet. Cost of construction $115,000. The institution was founded in 1801, by Robert Richard Randall of New York, who bequeathed 22 acres for this purpose in the 15th ward, which at that time was of comparatively little value, but now has increased to an immense estate. Connected with the building is a farm of 160 acres. In the yard fronting the edifice is an elegant monument to the memory of the founder. No worthy applicant has ever yet been rejected. There are here at present 110 of the sons of Neptune, many of whom having dropped their last anchor, have found a snug port for life.

NORTHFIELD is situated upon the NW. end of the island, and has a population of 2,747. The principal village, Port Richmond, contains 1 Baptist, 1 Methodist, and 1 Presbyterian church, and about 75 dwellings. Chelsea is a small village on Staten Island sound, opposite the mouth of Rahway river, containing a number of handsome dwellings.

SOUTHFIELD, on the SE. side of the island, has a population of 1,626. Richmond, the county seat, 13 miles from New York, is a neat but antiquated village, partly located in this town and in Northfield and Westfield. It contains 2 churches, 2 hotels, a courthouse and jail, and about 45 dwellings. At the Narrows are the forts Tompkins, Richmond, and Hudson, and the Signal Hill. At the termination of New Dorp lane on the shore is the "great elm," which serves as a landmark to the mariner out at sea. The village of Stapleton, which is but a continuation of Tompkinsville, is partly on the Castleton line. Here is located the "Seaman's retreat," a noble stone edifice. The heights in this vicinity are studded with numerous country seats.

WESTFIELD, at the SW. extremity of the island, has a population of 2,326. Rossville, named after Wm. E. Ross, Esq., is a small village 4½ miles N. of Richmond, and contains 32 dwelling-houses, 3 mercantile stores, and 181 inhabitants.

ROCKLAND COUNTY.

ROCKLAND COUNTY was taken from Orange in 1798; greatest length 23, greatest breadth 18 miles. It is situated in the extreme southern angle of the state, upon the west side of the Hudson. Its surface is generally much broken, and in the W. and NW. mountainous. The valleys are rich, extensive, and fertile. Dobbs Ferry, Stony Point, Fort Clinton, and the Pass, were noted in the annals of the revolution. "This county includes all that part of Orange which was settled when that county was erected, except so much thereof as fell to New Jersey, upon the determination of the boundary. Orangetown, now in Rockland, was the capital of the county until 1737, when a courthouse and jail were built at Goshen, in Orange, and the courts were holden at the two places alternately. About 1774, the courthouse and jail at Orangetown, having been destroyed by fire, and part of the village having been transferred to New Jersey, public buildings were erected at the 'New City' then in the precinct of Haverstraw." The New York and Erie railroad commences at Piermont, and running through Orangetown, Clarkstown, and Ramapo, enters Orange county in the town of Monroe. This county is divided into 4 towns. Pop. 11,874.

CLARKSTOWN, taken from Haverstraw in 1791, lies on the W. bank of the Hudson, opposite Tappan and Haverstraw bays, 28 miles N. of New York. Clarkstown and the New City are small villages, each several miles from the Hudson, the latter of which is the county seat. Pop. 2,538.

HAVERSTRAW, the northern town of the county, organized in 1788, is situated 36 miles N. of New York, on the Hudson. Pop. 3,348. Warren, upon the Hudson, near the S. line, contains about 60 dwellings. Sampsondale, 2 miles from the river, is a small village. Caldwells Landing is in the northern part of the town. Fort Clinton, of the revolution, was in the NE. angle, on the bank of the Hudson, the ruins of which are now visible. (For the attack on this fortress see p. 422.) Stony Point is at the NW. extremity of Haverstraw bay, above which is the Dunderberg or Thunder Mountain.

Northern view of Stony Point, on the Hudson.

The above is a northern view of Stony Point, as seen when passing down the Hudson. This place is a little rough promontory on the west bank of the Hudson, nearly a mile below the entrance of the Highlands, having a lighthouse on its summit. It was a fortified during the revolutionary war, and is distinguished by the celebrated assault made upon it on the 16th July, 1779, by Gen. Wayne. Verplanck's Point, on the opposite side of the river, is also a place distinguished in the history of the revolution. The following is an account of the storming of Stony Point as communicated in a letter from Gen. Wayne to Washington, dated Stony Point, July 17th, 1779.

" Sir,—I have the honor to give you a full and particular relation of the reduction of this Point, by the light infantry under my command.

" On the 15th instant at twelve o'clock we took up our line of march from Sandy Beach, distant fourteen miles from this place; the roads being exceedingly bad and narrow, and having to pass over high mountains, through deep morasses, and difficult defiles, we were obliged to move in single files the greatest part of the way. At eight o'clock in the evening the van arrived at Mr. Springsteels, within one mile and a half of the enemy, and formed into columns as fast as they came up, agreeably to the order of battle annexed; namely, Colonels Febiger's and Meigs' regiments, with Major Hull's detachment, formed the right column; Colonel Butler's regiment and Major Murfey's two companies the left. The troops remained in this position until several of the principal officers with myself had returned from reconnoitring the works. At half after eleven o'clock, being the hour fixed on, the whole moved forward. The van of the right consisted of one hundred and fifty volunteers, properly officered, who advanced with unloaded muskets and fixed bayonets, under the command of Lieutenant-Colonel Fleury; these were preceded by twenty picked men, and a vigilant and brave officer to remove the *abatis* and other obstructions. The van of the left consisted of one hundred volunteers, under the command of Major Stewart, with unloaded muskets and fixed bayonets, also preceded by a brave and determined officer, with twenty men, for the same purpose as the other.

"At twelve o'clock the assault was to begin on the right and left flanks of the enemy's works, whilst Major Murfey amused them in front; but a deep morass covering their whole front, and at this time overflowed by the tide, together with other obstructions, rendered the approaches more difficult than was at first apprehended, so that it was about twenty minutes after twelve before the assault began; previously to which I placed myself at the head of Febiger's regiment, or the right column, and gave the troops the most pointed orders not to fire on any account, but place their whole dependence on the bayonet, which order was literally and faithfully obeyed. Neither the deep morass, the formidable and double rows of *abatis*, nor the strong works in front and flank, could damp the ardor of the troops, who, in the face of a most tremendous and incessant fire of musketry, and from cannon loaded with grape-shot, forced their way at the point of the bayonet through every obstacle, both columns meeting in the centre of the enemy's works nearly at the same instant. Too much praise cannot be given to Lieutenant-colonel Fleury (who struck the enemy's standard with his own hand,) and to Major Stewart, who commanded the advanced parties, for their brave and prudent conduct.

"Colonels Butler, Meigs, and Febiger conducted themselves with that coolness, bravery, and perseverance, that will ever insure success. Lieutenant-colonel Hay was wounded in the thigh, bravely fighting at the head of his battalion. I should take up too much of your excellency's time, were I to particularize every individual who deserves it for his bravery on this occasion. I cannot, however, omit Major Lee, to whom I am indebted for frequent and very useful intelligence, which contributed much to the success of the enterprise; and it is with the greatest pleasure I acknowledge to you, that I was supported in the attack by all the officers and soldiers under my command, to the utmost of my wishes. The officers and privates of the artillery exerted themselves in turning the cannon against Verplanck's Point, and forced the enemy to cut the cables of their shipping, and run down the river.

"I should be wanting in gratitude were I to omit mentioning Captain Fishbourn and Mr. Archer, my two aids-de-camp, who on every occasion showed the greatest intrepidity, and supported me into the works after I received my wound in passing the last *abatis*.

"Enclosed are the returns of the killed and wounded of the light infantry, as also of the enemy, together with the number of prisoners taken, likewise of the ordnance and stores found in the garrison.

"I forgot to inform your excellency, that previously to my marching, I had drawn General Muhlenberg into my rear, who, with three hundred men of his brigade, took post on the opposite side of the marsh, so as to be in readiness either to support me, or to cover a retreat in case of accident; and I have no doubt of his faithfully and effectually executing either, had there been any occasion for him.

"The humanity of our brave soldiery, who scorned to take the lives of a vanquished foe calling for mercy, reflects the highest honor on them, and accounts for the few of the enemy killed on the occasion.

"I am not satisfied with the manner in which I have mentioned the conduct of Lieutenants Gibbons and Knox, the two gentlemen who led the advanced parties of twenty men each. Their distinguished bravery deserves the highest commendation. The former belongs to the sixth Pennsylvania regiment, and lost seventeen men killed and wounded in the attack; the latter belongs to the ninth Pennsylvania regiment, and was more fortunate in saving his men, though not less exposed. I have the honor to be, &c.

"ANTHONY WAYNE."

"The number of prisoners taken in the fort was *five hundred and forty-three*. By General Wayne's return the number of killed was sixty-three. In Colonel Johnson's official account of the transaction, his loss in killed is stated to have been only twenty. It is not easy to reconcile this discrepancy. The assailing party had fifteen killed and eighty-three wounded.

"Congress passed resolves highly complimentary to the officers and privates engaged in this enterprise, and confirming the promise of reward which had been previously made by General Wayne; and also directing the value of all the military stores taken at Stony Point to be ascertained and divided among the troops who were engaged in storming the fort.

"The rewards were as follows: to the first man who entered the enemy's works, five hundred dollars; to the second, four hundred dollars; to the third, three hundred; to the fourth, two hundred; to the fifth, one hundred; being fifteen hundred dollars in the whole. The ordnance and other stores were estimated at one hundred and fifty-eight thousand six hundred and forty dollars; which amount was divided among the troops in proportion to the pay of the officers and men.

"Three different medals, emblematical of the action, were struck by order of congress, bearing the names respectively of Wayne, Fleury, and Stewart."

ORANGETOWN was organized in 1788: it is 24 miles N. of New York. Pop. 2,771. Tappan 3, and Middletown 6 miles from the Hudson, are small villages. Piermont, on the river, is a thriving village, formerly known as the Sloat. The New York and Erie railroad commences here, by a pier in the river, nearly a mile in length. About a mile below Piermont, is Dobbs Ferry, a noted place in the revolution. Nyack, in the north part of the town, on the Hudson, is a flourishing place containing about 50 or 60 dwellings.

North view of the place where Andre was executed.

The place where Andre was executed is at the summit of a hill, about a quarter of a mile west of Tappan village, and overlooking to the east a romantic and fertile valley. A small heap of stones, thrown hastily together, with an upright stake and a few names carved rudely upon it, is the only monument to mark the spot of his execution and his grave. While in Tappan village, Andre was confined in an ancient stone mansion, at present occupied as a tavern by Mr. Thomas Wandle. His trial took place in the old Dutch church, which was torn down in 1836. A new one has since been erected on the same site. Washington's head-quarters were in the antiquated stone dwelling now occupied by Mr. Arthur Johnson.

The following account of the execution of Andre, which took place Oct. 2, 1780, is given by an eye-witness.

"I was at that time an artificer in Col. Jeduthan Baldwin's regiment, a part of which was stationed within a short distance of the spot where Andre suffered. One of our men, (I believe his name was Armstrong,) being one of the oldest and best workmen at his trade in the regiment, was selected to make his coffin, which he performed and painted black, agreeable to the custom in those times.

"At this time Andre was confined in what was called a Dutch church, a small stone building, with only one door, and closely guarded by six sentinels. When the hour appointed for his execution arrived, which I believe was 2 o'clock, P. M., a guard of three hundred men were paraded at the place of his confinement. A kind of procession was formed by placing the guard in single file on each side of the road. In front were a large number of American officers of high rank, on horseback; these were followed by the wagon containing Andre's coffin—then a large number of officers on foot, with Andre in their midst. The procession moved slowly up a moderately rising hill, I should think about a fourth of a mile to the west. On the top was a field without any enclosure; in this was a very high gallows, made by setting up two poles or crotches, laying a pole on the top. The wagon that contained the coffin was drawn directly under the gallows. In a short time Andre stepped into the hind end of the wagon—then on his coffin—took off his hat and laid it down—then placed his hands upon his hips, and walked very uprightly back and forth, as far as the length of his coffin would permit, at the same time casting his eyes upon the pole over his head and the whole scenery by which he was surrounded. He was dressed in what I should call a complete British uniform; his coat was of the brightest scarlet, faced or trimmed with the most beautiful green; his under clothes, or vest and breeches, were bright buff, very similar to those worn by military officers in Connecticut at the present day; he had a long and beautiful head of hair, which, agreeable to the fashion, was wound with a black riband, and hung down his back. All eyes were upon him, and it is not believed that any officer in the British army, placed in his situation, would have appeared better than this unfortunate man.

"Not many minutes after he took his stand upon the coffin, the executioner stepped into the wagon with a halter in his hand, on one end of which was what the soldiers in those days called a hangman's knot, which he attempted to put over the head and around the neck of Andre, but by a sudden movement of his hand this was prevented. Andre took off the handkerchief from his neck, unpinned his shirt collar, and deliberately took the end of the halter, put it over his head, and placed the knot directly under his right ear, and drew it very snugly to his neck; he then took from his coat pocket a handkerchief and tied it over his eyes. This done, the officer that commanded (his name I have forgotten) spoke in rather a loud voice, and said that his arms must be tied. Andre at once pulled down the handkerchief he had just tied over his eyes, and drew from his pocket a second one, and gave to the executioner, and then replaced his handkerchief. His arms were tied just above the elbows, and behind the back: the rope was then made fast to the pole overhead. The wagon was very suddenly drawn from under the gallows, which, together with the length of rope, gave him a most tremendous swing back and forth, but in a few moments he hung entirely still. During the whole transaction he appeared as little daunted as Mr. John Rogers, when he was about to be burnt at the stake; but his countenance was rather pale. He remained hanging, I should think, from 20 to 30 minutes, and during that time the chambers of death were never stiller than the multitude by which he was surrounded. Orders were given to cut the rope, and take him down without letting him fall; this was done, and his body carefully laid on the ground.—Shortly after, the guard was withdrawn and spectators were permitted to come forward to view the corpse, but the crowd was so great that it was some time before I could get an opportunity. When I was able to do this, his coat, vest, and breeches were taken off, and his body laid in the coffin, covered by some under clothes. The top of the coffin was not put on. I viewed the corpse more carefully than I had ever done that of any human being before. His head was very much on one side, in consequence of the manner in which the halter drew upon his neck. His face appeared to be greatly swollen and very black, much resembling a high degree of mortification; it was indeed a shocking sight to behold. There was at this time standing at the foot of the coffin, two young men of uncommon short stature—I should think not more than four feet high. Their dress was the most gaudy that I ever beheld. One of them had the clothes just taken from Andre hanging on his arm. I took particular pains to learn who they were, and was informed that they were his servants, sent up from New York to take care of his clothes, but what other business I did not learn.

"I now turned to take a view of the executioner, who was still standing by one of the posts of the gallows. I walked nigh enough to him to have laid my hand upon his shoulder, and looked him directly in his face. He appeared to be about twenty-five years of age, his beard of two or three week's growth, and his whole face covered with what appeared to me to be blacking taken from the outside of a greasy pot. A more frightful looking being I never beheld—his whole countenance bespoke him to be a fit instrument for the business he had been doing. Wishing to see the closing of the whole business, I remained upon the spot until scarce twenty persons were left, but the coffin was still beside the grave, which had previously been dug. I now returned to my tent, with my mind deeply imbued with the shocking scene I had been called to witness."

In August, 1831, the remains of Andre were disinterred and conveyed to London. The annexed narration of this event, is extracted from the account given by the British consul, J. Buchanan, Esq., to whom this duty was intrusted by the Duke of York.

" . . . . . . My next step was to proceed to Tappan, distant from this city [New York] twenty-four miles. Thither I went, accompanied by Mr. Moore, his majesty's agent for packets. Upon reaching the village, which does not contain above fifty or sixty houses, the first we inquired at proved to be the very house in which the major had been confined while a prisoner there, kept by one Dupuy, who was also postmaster, who took us to view the room which had been used as his prison. Excited as we were, it would be difficult to describe our feelings on entering this little chamber; it was then used as a milk and store room—otherwise unaltered from the period of his confinement—about twelve feet by eight, with one window looking into a garden, the view extending to the hill, and directly to the spot on which he suffered, as the landlord pointed out from the window, while in the room, the trees growing at the place where he was buried.

" Having inquired for the owner of the field, I waited on the Rev. Mr. Demarat, a minister residing in Tappan, to whom I explained the object of my visit, who generously expressed his satisfaction at the honor, ' which at length,' to use his words, ' was intended the memory of Major Andre,' and assured me that every facility should be afforded by him. Whereupon we all proceeded to examine the grave, attended by many of the inhabitants, who by this time had become acquainted with the cause of our visit; and it was truly gratifying to us, as it was honorable to them, that all were loud in the expressions of their gratification on this occasion.

" We proceeded up a narrow lane, or broken road, with trees at each side, which obscured the place where he suffered, until we came to the opening into the field, which at once led to an elevated spot on the hill. On reaching the mount, we found it commanded a view of the surrounding country for miles. General Washington's head-quarters, and the house in which he resided, was distant about a mile and a half or two miles, but fully in view. The army lay encamped chiefly also in view of the place, and must necessarily have witnessed the catastrophe. The field, as well as I could judge, contained from eight to ten acres, and was cultivated; but around the grave the plough had not approached nearer than three or four yards, that space being covered with loose stones thrown upon and around the grave, which was only indicated by two cedar trees about ten feet high. A small peach tree had also been placed at the head of the grave, by the kindly feeling of a lady in the neighborhood.

" Doubts were expressed by many who attended, that the body had been secretly carried to England, and not a few believed we should not find the remains; but their surmises were set aside by the more general testimony of the community. . . . . Arriving at Tappan by ten o'clock, A. M., though I was not expected until the following Tuesday, as I had fixed, yet a number of persons soon assembled, some of whom betrayed symptoms of displeasure at the proceeding, arising from the observations of some of the public journals, which asserted ' that any honor paid Major Andre's remains was casting imputation on General Washington, and the officers who tried him.' As these characters were of the lowest cast, and their observations were condemned by every respectable person in the village, I yet deemed it prudent, while the worthy pastor was preparing his men to open the grave, to resort to a mode of argument, the only one I had time or inclination to bestow upon them, in which I was sure to find the landlord a powerful auxiliary. I therefore stated to these noisy patriots, that I wished to follow a custom not unfrequent in Ireland, from whence I came, namely, of taking some spirits before proceeding to a grave. The landlord approved the Irish practice, and accordingly supplied abundance of liquor, so that in a short time, General Washington, Major Andre, and the object of my visit, were forgotten by them, and I was left at perfect liberty, with the respectable inhabitants of the place, to proceed to the exhumation, leaving the landlord to supply the guests, a duty which he faithfully performed, to my entire satisfaction.

"At twelve o'clock, quite an unexpected crowd assembled at the grave,—as our proceeding up the hill was seen by the inhabitants all around. The day was unusually fine; a number of ladies, and many aged matrons who witnessed his fall,—who had seen his person,—who had mingled tears with his sufferings,—attended, and were loud in their praises of the prince, for thus at length honoring one who still lived in their recollection with unsubdued sympathy. The laborers proceeded with diligence, yet caution. Surmises about the body having been removed were revived, and it would be difficult to imagine any event which could convey a degree of more intense excitement.

"As soon as the stones were cleared away, and the grave was found, not a tongue moved amongst the multitude,—breathless anxiety was depicted in every countenance. When, at length, one of the men cried out he had touched the coffin, so great was the enthusiasm at this moment, that I found it necessary to call in the aid of several of the ladies to form an enlarged circle, so that all could see the operation; which being effected, the men proceeded with the greatest caution, and the clay was removed with the hands, as we soon discovered the lid of the coffin was broken in the centre. With great care the broken lid was removed, and there to our view lay the bones of the brave Andre, in perfect order. I, among others, for the first time discovered that he had been a small man; this observation I made from the skeleton, which was confirmed by some then present. The roots of the small peach tree had completely surrounded the skull like a net. After allowing all the people to pass round in regular order, and view the remains as they lay, which very many did with unfeigned tears and lamentation, the bones were carefully removed, and placed in the sarcophagus, (the circle having been again formed;) after which I descended into the coffin, which was not more than three feet below the surface, and with my own hands raked the dust together, to ascertain whether he had been buried in his regimentals or not, as it was rumored among the assemblage that he was stripped; for, if buried in his regimentals, I expected to find the buttons of his clothes, which would have disproved the rumor;* but I did not find a single button, nor any article save a string of leather that had tied his hair, in perfect preservation, coiled and tied as it had been on his hair at the time. This string I forwarded to his sister in England. I examined the dust of the coffin so minutely (as the quantity would not fill a quart) that no mistake could have arisen in the examination. Let no unworthy motive be attributed to me for recording this fact; I state it as one which I was anxious to ascertain for the reason given. Having placed the remains in the sarcophagus, it was borne amidst the silent and unbought regret of the numerous assemblage, and deposited in the worthy pastor's house, with the intention of removing it to his majesty's packet, in New York city, on the Tuesday following.

"As soon as the removal of the sarcophagus to the packet was known in this city, it was not only honorable to the feelings of the citizens, but cheering to my mind, depressed as it had been, to find the sentiments which prevailed. Ladies sent me flowers; others, various emblematic devices, garlands, &c., to decorate the remains of the 'lamented and beloved Andre.' A beautiful and ornamented myrtle among those sent, I forwarded with the sarcophagus to Halifax, where Lieut. General Sir James Kempt, governor of Nova Scotia, caused every proper mark of respect to be paid to the remains. From thence they reached London, and were deposited near the monument which had been erected to his memory in the Abbey, and a marble slab placed at the foot of the monument, on which is set forth their removal by the order of his royal highness the Duke of York.

"Having represented to his royal highness the generous conduct of the Reverend Mr. Demarat, I recommended that his royal highness should convey to him a snuff-box, made out of one of the trees which grew at the grave, which I sent home. But my suggestion was far outdone by the princely munificence of his royal highness, who ordered a box to be made out of the tree, and lined with gold, with an inscription, 'From his Royal Highness the Duke of York, to the Rev. Mr. Demarat.' Whilst speaking of this act of liberality, I was unexpectedly honored with a silver inkstand, with the following inscription :—' The surviving sisters of Major Andre to James Buchanan, Esq., his Majesty's Consul, New York.' They also sent a silver cup, with a suitable inscription, to Mr. Demarat. I need not add, that I cherish this inkstand, (which I am now using,) and shall bequeath it to my children as a memorial which I prize with no ordinary feeling.

---

* It has since been ascertained, from an American officer present at the burial, that the regimentals of Major Andre were given to his servants, after his execution. This statement has satisfied Mr. Buchanan, and will account for the absence of any vestiges in his tomb.

"I omitted to mention, that I had the peach tree which had been planted on the grave, (the roots of which had surrounded the skull, as set forth,) taken up with great care, with as much of the clay as it was possible to preserve around the roots, and brought it to my garden in New York, where my daughters attended it with almost pious solicitude, shading it during the heat of the day, watering it in the cool of the evening, in the hope of preserving it to send to England. Had it reached his sisters, they would no doubt have regarded it as another Minerva; for, though it did not spring out of, yet it was nourished by their beloved brother's head.

"I have only to add, that, through the kind interference of my brother consul at Philadelphia, I obtained Major Andre's watch, which he had to part with when a prisoner during the early part of the war. This watch I sent to England lately; so that I believe every vestige connected with the subject of this narrative has been sent to the land of his birth, in the service of which his life was sacrificed."

RAMAPO, originally named New Hempstead, was taken from Haverstraw in 1791; centrally distant from New York 33 miles. The manufacturing village of Ramapo Works is situated in the *Pass*, which during the revolution was fortified. It is 13 miles W. from New City, the county seat, and contains 1 Presbyterian church and 80 dwellings. The names of the post-offices in this town are Ramapo, Scotland, and West Hempstead. Pop 3,217.

ST. LAWRENCE COUNTY.

ST. LAWRENCE COUNTY was taken from Oneida in 1802; distant from New York 350, from Albany NW. 206 miles. Greatest length on the St. Lawrence river, which bounds it on the N., 66 miles; greatest breadth 64. This county is larger by 1,000 square miles than any other in the state. That portion of it bordering upon the St. Lawrence, and extending 30 or 40 miles into the country, is agreeably diversified; waving in gentle swells and broad valleys, with extensive tracts of champaign. The soil is warm, rich, and productive, and equal to any of the uplands of the state. The southeastern part is broken and mountainous. These mountains abound with fine iron ore. The county is comparatively unsettled, but is now filling up rapidly. Since 1820, the population has more than trebled. This county extends 75 miles along the St. Lawrence. The many large streams, with their branches, furnish some internal navigation, with superabundance of hydraulic power. The St. Lawrence has a good sloop navigation from Lake Ontario to Ogdensburg. From Ogdensburg to Montreal, the navigation is dangerous on account of the rapids. This river is studded with numberless islands, rendering the scenery highly picturesque and beautiful. Wheat is raised upon the new lands, but there is danger of its being winter-killed in the long and almost unmitigated frosts. Rye, grass, and all the summer crops flourish luxuriantly; and it is obvious that the great source of wealth here will be found in grass farming and the culture of sheep. The county is divided into 25 towns. Pop. 56,676.

ST. LAWRENCE COUNTY.   483

BRASHER, taken from Massena in 1805; from Albany 250, and from Canton centrally distant NE. 39 miles. Pop. 2,118. Upon the forks of the St. Regis and North Deer rivers is the small post village of Helena, in the vicinity of which, on these streams, there is considerable hydraulic power.

CANTON was organized in 1805; from Albany 206 miles. Pop. 3,464. A natural canal, 6 miles long, and from 30 to 100 yards wide, connects in this town the Grasse with the Oswegatchie river. The "high falls" of the Grasse river are in the south part of the town, and

Western view of Canton.

near the northwest corner the falls of the Oswegatchie. The village of Canton, 18 miles from Ogdensburg, on the Grasse river, was made the county seat in 1828, previous to which time the courts were holden at Ogdensburg. The village contains the county buildings, an academy, 5 churches—1 Presbyterian, 1 Episcopal, 2 Methodist, 1 Baptist and Universalist united, called the Union church—and about 150 dwellings. This village was originally called "Foot's Falls," from Mr. Stillman Foot, who came here in the winter of 1799, and bought a mile square, comprising in its limits the site of the village. He erected a saw and a grist mill upon the ground now occupied by a saw-mill upon the west bank of the river. He was accompanied by George Foot, Jr., Amos Jones, and Medad Moody, all with their families, and originally from Middlebury, Vt. The Presbyterian, the first church erected here, was built in 1826. Mr. George Foot, the father of Stillman, was the first person who died in this town. His death occurred in 1800, and as there were no boards from which to construct a coffin, the body was wrapt in a blanket, enclosed in spruce bark, and buried.

DE KALB, on the Oswegatchie river, taken from Oswegatchie in 1806; from Albany 193 miles. Pop. 1,530. This town was purchased in 1803, by the late Judge Cooper of Cooperstown, Otsego county, and was settled by emigrants from Connecticut and Vermont. De Kalb village, formerly Cooper's village, 15 miles SE. from Ogdensburg, and Richville, are both small settlements.

DE PEYSTER was taken from De Kalb and Oswegatchie in 1825; from Ogdensburg centrally distant S. 9 miles. Pop. 1,032. De Peyster is a small settlement.

EDWARDS, taken from Fowler in 1827; centrally distant SE. from Ogdensburg 30 miles. Pop. 956. Edwardsville and South Edwards are small settlements.

FOWLER, taken from Rossie and Russel in 1816; from Albany 106 miles, comprising townships Nos. 7 and 11 of Great Tract No. 3 of Macomb's purchase. Centrally distant about 30 miles S. of Ogdensburg. Shingle Creek, Little York, and Fowlersville, are the names of the post-offices. Pop. 1,752.

GOUVERNEUR, named after Gouverneur Morris, taken from Oswegatchie in 1810; from Albany 180, from Ogdensburg centrally distant S. 25 miles. Pop. 2,529. "One of the ancient Indian works of fortification is in this town, on a farm of now or late Capt. Washburn, consisting of an embankment enclosing three acres, in which there are some remains of rude sculpture." Gouverneur is a small and pleasant village, and contains 2 churches and a flourishing academy. Washburnville is the name of a post-office.

HAMMOND, taken from Rossie and Morristown in 1827; from Albany 184, from Ogdensburg centrally distant SW. 22 miles. Hammond and South Hammond are small settlements. Pop. 1,845.

HERMON, originally named Depau, taken from Edwards and De Kalb in 1830; from Albany 180, centrally distant from Ogdensburg SE. 23 miles. Depauville is a small post village. Pop. 1,271.

HOPKINTON was organized in 1805. Pop. 1,149. Hopkinton, on Lyd brook, 234 miles from Albany, and 25 E. from Canton, is a small village. Port Jackson is a small settlement.

LAWRENCE, taken from Hopkinton and Brasher in 1828; from Albany 232, centrally distant E. from Ogdensburg 50 miles. Lawrenceville and Nicholville are small settlements. Pop. 1,835.

LISBON, organized in 1801; from Albany 211 miles. Pop. 3,508. On Stoney Island, in the St. Lawrence, a strong fort was built by the French, but was destroyed by Gen. Amherst in 1760. Three miles below Ogdensburg in this town was an Indian village of the Oswegatchie tribe, now in ruins. Rensselaerburg, formerly called Red Mills, on the St. Lawrence, is a considerable manufacturing village.

LOUISVILLE, taken from Massena in 1810; from Albany 231, centrally distant from Ogdensburg NE. 22 miles. Pop. 1,687. The battle at Williamsburg, in Canada, was fought opposite here, Nov. 11th, 1813. The town was settled in 1803, by eastern emigrants. Louisville post-office is on Grasse river. Churchville is a small settlement on the St. Lawrence.

MADRID, organized in 1802; from Albany 227, from Canton N. 15 miles. Pop. 4,510. This town belonged to Messrs. I. Waddington, D. A. Ogden, and T. L. Ogden. Waddington village, on the river St. Lawrence, 20 miles N. of Canton, has 8 mercantile stores, and 800 inhabitants. Columbiaville is a small village on the Grasse river.

MATILDAVILLE, recently formed; from Canton SE. centrally distant 17 miles. Matildaville is a small village.

MASSENA, organized in 1802; from Albany 238, centrally distant from Ogdensburg NE. 36 miles. Massena is a small village, and Massena Point a hamlet. Pop. 2,726.

MORRISTOWN, taken from Oswegatchie in 1821; NW. from Albany 190. Black Lake extends centrally across the town. Pop. 2,853. Morristown, on the St. Lawrence, 10 miles SW. from Ogdensburg, is a small but beautifully situated village.

NORFOLK was taken from Louisville in 1823; from Ogdensburg E. 26 miles. Pop. 1,132. There are two small villages on the Racket river in this town.

OSWEGATCHIE was organized in 1802, and is from Albany 200 miles. Pop. 5,719. The importance of this spot seems to have been discovered at an early day, the French having built a fort here at quite a remote period. On the maps published by them 100 years since, it is called *Fort Presentation*, afterward named Oswegatchie. It was situated either on or near the site of the ruins now standing, on the west bank of the river, near its mouth. Previous to 1796, there was not much of any settlement, when Judge Nathan Ford, an enterprising individual, from New Jersey, settled in the place. The British had had a garrison here, and the military works, then in a ruinous condition, were taken possession of by him in behalf of the proprietors. They consisted of 2 stone buildings of 2 stories, a bomb proof, a row of wooden barracks, and three or four other wooden structures. Ford gave a new spring to the settlement, and was soon followed by many New Englanders. The party who emigrated with him hired a Canadian batteaux, sailed up the Mohawk into the Wood creek, then down the Oswego river into Lake Ontario, and finally landed at the mouth of the Oswegatchie. Thomas Lee, now at an advanced age, (1840,) is the only person living of the party.

At this period there was a settlement of Indians at Indian Point, 4 miles down the St. Lawrence. They were very jealous of the judge, and made several attempts to drive him off, which would have succeeded had he not been a man of more than ordinary resolution. One night a party of them came to his house, built a fire in the centre of the floor, mastered his men, and were in the act of placing one of them on the fire, when the judge attacked them with a billet of wood, and being seconded by some of his men, was enabled to drive them off. The first frame building, a dwelling, was erected near where the Eagle Tavern now stands.

Ogdensburg, the port of this town, has a population of 2,555. It is 204 miles N. from Albany, 60 below Kingston, 130 from Montreal, 120 W. from Plattsburgh, 63 NE. from Sacketts Harbor, and 18 from Canton. This was formerly the county seat, but it has been re-

View of Ogdensburg.

moved to Canton. The above view was taken on the bank of the Oswegatchie river, near the ruins of the old barracks. The steeple seen on the left is that of the Presbyterian church; the one on the extreme right the old courthouse; the academy is next to it; and the square steeple is that of the Episcopal denomination. The first religious society organized was the Presbyterian; they held their meetings, as far back as 1811, in the old courthouse. In 1819, they erected their first church, a few rods southwest of where the present stone church now stands. There are here 1 Baptist, 1 Methodist, 1 Episcopal, 1 Roman Catholic, and 1 Presbyterian church, besides a society of Unitarians.

The proximity of the town to the Canada line made it an important place during the late war, and the scene of several minor military operations. The following is extracted from Thompson's History of the Late War.

<blockquote>
In retaliation for a daring exploit performed by Capt. Forsyth of the rifle regiment, in the destruction of an immense quantity of stores, &c., collected at the small village of Gananoque, in the town of Leeds, in Canada, "the enemy determined on attacking and destroying the town of Ogdensburg. Opposite to this is situated the Canadian village of Prescott, before which the British had a strong line of breastworks. On the 2d of October, 1812, they opened a heavy cannonading on the town from their batteries, and continued to bombard it with little intermission until the night of the 3d: one or two buildings only were injured. On Sunday, the 4th, having prepared forty boats, with from ten to fifteen armed men in each, they advanced with six pieces of artillery, to storm the town. General Brown commanded at Ogdensburg in person, and when the enemy had advanced within a short distance, he ordered his troops to open a warm fire upon them. The British, nevertheless, steadily approached the shore, and kept up their fire for two hours; during which, they sustained the galling fire of the Americans, until one of their boats was taken, and two others so shattered, that their crews were obliged to abandon them; they then relinquished the assault and fled to Prescott. There has been no engagement, perhaps, which exhibited more gallantry on both sides. In this attack, Gen. Brown had under his command about 400 men, the British 1000."
</blockquote>

The annexed account of the taking of this place on the 21st of February, 1813, is extracted from the same source as the above.

"The movements of the enemy at Prescott were indicative of an intention to attack Ogdensburg. Colonel Benedict was therefore induced to call out his regiment of militia, and arrangements were immediately made for the defence of the place. On the 21st of February, the enemy appeared before it, with a force of twelve hundred men, and succeeded in driving out Captain Forsyth and his troops. The British attacked in two columns, of six hundred men each, at 8 o'clock in the morning, and were commanded by Capt. M'Donnell of the Glengary light infantry, and Colonel Fraser of the Canadian militia. The American riflemen and militia received them with firmness, and contended for the ground upwards of an hour; when the superiority of numbers compelled them to abandon it, and to retreat to Black Lake, nearly nine miles from Ogdensburg, after losing twenty men in killed and wounded. The loss of the enemy, from the deliberate coolness with which the riflemen fired, was reputed to have been thrice that number. The British account, which claimed the capture of immense stores, none of which had ever been deposited there, admitted the loss of five distinguished officers. In consequence of this affair, a message was sent by the commandant of Fort George, to Colonel M'Feely, the commandant of Fort Niagara, informing him that a salute would be fired the next day in honor of the capture of the American village. Colonel M'Feely having received intelligence in the course of the same evening, of the capture of his majesty's frigate the Java, returned the message to the British commandant, by communicating to him his intention of firing a salute, at the same hour from Fort Niagara, in celebration of this brilliant event."

The following additional particulars respecting the taking of Ogdensburg were obtained by personal conversation with a resident at that time. The British landed in the northeast part of the village, near some barracks occupied by a detachment of militia under Captain Lytle, which he evacuated and then joined Col. Forsyth at the fort. The enemy marched up through Ford-street, and when the Americans had abandoned the fort, they crossed over on the ice opposite to the Eagle Hotel. Besides the public stores destroyed by them, they took away a large quantity of provisions, &c., private property, which they were much in need of, but for which they afterward paid full price. A barn is now standing on the SE. side of Ford-street, near the corner of Water-street, where holes made by grape shot fired from the fort are still to be seen. The Glengarian regiment, which was in the attack, was quite celebrated during the military operations on the frontier. This corps were from the county of Glengary, in Upper Canada. Their religion was Catholic, and they were the descendants of Scotch Highlanders.

The following is a view of Windmill Point and ruins in its vicinity. It is memorable as being the spot, where, during the recent struggle in Canada, a small body of men, under the unfortunate Van Schoultz, gallantly defended themselves against an overpowering force of British and Canadians. The following account of this affair, usually termed the "Battle of Prescott," is principally drawn from a work recently published by E. A. Theller, Esq., and entitled Canada in 1837–8.

Early in November, 1838, the patriots, (so called,) who had secretly rallied in clubs in and about Syracuse, Oswego, Sacketts Harbor, Watertown, Ogdensburg, French creek, and at other points on or near the American line, began to exhibit an intention of making a fresh demonstration at some point in Upper Canada. About the 10th, two schooners were noticed as being freighted from canal boats, which had come up the Oswego canal under suspicious circumstances, and to sail out of the harbor in a northern direction. On the 12th, the steamboat United States, which had been detained in port by a heavy gale, sailed for Sacketts Harbor. Here she took aboard about 250 patriots. The two schooners spoken of, were next discovered by the United States, lying in the river St. Lawrence; when Capt. Van Cleve complied with the request of a passenger of respectable appearance, to take them in tow; saying they were loaded with merchandise for Ogdensburg, which he

View of Windmill Point, Prescott, U. C.*

was desirous of getting into port the next morning. Accordingly the schooners were lashed one each side of the steamer. The boxes and barrels on their decks, with just men enough in sight to navigate them, exhibited no evidence of their being other than represented by the passenger. The captain was soon undeceived, by armed men climbing from the schooners on to his boat, to the number of some 200, and he determined to lay at Morristown, 10 miles above Ogdensburg, and give notice to the authorities. On arriving at that neighborhood, the patriots, after transferring about 100 of the boat's passengers, unfastened their vessels, and were found the next morning at anchor in the river, between Ogdensburg and Prescott, filled with armed men. Both towns were now the scene of excitement; for it was evident that Fort Wellington was the point of attack, and both shores were soon thronged with citizens. The Experiment, a British armed steamboat, was lying at the Prescott wharf, and by this time the United States had arrived at Ogdensburg. On her arrival, the people, with loud cheers, rushed on board and went to the relief of one of the schooners which by accident had got aground on the shoal in the river. Not succeeding in reaching her, they returned to the boat for a longer hawser. As she went out again, the Experiment came out and fired two shots, but without effect; and she passed down the river about a mile to Windmill Point, to the other schooner, which had succeeded in landing her forces, and was returning to take off the men from the grounded vessel. The Experiment followed her, and when the United States was covering her on her way up, kept up an irregular fire upon both, without effect. The United States having seen the schooner she was protecting anchored under the Ogdensburg shore, returned again to Windmill Point, where William Johnson with small boats landed 110 men. Meantime the American steam ferry-boat, Paul Pry, ran over to the stranded vessel, and hauled her off under a brisk fire from the Experiment, which the former returned with small-arms, killing 7 of the Experiment's men, but losing none. The United States was now returning, and again encountered the fire of the Experiment, breaking glass lights and doing other damage. Those who had remained after the disembarkation, about 25 in number, stood upon the promenade deck and cheered the discharges as they came. During this, a shot passing through the wheel-house, killed Mr. Solomon Foster, a young man, the helmsman of the boat. As the United States now went into port, she was surrendered to her owners, and immediately seized by the United States authorities, which completed the forenoon's operations.

"Commodore 'Bill Johnson' who had come on to Ogdensburg on the return of the United States, addressed 'the patriots' present, urging and beseeching them to go with him, and join those who had crossed. He succeeded in crossing with some, in one of the schooners, at two or three different times; whilst most of the afternoon and evening was occupied at Windmill Point, by the patriots, fortifying their position, and preparing for the contest. They had taken possession of the windmill, and other large stone buildings, to the number of about 200, which were increased by accessions from the small boats crossing over in the evening. It was seen that at Fort Wellington the British were also engaged in making preparations; but towards night there was scarcely a living soul seen in the streets of Prescott. There was no fighting that night. During the evening the steamboat

---

* The authors are indebted for the above view to Mr. Ellis, artist, of Ogdensburg.

Telegraph, with Col. Worth, of the United States army, had arrived, accompanied by two companies of United States troops, and by Mr. Garrow, a United States marshal, who immediately took into custody all the craft which had been employed by the patriots, including the United States, the two schooners, and the Paul Pry; and made effectual arrangements to cut off all further supplies of men, arms or provisions from the patriot camp, after which, all remained quiet during the night, except the report of cannon at long intervals. Early on the morning of the 13th, the British armed steamers Cobourg and Traveller, had arrived at Prescott with troops; and at about 7 o'clock, they, together with the Experiment, opened a discharge of cannon, and commenced throwing bombs at the patriots at the windmill, who discharged field-pieces from their battery on shore in return. At about 8 o'clock, a line of fire blazed along the summit of the hill, in the rear of the windmill, for about 80 or a 100 rods, and the crack of the rifles and muskets made one continuous roar. It appears that by the time the firing commenced in the morning, there were but 180 of those who had crossed left at Windmill Point; and that when they were attacked by land, in rear of their position, some 52 of these fled, leaving only 128 to face from 600 to 800 British regulars and volunteers. After a fight of about an hour, according to Theller's account, the British were driven back into their fort with a loss it is supposed of about 100 killed and many wounded. The patriots lost 5 men and 13 wounded. On the morning of the 14th little was done, and the British having sent a flag of truce for permission to bury the dead, the request was granted. Afterward when the patriots sent a flag, the bearer was shot. On the 15th, the British received a reinforcement of 400 regulars, with cannon and gun-boats, by steamboats from Kingston, and volunteers numbering in all about 2,000; who surrounded the mill by their gun-boats and steamers on the river, and by stationing cannon and troops on land; and keeping up a continual cannonading until Friday evening, when the patriots surrendered. At 5 o'clock, the same afternoon, a white flag was displayed from the mill, but no attention being paid to it, it was finally fastened on the outside; then 3 or 4 flags were sent out, and the bearers shot down as soon as seen. Immediately after the surrender, the British burnt 4 dwellings and two barns in the vicinity of the windmill. According to the account of Theller, 36 patriots were killed, 2 escaped, and 90 were made prisoners; and of the British about 150 men were killed and 20 officers, among whom was Capt. Drummond. The patriots were commanded by Van Schoultz, a Polander, who had fought for the freedom of his native land, and witnessed her expiring agonies at ill-fated Warsaw. When driven to desperation, he opposed the offering to the enemy the flag of truce, and besought his men to rush upon the enemy and die in the contest; but their ammunition and provisions were exhausted, and a five days' fatigue in active night and day defence had worn them out and made them indifferent to their fate. At the trials, Van Schoultz pleaded guilty and was sentenced to death, and was executed Dec. 9th, 1838, aged 31. Col. Dorephus Abbey, of Watertown, Jefferson county; Col. Martin Woodruff, of Salina, Onondaga county, and Daniel George, and others, suffered the same fate with Van Schoultz. A number of others were finally released, while the others were sentenced to transportation, and with those in a like situation, who had been respited, after their trials, and with Messrs. John G. Parker, Watson, and others, to the number of 23, were sent to England, and from thence, in company with 11 convicted felons, were transported to Van Diemen's Land."

PARISHVILLE, settled by the enterprise of Mr. David Parish; taken from Hopkinton in 1814; from Albany 195 miles. Pop. 2,251. Parishville, on the St. Regis river, and on the St. Lawrence and Malone turnpike, 39 miles SE. from Ogdensburg, is a small village. Lime and iron abound in the vicinity.

PIERREPOINT, taken from Hopkinton in 1814; from Albany 190, from Canton centrally distant SE. 10 miles. Pierrepoint is a small post village. Pop. 1,430.

PITCAIRN is a small and thinly settled town, recently formed. Pop. 396.

POTSDAM was taken from Madrid in 1806; from Albany 216, centrally distant from Canton NE. 10 miles. Pop. 4,460. The village of Potsdam is pleasantly situated at the falls of the Racket river, and contains several churches, a flourishing academy, numbering about 150 pupils, and about 130 dwellings. The annexed engraving shows

Western View of Potsdam.

the appearance of the village as entered from the west. The public building on the right is the Episcopal church; the two large edifices in the distance, with cupolas, are the academy buildings, each 4 stories in height; the buildings with spires between them are respectively the Methodist and Presbyterian churches, and the tall spire to the left is that of the Universalist church. This village was settled in 1803, by Benjamin Raymond, Esq., a native of Richmond, Berkshire county, Mass. He erected mills on the west side of Racket river. The first church erected was the Congregational, in 1822. James Chadwick was the first person who died in the village. He was killed in 1805, by the falling of a tree which he was chopping. During the late war, many left this section and vacated their farms from fear of the incursions of the British.

Rossie was taken from Russell in 1813; from Albany 178, from Ogdensburg centrally distant SW. 27 miles. Pop. 1,553. Rossie and Somerville are small villages in this town. The Rossie Iron Works were established in 1813. Exceedingly rich and valuable lead mines have here lately been discovered, and the reputation of the Rossie lead has now become widely spread.

Russell, named from Russell Atwater, by whom it was settled in 1805; organized in 1807; from Albany 194 miles. Russell, on the St. Lawrence turnpike and Grasse river, 12 miles S. from Canton, is a small village. Pop. 1,377.

Stockholm, taken from Massena in 1806; from Albany 227, from Ogdensburg, E., centrally distant 40 miles. Stockholm, West Stockholm, and Southville, are names of the post-offices. Pop. 2,993.

SARATOGA COUNTY.

SARATOGA COUNTY was taken from Albany in 1791; greatest length N. and S. 47, and greatest breadth E. and W. 30 miles. Centrally distant from Albany 36 miles. "Its name is supposed to be a corruption of the Indian word Sah-rah-ka, or the 'side hill.' The greater part of the lands in this tract were originally granted by the English crown to a company of 13 individuals, by the title of the patent of Kayaderosseras. Smaller portions were included in other patents. Thus Van Schaick's, of an earlier date, included the town of Waterford and adjacent country. The Saratoga patent embraced six miles square on the Hudson river north of Van Schaick's; and the apple patent, located on the Mohawk, extended 'three miles back into the woods,' towards Ballston Lake. The first recorded grant of lands in the Kayaderosseras patent was made in August, 1702. A good portion of the land is now held under a rent charge of from 15 to 20 cents an acre, derived originally from the above patent. Settlements were made in 1715 under that patent, and some probably earlier, along the Hudson, upon the patents of Van Schaick and Saratoga; but there was then none north of Fish creek, now Schuylersville, and few between that and the Mohawk. Until the conquest of Canada by the English, settlements were slowly made. After this, although rapidly formed, they were confined some years to the banks of the Hudson and Mohawk. The surface of the county presents a broad diversity, having the Kayaderosseras and Palmertown mountains in the northwest, and in the southeastern sandy plains, generally level, and along the Hudson and some of the smaller streams extensive tracts of rich alluvion. There are several small lakes, the largest of which are Saratoga, Ballston, or the Long Lake, Round Lake, Owl Pond, &c." This county is rich in historical incident. It has 20 towns. Pop. 40,542.

BALLSTON, organized in 1788; from Albany 25 miles. The first settlement here was made in 1763, by two brothers of the name of McDonald. The town has its name from the Rev. Eliphalet Ball, from Bedford, Westchester county, who, with a number of his congregation, settled about 2½ miles south of the springs. The Saratoga and Schenectady railroad runs through the town, and the Troy and Saratoga railroad enters it near the north boundary. Ballston Centre, East Line, and Burnt Hills are post-offices. Pop. 2,037.

CHARLTON, taken from Ballston in 1792; from Albany 25, from Ballston Spa SW. 8 miles. Pop. 1,937. Charlton is a small village, and West Charlton is a post-office.

CLIFTON PARK, taken from Half Moon in 1828; from Albany 15, from Ballston Spa S. 15 miles. Pop. 2,717. Willow Spring, on the Erie canal, Rexford Flats, Clifton Park, Vischer's Ferry, and Jonesville are post-offices.

CORINTH was taken from Hadley in 1818. It is N. from Albany 44, and from Ballston Spa N. 18 miles. Corinth, formerly Jesups Landing, is a small village; South Corinth is a post-office. The great falls of the Hudson are in this town, where there is a cataract of about 30 feet, and a rapid 1 mile above, with about the same descent. Above the falls there is a narrow place, about 12 feet wide and 20 feet long, where at low water the whole river passes through with astonishing rapidity. Pop. 1,365.

DAY, the northwestern town of the county, was originally named Concord and taken from Edinburgh and Hadley in 1819; from Albany 60, and from Ballston Spa NW. 35 miles. Day and West Day are post-offices. Pop. 943.

EDINBURGH, originally named Northfield, was taken from Providence in 1801; from Albany 50, and from Ballston Spa NW. 35 miles. Pop. 1,458. Edinburgh on the Scandanaga river is a small village.

GALWAY was taken from Ballston in 1792; from Albany 30, from Ballston Spa NW. 10 miles. Pop. 2,412. Galway's Corners and West Galway are small villages.

GREENFIELD, taken from Saratoga and Milton in 1793; centrally distant from Albany 36 miles. Pop. 2,807. West Greenfield 8 N., Greenfield Centre 10 miles N. from the Spa, and Porters Corners, are small settlements.

HADLEY, taken from Greenfield and Northumberland in 1801; from Albany 57, and from the Spa N. 27 miles. Pop. 865. Hadley on the Hudson river is a small settlement.

HALF MOON, bounded on the E. by the Hudson, was organized in 1788; from Albany 15, from Ballston Spa S. 16 miles. Middletown, Half Moon, and Mechanicsville are villages; the latter of which is noticed under Stillwater. The Champlain canal and Troy railroad run along the Hudson.

MALTA, taken from Stillwater in 1802; from Albany 25 miles. Pop. 1,459. The Troy and Ballston railroad crosses the town northwesterly. Dunning Street, 4 miles SE. from the Spa, and Maltaville, are small settlements.

MILTON, taken from Ballston in 1792; from Albany NNW. 30 miles. Pop. 3,149. Rock City, 6 miles NW., and Factory Village, 3 miles NW. from Ballston Spa, are small villages.

The village of Ballston Spa, the seat of justice for Saratoga county, was incorporated in 1807. It is 30 miles north from Albany, 15 from Schenectady, 24 from Troy, and 7 southwest from Saratoga Springs. The village is situated in a valley surrounded by hills, upon a branch of the Kayaderosseras creek, immediately around the mineral springs in the southeast corner of the town of Milton. The village contains about 180 dwellings, 3 churches—1 Presbyterian, 1 Baptist, and 1 Episcopal—a large courthouse of brick, and other county buildings, 2 newspaper printing offices, a number of hotels, of which the *Sans Souci* is the most prominent. This structure is of wood, having a front of 160 feet, and wings of 150 feet, and is three stories high.

View in Ballston.

"The mineral springs from which this village derives its importance and celebrity, were discovered in 1767. In 1772, Mr. Douglass erected a small log-house here for the accommodation of visiters. During the revolutionary war settlements in this part of the country were suspended, but about 1790 Mr. Douglass, enlarged his accommodations. In 1804, Nicholas Low, Esq., raised the well-known Sans Souci hotel. In 1807, several other springs, and in 1817, four springs of different qualities, were found near the great manufactory built by Mr. Low.

"The spring in the rear of the Sans Souci, and that in the rear of the village hotel, and the original spring at the west of the village, contain, as essential ingredients, the carbonates of soda, of lime, iron, and magnesia; the tonic qualities of the iron, and the sparkling and enlivening influence of the fixed air that they possess in an extraordinary degree, have a wonderful effect upon enervated, bilious, and debilitated constitutions.

"The use of the mineral waters here and at Saratoga is especially beneficial in all those affections termed bilious and dyspeptic, in calculous and nephritic complaints, in chronic rheumatism, gout, in ulcers and cutaneous disorders, scrofula, in mercurial diseases and strumous affections, in recent dropsy, paralysis, chlorosis, &c."

MOREAU, bounded on the E., N., and NW. by the Hudson, was taken from Northumberland in 1805; from Albany N. 50, from Ballston Spa NE. 21 miles. Pop. 1,575. Moreau, Reynolds Corners, and Clarksville are small settlements.

NORTHUMBERLAND, bounded E. by the Hudson, was taken from Saratoga in 1798; N. from Albany 40, and from Ballston Spa NE. 12 miles. Gansevoortville and Popes Corners are small settlements. Pop. 1,672.

PROVIDENCE, taken from Galway in 1796; from Albany NW. 36, from Ballston Spa NW. 18 miles. Pop. 1,512. Hagedorns Mills, Greensboro', and Johnsboro', are small settlements.

SARATOGA was organized in 1788; distant 15 miles N. from Ballston Spa, and 32 from Albany. Pop. 2,624. The surface of the township is moderately uneven on the Hudson, which forms the eastern boundary; there are some alluvial flats on the western border of the town around Saratoga lake; the soil is of a light sandy loam. Schuylerville, the principal village in the town, lies on the

Champlain canal near the mouth of Fish creek, which here flows into the Hudson, and consists of about 100 dwellings, 3 churches—1 Dutch Reformed, 1 Baptist, and 1 Methodist—and an academy, with several mills and factories.

Schuyler mansion-house, Schuylerville.

The above is a view of the mansion of the late Gen. Schuyler, in Schuylerville, which was built a short time after his house and mills at this place were destroyed by the army under General Burgoyne in 1777. This dwelling, the residence of George Strover, Esq., is a short distance south of the spot where Burgoyne surrendered his sword to General Gates. After the battle at Stillwater, Oct. 7th, he made an attempt to effect his retreat back to Fort Edward, but was unable to proceed any further than the mouth of Fish creek, where he was hemmed in by the American forces. The following account relative to the surrender of Burgoyne is from the 2d volume of Allen's American Revolution:—

"Previous to the action of the 7th, General Gates, anticipating the retreat of the enemy, had ordered Brigadier General Fellows, with 1,300 men, to cross the river, and take post on the heights opposite the Saratoga ford, supposing that he might be able to reinforce him before Burgoyne could reach the place. But the retreat of the British army being earlier than he expected, and the circumstances before related preventing him from pursuing immediately with the main army, or sending off any considerable detachment, General Fellows was placed in a critical situation, and nothing saved his detachment from destruction or capture, but the very slow movements of Burgoyne, occasioned by a heavy rain during the night of the 8th, and the badness of the roads, which compelled him to halt at Davocote, so that he did not reach Saratoga until the morning of the 9th. By this time General Fellows had received orders to recross the river and endeavor to oppose their passage, which he did just as the front of the British army entered Saratoga, and in time to post himself advantageously on the opposite bank of the river. On the evening before, his camp was so entirely unguarded, that Lieutenant-colonel Southerland, who had been sent forward by Burgoyne to reconnoitre, marched around it without meeting with a sentinel, and was so strongly impressed with the conviction that he could surprise him, that he solicited permission to attack him with his single regiment; and it was perhaps fortunate for General Fellows that Burgoyne refused.

"In the mean time several other bodies of militia were posted, to intercept the retreat of Burgoyne, in various directions, and one detachment was ordered to march immediately to Fort Edward, and take possession before any part of Burgoyne's troops could reach it. A rain on the 10th prevented General Gates from marching until the afternoon. When the front of the army reached Saratoga, about 4 o'clock, the British were encamped on the heights beyond the Fishkill, [Fish creek:] their boats lay at the mouth of the creek, and a fatigue party were at work in removing the baggage from the creek to the heights. General Fellows with his corps were on the opposite bank of the river, with a couple of small field-pieces on the plain, playing upon the enemy's fatigue party. General Gates on his arrival posted the army in several lines on the heights, about a mile in the rear of the Fishkill, with Colonel Morgan's corps in front. Under the idea that the enemy would retreat in the night, General Gates gave orders that the army should advance at *reveillee* in the morning of the 11th. A small detachment had been sent off by Burgoyne to possess themselves of Fort Edward, but finding it occupied by the Americans, had returned to camp: the movement of this detachment had given rise to the information which deceived General Gates, that the whole British army had moved off, leaving a small guard only in the camp to take care of the baggage and stores. Upon this intelligence it was determined to attack the camp early in the morning; and Brigadier-generals Nixon and Glover were ordered to cross the creek with their brigades for this purpose.

"Colonel Morgan advancing with his corps at daylight agreeably to orders, fell in with the enemy's picket, by whom he was fired upon, and lost a lieutenant and several privates. This induced him to suppose that the enemy had not moved as supposed, in which case his situation would be extremely critical, as the fog was so thick that nothing could be seen at the distance of twenty yards; a winding creek was in his rear, and he was unacquainted with the grounds. In this dilemma he was met by the Deputy Adjutant-general, Colonel Wilkinson, who had been sent out by the general for the purpose of reconnoitring. Wilkinson returned immediately to communicate this intelligence to the general, and Patterson's and Learned's brigades, both under the command of the latter, were sent to the support of Morgan. In the mean time the whole army had advanced as far as the ridge between the church and General Schuyler's house, where they halted. Generals Nixon and Glover were in advance, marching according to orders to the attack of the camp. Nixon had already crossed the creek, and Glover was preparing to follow him, when a deserter from the enemy was observed fording the creek, from whom information was received that Burgoyne with his whole army was still in his camp. This was confirmed by the capture of a reconnoitring party of a subaltern and 35 men, by the advance guard of 50 under Captain Goodale of Putnam's regiment, who discovered them through the fog just as he reached the bank of the creek, and making a resolute charge upon them, took them without firing a gun. The general was at this time a mile in the rear, and before this intelligence could be communicated to him, and orders received for the two brigades to desist and recross the river, the fog cleared up, and exposed to view the whole British army under arms. A heavy fire of artillery and small-arms was immediately opened upon Nixon's brigade, which was in advance, and they retreated in considerable disorder across the creek, with a trifling loss, and resumed their position.

"General Learned had in the mean time reached Morgan's corps with his two brigades, and was advancing rapidly to the attack, in obedience to a standing order which had been issued the day before, 'That in case of an attack against any point, whether front, flank or rear, the troops are to fall on the enemy at all quarters.' He had arrived within 200 yards of Burgoyne's strongest post, and in a few minutes more would have been engaged under great disadvantages, when Colonel Wilkinson reached him with intelligence that our right had given way, and that it would be prudent for him to retreat. Being without authority from the general to order it, the brave old general hesitated to obey, in opposition to the standing order, until Lieutenant-colonels Brooks and Tupper and some other officers coming up, a sort of council was held, and the proposition to retreat was approved. The moment they turned their backs, the enemy, who had been calmly expecting their advance, opened a fire upon them which was continued until they were masked by the wood. They retreated about half a mile, with Morgan on their left, and encamped in a strong position, which they held until the surrender of the British army."

On the 14th of October, Gen. Burgoyne sent Major Kingston to the head-quarters of Gen. Gates with a proposition for "a cessation of arms, during the time necessary to communicate the preliminary terms, by which in any extremity he and the army mean to abide." Gen. Gates had already prepared a schedule of the terms upon which he was willing to treat. This schedule evinced that he was well acquainted with the distresses of the British, and was drawn up in terms of extreme liberality. To the 9th article of Gen. Burgoyne's proposition, Gen. Gates affixed the following answer:

"'The *capitulation* to be finished by 2 o'clock, *this day*, the 15th, and the troops march from their encampment at 5, and be in readiness to move towards Boston to-morrow morning.' These preliminary articles and their answers being sent to General Burgoyne, produced the immediate return of his messenger with the following note. 'The eight first preliminary articles of Lieutenant-general Burgoyne's proposals, and the 2d, 3d, and 4th of those of Major-general Gates of yesterday, being agreed to, the formation of the proposed treaty is out of dispute, but the several subordinate articles and regulations necessarily springing from these preliminaries, and requiring explanations and precision, between the parties, before a definitive treaty can be safely executed, a longer time than that mentioned by General Gates in his answer to the 9th article, becomes indispensably necessary. Lieutenant-general Burgoyne is willing to appoint two officers immediately to meet two others from Major-general Gates to propound, discuss, and settle those subordinate articles, in order that the treaty in due form may be executed as soon as possible.'"

This meeting took place on the afternoon of the 15th, and the parties mutually signed articles of capitulation, or *convention*, as Gen. Burgoyne wished to have it designated. A copy of the convention was to be signed by Gen. Burgoyne and delivered the next morning. The following are the articles of convention.

Articles of Convention between Lieutenant-general Burgoyne and Major-general Gates.

"1st. The troops under Lieutenant-general Burgoyne to march out of their camp with the honors of war, and the artillery of the entrenchments, to the verge of the river where the old fort stood, where the arms and artillery are to be left; the arms to be piled by word of command from their own officers.

"2d. A free passage to be granted to the army under Lieutenant-general Burgoyne to Great Britain, on condition of not serving again in North America during the present contest; and the port of Boston is assigned for the entry of transports to receive the troops, whenever General Howe shall so order.

"3d. Should any cartel take place, by which the army under General Burgoyne, or any part of it, may be exchanged, the foregoing article to be void as far as such exchange shall be made.

"4th. The army under Lieutenant-general Burgoyne, to march to Massachusetts Bay, by the easiest, most expeditious, and convenient route; and to be quartered in, near, or as convenient as possible to Boston, that the march of the troops may not be delayed, when the transports arrive to receive them.

"5th. The troops to be supplied on their march, and during their being in quarters, with provisions, by General Gates' orders, at the same rate of rations as the troops of his own army; and if possible the officers' horses and cattle are to be supplied with forage at the usual rates.

"6th. All officers to retain their carriages, batt-horses and other cattle, and no baggage to be molested or searched; Lieutenant-general Burgoyne giving his honor that there are no public stores secreted therein. Major-general Gates will of course take the necessary measures for the due performance of this article. Should any carriages be wanted during the march, for the transportation of officers' baggage, they are, if possible, to be supplied by the country at the usual rates.

"7th. Upon the march, and during the time the army shall remain in quarters in Massachusetts Bay, the officers are not as far as circumstances will admit to be separated from their men. The officers are to be quartered according to rank, and are not to be hindered from assembling their men for roll-call and other necessary purposes of regularity.

"8th. All corps whatever of General Burgoyne's army, whether composed of sailors, batteauxmen, artificers, drivers, independent companies, and followers of the army, of whatever country, shall be included in the fullest sense and utmost extent in the above articles, and comprehended in every respect as British subjects.

"9th. All Canadians, and persons belonging to the Canadian establishment, consisting of sailors, batteauxmen, artificers, drivers, independent companies, and many other followers of the army, who come under no particular description, are to be permitted to return there; they are to be conducted immediately by the shortest route to the first British post on Lake George, are to be supplied with provisions in the same manner as the other troops, and are to be bound by the same condition of not serving during the present contest in North America.

"10th. Passports to be immediately granted for three officers not exceeding the rank of captains, who shall be appointed by Lieutenant-general Burgoyne, to carry despatches to

Sir William Howe, Sir Guy Carleton, and to Great Britain, by the way of New York; and Major-general Gates engages the public faith, that these despatches shall not be opened. These officers are to set out immediately after receiving their despatches, and are to travel the shortest route, and in the most expeditious manner.

"11th. During the stay of the troops in Massachusetts Bay, the officers are to be admitted on parole, and are to be allowed to wear their side-arms.

"12. Should the army under Lieutenant-general Burgoyne find it necessary to send for their clothing and other baggage to Canada, they are to be permitted to do it in the most convenient manner, and the necessary passports granted for that purpose.

"13. These articles are to be mutually signed and exchanged to-morrow morning, at 9 o'clock, and the troops under Lieutenant-general Burgoyne are to march out of their entrenchments at 3 o'clock in the afternoon.

(Signed) "HORATIO GATES, Major-general.
(Signed) "J. BURGOYNE, Lieutenant-general.

"Saratoga, Oct. 16th, 1777.

"To prevent any doubts that might arise from Lieutenant-general Burgoyne's name not being mentioned in the above treaty, Major-general Gates hereby declares, that he is understood to be comprehended in it, as fully as if his name had been specifically mentioned.
"HORATIO GATES."

"The brass artillery captured from Burgoyne at various times during the campaign, amounted to 42 pieces, constituting one of the most elegant trains ever brought into the field; 5,000 stand of arms, 6,000 dozen of cartridges; and a number of ammunition wagons, travelling forges, shot, carcasses, shells, &c., also fell into the hands of the Americans. The whole number of troops surrendered by the convention amounted to 5,763, which added to the number killed, wounded, and captured, in the several actions previous to the 17th October, amounting to near 5,000, makes Burgoyne's total loss of upwards of *ten thousand men.*

"On the morning of the 17th the troops of Burgoyne were marched out of their camp to the plain near the river, where their arms were deposited; and the victorious Americans took possession of their lines."

The annexed cut is a copy of the signature of General Burgoyne, attached to the articles of the convention now in possession of the New York Historical Society.

Fac-simile of Gen. Burgoyne's signature.

General Wilkinson's account of the interview between Gates and Burgoyne on the field of surrender is interesting.

"Early in the morning of the 17th, I visited General Burgoyne in his camp, and accompanied him to the ground, where his army was to lay down their arms, from whence we rode to the bank of the Hudson river, which he surveyed with attention, and asked me whether it was not fordable. 'Certainly, sir; but do you observe the people on the opposite shore?' 'Yes,' replied he, 'I have seen them too long.' He then proposed to be introduced to General Gates, and we crossed the Fishkill, and proceeded to head-quarters, General Burgoyne in front, with his adjutant-general Kingston, and his aids-de-camp Captain Lord Petersham, and Lieutenant Wilford behind him; then followed Major-general Philips, the Baron Reidesel, and the other general officers, and their suites, according to rank. General Gates, advised of Burgoyne's approach, met him at the head of his camp, Burgoyne in a rich royal uniform, and Gates in a plain blue frock; when they had approached nearly within sword's length, they reined up, and halted. I then named the gentlemen, and General Burgoyne, raising his hat most gracefully, said 'The fortune of war, General Gates, has made me your prisoner;' to which the conqueror, returning a courtly salute, promptly replied, 'I shall always be ready to bear testimony, that it has not been through any fault of your excellency.' Major-general Phillips then advanced, and he and General Gates saluted, and shook hands with the familiarity of old acquaintances. The Baron Reidesel, and the other officers, were introduced in their turn."

SARATOGA COUNTY.

Fac-simile of Philip Schuyler's signature.

" GEN. PHILIP SCHUYLER was born at Albany in 1731, of an ancient and respectable family. When quite young he became a member of the New York legislature, and was eminent for his intelligence and usefulness. To him and Governor Clinton it was chiefly owing that the province made an early and decided resistance to those British measures which terminated in the independence of the colonies. When the revolution commenced, he was appointed, June 19, 1775, a major-general, and was directed to proceed immediately from New York to Ticonderoga, to secure the lakes, and make preparations for entering Canada. Being taken sick in September, the command devolved upon Montgomery. On his recovery, he devoted himself zealously to the management of the affairs in the northern departments. He gave much attention to the superintendence of the Indian concerns. On the approach of Burgoyne, in 1777, he made every exertion to obstruct his progress; but the evacuation of Ticonderoga by St. Clair, occasioning unreasonable jealousies in regard to Schuyler, in New England, he was superseded by Gen. Gates in August; and an inquiry was directed by congress to be made into his conduct. He was afterward, though not in the regular service, very useful to his country in the military transactions of New York. He was a member of the old congress; and when the present government of the United States commenced its operation in 1789, he was appointed a senator in the national legislature. He was chosen a second time in 1797, to the same station. In the senate of New York, he contributed probably more than any other man to the code of laws adopted by the state. He died at his seat near Albany, Nov. 18, 1804, in the 73d year of his age. He possessed great strength of mind and purity of intention. In the contrivance of plans of public utility, he was wise and circumspect, and in their execution, enterprising and persevering. In his deportment he was dignified and courteous. He was a pleasant and instructive companion, and in all the functions of private life was highly exemplary."—*Encyclopedia Americana.*

View in the village of Saratoga Springs.

SARATOGA SPRINGS was taken from Saratoga in 1819. Pop. 2,624. The village of Saratoga Springs is 181 miles from New York, 36½ from Albany, and 6½ from Ballston Spa. It is located in a fertile country, and contains 6 churches, several literary institutions, and about 2,000 inhabitants. The above engraving was taken from near the circular railway, and exhibits the principal portion of the village, with a view of the elegant Grecian colonnade erected over the Congress spring, seen near the centre of the picture. This place derives its attractions from its medicinal springs. These are situated on the margin of a vale, bordering the village on the east, and are the continuation of a chain of springs discovering themselves about 12 miles to the south, in the town of Ballston. The springs in this vicinity are 18 or 20 in number, the principal of which are the Congress, the Iodine or Walton, Putnam's, Congress, the Monroe, the Hamilton, the Flat Rock, the High Rock, the Columbian, and the Washington. A new spring has lately been discovered, whose waters are gaining high favor with the public, and are said to be beneficial in consumption. The hotels in this place are numerous, and some of them truly elegant, built in good taste, with spacious piazzas, and yards ornamented with shrubbery. The facility with which it is visited, by railroads from Albany and Troy, with other thoroughfares, together with the numerous attractions of the place, has rendered Saratoga the summer resort of thousands from all parts of our wide-spread country.

Western view of the battle-ground, Stillwater.

STILLWATER was organized in 1788. It is centrally situated from Albany 22 miles. The general surface is level, and the river hills of a moderate height. Pop. 2,733. The village of Mechanicsville is situated on a section of land between Hudson river and the canal. It consists of about 50 or 60 dwellings, partly in this, and partly in the town of Half Moon, 2 or more churches, several mills and factories on Anthony's kill, which forms the southern boundary of the town. Stillwater is a small village on the canal, about 4 miles above Mechanicsville. This town is distinguished in history as being the battle-ground of the armies of Gens. Gates and Burgoyne in 1777.

The above shows the appearance of the battle-ground on Freeman's farm, as seen from near the front of Mr. J. Walker's house, 2½ miles from Pattison's tavern, and about 2 miles from Hudson river.

Freeman's house stood a few feet south of the southernmost building seen in the engraving; the line of trees or woods seen behind the buildings is the spot where Burgoyne formed his line on the brow of the elevated plain previous to the battle of Sept. 19th; Willard's mountain on the east side of the Hudson is seen in the distance. About 15 rods south from Mr. Walker's house, in what then was called a meadow, is the spot where Gen. Frazer was mortally wounded; it is a little west of a road running N. and S. which has since been made near this place. About 60 rods in a SW. direction was the hottest of the fight, on the 7th of October. Near the place where Frazer fell, a hole or grave was dug, into which the bodies of 40 soldiers were thrown, after being stripped of their clothing by the women of the camp. Maj. Ackland was wounded a little east of the present road. The following account of the battles is drawn from various sources.

"The army arrived at Stillwater on the 9th of September, fully determined to face the foe, and if necessary pursue him into his own confines. This was at first supposed to be an eligible position for throwing up a line of intrenchments, and a large party under the engineer Kosciusko were accordingly set to work for that purpose. But upon a more narrow inspection of the grounds, the general determined to change his position, and occupy Bemus's heights, which were taken possession of and fortified on the 12th. Burgoyne at this time lay opposite to Saratoga, occupying old Fort Miller and Battenkill; but what were his further intentions, Gen. Gates had no means of judging. In this situation the deputy adjutant-general, Col. James Wilkinson, volunteered to head a select reconnoitring party, and obtain if possible the desired information. He left the camp with 170 men, under cover of a dark night, and arrived by daylight at Davocote, about two miles from Saratoga. Here he posted the greater part of his men in a wood near the road, and proceeded himself to the heights of Fish creek; from which position he discovered a column of the enemy drawn up under arms, on the opposite bank of the creek, within 300 yards of him, and another column under march, descending the heights below Battenkill. Being satisfied from these circumstances that Gen. Burgoyne was advancing, Col. Wilkinson returned to camp with his party, bringing with him three prisoners, who confirmed the intelligence.

"On the 15th, Gen. Burgoyne having crossed the river some days before, had advanced as far as Davocote, where he halted 24 hours for the purpose of repairing the bridges and roads in his advance, for the more convenient march of his army. On the 18th, Gen. Arnold was sent out with 1,500 men, to harass and impede him, but returned without accomplishing any thing; Burgoyne continuing his march until he had arrived within 2 miles of Gen. Gates's camp. Here he encamped in a line extending from the river to a range of hills 600 yards distant, and upon which were posted the *elite* of his army. The position occupied by Gen. Gates, as described by an eye-witness, and one who knew it well, was as follows :—' His right occupied the brow of the hill near the river, with which it was connected by a deep intrenchment; his camp in the form of a segment of a great circle, the convex towards the enemy, extended rather obliquely to his rear, about three-fourths of a mile to a knoll occupied by his left; his front was covered from the right to the left of his centre, by a sharp ravine running parallel with his line, and closely wooded; from thence to the knoll at his extreme left, the ground was level and had been partially cleared, some of the trees being felled, and others girdled; beyond which, in front of his left flank, and extending to the enemy's right, there were several small fields in very imperfect cultivation, the surface broken and obstructed with stumps and fallen timber, and the whole bounded on the west by a steep eminence. The extremities of this camp were defended by strong batteries, and the interval was strengthened by a breastwork without intrenchments, constructed of the bodies of felled trees, logs and rails, with an additional battery at an opening left of the centre. The right was almost impracticable; the left difficult of approach.'"
—*Allen's Rev.*

While in this position, the battle of the 19th Sept. took place; the following account of which is from Gen. Wilkinson's Memoirs.

"This battle was perfectly accidental; neither of the generals meditated an attack at the time, and but for Lieut. Col. Colburn's report, it would not have taken place; Burgoyne's movement being merely to take ground on the heights in front of the great ravine, to give his several corps their proper places in line, to embrace our front and cover his transport, stores, provisions, and baggage, in the rear of his left; and on our side, the defences of our camp being not half completed, and reinforcements daily arriving, it was not Gen. Gates's policy to court an action. The misconception of the adverse chiefs put them on the defensive, and confined them to the ground they casually occupied at the beginning of the action, and prevented a single manœuvre, during one of the longest, warmest, and most obstinate battles fought in America.

"The theatre of action was such, that although the combatants changed ground a dozen times in the course of the day, the contest terminated on the spot where it began. The British line was formed on an eminence in a thin pine wood, having before it Freeman's farm, an oblong field, stretching from its centre towards its right, the ground in front sloping gently down to the verge of this field, which was bordered on the opposite side by a close wood. The sanguinary scene lay in the cleared ground, between the eminence occupied by the enemy, and the wood just described. The fire of our marksmen from this wood was too deadly to be withstood by the enemy in line, and when they gave way and broke, our men, rushing from their covert, pursued them to the eminence, where, having their flanks protected, they rallied, and, charging in turn, drove us back into the wood, from whence a dreadful fire would again force them to fall back; and in this manner did the battle fluctuate, like the waves of a stormy sea, with alternate advantage for four hours, without one moment's intermission. The British artillery fell into our possession at every charge, but we could neither turn the pieces upon the enemy, nor bring them off; the wood prevented the last, and the want of a match the first, as the linstock was invariably carried off, and the rapidity of the transitions did not allow us time to provide one. The slaughter of this brigade of artillerists was remarkable, the captain and 36 men being killed or wounded out of 48. It was truly a gallant conflict, in which death by familiarity lost his terrors, and certainly a drawn battle, as night alone terminated it; the British army keeping its ground in rear of the field of action, and our corps, when they could no longer distinguish objects, retiring to their own camp."

From the period this battle was fought, (Sept. 19th,) to October 7th, the time was spent by Gen. Burgoyne in strengthening his position, and by Gen. Gates in collecting reinforcements. Gen. Burgoyne is said to have planned an attack on the 20th and 21st of September, but fortunately it was delayed until the Americans were in the best situation to oppose him. Attacks on the British piquets took place almost every evening, and they were continually harassed. The following is Gen. Wilkinson's account of the battle of Oct. 7th.

"On the afternoon of October 7th, the advanced guard of the centre beat to arms; the alarm was repeated throughout the line, and the troops repaired to their alarm posts. I was at head-quarters when this happened, and with the approbation of the general, mounted my horse to inquire the cause; but on reaching the guard where the beat commenced, I could obtain no other satisfaction, but that some person had reported the enemy to be advancing against our left. I proceeded, over open ground, and ascending a gentle acclivity in front of the guard, I perceived, about half a mile from the line of our encampment, several columns of the enemy, 60 or 70 rods from me, entering a wheat field which had not been cut, and was separated from me by a small rivulet; and without my glass I could distinctly mark their every movement. After entering the field they displayed, formed the line, and set down in double ranks with their arms between their legs. Foragers then proceeded to cut the wheat or standing straw, and I soon after observed several officers mounted on the top of a cabin, from whence with their glasses they were endeavoring to reconnoitre our left, which was concealed from their view by intervening woods.

"Having satisfied myself, after fifteen minutes attentive observation, that no attack was meditated, I returned and reported to the general, who asked me what appeared to be the intentions of the enemy. 'They are foraging, and endeavoring to reconnoitre your left; and I think, sir, they offer you battle.' 'What is the nature of the ground, and what your opinion?' 'Their front is open, and their flanks rest on the woods, under cover of which they may be attacked; their right is skirted by a lofty height. I would indulge them.' 'Well, then, order on Morgan to begin the game.' I waited on the colonel, whose corps was formed in front of our centre, and delivered the order; he knew the ground and inquired the position of the enemy; they were formed across a newly cultivated field, their grenadiers with several field-pieces on the left, bordering on a wood and a small ravine formed by the rivulet before alluded to; their light infantry on the right, covered by a worm fence at the foot of the hill before mentioned, thickly covered with wood; their centre composed of British and German battalions. Col. Morgan, with his usual sagacity, proposed to make a circuit with his corps by our left, and under cover of the wood to gain the height on the right of the enemy, and from thence commence the attack, so soon as our fire should be opened against their left; the plan was the best which could be devised, and no doubt contributed essentially to the prompt and decisive victory we gained.

"This proposition was approved by the general, and it was concerted that time should be allowed the colonel to make the proposed circuit, and gain his station on the enemy's right before the attack should be made on their left; Poor's brigade was ordered for this service, and the attack was commenced in due season on the flank and front of the British grenadiers, by the New Hampshire and New York troops. True to his purpose, Morgan at this critical moment poured down like a torrent from the hill, and attacked the right of the enemy in front and flank. Dearborn, at the moment when the enemy's light infantry were attempting to change front, pressed forward with ardor, and delivered a close fire; then leaped the fence, shouted, charged, and gallantly forced them to retire in disorder; yet, headed by that intrepid soldier, the Earl of Balcarras, they were immediately rallied, and re-formed behind a fence in rear of their first position; but being now attacked with great audacity, in front and flanks, by superior numbers, resistance became vain, and the whole line, commanded by Burgoyne in person, gave way, and made a precipitate and disorderly retreat to his camp, leaving two twelve and six six pounders on the field, with the loss of more than 400 officers and men, killed, wounded and captured, and among them the flower of his officers—viz, brigadier-general Frazer; Major Ackland, commanding the grenadiers; Sir Francis Clark, his first aid-de-camp; Major Williams, commanding officer of the artillery; Captain Mooney, deputy quartermaster-general, and many others. After delivering the order to General Poor, and directing him to the point of attack, I was peremptorily commanded to repair to the rear, and order up Ten Broeck's regiment of New York militia, 3000 strong. I performed this service, and regained the field of battle at the moment the enemy had turned their backs—52 minutes after the first shot was fired. The ground which had been occupied by the British grenadiers, presented a scene of complicated horror and exultation. In the square space of twelve or fifteen yards lay eighteen grenadiers in the agonies of death, and three officers propped up against stumps of trees, two of them mortally wounded, bleeding and almost speechless. What a spectacle for one whose bosom glowed with philanthropy; and how vehement the impulse which excites men of sensibility to seek such scenes of barbarism! I found the courageous Colonel Cilley a-straddle on a brass twelve pounder, and exulting in the capture; whilst a surgeon, a man of great worth, who was dressing one of the officers, raising his blood-besmeared hands in the phrenzy of patriotism, exclaimed, 'Wilkinson, I have dipped my hands in British blood.' He received a sharp rebuke for his brutality; and with the troops I pursued the hard pressed flying enemy, passing over killed and wounded, until I heard one exclaim, 'Protect me, sir, against this boy.' Turning my eyes, it was my fortune to arrest the purpose of a lad thirteen or fourteen years old, in the act of taking aim at the wounded officer, who lay in the angle of a worm fence. Inquiring his rank, he answered, 'I had the honor to command the grenadiers.' Of course, I knew him to be Major Ackland, who had been brought from the field to this place, on the back of Captain Shrimpton, of his own corps, under a heavy fire, and was here deposited, to save the lives of both. I dismounted, took him by the hand, and expressed my hopes that he was not badly wounded. 'Not badly,' replied this gallant officer and accomplished gentleman, 'but very inconveniently. I am shot through both legs. Will you, sir, have the goodness to have me conveyed to your camp?' I directed my servant to alight, and we lifted Ackland into his seat, and ordered him to be conducted to head-quarters. I then proceeded to the scene of renewed action, which embraced Burgoyne's right flank defence, and extending to his left, crossed a hollow covered with wood, about 40 rods, to the intrenchment of the light infantry. The roar of cannon and small-arms, at this juncture, was sublime, between the enemy, behind their works, and our troops entirely exposed, or partially sheltered by trees, stumps, or hollows, at various distances, not exceeding 120 yards. This right flank defence of the enemy, occupied by the German corps of Breyman, consisted of a breastwork of rails piled horizontally between perpendicular pickets, driven into the earth, *en potence* to the rest of his line, and extended about 250 yards across an open field, and was covered on the right by a battery of two guns. The interval from the left to the British light infantry, was committed to the defence of the provincialists, who occupied a couple of log cabins. The Germans were encamped immediately behind the rail breastwork, and the ground in front of it declined, in a very gentle slope, for about 120 yards, when it sunk abruptly. Our troops had formed a line under this declivity, and covered breast high, were warmly engaged with the Germans. From this position, about sunset, I perceived Brigadier-general Learned advancing towards the enemy with his brigade, in open column, I think with Col. M. Jackson's regiment in front, as I saw Lieutenant-colonel Brooks, who commanded it, near the general when I rode up to him. On saluting this brave old soldier, he inquired, ' Where can I *put in* with most advantage?' I had particularly examined the ground between the left of the Germans and the light infantry, occupied by the provincialists, from whence I had observed a slack fire. I therefore recommended to General Learned to incline to his right, and attack at that point. He did so, with great gallantry; the provincialists abandoned their position and fled. The German flank was, by this means, left uncovered. They were assaulted vigorously, overturned in five minutes, and retreated in disorder, leaving their gallant commander, Lieutenant-colonel Breyman, dead on the field. By dislodging this corps, the whole British encampment was laid open to us; but the extreme darkness of the night, the fatigue of the men, and disorder incident to undisciplined troops, after so desultory an action, put it out of our power to improve the advantage; and in the course of the night, General Burgoyne broke up his camp, and retired to his original position, which he had fortified, behind the great ravine."

The following is from Allen's American Revolution:—

"The British lost in this action upwards of 400 killed, wounded, and prisoners, among whom were several of their most distinguished officers. Brigadier-general Frazer, and Lieutenant-colonel Breyman, who commanded the Germans, were both mortally wounded. Major Ackland, Sir Francis Clark, first aid-de-camp, Major Williams, who commanded the artillery, and the deputy quarter-master-general, Captain Money, were among the prisoners. Lieutenant-colonel Brooks, of General Learned's brigade, who commanded Jackson's regiment on this day, led his men into action with great spirit against the German grenadiers, who were posted behind a rail breastwork—the stockades were carried at the point of the bayonet, and the Germans forced to retreat. They were followed to their encampment, and again forced to fly, leaving their whole equipage to fall into the hands of the Americans. The Brunswickers showed great cowardice in the action, having fled before a man of them was killed or wounded. Besides their killed, wounded, and captured, the British lost eight brass field-pieces, a number of carts and tents, and a considerable quantity of baggage. Burgoyne himself narrowly escaped death, one shot having passed through his hat, and another through his waistcoat. He was on the field during the whole of the action, directing every movement; but neither gallantry nor skill could effect any thing against such a superiority of force. General Gates remained in camp during the whole action, that he might be the better enabled to order and regulate the various movements, as circumstances should require.

"The loss of the Americans did not exceed eighty men, killed and wounded. General Arnold was among the latter; who, though he had not been reinstated in his command since the dispute with General Gates, before mentioned, rode about the field giving orders in every direction, sometimes in direct contradiction to those of the commander, at others leading a platoon in person, and exposing himself to the hottest fire of the enemy. There seems to be little doubt, from the conduct of Arnold during the action, that he was in a state of intoxication. The mortifying situation in which he found himself at its commencement, without command or authority, sufficiently accounts for any extravagance in a spirit like his. At one time he dashed through two opposing lines, exposing himself to the fire of both sides, but miraculously escaped unhurt: at another time, placing himself at the head of a small platoon of Morgan's riflemen, he led them around into the rear of the enemy, at the moment they turned to retreat, under the hottest fire of the Americans. In this situation, his horse was killed under him, and his leg was broken. It would be doing injustice to General Arnold, traitor as he afterward proved, to deny that he deserved some credit on this day; but though he was brave almost beyond parallel, he was rash, impetuous and headstrong, and when it is considered, that these faults of his natural temper were aggravated and heightened by the peculiar circumstances of his situation, it will not perhaps be wrong to say, that he could not have rendered any very essential services to the American army, in this important contest.

"On the night of the battle, General Burgoyne deemed it prudent to change his position; for the Americans had followed them to within half a mile of their encampment, and continued to cannonade them without ceasing. He determined therefore to abandon his camp and move to the high grounds, which he effected in good order and without loss. On the morning of the 8th the American army moved forward and took possession of his abandoned camp, from which they kept up a random fire of artillery and small-arms during the whole day. Burgoyne's troops were all day under arms in expectation of another attack, and indicating by their movements that they intended a still further retreat. In the occasional skirmishes of the day, General Lincoln was shot in the leg by some of the enemy's marksmen."

House in which General Frazer died, Stillwater.

The annexed is a northeastern view of the house on the bank of the Hudson in Stillwater, in which General Frazer died.* This house was originally one story in height, and formerly stood about 25 rods westward of its present situation, at the foot of the hill north of the canal bridge seen in the rear of the house. It has since received an addition at both ends; the general expired near the first window to the right of the door. Beyond the bridge in the distance is seen an elevation about 100 feet in height. This spot is rendered interesting on account of its being the burial place of General Frazer. The grave† was between the two pine trees seen on the summit. During the last battle, the Americans had a few cannon on the rising ground above the eastern shore, from which shots were fired. This house appears to have been for a time the head-quarters of Burgoyne. Several ladies of distinction were also inmates at the time when the British troops were here, being the wives of some of the principal officers. The following is an extract from one of the letters of the Baroness Reidesel, originally published in Germany:—

"But severe trials awaited us, and on the 7th of October, our misfortunes began. I was at breakfast with my husband, and heard that something was intended. On the same day I expected Generals Burgoyne, Phillips, and Frazer to dine with us. I saw a great movement among the troops; my husband told me, it was merely a reconnoissance, which gave me no concern, as it often happened. I walked out of the house and met several Indians in their war dresses, with guns in their hands. When I asked them where they were go-

---

* The following are the circumstances of his death: In the midst of the sanguinary battle of Oct. 7th, Colonel Morgan took a few of his choice riflemen aside and said, "That gallant officer is General Frazer; *I admire and respect him, but it is necessary that he should die*; take your stations in that wood, and do your duty." Within a few moments Gen. Frazer fell mortally wounded. He was supported by two officers, till he reached his tent; he said he saw the man who shot him, that he was a rifleman posted in a tree.

† His remains were taken up some years since, and conveyed to England.

ing, they cried out, 'War! War!' (meaning they were going to battle.) This filled me with apprehension, and I scarcely got home before I heard reports of cannon and musketry, which grew louder by degrees, till at last the noise became excessive. About four o'clock in the afternoon, instead of the guests whom I expected, General Frazer was brought on a litter mortally wounded. The table, which was already set, was instantly removed and a bed placed in its stead for the wounded general. I sat trembling in a corner; the noise grew louder, and the alarm increased; the thought that my husband might perhaps be brought in, wounded in the same way, was terrible to me, and distressed me exceedingly. General Frazer said to the surgeon, '*Tell me if my wound is mortal; do not flatter me.*' The ball had passed through his body, and unhappily for the general, he had eaten a very hearty breakfast, by which the stomach was distended, and the ball, as the surgeon said, had passed through it. I heard him often exclaim with a sigh, 'Oh, fatal ambition! Poor General Burgoyne! Oh, my poor wife!' He was asked if he had any request to make, to which he replied, that 'If General Burgoyne would permit it, he should like to be buried at six o'clock in the evening on the top of a mountain, in a redoubt which had been built there.' I did not know which way to turn, all the other rooms were full of sick. Towards evening I saw my husband coming; then I forgot all my sorrows, and thanked God that he was spared to me. He ate in great haste with me and his aid-de-camp behind the house. We had been told that we had the advantage of the enemy, but the sorrowful faces I beheld told a different tale, and before my husband went away, he took me one side, and said every thing was going very bad, that I must keep myself in readiness to leave the place, but not to mention it to any one. I made the pretence that I would move the next morning into my new house, and had every thing packed up ready.

"Lady H. Ackland had a tent not far from our house; in this she slept, and the rest of the day she was in the camp. All of a sudden, a man came to tell her that her husband was mortally wounded and taken prisoner; on hearing this she became very miserable; we comforted her by telling her that the wound was only slight, and at the same time advised her to go over to her husband, to do which she would certainly obtain permission, and then she could attend him herself; she was a charming woman, and very fond of him. I spent much of the night in comforting her, and then went again to my children, whom I had put to bed. I could not go to sleep, as I had General Frazer and all the other wounded gentlemen in my room, and I was sadly afraid my children would awake, and by their crying disturb the dying man in his last moments, who often addressed me, and apologized '*for the trouble he gave me.*' About 3 o'clock in the morning I was told he could not hold out much longer; I had desired to be informed of the near approach of this sad crisis, and I then wrapped up my children in their clothes, and went with them into the room below. About 8 o'clock in the morning *he died.* After he was laid out and his corpse wrapped up in a sheet, we came again into the room, and had this sorrowful sight before us the whole day; and to add to this melancholy scene, almost every moment some officer of my acquaintance was brought in wounded. The cannonade commenced again; a retreat was spoken of, but not the smallest motion was made towards it. About 4 o'clock in the afternoon I saw the house which had just been built for me in flames, and the enemy was now not far off. We knew that General Burgoyne would not refuse the last request of General Frazer, though by his acceding to it, an unnecessary delay was occasioned, by which the inconvenience of the army was much increased. At 6 o'clock the corpse was brought out, and we saw all the generals attend it to the mountain; the chaplain, Mr. Brundell, performed the funeral service, rendered unusually solemn and awful, from its being accompanied by constant peals from the enemy's artillery. Many cannon balls flew close by me; but I had my eyes directed towards the mountain, where my husband was standing amid the fire of the enemy, and of course, I could not think of my own danger. General Gates afterward said, that if he had known it had been a funeral, he would not have permitted it to be fired on." Lady Harriet Ackland went to the American camp after the action, to take care of her husband, before the surrender, and the Baroness Reidesel afterward. They were both received with the greatest kindness and delicacy.

WATERFORD was taken from Half Moon in 1816. The village of Waterford, containing a population of about 1,600, is pleasantly situated at the junction of the Mohawk with the Hudson, 10 miles north of Albany. The annexed view was taken on the road to Cahoos Falls, about a mile west of the village. There are here 4 churches—viz, 1 Presbyterian, 1 Methodist, 1 Episcopal, and 1 Dutch Reformed—an academy, and a bank. It is favorably located for trade, being on

Western view of Waterford.

the lines of the Champlain canal and Rensselaer and Saratoga rail road. It also derives considerable importance from the navigation of small vessels on the Hudson. There is an outlet here from the canal by three locks, each 11 feet, to the Mohawk river. The agricultural and manufactured products exported from the village annually, amount to about a million of dollars. The water-power used in the large manufacturing establishments at this place is derived from the Mohawk. Pop. 1,824.

WILTON was taken from Northumberland in 1818. Pop. 1,438. Fortville, 19 miles NW. from Ballston Spa, and Wilton 15, are small settlements.

SCHENECTADY COUNTY.

SCHENECTADY COUNTY was taken from Albany in 1809; centrally distant from New York 163, from Albany 18 miles. Greatest length 25, greatest breadth 20 miles. The surface is much diversified by hills, plains, and valleys. The soil along the Mohawk and other streams is generally rich alluvion; on the hills, light sandy loam, sometimes fertile; and on the plains, clay and clayey loam, and sand, sometimes barren. Wherever practicable the country is generally well cultivated, chiefly by descendants of the primitive Dutch settlers, among whom are many wealthy farmers. The Mohawk river runs SE. through the county. The Schoharie kill, on the W., affords abundance of mill power. The Mohawk and Hudson, the Rensse-

---

* Since the drawing for the above engraving was taken, and while this work was in press, a destructive fire broke out and destroyed a large portion of this flourishing village.

laer and Saratoga, and the Utica and Schenectady railroads, and Erie canal, cross this county. The county is divided into five towns and the city of Schenectady. Pop. 17,233.

DUANESBURG was taken from Schenectady in 1801. Pop. 3,338. Duanesburg is a small village, 12 miles SW. from Schenectady. Eaton's Corners, Mariahville, and Quakers Street, are post-offices.

GLENVILLE originally formed the fourth ward of Schenectady, from which it was taken April 14, 1820. Pop. 3,068. It derives its name from the Glen family, who were early and large proprietors. It is centrally distant 5 miles from Schenectady. Glenville Church village, 9 miles from the city, contains a Dutch Reformed church and 6 or 8 dwellings. Scotia village lies on Sander's lake, about half a mile from Schenectady: it contains a Dutch Reformed church and about 30 dwellings.

Scotia, the ancient name of Scotland, was the name given by its first settler. This tract commences at a point nearly opposite the eastern extremity of the city, and extends westerly along the north side of the Mohawk about two miles. The first patent conveying it was granted Nov. 3, 1665, by Governor Richard Nichols to Sanders Lendertse Glen, (Anglice, Alexander Lindsay Glen.) Mr. Glen was an immediate descendant of the Earl of Crawford and Lindsay, whose family had been on the peerage roll since 1399. Mr. Glen took to wife Catharine McDonald, the daughter of a Highland chieftain. He left Scotland in the year 1645, to avoid persecution in consequence of the stand he had taken in reference to certain religious disputes which then agitated the country. He sided with the unfortunate Charles the First, who vainly strove to introduce the *English* liturgy into Scotland. Mr. Glen first emigrated into Holland, and engaged in mercantile pursuits for a number of years. He finally came to New York in company with a number of Dutch families. Here, and in Albany and Schenectady, he resided for a number of years. Some time previous to 1690, he moved to Scotia.

The country seat of Mr. Glen is still owned by his descendants, the Sanders family. Although it bears the advanced age of 123 years, it bids fair to outlive many of the flimsy structures which characterize the American architecture of the present century. The iron figures showing the date of its erection, (1713,) are still to be seen. During the French wars it was rendered defensible. At the foot of a small hillock, a few yards east of the mansion, tradition points to a spot where the Mohawks occasionally performed their sacrifices.

In the beginning of July, 1748, during the French and Indian war, a farmer named Daniel Toll, residing at Maulwyck, now Glenville, went in company with a favorite colored servant in search of some stray horses, at Boekendal, three miles from Schenectady. They soon heard, as they supposed, the trampling of horses, but on a nearer approach the sounds they mistook for that of horses' hoofs on the clayey ground proceeded from quoits with which some Indians were playing. Mr. Toll discovered his error too late, and fell pierced with the bullets of the savages. His servant escaped into Schenectady, and conveyed the news of the death of his master and the presence of the enemy. In less than an hour about 60 young men, the very *elite* of the city, were on their march as volunteers to the scene of action. Such was their zeal that they would not wait until the authorities had called out the militia, which they proposed to do in the afternoon of the day. Among the number, was a youth about twelve years of age, named Abraham Swits, whom they could not prevail upon without difficulty to return home. Without discipline or experience, and without a leader, they hastened to the Indian camp. Those in advance of the main body were attracted by a singular sight. They saw a man resembling Mr. Toll, sitting near a fence, in an adjoining field, and a crow flying up and down before him. On coming nearer they discovered it to be the corpse of Mr. Toll, with a crow attached to it by a string This proved to be a stratagem of the Indians to decoy their adversaries. The young men too readily fell into the snare, and were in a few moments surrounded by the Indians who had been laying in ambush. Their terrible war-cry was shouted,

"And rapid, rapid whoops, came o'er the plain."

Thus surprised, many were killed, and several taken prisoners ere they could make good their retreat. They however succeeded in reaching the dwelling of a Mr. De Graff, in the neighborhood, which had been deserted for some time. While retreating, they continued firing upon the enemy. On reaching the house, they bolted the doors, and ascended to the second story. Here they tore off all the boards near the eaves, and through the opening thus made, succeeded in firing upon the savages with success and keeping them at bay. In the mean time, one of the prisoners, Derick Vorst, who had been left in the charge of two young Indians, effected his escape.

The two youngsters were anxious to see the fight, and secured their prisoner (as they thought) by tying him to a tree; and then leaving him alone, he effected his escape by cutting the cord with his penknife. On the approach of the militia under Gen. Jacob Glen, the party were relieved from their perilous situation and the enemy retreated into Canada.

The corpses of the killed, thirty-two in number, were brought into Schenectady on the evening of the massacre, and deposited in the large barn of Abraham Mabee, being the identical one now on the premises of John Walton, Esq., in church-street. The relatives of the deceased repaired thither to claim their departed kindred, and remove them for interment.

> "Touched by the melting scene, no tearless eye was there;
> All eyes were veil'd, as pass'd each much loved shroud,
> While woman's softer soul in wo dissolved aloud."*

NESKAYUNA is derived from the Indian term, *Con-nes-ti-gu-ne*, signifying "*a field covered with corn.*" This is a small town, and was taken from Watervliet in 1809. Pop. 681. Its distance from Albany is 12, and from Schenectady 6 miles. This name was formerly borne by an extensive tract on both sides of the Mohawk, granted partly by the Nestiogine and partly by the Connestiogine patents, which embraced portions of Clinton Park, Half Moon, Watervliet, and the 1st ward of Schenectady. Near the Mohawk is the village church and a few dwellings. The Ballston turnpike crosses the Mohawk at Alexander's bridge, 4 miles below Schenectady, where are some falls, a low rolling dam across the river, and several mills. The Erie canal is carried over the Mohawk here by an aqueduct 748 feet long, 25 feet above the stream, and falls immediately after by 3 locks 21 feet.

The following are the names which tradition has preserved of a few of the chiefs of the Connestigiune band, who inhabited this section of country. *Ron-warrigh-wok-go-wa*, signifying in English, the great fault-finder, or grumbler. *Ka-na-da-rokh-go-wa*—a great eater. *Ro-ya-ner*—a chief. *As-sa-re-go*—big-knife. *A-roon-ta-go-wa*—big-tree. Of these, the first made the greatest objections to aliening their lands to the whites; and in every deed was careful to have a covenant inserted, by which the right of hunting and fishing was preserved to them. It was a common saying of his, that "after the whites have taken possession of our lands, they will make *Kaut-sore* (literally 'spoon food' or soup) of our bodies." Yet he was on the most friendly terms with the whites, and was never backward in extending to them his powerful influence and personal aid, during their expeditions against the Canadians during the French war. He took great delight in instructing the boys of the settlers in the arts of war. He was constantly complaining that the government did not prosecute the war against the French with sufficient vigor. The wittenagemote or council fire of the Connestigiune band was held about a mile south of the village.

Neskayuna was visited in 1687 by a spy from the Adirondacks, the allies of the French. Hunger drove him to the house of a Dutchman, by the name of Van Brakkle, where he devoured an enormous quantity of the food set before him, which happened to be *pork* and *peas*. Although his movements had been marked with more than usual caution, the eagle-eye of "the Grumbler" detected him. He waylaid him on leaving the house of his entertainer, and after a short conflict made him bite the dust. Having separated the head of the corpse from the body, he repaired to the house of Van Brakkle, and threw the head into the window, exclaiming to the owner, "*Behold the head of your Pea-eater.*"

---

* For the history of this town, Neskayuna, and other interesting matter relating to this region, we are indebted to a series of historical sketches written and published a few years since in the Schenectady Reflector, by Giles F. Yates, Esq., who was at the time its editor.

EASTERN VIEW OF SCHENECTADY, N. Y.

The above view shows the appearance of Schenectady from the elevated ground eastward of the city, near the Troy road. The ancient Union College building is seen in the central part, and on the extreme right the bridge over the Mohawk.

SCHENECTADY COUNTY.   509

The first white settlers in this town were the families of the Clutes, Vedders, Van Vrankens, Groots, Tymesens, Pearces, and Claas Jansen Van Buckhoven, who afterward moved to Schenectady. Tradition says this village was settled simultaneously with Schenectady, in 1640. From an old document it appears that Harmon Vedder obtained a patent for some land here in 1664.

PRINCETOWN, taken from Schenectady in 1798; from Albany 20 miles. Pop. 1,184. Netterville is a small village, 7 miles SW. of Schenectady.

ROTTERDAM, formerly the 3d ward of Schenectady; taken from the city in 1820. Pop. 2,274. The Erie canal by three locks passes the flats. Rotterdam is a small manufacturing village, 4 miles W. from Schenectady.

SCHENECTADY CITY was incorporated in 1798. Its name, pronounced by the Indians *Schagh-nac-taa-da,* signifying "*beyond the pine plains,*" was originally applied to Albany. The compact part of the city was in olden time the site of an Indian village called *Con-nugh-hariegugh-harie,* literally, "*a great multitude collected together.*" It is said that it was the principal seat of the Mohawks, even before the confederacy of the Iroquois, or Five Nations. It was abandoned by them at a very early period in the colonial history. Some time previous to 1620, it is stated that 15 or 20 persons, 12 of whom were direct from Holland, and the rest from Albany, settled here for the purpose of carrying on the fur trade. It appears from the Dutch records that the first grant of lands was made in 1661, to Arent Van Corlaer and others, on condition that they purchased the soil from the Indians. The deed was obtained in 1672, and signed by four Mohawk chiefs.

The compact part of Schenectady is on the SE. side of the Mohawk river, 15½ miles from Albany, and 15 SW. of Ballston springs. The plat is laid out on 20 streets crossing each other, running about one mile in one direction and half a mile in another, eight of which are diagonally intersected by the Erie canal. The city, which in some parts retains much of its ancient appearance, contains the county buildings, 1 Episcopal, 1 Dutch Reformed, 1 Presbyterian, 1 Baptist, 1 Cameronian, 1 Methodist, 1 Universalist, and 1 Catholic church, the Union College, Schenectady Lyceum, an academy, 3 banks, &c., &c. Pop. 6,688. The railroad from Albany to this place extends across a sandy plain covered with pines and shrubbery; it enters Schenectady by an inclined plane which descends 108 feet in half a mile. The Saratoga and Schenectady railroad passes through the city, crosses the Mohawk river on a substantial bridge between 8 and 900 feet long, and extends in a northerly direction over a heavy embankment for three fourths of a mile to a deep cut, where the Utica railroad diverges to the west, and the Saratoga to the northeast.

Union College, in this city, was incorporated by the regents in 1794, and has reached its present flourishing condition from a small beginning. In 1785, a small academy was erected by the consistory of the Reformed Dutch church, which after the establishment of

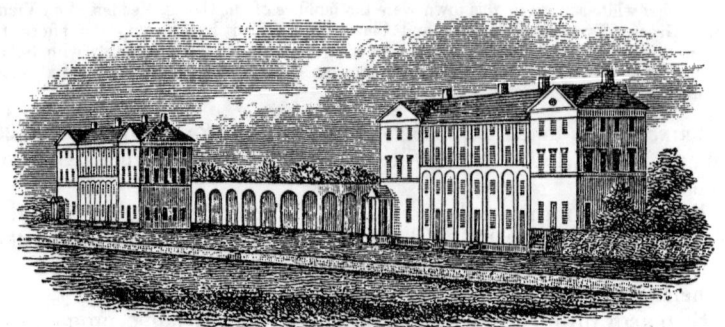

Union College Buildings, Schenectady.

Union College, was presented to its trustees, and used as a grammar school. Liberal donations from individuals, amounting to upwards of $30,000, raised a suite of edifices in the heart of the city, the principal one of which was afterward used as a courthouse, but having been repurchased by the institution, is now devoted to collegiate objects. In 1814, the trustees purchased a site on the rising ground overlooking the Mohawk valley, a little E. of the compact part of the city. Two edifices have been erected at this place, each 200 feet long, about 40 wide, 4 stories high, standing in a line 600 feet apart; a colonnade extending in the rear from each building 156 feet in length, by about 30 feet in width, and 2 stories high. The other college buildings are two boarding halls, farm-house, hospital house, for a professor, a number of tenements for servants, &c. The college has 6 professors and 4 assistant professors, and in its several libraries about 13,000 volumes. The total value of the college property is upwards of $448,000. There are here about 300 students.

The first clergyman of the Dutch church who settled at Schenectady was *Petrus Tasschemaker*, from Holland, who assumed the pastoral charge in 1684. The first edifice for public worship was erected at the south end of Church-street, near the head of Water-street, between the years 1684 and 1698. Previous to this time meetings for worship were probably held in private houses. In 1733, a more commodious edifice was erected in the centre of the street where Union and Church streets cross each other. This church was very similar in its appearance to the one now standing in Caughnawaga, in the town of Mohawk. [See page 281.]

"Before the settlement of Mr. Tasschemaker, the church-going people attended public worship in Albany; a journey to which place, going and coming, consumed more than two days. The road to Albany must have been very circuitous, as all the records of that day, when alluding to Schenectady, speak of it as being situated 'twenty miles west of Albany.'

"In February, 1690, when Schenectady was burnt by the French and Indians, Mr. Tasschemaker disappeared very mysteriously. In 1702, the Rev. Thomas Brower, also from Holland, received a call, and served until his death in 1728. The Rev. Bernardus Freeman and Rhynhard Erkson served next in order; but how long is not known. In 1740, we find the name of Cornelius Van Santvoord, who came from Staten Island, as the settled clergyman. Two years after his decease, viz., in 1754, the Rev. Barent Vrooman, a native of Schenectady, accepted a call and ministered until his decease in 1782. Mr. Vrooman received his education in Holland; as was the case with all the Dutch clergymen of that early day, before theological seminaries were established in this country. Mr. Vrooman was succeeded by the Rev. Derick Romeyn, from Hackensack and Schallenburgh, New Jersey. Mr. Romeyn died in 1804, and was succeeded by the Rev. John H. Myers, from Paltz, New Jersey. Mr. Myers died in 1806. His successor was the Rev. Cornelius Bogardus, who died in 1813, and was succeeded by the Rev. Jacob Van Vechten.

"The Episcopal church at Schenectady was founded by Mr. John W. Brown, who emigrated from England previous to 1762. About this time measures were taken to erect a chapel. The principal benefactors were Sir William Johnson and John Duncan, Esq. Previous to the revolution this church owned a valuable library, which, together with the organ and a greater part of the interior work of the building, was destroyed by a gang of lawless white freebooters and some Indians. Strange as it may seem, these freebooters were whigs, whose prejudices against England were so great as to extend to every thing English. That this church was called the *English* church, and was supposed to be under the English influence, formed a sufficient justification in their own view for its destruction. A project was set on foot to plunder Mr. Doty the pastor; but fortunately the projectors were not acquainted with his person or place of abode, and as nobody would inform them, he escaped.

"The Rev. William Andrews was probably the first pastor of this church. He was succeeded in 1773 by the Rev. Mr. Doty, who left this place about the year 1777, in the heat of the revolutionary contest. From this time there was no settled minister until 1791, when the Rev. Ammi Robbins took the pastoral charge and continued until 1798. After him came the Rev. Mr. Whitmore, whose ministration ended in 1804. The Rev. Cyrus Stebbins was the next pastor; and he was succeeded by the Rev. Pierre A. Proal in 1818."

The war during the reign of William and Mary, in England, commonly called "*King William's War*," commenced in 1690 and continued about 7 years. In the depth of winter, Count Frontenac, governor of Canada, fitted out three expeditions against the colonies —one against New York, a second against New Hampshire, and a third against the province of Maine. The following, relating to the destruction of Schenectady, is extracted from the account given in Mr. Drake's "Book of the Indians."

"After two-and-twenty days' march, the enemy fell in with Schenectady, February 8, 1690. There were about 200 French, and perhaps 50 Caughnewaga Mohawks, and they at first intended to have surprised Albany; but their march had been so long and tedious, occasioned by the deepness of the snow and coldness of the weather, that, instead of attempting any thing offensive, they had nearly decided to surrender themselves to the first English they should meet, such was their distressed situation, in a camp of snow, but a few miles from the devoted settlement. The Indians, however, saved them from the disgrace. They had sent out a small scout from their party, who entered Schenectady without even exciting suspicion of their errand. When they had staid as long as the nature of their business required, they withdrew to their fellows.

"Seeing that Schenectady offered such an easy prey, it put new courage into the French, and they came upon it as above related. The bloody tragedy commenced between 11 and 12 o'clock, on Saturday night; and, that every house might be surprised at nearly the same time, the enemy divided themselves into parties of 6 or 7 men each. Although the town was empaled, no one thought it necessary to close the gates, even at night, presuming the severity of the season was a sufficient security; hence the first news of the approach of the enemy was at every door of every house, which doors were broken as soon as the profound slumbers of those they were intended to guard. The same inhuman barbarities now followed, that were afterward perpetrated upon the wretched inhabitants of Montreal. 'No tongue,' said Col. Schuyler, ' can express the cruelties that were committed.' Sixty-three houses, and the church, were immediately in a blaze. *Enciente* women, in their expiring agonies, saw their infants cast into the flames, being first delivered by the knife of the midnight assassin! Sixty-three persons were put to death, and twenty-seven were carried into captivity.

"A few persons fled towards Albany, with no other covering but their night-clothes; the horror of whose condition was greatly enhanced by a great fall of snow; 25 of whom lost their limbs from the severity of the frost. With these poor fugitives came the intelligence to Albany, and that place was in a dismal confusion, having, as usual upon such occasions, supposed the enemy to have been seven times more numerous than they really were. About noon, the next day, the enemy set off from Schenectady, taking all the plunder they could carry with them, among which were 40 of the best horses. The rest, with all the cattle and other domestic animals, lay slaughtered in the streets.

"One of the most considerable men of Schenectady, at this time, was Capt. Alexander

Glen. He lived on the opposite side of the river, and was suffered to escape, because he had delivered many French prisoners from torture and slavery, who had been taken by the Indians in the former wars. They had passed his house in the night, and, during the massacre, he had taken the alarm, and in the morning he was found ready to defend himself. Before leaving the village, a French officer summoned him to a council, upon the shore of the river, with the tender of personal safety. He at length adventured down, and had the great satisfaction of having all his captured friends and relatives delivered to him; and the enemy departed, keeping good their promise that no injury should be done him."

Among those who made a successful defence and kept the foe at bay, was Adam Vrooman. Being well supplied with ammunition, and trusting to the strength of his building, which was a sort of a fort, he formed the desperate resolution to defend himself to the last extremity; and if it should prove his fate to perish in the ruins of his own domicil, to sell his own life and that of his children as dear as possible. Seconded in his efforts by one of his sons, who assisted in loading his guns, he kept up a rapid and continuous fire upon his assailants, and with the most deadly effect. His house was soon filled with smoke. His wife, nearly suffocated with it, cautiously, yet imprudently, placed the door ajar. This an alert Indian perceived, and firing through the aperture, killed her. In the mean time, one of his daughters escaped from the back hall door with his infant child in her arms. They snatched the little innocent from her arms, and dashed out its brains; and in the confusion of the scene the girl escaped. Their triumph here, however, was of short duration; Mr. Vrooman succeeded in securely bolting the door and preventing the intrusion of any of the enemy. On witnessing Mr. Vrooman's courage, and fearing greater havoc among their chosen band, the enemy promised, if he would desist, to save his life and not set fire to his building. This promise they fulfilled, but carried off two of his sons into captivity.

The following additional particulars respecting this event are drawn from the account given by Charlevoix, a learned French Jesuit, distinguished for his travels and authentic historical works.

"This party marched out before they had determined against what part of the English frontier they would carry their arms, though some part of New York was understood. Count Frontenac had left that to the two commanders. After they had marched 5 or 6 days, they called a council to determine upon what place they would attempt. In this council, it was debated, on the part of the French, that Albany would be the smallest place they ought to undertake; but the Indians would not agree to it. They contended that, with their small force, an attack upon Albany would be attended with extreme hazard. The French being strenuous, the debate grew warm, and an Indian chief asked them 'how long it was since they had so much courage.' To this severe rebuke it was answered, that, if by some past actions they had discovered cowardice, they should see that now they would retrieve their character; they would take Albany or die in the attempt. The Indians, however, would not consent, and the council broke up without agreeing upon any thing but to proceed on.

"They continued their march until they came to a place where their path divided into two; one of which led to Albany, and the other to Schenectady: here Mantet gave up his design upon Albany, and they marched on harmoniously for the former village. The weather was very severe, and for the following 9 days the little army suffered incredible hardships. The men were often obliged to wade through water up to their knees, breaking its ice at every step.

"At 4 o'clock in the morning, the beginning of February, they arrived within two leagues of Schenectady. Here they halted, and the Great Agnier, chief of the Iroquois of the falls of St. Louis, made a speech to them. He exhorted every one to forget the hardships they had endured, in the hope of avenging the wrongs they had for a long time suffered from the perfidious English, who were the authors of them; and in the close added, that they could not doubt of the assistance of heaven against the enemies of God, in a cause so just. Hardly had they taken up their line of march, when they met 40 Indian women, who gave them all the necessary information for approaching the place in safety. A Canadian, named Giguiere, was detached immediately with 9 Indians upon discovery, who acquitted himself to the entire satisfaction of his officers. He reconnoitred Schenectady at his leisure, and then rejoined his comrades. It had been determined by the party to put off the attack one day longer; but on the arrival of the scout under Giguiere, it was resolved to proceed without delay.

"Schenectady was then in form like that of a long square, and entered by two gates, one at each end. One opened towards Albany, the other upon the great road leading into the back country, and which was now possessed by the French and Indians. Mantet and St. Helene charged at the second gate, which the Indian women before mentioned had assured them was always open, and they found it so. D'Iberville and Repentigni passed to the left, in order to enter by the other gate, but, after losing some time in vainly endeavoring to find it, were obliged to return and enter with their comrades.

"The gate was not only open but unguarded, and the whole party entered without being discovered. Dividing themselves into several parties, they waylaid every portal, and then the war-whoop was raised. Mantet formed and attacked a garrison, where the only resistance of any account was made. The gate of it was soon forced, and all of the English fell by the sword, and the garrison was burned. Montigni was wounded, in forcing a house, in his arm and body by two blows of a halberd, which put him *hors du combat;* but St. Helene being come to his assistance, the house was taken, and the wounds of Montigni revenged by the death of all who had shut themselves up in it. Nothing was now to be seen but massacre and pillage in every place. At the end of about two hours, the chiefs, believing it due to their safety, posted bodies of guards at all the avenues, to prevent surprise, and the rest of the night was spent in refreshing themselves. Mantet had given orders that the minister of the place should be spared, whom he had intended for his own prisoner; but he was found among the promiscuous dead, and no one knew when he was killed, and all his papers were burned.

"After the place was destroyed, the chiefs ordered all the casks of intoxicating liquors to be staved, to prevent their men from getting drunk. They next set all the houses on fire, excepting that of a widow, into which Montigni had been carried, and another belonging to Major Coudre: they were in number about 40, all well built and furnished; no booty but that which could be easily transported was saved. The lives of about 60 persons were spared; chiefly women, children, and old men, who had escaped the fury of the onset, and 30 Indians who happened to be then in the place. The lives of the Indians were spared that they might carry the news of what had happened to their countrymen, whom they were requested to inform, that it was not against them that they intended any harm, but to the English only, whom they had now despoiled of property to the amount of four hundred thousand pounds."

The following ballad is an interesting relic of antiquity. It was written in 1690, to commemorate the destruction of Schenectady, and is composed something in the style of the celebrated "Chevy Chase."

"A BALLAD,

"In which is set forth the horrid cruellties practised by the French and Indians on the night of the 8th of last February. The which I did compose last night in the space of one hour; and am now writing, the morning of Fryday, June 12th, 1690. W. W.

"God prosper long our king and queen,
   Our lives and safeties all;
A sad misfortune once there did
   Schenectady befall.

From forth the woods of Canada
   The Frenchmen tooke their way,
The people of Schenectady
   To captivate and slay.

They marched for two and twenty daies,
   All through the deepest snow;
And on a dismal winter night,
   They strucke the cruel blow.

The lightsome sun that rules the day
   Had gone down in the west;
And eke the drowsie villagers
   Had sought and found their reste.

They thought they were in saftie all,
   And dreampt not of the foe:
But att midnight they all awoke,
   In wonderment and woe.

For they were in their pleasant beddes,
   And soundelie sleeping, when

Each door was sudden open broke
   By six or seven men.

The men and women, younge and olde,
   And eke the girls and boys,
All started up in great affright,
   Att the alarming noise.

They then were murther'd in their beddes,
   Without shame or remorse;
And soone the floors and streets were strew'd
   With many a bleeding corse.

The village soon began to blaze,
   Which shew'd the horrid sight:—
But, O, I scarce can beare to tell,
   The mis'ries of that night.

They threw the infants in the fire,
   The men they did not spare;
But killed all which they could find,
   Though aged or tho' fair.

O Christe! In the still midnight air,
   It sounded dismally;
The women's prayers, and the loud screams
   Of their great agony.

Methinks as if I hear them now
  All ringing in my ear;
The shrieks and groans and woeful sighs
  They uttered in their fear.

But some run off to Albany,
  And told the dolefull tale:
Yett though we gave our chearful aid,
  It did not much avail.

And we were horribly afraid,
  And shook with terror, when
They told us that the Frenchmen were
  More than a thousand men.

The news came on the Sabbath morn
  Just att the break of day,
And with a companie of horse
  I galloped away.

But soon we found the French were gone
  With all their great bootye;

Albany, 12th of June, 1690.

And then their trail we did pursue,
  As was our true dutye.

The Mohaques joynd our brave partye,
  And followed in the chase,
Till we came up with the Frenchmen,
  Att a most likelye place.

Our soldiers fell upon their rear,
  And killed twenty-five;
Our young men were so much enrag'd
  They took scarce one alive.

D'Aillebout them did commande,
  Which were but thievish rogues,
Else why did they consent and goe,
  With bloodye Indian dogges?

And here I end the long ballad,
  The which you just have redde;
I wish that it may stay on earth
  Long after I am dead.

WALTER WILIE.

The annexed novel marriage which occurred somewhere in this vicinity is well worthy of preservation.

About a century ago, saith tradition, when clergymen were not so plenty as they now are, a young gentlemen and his dulcinea were anxiously awaiting the happy day which was to see them united in the silken bands of matrimony. They resided on the north side of Tomhenick creek, and the clergyman who had been engaged to tie the knot lived on the south side of the same stream. As the fates would have it, heavy rains fell the night previous to the nuptial day, which rendered the creek impassable. Its waters were rising, and its current becoming more rapid every hour. The clergyman arrived at the appointed time at a place where he had been in the habit of fording the creek; but it was as much as his life was worth to attempt to cross it then. He turned his horse's head to return, when he was hailed by two voices on the opposite side of the stream—they were those of the groom and bride, who entreated him to stay. After some debate, it was agreed that the ceremony should proceed. In the mean time the friends of the betrothed arrived from the bride's house in the neighborhood. Then was presented a singular spectacle, "the like whereof was never seen before," and probably will not be again. The dominie read the marriage service, on the margin of the creek, while the parties stood on the opposite side. After the ceremony was over, the groom tossed a few guilders across the creek, which the dominie picked up and pocketed as his fee, mounted his horse and proceeded homewards, and the married couple did the same.

The following inscriptions are copied from a monument in the graveyard near the Presbyterian church.

"JONATHAN EDWARDS, S. T. D. North. reip. Mass., natus, A. D. 1745, coll. Nassov, A. B. 1765, et eodem tutor, 1767, ordinibus ecclesiæ sacris Nov. Port. Connect. reip. initiatus, 1769 iisdemq. Coluni, 1796, atque coll. Concord Schenect. N. Ebor præses, 1799.—Vir ingenio acri, justi tenax propositi, doctrina vere eximia maxime imbutus atque præditus, christianæ fidei intemeratæ defensor tum fervidus tum prævalidus, et in moribus intaminatis enituit magnum sui desiderium bonis omnibus reliquit, die 1 mo. Aug. anno salutis humanæ, 1801."

"MARIAE, Jonathani Edwards conjugis dilectissimæ, nec non memor hoc est etiam monumentum. Ipsa urbanitate, moribus, pietate, viro optimo dignissima, aquis, eheu! submersa fuit, Nov. Port. reip. Connect. Anno Domini, 1782. Eademque urbs reliquas ipsius habet."

[JONATHAN EDWARDS, D. D., born at Northampton, Mass., A. D. 1745; graduated at the college of New Jersey in 1765, where he was tutor in 1767; ordained to the ministry of the gospel at New Haven, Conn., in 1769, and also at Colebrook in 1796; and president of Union college at Schenectady, New York, in 1799. He was a man of acute mind, firm in his opinion, thoroughly versed and skilled in true learning, the intrepid defender, alike earnest and successful, of the Christian faith, and conspicuous for the purity of his life. He died amid the grief of all good men, on the first day of August, in the year of our Lord 1801.]

[MARIA, the beloved wife of Jonathan Edwards, is also commemorated by this monument. In urbanity, goodness, and piety, she was most worthy of that excellent man. In 1782, she was unfortunately drowned at New Haven, Connecticut, where her remains repose.]

SCHOHARIE COUNTY.

SCHOHARIE* COUNTY was taken from Albany and Otsego counties in 1795: greatest length N. and S. 30, greatest breadth E. and W. 25 miles. Centrally distant NW. from New York 150, from Albany W. 42 miles. In the western part of this county is the dividing ridge between the waters of the Mohawk and those of the Susquehannah and Delaware. In the eastern part it has the Cattskill and Helleberg† mountains. It has the valley of the Schoharie creek north and south through its centre, along which the alluvial flats are very extensive, with a soil of loam and vegetable mould, peculiarly rich and fertile. Much of the surface of this county is hilly, with some of a mountainous character. The soil of the uplands is of various qualities, generally better adapted to grass than to grain. The Schoharie creek, a large tributary of the Mohawk, has its rise in Green county, and flows northward through the centre of this county. In its course it receives several smaller streams, the principal of which are the Cobelskill on the west, and Foxes creek on the east. The Cattskill has its source in the eastern part of the county, and the Delaware and Susquehannah in the western. The county is well watered, and possesses many fine mill sites. In the towns of Summit, Jefferson, Blenheim, Broome, and the uplands of Middleburg and Fulton, the tenure of the soil is generally held by lease; the fee-simple being in proprietors of large tracts; but in these towns, there are many tracts upon the creek, which the Germans have taken up in fee, the common tenure of the northern towns. The towns of Schoharie, Cobelskill, Sharon, Fulton, Middleburg, and portions of Blenheim and Broome, have a population of German origin. The German language prevails among the older inhabitants, but their children are educated and converse in English. The early settlers suffered much from Indian hostilities, and during the revolution the country was overrun by the British and Indians under Sir John Johnson, Brant, and the infamous Walter Butler. The county is divided into 11 towns. At the commencement of the revolution this

---

* Schoharie, Indian name for driftwood.

† Helleberg, German—Helderburg, Dutch. The early settlers of Schoharie passed over this mountain on their route thither, and gave it this name, which signifies the "sightly hill."—*J. R. Simms.*

whole territory scarcely contained 1,000 inhabitants; the greater part of these inhabited the valley of the Schoharie river. The population in 1840 was 32,351.

BLENHEIM, organized in 1797; from Albany W. 44 miles. Pop. 2,726. North Blenheim, 15 miles S. from Schoharie, and Blenheim, are small villages.

BROOME, originally named Bristol, was organized in 1797; centrally distant S. from Schoharie 15 miles. Pop. 2,404. Gilboa, Broome, Livingstonville, Plattakill, and Smithtown, are small villages or settlements. The monument of David Williams, who died in this town, is at Livingstonville, and has the following inscription : "DAVID WILLIAMS, the only surviving captor of Andre, died August 1st, 1831, aged 77. Amor patriæ vincit," (the love of country conquers.)

CARLISLE, taken from Cobelskill and Sharon in 1807; from Schoharie NW. 10 miles. Pop. 1,850. Carlisle and Grosvenors Corners are small villages.

COBELSKILL* was formed from Schoharie in 1797. Near the brick meeting-house is one of those subterranean streams common to limestone countries. Cobelskill, 10 miles W. of Schoharie, Lawyersville, Punchkill, Richmondville, and Mann's Valley, are small villages.

In the summer of 1779, a party of Onondaga Indians, after the destruction of their town by Col. Van Schaick, made an incursion into this section, the account of which is thus given by Campbell in his Annals :—

"There was at this time a little settlement, consisting of only nineteen families, on the Cobleskill creek, ten miles west of Schoharie. Though they had erected no fortifications, they had prepared for defence, by organizing a company of militia, and procuring arms and ammunition. About the middle of May, it was reported at a meeting of the militia, that some straggling Indians had been seen in the neighborhood, and a scout of three men, one of whom was suspected of being secretly a royalist, was sent out into the forest. On the return of the scout, they met two Indians near the settlement, who accosting them in friendly terms, and pretending to be hunting, were suffered to pass. The Indians took a circuitous route, and in a short time met them again. The suspected individual had now disappeared, having taken a different path to the settlement. The Indians still pretended friendship; one of them familiarly took the musket from one of the men, and knocking out the flint, handed it back. The other attempted the same thing, but his adversary perceiving his intention, shot him. His companion fled, and the men returned to the settlement. This circumstance, together with a rumor that a large body of Indians were on their march for Schoharie, excited fears that this little settlement would be the first object of their revenge. They immediately despatched a messenger to Schoharie with the intelligence, and directed him to ask for assistance. A part of a company of continental soldiers, under the command of Captain Patrick, was sent the same day to Cobbleskill. The next morning a party of Indians were seen to cross the creek and return again into the woods. A small detachment of men were sent in pursuit. These were soon driven back by superior force. Captain Patrick then marched the whole of his little band, and 15 volunteers of the militia, to their support. The Indians were driven back, but soon made a stand, and after firing again retreated. They continued to retreat, disputing the ground at every step, evidently increasing in number, until the conflict became exceeding-

---

* Mr. Jephtha R. Simms, of Fultonville, who is at present writing a history of Schoharie county and its vicinity, for which object he has taken pains in collecting authentic and original information, in a letter to the authors thus alludes to the orthography of this name. "Cobelskill has been written Cobuskill, Cobbleskill, and as I write it. In the laws which record the formation of that town, it is spelled Cobelskill. The name of the man after whom it was called was Cobel."

ly fierce. Captain Patrick was at first wounded, and afterward killed, when his men sought safety in flight. The Indians immediately pursued them, and at the same instant the main body, which had been concealed in the thickets, rushed forth, and with deafening yells poured a shower of rifle balls upon the fugitives; their number, as afterward ascertained, was about 300.

"The death of Captain Patrick alone saved his men from entire destruction; in a few moments more they would have been surrounded, and their retreat cut off.

"The inhabitants of the settlement, as soon as they saw the fugitives emerging from the woods, pursued by the Indians, fled in an opposite direction, and all arrived safe at Schoharie; their escape was favored by the desperate resistance of seven of the soldiers, who, taking possession of a house, fired from the windows, and checked the pursuit of the enemy. The Indians at length succeeded in setting the house on fire, and six of its brave defenders perished in the flames; the other was afterward found a few rods distant, much burned, and horribly mutilated; a roll of continental money was put in his hand, as if in derision of the cause which he supported. The enemy set fire to the buildings in the vicinity, and after burying their dead and mangling the dead bodies of the soldiers, retired without pursuing the fugitives further. Of the 45 who went out, 21 escaped, 22 were killed, and 42 taken prisoners. The Indians suffered severely."

General James Dana moved into this town soon after the revolutionary war, and was a resident till his death. He was born in Ashford, Connecticut, October 10th, 1732. The following notice respecting this meritorious officer is from the manuscript of I. H. Tiffany, Esq., of Fultonville, which he has drawn up with care and accuracy. Most of the facts here stated were related to Mr. Tiffany by General Dana himself, January 7th, 1816.

He appears to have commenced his military career among the provincial troops, under Sir William Johnson. He assisted in building the fort at Lake George, and was at the battle of Lake Champlain, where the fortification was attacked by the French, and General Johnson wounded. At the commencement of the American revolution, he was a captain in Colonel Storr's regiment, in General Putnam's brigade of Connecticut militia. He arrived at the American camp at Cambridge, where General Ward commanded, immediately after the affair at Lexington. He was among the troops ordered to throw up a breastwork on Bunker's Hill. A half-moon fortification of facines and dirt was erected during the night. Colonel Prescott was the engineer; he requested Captain Dana's orderly sergeant to assist in laying out the fortification. The British embarked at Winnimesset ferry.

When the second division of 500 troops landed, they marched up Malden river to gain the rear of the American fortification. This movement was first perceived by Captain Dana, and communicated to General Putnam. By his orders, 500 of the Connecticut troops were marched down and took up their position, and formed two deep behind a fence. Captain (afterward Colonel) Knowlton commanded this detachment. Captain Dana was the second in command. Putnam, in giving his directions, said to these officers, "Do you remember my orders at Ticonderoga?" "*Yes*," was the reply: "*you told us not to fire till we could see the whites of the enemy's eyes.*" "Well," says Putnam, "I give the same orders now."

The British advanced with muffled drums and soft fifes; the officers and soldiers got over the fence south of the American line. Captain Dana was posted in the centre, towards which the British column was advancing. The order was, "death to any man who fired before Captain Dana." When the column was eight rods distant, Dana ordered the rear rank down flat. At this word the British officer faced about and ordered the column to display from the centre. At that instant Captain Dana, Lieutenant Grosvenor, and orderly-sergeant Fuller fired, and the British commanding officer (supposed to be Major Pitcairn) fell mortally wounded. The British troops broke and retreated, formed and advanced again, which probably occupied thirty minutes. When they arrived at the fence they fired. Lieutenant Grosvenor was wounded in the hand, and a bullet also passed through a rail and lodged in his shirt, flatted and harmless. Captain Knowlton's musket barrel was broken off by a cannon ball. Lieutenant Grosvenor bound up his hand and retired from the field. Within four or five minutes after Grosvenor was wounded, a cannon ball struck a rail against Dana's breast, which knocked him down breathless. He however recovered, and remained until the line was ordered off. When he arrived at his quarters, he was confined to his room, and unable to dress or undress himself for several days.

The first countersign given by General Washington after the battle of Bunker Hill was

"Knowlton," and the parole " Dana." In July, after the battle of Bunker Hill, an oration was delivered by Dr. Leonard, Washington's chaplain. After the oration and declaration had been pronounced, an aid of General Washington advanced from the head-quarters, bearing the American standard, with an order from the general directed to Captain Dana to receive it, and carry it three times around the front or interior circle of the army; furthermore, that in so doing he must not let the colors fall, as it would be considered as ominous of the fall of America. The captain declined, fearful of his ability to perform this duty in a proper manner. The aid returned to head-quarters with the apology: but soon came back with General Putnam, who, in his familiar way, clapped Captain Dana upon the shoulder, and said, " God curse it, Dana, you look like a white man; take the colors, clear away." The army immediately opened a passage to the right and left for his excellency General Washington, and the other officers. The next day the general in his orders expressed the most flattering approbation of the manner in which Captain Dana had performed the ceremony of displaying the flag.

Captain Dana was 6 feet and 1 inch in height, noble and commanding in his appearance, but modest and retiring in his manners. He was frequently offered promotion in the army, but uniformly declined. The celebrated General Eaton, afterward so distinguished in the war with Tripoli, was at the age of fifteen his waiter and secretary. He was put under Captain Dana at the request of his father. After the close of the revolution, Captain Dana removed to Cobelskill, where he occupied a small log-cabin or house till his death. Notwithstanding his humble circumstances, the legislature of New York, in consequence of his meritorious services in the revolution, appointed him a brigadier-general, being the first who held that office in the county of Schoharie.

CONESVILLE, taken from Broome in 1836, is the SE. corner town of the county; from Schoharie centrally distant 20 miles. Pop. 1,621. Conesville is a post-office. Strikersville is a small settlement near the western line.

FULTON, taken from Middleburg in 1828; from Albany 42 miles. On Stoney creek, in this town, there is a fall of nearly 100 feet perpendicular. Byrnville, 14 miles SW. from Schoharie, Fultonham, and Breakabeen, are small settlements. Pop. 2,146.

JEFFERSON, taken from Blenheim in 1803; from Albany 57, from Schoharie SW. 20 miles. Pop. 2,033. This town is inhabited by eastern emigrants and their descendants, who are extensively engaged in the dairy business and grazing. Lake Utsayanthe, a small pond here, is the source of the Mohawk branch of the Delaware. Jefferson is a small village.

MIDDLEBURG was taken from Schoharie in 1797; from Albany 37 miles. Pop. 3,841. The inhabitants are principally of Dutch or German origin. Middleburg, on the Schoharie river, 5 miles S. from Schoharie, is a village containing about 50 dwellings. Huntersland and Franklinton are small settlements.

Remains of the old Middle Fort, noted in the revolutionary annals, are now to be seen a short distance from Middleburg village, on the plain east of the road to Schoharie. The Upper Fort was 5 miles SE., near the margin of the Schoharie river, in the present limits of Fulton,—the lower was at the village of Schoharie, 5 miles N. This last was built for a church, and is at present used as such. [See Schoharie.] The annexed account of the attack on the Middle Fort by the British and Indians, is taken from the " Life and Adventures of Timothy Murphy, the Benefactor of Schoharie," a pamphlet published in 1839.

" In the fall of 1780, the enemy, about 800 strong, under Sir John Johnson, made preparations for destroying the valleys of Schoharie and the Mohawk. The forces, consisting of British regulars, loyalists, tories, and Indians, assembled on the Tioga, and marched thence up along the eastern branch of the Susquehannah, and crossed thence to Schoharie. On the 16th of October, they encamped about four miles above the upper fort. It was their intention to pass the upper fort in the night, and to attack the middle fort at daybreak: as it was expected that the upper fort would be the first object of attack, they hoped to surprise the middle fort by this unexpected movement. Sir John had ordered his troops to be put in motion at four in the morning, but from some mistake it was five before they began their march; consequently the rear guard was discovered by the sentinels of the upper fort, and the alarm gun was fired, which was quickly answered from the other forts, and 20 riflemen, under the supervision of Timothy Murphy,* were sent out from the middle fort to watch the motions of the enemy; they soon fell in with the advanced party, and retreated back. The firing of the alarm gun disappointed the enemy, and became the signal for them to commence the destruction of the settlement; houses, barns, and stacks of hay were burned, and cattle, sheep, and horses were killed or driven away.

"The Indians being in advance of the regular forces, were the first to approach the fort. Murphy, whose eye was ever watching the enemy, had stationed himself in a ditch a few rods south of the fort, that he might, unperceived, the better view the movements of the enemy. The Indians approached to within about eighty yards of the fort, when Murphy fired upon them; and as he arose the second time to fire, a bullet struck within a few inches of his face, and glanced over his head, throwing dirt in his eyes. He then ran into the fort, not however without bringing to the ground another Indian.

---

* Murphy, who was of great service to the inhabitants of Schoharie, was a native of Virginia, and had belonged to Morgan's rifle corps, in which he had distinguished himself as a marksman. After the capture of Burgoyne, the company to which he belonged was ordered to Schoharie, where it remained until their term of service expired. When the company was disbanded, Murphy and some others remained, and served in the militia; his skill in the desultory war which the Indians carry on, gave him so high a reputation, that though not nominally the commander, he usually directed all the movements of the scouts that were sent out, and on many important occasions the commanding officers found it dangerous to neglect his advice; his double rifle, his skill as a marksman, and his fleetness either in retreat or pursuit, made him an object both of dread and of vengeance to the Indians; they formed many plans to destroy him, but he always eluded them, and sometimes made them suffer for their temerity.

He fought the Indians in their own way, and with their own weapons. When circumstances permitted, he tomahawked and scalped his fallen enemy; he boasted after the war that he had slain forty of the enemy with his own hand, more than half of whom he had scalped; he took delight in perilous adventures, and seemed " to love danger for danger's sake." Tradition has preserved the account of many of his exploits; but there are so many versions of the same story, and so much evident fiction mixed with the truth, that we shall give but a single instance as a proof of the dread with which he was regarded by the Indians.

They were unable to conjecture how he could discharge his rifle twice without having time to reload; and his singular good fortune in escaping unhurt, led them to suppose that he was attended by some invisible being who warded off their bullets, and sped his with unerring certainty to the mark. When they had learned the mystery of his double-barrelled gun, they were careful not to expose themselves too much until he had fired twice, knowing that he must have time to reload his piece before he could do them further injury.

One day, having separated from his party, he was pursued by a number of Indians, all of whom he outran excepting one; Murphy turned round, fired upon this Indian, and killed him. Supposing that the others had given up the pursuit, he stopped to strip the dead, when the rest of his pursuers came in sight. He snatched the rifle of his fallen foe, and with it killed one of his pursuers; the rest, now sure of their prey, with a yell of joy heedlessly rushed on, hoping to make him their prisoner; he was ready to drop down with fatigue, and was likely to be overtaken, when, turning round, he discharged the remaining barrel of his rifle, and killed the foremost of the Indians; the rest, astonished at his firing three times in succession, fled, crying out that he could shoot all day without loading.—*Annals of Tryon county.*

" In stature, Murphy was about 5 feet 6 inches, and very well proportioned, with dark complexion, and an eye that would kindle and flash like the very lightning when excited. He was exceedingly quick in all his motions, and possessed an iron frame that nothing apparently could effect. And what is very remarkable, his body was never wounded or scarred during the whole war."

"About 8 o'clock the enemy commenced a regular attack on the fort, which was re turned with effect from the garrison. The regular troops fired a few cannon shot, and threw a number of shells, one of which burst in the air above the fort, doing no injury; another entered and burst in the upper loft of the fort, doing no other mischief than destroying a quantity of bedding, and nearly frightening to death a little Frenchman who had fled to the chamber for protection, and came running down stairs, at the same time exclaiming, '*de diable pe among de fedders.*' The interior of the fort was several times on fire, but was as often extinguished by the exertions of the women. The Indians retreated behind a row of willow trees, and kept up a constant fire, but at too great a distance to do effect. In the fort, all was gloom and despondency; the garrison only amounted to 150 regular troops, and about 100 militia. Their ammunition was nearly exhausted—to attempt to defend the fort, appeared to be madness;—to surrender, was to deliver up themselves, their wives and children to immediate death, or at least to a long captivity. Major Wolsey, who commanded the fort, was inclined to surrender on the first appearance of the enemy, but was prevented by the officers of the militia, who resolved to defend it or to die in the contest. Wolsey's presence of mind forsook him in the hour of danger; he concealed himself at first with the women and children in the house, and when driven out by the ridicule of his new associates, he crawled round the intrenchments on his hands and knees, amid the jeers and bravos of the militia, who felt their courage revive as their laughter was excited by the cowardice of the major. In times of extreme danger, every thing which has a tendency to destroy reflection by exciting risibility has a good effect.

"The enemy, perceiving that their shot and shells did little or no execution, formed under shelter of a small building near the fort, and prepared to carry the works by assault. While the preparations were making, a flag was seen to approach the fort; all seemed inclined to admit it, when Murphy and Bartholomew Vroman, who suspected that it was only an artifice to learn the actual strength of the garrison, and aware that for them at least there was no safety in capitulation, fired upon the flag. The flag retired, and some soldiers were ordered to arrest Murphy; but so great was his popularity among the soldiers, that no one dared to obey. The flag approached a second time, and was a second time driven back by Murphy and his adherents. A white flag was then ordered to be raised in the fort, but Murphy threatened with instant death any one who should obey. The enemy sent a flag the third time, and on Murphy's turning to fire upon it, Wolsey presented his pistol and threatened to shoot him if he did;—but not in the least intimidated by the major's threat, Murphy very deliberately raised his rifle, and pointing it towards him, firmly replied, 'I will die before they shall have me prisoner.' Major Wolsey then retired to his room, where he remained until Col. Vroman was despatched in search of him. He was found covered up in bed, trembling like a leaf. Col. Vroman accosted him, 'Was you sent here to sneak away so, when we are attacked by the tories and Indians? and do you mean to give up the fort to these bloody rascals?'—To which Major Wolsey made no reply, but consented to yield up the command to Col. Vroman. At this change of officers, unanimous joy pervaded the whole fort. And even the women* smiled to behold the portly figure of Col. Vroman stalking about the fort—directing and encouraging the soldiers in his melodious Low Dutch notes.

"The British officers now held a council of war, and after a short consultation withdrew; and then proceeded down the Schoharie creek, burning and destroying every thing that lay in their way. The loss of the garrison in this affair was only one killed and two wounded, one mortally. It is not known what loss the enemy sustained, or why they retreated so hastily."

SCHOHARIE was organized in 1788, as part of Albany county: it has a hilly surface, with extensive valleys on the Schoharie and Fox creeks. The Schoharie creek, at this place, is about 10 rods wide, and the flats on its borders are from 1 to 2 miles wide and of surpassing fertility. Pop. 5,532. Schoharie village, the county seat,

---

* "One of them," says Col. Stone, in his Life of Brant, "an interesting young woman, whose name yet lives in story among her own mountains, perceiving, as she thought, symptoms of fear in a soldier who had been ordered to a well without the works, and within range of the enemy's fire, for water, snatched the bucket from his hands, and ran forth for it herself. Without changing color, or giving the slightest evidence of fear, she drew and brought bucket after bucket to the thirsty soldiers, and providentially escaped without injury."

SCHOHARIE COUNTY.   521

Southeast view in the central part of Schoharie.

lies on the flats, near the junction of Schoharie and Fox creeks, 32 miles W. of Albany. It contains about 100 dwellings, the county buildings, 1 Lutheran and 1 Dutch Reformed church, and an academy. The above engraving is a SW. view in the central part of the village : the courthouse, a stone building 3 stories high, is seen on the right; the Lutheran church and the academy in the distance.

"In the year 1709, a number of families from the Palatinates in Germany, induced by the liberal offers made by Queen Anne, embarked for New York, and having proceeded up the Hudson as far as Albany, landed, and selected a few of their number to choose a place for a settlement. Of these, some went to Schenectady, and thence up the Mohawk, where a settlement of Germans had been formed a few years previous : the others, hearing of a beautiful country to the southwest, penetrated the wilderness in that direction; and after travelling through a hilly, and in some parts mountainous country, arrived the second day on the height of land east of the Schoharie creek.

"Here a scene of extraordinary beauty, and to them entirely new, burst upon their sight. At their feet, and far below them, was a plain of limited extent, embosomed by hills, in some places rising abruptly to the height of 1000 feet, and in others of more gentle ascent, and broken by deep ravines. The declivity of the hills was covered with a stinted growth of oak, too scanty to hide even from a distant view the rocks amid which they grew, and forming a striking contrast with the stately forest and luxuriant vegetation of the plain below. The valley had been partially cleared, and the alternate spots of woodland and meadow, interspersed with clumps of trees, added variety and richness to the landscape. Along its western boundary ran the Schoharie creek, now washing the base of the hill, now meandering through the flats; its course marked through the woodlands by the deep green of the trees along its bank, and through the meadows by the elms that lined its borders; sometimes its course was hidden from the view by the thick foliage, and again, as its channel spread out wider, or its course inclined to the east, its clear waters were seen glittering in the sunbeams. No traces of any occupants of this valley were seen, except here and there the ruins of a deserted wigwam.

"The travellers returned to Albany, and gave so flattering an account of the country which they had visited, that the whole company started immediately for Schoharie, without waiting for the return of their friends from the Mohawk. The place they chose for a settlement had formerly been occupied by a part of the Mohawk tribe of Indians; but they had most of them now left it. The settlers were illy provided with implements of husbandry, and with many of the necessaries of life, which wants were severely felt during many years. Whether they paid the Mohawks an equivalent for the land, tradition does not inform us. It was not, however, until several years after, that they obtained a grant

66

from government. A commission was sent to grant them a title in the name of the crown, and to extend to them the protection of the laws. Believing this to be a pretence for exacting taxes from them, and remembering their former oppression, they drove off the commissioners, and refused to accept his proposals. A part left the settlement, and went up the Mohawk, and the remainder were finally prevailed upon by threats and persuasion to accept the terms offered by the government agent."—*Annals of Tryon county.*

The following extracts are from a pamphlet publication by Mr. John M. Brown, entitled " A brief sketch of the first settlement of the county of Schoharie by the Germans," published in 1823.

" Schoharie was first inhabited by a French Indian prisoner, married to a Mohawk squaw. His name was Karigondonte, whose father-in-law sent him there, for fear that the Mohawk Indians would kill him when they got drunk, and gave him land, as the Mohawk bore a great enmity to the French. Other Indians, Mohawk, Mohegan, Discarora, Delaware, and Oneidas, flocked to him, so that he increased to a nation about 300 strong, and established chiefs among them; who then pretended to be the owners of all that vast territory of land, and granted conveyances thereof.

" Queen Anne having intended to settle America, sent her agent to purchase land from the natives; for which purpose she sent messengers to Germany, to invite people to come over and settle, and promised that they should have the land they possessed, free. In consequence whereof, many came over; and a purchase was made, beginning near little Schoharie creek, at high-water mark of the big Schoharie river, and at an oak stump, burned out hollow by the Indians to serve for stamping their corn; where a stone heap was erected which stands to this day. The Indian seal of a turtle and a snake was cut on the stump, (here I must digress a little, and mention that the said stump or stamp block, served the Germans for their first grist-mill,) from thence down to the north, including all the low land on both sides of the creek, for the space of about eight miles, containing 20,000 acres.

" . . . . Now being safe arrived, in the first week after three children were born, namely, Johanes Earhart, Wilhelmus Bouck, and Elizabeth Lawyer; they found the land good, and much of the flats clear. The Indians, who were all the people they found, having shifted, they went to work and planted corn, which they got of the natives; and in working the ground with their broad hoes, they found a potatoe-like root, which they called earth-acorns: also another, they called earth-beans, which they cooked or roasted, and so served them for food.

" In the fall of 1713, Lambert Sternbergh carried a spint of wheat along the Indian foot-path from Schenectady to Schoharie; there sowed or rather planted it over more than an acre of ground, which grew well; and the next year he reaped and threshed it, and measured 83 skipple out of it. This was the first wheat ever raised in Schoharie; and by about 40 years after, it was reckoned that one year in another, they carried 36,000 skipple, [27,000 bushels,] to Albany.

" Now the new inhabitants soon began to think themselves well off. By their industry, and great fertility of the soil, they soon got plenty to eat—wore moggisins, buckskin breeches and jackets of leather, which they plentifully obtained of the Indians. Nine of them owned the first horse, which was a gray. But now a new and very great difficulty was felt: they had no grist-mills, no teams, no horses, no roads fit for passage, but Indian foot-paths. They stamped, and also peeled their corn by help of lye, and then cooked it to eat. Their wheat they carried to Schenectady to grind, a space of 19 miles, every man about a skipple to his load: sometimes there would go 20 in a drove, often men and women together. This they had to do for 3 or four years. until a grist-mill was built by one William Fox.

" By now, the people began to think themselves very well off, having plenty to eat, began to have stock—used horses—made their own block sleighs for use at home, and wooden shod sleighs to go to Albany; but knew of no britsh collars, (which were an invention of Schenectady;) made a trip to Albany—back again in 5 days. Their wagons for summer use, were made of blocks sawed off, of a thick water beech tree, which we now call button-wood."

The following is an eastern view of the old stone church situated about a mile north of the courthouse in Schoharie, which was used as a fort during the revolutionary war. The view is taken from a painting executed about 17 years since, and now in the possession of Henry Hamilton, Esq., of Schoharie. Since that time the church

Ancient stone church in Schoharie.

has been somewhat altered, a tower having been erected in the place of the spire. It is very antiquated in its appearance. On many of the stones are carved various names, supposed to be those of persons who contributed towards its erection. In ancient times this church was surrounded with a picket fence. When Sir John Johnson ravaged the Mohawk valley in 1780, he visited Schoharie, and after making an unsuccessful attack on the Middle Fort, he proceeded to the Lower Fort, as this church was called.

"When they arrived at the Lower Fort, they showed little disposition to attack it, although its garrison did not amount to 100 men. They separated into two divisions, the regular troops marching along the bank of the creek, and the Indians filing off about half a mile to the east of the fort. The regulars fired a few cannon-shot without effect, one only lodging in the corner of the church;* and then, after sinking one of their field-pieces in a morass, marched round to the north of the fort, where they were joined by the Indians. Here they fired a few shot with small-arms, and a few of the Indians approached near enough to throw their bullets into the tower of the church, where some marksmen had been stationed. A discharge of grape from the fort drove them back, and they continued their march through the woods to Fort Hunter, on the Mohawk, near the mouth of Schoharie creek, where they arrived after dark.

"The beautiful valley of Schoharie creek presented a scene of devastation, on the night of the 17th of October, not easily described. Houses, barns, and numerous stacks of hay and grain, were consumed; domestic animals lay dead everywhere over the fields; a few buildings belonging to the royalists had been spared, but the militia, sallying out, set fire to them in revenge. After the burning of Schoharie, this settlement ceased to be so much an object of tory vengeance: and during the years 1781 and 1782, though there were frequent alarms, little damage was done by the enemy. The Indians appeared once in considerable numbers at Cobbleskill, burned a few buildings, killed one man, and carried off five prisoners; but the body of the inhabitants had taken refuge in a fort which they had built on their return from Schoharie in 1781, and were safe."—*Annals of Tryon County.*

Esperance, 8 miles N. of Schoharie courthouse, is a village of about 70 dwellings. Sloansville, Gallupville, and Smithville, are small villages or settlements in this town.

SEWARD was formed from the south part of Sharon in 1840; centrally distant from Schoharie NW. 20 miles. Pop. 2,086. Gardnersville and Hynesville are the names of the post-offices. In July, 1781, a battle was fought in this town between the Americans and a body of the enemy, principally Indians, under the command of a tory by the name of John Doxtader.

"Col. Willet, who now commanded at Fort Plain, in July sent Lieut. Gros, with 36 men, as a secret scout, into Durlagh, now the town of Sharon, [within the limits of the new town of Seward,] in Schoharie county. They discovered, near the borders of that settlement, an Indian trail, and followed it in the direction the Indians had gone. The scout fell in file alongside of the path made by the Indians, and by this means ascertained that the force of the enemy was very considerable. Three men were sent on to make further discoveries. After pursuing the trail a short distance, they arrived upon the borders of a thick cedar swamp, 5 or 6 miles NE. of Cherry Valley; here they found the camp of the enemy, in which a few sentinels only were stationed. The main body of the enemy were out on some expedition. One of the men stole up and took a blanket from beneath a tent, without being discovered. Having made the necessary observations, they followed the remainder of the scout back to Fort Plain. It was almost night when the scout arrived, but Col. Willet added 70 men, and ordered an immediate march. They were joined by Major Robert McKean, with about 30 men, making their force 150. McKean informed Col. Willet that the enemy were about 300 strong, principally Indians, under the command of a tory, by the name of John Doxtader—and that the day previous they had destroyed Currytown, a small settlement near the Mohawk, a short distance above Schenectady. The night was very dark, and there was no road, nothing but a path through the woods. About daylight they came in sight of the camp. A scout sent forward reported that the enemy had just returned. Col. Willet drew up his men in two parallel lines, and then ordered them to fall back and conceal themselves behind the trees. His plan was favored by the thick cedar swamp in the neighborhood of the enemy's camp. Major McKean with 50 men occupied the right, and Col. Willet commanded the left body, composed of his 100 men. Two men were then sent forward to pass over a piece of open ground in sight of the enemy. When discovered they were directed to lead in between the two lines. The expectations of Col. Willet were realized; the Indians, as soon as they saw these men, raised their war-cry and commenced an immediate pursuit. As they followed in, the troops of Major McKean opened a galling and destructive fire upon them, which was warmly seconded by Col. Willet's men on the left. The Indians were beaten at their own game; they sought shelter behind the trees, but were driven back and routed at the point of the bayonet. Col. Willet led the van, and waving his hat, cheered on his men. The camp of the enemy and all their plunder was taken. They retreated down towards the Susquehannah, and were pursued with considerable loss. Shortly after the first fire, Major McKean received two severe wounds, but he continued his command until the rout of the enemy was complete. His faithful soldiers carried him back to Fort Plain, where he survived but a day or two. The victory was dearly won by the loss of this brave and hardy chieftain."
—*Annals of Tryon County.*

SHARON, taken from Schoharie in 1797; from Albany 40 miles. Pop. 2,520. Sharon, 20 NW., and Leesville 24 miles from Schoharie, are small villages.

SUMMIT, taken from Cobelskill and Jefferson in 1819; from Albany 52 miles. This township comprises the highest mountains in the county, forming part of the water shed between the Susquehannah and Mohawk rivers. Summit Corners, 20 SW., and Charlotteville, 25 miles from Schoharie, are small settlements. Pop. 2,009.

SENECA COUNTY.

SENECA COUNTY was taken from Cayuga in 1804; since which other counties have been formed from it. Its greatest length N. and S. is 36 miles; medium width, 12. Centrally distant from New York 317, from Albany 172 miles. The land rises gently from the Cayuga and Seneca lakes, and the whole county is pleasantly diversified with hills and vales. The soil is well adapted to the culture of grain, grasses, and fruit trees, being principally a vegetable mould or calcareous loam. There is no stream of importance excepting the outlet of the Seneca lake, which from Waterloo to Seneca lake furnishes much hydraulic power. The lands of this county formed part of the military tract, and the titles therefore are derived from the state through patents to the soldiers of the revolution. The Erie canal just touches upon the county in the NE. part, in the town of Tyre. The Auburn and Rochester railroad passes through the towns of Waterloo and Seneca Falls. The county is divided into 10 towns. Pop. 24,868.

COVERT, taken from Ovid in 1817; from Albany 177, from Ovid SE. 9 miles. Pop. 1,744. Covert is a small village.

FAYETTE, originally named Washington, and taken from Romulus in 1800; from Albany 178 miles. Pop. 3,902. West Fayette, Canoga, and Bearysville, are small villages. Waterloo village lies partially in this town.

JUNIUS, taken from Fayette in 1803; from Albany 173 miles. Pop. 1,594. Dublin is a small settlement 7 miles northwest from Waterloo.

LODI, taken from Covert in 1826; from Albany 175 miles. Pop. 2,238. Lodi village, 4 miles S. from Ovid village, has about 35 dwellings. Townsendville and Ingersoll's Store are post-offices.

OVID, organized in 1789; bounds since altered; from Albany 171 miles. Pop. 2,719. Ovid, the half-shire seat, is about 17 miles SE. of Waterloo. It is delightfully situated on the Newburg turnpike. The village commands a view of a large part of both lakes, and of portions of 9 adjoining counties, the land rising gradually to it from the lakes, rich, arable, and finely cultivated in farms. There is here 1 Presbyterian and 1 Methodist church, a flourishing academy, and about 100 dwellings. Farmersville, 7 miles SE. from Ovid village, has about 40 dwellings.

ROMULUS was organized in 1789; from Waterloo centrally distant S. 13 miles. Romulus, Hoytes, and Bayleytown, are small settlements; the latter of which is upon Seneca lake, opposite Dresden, where there is a ferry. Pop. 2,066.

SENECA FALLS was taken from Junius in 1825. It is intersected centrally by the outlet of Seneca Lake. Pop. 4,101. Seneca Falls village is 4 miles E. of Waterloo, 11 from Geneva, 3 W. of Cayuga bridge, 85 from Utica, and 167 from Albany. This is a flourishing

East view of Seneca Falls village.

village, containing between 400 and 500 dwellings, 1 Baptist, 1 Presbyterian, 1 Episcopal, 1 Methodist, and 1 Catholic church, an academy, and 3 newspaper printing establishments. There is at this place a heavy water-power of 47 feet over 4 dams, putting in operation 7 extensive flour-mills, besides quite a number of other mills and manufacturing establishments. The above engraving is an eastern view of the village, the river, and the Cayuga and Seneca canal, with one of the locks, &c.

The first settlers at this place were Horatio Jones and Lawrence Van Clief, who fixed their residence here shortly after the revolutionary war. Van Clief was a soldier in Sullivan's expedition. The village of Seneca Falls was founded in 1815, by Col. Mynderse, who settled here in 1795, and built the first flouring mills in this section of the state. In 1827, the village contained only 265 inhabitants. Bridgeport, formerly called West Cayuga, at the W. end of Cayuga bridge, was formerly a place of some business, but at present is in a decayed state, the canals having diverted its trade to other places. In 1789, James Bennet settled at this spot, and in connection with Col. John Harris, on the opposite side of the lake, kept a ferry here, which was of great importance to the early settlers at the west.

Tyre was taken from Junius in 1829, centrally distant from Waterloo NE. 9, and from Albany 171 miles. Pop. 1,507. It has a level surface, and that part of the town bordering on the Clyde and Seneca rivers is marshy.

Varick, taken from Romulus in 1830. Pop. 1,971. It is centrally situated 13 miles S. from Waterloo. Varick is the name of the post-office. North Romulus, and Romulusville are small settlements.

Waterloo was taken from Junius in 1829. It has a level surface and fertile soil. Pop. 3,026. The flourishing village of Waterloo is situated on the Seneca outlet and the Seneca and Cayuga canal, 4 miles from Seneca Falls village, 7 from Geneva, and 167 from Alba-

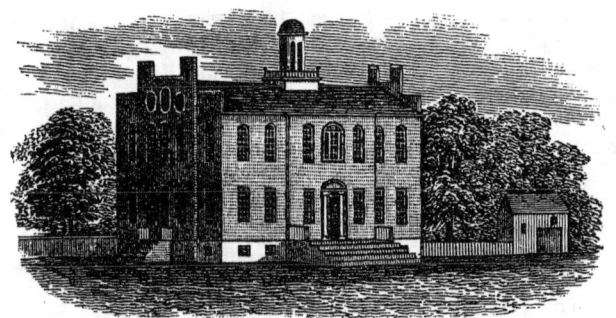

South view of the courthouse in Waterloo.

ny. It was founded in 1815, by the late Elisha Williams, of Columbia county, and was made a half-shire village in 1822. It contains about 300 dwellings, 4 churches—viz, 1 Episcopal, 1 Methodist, 1 Presbyterian, and 1 Baptist—and about 2,000 inhabitants. With the village of Seneca Falls, Waterloo possesses the advantage of the lateral canal uniting the Seneca and Cayuga lakes with the Erie canal. The water for the mills at this place is taken from the river and canal, and used under a head of 15 feet. The above engraving is a south view of the courthouse, built chiefly at the expense of Messrs. E. Williams and R. Swift, the former proprietors of the soil on which the village is erected.

STEUBEN COUNTY.

STEUBEN COUNTY, named in honor of Major-general Frederick William Baron de Steuben, the celebrated tactician of the revolutionary army, was taken from Ontario in 1796; boundaries since much altered; from Albany centrally distant SW. 216 miles, from New York W. 220; length and breadth 40 miles. The surface is broken and hilly, if not mountainous. Along the rivers, the general aspect of the county is uninviting, except that in some parts the alluvial flats are extensive and rich. The river hills are rocky, precipitous, and covered with evergreens; but the upland plains have a rich variety of trees, and fertile tracts principally of clayey loam. The staples of the county are lumber, grain, cattle, and wool. The lumbering is the chief business of the southern towns; but as the country is cleared of its forests, agriculture rises in importance. Chemung river is the great stream of the county; it was called by the Senecas *Cononque*, "horn in the water." Its flats are said to be superior in fertility to the Mohawk. This county, excepting the town of Reading on the western shore of the Seneca lake, was included in the extensive cession of New York to Massachusetts, and passed from that state, through Messrs. Phelps and Gorham and Robert Morris, to Sir William Pulteney. It was mostly settled by Pennsylvanians, excepting Prattsburg, which was settled by New Englanders. The county is divided into 27 towns. Pop. 45,985.

ADDISON, originally named Middletown, was organized in 1796. This town was settled in 1793. Its early inhabitants attended church at Canandaigua, 80 miles distant. Addison village, 16 miles S. from Bath, has about 40 dwellings. Rathbunville is the name of a post-office. Pop. 1,919.

BATH, organized in 1796; limits since much altered; from New York NW. 220, from Albany SW. 216 miles. Avoca, Kenadaville, and Mud Creek, are small settlements in this town. Pop. 4.796. Bath, the county seat, on the bank of the Conhocton* river, and 11 miles north of the N. York and Erie railroad, is one of the most pleasant villages in the western part of the state. The public square, laid out in 1792 by Capt. Charles Williamson, has the county and other public buildings, and several elegant private mansions.

View of the east side of Pulteney Square, Bath.

The above view of the eastern side of the square, shows on the right the Presbyterian church, built in 1822, being the first building erected with a steeple in the county. The one on the left is the Episcopal. There are in the village also, a courthouse, prison, a bank, a Methodist church, and about 200 dwellings. Bath was first settled in 1792, by Capt. Charles Williamson, the first agent of Sir William Pulteney, after whom the public square was named. Sir William, who was a noted English whig, was a large proprietor in this vicinity.

---

* Conhocton, in the Seneca language, means "trees in the water."

Capt. Williamson's party came here from Williamsport in Pennsylvania, and were obliged to cut a road all the way through the forest. In 1795, Capt. Williamson established a theatre at this place. He is represented to have been a scientific man, of liberal and extended views. Subsequently he was appointed governor of one of the West India islands; but died on his passage thither. As early as 1796, the various settlements in this region began to exhibit an appearance of respectability rarely instanced in so new a country. A printing office was then established here, and a newspaper printed, entitled the Bath Gazette. The number of inhabitants in Bath and 8 miles around numbered 800. There were also 2 schools, 1 grist-mill and 5 saw-mills.

The following, respecting the early history of this place is extracted from the Travels of Maude, an English gentlemen, who visited this region about the year 1800.

"Bath, which now contains about 40 families," says this traveller, "was laid out in 1792, the same year that Capt. Williamson forced a passage to this till then unknown country, through a length of wilderness which the oldest and most experienced woodmen could not be tempted to *assist* him to explore; tempted by an offer of more than 5 times the amount of their usual wages. Capt. Williamson was then accompanied by his friend and relative, Mr. Johnstone, and a servant—afterward a backwoodsman, was prevailed on to join the party. It was not till 1795 that this country could supply its inhabitants with food; for till then, their flour was brought from Northumberland, and their pork from Philadelphia; yet, so rapidly has the spirit of improvement gone forth in this country, so suddenly has plenty burst forth where so late was famine, and so quick the change of scene from dark tangled forests (whose death-like silence yielded to the growl of bears, the howl of wolves, and the yell of savages) to smiling fields, to flocks and herds, and to the busy hum of men, that instead of being indebted to others for their support, they will henceforth annually supply the low country, Baltimore especially, with many hundred barrels of flour and head of cattle. On Capt. Williamson's first arrival, where now is Bath, he built a small log-hut for his wife and family. If a stranger came to visit him, he built up a little nook for him to put his bed in. In a little time, a boarded or frame house was built to the left of the hut; this also was intended but as a temporary residence, though it then appeared a palace. His present residence, a very commodious, roomy, and well-planned house, is situated on the right of where stood the hut long since consigned to the kitchen fire. .... Bath is the capital of Steuben county, which county contains at present (1800) about 300 families. On the first settlement of the country these mountainous districts were thought so unfavorably of when compared with the rich flats of Ontario county, (or the Genesee country,) that none of the settlers could be prevailed upon to establish themselves here till Capt. Williamson himself set the example, saying, 'As Nature has done so much for the northern plains, I will do something for these southern mountains;' though the truth of the case was, that Capt. Williamson saw very clearly, on his first visit to the country, that the Susquehannah and not the Mohawk would be its best friend. Even now it has proved so; for at this day (1800) a bushel of wheat is better worth $1,00 at Bath than 60 cents at Geneva. This difference will grow wider every year; for little, if any, additional improvement can be made in the water communication with New York, while that to Baltimore will admit of very extensive and advantageous ones. Its present efforts are those of a child, compared with the manly strength it will soon assume. I visited Capt. Williamson's mills, a little west of Bath, on Conhocton creek, which before the winter sets in will be made navigable 15 miles higher up; at least a farmer there promises to send an ark down from thence in the spring. Should he succeed, Capt. Williamson promises him a gift of 30 acres of land. The navigation of the Susquehannah will then extend to within 6 miles of the Canandaigua lake."

The following inscriptions were copied from monuments in the graveyard in this place.

STEUBEN COUNTY.

"GEORGE C. EDWARDS, died Nov. 18th, 1837; born at Stockbridge, Mass., Sept. 28, 1787.—This monument records the affection and respect of the Members and Court of the Bar of Steuben county, for George C. Edwards.—Tribute to the memory of a just Judge, an able Lawyer, a good citizen, and an honest man.—The richest legacy to leave for posterity is a good name."

"Sacred to the memory of DUGALD CAMERON, a native of Invernesshire, Scotland, and a resident of this his adopted country from 1794 until his decease, which took place in the city of Albany whilst there as a member of the legislature of this state, on the 5th of March, 1828, aged 52 years. In his death the church was deprived of a liberal donor, the public of an useful and faithful representative, the poor and the wayfaring of a ready and benevolent friend.—'Mark the perfect man and behold the upright, for the end of that man is peace.'"

BRADFORD, recently formed; from Bath centrally distant E. 12 miles. Jersey is the post-office. Pop. 1,545.

CAMERON, taken from Addison in 1822; from Bath S. 8 miles. Pop. 1,349. The Canisteo river, which name in the Indian tongue signifies "board in the water," crosses the town. Cameron and South Cameron are the post-offices.

CAMPBELL, taken from Hornby in 1831; from Bath SE. 11 miles. Pop. 850. There is a post-office at Campbelltown village, and one at Hammond's mills.

CANISTEO, organized in 1796; from Albany 241, from Bath SW. 14 miles. Pop. 941. The rich flats of the Canisteo river in this town are about half a mile in width. This was the first settled place in the county. It was settled in 1790, by Solomon Bennett, 3 families by the name of Stevens, and Capt. Jemison. They came up the Chemung and Canisteo rivers from Athens, Pennsylvania. Canisteo and East Canisteo are post-offices.

CATON, the SE. town of the county, recently erected from Painted Post; centrally distant from Bath 28 miles. Pop. 797.

CONHOCTON, taken from Bath and Dansville in 1812; from Albany 215, from Bath NW. 16 miles. Pop. 2,985. Liberty is a small village; Blood's Corners and Patchin's Mills are small settlements.

DANSVILLE, organized in 1796; since altered in area; from Albany 240, from Bath NW. 24 miles. Pop. 2,725. South Dansville, Rogersville, Doty's Corners, and De Witts Valley, are post-offices.

ERWIN, taken from Painted Post in 1826; from Albany 212, from Bath SE. 20 miles. Near the mouth of the Conhocton river is the small village of Erwin, upon the Great Bend and Bath turnpike. Upon the rivers are rich alluvial flats, well cultivated, and a fine bridge across the Conhocton 300 feet long. There are post-offices at the village of Erwin and Painted Post. Pop. 782.

The celebrated "*painted post*," from which the town of Painted Post derived its name, formerly stood upon the bank of the river. There have been various stories in relation to its origin; the following account taken from the narrative of the captivity and sufferings of Gen. Freegift Patchin, who was taken prisoner by a party of Indians under Brant during the revolution, is probably correct. "Near this, we found the famous PAINTED POST, which is now known over the whole continent, to those conversant with the early history of our country; the origin of which was as follows. Whether it was in the revolution, or in the Dunmore battles with the Indians, which commenced in Virginia, or in the French war, I do not know; an Indian chief, on this spot, had been victorious in battle, killed and took prisoners to the number of about 60. This event he celebrated by causing a tree to be taken from the forest and hewed four square, painted red, and the number he killed, which was 28, represented across the post in black paint, without any heads, but those he took prisoners, which was 30, were represented with heads on in black paint, as the others. This post he erected, and thus handed down to posterity an account that here a battle was fought; but by whom, and who the sufferers were, is covered in darkness, except that it was between the whites and Indians."

GREENWOOD, taken from Troupsburg and Canisteo in 1827; from Albany 251; from Bath SW. 26 miles. Pop. 1,138.

HORNBY, taken from Painted Post in 1826; from Albany 199, from Bath SE. 20 miles. Pop. 1,048.

HORNELLSVILLE, taken from Canisteo in 1820; from Albany 236. Pop. 2,121. Hornellsville, so called from George Hornell, its first settler, lies on a branch of the Canisteo near the main stream, on the road from Bath to Angelica, 20 miles W. from the former, and on the line of the New York and Erie railroad; it contains 1 Presbyterian and 1 Methodist church, and about 50 dwellings. Arkport, on the Canisteo, and Purdy creek, are post-offices.

HOWARD, taken from Bath and Dansville in 1812; centrally distant W. from Bath 12 miles. Bennet's Flats, post village, contains 2 churches, an academy, and about 40 dwellings. The names of the post-offices are Howard, Goffs Mills, Towlesville, and Neil's Creek. Pop. 3,250.

JASPER, taken from Troupsburg and Canisteo in 1827; from Bath S. 24 miles. Pop. 1,187. Adamsport is a small village.

LINDLEY, recently formed from Erwin; from Bath SE. centrally distant 24 miles. Pop. 638. Erwin Centre and Lindleytown are the post offices. The limits of the town were early settled. At this

Early method of pounding corn.

period there being no mills in this section for grinding the grain of the inhabitants, they adopted a substitute for preparing their corn, not uncommon among the early settlements in this region. The above is a representation of this method, consisting of a stump hollowed out by fire as a mortar, with a log attached to the end of a young sapling bent over to act as a pestle. This process was slow and tedious, it being a day's work to convert half a bushel of corn into samp. The settlers who owned a few slaves employed them in this drudgery; hence the process was vulgarly termed "*niggering corn.*"

ORANGE, with Bradford, until recently comprehended one town, under the name of Jersey; 205 miles from Albany, from Bath centrally distant E. 15 miles. Pop. 1,822. Meads Creek and Sugar Hill are names of post-offices.

PAINTED POST, organized in 1796; from Albany 210, from Bath centrally distant SE. 22 miles. Pop. 1,672. This is a place much noted in the early history of this section of the country. The celebrated "*painted post,*" (for the history of which see Erwin in this county,) from which the place derived its name, stood within the old limits of this town. The flats on the Chemung river are very rich, and the adjoining hills covered with pine forests. The navigable feeder of the Chemung canal is supplied from the river at the "*chimney narrows,*" so called from several piles of rocks rising perpendicularly in various places from the hill-side, and having the appearance of chimneys. Within two miles of the western boundary of the town, on the Great Bend and Bath road and north bank of the Chemung river, is the little village of Centreville, which was formerly called Painted Post. This, including the village of Knoxville, with which it is nearly connected, contains 100 dwellings. The line of the Erie railroad runs in the valley of the Chemung river, which at the village of Corning, on the south bank of this stream, is intersected by the Corning and Blossburg railroad, communicating with the coal mines of Pennsylvania.

PRATTSBURG, named after a principal proprietor, was taken from Pulteney in 1813; from Albany 202, from Bath centrally distant N. 14 miles. Pop. 2,442. Prattsburg village has two churches, an incorporated academy, and about 80 dwellings.

PULTENEY, taken from Bath in 1808; from Albany 212, from Bath centrally distant NE. 18 miles. Pop. 1,782. Pulteney, Peltonville, and South Pulteney, are post-offices.

READING, the NE. town of the county, was taken from Frederickstown, then Wayne, in 1806; from Albany 186 miles. Pop. 1,535. Irelandville, 24 miles NE. from Bath, has about 50 dwellings. Jefferson or Savoy village, on the inlet of the lake, partly in Dix of Tioga county, has about 300 inhabitants. Rock Stream, near Seneca lake, has a cascade of 140 feet. There is a post-office called North Reading.

TROUPSBURG, settled in 1805; taken from Middletown and Canisteo in 1808; from Albany 247, and from Bath SW. 28 miles. Pop. 1,172. Troupsburg and West Troupsburg are the post-offices.

TYRONE, taken from Wayne in 1822; from Albany 194, from Bath NE. 16 miles; settled by emigrants from New England, New Jersey, and Orange county, New York. Tyrone, Tobanna, and Pine Grove, are post-offices. Pop. 2,098.

URBANA, taken from Bath in 1822; from Albany 207, centrally

distant from Bath NE. 8 miles. Pop. 1,889. "At the head of the Crooked Lake lies the flourishing village of Hammondsport, founded in 1826 by Lazarus Hammond, containing 1 Presbyterian and 1 Episcopal church, and about 100 dwellings. The village is favorably situated for trade, by reason of the lake. It must become the port of the county, whence much of its exports will seek a market in the centre of the state, and at the towns on the Hudson river. A steamboat daily plies between here and Penn Yan, the capital of Yates county; thence the Crooked Lake canal leads to the Seneca Lake, which is connected with the Erie canal by the Seneca and Cayuga canal, by which route there is an uninterrupted water communication with New York." Urbana, Cold Springs, and Mount Washington, are the names of the post-offices.

WAYNE, organized in 1796, under the name of Frederickstown; limits and name since altered; from Albany 199 miles. Pop. 1,377. Wayne, post village, at the north end of Little Lake, 18 miles NE. from Bath, has about 40 dwellings. There is a post-office at Wayne Four Corners.

WHEELER, taken from Bath and Prattsburg in 1820; from Albany 210, from Bath N. 10 miles. Pop. 1,305. Wheeler and West Urbana are post-offices.

WOODHULL, taken from Troupsburg and Addison in 1828; from Albany 236, from Bath centrally distant S. 22 miles. It is thinly inhabited. Pop. 820. Newville is a small settlement.

SUFFOLK COUNTY.

SUFFOLK COUNTY, which comprises about two thirds of Long Island, was organized in 1683, at which time the ridings were abolished, and Long Island was divided into three counties, as they have remained ever since. It is about one hundred and ten miles in length, and in some parts twenty in width. On the north side next the sound the land is considerably broken and hilly; in the interior, and on the south side it is mostly a sandy plain, covered for the greater part with forests of pine, in which the wild deer is still an inhabitant. The county is not well watered, the streams being few and small. The chief business of the inhabitants is agriculture and fishing; they also send large quantities of pine wood to market. The original settlers of the county were mostly from New England, and the inhabitants have ever retained to a great degree the habits and manners of the Puritans. The county is divided into 9 towns, all of which, except Riverhead, were organized in 1788. Pop. 32,468.

BROOKHAVEN, the largest town in the county, embraces the whole width of the island. It contains more than 103,000 acres, of which only about 35,000 are improved. The greater part of the inhabitants are distributed along the villages on the sound and the ocean. The middle portion is for the most part covered with pine forests, in which deer abound. Pop. 7,050.

"The first settlement in the town was commenced at Setauket, in 1655, by which name the town was at first called. Most, if not all, the original planters came from Boston and its vicinity. The civil affairs of the settlement were conducted by magistrates elected from among themselves, and by rules and ordinances adopted in the primary assemblies of the people. After the conquest of New York in 1664, a patent of confirmation for their purchases of the natives was obtained from Governor Nicol. The first minister, Rev. Nathaniel Brewster, was settled here in 1665. He was a grandson of Elder William Brewster, one of the founders of the Plymouth colony, who came over in the May Flower, in 1620. Mr. Brewster died in 1690. It would seem that from age or some other infirmity, he was unable to discharge his pastoral duties for some years before his death; for at a town meeting held October 31, 1685, Samuel Eburne was chosen by vote to be minister of the town, 'and it being proposed unto him, that in regard of some *tender consciences*, he would omit the *ceremony* in the book of common prayer, the said Samuel promised, that according to their desire, in regard of their *tender consciences*, to omit and not use the aforesaid *ceremonies* in the public worship, *except to such as should desire the same*.' The next minister, Rev. George Phillips, came to Setauket in 1697, and continued here till his death in 1739. The next minister was Rev. David Youngs: his successor, Rev. Benjamin Tallmadge, was settled here in 1754. Mr. Tallmadge was succeeded by Rev Noah Wetmore, who came here in 1786: Rev. Zachariah Greene was his successor. The following relative to seating the meeting-house, recorded on the town books, is a curious relic of olden times:—

"At a meeting of the trustees of Brookhaven, August 6th, 1703: Whereas there hath been several rude actions of late happened in our church by reason of the people not being seated, which is much to the dishonor of God and the discouragement of virtue. For preventing the like again, it is *ordered* that the inhabitants be seated after the manner and form following: All freeholders that have or shall subscribe within a month to pay 40 shillings to Mr. Phillips towards his sallary shall be seated at the table, and that no *women* are permitted to set there, except Col. *Smith's lady*, nor any *women kind*; And that the President for the time being shall sit in the right-hand seat under the pulpit, and the clerk on the left: the trustees in the front seat, and the Justices that are inhabitants of the town, are to be seated at the table, whether they pay 40 shillings or less. And the pew, No. 1, all such persons as have or shall subscribe 20 shillings; and the pew, No. 2, such as subscribe to pay 15 shillings; in pew, No. 3, such as subscribe to pay 10 shillings; No. 4, 8 shillings; No. 5, 12 shillings; No. 6, 9 shillings; No. 7, for the young men; No. 8, for the boys; No. 9, for ministers' widows and wives; and for those women whose husbands pay 40 shillings, to sit according to their age; No. 11, for those men's wives that pay from 20 to 15 shillings. The alley fronting the pews to be for such maids whose parents or selves shall subscribe for two, 6 shillings; No. 12, for those men's wives who pay from 10 to 15 shillings; No. 13, for maids; No. 14, for girls; and No. 15, free for any. Captain Clark and Joseph Tooker to settle the inhabitants according to the above order."

Caroline church, in Setauket, the first Episcopal church on Long Island, was erected in 1730. This building, after having been repeatedly altered and repaired, is still standing. The Congregational church at Old Mans, was first erected in 1720, and rebuilt in 1805. The Presbyterian church was built in 1800, at Middletown, and another at Fire-place, in 1828; the first church at this latter place was erected in 1740. The first Congregational church at Patchogue was built in 1767, the present in 1822. The Methodist church at this place was erected in 1830. The Baptist church at Corum has stood about ninety years. The Methodist church at Stonybrook was erected in 1817.

Setauket, the oldest and one of the most populous villages in the town, received its name from its being the residence of the Seatalcott tribe of Indians. It is situated on both sides of the harbor, occupying about two square miles. The village of Stonybrook is on the western side of the town adjoining the sound, and has one of the best harbors in this part of the island. There are about 60 dwellings; shipbuilding to a considerable extent is carried on in this place. Port Jefferson and Millers Place are small villages.

Corum is near the centre of the town, and has been the seat of the town business for more than 60 years. It is a small village containing about 150 inhabitants. In, or near the village, the British had accumulated a large quantity of forage in the winter of 1780, which was destroyed by Colonel Tallmadge, a native of Setauket. The plan of this expedition was approved of by a communication from General Washington.

"In pursuance of this communication, Major Tallmadge ordered the detachment to repair to Fairfield. Here being met by other troops, the party embarked, the 21st of November, 1780, at four o'clock, P. M., in eight whale-boats. The whole number, including the crews of the boats, amounted to eighty men. They crossed the sound in four hours, and landed at Old Mans at nine o'clock. The troops had marched about five miles, when it beginning to rain, they returned, and took shelter under their boats, and lay concealed in the bushes all that night and the next day. At evening the rain abating, the troops were again put in motion, and at three o'clock in the morning were within two miles of the fort. Here he divided his men into three parties, ordering each to attack the fort at the same time at different points. The order was so well executed, that the three divisions arrived nearly at the same moment. It was a triangular enclosure of several acres, strongly stockaded, well barricaded houses at two of the angles, and at the third a fort, with a deep ditch and wall, encircled by an abatis of sharpened pickets, projecting at an angle of forty-five degrees. The stockade was cut down, the column led through the grand-parade, and in ten minutes the main fort was carried by the bayonet. The vessels near the fort, laden with stores, attempted to escape, but the guns of the fort being brought to bear upon them, they were secured and burnt, as were the works and stores. The number of prisoners was fifty-four, of whom seven were wounded. While they were marched to the boats under an escort, Major Tallmadge proceeded with the remainder of his detachment, destroyed about three hundred tons of hay collected at Corum, and returned to the place of debarkation just as the party with the prisoners had arrived, and reached Fairfield by eleven o'clock the same evening; having accomplished the enterprise, including a march of forty miles by land and as much by water, without the loss of a man. Congress passed a resolve complimentary to the commander and troops engaged in this expedition, which was said by them to have been planned and conducted with wisdom and great gallantry by Major Tallmadge, and executed with intrepidity and complete success by the officers and soldiers of his detachment."

View of Patchogue in Brookhaven, Long Island.

The above is a view taken at the western entrance into the village of Patchouge; the Congregational and Methodist churches are seen on the left, and the compact part of the village in the distance on the right. The village is named after the Patchogue tribe of Indians, who once possessed the territory in this part of the island. It contains about 75 dwellings, the greater part of which have been erected within a few years. It is 28 miles from Riverhead, and 60 from New York, upon the great thoroughfare from Brooklyn to Sagg Harbor. Four miles east is the recently built village of Bell Port, containing about 30 dwellings, an academy, 2 ship-yards, &c. Five miles east of here is a small settlement called Fire-place, known as a rendezvous for sportsmen. Moriches is in the east part of the town, extending east from Mastic river. The groves of Mastic are somewhat celebrated.

EASTHAMPTON, the most easterly town on Long Island, includes the peninsula of Montauk and Gardiner's Island. It is centrally distant from New York 110 miles. Pop. 2,076. The town was settled in 1649 by about thirty families from Lynn, Massachusetts, and the towns adjacent. The town continued an independent plantation or community till 1657, when they put themselves under the jurisdiction of Connecticut. The Rev. Thomas James was the first minister in the town; he died in 1696, and was succeeded by Rev. Nathaniel Hunting. Mr. Hunting was succeeded by Rev. Samuel Buell in 1746. The fourth minister was Rev. Lyman Beecher, who was settled here in 1799. Mr. Beecher is now the President of the Lane Seminary in Ohio. The village of Easthampton is confined to a single street, of about a mile in length, having about 100 dwellings, mostly of an antiquated appearance, a church, and the Clinton academy, erected here in 1785, being the first institution of the kind on Long Island. The village of Amagansett, containing about 50 houses, is three miles to the east. Wainscott is a small village in the SW. part.

Gardiner's Island contains about 3,300 acres, with a soil mostly of a good quality; the nearest point of distance to Long Island is three miles. Lyon Gardiner, the first settler on the island, was a native of Scotland. He belonged to the republican party, with the illustrious Hampden, Cromwell, and others. His family bible, now in possession of his descendants on the island, contains the following, written in his own hand:—

"In the year 1635, the 10th day of July, came I, Lyon Gardiner, and Mary my wife, from Woden, a town of Holland, where my wife was born, being the daughter of one Diricke Willemson; her mother's name was Hachir, and her aunt, sister of her mother, was the wife of Wouter Leanderson, Old Burger Muster, dwelling in the Hostade, over against the Bruser, in the Unicorne's Head; her brother's name was Punce Garretson, also old Burger Muster. We came from Woden to London, and from thence to New England, and dwelt at Saybrook fort four years; it is at the mouth of Connecticut River, of which I was commander; and there was born to me a son, named David, the first born in that place; and in 1638 a daughter was born, named Mary, 30th of August, and then I went to an island of my own, which I had bought of the Indians, called by them Manchonock, by us Isle of Wight, and there was born another daughter the 14th of September, 1641, she being the first child of English parents born there."

The notorious pirate William Kidd visited this island and buried a valuable treasure. From this circumstance, doubtless, has arisen the numerous legends respecting the burial of "Kidd's money," in many places along the coast. The following is a brief account of Kidd:—

"William Kidd, the famous freebooter and pirate, was the commander of a merchant vessel which sailed between New York and London, and celebrated for his nautical skill and enterprise: on which account he was strongly recommended by Mr. Livingston of New York, then in London, as a proper person to take charge of a vessel which Lord Romney and others had purchased, and were then fitting out against the hordes of marauders which infested the Indian seas, and preyed upon the commerce of all nations. The expense of this expedition was £6000 sterling. It was a joint fund, to which the King, Lord Somers, the Earl of Rumsey, the Duke of Shrewsbury, the Earl of Oxford, Lord Bellamont, and Mr. Livingston were contributors. Kidd agreed to be concerned to the amount of one-fifth of the whole, and Mr. Livingston became his surety for the sum of £600. He soon set sail, and arrived on the American coast, where he continued for some time, and was useful in protecting our commerce, for which he received much public applause; and the assembly of this state voted him the sum of £250 as an acknowledgment of his services. He soon after established himself at the Island of Madagascar, where he lay like a shark, darting out at pleasure, and robbing with impunity the vessels of every country. Having captured a larger and better vessel than his own, he burnt the one in which he had sailed, and took command of the other; in which he ranged over the Indian coast from the Red Sea to Malabar, and his depredations extended from the Eastern Ocean, back along the Atlantic coast of South America, through the Bahamas, the whole West Indies, and the shores of Long Island. The last of which were selected as the fittest for depositing his ill-gotten treasures. He is supposed to have returned from the east with more valuable spoil than ever fell to the lot of any other individual. On his homeward passage from the West Indies to Boston, where he was finally apprehended, he anchored in Gardiner's bay, and in the presence of the owner of the island, Mr. Gardiner, and under the most solemn injunctions of secrecy, buried a pot of gold, silver, and precious stones. On the 3d of July, 1699, he was summoned before Lord Bellamont at Boston, and ordered to report his proceedings while in the service of the company; which refusing to do, he was immediately arrested and transported to England, where he was tried, convicted, and executed at "Execution Dock" on the 12th of May, 1701. He was found guilty of the murder of William Moore, gunner of the ship, and was hung in chains. Mr. John G. Gardiner has a small piece of gold cloth, which his father received from Mrs. Wetmore, who gave also the following account of Kidd's visit to the island. 'I remember, (she says,) when very young, hearing my mother say that her grandmother was the wife to Lord Gardiner when the pirate came to that island. He wanted Mrs. Gardiner to roast him a pig; she being afraid to refuse him, roasted it very nice, and he was much pleased with it. He then made her a present of this cloth, which she gave to her two daughters; what became of the other know I not; but this was handed down to me, and is, I believe, as nice as when first given, which must be upwards of a hundred years.'

"It having been ascertained that he had buried treasures upon this island, commissioners were sent by Governor Bellamont, who obtained the same, and for which they gave the following receipt:—

"A true account of all such gold, silver, jewels, and merchandize, late in the possession of Captain William Kidd, which had been seized and secured by us pursuant to an order from his Excellency, Richard Earl of Bellamont, bearing date July 7, 1699.

Received, the 17th instant, of Mr. John Gardiner, viz.   ounces.
No. 1. One bag of dust-gold, - - - - - - - - - - - - - - - -   63 3-4
     2. One bag of coined gold,
        and one in silver, - - - - - - - - - - - - - - - - -   11
                                                                                124
     3. One bag of dust-gold, - - - - - - - - - - - - - - -   24 3-4
     4. One bag of silver rings, and sundry precious stones, - - - -   4 7-8
     5. One bag of unpolished stones, - - - - - - - - - -   12 1-2
     6. One piece of crystal, carnelian rings, two agates, two amethysts.
     7. One bag silver buttons and lamps, - - - - - - -
     8. One bag of broken silver, - - - - - - - - - - - -   173 1-2
     9. One bag of gold bars, - - - - - - - - - - - - -   353 1-4
    10. One do. - - - - - - - - - - - - - - - - - - -   238 1-2
    11. One bag of dust-gold, - - - - - - - - - - - - -   59 1-2
    12. One bag of silver bars, - - - - - - - - - - - -   309

        Samuel Sewall, Nathaniel Byfield,
        Jeremiah Dummer, Andrew Belcher,
                                        Commissioners."

View of Montauk Point, Long Island.

The peninsula of Montauk contains 9,000 acres. The land is owned by about forty individuals, as tenants in common. The Indians have non-fructuary interest in a portion of the land; but as the race is nearly extinct, this incumbrance must be of short duration. The soil is generally good, and is used as pasture land. The surface is rough, and in some places precipitous. "There is a sublimity and wildness, as well as solitariness here, which leave a powerful impression on the heart. In a storm, the scene which the ocean presents is awfully grand and terrific. On the extreme point stands the tall white column erected by the government for a lighthouse in 1795, at an expense of $22,300. It is constructed of stone, in the most substantial manner." Within five or six miles of this place the Spanish schooner Amistad, in possession of a company of African slaves, was captured and carried into New London. The following particulars respecting the schooner, &c., was written by one of the officers of the United States brig Washington:—

New London, August 26, 1839.

"While this vessel was sounding this day between Gardiner's and Montauk Points, a schooner was seen lying in-shore off Culloden Point, under circumstances so suspicious as to authorize Lieutenant-commandant Gedney to stand in to see what was her character: seeing a number of people on the beach with carts and horses, and a boat passing to and fro, a boat was armed and despatched with an officer to board her. On coming alongside, a number of negroes were discovered on her deck, and twenty or thirty more were on the beach—two white men came forward and claimed the protection of the officer. The schooner proved to be the 'Amistad,' Captain Ramonflues, from the Havanna, bound to Guanajah, Port Principe, with 54 blacks and two passengers on board; the former, four nights after they were out, rose and murdered the captain and three of the crew—they then took possession of the vessel, with the intention of returning to the coast of Africa. Pedro Montez, passenger, and Jose Ruiz, owner of the slaves and a part of the cargo, were only saved to navigate the vessel. After boxing about for four days in the Bahama channel, the vessel was steered for the Island of St. Andrews, near New Providence—from thence she went to Green Key, where the blacks laid in a supply of water. After leaving this place the vessel was steered by Pedro Montez for New Providence, the negroes being under the impression that she was steering for the coast of Africa—they would not however permit her to enter the port, but anchored every night off the coast. The situation of the two whites was all this time truly deplorable, being treated with the greatest severity, and Pedro Montez, who had charge of the navigation, was suffering from two severe wounds, one on the head and one on the arm, their lives being threatened every instant. He was ordered to change the course again for the coast of Africa, the negroes themselves steering by the sun in the daytime, while at night he would alter their course so as to bring them back to their original place of destination. They remained three days off Long Island, to the eastward of Providence, after which time they were two months on the ocean, sometimes steering to the eastward, and whenever an occasion would permit, the whites would alter the course to the northward and westward, always in hopes of falling in with some vessel of war, or being enabled to run into some port, when they would be relieved from their horrid situation.

"Several times they were boarded by vessels; once by an American schooner from Kingston; on these occasions the whites were ordered below, while the negroes communicated and traded with the vessels; the schooner from Kingston supplied them with a demijohn of water for the moderate sum of one doubloon—this schooner, whose name was not ascertained, finding that the negroes had plenty of money, remained lashed alongside the 'Amistad' for twenty-four hours, though they must have been aware that all was not right on board, and probably suspected the character of the vessel—this was on the eighteenth of the present month; the vessel was steered to the northward and westward, and on the 20th instant, distant from New York 25 miles, the pilot-boat No. 3 came alongside and gave the negroes some apples. She was also hailed by No. 4; when the latter boat came near, the negroes armed themselves and would not permit her to board them; they were so exasperated with the two whites for bringing them so much out of their way, that they expected every moment to be murdered. On the 24th they made Montauk light, and steered for it in the hope of running the vessel ashore, but the tide drifted them up the bay, and they anchored where they were found by the brig Washington, off Culloden point. The negroes were found in communication with the shore, where they laid in a fresh supply of water, and were on the point of sailing again for the coast of Africa. They had a good supply of money, some of which it is likely was taken by the people on the beach. After disarming and sending them on board from the beach, the leader jumped overboard with three hundred doubloons about him, the property of the captain, all of which he succeeded in losing from his person, and then submitted himself to be captured. The schooner was taken in tow by the brig and carried into New London."

The Africans were afterward taken to New Haven; and an investigation was had before the United States court at Hartford. In January, 1840, their case was tried before the United States district court. Judge Judson decided that they should be delivered up to the President of the United States to be sent back to Africa. The United States attorney having appealed from this decision, the case was referred to the Supreme Court, at Washington, which set in January, 1841. This court declared the freedom of the Africans.

HUNTINGTON, the westernmost town in the county, is bounded on the N. by the sound, and S. by the ocean. The surface in the N. is rough and hilly, in the centre a high sandy plain, covered with pines and shrub oaks. The South Bay has on its northern shore a strip of salt meadow nearly a mile wide. The soil near the sound, and particularly upon the necks, is the best in the town. Pop. 6,562. The earliest deed for land in this town was given to Gov. Eaton, of New Haven, for Eaton's Neck, in 1646, the first Indian deed to the original settlers of Huntington, and comprised six square miles.

"In an early period of the settlement, in this town as well as in others, almost all domestic trade was carried on by means of exchange. Contracts were made to be satisfied in produce, and even the judgments given in the courts, were made payable in grain, at fixed prices, or in *merchantable pay at the current price*. The prices were established by the governor and court of assize; and in 1665 the assessors were ordered to fix an estimate for stock. Accordingly, a horse or mare four years old and upward, was to be taken in pay at twelve pounds; a cow four years old and upward, at five pounds; an ox or bull of the same age, at six pounds; and other articles, as pork, wheat, corn, &c., at proportionate prices. In the draft of a contract between the town and a schoolmaster in 1657, the salary was to be paid in *current pay;* and in 1686 the town contracted with a carpenter to make an addition to the meeting-house, to be paid in produce. Even executions issued by the magistrates, were satisfied in the same way. 'At a town meeting, April 4, 1661, it was agreed that a *firkin of butter* should be paid in, at Stephen Jarvis's house by the middle of June, for the satisfaction of a debt due from ye town to Ensigne Briant.' The more effectually to preserve the public morals, the people excluded from society those whom they thought likely to injure them. In 1662, they appointed, by a vote at town meeting, a committee, consisting of the minister and six of their most respectable citizens, to examine the characters of those coming to settle among them; with power to admit or reject, as they judged most likely to benefit or injure society, with a proviso, that they should not exclude any 'that were honest, and well approved by honest and judicious men;' and forbid any inhabitant to sell or let house or land to any one not approved by the committee, under the penalty of ten pounds, to be paid to the town. In 1653, the town forbade any inhabitant to entertain a certain obnoxious individual longer than the space of a week, either gratuitously or for pay, under the penalty of forty shillings."

In 1660, the town put themselves under the jurisdiction of Connecticut, and in 1662, elected two deputies to attend the general court at Hartford. The connection was dissolved on the conquest of New York, in 1664. The first minister of the town was William Leveridge, who was established here 1658. He was succeeded by Rev. Eliphalet Jones in 1677. Mr. Jones was succeeded by Ebenezer Prime, who died in 1779, who was succeeded by Rev. Nathan Woodhull, and the latter by the Rev. William Schenck.

The following shows the appearance of the village of Huntington as it is entered from the westward. The Presbyterian church and academy are seen in the distance, near the central part of the engraving. The Universalist church is seen near the burying ground on the right. There are about one hundred dwellings in the vicinity of the churches. A newspaper is published in this place. This village is 40 miles W. from Riverhead, and about 45 from New York. The thriving village of Babylon, 40 miles from New York, on the south side of the island, in full view of the bay and ocean, contains about 250 inhabitants. It is situated upon *Sunquams Neck*, and has a fine stream of water on either side, upon which mills have long been

Western view of Huntington Village.

erected. The village of Little Cow Harbor is now called Centre Port, and the name of Great Cow Harbor changed to North Port. The steamer Lexington was burnt near Eaton's Neck, Jan. 13, 1840.

ISLIP. This town, on the S. side of the island, is centrally distant about 45 miles from New York. It received its name from the first settlers, many of whom came from Islip, in Oxfordshire, England. It has a level surface and a light and sandy soil, rendered productive by manures of sea-weed and fish. The bay on the south is 4 or 5 miles wide, containing an inexhaustible variety of fish, and is visited by a vast number of wildfowl. Pop. 1,909. The extensive domain known as Nicol's Patent, includes more than sixty square miles of land, and has, since its first purchase from the Indians in 1683 by William Nicol, been by successive entailment preserved as one estate.

RIVERHEAD, the shire town, was taken from Southold in 1792. Only a comparatively small portion of the town is under improvement; much of its territory is covered with wood, which has for a long period been a staple article for transportation.

The following is a southern view of the central part of the village of Riverhead, as seen from the residence of Mr. J. P. Terry, about 50 rods S. from the courthouse. The village is situated upon Peconic creek or river, a mill stream, about 2 miles above Peconic bay, about 90 miles from New York, 24 from Sagg Harbor, and 23 from Greenport. The village contains about 70 dwellings, a large proportion of which are one story in height, 1 Methodist, 1 Congregational, and 1 Swedenbourg or New Jerusalem church, an academy, and about 500 inhabitants. The courthouse, seen in the central part of the engraving with a small spire, has stood more than a century. James Port is a recent village E. of Riverhead. Old Aquabogue, Upper Aquabogue, Fresh Pond, Baiting Hollow, and Wading River, are small villages.

South view of the central part of Riverhead.

SHELTER ISLAND is a town comprehending the island of that name in Gardiner's bay. It is about six miles long and four broad, containing about 8,000 acres, divided into several farms. Pop. 379. The surface of the island is generally undulating, and covered in part by oak and other timber. The Indian name of this island was *Manhansack-aha-qushu-wamock,* meaning *an island sheltered by other islands.* It was originally purchased by James Farret from the Indians; it afterward became the property of Nathaniel and Constant Sylvester and Thomas Middleton. In 1674, the rights of these two last persons were confiscated by the Dutch government, and sold to the first for £500, the payment of which was enforced by a party of soldiers. The first church on the island was erected by the Presbyterians in 1733: it was taken down in 1816, and the present church erected on the same spot.

SMITHTOWN is centrally distant from New York 47 miles. Pop. 1,932. The town is nearly 10 miles square: the surface on the north is broken and hilly, and on the south a perfectly level plain. The inhabitants are much scattered over the surface. There are several small villages, the most considerable of which are the *Branch* and the settlement called *Head of the River.*

This town derives its name from Richard Smith, the patentee. The annexed account of this individual has been obligingly communicated by J. W. Blydenburgh, Esq.

" Smithtown takes its name from the original patentee, Richard Smith, jr., of Narragansett, who with his father Richard Smith, sen., and other relatives, came from Gloucestershire, England, to Boston in 1630. Smith married at Boston, and settled with his father at Taunton, 1637, where he remained until 1641, when he purchased a tract of the Narragansett sachems ' among the thickest of the Indians,' computed at 30,000 acres, erected a house for trade, and gave free entertainment to travellers,—it being the great road of the country. The dwelling of Smith stood on the present site of the Updike house in North Kingston, and it is said that the present dwelling contains some of the materials of the old. Smith's was the first house built in Narragansett, and was probably a blockhouse. Roger Williams, Wilcox and others, built soon after, and Williams sold out to Smith in 1651. Smith afterward made many purchases of the Indians, and March 8, 1656, Coginiquant leased them for 60 years an immense tract south of his dwelling. June 8, 1659, the same sachem leased them for a thousand years an enlarged tract, which gave rise to great disputes, which were the final cause of his removal to Long Island and the settlement of Smithtown. In 1654, the war broke out between the Nini-

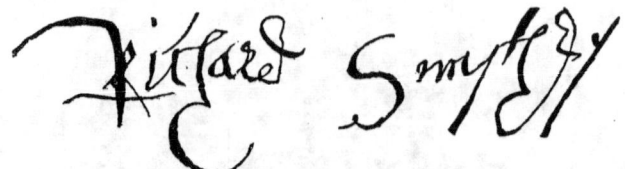

Fac-simile of Richard Smythe's signature. *

gret and the Long Island Indians, which continued with various success for several years. In one of the expeditions made to Long Island by Ninigret, he took among other captives 14 of their chief women, one of whom proved to be the daughter of Wyandanch, chief sachem of the Montaugs. These squaws were taken by Lyon Gardiner, lieutenant of Lord Say, to Smith's house, where the Indian princess remained until she was restored to her father by Gardiner, who gave as her ransom a grant of all the Nessaquake lands, since called Smithtown. Smith's house at Wickford, now North Kingston, R. I., was the rendezvous of the whites, during all the Indian wars, and the great swamp fight took place a short distance therefrom. Smith became very influential with the Indian chiefs. He negotiated and signed the treaty for Connecticut; several times made peace between the Narragansetts and the Massachusetts colonists, until his eastern neighbors became jealous of his power, and actually indicted him in their court, ordered him to be arrested and carried to Newport for trial. They attempted to defeat his lease of the Narragansett lands, which occasioned Roger Williams to interfere in his behalf, and write a very complimentary letter to King Charles the 2d concerning him. In disgust at their conduct, he purchased of Lyon Gardiner, the Nessaquake lands on Long Island, whither he removed and left his eastern possessions with his relatives. On the arrival of Col. Richard Nicol, he received a patent for his Smithtown tract, and after a successful lawsuit in the general court of assize respecting his boundary, he at length secured from Sir Edmund Andross a confirmatory patent, under the title of Smithtown, or Smithfield, dated 25th March, 1677.

"Richard Smith, patentee of Smithtown, made his will March 5th, 1691, and died soon after. His will was proved, 1692. He gave to Lodovica Updike all his homestead, as far south as was then fenced in, with his Sagoge land, on condition of surrendering his West Quoge farm. To Daniel and James Updike, the land south of Wickford, then occupied by Jacob Pindor and John Thomas. To Israel and James Newton, the West Quoge farm. To Thomas Newton, Hay Island and his house in Bristol. To Elizabeth Pratt, alias Newman, the Boston neck land, on which Alexander King lived. He gave legacies to Richard, son of Lodovica Updike, and Smith, son of Thomas Newton, &c., &c., leaving his town on Long Island to his seven children in equal shares. His son, Obadiah, was drowned in crossing Nessaquake river, August 20th, 1680, and six sons and a daughter survived him, as follows: Jonathan, who married Mary Brewster, who left two children—Richard, who married Elizabeth Tucker, and left 5 children—Job, who married Elizabeth Thompson, and left 7 children—Adam, who married Elizabeth Brown, and left 1 child—Samuel, who married Hannah Longbotham, and left 6 children—Daniel, who married Ruth Tucker, and left 7 children—and Deborah, who married William Lawrence, and left 6 children.

"On the 13th March, 1735, his grandchildren entered into an agreement to divide the town according to the proprietary rights of their parents, the seven children, and it was surveyed and laid out in pursuance of such agreement.

"Smith was buried at Nessaquake, near his residence, on land now or late in the possession of Jesse W. Floyd."

"It is probable," says Thompson, in his History of Long Island, "that horses were very rare during the first settlement of this town, or that they had not as yet been introduced; which accounts for Mr. Smith's having made use of a large bull for many purposes for which horses were afterward used, which occasioned him to be designated as the *bull-rider*, and his posterity to this day as the *Bull Smiths*, while the descendants of Col. William Smith of Brookhaven are as familiarly known as the *Tangier Smiths*, he having once filled the office of governor of Tangier. There are also upon the island two other distinct races of families by the name of Smith, the one called *Rock Smiths* and the other *Blue Smiths*, the origin of which is matter of conjecture. Many singular traits of character, and not a few strange stories, are related concerning this famous progenitor of the Smiths of Smithtown, the records of which have too much the semblance of fiction to be worth perpetuating"

The first minister of the town was the Rev. Abner Reeve, who was employed here about 1735. He was the father of the Hon. Tappan Reeve, the founder of the celebrated law school at Litchfield, Conn. His successor, the Rev. Napthali Daggett, was settled here in 1751. Mr. Daggett afterward became President of Yale College. The next clergymen were Thomas Lewis, Joshua Hart, and Luther Gleason.

"In a note to Moulton's History of New York, it is stated that an obituary appeared in a

---

* The above fac-simile is taken from the deed given by Richard Smith to his grandson Obadiah; from which it appears that he spelt his name unlike his posterity.

newspaper, printed in 1739, of the death of a negro at Smithtown, Long Island, reputed to have been *one hundred and forty years old*, who declared that he well remembered when there were but *three houses* in New York. The memory, therefore, of this remarkable individual must have extended back to the first settlement of New Amsterdam, (as New York was then called,) in 1626."

Northern view of Sagg Harbor, Long Island.

SOUTHAMPTON, called by the natives Agawam, was settled in 1640, principally by about forty families from Lynn, Mass. Its name was given in remembrance of Southampton, Eng. The surface of the township is generally level, in the W. and N. the soil is light and sandy, in the S. mixed with loam, and when properly manured, produces good crops. Pop. 6,205. The people of this town early sought an alliance with Connecticut, and were received into their jurisdiction in 1644. They were represented by deputies in the general court at Hartford. The Rev. Abraham Pierson was the first minister; he was succeeded by the Rev. Robert Fordham in 1649, who was succeeded by Rev. Joseph Taylor in 1680, and Rev. Joseph Whiting in 1682. Rev. Samuel Gelston settled here in 1717, and remained about 10 years.

The village of Southampton is built on a single street, 18 miles from Riverhead. Bridgehampton, Westhampton, Good Ground, Flanders Speunk, Quogue, Canoe Place, and Beaverdam, are names of localities and villages. Shinnecock, or Southampton bay, is a fine sheet of water, 10 miles long, and from 3 to 4 wide. The territory of Shinnecock, containing some thousands of acres, is little else than a collection of sand hills. A small remnant of the Shinnecock tribe of Indians still linger on the SE. part of this tract, where they have a small church and a few dwellings.

The above is a northern view of Sagg Harbor, situated in the NE corner of the town, 100 miles from New York. It has a good harbor, lying on an arm of Gardiner's bay. The village contains 400 dwellings, 1 Presbyterian, 1 Methodist, 1 Catholic, and 1 African church, 2 printing offices, and about 3,000 inhabitants. The wealth and trade of the place may with propriety be said to be founded on the whaling business.

"*Sagg Harbor* is the most populous, wealthy, and commercial place in the county, and may therefore not improperly be considered the emporium of Suffolk. The capital employed in trade here probably exceeds that of the whole county besides, there being nearly a million of dollars invested in the whale-fishery alone, employing a tonnage of more than six thousand, exclusive of several fine packets and other vessels engaged in the coasting business. It is supposed that no permanent settlement was attempted here previous to 1730, and then only a few small cottages were erected near the head of the present wharf, for the convenience of those engaged in fishing. Most of the land in the vicinity was then covered with timber and forest, and it is probable also that no inconsiderable number of Indians dwelt in the vicinity. In 1760, several respectable families established themselves here, perceiving that it possessed many local advantages, and built for themselves comfortable houses. In 1767, the number of inhabitants had so increased, that it was resolved to erect a house for public worship, and without the advantage of regular preaching, the people were accustomed to assemble on the Sabbath at the *beat of drum*, and hear a sermon read by one of the congregation. They began soon after more largely to appreciate the commercial facilities offered by the adjacent waters, and fresh efforts were made to improve upon the old practice of *boat-whaling*. For this end small sloops were fitted out, and ranged the ocean at some distance from the coast; but when a whale was caught, it became necessary to return to port for the purpose of boiling out the oil upon the shore. The business had made but little progress when hostilities commenced between the mother country and her colonies in 1775; and this island being the next year abandoned to the enemy, commerce of every kind was of course suspended till the close of the contest in 1783. Several British ships took their stations in the bay, and this village was made not only a depot for military stores, but the garrison for a considerable body of soldiers. During the war it became the theatre of one of the most extraordinary feats that was accomplished during the revolution. It has generally been denominated *Meig's Expedition*, and the circumstances are thus related by the historians of that period :

"'In retaliation for the burning of Ridgefield in Connecticut, by General Arnor and the wretches under his command, in April, 1777, a few soldiers from Newhaven went on a predatory excursion to Long Island. A quantity of provisions had been collected at Sagg Harbor, and to destroy these was the object of the expedition. The enterprise was one of the most spirited and successful of that eventful period. General Parsons conceived it possible to surprise the place, and confided the execution of it to Lieutenant-colonel Meigs, who embarked from Newhaven, May 21, 1777, with two hundred and thirty-four men, in thirteen whale-boats. He proceeded to Guilford, but on account of the roughness of the sea, could not pass the sound till the twenty-third. On that day, at one o'clock in the afternoon, he left Guilford with one hundred and seventy men, under convoy of two armed sloops, and crossed the sound to Southold, where he arrived at six o'clock. The enemy's troops on this part of the island had marched for New York two or three days before, but it was reported that there was a party at Sagg Harbor on the south branch of the island about fifteen miles distant. Colonel Meigs ordered the whale-boats to be transported over the land to the bay between the north and south branches of the island, where one hundred and thirty men embarked, and at twelve o'clock at night arrived safely on the other side of the bay within four miles of Sagg Harbor. Here the boats were secured in a wood, under a guard, and the remainder of the detachment marched quickly to the harbor, where they arrived at two o'clock in the morning, in the greatest order, attacking the outpost with fixed bayonets, and proceeding directly to the shipping at the wharf, which they found unprepared for defence. The alarm was given, and an armed schooner with twelve guns and seventy men began to fire upon them at the distance of one hundred and fifty yards, which continued three quarters of an hour, but did not prevent the troops from executing their design with the greatest intrepidity and effect. Twelve brigs and sloops, one of which was an armed vessel of twelve guns, and one hundred and twenty tons of hay, corn, oats, ten hogsheads of rum, and a large quantity of merchandise, were entirely destroyed. Six of the enemy were killed and ninety taken prisoners. Not one of Colonel Meig's men was either killed or wounded. He returned to Guilford at two o'clock in the afternoon, having been absent only twenty-five hours; and in that time had transported his troops by land and water full ninety miles, and completed his undertaking with the most entire success.'

"On the declaration of war against Great Britain in 1812, preparations were made to protect this place against the enemy, and a small detachment of militia was stationed here, who employed themselves in erecting a fortification upon the high ground overlooking the harbor. No regular garrison was established, however, till the summer of 1813, when the British ships, taking their station in Gardiner's Bay, threatened to land at several points in the vicinity of this port. At that time three or four hundred men were placed here, and were continued till the end of the war. Some part of the time a company of artillery, and another of regular troops, were stationed here: and in 1814 one or more companies of sea fencibles. But at no time was the number of soldiers sufficient to have effectually defended the place against the enemy, had the capture of it been considered by them an object of sufficient importance to have warranted the attempt. It was wholly impossible to have prevented their landing at various places bordering upon the bay, and they accordingly visited at pleasure Gardiner's Island, Montauk, and Oyster Ponds; taking such provisions as their necessities required, and for which, it is believed, they generally paid an equivalent. In June, 1813, a launch and two barges, with about one hundred men from the squadron of Commodore Hardy, attempted to land at the wharf in the night; but being timely discovered, the alarm was sounded, and the guns of the fort brought to bear in the direction of the boats; so successful was the means used, that the designs of the enemy were effectually frustrated. They had only time to set fire to a sloop which they took from the wharf, when a shot from the fort raked her fore and aft, and obliged them to abandon her. The Americans going on board, extinguished the flames, when they found a quantity of guns, swords, pistols, and other instruments, which the invaders, (deeming discretion to be the better part of valor,) had left in their hurry to escape."

SOUTHOLD embraces the N. branch of Long Island, and includes Fisher's, Plumb, Robins, and Gull islands. It is centrally situated 17 miles from Riverhead, and 103 from New York. The surface is generally level, and the soil a sandy loam, and productive under careful cultivation. Pop. 3,907. The inhabitants are principally settled along the great road which passes centrally through the town in a number of thickly settled neighborhoods or villages, as at Mattatuc, Cutchogue, Southold, Oyster Ponds, or Orient, forming almost a continued village.

Southern view of Greenport, in Southold.

Greenport, the largest village in the town, is situated at what is called Southold harbor, a part of the great Peconic bay, 23 miles from the courthouse at Riverhead. It is laid out into streets and building lots, and contains about 100 dwellings, 1 Baptist, 1 Methodist, and 1 Presbyterian church, and wharves and railways for the accommodation of vessels. The water is of sufficient depth for large ships, and well sheltered from storms. The village was commenced by a few spirited individuals in 1827. The ancient village of Southold contains 1 Presbyterian and 1 Universalist church, and an academy. The peninsula of Oyster Ponds is the eastern extremity of the island; the village, now called Orient, contains two churches, two docks or wharves, and upwards of 500 inhabitants. *Fisher's Island*, belonging to this town, is 9 miles from New London, Conn., and 4 from Stonington. It is about 9 miles long, and has a medial width of one mile, containing about 4,000 acres. This island was purchased by Gov. Winthrop, of Connecticut, in 1664, and has been in possession of the Winthrop family ever since. The staple articles raised on the island are wool, butter, and cheese. There are about 45 persons of all ages upon the island. *Plumb Island* contains about 800 acres of land, and has a population of about 75 persons. *Great* and *Little Gull islands* are situated in what is called the *Race*, on account of the swiftness of the current. Great Gull contains 15 acres; Little Gull one acre, mostly a solid rock. Upon this last island a lighthouse has been erected, which is of much importance to the navigation of the sound.

"The Indian name of this town is **Yennecock**, and was purchased from the Corchougs, a tribe that possessed this part of the island, in the summer of 1640. Most of the first planters were originally from Hingham, in Norfolk, England, and came here by the way of New Haven. The Rev. John Youngs, who had been a preacher in England, was their leader. He organized a church at New Haven, and they, with others willing to accompany them, commenced the settlement of this town. The principal men among them, besides Mr. Youngs, were William Wells, Barnabas Horton, Thomas Mapes, John Tuthill, and Matthias Corwin. The governor of New Haven, Theophilus Eaton, and the authorities there, had not only aided the first settlers in their negotiations about the purchase of the soil, but actually took the conveyance in their own names, and exercised a limited control over the territory for several years, which eventually occasioned some dissatisfaction among the inhabitants. The civil and ecclesiastical concerns of the settlement were conducted in a similar manner with the other plantations under the jurisdiction of New Haven. All government was reputed to be in the church, and none were admitted to the entire privileges of freemen, or free burgesses as they were called, except church members; a court was in like manner instituted, which was authorized to hear and determine all causes, civil and criminal, and whose decisions were to be according to the laws of God as contained in the holy scriptures. In the general court, (or town meeting,) consisting also of church members, was transacted the ordinary business of the plantation. In these, orders were made in relation to the division of lands, the enclosure or cultivation of common fields, the regulation of fences, highways, and the time and manner of permitting cattle and sheep to go at large upon the common lands; and such further measures as were required for the mutual defence of the settlement from hostile attacks on every side. One of the first ordinances required every man to provide himself with arms and ammunition, and to assemble at an appointed place, whenever warned so to do, under a certain penalty for neglect in any of these respects. The plantation made early provision for the education of children, the preservation of good morals, and the support of religion. A committee was appointed to regulate the admission of new settlers, and no one could become an inhabitant without their approbation; and no planter could sell or let his house or land to a stranger, but only to such as were approved by the said committee, under a heavy penalty."

SULLIVAN COUNTY.

SULLIVAN COUNTY was erected in March, 1809, from Ulster county, and received its name in honor of General Sullivan, an officer of the revolutionary army. It is centrally distant from New York about 100 miles NW., and, by the routes usually travelled, 112 SW. of Albany. Greatest length NW. and SE. 45, and greatest breadth NE. and SW. 37 miles. The county of Sullivan is situated on the Delaware river, W. of Ulster county, in a region of broken land. It contains a large proportion of mountainous country. The Newburg and Cochecton turnpike runs centrally and westerly across the county; and on this road and the Delaware river are the principal settlements. The New York and Erie railroad runs through the southern portion. The northern part is the wildest and least settled. The Delaware and Hudson canal passes through the valley of Bashe's kill into Orange, and returns from that county by the valley of the Delaware, along which it extends in this county about 15 miles, to the dam opposite the Laxawaxen river. The country along the Delaware is not favorable for agriculture; generally the highlands are preferred for cultivation, being more dry, and productive of finer grass than the valleys, which are commonly wet and cold. Upon the Delaware, and the streams which flow into it, the inhabitants are chiefly engaged in lumbering. With the exception of a small tract on the southeast, in the Minisink patent, the whole county was covered by the Hardenburg patent, under which there are now some extensive landholders. The inhabitants are chiefly of Dutch and New England descent. About one tenth of the county only is improved. It is divided into 10 towns. Pop. 15,630.

BETHEL, taken from Lumberland in 1809; centrally distant from New York 135, from Albany 121, and from Monticello W. 8 miles. Pop. 1,483. Whitelake and Bethel are post-offices.

COCHECTON, taken from Bethel in 1828; from New York 118, from Albany 130 miles. Pop. 622. Cochecton is a small village upon the Delaware, 21 miles NW. of Monticello. Fosterdale is a post-office.

FALLSBURG, organized in 1826; from New York 108, from Albany 102, from Monticello centrally distant NE. 8 miles. Pop. 1,782. Fallsburg and Woodburn are small post villages.

FORESTBURG, recently formed, is centrally distant from Monticello S. 8 miles. Forestburg is a small village. Pop. 433.

LIBERTY, taken from Lumberland in 1807; NW. from New York 110, from Albany SW. 110, from Monticello to the settled portion of the town N. 10 miles. Liberty is a small village of about 40 dwellings. Pop. 1,570.

LUMBERLAND, taken from Mamakating in 1798; from New York 115, from Albany 130, and from Monticello centrally distant SW. 20 miles. Pop. 1,205. Lumbering is the principal business of the inhabitants. Barryville and Lumberland are post-offices. Narrowsburg is a small village.

MAMAKATING, organized in 1798; since divided; centrally distant from New York 85, and from Albany 100 miles. Pop. 3,418. Bloomingsburg, upon the eastern foot of the Shawangunk mountain, on the Newburg and Cochecton turnpike, 13 miles SE. from Monticello, incorporated in 1833, has about 60 dwellings. Wurtsborough on the canal, 43 miles from Eddyville, and 11 miles from Monticello, has about 60 dwellings. Near here is a valuable lead mine. Philipsport is a small village on the canal, 4 miles N. from Wurtsborough. Burlingham is a small village on the Shawangunk creek, 4 miles below Bloomingsburg. Mount Vernon and West Brookville are post-offices. This town was settled by the Dutch about a century since.

NEVERSINK, organized in 1798; since altered in area; from New York 115, from Albany 104, and from Monticello N. 13 miles. Pop. 1,681. Neversink and Grahamsville are post-offices.

ROCKLAND, taken from Neversink in 1798; from New York 125, from Albany 116, and from Monticello N. 23 miles. Pop. 826. Rockland, Little Beaver Kill, and Purvis, are post-offices.

THOMPSON, taken from Mamakating; from New York 100, and from Albany 110 miles. Pop. 2,610.

Western entrance into Monticello.

Monticello, the county seat, on the Newburg and Cochecton turnpike, named after Jefferson's residence, was founded in 1804, by Messrs. Samuel F. and J. P. Jones, from New Lebanon, Columbia county, who were proprietors of most of the lands in the vicinity. Judge Platt Pelton built the second frame house here in 1806. The above view was taken near the residence of Mr. E. W. Edmonds, and shows on the right the steeple of the Episcopal church, and on the left the Presbyterian church and the courthouse. There are about 60 dwellings in the village and vicinity. Thompsonville is a small post village. Bridgeville and Gales are post-offices.

TIOGA COUNTY.

TIOGA COUNTY, taken from Montgomery in 1794; bounds since much altered: still further reduced in 1836, by the erection of Chemung county from its western portion. Greatest length E. and W. 31, greatest breadth N. and S. 29 miles. This, with Chemung county, is part of the broad and long belt extending westerly from Ulster and Green counties to the vicinity of Lake Erie, preserving for a great part of the distance a mean height of about 1,600 feet above the level of the ocean. The soil of the county consists generally of sandy and gravelly loam, interspersed with patches of mud and clay. The uplands are commonly better adapted to grass than grain; but the valleys give fine crops of wheat and corn; oats, barley, peas, beans, and hops thrive almost everywhere. The Susquehannah is the principal stream of the county. The New York and Erie railroad crosses the county E. and W.; and the railroad from Owego to Ithaca N. and S. The county is divided into 9 towns. Pop. 20,351.

BARTON, taken from Tioga in 1824; from Albany 181 miles, from Owego W. 16. Factoryville, 17 miles SE. from Elmira, is a small village on Cayuta creek. Barton and North Barton are post-offices. Pop. 2,305.

BERKSHIRE, taken from Tioga in 1808; from Albany 148, from Owego N. 14 miles. Berkshire is a small village. Pop. 955.

CANDOR, taken from Spencer in 1811; from Albany 177, from Owego N. 8 miles. Pop. 3,367. This town was settled in 1796, by emigrants from Hartford county, Conn. Candor village, centrally situated, has about 370 inhabitants. The northern portion of this town once belonged to the Connecticut school fund. Willseyville is the name of a post-office, around which there is a settlement.

NEWARK, originally named Westville, and taken from Berkshire in 1823; from Albany 167, from Owego NE. 8 miles. Pop. 1,616. Newark Valley is a pleasant and thriving village.

NICHOLS, taken from Tioga in 1824; from Albany 167, from Owego SW. 10 miles. Rushville, in the valley of the Susquehannah, has about 400 inhabitants. Canfield's Corners is a small settlement. Pop. 1,986.

OWEGO was organized in 1791; distant NW. from New York city 177, from Albany SW. 167, from Elmira E. 36 miles. Pop. 5,329. Owego village, the county seat, is pleasantly and advantageously situated for trade upon the Susquehannah river, and upon the line of the New York and Erie railroad, 30 miles SE. from Ithaca. The name Owego is of Indian origin, signifying *swift* or *swift river*, and was applied to the Owego creek, which empties into the Susquehannah about half a mile from the village. About the year 1783 or 1784, James McMaster and Amos Draper purchased of the Indians what they called a half township, comprising 11,500 acres, and embracing the site upon which the village now stands. "In 1785, McMaster, and William Taylor, still living in Owego, and then a bound boy to McMaster, came and cleared in one season 10 or 15 acres of land, and through the summer planted and raised a crop of corn from the same. This was the first *transition* of the ground, where Owego now stands, from a wilderness state. In 1794 or 1795, McMaster and Hudson, a surveyor, laid out the village into streets and lots, and thus laid the foundation of what Owego now is or shall be hereafter. .... The sources of wealth, as the village grew up, were salt from Salina, brought to the place and carried down the river in arks for the Pennsylvania and Maryland markets, wheat from the north, which was also transported down the river, lumber, also, and plaster."*

"Between Owego and Tioga Point there were a number of Indians lived on the river plain for a length of time after its settlement by the whites. They demanded a yearly rent of the settlers for their land, until a treaty was held with them at Tioga, 3 or 4 years after the first settlement. An Indian, called Captain John, was their chief, or passed as such. They were always pleased to have white people eat with them; and would appear offend-

---

* See Annals of Binghampton and of the country connected with it, from which the early history of this place is extracted.

ed, if, when calling at their wigwams when they were eating, they refused to eat with them. In seeking their rent, which they expected to be paid in grain, or when they wished to borrow, or buy, or beg, they never would ask for wheat, but always for *corn*. It is said, that some of the squaws could make an excellent kind of cake, out of fine Indian meal, dried berries, and maple sugar. When they wished to beg something to eat, instead of expressing it in words, they would place their hand first on their *stomach* and then to their *mouth*. This mute language must have been a powerful appeal to the hospitality and sympathies of their more fortunate brethren. When they had bad luck, it is said, they would eat some kind of root which made them very sick and vomit, that they might, as they said, have better luck in future.

"A few years after the country was settled, there prevailed an extensive and serious famine. It was felt more particularly in the region between Owego and Elmira, embracing Tioga. It was experienced even down to Wyoming. For 6 weeks or more the inhabitants were entirely without *bread* or its kind. This season of famishing occurred immediately before the time of harvesting. So far as the cause of this destitution was accounted for, it was supposed to result from a greater number, than usual, of new settlers coming in, and also a great scarcity prevailing in Wyoming that season. This being a much older settled country, a scarcity here would materially affect the newer parts. During the prevalency of this want of bread, the people were languid in their movements, irresolute and feeble in what they undertook, emaciated and gaunt in their appearance. The inhabitants, as a substitute for more substantial food, gathered, or rather, it is believed, *dug* what were called wild beans; which, it seems, were found in considerable quantities. These they boiled and ate, with considerable relish. They would also gather the most nutritious roots and eat. As soon as their rye was in the milk, it was seized upon, and by drying it over a moderate fire, until the grain acquired some consistency, they were enabled to pound it into a sort of meal, out of which they made *mush*. This was a very great relief, although the process was tedious, and attended with much waste of the grain. In the early part of the scarcity, while there was a possibility of finding grain or flour of any kind abroad, instances were not unfrequent, of families tearing up their feather-beds, and sending away the feathers in exchange for bread; and instances also of individuals riding a whole day and not obtaining a *half* of a loaf. During the time of this great want, however, none died of hunger. There were two young men that died in consequence of eating to *excess*, when their hunger came to be relieved by the green rye."

West view of the courthouse and other buildings, Owego.

The above view was taken near the residence of Dr. Lucius Allen. The building with a cupola near the centre of the drawing is the courthouse, the one on the right the academy, both of which face the public square. The building seen in the distance is the Baptist church. Besides the above, there are in the village 1 Presbyterian and 1 Methodist church, the Owego bank, capital $200,000, 3 fine hotels, and about 200 dwellings. The railroad which extends from here to Ithaca, was the second chartered in the state, (1828,) and is 29½ miles in length. East Owego and Flemingville are names of post-offices in this town.

The following inscription was copied from a monument in the village graveyard.

"In memory of COL. DAVID PIXLEY, who departed this life Aug. 25th, 1807, in the 67th year of his age.—He was an officer of the revolution at the siege of Quebec in 1775, under Gen. Montgomery, was the first settler of Owego in 1790, and continued its father and friend until his death."

RICHFORD, taken from Berkshire in 1833; from Owego N. 18 miles. Richford is a neat but small village centrally situated. Pop. 938.

SPENCER was taken from Owego in 1806; from Owego NW. 13 miles. Pop. 1,532. Spencer, on the Cattotong creek, has several churches and about 450 inhabitants. It was previous to 1822 the seat of justice of the county. The courthouse having been burnt, it was removed to the then half-shire towns of Owego and Elmira, the latter of which is now the seat of justice for Chemung county. East Spencer is a post-office.

TIOGA was formed in 1800; from Albany 176 miles. Pop. 2,323. Smithborough, 12 miles SW. from Owego, and Ransomville, are small villages.

TOMPKINS COUNTY.

TOMPKINS COUNTY, named in honor of the Hon. Daniel D. Tompkins, formerly Vice-president of the United States, was taken from Cayuga and Seneca counties in 1817; limits since changed. Greatest length E. and W. 34, greatest breadth N. and S. 28 miles; centrally distant from New York 212, and from Albany 163 miles. This county forms part of the high land in the southwestern portion of the state. Its summit generally is elevated from 1,200 to 1,400 feet, but the singular and deep basins in which lie the Cayuga and Seneca lakes, have given a peculiar formation to its surface, and to the course and character of its streams. The Cayuga lake indents it on the N. about 18 miles; the Seneca lake extends southerly on its western border 12 miles. The greater portion of the country declines from all sides towards the Cayuga lake. The ascent from the shores of the lake is gradual and smooth to the eye, yet it is rapid, and attains within 2 miles the height of at least 500 feet. This gives to the streams a precipitous character. The towns of Newfield, Danby, and Caroline, were purchased from the state by Messrs. Watkins and Flint. The towns north of these, excepting a small portion in the northeastern part of Dryden, belong to the military tract. That portion was in the cession to Massachusetts. The county is chiefly settled by New England emigrants. The New York and Erie railroad passes through the county. Tompkins county is divided into 10 towns. Pop. 38,113.

CAROLINE, taken from Spencer in 1811; W. from Albany 165, centrally distant from Ithaca SE. 11 miles. Caroline, Speedville, Mott's Corners, and Slatersville, are small post villages, of which the latter is the largest. Pop. 2,459.

DANBY, taken from Spencer in 1811; from Albany 172 miles. The Ithaca and Owego railroad crosses the northeastern border of the town. Danby is a small village 6 miles S. of Ithaca, upon the Owego turnpike. South Danby is a post-office. Pop. 2,570.

DRYDEN, taken from Ulysses in 1803; from Albany 153 miles. Dryden is a neat village 11 miles NE. of Ithaca, containing about 50 dwellings. Etna, Verna, and West Dryden, are smaller settlements. Pop. 5,433.

ENFIELD was taken from Ulysses in 1821; from Albany 171, centrally distant 6 miles W. of Ithaca. West Enfield and Enfield are the names of the post-offices. Pop. 2,343.

GROTON, originally named Division, was organized in 1817; from Albany W. 160, from Ithaca centrally distant NE. 14 miles. McLeansville, Groton, Peruville, Fall Creek, and West Groton are small post villages. Pop. 3,618.

HECTOR was taken from Ovid in 1802; from Ithaca W. 16 miles. Burdette, Mecklenburg, Reynoldsville, and Searsburg, are small post villages. There are one or two other post-offices and small settlements in the town. Pop. 5,654. The Hector Falls, a beautiful cascade of 20 feet, are upon a stream which empties into the Seneca lake, near the village of Burdette.

ITHACA was taken from Ulysses in 1821. Pop. 5,811. Around the head of the Cayuga lake, which extends about two miles within the limits of the town, are several thousand acres of alluvial flats. From this plain, the hills rise on three sides in the form of an amphitheatre, to the height of 500 feet, exhibiting uncommonly beautiful and magnificent scenery. To the lover of nature, few places afford scenes of more interest than Ithaca. There are several splendid cataracts within the space of a very few miles, each of which has its peculiar attractions, among which are the Cascadilla, Eagle, Lucifer, Taghcanic, and those on Fall creek, about a mile distant from the village of Ithaca. These last are the most visited, and derive an additional interest from the tunnel, a subterraneous work of art, 200 feet in length, from 10 to 12 wide, and 13 feet in height, which conducts the water from a point a few rods above the first fall to a mill site at the bridge below.

The village of Ithaca was founded by the late Simeon De Witt, surveyor-general of the state. It is beautifully situated about a mile and a half above the Cayuga lake, partially upon the flats and partially upon the hill. It is distant 163 miles from Albany, 40 SE. from Geneva, and 29 from Owego. The Cayuga inlet is navigable to the

EASTERN VIEW OF ITHACA, TOMPKINS COUNTY, N. Y.

lake for boats of 50 tons. Ithaca is well located for trade. It communicates with the Erie canal by the lake and Seneca canal, and with the Susquehannah river and the line of the Erie railroad, by the Owego railroad. The village contains upwards of 700 dwellings, 1 Presbyterian, 1 Methodist, 1 Episcopal, 1 Baptist, and 1 Dutch Reformed church, the Ithaca Academy, 2 banks, several printing offices, a very extensive map-publishing establishment, a variety of mills and manufactories, and about 4,000 inhabitants. The Ithaca and Owego railroad, the second chartered in the state, (1828,) is $29\frac{1}{2}$ miles in length. It ascends from the level of the lake by two inclined planes; the first, $1,733\frac{1}{2}$ feet long, rises 1 foot in 4.28, or 405 feet; the other, 2,225 feet long, ascends 1 foot in 21 feet. The whole elevation above the lake overcome, is 602 feet within 8 miles; after which there is a descent of 376 feet to Owego. Stationary steam-power is used upon the first, and horse-power upon the second plane and other portions of the road.

The Presbyterian church was erected in 1817; the society which worships in this house is the oldest in the village, having been organized in 1804 or 1805. They worshipped in a common school-house until 1816, which being demolished in a riot, the congregation were obliged for a season to meet in an old barn. Their first pastor was the Rev. Mr. Mandeville, who officiated till 1816. William Wisner, A. E. Campbell, and John W. McCullough, have been succeeding ministers. The Methodist Episcopal church was erected in 1819, and enlarged in 1826. The Episcopal church was built in 1824. The first Baptist society was constituted in Oct. 1826; their church was opened for worship in Jan. 1831. The Reformed Dutch church was organized in 1830; their meeting-house was completed in 1683. The Ithaca Journal, the oldest newspaper in the county, was established by Ebenezer Mack, in 1818.

LANSING was taken from Genoa of Cayuga county in 1817. Ludlowville, 10 miles N. of Ithaca, has about 60 dwellings. Lansingville 12, North Lansing 10, and South Lansing 8 miles from Ithaca, are small villages. Pop. 3,673.

NEWFIELD was originally named Spencer, and organized in 1811 as part of Tioga county. Newfield, 7 miles SW. of Ithaca, is a small post village, containing 2 churches and about 60 dwellings. It was founded in 1820. Pop. 3,572.

ULYSSES was organized in 1801. Trumansburg, 11 miles NW. from Ithaca, has 1 Baptist, 1 Methodist, and 1 Presbyterian church, and about 100 dwellings. Jacksonville, Waterburg, and Halseyville, are small settlements. On Halsey creek, about 10 miles from Ithaca, are the Taghcanic Falls, shown in the following engraving. This cataract is about 200 feet in height, and the rocks tower 100 feet above the top. Viewed from above or beneath, the scene is one of sublimity. The latter, however, is the best. To witness this, the visiter is obliged to go down the stream about a mile, and return by the valley, which is bounded by a rocky gorge, with perpendicular rocks rising in some places 400 or 500 feet above the bed of the

Taghcanic or Goodwin's Falls, Ulysses.

creek, when the scene bursts suddenly upon him in all its wildness and majesty.

The following account of an adventure with a bear, at this place, communicated by Mr. George Weyburn, a resident in this vicinity, shows that not many years have elapsed since this was a spot

" Where beasts with man divided empire claimed."

One Sunday evening in October, about 47 years since, as my father, Mr. Samuel Weyburn, was returning from feeding his horse on the north side of the creek, near where the distillery now stands, his dog started up a bear and her two cubs. They followed their course up the hill on the south side of the creek until near the summit, a few rods above the mill-site fall, where the cubs took to a tree. My father ran to the house, and, having obtained his gun, pursued. Being directed by the barking of the dog, he passed about 20 rods beyond the tree in which the cubs were, and there he found the bear with her back against a tree standing on the brink of the gulf, defending herself from the attacks of the dog. He fired, and, as it afterward proved, broke one of her fore legs. The animal retreated into the gulf, and was seen no more that night. In the mean time my mother, brother, and myself, who had followed in the pursuit, came to the tree into which the cubs had retreated, who, being frightened at the report of the gun and the sound of our voices, began to cry *mam! mam!* in the most affecting tones, strongly resembling the human voice. My mother having called my father, he shot the cubs and returned home. The next morning, my father thinking that he had either killed or severely wounded the animal, for the want of a better weapon, (having expended his only charge of gunpowder the evening previous,) took a pitchfork and proceeded in quest of the enemy, accompanied by myself and brother. I was armed with a small axe; but my brother, not being equipped for war, was allowed to accompany us *bare*-handed. Thus accoutred and followed by our dog, we proceeded to within about 40 rods of the great fall, when my father, apprized of the nearness of the enemy by the barking of the dog, ran and left us in the rear. We soon came in sight of the bear and dog, who were passing from the left wall of the precipice across the basin to the right, and ascended up almost to the perpendicular rock, a distance of 80 or 100 feet. My father, climbing up lower down, was enabled to intercept her passage in consequence of her broken limb. Here the action again commenced by his giving her three thrusts with the fork. The first and second were near the heart, the third struck her shoulder-blade, when she turned upon him and he met her with a thrust in her face, putting out one of her eyes with one prong and tearing her tongue with the other. She then rushed towards him, his feet gave away, and as he fell she caught him by the clothes, near his breast. At this juncture, he seized her and threw her below him. This he repeated two or three times in their descent towards the bottom of the ravine, during which she bit him in both his legs and in his arms. At the bottom, in the creek, lay a stone whose front was not unlike the front of a common cooking stove, the water reaching to the top. Near this, 4 or 5 feet distant, stood a rock on the bank. Into this snug notch it was his good luck to throw his antagonist, with her feet and claws towards the rock in the stream. In this situation he succeeded in holding her with his back to hers, and braced between the rocks. With his left hand he held her by the back, and with his right clenched her by the neck until I came up. I struck her with all my might on the back with the axe. At this my father sprang from her and seized his fork. The bear turned towards us with a shake and a snort—I gave her a severe blow. She fell, but recovering herself, endeavored to retreat. We renewed the conflict, and ere long the lifeless corpse of the animal proclaimed us masters of the field. The victory was dearly bought, the blood was running in streams from my father's hands, and from his limbs into his shoes. On examination, he found that she had bitten him in each limb, inflicting four ugly wounds at each bite, besides a slit in his wrist, supposed to have been done by one of her claws."

ULSTER COUNTY.

ULSTER, an original county, was organized in 1683. It is from New York centrally distant N. 110, and from Albany S. 60 miles. Greatest length E. and W. 50, breadth N. and S. 40 miles. The face of the country is mountainous. The Shawangunk mountain enters the county from Orange, and running NE. nearly 30 miles, sinks into low and irregular hills in Hurley; but its continuity is preserved to Kingston near the Hudson. Northward of that village it again rises, until it is identified with the Catskill mountains. Between the Blue and Shawangunk mountains is a broad valley through which winds the Rondout river, a stream whose name is a corruption of the word Redoubt, so named after a fortification built upon the stream by the early Dutch settlers. The Wallkill runs a northeast course south of the Shawangunk mountain, receiving the Shawangunk creek, and uniting with the Rondout, 8 miles from its mouth. The three streams above noticed are the great drains of the county, and afford very advantageous mill power, within a few miles of the tide, much of which is yet unemployed. In the west the Nevisink river and other tributaries of the Delaware have their sources. The Delaware and Hudson canal enters the county at its southwest border, and passing through the towns of Wawarsing, Rochester, Marbletown, and Hurley, unites in the town of Kingston with the Rondout, 2½ miles from the Hudson. The inhabitants are much engaged in manufacturing, and much attention has been given to the raising of sheep and cattle, for which purpose few counties are better adapted. The county was settled by the Dutch as early as 1616. Tradition says that at a very early period there were settlers upon the Minisink on the Delaware, who transported some valuable minerals by the road along the

Rondout to the North river. This county appears to have suffered more from Indian hostilities than any other portion of the country while under the Dutch. The county is divided into 14 towns. Pop. 45,724.

ESOPUS, formerly called Kline or Little Esopus, taken from Kingston in 1810; from Albany 69, from Kingston S. 6 miles. Elmores Corners is a small post village, half a mile west of the Hudson. Pop. 1,927.

HURLEY, organized in 1788; from Albany 64 miles. The inhabitants are chiefly descendants from the early Dutch settlers and New England emigrants, and their progeny. Pop. 2,201. Hurley, on the right bank of the Esopus, 3 miles SW. from Kingston, and Rosendale, 8 miles SW., are small villages. At the latter place a large quantity of lime is manufactured, celebrated for its strength and durability. Pop. 2,201.

Eastern view of Kingston.

KINGSTON was organized in 1788. It has a rolling surface, and generally a good soil. Pop. 5,824. It was one of the earliest Dutch settlements in the state, having commenced in 1616, and is said to have been the third place settled in New York. In 1662, it had a settled minister, and the county records commence about that period. Kingston village, formerly called Esopus, was incorporated in 1805. The above engraving shows the appearance of the village as viewed from the residence of J. H. Rutzer, Esq., which is situated on a gentle eminence a few rods south of the Rondout road. The Catskill mountains are seen in the extreme distance. The village is regularly laid out on ten streets, and beautifully situated on the fertile pine flats elevated about 40 feet above the Esopus creek. These flats commence at Kingston and extend to Saugerties, about ten or twelve miles, and are from 2 to 2½ miles in width. The village contains the county buildings, 1 Dutch Reformed, 1 Episcopal, 1 Methodist, and 1 Baptist church, an academy, 2 banks, 3 newspaper establishments, a large iron foundry, and about 275 dwellings, many of which are built of blue limestone. It is 58 miles from Albany, 93 from New York, and about 3 from the landing on Hudson river. The village of Rondout, about a mile from the Hudson, was founded in 1828 by the Delaware and Hudson Canal Company, being a place of deposit for their coal. It contains a church and about 75 dwellings. Eddysville, a small village partly in Esopus and partly in Kingston, is at the head of navigation on Rondout creek, 4 miles above its mouth, at the commencement of the Hudson and Delaware canal.

"In the year 1663, the Indians near Esopus, (now Kingston,) who had for some time evinced discontent with their Dutch neighbors, seem to have united in a plan for exterminating the whites. In the month of June, while they amused the people with a negotiation for better neighborhood, they seized the opportunity, while the men of the village were at their agricultural employment abroad, to enter, as 'tis said, under pretence of trade, and in a very short time killed or carried off captive sixty-five persons. The Netherlanders, who from anterior hostilities had been induced to erect a fort, rallied and seized their arms; but the natives, as if intending further aggression, likewise erected a palisaded fortification, and were probably increasing in force, when Martin Crygier arriving from New Amsterdam with troops sent by Governor Stuyvesant, the red men fled to the mountains.

"During part of this summer the director-general repaired to Esopus, and by sending out parties, not only kept the superior numbers of the enemy in check, but made inroads among the hill fastnesses, destroyed the Indian villages and forts, laid waste and burnt their fields and magazines of maize, killed many of their warriors, released the Dutch captives to the number of twenty-two, and captured eleven of the enemy. These vigorous operations were followed by a truce in December, and a treaty of peace the May following."

The village of Kingston was one of the largest places in the province of New York previous to the revolution. It was laid in ashes by the British under General Vaughan in October, 1777, and a large quantity of public stores were destroyed. It is stated that at that period the village was nearly as large as it is at the present time. Every house, excepting one in which Mrs. Hammersly resided, was destroyed. This lady being acquainted with some of the British officers, it was spared on her account. The following account of the burning of this place is from the Connecticut Journal of Oct. 27:—

"In our last we observed that the British proceeded up the river past this place. As they went along, they burnt a few mills, houses, and boats. On Friday they reached Esopus, and there landed a number of men, who marched up to the defenceless town of Kingston, about two miles from the river, and immediately set it on fire; the conflagration was general in a few minutes, and in a short time that pleasant and wealthy town was reduced to ashes; only one house escaping the flames. Thus by the wantonness of power, the third town in this state for size, elegance, and wealth is reduced to a heap of rubbish; and the once happy inhabitants, (who are chiefly of Dutch descent,) obliged to solicit for shelter among strangers, and those who possessed lately elegant and convenient dwellings, obliged to take up with such huts as they find can defend them from the cold blasts of approaching winter. We learn that the inhabitants saved the best part of their movable property, but some lost the best part of their temporal all. 'Tis said the enemy took little time to plunder, being told that General Clinton was at hand with 1,500 men, but unluckily not so near as to save the town. They burnt several vessels and houses at the landing, then scampered off precipitately to their vessels. Next day they burnt several houses at Rhynebeck Flatts, and proceeded as far as Livingston's manor, where they burnt a few more; our troops are now up with them. It is hoped they will be able to put a stop to these depredations."

The following is an eastern view of the house of James W. Baldwin, Esq., recently standing on the corner of Maiden-lane and Fair-street,

The building in which the Constitution of New York was formed.

in the village of Kingston. It is built of blue limestone, which was procured in the vicinity. It was in a chamber in this building that the convention met and formed the first constitution of the state of New York, which was adopted April 20th, 1777. "It embraced the outlines of a state government; defined the powers and duties of the executive, legislative, judicial, and military departments; prescribed the mode of elections, and secured to the citizens their natural and unalienable rights. From the adoption of this instrument to the present day, the state of New York has been under the empire of laws either framed or adopted by representatives elected by the spontaneous suffrages of her citizens."

During the revolutionary war a number of royalists were executed in this town for treason. Judge Hasbrouck of Kingston, who was at that time a lad, says that two of them were executed on the first hill from the landing. It appears that these unfortunate men expected to be reprieved; when they drew near the gallows, and saw the preparation for their execution, they became overwhelmed with a sense of their awful situation, and exclaimed, *" O heer! vergeeven onze zonde,"* (O Lord! forgive our sins.) The father of Judge Hasbrouck, one of the principal men of the place, although a firm friend to the American cause, was opposed to the execution, and suffered much anguish of mind on account of these harsh and bloody measures. These men, although tories, were persons of respectability, who had families. Between 20 and 30 royalists who were taken up, enlisted in the American army, and thus saved their lives.

MARBLETOWN, organized in 1788; from Albany S. 66 miles. Marble of a superior quality abounds. Marbletown 7 miles SW. of Kingston, Stony Ridge 10 SW., and High Falls on the Rondout 12 miles from Kingston, are small settlements. Yaughcripple Bush, 12 miles from Kingston, is a hamlet. Pop. 3,812.

MARLBOROUGH, organized in 1788; from Albany 75 miles. The inhabitants are more generally of English origin than any other town in the county. Marlborough, 26 miles S. of Kingston, and Milton

22 miles, are both on the Hudson, and have each about 30 dwellings. Latintown is a small village centrally situated. Pop. 2,534.

NEW PALTZ was organized in 1788; from Albany S. 70 miles. The inhabitants are descendants of the primitive Dutch settlers. Pop. 5,412. New Paltz, on the Wallkill, 16 miles SW. from Kingston, has about 30 dwellings, principally of stone, in the ancient Dutch style, and an incorporated academy. New Paltz Landing, on the Hudson opposite Poughkeepsie, 20 miles S. of Kingston, is a small settlement. Dashville and Springtown are small villages on the Wallkill.

OLIVE, taken from Marbletown, Hurley, and Shandanken in 1823; from Albany S. 64 miles. "The City" and Caseville, 14 miles W. of Kingston, are small settlements. Pop. 2,023.

PLATTEKILL, taken from Marlborough in 1800; from Albany 76 miles. Pleasantville, 26 miles S. from Kingston, and Modena, are small settlements. Pop. 2,123.

ROCHESTER, organized in 1788; from Albany 75, from Kingston SW. centrally distant 17 miles. This town was originally named Mombackus, meaning Indian face. Accord and Kyserike are post-offices. Pop. 2,674. Rochester is a small settlement.

SAUGERTIES, taken from Kingston in 1811. Pop. 6,119. Malden, on the Hudson, 13 miles N. of Kingston, is a place of considerable business, and has an academy and about 40 dwellings. Glasgo, on the river, 9 miles N. from Kingston, is a small settlement.

Ulsterville, (late Saugerties,) at the confluence of the Esopus creek with the Hudson, 100 miles N. of New York, 44 S. from Albany, and 10 from Kingston. "This place, now one of the most thrifty on the river, was undistinguished until the year 1826, when Mr. Henry Barclay, of New York, duly appreciating the value of the water-power, became the purchaser of it and several farms in the vicinity. By a strong dam and a raceway, cut 65 feet perpendicularly through the rock, there has been obtained the use of the water under a fall of 47 feet, which may be applied twice in its descent. The enterprising proprietor established a large paper mill, extensive iron works, and erected a building for calico printing, since converted into a paint manufactory. The business of the country now centres here; and the trade employs 30 or 40 sloops and schooners, of from 80 to 150 tons burden. In 1825, there was not a single church here: there are now five neat edifices for public worship." Five miles above Ulster village, upon the creek at Whittaker's Falls, there is a very flourishing manufacturing village.

SHANDAKEN, a name signifying in Indian, "rapid waters," and as the old settlers report, the name of an Indian who anciently resided there. This town is in the NW. extremity of the county, and was taken from Woodstock in 1804; from Kingston NW. 30 miles. Pop. 1,464. Shandaken, Shandaken Corners, and Pine Hill, are the post-offices.

SHAWANGUNK. *Shawan*, in the language of the Mohegan Indians, means white salt, and *Gunk*, rocks or piles of rocks. The term Shawangunk, is said to have been applied by them to a precipice of white rocks of the mill-stone kind, near the top of these mountains, and facing the east. This town was organized in 1788; distant from Albany S. 91, from Kingston SW. 28 miles. In this and the adjoining towns the skeletons of 9 mammoths have been dug up; one of which has been sent entire to Europe, and the other exhibited in a museum at Philadelphia. The one at Philadelphia must have been 4 or 5 times as large as an elephant. Shawangunk, New Henly, Bruynswick, and Ulsterville, are names of post-offices. Pop. 3,885.

WAWARSING was taken from Rochester in 1806; from Albany SW. 80 miles. *Waa-wa-sing*, in the Indian language, means blackbird's nest. At the Hong Falls upon the river, there is a descent of 64 feet nearly perpendicular, and one mile below them, near the village of Napanock, is another cascade, and, including the rapids, a fall of 200 feet. Iron ore and plumbago of good quality are found here. Wawarsing, 24 miles SW. from Kingston, and Port Hixon, on the canal, are small settlements. Ellenville, Napanock, and Port Benjamin, all on the Hudson and Delaware canal, are small villages. Pop. 4,044.

The following are extracts from ancient newspapers:

From the Connecticut Journal, Sept. 2, 1778.

"POUGHKEEPSIE, AUG. 17.—We have also certain accounts that Andrieson and Osterhout, who were taken by the Indians and tories at Leghewegh, in Ulster county, some time ago, made their escape from them when within one day's march of Niagara, and are returned home. They were committed to the charge of three Indians, one a captain, and two squaws, who treated them with great severity, threatened to kill Osterhout, who from fatigue and hunger could not travel as fast as they would have him. At night, the Indians thinking themselves secure from their great distance back into the country, went to sleep; when Andrieson proposed to Osterhout to seize the opportunity of putting them to death; which (Osterhout declining,) he executed himself by very expeditiously tomahawking the three Indians before they were so far recovered from their sleep as to make any effectual resistance. The squaws waking with the noise, took to their heels and escaped. Whereupon Andrieson and Osterhout, possessing themselves of the Indians' provisions, consisting of 3 or 4 ducks and 2 quarts of samp, with the most valuable part of the Indians' plunder, consisting of some fine linen shirts, a laced beaver hat, with other articles of clothing, and some silver, with each of them a gun, set out for home, where they arrived after 17 days' march, much worn out with fatigue and hunger, but in high spirits."

From the Connecticut Journal of May 19, 1779.

"We have advice from Warwasink in Ulster county, that on Tuesday last, the 4th inst., a party of the enemy, supposed to be mostly tory inhabitants, burnt four dwelling-houses and five barns in that neighborhood at the Fantine Kill, and killed six people, besides three or four more who are supposed to be burnt in their houses. Advice of the mischief being brought to Col. Cortlandt, stationed there with his regiment, he immediately marched in pursuit of the enemy, whom he twice got sight of on a mountain, exchanged some shots with them, though at too great a distance, and endeavored to surround them, but in vain; they all made their escape. In their flight they left a young woman whom they had taken, from whom we received the account, that their number was 3 Indians, and 27 white savages."

From the Connecticut Journal, Oct. 11, 1781.

"Early in the morning of the 22d ult., a party of Indians and tories, consisting of about 400, entered the beautiful settlement of Warwarsing, situated on the great road leading from Minisink to Esopus, about 35 miles from the former; at their first coming to the place, they were hailed by a sentinel who was at the gate of a piquet fort where was a sergeant's guard kept, (which were the only soldiers in that quarter;) they not making any answer, induced the sentinel to fire and run within the fort, which alarmed the garrison. The enemy kept up a constant fire upon the fort for some time, but without effect, and at last retired in confusion, with the loss of three killed and two wounded. They then proceeded to burning and plundering the place. The inhabitants being alarmed by the firing at the fort, all made their escape, except one John Kettle, whom they killed. The loss of these poor people is very great; the fate of an hour reduced them from a state of ease and affluence to want and beggary. Thirteen elegant dwelling-houses, with all the out-buildings and furniture, 14 spacious barns filled with wheat, besides barracks, stables, stacks of hay and grain, were all consumed. Between 60 and 70 horses, mostly very fine, a great number of cattle, sheep, and hogs, were driven off. Col. Pauling, getting intelligence of the above, immediately collected about 200 New York levies and militia, and pursued them about 40 miles; but was not able to overtake them.* It appeared that they fled in confusion, as they left a considerable quantity of plunder behind them in many places. By a white man who has been with them 3 years, and made his escape while Warwarsing was in flames, we learn that this party was from Niagara, and that they were 4 weeks and 3 days on their way; that they were exceedingly distressed for want of provisions, insomuch that they eat up their pack-horses and dogs. He adds that the garrison of Niagara was in a melancholy situation for the want of provisions and the necessaries of life, and that the tories there most bitterly execrate the day they were deluded by the tyrant's emissaries to take up arms against their native country."

WOODSTOCK, organized in 1788; from Albany SW. 50, from Kingston NW. centrally distant 12 miles. Bristol and Woodstock are small villages. Pop. 1,692.

WARREN COUNTY.

WARREN COUNTY, taken from the NW. part of Washington county in 1813. It is principally situated on the west side of Lake George, centrally distant from New York 240, and from Albany 75 miles. Greatest length N. and S. 44, greatest breadth E. and W. 40 miles. With the exception of a small district on the SE., the whole county is mountainous. The mountains, which are of primitive formation, are covered with a heavy growth of trees, and contain it is said abundance of iron ore of good quality, but have very small portions of arable soil. The valleys, which are narrow, contain some fertile alluvion, on secondary limestone. The principal employment of the inhabitants is getting lumber, which is sent to market by the rivers, lake, and Champlain canal. This county embraces about one half

* Col. Pauling arrived at the outskirts in time to catch a glimpse of the enemy's rear, and to relieve some of the inhabitants, among whom were a man and his wife, who had conducted themselves with distinguished bravery. His house was constructed of unhewn logs, in the woods, and in advance of all others. On the appearance of the foe, he fled to his castle with his wife, and securing it in the best manner he could, gave battle to a party of the Indians who laid siege to his fortress. Being well armed, he defended himself with so much spirit, that they recoiled with loss. Finding, after several attempts, that they could not force an entrance, the Indians collected a heap of combustibles, and set fire to the premises. Retiring a short distance to see the result, the man watched his opportunity, and rushing out with a couple of buckets, he procured water, which was close at hand, and extinguished the fire. The Indians, of course, ran down upon him; but not being quick enough of foot to prevent his gaining the door, hurled their tomahawks at his head—happily without effect. He entered his castle, made fast his sally-port, and re-commenced his defence. Just at this moment Col. Pauling with his troops appeared in sight, whereupon the Indians raised the siege and departed.—*Life of Brant.*

of the Horicon or Lake George, the greater part of Schroon lake, the whole of Brant lake, and many smaller ones. The Horicon is a beautiful sheet of water 33 miles long, and about 2 wide, and discharges its waters northward into Lake Champlain at Ticonderoga. Its waters are very deep and clear, and abound with the finest fish. The mountain scenery of this lake is excelled in its romantic beauties by none in the world. Schroon and Brant lakes are beautiful sheets of water, and abound with fish similar to Lake George. The county is divided into 10 towns. Pop. 13,470.

ATHOL, originally called Thurman; distant from Albany 70, and from Caldwell WNW. 18 miles. Pop. 1,210.

BOLTON, bounded on the east by Lake George, from Caldwell N. 9 miles. Pop. 1,153.

CALDWELL, the shire town of Warren county, was organized in 1810, and named in honor of James Caldwell, Esq., a principal pro-

View of Caldwell, on Lake George.

prietor and benefactor. It has a mountainous surface, and embraces the south end of Lake George. Pop. 635. Caldwell village lies at the head of Lake George, 62 miles from Albany, 9 from Glenn's Falls, and 27 from Saratoga springs. The village consists of about 50 dwellings.

The scenery in this vicinity is of a wild and picturesque character, similar to the Highlands of Scotland. Westward, rises a range of mountains, the highest of which is Prospect or Rattlesnake Hill, which is an elevation of about 1,500 feet. Remains of forts William Henry and George, are still to be seen at the head of the lake, a short distance east of the courthouse.

This village and the lake has become quite a fashionable place of resort during the warm season of the year. Besides the attractions of the natural scenery, it is rendered interesting from having been the theatre of important military operations. The celebrated "Battle of Lake George," on Sept. 8th, 1755, was fought in the vicinity of *Bloody Pond*, so called from the fact that corpses of the slain were thrown into it. The battle was between the provincial troops under Major-general, afterward Sir William Johnson, aided by a body of Indians under Hendrick the Mohawk chieftain, and a body of French Canadians and Indians under Baron Dieskau, a French nobleman. The baron embarked at Fort Frederick, at Crown Point, with 2,000 men in batteaux, and landed at Skeensboro, now Whitehall. Having understood that Johnson lay carelessly encamped at the head of Lake George, he determined to attack him.

The following account of the conflict that ensued, is given by Dr. Dwight, who received much of his information from eye-witnesses of the action.

On the night of Sunday, Sept. 7, at 12 o'clock, information was brought, that the enemy had advanced 4 miles on the road from Fort Edward to Lake George; or half way between the village of Sandy-Hill and Glenn's falls. A council of war was held early in the morning, at which it was resolved to send a party to meet them. The number of men, determined upon at first, was mentioned by the general to Hendrick; and his opinion was asked. He replied, "If they are to fight, they are too few. If they are to be killed, they are too many." The number was accordingly increased. Gen. Johnson also proposed to divide them into 3 parties. Hendrick took 3 sticks, and, putting them together, said to him, "Put these together, and you can't break them. Take them one by one, and you will break them easily." The hint succeeded, and Hendrick's sticks saved the party, and probably the whole army, from destruction.

The party detached consisted of 1,200, and were commanded by Col. Ephraim Williams, a brave and skilful officer, greatly beloved by the soldiery, and greatly respected by the country at large. Lieut. Col. Whiting, of New Haven, was second in command, and brought up the rear. Col. Williams met the enemy at Rocky brook, 4 miles from Lake George. Dieskau had been informed of his approach by his scouts, and arranged his men in the best possible order to receive them, extending his line on both sides of the road in the form of a half-moon. Johnson did not begin to raise his breastwork until after Williams had marched; nor, as a manuscript account of this transaction, now before me, declares, until after the rencounter between Williams and the enemy had begun.

Williams marched his men directly into the hollow of the half-moon. This will be explained by the fact, that the whole country was a deep forest. When the enemy saw them completely within his power, he opened a fire of musketry on the front and on both flanks of the English at the same moment. The English fell in heaps; and at the head of them their gallant commander. Hendrick, also, was mortally wounded, fighting with invincible courage in the front of his people. He was shot in the back: a fact which filled him with disdain and anguish; as he thought, that he should be believed to have fled from the enemy. The truth was, the horns of the half-moon were so far advanced, that they in a great measure enclosed the van of the English, and fired upon them from the rear. From this fire Hendrick received the wound which terminated his life.

Upon the death of Col. Williams, Lieut. Col. Whiting succeeded to the command of the detachment. He was an officer of great merit, and had gained much applause at the reduction of Louisburgh; and, in consequence of his gallant conduct at that siege, had been made a captain in the regular British service. Whiting, seeing the danger of his men, immediately ordered a retreat; and conducted it so judiciously, that he saved the great body of them from destruction, in circumstances of extreme peril; in which their own confusion and alarm, and the situation of the ground, threatened their extermination no less than the superior numbers of the enemy.

The noise of the first fire was heard at Lake George. Efforts began then to be made in earnest by the general for the defence of the camp: and a party of 300 men were despatched under Lieut. Col. Cole, to support the retreating corps. A few stragglers, both English and Indians, came into the camp, and announced, what had indeed been already sufficiently evident from the approaching sound of the musketry, that the French army was superior in numbers and strength to Col. Williams' corps, and was driving them towards the camp. Some time after "the whole party that escaped," says Gen. Johnson, "came in in large bodies;" a decisive proof of the skill and coolness with which Lieut. Col. Whiting conducted this retreat. These men also arranged themselves in their proper places, and took their share in the engagement which followed.

About half after 11 o'clock, the enemy appeared in sight marching up the road in the best order towards the centre of the English. When they came to the bottom of an open valley, directly in front of the elevation, on which Fort George was afterward built, and on which the centre of the English army was posted, Dieskau halted his men about 15 minutes, at the distance of little more than 150 yards from the breastwork. I have never seen a reason assigned for this measure. I think I can assign one. The Indians were sent out on the right flank, and a part of the Canadians on the left, intending to come in upon the rear of the English, while the main body attacked them in front. The ground was remarkably favorable to this design; being swampy, thickly forested, and, therefore, perfectly fitted to conceal the approach of these parties. The Indians, however, were soon discovered by Lieut. Col. Pomeroy, who immediately mentioned the fact to the general; and, observing to him, that these people were extremely afraid of cannon, requested that one or two pieces might be pointed against them. They were then near the ground on which Fort William Henry was afterward built. The general approved of the proposal. A shell was instantly thrown among them from a howitzer, and some field-pieces showered upon them a quantity of grape-shot. The Indians fled.

The baron, in the mean time, led up his main body to attack the centre. They began the engagement by firing regularly in platoons; but at so great a distance, that they did very little execution. This circumstance was favorable to the English; and soon recovering from the panic into which they had been thrown by the preceding events of the day, they fought with great spirit and firmness.

Gen. Johnson, at the commencement of the battle, received a flesh wound in his thigh, and the ball lodged in it. He bled freely, but was able to walk away from the army to his tent. Gen. Lyman then took the command, and continued in it during the action. This gentleman, who seemed to have no passions, except those which are involved in the word *humanity*, immediately stationed himself in the front of the breastwork; and there, amid the thickest danger, issued his orders, during 5 hours, to every part of the army, as occasion demanded, with a serenity which many covet, and some boast, but very few acquire. The main body of the French kept their ground, and preserved their order, for a considerable time; but the artillery, under the command of Capt. Eyre, a brave English officer, who performed his part with much skill and reputation, played upon them with such success, and the fire from the musketry was so warm and well-directed, that their ranks were soon thinned, and their efforts slackened sufficiently to show that they despaired of success in this quarter. They then made another effort against the right of the English, stationed between the road and the site of Fort William Henry, and composed of Ruggles' regiment, Williams', now commanded by Lieut. Col. Pomeroy, and Titcomb's. Here a warm fire was kept up on both sides about an hour; but on the part of the enemy was unavailing.

At 4 o'clock, the English, and the Indians who fought with them, leaped over their breastwork, and charged the enemy. They fled, and were vigorously pursued for a short distance. A considerable number were slain in the pursuit. The wounded, and a very few others, were made prisoners. Among these was Dieskau. He was found by a soldier, resting on a stump, with hardly an attendant. As he was feeling for his watch, in order to give it to the soldier, the man, suspecting that he was searching for a pistol, discharged the contents of his musket through his hips. He was carried into the camp in a blanket by 8 men, with the greatest care and tenderness, but evidently in extreme distress.

Hendrick had lived to this day with singular honor, and died fighting with a spirit not to be excelled. He was at this time from 60 to 65 years of age. His head was covered with white locks: and what is uncommon among Indians, he was corpulent. Immediately before Col. Williams began his march, he mounted a stage, and harangued his people. He had a strong masculine voice; and, it was thought, might be distinctly heard at the distance of half a mile; a fact which, to my own view, has diffused a new degree of probability over Homer's representations of the effects produced by the speeches and shouts of his heroes. Lieut. Col. Pomeroy, who was present, and heard this effusion of Indian eloquence, told me, that, although he did not understand a word of the language, yet such was the animation of Hendrick, the fire of his eye, the force of his gesture, the strength of his emphasis, the apparent propriety of the inflections of his voice, and the natural appearance of his whole manner, that himself was more deeply affected with this speech, than with any other which he had ever heard. In the Pennsylvania Gazette, Sept. 25, 1755, he is styled " this famous Hendrick, a renowned Indian warrior among the Mohawks;" and it is said that his son, being told that his father was killed, giving the usual Indian groan upon such occasions, and suddenly putting his hand on his left breast, swore, that his father was still alive in that place, and that there stood his son. Baron Dieskau was conveyed from Albany to New York, and from thence to England; where soon after he died.

The capture of Fort William Henry, at this place, Aug. 9th, 1757, and the massacre by the Indians, created a great sensation in all the northern states. The following account of the capture of the fort, is extracted from Professor Silliman's Tour.

The Marquis de Montcalm, after three ineffectual attempts upon Fort William Henry, made great efforts to besiege it in form, and in August, 1757, having landed ten thousand men near the fort, summoned it to surrender. The place of his landing was shown me, a little north of the public house; the remains of his batteries and other works are still visible; and the graves and bones of the slain are occasionally discovered.

He had a powerful train of artillery, and although the fort and works were garrisoned by three thousand men, and were most gallantly defended by the commander, Colonel Monroe, it was obliged to capitulate; but the most honorable terms were granted to Colonel Monroe, in consideration of his great gallantry. The bursting of the great guns, the want of ammunition, and above all, the failure of General Webb to succor the fort, although he lay idle at Fort Edward with four thousand men, were the causes of this catastrophe.

The capitulation was, however, most shamefully broken; the Indians attached to Moncalm's army, while the troops were marching out of the gate of the fort, dragged the men from the ranks, particularly the Indians in the English service, and butchered them in cold blood—they plundered all without distinction, and murdered women and little children, with circumstances of the most aggravated barbarity.* The massacre continued all along the road, through the defile of the mountains, and for many miles, the miserable prisoners, especially those in the rear, were tomahawked and hewn down in cold blood; it might well be called the *bloody defile*, for it was the same ground that was the scene of the battles, only two years before, in 1755. It is said that efforts were made by the French to restrain the barbarians, but they were not restrained, and the miserable remnant of the garrison with difficulty reached Fort Edward pursued by the Indians, although escorted by a body of French troops. I passed over the whole of the ground, upon which this tragedy was acted, and the oldest men of the country still remember this deed of guilt and infamy.

Fort William Henry was levelled by Montcalm, and has never been rebuilt. Fort George was built as a substitute for it, on a more commanding site, and although often mentioned in the history of subsequent wars, was not I believe the scene of any very memorable event.

CHESTER, taken from Thurman; from Albany 80, and from Caldwell N. 18 miles. Chester is a village having about 40 dwellings, 6 mercantile stores, 3 churches—1 Presbyterian, 1 Baptist, and 1 Methodist. It is situated on the Canada road, near the outlet of Friends and Loon lakes. The land in the vicinity is fertile. Pottersville is a post-office in the N. part. Pop. 1,623.

HAGUE, originally named Rochester, and taken from Bolton in 1807; from Caldwell NE. 30 miles. Pop. 610.

"Rogers Rock is on the west side of Lake George, in the northeastern border of the town, 2 miles from the outlet. It rises out of the water at an angle of more than forty-five degrees to the height of 3 or 400 feet. The face of the rock for more than 100 feet is a perfectly smooth slide, reaching from top to bottom. This rock derives its name from the following incident. During the winter of 1758, Major Rogers was one of a party which was surprised and put to flight by the Indians at the outlet of the lake. Rogers came alone to the summit of this rock, whither he knew the Indians would follow him by his tracks in the snow, and where he could prevent pursuit by a singular stratagem. Throwing his pack down the precipice, he slipped off his snow shoes, and without changing their position, turned himself about and again put them on his feet. Thus equipped, he retreated several rods along the southern brow of the rock. The Indians coming to the spot went no further, as they saw the two tracks both leading the same way and apparently made by two persons who had come to the precipice, and chosen to throw themselves off rather than to fall into the hands of their pursuers. Meanwhile Rogers made good his descent to the foot of the rock, where he resumed his pack, and escaped on the ice to the head of the lake.

"*Sabbath-day Point* is a low neck of land stretching into Lake George from the western shore, 3 miles from the little village of Hague. On Sabbath-day Point, Lord Amherst with his army stopped for refreshment upon the morning of the Sabbath, and gave this beautiful spot the name by which it is known. It is a charming place, and susceptible of great embellishment. In the summer of 1756, a small body of provincials who had retreated to this point defeated a superior force of French and Indians, who had attacked them in gun-boats."

HORICON, recently formed from Hague and Bolton; centrally dis-

---

* Men and women had their throats cut, their bodies ripped open, and their bowels, with insult, thrown in their faces. Infants and children were barbarously taken by the heels, and their brains dashed out against stones and trees. The Indians pursued the English nearly half the way to Fort Edward, where the greatest number of them arrived in a most forlorn condition.

tant N. from Caldwell 24 miles. Pop. 663. Horicon post-office is in the SW. part, on the Schroon branch of the Hudson.

JOHNSBURG, the NW. corner town, taken from Thurman in 1805; from Albany 85, from Caldwell NW. 21 miles. Johnsburg is a small settlement, and lies about 3 miles west of the Hudson. Pop. 1,156.

LUZERNE, first settled about 1770, taken from Queensbury in 1808; from Albany 55, centrally distant SW. from Caldwell 8 miles. Luzerne is a small village on the Hudson. Hadley's and Jessup's falls are in this town. Pop. 3,664.

QUEENSBURY was organized in 1788. The soil in the E. part of the town is a strong and productive loam, in the W. it is sandy. Pop. 3,664. The village of Glenn's Falls, in this town, lies on the N. bank of the Hudson, 53 miles from Albany, 3 W. from Sandy Hill, and 17 from Saratoga. It received its name from from a Mr. Glenn, the first settler, whose house is still standing about 20 rods from the falls.

Distant view of the village of Glenn Falls.

The above is a SE. view of the village as seen from the S. bank of the Hudson. There are here about 120 dwellings, 1 Presbyterian, 1 Methodist, and 1 Baptist church, a female seminary, a printing office, and about a dozen mills on both sides of the river for sawing lumber and marble. The Presbyterian and Methodist churches and the academy are seen on the right, and part of the bridge over the Hudson at the falls, on the left.

<small>These falls have a total descent of about 70 feet. The water flows in one sheet over the brink of the precipice, 900 feet in length, and when in full flood, rushes in one mass down the cataract, filling the mind of a spectator on the bridge with awe and admiration. In ordinary seasons the river is divided at the falls by rocks into three channels, which have an angular descent of several hundred feet. These falls have evidently receded from a position lower down the stream. The banks below are in some places 70 feet in perpendicular height, formed of rocks, in which the stratification is beautifully disposed, containing many organic remains. The navigable feeder of the Champlain canal is taken from the river, two miles above, and passes along the elevated bank of the river seen in the engrav</small>

ing. It is believed that as many as eighteen or twenty persons have been drawn over the falls, within the memory of those now living, only two of whom escaped death. Animals are frequently drawn over, and almost invariably perish.

WARRENSBURG, formed in 1813; N. from Albany 68 miles. It is a mountainous district, covered with wood and abounding in iron ore. The main branch of the Hudson flows on the west boundary, and the Schroon branch on the E. and S., uniting with the former in the SW. Warrensburg, on the Schroon branch, 6 miles N. of Caldwell, is a village containing two churches and about 60 dwellings. Pop. 1,469.

WASHINGTON COUNTY.

WASHINGTON COUNTY received its present name in 1784, having previously been called Charlotte county, when it claimed to include a part of the present state of Vermont. Its greatest length is 64 miles; average breadth to South Bay, of Lake Champlain, 17 miles; and thence on the N. 6 miles. Centrally distant from New York 210, from Albany 60 miles.

The face of the country is very much diversified. That around Lake George is generally rugged and mountainous, presenting summits from 600 to 1200 feet in height. All the northern part is broken and hilly. The southern part, though considerably uneven, presents a very large proportion of arable land, well adapted for the various products of agriculture. In the northern part, which is comparatively new, the pine forests supply large quantities of lumber. The county is abundantly watered. As a whole, it holds a respectable rank in agriculture, producing much wheat, but is better adapted to grass. A large proportion of the population is from New England, and large emigrations are yearly making from Vermont. The county is divided into 17 towns. Pop. 41,095.

ARGYLE, organized in 1788; N. from Albany 44 miles. The tract comprised in the original town of Argyle, was granted by George II., in 1742, to 141 Scotch emigrants, who severally drew a farm lot of from 150 to 600 acres, with a town lot of from 15 to 16 acres. Argyle, 8 miles SE. from Sandy Hill, has about 50 dwellings. North Argyle 5, and South Argyle 11 miles from Sandy Hill, are small settlements. Pop. 3,113.

CAMBRIDGE, organized in 1788; N. from Albany 35 miles. Cambridge, a large but scattered village, has an academy for qualifying young men as teachers, and about 120 dwellings. Buskirk's Bridge, upon Hoosick river, partly in Pittstown, Rensselaer county, has from 30 to 40 dwellings. Centre Cambridge is a small village centrally situated. Pop. 2,004.

DRESDEN, taken from Putnam in 1822, by the name of South Bay, from Albany 72, and from Sandy Hill N. 20 miles. It is situated in a mountainous and wild country, between lakes Champlain and George. In the forests deer and wolves are said to be common. Pop. 697.

EASTON, taken from Stillwater and Saratoga; from Albany N. 27, from Salem SW. 16 miles. Union village is partly in this town and partly in Greenwich. Easton is a post village, containing about 50 dwellings. North Easton and South Easton are small settlements with post-offices. Pop. 3,002.

FORT ANN was originally organized by the name of Westfield; it received its present name in 1808. The face of the township is diversified with mountains and valleys. On Wood creek there are fertile alluvial flats and plains, but a great part of this extensive township is sterile and barren. Pop. 3,559. The village of Fort Ann, which gives its name to the township, on Wood creek and the canal, 58 miles from Albany and 10 S. from Whitehall, contains about 50 dwellings and 3 churches. It is situated on the site of old Fort Ann erected in 1757, and was a place of some importance during the colonial wars. About two miles south of the village, vestiges of Burgoyne's road, constructed of logs, &c., in 1777, are still to be seen.

Professor Silliman in his tour gives the following account of a severe battle fought near this place, between a detachment of the British and one of the American army, July 8th, 1777:—

At a narrow pass between some high rocks and the river, we were shown the place where, on the 8th of July, 1777, the 9th British regiment, belonging to General Burgoyne's army, sustained a heavy loss, by a conflict with the Americans under Colonel Long.

After the surrender of Ticonderoga, General Burgoyne endeavored to keep up the alarm, by spreading his parties over the country. With this view, Colonel Hill, at the head of the 9th regiment, was despatched after Colonel Long, who, with four or five hundred men, principally the invalids and convalescents of the army, had taken post at Fort Anne, and was directed by General Schuyler to defend it. Colonel Long, with his party, did not wait an attack from the enemy, but boldly advanced to meet them. "At half past ten in the morning, (says Major Forbes, of the British regiment,) they attacked us in front, with a heavy and well-directed fire; a large body of them passed the creek on the left, and fired from a thick wood across the creek on the left flank of the regiment: they then began to recross the creek and attack us in the rear; we then found it necessary to change our ground, to prevent the regiment's being surrounded; we took post on the top of a hill to our right. As soon as we had taken post, the enemy made a very vigorous attack, which continued for upwards of two hours; and they certainly would have forced us, had it not been for some Indians that arrived and gave the Indian whoop, which we answered with three cheers; the rebels soon after that gave way." The giving way of the Americans was, however, caused, not by the terror of the war-whoop, but by the failure of their ammunition. The fact was, the British regiment was worsted, and would probably have been taken or destroyed, had Colonel Long been well supplied with ammunition. It was said by Captain Money, another British officer, that the fire was even heavier than it was in the obstinate battle of September 19th, on Bemus' heights. The scene of this battle is very correctly described above, by Major Forbes.

On leaving the street of Fort Anne village, we crossed a bridge over Wood creek, and were now on its left bank. Immediately after, we came to a narrow pass, only wide enough for the carriage, and cut, in a great measure, out of a rocky ledge, which terminates here, exactly at the creek. This ledge is the southern end of a high rocky hill, which converges towards Wood creek, and between the two is a narrow tract of level ground, which terminates at the pass already mentioned. On this ground the battle took place, and the wood on the right bank of the creek, from which the Americans fired upon the left flank of the British, is still there, and it was up this rocky hill that they retreated and took their stand.

General Burgoyne, as usual, claimed a victory in this affair, which is understood to have been a bloody contest, as indeed it obviously must have been, from the narrowness of the defile, and the consequent nearness of the contending parties. Captain Montgomery, of Colonel Hill's regiment, was left wounded on the field, and taken prisoner by the Americans, which could not have been the fact, had the royal party been victorious."

FORT EDWARD was taken from Argyle in 1818. The surface of the town is level or gently undulating, and the soil mostly of a good quality. Pop. 1,728. Fort Edward is a small village, situated on the Hudson river and Champlain canal, 47 miles from Albany, and about 3 from Sandy Hill. There is a dam above the village 900 feet long and 27 high, which supplies a feeder to the canal. Fort Miller and Fort Edward Centre, also on the Champlain canal and Hudson river, are small settlements.

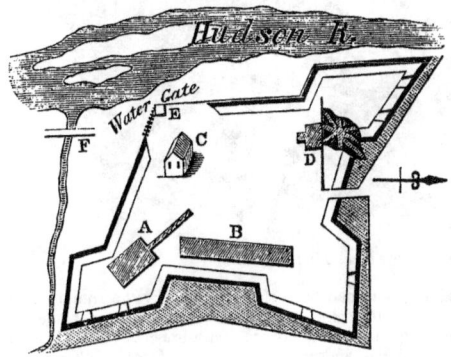

Fort Edward—references: A. magazine, B. barracks, C. storehouse, D. Hospital, E. a flanker, F. Colonel Bagly's bridge.

Fort Edward, from which this town derives its name, was built in 1755, of timber and earth, 16 feet high, 22 feet thick, and had six cannon on its ramparts. It had a deep fosse in front; it was situated about half a mile south of the lock of the Champlain canal, in the village, and was at first called Fort Lyman, from General Lyman, a distinguished officer in the French war. This spot was also named the *first carrying place*, being the point where, in the expeditions against Canada, the troops, stores, &c., were landed and carried to Wood creek, a distance of 12 miles, where they were again embarked.

The village of Fort Edward is rendered memorable as being the spot where Miss M'Crea met with her tragical fate. This unfortunate young woman lived about four miles south from Fort Edward, on the west bank of the Hudson. Her lover, a Mr. Jones, lived about a mile south of the fort. When Burgoyne with his army from Canada had arrived in this vicinity, Mr. Jones left the American army, and with many of his neighbors joined the forces under Burgoyne. For his loyalty he was made a major. As the place where Miss M'Crea resided was exposed to the hostile incursions of both armies, Mr. Jones, being anxious for her safety, found means to convey intelligence to her that he would take measures to have her brought into the British camp. For this purpose she was directed to come to Mrs. Campbell's, a relative of hers who lived in a house now standing in Fort Edward village. Here she was to wait till he sent a convoy for her safety. Miss M'Crea left her home in the morning, crossed the river by Mr. Jones' house, took breakfast " at the old Baldwin house," near by Fort Edward, and from thence went to Mrs. Campbell's.

It appears that Mr. Jones, by offering a quantity of rum as a reward, induced a party of Indians to go for Miss M'Crea, and bring her into the British camp. Some accounts state that when the Indians came near the house they held up a letter to allay her fears, which being from her lover, she did not hesitate to venture herself with them. The Indians also took Mrs. Campbell with them. When this party had proceeded but a short distance, about half way up the elevation north of the village, they were met by another party of Indians. It is stated that the latter, hearing of the offer of Mr. Jones, determined to share a portion of the reward. This brought on a contention between them, which rose to such a height, that an aged Indian chief, fearful of the consequences, determined to end the dispute. Approaching Miss M'Crea, he shot her dead as she sat on her horse. He then sprang forward, sunk his tomahawk into her head, and then scalped her. "Tradition reports, that the Indians divided the scalp, and that each party carried half of it to the agonized lover."

She was now stripped of her clothing and dragged about thirty rods west of the place where she was killed, and laid under a log by the side of the ancient pine represented in the engraving. It is stated by those who saw her remains, that they exhibited a most shocking spectacle; her limbs were much swollen, and covered with dust and blood.

The Jane M'Crea tree, Fort Edward.

An American officer, Lieutenant Palmer, who had been slain that day by the Indians with 18 of his men, about 80 rods northwest of the pine tree, was also thrown under the log near Miss M'Crea, and the remains of both partially covered with brushwood and bushes. The engraving shows the appearance of the spot where the body of Miss M'Crea was found. The pine tree which was then standing, still remains, having a venerable and ancient appearance. Her name is inscribed on the tree, with the date 1777, and "no traveller passes this spot without spending a plaintive moment in contemplating the untimely fate of youth and loveliness." At its root it is about 5 feet in diameter, standing about four rods west from the road to Sandy Hill, and about 80 rods north of the village, on the side of a sandy ridge. A fine spring issues a few feet below this tree. The bodies of Miss M'Crea and Lieutenant Palmer were taken and buried three miles below the fort, near what was called the "*black house.*" About 18 years since, her remains were taken up and re-interred in a village burying ground at Fort Edward; the Rev. Mr. Cummings, of Albany, preached a funeral sermon on the occasion. At the time of her death she was about twenty years of age, and is represented as having been of a middling stature, finely formed, dark hair, and uncommonly beautiful. Mr. Jones, who was about twenty-five, survived her death but a short period, and it is said his hair turned gray the first night after receiving the fatal news.

GRANVILLE was organized in 1788. The township is handsomely diversified, and the soil is of a superior quality, well watered by springs, rivulets, &c. Pop. 3,846. The town was principally settled by emigrants from the New England states. There are 3 villages having post-offices. Granville village, or Granville Corners, 63 miles from Albany, 17 from Salem, and 21 from Sandy Hill, is the most compact settlement; it consists of about 75 dwellings, having 1 Methodist, 1 Episcopal, and 1 Friends church, an academy, a woollen factory, &c.

The following is a northwestern view of the central part of Middle Granville, about 2 miles north of Granville Corners village. The village consists of about 30 dwellings, 1 Congregational, and 1 Pres-

Northwest view of the central part of Middle Granville.

byterian church, a number of mills, &c. The Congregational church and school-house are seen on the right of the engraving; the mountainous elevations seen in the extreme distance are in the town of Pawlet, in the state of Vermont, about six miles distant. North or West Granville, 18 miles from Sandy Hill, has a church, an academy, and is a substantial village scattered for a considerable distance along the road. South Granville is a small village.

Southeastern view of Union Village.

GREENWICH was taken from Argyle in 1803. The surface of the township is moderately uneven; the soil is principally a gravelly loam, and is under good cultivation. Pop. 3,379.

The above engraving shows the appearance of Union village,

as seen from the elevated ground near the school-house, on the Easton side of the Battenkill. This flourishing village is 35 miles from Albany, 12 from Salem, and about 5 E. from Schuylerville. It contains 4 churches—1 Baptist, 1 Dutch Reformed, 1 Congregational, and 1 Methodist—an academy, a bank, a newspaper printing office, a number of mills and factories, and about 1,500 inhabitants. The Baptist church, the oldest in the village, is seen on the right of the engraving; a few rods westward is the Methodist church; the Dutch Reformed church is in the central part; and on the extreme left is seen part of the front of the Congregational church, which is without a spire. The village was founded in 1809. Battenville and Franklinton are small manufacturing villages, on the Battenkill. North and East Greenwich and Lake, are post-offices, with settlements.

HAMPTON, from Albany NE. 70, from Salem N. 25, and from Sandy Hill NE. 25 miles. Hampton and Low Hampton are post-offices. Pop. 972.

HARTFORD, taken from Westfield, originally the name of Fort Ann, in 1793; from Albany NE. 54 miles. Hartford, 13 miles NE. from Sandy Hill, and South Hartford, 2 miles south of the former, are small post villages. Pop. 2,158.

HEBRON is centrally distant north of Salem 7 miles. Pop. 2,498. Hebron, North Hebron, and South Hebron, are small post villages.

JACKSON, taken from Cambridge in 1815; from Albany NE. 40, from Salem S. 6 miles. Jackson and Anaquascook are post-offices. Pop. 1,730.

KINGSBURY was organized in 1788. It has a surface generally level and well cultivated, and in former times was mostly covered with fine groves of white pines. Pop. 2,773. This town has three villages— viz, Sandy Hill, Kingsbury, and Adamsville. Sandy Hill, on the north bank of the Hudson, is the half-shire village of the county, and was incorporated in 1810. It is situated upon a high sandy plain, about 100 feet above the river, opposite Baker's Falls, where, in the course of 60 rods, the river descends 76 feet. The contemplated railroad from Saratoga to Whitehall is to cross the Hudson here by a viaduct 1,100 feet in length.

The following is a south view of the central part of the village of Sandy Hill, 48 miles from Albany. In the central part of the engraving is seen a triangular enclosure, set out with ornamental trees and shrubbery. The courthouse is on the right, and the church on the left. The village contains a Presbyterian and Episcopal church and upwards of 100 dwelling-houses. James Bradshaw was the first settler in the village, and the second was Albert Baker, who came here in 1768. His family was the 11th which settled in Kingsbury. Kingsbury village, 5 miles from Sandy Hill, is situated on the road to Fort Ann, and has 1 Baptist church and about 30 dwellings. Adamsville, 6 miles from Sandy Hill, is a village containing a Baptist church and 25 dwellings.

The first minister settled in the town was Francis Baylor, a Moravian. He remained but a short time, and left in the year 1777. The first meeting-house was built soon after the revolu-

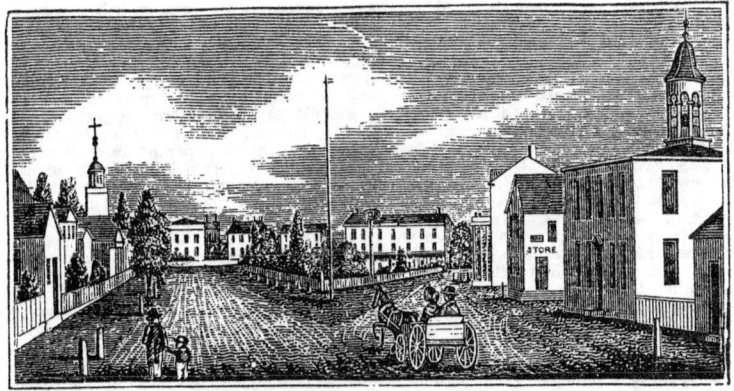

Southern view of the central part of Sandy Hill.

tion, and is still standing and occupied by the Baptists. During the war the town was burnt by Burgoyne's army, which lay encamped here about six weeks. The Hessians occupied the ground in the vicinity of the new burying-yard at Sandy Hill, while the Grenadiers lay at Moss Street, 2 miles north, and the light infantry under Frazer at Fort Edward Hill.

The site on which stands the village of Sandy Hill, was formerly the scene of Indian barbarities. The following anecdote is related by Professor Silliman, in his Tour from Hartford to Quebec in the autumn of 1819.

From Mr. H., a very respectable inhabitant, I learned the following singular piece of history Old Mr. Schoonhoven, recently living in this vicinity, and probably still surviving, although at the great age of more than fourscore, informed Mr. H. that during the last French war, he and six or seven other Americans coming through the wilderness, from Fort William Henry, at the head of Lake George, to Sandy Hill, had the misfortune to be taken prisoners by a party of the savages. They were conducted to the spot which is now the central green of Sandy Hill, and ordered to sit down in a row, upon a log. Mr. Schoonhoven pointed out to Mr. H. the exact place where the log lay; it was nearly in front of the house where we dined. The Indians then began, very deliberately, to tomahawk their victims, commencing at one end of the log, and splitting the skulls of their prisoners, in regular succession; while the survivors, compelled to sit still, and to witness the awful fate of their companions, awaited their own, in unutterable horror. Mr. Schoonhoven was the last but one, upon the end of the log, opposite to where the massacre commenced; the work of death had already proceeded to him, and the lifted tomahawk was ready to descend, when a chief gave a signal to stop the butchery. Then approaching Mr. Schoonhoven, he mildly said, "Do you not remember that (at such a time) when your young men were dancing, poor Indians came, and wanted to dance too; your young men said, 'No!—Indians shall not dance with us;' but you (for it seems this chief had recognised his features only in the critical moment) you said, Indians shall dance—now I will show you that Indians can remember kindness." This chance recollection (*providential*, we had better call it) saved the life of Mr. Schoonhoven, and of the other survivor.

Strange mixture of generosity and cruelty! For a trifling affront, they cherished and glutted vengeance, fell as that of infernals, without measure of retribution, or discrimination of objects; for a favor equally trifling, they manifested magnanimity exceeding all correspondence to the benefit, and capable of arresting the stroke of death, even when falling with the rapidity of lightning.

Two miles north of the village of Kingsbury is the spot where a bloody battle was fought in the French war, between a body of troops under Putnam and Rogers, and 500 French and Indians commanded by Molang.

"In the month of August, 1758, five hundred men were employed, under the orders of Majors Rogers and Putnam, to watch the motions of the enemy near Ticonderoga. At South Bay they separated the party into two equal divisions, and Rogers took a position on Wood Creek, twelve miles distant from Putnam.

"Upon being, some time afterward, discovered, they formed a reunion, and concerted measures for returning to Fort Edward. Their march through the woods was in *three divisions*, *by* FILES: the right commanded by Rogers, the left by Putnam, and the centre by Captain D'Ell. The first night they encamped on the banks of *Clear River*, about a mile from old Fort Ann, which had been formerly built by General Nicholson. Next morning Major Rogers, and a British officer named Irwin, incautiously suffered themselves, from a spirit of false emulation, to be engaged in firing at a mark. Nothing could have been more repugnant to the military principles of Putnam than such conduct, or reprobated by him in more pointed terms. As soon as the heavy dew which had fallen the preceding night would permit, the detachment moved in one body, Putnam being in front, D'Ell in centre, and Rogers in the rear. The impervious growth of shrubs and under-brush that had sprung up, where the land had been partially cleared some years before, occasioned this change in the order of march. At the moment of moving, the famous French partisan Molang, who had been sent with five hundred men to intercept our party, was not more than one mile and a half distant from them. Having heard the firing, he hastened to lay an ambuscade precisely in that part of the wood most favorable to his project. Major Putnam was just emerging from the thicket, into the common forest, when the enemy rose, and with discordant yells and whoops, commenced an attack upon the right of his division. Surprised, but undismayed, Putnam halted, returned the fire, and passed the word for the other divisions to advance for his support. D'Ell came. The action, though widely scattered, and principally fought between man and man, soon grew general and intensely warm. It would be as difficult as useless to describe this irregular and ferocious mode of fighting. Rogers came not up; but, as he declared afterward, formed a circular file between our party and Wood creek, to prevent their being taken in rear or enfiladed. Successful as he commonly was, his conduct did not always pass without unfavorable imputation. Notwithstanding, it was a current saying in the camp, 'that Rogers always *sent*, but Putnam *led* his men to action,' yet, in justice, it ought to be remarked here, that the latter has never been known, in relating the story of this day's disaster, to affix any stigma upon the conduct of the former.

"Major Putnam, perceiving it would be impracticable to cross the creek, determined to maintain his ground. Inspired by his example, the officers and men behaved with great bravery: sometimes they fought aggregately in open view, and sometimes individually under cover; taking aim from behind the bodies of trees, and acting in a manner independent of each other. For himself, having discharged his fuzee several times, at length it missed fire, while the muzzle was pressed against the breast of a large and well proportioned savage. This *warrior*, availing himself of the indefensible attitude of his adversary, with a tremendous war-whoop, sprang forward, with his lifted hatchet, and compelled him to surrender; and having disarmed and bound him fast to a tree, returned to the battle.

"The intrepid Captains D'Ell and Harman, who now commanded, were forced to give ground for a little distance: the savages conceiving this to be the certain harbinger of victory, rushed impetuously on, with dreadful and redoubled cries. But our two partisans, collecting a handful of brave men, gave the pursuers so warm a reception as to oblige them, in turn, to retreat a little beyond the spot at which the action had commenced. Here they made a stand. This change of ground occasioned the tree to which Putnam was tied to be directly between the fire of the two parties. Human imagination can hardly figure to itself a more deplorable situation. The balls flew incessantly from either side, many struck the tree, while some passed through the sleeves and skirts of his coat. In this state of jeopardy, unable to move his body, to stir his limbs, or even to incline his head, he remained more than an hour So equally balanced, and so obstinate was the fight! At one moment, while the battle swerved in favor of the enemy, a young savage chose an odd way of discovering his humor. He found Putnam bound. He might have despatched him at a blow. But he loved better to excite the terrors of the prisoner, by hurling a tomahawk at his head, or rather it should seem his object was to see how near he could throw it without touching him—the weapon struck in the tree a number of times at a hair's breadth distance from the mark. When the Indian had finished his amusement, a French bas-officer (a much more inveterate savage by nature, though descended from so humane and polished a nation) perceiving Putnam, came up to him, and, levelling a fuzee within a foot of his breast, attempted to discharge it—it missed fire. Ineffectually did the intended victim solicit the treatment due to his situation, by repeating that he was a prisoner of war. The degenerate Frenchman did not understand the language of honor or of nature: deaf to their voice, and dead to sensibility, he violently, and repeatedly, pushed the muzzle of his gun against Putnam's ribs, and finally gave him a cruel blow on the jaw with the butt-end of his piece. After this dastardly deed he left him.

"At length the active intrepidity of D'Ell and Harman, seconded by the persevering valor of their followers, prevailed. They drove from the field the enemy, who left about ninety dead behind them. As they were retiring, Putnam was untied by the Indian who had made him prisoner, and whom he afterward called master. Having been conducted for some distance from the place of action, he was stripped of his coat, vest, stockings, and shoes; loaded with as many of the packs of the wounded as could be piled upon him; strongly pinioned, and his wrists tied as closely together as they could be pulled with a cord. After he had marched, through no pleasant paths, in this painful manner, for many a tedious mile, the party (who were excessively fatigued) halted to breathe. His hands were now immoderately swelled from the tightness of the ligature; and the pain had become intolerable. His feet were so much scratched, that the blood dropped fast from them. Exhausted with bearing a burden above his strength, and frantic with torments exquisite beyond endurance, he entreated the Irish interpreter to implore, as the last and only grace he desired of the savages, that they would knock him on the head and take his scalp at once, or loose his hands. A French officer, instantly interposing, ordered his hands to be unbound, and some of the packs to be taken off. By this time the Indian who captured him, and had been absent with the wounded, coming up, gave him a pair of moccasins, and expressed great indignation at the unworthy treatment his prisoner had suffered.

"That savage chief again returned to the care of the wounded, and the Indians, about two hundred in number, went before the rest of the party to the place where the whole were that night to encamp. They took with them Major Putnam, on whom, besides innumerable other outrages, they had the barbarity to inflict a deep wound with the tomahawk in the left cheek. His sufferings were in this place to be consummated. A scene of horror, infinitely greater than had ever met his eyes before, was now preparing. It was determined to roast him alive. For this purpose they led him into a dark forest, stripped him naked, bound him to a tree, and piled dry brush, with other fuel, at a small distance, in a circle round him. They accompanied their labors, as if for his funeral dirge, with screams and sounds inimitable but by savage voices. Then they set the piles on fire. A sudden shower damped the rising flame. Still they strove to kindle it, until, at last, the blaze ran fiercely round the circle. Major Putnam soon began to feel the scorching heat. His hands were so tied that he could move his body. He often shifted sides as the fire approached. This sight, at the very idea of which all but savages must shudder, afforded the highest diversion to his inhuman tormentors, who demonstrated the delirium of their joy by correspondent yells, dances, and gesticulations. He saw clearly that his final hour was inevitably come. He summoned all his resolution, and composed his mind, as far as the circumstances could admit, to bid an eternal farewell to all he held most dear. To quit the world would scarcely have cost a single pang; but for the idea of home, but for the remembrance of domestic endearments, of the affectionate partner of his soul, and of their beloved offspring. His thought was ultimately fixed on a happier state of existence, beyond the tortures he was beginning to endure. The bitterness of death, even of that death which is accompanied with the keenest agonies, was, in a manner, past—nature, with a feeble struggle, was quitting its last hold on sublunary things—when a French officer rushed through the crowd, opened a way by scattering the burning brands, and unbound the victim. It was Molang himself—to whom a savage, unwilling to see another human sacrifice immolated, had run and communicated the tidings. That commandant spurned and severely reprimanded the barbarians, whose nocturnal powwos and hellish orgies he suddenly ended. Putnam did not want for feeling or gratitude. The French commander, fearing to trust him alone with them, remained until he could deliver him in safety into the hands of his master.

"The savage approached his prisoner kindly, and seemed to treat him with particular affection. He offered him some hard biscuit; but finding that he could not chew them, on account of the blow he had received from the Frenchman, this more humane savage soaked some of the biscuit in water, and made him suck the pulp-like part. Determined, however, not to lose his captive (the refreshment being finished) he took the moccasins from his feet, and tied them to one of his wrists: then directing him to lie down on his back upon the bare ground, he stretched one arm to its full length, and bound it fast to a young tree; the other arm was extended and bound in the same manner—his legs were stretched apart and fastened to two saplings. Then a number of tall, but slender poles were cut down, which, with some long bushes, were laid across his body from head to foot: on each side lay as many Indians as could conveniently find lodging, in order to prevent the possibility of his escape. In this disagreeable and painful posture he remained until morning. During this night, the longest and most dreary conceivable, our hero used to relate that he felt a ray of cheerfulness come casually across his mind, and could not even refrain from smiling when he reflected on this ludicrous group for a painter, of which he himself was the principal figure.

"The next day he was allowed his blanket and moccasins, and permitted to march without carrying any pack, or receiving any insult. To allay his extreme hunger, a little bear's meat was given, which he sucked through his teeth. At night the party arrived at Ticonderoga, and the prisoner was placed under the care of a French guard. The savages, who had been prevented from glutting their diabolical thirst for blood, took other opportunity of manifesting their malevolence for the disappointment, by horrid grimaces and angry gestures; but they were suffered no more to offer violence or personal indignity to him.

"After having been examined by the Marquis de Montcalm, Major Putnam was conducted to Montreal by a French officer, who treated him with the greatest indulgence and humanity."
—*Humphrey's Life of Putnam.*

PUTNAM, the extreme northern town of the county, was taken from Westfield in 1806; from Albany 90, and from Sandy Hill N. 30 miles. Pop. 785. Palmerston mountain, in this town, rises to the height of 1,500 feet.

SALEM was organized in 1788; has a hilly surface with narrow valleys and plains, and generally a fertile soil. Pop. 2,855.

The following is a view of Salem, the half-shire village of Washington county, as seen from an elevation on the main road at the northern extremity of the village, showing the principal street and the public

North view of Salem village.

buildings. The village is 46 miles from Albany and 21 from Sandy Hill, and consists of upwards of 100 dwellings, 1 Presbyterian, 1 Associate Reformed Congregational church, an academy, the county buildings, offices, stores, printing office, &c. The Presbyterian church and courthouse are seen on the left of the engraving, the Congregational near the centre, and the academy on the extreme right. The village was incorporated in 1803; the academy in this place has been incorporated for about half a century, and is a very respectable institution, where quite a number of eminent men have been educated.

Salem was first setttled about the year 1756, by two companies of emigrants, one from Scotland and Ireland, the other from New England. They worshipped together under the ministry of the Rev. Thomas Clark, an Irish preacher, till differences arose about " occasional communion," and about " receiving the covenant of the three kingdoms." This controversy occasioned a separation in 1769. A Presbyterian church was formed, and the Rev. John Warford, the first minister, was installed in 1789. He labored about 14 years, and was succeeded by Rev. Samuel Tomb, who continued in the ministry till his death in 1832. His successors have been Rev. John Whiton and Rev. A. B. Lambert. The first Presbyterian church was built in 1774, and for three years it was used for barracks and a storehouse. It was burnt by the royalists in 1778. The next house was built immediately after the war, and was burnt by accident in 1836. The third, erected at a cost of $10,000, was burnt in April, 1840; another is now erecting.

The following inscription is copied from a monument in the village graveyard.

"Here lie the earthly remains of the Rev. James Proudfit, pastor of the Ass. Ref. Congregation, Salem, who, after manifesting the most ardent zeal and disinterested faithfulness in the gospel of his Master during the period of fifty years, fell asleep in Jesus Oct. 22d, 1802.—'Well done ! good and faithful servant, enter thou into the joy of thy Lord.' 'They that turn many to righteousness shall shine as the stars forever.' 'To him that overcometh will I grant to sit with me in my throne, even as I also overcame, and am set down with my Father in his throne.' "

White Creek, the SE. town of the county, was taken from Cambridge in 1815; centrally distant S. from Salem 12 miles. Pop. 2,204. North White Creek and Little White Creek are small post villages. White Creek Centre and Wait's Corners are small settlements.

WHITEHALL, organized in 1788, has a great diversity of surface. The soil is principally a stiff clay, well adapted to grass. Pop. 3,810.

Northern view of Whitehall.

The above engraving shows the appearance of the village of Whitehall as seen from the rocky eminence which rises perpendicularly from the waters of Lake Champlain, a short distance to the north, overlooking the harbor. The village is compactly built, and lies in a rocky ravine, at the junction of Wood creek and the Champlain canal with the waters of Lake Champlain, 73 miles from Albany and 21 from Sandy Hill. The mouth of the creek and canal are seen in the central part of the engraving. The waters of the canal descend a distance of 26 feet by three locks. There is a steamboat communication with this place and St. Johns in Canada, 150 miles distant. The steamboat landing is seen on the left at the foot of a rocky eminence about 200 feet high; the Presbyterian and Episcopal churches are on the right. The village, which is a place of extensive business, consists of about 150 dwellings, a number of mills, many warehouses for the commission and forwarding business, a number of churches, and a bank. In the vicinity are the decaying hulks of the British vessels captured by Com. McDonough during the last war off Plattsburg.

The Indian name of this place was *Kah-cho-quah-na*, "*the place where dip-fish.*" It was formerly called *Skenesborough*, so named from Maj. Skene, a royalist, who resided here previous to the revolution. The pass at this place was seized by a detachment of volunteers from Connecticut in May, 1775. Maj. Skene and his family, with a number of soldiers and several small pieces of cannon, were taken. When Ticonderoga was abandoned on the approach of Burgoyne, the public stores were embarked on board of 200 batteaux and sent up the lake to Skenesborough under a convoy of 5 galleys. They were pursued by a British brigade of gun-boats and overtaken at Skenesborough. Two of the galleys were taken, and the other three blown up, and the Americans being unable to make an effectual stand, set fire to the works, fort, mills, batteaux, and escaped as they could to Fort Ann. This place was occupied by Burgoyne as his head-quarters for a considerable time while his troops were clearing a road to Ford Edward. On the heights overlooking the harbor are the remains of a battery and blockhouse.

WAYNE COUNTY.

WAYNE COUNTY was taken from the NW. corner of Ontario, and the N. of Seneca counties in 1823. Greatest length from E. to W. 35 miles; greatest breadth N. and S. 30.

The surface is much diversified; on the N. the ancient beach of Lake Ontario extends with the lake E. and W. from it 4 to 8 miles; forming in its whole course a road through the county, known as the "*ridge road.*" The Erie canal, for nearly the whole of its devious course of forty-three miles through the county, keeps the valley of Mud creek and the Clyde. The soil is generally highly fertile. The greater portion of the county on the west, including one fourth of the towns of Galen, Rose, and Huron, was in the grant to Massachusetts and in Phelps and Gorham's purchase, passing from those gentlemen to Robert Morris, and from him to Sir William Pulteney, from whom the present possessors derive title. The remnant in the east pertained to the military tract. The county is divided into 15 towns. Pop. 42,068.

ARCADIA, taken from Lyons in 1825; from Albany 186 miles. Newark, 6 miles W., and Lockville 5 miles W. of Lyons, each on the canal, are villages. Fairville is a post-office. Pop. 4,982.

BUTLER, taken from Wolcott in 1826; from Lyons NE. centrally situated 14 miles. Butler and South Butler are post-offices. Pop. 2,287.

GALEN, organized as part of Seneca county, and taken from Junius in 1812; NW. from Albany 172 miles. Pop. 4,245. Clyde, incorporated in 1835, is situated upon the Erie canal, 8 miles E. from

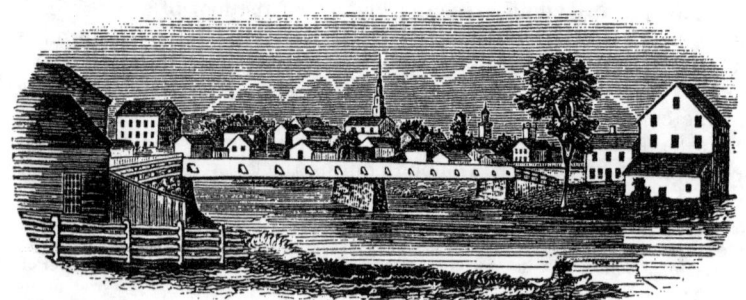

Southern view of Clyde.

Lyons. The above view was taken on the S. side of the Clyde river, and shows the principal portion of the village. The steeple in the centre of the view is that of the Methodist church, the one to the left the Presbyterian, and that to the right the Baptist. The village is a place of much business, and contains about 130 dwellings.

WAYNE COUNTY.

HURON, taken from Wolcott in 1826, by the name of Port Bay; from Albany 193, from Lyons NE. 15 miles. Pop. 2,020.

LYONS was taken from the S. end of Sodus in 1811; area since diminished. The surface of the township is hilly, and the soil of an excellent quality. Pop. 4,300.

Eastern entrance into Lyons.

Lyons, the shire village, was incorporated in 1831. It is situated at the junction of Mud creek with the Canandaigua outlet, (below which the stream takes the name of Clyde river,) and on the Erie canal, 181 miles from Albany, 34 from Rochester, 15 N. of Geneva, and 16 S. of Sodus Point. The village contains about 250 dwellings, 1 Presbyterian, 1 Lutheran, 1 Methodist, 1 Baptist, and 1 Episcopal church, the county buildings, a bank, 2 newspaper printing offices, a number of mills, &c. The accompanying view was taken at the bridge over the Erie canal, at the eastern entrance into the village, and shows in the distance a number of public buildings. The village was originally laid out by C. Williamson, agent for the Pulteney estate, and is said to have derived its name from the similarity of its situation to the city of that name in France. The first settlement was commenced in June, 1798, by emigrants from New Jersey and Maryland. Mr. Van Wickle, from New Jersey, "moved in, along with 40 persons." Alloway is a small manufacturing village.

"In 1834, a white oak tree was cut in this town, two miles west of Lyons, measuring 4½ feet in diameter. In the body of the tree, about 3½ feet from the ground, was found a large and deep cutting by an axe, severing the heart of the tree, and exhibiting with perfect distinctness the marks of the axe at the present time. The whole cavity thus created by the original cutting was found to be encased by 460 years' growth of the wood, i. e., it was concealed beneath 460 layers of the timber, which had grown over it subsequently to the cutting. Consequently the original cutting must have been in the year 1372, or 118 years *before the discovery of America by Columbus.* The tree was cut by James P. Bartle of Newark, a forwarding merchant, and the timber used by him in building the boat Newark, now belonging to the Detroit line. The cutting was at least six inches deep."

MACEDON, taken from Palmyra in 1823. Macedon Centre, 22 miles NW., and Macedon on the canal, 20 miles W. of Lyons, are small settlements. Pop. 2,397.

WAYNE COUNTY.

MARION, originally named Winchester, and taken from Williamson in 1825; from Lyons centrally distant NW. 13 miles. Marion Corners is a small settlement. Pop. 2,158.

ONTARIO, originally named Freetown, and taken from Williamson, was organized as part of Ontario county; centrally distant from Lyons NW. 24 miles. Ontario and West Ontario are the post-offices. Pop. 1,903.

PALMYRA was organized by the general sessions of Ontario county, pursuant to the act of 27th of Jan. 1789; since modified. It comprised two townships of Phelps and Gorham's purchase, being No. 12, in the 2d and 3d ranges. The surface of the town is gently undulating, and the soil of a superior quality. Pop. 3,550.

Eastern view in Main-street, Palmyra.

The village of Palmyra is situated on Mud creek and the Erie canal, 196 miles distant from Albany by the post route, 11 from Lyons, 13 from Canandaigua, and 22 from Rochester. It is a place of considerable business, containing about 250 dwellings, 1 Presbyterian, 1 Episcopal, 1 Methodist, and 1 Baptist church, a bank, 2 newspaper printing offices, a number of mills, &c. The accompanying engraving shows part of Main-street, looking westward.

Joseph Smith, the founder of the Mormon sect, began his public career in and near this village. The following account of Smith, and his operations, is derived from authentic sources of information.

Joseph Smith, the founder of Mormonism, was born in Royalton, Vt., and removed to Manchester, Ontario county, N. Y., about the year 1820, at an early age, with his parents, who were in quite humble circumstances. He was occasionally employed in Palmyra as a laborer, and bore the reputation of a lazy and ignorant young man. According to the testimony of respectable individuals in that place, Smith and his father were persons of doubtful moral character, addicted to disreputable habits, and moreover extremely superstitious, believing in the existence of witchcraft. They at one time procured a mineral rod, and dug in various places for money. Smith testified that when digging he had seen the pot or chest containing the treasure, but never was fortunate enough to get it into his hands. He placed a singular looking stone in his hat, and pretended by the light of it to make many wonderful discoveries of gold, silver, and other treasures, deposited in the earth. He commenced his career as the founder of the new sect when about the age of 18 or 19, and appointed a number of meetings in Palmyra, for the purpose of declaring the divine revelations which he said were made to him. He was, however, unable to produce any excitement in the village; but very few had curiosity sufficient to listen to him. Not having the means to print his revelations, he applied to Mr. Crane, of the society of Friends, declaring that he was moved by the spirit to call upon him for assistance. This gentleman bid him to go to work, or the state prison would end his career. Smith had better success with Martin Harris, an industrious and thrifty farmer of Palmyra, who was worth about $10,000, and who became one of his leading disciples. By his assistance, 5,000 copies of the Mormon Bible, (so called,) were published at an expense of about $3,000. It is possible that Harris might have made the advances with the expectation of a profitable speculation, as a great sale was anticipated. This work is a duodecimo volume, containing 590 pages, and is perhaps one of the weakest productions ever attempted to be palmed off as a divine revelation. It is mostly a blind mass of words, interwoven with scriptural language and quotations, without much of a leading plan or design. It is in fact such a production as might be expected from a person of Smith's abilities and turn of mind. The following is a copy of the title page:

"THE BOOK OF MORMON: AN ACCOUNT WRITTEN BY THE HAND OF MORMON, UPON PLATES TAKEN FROM THE PLATES of NEPHI.

" Wherefore it is an abridgment of the record of the people of Nephi, and also of the Lamanites; written to the Lamanites, which are a remnant of the house of Israel, and also to the Jew and Gentile, written by way of commandment, and also by the spirit of Prophecy and Revelation. Written and sealed up and hid up to the LORD that they may not be destroyed, to come forth by the gift and power of God unto the interpretation thereof, sealed by the hand of Moroni and hid up unto the LORD to come forth in due time by the way of the Gentile: the interpretation thereof by the gift of God, an abridgment taken from the book of Ether. Also, which is a Record of the People of Jared, which were scattered at the time the LORD confounded the language of the people when they were building a tower to get to Heaven, which is to shew unto the remnant of the house of Israel how great things the LORD hath done unto their fathers, and that they may know the covenants of the LORD, and that they are not cast off forever; and also to the convincing of the Jew and Gentile, that JESUS is the CHRIST, the ETERNAL GOD, manifesting Himself unto all nations. And now if there are faults it be the mistake of men, wherefore condemn not the things of God that ye may be found spotless at the judgment seat of Christ.

" By Joseph Smith, Junior, Author and Proprietor, Palmyra. Printed by E. B. Grandin, for the Author, 1830."

At the close of the book is " the testimony of three witnesses," viz: Oliver Cowdery, David Whitmer, and Martin Harris, in which they state unto all nations, kindreds, tongues and people, that they have seen the plates containing the record, and the engravings upon them, &c. On the last page is contained the testimony of eight witnesses, of which the following is a copy:

" Be it known unto all nations, kindred, tongues, and people, unto whom this book shall come, that Joseph Smith, Jr., the Author and Proprietor of this work, hath shewed unto us the plates of which hath been spoken, which have the appearance of gold; and as many of the leaves as the said Smith has translated we did handle with our hands, and we also saw the engravings thereof, all of which had the appearance of ancient work and of curious workmanship. And this we bear record, with words of soberness, that the said Smith has shown unto us. for we have seen and HEFTED, and know of a surety that the said Smith has got the plates of which we have spoken. And we give our names unto the world that which we have seen and we lie not, God bearing witness of it. Christian Whitmer, Jacob Whitmer, Peter Whitmer, Jr., John Whitmer, Hiram Page, Joseph Smith, Senior, Hyrum Smith, Samuel H. Smith."

In the preface, Smith states " that the plates of which have been spoken, were found in the township of Manchester, Ontario county, New York."

It is stated by persons in Palmyra, that when he exhibited these plates to his followers, they were done up in a canvas bag, and Smith made the declaration, that if they uncovered them, the Almighty would strike them dead. It is said that no one but Smith could read what was engraved upon them; which he was enabled to do by looking through a peculiar kind of spectacles found buried with the plates.

Soon after the publication of the Mormon Bible, one Parley B. Pratt, a resident of Lorrain county, Ohio, happening to pass through Palmyra, on the canal, hearing of the new religion, called on the prophet and was soon converted. Pratt was intimate with Sidney Rigdon, a very popular preacher of the denomination called " Reformers" or " Disciples." About the time of the arrival of Pratt at Manchester, the Smiths were fitting out an expedition for the western country, under the command of Cowdery, in order to convert the Indians or Lamanites, as they termed them. In October, 1830, this mission, consisting of Cowdery, Pratt, Peterson, and Whitmer, arrived at Mentor, Ohio, the residence of Rigdon, well supplied with the new Bibles. Near this place, in Kirtland, there were a few families belonging to Rigdon's congregation, who having become extremely fanatical, were daily looking for some wonderful event to take place in the world. Seventeen of these persons readily believed in Mormonism, and were all re-immersed, in one night, by Cowdery. By

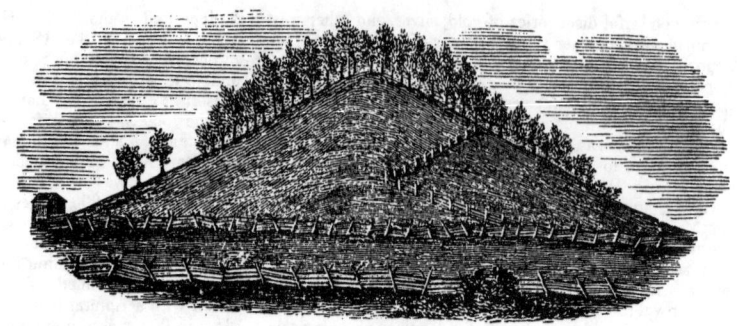

The Mormon Hill.

[The above is a northern view of the Mormon Hill in the town of Manchester, about 3 miles in a southern direction from Palmyra. It is about 140 feet in height, and is a specimen of the form of numerous elevations in this section of the state. It derives its name from being the spot, (if we are to credit the testimony of Joseph Smith,) where the plates containing the Book of Mormon were found.]

the conversion of Rigdon, soon after, Mormonism received a powerful impetus, and more than one hundred converts were speedily added. Rigdon visited Smith at Palmyra, where he tarried about two months, receiving revelations, preaching, &c. He then returned to Kirtland, Ohio, and was followed a few days after by the prophet Smith and his connections. Thus from a state of almost beggary, the family of Smith were furnished with the "fat of the land" by their disciples, many of whom were wealthy.

A Mormon temple was erected at Kirtland, at an expense of about $50,000. In this building, there was a sacred apartment, a kind of holy of holies, in which none but the priests were allowed to enter. An unsuccessful application was made to the legislature for the charter of a bank. Upon the refusal, they established an unchartered institution, commenced their banking operations, issued their notes, and made extensive loans. The society now rapidly increased in wealth and numbers, of whom many were doubtless drawn thither by mercenary motives. But the bubble at last burst. The bank being an unchartered institution, the debts due were not legally collectable. With the failure of this institution, the society rapidly declined, and Smith was obliged to leave the state to avoid the sheriff. Most of the sect, with their leader, removed to Missouri, where many outrages were perpetrated against them. The Mormons raised an armed force to "drive off the infidels;" but were finally obliged to leave the state. By the last accounts, they were establishing themselves at Nauvoo, Illinois; and it is said are now in a more flourishing condition than ever, rapidly making converts by means of their itinerant preachers in various sections of our own country and even in England.

Rose, taken from Wolcott in 1826; from Albany 177 miles. Rose Valley is a small post village, 10 miles NE. from Lyons. Pop. 2,031.

Savannah, taken from Galen in 1824; from Lyons centrally situated E. 13 miles. Pop. 1,707.

Sodus was organized in 1789; bounds since altered; from Albany 180 miles. Sodus, on the Ridge road, 13 miles NW., and Sodus Point, 15 miles from Lyons, are small villages. At Nicholas Point, on Sodus bay, a body of Shakers settled in 1825. They have a a church, but are few in number. At Sodus bay, on Lake Ontario, the United States have made a pier for the improvement of the harbor, of about a mile in length. The lake steamers enter the harbor and bay. Pop. 4,393.

The following is extracted from Thompson's History of the late War:

"On the 18th of June, 1813, the British fleet appeared before the town of Sodus, on a bay of that name, which is formed on the American side of Lake Ontario, between Genesee and Oswego rivers. General Burnet, of the New York militia, suspecting that they intended to land their troops, and capture a quantity of provisions, ordered out a regiment from the county of Ontario. The militia collected in great haste, and arrived at Sodus on the following morning. But the enemy, well knowing that his appearance would excite the alarm of the inhabitants, drew off his forces until their apprehensions should be subsided, and re-appeared in the evening of the 19th, a few hours after the militia had been discharged. In contemplation of his return, the inhabitants had removed all the public stores from the buildings on the water's edge, to a small distance in the woods, and on the re-appearance of the hostile squadron, a second alarm was immediately given, and expresses sent after the discharged militia, which overtook and brought them back, with a large reinforcement. Before their return, the enemy had landed, and finding that the provisions had been removed, they set fire to all the valuable buildings in the town, and destroyed most of the private property of every description. They then agreed to stipulate with the inhabitants, to desist from destroying the remaining houses, on condition of their surrendering the flour and provisions, which they knew had been deposited at that place. These articles were then not more than two hundred yards from the village, yet the enemy did not choose to attempt their capture, lest he might be drawn into an ambuscade; but he threatened the entire destruction of every house in the town, if they were not immediately delivered over to him. The appearance of the militia prevented the execution of this threat, and the enemy immediately returned to his shipping, and moved up the lake on the following morning."

WALWORTH, taken from Ontario in 1829; from Albany 208, from Palmyra NW. 6 miles. Walworth Corners is a small village. Pop. 1,734.

WILLIAMSON, taken from Sodus in 1802; area since altered; from Albany 206 miles. Pop. 2,147. Pulteneyville, 21 miles NW. from Lyons, on Lake Ontario, and Williamson Corners, are small post villages.

The following account of the invasion of Pulteneyville, May 15th, 1814, by the British, is from the Ontario Messenger, published at that time at Canandaigua:—

" General Porter has received a letter from General Smith, communicating the particulars of the late visit of the enemy to that place, of which the following is a summary : ' On Saturday evening, 15th ult., the British squadron was discovered making towards Pulteneyville, and information sent to General Swift, who repaired thither in the course of the succeeding night with 130 volunteers and militia. On Sunday a flag was sent on shore demanding a peaceable surrender of all public property, and threatening an immediate destruction of the village, (which is on the margin of the lake,) in case of refusal. General Swift returned for answer that he should oppose any attempt to land, by all means in his power. Soon after the return of the flag, General Swift was induced, by the pressing solicitations and entreaties of the inhabitants of the town, to permit one of the citizens to go to the enemy with a flag, and offer up the surrender of the property contained in a storehouse at the water's edge, consisting of about 100 barrels of flour, considerably damaged, on condition that the commanding officer would stipulate not to take any other, nor molest the inhabitants. Before the return of the flag, the enemy sent their boats with several hundred men on shore, who took possession of the flour in the store and were proceeding to further depredations. General Swift, whose force was too inferior to justify an open attack, (and which, if attempted, must have exposed his men to the guns of the whole fleet,) commenced a fire upon them from an adjacent wood, which wounded several, and became so harassing as to induce them to re-embark, whence they commenced a cannonade from the fleet upon the town, which was continued for some time, but with no other injury than a few shot-holes through the houses. Three hundred barrels of good flour had been removed back from the storehouse a few days before, leaving the damaged flour, which was the only booty obtained by the enemy. The three hundred barrels of flour were deposited about a mile back of the town, of which the enemy were apprized by some prisoners they took. But they chose to forego the plunder of it, rather than trust themselves in the woods with General Swift and his riflemen.' "

WOLCOTT, taken from Junius, and organized as part of Seneca county in 1807; area since altered; from Albany 184 miles. Wolcott

18 miles NE. from Lyons, is a village of about 60 dwellings. Rea Creek is a small settlement, 26 miles from Lyons. Pop. 2,482.

WESTCHESTER COUNTY.

WESTCHESTER COUNTY is of ancient date. It was represented in the first legislative assembly in the colony, which met at New York in 1691. And it has constituted one county to this time, having been organized as such by the general acts of 1788 and 1801. This county comprises a very important section of the state. Washed on the west by the Hudson, and on the south by the East river and Long Island sound, it enjoys very superior advantages for trade and commerce. The county generally exhibits a beautiful diversity of surface. The northwestern corner is considerably broken by the SE. border of the Highlands, of a mountain character, and a range of hills of moderate height extends from York Island towards the NE. extremity, on which are situated the heights and hills much known in the revolution. Based upon primitive rock, the soil is naturally sterile, but is rendered productive by careful and painful cultivation. Of wheat it produces little, and the inhabitants import a large portion of their bread-stuffs. Summer crops are good, and by the use of plaster, valuable returns in grass are obtained. The chief business of the inhabitants consists in supplying New York city with garden stuffs, field vegetables, butter, poultry, &c.

This county suffered severely during the revolution. The whole southern part was marked by the marches, works of defence, or skirmishes and battles of hostile armies. And, indeed, the active operations of the war in 1776, were principally confined to this region, and in the autumn to this county, where the two armies were in full force, constantly on the alert, and under the eyes of their respective commanders. The county is divided into 21 towns, all of which were organized under the act of March 7th, 1788, excepting New Castle. Pop. 48,687.

BEDFORD, from New York NE. 44 miles, was first settled under a Connecticut license in 1681 or 1682, at a place called the hop-ground. on account of its natural product. The original patent, dated 1697, bears the Connecticut seal, and it was not until 1700 that the settlement was attached to New York by order of King William. Bedford, the half-shire town, has a courthouse and about 45 dwellings. Whitlockville is a small village. John Jay during the latter part of his life resided in the northern part of this town. The annexed sketch of his life is from Blake's Biographical Dictionary :—

"JOHN JAY, LL. D., first chief-justice of the United States under the constitution of 1789, graduated at Kings, (now Columbia college,) 1764, and in 1768 was admitted to the bar. He was appointed to the first American congress in 1774. Being on the committee with Lee and Livingston to draft an address to the people of Great Britain, he was the

The residence of the late Chief-Justice Jay, Bedford.

writer of that eloquent production. In the congress of 1775, he was on various important committees, performing more service perhaps than any other member except Franklin and John Adams. In May, 1776, he was recalled to assist in forming the government of New York, and in consequence his name is not attached to the Declaration of Independence; but July 9th, he reported resolutions in the provincial convention in favor of the declaration. After the fall of New York and the removal of the provincial assembly to Poughkeepsie, Mr. Jay retained his resolute patriotism. The very eloquent address of the convention to the people of New York, dated Fishkill, December 23, 1776, and signed by A. Ten Broeck, as president, was written by him. March 12, 1777, he reported to the convention of New York the draft of a form of government, which was adopted, and many of the provisions of which were introduced into the constitution of other states. From May 3, 1777, to August 18, 1779, he was chief-justice of the state, but resigned that office in consequence of his duties as president of congress. The glowing address of that body to their constituents, dated September 8, 1779, was prepared by him. On the 29th of September, he was appointed minister plenipotentiary to the court of Spain. He was one of the commissioners to negotiate peace with Great Britain, and signed the definitive treaty of peace at Paris, September 3, 1783. He returned to America in 1784. Congress had previously appointed him secretary of state for foreign affairs. In the difficult circumstances of the country, the secretary was in effect the head of the government. Mr. Jay's services were of great importance. He drew up, October 13, 1776, an elaborate report on the relations between the United States and Great Britain. Though not a member of the convention which formed the constitution of the United States, he was present at Annapolis, and aided by his advice. He also assisted Madison and Hamilton in writing the Federalist. In the convention of New York he contributed to the adoption of the constitution. He was appointed chief-justice by Washington, September 26, 1789. In 1794, he was appointed minister plenipotentiary to Great Britain, and succeeded in negotiating the treaty which still goes by his name. He was governor of the state of New York from 1795 to 1801. The remainder of his life he passed in retirement. He died in 1829, aged 84."

CORTLAND. The surface of this town on the north is covered by the highlands, and has some lofty summits, the principal of which is the Colleberg and Anthony's nose. The town has a considerable portion of arable land. Pop. 5,592. Croton and Cortlandtown are small post villages.

Peeksville village was incorporated in 1826. It is situated 12 miles north of Sing Sing, and immediately south of the southern termination of the highlands. The annexed engraving shows the appearance of the village as seen from an elevation a few rods northward from the road to Carmel. The old Dutch Reformed and the Epis-

East view of Peekskill.

copal church are discernible on the right; the Methodist and the Presbyterian church, having a small tower, are on the extreme left. The elevated spire of the new Dutch Reformed church is in the central part of the view. Hudson river, with the towering highlands, is seen in the distance. The village represented in the engraving is situated on an elevation 200 feet above the level of the river, half a mile from the landing, on both sides of a deep ravine, in which flows Gregory's brook, a rapid stream. There are in the village a bank, 2 printing-offices, 2 large iron foundries, &c. There is an academy, a large edifice, situated on a commanding eminence at the south. It was erected by subscription, at an expense of $7,000. The village, including the landing, contains upwards of 200 dwellings, and 2 churches for Friends, besides those mentioned above. There is a steamboat ferry at this place to Caldwell's landing, on the opposite side of the Hudson, two miles distant. Verplanck's point and Continental village, places distinguished in the revolutionary war, are within the limits of this town. This latter place, which had barracks for 2,000 men, was burnt by the British in October, 1777; the following account of which is extracted from the Connecticut Journal of April 2d, 1777.

Fishkill, March 27.—Our post at Peck's-kill, since the removal of the militia of the eastern states, has been in a manner in a defenceless situation, there being only part of 2 regiments stationed there under the care of Gen. McDougal amounting to about 250 men. The enemy having received intelligence of this, formed an expedition thither with a view to take or destroy the stores belonging to the continentals that were deposited there. Accordingly on Sunday last they appeared with a frigate, four transports, and several other small vessels in the bay, and landed about 1,000 men, with several pieces of cannon. General McDougal not thinking it prudent to hazard a battle with such an unequal force, and not having seasonable advice of the enemy's movement, was under the necessity of destroying their stores in order to prevent their falling into their hands, and retired about two miles into the pass in the Highlands, carrying with him his baggage and military stores; his advanced guard being stationed at Cortlandt's house in the valley. The enemy the same day took possession of the village, and remained close in their quarters until the next day in the afternoon, when a party of them, consisting of about 200 men, possessed themselves of a height a little south of Cortlandt's. The general having received a reinforcement from Col. Gansevoort's regiment, of about 80 men, under the command of Lieut. Col. Willet, permitted them to attempt to dispossess the enemy from that eminence. Col. Willet having accordingly made the necessary disposition, advanced with his small party with the greatest firmness and resolution, and made the attack. The enemy instantly fled with the greatest precipitation, leaving three men dead on the field, and the whole body, panic-struck, betook themselves to their shipping, embarking under cover of the night; and by the last accounts they had sailed down the river. Before they embarked, they gave out they intended to stop at Tarrytown, on their way down, and attempt to destroy our magazine of forage at Wright's mills. Upon their evacuating the place, Gen. McDougal took possession of his former quarters, and detached a party of men to watch their motions The enemy on this occasion have been exceedingly disappointed, as they have not been able to carry off any stores left behind by our men, and no other flock than about 40 sheep and 8 or 10 head of cattle, with which they were supplied by our good friends the tories. Never did troops exhibit more firmness and resolution than did our army on this occasion. Notwithstanding the disparity of numbers was great, and the measure absolutely necessary, it was with the utmost reluctance they retired to the pass. As usual, these heroes of 'Britain have burnt some houses, plundered the inhabitants of what they could conveniently take with them, frightened the women and children, and raised the spirits of their tory brethren in that quarter, but which, alas, as is always the case when unnaturally elevated, are now again proportionably depressed.

Peekskill is the birthplace of John Paulding, the American farmer, who intercepted Andre, the British spy, at Tarrytown, some fifteen miles below this place. His monument is situated about two miles to the north of the village. It is built of marble, of a pyramidal shape, about fifteen feet in height, and running to a point. It is enclosed in an iron railing about twelve feet square. The main inscription is on the south side, and runs thus:—

"Here repose the mortal remains of JOHN PAULDING, who died on the 18th day of February, 1818, in the 60th year of his age. On the morning of the 23d of September, 1780, accompanied by two young farmers of the county of Westchester, (whose names will one day be recorded on their own deserved monuments,) he intercepted the British spy, Andre. Poor himself, he disdained to acquire wealth by sacrificing his country. Rejecting the temptation of great rewards, he conveyed his prisoner to the American camp, and by this act of noble self-denial, the treason of Arnold was detected; the designs of the enemy baffled; West Point and the American army saved, and these U. S., now by the grace of God free and independent, rescued from imminent peril." On the opposite side is written—"The corporation of the city of New York erect this tomb as a memorial raised to public gratitude." On the east side is a beautiful wreath engraved on the marble, with the word, "Fidelity."

EAST CHESTER. The village of East Chester is situated at the head of a bay on Long Island sound, 16 miles NE. from New York, on the old turnpike and stage road to Boston, and contains an Episcopal church and about 25 dwellings. Bronx is the name of a small settlement and post-office in the northern part of the town, in the vicinity of which are valuable marble quarries. Pop. 1,502.

GREENSBURGH is pleasantly situated on the Hudson, 22 miles N. of the city of New York. Pop. 3,361. On the banks of the river are splendid sites for country residences, many of which are occupied by the wealthy. About two miles below the village of Tarrytown, beautifully situated on the Hudson, is the country residence of Washington Irving, Esq., and well known as the "Van Tassel house." Dobbs' Ferry, a noted place in the revolution, is situated on the Hudson, 22 miles N. of New York, and opposite the northern termination of the Palisades. There is here a village containing 2 churches, and about 30 dwellings. Hastings is a small settlement and landing on the Hudson, 2 miles below Dobbs' Ferry: 3 miles E. of Tarrytown, is the small village of Greensburgh, where there is a store, a tavern, a few neat dwellings, and a Presbyterian church, in whose cemetery rest the remains of Isaac Van Wart, one of the captors of Andre; over which is a marble monument, consisting of a base and pyramid, with the following inscription:

Van Tassel house, the residence of Washington Irving.

"Here repose the mortal remains of Isaac Van Wart, an elder of the Greenburgh church, who died on the 23d of May, 1828, in the 69th year of his age. Having lived the life, he died the death of the Christian.—The citizens of the county of Westchester erected this tomb, in testimony of the high sense they entertained for the virtuous and patriotic conduct of their fellow-citizen, and as a memorial sacred to public gratitude.—Vincit Amor Patriæ.—Nearly half a century before this monument was built, the conscript fathers of America had, in the senate chamber, voted that Isaac Van Wart was a faithful patriot—one in whom the love of country was invincible, and this tomb bears testimony that the record is true.—Fidelity. On the 23d of Sept. 1780, Isaac Van Wart, accompanied by John Paulding and David Williams, all farmers of the county of Westchester, intercepted Major Andre on his return from the American lines in the character of a spy, and notwithstanding the large bribes offered them for his release, nobly disdained to sacrifice their country for gold, secured and carried him to the commanding officer of the district, whereby the dangerous and traitorous conspiracy of Arnold was brought to light, the insidious designs of the enemy baffled, the American army saved, and our beloved country freed," &c.

Tarrytown is pleasantly situated, 28 miles N. of New York, on an elevation overlooking the Hudson, opposite the widest part of Tappan bay. The village contains 4 churches, 80 or 90 dwellings, and about 1,000 inhabitants. The above is a view of the place, situated about one fourth of a mile N. of the village where Andre was taken prisoner, in Sept. 1780, by three militiamen. The road at that time ran a little to the west of its present location. The three were playing cards in the field on the right of the engraving, which was then covered with trees and shrubbery, when their attention was arrested by the clattering of a horse's hoofs over a wooden bridge thrown across the little brook seen in the foreground. They left their cards, and arrested Andre in the vicinity of the place where now stands a small pine tree, near which a human figure is placed in the engraving.

The annexed account of the taking of Andre, is from a manuscript in the possession of Isaac H. Tiffany, Esq., of Fultonville ; being the notes of a personal conversation which he had with David Williams,

North view of the place where Andre was taken prisoner.

one of the actors in the scene at Broome, Schoharie county, Feb. 13, 1817.

Williams, Van Wart, and Paulding, (Williams aged between 22 and 23, the other two being younger,) were going to see some relations 20 miles below. The three were seated beside the road in the bushes, amusing themselves at cards, when their attention was arrested by the galloping of a horse. On approaching the road, they saw a gentleman riding towards them, seated on a large brown horse, which was afterward observed to have marked on the near shoulder the initials U. S. A. The rider was a light, trim-built man, about 5 feet 7 inches in height, with a bold military countenance and dark eyes, and was dressed in a round hat, blue surtout, crimson coat, with pantaloons and vest of nankeen. As he neared them, the three cocked their muskets and aimed at the rider, who immediately checked his horse, and the following conversation ensued:

Andre. "Gentlemen, I hope you are of our party!"
Paulding. "What party?"
Andre. "The lower party."
Paulding. "We do."
Andre. "I am a British officer; I have been up in the country on particular business, and would not wish to be detained a single moment."

He thereupon pulled out a gold watch, and exhibited it as an evidence that he was a gentleman, and returned it again to his fob. Paulding thereupon remarked, "*We are Americans.*"

Andre. "God bless my soul! a man must do any thing to get along—I am a continental officer, going down to Dobbs Ferry to get information from below."

Andre then drew out and presented a pass from General Arnold, in which was the assumed name of John Anderson. Seizing hold upon the reins of the horse, they ordered him to dismount. Andre exclaimed, "You will bring yourself into trouble!" "We care not for that," was the reply. They took him down ten or fifteen rods beside a run of water, and Williams proceeded to search the hat, coat, vest, shirt, and pantaloons, in which they found $80 in continental money; and at last ordered him to take off his boots. At this, he changed color. Williams drew off the left boot first, and Paulding seizing it exclaimed, "My God! here it is!" In it three half sheets of written paper were found enveloped by a half sheet, marked, "contents West Point." Paulding again exclaimed, "*My God! he's a spy!*" On pulling off the other boot, a similar package was found.

Andre was now allowed to dress, and they marched him across the road into the field about twenty rods. The young men winked to each other to make further discoveries, and inquired from whom he got the papers? "Of a man at Pine's bridge, a stranger to me," replied Andre. He then offered them for his liberty, his horse and equipage, watch, and 100 guineas. This they refused to take, unless he informed them where he obtained the manuscript. He refused to comply, but again offered his horse, equipage, and one thousand guineas. They were firm in their denial, and Andre increased his offer to ten thousand guineas and as many drygoods as they wished, which should be deposited in any place desired,—that they might keep him and send some one to New York with his order, so that they could obtain them unmolested. To this they replied, "that it did not signify for him to make any offer, for he should not go." They then proceeded to the nearest military station, which was at North Castle, about twelve miles distant. On the way, Andre gave them his watch, telling them that "it was a prize." On delivering him to Colonel Jamieson, the commanding officer, that gentleman enjoined the strictest secrecy, at the same time expressing an opinion that there were others doubtless concerned in the plot. Major Tallmadge, who had commanded a guard, received Andre at Col. Jamieson's quarters, and afterward, with about twenty men, conducted him to Col. Sheldon, at Salem. The three accompanied Andre part of the way, and then left. During the night, Tallmadge caused Andre to be tied to a tree at Comyen hill. From Salem he was conveyed to West Point, and from thence to Tappan.

Williams, Paulding, and Van Wart, stood within the ring when Andre was hung. When the officer informed him that his time had nearly expired, and inquired if he had any thing to say, he answered, "Nothing but for them to witness to the world that he died like a brave man." The hangman, who was painted black, offered to put on the noose—"Take off your black hands!" said Andre; then putting on the noose himself, took out his handkerchief, tied it on, drew it up, bowed with a smile to his acquaintances, and died.

David Williams, now (Feb. 13, 1817,) aged 61, was born at Tarrytown, of Dutch extraction, and speaks that language. Paulding and Van Wart were also Dutch; neither of the three spoke English well. Congress gave each a farm in Westchester county, of the value of £500, an annuity of $200 through life, together with an elegant silver medal, on one side of which was the inscription, "*Fidelity*," and on the reverse, the motto "*Amor patriæ vincit*," (the love of country conquers.)

HARRISON is 28 miles N. of New York and 3 east of White Plains. Pop. 1,139. This is a fertile township, mostly inhabited by Friends. Harrison Purchase is a thickly settled agricultural vicinage, where is located a meeting-house and a post-office.

LEWISBORO, originally South Salem, received its present name in 1840; centrally distant NE. from Bedford 6, and from New York 50 miles. Pop. 1,619. Cross River, South Salem, Vista, and Golden's Bride, are names of the post-offices. At Cross River there are 2 churches and about 20 dwellings.

Sarah Bishop, the hermitess, resided near the boundary line of Lewisboro and the state of Connecticut. She lived on Long Island at the time of the revolutionary war. Her father's house was burnt by the British, and she was cruelly treated by a British officer. She then left society and wandered among the mountains near this part of the state, where she found a cave near Ridgefield, in which she resided till about the time of her death, which took place in 1810. She sometimes came down to the adjoining town of Ridgefield, Conn., to attend public worship on the Sabbath. It is said that the wild animals were so accustomed to see her, that they were not afraid of her presence. The following account of a visit to this hermitess, is taken from a newspaper printed at Poughkeepsie, in 1804.

"Yesterday I went in the company of two Capt. Smiths of this town to the mountain, to visit the hermitage. As you pass the southern, an elevated ridge of the mountain, and begin to descend the southern steep, you meet with a perpendicular descent of a rock, in the front of which is this cave. At the foot of this rock is a gentle descent of rich and fertile ground, extending about ten rods, when it instantly forms a frightful precipice, descending half a mile to the pond called Long pond. In the front of the rock, on the north, where the cave is, and level with the ground, there appears a large frustum of the rock, of a double fathom in size, thrown out by some unknown convulsion of nature, and lying in the front of the cavity from which it was rent, partly enclosing the mouth, and forming a room: the rock is left entire above, and forms the roof of this humble mansion. This cavity is the habitation of the hermitess, in which she has passed the best of her years, excluded from all society; she keeps no domestic animal, not even fowl, cat, or dog. Her little plantation, consisting of half an acre, is cleared of its wood, and reduced to grass, where she has raised a few peach trees, and yearly plants a few hills of beans, cucumbers, and potatoes; the whole is surrounded with a luxuriant grape vine, which overspreads the surrounding wood, and is very productive. On the opposite side of this little tenement, is a fine fountain of excellent water. At this fountain we found the wonderful woman, whose appearance it is a little difficult to describe; indeed, like nature in its first state, she was without form. Her dress appeared little else than one confused and shapeless mass of rags, patched together without any order, which obscured all human shape, excepting her head, which was clothed with a luxuriancy of lank gray hair depending on every side, as time had formed it, without any covering or ornament. When she discovered our approach, she exhibited the appearance of a wild and timid animal: she started and hastened to her cave, which she entered, and barricadoed the entrance with old shells, pulled from the decayed trees. We approached this humble habitation, and after some conversation with its inmate, obtained liberty to remove the pallisadoes and look in; for we were not able to enter, the room being only sufficient to accommodate one person. We saw no utensil either for labor or cookery, save an old pewter basin and a gourd shell; no bed but the solid rock, unless it were a few old rags, scattered here and there; no bed-clothes of any kind; not the least appearance of food or fire. She had, indeed, a place in one corner of her cell, where a fire had at some time been kindled, but it did not appear there had been one for some months. To confirm this, a gentleman says he passed her cell 5 or 6 days after the great fall of snow in the beginning of March, that she had no fire then, and had not been out of her cave since the snow had fallen. How she subsists during the severe season, is yet a mystery; she says she eats but little flesh of any kind; in the summer she lives on berries, nuts, and roots. We conversed with her for some time, found her to be of a sound mind, a religious turn of thought, and entirely happy in her situation; of this she has given repeated proofs by refusing to quit this dreary abode. She keeps a Bible with her, and says she takes much satisfaction, and spent much time in reading it."

MAMARONECK has a hilly surface, and the township is generally under good cultivation. Pop. 1,416. The village of Mamaroneck is about 24 miles from New York, and 161 from Albany. It is situated on a bay about one mile from the sound, which admits vessels of 100 tons burden. The village contains 2 churches, 2 cotton factories, and about 50 dwellings.

The following letter of Gen. Samuel Parsons, dated at Mamaroneck, Nov. 21st, 1777, to Gov. Tryon, with his answer, is copied from a newspaper printed at the time.

"SIR,—Adding to the natural horrors of war the most wanton destruction of property, is an act of cruelty unknown to civilized nations, and unaccustomed in war, until the servants of the king of Great Britain have convinced the impartial world, no act of inhumanity, no stretch of despotism, are too great to exercise towards those they term *rebels*.

"Had any apparent advantage been derived from burning the house on Philips' manor, last Monday, there would have been some reason to justify the measure; but when no benefit whatever can be proposed, by burning those buildings and stripping the women and children of necessary apparel, to cover them from the severity of a cold night, and captivating and leading in triumph to your lines, in the most ignominious manner, the heads of those families, I know not what justifiable cause to assign for those acts of cruelty; nor can I conceive a necessity for your further order to destroy Tarrytown.

"You cannot be insensible it is every day in my power to destroy the houses and buildings of Col. Philips, and those belonging to the family of Delancy, each as near your lines as those buildings were to my guards; and notwithstanding your utmost diligence, you cannot prevent the destruction of every house this side of King's bridge. It is not fear, it is not want of opportunity that has preserved those buildings; but a sense of the injustice and savageness of such a line of conduct has saved them: and nothing but necessity will induce me to copy examples of this sort so often set by your troops.

"It is not my inclination, sir, to war in this manner, against the inhabitants within your lines, who suppose themselves within your king's protection. But necessity will oblige me to retaliate in kind upon your friends, to procure the exercise of that justice which humanity used to dictate: unless your explicit disavowal of your two captains, Emmerick and Barns, shall convince me these houses were burned without your knowledge and against your order. I am, sir, your humble servant, SAMUEL H. PARSONS."

Governor Tryon's answer, dated King's bridge camp, Nov. 23d, 1777.

"SIR,—Could I possibly conceive myself accountable to any revolted subject of the king of Great Britain, I might answer your letter received by the flag of truce yesterday, respecting the conduct of the party under Capt. Emmerick's command upon the taking of Peter and Cornelius Van Tassell; I have, however, candor enough to assure you, as much as I abhor every principle of inhumanity, or ungenerous conduct, I should, were I in more authority, burn every committee man's house within my reach, as I deem those agents the wicked instruments of the continued calamities of this country: and in order sooner to purge this country of them, I am willing to give twenty-five dollars for every *acting* committee man, who shall be delivered up to the king's troops: I guess before the end of next campaign, they will be torn in pieces by their own countrymen, whom they have forcibly dragged in opposition to their principles and duty (after fining them to the extent of their property) to take up arms against their lawful sovereign, and compelling them to exchange their happy constitution, for paper, rags, anarchy, and distress.

"The ruins from the conflagration of New York, by the emissaries of your party last year, remain a memorial of their tender regard for their fellow beings exposed to the 'severity of a cold night.'

"This is the first correspondence I have held with the king's enemies, on my part in *America*, and as I am immediately under the command of Sir Henry Clinton, your future letters, dictated with decency, would be more properly directed to his excellency.

"I am, sir, your most obedient servant,   WILLIAM TRYON, Major Gen.
"To Gen. Parsons."

This came on Sunday the 23d inst., and by some means or other Gen. Delancy's house at Bloomingdale, on York Island, took fire on the 25th at night.

From the Connecticut Journal, Dec. 10, 1777.

"James Delancy, late sheriff of Westchester, and colonel of the enemy's militia, was taken last week by one of our scouts; the colonel was found under a bed, and for a better defence, had surrounded himself with a bulwark of baskets. He was dragged from his humble redoubt, put under a proper guard, and sent to a place better secured."

The following relative to the situation of this county in 1777, is taken from the 3d vol. of Dr. Dwight's Travels.

"In the autumn of 1777, I resided for some time in this county. The lines of the British were then in the neighborhood of King's bridge; and those of the Americans at Byram river. These unhappy people were, therefore, exposed to the depredations of both. Often they were actually plundered; and always were liable to this calamity. They feared everybody whom they saw, and loved nobody. It was a curious fact to a philosopher, and a melancholy one to a moralist, to hear their conversation. To every question they gave such an answer, as would please the inquirer; or, if they despaired of pleasing, such an one as would not provoke him. Fear was, apparently, the only passion by which they were animated. The power of volition seemed to have deserted them. They were not civil, but obsequious; not obliging, but subservient. They yielded with a kind of apathy, and very quietly, what you asked, and what they supposed it impossible for them to retain. If you treated them kindly, they received it coldly; not as kindness, but as a compensation for injuries done them by others. When you spoke to them, they answered you without either good or ill-nature, and without any appearance of reluctance or hesitation: but they subjoined neither questions, nor remarks, of their own; proving to your full conviction, that they felt no interest either in the conversation, or in yourself. Both their countenances, and their motions, had lost every trace of animation and of feeling. Their features were smoothed, not into serenity, but apathy; and instead of being settled in the attitude of quiet thinking, strongly indicated, that all thought, beyond what was merely instinctive, had fled their minds forever.

"Their houses, in the mean time, were in a great measure scenes of desolation. Their furniture was extensively plundered, or broken to pieces. The walls, floors, and windows, were injured both by violence and decay; and were not repaired, because they had not the means of repairing them, and because they were exposed to the repetition of the same injuries. Their cattle were gone. Their enclosures were burnt, where they were capable of becoming fuel; and in many cases thrown down, where they were not. Their fields were covered with a rank growth of weeds and wild grass. Amid all this appearance of desolation, nothing struck my own eye more forcibly than the sight of this great road—the passage from New York to Boston. Where I had heretofore seen a continual succession of horses and carriages, and life and bustle lent a sprightliness to all the environing objects, not a single, solitary traveller was visible from week to week, or from month to month. The world was motionless and silent; except when one of these unhappy people ventured upon a rare and lonely excursion to the house of a neighbor, no less unhappy; or a scouting

WESTCHESTER COUNTY. 593

party, traversing the country in quest of enemies, alarmed the inhabitants with expectations of new injuries and sufferings. The very tracks of the carriages were grown over, and obliterated: and, where they were discernible, resembled the faint impressions of chariot wheels said to be left on the pavements of Herculaneum. The grass was of full height for the scythe; and strongly realized to my own mind, for the first time, the proper import of that picturesque declaration in the Song of Deborah: 'In the days of Shamgar, the son of Anath, in the days of Jael, the highways were unoccupied; and the travellers walked through by-paths. The inhabitants of the villages ceased: they ceased in Israel.'"

MOUNT PLEASANT is a large and fine township, diversified with hills and valleys. Pop. 7,308. Beds of marble abound in this vicinity, and are extensively quarried at Sing Sing and other places. Sing Sing, Pleasantville, Sparta, and Unionville, are villages. The village of Sing Sing, 34 miles from New York, and 111 from Albany, was incorporated in 1813. Its name is derived from the Chinese *Tsing-sing*, the title of a celebrated governor, in China, of a city so called. It is said to have been brought to this country by a Dutch settler who had traded with China. The village is situated on an uneven spot of ground, and is quite diversified in its appearance; and is a thriving place, having 4 churches, an academy for males, an institution for females, a number of mills, and upwards of 200 dwellings.

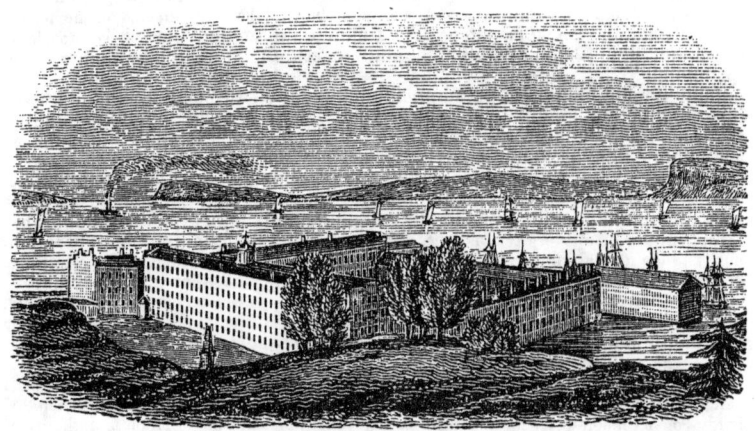

Sing Sing Prison.

The above is a view of the State Prison on the bank of the Hudson in Sing Sing village, which usually contains from 800 to 900 convicts. The following, relative to the history of the prison, &c., is taken from an article published in the N. Y. Express, April 13th, 1841.

"In 1823, the solitary system of imprisonment was abandoned at the Auburn prison, and was succeeded in 1824 by the present system of shutting up the convicts in separate cells by night, and compelling them to labor diligently during the day.

"The adoption of this system rendered the Auburn prison, which in 1824 contained but 550 separate cells, insufficient for the accommodation of all the convicted felons in the state, and an act of the legislature was passed in March, 1824, for the erection of a new state prison in the first or second senatorial districts, which the commissioners appointed for the purpose thought proper to locate in Mount Pleasant, Sing Sing, owing to its exhaustless bodies of marble, its healthy situation, and its accessibility by water. On the 14th of May, 1826, Capt. E. Lynds, former agent of the Auburn prison, with 100 convicts, in obedience to instructions, proceeded to Sing Sing, and commenced the erection of the state prison there. This was completed in 1829, and contained 800 cells. By the addition of several additional counties to this prison district, greatly increasing the number of convicts, it was discovered that these accommodations were insufficient, and 200 more cells were ordered to be added, which result was obtained by adding another, or fifth story to the prison building—which addition was completed in 1831.

" In May, 1828, the convicts then in the old state prison in this city were removed to Sing Sing, and the old prison here was emptied of its inmates, and abandoned forever as a prison.

" The Mount Pleasant prison at Sing Sing is 33 miles from this city on the eastern shore of the Hudson river, and the ground on which it stands is about 10 feet above high-water mark. The prison grounds contain 130 acres, and the wharf is approachable by vessels drawing 12 feet of water. The prison, keeper's house, workshops, &c., are built of rough dressed stone. The prison for the males is 480 feet in length from north to south, and 44 in width, fronting towards the west, or the Hudson river. This building is five stories high, containing a line of 100 cells in each story on the west side, and as many more on the east side, making 1,000 cells in all. The western yard is enclosed by two buildings 40 feet wide, and 2 stories high, which are occupied as the kitchen, hospital, chapel, workshops, storehouses, &c., and extend from the prison westerly to the edge of the water. The south wing adjoins the prison, but communicates with it only through the hospital. The north wing connects with the prison by a wall 20 feet in height, running north and south 10 feet, enclosing together an area of 494 feet by 412. In the centre of the west yard is a range of shops, 40 feet wide, fronting on the Hudson, and running parallel with the prison 276 feet, with wings extending easterly towards the prison 140 feet, which are occupied as stone shops. The guard-house is on the bank or height on the east side of the prison, about 170 feet above the level of the yard, commanding a perfect view of the east yard, and most of the west. Within the last few years, an additional building has been erected on the heights east of the main prison for the purposes of a female prison exclusively, which is capable of containing about 72 female convicts, one in each cell, and in which that number is now confined.

" The officers of the prison, or those connected with its government, business, interests, health, and morals, are—five inspectors, a principal keeper, agent, clerks, physician, and chaplain, 25 assistant keepers, and 26 guards. These, except the clerk, are appointed by the Board of Inspectors, and hold their offices during their pleasure. The clerk is appointed by the governor and senate, and holds his office for four years. The inspectors are appointed every two years by the governor and senate, and on them the government of the prison, its discipline, police, its moneyed concerns, contracts, &c., by law devolves. They are required to meet every two months, and inspect the prison, and to make a report annually to the legislature soon after it convenes. The duties of the principal officers are defined by law, and are such as the good government and welfare of the institution require.

" In this prison the convicts are compelled to labor in silence—no conversation by word, look, or gesture being allowed between or amongst them. If any information is needed by the prisoner in regard to his business. he modestly applies to, and obtains it of his keeper, one of whom is always near him in each department of labor.

" The utmost harmony of movement in the various businesses conducted, and the most perfect order reigns. The whole internal machinery of the prison, with its more than 800 hardy convict laborers, resembles more the quiet industry and subordination to authority of a well-regulated family, than an institution for the punishment of hardened offenders.

" The hours of labor are not more than laboring men out of prison generally labor. The food afforded is ample. The ration for each day consists of either 16 ounces of good prime beef, or 12 ounces of prime pork, 8 ounces of rye flour, 12 ounces of sifted Indian meal, and half a gill of molasses per man; and three bushels of potatoes, or 40 pounds of rice, 4 quarts of rye in the grain for coffee, 2 quarts of vinegar, and two ounces of pepper to every 100 rations. This is all weighed or measured out each day by the superintendent of the kitchen. The bread is well baked, and the provisions well cooked by some of the convicts employed for that purpose. Their provisions are put in small wooden vessels called kids, which are placed on racks, one of which each prisoner takes as he retires from labor to his cell, in which he is locked, and where silently he eats his repast. If any convict requires more food, on making his wants known, he is supplied from the kitchen.

" At the close of the day, in long lines they march to their respective cells, accompanied by their keepers, and being locked in, partake of their food and indulge in repose. Each cell has a bunk of wood or frame, made of pine, 6 feet long and two wide, 4 or 6 inches from the floor, 4 blankets, a bible, pint-cup for their coffee, small tin cup for vinegar, an iron spoon, a comb, and a towel. These are all kept clean, or made so when they are otherwise. From 12 to 14 convicts are employed in washing the clothes and bedding of the prisoners;

some others do the cooking; and once a week they are all shaved by a convict who acts as barber.

"The tailoring is done by convict tailors, who make and repair all the prisoners' garments. Clean underclothes are placed in their cells each week. At night they are carefully watched by a keeper and four armed guards, who pace the galleries noiselessly, with socks on their feet—observe that all is safe—notice every noise; and are prepared to quell any disturbance that might possibly arise. This latter is, however, almost impossible, as each prisoner is in a small cell by himself, and secured by powerful bolts and bars.

"The moral and religious condition of the prisoners is also carefully attended to. Prayer generally at night, and a sermon and prayers every Sabbath morning by the chaplains in the chapel, a bible, and latterly other religious books in the cells, constitute a portion of their spiritual privileges. A Sunday school, attended by some 250 convicts as pupils, and a bible-class of 120 or more of them, are also in active operation each Sabbath in the chapel. The effects of these united means of mental and moral culture on many of the convicts, are highly beneficial, and promissory of good fruits at a future day. They render the convicts more orderly and sober-minded, and divert their attention from less profitable subjects."

The famous *Sleepy Hollow*, the noted location described in the "*Sketch Book*" by Washington Irving, is situated in the south part of this township, near Tarrytown; it is a long ravine of 2 or 3 miles, through which a road passes on which is situated several romantic dwellings.

Ancient Dutch church.

The above is a northwestern view of the old Dutch Reformed church situated in the southern part of this town, about a mile north of the place where Andre was taken in Tarrytown. It is believed to be the oldest church now standing in the state. A tablet placed on the church bears the inscription, "Erected and built by Frederick Philips,* and Catharine Van Cortlandt, his wife, in 1699." The pulpit and communion table were brought from Holland at the time of the

---

* Frederick Philips was the original patentee of Philips' Patent, a very extensive tract in this county, originally comprising no less than 20 miles square, bounded west by the Hudson, and lying south of the mouth of the Croton. Mr. Philips' settled on his manor about the year 1680, and built his dwelling, a stone mansion, a few rods west of the church.

erection of the church. The building has latterly undergone some repairs internally and externally, by which it has lost considerable of its venerable appearance. Unfortunately, the pulpit has not escaped the hand of modern innovation, but the communion table still remains unchanged, a venerable relic of a former age. This church and vicinity has been made celebrated by Irving's well-known "Legend of *Sleepy Hollow*."

"The sequestered situation of this church," says the author of this legend, "seem always to have made it a favorite haunt of troubled spirits. It stands on a knoll surrounded by locust trees and lofty elms, from among which its decent whitewashed walls shine modestly forth like Christian purity beaming through the shades of retirement. A gentle slope descends from it to a silver sheet of water, bordered by high trees, between which, peeps may be caught at the blue hills of the Hudson. To look upon its grass-grown yard, where the sunbeams seem to sleep so quietly, one would think that there at least the dead might rest in peace. On one side of the church extends a wide woody dell, along which laves a large brook among broken rocks and trunks of fallen trees. Over a deep black part of the stream, not far from the church, was formerly thrown a wooden bridge; the road that led to it and the bridge itself were thickly shaded by overhanging trees, which cast a gloom about it even in the daytime, but occasioned a fearful darkness at night."

It was in this church that the never-to-be-forgotten Yankee pedagogue Ichabod Crane, in rivalry to the old Domine, led off the choir, making the welkin ring with the notes of his nasal psalmody. It was too in the ravine just back of the church, that this redoubtable hero, Ichabod, had his fearful midnight encounter with the *headless horseman*, and forever disappeared from the sight of the goodly inhabitants of Sleepy Hollow.

NEWCASTLE was organized from Northcastle in 1791; from New York N. 37, from Bedford W. 6 miles. Pop. 1,529. Newcastle is a small post village, in the northeast angle of the town.

NEW ROCHELLE is situated on Long Island sound, 20 miles northeast of New York. Pop. 1,816. Settlements were early made in this town by Huguenots, who fled from France after the repeal of the edict of Nantz. The village of New Rochelle is delightfully situated in sight of the sound, on the turnpike road from New York to Connecticut, and contains 4 churches, several hotels, and about 60 dwellings. There is a small settlement at the landing on the sound containing an elegant hotel, &c.

NORTHCASTLE is 36 miles NE. from New York, and centrally distant 5 SW. of Bedford. Pop. 2,058. Northcastle is a post-office, around which there is a small settlement.

NORTH SALEM is in the NE. corner of the county, 55 miles from New York, and 12 from Bedford. Pop. 1,161. North Salem, post village, has 3 churches, several mills and stores, and in its vicinity about 40 dwellings.

PELHAM is situated on the sound, 18 miles NE. from New York. Pop. 789.

This dwelling was fortified against the Indians, and went by the name of Castle Philips. It is now standing, and is occupied by his great grand-daughter, Mrs. Cornelia Beekman. Although the mansion has been modernized, remains of the port-holes are still to be seen in the stone walls of the cellar.

POUNDRIDGE is situated 4 miles E. from Bedford. Pop. 1,407. Poundridge, post village, centrally situated, contains 1 Presbyterian, 1 Methodist Episcopal church, and about 15 dwellings.

RYE, the southeast town of the county, is distant from New York 26 miles. Pop. 1,803. Port Chester, post village, formerly called Sawpits, is on the New York and Connecticut turnpike, and west side of Byram river, which is here the boundary line of Connecticut and New York; it is pleasantly situated, and contains 3 churches, and about 100 dwellings. This place possesses a convenient landing for steamboats and sloops. The village of Rye, on the New York turnpike, 1 mile from the sound, contains 3 churches, 2 academies, and about 30 dwellings. The old Jay mansion is situated in the western part of the town.

SCARSDALE is 24 miles from New York, and 3 S. of White Plains. Pop. 255.

SOMERS is on the north line of the county, 50 miles NE. of New York, and 10 east of Peekskill. Pop. 2,082. Somers is a neat post village, containing 2 churches and about 40 dwellings. Owensville is a post village, where there are located several factories and about 30 dwellings.

WESTCHESTER has an uneven surface, and a soil which will sustain a high degree of cultivation. Pop. 4,154. This town was probably first settled in 1642, by a Mr. Throckmorton and 35 associates, who came from New England with the approbation of the Dutch authorities. It was called by the Dutch, Eastdorp. The manor of Morrisiana, originally containing about 3,000 acres, belongs to the distinguished family of Morris; it is in the SW. corner of the town, opposite Hell Gate. This manor gave name to a town from 1788 to 1791, part of the present town of Westchester. Westchester village, at the head of navigation of Westchester creek, 2 miles from the sound, and 14 NE. from New York, contains about 50 dwellings. West Farms, on the Bronx river at the head of navigation, 3 miles from the sound and 12 from New York, contains about 60 dwellings.

"GOUVERNEUR MORRIS was born at Morrisiana, Jan. 31, 1752. He graduated at Kings college, New York, in 1768. He was bred to the law, in which he obtained a great reputation. In 1775, he was a delegate to the provincial congress in New York. In 1776, (Dec.) he acted as one of the committee for drafting a constitution for the State of New York, which was reported in March, 1777, and adopted in April of that year, after repeated and very able debates. He was employed in the public service in various capacities, during the revolutionary contest, in all of which he displayed great zeal and ability. After the revolution, he retired from public life, and passed a number of years in private pursuits, excepting being a very active member of the convention which framed the constitution of the United States. In 1792, he was appointed minister to France, and remained there in that capacity until Oct. 1794. He returned to America in 1798, and in 1800 was chosen a senator from New York. In the summer of 1810, he examined the route for the Erie canal, and took a prominent part in originating and promoting that noble work. He died at Morrisiana, Nov. 5, 1816. He passed the latter years of his life at Morrisiana, exercising an elegant and munificent hospitality, reviewing the studies of his early days, and carrying on a very interesting correspondence with statesmen and literati in Europe and America. The activity of his mind, the richness of his fancy, and the copiousness of his eloquent conversation, were the admiration of all his acquaintance; and he was universally admitted to be one of the most accomplished and prominent men of our country."

Southeast view o White Plains village, (central part.)

WHITE PLAINS has a hilly, but mostly an arable soil. well adapted for grazing. Pop. 1,087. The half-shire village of White Plains is situated on the old post road to Boston, 27 miles NE. from New York, 125 from Albany, and 14 miles SW. from Bedford. It contains 2 Methodist, 1 Presbyterian, 1 Episcopal, and 1 Baptist church, the county buildings, an academy, 70 or 80 dwellings, and about 550 inhabitants. The above view shows the appearance of the central part of the village: the courthouse, an ancient building, is seen on the left, the spire of the academy on the extreme right.

The following account of the military operations in this town and its vicinity in Oct. 1776, and the events which followed, is from Botta's American Revolution.

"The English general remained several days at Frogs Neck, as well to repair the bridges which the enemy had broken, as to wait for a considerable reinforcement which he had called from Staten Island. The road from Frogs Neck to Kingsbridge is excessively rough with continual masses of small stones, and the Americans had also obstructed it in many places. Washington, who had assembled all his army at Kingsbridge, sent forward his light infantry to scour the country, and to harass the enemy in his march.

"Gen. Howe, having received his reinforcements, put himself in motion with all his troops; he crossed Pelham Manor, and went to encamp at New Rochelle, where he was joined by the second division of Hessians, and of the troops of Waldeck under Gen. Knyphausen, and by a regiment of cavalry lately arrived at New York from Ireland. As the principal project of the expedition was to intercept the communication of Washington with the eastern provinces, and then, if he declined to venture an engagement, to shut him up on the island of New York, consequently it was necessary to occupy the two roads leading into Connecticut; the one upon the coast of the sound, and the other more inland. The first was already in the power of the English; but in attempting to occupy the second, it was requisite to traverse the difficult country of which we have already made mention, in order to secure the post of the highlands, known by the name of White Plains, upon the rear of Kingsbridge.

"Gen. Howe determined to take this route; he marched, however, slowly and with extreme caution, after leaving at New Rochelle the German corps, lately arrived, to secure the lower road, and the communication with those places whence stores and necessaries were to arrive.

"Washington examined, with attention, the danger of his position. He penetrated the designs of the enemy, and consequently decided to abandon, with the main body of his army, the encampment of Kingsbridge. Extending, therefore, his left wing, he took post with it in the White Plains, while the right occupied the heights of Valentine's Hill, near

Kingsbridge; the centre exactly filled the space comprehended between these two points. Here he intrenched himself with the greatest care. His army thus formed a well secured line, parallel to the river Bronx, which lay on its front, and separated it from the English, who marched up along the left bank of this stream.

"Washington had behind him the great river Hudson, into which the English frigates had not yet been able to penetrate so far as to intercept the supplies of provisions which he received from the upper parts. With his left wing he occupied the upper road of Connecticut, by which he was also abundantly supplied with provisions and munitions. He had left sufficient garrisons at Kingsbridge, at Harlem, and in Fort Washington; in this last place, however, against his own opinion. Meanwhile, he detached numerous parties, over the Bronx, in order to retard the motions of the enemy. Hence frequent skirmishes ensued, and though the royalists had generally the advantage in these rencounters, they still served to dissipate the terror of the Americans, who every day showed themselves more bold in defying the enemy.

"Upon the approach of the English to the White Plains, Washington, all at once, called in his detachments, and abandoning the positions he had occupied along the Bronx, assembled all his troops in a strong camp upon the heights, near these plains, in front of the enemy. His right flank was protected by the Bronx, which, by its windings, also covered the front of the right wing. The main body was nearly parallel to the river, and the left wing being placed at a right angle upon the centre, and consequently parallel to the right, extended towards the north upon the hills, as much as was necessary to guard the defiles leading to the upper mountainous regions, into which the army, if expedient, might retire. But the right wing, being posted in more level and less difficult ground, found itself more exposed; wherefore Gen. McDougall was ordered to occupy, with a strong detachment, a mountain about a mile distant from the camp; he intrenched himself there as well as the time would admit of.

"Such was the position of the American army when the English arrived within 7 or 8 miles of White Plains, and prepared themselves to attack without loss of time. On the morning of the 28th of Oct. they advanced in 2 columns, the right commanded by Gen. Clinton, and the left by Gen. Heister. At noon, all the outposts being driven back by the English and Hessian light infantry, the British army appeared before the American camp. Immediately there ensued a cannonade, but to very little effect. The English drew up in order of battle; their right occupied the road which leads to Marrineck, about a mile distant from the centre of the enemy; while the left, equally distant from his right, bordered the Bronx. The English general having observed the importance of the position taken by Gen. McDougall, and being persuaded that the right of the enemy, which was his only assailable point, could not be forced so long as it should be protected by a post of such strength, resolved to wrest it from the Americans. He ordered a Hessian regiment, commanded by Col. Ralle, to ford the Bronx, and by a circuitous movement to fall upon the flank of Gen. McDougall, while Gen. Leslie should attack him in front with a brigade of English and Hessians. Col. Ralle having arrived at the point indicated, Leslie, who had also crossed the Bronx, furiously assaulted the intrenchments of McDougall. The militia soon fled, but the regular troops made a valiant resistance. A regiment of Maryland, conducted by Col. Smallwood, and a regiment of New York, under Col. Ratzemar, ventured even to come out of the lines and to charge the enemy at the very foot of the mountain, but they were overpowered by numbers and forced to retire. Then the English and Hessians ascended the heights with singular intrepidity, and took possession of them after a vigorous struggle. The Americans, however, continued for some time to fire from behind the walls of enclosures, and thus retarded the progress of the assailants. But Gen. Putnam, who had been sent to their succor, could not arrive in season. The loss of men in this action was great on the one part as well as on the other.

"Washington, calmly expecting that the enemy would come to attack him next, had already sent into his rear the sick and the baggage; but as it grew towards the close of day, the English general determined to defer the assault till the next morning. He caused his troops to encamp within cannon-shot of the American lines. Washington took advantage of the night to strengthen them with additional works, and to occupy a stronger position in the rear with his left wing, which, by the loss of the mountain, had become more exposed. When the light appeared, Gen. Howe reconnoitred the intrenchments of the enemy, and found them sufficiently formidable to determine him to wait the arrival of some battalions that had been left at New York, under the command of Lord Percy, and of several companies from Marrineck. These reinforcements being received on the evening of the 30th, he appointed the following morning for the assault, but the excessive rain which fell during the night and also in the morning, compelled him to defer it. The American general, in the mean time, examined his position with his accustomed prudence; he was decided not to risk a pitched battle without the strongest hope of success. He perceived that the English had already erected 4 or 5 batteries, and that by turning his right flank they might get possession of the heights situated upon his rear. He concluded, therefore, to break up his camp in the night of the 1st of November. He removed into a country still more mountainous in the vicinity of North Castle; having previously set fire to the houses in White Plains and the neighborhood, and to the forage that was found in the camp. He immediately detached a strong corps to occupy the bridge over the Croton river, which leads to the upper parts of the Hudson. On the following morning the English took possession of the American camp.

"Gen. Howe, perceiving that his enemy declined an engagement, and that from the situation of the country, and his knowledge of every advantageous position, it would be impossible to compel him to fight but upon the most unequal and hazardous terms, took the determination to discontinue the pursuit, and to turn his attention to the reduction of the forts and fastnesses still occupied by the Americans in the neighborhood of New York. His views were particularly directed upon Fort Washington, which was its principal bulwark. But, though the ground where this fortress had been erected was very rough and difficult, its fortifications were not sufficiently strong to resist heavy artillery. It was incapable, from its little extent, of containing more than a thousand defenders; the outworks that surrounded it, especially to the south, towards New York, might lodge, it is true, a much stronger garrison.

"The commander-in-chief, as if he had foreseen the event, had written to Gen. Greene, who commanded in this part, enjoining him to reflect maturely upon his position, and in case he should find that Fort Washington was not in a situation to sustain an assault, to cause it to be forthwith evacuated; and to transport the garrison to the right bank of the Hudson. But this general, either believing that the strength of the place and the valor of the troops would assure him a long defence, or from the apprehension that his retreat would increase the already too general discouragement of the Americans, took the resolution to hold out to the last. He was herein the more easily determined, as he believed that the garrison would always be able to retreat into Fort Lee, situated upon the other bank of the river. But Washington judged less favorably of the future; he was persuaded that the English would not remain satisfied with the reduction of the first fort; but that crossing the river, and making themselves masters of the second, which was not tenable, they would spread themselves in the province of New Jersey. He left therefore Gen. Lee, with the militia of the eastern provinces, upon the left bank of the Hudson, and having secured the strong positions towards the Croton river, and especially that of Peeks Kill, near the Hudson itself, he crossed that river with the main body of his army, and went to rejoin Gen. Greene in his camp under Fort Lee. Gen. Lee himself had orders to come with all speed and join him, in case the enemy, after having taken the fort, should show himself upon the right bank of the Hudson. He afterward wrote to the governor of New Jersey, requesting him to remove the magazines of provisions into the most remote parts, and to call out all the militia. All these dispositions being made to his wish, Washington watched with an attentive eye the movements of the enemy.

"Meanwhile, Gen. Howe had ordered Gen. Knyphausen to march from New Rochelle, and to occupy Kingsbridge. This he executed without obstacles, the Americans, who guarded this position, having fallen back upon Fort Washington. The corps of Gen. Knyphausen consequently penetrated into the island of New York, and proceeded to invest the fort, on the part of the north.

"A short time after, the English general himself abandoned the White Plains, and descending along the banks of the Hudson, conducted the rest of the army to Kingsbridge. He pitched his camp upon the heights of Fordham, his right wing being covered by the Hudson, and his left by the Bronx.

"The royalists then prepared to attack Fort Washington; its interior and appurtenances were defended by full 3,000 men, under the command of Col. Magaw, a brave and experienced officer. He was summoned in vain to surrender. The besiegers proceeded to the assault in four divisions, the first from the north, commanded by Gen. Knyphausen, and consisting of Hessians and the troops of Waldeck; the second from the east, composed of English light infantry and two battalions of guards, conducted by Gen. Matthews. This corps was to attack the intrenchments which extended from Fort Washington almost to the East river; the third, commanded by Col. Sterling, was destined to pass this river lower down than the second, in order to assail the fort more to the south; but this was only a feint. The fourth, which obeyed the orders of Lord Percy, a very strong corps, was directed to aim its assault against the western flank of the fortress. These different divisions were provided with a numerous and excellent artillery. The Hessians, under Gen. Knyphausen, were to pass through a very thick forest, where Col. Rawlings was already posted with his regiment of riflemen. An extremely warm affair was engaged, in which the Germans sustained a severe loss. The Americans, ambushed behind the trees and rocks, fired in security; but at last, the Hessians redoubling their efforts, gained a very steep ascent, whence they came down upon the enemy with an irresistible impetuosity; the divisions which followed them were thus enabled to land without molestation. Col. Rawlings retreated under the cannon of the fort. Lord Percy, on his part, had carried an advanced work, which facilitated the debarkation of the party under Col. Sterling, who, the moment he had landed, forced his way up a difficult height, which was very resolutely defended; he gained the summit, where he took a considerable number of prisoners, notwithstanding their gallant resistance. Col. Cadwallader, who was charged with the defence of this part, retired also into the fort.

"Col. Ralle, who led the right column of Gen. Knyphausen's attack, surmounted all obstacles with admirable valor, and lodged his column within 100 yards of the fort. Soon after, Gen. Knyphausen joined him with the left column; having at length extricated himself from the difficulties encountered in the forest. The garrison having thus lost, though not without glory, all their advanced works, found themselves closely invested within the body of the fortress. The besiegers then summoned Col. Magaw to surrender. He had already consumed nearly all his ammunition. The very multitude of defenders pressed into so narrow a space, was prejudicial to defence, and every thing demonstrated that he could not sustain an assault. Accordingly he decided to capitulate. The garrison, amounting to 2,600 men, inclusive of the country militia, surrendered prisoners of war. The Americans had few killed; the royalists lost about 800, the greater part Germans. The reduction of Fort Washington thus gave the royal army entire possession of the island of New York."

Yonkers is centrally distant 16 miles N. of New York. Pop. 2,968. Yonkers village, formerly called Philipsburg, is situated upon the Hudson, and contains 2 churches, a female seminary, and about 50 dwellings. This place is a favorite summer resort for the citizens of New York. Kingsbridge, 13 miles N. of the city hall, New York, is on Spuyten Duyvel creek, or Harlem river, and contains about a dozen dwellings. The bridge at this place is of wood, about 60 feet long. This neighborhood was the scene of important military operations during the revolution.

Yorktown is 45 miles N. of New York, and 6 E. of Peekskill. Pop. 2,819. Crompond is a small village containing 2 churches and about a dozen dwellings. The names of the post-offices are Yorktown, Pine Bridge, and Shrub Oak. Through the south part flows the Croton river, where is located the great dam and reservoir for the Croton aqueduct. [See p. 336.] This river was named after an ancient sachem, Croton, who resided on its banks at the first settlement of the country.

WYOMING COUNTY.

Wyoming county was formed from the southern portion of Genesee county in 1841; length E. and W. 25, breadth N. and S. 18 miles; centrally distant from New York 325, and from Albany 264 miles. The surface of the county is but gently undulated, and the general character of the soil is a most sandy or gravelly loam, well adapted to the culture of grain and grass. The Genesee river touches the southeastern corner in the town of Castile. Allen's creek, so named from the infamous Indian Allen, who committed many murders on the frontier inhabitants in this region, rises in this county, and flowing northeasterly through a portion of the county of Genesee empties into the Genesee river in the town of Wheatland, Monroe county. The Holland Land Company, to whom this country originally belonged, still own some small tracts. It is divided into 13 towns, and has a population of about 30,000.

ATTICA, taken from Sheldon in 1821; centrally distant NW. from Warsaw, the county seat, 8 miles. Pop. 2,709. Attic, a post village in the northern part, contains 2 churches, a printing office, several mills, stores, and about 125 dwellings. Attica Centre is a smaller village.

BENNINGTON, the NW. corner town, was taken from Sheldon in 1818; centrally distant NW. from Warsaw 14 miles. Pop. 2,367. Bennington and Cowlesville are small post villages.

CASTILE, the SE. corner town, was taken from Perry in 1821; centrally distant SE. from Warsaw 7 miles. Pop. 2,828. Castile and St. Helena are small villages, the latter of which is on the Genesee river. Silver Lake is a post-office near the Silver Lake.

" The Gardow Reservation, which lies partly in this town, was a tract of 10,000 acres, which the Seneca Indians reserved in their sale to Robert Morris in 1797, conferring it upon Mary Jemison, the celebrated " *White Woman*," who resided upon it until her decease, at a very advanced age, in Sept. 1833. Mary Jemison was truly a remarkable woman. She was of Irish parents, and was born at sea, on their passage to America in 1742 or '43. Her parents settled on what was at that time the frontier of Pennsylvania. She had an uncle in the command of Washington, who ' fell at Braddock's defeat. In the spring of 1755, Mary, her parents, two brothers, and several inmates of the house, were made prisoners by a party of half a dozen Seneca Indians and four Frenchmen. They were all hurried off into the woods, and the whole party murdered, Mary alone excepted. She was exposed to all the hardships and privations of a prisoner until her arrival at a Seneca town, where she was adopted into an Indian family as a daughter, and henceforward treated with kindness,—leading a roving life, and for a season meditating upon the means of escape. These being frustrated, she at length resigned herself entirely to the Indian life and customs. At a proper age, she was married to a Delaware Indian, whom she loved, and by whom she had one or more children. She visited Fort Pitt several times, and occasionally resided among the Shawnee Indians.

" Her husband died, and she afterward married a Seneca chief, living in the Genesee valley, at about the beginning of the revolution. Her Seneca husband was a man of blood, but kind and affectionate to her. She retained her family name, Jemison, and also the English language, which she spoke fluently until the day of her death. But although she had been religiously instructed by her parents, she embraced the religion of the Indians, and became thoroughly Indianized—adopting and becoming enamored of all their manners, habits, and customs, throughout. Her life was full of incident and wild adventure. The Indians ever entertained an exalted esteem for her, as was evinced by the grant of the Gardow tract—embracing a rich section, both of intervale and upland, upon which she resided until within a few years before her death, which took place at the Buffalo Creek Reservation. [See Buffalo.] In obtaining this grant or reservation, moreover, she showed all the cunning of her adopted people. Mr. Thomas Morris, who conducted the treaty for his father, has told me that when a request was made to him for a reservation for the " White Woman," he supposed that they meant only a farm of some 200 or 300 acres, but that the woman herself by artfully indicating certain bounds, with which he was not exactly familiar, actually overreached him and obtained the large tract already mentioned; including the whole of the Gardow Flats, and the romantic walls of rock and hill within which they are sequestered.

" During the revolution, her house was often the quarters of Brant and Col. John Butler, when making their inroads upon the frontiers of the colonies. She attended the treaty of

WYOMING COUNTY. 603

Genesee Flats, held by Gen. Schuyler in 1775; and her life, taken down in writing, from her own lips in 1823, was full of incident and adventure. She would not throw off her Indian costume, even after the white population had completely surrounded her residence, but adhered to her Indian customs with the utmost tenacity to the last. She was rich, not only in lands, but in herds and flocks, and had tenants who worked her lands. One of her sons was educated a physician, and obtained a surgeon's commission in the navy—dying a few years ago on the Mediterranean station. In many respects, Mary was a valuable woman—humane and benevolent—and doing great good among the people of her adoption."—*New York Commercial Advertiser.*

CHINA, the SW. town of the county, was taken from Sheldon in 1818; from Warsaw centrally distant SW. 17 miles. Pop. 1,437. Arcade is a small post village, containing about 60 dwellings. East China is a post-office, around which there is a settlement.

COVINGTON, the NE. corner town, was taken from Le Roy and Perry in 1817. Its limits were reduced in 1841, at the time of the division of Genesee county by the erection of Pavilion from its northern portion. It is centrally distant from Warsaw NE. 10 miles. Covington and La Grange are small post villages.

GAINESVILLE was originally named Hebe, and taken from Warsaw in 1814; centrally distant 6 miles. Pop. 2,367. Gainesville Centre, East Gainesville, and Gainesville, are small post villages.

JAVA was taken from China in 1832; centrally distant SW. of Warsaw 15 miles. Pop. 2,331. Java, Java Centre, and Java village, are small post villages.

MIDDLEBURY was taken from Warsaw in 1812; centrally distant N. of Warsaw 6 miles. Pop. 2,447. Wyoming, post village, near the eastern boundary on Allen's creek, is 14 miles SE. of Batavia, and contains 1 Baptist, 1 Presbyterian, and 1 Methodist church, 61 dwellings, 3 mercantile stores, and about 450 inhabitants. The Middlebury academy is a flourishing institution in this place. Middlebury, a post-office, is in the northern part of the town.

ORANGEVILLE was taken from Attica in 1816; centrally distant W. from Warsaw 6 miles. Pop. 1,949. Orangeville, East Orangeville, and Johnsonburgh, are small post villages.

PERRY was taken from Leicester in 1814; centrally distant E. of Warsaw 6 miles. Pop. 3,087.

The following is a view in the central portion of Perry village, incorporated in 1830, and situated about 7 miles E. of Warsaw. It is a place of considerable mercantile and manufacturing business, and contains an academy, 3 churches, and about 150 buildings. It is situated on the outlet of Silver lake, which is a beautiful sheet of water 3 miles in length, and well stocked with fish. The outlet furnishes much hydraulic power for the mills and factories in this vicinity. Perry Centre is much smaller, though incorporated. It is situated about 2 miles to the north.

SHELDON was taken from Batavia in 1808; centrally distant from Warsaw W. 12 miles. Pop. 2,366. Sheldon Centre, Strykersville, and Varysburgh, are small post villages. North Sheldon is the name of a post-office.

South view in Perry village.

WARSAW was formed from Batavia in 1808; from Albany W. 248 miles. Pop. 2,852. The village of Warsaw is situated 22 miles S. from Batavia, at the head of "Allen's Creek Valley," and on Allen's creek, nearly equidistant from Rochester, Canandaigua, Buffalo, and Olean. By the act of the commissioners appointed by the legislature, the courthouse, clerk's office, and jail of Wyoming county were located at this place, July 10, 1841. There are here 1 Presbyterian, 1 Baptist, 1 Methodist, and 1 Congregational church, 100 dwellings, 1 printing office, 1 tannery, 6 mercantile stores, 26 mechanical shops, 2 iron foundries, 2 carding works, 1 woollen factory, 1 grist-mill, and about 800 inhabitants. The town was settled in 1801, principally by emigrants from New England; and its present inhabitants are noted for their morality and fondness for literature. The oldest church erected in the state west of the Genesee river, is yet standing in the centre of the village of Warsaw. South Warsaw is a small village in the south part of the town.

WETHERSFIELD was taken from Orangeville in 1823; centrally distant SW. from Warsaw 8 miles. Pop. 1,731. Hermitage, Wethersfield, and Wethersfield Springs, are small post villages. North Wethersfield is the name of a post-office.

YATES COUNTY.

YATES COUNTY was taken from Ontario in 1823; centrally distant from New York via Albany 330, and from Albany 185 miles; greatest length E. and W. 24, greatest breadth N. and S. 20 miles. The surface of this county is agreeably diversified; the northern part is gently undulating, and the southern hilly. The soil is in many places composed of a warm rich mould, yielding abundant crops, though as a whole it is more of a grazing than a grain country. The climate is temperate, and for the cultivation of fruit is not exceeded by any portion of the state. It lies wholly in the tract ceded to Massachusetts, and in that portion of it which passed through Messrs. Gorham, Phelps, and Robert Morris to Sir William Pulteney. It is divided into eight towns. Pop. 20,442.

BARRINGTON, taken from Wayne in 1822; centrally distant from Penn Yan S. 11 miles. Warsaw is a small post village. Barrington is a post-office. Pop. 1,869.

BENTON, taken from Jerusalem in 1803. Pop. 3,911. Dresden, on the Seneca Lake, 7 miles E. of Penn Yan, Benton, 8 miles NE., and Benton Centre, 4 miles N., are villages containing from 40 to 60 dwellings each. Hopeton is a small settlement near Dresden.

ITALY, taken from Naples of Ontario county in 1815; from Penn Yan SW. 15 miles. Italy Hill, and Italy Hollow, are the post-offices. Pop. 1,663.

South view of the Jemima Wilkinson house.

JERUSALEM, organized by general sessions of Ontario county; area since altered. Pop. 2,934. Branchport, 7 miles SW. of Penn Yan, and Yatesville, partly in the town of Potter, are small villages. Jerusalem is a post-office centrally situated. Bluff Point is a place notable for the singularity of its position, as embraced by the arms of the Crooked Lake, for its high and rolling surface, and for having been the residence and death-place of Jemima Wilkinson, self-styled the " Universal Friend," and founder of a religious sect.

The above is a view of the Jemima Wilkinson house, situated at what is generally called the Friends settlement. It is a large and commodious mansion, and is still occupied by a few persons, the sole remnant of her followers. The dwelling is occasionally visited by strangers; though there is not any thing of interest excepting a portrait of the " Universal Friend," which is said to be a faithful representation, and exhibits a countenance, intellectual, uncommonly beautiful, and apparently beaming with benevolence. The followers of

Jemima Wilkinson first settled about the year 1790 at Milo, in this county, near the Seneca Lake, and subsequently removed to this place. Their settlement at Milo was at that time the largest in the whole Genesee country, numbering about forty families. A highly intelligent gentleman, who visited them many years since, in the season of their greatest prosperity, describes them as being distinguished for their frugality, honesty, and industry, living retired from the world, and devoting much of their time to religious exercises. The "Universal Friend" he represented as having been beautiful and dignified in her person, but illiterate in her conversation, and so ignorant of worldly concerns as scarcely to be enabled to understand a common newspaper. Her memory, however, was retentive, and her knowledge of the Bible truly wonderful. Many of the extravagances of which she is said to have been guilty, may be attributed to the high-wrought enthusiasm so often seen among religionists of her stamp at the present day.

"Jemima Wilkinson, or the 'Universal Friend,' was born in Cumberland, Rhode Island, about the year 1753. She was educated among the Friends. Recovering from an apparent suspension of life which she experienced when about twenty-three years of age, during a fit of sickness, she gave out that she had been raised from the dead, and claimed to be invested with divine attributes and authority to instruct mankind in religion. It is also said, she pretended to foretell future events, to discern the secrets of the heart, and to have the power of healing diseases; and if any person who made application to her was not healed, she attributed it to a want of *faith*. She asserted that those who refused to believe these exalted things concerning her, will be in the state of the unbelieving Jews, who rejected the counsel of God against themselves; and she told her hearers that that was the eleventh hour, and the last call of mercy that ever should be granted to them; for she heard an inquiry in Heaven saying, 'Who will go and preach to a dying world?' and she said she answered, 'Here am I—send me;' and that she left the realms of light and glory and the company of the heavenly hosts, who are continually praising and worshipping God, in order to descend upon earth, and pass through many sufferings and trials for the happiness of mankind. She professed to be able to work miracles, and offered to demonstrate it by walking on the water in imitation of our Saviour; accordingly a frame was constructed for the purpose on the banks of the Seneca Lake, at Rapelyea's ferry, 10 miles south of Dresden. At the appointed time, having approached within a few hundred yards of the lake shore, she alighted from an elegant carriage, and the road being strewed by her followers with white handkerchiefs. She walked to the platform, and having announced her intention of walking across the lake on the water, she stepped ankle deep into the clear element, when suddenly pausing she addressed the multitude, inquiring whether or not they had *faith* that she could pass over, for if otherwise she could not; and on receiving an affirmative answer returned to her carriage, declaring as they believed in her power it was unnecessary to display it. She died in 1819."

The following description of Jemima's personal appearance is from the Freeman's Journal, published at Philadelphia, in 1787:—

"There are now in this city a number of the disciples of a certain JEMIMA WILKINSON, a native Rhode Island, a person who professes that 'she is Christ come again in the flesh a second time without sin unto salvation;' though it should be noticed that her followers do not admit she is a woman, as a female Messiah appears an incongruity, and they therefore of consequence deny her name, and appear to resent it as an affront when she is called Jemima Wilkinson, and declare in the most solemn manner they know no such person. Some of the society when asked to explain themselves, do it in the following manner, ' that the names of persons most properly belong to the soul; but when a person dies and the soul leaves the body, the body can no more be called by its former name. Now some years ago, there was a person called Jemima Wilkinson, but she died and her soul went to heaven; after which the Divine Spirit re-animated that same body, and it arose from the dead: now this Divine inhabitant is Christ Jesus our Lord, the friend of all mankind, and gives the name to the body to which he is united, and therefore body and spirit conjointly is the Universal Friend.' To complete the character of so extraordinary a personage, she has her attendants of the extraordinary kind also, and those attendants are said to be two witnesses which are prophesied by St. John the Divine, in the Revelations. (See chap. xi. from the 3d to the 13th verse.) The Universal Friend, as she is styled, appears to be about 30 years of age, of the middle size of women, not genteel in person, and rather awkward in her carriage, her complexion good, her eyes black and remarkably brilliant, her hair black, and waving in beautiful ringlets upon her neck and shoulders, her features regular, and her face thought by many to be perfectly beautiful. As she is not to be supposed to be of either sex, so this neutrality is manifested in her external appearance; she wears no cap, letting her hair hang down as above described upon her neck and shoulders. Her neckcloth she wears like a man, her shift buttons around her neck, and her shift sleeves are brought down to her hands, and buttoned as is common with men. Her outside garment is a loose robe that resembles a morning-gown, such as both men and women commonly wear; under this it is said her apparel is very expensive, and the form of them conveys the same idea as her external appearance, of her being neither man nor woman. Her understanding is not deficient, except touching her religious fanaticism. She is very illiterate; yet her memory is very great. She is artful in discovering many circumstances which fall out among her disciples, and in making them believe that, as she is divine, nothing can be hid from her. On all occasions she requires the most extraordinary attendance that can be bestowed upon her, having little regard to the convenience of families wherever she happens to be; and one or two disciples usually attend her and perform the most menial service. Her voice is masculine, and her pronunciation in the usual dialect of the most illiterate of the country people of New England. Her preaching has but very little connection, and is frequently very lengthy, standing at times for several hours. Sometimes cold and languid, at others it is said she is lively, and discovers that kind of zeal and animation which give reason to suppose she may really apprehend herself to be a person that is divine. She is commonly reserved to strangers, and only grows familiar as she discovers in them a great respect for her: and as she is very attentive to the disposition of those about her, she soon discovers such as are affected by her peculiar manner. Her first address to strangers is usually in a grum, masculine, authoritative tone of voice, with expressive countenance and piercing eyes; and these are the effects of her spiritual pride. Yet she often strikes the beholder with a profound awe, and the immoral are sometimes convicted before her, which she is artful to improve, so as to raise in them a great veneration for her; and when she discovers any one properly prepared in this way, she usually puts some question to them relating to her own imagined divinity."

MIDDLESEX was organized in 1789 as part of Ontario county, by the name of Augusta; from Penn Yan centrally distant NW. 12 miles. Pop. 1,439. Middlesex is the name of a post-office.

MILO was taken from Benton in 1818; from Albany W. 189 miles. Pop. 3,985. The thriving incorporated village of Penn Yan, the county seat, which is principally built on a street about a mile in length, is situated at the northern termination of the eastern arm of the Crooked Lake. It was founded by Mr. Abraham Waggener, and derives its name from the circumstance that its early settlers were Pennsylvanians and Yankees, in nearly equal numbers. The annexed view was taken from an eminence about a third of a mile east of the village. The first building with a steeple on the right is the Presbyterian church, the one next on the left with a cupola, the courthouse, and the third and fourth, the Baptist and Methodist churches. Crooked or Keuka Lake is partially seen in the distance. The other public buildings in the village are an Episcopal church, an academy, a prison, a bank, and the county clerk's office. The place is one of much business, and has many mercantile stores and about 300 dwellings. Milo Centre, 4 miles SE. of Penn Yan, and Milo 6 miles, are small villages.

POTTER was taken from Middlesex in 1832. Pop. 2,245. Rushville is a thriving village of 60 or 80 dwellings in the north portion of

Northeastern view of Penn Yan.

the town, partly in Gorham of Ontario county, and lies 10 miles SW. of Canandaigua. Yatesville is a small village near the southeastern corner, and partly in Jerusalem. Potter and North Middlesex are names of post-offices.

STARKEY, the southeastern corner town of the county, was taken from Reading of Steuben county in 1824. Pop. 2,426. Starkey, including Eddyville 14 miles SE. of Penn Yan, are settlements scattered along the road for about two miles, and containing about 60 or 70 dwellings. Dundee, late Harpendings Corners, is a thriving village, 14 miles S. of Penn Yan, containing 4 churches and about 80 dwellings. Big Stream and Rock Stream are names of post-offices in the south part, the former of which is on Seneca Lake. The falls of the Big Stream in this town are one hundred and forty feet perpendicular. This cataract is situated at the foot of a rapid half a mile in length, whence the stream comes dashing over craggy rocks of slate, and leaps into a basin eight or ten rods in diameter, separated from the lake by a channel some eighty rods in length.

THE END.

www.ingramcontent.com/pod-product-compliance
Lightning Source LLC
Chambersburg PA
CBHW070905300426
44113CB00008B/939